Old and Middle English

BLACKWELL ANTHOLOGIES

Old and Middle English: An Anthology

Edited by Elaine Treharne

Editorial Advisers

Rosemary Ashton, University of London; Gillian Beer, University of Cambridge; Gordon Campbell, University of Leicester; Terry Castle, Stanford University; Margaret Ann Doody, Vanderbilt University; Richard Gray, University of Essex; Joseph Harris, Harvard University; Karen L. Kilcup, University of North Carolina, Greensboro; Jerome J. McGann, University of Virginia; David Norbrook, University of Oxford; Tom Paulin, University of Oxford; Michael Payne, Bucknell University; Elaine Showalter, Princeton University; John Sutherland, University of London; Jonathan Wordsworth, University of Oxford.

Blackwell Anthologies are a series of extensive and comprehensive volumes designed to address the numerous issues raised by recent debates regarding the literary canon, value, text, context, gender, genre and period. While providing the reader with key canonical writings in their entirety, the series is also ambitious in its coverage of hitherto marginalized texts, and flexible in the overall variety of its approaches to periods and movements. Each volume has been thoroughly researched to meet the current needs of teachers and students.

OLD AND MIDDLE ENGLISH

AN ANTHOLOGY

EDITED BY **ELAINE TREHARNE**

BLACKWELL
Publishers

Copyright © Blackwell Publishers Ltd 2000

Editorial matter, Old English translations, selection and organization of whole volume
copyright © Elaine Treharne 2000

First published 2000

2 4 6 8 10 9 7 5 3 1

Blackwell Publishers Ltd
108 Cowley Road
Oxford OX4 1JF
UK

Blackwell Publishers Inc.
350 Main Street
Malden, Massachusetts 02148
USA

British Library Cataloguing in Publication Data

A CIP catalogue record for this book is available from the British Library.

Library of Congress Cataloging-in-Publication Data

Old and Middle English : an anthology / edited by Elaine Treharne.
     p.   cm. — (Blackwell anthologies)
    Texts in Old and Middle English, with translations and commentary
in Modern English.
    Includes bibliographical references and index.
    ISBN 0-631-20465-2 (alk. paper). — ISBN 0-631-20466-0 (pbk. :
alk. paper)
    1. English literature—Old English, ca. 450–1100.   2. English
literature—Old English, ca. 450–1100 Modernized versions.
3. English literature—Middle English, 1100–1500 Modernized
versions.   4. English literature—Middle English, 1100–1500.
5. Middle Ages—Literary collections.   6. Manuscripts, Medieval—
England.   I. Treharne, Elaine M.   II. Series.
PR1120.O4   2000
829'.08—dc21   99-34413
                                          CIP

Commissioning Editor: Andrew McNeillie
Development Editor: Alison Dunnett
Desk Editor: Fiona Sewell
Production Manager: Lisa Eaton
Text Designer: Lisa Eaton
Picture Researcher: Leanda Shrimpton

Typeset in 9½ on 11 pt Garamond 3
by Ace Filmsetting Ltd, Frome, Somerset
Printed in Great Britain by T.J. International, Padstow, Cornwall

This book is printed on acid-free paper.

Contents

Alphabetical List of Authors and Works

Preface and Acknowledgements

I am grateful for the assistance of the librarians and curators, especially at the Bodleian Library, Oxford; Corpus Christi College, Cambridge; Trinity College, Cambridge; the British Library (expecially Andrew Prescott); and the British Library's lending service at Boston Spa. I should like to thank the staff at Leicester University Library, particularly in the Inter-Library Loans section, for their assistance, and the Faculty of Arts at Leicester University, which has been generous in funding some of my library visits. Many thanks are due to the following colleagues: Bob Bjork, Graham Caie, Patrick Conner, Joyce Hill, Susan Irvine, Patrizia Lendinara, Kathryn Lowe, Hugh Magennis, Richard Marsden, John McGavin, Bella Millett, Gale Owen-Crocker, Susan Rosser, David Salter, Hans Sauer, William Schipper, Mary Swan, Elizabeth Tyler and Gernot Wieland, all of whom made many useful suggestions and criticisms of this volume in its initial stages. Thanks especially to Jill Frederick, Roy Liuzza and Phillip Pulsiano, for their friendship, support and numerous helpful comments. I have not produced precisely the volume that anyone requested, but hope there is something in here to suit most colleagues. For the inevitable errors, I am, of course, completely responsible.

I should particularly like to thank Andrew McNeillie of Blackwell's for suggesting this volume in the first place, and for his support throughout its preparation; and at Blackwell's too, Ally Dunnett and Lisa Eaton have kept this project on the rails. Many thanks, too, to Fiona Sewell, my desk editor. At Leicester, Gordon Campbell, Vincent Newey and John V. Gough have provided encouragement and support throughout this and other projects. Those to whom I owe most thanks are Greg Walker, who has been a source of constant help and friendship; my mum, Iola Treharne; and Don Scragg, the *magister*.

This book is dedicated to my husband and son: Andy and Jonathan Fryett. I thank Andy for his help during the preparation of this volume; he has put up with me in the best and worst of times, as indeed has my son, Jonathan, whose smile is enough to remind me what life is about.

And as for this *Anthology*, the closing words of the author of *Ancrene Wisse* seem highly appropriate:

Me were leovere, Godd hit wite, do me toward Rome, þen forte biginnen hit eft forte donne.

Chronology of Events and Literary Landmarks

Historical events	*Literary landmarks*
From *c*.449: Anglo-Saxon settlements	
597: St Augustine arrives to convert Anglo-Saxons	
664: Synod of Whitby	
	c.670? Cædmon's *Hymn*
	731: Bede finishes *Ecclesiastical History*
735: Death of Bede	
793: Vikings raid Lindisfarne	
869: Vikings kill King Edmund of East Anglia	
871–99: Alfred reigns as king of Wessex	from *c*.890: *Anglo-Saxon Chronicle*
	Alfredian translations of Bede's *Ecclesiastical History*; Gregory's *Pastoral Care*; Orosius; Boethius's *Consolation of Philosophy*; Augustine's *Soliloquies*
937: Battle of Brunanburh	
from *c*.950: Benedictine reform	
	c.970: Exeter Book copied
959–75: King Edgar reigns	c.975: Vercelli Book copied
978–1016: Æthelred 'the Unready' reigns	990s: Ælfric's *Catholic Homilies* and *Lives of Saints*
	c.1000: *Beowulf*-manuscript copied
c.1010: death of Ælfric	c.1010?: Junius manuscript copied
	c.1014: Wulfstan's *Sermo Lupi ad Anglos*
1016–35: Cnut, king of England	
1023: death of Wulfstan	
1042–66: Edward the Confessor reigns	*Apollonius of Tyre*
1066: Battle of Hastings	
1066–89: William the Conqueror reigns	
1135: Stephen becomes king	Geoffrey of Monmouth's *Historia Regum Britanniae*
1135–54: civil war between King Stephen and Empress Matilda	*Peterborough Chronicle* continuations
1154–89: Henry II reigns	1155: Wace's *Roman de Brut*
	1170-90: Chrétien de Troyes's *Romances*
	c.1170s: The *Orrmulum*

Poema Morale

1180s: Marie de France's *Lais*

1189–99: Richard I reigns

*c.*1190-1200? Trinity Homilies

1199–1216: John reigns

*c.*1200? *Hali Meiðhad*

1204: loss of Normandy

1215: Magna Carta

1215: fourth Lateran Council

1216–72: Henry III reigns

*c.*1220 Laȝamon's *Brut*

1224: Franciscan friars arrive in England

*c.*1225: *Ancrene Wisse*

*c.*1225: *King Horn*

1272–1307: Edward I reigns

Manuscript Digby 86 copied

Manuscript Jesus 29 copied

Manuscript Cotton Caligula A. ix copied

Manuscript Arundel 292 copied

Manuscript Trinity 323 copied

South English Legendary composed

*c.*1300: *Cursor Mundi*

1303: Robert Mannyng of Brunne begins
    Handlyng Synne

1307–27: Edward II reigns

1327–77: Edward III reigns

Auchinleck Manuscript copied

Manuscript Harley 2253 copied

1337(–1454): Hundred Years War with France

1338: Robert Mannyng of Brunne's *Chronicle*

1340: *Ayenbite of Inwit*

*c.*1343: Geoffrey Chaucer born

Ywain and Gawain translated

1349: Black Death comes to England

1349: Richard Rolle dies

1355–80: *Athelston*

Wynnere and Wastoure written

1362: English displaces French as language of
    lawcourts and Parliament

1377: Richard II accedes to throne

Introduction

The Anthology

The aim of this anthology is to provide an extensive selection of literary texts that effectively covers the earliest writings in the vernacular up to the time of Chaucer. This time-span of almost seven centuries is greater than that from Chaucer to the present day, and encompasses the foundation and consolidation of literature written in English. The volume therefore aims to demonstrate both the continuities and changes in the evolution of this literature; and to give sufficient explanatory annotation and bibliographical information for students to begin their studies on particular texts within the volume. There has been no conscious attempt to divide the volume proportionally between the periods traditionally known as Old English and Middle English, though inevitably rather more is included from the later centuries by virtue of the fact that more survives. It is hoped that this anthology will allow the student to view the earlier medieval period as a whole, creating links between genres and themes, for example, that span the centuries. Such genres might include historical writings (*The Anglo-Saxon Chronicle*, Laȝamon's *Brut* and Robert Mannyng of Brunne's *Chronicle*); the homiletic and hagiographic (Vercelli Homily X, Ælfric's Homily on the Nativity of the Innocents, Ælfric's *Passion of St Edmund*, the *Orrmulum* and *The South English Legendary's Life of St Wulfstan*); and the Romance (*Apollonius of Tyre*, *Kyng Alisaunder*, *Ywain and Gawain*, *Athelston*). Themes might include the transience of life (*The Wanderer* and *The Seafarer*, the Digby, Trinity or Harley Lyrics); the heroic (*Beowulf*, *Judith*, *The Battle of Maldon*, *King Horn*); writings by or for women (*The Wife's Lament*, *Wulf and Eadwacer*, *Hali Meiðhad*, *Ancrene Wisse*, Richard Rolle's *Ego Dormio*); and the treatment of sin and the devil (Vercelli Homily X, Wulfstan's *Sermo Lupi ad Anglos*, the Trinity Homily on Psalm 119, and Richard Rolle's *Handlyng Synne*).

The method of organization has proved a complex issue, and because the majority of texts, particularly poetic texts, in Old and earlier Middle English are not securely dated, the volume is organized by extant manuscript date, rather than by approximate textual date. For the pre-Conquest period, the four major poetic codices are dated within a half-century or so, and are later than the Alfredian prose manuscripts, making the sequence of the texts relatively straightforward. For the post-Conquest period, most texts in the book are where one might expect to find them in terms of chronology; some, however, such as *King Horn* or Laȝamon's *Brut*, occur after texts that are later in terms of compositional date. *King Horn* is edited from London, British Library, Harley 2253, a fourteenth-century manuscript; and while the text itself probably dates to the thirteenth century, it has nevertheless been placed in the order of its manuscript's date. This organization may seem unnecessarily problematic, but the issues that it raises are crucial to our understanding of the ways in which medieval texts operate both contemporaneously and in the present day inasmuch as many texts are anonymous and undated: the concepts of authorship and textual dating in the medieval period are quite removed from modern practices. Some texts will have circulated orally before being committed to written form and will thus be much earlier in terms of date of origin than the manuscript context might imply; other texts may have been composed in written format immediately. While texts like Robert Mannyng of Brunne's *Handlyng Synne* are known to date from the beginning of the fourteenth century, there is substantial controversy about the dates of numerous other medieval texts, such as *Beowulf*, *Exodus*, *The Proverbs of Alfred*, *The Owl and the Nightingale* and *Athelston*. This volume does not seek to impose a date of composition on the undated texts that are included; however, texts that are incontrovertibly dated are included in their logical chronological sequence.

In addition, many texts such as Cædmon's *Hymn* and *The Owl and the Nightingale* have undergone editorial changes in the process of being copied by scribes; others, such as the *Orrmulum* and the *Ayenbite of Inwit*, survive in copies written by the author himself. The manuscript context becomes crucial to an understanding of the nature of the text and the ways in which that text was viewed by a medieval author, scribe or manuscript compiler. *The Wife's Lament*, for example, is incorporated into the tenth-century Exeter Book amidst a variety of Riddles; *The Dream of the Rood* is copied into the tenth-century Vercelli Book, which includes over twenty prose homilies; and *The Proverbs of Alfred* are copied with a number of penitential and devotional texts into a thirteenth-century manuscript. By seeking to comprehend the perceived nature of the text in its own time, readers may come to appreciate the multitude of interpretations yielded by these texts both from the modern perspective and from a more medieval one.

The texts that are edited here are those deemed most necessary for all students of medieval literature to know, supplemented by those that it would be useful to know. Many of the texts are those that one would expect to find, and indeed will find, in all such collections, but some are less common, and some are edited for the first time in anthology format. It is the case that the majority of the texts included are edited in their entirety; where extracts have had to be selected because the length of the work precludes its complete inclusion, the extracts are usually episodes or whole sections. Where extracts are given, the context of that selection is generally provided.

Each text begins with a headnote that incorporates information about the manuscript, the date, the literary context, possible interpretations, bibliographical matter and dialect. Explanatory notes are usually only given to clarify a reading. Textual emendations occur at the back of the volume, followed by a select bibliography, and a number of indexes to assist in using the anthology.

General Historical and Literary Background

In *c.*410, Rome was under threat of invasion from northern tribes such as the Goths. Legions that were posted in the many provinces of the Roman Empire were recalled to defend the capital and its environs. In the parts of Britain where the Romans had maintained authority for four centuries, the Celts, Picts and Irish were left to fight among themselves for political power. As Bede relates in his *Ecclesiastical History*, chapter I.xv, in the late 440s, Vortigern, king of the Celts, invited Anglo-Saxon mercenaries to assist him in his wars, and chief among the warriors who arrived were two brothers, Hengest and Horsa. This was the legendary beginning of the Anglo-Saxon settlement of the area that has become modern-day England.

'The Anglo-Saxons' is a convenient label for a number of different tribes from the Low Countries, Jutland in Denmark, and parts of Germany. The Angles, Saxons and Jutes are those whom Bede mentions, but it is likely that settlers came from other tribes such as the Frisians. The Anglo-Saxons pushed the Celts back to the western fringes of Britain – to Wales, Cumbria, Cornwall, and across the Channel to Britanny – and took control of England. These Anglo-Saxon tribes settled in various parts of England where they created their own kingdoms; for example, Sussex, Essex, Middlesex and Wessex were settled by the Saxons; East Anglia, Northumbria and parts of the Midlands by the Angles. In this early period, and for some centuries to come, there was no single kingdom of England; rather, the different kings controlled their own regions, and each sought to obtain political hegemony. In the eighth century, Northumbria and Mercia were dominant; by the late ninth century, Wessex was the most powerful kingdom.

When the Anglo-Saxons arrived in the fifth and sixth centuries, they were not Christian but pagan. They shared the same religion as the related Germanic tribes on the continent. The country that the

Anglo-Saxons conquered, however, had been Christian since the fourth century when Constantine declared that the Roman Empire was to adopt Christianity, although Bede relates that Christianity had fallen into decline and that the defeat of the Celts at the hands of the Anglo-Saxons was a result of their sins against God. It was not until 597, and the arrival in Kent of Augustine, that the long process of converting the Anglo-Saxons began in the south of the country. Augustine, sent by Pope Gregory, converted King Ethelberht of Kent, and throughout the seventh century this process of Christianizing the population of Anglo-Saxon England continued. In the north of the country, Christianity was simultaneously being spread by the Celtic missionaries from Ireland and Scotland. In 664, at the Synod of Whitby, the Roman and Celtic Christians came together to decide upon the course of Christianity in England: the Roman advocates won the day, and from that time onwards, Roman methods of organizing the church prevailed.

The arrival of Christianity had important implications for the production and survival of literature in Latin and, later, Old English. Christianity, by virtue of the fact that it is a religion dependent on the word of God in the Bible, necessarily required the production of preaching and teaching materials. In the period up to the ninth century, these materials were written in Latin, though this does not mean that composition in Old English did not occur; on the contrary, English was spoken by the ordinary population, and used for the oral recitation of poetry, but it was not yet considered a language suitable for writing. The earliest piece of Old English to survive in a contemporary manuscript is Cædmon's *Hymn*, transcribed into two manuscripts of Bede's Latin *Ecclesiastical History* in the 730s. This poem in praise of God employs the form of alliterative poetry used by all the Germanic tribes to relate their legends of heroes and battles, but that form is used now by Cædmon to impart a Christian message.

While Latin works and manuscripts were written and produced throughout the eighth and ninth centuries, the major task of the English kings in the ninth century was to fend off the Viking incursions that had begun in 793 with the sacking of Lindisfarne in Northumbria. The Vikings, who, like the Anglo-Saxons, were Germanic peoples, eventually settled in the kingdoms of Northumbria, East Anglia and parts of Mercia (in the Midlands).[1] It is during the reign of King Alfred of Wessex (871–99) that this division of the country was recognized by the creation of the Danelaw ruled by the Vikings.[2] It was also in Alfred's reign that Old English became authorized as a language for written texts. During the latter years of his reign, Alfred, distraught by the decline of learning in England, initiated his programme of education in the vernacular.[3] To achieve this objective, Alfred obtained assistance from abroad and from neighbouring kingdoms (Wales and Mercia, for example) in determining the books most necessary for all people to know, and for aid in translating these books into English. The books at the top of Alfred's educational agenda were: St Augustine's *Soliloquies*; Gregory's *Cura Pastoralis* and *Dialogues*; Bede's *Ecclesiastical History*; Orosius's *Historiae adversum paganos*; and Boethius's *Consolation of Philosophy*. Each of these works was considered throughout the medieval period to be fundamental to the acquisition of Christian knowledge and to a wider knowledge of the world and its history. And it was also during this reign of Alfred that the *Anglo-Saxon Chronicle* recording the history of the English was started; the earliest manuscript, *The Parker Chronicle*, written in Winchester, dates from the last decade of the ninth century.

The first half of the tenth century saw far less activity in the continuation of the *Chronicle* and in the production of English prose in general. By the middle of the century, however, a significant religious reform was under way in Wessex and southern England, deriving its impetus in part from the Carolingian reforms on the continent. The Benedictine reform movement, supported by King Edgar (959–75), was crucial in reviving learning and the production of manuscripts in the second half of the tenth century. The major figures in England within this reform of the Benedictine monastic system were Dunstan, archbishop of Canterbury (959–88), Oswald, bishop of Worcester (961–92) and archbishop of York (971–92), and Æthelwold, bishop of Winchester (963–84). While in exile abroad, Dunstan had seen at first hand the results of the Benedictine reforms, and, on his return to England, he was instrumental in

---

1 In 869, for example, Edmund, king of East Anglia, was killed by the Vikings, who thus took control of his kingdom. See Ælfric's *Passion of St Edmund*.
2 In the Treaty of Wedmore, 878, between Guthrum, the Danish king, and Alfred. Guthrum had to convert to Christianity to obtain this treaty.
3 See Alfred's *Preface* to Gregory's *Pastoral Care* for the motives and methods behind this programme.

putting the practices of the reform into place. New monasteries, such as Ramsey, were established during this period, and existing monasteries were improved. The *Regularis Concordia*, an adaptation of the Benedictine Rule for English religious houses, became the principal reform document.

The Benedictine reform fostered education within the monastic system. The four major poetic codices, the Exeter Book, the Vercelli Book, the *Beowulf* or Nowell codex and the Junius manuscript, were compiled during this period, and can be dated variously from the second half of the tenth century to the first quarter of the eleventh. Together with other surviving fragments and texts – *The Battle of Maldon*, for example – this corpus of work represents the largest and most significant body of poetry in any vernacular from this period.[4] A substantial amount of the surviving Old English poetry (and some prose) copied during these decades concerns the adaptation and versification of biblical stories; for example, *The Fates of the Apostles*, *Judith* and *Exodus*. This religious poetry often concerns the presentation of the heroic code in action through the Christian protagonist. Side by side with this is the depiction of the heroic code portrayed through the battles of English or Germanic heroes, and this material in many ways reflects the Germanic origins of the Anglo-Saxons themselves. The major themes of this heroic poetry concern the *comitatus* (the lord and his loyal band of warriors), the loyalty of kinship and kingship, often contradictory, as in *Beowulf* and in *Cynewulf and Cyneheard*, the feasting and glory of the beerhall, the dedication and courage to a lord in battle, the boasting of bravery in battle and living up to that boast in a public display of valour, fighting to the death and urging other comrades to do the same, the giving and receiving of treasure as a reward, and the desire to achieve immortal glory and praise.

The re-emergence of prose is also seen in this period of the later tenth and early eleventh centuries with the production of the Vercelli Homilies (in the Vercelli Book) and the Blickling Homilies, two collections of anonymous religious writings, parts of which are based on apocryphal sources, and influenced by the Hiberno-Latin tradition. It was partially the existence of such non-orthodox collections that inspired Ælfric, the greatest prose writer from the earlier medieval period, to compile his orthodox vernacular sermons and saints' lives in the 990s and early eleventh century.[5] Ælfric was very much a product of the Benedictine reform, having been educated under Æthelwold at Winchester. He, along with his contemporary, Wulfstan, bishop of Worcester and archbishop of York (1002–16; d. 1023), provided a substantial body of prose that surpasses in quantity and quality any other prose writings in any vernacular at this time.

During the eleventh century, Old English prose continued to be copied into manuscripts, the *Anglo-Saxon Chronicle* continued, and there were some additional translations written such as *Apollonius of Tyre*. Norman influence was already being felt during the reign of Edward the Confessor (1042–66), who had been brought up in Normandy by his mother, Emma, and it was his promise of the English throne to William, duke of Normandy, that precipitated the events of 14 October 1066.[6] Following the death of Edward on 5 January 1066, Harold Godwineson, ruler of East Anglia and Wessex, laid claim to the throne of England and was crowned king on 6 January 1066. Harold had allegedly pledged his support some years earlier to William in his claim on the throne, and thus William attacked to regain his crown.[7]

In 1066, 5,000 Normans invaded, and between 1066 and 1100, another 20,000 Normans settled in England. If, as suggested by the *Doomsday Book*, compiled in 1087 by William as a stock-take on his English lands, the population of England was some 1.5 million, the Norman settlers represented initially only a very small percentage of the population. The crucial aspect of the Norman conquest of England, though, was that the Conqueror placed his men in all the positions of power – in the church,[8] in central and local government and administration, in the court, and as local magnates.

---

4 A major point to bear in mind is that although the majority of poetry copied into the four main poetic codices can be dated to c.970–1025, that dating represents the period in which the texts were committed to writing. It is extremely difficult to determine the date of actual, original composition of many of these poetic texts, and this aspect of Old English literature has occupied critics for generations. Many linguistic features, presumably contained within the original text, will have been eradicated in the process of copying – especially so since copying took place in the literary standard West Saxon dialect.

5 Ælfric wrote, among other things, two series of *Catholic Homi-*

lies, the *Lives of Saints*, a *Colloquy* (in Latin), a *Grammar*, and a number of *Pastoral Letters* for his colleagues. See the bibliography under 'Ælfric'.

6 Emma was the great-aunt of William the Conqueror, providing him with another reason to make a claim on the throne after Edward died.

7 See Robert Mannyng of Brunne's account of the Conquest in his *Chronicle*, below.

8 The longest surviving Anglo-Saxon bishop was Wulfstan of Worcester, who died in 1095. See below for his *Life* from the *South English Legendary*.

The result of this for the production of literature in the period is that, essentially, English ceased to be the language of the monarchy and its related administrative bodies. Latin continued, as it always had done, in its role as the main language of learning and religious writings; French was used for administration, later law, and the production of literature for the aristocratic, the aspiring gentleperson and the educated. English did continue to be copied throughout the period; numerous manuscripts survive from the second half of the eleventh century into the late twelfth and beyond. The majority of the manuscripts produced between *c*.1070 and *c*.1170 tend to be adaptations and copies of earlier Old English religious prose texts, but there was also some new composition and translation in English. *The Peterborough Chronicle*, one of the *Anglo-Saxon Chronicle* manuscripts, continued to record events with some detail up until 1154, the end of Stephen's reign; the *Lives* of St Nicholas and St Giles were translated in the half-century after the Conquest; and it is to this period that numerous homilies and didactic writings can be assigned.

In the last quarter of the twelfth century, English was used for the composition of important, original texts such as the *Poema Morale*, the Trinity Homilies and the *Orrmulum*, and by the beginning of the thirteenth century, English was used for many writings[9] originating in the West Midlands area, a region that had retained a nationalistic pride, and had continued the prose literary traditions of the Anglo-Saxon past.

During the twelfth century, education and many aspects of intellectual culture throughout Europe underwent something of a renaissance. Universities were created in Paris, Bologna and Oxford, complementing and eventually overtaking the education given in the monastic and cathedral schools. The scholasticism of the period gave rise to great scholars who produced works that were to have a lasting effect on the development of literature, religion and philosophy. For example, key figures are Anselm, archbishop of Canterbury; Peter Abelard; Bernard of Clairvaux; John of Salisbury; and Geoffrey of Monmouth. The last scholar, in writing his Latin *Historia Regum Britanniae*, effectively began the widespread dissemination of the legend of Arthur that spawned numerous Romances and histories in many vernaculars. The focus on Arthur as the greatest of heroes in terms of 'Matter of Britain' Romances was part of the new trend of Romance and the lyric, both of which were transmitted from France. Henry II's marriage to Eleanor of Aquitaine in the middle of the twelfth century had important implications for the emergence of these new trends in England. For example, the Anglo-Norman *Brut* of Wace written in *c*.1155, a verse history of England derived from Geoffrey of Monmouth, was presented to Eleanor, and it formed one of the sources for Laȝamon's English *Brut* some fifty years later. The Arthurian Romances of Chretién de Troyes in the second half of the twelfth century were to influence numerous successors, including the fourteenth-century *Ywain and Gawain*; the love poetry of the French troubadours and trouveres was fundamental in influencing English lyric poetry; and the Breton lays of Marie de France, composed in the second half of the twelfth century, provided the generic impetus for later English Breton lays such as *Sir Orfeo*.

The influence of Romance and texts dedicated to chivalry and the exploits of great heroes is seen very quickly in English texts. In the *Ancrene Wisse*, book 7, for example, the love of Christ for the anchoress is described in terms of the knight's love for his lady; in the English lyrics written in the thirteenth century, French lyrical forms such as the *pastourelle*, the *reverdie* and the *chansons d'aventure* are employed. In many of the texts, therefore, there is a distinct movement away from Germanic motifs of the lord and his *comitatus*, the public duty of the hero to his subjects, to those of Romance and the personal quest of the individual; his self-development and deeds of bravery for his own, as well as his king's and, occasionally, lady's, glory.

These features that were to dominate secular literature are also felt in religious life and texts. There is far greater emphasis on the individual's relationship with God, on the personal and loving closeness that could be obtained through penitence and contemplation. Many religiously inclined people from the twelfth century onwards sought to develop this relationship by undertaking a solitary life – that of the hermit, anchorite or anchoress; or via a conventual community dedicated to God. The result of this movement in terms of literature is the emergence of instructive texts such as the *Ancrene Wisse*, and of devotional and penitential lyrics, spoken by the sinner directly to God, or the major intercessor, the Virgin Mary.

---

9   For example, *Hali Meiðhad*, Laȝamon's *Brut* and the *Ancrene Wisse*.

As well as these new trends in literature, later medieval attitudes to and thoughts about the world and the afterlife are represented in terms of traditions in literature already established in the Anglo-Saxon period. The *'Ubi sunt?'* motif, seen in poems such as *The Wanderer*, is very prevalent in the later period, not only in penitential lyrics, but also in Romances such as *Sir Orfeo*. The hero of Anglo-Saxon poems such as *The Battle of Maldon* or *Beowulf* is transformed into the armoured knight of *King Horn* or the adventurous Arthurian knight seeking to prove his chivalric prowess in *Ywain and Gawain*. The tradition of vernacular homilies and saints' lives of Ælfric and Wulfstan is reflected in the great religious works of the period: the *South English Legendary*, *Cursor Mundi* and others. And the confessionals and penitentials that were produced primarily in Latin in the pre-Conquest period now appear in the vernacular in Robert Mannyng of Brunne's *Handlyng Synne* and Dan Michel of Northgate's *Ayenbite of Inwit*. These latter texts were probably inspired by the dictates of the Fourth Lateran Council in 1215, which stipulated that priests and bishops were to ensure that regular confession and attendance at mass occurred for the congregation, and that instruction and confession should be made more accessible by the use of the vernacular.

The period as a whole, then, sees transitions in the vernacular that reflect major social events and concerns. Much of the religious literature comments explicitly or implicitly on the corruptions of society, and on the need to reform. This depiction of society's corruption is found in thirteenth- and four-teenth-century satirical literature such as *The Land of Cockayne*, or *Wynnere and Wastoure*. The secular Romance literature provides examples of the heroes whose behaviour represented the epitome of the courtly and the chivalric: a behaviour to be emulated by the aristocratic and expanding aspiring middle classes. From this literature, the anxieties, concerns and mores of the English can be deduced, and the thoughts, aspirations and lives of many understood more fully.

Manuscript Culture

All of the literature edited in this volume survives only in manuscript form. Printing in England did not begin until the end of the fifteenth century, and there is no comparable mass-production of written materials prior to this invention. Literacy in the Anglo-Saxon period was confined to relatively few people: those of the aristocratic stratum of society, and those who chose to enter a monastic or regular religious life. In the post-Conquest period, literacy became more widespread, and the demand for litera-ture in the three languages of French, Latin and English grew. By the thirteenth and fourteenth centu-ries, considerably more manuscripts were produced than in previous centuries as a result of this increase in literacy and the greater accessibility of education.[10] Manuscripts were, though, costly in terms of labour and resources to produce, and only relatively wealthy individuals and institutions, or educated people, owned or had access to them.

What survives from the medieval period probably represents only a small proportion of what existed: much literature has perished, either as a result of its unintelligibility and subsequent destruction; or by accident, such as the fires that broke out in Canterbury Cathedral in the late eleventh century, and in 1731 in the library housing the medieval manuscripts of Sir Robert Cotton. All of the texts from these centuries survive in manuscript form, written out by a scribe on vellum or parchment and incorporated into a unified codex, or a composite manuscript containing disparate material. Many of the texts, indeed, survive in only one copy; for example, most of the poems in the Exeter Book, *Beowulf* and *Judith*, the *Orrmulum*, the *Ayenbite of Inwit* and *Athelston*. Very few manuscripts are written by the author him or herself; the *Orrmulum* and the *Ayenbite of Inwit* are two such examples. This issue of authorial control is one of great importance: scribes not only copied material, but they also often acted as editors; indeed, Ælfric asked for the integrity of his work to be maintained, but almost immediately, his texts are copied into manuscripts with the anonymous homilies that he appears to have despised. Because scribes, or the compilers of manuscripts, often acted in an editorial capacity, we cannot always be sure that what we are reading is what the author actually intended. What we can be sure of is that the editions of texts such as those that follow in this volume represent one more step away from the authorial composition of the work.

---

10   See especially M. T. Clanchy, *From Memory to Written Record: England 1066–1307*, 2nd edn (Oxford, 1993).

Where texts exist in more than one copy, variant readings can often be used to present a fuller under-standing of the text. One often finds, however, considerable irregularity of spelling and lexis that com-plicates this reconstruction. *The Owl and the Nightingale*, for example, exists in two manuscripts both of which can be dated to the last quarter of the thirteenth century. Neither manuscript is a copy of the other, and there are a number of differences, in spelling and in vocabulary, that complicate the construc-tion of the original text.

In addition, the anonymity of the greater proportion of authors in the medieval period imposes an immediate distance between the reader and the text. If little or nothing is known about the author, we cannot always be sure about the date of the text's composition, the agenda and methods of the author, and his or her intended audience, and thus the probable interpretation of the text. This is true of much Old English poetry such as *The Wife's Lament* as well as later material such as *Athelston*.

Forms of Poetry

Many Anglo-Saxon poems may have existed in oral form first. This form operates through alliteration and stress, reflecting the patterns of natural speech and thus being wholly appropriate to oral per-formance. This alliterative verse is common to all the Germanic tribes, though few texts survive in vernaculars other than English. The first recorded example of this alliterative poetry is Cædmon's *Hymn*, which appropriates the Germanic heroic form and combines it with a Christian content, praising God the creator.

Nu we sculen **herigean**   heofonrices Weard,
Meotodes meahte,   ond his **modgeþanc**,
weorc **Wuldorfæder**,   swa he **wundra** gehwæs,
ece Drihten,   or onstealde.
He **ærest** sceop   eorðan bearnum
heofon to hrofe,   halig Scyppend;
þa **middangeard**   moncynnes Weard,
ece Drihten,   æfter teode
firum foldan,   Frea ælmihtig.

In Cædmon's *Hymn*, alliteration occurs on stressed syllables; that is, on the important and emphatic words in the verse-line. The poetry can be described as two half-lines (a and b), each linked by the alliteration which runs across the verse-line. In the first line, alliteration falls on the <w> of *we* and *Weard*, and on the <h> of *herigean* and *heofonrices*. The caesura in the middle represents the break between the two half-lines: the natural pause for emphasis. For this kind of poetry, the poet needs a stock of vocabulary; here, Cædmon required a variety of epithets for the Deity. In other poems, such as *Beowulf*, the poet needs an alliterating stock of words for 'warrior', 'hero', 'battle', 'sword' and so on. In *The Dream of the Rood*, there are a number of different words for wood or tree or cross: *treow, sigebeam, beacen, gealga, tacen, rod*. Each word highlights a particular aspect of the cross's metamorphic appearance and significa-tion.

This alliterative poetry continues, albeit in a less regular metrical and alliterative form, into the fourteenth century, particulary in the West Midlands region with works such as Laȝamon's *Brut* and *Wynnere and Wastoure*. In addition to this native tradition of alliterative verse, the thirteenth century sees the use in English of patterns of prosody associated originally with French Romance. The octosyllabic rhyming couplet, for example, is used by the poets of *The Owl and the Nightingale*, *The Fox and the Wolf* and *Sir Orfeo*; in *King Horn*, a short rhyming couplet of two or three stresses is used; while later, in the fourteenth century, the tail rhyme stanzas of *Athelston* represent a form common to East Anglian texts. Other varied types of metre are illustrated particularly by the Digby, Trinity and Harley Lyrics.

Language

English ultimately derives from a language called proto-Indo-European spoken many thousands of years ago. This original language, one of a number in the world, is the parent of various language families such as Germanic (German, Scandinavian languages, etc.), Celtic (Welsh, Gaelic, etc.), Hellenic (Greek), Italic (Italian, French, Spanish, etc.) and Indo-Iranian (Hindi, Bengali, etc.).[11] These different branches were formed as tribes moved throughout Europe, settling in different areas, and forming their own versions of the original. Over time, these languages became quite divergent to the point where they appear, *prima facie*, to be unrelated.

English belongs to the Germanic branch of Indo-European, specifically to the West Germanic dialect. In simplified terms, the Angles, the Saxons and the Jutes brought versions of this dialect with them when they settled in the fifth century in what came to be known as England. As these peoples were essentially three different tribes, and as they settled in different areas of England, four dialects emerged in the Anglo-Saxon period: West Saxon, Northumbrian, Kentish and Mercian. These four dialects are often subsumed under the label of Old English.[12] Old English is the language used in speech by the Anglo-Saxons from the fifth century to the twelfth. In the case of written records, Old English was used regularly from the ninth century, although there are some texts surviving from the eighth. The Anglo-Saxons already had an alphabet, prior to their arrival in England, which was common to the Germanic peoples and which consisted of Runic characters. Some of these letter-forms were used in conjunction with the Roman alphabet. These graphs are æ (as in <cat>) þ, ð (pronounced as in <thin> and <the>) and wyn (<w>). Of these, the first three are retained in the editions below. Written English saw the loss of æ, ð and wyn in the alphabet by the thirteenth century, but þ is retained for many centuries. From the twelfth century, another letter-form, yogh (ȝ), which was derived from the Old English form of *g*, became commonly used for the initial sound in words such as <yet> and for the sound of *gh* in <knight>.

During the twelfth century, in particular, changes that had been apparent in Old English from much earlier but which had been disguised by the use of the literary standard, West Saxon, came to the fore. While throughout the centuries of Anglo-Saxon rule, Latin had been used widely in addition to English as an official and literary language in England for a variety of administrative, ecclesiastical and scholarly writings,[13] after the Conquest, Latin and French displaced English as an official language. Thus there was no longer a standard English literary version for scribes to adhere to in their writings.

Writings that survive in English from *c.*1070 to *c.*1170 tend to be reworkings of earlier West Saxon material. As the West Saxon dialect was slightly archaic by the twelfth century, some English scribes imposed features of their own spelling, pronunciation and vocabulary that are more representative of contemporary twelfth-century language use onto the material they were copying. When original writings in English,[14] or translations from Latin into English, were made in this period, these language changes are much more obvious than in copied material: the twelfth century is the transitional phase, as Old English becomes early Middle English. Once we reach the Middle English period proper (*c.*1170–*c.*1450), because there was no longer a standard literary dialect, texts that survive are written in a variety of different dialects (Kentish, Southern, East Midland, West Midland, Northern). These dialects are represented in Middle English by different spellings of the same word (e.g., *sche* and *heo* both mean 'she', as does *he* in some texts), by different inflexions, or endings, on nouns, adjectives and verbs, and by different vocabulary. Thus, towards the end of the period, in 1385, John of Trevisa, translating Ranulph Higden's *Polychronicon* into English, said:

> Therefore it is that people of the Midlands are, as it were, partners of the ends [of England], and understand those languages from either side, North and South, better than the Northerners and Southerners understand

11   For an excellent discussion of the origin of English and its subsequent history to modern times see A. C. Baugh and T. Cable, *A History of English Language*, 3rd edn (London, 1978). The comprehensive *Cambridge History of the English Language*, volumes 1 and 2, discusses the Old and Middle English periods in detail. The relationships between these numerous dead and living languages are explained by comparative philology. In essence, this language science analyses similarities in vocabulary and phonology to determine how languages are related, and from examining the analogies, the probable forms of Indo-European itself can be reconstructed.

12   It should be borne in mind that the majority of written material that survives from this period is composed in the West Saxon

dialect, the standard literary language of Anglo-Saxon England from the tenth century until the twelfth. Some texts in the other dialects do survive, but, in relative terms, there are few of them.

13   See M. Lapidge, 'The Anglo-Latin Background', in *A New Critical History of Old English Literature*, eds S. B. Greenfield and D. G. Calder (London, 1986), pp. 5–37. A significant number of Latin loanwords have helped to shape English during its evolution. These include numerous religious words ('monk', 'disciple', 'candle', 'episcopal'); legal words ('subpoena', 'penalty', 'legal'); and many scholarly and administrative terms.

14   Such as *The Peterborough Chronicle*.

each other. The language of Northumbria, and especially at York, is so sharp, grinding and piercing, and ill formed, that we Southern people can only understand that language with difficulty.[15]

This complaint about the unintelligibility of different dialects is one that is still heard in England today; Trevisa's comments summarize well the difficulties that arose from the diversity of spoken and written language in the Middle English period. This extends into the fifteenth century when the beginning of Standard English can be traced, influenced primarily by dialects from the East Midlands and London area, and initiated by Chancery scribes, among others.

Old and Middle English are therefore a continuum in the development of the English language as a whole, before the period in which a standard literary form of the language arose. In the period covered by this volume we are dealing with language that not only looks very different from Modern English, but which also can look different from one text to the next. To begin with, the spelling of Old and Middle English is often quite unlike that of Modern English. In addition, much of the vocabulary of this earlier form of the language has died out. Furthermore, Old English can be labelled for convenience as a synthetic or inflected language (although it is not completely synthetic), while Middle English shows far fewer inflexions, but a much wider variety of dialectal forms.

Word order was more flexible in this earlier period too. In Modern English, word order in declarative clauses tends to be Subject-Verb-Object (SVO) as in 'Andy opens the parcel'; but in Old English, for example, word order could be Verb-Subject (*Þa sende se cyning* – 'then sent the king') or Subject-Object-Verb (usually in dependent clauses such as *Ða ic ða ðis eall gemunde* – 'When I then this all remembered') although SVO is common (*Hi wæron þæs Hælendes gewitan* – 'they were the Saviour's witnesses'). Throughout the medieval period, the tendency was increasingly towards use of SVO, but variations did exist particularly in poetic texts when the demands of the metre or alliteration often outweighed syntactic considerations.

The flexibility of word order is related to the use of inflexions to an extent. In a language that is inflected (such as modern German), one can determine the role each part of speech plays in a clause by its inflexion or overall spelling. Each noun, pronoun, demonstrative article ('the, that, this') and adjective in Old English was a particular grammatical gender – feminine, masculine, neuter – and declined, or changed its spelling, according to this gender and the grammatical role within the sentence. Thus, each part of speech can be labelled as a particular case depending on the word's use in a clause (subject, object, indirect object and possessive object), and whether it indicates a singular or plural number. For example, in Modern English, in a sentence such as 'That man overtook the woman with the policeman's car' we have four cases and a verb:

The man	= subject (or nominative)
overtook	= verb
the woman	= direct object (or accusative)
with	= preposition
the policeman's	= possessive (or genitive)[16]
car.	= indirect object (or dative)

All Old English nouns, pronouns, demonstrative articles and adjectives can be any one of these four cases depending on its role in a clause.[17] This is also true in Modern English, of course, except that the forms of the words often look the same irrespective of whether the word is a subject or object. In Old English, however, the case can usually be determined by its inflexion, or by the inflexion of the accompanying demonstrative article ('*the* man'), or by the inflexion of a modifying adjective ('the *good* man'). In Old English, these elements, article + adjective + noun, can be said to be in concord: that is, they will always agree with each other in gender (feminine, masculine, neuter), number (singular or plural)

15   My translation from the text as edited by F. Mossé, ed., *A Handbook of Middle English*, trans. J. A. Walker (Baltimore, 1952), pp. 285–89, at p. 289.

16   The Modern English possessive or genitive case retains its inflexion of the apostrophe *s*, derived from the Old English genitive singular *–es* inflexion; for example, *the cat's bowl*.

17   There is a fifth, known as the instrumental case, that is used to express time, accompaniment or manner. See B. Mitchell and F. C. Robinson, *A Guide to Old English*, 5th edn (Oxford, 1995), § 192. See Mitchell and Robinson, pp. 17–35, for more detailed information about these matters; see also R. Quirk and C. L. Wrenn, *An Old English Grammar*, 2nd edn (London, 1957; repr. 1989).

and case (nominative, accusative, etc.). Some examples of this concord in a masculine noun[18] would be:

se tila mann	= 'the good man' (nominative singular)
þone tilan mann	= 'the good man' (accusative singular)
þæs tilan mannes	= 'of the good man'/'the good man's' (genitive singular)
þæm tilan menn	= 'to, with, by, from etc. the good man' (dative singular)
þa tilan menn	= 'the good men' (nominative plural)
þa tilan menn	= 'the good men' (accusative plural)
þara tilra manna	= 'of the good men'/'the good men's' (genitive plural)
þæm tilum mannum	= 'to, with, by, from etc. the good men' (dative plural)

A full nominal (noun or pronoun) declension can be shown by the following two examples from the feminine declension and the neuter declension:

Glof 'glove' (a feminine noun)

	Singular	Plural
Nominative	seo glof (the glove etc.)	þa glofa (the gloves etc.)
Accusative	þa glofe	þa glofa
Genitive	þære glofe	þara glofa
Dative	þære glofe	þæm glofum

Wif 'woman' (a neuter noun)

	Singular	Plural
Nominative	þæt wif (the woman etc.)	þa wif (the women etc.)
Accusative	þæt wif	þa wif
Genitive	þæs wifes	þara wifa
Dative	þæm wife	þæm wifum

The declensions given so far are relatively simple. There are numerous other types of nouns, feminine, masculine and neuter, that belong to other strong and weak declensions.[19] Apart from the demonstrative article (given above in concord with the nouns), which is the single most important declension for providing information about the part of speech of the subsequent noun, the declensions of the first, second and third person personal pronouns are very useful to know and are actually quite similar to their forms in Modern English:[20]

First person personal pronoun

	Singular	Plural
Nominative	ic (I)	we (we)
Accusative	me, mec (me)	us (us)
Genitive	min (my)	ure (our)
Dative	me (to, with me)	us (us)

---

18   The declension given here is only one of a number of masculine noun declensions. It shows demonstrative article + weak adjective + noun. There are also strong adjectives that are used in conjunction with a noun only, and these decline differently.

   Another very common declension would be that of the masculine noun *cyning* 'king'. The endings for this are:

	Singular	Plural
Nominative	cyning	cyningas
Accusative	cyning	cyningas
Genitive	cyninges	cyninga
Dative	cyninge	cyningum

19   For example, *nama* 'name' is a weak masculine noun. In this declension, the accusative, dative, genitive singular, nominative and accusative plural forms are all spelt *naman*. The nominative singular is *nama*; genitive plural *namena*; and dative plural *namum*.

20   Unlike Modern English, Old English had a form of first and second person personal pronoun that was specific to two people: 'we two' or 'you two'. It declines as follows:

	First person	Second person
Nominative	wit (we two)	git (you two)
Accusative	unc (us two)	inc (you two)
Genitive	uncer (of both of us)	incer (of you both)
Dative	unc (to, with us two)	inc (to, with you two)

Second person personal pronoun

	Singular	*Plural*
Nominative	þu (you)	ge (you)
Accusative	þe, þec (you)	eow (you)
Genitive	þin (your)	eower (your)
Dative	þe (to, with you)	eow (to, with you)

Third person personal pronoun

	Singular			*Plural*
	Masculine	*Feminine*	*Neuter*	*All genders*
Nominative	he (he)	heo (she)	hit (it)	hie, hi (they)
Accusative	hine (him)	hie, hi (her)	hit (it)	hie, hi (them)
Genitive	his (his)	hire (of her)	his (of it)	heora (their)
Dative	him (to him)	hire (to her)	him (to it)	him, heom (to them)

In the following sentence, it is clear that knowledge of the third person personal pronoun declension would help in understanding who is the subject of the clause and who is the object:

> Ond **hiene**[21] þa Cynewulf on Andred adræfde, ond he þær wunade oþ þæt **hiene** an swan ofstang æt Pryfetes flodan.

> And **him** then Cynewulf into Andred drove, and he there lived until **him** a swineherd killed at the stream at Privett.

It is clear that *hiene* (or *hine* as it is usually spelt) is the accusative case, the object in this clause, and thus Cynewulf (nominative or subject) is exiling 'him' (a person called Sigebryht). In the second clause, Sigebryht 'he' lives in Andred until a swineherd (nominative or subject) kills *hiene* 'him' (accusative or object; i.e. Sigebryht).

This type of sentence construction is often confusing for a student to translate. As we are accustomed in Modern English to SVO word order, we expect the subject to come first. In the sentence given here, the subjects (*Cynewulf, an swan*) in both clauses come after the object (*hiene*), and thus in this instance it is important to know that *hiene* is the object case of this pronoun.

While these inflexions are a fundamental aspect of Old English language, then, it is obvious from examples such as *wif* (where the nominative or accusative, singular or plural, are spelt the same) that the inflectional system is not the most efficient. Levelling of inflexions, or non-differentiation of cases by spelling, was already becoming common during the Anglo-Saxon period. This levelling continued throughout the transitional and Middle English periods, though not simultaneously in all regions of England. Inflexions became increasingly simplified, endings for the grammatical gender of nouns became indistinct, and in tandem with this, SVO word order came to dominate to make up for the possible confusion of cases.[22] By the twelfth century, in a text such as *The Peterborough Chronicle*, the dative plural *for ure sinnes* ('for our sins') shows that the *-um* ending of Old English (*for urum synnum*) had been lost. This levelling of inflections gives rise in Middle English to much simpler noun declensions that will be more familiar to Modern English speakers:

	Singular	*Plural*
Nominative	wyf (woman)	wyves (women)
Accusative	wyf	wyves
Genitive	wyves (woman's)	wyves
Dative	wyve	wyves

---

21 *hiene* is another way of spelling *hine*, the masculine accusative singular pronoun.

22 For more detail about Middle English language, see Mossé, *A* *Handbook of Middle English*, pp. 44–130; J. A. Burrow and T. Turville-Petre, eds, *A Book of Middle English* (Oxford, 1992), pp. 20–55.

	Singular	*Plural*
Nominative	king (king)	kinges (kings)
Accusative	king	kinges
Genitive	kinges (king's)	kinges
Dative	king(e)	kinges

The Modern English inflexions, apostrophe *'s* to denote possession (genitive 'dog*'s* bowl') and *-s* to denote plural ('dogs'), derive directly from these Middle English, and thus Old English, case endings.

Like nouns, adjectives too become simplified in the Middle English period. Most adjectives were spelt the same irrespective of their case or position in a sentence: *fre* ('generous'), *dere* ('dear') etc. Some adjectives ending in a consonant retained weak and strong forms but these will cause no problems to the reader: for example, the strong form of *god* ('good') is *god* in the singular and *gode* in the plural; its weak form is invariably *gode*.

The demonstrative article, so useful for determining noun cases in Old English, follows this general tendency towards simplification. The Old English forms *se* and *seo* (masculine and feminine nominative singular) disappeared to be replaced with *þe* (as in Modern English 'the'). Other cases still often showed some kind of inflexion, which varied according to the dialect in which the text was written. For example, *þene*, the accusative singular masculine in West Midlands texts is spelt *þane* in texts from southeastern regions; *þa*, the plural form in West Midlands texts, is spelt *þo* in texts from south-eastern regions; the genitive singular is usually *þas*; the dative singular is *þan* or *þon*; and the genitive and dative plurals are *þere* or *þare*.

Very similar to the declensions of Old English, and indeed to Modern English, are the Middle English first and second person personal pronouns. The forms of these are:

	Singular		*Plural*	
	1st Person	*2nd Person*	*1st Person*	*2nd Person*
Nominative	ich, I	þu	we	ʒe
Accusative	me	þe	us	ow
Genitive	min, mi	þin	ure	ower
Dative	me	þe	us	ow

The least straightforward declension is that of the third person personal pronoun. Its forms vary according to where or in which dialect a text was written:[23]

		Singular	
	Masculine	*Feminine*	*Neuter*
Nominative	he, hee, ha, a	heo, hue, ho/a/e/i, sche,[24] scho	hit, it, a
Accusative	hine, hin	hire, hir, hure	hit, it
Genitive	his, hise, hys	hire, her(e), hore, hir	his, hys
Dative	him	hire, hir, hure	him

Plural: all genders

Nominative	hy, heo, ho, he, ha, a (South); þai, þay, thai, þei, þeʒ (North and Midlands)
Accusative	hi, his(e), heom, hem (South); þaim, thame, þaim (North and Midlands)
Genitive	her(e), heore, hor, hure, hire (South); þeʒre, þayr (North and Midlands)
Dative	heom, hem, hom, ham (South); þaim, thame, þaim (North and Midlands)

As well as nouns, adjectives and demonstrative articles operating through a system of inflections in Old and Middle English, verbs too were considerably more inflected in this period than they are today. Essentially, there are two types of main verb: strong and weak. Strong verbs form their past tense with a

---

23   This is a simplified tabulation of these very important linguistic variants. The forms beginning with þ (pronounced 'th'), such as *þai* ('they') and *þayr* ('their'), are Scandinavian in origin. They eventually replaced the native third person plural pronouns, but this was a gradual process that took place at different rates according to where Scandinavian influence was initially strongest. We see these forms,

for example, in texts from the East Midlands from the thirteenth century.

24   The form *sche* (Modern English 'she') 'was adopted at very different times in different parts of the country': Burrow and Turville-Petre, *A Book of Middle English*, p. 27.

change of vowel or diphthong in the middle of the word (as in Modern English, 'I sing', 'I sang', 'I have sung'), while weak verbs form the past tense by using a dental suffix, or ending using <t> or <d>. Weak verbs in Modern English include 'walk' ('I walk', 'I walked') and 'spell' ('I spell', 'I spelt'). There are also anomalous verbs in Old and Middle English, such as 'to be', which are still irregular in Modern English. In addition, there are separate paradigms in Old and Middle English for the subjunctive mood, which expresses uncertainty or possibility. In Modern English, the subjunctive mood is expressed by using a modal verb: 'I might go out', 'the bus should be here soon'; but in medieval English the subjunctive is formed by the use of particular inflections. The paradigms given below of the weak verb 'to hear' demonstrate these inflections:

Old English		Middle English[25]
Infinitive	hieran ('to hear')	heren ('to hear')
Present Indicative		*Present Indicative*
Singular 1	hiere	here ('I hear')
Singular 2	hierst	herest ('you hear')
Singular 3	hierþ	hereð ('he, she, it hears')
Plural	hieraþ	hereð ('we, you, they hear')
Imperative		
Singular	hier	her ('Hear!')
Plural	hieraþ	hereð ('Hear!')
Present Subjunctive		
Singular	hiere	here ('I, you, (s)he, it may hear')
Plural	hieren	heren ('we, you, they may hear')
Preterite (Past) Indicative		
Singular 1	hierde	herde ('I heard')
Singular 2	hierdest	herdest ('you heard')
Singular 3	hierde	herde ('(s)he, it heard')
Plural	hierdon	herden ('we, you, they heard')
Preterite Subjunctive		
Singular	hierde	herde ('I etc. may have heard')
Plural	hierden	herden ('we may have heard')
Pres. Participle	hierende	herinde ('hearing')
Past Participle	(ge)hiered	iherd ('heard')

There are numerous other differences between the types and forms of verbs in medieval English that are too complex to outline here. Students should refer to any one of the numerous good Old and Middle English grammars for details,[26] and should use these grammars in conjunction with the translations and glosses provided in this volume to inform their own interpretation of the original texts.

Editorial and Translation Policies

Selecting texts for an anthology is an ordeal by fire. The texts selected here have been chosen for the following reasons: they are essential teaching texts (Alfred's *Preface* to Gregory's *Pastoral Care*; *The Wanderer*; Ælfric's *Catholic Homilies*; *The Owl and the Nightingale*; *Sir Orfeo*, etc.); they are representative texts

25   This is a thirteenth-century West Midlands paradigm. Other dialects from later periods will differ. See Burrow and Turville-Petre, *A Book of Middle English*. For Old English, see Mitchell and Robinson, *A Guide to Old English*.

26   See the bibliography, under 'Language'.

(Bede, Riddles and Lyrics, the Trinity Homily, etc.); or they are simply enjoyable and instructive texts (*Apollonius of Tyre, The Fox and the Wolf, Cursor Mundi, Kyng Alisaunder*). Many of the texts in this edition appear elsewhere: there will always be a core of canon works that cannot be ignored. Some of the texts and excerpts here, however, are not usually edited in anthologies; many of these are personal favourites that I believe have a use in courses of medieval literature.

This book is aimed primarily at literature students. For that reason, there is not a great deal of language information in this volume. I deliberately decided against providing a substantial glossary (of enormous proportions), and instead chose to translate and gloss. This will not be to everyone's taste, but it does make these texts accessible to students who are not language specialists. There are excellent translations currently in print (such as S. A. J. Bradley's *Anglo-Saxon Poetry*)[27] but these do not generally provide the original text. Students ought to be able to study the Modern English alongside the original as a starting point in their study of early literature.

I have chosen to adopt what I believe is a sensible mixed translation policy for the texts, providing full translations for all the Old and earlier Middle English material, and only marginal glosses for the later texts. I have endeavoured to translate the texts accurately, generally using Clark Hall and Meritt, *A Concise Anglo-Saxon Dictionary*, for the Old English and *The Middle English Dictionary*, eds Kurath and Kuhn et al., for the Middle English.[28] I have also frequently used the glossaries supplied by editors of anthologies and individual texts. My debt to the work of earlier editors is referenced throughout the volume, and this book builds on the scholarship of many excellent medievalists for which I have been very grateful.

As the translations adhere closely to the original wherever possible, this has sometimes resulted in a rather syntactically stilted Modern English version with the inevitable loss of the poetic poise of the Old or earlier Middle English. In addition, translating an individual, often polysemic, medieval word into a Modern English 'equivalent' results in a single interpretation that may not be to everyone's satisfaction.[29] However, a close, semi-literal translation means that a student engaged in a reading of the original text should be able to follow the text with ease. With the additional assistance of a dictionary and grammar, students ought to be able to interpret the text for themselves, as I hope that they might wish to do.

Students should be aware that editing the material in the first place puts the edited version at one substantial remove from the actual text. There can be no substitute for returning to the manuscript, and putting trust in the scribe rather than in the editor's mediation. For much of the Old English material, in particular, I have had recourse to printed editions and editorial emendations, and for many texts, such as *Beowulf* and *Hali Meiðhad*, the work of previous scholars has proved invaluable. Textual emendations are listed towards the end of the volume. My principle is always to provide the manuscript reading rather than to emend; emendation only occurs when the scribe's form makes no sense or is illegible.

I have generally chosen to follow the manuscript version of a text employed by the editor of the relevant scholarly edition. This is partially for ease of reference for the student, but also because the base text of earlier editions is usually the most satisfactory. Where a text exists in more than one version, I do not provide a collated text; I adhere to a single manuscript copy.

Within the editions in this volume, I have provided no standardization of the host of orthographic variations in this period of literature. I have not normalized <þ> or <ð>, <æ> or <ȝ>, to <th>, <a/e> or <y/gh> as I believe this misleads the student and makes the subsequent study of Old and Middle English more difficult. I have, however, provided modern punctuation, capitalizing the first person personal pronoun, and the names of the Deity and personal pronouns. I have normalized the letters <u/v> and <i/j> throughout the texts as I believe them to represent graphemic rather than phonetic convention; following that principle, I have not emended <u> for <w> as in *suete*, for example, as this use of

27   S. A. J. Bradley, *Anglo-Saxon Poetry*, 2nd edn (London, 1995).

28   J. R. Clark Hall ed., *A Concise Anglo-Saxon Dictionary*, supp. H. D. Meritt, 4th edn (Toronto, 1960); H. Kurath and S. M. Kuhn et al., eds, *The Middle English Dictionary* (Ann Arbor, 1956–).

29   See E. G. Stanley's exemplary discussion of the difficulties of interpreting the semantic range of individual Old English words in

'Some Problematic Sense-Divisions in Old English: "glory" and "victory"; "noble", "glorious", and "learned" ', in *Heroic Poetry in the Anglo-Saxon Period: Studies in Honor of Jess B. Bessinger, Jr.*, eds H. Damico and J. Leyerle, *Studies in Medieval Culture* 32 (Kalamazoo, 1993), pp. 171–226.

<u> here is clearly phonetic. I have expanded all abbreviations silently, and set verse into its now conventional format for both the Old and Middle English texts.

The edition necessarily becomes my interpretation of the text. This, together with the provision of selective translations and glosses, imposes a subjective reading on the Old and Middle English that cannot, in any way, be regarded as the ideal substitute for the student's own reading of the original text.

Bede's *Ecclesiastical History*

CÆDMON'S *HYMN*

St Petersburg, Saltykov-Schedrin Public Library, Q. v. I. 18, contains at the bottom of f. 107r arguably the earliest surviving written record of oral Old English poetry: Cædmon's *Hymn*. It is included as an addition to Bede's Latin *Historia Ecclesiastica Gentis Anglorum*, 'Ecclesiastical History of the English People', which was copied into this manuscript (known as the Leningrad Bede) *c*.735, at Monkwearmouth-Jarrow where Bede was a monk. Bede completed his *Historia* in 731, and it is, without doubt, one of the most important sources for the history of the period. In relating the life-story of Abbess Hild, Bede recounts an event about a certain Cædmon, a lay worker at the abbey of Whitby during the abbacy of Hild in the late seventh century. He was unable to participate in the traditional entertainment at the feast – reciting poetry to the accompaniment of the harp – because he had never learned the art of composing songs in verse. One night, as the harp player approached him, he left and went to the cattle-shed to look after the animals in his care. He had a vision in which a celestial visitor asked him to sing. He replied that he could not sing. The visitor insisted that Cædmon should sing something about the Creation. Immediately, Cædmon was able to compose a poem praising God, the creator of all things.

At this point in the *Historia*, Bede paraphrases Cædmon's hymn of praise in Latin, and then goes on to narrate that the following day, Cædmon was able to recall and expand on the hymn he had sung. His miraculous powers were made known to the abbess, and from that time on, Cædmon, who became a monk, was able to turn into poetry all the scriptural stories read to him by the brothers at Whitby.

In some of the manuscripts that contain the Latin *Historia*, Cædmon's *Hymn* has been rendered into Old English in the margin or at the bottom of the relevant page. In St Petersburg, Q. v. I. 18, as mentioned above,

it is written in three lines in the lower margin of folio 107 recto. It is composed in the Northumbrian dialect, as are four other versions of the *Hymn*. In other manuscripts dating from the late ninth century onwards, Bede's *Historia* was itself translated into Old English as part of Alfred's educational programme, and thus the *Hymn* appears in Old English within the text.[1] The remaining versions of the poem are written in the more commonly recorded West Saxon dialect, and one of these versions of the story and *Hymn* is edited in the text following this.

The form and interpretation of the *Hymn* have been discussed in many critical commentaries.[2] The *Hymn* is the earliest recorded poem that employs the structure and method of oral poetic composition traditional to the Germanic peoples. The form, the four-stressed alliterative verse-line divided structurally into two halves by the caesura (though this is not visually recorded in manuscript copies of poetic texts), was that used previously solely for composing heroic verse. Here, documented for the first time, is the heroic verse form employed to praise the Christian God. Fred Robinson points out that the opening word of the poem, *Nu*, marks this text as of especial importance.[3] Verse previously used for the praising or eulogizing of heroic deeds, kings, and legendary episodes in history was from this period onwards to be adapted for use in praising the Christian God: a new age for the Anglo-Saxons. Among other things, it is this combination of the Germanic form of poetic composition with the religious content that makes the poem so important in the history of English literature.

Below, the Northumbrian *Hymn* from the eighth-century manuscript, St Petersburg, Saltykov-Schedrin Public Library, Q. v. I. 18, is presented. A second, West Saxon version from the tenth-century manuscript, Oxford, Bodleian Library, Tanner 10, follows in the next pair of texts, within its Old English context, for comparison.

1   K. O'Brien O'Keeffe discusses the implications of manuscript layout and punctuation in the extant versions of Cædmon's *Hymn* in 'Orality and the Developing Text of Cædmon's *Hymn*', in *Anglo-Saxon Manuscripts: Basic Readings*, ed. M. P. Richards (New York, 1994), pp. 221–50, and in her *Visible Song: Transitional Literacy in Old English Verse*, Cambridge Studies in Anglo-Saxon England 4 (Cambridge, 1990).
2   See for example S. B. Greenfield and D. G. Calder, eds, *A New Critical History of Old English Literature* (London, 1986), pp. 227–31;

F. P. Magoun, 'Bede's Story of Cædmon: The Case-History of an Anglo-Saxon Oral Singer', *Speculum* 30 (1955), 49–63; P. R. Orton, 'Cædmon and Christian Poetry', *Neuphilologische Mitteilungen* 84 (1983), 163–70.
3   F. C. Robinson, 'The Accentuation of *Nu* in *Cædmon's Hymn* ', in *Heroic Poetry in the Anglo-Saxon Period: Studies in Honor of Jess B. Bessinger, Jr.*, eds H. Damico and J. Leyerle (Kalamazoo, 1993), pp. 115–20.

Cædmon's *Hymn*

Nu scilun herga   hefenricæs Uard,
Metudæs mehti   and his modgithanc,
uerc Uuldurfadur,   sue he uundra gihuæs,
eci Dryctin,   or astelidæ.
5   He ærist scop   aeldu barnum
hefen to hrofæ,   halig Sceppend;
tha middingard   moncynnæs Uard,
eci Dryctin,   æfter tiadæ
firum foldu,   Frea allmehtig.

The Settlement of the Angles, Saxons and Jutes; The Life of Cædmon

During the reign of King Alfred (871–99), Bede's *Ecclesiastical History* was translated into Old English as part of Alfred's programme of educational reform outlined in his own *Preface* to Gregory's *Pastoral Care*. Scholars agree that Alfred did not translate this version of Bede himself, partly because of the occurrences of Anglian dialectal forms in the text, but it is possible that one of Alfred's circle of advisors and scholars was responsible for it. There are five extant manuscripts of the work in varying states of completeness: Oxford, Bodleian Library, Tanner 10, dated to the first half of the tenth century, and from which the story of Cædmon is edited; Cambridge, Corpus Christi College, 41, from the first half of the eleventh century; the burnt manuscript, London, British Library, Cotton Otho B. xi (mid-tenth century); Oxford, Corpus Christi College, 279, part II (beginning of the eleventh century); and Cambridge University Library Kk. 3. 18, from the second half of the eleventh century, and from which 'The Settlement of the Angles, Saxons and Jutes' is edited. The Old English version of the text abbreviates Bede's original to concentrate on matters specifi-

cally relevant to the English, and it tends to focus on the miraculous and religious events of Bede's original. The syntax of the translation is occasionally convoluted, as the first fifteen or so lines of the account of Cædmon below amply show, but it is also often clear and relatively poetic in its diction. The first text edited here is extracted from the *Ecclesiastical History*, book 1, chapter xv, and recounts the arrival of the Anglo-Saxon settlers in the fifth century. Bede's account is one of the most important for this period of history.

The second extract, the story of Cædmon (who died *c*.670), is told as an important incident in the narration of Abbess Hild's life (book 4, chapter xxiv).[4] Printed as the first text in this volume is the eighth-century Northumbrian version of the poem for comparison. This incident in the narration of Hild's life is usually provided in anthologies because of the information the story provides about the first named Old English poet, and the methods of oral poetic composition that can be inferred from it.

The Settlement of the Angles, Saxons and Jutes

Ða wæs ymb feower hund wintra and nigon and feowertig fram ures Drihtnes menniscnysse þæt
Martianus casere rice onfeng and vii gear hæfde. Se wæs syxta eac feowertigum fram Agusto þam
casere. Ða Angelþeod and Seaxna wæs geladod fram þam foresprecenan cyninge, and on Breotone
com on þrim myclum scypum, and on eastdæle þyses ealondes eardungstowe onfeng þurh ðæs
5   ylcan cyninges bebod, þe hi hider geladode, þæt hi sceoldan for heora eðle compian and feohtan.
And hi sona compedon wið heora gewinnan, þe hi oft ær norðan onhergedon; and Seaxan þa sige
geslogan. Þa sendan hi ham ærenddracan and heton secgan þysses landes wæstmbærnysse and
Brytta yrgþo. And hi þa sona hider sendon maran sciphere strengran wihgena; and wæs
unoferswiðendlic weorud, þa hi togædere geþeodde wæron. And him Bryttas sealdan and geafan
10   eardungstowe betwih him, þæt hi for sibbe and for hælo heora eðles campodon and wunnon wið
heora feondum, and hi him andlyfne and are forgeafen for heora gewinne.

Comon hi of þrim folcum ðam strangestan Germanie, þæt of Seaxum and of Angle and of

4   See B. Colgrave and R. A. B. Mynors, eds, *Bede's Ecclesiastical History of the English People*, Oxford Medieval Texts (Oxford, 1969), pp. 414–21.

Cædmon's *Hymn*

Now we ought to praise the Guardian of the heavenly kingdom,
the might of the Creator and his conception,
the work of the glorious Father, as he of each of the wonders,
eternal Lord, established the beginning.
5   He first created for the sons of men[5]
heaven as a roof, holy Creator;
then the middle-earth, the Guardian of mankind,
the eternal Lord, afterwards made
the earth for men, the Lord almighty.

The Settlement of the Angles, Saxons and Jutes

It was about four hundred and forty-nine years after our Lord's incarnation that the Emperor Martian acceded to the throne and he held it for seven years. He was also the forty-sixth after the Emperor Augustus. Then the people of the Angles and Saxons were invited by the aforesaid king [Vortigern] and came to Britain in three large ships, and they received a place to live in the east part of the island through the instruction of that same king who invited them here, so that they might battle and fight on behalf of the homeland. And immediately, they fought against their enemies who had often previously attacked them from the north; and the Saxons won the victory. Then they sent a messenger home and instructed him to speak about the fertility of this land and the cowardice of the Britons. And straightaway they sent here more naval forces with stronger warriors; and this was to be an invincible army when they were united together. And the Britons offered and gave them a place to live among themselves, so that for peace and for prosperity they would fight and battle for their homeland against their enemies, and they gave them provisions and property because of their battles.

5   *ældu barnum*, 'the sons/children of men', becomes *eorðan bearnum*,
'the children of earth', in the West Saxon version.

Geatum. Of Geata fruman syndon Cantware and Wihtsætan; þæt is seo ðeod þe Wiht þæt ealond
oneardað. Of Seaxum, þæt is, of ðam lande þe mon hateð Ealdseaxan, coman Eastseaxan and
15 Suðseaxan and Westseaxan. And of Engle coman Eastengle and Middelengle and Myrce and eall
Norðhembra cynn; is þæt land ðe Angulus is nemned, betwyh Geatum and Seaxum; is sæd of
ðære tide þe hi ðanon gewiton oð todæge þæt hit weste wunige. Wæron ða ærest heora latteowas
and heretogan twegen gebroðra, Hengest and Horsa. Hi wæron Wihtgylses suna, þæs fæder wæs
Wihta haten, and þæs Wihta fæder wæs Woden nemned, of ðæs strynde monigra mægða
20 cyningcynn fruman lædde. Ne wæs ða ylding to þon þæt hi heapmælum coman maran weorod of
þam þeodum þe wæ ær gemynegodon. And þæt folc ðe hider com ongan weaxan and myclian to
þan swiðe þæt hi wæron on myclum ege þam sylfan landbigengan ðe hi ær hider laðedon and
cygdon.

Æfter þissum hi ða geweredon to sumre tide wið Pehtum, þa hi ær ðurh gefeoht feor adrifan.
25 And þa wæron Seaxan secende intingan and towyrde heora gedales wið Bryttas. Cyðdon him
openlice and sædon, nemne hi him maran andlyfne sealdon, þæt hi woldan him sylfe niman and
hergian, þær hi hit findan mihton. And sona ða beotunge dædum gefyldon; bærndon and hergedon
and slogan fram eastsæ oð westsæ, and him nænig wiðstod. Ne wæs ungelic wræcc þam ðe iu
Chaldeas bærndon Hierusaleme weallas and ða cynelican getimbro mid fyre fornaman for ðæs
30 Godes folces synnum. Swa þonne her fram þære arleasan ðeode, hwæðere rihte Godes dome, neh
ceastra gehwylce and land wæs forheriende. Hrusan afeollan cynelico getimbro somod and anlipie,
and gehwær sacerdas and mæssepreostas betwih wibedum wæron slægene and cwylmde; biscopas
mid folcum buton ænigre are sceawunge ætgædere mid iserne and lige fornumene wæron. And
ne wæs ænig se ðe bebyrignysse sealde þam ðe swa hreowlice acwealde wæron. And monige ðære
35 earman lafe on westenum fanggene wæron and heapmælum sticode. Sume for hungre heora feondum
on hand eodon and ecne þeowdom geheton wið ðon þe him mon andlyfne forgeafe; sume ofer sæ
sorgiende gewiton; sume forhtiende on eðle gebidan, and þearfendum life on wuda westene and
on hean clifum sorgiende mode symle wunodon.

The Life of Cædmon

In ðeosse abbudissan mynstre wæs sum broðor syndriglice mid godcundre gife gemæred ond
geweorðad, for þon he gewunade gerisenlice leoð wyrcan, þa ðe to æfæstnisse ond to arfæstnisse
belumpen, swa ðætte, swa hwæt swa he of godcundum stafum þurh boceras geleornode, þæt he
æfter medmiclum fæce in scopgereorde mid þa mæstan swetnisse ond inbryrdnisse geglængde
5 ond in Engliscgereorde wel geworht forþbrohte. Ond for his leoþsongum monigra monna mod
oft to worulde forhogdnisse ond to geþeodnisse þæs heofonlican lifes onbærnde wæron. Ond eac
swelce monige oðre æfter him in Ongelþeode ongunnon æfæste leoð wyrcan; ac nænig hwæðre
him þæt gelice don meahte, for þon he nales from monnum ne þurh mon gelæred wæs, þæt he
þone leoðcræft leornade, ac he wæs godcundlice gefultumed ond þurh Godes gife þone songcræft
10 onfeng. Ond he for ðon næfre noht leasunge ne idles leoþes wyrcan meahte, ac efne þa an þa ðe to
æfæstnesse belumpon, ond his þa æfestan tungan gedafenode singan.

Wæs he se mon in weoruldhade geseted oð þa tide þe he wæs gelyfdre ylde, ond næfre nænig
leoð geleornade. Ond he for þon oft in gebeorscipe, þonne þær wæs blisse intinga gedemed, þæt
heo ealle sceoldon þurh endebyrdnesse be hearpan singan. Þonne he geseah þa hearpan him nealecan,
15 þonne aras he for scome from þæm symble ond ham eode to his huse. Þa he þæt þa sumre tide
dyde, þæt he forlet þæt hus þæs gebeorscipes, ond ut wæs gongende to neata scipene, þara heord
him wæs þære neahte beboden, þa he ða þær in gelimplice tide his leomu on reste gesette ond
onslepte, þa stod him sum mon æt þurh swefn ond hine halette ond grette ond hine be his noman
nemnde: 'Cedmon, sing me hwæthwugu.' Þa ondswarede he ond cwæð: 'Ne con Ic noht singan;

They came from among the three most powerful Germanic tribes, those of the Saxons, the Angles and the Jutes. Of Jutish origins are the people in Kent and people of the Isle of Wight: that is the people who inhabit the Isle of Wight. From the Saxons, that is from that land which is called Saxony, come those in Essex, Sussex and Wessex. And from the Angles come the East Anglians and Middle Anglians and Mercians and all the people of Northumbria. That land which is called Angeln[6] is between Jutland and Saxony; it is said that from the time they left there until the present day that it remains deserted. The first of their leaders and commanders were two brothers, Hengest and Horsa. They were the sons of Wihtgyls, whose father was called Wihta, this Wihta's father was named Woden, from whose lineage many tribes of royal races claimed their origin. It was not long before more troops came in crowds from those people that we mentioned before. And the people who came here began to expand and grow to the extent that they were a great terror to those same inhabitants who had previously invited and summoned them here.

After this, they were united by agreement with the Picts,[7] whom they had previously driven far away through battle. And then the Saxons were seeking a cause and opportunity for their separation from the Britons. They informed them openly and said to them that unless they gave them more provisions they would take it and plunder it themselves wherever they might find it. And immediately the threat was carried out; they burned and ravaged and murdered from the east coast to the west, and no one withstood them. This was not unlike the former vengeance of the Chaldeans when they burned the walls of Jerusalem and destroyed the royal buildings with fire because of the sins of the people of God.[8] Thus here because of the graceless people, yet with the righteous judgement of God, nearly every city and land was ravaged. Royal private buildings were razed to the ground, and everywhere priests and mass-priests were murdered and killed among their altars; bishops with the people, without being shown any mercy, were destroyed with sword and fire together. And nor was there any burial given to those who were so cruelly killed. And many of the wretched survivors were captured in the wastelands and stabbed in groups. Because of hunger, some went into the hands of the enemy and promised perpetual slavery with the provision that they be given sustenance; some went sorrowing over the sea; some remained, always fearful, in their native land, and lived in deprivation in the deserted woods or dwelled on high cliffs, always with a mournful mind.

The Life of Cædmon

In this abbess's monastery was a certain brother made especially famous and honoured with a divine gift, because he was accustomed to producing suitable poetry which pertained to religion and piety, such that, whatever he learned from divine scriptures through scholars, he was able to transpose into poetry after a short period of time adorned with the most sweetness and inspiration, and to produce it well made in the English language. And because of his poetry, the minds of many men were often inspired towards contempt of the world and towards the joining of the heavenly life. And also, similarly, after him, many others among the English began to compose pious poems; but, however, none of them was able to do it like him, because he was not taught the poetic skill that he learned from men or by anyone at all, but he was divinely aided and received his skill at recitation through a gift of God. And because of this, he would never create fables or worthless poetry, but only that which concerned piety, and that was suitable for his pious tongue to sing.

He was established in the secular life until a time when he was advanced in years, and he had never learned any poetry. And he was often in drinking parties, when there was decreed, as a cause for joy, that they should all sing in turns to the accompaniment of the harp. When he saw the harp approach him, he rose up for shame from that feast and went home to his house. On a certain occasion when he did just that, he left the building of the drinking party, and went out to the animal shed, the care of which had been given to him that night. Then, in due time, he got himself settled in rest and slept, and a man stood before him as if in a dream and called him and greeted him and spoke to him by his name: 'Cædmon, sing me something.' Then he answered and said: 'I cannot sing; and therefore I left the party

---

6   i.e. Slesvig.

7   The Picts were a 'confederation of tribes living north of the Antonine Wall', as Isabel Henderson states s.v. 'Picts', in *The Blackwell*

Encyclopaedia of Anglo-Saxon England (Oxford, 1998), pp. 365–6.

8   4 Kings 25.8–10.

20   ond Ic for þon of þeossum gebeorscipe ut eode, ond hider gewat, for þon Ic naht singan ne cuðe.'
Eft he cwæð, se ðe wið hine sprecende wæs: 'Hwæðre þu me aht singan.' Þa cwæð he: 'Hwæt sceal
Ic singan?' Cwæð he: 'Sing me frumsceaft.' Þa he ða þas andsware onfeng, þa ongon he sona singan
in herenesse Godes Scyppendes þa fers ond þa word þe he næfre gehyrde, þære endebyrdnesse þis is:

Nu sculon herigean   heofonrices Weard,
25   Meotodes meahte   ond his modgeþanc,
weorc Wuldorfæder,   swa he wundra gehwæs,
ece Drihten,   or onstealde.
He ærest sceop   eorðan bearnum
heofon to hrofe,   halig Scyppend;
30   þa middangeard   moncynnes Weard,
ece Drihten,   æfter teode
firum foldan,   Frea ælmihtig.

Þa aras he from þæm slæpe, ond eal þa þe he slæpende song fæste in gemynde hæfde, ond þæm
wordum sona monig word in þæt ilce gemet Gode wyrðes songes to geþeodde. Þa com he on
35   morgenne to þæm tungerefan, þe his ealdormon wæs; sægde him hwylce gife he onfeng. Ond he
hine sona to þære abbudissan gelædde ond hire þa cyðde ond sægde. Þa heht heo gesomnian ealle
þa gelæredestan men ond þa leorneras, ond him ondweardum het secgan þæt swefn ond þæt leoð
singan, þæt ealra heora dome gecoren wære hwæt oððe hwonon þæt cuman wære. Þa wæs him
eallum gesegen, swa swa hit wæs, þæt him wære from Drihtne sylfum heofonlic gifu forgifen. Þa
40   rehton heo him ond sægdon sum halig spell ond godcundre lare word, bebudon him þa, gif he
meahte, þæt he in swinsunge leoþsonges þæt gehwyrfde. Þa he ða hæfde þa wisan onfongne, þa
eode he ham to his huse, and cwom eft on morgenne, ond þy betstan leoðe geglenged him asong,
ond ageaf þæt him beboden wæs.

Ða ongan seo abbudisse clyppan ond lufigean þa Godes gife in þæm men. Ond heo hine þa
45   monade ond lærde þæt he woruldhade anforlete ond munuchad onfenge; ond he þæt wel þafode.
Ond heo hine in þæt mynster onfeng mid his godum, ond hine geþeodde to gesomnunge þara
Godes þeowa, ond heht hine læran þæt getæl þæs halgan stæres ond spelles. Ond he eal þa he in
gehyrnesse geleornian meahte mid hine gemyndgade, ond swa swa clæne neten eodorcende, in
þæt sweteste leoð gehwerfde. Ond his song ond his leoð wæron swa wynsumu to gehyranne þætte
50   seolfan þa his lareowas æt his muðe wreoton ond leornodon.

Song he ærest be middangeardes gesceape ond bi fruman moncynnes ond eal þæt stær Genesis:
þæt is seo æreste Moyses booc. Ond eft bi utgonge Israhela folces of Ægypta londe ond bi ingonge
þæs gehatlandes ond bi oðrum monegum spellum þæs halgan gewrites canones boca. Ond bi
Cristes menniscnesse ond bi his þrowunge ond bi his upastignesse in heofonas, ond bi þæs Halgan
55   Gastes cyme ond þara apostola lare; ond eft bi þæm dæge þæs toweardan domes, ond bi fyrhtu
þæs tintreglican wiites ond bi swetnesse þæs heofonlecan rices he monig leoð geworhte. Ond
swelce eac oðer monig be þæm godcundan fremsumnessum ond domum he geworhte. In eallum
þæm he geornlice gemde þæt he men atuge from synna lufan ond mandæda, ond to lufan ond to
geornfulnesse awehte godra dæda; for þon he wæs se mon swiþe æfæst ond regollecum þeodscipum
60   eaðmodlice underþeoded. Ond wið þæm þa ðe in oðre wisan don woldon, he wæs mid welme
micelre ellenwodnisse onbærned. Ond he for ðon fægre ænde his lif betynde ond geendade.

For þon þa ðære tide nealæcte his gewitenesse ond forðfore, þa wæs he feowertynum dagum ær,
þæt he wæs lichomlicre untrymnesse þrycced ond hefgad, hwæðre to þon gemetlice þæt he ealle
þa tid meahte ge sprecan ge gongan. Wæs þær in neaweste untrumra monna hus, in þæm heora
65   þeaw wæs þæt heo þa untrumran ond þa ðe æt forðfore wæron inlædan sceoldon, ond him þær
ætsomne þegnian. Þa bæd he his þegn on æfenne þære neahte þe he of worulde gongende wæs
þæt he in þæm huse him stowe gegearwode, þæt he gerestan meahte. Þa wundrode se þegn for
hwon he ðæs bæde, for þon him þuhte þæt his forðfor swa neah nære; dyde hwæðre swa swa he
cwæð ond bibead.
70   Ond mid þy he ða þær on reste eode, ond he gefeonde mode sumu þing mid him sprecende

and came here, because I am not able to sing anything.' Again, the one who was speaking with him said: 'Nevertheless, you must sing something for me.' Then Cædmon said: 'What shall I sing?' He said: 'Sing to me about creation.' When he got this answer, he began to sing straightaway in praise of God the Creator, in verse and words that he had never heard, of which the arrangement is:

> Now praise the Guardian of the heavenly kingdom,
> the might of the Creator and his conception,
> the work of the glorious Father, as he established the beginning,
> eternal Lord, of each of the wonders.
> He first created for the children of earth
> heaven as a roof, holy Creator;
> then the middle-earth, the Guardian of mankind,
> eternal Lord, afterwards adorned
> the world for people, the Lord almighty.

Then he arose from sleeping, and all that he had sung while sleeping was secure in his memory, and immediately he added many words in the same metre to the words of the worthy poem to God. In the morning, he came to the estate's reeve who was his superior; he told him about the gift that he had received. And straightaway the reeve led him to the abbess and he informed and told her. Then she instructed that all the most learned men and students should be gathered together, and she asked Cædmon to tell them his dream and sing the poem, so that all of them who were selected might judge what the poem was and where it came from. And they all said, just as it was the case, that it seemed that he had been given a heavenly gift from God himself. When they narrated and told him a holy story and words of divine instruction, they asked him to turn it into harmonious poetry, if he was able. When he had absorbed that information, he went back to his house, and returned again in the morning and sang them the most ornate poem and by that, gave back what had been asked of him.

Then the abbess began to embrace and love God's gift in that man. And she advised and instructed him to leave the secular order and take up a monastic life; and he consented to do that. And she received him and all his possessions into that monastery, and he was joined with the community of God's servants, and she instructed him to learn the sequence of holy history and all its stories. And everything that he was able to learn by listening, he ruminated upon, just as a clean beast chewing the cud, and turned into the sweetest poetry. And his songs and poems were so joyful to hear that the self-same men who were his teachers wrote down what came from his mouth and studied it.

First he sang of the creation of this middle-earth and of the beginning of humanity and all that story of Genesis: that is, the first book of Moses. And afterward he sang about the Israelites' journey out of Egypt and entry into the promised land, and about many other sacred stories written in the canonical book. And he composed about Christ's incarnation, and about his suffering and his ascension to heaven, and about the advent of the Holy Ghost, and of the Apostles' teaching; and afterward, he composed many others about the future Day of Judgement, and the horror of tormenting punishment, and the sweetness of the heavenly kingdom. And likewise, he composed many others about divine benefits and judgements. In all his poetry he eagerly took care to draw men away from the love of sin and wickedness, and to arouse them towards love and desire of good deeds; this was because he was a very pious man, humbly devoted to monastic discipline. And to those who wished to act in other ways, he was very fervently inspired in his zealous aim. And therefore, he concluded and finished his life with a good death.

Thus, the time of his death and going forth drew near, when for fourteen days previously, he was physically oppressed and weighed down with infirmity, but in such a way that he could at all times both speak and walk. Nearby, there was a house for sick people, into which it was their custom to bring the infirm and those who were near to death, and to care for them there. Then he asked his servant on the evening of the night when he would be going from this world to get a place ready for him in that house, so that he might stay there. The servant wondered why Cædmon asked this, for it did not seem to him that his death was so near; even so, he did as he had said and asked.

And with that he went there to rest, and, rejoicing in mind, he was talking and laughing about things

ætgædere ond gleowiende wæs, þe þær ær inne wæron. Þa wæs ofer middeneaht þæt he frægn hwæðer heo ænig husl inne hæfdon. Þa ondswarodon heo ond cwædon: 'Hwylc þearf is ðe husles? Ne þinre forþfore swa neah is, nu þu þus rotlice ond þus glædlice to us sprecende eart.' Cwæð he eft: 'Berað me husl to.' Þa he hit þa on honda hæfde, þa frægn he hwæþer heo ealle smolt mod ond buton eallum incan bliðe to him hæfdon. Þa ondswaredon hy ealle ond cwædon þæt heo nænigne incan to him wiston, ac heo ealle him swiðe bliðemode wæron. Ond heo wrixendlice hine bædon þæt he him eallum bliðe wære. Þa ondswarade he ond cwæð: 'Mine broðor, mine þa leofan, Ic eom swiðe bliðemod to eow ond to eallum Godes monnum.' Ond swa wæs hine getrymmende mid þy heofonlecan wegneste ond him oðres lifes ingong gegearwode. Þa gyt he fraegn hu neah þære tide wære þætte þa broðor arisan scolden ond Godes lof ræran ond heora uhtsong singan. Þa ondswaredon heo: 'Nis hit feor to þon.' Cwæð he: 'Teala, wuton we wel þære tide bidan.' Ond þa him gebæd ond hine gesegnode mid Cristes rodetacne, ond his heafod onhylde to þam bolstre, ond medmicel fæc, onslepte. Ond swa mid stilnesse his lif geendade. Ond swa wæs geworden þætte swa swa he hluttre mode ond bilwitre ond smyltre wilsumnesse Drihtne þeode, þæt he eac swylce swa smylte deaðe middangeard wæs forlætende, ond to his gesihðe becwom. Ond seo tunge, þe swa monig halwende word in þæs Scyppendes lof gesette, he ða swelce eac þa ytmæstan word in his herenisse, hine seolfne segniende ond his gast in his honda bebeodende, betynde. Eac swelce þæt is gesegen þæt he wære gewis his seolfes forðfore, of þæm we nu secgan hyrdon.

together with those who were already there. Then just after midnight, he asked whether they had any consecrated bread and wine there. They answered him and said: 'Why do you have need of the Eucharist? Your departure cannot be so near, now that you are speaking so cheerfully and happily to us.' So he said once again: 'Bring me the Eucharist.' Then when he had it in his hand, he asked whether they all had a peaceful and friendly mind without any complaint against him. And they all answered and said that they had nothing to complain of about him, but they all felt very peaceably towards him. And they asked him in turn if he felt happy with all of them. Then he answered them saying: 'My brothers, my dearest men, I feel very contented towards you and towards all men of God.' And so he was strengthened with the heavenly viaticum,[9] and prepared himself for entry into another life. And still he asked how soon would it be time for the monks to rise to celebrate God's love and to sing their matins.[10] And they answered: 'It isn't long until then.' He said: 'Oh well, let us bide the time well.' And then he prayed and crossed himself with the sign of Christ's cross, and laid his head on the pillow, and within a short time, he fell asleep. And thus with peace his life ended. And thus it happened that just as he had served God with a pure mind and innocent and serene devotion, so he was likewise released from this earth with a serene death, and came to his sight. And his tongue, that had composed so many salutary words in praise of the Creator, likewise spoke its last words in his praise, as, crossing himself and commending his spirit into his hands, he died. So, similarly, it can be seen from what we have now heard said that he was aware of his own death.

---

9 The viaticum is the Eucharist given to those who are about to die: effectively, the last rites.

10 Matins is the first service of prayer in the monastic daily office, occurring at 6 a.m. in the winter, and 3.30 or 4 a.m. in summer.

Alfred

PREFACE TO THE TRANSLATION OF GREGORY'S PASTORAL CARE

One of the first works that Alfred included for translation in his programme of educational reform was Pope Gregory's *Cura Pastoralis*. This book, written in the 590s, advises ecclesiastical officers on the qualities that were fundamental in administering their pastoral duties, and on the kinds of activities and people that the bishop was likely to encounter. Alfred recognized the applicability of much of Gregory's work to a secular leader like himself, and, keenly aware of the responsibilities of the king and his bishops, outlined his reasons for translating this book, and others, in his letter to Bishop Wærferth which forms the *Preface* as edited below. Keynes and Lapidge rightly comment that 'this preface is considered a cardinal document in our understanding of King Alfred and of the literary culture of late Anglo-Saxon England in general'.[1] In the *Preface*, composed *c*.890, Alfred speaks of the decayed state of learning in England at the time of his accession to the throne and his proposed methods for remedying this situation. His intention to raise the standards of literacy among the clergy and freeborn men of England is a remarkable innovation, and essentially created the earliest sustained use of the vernacular as an official literary language. Alfred intended to send every bishopric in his kingdom a copy of the *Pastoral Care*, together with an 'æstel' (probably a pointer) worth fifty mancuses. To assist him in his overall plan, Alfred enlisted the help of a number of scholars from England and

abroad in the 880s: Plegmund, from Mercia, who became archbishop of Canterbury in 890; Asser, a Welsh bishop who wrote the *Life of King Alfred*;[2] Grimbold, from St Bertin in Flanders; John, a Saxon, who became abbot of Athelney; Wærferth, bishop of Worcester; and Æthelstan and Werwulf, Mercian priests.

There are six surviving manuscripts of the translation of the *Pastoral Care*, one of which (Cambridge, Trinity College, R. 5. 22, dated to the end of the tenth or beginning of the eleventh century) does not contain the *Preface*. Of the five that do, two were very badly damaged in the fire in Sir Robert Cotton's library in Ashburnham House in London in 1731.[3] These are London, British Library, Cotton Tiberius B. xi, dated to the end of the ninth century, and Cotton Otho B. ii, dated to the tenth century. Cambridge, Corpus Christi College 12, written at the beginning of the tenth century, and Cambridge, University Library Ii. 2. 4, written in the mid-eleventh century, contain complete copies of the text. It is Oxford, Bodleian Library, Hatton 20, however, that is considered the base manuscript for this work, and which is especially important for the evidence that it provides of the dialect of West Saxon in this period. It is dated to the end of the ninth century, and is the copy of the text that Alfred sent to the bishopric of Worcester. The following edition of the *Preface* is based on this manuscript.

Preface to the Translation of Gregory's *Pastoral Care*

Deos boc sceal to Wigora ceastre

Ælfred kyning hateð gretan Wærferð biscep his wordum luflice ond freondlice; ond ðe cyðan hate
ðæt me com swiðe oft on gemynd, hwelce wiotan iu wæron giond Angelcynn, ægðer ge godcundra
hada ge woruldcundra; ond hu gesæliglica tida ða wæron giond Angelcynn; ond hu ða kyningas
ðe ðone onwald hæfdon ðæs folces Gode ond his ærendwrecum hiersumedon; ond hu hie ægðer ge
5   hiora sibbe ge hiora siodo ge hiora onweald innanbordes gehioldon, ond eac ut hiora eðel gerymdon;
ond hu him ða speow ægðer ge mid wige ge mid wisdome; ond eac ða godcundan hadas, hu
giorne hie wæron ægðer ge ymb lare ge ymb liornunga, ge ymb ealle ða ðiowotdomas ðe hie Gode
don scoldon; ond hu man utanbordes wisdom ond lare hieder on lond sohte; ond hu we hie nu
sceoldon ute begietan, gif we hie habban sceoldon. Swæ clæne hio wæs oðfeallenu on Angelcynne
10   ðæt swiðe feawa wæron behionan Humbre ðe hiora ðeninga cuðen understondan on Englisc oððe
furðum an ærendgewrit of Lædene on Englisc areccean; ond Ic wene ðætte noht monige begiondan
Humbre næren. Swæ feawa hiora wæron ðæt Ic furðum anne anlepne ne mæg geðencean be suðan
Temese ða ða Ic to rice feng. Gode ælmihtegum sie ðonc ðætte we nu ænigne onstal habbað

1 S. Keynes and M. Lapidge, eds, *Alfred the Great: Asser's Life of King Alfred and Other Contemporary Sources* (London, 1983), p. 124.
2 See Keynes and Lapidge, *Alfred the Great*, for all of this information plus a good selection of translated texts relating to Alfred's reign.
3 For the catastrophic events of 23 October 1731 at Ashburnham House, and the subsequent attempts to reconstitute damaged manuscripts, see A. Prescott, 'The Ghost of Asser', in *Anglo-Saxon Manuscripts and their Heritage*, eds P. Pulsiano and E. M. Treharne (Aldershot, 1998), pp. 255–91, and references therein.

Preface to the translation of Gregory's *Pastoral Care*

This book shall go to Worcester

King Alfred sends greetings to Bishop Wærferth with his loving and friendly words, and bids you know that it has very often come to my mind what wise men there were formerly throughout the English people, both in sacred and in secular orders; and how there were happy times then throughout England; and how the kings who had authority over the people were obedient to God and his messengers; and how they both maintained their peace and their morality and their authority at home, and also enlarged their territory abroad; and how they prospered both in warfare and in widsom; and also how zealous the sacred orders were both about teaching and about learning as well as all the services that they had to perform for God; and how people from abroad came here to this country in search of knowledge and instruction, and how we should now have to get them from abroad, if we were to acquire them. So complete was learning's decay among the English people that there were very few this side of the Humber who could understand their services in English, or even translate a letter from Latin into English; and I imagine that there were not many beyond the Humber. There were so few of them that I cannot even remember a single one south of the Thames when I succeeded to the kingdom. Thanks be to

lareowa. Ond for ðon Ic ðe bebiode ðæt ðu do swæ Ic geliefe ðæt ðu wille: ðæt ðu ðe ðissa
woruldðinga to ðæm geæmetige, swæ ðu oftost mæge, ðæt ðu ðone wisdom ðe ðe God sealde ðær
ðær ðu hiene befæstan mæge, befæste. Geðenc hwelc witu us ða becomon for ðisse worulde, ða ða
we hit nohwæðer ne selfe ne lufedon, ne eac oðrum monnum ne lefdon; ðone naman ænne we
lufodon ðætte we Cristne wæren, ond swiðe feawa ða ðeawas.

Ða Ic ða ðis eall gemunde, ða gemunde Ic eac hu Ic geseah – ær ðæm ðe hit eall forhergod wære
ond forbærned – hu ða ciricean giond eall Angelcynn stodon maðma ond boca gefyldæ, ond eac
micel mengeo Godes ðiowa. Ond ða swiðe lytle fiorme ðara boca wiston, for ðæm ðe hie hiora
nanwuht ongiotan ne meahton, for ðæm ðe hie næron on hiora agen geðiode awritene. Swelce hie
cwæden: 'Ure ieldran, ða ðe ðas stowa ær hioldon, hie lufodon wisdom, ond ðurh ðone hie begeaton
welan ond us læfdon. Her mon mæg giet gesion hiora swæð, ac we him ne cunnon æfter spyrigean.
Ond for ðæm we habbað nu ægðer forlæten ge ðone welan ge ðone wisdom, for ðæm ðe we noldon
to ðæm spore mid ure mode onlutan.'

Ða Ic ða ðis eall gemunde, ða wundrade Ic swiðe swiðe ðara godena wiotena ðe giu wæron
giond Angelcynn, ond ða bec eallæ be fullan geliornod hæfdon, ðæt hie hiora ða nænne dæl
noldon on hiora agen geðiode wendan. Ac Ic ða sona eft me selfum andwyrde, ond cwæð: 'Hie ne
wendon ðætte æfre menn sceolden swæ reccelease weorðan ond sio lar swæ oðfeallan: for ðære
wilnunga hie hit forleton, ond woldon ðæt her ðy mara wisdom on londe wære ðy we ma geðeoda
cuðon.' Ða gemunde Ic hu sio æ wæs ærest on Ebriscgeðiode funden, ond eft, ða hie Creacas
geliornodon, ða wendon hie hie on heora agen geðiode ealle, ond eac ealle oðre bec. Ond eft
Lædenware swæ same, siððan hie hie geliornodon, hie hie wendon ealla ðurh wise wealhstodas on
hiora agen geðiode. Ond eac ealla oðræ Cristnæ ðioda sumne dæl hiora on hiora agen geðiode
wendon.

For ðy me ðyncð betre, gif iow swæ ðyncð, ðæt we eac sumæ bec, ða ðe niedbeðearfosta sien
eallum monnum to wiotonne, ðæt we ða on ðæt geðiode wenden ðe we ealle gecnawen mægen,
ond gedon, swæ we swiðe eaðe magon mid Godes fultume, gif we ða stilnesse habbað, ðætte eall
sio gioguð ðe nu is on Angelcynne friora monna, ðara ðe ða speda hæbben ðæt hie ðæm befeolan
mægen, sien to liornunga oðfæste, ða hwile ðe hie to nanre oðerre note ne mægen, oð ðone first ðe
hie wel cunnen Englisc gewrit arædan. Lære mon siððan furður on Lædengeðiode ða ðe mon
furðor læran wille ond to hieran hade don wille.

Ða Ic ða gemunde hu sio lar Lædengeðiodes ær ðissum afeallen wæs giond Angelcynn, ond
ðeah monige cuðon Englisc gewrit arædan, ða ongan Ic ongemang oðrum mislicum ond
manigfealdum bisgum ðisses kynerices ða boc wendan on Englisc ðe is genemned on Læden
Pastoralis, ond on Englisc 'Hierdeboc', hwilum word be worde, hwilum andgit of andgiete, swæ
swæ Ic hie geliornode æt Plegmunde minum ærcebiscepe, ond æt Assere minum biscepe, ond æt
Grimbolde minum mæsseprioste, ond æt Johanne minum mæssepreoste. Siððan Ic hie ða geliornod
hæfde, swæ swæ Ic hie forstod, ond swæ Ic hie andgitfullicost areccean meahte, Ic hie on Englisc
awende; ond to ælcum biscepstole on minum rice wille ane onsendan; ond on ælcre bið an æstel,
se bið on fiftegum mancessa. Ond Ic bebiode on Godes naman ðæt nan mon ðone æstel from ðære
bec ne do, ne ða boc from ðæm mynstre. Uncuð hu longe ðær swæ gelærede biscepas sien, swæ
swæ nu, Gode ðonc, welhwær siendon. For ðy Ic wolde ðætte hie ealneg æt ðære stowe wæren,
buton se biscep hie mid him habban wille, oððe hio hwær to læne sie, oððe hwa oðre bi write.

almighty God that now we have any supply of teachers at all. And therefore I urge you to do as I believe you wish to: disengage yourself as often as you can from the affairs of this world, so that you can apply the wisdom that God has given you wherever you are able to apply it. Think what punishments came upon us in this world then when we neither loved learning ourselves nor allowed it to other men: we loved only to be called Christians, and very few loved the virtues.

When I remembered all this, then I also recollected how – before it was all ravaged and burnt – I had seen how the churches throughout all England stood filled with treasures and books, and there was also a great multitude of God's servants. They had very little benefit from those books, because they could not understand anything of them, since they were not written in their own language. It is as if they had said: 'Our forefathers who formerly held these places loved knowledge, and through it they acquired wealth and left it to us. One can see their footprints here still, but we cannot follow after them. And therefore we have now lost both the wealth and the knowledge because we would not set our mind to that course.'

When I remembered all this, then I wondered greatly why those good wise men who formerly existed throughout England, and had fully studied all those books, did not wish to translate any part of them into their own language. But I immediately answered myself then, and said: 'They did not imagine that men would ever become so careless and learning so decayed; they refrained from it by intention and hoped that there would be the greater knowledge in this land the more languages we knew.' Then I remembered how the law was first found in the Hebrew language, and afterwards, when the Greeks learned it, they translated it all into their own language, and all the other books as well. And afterwards in the same way the Romans, when they had learned them, they translated them all into their own language through learned interpreters. And all other Christian nations also translated some part of them into their own language.

Therefore it seems better to me, if it seems so to you, that we also should translate certain books which are most necessary for all men to know into the language that we can all understand, and also arrange it, as with God's help we very easily can if we have peace, so that all the young freeborn men now among the English people, who have the means to be able to devote themselves to it, may be set to study for as long as they are of no other use, until the time they are able to read English writing well. Afterwards one may teach further in the Latin language those whom one wishes to teach further and wishes to promote to holy orders.

Then when I remembered how the knowledge of Latin had previously decayed throughout the English, and yet many could read English writing, I began among other various and manifold cares of this kingdom to translate into English the book which is called *Pastoralis* in Latin and 'Shepherd's Book' in English, sometimes word for word, sometimes in a paraphrase, as I learned it from my archbishop Plegmund, and my bishop Asser, and my mass-priest Grimbold and my mass-priest John. When I had learned it, I translated it into English as I understood it and as I could interpret it most intelligibly; and I will send one to every bishopric in my kingdom; and in each there will be an *æstel* worth fifty mancuses. And in the name of God, I command that no one remove the *æstel* from the book, nor the book from the minster. It is uncertain how long there may be such learned bishops, as now, thanks be to God, there are almost everywhere. Therefore I desire that they should always be at that place, unless the bishop wants to have it with him, or it is somewhere on loan, or anyone is copying it.

TRANSLATION OF BOETHIUS'S *CONSOLATION OF PHILOSOPHY*

One of the works that King Alfred thought 'most necessary for all men to know' is Boethius's *De Consolatione Philosophiae*. Written in the sixth century in prose and verse by Boethius (alias St Severinus), this work became one of the most widely known, read and translated books in the Middle Ages and its possible influence on works such as the Old English poems *Deor* and *The Wanderer* has been often discussed. Alfred created two versions of this classic text, a prose version, followed by a poetic version (the *Meters of Boethius*). Although Boethius was a Christian, his work is primarily infused with a neo-Platonic philosophy and a stoicism in the face of his own adversity that results in his view of a universe where a temporal fate seems to govern, but eternal providence (God) is ultimately in control. Boethius's *Consolation* centres on the dialogue between the personification, Lady Philosophy, a figure that Alfred recreates as Wisdom, and Boethius, who appears in Alfred's text as 'Mind'. Alfred's translation is, in fact, far more than the word 'translation' implies: it is essentially an adaptation or recomposition of the original. Alfred's version is explicitly Christian in outlook, aiming to edify and educate his audience; it contains concrete examples where Boethius gives abstract examples; historical references are supplied by Alfred to aid his audience's understanding; Alfred interpolates, expands, refocuses, and adds new details and fresh images.

Alfred's version of the *Consolation* exists in two manuscripts and a fragment. London, British Library, Cotton Otho A. vi, is dated to the mid-tenth century and consists of the Old English *Meters*, containing both prose and verse. This manuscript was badly damaged by the fire at Ashburnham House in London in 1731,[4] but a partial transcript had been made of it before this by Franciscus Junius, a seventeenth-century philologist and Old English specialist, and this survives as Oxford,

Bodleian Library, Junius 12. A later manuscript dating to the twelfth century, Oxford, Bodleian Library, Bodley 180, contains the Old English text copied as prose. A full text, collated from the existing manuscripts, is edited by W. J. Sedgefield.[5] Three extracts are given here: the 'Proem' to the work, which is based on Bodley 180 as it does not survive in Otho A. vi; 'On Government', which is based on Bodley 180; and 'Orfeus and Eurydice', which is based on Otho A. vi.

The 'Proem' is Alfred's authorial preface briefly outlining how he translated the work, and beseeching his audience to forgive his shortcomings (a typical authorial modesty *topos*). The second extract, 'On Government', occurs as chapter XVII, and derives its inspiration from book II, prose 7. It is Alfred's imagined response of Boethius to Wisdom, discussing the means by which a virtuous king rules. This extract is widely known and translated as it appears to be an important personal statement by Alfred, expanding on his source in the *Consolation*. 'Orfeus and Eurydice' occurs in chapter XXXV, and is based on book III, metre 12, in Boethius's *Consolation*. While it relates the very familiar story of the famous classical figures, this version alters the significance of the legend as told by Boethius. In Boethius the story ends with the moral that one should avoid looking back at hell. In Alfred's version, this becomes overtly Christian and didactic. In Boethius's account, Eurydice represents transient earthly happiness; in Alfred's adaptation, she represents man's previous sins. Orfeus becomes an example of a reformed sinner who falls once more into his bad habits by looking back at his sins committed earlier. Alfred ends with the admonition that it is dangerous to return to sinful ways; one must fully repent of them. For another version of 'Orfeus and Eurydice', dramatically and effectively transformed into a romance, see the Middle English text *Sir Orfeo*.[6]

Translation of Boethius's *Consolation of Philosophy*

Proem

Ælfred kuning wæs wealhstod ðisse bec: ond hie of Boclædene on Englisc wende, swa hio nu is gedon. Hwilum he sette word be worde, hwilum angit of andgite, swa swa he hit þa sweotolost ond andgitfullicast gereccan mihte, for þam mistlicum ond manigfealdum weoruldbisgum þe hine oft ægðer ge on mode ge on lichoman bisgodan. Đa bisgu us sint swiþe earfoþrime þe on his

5   dagum on þa ricu becoman þe he underfangen hæfde; ond þeah, ða þas boc hæfde geleornode ond of Lædene to Engliscum spelle gewende, ond geworhte hi eft to leoðe, swa swa heo nu gedon is. Ond nu bit ond for Godes naman he halsað ælcne þara þe þas boc rædan lyste, þæt he for hine gebidde, ond him ne wite gif he hit rihtlicor ongite þonne he mihte: for þam þe ælc mon sceal be his andgites mæðe, ond be his æmettan sprecan þæt he sprecð, ond don þæt þæt he deþ.

4 See note 3 on Alfred's *Preface* to Gregory's *Pastoral Care*.

5 W. J. Sedgefield, ed., *King Alfred's Old English Version of Boethius, De Consolatione Philosophiae* (Oxford, 1899).

6 For other extracts and contemporary texts in translation con-

cerned with the reign of King Alfred, see S. Keynes and M. Lapidge, eds, *Alfred the Great: Asser's Life of King Alfred and Other Contemporary Sources* (London, 1983).

Translation of Boethius's *Consolation of Philosophy*

Proem

King Alfred was the translator of this book, and turned it from Latin into English, as it is now done. Sometimes he translated word for word, sometimes sense for sense, as he was able to explain it in the clearest and most meaningful way, despite the various and manifold worldly occupations that frequently beset him in both mind and body. These occupations, which befell him in those days when he had succeeded to that kingdom, are very difficult for us to count; and yet, when he had mastered this book and translated it from Latin into English prose, he rendered it again into poetry, just as it is now done. And now he prays and entreats in God's name each one of those who might desire to read this book, that he will pray for him, and will not blame him if they are able to interpret it more accurately than he could: for each person must, by the measure of his own understanding and at his leisure, say what he says and do what he does.

On Government

Þa andswarode þæt Mod ond þus cwæð: 'Eala, Gesceadwisnes, hwæt, þu wast þæt me næfre seo gitsung ond seo gemægð þisses eorðlican anwealdes forwel ne licode, ne Ic ealles forswiðe ne girnde þisses eorðlican rices, buton tola Ic wilnode þeah ond andweorces to þam weorce þe me beboden was to wyrcanne. Þæt was þæt Ic unfracodlice ond gerisenlice mihte steoran ond reccan
5 þone anweald þe me befæst wæs.

Hwæt, þu wast þæt nan mon ne mæg nænne cræft cyðan, ne nænne anweald reccan ne stioran butun tolum ond andweorce. Þæt bið ælces cræftes andweorc þæt mon þone cræft butun wyrcan ne mæg. Þæt bið þonne cyninges andweorc ond his tol mid to ricsianne: þæt he hæbbe his land fullmonnad; he sceal habban gebedmen ond fyrdmen ond weorcmen. Hwæt, þu wast þætte butan
10 þisum tolum nan cyning his cræft ne mæg cyðan. Þæt is eac his andweorc: þæt he habban sceal to þam tolum þam þrim geferscipum biwiste. Þæt is þonne heora biwist: land to bugianne, ond gifta ond wæpnu ond mete ond ealo ond claþas, ond gehwæt þæs ðe þa þre geferscipas behofiað.

Ne mæg he butan þisum þas tol gehealdan, ne buton þisum tolum nan þara þinga wyrcan þe him beboden is to wyrcenne. For þy Ic wilnode andweorces mid to reccenne, þæt mine cræftas
15 ond anweald ne wurden forgitene ond forholene: for þam ælc cræft ond ælc anweald bið sona forealdod ond forswugod gif he bið buton wisdome; for þæm ne mæg non mon nænne cræft forðbringan buton wisdome. For þæm þe swa hwæt swa þurh dysig gedon bið, ne mæg hit mon næfre to cræfte gerecan. Þæt is nu hraþost to secganne, þæt Ic wilnode weorðfullice to libbanne þa hwile þe Ic lifede, ond æfter minum life þæm monnum to læfanne þe æfter me wæren min
20 gemynd on godum weorcum.'

Orfeus and Eurydice

Hit gelamp gio ðætte an hearpere wæs on ðære ðiode ðe Ðracia hatte, sio wæs on Creca rice; se hearpere wæs swiðe ungefræglice good, ðæs nama wæs Orfeus. He hæfde an swiðe ænlic wif, sio wæs haten Eurudice. Ða ongon mon secgan be ðam hearpere þæt he meahte hearpian þæt se wudu wagode, ond þa stanas hi styredon for ðy swege, ond wildu dior ðær woldon to irnan ond stondan
5 swilce hi tamu wæren, swa stille – ðeah him men oððe hundas wið eoden – ðæt hi hi na ne onscunedon. Ða sædon hi þæt ðæs hearperes wif sceolde acwelan, ond hire saule mon sceolde lædan to helle. Ða sceolde se hearpere weorðan swa sarig þæt he ne meahte ongemong oðrum mannum bion, ac teah to wuda, ond sæt on ðæm muntum ægðer ge dæges ge nihtes, weop ond hearpode ðæt ða wudas bifedon, ond þa ea stodon, ond nan heort ne onscunode nænne leon, ne
10 nan hara nænne hund, ne nan neat nyste nænne andan ne nænne ege to oðrum, for ðære mergðe ðæs sones.

Ða ðæm hearpere ða ðuhte ðæt hine nanes ðinges ne lyste on ðisse worulde, ða ðohte he ðæt he wolde gesecan helle godu, ond onginnan him oleccan mid his hearpan, ond biddan þæt hi him agefan eft his wif. Þa he ða ðider com, ða sceolde cuman ðære helle hund ongean hine, þæs nama
15 wæs Cerverus, se sceolde habban þrio heafdu, ond onfægnian mid his steorte ond plegian wið hine for his hearpunga. Ða wæs ðær eac swiðe egeslic geatweard, ðæs nama sceolde bion Caron, se hæfde eac þrio heafdu, ond wæs swiðe oreald. Ða ongon se hearpere hine biddan þæt he hine gemundbyrde ða hwile þe he ðær wære, ond hine gesundne eft ðonan brohte. Ða gehet he him ðæt, for ðæm he wæs oflyst ðæs seldcuðan sones. Ða eode he furður oð he mette ða graman metena
20 ðe folcisce men hatað Parcas, ða hi secgað ðæt on nanum men nyton nane are, ac ælcum men wrecen be his gewyrhtum; þa hi secgað ðæt walden ælces mannes wyrde. Ða ongon he biddan heora blisse, ða ongunnon hi wepan mid him.

On Government

Then the Mind[7] answered and said this: 'Listen, Wisdom,[8] indeed, you know that greed and ambition for this earthly power never pleased me very well, nor of all things did I unduly desire this earthly kingdom, except though that I wished for tools and materials in order to accomplish whatever work was required from me. This was that I should virtuously and suitably guide and direct the power that had been entrusted to me.

Indeed, you know that no one can make known any skill, nor steer nor direct any authority without tools and materials. Thus it is that a man cannot perform any enterprise without the material for that task. This is, then, the king's material and his tool with which to rule: that he has his land manned fully; he must have praying men and fighting men and working men.[9] Indeed, you know that without these tools no king is able to make his skill known. There are also his materials: that he must have for those tools, sustenance for the three communities of men. Their sustenance thus consists of this: land on which to live, and gifts and weapons and food and ale and clothes and whatever else might be required by the three communities.

And without these things, he cannot maintain these tools, nor without these tools can he do any of the things he is charged to do. Consequently, I desired materials with which to rule, so that my skills and power would not be forgotten and hidden: because each skill and each power is soon decayed and passed over in silence if it is without wisdom; because no man can produce any skill without wisdom. Therefore whatever is done through foolishness cannot be considered by man to be a skill. To be brief, I may say that I desired to live worthily while I lived, and that after my life, to leave to men who came after me the memory of me in good works.'

Orfeus and Eurydice

It happened years ago that there was a harper among the nation known as the Thracians, which was in the kingdom of Greece; the harper was most unusually good, and his name was Orfeus; he had a most excellent wife who was called Eurydice. Then men began to say about the harper that he could harp until the trees moved, and that stones would stir because of the melody, and that wild animals would run to him there and stand as if they were tame, just as still – though men or dogs came against them – as if they were not afraid. Then it is said that this harper's wife died and her soul was led to hell. Then the harper became so sorrowful that he could not live among other men, but went into the woods, and sat on the hills both by day and by night, crying and playing the harp, so that the trees trembled and the river stood still, and no stag feared any lion, nor the hare the hound, nor did any animal bear any malice or fear against any other, because of the joyfulness of that sound.

Then the harper reflected that there was nothing in this world that he desired, and he thought that he would seek the gods of hell, and begin to soothe them with his harp, and to pray that his wife might be returned to him. When he came there, then the hound of hell came towards him, whose name was Cerverus, and he had three heads; and he fawned on him and played with him because of his harping. There was also a terrible gate-warden there, the name of whom was Caron, and he also had three heads and was very old. Then the harper began to ask him if he would protect him while he was there and would bring him unhurt again from that place. Then Caron promised him that because he was delighted by the rare sound of music. Then he went on further until he found the fierce goddesses who are popularly called Parcas, and who are said to have no mercy on any man, but will punish each man as he deserves; they are said to control the fate of every man. When he prayed for their kindness, they began to weep with him.

Then he went on further, and all the inhabitants of hell ran towards him and led him to their king and all of them began to speak with him, asking what it was that he requested. And that restless wheel to

---

7   The Mind is Boethius, although the words here are those of King Alfred.

8   Alfred alters Boethius's Lady Philosophy to the personification 'Wisdom'.

9   Commonly referred to as the 'three estates', this division of soci-

ety became very common in the later medieval period. Alfred's use of this idea is the first recorded instance. See T. E. Powell, 'The "Three Orders" of Society in Anglo-Saxon England', *Anglo-Saxon England* 23 (1994), pp. 103–32.

Ða eode he furður, ond him urnon ealle hellwaran ongean ond læddon hine to hiora cininge, ond ongunnon ealle sprecan mid him ond biddan þæs ðe he bæd. Ond þæt unstille hweol ðe Ixion wæs to gebunden, Levita cyning, for his scylde, ðæt oðstod for his hearpunga. Ond Tantulus se cyning, ðe on ðisse worulde ungemetlice gifre wæs, ond him ðær ðæt ilce yfel filgde ðære gifernesse,
25   he gestilde. Ond se ultor sceolde forlætan ðæt he ne slat ða lifre Tyties ðæs cyninges, ðe hine ær mid ðy witnode; ond eall hellwara witu gestildon ða hwile þe he beforan ðam cyninge hearpode. Ða he ða longe ond longe hearpode, ða cleopode se hellwara cyning ond cwæð: 'Wuton agifan ðæm esne his wif for ðæm he hi hæfð geearnad mid his hearpunga.' Bebead him ða ðæt he geare wisse, ðæt he hine næfre under bæc ne besawe, siððan he ðonanweard wære, ond sæde, gif he hine
30   under bæc besawe ðæt he sceolde forlætan ðæt wif. Ac ða lufe mon mæg swiðe uneaðe oððe na forbeodan: weilawei! Hwæt, Orpheus ða lædde his wif mid him oð he com on ðæt gemære leohtes ond ðiostro; ða eode þæt wif æfter him. Ða he furðum on ðæt leoht com, ða beseah he hine under bæc wið ðæs wifes. Ða losade hio him sona.

Ðas leasan spell læraþ gehwylcne mon ðara ðe wilnað helle ðiostro to flionne, ond to ðæs soðan
35   Godes liohte to cumanne, ðæt he hine ne besio to his ealdan yflum, swa ðæt he hi eft swa fullice fullfremme swa he hi ær dyde. For ðæm swa hwa swa mid fulle willan his mod went to ðæm yflum ðe he ær forlet, ond hi ðonne fullfremeð, ond hi him ðonne fullice liciað, ond he hi næfre forlætan ne ðenceð, ðonne forlyst he eall his ærran good, buton he hit eft gebete. Her endað nu sio þridde boc Boeties, ond onginneð sio fiorðe.
40

which Ixion, the king of the Lapithae, was bound for his sin stood still because of Orfeus's harping. And Tantalus the king, who was excessively greedy in this world, and who was pursued there by that same evil of greediness, ceased. And the vulture was obliged to abandon his task so that he did not tear the liver of Tyties the king, which he had tormented him with before. And all the inhabitants of hell ceased their torments while he harped in front of the king. When he had harped for longer and longer, the king of hell called out, and said: 'Let us give this man his wife for he has earned her with his harping.' He commanded him that he should know surely that he might never look back after he had gone from there, and he said if he did look back, then he would lose his wife. But one can scarcely forbid love, or not at all: alas! Indeed then Orfeus led his wife away with him, until he came to the boundary between light and darkness; his wife came after him. When he came forth into that light, he looked behind himself towards his wife. She was lost to him immediately.

These untruthful stories teach every one of those who wish to flee from the darkness of hell, and to come to the light of the true God, that he should not look back at his old sins, lest he again complete them as fully as he did before. Therefore, whoever turns his mind with complete desire to those evils that he previously abandoned, and then he perfects them, and finds that they are very pleasing to him, and he never ceases to think of them, then he is deprived of all his previous good deeds, unless he atones for it afterwards. Here now ends the third book of Boethius, and the fourth begins.

The Anglo-Saxon Chronicle

ANNAL 755: CYNEWULF AND CYNEHEARD; ANNALS 855–78: THE DEATH OF EDMUND; ALFRED'S BATTLES WITH THE VIKINGS

The seven independent manuscripts collectively known as *The Anglo-Saxon Chronicle* constitute the most important historical sources for the period. Between them, they cover the history of England from the arrival of Julius Caesar to the end of King Stephen's reign in 1154. One theory links the *Chronicle*'s origins with the desire of King Alfred to raise the historical, literary and religious awareness of his subjects. As such, the earliest manuscript of the *Chronicle*, Cambridge, Corpus Christi College 173, known as Manuscript A, 'The Winchester Manuscript', or 'The Parker Chronicle', may have resulted from the programme of educational reform instigated by Alfred in the latter years of his reign. This manuscript, written at Winchester in the 990s, probably derives from an earlier version which was sent to other centres in England for copying and adaptation. 'The Parker Chronicle' itself contains entries of varying length and styles from '60 years before the Incarnation of Christ' to 1070, when the archbishop of York, Thomas, made obeisance to Lanfranc, archbishop of Canterbury. J. Bately edits *MS A* in the continuing series, *The Anglo-Saxon Chronicle: A Collaborative Edition*; and the complete texts are translated in M. Swanton, *The Anglo-Saxon Chronicle*.[1]

The Anglo-Saxon Chronicle stems from the practice of entering important events into Easter tables.[2] It is thus organized by annal entries, with the year in roman numerals in the margin, followed by the entry. The entries range from those for the year 734: 'Here Æthelbald captured Somerton; and the sun grew dark',[3] to the much longer entries given below. The *Chronicle* is a selective history in that it records events and persons (mostly men) of national importance. Stylistically, it varies from abrupt, objective phrases for some years to lengthy, more subjective annals. Regional interests are also prevalent in most of the versions, such as Manuscript D, the Worcester Chronicle.[4]

Edited from 'The Parker Chronicle' here are two extracts. The first, from folio 10, is a narrative account of an event that took place in AD 755, and which is known as 'Cynewulf and Cynheard'. This episode is one of the most famous Old English prose texts. Commentators regard it as an interpolation into the *Chronicle* that serves to highlight the heroic code of the Anglo-Saxons: the conflict between political opponents; the demands of kinship versus the demands of loyalty to the lord of the *comitatus*; and the ultimately heroic action of the central protagonists. I have curtailed the annal entry slightly by omitting the genealogy of Offa that comes at the end.

The second extract is perhaps more representative of the *Chronicle* as a whole, and comes from folios 13 recto to 15 recto. It contains the annal entries for the years 855–878 that include the death of Edmund and Alfred's wars against the Danes, culminating in the baptism of the Danish king, Guthrum, at the court of Alfred. Notable in this extract is the genealogy that provides an authoritative ancestry for Alfred, and which reflects the Anglo-Saxon nobles' desire to root themselves within a worthy lineage.

Annal 755: Cynewulf and Cyneheard

755   Her Cynewulf benam Sigebryht his rices ond Westseaxna wiotan for unryhtum dædum, buton Hamtunscire; ond he hæfde þa oþ he ofslog þone aldormon þe him lengest wunode. Ond hiene þa Cynewulf on Andred adræfde; ond he þær wunade oþþæt hiene an swan ofstang æt Pryfetesflodan; ond he wræc þone aldormon Cumbran. Ond se Cynewulf oft miclum gefeohtum

5   feaht uuiþ Bretwalum; ond ymb xxxi wintra þæs þe he rice hæfde, he wolde adræfan anne æþeling se was Cyneheard haten, ond se Cyneheard wæs þæs Sigebryhtes broþur. Ond þa geascode he þone cyning lytle werode on wifcyþþe on Merantune, ond hine þær berad, ond þone bur utan beeode ær hine þa men onfunden þe mid þam kyninge wærun.

        Ond þa ongeat se cyning þæt, ond he on þa duru eode, ond þa unheanlice hine werede oþ he on

10   þone æþeling locude, ond þa ut ræsde on hine ond hine miclum gewundode; ond hie alle on þone cyning wærun feohtende oþþæt hie hine ofslægenne hæfdon. Ond þa on þæs wifes gebærum onfundon þæs cyninges þegnas þa unstilnesse, ond þa þider urnon swa hwelc swa þonne gearo

1   J. Bately, ed., *MS A. The Anglo-Saxon Chronicle: A Collaborative Edition* 3 (Cambridge, 1986); M. Swanton, trans. and ed., *The Anglo-Saxon Chronicle* (London, 1996).

2   See S. B. Greenfield and D. G. Calder, eds, *A New Critical History of Old English Literature* (London, 1986), pp. 59–61.

3   Swanton, *Anglo-Saxon Chronicle*, p. 44.

4   G. P. Cubbin, ed., *MS D. The Anglo-Saxon Chronicle: A Collaborative Edition* 6 (Woodbridge, 1996).

Annal 755: Cynewulf and Cyneheard

755   In this year Cynewulf and the West Saxon witan deprived Sigebryht of his kingdom, except for Hampshire; and he retained that until he killed the ealdorman who had lived with him longest. And then Cynewulf drove him into the Weald, and Sigebryht lived there until a swineherd killed him at the stream at Privett; and by this he avenged the ealdorman Cumbra. And Cynewulf often fought great battles against the Britons. And about thirty-one years after he had the kingdom, he wanted to drive out a prince who was called Cyneheard; and this Cyneheard was the brother of Sigebryht. And then Cyneheard discovered the king with a small troop in the company of a mistress at Merton, and he rode there and surrounded the burh before the men who were with the king discovered him.

   And then the king perceived that, and he went through the door and then valiantly defended himself until he looked upon the prince, and then he rushed out against him and severely wounded him; and they all continued fighting against the king until they had killed him. And then because of the woman's cries, the king's thanes discovered that disturbance, and they quickly ran there whoever was ready the quickest.

wearþ, ond radost. Ond hiera se æþeling gehwelcum feoh ond feorh gebead, ond hiera nænig hit
geþicgean nolde; ac hie simle feohtende wæran oþ hie alle lægon butan anum Bryttiscum gisle,
15   ond se swiþe gewundad wæs.

Þa on morgenne gehierdun þæt þæs cyninges þegnas, þe him beæftan wærun, þæt se cyning
ofslægen wæs. Þa ridon hie þider, ond his aldormon Osric, ond Wiferþ his þegn, ond þa men þe
he beæftan him læfde ær, ond þone æþeling on þære byrig metton þær se cyning ofslægen læg,
ond þa gatu him to belocen hæfdon, ond þa þærto eodon. Ond þa gebead he him hiera agenne
20   dom feos ond londes, gif hie him þæs rices uþon; ond him cyþdon þæt hiera mægas him mid
wæron, þa þe him from noldon. Ond þa cuædon hie þæt him nænig mæg leofra nære þonne hiera
hlaford, ond hie næfre his banan folgian noldon. Ond þa budon hie hiera mægum þæt hie gesunde
from eodon; ond hie cuædon þæt tæt ilce hiera geferum geboden wære þe ær mid þam cyninge
wærun. Þa cuædon hie þæt hie hie þæs ne onmunden 'þon ma þe eowre geferan þe mid þam
25   cyninge ofslægene wærun'. Ond hie þa ymb þa gatu feohtende wæron oþþæt hie þærinne fulgon
ond þone æþeling ofslogon ond þa men þe him mid wærun, alle butan anum, se wæs þæs
aldormonnes godsunu; ond he his feorh generede ond þeah he wæs oft gewundad. Ond se Cynewulf
ricsode xxxi wintra ond his lic liþ æt Wintanceastre, ond þæs æþelinges æt Ascanmynster; ond
hiera ryhtfæderencyn gæþ to Cerdice.
30   Ond þy ilcan geare mon ofslog Æþelbald Miercna cyning on Seccandune, ond his lic liþ on
Hreopadune; ond Beornræd feng to rice, ond lytle hwile heold ond ungefealice. Ond þy ilcan
geare Offa feng to rice, ond heold xxxviiii wintra, ond his sunu Ecgferþ heold xli daga ond c daga.

Annals 855–78: The Death of Edmund; Alfred's Battles with the Vikings

855   Her hæþne men ærest on Sceapige ofer winter sætun. Ond þy ilcan geare gebocude Æþelwulf
cyning teoþan dæl his londes ofer al his rice Gode to lofe ond him selfum to ecere hælo, ond þy
ilcan geare ferde to Rome mid micelre weorþnesse ond þær was xii monaþ wuniende ond þa him
hamweard for. Ond him þa Carl Francna cyning his dohtor geaf him to cuene, and æfter þam to
5   his leodum cuom and hie þæs gefægene wærun. Ond ymb ii gear þæs ðe he of Francum com he
gefor, ond his lic liþ æt Wintanceastre, ond he ricsode nigonteoþe healf gear. Ond se Æþelwulf
wæs Ecgbrehting, Ecgbryht Ealhmunding, Ealhmund Eafing, Eafa Eopping, Eoppa Ingilding;
Ingild wæs Ines broþur Westseaxna cyninges, þæs þe eft ferde to Sancte Petre ond þær eft his
feorh gesealde; ond hie wæron Cenredes suna, Cenred wæs Ceolwalding, Ceolwald Cuþaing, Cuþa
10   Cuþwining, Cuþwine Ceaulining, Ceawlin Cynricing, Cynric Cerdicing, Cerdic Elesing, Elesa
Esling, Esla Giwising, Giwis Wiging, Wig Freawining, Freawine Friþogaring, Friþogar Bronding,
Brond Bældæging, Bældæg Wodening, Woden Friþowalding, Friþuwald Frealafing, Frealaf
Friþuwulfing, Friþuwulf Finning, Fin Godwulfing, Godwulf Geating, Geat Tætwaing, Tætwa
Beawing, Beaw Sceldwaing, Sceldwea Heremoding, Heremod Itermoning, Itermon Hraþaing, se
15   wæs geboren in þære earce: Noe, Lamach, Matusalem, Enoh, Jaered, Maleel, Camon, Enos, Sed,
Adam *primus homo; et pater noster est Christus.* Amen.

Ond þa fengon Æþelwulfes suna twegen to rice, Æþelbald to Wesseaxna rice ond Æþelbryht to
Cantwara rice ond to Eastseaxna rice ond to Suþrigea ond to Suþseaxna rice; ond þa ricsode Æþelbald
v gear.

20   860   Her Æþelbald cyng forþferde, ond his lic liþ æt Sciraburnan, ond feng Æþelbryht to allum
þam rice his broþur, ond he hit heold on godre geþuærnesse ond on micelre sibsumnesse. Ond on
his dæge cuom micel sciphere up ond abræcon Wintanceaster, ond wiþ þone here gefuhton Osric
aldorman mid Hamtunscire ond Æþelwulf aldorman mid Bearruscire, ond þone here gefliemdon
ond wælstowe gewald ahton. Ond se Æþelbryht ricsode v gear ond his lic liþ æt Scireburnan.

25   865   Her sæt hæþen here on Tenet ond genamon friþ wiþ Cantwarum, ond Cantware him feoh
geheton wiþ þam friþe, ond under þam friþe ond þam feohgehate se here hiene on niht up bestæl,
ond oferhergeade alle Cent eastewearde.

And the prince offered each of them money and life, but not one of them would accept it; but they continued fighting until they all lay dead except for one British hostage, and he was severely wounded.

Then in the morning, the king's thanes who had been left behind heard that their king lay dead. They rode there then, his ealdorman Osric, and Wiferþ his thane, and the men who had been left behind him before, and encountered the prince in that burh where the king lay dead (and the gates had been locked against them) and then they went there. And then Cyneheard offered them their own judgement of money and land if they granted him the kingdom, and revealed to them their kinsmen were with him who did not wish to leave him. And then Cynewulf's men said that no kinsman could be dearer to them than their lord and that they would not follow his murderer. And then they offered their kinsman the chance to go unharmed from there. And Cyneheard's men said that the same thing had been offered to their own comrades who had been with the king before. They said that they would take no heed of that 'any more than did your companions who were killed with the king.' And then they continued fighting around the gates until they had penetrated in there and they killed the prince and the men who were with him, all except one, who was the godson of the ealdorman; and his life was saved, even though he had been wounded many times. And Cynewulf had reigned for thirty-one years and his body lies at Winchester, and the prince's lies at Axminster; and their direct paternal ancestry goes back to Cerdic.

And in the same year, Æþelbald the Mercian king was killed at Seckington, and his body lies at Repton; and Beornræd succeeded to the kingdom and held it for a short time unhappily. And that same year, Offa succeeded to the kingdom and held it for thirty-nine years, and his son Ecgferþ held it for one hundred and forty-one days.

Annals 855–78: The Death of Edmund; Alfred's Battles with the Vikings

855   In this year, for the first time, the heathen men settled in Sheppey during the winter. And in the same year King Æþelwulf granted a tenth part of his land by charter over all his kingdom, to the glory of God and for his own perpetual salvation. And in the same year he went to Rome with great splendour, and he stayed there for twelve months, and then journeyed homewards. And then Charles, king of the Franks, gave him his daughter for a queen, and after that he came back to his people and they were happy at that. And about two years after he came back from Francia, he died, and his body lies at Winchester; and he ruled for eighteen and a half years. And this Æþelwulf was Egbert's offspring, Egbert Ealhmund's offspring, Ealhmund Eafa's offspring, Eafa Eoppa's offspring, Eoppa Ingeld's offspring; Ingeld was the brother of King Ine of Wessex, who went afterwards to St Peter's and thereafter he gave up his life; and they were Cenred's sons. Cenred was Ceolwald's offspring, Ceolwald Cuþa's offspring, Cuþa was Cuþwine's offspring, Cuþwine was Ceawlin's offspring, Ceawlin Cynric's offspring, Cynric was Cerdic's offspring, Cerdic Elesa's offspring, Elesa Esla's offspring, Esla Gewis's offspring, Gewis was Wig's offspring, Wig was Freawine's offspring, Freawine Friþogar's offspring, Friþogar Brand's offspring, Brand Bældæg's offspring, Bældæg Woden's offspring, Woden was Friþowald's offspring, Friþowald Frealalf's offspring, Frealaf Friþuwulf's offspring, Friþuwulf Finn's offspring, Finn was Godwulf's offspring, Godwulf Geat's offspring, Geat Tætwa's offspring, Tætwa Beaw's offspring, Beaw was Sceldwa's offspring, Sceldwa Heremod's offspring, Heremod Itermon's offspring, Itermon Hraþra's offspring, he was born in the ark: Noah, Lamech, Methuselah, Enoch, Jared, Mahalaleel, Cainan, Enos, Seth, Adam the first man, and our father that is Christ. Amen.

And then Æþelwulf's two sons succeeded to the kingdom: Æþelbald to the kingdom of the West Saxons, and Æþelberht to the kingdom of the people of Kent and to the kingdom of the East Saxons, and to Surrey and to the kingdom of the South Saxons; and then Æþelbald ruled for five years.

860   Here King Æþelbald died, and his body lies at Sherborne; and Æþelberht, his brother, succeeded to the whole kingdom, and he held it in good peace and in much concord. And during his days a great fleet came up and destroyed Winchester; and against that Viking army Ealdorman Osric fought with the Hampshire men, and Ealdorman Æþelwulf with those of Berkshire; and they drove away the Viking army and controlled that place of slaughter. And Æþelberht ruled for five years, and his body lies at Sherborne.

866 Her feng Æþered Æþelbryhtes broþur to Wesseaxna rice; ond þy ilcan geare cuom micel here on Angelcynnes lond, ond wintersetl namon on Eastenglum ond þær gehorsude wurdon ond hie him friþ wiþ namon.

867 Her for se here of Eastenglum ofer Humbre muþan to Eoforwicceastre on Norþhymbre, ond þær wæs micel ungeþuærnes þære þeode betweox him selfum, ond hie hæfdun hiera cyning aworpenne Osbryht ond ungecyndne cyning underfengon Ællan; ond hie late on geare to þam gecirdon þæt hie wiþ þone here winnende wærun, ond hie þeah micle fierd gegadrodon ond þone here sohton æt Eoforwicceastre ond on þa ceastre bræcon ond hie sume inne wurdon; ond þær was ungemetlic wæl geslægen Norþanhymbra, sume binnan, sume butan, ond þa cyningas begen ofslægene, ond sio laf wiþ þone here friþ nam. Ond þy ilcan geare gefor Ealchstan biscep, ond he hæfde þæt bisceprice l wintra æt Scireburnan, ond his lic liþ þær on tune.

868 Her for se ilca here innan Mierce to Snotengaham ond þær wintersetl namon. Ond Burgræd Miercna cyning ond his wiotan bædon Æþered Westseaxna cyning ond Ælfred his broþur þæt hie him gefultumadon, þæt hie wiþ þone here gefuhton. Ond þa ferdon hie mid Wesseaxna fierde innan Mierce oþ Snotengaham ond þone here þær metton on þam geweorce, ond þær nan hefelic gefeoht ne wearþ, ond Mierce friþ namon wiþ þone here.

869 Her for se here eft to Eoforwicceastre ond þær sæt i gear.

870 Her rad se here ofer Mierce innan Eastengle ond wintersetl namon æt Þeodforda. Ond þy wintra Eadmund cyning him wiþ feaht ond þa Deniscan sige namon ond þone cyning ofslogon ond þæt lond all geeodon. Ond þy geare gefor Ceolnoþ ærcebiscep; ond Æþered Wiltunscire biscop wearþ gecoren to ærcebiscope to Cantuareberi.

871 Her cuom se here to Readingum on Westseaxe, ond þæs ymb iii niht ridon ii eorlas up. Þa gemette hie Æþelwulf aldorman on Englafelda, ond him þær wiþ gefeaht, ond sige nam. Þæs ymb iiii niht Æþered cyning ond Ælfred his broþur þær micle fierd to Rædingum gelæddon, ond wiþ þone here gefuhton; ond þær wæs micel wæl geslægen on gehwæþre hond, ond Æþelwulf aldormon wearþ ofslægen; ond þa Deniscan ahton wælstowe gewald.
  Ond þæs ymb iiii niht gefeaht Æþered cyning ond Ælfred his broþur wiþ alne þone here on Æscesdune. Ond hie wærun on twæm gefylcum: on oþrum wæs Bachsecg ond Halfdene, þa hæþnan cyningas; ond on oþrum wæron þa eorlas. Ond þa gefeaht se cyning Æþered wiþ þara cyninga getruman, ond þær wearþ se cyning Bagsecg ofslægen; ond Ælfred his broþur wiþ þara eorla getruman, ond þær wearþ Sidroc eorl ofslægen se alda, ond Sidroc eorl se gioncga, ond Osbearn eorl, ond Fræna eorl, ond Hareld eorl; ond þa hergas begen gefliemde, ond fela þusenda ofslægenra, ond onfeohtende wæron oþ niht.
  Ond þæs ymb xiiii niht gefeaht Æþered cyning ond Ælfred his broður wiþ þone here æt Basengum, ond þær þa Deniscan sige namon.
  Ond þæs ymb ii monaþ gefeaht Æþered cyning ond Ælfred his broþur wiþ þone here æt Meretune, ond hie wærun on tuæm gefylcium, ond hie butu gefliemdon, ond longe on dæg sige ahton; ond þær wearþ micel wælsliht on gehwæþere hond; ond þa Deniscan ahton wælstowe gewald; ond þær wearþ Heahmund biscep ofslægen, ond fela godra monna. Ond æfter þissum gefeohte cuom micel sumorlida.
  Ond þæs ofer Eastron gefor Æþered cyning; ond he ricsode v gear, ond his lic liþ æt Winburnan.
  Þa feng Ælfred Æþelwulfing his broþur to Wessaxna rice. Ond þæs ymb anne monaþ gefeaht Ælfred cyning wiþ alne þone here lytle werede æt Wiltune, ond hine longe on dæg gefliemde, ond þa Deniscan ahton wælstowe gewald.
  Ond þæs geares wurdon viiii folcgefeoht gefohten wiþ þone here on þy cynerice be suþan Temese, ond butan þam þe him Ælfred þæs cyninges broþur ond anlipig aldormon ond cyninges þegnas oft rade on ridon þe mon na ne rimde; ond þæs geares wærun ofslægene viiii eorlas ond an cyning. Ond þy geare namon Westseaxe friþ wiþ þone here.

865   In this year the heathen Viking army remained in Thanet, and made a peace with the people of Kent; and the people of Kent promised them money in order to have that peace. And under the peace and the promise of money, the Viking army moved away stealthily by night and ravaged all of eastern Kent.

866   In this year Æþelred, Æþelberht's brother, succeeded to the kingdom of the West Saxons; and in the same year a great Viking army arrived in the land of the English and took winter quarters in East Anglia, and there they were given horses, and they made peace with them.

867   In this year the Viking army travelled from East Anglia over the mouth of the River Humber to the city of York in Northumbria; and there was great conflict of that people among themselves; and they had deposed Osberht their king and accepted an alien king, Ælla. And it was late in that year when they turned their attention to fighting against the Viking army, and even so, they gathered a great army and went after the Viking army at York and stormed the city, and some of them got inside; and there was violent slaughter of the Northumbrians there, some inside, some outside, and the kings were both killed, and those who survived made peace with the Viking army. And in the same year, Bishop Ealhstan died, and he held that see for fifty years at Sherborne, and his body lies there in the town.

868   In this year that same Viking army travelled into Mercia to Nottingham, and took winter quarters there. And Burhred, king of the Mercians, and his witan asked Æþelred, king of Wessex, and Ælfred, his brother, that they help them fight against the Viking army. And then they travelled with the West Saxon army into Mercia up to Nottingham, and there they met the Viking army in that fortified place, and no serious battle happened there, and the Mercians made a peace with the Viking army.

869   In this year the Viking army went to York again, and remained there for one year.

870   In this year the Viking army rode through Mercia into East Anglia, and took winter quarters at Thetford. And that winter King Edmund fought against them, and the Danes gained the victory, and murdered the king, and occupied the entire region. And in that year Archbishop Ceolnoþ died; and Æþelred, bishop of Wiltshire, was chosen as archbishop of Canterbury.

871   In this year the Viking army arrived in Reading in Wessex, and three days after, two eorls rode up. Then Ealdorman Æþelwulf met them at Englefield, and fought against them there, and possessed the victory. Four days after this, King Æþelred and Ælfred, his brother, led a great army there to Reading, and fought against the Viking army; and there was great slaughter on either side, and Ealdorman Æþelwulf was killed; and the Danes controlled the place of slaughter.

And about four days after this, King Æþelred and Ælfred, his brother, fought against the entire Viking army at Ashdown. And the Vikings were in two divisions: in one were Bachsecg and Halfdene, the heathen kings, and in the other were the eorls. And then King Æþelred fought against the troop of the king, and King Bachsecg was killed there; and Ælfred, his brother, was against the eorls' troop, and Eorl Sidroc the Old was killed there, and Eorl Sidroc the Young, and Eorl Osbern, and Eorl Fræna and Eorl Hareld. And the Viking armies both fled, and many thousands were killed, and the fighting continued until night.

And about fourteen days after this, King Æþelred and Ælfred, his brother, fought against a Viking army at Basing, and there the Danes controlled the place of slaughter.

And about two months after this, King Æþelred and Ælfred, his brother, fought against the Viking army at Merton, and they were in two divisions, and they both fled, and for long into the day they possessed the victory. And there was great slaughter on either side, and the Danes controlled the place of slaughter; and there Bishop Heahmund was killed, and many good men. And after this battle a great summer army came.

And after this, over Easter, King Æþelred died; and he ruled for five years, and his body lies at Wimborne.

Then his brother Ælfred, Æþelwulf's offspring, succeeded to the kingdom of Wessex. And about one

872   Her for se here to Lundenbyrig from Readingum ond þær wintersetl nam, ond þa namon Mierce friþ wiþ þone here.

873   Her for se here on Norþhymbre ond he nam wintersetl on Lindesse æt Turecesiege, ond þa namon Mierce friþ wiþ þone here.

80   **874**   Her for se here from Lindesse to Hreopedune ond þær wintersetl nam, ond þone cyning Burgræd ofer sæ adræfdon ymb xxii wintra þæs þe he rice hæfde ond þæt lond all geeodon. Ond he for to Rome ond þær gesæt ond his lic liþ on Sancta Marian ciricean on Angelcynnes scole. Ond þy ilcan geare hie sealdon anum unwisum cyninges þegne Miercna rice to haldanne, ond he him aþas swor ond gislas salde þæt he him gearo wære swa hwelce dæge swa hie hit habban
85   wolden ond he gearo wære mid him selfum ond on allum þam þe him læstan woldon to þæs heres þearfe.

875   Her for se here from Hreopedune, ond Healfdene for mid sumum þam here on Norþhymbre ond nam wintersetl be Tinan þære ei, ond se here þæt lond geeode ond oft hergade on Peohtas ond on Stræcled-Walas. Ond for Godrum ond Oscytel ond Anwynd, þa iii cyningas, of Hreopedune to
90   Grantebrycge mid micle here ond sæton þær an gear. Ond þy sumera for Ælfred cyning ut on sæ mid sciphere ond geafeaht wiþ vii sciphlæstas, ond hiera an gefeng ond þa oþru gefliemde.

876   Her hiene bestæl se here in Werham Wesseaxna fierde, ond wiþ þone here se cyning friþ nam, ond him þa aþas sworon on þam halgan beage, þe hie ær nanre þeode noldon, þæt hie hrædlice of his rice foren; ond hie þa under þam hie nihtes bestælon þære fierde, se gehorsoda
95   here, into Escanceaster. Ond þy geare Healfdene Norþanhymbra lond gedælde ond ergende wæron ond hiera tilgende.

877   Her cuom se here into Escanceastre from Werham, ond se sciphere sigelede west ymbutan, ond þa mette hie micel yst on sæ, ond þær forwearþ cxx scipa æt Swanawic. Ond se cyning Ælfred æfter þam gehorsudan here mid fierde rad oþ Exanceaster ond hie hindan ofridan ne meahte ær
100   hie on þam fæstene wæron, þær him mon to ne meahte; ond hie him þær foregislas saldon, swa fela swa he habban wolde, ond micle aþas sworon, ond þa godne friþ heoldon. Ond þa on hærfeste gefor se here on Miercna lond ond hit gedældon sum ond sum Ceolwulfe saldon.

878   Her hiene bestæl se here on midne winter ofer tuelftan niht to Cippanhamme, ond geridon Wesseaxna lond ond gesæton, ond micel þæs folces ofer sæ adræfdon, ond þæs oþres þone mæstan
105   dæl hie geridon ond him to gecirdon buton þam cyninge Ælfrede: ond he lytle werede unieþelice æfter wudum for ond on morfæstenum.

Ond þæs ilcan wintra wæs Inwæres broþur ond Healfdenes on Westseaxum on Defenascire mid xxiii scipum; ond hiene mon þær ofslog, ond dccc monna mid him, ond xl monna his heres.

Ond þæs on Eastron worhte Ælfred cyning lytle werede geweorc æt Æþelinga-eigge; ond of
110   þam geweorce wæs winnende wiþ þone here, ond Sumursætna se dæl se þær niehst wæs.

Þa on þære seofoðan wiecan ofer Eastron, he gerad to Ecgbryhtes stane be eastan Sealwyda. Ond him to coman þær ongen Sumorsæte alle, ond Wilsætan, ond Hamtunscir (se dæl se hiere behinon sæ wæs), ond his gefægene wærun. Ond he for ymb ane niht of þam wicum to Iglea, ond þæs ymb ane to Eþandune; ond þær gefeaht wiþ alne þone here ond hiene gefliemde, ond him æfter rad
115   oþþæt geweorc, ond þær sæt xiiii niht. Ond þa salde se here him foregislas ond micle aþas þæt hie of his rice uuoldon; ond him eac geheton þæt hiera kyning fulwihte onfon wolde: ond hie þæt gelæston swa. Ond þæs ymb iii wiecan com se cyning to him Godrum, þritiga sum þara monna þe in þam here weorþuste wæron æt Alre, ond þæt is wiþ Æþelingga-eige; ond his se cyning þær onfeng æt fulwihte, ond his crismlising wæs æt Weþmor. Ond he was xii niht mid þam cyninge;
120   ond he hine miclum ond his geferan mid feo weorðude.

month after this, King Ælfred fought with a small troop at Wilton against the entire Viking army, and long in the day they put him to flight, and the Danes controlled the place of slaughter.

And that year there were nine general engagements against the Viking army in the kingdom south of the Thames, besides those raids which Ælfred, the king's brother, and a single ealdorman and the king's thanes often rode to which no one ever counted. And that year nine eorls and one king were killed; and in the same year, the West Saxons made peace with the Viking force.

872   In this year the Viking army travelled from Reading to London, and made their winter quarters there, and then the Mercians made peace with the Viking force.

873   In this year the Viking army travelled into Northumbria, and it made winter quarters at Torksey in Lindsey, and the Mercians made peace with the Viking force.

874   In this year the Viking army travelled from Lindsey to Repton and took winter quarters there, and drove out King Burgræd over the sea about twenty-two years after he had acceded to the kingdom; and they overran that entire region. And he journeyed to Rome and settled there, and his body lies in St Mary's church in the English area. And in that same year, they gave the kingdom of Mercia to a foolish king's thane[5] to control, and he swore oaths to them and gave hostages, so that the kingdom would be ready for them on whatever day they might want to have it, and he himself would be ready with all those who would serve him whenever the Viking army had need.

875   In this year the Viking army travelled from Repton, and Healfdene went with some of the army into Northumbria, and took winter quarters by the River Tyne; and the Viking force overran that region and often raided among the Picts and among the Britons of Strathclyde. And Guthrum and Oscytel and Anwynd, the three kings, travelled from Repton to Cambridge with a great Viking army, and stayed there for a year. And in that summer King Ælfred journeyed out on the sea with a ship-army and fought against seven crews, and captured one of them and made the others flee.

876   In this year the Viking army moved stealthily away from the West Saxon army into Wareham. And the king made peace with the Viking force, and they swore oaths to him on a holy ring, which previously they would not do with any nation, that they would go quickly from his kingdom; and then with that, they moved stealthily in the night away from the English army, the mounted Viking troops, into Exeter. And in that year Healfdene split up the region of Northumbria; and they were ploughing and providing for themselves.

877   In this year the Viking army travelled from Wareham into Exeter, and the fleet sailed around to the west, and then they came across great storms at sea, and there one hundred and twenty ships were lost at Swanage. And King Ælfred rode after the mounted Viking force with his army up to Exeter, and they could not overtake them from behind before they were in the fortress where one could not get at them. And they gave him there preliminary hostages, as many as he wished to have, and swore great oaths, and then held a good peace. And then at harvest-time the Viking army travelled into the region of Mercia, and they divided up some of it and they gave some to Ceolwulf.

878   In this year the Viking army moved secretly away in midwinter after Twelfth Night to Chippenham, and overran the region of Wessex and occupied it, and drove many of the people over the sea. The other greater part they overran and they turned the people to them, except for King Ælfred, and he went with a small troop far through the woods and onto the inaccessible moors with difficulty. And that same winter Inwar's brother Healfdene was in Wessex, in Devonshire, with twenty-three ships; and he was killed there and eight hundred men with him, and forty men of his warband.

And at Easter, King Ælfred with a small troop built a fortified dwelling at Athelney; and from that fort they were fighting against the Viking army, with the help of the men of Somerset who were nearest.

5   To a thane called Ceolwulf.

The Reign of Æðelstan and *The Battle of Brunanburh*

The following text covers annals 924 to 940 of *The Anglo-Saxon Chronicle*, the reign of King Æðelstan of Wessex, grandson of Alfred. This part of the *Chronicle* is probably best known for its inclusion of the heroic poem *The Battle of Brunanburh*. It survives in four of the manuscripts that make up the collective *Anglo-Saxon Chronicle*; the version below is from Manuscript A, 'The Parker Chronicle', folios 26 recto to 27 recto. The poem, which forms the annal entry for 937, is written as prose in the manuscript but a single point is usually placed after half-lines; here, it is edited as verse. The major scholarly edition of the poetic text is that of A. Campbell, *The Battle of Brunanburh*.[6] Campbell terms the poem and the other surviving poems contained in the *Chronicle* manuscripts as 'panegyrics upon royal persons, arising out of the com-memoration of events in which they were concerned'.[7] The poet certainly lauds his English protagonists and glorifies their abilities as warriors to the detriment of the Norse opponents, who are made to appear somewhat cowardly in their retreat to Ireland; and whose fragmentation and loss is emphasized by the unity of the rejoicing brothers' return to Wessex. Many typical motifs of Old English heroic poetry are incorporated into this poem, from the vocabulary of weaponry to the depiction of the enjoyment of the birds and beasts of battle of their gruesome prey. The author of the prose *Chronicle* account that surrounds the poem is noticeably controlled in his praise of the king, preferring to create a sense of objectivity and historical restraint; the poem is the more effective precisely because of its context.

The Reign of Æðelstan and *The Battle of Brunanburh*

924   Her Eadweard cing forþferde, ond Æþelstan his sunu feng to rice. Ond Sancte Dunstan wearð akænned, ond Wulfelm feng to þan arcebiscoprice on Cantuarebyri.

931   Her mon hadode Byrnstan bisceop to Wintanceastre .iiii. kalendas Junii, ond he heold þridde healf gear bisceopdom.

5   932   Her forþferde Fryþestan bisceop.

933   Her for Æþelstan cyning in on Scotland, ægþer ge mid landhere ge mid scyphere, ond his micel oferhergade. Ond Byrnstan bisceop forþferde on Wintanceastre to Omnium Sanctorum.

934   Her feng Ælfheah bisceop to bisceopdome.

937   Her Æþelstan cyning,   eorla dryhten,
10   beorna beahgifa,   ond his broþor eac,
          Eadmund æþeling,   ealdorlangne tir
          geslogon æt sæcce   sweorda ecgum
          ymbe Brunnanburh.   Bordweal clufan,
          heowan heaþolinde   hamora lafan,
15   afaran Eadweardes,   swa him geæþele wæs
          from cneomægum,   þæt hi æt campe oft

6   A. Campbell, ed., *The Battle of Brunanburh* (London, 1938).   7   Ibid., p. 37.

Then in the seventh week after Easter Ælfred rode to Ecgbert's Stone, east of Selwood. And then all those of Somerset and those of Wiltshire and Hampshire (the part on this side of the sea) came to meet him there and were glad of his coming. And one day after this, he went from that camp to Island Wood, and about one day later to Edington; and there he fought against the entire Viking force, and put it to flight, and rode after it up to the fort, and besieged them there for fourteen days. And then the Viking army gave him hostages and great oaths that they would go from his kingdom; and they also promised that their king would receive baptism; and they carried out just that. And about three weeks later, King Godrum came to him, one of thirty of the men who were the most worthy in the Viking army, at Aller (and that is near Athelney); and the king received him at baptism there; and his removal of the baptism robe was at Wedmore. And he stayed twelve days with the king; and he greatly honoured him and his companions with property.

The Reign of Æðelstan and *The Battle of Brunanburh*

924 In this year King Edward died, and Æþelstan his son succeeded to the kingdom. And Saint Dunstan was born, and Wulfelm succeeded to the archbishopric of Canterbury.

931 In this year Byrnstan was consecrated bishop of Winchester on 29 May, and he held that see for two and a half years.

5   **932** In this year Bishop Fryþestan died.

933 In this year King Æþelstan went into Scotland with both an army and a fleet, and ravaged much of it. And Bishop Byrnstan died in Winchester on All Saints' Day.

934 In this year Bishop Ælfheah succeeded to the see [of Winchester].

937 In this year King Æþelstan, lord of warriors,
10   ring-giver of men, and also his brother,
         atheling Edmund, obtained eternal glory
         by fighting in battle with the edges of swords
         around Brunanburh. They split the shield-wall,
         cut down the lime-shields with the remnants of hammers,[8]
15   Edward's offspring, as was natural for them
         because of their ancestors, that they should often defend

---

8   i.e. swords.

wiþ laþra gehwæne   land ealgodon,
hord ond hamas.   Hettend crungun,
Sceotta leoda   ond scipflotan

20   fæge feollan.   Feld dænnede
secgas hwate,   siðþan sunne up
on morgentid;   mære tungol
glad ofer grundas,   Godes condel beorht,
eces Drihtnes,   oð sio æþele gesceaft

25   sah to setle.   Þær læg secg mænig
garum ageted,   guma norþerna
ofer scild scoten;   swilce Scittisc eac,
werig, wiges sæd.   Wesseaxe forð
ondlongne dæg   eorodcistum

30   on last legdun   laþum þeodum,
heowan herefleman   hindan þearle
mecum mylenscearpan.   Myrce ne wyrndon
heeardes hondplegan   hæleþa nanum
þæ mid Anlafe   ofer æra gebland

35   on lides bosme   land gesohtun,
fæge to gefeohte.   Fife lægun
on þam campstede,   cyninges giunge,
sweordum aswefede;   swilce seofene eac
eorlas Anlafes,   unrim heriges,

40   flotan ond Sceotta.   Þær geflemed wearð
Norðmanna bregu,   nede gebeded,
to lides stefne   litle weorode;
cread cnear on flot,   cyning ut gewat
on fealene flod: feorh generede.

45   Swilce þær eac se froda   mid fleame com
on his cyþþe norð,   Costontinus,
har hilderinc,   hreman ne þorfte
mæcan gemanan;   he wæs his mæga sceard,
freonda gefylled   on folcstede,

50   beslagen æt sæcce;   ond his sunu forlet
on wælstowe   wundun fergrunden,
giungne æt guðe.   Gelpan ne þorfte
beorn blandenfeax   bilgeslehtes,
eald inwidda,   ne Anlaf þy ma;

55   mid heora herelafum   hlehhan ne þorftun
þæt heo beaduweorca   beteran wurdun
on campstede   cumbolgehnastes,
garmittinge,   gumena gemotes,
wæpengewrixles,   þæs hi on wælfelda

60   wiþ Eadweardes   afaran plegodan.
    Gewitan him þa Norþmen   nægledcnearrum,
dreorig daraða laf,   on Dingesmere
ofer deop wæter   Difelin secan,
ond eft Hiraland,   æwiscmode.

65   Swilce þa gebroþer   begen ætsamne,
cyning ond æþeling,   cyþþe sohton,
Wesseaxena land,   wiges hremige.

their land, at battle against every enemy,
treasure and homes. The enemies perished,
the people of the Scots and the sailors
20 fell doomed. The field was darkened
with the blood of warriors, after the sun rose
in the morning time; the glorious heavenly body
glided over the land, the bright candle of God,
of the eternal Lord, until that noble creature
25 sank in setting. There lay many a warrior
destroyed by spears, men of the north
shot above the shield; likewise the Scottish too,
weary, sated with war. The West Saxons went forward
the whole length of the day with the troops,
30 pressed on in the track of the hostile people,[9]
cut down fugitive soldiers severely from behind
with file-sharpened swords. The Mercians did not refuse
hard battle to any of the heroes
who with Anlaf over the turmoil of the seas
35 in the ship's bosom sought land,
doomed in battle. Five lay
on the battlefield, young kings,
put to sleep by swords; similarly another seven
jarls of Anlaf, a countless number of the army,
40 sailors and Scots. There, put to flight,
was the prince of the Norsemen, compelled by force
into the prow of the ship with a small troop;
the ship was driven onto water, the king sailed out
onto the fallow sea: he saved his life.
45 Likewise there too the old Costontinus
with flight came into his northern native land;
this grey-haired warrior had no cause to exult
in the meeting of swords; he was deprived of kinsmen,
of friends, killed on the battlefield,
50 deprived by the strife; and he left his son
on the slaughter-field ground down by wounds,
young in battle. The grey-haired warrior
had no reason to boast there of the sword-clash,
the old wicked man, no more than did Anlaf;
55 with their remnant of an army they had no cause to rejoice
that they would be the better in deeds of war
on the battlefield in the clash of banners,
in the meeting of spears, in the confrontation of men,
in the hostile encounter, when they played on the slaughter-field
60 with Edward's descendants.
    Then the Norsemen departed in nailed ships,
mournful survivors of spears, into Dingesmere
over deep water to seek Dublin,
and Ireland again, ashamed.
65 Likewise, both brothers together,[10]
the king and the prince, sought their native land,
the country of the West Saxons, exultant in battle.

---

9 As Campbell, *Battle of Brunanburh*, p. 105.   10 Æþelstan and Edmund.

Letan him behindan   hræw bryttian
saluwigpadan,   þone sweartan hræfn,
70   hyrnednebban,   ond þane hasewanpadan,
earn æftan hwit,   æses brucan,
grædigne guðhafoc,   ond þæt græge deor,
wulf on wealde.   Ne wearð wæl mare
on þis eiglande   æfer gieta
75   folces gefylled   beforan þissum
sweordes ecgum,   þæs þe us secgað bec,
ealde uðwitan,   siþþan eastan hider
Engle ond Seaxe   up becoman,
ofer brad brimu   Brytene sohtan,
80   wlance wigsmiþas,   Weealles ofercoman,
eorlas arhwate   eard begeatan.

940   Her Æþelstan cyning forðferde on vi kalendas Novembris ymbe xl wintra butan anre niht þæs þe Ælfred cyning forþferde, ond Eadmund æþeling feng to rice, ond he wæs þa xviii wintre. Ond Æþelstan cyning rixade xiiii gear ond x wucan. Þa was Wulfelm arcebiscop on Cantwarebyri.

They left behind them to enjoy the corpses
the dark-coated one, the black raven,
70   the horny-beaked one, and the dun-coated one,
the eagle, white from behind, to enjoy the carrion,
the greedy bird of war, and the grey animal,
the wolf in the wood. Never was there a greater slaughter
of people killed on this island
75   by the sword's edge, even up until now
or before this, of which books
tell us, since from the east
the Angles and Saxons arrived up
over the broad seas to seek Britain,
80   proud warmongers, they overcame the Welsh,
noble warriors, eager for glory, they conquered the country.

940   In this year King Æþelstan died on 27 October about forty years less one night after King Ælfred died, and Prince Edmund succeeded to the kingdom, and he was then eighteen years old. And King Æþelstan reigned for fourteen years and ten weeks. Wulfelm was archbishop of Canterbury at the time.

The Exeter Book

The Exeter Book, Exeter, Cathedral Library, 3501, folios 8–130, is one of four major poetic codices surviving from Anglo-Saxon England. It dates from around the 960s or 970s and was probably acquired for Exeter Cathedral by Bishop Leofric in the eleventh century. A donation list, datable to 1069–72, shows that among the manuscripts Leofric left to his secular cathedral was a 'mycel Englisc boc be gehwilcum þingum on leoðwisum geworht' (a 'large English book about many things written in verse'). This entry is generally thought to refer to the Exeter Book. Although the manuscript was at Exeter by the third quarter of the eleventh century, and has remained there ever since, this need not imply that it originated at Exeter. Some scholars believe the book was written at Exeter,[1] others believe that its origin may lie elsewhere, such as Crediton,[2] or Glastonbury.[3]

Wherever the manuscript was written, it remains one of the most important extant volumes from the period because it contains a large number of unique Old English secular and religious poetic texts. One scribe who copied the collection from a number of different exemplars writes the manuscript. The texts appear, *prima facie*, to be diverse in nature, complex and interesting. The book is, though, organized into sections which reflect themes and issues appropriate to the later tenth-century monastic milieu.[4] Some leaves of the manuscript have been damaged over the centuries; this is particularly the case with folios 117–30 where it is thought that a fire brand fell onto the back of the book. This damage severely affects the reading of most of the texts concerned.

The Exeter Book, reproduced in facsimile by R. W. Chambers,[5] contains over thirty individual poetic texts as well as more than ninety riddles. Conner argues for the classification of these works into numerous genres, organized into three booklets, written in the order 2, 3, 1.[6] The second booklet demonstrates connections with continental culture, and contains narrative and catalogue poetry, allegory and elegy, among others (for example, *Juliana*, *The Gifts of Men*, *Maxims I*, *The Whale* and *The Wanderer*). The third booklet reflects clerical as well as monastic interests, and represents the amalgamation of two separate collections.[7] This third booklet contains the Riddles as well as religious and elegiac material, such as *The Descent into Hell*, *Soul and Body II*, *Deor*, *Wulf and Eadwacer*, *The Wife's Lament*, *The Husband's Message*, *Resignation A and B*. The first booklet (containing the three *Christ* poems, and *Guthlac A and B*) is concerned with salvation and how to obtain it. While not all critics agree with Conner's division of the Exeter Book into three sections,[8] this approach usefully suggests ways in which the manuscript can be shown to be an organized and coherent collection, rather than an assemblage of disparate poetic texts.

From the wide choice of material available for inclusion here, I have selected a number of texts that show something of the diversity of poetry in this collection. Some of these are among the most commonly discussed works from the Anglo-Saxon poetic corpus (*The Wife's Lament*, *The Wanderer*, for example). Others are less familiar, but no less worthy of study (*Advent Lyrics VII and VIII*, *The Whale*). It should be noted that the titles of these poems are not supplied in the manuscript itself, but have been provided by editors from the nineteenth century up to the present day.

1 P. W. Conner, *Anglo-Saxon Exeter: A Tenth-Century Cultural History* (Woodbridge, 1993).

2 B. Muir, *The Exeter Book Anthology of Old English Poetry: An Edition of Exeter, Dean and Chapter MS 3501*, 2 vols (Exeter, 1994). He also sees Exeter as a possibility.

3 Tentatively suggested by R. Gameson, 'The Origin of the Exeter Book of Old English Poetry', *Anglo-Saxon England* 25 (1996), 135–87.

  Gameson also suggests, however, that we may never know where the manuscript was written.

4 See Muir, *Exeter Book Anthology*, I, pp. 18–27, and especially Conner, *Anglo-Saxon Exeter*, ch. vi.

5 R. W. Chambers, ed. (Facsimile) *The Exeter Book of Old English Poetry* (London, 1933).

6 Conner, *Anglo-Saxon Exeter*, ch. vi.

7 Conner, *Anglo-Saxon Exeter*, pp. 159–62.

8 See Muir, *Exeter Book Anthology*, for example.

ADVENT LYRICS VII AND *VIII* (FROM *CHRIST I*)

The *Advent Lyrics*, or *Christ I* as this sequence is also known, are the opening lines of Old English poetry in the Exeter Book. Together with *Christ II* (the Ascension) and *Christ III* (Judgement Day), the *Advent Lyrics* form part of the revelation of the whole of salvation history, in particular, the meaning that Christ's birth has for humanity. There are twelve lyrics in all, written in the manuscript in five sections (not as twelve individual poems). They are 'inspired by particular Advent antiphons, which were either chanted or recited at Vespers, usually before and after the Magnificat'.[9] Conner sees the *Advent Lyrics* as 'a celebration of the images and symbols which make monasticism possible: the Incarnation, which gave the monk his model in Christ; the Virgin-birth, which provided the monk with the highest precedent for personal intimacy with God; and the fellowship of angels, which justified the monk's labour in the divine service, just as angels' labours are spent in praising the Godhead'.[10] The text is therefore very much a product of the Benedictine reform of the tenth century.

Edited here are lines 164–274, from folios 10 recto to 11 verso. These lines are generally divided into *Lyrics VII* and *VIII*, which together form the third section of the poem as it occurs in the manuscript. These two lyrics concern the exchange between Mary and Joseph in which Christ's divinity is revealed in accordance with the prophets, and the prayer to Christ the redeemer that emphasizes the eternity of Christ's existence, and expresses a longing for the return of the Messiah. The relevant antiphon for *Lyric VII* is 'O Joseph, why did you believe what before you feared? Why indeed? The One whom Gabriel announced would be coming, Christ, is begotten in her by the Holy Spirit.' The antiphon for *Lyric VIII* is 'O King of Peace, you who were born before the ages: come forth through the golden gate, visit those you have redeemed, and summon them back to that place from which they rushed headlong through sin.'

Advent Lyric VII consists almost wholly of a dialogue between Mary and Joseph that Bradley points out is similar in form to liturgical drama.[11] He states that: 'the poet of *Lyric 7* merits at least a footnote in the history of the first emergence of medieval religious drama in England'. There has been some controversy about the ascription of the speeches to Mary and Joseph.[12] Here, Mary speaks at lines 1–4a, 13b–18a and 34a–49; Joseph speaks all other lines, apart from 32b–33, spoken by the poet.

Advent Lyric VII

'Eala Joseph min,   Jacobes bearn,
mæg Davides   mæran cyninges,
nu þu freode scealt   fæste gedælan,
alætan lufan mine.'   'Ic lungre eam
5   deope gedrefed,   dome bereafod,
forðon Ic worn for þe   worde hæbbe
sidra sorga   ond sarcwida,
hearmes gehyred,   ond me hosp sprecað,
tornworda fela.   Ic tearas sceal
10   geotan geomormod.   God eaþe mæg
gehælan hygesorge   heortan minre,
afrefran feasceaftne.   Eala fæmne geong,
mægð Maria!'   'Hwæt bemurnest ðu,
cleopast cearigende?   Ne Ic culpan in þe,
15   incan ænigne   æfre onfunde,
womma geworhtra,   ond þu þa word spricest
swa þu sylfa sie   synna gehwylcre
firena gefylled.'   'Ic to fela hæbbe
þæs byrdscypes   bealwa onfongen.
20   Hu mæg Ic ladigan   laþan spræce
oþþe ondsware   ænige findan
wraþum towiþere?   Is þæt wide cuð

9 Muir, *Exeter Book Anthology*, II, p. 386.
10 Conner, *Anglo-Saxon Exeter*, p. 162.
11 S. A. J. Bradley, *Anglo-Saxon Poetry*, 2nd edn (London, 1995), p. 204.

12 Muir, *Exeter Anthology*, II, p. 387.

Advent Lyric VII

'Oh my Joseph, Jacob's son,
kinsman of David the famous king,
now you intend to separate our affection completely,
to renounce my love.' 'I am suddenly
5   deeply troubled, deprived of reputation,
because I have listened to a number
of painful words and taunts for you,
damaging remarks, and they speak to me in insults,
in many offensive expressions. Sorrowful,
10   I must shed tears. God might easily
heal my anxious heart,
comfort me, helpless. Alas young woman,
Mary the virgin!' 'Why do you mourn,
calling out as one so sad? I have never found fault with you,
15   nor have I ever found suspicion
of you doing wrong, and you speak those words
as if you yourself were filled
with every sin and crime.' 'I have received too many
injuries because of this pregnancy.
20   How can I dispute the hateful rumours
or find any response
in answer to these hostile ones? It is widely known

þæt Ic of þam torhtan   temple Dryhtnes
onfeng freolice   fæmnan clæne,
25   womma lease,   ond nu gehwyrfed is
þurh nathwylces.   Me nawþer deag,
secge ne swige.   Gif Ic soð sprece,
þonne sceal Davides   dohtor sweltan,
stanum astyrfed.   Gen strengre is
30   þæt Ic morþor hele;   scyle manswara
laþ leoda gehwam   lifgan siþþan,
fracoð in folcum.'   Þa seo fæmne onwrah
ryhtgeryno,   ond þus reordade:
'Soð Ic secge   þurh Sunu Meotudes,
35   gæsta Geocend,   þæt Ic gen ne conn
þurh gemæcscipe   monnes ower
ænges on eorðan;   ac me eaden wearð,
geongre in geardum,   þæt me Gabrihel,
heofones heagengel,   hælo gebodade.
40   Sægde soðlice   þæt me swegles gæst
leoman onlyhte,   sceolde Ic lifes þrym
geberan, beorhtne Sunu,   bearn eacen Godes,
torhtes Tirfruma.   Nu Ic his tempel eam,
gefremed butan facne,   in me frofre gæst
45   geeardode.   Nu þu ealle forlæt
sare sorgceare.   Saga ecne þonc
mærum Meotodes Sunu   þæt Ic his modor gewearð,
fæmne forð seþeah,   ond þu fæder cweden
woruldcund bi wene.   Sceolde witedom
50   in him sylfum beon   soðe gefylled.'

Advent Lyric VIII

Eala þu soða   ond þu sibsuma
ealra cyninga Cyning,   Crist ælmihtig,
hu þu ær wære   eallum geworden
worulde þrymmum   mid þinne Wuldorfæder,
55   cild acenned   þurh his cræft ond meaht.
Nis ænig nu   eorl under lyfte,
secg searoþoncol,   to þæs swiðe gleaw
þe þæt asecgan mæge   sundbuendum,
areccan mid ryhte,   hu þe rodera Weard
60   æt frymðe genom   him to freobearne.
Þæt wæs þara þinga   þe her þeoda cynn
gefrugnen mid folcum,   æt fruman ærest
geworden under wolcnum,   þæt witig God,
lifes Ordfruma,   leoht ond þystro
65   gedælde dryhtlice,   ond him wæs domes geweald,
ond þa wisan abead   weoroda Ealdor:
'Nu sie geworden forþ   a to widan feore
leoht, lixende gefea,   lifgendra gehwam
þe in cneorissum   cende weorðen.'
70   Ond þa sona gelomp,   þa hit swa sceolde,
leoma leohtade   leoda mægþum,
torht mid tunglum,   æfter þon tida bigong.

that from the noble temple of the Lord
I freely received a pure woman,
25 free from sin, and now she is changed
because of someone unknown. Neither will avail me,
speaking nor silence. If I speak the truth,
then David's daughter will die,
killed with stones. Yet it is worse
30 that I conceal this mortal sin; the perjurer must
live afterwards hated by every person,
a criminal among people.' Then the virgin revealed
the true miracle, and thus said:
    'I will tell the truth through the Son of the Creator,
35 the Saviour of souls, that I still do not know
any man through a sexual relationship
anywhere on earth; but it was granted to me,
a young woman at home, that Gabriel,
heaven's archangel, announced his greeting.
40 He said truthfully that the heavenly spirit
would illuminate me with light, that I would bear
the glory of life, the bright Son, the mighty child of God,
the radiant Prince of glory. Now I am his temple,
made so without blemish, in me the comforting spirit
45 had resided. Now you should abandon all
sorrowful mourning. Say eternal thanks
to the excellent Son of the Creator that I become his mother,
while yet remaining a virgin, and you, it is said,
have become his worldly father. Truly,
50 that prophecy had to be fulfilled in him, himself.'

Advent Lyric VIII

O you true and peace-loving
King of all kings, Christ almighty,
you were in existence before all
the world's multitudes with your glorious Father,
55 born a child through his strength and might.
There is now no man under the sky,
no shrewd person, who is prudent to the extent that
he can reveal to mankind,
explain correctly how the Guardian of heaven
60 in the beginning undertook you to him as noble-born son.
That was one of the things that humans here
heard tell among the people, that first at the creation
it happened under the clouds that the wise God
the Creator of life, parted light and dark
65 in a lordly way, and the power of supremacy was with him,
and the Lord of hosts decreed this ordinance:
'Now let there shine forth for ever and ever
light, a splendid joy for each living thing
which may be produced in posterity.'
70 And this immediately happened, just as it had to be,
the radiance lit the families of people,
glorious among the stars, throughout the passing of time.

Sylfa sette   þæt þu Sunu wære
efeneardigende   mid þinne engan Frean
75 ærþon oht þisses   æfre gewurde.
Þu eart seo snyttro   þe þas sidan gesceaft
mid þi Waldende   worhtes ealle.
Forþon nis ænig þæs horsc,   ne þæs hygecræftig,
þe þin fromcyn mæge   fira bearnum
80 sweotule geseþan.   Cum, nu, sigores Weard,
Meotod moncynnes,   ond þine miltse her
arfæst ywe.   Us is eallum neod
þæt we þin medrencynn   motan cunnan,
ryhtgeryno,   nu we areccan ne mægon
85 þæt fædrencynn   fier owihte.
Þu þisne middangeard   milde geblissa
þurh ðinne hercyme,   hælende Crist,
ond þa gyldnan geatu,   þe in geardagum
ful longe ær   bilocen stodan,
90 heofona Heahfrea,   hat ontynan,
ond usic þonne gesece   þurh þin sylfes gong
eaðmod to eorþan.   Us is þinra arna þearf:
hafað se awyrgda   wulf tostenced,
deor dædscua,   Dryhten, þin eowde,
95 wide towrecene.   Þæt ðu, Waldend, ær
blode gebohtes,   þæt se bealofulla
hyneð heardlice,   ond him on hæft nimeð
ofer usse nioda lust.   Forþon we, Nergend, þe
biddað geornlice   breostgehygdum
100 þæt þu hrædlice   helpe gefremme
wergum wreccan,   þæt se wites bona
in helle grund   hean gedreose,
ond þin hondgeweorc,   hæleþa Scyppend,
mote arisan   ond on ryht cuman
105 to þam upcundan   æþelan rice,
þonan us ær þurh synlust   se swearta gæst
forteah ond fortylde,   þæt we, tires wone,
a butan ende   sculon ermþu dreogan,
butan þu usic þon ofostlicor,   ece Dryhten,
110 æt þam leodsceaþan,   lifgende God,
Helm alwihta,   hreddan wille.

He himself established that you, the Son, were
dwelling together with your one Lord
75   before any of this had ever been achieved.
You are the wisdom who made all of this
entire creation with the Ruler.
Therefore, there is no one so wise, nor so prudent,
who can clearly prove your origin
80   to the children of men. Come now, Lord of victory,
Ruler of mankind, and show here your mercy
and compassion. It is necessary for us all
that we might know your mother's family,
that true miracle, since we cannot explain
85   your father's ancestry any further at all.
Mercifully bless this earth
through your advent, saviour Christ,
and command to be opened the golden gates,
which previously in days of old for a very long time
90   stood locked, high Lord of the heavens,
and then seek us through your own arrival
as a humble one on earth. We have great need of your favours:
the cursed wolf, the wild beast and spirit of death
has driven apart, Lord, your flock,
95   and scattered it widely. Lord, that which
you bought with your blood before, the wicked one
seriously injures and seizes into bondage for himself
against the earnestness of our desires. Therefore, Saviour, we
fervently pray you in the thoughts of our hearts
100   that you give help quickly
to us, weary exiles, so that the torturing slayer
might fall despised into the pit of hell,
and your handiwork, Creator of men,
might rise up and come rightly
105   to the heavenly noble kingdom,
from where previously, through a lust for sin, the dark spirit
misled and seduced us, such that we, deprived of glory,
must suffer miseries forever without end,
unless you are the quicker, eternal Lord,
110   living God, Protector of all things,
in your desire to save us from the people's enemy.

THE WANDERER

The Wanderer is usually thought of as an elegy or wisdom poem, the first of a number of such poems included in the Exeter Book at folios 76 verso to 78 recto. There has been a great deal of critical debate surrounding the structure of the text. It may be a single dramatic monologue spoken by a solitary person, or a narrated poem consisting of a monologue enclosed within the framework of narratorial comments (at lines 1–7, 110–15). The *anhaga* 'solitary one' of line 1 is bereft of friends and worldly comforts, although some consolation is found in faith in the *Fæder in heofonum* ('Father in heaven'). This consolation, coming as it does at the end of the poem, seems overshadowed by the personal hardships that the *eardstapa* ('earth-stepper') so vividly describes. The loneliness of the solitary's position is emphasized by the nostalgic thoughts of previous days in the company of others; he is now lordless, unprotected and forced to exist alone, in extreme discomfort. The harsh weather heightens the predicament of the *anhaga*. The necessity to keep thoughts private, and the metaphors of imprisonment and binding, reinforce the feeling that it is *wyrd* ('fate') that has caused the present circumstances, not the voluntary actions of a self-imposed exile (unlike the Seafarer).

If this text is viewed as an extended interior monologue, one can see the progression of the *anhaga* from the misery and loneliness of his personal story (lines 1–57) to a general reflection on the transience of temporal things (themes familiar in *The Seafarer* too), and the need to reflect on virtuous and heroic behaviour at lines 58–114a in order to achieve heavenly comfort (lines 114b–15). Thus the individual situation extends into the universal and the *anhaga*'s experience becomes a lesson for all. This theme of consolation may have been influenced by Boethius's *Consolation of Philosophy*. It may also result from the spiritual advancement of the *anhaga* gaining the perspective of the *snottor* ('wise man'): that all earthly things are transitory, and that it is only in the next life that *fæstnung* ('permanence, stability', line 115) can be achieved.

The Wanderer and *The Seafarer* are often regarded as companion texts by scholars, and thus much criticism treats the two works together. Some of the major commentaries on *The Wanderer* are listed in the bibliography in this volume; many others can be found in Muir.[13]

The Wanderer

    Oft him anhaga are gebideð,
    Metudes miltse, þeah þe he modcearig
    geond lagulade longe sceolde
    hreran mid hondum hrimcealde sæ,
5   wadan wræclastas. Wyrd bið ful aræd.
     Swa cwæð eardstapa, earfeþa gemyndig,
    wraþra wælsleahta, winemæga hryre:
     'Oft Ic sceolde ana uhtna gehwylce
    mine ceare cwiþan. Nis nu cwicra nan
10 þe Ic him modsefan minne durre
    sweotule asecgan. Ic to soþe wat
    þæt biþ in eorle indryhten þeaw
    þæt he his ferðlocan fæste binde,
    healde his hordcofan, hycge swa he wille.
15 Ne mæg werig mod wyrde wiðstondan,
    ne se hreo hyge helpe gefremman.
    Forðon domgeorne dreorigne oft
    in hyra breostcofan bindað fæste.
    Swa Ic modsefan minne sceolde,
20 oft earmcearig, eðle bidæled,
    freomægum feor feterum sælan,
    siþþan geara iu goldwine minne
    hrusan heolstre biwrah ond Ic hean þonan
    wod wintercearig ofer waþema gebind,
25 sohte seledreorig sinces bryttan,
    hwær Ic feor oþþe neah findan meahte

---

13   Muir, *Exeter Book Anthology*, bibliography.

The Wanderer

Often the solitary man himself experiences favour,
the mercy of the Lord, although sorrowful in heart he
must long throughout the waterways
stir with his hands the ice-cold sea,
5   the paths of an exile. Fate is very inflexible.
   So spoke the earth-stepper, mindful of miseries,
of the cruel battles, the deaths of kinsmen:
   'Often, at every dawn, I alone must
lament my sorrows. There is now no one living
10   to whom I might dare to reveal clearly
my heart. I know too truly
that it is a noble custom that a man
should bind fast his breast,
should hold fast his thoughts, think as he will.
15   Nor can the weary mind withstand fate,
nor the turbulent mind find help.
Therefore those eager for glory must often
bind a heavy heart fast.
Thus I have had to bind my heart with fetters,
20   often wretched and sad, deprived of my homeland,
far from noble kinsmen,
since years ago my generous lord
I covered in the earth's hiding-place, and wretched I
went from there winter-sorrowing over the binding waves,
25   sad at the loss of the hall, sought a giver of treasure,
where I might find near or far

þone þe in meoduhealle   mine wisse,
oþþe mec freondleasne   frefran wolde,
wenian mid wynnum.   Wat se þe cunnað
30   hu sliþen bið   sorg to geferan
þam þe him lyt hafað   leofra geholena;
warað hine wræclast,   nales wunden gold,
ferðloca freorig,   nalæs foldan blæd.
Gemon he selesecgas   ond sincþege,
35   hu hine on geoguðe   his goldwine
wenede to wiste.   Wyn eal gedreas.
    Forþon wat se þe sceal   his winedryhtnes
leofes larcwidum   longe forþolian,
ðonne sorg ond slæp   somod ætgædre
40   earmne anhogan   oft gebindað,
þinceð him on mode   þæt he his mondryhten
clyppe ond cysse,   ond on cneo lecge
honda ond heafod,   swa he hwilum ær
in geardagum   giefstolas breac.
45   Ðonne onwæcneð eft,   wineleas guma,
gesihð him biforan   fealwe wegas,
baþian brimfuglas,   brædan feþra;
hreosan hrim ond snaw   hagle gemenged.
Þonne beoð þy hefigran   heortan benne,
50   sare æfter swæsne.   Sorg bið geniwad
þonne maga gemynd   mod geondhweorfeð;
greteð gliwstafum;   georne geondsceawað
secga geseldan;   swimmað oft on weg.
Fleotendra ferð   no þær fela bringeð
55   cuðra cwidegiedda.   Cearo bið geniwad
þam þe sendan sceal   swiþe geneahhe
ofer waþema gebind   werigne sefan.
    Forþon Ic geþencan ne mæg   geond þas woruld
for hwan modsefa   min ne gesweorce
60   þonne Ic eorla lif   eal geondþence,
hu hi færlice   flet ofgeafon,
modge maguþegnas.   Swa þes middangeard
ealra dogra gehwam   dreoseð ond fealleþ.
Forþon ne mæg wearþan wis   wer ær he age
65   wintra dæl in woruldrice.   Wita sceal geþyldig:
ne sceal no to hatheort,   ne to hrædwyrde,
ne to wac wiga,   ne to wanhydig,
ne to forht, ne to fægen,   ne to feohhgifre,
ne næfre gielpes to georn,   ær he geare cunne.
70   Beorn sceal gebidan   þonne he beot spriceð,
oþþæt collenferð   cunne gearwe
hwider hreþra gehygd   hweorfan wille.
Ongietan sceal gleaw hæle   hu gæstlic bið
þonne ealle þisse worulde wela   weste stondeð,
75   swa nu missenlice   geond þisne middangeard
winde biwaune   weallas stondaþ,
hrime bihrorene,   hryðge þa ederas.
Woriað þa winsalo.   Waldend licgað
dreame bidrorene;   duguþ eal gecrong

he who might show me affection in the meadhall,
or would comfort me, friendless,
entertain me with joys. He knows, he who is able to know,
30   how cruel sorrow is as a companion
to him who has few beloved confidants;
the paths of an exile occupy his mind, not wound gold at all,
a frozen heart, not the riches of the earth at all.
He remembers retainers and the receiving of treasure,
35   how in his youth his gold-giving lord
accustomed him to feasting. Joy has entirely gone.
      Therefore he knows, who must long forgo
his beloved lord's counsel,
when sorrow and sleep both together
40   often bind the wretched solitary man,
it seems to him in his mind that he embraces and kisses
his lord, and on his knee might lay
hands and head, as before he sometimes
enjoyed the gift-stool in days of old.
45   Then he awakes again, the friendless man,
sees before him fallow waves,
bathing seabirds, with spread feathers;
falling frost and snow are mixed with hail.
Then the wounds of the heart are the more heavy,
50   sorrowful for the beloved. Sorrow is renewed
when the memory of kinsmen pervades the mind;
he greets them joyfully; eagerly surveys
the companions of men; they often swim away again.
The spirits of seabirds do not bring many
55   familiar utterances there. Sorrow is renewed
to those who must send a weary heart
frequently over the binding waves.
      Therefore I cannot think throughout this world
why my mind should not grow dark
60   when I meditate on the lives of earls,
how they quickly left the floor of the hall,
brave young warriors. So this middle-earth
each and every day declines and falls.
Therefore no man may become wise, before he has had
65   his share of winters in the worldly kingdom. A wise man shall be patient:
he shall not be too hot-hearted, not too hasty of speech,
nor too weak a warrior, not too reckless,
nor too timorous nor too eager, nor too greedy for riches
nor ever too desirous of boasting, before he clearly may have knowledge.
70   A warrior shall wait when he speaks a boast,
until, stout-hearted, he knows clearly
where the thoughts of his heart might tend.
The wise warrior is able to perceive how ghostly it will be
when all this world's wealth stands waste,
75   just as now in various places throughout this middle-earth
walls stand blown by wind,
covered with frost, the buildings snow-swept.
The wine-halls topple. The rulers lie
deprived of joys; mature men all perished

80   wlonc bi wealle.   Sume wig fornom,
ferede in forðwege;   sumne fugel oþbær
ofer heanne holm;   sumne se hara wulf
deaðe gedælde;   sumne dreorighleor
in eorðscræfe   eorl gehydde.

85   Yþde swa þisne eardgeard   ælda Scyppend
oþþæt burgwara   breahtma lease,
eald enta geweorc   idlu stodon.

    Se þonne þisne wealsteal   wise geþohte
ond þis deorce lif   deope geondþenceð,

90   frod in ferðe,   feor oft gemon
wælsleahta worn,   ond þas word acwið:
"Hwær cwom mearg? Hwær cwom mago?   Hwær cwom maþþumgyfa?
Hwær cwom symbla gesetu?   Hwær sindon seledreamas?
Eala beorht bune!   Eala byrnwiga!

95   Eala þeodnes þrym!   Hu seo þrag gewat,
genap under nihthelm   swa heo no wære.
Stondeð nu on laste   leofre duguþe
weal wundrum heah,   wyrmlicum fah.
Eorlas fornoman   asca þryþe,

100   wæpen wælgifru,   wyrd seo mære,
ond þas stanhleoþu   stormas cnyssað,
hrið hreosende   hrusan bindeð
wintres woma,   þonne won cymeð,
nipeð nihtscua,   norþan onsendeð

105   hreo hæglfare   hæleþum on andan.
Eall is earfoðlic   eorþan rice;
onwendeð wyrda gesceaft   weoruld under heofonum.
Her bið feoh læne;   her bið freond læne;
her bið mon læne;   her bið mæg læne.

110   Eal þis eorþan gesteal   idel weorþeð.'"
    Swa cwæð snottor on mode,   gesæt him sundor æt rune.
Til biþ se þe his treowe gehealdeþ: ne sceal næfre his torn to rycene
beorn of his breostum acyþan,   nemþe he ær þa bote cunne,
eorl mid elne gefremman.   Wel bið þam þe him are seceð,

115   frofre to Fæder on heofonum,   þær us eal seo fæstnung stondeð.

80   proud by the wall. Battle destroyed some,
            carried them off on the way; a bird carried one away
            over the high sea; a hoary wolf
            shared one in death; one a sad-faced warrior
            concealed in an earth-cave.
85   The Creator of men thus laid waste this earth
            until deprived of the joy of its inhabitants,
            the ancient work of giants stood empty.
               Then he who wisely reflects upon this foundation
            and deeply meditates on this dark life,
90   wise in mind, far off remembers
            a large number of slaughters, and utters these words:
            "Where has the horse gone? Where has the man gone? Where have the treasure-givers gone?
            Where has the place of banquets gone? Where are the joys of the hall?
            Alas the gleaming cup! Alas the armoured warrior!
95   Alas the prince's glory! How the time has passed away,
            grown dark under the helm of the night, as if it never were.
            There stands now in the track of the dear retainer
            a wall, wondrously high, adorned with serpent-patterns.
            The might of ash-spears snatched away noble men,
100   weapons greedy for carnage, notorious fate,
            and storms beat the stone-heaps,
            hailstorms falling binds the earth,
            winter's chaos, then the darkness comes,
            night-shadows spread gloom, sending from the north
105   fierce hailstorms to the terror of men.
            All is hardship in the earthly kingdom;
            the operation of fate changes the world under the heavens.
            Here, wealth is transitory; here a friend is transitory;
            here a man is transitory; here a kinsman is transitory.
110   All this earth's foundation will become empty." '
               So spoke the wise man in his mind, he sat apart in secret meditation.
            It is good for him who retains his faith: never shall a man express too quickly
            the grief from his heart, unless beforehand he might know how to bring about
            the cure, an earl with courage. It will be well for him who seeks mercy,
115   consolation from the Father in heaven, where for us all security stands.

The Seafarer

The Seafarer is contained in folios 81 verso to 83 recto of the Exeter Book. Often labelled as an elegy, it is one of the most evocative of the Old English short poems. The poem is related as a reflective monologue, like *The Wanderer*: its speaker is one who suffers in exile at the hands of inhospitable elements; who ponders life's meaning, describing it as *deade* ('dead') and *læne* ('transitory'); and the way by which we might progress to something more, to *ecan eadignesse*, 'eternal bliss'. This progression, life's journey, is not simply an end in itself, but the means by which to develop spiritually. From line 64b, the motif of a personal seafaring experience (from which the poem was given its title in the nineteenth century) evolves into a universal debate on the mortality of mankind, the futility of earthly wealth, the morality of Christian living, and the need to be judged worthy of *lof* ('praise').

There are many editions of this text, and a substantial amount of critical commentary. Some critics interpret this poem allegorically: the voyaging theme representing an ascetic *peregrinatio pro amore Dei* ('pilgrimage for the love of God') in which the Christian subject strives to reach his heavenly home, exiled as he is in this mortal world. This, and other readings,[14] accounts also for the use of the *Ubi sunt?* motif (seen also in *The Wanderer*) where the death of those who have previously lived gives rise to a recognition that all earthly things are transient.[15] The homiletic ending of the poem urging the speaker and reader forward to discover where our home might be offers a consolation for the vicissitudes of this world and a hope for better things to come. There is much in this work that will strike a chord with its readers.

The Seafarer

Mæg Ic be me sylfum   soðgied wrecan,
siþas secgan,   hu Ic geswincdagum
earfoðhwile   oft þrowade.
Bitre breostceare   gebiden hæbbe,
5   gecunnad in ceole   cearselda fela,
atol yþa gewealc,   þær mec oft bigeat
nearo nihtwaco   æt nacan stefnan
þonne he be clifum cnossað.   Calde geþrungen
wæron mine fet,   forste gebunden
10   caldum clommum,   þær þa ceare seofedun
hat ymb heortan.   Hungor innan slat
merewerges mod.   Þæt se mon ne wat
þe him on foldan   fægrost limpeð:
hu Ic, earmcearig,   iscealdne sæ
15   winter wunade   wræccan lastum,
winemægum bidroren,
bihongen hrimgicelum;   hægl scurum fleag.
Þær Ic ne gehyrde   butan hlimman sæ,
iscaldne wæg.   Hwilum ylfete song
20   dyde Ic me to gomene,   ganetes hleoþor,
ond huilpan sweg   fore hleahtor wera;
mæw singende   fore medodrince.
Stormas þær stanclifu beotan,   þær him stearn oncwæð
isigfeþera;   ful oft þæt earn bigeal,
25   urigfeþra.   Ne ænig hleomæga
feasceaftig ferð   frefran meahte.
Forþon him gelyfeð lyt,   se þe ah lifes wyn,

---

14   See, for example, A. Klinck, ed., *The Old English Elegies: A Critical Edition and Genre Study* (London, 1992), pp. 35–40, for a synopsis of interpretations of *The Seafarer*. Klinck herself, at p. 37, interprets the poem symbolically: 'the Seafarer's life is deliberately strenuous and ascetic; he rejects the illusory blandishments of this world because the joys of the Lord are warmer to him . . . the desired voyage

. . . is a quest for transcendental good, a quest which in this poem takes the form of seafaring'.
15   See Ida Gordon, ed., *The Seafarer* (London, 1960), pp. 12–27, for an excellent discussion of these themes, and the wider literary and intellectual setting.

The Seafarer

I can narrate a true story about myself,
speak of the journey, how, in days of toil, I
often suffered a time of hardship.
Grievous heartfelt anxiety I have experienced,
5   explored in a boat many places of sorrow,
dreadful tossing of waves, where the anxious night-watch
often held me at the prow of the boat
when it crashes beside the cliffs. Afflicted by cold
were my feet, frost bound
10   by cold fetters, where the sorrows surged
hot about the heart. Hunger within tore
the spirit of the sea-weary. The man who lives most happily
on land does not know this:
how I, wretched and sad, dwelt a winter
15   on the ice-cold sea on the paths of the exile,
deprived of dear kinsmen,
hung round with icicles; hail flew in storms.
There I heard nothing but the roar of the sea,
the ice-cold wave. Sometimes, the song of the swan
20   I had as my entertainment, the cry of the gannet,
and the curlew's sound instead of the laughter of men;
the seagull singing in the place of mead-drinking.
Storms beat the rocky cliffs there, where the tern calls out to them
icy-feathered; very often that sea-eagle cries in response,
25   wet-feathered. No protective kinsman
might comfort the desolate spirit.
    Thus he little believes, he who possesses life's joy,

gebiden in burgum,   bealosiþa hwon,
wlonc ond wingal,   hu Ic werig oft
30   in brimlade   bidan sceolde.
Nap nihtscua,   norþan sniwde,
hrim hrusan bond,   hægl feol on eorþan,
corna caldast.   Forþon cnyssað nu
heortan geþohtas   þæt Ic hean streamas,
35   sealtyþa gelac   sylf cunnige;
monað modes lust   mæla gehwylce
ferð to feran,   þæt Ic feor heonan
elþeodigra   eard gesece.
Forþon nis þæs modwlonc   mon ofer eorþan,
40   ne his gifena þæs god,   ne in geoguþe to þæs hwæt,
ne in his dædum to þæs deor,   ne him his dryhten to þæs hold,
þæt he a his sæfore   sorge næbbe
to hwon hine Dryhten   gedon wille.
Ne biþ him to hearpan hyge   ne to hringþege,
45   ne to wife wyn   ne to worulde hyht,
ne ymbe owiht elles   nefne ymb yða gewealc;
ac a hafað longunge   se þe on lagu fundað.
    Bearwas blostmum nimað,   byrig fægriað,
wongas wlitigiað,   woruld onetteð;
50   ealle þa gemoniað   modes fusne
sefan to siþe,   þam þe swa þenceð
on flodwegas   feor gewitað.
Swylce geac monað   geomran reorde,
singeð sumeres weard,   sorge beodeð
55   bitter in breosthord.   Þæt se beorn ne wat,
esteadig secg,   hwæt þa sume dreogað,
þe þa wræclastas   widost lecgað.
    Forþon nu min hyge hweorfeð   ofer hreþerlocan,
min modsefa   mid mereflode
60   ofer hwæles eþel   hweorfeð wide,
eorþan sceatas;   cymeð eft to me
gifre ond grædig;   gielleð anfloga,
hweteð on wælweg   hreþer unwearnum,
ofer holma gelagu.   Forþon me hatran sind
65   Dryhtnes dreamas   þonne þis deade lif,
læne on londe.   Ic gelyfe no
þæt him eorðwelan   ece stondeð.
Simle þreora sum   þinga gehwylce,
ær his tidege,   to tweon weorþeð:
70   adl oþþe yldo   oþþe ecghete
fægum fromweardum   feorh oðþringeð.
Forþon bið eorla gehwam   æftercweþendra
lof lifgendra   lastworda betst
þæt he gewyrce   ær he on weg scyle,
75   fremman on foldan   wið feonda niþ,
deorum dædum   deofle togeanes
þæt hine ælda bearn   æfter hergen,
ond his lof siþþan   lifge mid englum,
awa to ealdre   ecan lifes blæd,
80   dream mid dugeþum.   Dagas sind gewitene

lives in the city, free from dangerous journeys,
proud and merry with wine, how, weary, I had often
30   to survive in the sea-path.
The shadow of night grew dark, it snowed from the north,
frost gripped the earth, hail fell on the ground,
the coldest of grains. Therefore now the thoughts of my heart
are troubled whether I should try out for myself
35   the deep seas, the tossing of salty waves;
the mind's desire at all times prompts
the spirit to travel so that I, far from here,
might seek the home of those living in a foreign land.
Therefore there is no man so proud-hearted on the earth,
40   so generous of his gifts, so keen in youthfulness,
in his deeds so brave, so loyal to his lord,
that he will never be anxious in his sea voyage
about what the Lord will bring to him.
Nor is his thought on the harp nor on the receiving of rings,
45   nor on pleasure in a woman nor the joy of worldly things,
nor about anything else except the tossing of the waves;
but he always has a longing who sets out on the sea.
    The groves assume blossoms, they adorn the cities,
the meadows grow beautiful, the world quickens;
50   all of this urges those eager of spirit,
the spirit to the journey, to him who is so inclined
to venture far on the paths of the sea.
Likewise the cuckoo urges him with a melancholy voice,
the watchman of summer sings, announces sorrow
55   bitter in his heart. This the warrior does not know,
the man blessed with luxury, what some endure,
those who travel furthest on the paths of exile.
    And yet now my spirit roams beyond the enclosure of the heart,
my thought of mind, along with the sea-flood,
60   travels widely over the whale's haunt,
over the world's expanse; it comes again to me
eager and greedy; the solitary flier yells,
incites the spirit irresistibly on the whale's path
over the sea's expanse. Thus the joys of the Lord are
65   warmer to me than this dead life,
transitory on land. I do not believe
that earthly happiness will endure eternally.
Always, in all conditions, one of three things
hangs in the balance before his final day:
70   disease or old age or attack by the sword
will wrest life from those doomed to die, on their way hence.
Therefore for every man, praise from those who speak of him afterwards,
from the living, is the best memorial
that he might earn before he must depart,
75   achievements on earth against the wickedness of enemies,
opposing the devil with brave deeds
so that the children of men might praise him afterwards,
and his glory will live then among the angels,
always forever in the glory of eternal life,
80   joy among the host. The days are gone

ealle onmedlan   eorþan rices;
næron nu cyningas   ne caseras
ne goldgiefan   swylce iu wæron,
þonne hi mæst mid him   mærþa gefremedon
85   ond on dryhtlicestum   dome lifdon.
Gedroren is þeos duguð eal;   dreamas sind gewitene.
Wuniað þa wacran   ond þas woruld healdaþ,
brucað þurh bisgo.   Blæd is gehnæged.
Eorþan indryhto   ealdað ond searað,
90   swa nu monna gehwylc   geond middangeard:
yldo him on fareð,   onsyn blacað,
gomelfeax gnornað;   wat his iuwine,
æþelinga bearn,   eorþan forgiefene.
Ne mæg him þonne se flæschoma,   þonne him þæt feorg losað,
95   ne swete forswelgan   ne sar gefelan,
ne hond onhreran,   ne mid hyge þencan.
Þeah þe græf wille   golde stregan
broþor his geborenum,   byrgan be deadum
maþmum mislicum   þæt hine mid wille,
100   ne mæg þære sawle   þe biþ synna ful
gold to geoce   for Godes egsan,
þonne he hit ær hydeð   þenden he her leofað.
    Micel biþ se Meotudes egsa,   forþon hi seo molde oncyrreð;
se gestaþelade   stiþe grundas,
105   eorþan sceatas   ond uprodor.
Dol biþ se þe him his Dryhten ne ondrædeþ: cymeð him se dead unþinged.
Eadig bið se þe eaþmod leofaþ: cymeð him seo ar of heofonum.
Meotod him þæt mod gestaþelað   forþon he in his meahte gelyfeð.
Stieran mon sceal strongum mode,   ond þæt on staþelum healdan,
110   ond gewis werum,   wisum clæne.
Scyle monna gehwylc   mid gemete healdan
wiþ leofne   ond wið laþne bealo,
þeah þe he hine wille fyres   fulne
oþþe on bæle   forbærnedne
115   his geworhtne wine.   Wyrd biþ swiþre,
Meotud meahtigra   þonne ænges monnes gehygd.
    Uton we hycgan   hwær we ham agen,
ond þonne geþencan   hu we þider cumen;
ond we þonne eac tilien,   þæt we to moten
120   in þa ecan   eadignesse,
þær is lif gelong   in lufan Dryhtnes,
hyht in heofonum.   Þæs sy þam Halgan þonc,
þæt he usic geweorþade,   wuldres Ealdor,
ece Dryhten,   in ealle tid. Amen.

of all the pomp of the kingdoms of earth;
there are now no kings or emperors
or gold-givers such as there formerly were,
when they most performed glorious deeds among themselves,
85   and lived in magnificent renown.
The whole of this noble band has fallen; joys are departed.
Inferior ones live and possess the world,
they enjoy it by way of toil. Glory is brought low.
The earth's nobility grows old and withers,
90   as does each man now throughout the earth:
old age overtakes him, his face grows pale,
a grey-haired one laments; he knows that his friends of old,
the children of princes, have been consigned to the earth.
Nor when his life is lost will his body
95   taste sweetness or feel pain,
or move a hand, or think with the mind.
Though a brother might wish to scatter the grave
with gold for his sibling, to bury with the dead
various treasures that he would like to have with him,
100   the gold that he hid before while he lived here
cannot be a help to the soul which is full of sins
when it comes into the presence of the terrible power of God.
    Great is the terrible power of the Ordainer before which the earth will quake;
he established the firm ground,
105   the expanse of the earth and the heavens above.
Foolish is he that does not fear his Lord: death will come to him unexpectedly.
Blessed is the man who lives humbly: the favour of heaven will come to him.
God establishes that spirit in him because he believes in his power.
A man must control a headstrong spirit and hold that firmly,
110   reliable in his pledges and clean in his ways.
Every man should act with restraint
towards both friend and foe,
although he might want him filled with fire,
or consumed on the pyre,
115   this friend that he has made. Fate is greater,
the Lord more mighty than any man's conception.
    Let us consider where we might have a home,
and then reflect upon how we could come there
and then we may also strive so that we should come there
120   into that eternal blessedness,
where there is life to be obtained in the love of God,
hope in heaven. Thanks be to the Holy One
that he has exalted us, Prince of glory,
eternal Lord, through all time.   Amen.

THE WHALE

The Whale occurs at folios 96 verso to 97 verso in the Exeter Book. It is one of a group of three poems in the manuscript that are allegorical in nature (there is also a fourth allegorical text, *The Phoenix*, at folios 55–65), and derived from the Latin *Physiologus*, a popular medieval bestiary with a lengthy textual history. In the Exeter Book, *The Panther* precedes *The Whale*, the former symbolizing Christ and his attributes, the latter, the devil and his characteristics. These are followed by an incomplete poem that probably refers to *The Partridge*, perhaps symbolizing the soul; thus the essential elements of earth, sea and air are alluded to in this group of works that deal with salvation and damnation.

The whale, a partially mythical creature, is renowned for its deceitfulness. As it looks like a rocky island, it lures sailors onto it, before diving to the depths and drowning them. In this it resembles the devil who lures mankind by seeming to be a secure bet. The whale also emits from its mouth a sweet smell that attracts fish to their death; this alludes to the false pleasures of the devil to which people are attracted and subsequently damned. In *The Panther*, at lines 44–54, the animal is said to emit a sweet smell after singing which attracts many people towards it; this is likened to the sweet fragrance of Christ's resurrection at lines 64–5. The same attribute of perfume is thus used in these two poems to demonstrate how easy it is to be deceived by the devil's trickery in this instance, and to show that good and evil are in direct opposition to each other.

The following text can be compared to the Middle English version of *The Whale* from the late thirteenth-century manuscript, London, British Library, Arundel 292, given later in this anthology.

The Whale

    Nu Ic fitte gen   ymb fisca cynn
    wille woðcræfte   wordum cyþan
    þurh modgemynd   bi þam miclan hwale.
       Se bið unwillum   oft gemeted,
5   frecne ond ferðgrim   fareðlacendum
    niþþa gehwylcum;   þam is noma cenned,
    fyrnstreama geflotan,   Fastitocalon.
    Is þæs hiw gelic   hreofum stane
    swylce worie   bi wædes ofre
10   sondbeorgum ymbseald,   særyrica mæst,
    swa þæt wenaþ   wægliþende
    þæt hy on ealond sum   eagum wliten;
    ond þonne gehydað   heahstefn scipu
    to þam unlonde   oncyrrapum,
15   setlaþ sæmearas   sundes æt ende,
    ond þonne in þæt eglond   up gewitað
    collenferþe;   ceolas stondað
    bi staþe fæste,   streame biwunden.
    Ðonne gewiciað   werigferðe,
20   faroðlacende,   frecnes ne wenað.
    On þam ealonde   æled weccað,
    heahfyr ælað;   hæleþ beoþ on wynnum,
    reonigmode,   ræste geliste.
    Þonne gefeleð   facnes cræftig
25   þæt him þa ferend on   fæste wuniaþ,
    wic weardiað   wedres on luste,
    ðonne semninga   on sealtne wæg
    mid þa noþe   niþer gewiteþ,
    garsecges gæst,   grund geseceð,
30   ond þonne in deaðsele   drence bifæsteð,
    scipu mid scealcum.   Swa bið scinna þeaw,
    deofla wise,   þæt hi drohtende

The Whale

Now, in a song about a species of fish,
I will relate in words with the art of speech
consistent with my thoughts, about the great whale.
   He is often encountered accidentally,
5   dangerous and savage to sailors
in each attack; to him, floater of the oceans,
is the name given, Fastitocalon.
His appearance is like a rough rock
that crumbles by the water's edge
10   surrounded by sand-dunes, the largest bank,
so that seafarers believe
that they have observed some island with their eyes;
and then they fasten the high-prowed ships
to that supposed land with anchor-ropes,
15   position the sea-steeds at the ocean's limit,
and then go boldly up on to the island;
the ships remain fast by the shore,
rolled by the current.
Then, weary-hearted, the sailors encamp,
20   not thinking of danger.
On that island they kindle a flame
and light a great fire; the men are joyful,
weary and longing for rest.
When, crafty in his deceit, he feels
25   that the travellers are resting safe on him,
and are keeping to camp longing for fair weather,
then suddenly into the salty flood
he daringly goes down with them,
the demon of the ocean, seeking out the seabed,
30   and then in the halls of death dispatches them in drowning, the ships with the crew.
Just so is the custom of evil spirits,
the way of devils, who through hidden strength

þurh dyrne meaht   duguðe beswicað,
ond on teosu tyhtaþ   tilra dæda,
35   wemað on willan,   þæt hy wraþe secen,
frofre to feondum,   oþþæt hy fæste ðær
æt þam wærlogan   wic geceosað.
     Þonne þæt gecnaweð   of cwicsusle
flah feond gemah   þætte fira gehwylc
40   hæleþa cynnes   on his hringe biþ
fæste gefeged,   he him feorgbona
þurh sliþen searo   siþþan weorþeð,
wloncum ond heanum,   þe his willan her
firenum fremmað.   Mid þam he færinga,
45   heoloþhelme biþeaht,   helle seceð,
goda geasne,   grundleasne wylm
under mistglome,   swa se micla hwæl,
se þe bisenceð   sæliþende,
eorlas ond yðmearas.   He hafað oþre gecynd,
50   wæterþisa wlonc,   wrætlicran gien.
Þonne hine on holme   hungor bysgað
ond þone aglæcan   ætes lysteþ,
ðonne se mereweard   muð ontyneð,
wide weleras;   cymeð wynsum stenc
55   of his innoþe,   þætte oþre þurh þone,
sæfisca cynn   beswicen weorðaþ,
swimmað sundhwate   þær se sweta stenc
ut gewitað.   Hi þær in farað
unware weorude,   oþþæt se wida ceafl
60   gefylled bið;   þonne færinga
ymbe þa herehuþe   hlemmeð togædre
grimme goman.   Swa biþ gumena gehwam,
se þe oftost his   unwærlice
on þas lænan tid   lif bisceawað,
65   læteð hine beswican   þurh swetne stenc,
leasne willan,   þæt he biþ leahtrum fah
wið Wuldorcyning.   Him se awyrgda ongean
æfter hinsiþe   helle ontyneð,
þam þe leaslice   lices wynne
70   ofer ferhtgereaht   fremedon on unræd.
     Þonne se fæcna   in þam fæstenne
gebroht hafað,   bealwes cræftig,
æt þam edwylme,   þa þe him on cleofiað,
gyltum gehrodene,   ond ær georne his
75   in hira lifdagum   larum hyrdon,
þonne he þa grimman   goman bihlemmeð
æfter feorhcwale   fæste togædre,
helle hlinduru.   Nagon hwyrft ne swice
utsiþ æfre   þa þær in cumað,
80   þon ma þe þa fiscas   faraðlacende
of þæs hwæles fenge   hweorfan motan.
Forþon is eallinga[16]
dryhtna Dryhtne,   ond a deoflum wiðsace

---

16   At least one half-line is missing in the manuscript at this point.

deceive people associating with them,
and persuade them from good works into ruin,
35 lead them astray in their purpose, so that, evil, they seek
comfort from their enemies, until there they
choose secure lodgings with the treacherous one.
    When in his hell-torment the deceitful and shameless foe
perceives that any of the people
40 of the human race are tied up securely
in his fetters, then he afterwards becomes
a murderer to them, through cruel treachery,
to the proud and to the despised, who here
wickedly perform his will. With those he suddenly
45 makes for hell, concealed by the helmet of invisibility,
bereft of virtues, to the bottomless ferment
under the misty gloom, just like the great whale,
he who sinks sailors,
men and their sea-steeds. He has another trait,
50 this proud whale, yet more curious.
When hunger afflicts him at sea
and provokes the monster with a desire for food,
then the sea-warden opens his mouth,
his wide lips; a pleasant fragrance
55 comes out from his innards, so that through that
other kinds of sea-fish are deceived by it,
and those good at swimming swim to where the sweet smell
is coming from. They enter in there
an unwary troop, until the wide jaw
60 is filled; then suddenly,
around the prey the savage jaws
crash together. So it is with any man
who most often regards his life
heedlessly in this transitory time,
65 allows himself to be deceived by the sweet smell,
a false desire, so that he is stained with sins
against the King of glory. Towards them the accursed one
opens hell after their departure from here,
those who have falsely and ill-advisedly
70 advanced the pleasures of the body over the rights of the spirit.
    When the traitor, crafty in his treachery,
has brought into that prison,
into that whirlpool of fire, those who cling to him,
covered with sins, who previously eagerly obeyed
75 his teachings in the days of their life,
then he crashes together securely
those grim jaws after the death of the living,
the barred doors of hell. There is no right to a way out or an escape
or a departure ever for those who enter in there,
80 any more than the seafaring fish
are able to get out of the whale's grasp.
Therefore it is of all things. . .
the Lord of lords, and oppose the devils always

wordum ond weorcum,   þæt we Wuldorcyning
85   geseon moton.   Uton a sibbe to him
on þas hwilnan tid   hælu secan,
þæt we mid swa Leofne   in lofe motan
to widan feore   wuldres neotan.

85

with words and with deeds, so that we might see
the King of glory. Let us always look to him
for love and for salvation in this transitory time,
so that with the Beloved One in glory
we may enjoy splendour in life everlasting.

Deor

Deor is contained on folio 100 in the Exeter Book. It is a monologic poem spoken by a *scop* (a poet) who has been through life's experiences and reflects with ironic detachment on misfortune and the mutability of all things. The poem harks back to the heroic age of the Anglo-Saxons' Germanic past, concisely and elusively referring to once famous legendary figures, all of whom were involved in personal tragedy from which some consolation could nevertheless be sought. The poet, who names himself as Deor, is lordless, and, in comparing his personal situation with those of his much more notorious predecessors, he finds solace in the thought that his fortunes may change for the better as rapidly as they had changed for the worse. This encouragement arises chiefly from the gnomic refrain, *Þæs ofereode, þisses swa mæg* ('As that passed over, so can this'), which offers a brave response to the apparent indifference of fate; and from the last stanza in which a *witig Dryhten* ('wise Lord') is introduced as ultimately controlling man's destiny.

Deor has been variously interpreted as, for example, a begging poem, advertising the profession of the *scop*; a charm against bad fortune; and a poem with the central function of celebrating or cataloguing the Germanic traditions and identity. Some critics have directly linked *Deor* to the subsequent poem in the Exeter Book, *Wulf and Eadwacer*, but there is not a great deal of contextual evidence to support this reading. Both are, however, riddlic in nature and are compact utterances revolving around relatively obscure referents, presupposing that the audience will have a certain amount of knowledge of the legends discussed.

The date of this poem is unknown, but it may have been composed by one of King Alfred's circle of scholars towards the end of the ninth century.[17] Its stanzaic form is rare in the corpus of Old English poetry; each stanza briefly tells a complete tale. Weland, in the first stanza, was smith to the gods, whose skills were famed in Germanic legend. He was forced to remain in service as a smith to King Niðhad, who had Weland's hamstrings cut. This is the Weland mentioned in King Alfred's translation of Boethius's *Consolation of Philosophy*, book 2, metre 7, where he forms the focus for an *'Ubi sunt?'* question: 'Where now are the bones of the famous and wise goldsmith, Weland?' replacing the 'Fabricius' of the Boethian original.[18] Weland also appears as one of the figures carved into the ivory Franks Casket, dated to the eighth century.

In the second stanza of *Deor*, the story of Beadohild, Niðhad's daughter is enigmatically outlined. Weland raped her and killed her brothers in revenge for his own mistreatment by her father. In the poem, Beadohild discovers she is pregnant; later she gave birth to Widia, a great hero, and she and Weland were reunited. Mæðhild, mentioned in the third stanza, is presumably a lovelorn woman of legend. Nothing is known of this particular story or about who Geat might be. Theodoric, the focus of the next stanza, is, like Eormanric the tyrant of stanza five, a cruel ruler. The former king may be Theoderic the Goth who imprisoned and executed Boethius. Eormanric was a fourth-century king, whose cruelty was legendary. The poet highlights the misfortunes of these figures and their victims, seemingly to demonstrate that all hardships can be overcome or will pass away (*ofereode* in the refrain can mean 'overcome' as well as 'pass over').

Deor

Welund him be wurman   wræces cunnade,
anhydig eorl,   eorfoþa dreag;
hæfde him to gesiþþe   sorge ond longaþ,
wintercealde wræce,   wean oft onfond,
5   siþþan hine Niðhad on   nede legde,
swoncre seonobende   on syllan monn.
Þæs ofereode,   þisses swa mæg.

Beadohilde ne wæs   hyre broþra deaþ
on sefan swa sar   swa hyre sylfre þing:
10   þæt heo gearolice   ongieten hæfde
þæt heo eacen wæs;   æfre ne meahte
þriste geþencan   hu ymb þæt sceolde.
Þæs ofereode,   þisses swa mæg.

---

17   See Klinck, *Old English Elegies*, p. 161.
18   Cited in S. B. Greenfield and D. G. Calder, eds, *A New Critical History of Old English Literature* (London, 1986), p. 50.

Deor

Weland knew the torment of the serpents upon him,
resolute man, he had suffered hardships;
he had sorrow and longing for his companions,
the pain of winter-cold, he often encountered misfortune
5   since Niðhad had laid constraints upon him,
supple sinew-bonds upon the better man.
As that passed over, so can this.

Beadohild was not so pained in spirit
about her brothers' death as about her own situation:
10 that she had perceived clearly
that she was pregnant; she could not ever consider
without fear what she should do about that.
As that passed over, so will this.

We þæt Mæðhilde   monge gefrugnon:
15   wurdon grundlease   Geates frige,
þæt him seo sorglufu   slæp ealle binom.
Þæs ofereode,   þisses swa mæg.

Ðeodric ahte   þritig wintra
Mæringa burg.   Þæt wæs monegum cuþ.
20   Þæs ofereode,   þisses swa mæg.

We geascodan   Eormanrices
wylfenne geþoht;   ahte wide folc
Gotena rices.   Þæt wæs grim cyning!
Sæt secg monig   sorgum gebunden,
25   wean on wenan,   wyscte geneahhe
þæt þæs cynerices   ofercumen wære.
Þæs ofereode,   þisses swa mæg.

Siteð sorgcearig   sælum bidæled,
on sefan sweorceð;   sylfum þinceð
30   þæt sy endeleas   earfoða deal.
Mæg þonne geþencan   þæt geond þas woruld
witig Dryhten   wendeþ geneahhe:
eorle monegum   are gesceawað,
wislicne blæd;   sumum weana dæl.
35   Þæt Ic bi me sylfum   secgan wille,
þæt Ic hwile wæs   Heodeninga scop,
dryhtne dyre;   me wæs Deor noma.
Ahte Ic fela wintra   folgað tilne,
holdne hlaford,   oþþæt Heorrenda nu,
40   leoðcræftig monn,   londryht geþah
þæt me eorla hleo   ær gesealde.
Þæs ofereode,   þisses swa mæg.

Many of us have heard about that business of Mæðhilde:
15   the passion of Geat was bottomless,
so that this sorrowful love deprived her of all sleep.
As that passed over, so will this.

Theodric possessed the city of the Mærings
for thirty winters. That was known to many.
20   As that passed over, so will this.

We have discovered the wolfish thought
of Eormanric; he widely ruled the people
of the kingdom of the Goths. That was a cruel king!
Many men sat bound by sorrows,
25   in expectation of misfortune, would often wish
that his kingly power would be overcome.
As that passed over, so will this.

Filled with anxiety and care, he sits, deprived of happy times,
grows dark in spirit; it seems to him that
30   his share of hardships is endless.
Then he is able to consider that throughout this world
the wise Lord often causes change:
he shows favour to many men,
certain prosperity; to some a portion of misfortune.
35   I want to reveal about myself
that I was the scop of the Heodenings for a while,
dear to my lord; my name was Deor.
I had a good position in service for many winters,
a loyal lord, until now Heorrenda,
40   a man skilled in poetic craft, has received the land-rights
that my protector of men formerly gave to me.
As that passed over, so will this.

WULF AND EADWACER

This short poem occurs at folios 100 verso to 101 recto, and immediately precedes the Riddles in the Exeter Book. Although it is only nineteen lines long, it is one of the most challenging Old English poems to interpret satisfactorily. The multitude of meanings that can be derived from a translation have led to a variety of critical readings. The first two lines, for example, have been translated as 'To my people it is as though one might present them with a sacrifice: they want to destroy him if he comes under subjugation'[19] and 'Prey, it's as if my people have been handed prey. They'll tear him apart if he comes with a troop'.[20] The possibilities for such different readings are a result of the polysemous nature of the text (in line 1, for example, *lac* can mean 'battle, sacrifice, gift', while *gife*, the present third singular indicative of *giefan*, can mean 'bestow, commit, devote, give, present'). This polysemy, together with the fact that the speaker appears to be female (the adjective *reotugu*, line 10, has a feminine ending), has led to this poem's classification as a 'woman's song', part of the *frauenlieder* tradition. Its short lines, refrains, and almost stream-of-consciousness narration have made it ideal for feminist readings.[21]

There are many other interpretations of this poem and the characters who appear in it. In this translation, it is suggested that the female speaker may have a husband (*Eadwacer*: lit. 'property watcher'), and a lover (Wulf) by whom she has a child. She is separated from her lover, it seems forcibly so, and is suffering hardship and misery as a result. She worries for her lover's safety at the hands of a hostile troop, possibly her husband's people. The lament that she makes is one of the most powerful and emotive texts in Old English: it cannot fail to impress and perplex its readers.

Wulf and Eadwacer

Leodum is minum   swylce him mon lac gife.
Willað hy hine aþecgan   gif he on þreat cymeð.
Ungelic is us.
Wulf is on iege,   Ic on oþerre.
5   Fæst is þæt eglond,   fenne biworpen.
Sindon wælreowe   weras þær on ige.
Willað hy hine aþecgan   gif he on þreat cymeð.
Ungelice is us.
Wulfes Ic mines widlastum   wenum dogode,
10   þonne hit wæs renig weder,   ond Ic reotugu sæt.
Þonne mec se beaducafa   bogum bilegde:
wæs me wyn to þon;   wæs me hwæþre eac lað.
Wulf, min Wulf,   wena me þine
seoce gedydon,   þine seldcymas,
15   murnende mod,   nales meteliste.
Gehyrest þu, Eadwacer?   Uncerne earmne hwelp
bireð wulf to wuda.
Þæt mon eaþe tosliteð   þætte næfre gesomnad wæs,
uncer giedd geador.

19   Bradley, *Anglo-Saxon Poetry*, p. 366.
20   K. Crossley-Holland, *The Anglo-Saxon World* (Oxford, 1984), p. 59.
21   See P. Belanoff, 'Women's Songs, Women's Language: *Wulf and Eadwacer* and *The Wife's Lament*', in *New Readings on Women in Old English Literature*, eds H. Damico and A. Hennessey Olsen (Bloomington, IN, 1990), pp. 193–203.

Wulf and Eadwacer

It is to my people as if someone would give him a gift.
They will consume him if he comes into their troop.
It is different with us.
Wulf is on an island, I on another.
5   That island is secure, surrounded by fen.
There are bloodthirsty men on the island.
They will consume him if he comes into their troop.
It is different with us.
I pursued in my hopes the far journeys of Wulf,
10   when it was rainy weather, and I sat, sorrowful.
Then the battle-bold one laid his arms around me:
there was joy to me in that; yet it was also hateful to me.
Wulf, my Wulf, my hopes of you
have made me sick, your rare visits,
15   a mourning mind, and this is not at all from lack of food.
Do you hear me, Eadwacer? The wolf bears our wretched whelp
to the woods.
That may be easily separated which was never bound,
the riddle of us two together.

EXETER BOOK RIDDLES 5, 7, 12, 26, 29, 30, 43–6, 55

There are over ninety Riddles in the Exeter Book, appearing in two main groups at folios 101 recto to 115 recto, and 124 verso to 130 verso, with two Riddles at folios 122 verso to 123 recto. The folios containing Riddles and other texts such as *The Husband's Message* at the end of the manuscript have been damaged by fire. As the scribe did not always make clear where the textual divisions of the Riddles were, some scholars believe there are ninety-five individual texts[22] and some that there are ninety-four[23]. These Riddles are a diverse genre, covering a wide variety of subjects from the biblical to the scurrilous, from natural phenomena to weapons of war, in no particular thematically linked order (as can be seen from the examples from Riddles 43–55 below). Riddles have been a popular and entertaining test of intelligent lateral thinking throughout history, and were favoured in the Anglo-Saxon period in both Latin and Old English.[24]

A few of the Old English Riddles are, in fact, derived from earlier Latin texts. In some of the Riddles, a more personal side to Anglo-Saxon life than in most other texts can be seen; in Riddle 5, for example, it is the horrors of war and injury that are revealed rather than the public, heroic version of warfare. As a contrast, the humour of the Anglo-Saxons is revealed in the scurrilous Riddles such as 44–5, etc.; and individual details of everyday life, as well as intellectual pursuits, are brought to life (in Riddles 12 and 26, for instance).

The Riddles take the form of relatively short, usually first person revelations which provide ambiguous clues about the object concerned, or a first person revelation by the object itself. The poetry is often dense, paradoxical, always ambivalent, and full of metaphorical description (such as *lyftfæt*, 'light-vessel' at Riddle 29, line 3, or *Hrægl*, 'garment,' at Riddle 7, line 1) and kennings, or condensed metaphors (as in *fugles wyn*, 'bird's joy', at Riddle 26, line 7, meaning 'feather', and thus 'quill'). There are two main modes of expression: in the first four Riddles given here, for instance, the object speaks about itself directly, *Ic* 'I', or *mec* 'me'. In Riddle 5, the subject begins with *Ic eom*, 'I am', and follows this with circumlocutory detail about its nature. Sometimes, this type of Riddle ends with a demand – *Saga hwæt Ic hatte*, 'Say what I am called.' Other Riddles, such as 29 and 43, are in the voice of the Riddler, revealing *Ic geseah*, 'I saw', or *Ic wat*, 'I know', with a demand at the end, as in 43, for someone with courage or knowledge to solve the clues and speak the answer.

The Riddles have attracted a great deal of critical commentary probably because, as no solutions are given in the untitled texts in the manuscript, many remain to be solved. Indeed, numerous Old English Riddles still have no universally accepted solution. Those that are edited here give a flavour of the Riddles as a whole, and do have solutions that seem to be satisfactory. The answers proposed are: Riddle 5, Shield, which occurs at folio 102 verso;[25] Riddle 7, Swan (folio 103 recto); Riddle 12, Leather (folios 103 verso to 104 recto); Riddle 26, Gospel-Book (folio 107); Riddle 29, Sun and Moon (folios 107 verso to 108 recto); Riddle 30, Cross (folio 108 recto); Riddle 43, Soul and Body (folio 112); Riddle 44, Key (folio 112 verso); Riddle 45, Dough (folio 112 verso); Riddle 46, Lot (folio 112 verso); Riddle 55, Cruciform Sword-Rack (folio 114 recto).

Riddle 5

Ic eom anhaga,   iserne wund,
bille gebennad,   beadoweorca sæd,
ecgum werig.   Oft Ic wig seo,
frecne feohtan.   Frofre ne wene,
5   þæt me geoc cyme   guðgewinnes
ær Ic mid ældum   eal forwurðe;
ac mec hnossiað   homera lafe,
heardecg heoroscearp,   ondweorc smiþa,
bitað in burgum;   Ic abidan sceal
10   laþran gemotes.   Næfre læcecynn
on folcstede   findan meahte

---

22 E.g., F. Tupper, ed., *The Riddles of the Exeter Book* (Darmstadt, 1968).
23 E.g., Muir, *Exeter Anthology*.
24 See M. Lapidge, 'The Anglo-Latin Background', in Greenfield and Calder, *New Critical History of Old English Literature*, for the *Enigmata* of Aldhelm and Tatwine, for example.

25 For an alternative solution see Wim Tigges, 'Snakes and Ladders: Ambiguity and Coherence in the Exeter Book Riddles and Maxims', in *Companion to Old English Poetry*, eds H. Aertsen and R. H. Bremmer (Amsterdam, 1994), pp. 100–1.

Riddle 5

I am a solitary being, wounded by iron,
maimed by the sword, wearied with battle-deeds,
exhausted by sword-edges. Often I see battle,
terrible enemies. I expect no comfort,
5   no help will come to me in the battle
before at last I am done to death;
but the leavings of hammers, hard-edged,
war-sharp, the handiwork of smiths, bite deeply into me,
in the stronghold of the city; I can but await
10   a more fearsome encounter. I am never
able to find physicians in the city

þara þe mid wyrtum   wunde gehælde,
ac me ecga dolg   eacen weorðað
þurh deaðslege   dagum ond nihtum.

Riddle 7

Hrægl min swigað   þonne Ic hrusan trede
oþþe þa wic buge   oþþe wado drefe.
Hwilum mec ahebbað   ofer hæleþa byht
hyrste mine   ond þeos hea lyft,
ond mec þonne wide   wolcna strengu
ofer folc byreð.   Frætwe mine
swogað hlude   ond swinsiað,
torhte singað,   þonne Ic getenge ne beom
flode ond foldan,   ferende gæst.

Riddle 12

Fotum Ic fere,   foldan slite,
grene wongas,   þenden Ic gæst bere.
Gif me feorh losað,   fæste binde
swearte Wealas;   hwilum sellan men.
Hwilum Ic deorum   drincan selle
beorne of bosme,   hwilum mec bryd triedeð
felawlonc fotum;   hwilum feorran broht
wonfeax Wale   wegeð ond þyð,
dol druncmennen,   deorcum nihtum,
wæteð in wætre,   wyrmeð hwilum
fægre to fyre;   me on fæðme sticaþ
hygegalan hond,   hwyrfeð geneahhe,
swifeð me geond sweartne.   Saga hwæt Ic hatte
þe Ic lifgende   lond reafige,
ond æfter deaþe   dryhtum þeowige.

Riddle 26

Mec feonda sum   feore besnyþede,
woruldstrenga binom;   wætte siþþan
dyfde on wætre;   dyde eft þonan,
sette on sunnan   þær Ic swiþe beleas
herum þam þe Ic hæfde.   Heard mec siþþan
snað seaxses ecg,   sindrum begrunden;
fingras feoldan,   ond mec fugles wyn
geondsprengde speddropum,   spyrede geneahhe.
Ofer brunne brerd   beamtelge swealg
streames dæle,   stop eft on mec,
siþade sweartlast.   Mec siþþan wrah
hæleð hleobordum,   hyde beþenede,

who could heal my wounds with herbs,
but for me the sword wounds become wider
through death blows by day and by night.

Riddle 7

My garment is silent when I tread upon the earth
or reside in my dwelling or stir up the waters.
Sometimes my apparel and this high air
lift me over the dwellings of men,
and the strength of the clouds carries me far
over the people. My ornaments
resound loudly and make music,
sing clearly, when I am not resting on
water and ground, a travelling spirit.

5

Riddle 12

I travel by foot, trample the ground,
the green fields, as long as I carry a spirit.[26]
If I lose my life, I bind fast
dark Welshmen; sometimes better men.
On occasion, I give a brave warrior drink
from within me, sometimes a very stately bride treads
her foot on me; sometimes a dark-haired slave-girl
brought far from Wales shakes and presses me,
some stupid, drunken maidservant, on dark nights
she moistens with water, she warms for a while
by the pleasant fire; on my breast she thrusts
a wanton hand and moves about frequently,
then sweeps me within the blackness. Say what I am called
who, living, ravages the land,
and after death, serves the multitudes.

5

10

15

Riddle 26

An enemy took my life, deprived me
of my physical strength; then he moistened me,
he dipped me in water; took me out again,
and set me in the sun where I rapidly lost
all of the hairs that I had. Then the knife's hard edge
cut into me, ground away with cinders;[27]
fingers folded me, and the bird's joy[28]
went over me with useful drops, made tracks repeatedly.
Over the brown rim it swallowed more tree-dye,
a measure of the liquid, again it stepped on me,
leaving its black tracks. Then a man covered me,
with boards, stretched skin over me,

5

10

26   i.e. as long as I am living
27   *sindrum begrunden* is often taken to mean 'ground off all impurities', but it has been argued (as discussed by Muir, *Exeter Anthology*, II, p. 592) that this phrase, 'ground away with cinders', refers to the process of rubbing down the vellum or parchment with pumice as part of the preparation for making a manuscript.
28   A bird's joy is its feathers.

gierede mec mid golde;   forþon me gliwedon
wrætlic weorc smiþa,   wire befongen.
15   Nu þa gereno   ond se reada telg
ond þa wuldorgesteald   wide mære
dryhtfolca Helm,   nales dol wite.
Gif min bearn wera   brucan willað,
hy beoð þy gesundran   ond þy sigefæstran,
20   heortum þy hwætran,   ond þy hygebliþran,
ferþe þy frodran;   habbaþ freonda þy ma,
swæsra ond gesibbra,   soþra ond godra,
tilra ond getreowra,   þa hyra tyr ond ead
estum ycað,   ond hy arstafum
25   lissum bilecgað   ond hi lufan fæþmum
fæste clyppað.   Frige hwæt Ic hatte,
niþum to nytte;   nama min is mære,
hæleþum gifre   ond halig sylf.

Riddle 29

Ic wiht geseah   wundorlice
hornum bitweonum   huþe lædan,
lyftfæt leohtlic,   listum gegierwed,
huþe to þam ham   of þam heresiþe:
5   walde hyre on þære byrig   bur atimbran,
searwum asettan,   gif hit swa meahte.
Ða cwom wundorlicu wiht   ofer wealles hrof —
seo is eallum cuð   eorðbuendum —
ahredde þa þa huþe,   ond to ham bedraf
10   wreccan ofer willan;   gewat hyre west þonan
fæhþum feran;   forð onette.
Dust stonc to heofonum,   deaw feol on eorþan,
niht forð gewat.   Nænig siþþan
wera gewiste   þære wihte sið.

Riddle 30

Ic eom legbysig,   lace mid winde
bewunden mid wuldre,   wedre gesomnad,
fus forðweges,   fyre gebysgad,
bearu blowende,   byrnende gled.
5   Ful oft mec gesiþas   sendað æfter hondum
þæt mec weras ond wif   wlonce cyssað.
Þonne Ic mec onhæbbe,   ond hi onhnigaþ to me
monige mid miltse;   þær Ic monnum sceal
ycan upcyme   eadignesse.

adorned me with gold; therefore I am decorated
with the smith's artistic works, enveloped in filigree.
15   Now the ornaments and the red dye
and these glorious attributes celebrate widely
the Protector of the people, the punishment of the foolish no less.[29]
If the children of men would use me,
they will be the safer and the more victorious,
20   their hearts will be bolder, their thoughts gladder,
their minds wiser; they will have more friends,
dear and near, true and virtuous,
good and faithful, who will gladly increase
their honour and happiness, and with kindness they
25   will envelop them with joy, and clasp them fast
in the embrace of love. Ask what I am called,
that is of use to men; my name is famous,
useful to men, and itself holy.

Riddle 29

I saw a creature wondrously
carrying booty between his horns,
a shining air-vessel skilfully adorned,
taking booty to his home from that war raid:
5   he wanted to build a bower for it in that city,
to artfully place it, if he might have done so.
Then a wondrous creature came over the roof of the wall –
one who is known to all earth-dwellers –
and snatched away the booty, and drove home
10   the wretch, against his will; she departed west from there
to journey from her feud; she hastened forth.
Dust leapt to the heavens, dew fell to the earth,
night went away. Afterwards, none among men
knew where the creature went.

Riddle 30[30]

I am beset with flames, fighting with the wind,
wound round with splendour, united with the elements,
eager for the onward journey, agitated by fire,
blooming in a wood, a burning flame.
5   Very often companions pass me from hand to hand
so that proud men and women can kiss me.
Then I raise myself up, and they bow to me
many with reverent joy; there I shall
increase the ascendancy of blessedness among people.

---

29   *nales dol wite* is variously translated and, in Tupper, *Riddles of the Exeter Book*, p. 20, emended to *nales dolwite*, 'not the pains of hell'. In the translation given above, I follow Bradley, *Anglo-Saxon Poetry*, p. 374.

30   This Riddle can be compared to the depiction of the Rood in *The Dream of the Rood*. Like the latter, this object is mutable in its nature, contending with natural forces, and simultaneously eager for the spiritual journey, and a symbol of salvation for mankind.

Riddle 43

Ic wat indryhtne   æþelum deorne
giest in geardum,   þam se grimma ne mæg
hungor sceððan,   ne se hata þurst,
yldo ne adle.   Gif him arlice
esne þenað   se þe agan sceal
on þam siðfate,   hy gesunde æt ham
findað witode him   wiste ond blisse,
cnosles unrim;   care, gif se esne
his Hlaforde   hyreð yfle,
Frean on fore,   ne wile forht wesan
broþor oþrum;   him þæt bam sceðeð,
þonne hy from bearme   begen hweorfað
anre magan,   ellorfuse,
moddor ond sweostor.   Mon, se þe wille,
cyþe cynewordum   hu se cuma hatte,
eðþa se esne,   þe Ic her ymb sprice.

5

10

15

Riddle 44

Wrætlic hongað   bi weres þeo,
frean under sceate.   Foran is þyrel,
bið stiþ ond heard,   stede hafað godne.
Þonne se esne   his agen hrægl
ofer cneo hefeð,   wile þæt cuþe hol
mid his hangellan   heafde gretan
þæt he efenlang ær   oft gefylde.

5

Riddle 45

Ic on wincle gefrægn   weaxan nathwæt,
þindan ond þunian,   þecene hebban.
On þæt banlease   bryd grapode
hygewlonc hondum;   hrægle þeahte
þrindende þing   þeodnes dohtor.

5

Riddle 46

Wær sæt æt wine   mid his wifum twam
ond his twegen suno   ond his twa dohtor,
swase gesweostor   ond hyre suno twegen,
freolico frumbearn;   fæder wæs þær inne
þara æþelinga,   æghwæðres mid
eam ond nefa.   Ealra wæron fife
eorla ond idesa   insittendra.

5

Riddle 55

Ic seah in healle,   þær hæleð druncon,
on flet beran   feower cynna,
wrætlic wudutreow,   ond wunden gold,
sinc searobunden,   ond seolfres dæl,

Riddle 43

I know a noble guest, virtuous and excellent,
in a dwelling, who fierce hunger
cannot harm, nor fiery thirst,
nor old age nor disease. If the man who keeps him
honourably attends him as a servant
on their journey, they will find, safe at their destination,
appointed to them sustenance and happiness,
innumerable kin; it will be sorrow, if the man
badly obeys his Lord
and Master upon the journey, or will not live in fear
of the other brother; the latter will injure them both
when they both depart from the breast
of their only kinswoman, eager for the journey,
their mother and their sister. Let the man who wishes to,
reveal in fitting words what the visitor is called,
or the man, of whom I have spoken about here.

Riddle 44

A curious thing hangs by a man's thigh,
under the lap of its lord. In its front it is pierced,
it is stiff and hard, it has a good position.
When the man lifts his own garment
above his knee, he intends to greet
with the head of his hanging object that familiar hole
which is the same length, and which he has often filled before.

Riddle 45

I have heard of something that grows in a corner,
swelling and standing up, lifting up its covering.
Upon that boneless thing a proud-minded woman
gripped with her hands; with her garment a lord's daughter
covered the swollen thing.

Riddle 46

A man sat at wine with his two wives
and his two sons and his two daughters,
dear sisters, and their two sons,
noble and firstborn children; in there was the father
of these noble boys, with each of them
uncle and nephew. In all there were five
men and women sitting within.

Riddle 55

I saw in a hall, where heroes drank,
on the floor made of four kinds of wood,
a wondrous forest tree, and twisted gold,
skilfully fastened treasure, and part of it in silver,

5   ond rode tacn þæs us to roderum up
        hlædre rærde, ær he helwara
        burg abræce. Ic þæs beames mæg
        eaþe for eorlum æþelu secgan:
        þær wæs hlin ond acc, ond se hearda iw,
10   ond se fealwa holen; frean sindon ealle
        nyt ætgædre; naman habbað anne,
        wulfheafedtreo, þæt oft wæpen abæd
        his mondryhtne, maðm in healle,
        goldhilted sweord. Nu me þisses gieddes
15   ondsware ywe, se hine on mede
        wordum secgan hu se wudu hatte.

5

and the symbol of the cross of him who raised us up
to the heavens by that ladder, before he broke down that city
of the inhabitants of hell. I can easily reveal
the nature of that hero's tree:
there was maple and oak, and hard yew,

10

and the yellowish holly; to the lord are all
of these useful together; it has a certain name,
wolf's head tree, that often restrained a weapon
for its lord, treasure in the hall,
the gold-hilted sword. Now reveal to me

15

the answer of this riddle, he who with courage
will say in words what this wood is called.

THE WIFE'S LAMENT

The Wife's Lament, contained without a title at folio 115 in the Exeter Book, and immediately following Riddle 59, is one of the most extensively discussed of the Old English elegiac poems. A substantial number of interpretations of the status of the speaker and the referent have been proposed ranging from the allegorical (Christ and the church; the body and the soul) to the literal (a woman's lament about a man or two men; a retainer's lament about his lost lord). As the inflexions on *geomorre*, line 1, and *minre sylfre* in line 2 are clearly feminine singular endings, there is every reason to think that the speaker is a woman. This poem, like *Wulf and Eadwacer*, has been linked to the *frauenlieder* tradition of women's songs.[31] *The Wife's Lament* has also been linked with *The Husband's Message*, a text that occurs some eight folios later in the manuscript.

The lament of the woman in *The Wife's Lament* centres on the loss of her *leodfruma* ('leader of the people'). Though her precise relationship with this man is not clearly established, it can be assumed that he is her husband or lover. With these suppositions in mind, the poem becomes a revelation of an enigmatic personal tragedy: the woman has been exiled, isolated from all other people; she is forced to live out her lonely life in a desolate and unfriendly place, where her thoughts are her only companions. Her reflections on the vicissitudes of life and the cruelties of others cause her to utter general, somewhat gnomic statements, about the need for discretion, and the inevitable grief that comes after losing love. Much else in this poem is ambiguous; and that ambiguity stems not only from the deliberate evasiveness of the poet but also from the polyvalency of the language used. Since many of the words in this text have a range of interpretative possibilities, translation becomes a subjective exercise. As is the case with the poem *Wulf and Eadwacer*, readers should thus be aware that the Modern English interpretation offered here is one version of the original only, and that there is no substitution for individual translation.

The Wife's Lament

Ic þis giedd wrece   bi me ful geomorre,
minre sylfre sið.   Ic þæt secgan mæg,
hwæt Ic yrmþa gebad   siþþan Ic up weox,
niwes oþþe ealdes,   no ma þonne nu.
5   A Ic wite wonn   minra wræcsiþa.
   Ærest min hlaford gewat   heonan of leodum
ofer yþa gelac;   hæfde Ic uhtceare
hwær min leodfruma   londes wære.
Ða Ic me feran gewat   folgað secan,
10   wineleas wræcca   for minre weaþearfe.
Ongunnon þæt þæs monnes   magas hycgan
þurh dyrne geþoht   þæt hy todælden unc,
þæt wit gewidost   in woruldrice,
lifdon laðlicost;   ond mec longade.
15   Het mec hlaford min   her heard niman.
Ahte Ic leofra lyt   on þissum londstede,
holdra freonda;   forþon is min hyge geomor.
Ða Ic me ful gemæcne   monnan funde
heardsæligne,   hygegeomorne,
20   mod miþendne,   morþor hycgendne,
bliþe gebæro.   Ful oft wit beotedan
þæt unc ne gedælde   nemne deað ana,
owiht elles;   eft is þæt onhworfen.
Is nu   swa hit no wære
25   freondscipe uncer.   Sceal Ic feor ge neah

---

31   See Belanoff, 'Women's Songs, Women's Language'.

The Wife's Lament

I relate this very mournful riddle about myself,[32]
about my own journey. I am able to relate
those miseries that I endured since I grew up,
of new and old ones, never more than now.
5   Forever I have suffered the torment of my exile.
   First my lord went away from the people
over tossing waves; I had anxiety at dawn[33]
about where in the land my leader of the people might be.
Then I departed on my journey to seek a refuge,
10   a friendless exile because of my woeful need.
The kinsmen of the man began to think,
through secret consideration, that they would separate us,
so that we two would live furthest apart in this worldly kingdom,
most hatefully; and yearning occupied me.
15   My cruel lord commanded me to be taken here.[34]
I possessed few dear ones in this region,
loyal friends; because of that my mind is mournful.
Then I found a very suited man to be
ill-fated, sad at heart,
20   having a concealing mind, intending violent crime,
but with a cheerful bearing. Very often, we two vowed
that nothing would part the two of us
except death alone; afterwards, that has turned around.
It is now as if it never were
25   the friendship of us two. Far and near I shall endure

---

32   Or 'this song about my very sad self'.
33   'anxiety at dawn', translating *uhtceare*, suggests that the speaker has had a sleepless night. Dawn is a period when even the smallest worries take on an exaggerated aspect.
34   *her eard* is a common emendation: 'My lord commanded me to take up a dwelling here.'

mines felaleofan   fæhðu dreogan.

  Heht mec mon wunian   on wuda bearwe,
under actreo   in þam eorðscræfe.
Eald is þes eorðsele;   eal Ic eom oflongad.

30   Sindon dena dimme,   duna uphea,
bitre burgtunas   brerum beweaxne:
wic wynna leas.   Ful oft mec her wraþe begeat
fromsiþ frean.   Frynd sind on eorþan,
leofe lifgende,   leger weardiað,

35   þonne Ic on uhtan   ana gonge
under actreo   geond þas eorðscrafu.
Þær Ic sittan mot   sumorlangne dæg
þær Ic wepan mæg   mine wræcsiþas,
earfoþa fela;   forþon Ic æfre ne mæg

40   þære modceare   minre gerestan,
ne ealles þæs longaþes   þe mec on þissum life begeat.
  A scyle geong mon   wesan geomormod,
heard heortan geþoht,   swylce habban sceal
bliþe gebæro   eac þon breostceare,

45   sinsorgna gedreag,   sy æt him sylfum gelong
eal his worulde wyn,   sy ful wide fah
feorres folclondes,   þæt min freond siteð
under stanhliþe   storme behrimed,
wine werigmod,   wætre beflowen

50   on dreorsele.   Dreogeð se min wine
micle modceare;   he gemon to oft
wynlicran wic.   Wa bið þam þe sceal
of langoþe   leofes abidan.

that feud of my beloved.

   He commanded me to dwell in the wood's grove
under an oak tree in the earth-cave.
Old is this hall in the earth; I am all worn out with longing.
There are dark valleys, high hills,
bitter enclosures overgrown with briars:
a dwelling place deprived of joy. Very often here the departure of my lord
cruelly laid hold of me. Beloved ones are on the earth,
loved ones living, occupying a bed,
while I walk alone at dawn
under the oak tree through these earth-dwellings.
There I must sit the summer-long day,
where I can only weep about my exile,
about many hardships; because of this I cannot ever
rest from the sadness of my heart,
or from all the longing which takes hold of me in this life.
   The young man may always be sad in mind,
hard-hearted in thought, just as he must have
a happy appearance despite the grief in his breast
of a multitude of perpetual sorrows, whether it is that all his
joy in the world is at his own disposal, or whether far and wide
he is outlawed in a distant country, so that my beloved sits
under rocky cliffs assaulted by a storm,
a lord sad at heart, surrounded by water,
in a dismal hall. My beloved suffers
much mental torment; he remembers too often
a more joyful dwelling. It is misery for those who, longing,
have to wait for a loved one.

THE HUSBAND'S MESSAGE

The Husband's Message, coming as it does towards the end of the Exeter Book at folio 123, has been made illegible in places by fire damage. As it is a unique text, there is no other version that can be used to aid in interpreting this poem. In spite of this, J. C. Pope proposed an interesting conjectural reconstruction of the text.[35] I have presented the poem as it is now extant in the manuscript as much to demonstrate how fortuitous is the survival of any Old English text as to be faithful to what remains in the Exeter Book itself.

As the poem is incomplete, its interpretation is made the more complex. A messenger arrives by ship to reveal to a woman that her lord waits for her across the sea, and is anticipating that she will join him. The messenger in the text either brings to the woman a piece of wood carved with runes that represent a former vow, or, the poem is actually spoken by an animated piece of carved wood. As Klinck points out,[36] this latter interpretation would link the poem to the Old English Riddles that precede it in the Exeter Book.

A number of critical readings of *The Husband's Mes-sage* have been published that link it explicitly with Riddle 60, which comes immediately before *The Husband's Message* in the Exeter Book, and which has a possible solution of 'wood engraved with runes'. Other commentators see in *The Husband's Message* a response to *The Wife's Lament*, which makes of these two poems a pair that is concerned with the separation of the same lovers. *The Husband's Message* is an altogether more formal and optimistic poem, though, and there is little evidence to suggest that the two texts concern themselves with a shared experience. While other interpretations of this poem include the allegorical (the longed-for future reunion of Christ with his church), what is certain is that the central figure being spoken of by the messenger is a lord who has been exiled from his homeland and from the woman with whom he has a pledge of love. He calls for this woman to join him and make his sojourn overseas one of happiness. Familiar motifs of loneliness, seafaring and loyalty are key themes in this arguably elegiac poem, as they are in others such as *The Wanderer*.

The Husband's Message

Nu Ic onsundran þe   secgan wille
. . . treocyn   Ic tudre aweox.
In mec æld . . .   . . . sceal
ellor londes   settan . . .
5   sealte streamas   . . . sse.
       Ful oft Ic on bates . . .   . . . gesohte
þær mec mondryhten   min . . .
ofer heah hafu.   Eom nu her cumen
on ceolþele,   ond nu cunnan scealt
10   hu þu ymb modlufun   mines frean
on hyge hycge.   Ic gehatan dear
þæt þu þær tirfæste   treowe findest.
Hwæt, þec þonne biddan het   se þisne beam agrof
þæt þu, sinchroden,   sylf gemunde
15   on gewitlocan   wordbeotunga
þe git on ærdagum   oft gespræcon,
þenden git moston   on meoduburgum
eard weardigan,   an lond bugan,
freondscype fremman.   Hine fæhþo adraf
20   of sigeþeode.   Heht nu sylfa þe
lustum læran   þæt þu lagu drefde,
siþþan þu gehyrde   on hliþes oran
galan geomorne   geac on bearwe.

35 J. C. Pope, 'Palaeography and Poetry: Some Solved and Unsolved Problems of the Exeter Book', in *Medieval Scribes, Manuscripts and Libraries: Essays Presented to N. R. Ker*, eds M. B. Parkes and A. G. Watson (London, 1978), pp. 25–65.

36 s.v. *The Husband's Message* in M. Lapidge, J. Blair, S. Keynes and D. Scragg, eds, *The Blackwell Encyclopaedia of Anglo-Saxon England* (Oxford, 1998), p. 245.

The Husband's Message

Now, in private, I will reveal
the kind of wood I grew up as from a young offspring.
In me men . . . have other land
to establish . . .
5   salty seas . . .
Very often in a boat I . . . sought
where my lord . . .
over the high seas. I have now come here
on the deck of a ship, and now you shall know
10   how you might think in your heart about
the heartfelt love of my lord. I dare promise
that you will find there a gloriously assured commitment.
Indeed, he who engraved this wood instructed me to ask
that you, adorned with jewels, yourself remember
15   in your mind the spoken vows
that you two often spoke in former days,
while you were permitted to occupy a home
in the cities where mead was drunk, inhabit the same land,
and show your friendship. A feud drove him away
20   from the victorious people. Now he himself has asked me
to instruct you joyfully that you should stir up the water,
after you have heard on the edge of the cliff
the mournful cuckoo sing in the wood.

Ne læt þu þec siþþan   siþes getwæfan,
25   lade gelettan   lifgendne monn.
Ongin mere secan   mæwes eþel,
onsite sænacan   þæt þu suð heonan
ofer merelade   monnan findest,
þær se þeoden is   þin on wenum.
30   Ne mæg him worulde   willa . . .
mara on gemyndum,   þæs þe he me sægde,
þonne inc geunne   alwaldend God
. . . ætsomne   siþþan motan
secgum ond gesiþum,   . . .
35   næglede beagas.   He genoh hafað
fædan goldes   . . .
. . . elþeode   eþel healde,
fægre foldan   . . .
. . . ra hæleþa,   þeah þe her min wine . . .
40   . . . .

nyde gebæded,   nacan ut aþrong,
ond on yþa . . .   . . . sceolde
faran on flotweg,   forðsiþes georn,
mengan merestreamas.   Nu se mon hafað
45   wean oferwunnen;   nis him wilna gad,
ne meara ne maðma,   ne meododreama,
ænges ofer eorþan   eorlgestreona,
þeodnes dohtor,   gif he þin beneah.
Ofer eald gebeot   incer twega,
50   gehyre Ic ætsomne   [sigel] [rad] geador
[ear] [wen] ond [monn]   aþe benemnan
þæt he þa wære   ond þa winetreowe
be him lifgendum   læstan wolde
þe git on ærdagum   oft gespræconn.

Then, do not let any living man
25   keep you from the voyage or hinder your journey.
Begin to seek the ocean, the native land of seagulls,
board a seaworthy ship so that south from here
you may find the man beyond the ocean-path,
where your lord is in expectation of you.
30   Nor can he in all the world desire . . .
more in his mind, as he told me,
than that the all-ruling God might grant that you two
. . . together may afterwards
[give] to men and to retainers,
35   studded circlets. He has enough
decorated gold. . ...
. . . [though] he must hold his land from a foreign country,
a pleasant land . . .
. . . of heroes, even though my lord was
40   . . . .
forced here by necessity, urged his ship out,
and upon the waves . . . . . . had to
journey upon the path of the sea, eager for the journey away,
and to stir up the sea currents. Now the man has
45   overcome his trouble; he has no lack of joy,
or of horses or treasures, or the pleasures of mead,
or of any of the noble treasures upon earth,
prince's daughter, if he possesses you.
In accordance with the past vow of the two of you,
50   I hear S join together with R
and EA and W and M to declare an oath[37]
that he would keep the pledge
and the vow of friendship as long as he lives,
that which in former days you two often uttered.

---

37   These single letters are actually written as runes in the manuscript. Translated they may mean Sun, Road, Sea, Joy, Man, which
have been interpreted in a variety of different ways: for example, as
indirectly indicating heaven, earth and man (the elements used to
guarantee the efficacy of oaths). See Klinck, *Old English Elegies*, p.
208.

THE RUIN

This badly damaged text is, in the words of Mitchell and Robinson, 'something of a ruin itself'.[38] What remains to us of the fire-damaged *Ruin* at folios 123 verso to 124 verso of the Exeter Book is sufficient to understand the general thrust of the poem – the glorious past reflected in present decay; but insufficient to build a clearer picture of the final intended effect. Like the authors of *The Wanderer*, *The Seafarer*, *The Wife's Lament* and other short poems that are often labelled as elegies, the poet of *The Ruin* contemplates the transience of human life and human endeavour. Unlike these other texts, though, there is no first person narrator relating the lines; instead, this is a descriptive piece that visually and imaginatively recreates a picture of a splendid stronghold, left to deteriorate once its inhabitants were gone. In this, it is reminiscent of Latin works, such as Venantius Fortunatus's *The Destruction of Thuringia*[39] and other, earlier texts. In the Anglo-Saxon poet's focus on a ruined

site, perhaps one that had been built by the Romans, some critics have interpreted the stronghold literally as Bath with its Roman buildings and bath-houses. Others have proposed an allegorical interpretation, with the stronghold representing a hedonistic city, destined to fall, such as Babylon.[40]

In many respects, it matters little whether the ruins being described can be identified, for the detailed depiction created from the poet's account can bring to mind the splendour of previous cultures, of once-magnificent buildings and peoples. The deictic forms of 'here', 'this' and 'that' urge the reader to participate with the poet as the observations are made. Here, there is no sense of a consolation being offered for the continual passing away of people and places; rather, a sense of appreciation for the achievements of past generations, and the startling contrast between the previous splendour and present deterioration of the buildings, is uppermost.

The Ruin

Wrætlic is þes wealstan,   wyrde gebræcon.
Burgstede burston,   brosnað enta geweorc.
Hrofas sind gehrorene,   hreorge torras,
hrimgeat berofen,   hrim on lime,
5   scearde scurbeorge,   scorene, gedrorene,
ældo undereotone.   Eorðgrap hafað
waldendwyrhtan   forweorone, geleorene,
heardgripe hrusan,   oþ hund cnea
werþeoda gewitan.   Oft þæs wag gebad,
10   ræghar ond readfah,   rice æfter oþrum,
ofstonden under stormum,   steap geap gedreas.
Wonað giet se . . .   . . . num geheapen
felon . . .
grimme gegrunden . . .
15   . . . scan,   heo . . .
. . . g orþonc   ærsceaft . . .
. . . g.   lamrindum beag
mod mo . . .   . . . ne swiftne gebrægd,
hwætred in hringas,   hygerof gebond
20   weall walanwirum   wundrum togædre.
Beorht wæron burgræced,   burnsele monige,
heah horngestreon,   heresweg micel,
meodoheall monig   mondreama full –
oþþæt þæt onwende   wyrd seo swiþe.
25   Crungon walo wide;   cwoman woldagas.

38   B. Mitchell and F. C. Robinson, *A Guide to Old English*, 5th edn (Oxford, 1995), p. 254.
39   D. G. Calder and M. J. B. Allen, *Sources and Analogues of Old English Poetry 1: The Major Latin Texts in Translation* (Cambridge, 1976), pp. 137–41.

40   C. Fell, 'Perceptions of Transience', in *The Cambridge Companion to Old English Literature*, eds M. Godden and M. Lapidge (Cambridge, 1991), pp. 179–82.

The Ruin

Wondrous is this stone wall, smashed by fate.
The buildings have crumbled, the work of giants decays.
Roofs have collapsed, the towers in ruin,
the frosted gate is unbarred, hoar-frost on mortar,
5   the storm-protection mutilated, cut down, declined,
undermined by age. The earth's grip holds
the powerful makers, decayed, passed away,
the hard grasp of the earth, until a hundred generations
of the nation of men have passed away. Often this wall has survived,
10   grey with lichen and stained with red, one kingdom after another,
endured under storms, high and arched, it perished.
It decays yet . . . . . . heaped
persisted . . .
fiercely sharpened . . .
15   . . . it shone, they . . .
. . . ingenious ancient work . . .
. . . ringed with crusted mud
the mind . . . a clever idea, one quick-minded,
sharp in thought, the stout-hearted one, ingeniously bound
20   the wall-supports together with wires into rings.
Bright were the stronghold's buildings, the many bath-houses,
the abundance of high arched structures, the great sound of warriors,
many a meadhall full of the celebrations of men –
until fate, the mighty one, changed that.
25   Those slain in battle fell far and wide; the days of pestilence came.

Swylt eall fornom   secgrofra wera,
wurdon hyra wigsteal   westen staþolas,
brosnade burgsteall.   Betend crungon
hergas to hrusan.   Forþon þas hofu dreorgiað,
30   ond þæs teaforgeapa   tigelum sceadeð,
hrostbeages rof.   Hryre wong gecrong
gebrocen to beorgum,   þær iu beorn monig
glædmod ond goldbeorht   gleoma gefrætwed,
wlonc ond wingal,   wighyrstum scan;
35   seah on sinc, on sylfor,   on searogimmas,
on ead, on æht,   on eorcanstan,
on þas beorhtan burg   bradan rices.
  Stanhofu stodan;   stream hate wearp,
widan wylme.   Weal eall befeng
40   beorhtan bosme,   þær þa baþu wæron,
hat on hreþre.   Þæt wæs hyðelic.
Leton þonne geotan . . .
ofer harne stan   hate streamas
un . . .
45   . . . þþæt hringmere   hate . . .
  . . .   þær þa baþu wæron.
Þonne is . . .
. . . re;   þæt is cynelic þing
hu se . . .   burg . . .

Death carried off all of the sword-brave men,
their battle places became deserted sites,
the site of the city crumbled. The repairers,
the armies, fell to the earth. Therefore, these dwellings fall down,
30   and this red-arch comes away from the tiles,
the roof of the pillared vault. The place fell into ruin
broken into mounds, where once many a warrior
joyful-hearted and bright with gold, brightly adorned,
proud and elated with wine, shone in his war-trappings;
35   he looked upon treasure, on silver, on elaborately made jewels,
on riches, on possessions, on precious stones,
on that bright stronghold of the broad kingdom.
   Stone buildings were standing; the flowing water threw out heat,
a wide surge. The wall entirely encompassed it
40   within its bright breast, where the baths were,
hot to the core. That was convenient.
They let out the . . .
hot streams then to gush over the grey stone
un- . . .
45   . . . until the hot circular pool . . .
. . . where the baths were.
Then it is . . .
. . . ; that is a splendid thing
how the . . . stronghold . . .

The Vercelli Book

The 135 leaves of the Vercelli Book, Vercelli, Biblioteca Capitolare cxvii, written by one scribe, contain twenty-three prose texts that are homiletic or hagiographic in content. These are interspersed with six poetic texts: *Andreas* (folios 29 verso to 52 verso), *The Fates of the Apostles* (folios 52 verso to 54 recto), *Soul and Body I* (folios 101 verso to 103 verso; and another version of which is in the Exeter Book), *Homiletic Fragment I* (folio 104), *The Dream of the Rood* (folios 104 verso to 106 recto), and *Elene* (folios 121 recto to 133 verso). Portions of some of the texts are missing because of the loss of manuscript leaves; for example, part of Andreas is missing as one leaf has been lost after folio 42; and part of Homily IX is lost between the current folios 63 and 64. C. Sisam has published the entire manuscript in facsimile and discusses its physical make-up and contents in her introduction.[1]

The manuscript is generally assigned to the second half of the tenth century, and to the south east of England. D. G. Scragg proposes that three of the homilies, XIX, XX and XXI, were compiled by an author working in Canterbury during the period when Dunstan was archbishop (959–88).[2] These three texts, and the others included in the Vercelli Book, may have been found and copied by the manuscript's compiler at St Augustine's, Canterbury.[3]

The Vercelli Book appears then to have been put together from a number of different exemplars with no apparent overall design in mind.[4] The manner in which the scribe did the copying is relatively mechanical. In most cases, he copied the dialect and the manuscript punctuation that was found in the original texts, and these aspects therefore aid in reconstructing the variety of exemplars.[5] The texts therefore range in date for although they were all copied in the later tenth century, they need not all have been written in this period. Indeed, some, such as those poems attributed to Cynewulf (*The Fates of the Apostles* and *Elene* in this manuscript), could be much earlier in date of origin.

Although the exemplars are diverse, and no apparent chronological or formal arrangement can be discerned, the texts suggest the compiler was someone 'in a monastic setting' who wished 'to illustrate his personal interest in penitential and eschatalogical themes and to glorify the ascetic way of life'.[6] The homilies represent part of the anonymous tradition of religious prose writing in Anglo-Saxon England. This tradition, which preceded the authored tradition of Ælfric and Wulfstan, is often marked by a Celtic influence and by an emphasis in some homilies on apocryphal material.[7] The homilies concern themselves with central Christian events such as Judgement Day, and with admonitions warning of the need to beware of the devil, to refrain from sin, to live a good Christian life, to give alms, and to save the soul. These concerns are reinforced by hagiographic texts, *Andreas*, *The Fates of the Apostles* and Homilies XVIII and XXIII (about Saints Martin and Guthlac respectively), which provide examples of Christianity in action.

It is not clear how the manuscript made its way to Vercelli in northern Italy, but it seems to have been there since the twelfth century.[8] The Vercelli Book was only discovered in the nineteenth century when a German, Friedrich Blume, who was looking for legal manuscripts, came across it in the Vercelli library. It remains there to this day.

1   C. Sisam, intro., *The Vercelli Book: A Late Tenth-Century Manuscript Containing Prose and Verse, Vercelli Biblioteca Capitolare CXVII*, EEMF 19 (Copenhagen, 1976).
2   D. G. Scragg, ed., *The Vercelli Homilies and Related Texts*, EETS o.s. 300 (London, 1992), pp. xli–lii.
3   Ibid. pp. lxxviii–lxxix.
4   Ibid., pp. xxiv–xxv; Sisam, *Vercelli Book*, pp. 37–44.
5   See K. O'Brien O'Keeffe, *Visible Song: Transitional Literacy in Old English Verse*, Cambridge Studies in Anglo-Saxon England 4 (Cambridge, 1992), pp. 165–72, for the manuscript's verse punctuation and layout.

6   S. B. Greenfield and D. G. Calder, eds, *A New Critical History of Old English Literature* (London, 1986), p. 74, following M. McC. Gatch.
7   See C. D. Wright, *The Irish Tradition in Old English Literature*, Cambridge Studies in Anglo-Saxon England 6 (Cambridge, 1993); M. McC. Gatch, *Preaching and Theology in Anglo-Saxon England: Ælfric and Wulfstan* (Toronto, 1977).
8   Scragg, *Vercelli Homilies*, p. xxiv.

THE FATES OF THE APOSTLES

The Fates of the Apostles survives only in the Vercelli Book at folios 52 verso to 54 recto. Little is known about Cynewulf, the probable author of this poem. He may have been a Mercian or a Northumbrian in religious orders who lived sometime between the late eight and late tenth centuries.[9] He is thought to have composed up to four poems in Old English: *Christ II* (The Ascension), *Elene, Juliana* and *The Fates of the Apostles*. This attribution is made on the basis of signatures written in runes that are integrated into the final sections of the poems.[10] Although the meaning of each rune is open to a variety of interpretations, the critical consensus is that each riddle points to this Cynewulf. His disguised signature attempts to guarantee both the survival of his name as author in a period when very few individual authors are known, and the intact transmission of his texts. These efforts to preserve the poet's authority over his writings suggests a transition from the period of oral and anonymous vernacular literature to a society in which text was committed to writing at the level of original composition.[11] The signatures also encapsulate Cynewulf's envisaged relationship with his inscribed audience, a first person plea for his readers' and listeners' prayers, and an insistence on appreciation for and engagement with his claimed writings.

The four poems traditionally assigned to Cynewulf deal with New Testament and early Christian events, and they are each influenced by and refer to significant feasts in the Church calendar. A possible source or inspiration for *The Fates of the Apostles* is the *Breviarium Apostolorum*.[12] This is an early eighth-century liturgical text that lists the twelve apostles and their feast days but in an order

that differs from the poem. Church litanies (supplicatory prayers) also contain the apostles in their lists, as do martyrologies (books containing brief lives of those who died as witnesses to the Christian faith). Both of these types of service book may have influenced the composition and the intended use of the poem, and it is perhaps because of these associations and the relatively simple diction of *The Fates of the Apostles* that it is underrated. It is, in fact, a good example of a short instructional and meditative text combining the vocabulary of the heroic tradition with a Christian content, and developing structurally from the centuries-old events of the apostles' lives to an inspired personal reflection. Bradley suggests that *The Fates of the Apostles* may be 'regarded as a mnemonic list . . . an aid to meditation upon exemplary Christian witness, faithful unto death'.[13] It can certainly be seen as didactic in its emphasis on the courage of the apostles in the face of persecution, each individual encompassing the ideals of the 'soldier of Christ' motif, to be emulated in some small way by the Christian audience. The lives of the apostles are viewed as a conflict, a struggle between the good warriors of Christ and the heathen persecutors. The penitential poet links himself to these apostles by revealing his own spiritual struggle with the fear of the journey he must make from this world to the next. The fact that he must make this journey to an unknown land alone parallels the travels of the apostles; the poet's evangelizing through his text mirrors that of Christ's retainers; and the search for immortality, not only in heaven, but in this world – through the use of the inscription – represents a human desire to emulate the fame of 'the twelve good men'.

The Fates of the Apostles

Hwæt! Ic þysne sang   siðgeomor fand
on seocum sefan;   samnode wide,
hu þa æðelingas   ellen cyðdon,
torhte ond tireadige.   Twelfe wæron,
5   dædum domfæste,   Dryhtne gecorene,
leofe on life.   Lof wide sprang,
miht ond mærðo,   ofer middangeard,
Þeodnes þegna –   þrym unlytel.
Halgan heape   hlyt wisode
10   þær hie Dryhtnes æ   deman sceoldon,

9   See R. E. Bjork, 'Cynewulf', in *The Garland Medieval Encyclopaedia*, ed. P. E. Szarmach (New York, 1998).

10   See D. Warwick Frese, 'The Art of Cynewulf's Signatures', repr. in *Cynewulf: Basic Readings*, ed. R. E. Bjork, Basic Readings in Anglo-Saxon England 4 (New York, 1996), pp. 323–45. These runes occur at lines 98–104 here.

11   See R. Woolf, ed., *Cynewulf's Juliana*, 2nd edn (Exeter, 1993), pp. 8–9.

12   Included in D. G. Calder and M. J. B. Allen, *Sources and Analogues of Old English Poetry 1: The Major Latin Texts in Translation* (Cambridge, 1976), pp. 37–9.

13   S. A. J. Bradley, *Anglo-Saxon Poetry*, 2nd edn (London, 1995), p. 154.

The Fates of the Apostles

Listen! I found this song journey-weary,
sick at heart; assembled it from far and wide,
about how these noble men revealed their courage,
glorious and famous. They were twelve,
renowned in deeds, chosen by the Lord,
beloved in their life. Their fame spread widely,
over the earth, the power and glory
of these thanes of the Lord – not a small glory.
The holy band's duty led
them to where they should preach the law of God,

5

10

reccan fore rincum.   Sume on Romebyrig,
frame, fyrdhwate,   feorh ofgefon
þurg Nerones   nearwe searwe:
Petrus ond Paulus.   Is se apostolhad
15   wide geweorðod   ofer werþeoda.
            Swylce Andreas   in Achagia
for Egias   aldre geneðde.
Ne þreodode he fore þrymme   ðeodcyninges,
æniges on eorðan,   ac him ece geceas,
20   langsumre lif,   leoht unhwilen,
syþþan hildeheard,   heriges byrhtme,
æfter guðplegan   gealgan þehte.
            Hwæt, we eac gehyrdon   be Johanne
æglæawe menn   æðelo reccan.
25   Se manna wæs,   mine gefrege,
þurh cneorisse,   Criste leofast
on weres hade,   syððan wuldres Cyning,
engla Ordfruma,   eorðan sohte
þurh fæmnan hrif,   Fæder manncynnes.
30   He in Effessia   ealle þrage
leode lærde;   þanon lifes weg
siðe gesohte,   swegle dreamas,
beorhtne boldwelan.   Næs his broðor læt
siðes sæne,   ac ðurh sweordes bite
35   mid Judeum   Jacob sceolde,
fore Herode   ealdre gedælan,
feorh wið flæsce.   Philipus wæs
mid Asseum;   þanon ece lif
þurh rode cwealm   ricene gesohte,
40   syððan on galgan   in Gearapolim
ahangen wæs   hildecorðre.
            Huru, wide wearð   wurd undyrne
þæt to Indeum   aldre gelædde,
beaducræftig beorn,   Bartholameus.
45   Þone heht Astrias   in Albano,
hæðen ond hygeblind,   heafde beneotan,
forþan he ða hæðengild   hyran ne wolde,
wig weorðian.   Him wæs wuldres dream,
lifwela leofra   þonne þas leasan godu.
50   Swylce Thomas eac   þriste geneðde
on Indea   oðre dælas,
þær manegum wearð   mod onlihted,
hige onhyrded,   þurh his halig word.
Syððan, collenferð,   cyninges broðor
55   awehte for weorodum,   wundorcræfte,
þurh Dryhtnes miht,   þæt he of deaðe aras
geong ond guðhwæt,   ond him wæs Gad nama.
Ond ða þæm folce   feorg gesealde,
sin æt sæcce: sweordræs fornam
60   þurh hæðene hand   þær se halga gecrang,
wund for weorudum;   þonon wuldres leoht
sawle gesohte   sigores to leane.
            Hwæt, we þæt gehyrdon   þurg halige bec,

to interpret it before the people. Some, in the city of Rome,
bold, warrior-like, gave up their lives
because of Nero's oppressive treachery:
Peter and Paul. That order of apostles is
15 widely honoured by the nations.
    Likewise, Andrew, in Achaia,
risked his life before Ægeas.
He did not waver in front of the might of a monarch,
of any of them on earth, but he chose for himself the eternal,
20 perpetual life, long-lasting light,
when bold in battle, to the noise of the hostile crowd,
after the conflict he mounted the gallows-cross.
    Listen, we have also heard about John
from men that know the scriptures, who tell of his noble family.
25 He was of all people, as I have heard it said,
through his family, the dearest to Christ
of all the race of men, after the King of glory,
Creator of angels, had come to earth
through a virgin's womb, the Father of mankind.
30 In Ephesus, all the time, John
taught the people; from there he sought
the way of life in death, heavenly joys,
the beautiful paradise. His brother was not reluctant
or cowardly in dying, but through the bite of the sword
35 among the Jews, and in front of Herod,
James had to dispense with life,
his soul separated from his body. Philip was
with the Asians; from there he quickly sought
eternal life through death on the cross,
40 after he was hanged on the cross
in Hierapolis by a crowd intent on conflict.
    Truly, far and wide, it was a clearly known fact
that in India the warlike warrior,
Bartholomew, passed his life.
45 Then, at Albanopolis, the heathen and spiritually blind Astrages
commanded that Bartholomew's head be cut off
because he would not subject himself to idols,
would not worship an image. The joy of heaven was, to him,
riches more valuable than those false gods.
50 Likewise, Thomas also boldly ventured
into other parts of India,
where through his holy word the minds of many
became enlightened, resolve strengthened.
Then, emboldened in spirit, he raised the king's brother up
55 in front of the crowds, a miraculous ability
through the power of the Lord, so he arose from death
young and fierce in battle, and his name was Gad.
And then Thomas gave his life for the people
in a conflict: a sword-attack at the hands of a heathen
60 overcame him where the saint fell,
wounded in front of the crowds; from there his soul sought
the radiance of heaven as a reward for his triumph.
    Listen, we have heard through holy books

þæt mid Sigelwarum   soð yppe wearð,
65   dryhtlic dom Godes.   Dæges or onwoc,
leohtes geleafan;   land wæs gefælsod
þurh Matheus   mære lare
þone het Irtacus,   ðurh yrne hyge,
wælreow cyning,   wæpnum aswebban.
70   Hyrde we þæt Jacob   in Jerusalem
fore sacerdum   swilt þrowode.
Þurg stenges sweng   stiðmod gecrang,
eadig for æfestum.   Hafað nu ece lif
mid Wuldorcining   wiges to leane.
75   Næron ða twegen   tohtan sæne
lindgelaces;   land Persea
sohton siðfrome: Simon ond Thaddeus,
beornas beadorofe.   Him wearð bam samod
an endedæg: æðele sceoldon
80   ðurh wæpenhete   weorc þrowigan
sigelean secan   ond þone soðan gefean,
dream æfter deaðe,   þa gedæled wearð
lif wið lice,   ond þas lænan gestreon,
idle æhtwelan,   ealle forhogodan.
85   Ðus ða æðelingas   ende gesealdon,
XII tilmodige.   Tir unbræcne
wegan on gewitte   wuldres þegnas.
Nu Ic þonne bidde   beorn se ðe lufige
þysses giddes begang   þæt he geomrum me
90   þone halgan heap   helpe bidde,
friðes ond fultomes.   Hu, Ic freonda beþearf,
liðra on lade,   þonne Ic sceal langne ham,
eardwic uncuð,   ana gesecan;
lætan me on laste   lic, eorðan dæl,
95   wælreaf wunigean   weormum to hroðre.
Her mæg findan   foreþances gleaw,
se ðe hine lysteð   leoðgiddunga,
hwa þas fitte fegde: [feoh] þær on ende standeþ;
eorlas þæs on eorðan brucaþ.   Ne moton hie awa ætsomne
100   woruldwunigende.   [Wen] sceal gedreosan,
[ur] on eðle,   æfter tohreosan
læne lices frætewa,   efne swa [lagu] toglideð.
Þonne [cen] ond [yr]   cræftes neotad,
nihtes nearowe   on him [nyd] ligeð,
105   cyninges þeodom.   Nu ðu cunnon miht
hwa on þam wordum wæs   werum oncyðig.
Sie þæs gemyndig,   mann se ðe lufige
þisses galdres begang,   þæt he geoce me
ond frofre fricle.   Ic sceall feor heonan
110   an elles forð   eardes neosan,
sið asettan —   nat Ic sylfa hwær —
of þisse worulde.   Wic sindon uncuð,
eard ond eðel,   swa bið ælcum menn
nemþe he godcundes   gastes bruce.
115   Ah utu we þe geornor   to Gode cleopigan,
sendan usse bene   on þa beorhtan gesceaft

that among the Ethiopians the truth was revealed,
65 the divine glory of God. At the beginning of the day arose
the light of faith; the land was cleansed
through the holy teaching of Matthew
when Irtacus, that bloodthirsty king,
with an angry mind, ordered him to be killed with weapons.
70   We have heard that James suffered death
in Jerusalem in front of the priests.
Resolute, he fell through the cudgel's blow,
happy despite this malice. Now he has eternal life
with the King of glory as a reward for his battle.
75   These two were not cowardly in the campaign
of this battle; the land of the Persians
they sought, ready for the journey: Simon and Thaddeus,
warriors renowned in war. To both of them together came
a single end-day: these noble men had
80 to suffer pain through armed hate
to seek the reward of glory and the true bliss,
joy after death, when life was separated
from the body, and these temporary treasures,
idle wealth, were entirely rejected.
85   Thus these noble men gave up their lives,
twelve good men. Unassailable glory
was sustained in the senses of heaven's thanes.
    Now I ask that the person who may approve
of the course of this poem should pray for my grief
90 to that holy band for help,
for refuge and for support. Indeed, I will have need of friends,
of kind ones, on that journey, when alone I have to seek
a permanent home, an unknown dwelling;
have to leave behind my body, this portion of earth,
95 the spoils of death, to remain as a treat for the worms.
Here a person wise in forethought may discover,
he who enjoys the recitation of poems,
who composed this song: [wealth] stands there at the end;
earls enjoy this on earth. They will not be allowed to be together forever
100 dwelling in the world. The [pleasure] that is [male strength]
shall decline in this homeland, after the body's
temporary ornaments decay, just as the [ocean] will glide away.
While the [torch] and the [bow] use their skill,
[need] lies on them in the anxious night,
105 the servitude of the king. Now you might know
who has been made known to men by these words.
Let him, the man who is fond of the performance of this song,
be mindful of this, so that he might help me
and seek comfort for me. Alone from here I must travel
110 away elsewhere to search for the native land,
to set out on a journey – I myself do not know where –
away from this world. The places are unknown,
the land and the home, just as they are to each man
unless he possesses a divine spirit.
115   We ought ever to call out to God more earnestly,
send our prayers into that bright creation

þæt we þæs botles   brucan motan,
hames in hehðo,   þær is hihta mæst,
þær Cyning engla   clænum gildeð
120   lean unhwilen.   Nu a his lof standeð,
mycel ond mære,   ond his miht seomaþ,
ece ond edgiong,   ofer ealle gesceaft. *Finit*.

so that we might be allowed to enjoy that palace,
a home in the heavens, where there is the most joy,
where the King of angels pays the virtuous
120 a perpetual reward. Now and forever his glory remains,
great and splendid, and his strength will continue,
eternal and invigorating, throughout all creation. *Finit.*

Vercelli Homily X

This lengthy penitential homily occurs not only in the Vercelli Book at folios 65 recto to 71 recto, but also in other manuscripts dating from the eleventh to the twelfth centuries. Complete versions of the same homily (but without the first seven lines) survive in Cambridge, Corpus Christi College 419 and 421 (first half of the eleventh century), and Cambridge, Corpus Christi College 302 (early twelfth century). An incomplete version also exists in Princeton, University Library, Scheide Collection 71, a manuscript known as *The Blickling Homilies*. In addition, parts of the homily are found as sections of other prose pieces.[14] Thus it can be assumed that texts of this homily circulated fairly widely in late Anglo-Saxon and post-Conquest England, and that the contents were of interest and use to a number of manuscript compilers.

Homily X is a well-structured, effective piece of didactic and admonitory literature. Its central themes are the events of Judgement Day and the transience of life, both of which are thematic concerns of many Old and Middle English texts. A number of different Latin sources inspired the author, including Paulinus of Aquileia's *Liber exhortationis ad Henricum comitem* for the Judgement Scene, and Isidore of Seville's *Synonyma* for the transitoriness of worldly glories.[15] But the author of the Old English expands considerably on these sources, weaving them into an original and compelling work. The homily is rhetorically skilled, using direct speech, alliterative prose, various devices of repetition, rhetorical questions, and figurative and legal language to impart its instructive messages while maintaining the audience's interest.

Vercelli Homily X

Her sagað on þyssum halegum bocum be ælmihtiges Dryhtnes godspelle, þe he him sylfum þurh his ða halegan mihte geworhte mannum to bysene and to lare. And he sylf gecwæð his halegan muðe: 'Þeah man anum men godspel secge, þonne bio Ic þæron middan.' And þam bioð synna forgifena þe ðæt godspel segð and gecwið, and synna þam bioð forgifene þe hit for Godes naman
5   lustlice gehyreð; and þam bið wa æfre geworht þe secgan can and nele, for ðam men sculon þurh ða godcundan lare becuman to life.

We þonne, men þa leofestan, we gehyrdon oft secgan be ðam æðelan tocyme usses Dryhtnes, and hu him man in ða woruld wiðþingian ongan. Þæt heahfæderas bodedon and cyðdon, þæt witegan witegedon and heredon, þæt sealmscopas sungon and sædon þæt se wolde of ðam rice
10   cuman and of ðam cynestole and of ðam þrymrice hyder on þas eorðan, and him þas cynerico on his anes æht ealle geagnian. And eall ðæt wæs gelæsted siððan heofenas tohlidon and sio heahmiht on þysne wang astah, and se Halega Gæst wunode in þam æðelan innoðe and in þam betstan bosme and in þam gecorenan hordfate. And in þam halegan breostum he eardode nigon monoð, and þa ealra fæmnena wuldor cende þone soðan Scyppend and ealles folces Frefrend, and ealles
15   middangeardes Hælend and ealra gasta Nerigend and eallra sawla Helpend, ða se ælmihtega Dryhten in þas woruld becwom and menniscne lichoman onfeng æt Sancte Marian. Þurh þa byrðran we wæron gehælede, and þurh þæt gebiorðor we wurdon alysede, and þurh ða gesamnunge we wæron gefrioðode and gewelgode. And syððan he, Dryhten Crist, her on worlde wunode mid mannum, and feala wundra mannum cyðde, and beforan worhte, and him liðelice hælo sealde,
20   and his mildheortnesse tæhte.

Ær hie wæron stænenre heortan and blinde þæt hie þæt ongitan ne meahton þæt hie ðær gesawon, ac þa se ælmihtega Dryhten afyrde him þæt unrihte wrigels of hyra heortan, and onbyrhte hie mid leohte andgyte, þa hie þæt ongeaton and oncnawan meahton hwa him to helpe and to feorhnere on þas woruld astah, syðþan he him mildheortnesse earan ontynde, and hie to geleafan
25   onbyrgde, and his miltse him onwreah and his mægensybbe gecyðde.

Ær þan we wæron steopcild gewordene ða we wæron bewerede þæs hiofoncundan rices, and we wæron adilgode of þam þryðfullan frumgewrite ða we wæron to hiofonum awritene. Wæron we nu syðþan amearcode þurh þone soðan Scyppend and þurh þone lyfigendan God and þurh þone acennedan sunu, urne Dryhten, to þan gefean neorxnawanges. Ne gelette us þæs siðes se frecna
30   feond, ne us ðæs wilweges ne forwyrne, ne us þa gatu betyne þe us opene standaþ, ne us þære

---

14 See Scragg, *Vercelli Homilies*, pp. 191–218, for a collated edition of this homily, and pp. 192–5 for the history of the text's transmission.

15 See ibid., pp. 191–213, for these sources.

Vercelli Homily X

Here it says in this book about the almighty Lord's gospel, which he himself through his holy power made as an example and lesson for humanity. And he himself said through his holy mouth: 'Even if one man tells the gospel to one person, then I am in the midst of them.'[16] And their sins will be forgiven to those who speak and relate that gospel, and sins are forgiven to those who hear it eagerly for God's name; and misery will always be the result for those who can tell it and will not, because people will come to life through the divine scriptures.

Then we, dearest people, we have often heard it said about the noble advent of our Lord, and how people in this world began to become reconciled with him. The patriarchs announced and made known, the prophets prophesied and praised, the psalmists sung and related that he would come from that kingdom and from that throne and from that glorious kingdom here to this earth, and he would claim all of these kingdoms for his ownership alone. And all that was fulfilled after the heavens burst open and the great power descended into this world and the Holy Spirit dwelled in the noble womb and in the best breast and in the chosen precious vessel. And in that holy breast he dwelled for nine months, and then the glory of all women gave birth to the true Creator and the Comforter of all people, and the Saviour of the entire earth and the Preserver of all spirits, and the Helper of all souls, the almighty Lord came into this world and received the body of a man from Saint Mary. Through this bearer we were healed, and through that child we were saved, and through that coming together we were rescued and enriched. And afterwards, he, the Lord Christ, dwelt here in this world amongst people, and showed many miracles to humanity, and performed them in front of them, and gave them salvation mercifully, and taught them about his mercy.

Before, they were more stone-hearted and blind, so that they could not perceive what they saw there, but then the almighty Lord removed that unrighteous covering from their hearts, and illuminated them with clear understanding, so that they might perceive and know who descended into this world as a help and comfort to them, after he opened their ears to mercy, and they partook in faith, and uncovered his mercy to them and revealed the power of God's love.

Before this we had become orphans when we were deprived of the kingdom of heaven, and we were erased from that glorious first charter on which we were enrolled into heaven.[17] Afterwards, we were appointed through the true Creator and through the living God and through the begotten son, our Lord, to the joy of paradise. The dangerous enemy does not prevent us from that journey, nor deny to us that desired path, nor close the gates that stand open to us, nor withhold us from that city through his false

---

16   Matthew 18.20: 'For, where there are two or three gathered together in my name, there am I in the midst of them.'

17   This refers to the expulsion of humanity from Paradise: the Fall of Man, in Genesis 3.23.

byrig ne ofteo þurh his lease brægdas, ne us ðæs rices ne forwyrne þe we to gesceapene syndon, ne us ne dwelle þæs rihtan geleafan þe we to gelærede syndon. And we ða Dryhtenlycan wære gehealden, and þa syblycan lufan Godes and manna. Ne syn we to gifre, ne to frece ne to fyrenlusteorne, ne to æfestige ne to inwitfulle, ne to tælende ne to twyspræce, ne morðor to
35 fremmanne ne leasunga to secganne ne þeofða to beganganne ne wirignessa to fyligenne, ne heafodlice leahtras. Ne lufien we ne scincræftas, ne herien we ne galdorsangas; ne unriht lyblac ne onginnen we, ne to yðbylge, ne to langsum yrre næbben we; ac þas uncysta ealle we us bebiorgen þa ðe Gode laðe syndon, and we þurh þæt þone awyrigedan gast aflymen and þurh ða heahmyhte ures Dryhtnes.

40 Forðan we a sculon bion ymbhydige ure sawle rædes, and ure hiortan reccen and gestaðeligen Gode to willan, and geþencen þæne dom þe we to geladode syndon, and ðone Deman þe to þam dome cymeð: he demð rihtne dom. Ne bioð þær cyninga setl þrymmum gefrætewod – butan þam anum þe ofer ealle a rixað. Ne bið þær forðborene gyldene beagas, ne bið þær hyra heafodgold ne woruldgestreon boren to þam Sigedeman. Ac on þam gemote standeð anra gehwylces mannes
45 sawl. Hio bið forðlædende ealle þa wiorc þe hio gefremede, godes oððe yfeles. Gif ðær þænne bið þara misdædena ma and þæs godes to lyt, þonne wynsumaþ se wiðerwearda feond and se awirigeda gæst on gesyhðe þæs reðan cyninges.

And he ðonne bealdlice cliopaþ to ðam hean Deman and ðus cwið: 'Dem, la Dema, rihtne dom and emne dom. Dem be ðam þe þine bebodu forhogodon, and þine æ abræcon, and symle hie
50 besmiton mid synnum and gebysmeredon. Gearalice we witon þas heregas þry ðe mid þe wæron: an is se heofoncunda se ðe mid fereð and þe þenaþ; oðer is ðæt eorðlice mægen þe þu her somnost and to þrymdome cumen is; ðridde is þæt hellcunde werod þe hyder cwom to þan þæt hie woldon þine domas gehyran, hu þu þam forworhtum scrifan woldest. Eall þis mægen wat, þe her to þys gemote com, þæt heahsetl is þrymmes anes eall afylled and mid soðfæstnesse and mid rihtwisnesse
55 geseted.

Dem, la Dryhten, rihte domas, and forlæt me mines rihtes wyrðe þæs ðe Ic me sylf begiten hæbbe. Þæt wæron mine: þa ðe to þe noldon. Min riht is þæt Ic þa mid witum þreage þa þe þine hyrnesse forhogodon. Hie hie scyrpton minum reafum, nals ðam gewædum þe ðu hie hete. Hie wæron ungemetfæste eallum tidum and oferhidum to fulle and mines willan to georne. Þonne hie
60 gehyrdon þine bec rædan and þin godspel secgan, and hira lif rihtan and him ecne weg cyðan, hy symle hiera earan dytton and hit gehyran noldon. Ac ðonne Ic mine hearpan genam and mine strengas styrian ongan, hie ðæt lustlice gehyrdon, and fram þe cyrdon and to me urnon. And Ic hie mine leahtras lærde, and hie me hyrdon georne. And Ic hie to þeofðum tyhte and to geflite scyrpte and to inwitfullum geðancum, þæt Ic wolde þæt hy þe afremdedon. Ac, hwæt, woldon
65 hie in minon hordcofan, and þin cynerice eal forgeaton. Æt me hie leornodon scondword and lease brægdas, and þine soðfæsten lare hie forgeaton and þinne dom ne gemundon; ac minre neaweste a wilnodon and þine forhogodon.

Dem la, ealra gesceafta Reccend and Scippend and Steorend, dem rihtne dom. Hwæt, ðu þe sylfne geeadmeddest for hyra ealra lufan and for urre læððo. Þin feorh for hyra in deað þu gesealdest,
70 and þu þe sylf on rode astige ðær ðu ðæt þin halige blod on eorðan agute for him, and mid þine þe æðelan swate gebohtest; and mid þine þy deorwyrðan blode alysdest and gefreoðodest; and hie þe þæs leanes ealles forgeaton. Þa hie to me cyrdon, næfre Ic him are ne gefremede, ne næfre helpes geuðe; ac forlæt hie me in wite gelædan and in susle cwelman, and þa mishyrnesse gewrecan þe hie wið ðe worhton.'

75 Hwæt, we nu gehyrdon secgan, men ða leofestan, hu bealdlice spreceð þæt dioful to þam Hælende, and þa misdæda stæleð on þa gæstas. He þonne ofer eaxle besyhð, se soðfæsta Dema and se rihtwisa, to ðam scyldegum, and þus cwið worda grimmost: 'Nelle Ic eow habban on minre geferrædenne, ac ge fram me gewitað, wuldres bedælede, freondum afyrde, feondum betæhte, in þam hatan wylme helle fyres þær ge awirgedan sculon sincan and swincan in ðam hatan hellebrogan
80 and in þam witum wunigan a butan ende.' Þænne bið Dryhtnes word hraþe gehyred þam synfullan strengest: bið se Dema þearl.

tricks, nor deny us that kingdom for which we are created, nor lead us from dwelling in that true faith that we have learned. And we ought to hold to the Lordly covenant, and the peacemaking love of God and humanity. Neither should we be too greedy, nor too bold to satisfy evil desires, nor too envious nor crafty, nor too censorious nor hypocritical, nor should we commit murder nor tell lies nor practise stealing nor follow blasphemy, or the capital sins. We should not love sorcery, neither should we utter incantations; neither should we begin witchcraft, nor be too easily angered, nor to have too protracted an anger; but we should guard against all these sins that are hateful to God, and through that, we can put to flight the damned spirit because of the great strength of our Lord.

Therefore we should always be mindful of the benefit of our souls, and guide and fix our hearts towards the will of God, and consider the judgement to which we will be led, and the Judge who will come to that judgement: he will judge a just judgement. Nor will there be kings' seats adorned with glory there – except the one that rules over all forever. Nor will there be golden rings carried forth there, nor will there be crowns nor worldly wealth carried to the victorious Judge. But in that assembly the soul of each person will stand. It will be led forth by all the works that it performed, good or evil. If there are more misdeeds there and too few that were good, then the hostile fiend and the damned spirit will rejoice in the sight of the cruel king.

And then he boldly calls out to the high Judge and says this: 'Judge then, Lord, just judgement and exact judgement. Judge those who despised your commands, and broke your law, and they defiled and insulted them continually with sins. Readily the three hosts who are with you understand: one is the heavenly host who travel with you and serve you; the other is that earthly host that you assembled here and that has come to glory; the third is the host of hell who come here so that they are able to hear your judgements, how you would estimate the wicked. All this assembly knows, who come here to this meeting, that the throne is filled up with one glory and established with truth and with righteousness.

Judge then, Lord, just judgements, and let me be worthy of my justice, which I have obtained for myself. They were mine: those who would not turn to you. My right is that I should torment those who despised your teaching with punishments. They dressed themselves in my garments, not those clothes that you commanded of them. They were immoderate at all times and too full of pride and too eager for my desire. When they heard your book read out and your gospel spoken, and their life made right and the eternal way revealed, they always closed their ears and would not hear it. But when I took up my harp and began to stir the strings, they heard that lustily, and turned from you and ran to me. And I taught them my sins, and they eagerly heard me. And I persuaded them towards stealing and incited them towards strife and towards wicked thoughts, because I wanted them to be alienated from you. But, indeed, they wanted to be in my private chamber, and entirely forgot your kingdom. From me they learned abusive speech and false tricks, and they forgot your true teaching and did not recall your judgement; but they always desired my companionship and forgot about you.

Judge then, Ruler and Creator and Steersman of all things, judge just judgement. Listen, you humbled yourself for the love of all of them and for our hatred. You gave your life for them in death, and you yourself ascended the cross where you spilt your holy blood on the ground for them, and bought them with your noble sweat; and with your precious blood you redeemed and rescued them; and they have forgotten all about the reward. When they turned to me, I never advanced them any honour nor ever offered help; but allow me to lead them into hardship and kill them in torment, and avenge the disobedience that they performed against you.'

Indeed, we have heard tell, dearest people, how boldly that devil will speak to the Saviour, and will lay charges of misdeeds on the souls. He then, the true and the righteous Judge, will look over his shoulder to the sinners, and say the most terrible of words, thus: 'I will not have you in my company, but you will depart from me, deprived of glory, separated from friends, delivered to fiends, in the hot flames of hell fire where you condemned ones will sink and suffer into the hot terror of hell and dwell in those torments for ever without end.'[18] Then the Lord's word is immediately heard by the sinful to be most powerful: the Judge is severe.

We have then, dearest people, great necessity that we are not with the guilty but with the chosen and those pleasing to Christ. We should earn his mercy then so that we might have his merciful judgement

18   Matthew 25.41.

Habbað we þænne, men þa leofestan, micele nydþearfe þæt we ne syn mid þam scyldegum ac mid þam gecorenum and mid ðam gedefum Cristes. We ðonne sculon his mildheortnesse geearnigan þæt we eft mildne deman hæbben. We wæron oft gemyndgode to ures Dryhtnes gehyrsumnesse,

85 þæt we scoldon his willan wyrcan and his bebodu healdan, and rummode bion rihtra gestreona and þearfendum arfulle, and wydewena helpend and steopcilda frefrend, and earmra retend and wependra frefrend. And gif we ðas weorc ongynnað and gelæstað, þonne bioð we Godes dyrlingas in hiofenum. Nis urum Hælende nanuht behyddes ne gediglodes þæs ðe men wyrcað on þysse worlde, forþan his eagan ofer eall gesioð.

90 Swa sanctus Jacobus sæde, Cristes apostol, hu se Hælend spræc to sumum welegum men þe he mid glengo and mid wiste gegodod hæfde. Ac he wæs ormod and swar, and him wæs lað þearfendum mannum aht to syllanne, and him wæs unyðe þæt he for Gode aht dælde, oððe þam sealde þe hit him ær eal forgeaf. Ac hyne se Hælend eft þara leana myndgode ða he cwæð: 'Ne gemundest ðu na Salomones cwide þe he cwæð: "Do ælmyssan under þæs þearfan sceat se cliopað to me and Ic hine

95 symle gehyre and mine miltse ofer þone sende"? Emne hit bið gelice swa man mid wætere þone weallendan wylm agiote þæt he rixian ne mote, swa man mæg mid ælmyssan ealla synna gebetan and þa gyltas gehælan. Þonne ðu, welega, hwi noldest ðu mine bebodu healdan? Ac se min þearfa aswæmde æt þinre handa. Hwi noldest þu geþencan hwa hit þe sealde? Þonne he cliopade earmre stemne, þu wiðsoce þæt ðu hiene ne gehyrdest. Ac Ic his giomrunga gehyrde and geseah hwæt ðu

100 dydest minum þearfan þam þe þe mildheortnesse bædon. And þu hie oferhogodest and geunrotsodest and þinne andwlitan fram him awendest, and ne gemundest no hwæt se witega cwæð: "Se ðe his andwlitan fram þam þearfan awendeð þonne he hluddost cliopað, Dryhten hyne gehyreð þonne se man nele þone oðerne gehyran."'

Swa se Hælend cwæð to þam wlancan: 'To hwan wurd ðu swa heamul minra goda þe Ic ðe dyde

105 and sealde? To hwan areceleasodest ðu ðære gife þe Ic þe geaf? Ic þe nu afyrre fram mine sylene þe Ic þe ær forgeaf; þonne bist ðu wædla in woruldrice. For hwan noldest geþencean þæt Ic wille forgildan æghwylce gode dæde þe for minon naman man gedeð? Ic hit forgilde swa hit is on minon godspelle gecweden: "Swa lange swa ge hit doð, and swa oft swa ge hit syllað anum minum læstum, ge hit symle me syllað, and Ic eow sylle ecne gefean in heofonum".

110 Þonne ðu, man, to hwan eart ðu me swa unþancul minra goda and minra gifa? Hwæt, Ic þe gesceop and geliffæste, and æghwæt þæs ðe ðu hafast, Ic þe sealde. Eall hit is min, and þin Ic afyrre fram þe. Ðu liofa butan me gif ðu mæge. Þe Ic hit sealde to ðan þæt ðu hit sceoldest þearfum dælan. And Ic swerige þurh me sylfne þæt Ic eom se ilca God se ðe weligne gedyde. And þearfendan Ic geworhte mid minum handum, þæt Ic wolde þæt ðu mine þearfan fedde þonne hie

115 wæron þe biddende minra goda. Þu him symle tiðe forwyrndest. For hwan noldest ðu hit geþencan, gif ðu him mildheortnesse an gecyðdest, þonne ne sceoldest ðu ðæs naht forliosan ðæs ðu him dydest, ne me mid þære sylene abelgan mines agenes? To hwan feddest ðu þe ænne of ðam þe Ic inc bæm gesceop, to welan and to feorhnere? To hwan heold ðu hit þe sylfum and þinum bearnum, þæt meahte manegum mannum genihtsumian? Unyðe þe wæs þæt ðu hit eal ne meahtest

120 gefæstnigan, ne mid insigelum eal beclysan. Wenst ðu ðæt hit þin sie þæt sio eorðe forðbringeð, hio þe groweð and bloweð and sæd lædeð and onlifan bringeð? Eall Ic nu afyrre minne fultum fram ðe. Hafa æt þinum gewinne þæt ðu mæge and on þinum geswince. Ic ofteo mine renas þæt hie þine eorðan ne onhrinað, and Ic afyrre fram þe mine mildheortnesse, and þonne bið sona gecyðed and ætiewed þinra yrmða dæl. Gif ðu wene þæt hit þin bocland sie and on agene æht

125 geseald, hit þonne wæron mine wæter þa ðe on heofonum wæron þanon Ic mine gife dæle eorðwærum. Gif ðu mihta hæbbe, dæl regnas ofer þine eorðan. Gif ðu strang sy, syle wæstm þinre eorðan. Ic ahyrde mine sunnan and hie gebyrhte; þone forbærneð hio ealle þine æceras; þonne bist ðu dælleas mines renes, and þe þin eorðe bið idel and unnyt goda gehwylces.

Mine þearfan lifiað bi me. Gif ðu mæge, wuna butan me. Mine þearfan me ealne weg habbað,

130 and Ic hie næfre ne forlæte. Mine þearfan me lufiað and hie cygeað me hyra Dryhten – and hine gelomlice nemnaþ and lufiað, and him ege to habbað swa men sculon to hiera Hlaforde. Þonne þu, welega, ne þu þinne Dryhten lufast, ne ðu him miltse æt hafast, ne ðu, yrming, ne most lifian

afterwards. We were often reminded about obedience to our Lord, that we should perform his will and hold his command, and be generous with proper possessions and generous to the needy, and the helper of widows and comforter of orphans, and comforter of the poor and consoler of those who weep. And if we begin and sustain this work, then we will be God's darlings in heaven. Nothing that people do in this world is hidden from our Lord or secret, because his eyes see over everything.

It is just as Saint James, Christ's apostle, narrated how the Saviour spoke to a certain wealthy man whom he had enriched with wealth and with food.[19] But he was very proud and mean, and he was loath to give anything to needy men, and it was grievous to him that he should give anything for God's sake, unless it was given to those who had previously given to him. But the Saviour reminded him again of the reward when he said: 'Do you not remember Solomon's words when he said: "Put alms under the cloak of the beggar who calls to me and I will always hear him and send my mercy over him"? Again it is like the man who put out the burning flame that he could not control with water, so one can remedy all sins and heal all guilt with alms-giving. Then you, a prosperous man, why didn't you obey my command? For this is my beggar who wasted away at your hand. Why didn't you consider what you might give him? When he called out in a wretched voice, you denied that you could hear him. But I heard his lament and saw what you did to my beggar who asked you for mercy. And you despised and afflicted him and turned your face from him, and did not remember what the prophet said: "He who turns his face from the needy when he calls out loudest, when that other man will not heed him, the Lord will hear him then."'

Thus the Saviour will say to the proud man: 'Why were you so miserly with my benefits, which I did for you and gave you? Why were you so careless with that gift that I gave you? I remove you now from my gift that I had previously given you; then you will become a poor man within this worldly kingdom. Why did you not consider that I would reward each good deed that is done in my name? I reward it just as it is stated in my gospel: "As long as you do this, and as often as you give this to one of my least ones, you always give it to me, and I will give you eternal reward in heaven."[20]

Then you, man, why are so ungrateful to me for my benefits and my gifts? Listen, I made you and gave life to you, and everything that you have, I gave to you. All of it is mine, and I can take yours from you. Live without me if you can. I gave it to you so that you could share it out with the needy. And I myself swear that I am that same God who made you wealthy. And I made the beggar with my hands because I wanted you to feed my needy when they were asking you for my benefits. You always refused that gift to them. Why did you not consider, if you showed them some mercy, then you would not lose any of that which you gave to them, nor would you anger me with the gift of my property? Why did you feed yourself alone from that which I created for the prosperity and comfort of both of you? Why did you retain for yourself and your children that which might be plentiful for many men? It was hard on you that you could not hold onto it all, nor enclose it all with seals. Do you think that what the earth brings forth is yours, that it grows and flowers and produces seed and brings food for you? I take all of my support away from you now. Get whatever you can from your toil and from your work. I withhold my rain so that it will not touch the earth, and I take my mercy from you, and then immediately your share of miseries will be revealed and made clear. If you think that hereditary land might be yours, and given into your own possession, then it was my waters that were in the heavens from where I gave my gift to the inhabitants of earth. If you have the power, dispense rain over the earth. If you are that strong, obtain produce from your earth. I will intensify my sun and it will brighten; then it will burn up all your fields; then you will not have a drop of my rain, and your earth will be empty and idle of each benefit.

My beggars live near by me. If you can, live without me. My needy have me all the way, and I will never abandon them. My needy love me and they call me their Lord – and frequently they call that name and love it, and they have fear just as men ought to fear their Lord. Whereas you, wealthy man, you do not love your Lord, nor will you receive mercy from him, nor, wretch, will you be allowed to live long at all. Indeed, did you think, proud man, if you gave me anything of yours that you would always be decreasing your transitory riches? Sadly, you thought too little about the end of your life. You were too stupid when you thought that there would be no end to your possessions. I know, though, that your life

---

19 See James 2, for this concept of faith with good works.   20 Matthew 10.42.

naht lange. Hwæt, wendest ðu, wlanca, gif ðu me sealde þines awiht þæt þe þonne wære þin woruldgestreon a gelytlod? Eala, þæt ðu lyt hogodest ymb þone ende þines lifes. To dol ðu wære,
135   þa ðu wendest ðæt þinra feohgestreona ende ne wurde. Ic wat, hwæðre, þæt lif bið geendod þonne ðu his ne wenst. Þu, welega, to hwan getruwedest ðu in þine wlenceo and in þine oferflownessa þinra goda, and na on me þe hit þe eal forgeaf þæt ðu on wære?'

And he ða, Dryhten Crist, cwæð to ðam welegan men: 'Eawla, ðu, dysega and gedwealda, to hwy getruwedest ðu ðe on þine speda and on þine æhta? Þin sawl on þisse ilcan niht bið be minre
140   hæse of ðinum lichoman alæded; ac hwa fehð þonne to þam þe þu lange stryndest? Oððe hwam gearwodest þu þin botl oððe þine getimbro, nu þine yrfeweardas leng lyfian ne moton, for þan þu me noldest nanne þanc don minra goda?'

Men þa leofestan, sceoldon þa word bion ealle cuðlice gelæste þe se Hælend cwæð. Sona þa on þone welegan mann on þære ilcan nihte deaþ on becwom, and on his bearn ealle. Fengon þa to
145   gestreonum fremde syþþan.

Hwæt, we nu magon be þysan ongitan and oncnawan þæt se ælmihtiga God nele þæt his gifena man þanc nyte. Ne ðurfon we þæs wenan þæt he us nelle þara leana gemanigan þe he us her on eorðan to gode forgifeð. Swa we him mærlycor þancian sculon: a swa þrymlycor ar swa mare eadmodnes. Þam þe Dryhten mycel syleð, myceles he hine eac eft manað. Þam þe he micel to
150   forlæteð, mycel he to þam seceð.

Æghwylc heah ham her in worulde bið mid frecennesse ymbseald; emne swa ða woruldgeþingu bioð maran, swa bioð þa frecennessa swiðran. Swa ge magon bi ðan þa bysene oncnawan and ongitan: þæt treow, þonne hit geweaxeð on ðam wudubearwe and hit hlifað up ofer þa oðre ealle and brædeþ, and hit þonne se stranga wind gestandeð, hit bið swiðlicor geweged and geswenced
155   þonne se oðer wuda. Swa bið eac gelic be ðam hean clifum and torrum, þonne hie feorran ofer ða oðre eorþan hlifiað, and hie þonne semninga feallan onginnaþ and ful heardlice hrioseð to foldan. Swylce eac be ðam micelum muntum and dunum, þa þe hyhst standaþ and goriað ofer ealne middangeard, and þeahhwæðere hi wite habbað þæs ealdordomes þæt hie bioð geneahhe mid heofonfyre geþread and geþræsted, and geslægen mid lige. Swa ða hean myhta her in worulde
160   hreosaþ and feallað and to lore wiorð; þysse worulde welan wiorð to nahte; and þas eorðlican wuldor wiorð to sorge. Þeah we þysse worulde glenga tiligen swiðe and we in wuldre scinan swiðe, and þeah we us scyrpen mid þam readdestan godewebbe and gefrætewigen mid ðam biorhtestan golde, and mid þam diorwyrðan gimstanum utan ymbhon, hwæðere he sceal in nearonesse ende gebidan. And þeah þa strengestan and þa ricestan hatan him reste gewyrcan of
165   marmanstane and of oðrum goldfrætewum, and mid gimcynnum eal astæned and mid seolfrenum ruwum and beddum eal oferwreon, and mid dieorwyrðum wyrtgemengnessum eall geseted and mid goldleafum geþread ymbutan, hwæðere se bitera deaþ þæt todæleð eall. Þonne bið sio gleng agoten, and se þrym tobroden, and þa gimmas toglidene and þæt gold toscæned, and þa lichaman gebrosnode and to duste gewordene.

170   Forþan nis naht þysses middangeardes wlite and þysse worulde wela; he is hwilendlic and yfellic and forwordenlic, swa ða rican syndon her in worulde. Hwær syndon þa rican caseras and cyningas þa þe gio wæron, oððe þa cyningas þe we io cuðon? Hwær syndon þa ealdormen þa þe bebodu setton? Hwær is demera domstow? Hwær is hira ofermetto, butan mid moldan beþeahte and in witu gecyrred? Wa is woruldescriftum, butan hie mid rihte reccen. Nis þam leornerum na
175   sel þonne leornendum, butan hie mid rihte domas secen. Hwær coman middangeardes gestreon? Hwær com worulde wela? Hwær cwom foldan fægernes? Hwær coman þa þe geornlicost æhta tiledon and oðrum eft yrfe læfdon? Swa læne is sio oferlufu eorðan gestreona: emne hit bið gelice rena scurum, þonne he of heofenum swiðost dreoseð and eft hraðe eal toglideð; bið fæger weder and beorht sunne. Swa tealte syndon eorðan dreamas, and swa todæleð lic and sawle. Þonne is us
180   uncuð hu se Dema ymb þæt gedon wylle.

Forþan nis naht ne selre þonne we lufigen urne Dryhten mid ealle mode, and mid ealle mægene, and of eallum urum ingehiedum. Swa hit awriten is, and he sylf cwæð: 'Se ðe hæfð minne lufan in him and his bene to me sendeð, Ic hine symle gehyre and mine miltse ofer hyne sende. And þa þe

will be ended when you do not expect it. You, rich man, why did you trust in your pride and in the abundance of your riches, and not in me, who gave you everything that was in you?'

And then he, the Lord Christ, will say to the rich person: 'Alas, you, foolish and misguided person, why did you trust in your riches and in your possessions? On this same night, your soul will be led from your body at my command; who will then take what you have amassed? Or for whom did you prepare your mansion or your building now that your heirs will not be allowed to live for long, because you would not give any thanks for my benefits?'

Dearest people, these words that the Saviour spoke shall all be clearly fulfilled. Immediately, death came upon that rich man and all his children on that same night. Strangers took the treasures afterwards.

Indeed, by this, we may now understand and perceive that almighty God does not want man to be unaware of his gifts. Nor need we think that he will not remind us of the rewards that he has given us here on earth as a benefit. So we should thank him more richly: always, the more glorious the honour, the greater the humility. From those to whom the Lord gives much, he will also claim much afterwards. From those to whom he has allowed much, much he will seek for that.

Every lofty home here in the world is surrounded with danger; even as worldly things are the greater, so are the dangers worse. Thus you may understand and perceive by example: the tree, when it grows in the grove and lifts itself up above all the others and spreads out, when a strong wind comes along, it is more troubled and afflicted than the other trees. It is just the same with the high cliffs and towers, when they rise further than others above the earth, then they might suddenly begin to fall and very terribly crash to the ground. It is likewise also with great mountains and hills when they stand highest and most visible over all the earth, yet they have the torment of superiority in that they are often threatened and checked with lightning, and struck with flames. So the high powers here in the world collapse and fall and come to destruction; the wealth of the world comes to nothing; and this earthly glory turns to sorrow. Though we might work hard for honours in this world and shine greatly in glory, and though we might dress ourselves with the finest materials and adorn ourselves with the brightest gold, and deck ourselves out with the most precious gems, yet one must endure an end in narrowness. And though the strongest and most powerful person commands a tomb to be made from marble and from other precious materials, all decorated with jewels and covered with silver hangings and bed-linen, and all strewn with the most precious spices and impressed all about with gold leaf, yet bitter death parts us from all that. Then the glory will be lost and the power shattered, and the gems torn off and the gold destroyed, and the body decayed and turned to dust.

Therefore this earth's glory and this world's wealth is as nothing; it is transitory and evil and perishable, as are the powerful here in the world. Where are the powerful emperors and kings who once were, or the kings that we knew formerly? Where are the ealdormen who established the laws? Where is their judgement hall? Where is their pride, except covered with earth and turned into torment? Misery is the lot of secular judges unless they should rule with justice. It is not any better for the scholar than for the one who learns, unless they should seek judgement with justice. Where have the possessions of the earth gone? Where has the world's wealth gone? Where has the beauty of the earth gone? Where have those that most eagerly sought for possessions and left them to others as an inheritance? So transitory is excessive love of the things of the earth: it is just like showers of rain when they fall hardest from heaven and then quickly disappear altogether; then there is fair weather and bright sunshine. Just as the joys of the earth are precarious, so the body and soul are parted. Then it is unknown to us how the Judge will act about that.

Therefore, there is nothing better than that we should love our Lord with all our minds, and with all strength, and with all of our understanding. As it is written and as he himself said: 'He who has my love in him and sends his request to me, I will always hear him and send my mercy over him.[21] And those who turn away from their sins to me, and make confession in my name, and perform penance with fasting and with tears and with prayers, then I will give my mercy to them, and will give forgiveness, and grant my kingdom, and teach them the heavenly path, where there is always benefit and the most joy and great reward.

---

21 Similar doctrine is expressed in Matthew 10.32.

to me cyrraþ fram hyra gyltum, and geandettaþ on minum naman, and bote mid fæstenum doð
185 and mid tearum and mid gebedum, þonne Ic him forlæte mine miltse to, and forgifenysse sylle,
and min rice alyfe, and heofonlice weg tæce, þær bið a god and sio hea blis and sio mycle med.

For þam iorðlicum Ic sylle þa heofonlican, for þyssum hwilendlicum þa ecan, for þyssum lænan
life þæt unlæne, for þyssum uncorenan life þæt gecorene, for þyssum earmlican life þæt eadige.
Gesælige bioð þa ðe þæt rice gemunað: unlæde bioð þa þe þam wiðsacaþ. Hwæt hylpeð þam men
190 aht, þeah þe he ealne middangeard on his anes æht eal gestryne, gif eft þæt dioful genimeð þa
sawle? Ne him no þe bet ne bið, þeah he her on life lifige þusend wintra, gif he æfter his deaþe bið
læded on helle and þær on witum wunaþ a butan ende.'

Utan we þænne wendan to þam beteran and gecyrran to þam selran. Þonne we moton gesion
soðne Dryhten, and on gefean faran to Fæder rice. Þær is sio hea ar, and þær is sio frætewednes þæs
195 Æðelinges. Þær is Cyninges þrym gesyne, and þær is arwyrðnes witegna. And þær is gestæðþignes
gioguðe, and þær is ar and fægernes werum and wifum, and geswæsscipe engla, and geferræden
apostola and heahfædera and witegena; and eadige gefioð and wynsumiaþ on lisse and on blisse
and on ecum gefean. Þær is sang and swinsung and Godes lof gehyred, and þæs hyhstan Cyninges
gehyrnes. And sio biorhtu þara haligra sawla and þara soðfæstra scinaþ swa sunne, and þa men
200 rixiað swa englas on heofenum. And we syndon þyder gelaðode and gehatene to þan halegan ham
and to þam cynelycan friðstole þær Drihten Crist wunaþ and rixað mid eallum halegum a butan
ende. Amen.

For the earthly I give the heavenly, for this temporary the eternal, for this transitory life the everlasting, for this involuntary life the chosen, for this wretched life the blessed. Happy are those who remember that kingdom: wretched are those who forsake it. What help will it be to that man at all, though he entirely amass the world into his own ownership, if the devil takes his soul afterwards? There will be no remedy for him, though he lived a thousand winters in life here, if he is led into hell after his death and dwells there in torment forever without end.'

Then let us turn to the better and choose the preferred. Then we might see the true Lord, and, in joy, journey to the Father's kingdom. There will be high honour, and there will be the adornment of the Prince. There the glory of the King is seen, and there is the dignity of the prophets. And there is stability for the youth, and there is honour and beauty for the man and the woman, and the fellowship of angels, and the companionship of the Apostles and the patriarchs and the prophets; and the blessed rejoice and enjoy love and bliss and eternal joy. Song and melody and God's praise is heard there, and obedience to the highest King. And the brightness of the holy souls and of the faithful shines like the sun, and men rule as angels in heaven. And we are summoned there and called to the holy home and to the royal refuge where the Lord Christ lives and reigns with all the saints forever without end. Amen.

THE DREAM OF THE ROOD

The Dream of the Rood, or *A Vision of the Cross* as it is sometimes more appropriately titled, is justly one of the most
critically acclaimed poems in English. It survives in the
Vercelli Book, folios 104 verso to 106 recto. Parts of the
text are among the oldest surviving poetic expressions
in the vernacular. Carved in runes into the shaft of the
early eighth-century Northumbrian Ruthwell Cross are
lines of poetry that, in the tenth century, reappear in *The
Dream of the Rood*. The lines on the Ruthwell Cross form
the marginal text to elaborate carved depictions of the
Tree of Life. They correspond to lines 39–42, 44–5, 48–
9, 56–9, and 62–4 of the unique Vercelli Book text.[22]

The Dream of the Rood is riddlic (see also Exeter Book
Riddle 30 on the Cross), penitential, eschatalogical (that
is, concerned with death, judgement and the afterlife),
and evangelical. It is the first dream-vision poem in English. The poet speaks in the first person to relate the vision, creating a sense of immediacy and urgency in the
narration. The precise nature of this vision is only gradu-
ally revealed, as in a riddle. When it is made known that
syllicre treow ('a more wonderful tree', line 4), this *beam*
'wood', refers to the Saviour's tree, the immediacy of the
text is increased by the startling poetic device of
prosopopeia through which the inanimate object is
brought to life and given a voice of its own. The Cross is
Christ's retainer, serving its lord as a Germanic comitatus member would serve; but it is also Christ's *bana*,
'slayer' (line 66), a role that goes against all that the heroic code advocates. The reader or listener of the poem
observes the Cross with the poet through a rich visual
depiction: the Cross is mutable, covered in gems, then
covered in blood. This duality represents the central paradox of the Cross. The audience is made to participate in
the Crucifixion and its aftermath, seeing the events
through the eyes of the witness Cross. In this way, the
revelations bring about repentance in the audience for
the sins committed that compelled Christ to become
mortal and redeem mankind. Christ's mortality, the issue of his divine humanity, was the focus of considerable
theological controversy in the earlier medieval period.
The poet deftly retains complete orthodoxy by inscribing the sufferings of Christ onto the Cross: the Cross
speaks of its pain, its torment, not of that belonging to
Christ himself. At the same time, Christ is a divine being, and an heroic Germanic lord, one who dies to save
his troop. He voluntarily ascends the Cross, indeed, 'embraces' the instrument of his death. Neither does the Cross
talk of Christ's death: Christ rests, 'weary after the battle'. The victory of resurrection complete, the Cross continues with its biography – its discovery by Helena,
Constantine's mother (for which see 'The History and
Invention of the True Cross' from *The South English Legendary* at pp. 427–34), and how it is now a symbol of
Christ's salvation and judgement, a token of faith and,
as in the case of the Ruthwell Cross, an object of devotion. This leads into the final homiletic section of the
poem in which the poet himself, initially impelled to
contrition, then to a revitalized faith, determines to seek
the heavenly home.

Within the structural framework of the text, phrasal
parallels draw together the three central characters in
the work: the poet, the Cross and Christ. These verbal
links emphasize God's desire for mankind to be united
with him and his church and repatriated in heaven by
following *lifes weg* ('the way of life', line 88b). This poem
is a unique reading of the central event in salvation history – the Crucifixion – and is not confined to present or
past or future; it is a timeless text that continues to move
readers more than a thousand years after its creation.

The Dream of the Rood

> Hwæt, Ic swefna cyst   secgan wylle
> hwæt me gemætte   to midre nihte,
> syðþan reordberend   reste wunedon.
>   Þuhte me þæt Ic gesawe   syllicre treow
> 5   on lyft lædan,   leohte bewunden,
> bearma beorhtost.   Eall þæt beacen wæs
> begoten mid golde;   gimmas stodon
> fægere æt foldan sceatum,   swylce þær fife wæron
> uppe on þam eaxlegespanne.   Beheoldon þær engel Dryhtnes ealle
> 10   fægere þurh forðgesceaft.   Ne wæs ðær huru fracodes gealga;
> ac hine þær beheoldon   halige gastas,

---

22   For the texts arranged *en face*, and a good discussion of the artistic scheme of the Ruthwell Cross, see M. Swanton, ed., *The Dream of
the Rood* (Manchester, 1970).

The Dream of the Rood

Listen, I will tell the best of visions,
what came to me in the middle of the night,
when voice-bearers dwelled in rest.
    It seemed to me that I saw a more wonderful tree
5 lifted in the air, wound round with light,
the brightest of beams. That beacon was entirely
cased in gold; beautiful gems stood
at the corners of the earth, likewise there were five
upon the cross-beam. All those fair through creation
10 gazed on the angel of the Lord there. There was certainly no gallows of the wicked;
but the holy spirits beheld it there,

men ofer moldan   ond eall þeos mære gesceaft.
Syllic wæs se sigebeam   ond Ic synnum fah,
forwunded mid wommum.   Geseah Ic wuldres treow

15 wædum geweorðode,   wynnum scinan,
gegyred mid golde;   gimmas hæfdon
bewrigene weorðlice   wealdes treow.
    Hwæðre, Ic þurh þæt gold   ongytan meahte
earmra ærgewin,   þæt hit ærest ongan

20 swætan on þa swiðran healfe.   Eall Ic wæs mid sorgum gedrefed.
Forht Ic wæs for þære fægran gesyhðe;   geseah Ic þæt fuse beacen
wendan wædum ond bleom: hwilum hit wæs mid wætan bestemed,
beswyled mid swates gange;   hwilum mid since gegyrwed.
    Hwæðre Ic þær licgende   lange hwile,

25 beheold hreowcearig   Hælendes treow,
oððæt Ic gehyrde   þæt hit hleoðrode;
ongan þa word sprecan   wudu selesta:
    'Þæt wæs geara iu,   Ic þæt gyta geman,
þæt Ic wæs aheawen   holtes on ende,

30 astyred of stefne minum.   Genaman me ðær strange feondas,
geworhton him þær to wæfersyne,   heton me heora wergas hebban.
Bæron me ðær beornas on eaxlum,   oððæt hie me on beorg asetton,
gefæstnodon me þær feondas genoge.   Geseah Ic þa Frean mancynnes
efstan elne mycle   þæt he me wolde on gestigan.

35 Þær Ic þa ne dorste   ofer Dryhtnes word
bugan oððe berstan,   þa Ic bifian geseah
eorðan sceatas.   Ealle Ic mihte
feondas gefyllan;   hwæðre Ic fæste stod.
Ongyrede hine þa geong hæleð –   þæt wæs God ælmihtig–

40 strang ond stiðmod;   gestah he on gealgan heanne,
modig on manigra gesyhðe,   þa he wolde mancyn lysan.
Bifode Ic þa me se beorn ymbclypte;   ne dorste Ic hwæðre bugan to eorðan,
feallan to foldan sceatum,   ac Ic sceolde fæste standan.
Rod wæs Ic aræred.   Ahof Ic ricne Cyning,

45 heofona Hlaford;   hyldan me ne dorste.
Þurhdrifan hi me mid deorcan næglum;   on me syndon þa dolg gesiene,
opene inwidhlemmas;   ne dorste Ic hira nænigum sceððan.
Bysmeredon hie unc butu ætgædere.   Eall Ic wæs mid blode bestemed
begoten of þæs guman sidan   siððan he hæfde his gast onsended.

50   Feala Ic on þam beorge   gebiden hæbbe
wraðra wyrda.   Geseah Ic weruda God
þearle þenian.   Þystro hæfdon
bewrigen mid wolcnum   Wealdendes hræw,
scirne sciman.   Sceadu forð eode

55 wann under wolcnum.   Weop eal gesceaft,
cwiðdon Cyninges fyll.   Crist wæs on rode.
    Hwæðere þær fuse   feorran cwoman
to þam æðelinge;   Ic þæt eall beheold.
Sare Ic wæs mid sorgum gedrefed;   hnag Ic hwæðre þam secgum to handa,

60 eaðmod elne mycle.   Genamon hie þær ælmihtigne God,
ahofon hine of ðam hefian wite.   Forleton me þa hilderincas,

men over the earth and all this glorious creation.
Wondrous was the victory-tree, and I stained with sins,
wounded with guilts. I saw the tree of glory,
15 honoured with garments, shining with joys,
covered with gold; gems had
covered magnificently the tree of the forest.
    Nevertheless, I was able to perceive through that gold
the ancient hostility of wretches, so that it first began
20 to bleed on the right side. I was all drenched with sorrows.
I was frightened by the beautiful vision; I saw that urgent beacon
change its covering and colours: sometimes it was soaked with wetness,
stained with the coursing of blood; sometimes adorned with treasure.
Yet as I lay there a long while
25 I beheld sorrowful the tree of the Saviour,
until I heard it utter a sound;
it began to speak words, the best of wood:
    'That was very long ago, I remember it still,
that I was cut down from the edge of the wood,
30 ripped up by my roots. They seized me there, strong enemies,
made me a spectacle for themselves there, commanded me to raise up their criminals.
Men carried me there on their shoulders, until they set me on a hill,[23]
enemies enough fastened me there. I saw then the Saviour of mankind
hasten with great zeal, as if he wanted to climb up on me.
35 There I did not dare, against the word of the Lord,
bow or break, when I saw the
corners of the earth tremble. I might have
felled all the enemies; even so, I stood fast.
He stripped himself then, young hero – that was God almighty–
40 strong and resolute; he ascended on the high gallows,
brave in the sight of many, when he wanted to ransom mankind.
I trembled when the warrior embraced me; even then I did not dare to bow to earth,
fall to the corners of the earth, but I had to stand fast.
I was reared a cross. I raised up the powerful King,
45 the Lord of heaven; I did not dare to bend.
They pierced me with dark nails; on me are the wounds visible,
the open wounds of malice; I did not dare to injure any of them.
They mocked us both together. I was all drenched with blood
poured out from that man's side after he had sent forth his spirit.
50   I have experienced on that hillside many
cruelties of fate. I saw the God of hosts
violently stretched out. Darkness had
covered with clouds the Ruler's corpse,
the gleaming light. Shadows went forth
55 dark under the clouds. All creation wept,
lamented the King's fall. Christ was on the cross.
    Yet there eager ones came from afar
to that noble one; I beheld all that.
I was all drenched with sorrow; nevertheless I bowed down to the hands of the men,
60 humble, with great eagerness. There they took almighty God,
lifted him from that oppressive torment. The warriors forsook me then

23 The hill is Golgotha or Calvary on which Christ was crucified.
See John 19.17–42 for one of the accounts of Good Friday.

standan steame bedrifenne;   eall Ic wæs mid strælum forwundod.
Aledon hie ðær limwerigne,   gestodon him æt his lices heafdum,
beheoldon hie ðær heofenes Dryhten,   ond he hine ðær hwile reste,

65   meðe æfter ðam miclan gewinne.   Ongunnon him þa moldern wyrcan,
beornas on banan gesyhðe;   curfon hie ðæt of beorhtan stane,
gesetton hie ðæron sigora Wealdend.   Ongunnon him þa sorhleoð galan
earme on þa æfentide;   þa hie woldon eft siðian
meðe fram þam mæran Þeodne.   Reste he ðær mæte weorode.

70   Hwæðere we ðær reotende   gode hwile
stodon on staðole,   syððan stefn up gewat
hilderinca.   Hræw colode,
fæger feorgbold.   Þa us man fyllan ongan
ealle to eorðan: þæt wæs egeslic wyrd.

75   Bedealf us man on deopan seaþe;   hwæðre me þær Dryhtnes þegnas,
freondas gefrunon,
gyredon me   gold ond seolfre.
     Nu þu miht gehyran,   hæleð min se leofa,
þæt Ic bealuwara weorc   gebiden hæbbe,

80   sarra sorga.   Is nu sæl cumen
þæt me weorðiað   wide ond side
menn ofer moldan   ond eall þeos mære gesceaft;
gebiddaþ him to þyssum beacne.   On me Bearn Godes
þrowode hwile;   forþan Ic þrymfæst nu,

85   hlifige under heofenum,   ond Ic hælan mæg
æghwylcne anra   þara þe him bið egesa to me.
Iu Ic wæs geworden   wita heardost,
leodum laðost,   aerþan Ic him lifes weg
rihtne gerymde,   reordberendum.

90   Hwæt, me þa geweorðode   wuldres Ealdor
ofer holmwudu,   heofonrices Weard,
swylce swa he his modor eac,   Marian sylfe,
ælmihtig God,   for ealle menn
geweorðode   ofer eall wifa cynn.

95   Nu Ic þe hate,   hæleð min se leofa,
þæt ðu þas gesyhðe   secge mannum:
onwreoh wordum   þæt hit is wuldres beam
se ðe ælmihtig God   on þrowode
for mancynnes   manegum synnum

100 ond Adomes   ealdegewyrhtum.
Deað he þær byrigde;   hwæðere eft Dryhten aras
mid his miclan mihte   mannum to helpe.
He ða on heofenas astag.   Hider eft fundaþ
on þysne middangeard   mancynn secan

105 on domdæge   Dryhten sylfa,
ælmihtig God,   ond his englas mid,
þæt he þonne wile deman,   se ah domes geweald,
anra gehwylcum   swa he him ærur her
on þyssum lænum   life geearnaþ.

110 Ne mæg þær ænig   unforht wesan

standing covered with moisture; I was all wounded with arrows.
They laid the weary-limbed one down there, they stood at the head of his body,
they beheld the Lord of heaven there, and he himself rested there a while,
65   weary after the great battle. They began to fashion a tomb for him,
warriors in the sight of the slayer; they carved that from bright stone,
they set the Lord of victories in there. They began to sing the sorrow-song for him,
wretched in the evening-time; then they wanted to travel again,
weary from the glorious Lord. He rested there with little company.[24]
70   Nevertheless, weeping, we[25] stood there a good while
in a fixed position, after the voice departed up
of the warriors. The corpse grew cold,
the fair life-dwelling. Then men began to fell us
all to the ground: that was a terrible fate.
75   Men buried us in a deep pit; nevertheless the Lord's thanes,
friends,[26] discovered me there,
adorned me with gold and silver.
Now you might hear, my beloved hero,
that I have experienced the work of evil-doers,
80   grievous sorrows. Now the time has come
that I will be honoured far and wide
by men over the earth and all this glorious creation;
they will pray to this beacon. On me the Son of God
suffered for a while; because of that I am glorious now,
85   towering under the heavens, and I am able to heal
each one of those who is in awe of me.
Formerly I was made the hardest of punishments,
most hateful to the people, before I opened for them,
for the voice-bearers, the true way of life.
90   Listen, the Lord of glory, the Guardian of the kingdom of heaven,
then honoured me over the forest trees,
just as he, almighty God, also honoured
his mother, Mary herself, for all men,
over all womankind.
95   Now I urge you, my beloved man,
that you tell men about this vision:
reveal with words that it is the tree of glory
on which almighty God suffered
for mankind's many sins
100   and Adam's ancient deeds.
Death he tasted there; nevertheless, the Lord rose again
with his great might to help mankind.
He ascended into heaven. He will come again
to this earth to seek mankind
105   on doomsday, the Lord himself,
almighty God, and his angels with him,
so that he will then judge, he who has the power of judgement,
each one of them, for what they themselves have
earned here earlier in this transitory life.
110   Nor may any of them be unafraid there

---

24   Litotes, meaning 'alone'.
25   'we' are the three crosses: that of Christ and those of the two
thieves crucified with him.

26   Helena, mother of Constantine, and Saint Cyriac discovered
the Cross in the fourth century.

for þam worde   þe se Wealdend cwyð:
frineð he for þære mænige   hwær se man sie,
se ðe for Dryhtnes naman   deaðes wolde
biteres onbyrigan,   swa he ær on ðam beame dyde.

115   Ac hie þonne forhtiað   ond fea þencaþ
hwæt hie to Criste   cweðan onginnen.
Ne þearf ðær þonne ænig   unforht wesan
þe him ær in breostum bereð   beacna selest.
Ac ðurh ða rode sceal   rice gesecan
120   of eorðwege   æghwylc sawl
seo þe mid Wealdende   wunian þenceð.'
     Gebæd Ic me þa to þan beame   bliðe mode,
elne mycle,   þær Ic ana wæs
mæte werede.   Wæs modsefa
125   afysed on forðwege;   feala ealra gebad
langunghwila.   Is me nu lifes hyht
þæt Ic þone sigebeam   secan mote
ana oftor   þonne ealle men,
well weorþian.   Me is willa to ðam
130   mycel on mode,   ond min mundbyrd is
geriht to þære rode.   Nah Ic ricra feala
freonda on foldan;   ac hie forð heonon
gewiton of worulde dreamum,   sohton him wuldres Cyning;
lifiaþ nu on heofenum   mid Heahfædere,
135   wuniaþ on wuldre.   Ond Ic wene me
daga gehwylce   hwænne me Dryhtnes rod,
þe Ic her on eorðan   ær sceawode,
on þysson lænan   life gefetige
ond me þonne gebringe   þær is blis mycel,
140   dream on heofonum,   þær is Dryhtnes folc
geseted to symle,   þær is singal blis;
ond he þonne asette   þær Ic syþþan mot
wunian on wuldre   well mid þam halgum
dreames brucan.   Si me Dryhten freond,
145   se ðe her on eorþan   ær þrowode
on þam gealgtreowe   for guman synnum.
He us onlysde   ond us lif forgeaf,
heofonlicne ham.   Hiht wæs geniwad
mid bledum on mid blisse   þam þe þær bryne þolodan.
150   Se Sunu wæs sigorfæst   on þam siðfate,
mihtig ond spedig,   þa he mid manigeo com,
gasta weorode,   on Godes rice,
Anwealda ælmihtig,   englum to blisse
ond eallum ðam halgum   þam þe on heofonum ær,
155   wunedon on wuldre,   þa heora Wealdend cwom,
ælmihtig God,   þær his eðel wæs.

because of the words which the Saviour will speak:
he will ask in front of the multitude where the person might be
who for the Lord's name would
taste bitter death, just as he did before on that tree.
115   But then they will be fearful and little think
what they might begin to say to Christ.
Then there will be no need for any of those to be very afraid
who bear before them in the breast the best of trees.
But by means of the rood each soul
120   who thinks to dwell with the Ruler
must seek the kingdom from the earthly way.'
    I prayed to the tree with a happy spirit then,
with great zeal, there where I was alone
with little company. My spirit was
125   inspired with longing for the way forward; I experienced in all
many periods of longing. It is now my life's hope
that I might seek the tree of victory
alone more often than all men,
to honour it well. My desire for that is
130   great in my mind, and my protection is
directed to the cross. I do not have many wealthy
friends on earth; but they have gone forward from here,
passed from the joys of this world, sought for themselves the King of glory;
they live now in heaven with the High Father,
135   they dwell in glory. And I myself hope
each day for when the Lord's cross,
that I looked at here on earth,
will fetch me from this transitory life,
and then bring me where there is great bliss,
140   joy in heaven, where the Lord's people
are set in feasting, where there is unceasing bliss;
and then will set me where I might afterwards
dwell in glory fully with the saints
to partake of joy. May the Lord be a friend to me,
145   he who here on earth suffered previously
on the gallows-tree for the sins of man.
He redeemed us, and gave us life,
a heavenly home. Hope was renewed
with dignity and with joy for those who suffered burning there.
150   The Son was victorious in that undertaking,[27]
powerful and successful, when he came with the multitudes,
a troop of souls, into God's kingdom,
the one Ruler almighty, to the delight of angels
and all the saints who were in heaven before,
155   who dwelled in glory, when their Ruler came,
almighty God, to where his native land was.

27   This 'undertaking' refers to the Harrowing of Hell, when Christ rescued the souls who had been condemned to hell following the centuries after the Fall of Man. This apocryphal event took place in the days between Christ's Crucifixion and Resurrection.

Ælfric

OLD ENGLISH PREFACE TO HIS FIRST SERIES OF
CATHOLIC HOMILIES

Ælfric composed his two series of *Catholic Homilies* from the late 980s to 995, with the First Series dated to 989, as a result of his desire to see orthodox religious writings available for delivery to lay congregations. He believed that his era was one of affliction and turmoil, that would see the end of the world, and thus the need for Christians to save themselves was great. The *Catholic Homilies* are comprised of forty homilies and hagiographies in each series that follow the order of the services of the church year, and often expand on a doctrinal point raised in the Gospel pericope for a Sunday, or are meant to be read on a particular saint's day. The texts include a great variety of Christian subject matter, and are always written with clarity and comprehension in mind. To these two collections, Ælfric subsequently added his *Lives of Saints*. His desire to create a body of vernacular didactic prose marks him out as a remarkable author in this period, and he clearly allies his educational aims with those of King Alfred in his programme of translating essential Latin works into the native tongue.

Over thirty manuscripts containing the *Catholic Homilies* survive. The most reliable witness to Ælfric's work is London, British Library, Royal 7 C.xii, written in 990 at Cerne Abbas, where Ælfric was a monk and teacher.[1] The manuscript contains the First Series of *Catholic Homilies*, but not the Latin and Old English Prefaces to the work (the Old English edition of the Preface below comes from Cambridge University Library, Gg. 3. 28, folios 1 verso to 2 verso, dated to the end of the tenth century or

beginning of the eleventh). The large number of manuscript witnesses, dating right up to the end of the twelfth century, clearly demonstrate the authority and popularity of Ælfric's writings. The *Catholic Homilies* were copied, adapted, extracted, and used by manuscript compilers to provide vernacular religious prose for the edification of their Christian audience.

The major scholarly edition of Ælfric's First Series of *Catholic Homilies* is that by P. Clemoes.[2] Clemoes edits both the Latin and Old English Prefaces, as does J. Wilcox in his *Ælfric's Prefaces*.[3] This latter edition contains an excellent introduction to Ælfric, his life and his work. Numerous other essential books and articles on Ælfric are listed in the bibliography.

In the Old English Preface, Ælfric's concerns about the imminent arrival of the Antichrist are made apparent. These concerns appear to have been a major impetus in the composition of the First Series of *Catholic Homilies*, together with the author's desire to secure the salvation of his own and other Christians' souls. Ælfric also demonstrates his dissatisfaction at the appearance of non-orthodox religious writings in English (material that may have been similar to some of the Blickling or Vercelli Homilies, perhaps) that he is sure will mislead and harm the unlearned Christian. His work aims to rectify this situation by providing a series of orthodox and authoritative writings that will be intelligible to his perceived lay audience.

Old English Preface to his First Series of *Catholic Homilies*

Ic, Ælfric, munuc and mæssepreost, swa ðeah waccre þonne swilcum hadum gebyrige, wearð asend on Æþelredes dæge cyninges fram Ælfeage biscope, Aðelwoldes æftergengan, to sumum mynstre, ðe is Cernel gehaten, þurh Æðelmæres bene ðæs þegenes, his gebyrd and goodnys sind gehwær cuðe. Þa bearn me on mode, Ic truwige ðurh Godes gife, þæt Ic ðas boc of Ledenum
5 gereorde to Engliscre spræce awende, na þurh gebylde micelre lare, ac for ðan ðe Ic geseah and gehyrde mycel gedwyld on manegum Engliscum bocum, ðe ungelærede menn ðurh heora bilewitnysse to micclum wisdome tealdon. And me ofhreow þæt hi ne cuðon ne næfdon ða godspellican lare on heora gewritum, buton ðam mannum anum ðe þæt Leden cuðon, and buton þam bocum ðe Ælfred cyning snoterlice awende of Ledene on Englisc, ða synd to hæbbenne. For
10 ðisum antimbre Ic gedyrstlæhte, on Gode truwiende, þæt Ic ðas gesetnysse undergann, and eac for ðam ðe menn behofiað godre lare swiðost on þisum timan, þe is geendung þyssere worulde. And beoð fela frecednyssa on mancynne ær ðan þe se ende becume, swa swa ure Drihten on his

1 A full facsimile of this manuscript has been edited by N. E. Eliason and P. Clemoes as *Ælfric's First Series of Catholic Homilies: British Museum Royal 7 C. xii*, EEMF 13 (Copenhagen, 1966).

2 P. Clemoes, ed., *Ælfric's Catholic Homilies: The First Series*, EETS s.s. 17 (Oxford, 1997).

3 Ibid., pp. 173–7; J. Wilcox, ed., *Ælfric's Prefaces*, Durham Medieval Texts 9 (Durham, 1994), pp. 107–10.

Old English Preface to his First Series of *Catholic Homilies*

I, Ælfric, monk and mass-priest, even though more insignificant than is fitting for such an order, was sent in the days of King Æthelred from Bishop Ælfeage, Æthelwold's successor, to a certain monastery, which is called Cerne, by the request of Æthelmær the thane, whose parentage and goodness are known everywhere.[4] Then it came into my mind, I believe through the grace of God, that I should translate this book from the language of Latin into English speech, not through the confidence of great learning, but because I saw and heard much heresy in many English books,[5] which unlearned people through their simplicity esteemed as great wisdom. And it grieved me that they did not know nor did they have teaching of the gospels in their writing, except via those men alone who understood Latin, and except for those books which King Alfred wisely translated from Latin into English, which we still have. For this reason I presumed, trusting in God, to undertake this composition, and also because men have need of good teachings above all at this time, which is the ending of this world. And there are many dangers to mankind before the end comes, just as our Lord said in his gospel to his disciples: 'Then there will be

4 Ælfric was sent to Cerne Abbas probably in 987 or thereabouts when Ælfheah, bishop of Winchester ordered this, at the request of the nobleman Æthelmær, a patron of the monastery. See Wilcox, *Ælfric's Prefaces*, pp. 10–11.

5 Ælfric might be referring here to collections of homilies such as those of the Vercelli and Blickling books that contained some material not regarded as orthodox.

godspelle cwæð to his leorningcnihtum: 'Þonne beoð swilce gedreccednyssa swilce næron næfre
ær fram frymðe middangeardes. Manega lease Cristas cumað on minum naman, cweðende, "Ic
15 eom Crist", and wyrcað fela tacna and wundra to bepæcenne mancynn and eac swylce ða gecorenan
men, gif hit gewurðan mæg. And butan se ælmihtiga God ða dagas gescyrte, eall mennisc forwurde;
ac for his gecorenum he gescyrte ða dagas.'

Gehwa mæg þe eaðelicor þa toweardan costnunge acuman ðurh Godes fultum, gif he bið þurh
boclice lare getrymmed, for ðan ðe ða beoð gehealdene, þe oð ende on geleafan þurhwuniað. Fela
20 gedreccednyssa and earfoðnyssa becumað on ðissere worulde ær hire geendunge, and þa sind ða
bydelas þæs ecan forwyrdes on yfelum mannum, þe, for heora mandædum, siððan ecelice ðrowiað
on ðære sweartan helle. Þonne cymð se Antecrist – se bið mennisc mann and soð deofol, swa swa
ure Hælend is soðlice mann and God on anum hade – and se gesewenlica deofol þonne wyrcð
ungerima wundra, and cwyð þæt he sylf God beo, and wile neadian mancynn to his gedwylde; ac
25 his tima ne bið na langsum, for ðan ðe Godes grama hine fordeð, and ðeos weoruld bið siððan
geendod.

Crist ure Drihten gehælde untrume and adlige, and þes deofol þe is gehaten Antecrist (þæt is
gereht 'ðwyrlic Crist') aleuað and geuntrumað þa halan, and nænne ne gehæld fram untrumnyssum,
buton þam anum þe he sylf ær awyrde. He and his gingran awyrdað manna lichaman digellice
30 ðurh deofles cræft, and gehælað hi openlice on manna gesihðe; ac he ne mæg nænne gehælan þe
God sylf ær geuntrumode. He neadað þurh yfelnysse þæt men sceolon bugan fram heora Scyppendes
geleafan to his leasungum, se ðe is ord ælcere leasunge and yfelnysse. Se ælmihtiga God geðafað
þam arleasan Antecriste to wyrcenne tacna and wundra and ehtnysse to feorðan healfan geare, for
ðan ðe on ðam timan bið swa micel yfelnyss and þwyrnys betwux mancynne þæt hi wel wyrðe
35 beoð þære deoflican ehtnysse: to ecum forwyrde þam ðe him onbugað, and to ecere myrhðe þam
þe him þurh geleafan wiðcweðað. God geðafað eac þæt his gecorenan ðegenas beon aclænsade
fram eallum synnum ðurh ða ormatan ehtnyssa, swa swa gold bið on fyre afandod. Þa ofslihð se
deofol ðe him wiðstandað, and hi ðonne farað mid halgum martyrdome to heofenan rice. Þa ðe his
leasungum gelyfað, þam he arað, and hi habbað syððan þa ecan susle to edleane heora gedwyldes.

40 Se arleasa deð þæt fyr cymð ufan swilce of heofonum on manna gesihðe, swilce he God ælmihtig
sy, ðe ah geweald heofenas and eorðan; ac þa Cristenan sceolon beon þonne gemyndige hu se
deofol dyde, ða ða he bæd æt Gode þæt he moste fandian Jobes. He gemacode ða þæt fyr com ufan
swilce of heofenum, and forbærnde ealle his scep ut on felda and þa hyrdas samod, buton anum þe
hit him cyðan sceolde. Ne sende se deofol ða fyr of heofenum, þeah ðe hit ufan come, for ðan ðe he
45 sylf næs on heofonum syððan he for his modignysse of aworpen wæs. Ne eac se wælhreowa Antecrist
næfð þa mihte þæt he heofenlic fyr asendan mæge, ðeah ðe he þurh deofles cræft hit swa gehiwige.
Bið nu wislicor þæt gehwa ðis wite and cunne his geleafan, weald hwa ða micclan yrmðe gebidan
sceole.

Ure Drihten bebead his discipulum þæt hi sceoldon læran and tæcan eallum þeodum ða ðing
50 þe he sylf him tæhte; ac ðæra is nu to lyt ðe wile wel tæcan and wel bysnian. Se ylca Drihten
clypode þurh his witegan Ezechiel: 'Gif ðu ne gestentst þone unrihtwisan and hine ne manast þæt
he fram his arleasnysse gecyrre and lybbe, þonne swelt se arleasa on his unrihtwisnysse and Ic
wille ofgan æt ðe his blod': þæt is his lyre. 'Gif ðu ðonne þone arleasan gewarnast, and he nele
fram his arleasnysse gecyrran, þu alysdest þine sawla mid þære mynegunge, and se arleasa swylt
55 on his unrihtwisnysse.' Eft cwæð se Ælmihtiga to þam witegan Isiam: 'Clypa and ne geswic ðu,
ahefe ðine stemne swa swa byme, and cyð minum folce heora leahtras, and Jacobes hirede heora
synna.' For swylcum bebodum wearð me geðuht þæt Ic nære unscyldig wið God gif Ic nolde
oðrum mannum cyðan, oþþe þurh gewritu, ða godspellican soðfæstnysse, þe he sylf gecwæð and
eft halgum lareowum onwreah.

60 Forwel fela Ic wat on ðisum earde gelæredran þonne Ic sy, ac God geswutelað his wundra ðurh
ðone ðe he wile: swa swa ælmihtig Wyrhta, he wyrcð his weorc þurh his gecorenan, na swylce he
behofige ures fultumes, ac þæt we geearnion þæt ece lif þurh his weorces fremminge. Paulus se

such afflictions as there never were before since the creation of the earth. Many false Christs will come in my name, saying, "I am Christ", and will perform many signs and wonders to deceive mankind and likewise the chosen people, if it is possible. And unless almighty God will cut short those days, all people would perish; but because of his chosen people he will cut short those days.'[6]

Everyone may more easily withstand future temptation through God's help, if they are strengthened through scholarly teaching, because they will be protected, who persevere in faith until the end. Many calamities and difficulties will come into this world before its ending, and those are the heralds of the eternal destruction of evil men, who, because of their crimes, will afterwards suffer eternally in dark hell. Then the Antichrist will come – he is mortal man and true devil, just as our Saviour is truly man and God in one person – and the visible devil will then perform countless wonders, and will say that he himself is God, and will coerce mankind to his heresy; but his time will not be protracted at all, because God's anger will destroy him, and this world will be finished afterwards.

Christ our Lord healed the infirm and the sick, and this devil that is called Antichrist (that is interpreted as 'adverse Christ') maims and makes the healthy ill, and heals no one from this infirmity, except those alone whom he himself had injured before. He and his followers injure people's bodies secretly through devilish skills, and they openly heal them in the sight of men; but he cannot heal any of those whom God himself weakened before. He will insist through evilness that people should turn away from their God's faith to his lies, he who is the source of each falsehood and wickedness. The almighty God will allow the wicked Antichrist to perform signs and miracles and persecution for three and a half years, because in that time there will be so much evil and depravity among mankind that they are well worthy of that diabolical persecution: to everlasting destruction for those who bow down to him, and to eternal joy for those who resist him through their faith. God will also allow his chosen thanes to be cleansed from all sins through that enormous persecution, just as gold is tested in the fire. Then the devil will murder those who withstand him, and they will journey with holy martyrdom to the heavenly kingdom. Those who believe his falsehoods he will favour, and they afterwords will have eternal torment as a reward for their heresy.

The impious one makes it so that fire comes from above as if from heaven in the sight of people, as if he were God almighty, he who possesses the power of heaven and earth; but then the Christian must be mindful what the devil did when he asked God that he might test Job. Then he made fire come from above as if from heaven, and completely burned his sheep and the shepherds out in the field, except for one who should make it known to him. Nor did the devil send fire from heaven, even though it came from above, because he himself was not in heaven after he was thrown out from there for his pride. Nor also did the bloodthirsty Antichrist have the power to be able to send heavenly fire, even though he was able to make it appear so through devilish skill. Be now the wiser so that everyone might know this and understand his faith, in case someone should experience great misery.

Our Lord commanded his disciples that they should instruct and teach all people these things that he himself taught; but of these there are now too few who wish to teach well and instruct by example. The same Lord called out through his prophet Ezekiel: 'If you do not take a stand against the unrighteous one and do not admonish him that he turn away from his wickedness and live, then the wicked one will die in his unrighteousness and I will require from you his blood': that is his destruction. 'If you warn the wicked one then, and he will not turn from his wickedness, you have saved your soul with that admonition, and the wicked one will die in his unrighteousness.'[7] Again, the Almighty said to the prophet Isaiah: 'Call out and do not cease, raise your voice like a trumpet, and tell my people of their sins, and of the sins of Jacob's family.'[8] Because of such commands it seems to me that I might not be guiltless with God if I do not make it known to other people, or through my writings, the truth of the gospels, which he himself spoke and afterwards disclosed to the holy teachers.

I know very well that in this land there are many more learned men than I, but God reveals his miracles through whomever that he desires: likewise, the almighty Creator performs his work through his chosen, not because he has need of our help at all, but so that we earn that eternal life through performing his work. Paul the Apostle said: 'We are God's helpers',[9] and even so, we do not do anything for God without God's help.

---

6   Matthew 24.21, 5, 24, 22.   8   Isaiah 58.1.
7   Ezekiel 3.18–19.   9   I Corinthians 3.9.

apostol cwæð: 'We sind Godes gefylstan', and swa ðeah, ne do we nan ðing to Gode buton Godes fultume.

65   Nu bydde Ic and halsige on Godes naman, gif hwa þas boc awritan wylle, þæt he hi geornlice gerihte be ðære bysene, þy læs ðe we ðurh gymelease writeras geleahtrode beon. Mycel yfel deð se ðe leas writ, buton he hit gerihte, swylce he gebringe þa soðan lare to leasum gedwylde; forði sceal gehwa gerihtlæcan þæt þæt he ær to woge gebigde gif he on Godes dome unscyldig beon wile.

        Quid necesse est in hoc codice capitula ordinare, cum prediximus quod quadraginta sententias in se contineat
70   *(excepto quod Æþelwerdus dux vellet habere xl quattuor in suo libro)?*

Now I pray and entreat in God's name, that if anyone wishes to copy this book, he earnestly correct it by the exemplar, lest we be blamed because of careless scribes. He who writes falsely does great evil unless he corrects it, so that he brings the true teaching to false heresy; therefore, each one should put right what he previously distorted with error if he wishes to be blameless at God's judgement.

What necessity is there to list a table of contents in this volume, when we have previously said that it contains forty pieces (except that Ealdorman Æthelweard wishes to have forty-four in his book)?

Homily on the Nativity of the Innocents

Ælfric wrote this homily as part of the First Series of *Catholic Homilies* to commemorate the deaths of the babies killed by Herod after the birth of Christ, as related in Matthew 2.16–18. The festival for which this homily was composed falls in the week after Christmas, on 28 December. Ælfric uses as his sources for this homily a number of Latin writers such as Haymo and Severianus, but these sources would probably have been mediated through one of the collections of Latin homiletic texts used by Ælfric, such as that of Paul the Deacon.

To any audience, medieval or modern, the slaughter of male children under two years old would be an emotional subject: why would a loving God allow such an act to occur? Ælfric appears to be keenly aware that the pericope for this particular homily has to be treated with special care. The style of the text is directed towards distancing the audience from the massacre on the one hand, while retaining the pathos of the subject; and, on the other hand, engaging the audience's emotions in his vivid depiction of the suffering and death of the damned King Herod. These two contrasting sections of the homily serve to highlight the polarity between good and evil, a typical sermon technique of the period.

The beginning of the text recounts the events, as told in Matthew 2, surrounding Christ's birth. The first half of the homily then relates the massacre, and emphasizes not the horror of the killings, but the salvation of those children murdered: that they died as 'glorious martyrs',

suffering death for the sake of Christ, and that they are 'blessed' in their innocence. Their closeness to Christ in dying for his life is confirmed by the final paragraph of the homily, in which their proximity to Christ in heaven becomes literal. Ælfric utilizes many of his rhetorical skills of balance, paradox and occasional alliteration to maintain audience understanding and sympathy for the small victims, while not seeking to shock. The fully developed simile of the children as blossoms not yet ripe is effective in its simple beauty, but sophisticated enough to detach the audience from the horror of the event. This is in sharp contrast to the detailed, realistic depiction of the suffering and torment of the living Herod, which, as Ælfric is sure to let us know, is but a taste of the eternal torture of hell.

The text is a carefully structured, highly effective piece of didactic prose. In terms of the canon of Ælfric's writings this is an early composition that does not illustrate the alliterative prose style as consistently as his later works do. Even so, it is an excellent example of the author's ability to vary his style to suit his purpose and ensure that his orthodox Christian teaching is understood by all of his audience.

This homily survives in a number of different manuscripts,[10] and the edition that follows is based on Cambridge University Library Gg. 3. 28, dated to the end of the tenth or beginning of the eleventh century, where the text occurs at folios 17 recto to 20 recto.

Ælfric's Homily on the Nativity of the Innocents

Nu todæg Godes geladung geond ealne ymbhwyrft mærsað þæra eadigra cildra freolstide þe se wælhreowa Herodes for Cristes acennednysse mid arleasre ehtnysse acwealde, swa swa us seo godspellice racu swutellice cyð.

Matheus awrat on þære forman Cristes bec ðysum wordum be ðæs Hælendes gebyrdtide, and
5   cwæð: 'Þa ða se Hælend acenned wæs on þære Judeiscan Bethleem, on Herodes dagum cyninges, efne ða comon fram eastdæle middangeardes þry tungelwitegan to ðære byrig Hierusalem, þus befrinende: "Hwær is Judeiscra leoda cyning se ðe acenned is? We gesawon soðlice his steorran on eastdæle, and we comon to ði þæt we us to him gebiddon."' Hwæt, ða Herodes cyning þis gehyrende wearð micclum astyred, and eal seo burhwaru samod mid him. He ða gesamnode ealle þa
10   ealdorbiscopas and ðæs folces boceras, and befran hwær Cristes cenningstow wære. Hi sædon, on ðære Judeiscan Bethleem. Þus soðlice is awriten þurh ðone witegan Micheam: 'Eala þu Bethleem, Judeisc land, ne eart ðu nateshwon wacost burga on Judeiscan ealdrum: of ðe cymð se heretoga se ðe gewylt and gewissað Israhela folc.' Ða clypode Herodes þa ðry tungelwitegan on sunderspræce, and geornlice hi befran to hwilces timan se steorra him ærest æteowode, and asende hi to Bethleem,
15   ðus cweðende: 'Farað ardlice, and befrinað be ðam cilde, and þonne ge hit gemetað, cyðað me, þæt Ic mage me to him gebiddan.'

Þa tungelwitegan ferdon æfter þæs cyninges spræce, and efne ða se steorra þe hi on eastdæle gesawon glad him beforan, oð þæt he gestod bufon þam gesthuse þær þæt cild on wunode. Hi

10   For which see Clemoes, *Ælfric's Catholic Homilies: The First Series*.

Homily on the Nativity of the Innocents

Now, today, God's congregation throughout the world proclaim the festival of the blessed children whom the cruel Herod killed with wicked persecution because of Christ's birth, just as the gospel narrative clearly reveals.

Matthew wrote in the first book of Christ these words about the Saviour's birth, and said: 'When the Saviour was born in Bethlehem in Judah, in the days of King Herod, behold there came from the eastern part of the world three astrologers to the city of Jerusalem, asking thus: "Where is the king of the Jewish nation who has been born? We truly saw his star in the east, and we have come so that we might pray to him." '[11] Indeed on hearing this, King Herod became very agitated, as did all the citizens together with him. He then gathered all the chief bishops and the nation's scribes, and asked where Christ's birthplace was. They said, in Bethlehem in Judah. Thus truly it is written in the prophet Micah: 'Lo, you Bethlehem, in Judah, you are not the most insignificant of the princes of Judah: from you will come the leader who will rule and guide the people of Israel.'[12] Then Herod called the three astrologers into private conversation, and eagerly asked them at what time the star had first appeared to them, and he sent them to Bethlehem, saying this: 'Go quickly and ask about the child, and when you meet him, tell me, so that I might pray to him myself.'

After the king's speech, the astrologers went and indeed then the star that they had seen in the east went before them, until it stood above the inn where that child was staying. They saw the star and greatly rejoiced. Then they went into the inn, and met that child with his mother Mary, and, kneeling

---

11 Matthew 2.2.   12 Micah 5.2.

gesawon ðone steorran and þearle blissodon. Eodon ða inn, and þæt cild gemetton mid Marian his
20   meder, and niðer feallende hi to him gebædon. Hi geopenodon heora hordfatu, and him lac
geoffrodon, gold, and recels, and myrran. Hwæt, ða God on swefne hi gewarnode, and bebead þæt
hi eft ne gecyrdon to ðan reðan cyninge Herode, ac þurh oðerne weg hine forcyrdon, and swa to
heora eðele becomon.

Efne ða Godes engel æteowode Josepe, ðæs cildes fosterfæder, on swefnum, cweðende: 'Aris,
25   and nim þis cild mid þære meder, and fleoh to Egypta lande, and beo þær oð þæt Ic þe eft secge:
soðlice toweard is þæt Herodes smeað hu he þæt cild fordo.' Joseph ða aras nihtes, and þæt cild
mid þære meder samod to Egypta lande ferede, and þær wunode oð þæt Herodes gewat, þæt seo
witegung wære gefylled, þe be ðære fare ær ðus cwæð: 'Of Egypta lande Ic geclypode minne
sunu.'

30   Nu secgað wyrdwriteras þæt Herodes betwux ðisum wearð gewreged to þam Romaniscan
casere, þe ealne middangeard on þam timan geweold. Þa gewende he to Rome be ðæs caseres
hæse, þæt he hine betealde, gif he mihte. Þa betealde he hine swiðe geaplice, swa swa he wæs
snotorwyrde to ðan swiðe þæt se casere hine mid maran wurðmynte ongean to Judeiscum rice
asende. Þa þa he ham com, þa gemunde he hwæt he ær be ðan cilde gemynte, and geseah þæt he
35   wæs bepæht fram ðam tungelwitegum, and wearð þa ðearle gegremod. Sende ða his cwelleras,
and ofsloh ealle ða hysecild þe wæron on þære byrig Bethleem, and on eallum hyre gemærum,
fram twywintrum cilde to anre nihte, be ðære tide þe he geaxode æt ðam tungelwitegum. Þa wæs
gefylled Hieremias witegung, þe ðus witegode: 'Stemn is gehyred on heannysse, micel wop and
ðoterung; Rachel beweop hire cildru, and nolde beon gefrefrod, for ðan ðe hi ne sind.'

40   On ðam twelftan dæge Cristes acennednysse comon ða ðry tungelwitegan to Herode, and hine
axodon be ðam acennedan cilde; and þa þa hi his cenningstowe geaxodon, þa gewendon hi wið
þæs cildes, and noldon ðone reðan cwellere eft gecyrran, swa swa he het. Þa ne mihte he forbugan
þæs caseres hæse, and wæs ða þurh his langsume fær þæra cildra slege geuferod swiðor þonne he
gemynt hæfde. And hi wurdon ða on ðysum dægþerlicum dæge wuldorfullice gemartyrode; na
45   swa ðeah þæs geares þe Crist acenned wæs, ac æfter twegra geara ymbryne æfter ðæs wælhreowan
hamcyme.

Næs he æðelboren, ne him naht to þam cynecynne ne gebyrode; ac mid syrewungum and
swicdome he becom to ðære cynelican geðincðe, swa swa Moyses be ðam awrat, þæt ne sceolde
ateorian þæt Judeisce cynecynn oþþæt Crist sylf come. Ða com Crist on ðam timan þe seo cynelice
50   mæigð ateorode, and se ælfremeda Herodes þæs rices geweold. Þa wearð he micclum afyrht and
andracode þæt his rice feallan sceolde þurh tocyme þæs soðan Cyninges. Þa clypode he ða
tungelwitegan on sunderspræce, and geornlice hi befran on hwilcne timan hi ærest þone steorran
gesawon for ðan ðe he ondred, swa swa hit gelamp, þæt hi eft hine ne gecyrdon. Þa het he for ðy
acwellan ealle ða hysecild þære burhscire, fram twywintrum cilde oð anre nihte: ðohte gif he hi
55   ealle ofsloge, þæt se an ne ætburste þe he sohte. Ac he wæs ungemyndig þæs halgan gewrites ðe
cwyð: 'Nis nan wisdom ne nan ræd naht ongean God.'

Se swicola Herodes cwæð to ðam tungelwitegum: 'Farað and geornlice befrinað be ðam cilde,
and cyðað me, þæt Ic eac mage me to him gebiddan.' Ac he cydde syððan his facenfullan syrewunge,
hu he ymbe wolde, gif he hine gemette, ða ða he ealle his efenealdan adylegode for his anes
60   ehtnysse. Þearflæs he syrwde ymbe Crist: ne com he for ðy þæt he wolde his eorðlice rice, oþþe
æniges oðres cyninges mid riccetere him to geteon; ac to ði he com þæt he wolde his heofenlice
rice geleaffullum mannum forgyfan. Ne com he to ðy þæt he wære on mærlicum cynesetle ahafen,
ac þæt he wære mid hospe on rodehengene genæglod. He wolde ðeah þæs wælhreowan syrwunge
mid fleame forbugan, na for ði þæt he deað forfluge, se ðe sylfwilles to ðrowienne middangearde
65   genealæhte; ac hit wære to hrædlic, gif he ða on cildcradole acweald wurde, swilce ðonne his
tocyme mancynne bediglod wære. Þi forhradode Godes engel þæs arleasan geþeaht, and bebead
þæt se fosterfæder þone heofenlican Æðeling of ðam earde ardlice ferede.

Ne forseah Crist his geongan cempan, ðeah ðe he lichamlice on heora slege andwerd nære; ac down, they prayed to him. They opened their coffers and offered him treasure, gold, and frankincense and myrrh. Indeed, then God warned them in a dream and commanded that they should not return again to the cruel King Herod, but avoid him by taking another road, and in that way they came to their native land.

Behold, then God's angel appeared in a dream to Joseph, the foster-father of the child, saying: 'Arise and take this child with his mother, and flee to Egypt, and stay there until I speak to you again: truly, in the future, Herod is considering how he might destroy the child.'[13] Joseph then arose by night and went to Egypt together with the child and his mother, and stayed there until Herod died, so the prophecy that had been spoken previously about this journey was fulfilled: 'Out of the land of Egypt I have called my son.'[14]

Now historians say that during this, Herod was betrayed to the Roman emperor, who at this time ruled the whole world. Then he went to Rome at the command of the emperor so that he might exonerate himself, if he could. Then he exonerated himself very cunningly, for he was so eloquent that the emperor sent him back to Judea with great honour. Then, when he arrived home, he remembered what he had intended to do about the child before; and he realized that he had been deceived by the astrologers, and became very angry. So he sent his killers and murdered all the male children who were in the town of Bethlehem and all its environs from two years old to one night, at the time when he had sought information from the astrologers. So the prophecy of Jeremiah was fulfilled who thus prophesied: 'A voice is heard on high, great weeping and wailing; Rachel wept for her children, and would not be comforted, because they are not.'[15]

On the twelfth day after Christ's birth, the three astrologers came to Herod, and they asked him about the birth of the child; and then when they had discovered his birthplace, they went to the child, and would not return again to the cruel killer as he had commanded. Then he could not avoid the emperor's command, and because of his long journey, he was delayed in the killing of the children more than he had intended to be. And they became gloriously martyred on this very day; not, however, in the year in which Christ was born, but after two years had lapsed following the cruel one's homecoming.

Herod was not noble by birth, neither was he connected in any way with the royal family; but with treachery and deceit he came to appear noble. This is just as Moses wrote that the royal line of Judah would not fail until Christ himself came. Then Christ came at the time when the noble family had ceased, and the foreigner Herod had power over the kingdom. Then he became terribly afraid and dreaded that his kingdom should fall because of the arrival of the true King. Then he called the astrologers into a private conversation, and earnestly asked them at which time they first saw the star because he feared, just as it happened, that they would not return again to him. Therefore he then commanded all the male children in the area to be killed, those children aged from two years to one night: he thought that if he murdered them all, the one that he sought would not escape. But he was not mindful of the holy scriptures that say: 'There is no wisdom nor any plan against God.'

The deceitful Herod said to the astrologers: 'Go and diligently ask about the child and tell me so that I might also pray to him.' But he revealed afterwards his treacherous perfidy concerning what he would do if he found him, when he destroyed all those of equal age through his persecution of the one. Needlessly, he plotted against Christ: he did not come because he wanted Herod's earthly kingdom, or with the ambition to take those of any of the other kings; but he came so that he could grant his heavenly kingdom to faithful men. He did not come so that he was raised up on a glorious throne, but so that he would be, with insult, nailed upon the cross. He wanted, nevertheless, to escape the treachery of the cruel one by flight, not because he avoided death, he who voluntarily came to earth to suffer; but it was too soon, if he were killed in the cradle, because his arrival was not known to mankind. Thus, God's angel anticipated the plan of the evil Herod, and commanded that the foster-father of the heavenly Prince journey from that land quickly.

Christ did not despise his young warriors, although he was not present physically at their slaying; but he sent them from this wretched life to his eternal kingdom. Blessed they were born that they were able to suffer death for his sake. Blessed is their age, which, although it could not yet confess

13   Matthew 2.13.

14   Matthew 2.15, referring to Osee 11.1.

15   Matthew 2.18, referring to Jeremiah 31.15.

70 he asende hi fram þisum wræcfullum life to his ecan rice. Gesælige hi wurdon geborene þæt hi
moston for his intingan deað þrowian. Eadig is heora yld, seo ðe þa gyt ne mihte Crist andettan,
and moste for Criste þrowian. Hi wæron þæs Hælendes gewitan, ðeah ðe hi hine ða gyt ne cuðon.
Næron hi geripode to slege, ac hi gesæliglice þeah swulton to life. Gesælig wæs heora acennednys,
for ðan ðe hi gemetton þæt ece lif on instæpe þæs andweardan lifes. Hi wurdon gegripene fram
moderlicum breostum, ac hi wurdon betæhte þærrihte engellicum bosmum. Ne mihte se manfulla
75 ehtere mid nanre ðenunge þam lytlingum swa micclum fremian swa micclum swa he him fremode
mid ðære reðan ehtnysse hatunge.

Hi sind gehatene martyra blostman, for ðan ðe hi wæron swa swa upaspringende blostman on
middeweardan cyle ungeleaffulnysse, swilce mid sumere ehtnysse forste forsodene. Eadige sind þa
innoðas þe hi gebæron, and ða breost þe swylce gesihton. Witodlice ða moddru on heora cildra
80 martyrdome þrowodon; þæt swurd ðe þæra cildra lima þurharn becom to ðæra moddra heortan;
and neod is þæt hi beon efenhlyttan þæs ecan edleanes, þonne hi wæron geferan ðære þrowunge.
Hi wæron gehwæde and ungewittige acwealde, ac hi arisað on þam gemænelicum dome mid
fullum wæstme and heofenlicere snoternysse. Ealle we cumað to anre ylde on þam gemænelicum
æriste, þeah ðe we nu on myslicere ylde of þyssere worulde gewiton.

85 Þæt godspel cweð þæt Rachel beweop hire cildra and nolde beon gefrefrod, for ðan þe hi ne
sind. Rachel hatte Jacobes wif ðæs heahfæderes, and heo getacnode Godes gelaðunge, þe bewypð
hire gastlican cild; ac heo nele swa beon gefrefrod þæt hi eft to woruldlicum gecampe gehwyrfon
þa þe æne mid sygefæstum deaðe middangeard oferswiððon, and his yrmða ætwundon to
wuldorbeagienne mid Criste.

90 Eornostlice ne breac se arleasa Herodes his cynerices mid langsumere gesundfulnysse, ac buton
yldinge him becom seo godcundlice wracu, þe hine mid menigfealdre yrmðe fordyde, and eac
geswutelode on hwilcum suslum he moste æfter forðsiðe ecelice cwylmian. Hine gelæhte
unasecgendlic adl: his lichama barn wiðutan mid langsumere hætan, and he eal innan samod
forswæled wæs and toborsten. Him wæs metes micel lust, ac ðeah mid nanum ætum his gyfernysse
95 gefyllan ne mihte. He hriðode, and egeslice hweos, and angsumlice siccetunga teah, swa þæt he
earfoðlice orðian mihte. Wæterseocnyss hine ofereode beneoðan þam gyrdle to ðan swiðe þæt his
gesceapu maðan weollon, and stincende attor singallice of ðam toswollenum fotum fleow.
Unaberendlic gyhða ofereode ealne ðone lichaman, and ungelyfendlic toblawennys his innoð
geswencte. Him stod stincende steam of ðam muðe, swa þæt earfoðlice ænig læce him mihte
100 genealæcan. Fela ðæra læca he acwealde: cwæð þæt hi hine gehælan mihton, and noldon. Hine
gedrehte singal slæpleast, swa þæt he þurhwacole niht buton slæpe adreah. And gif he hwon
hnappode, ðærrihte hine drehton nihtlice gedwimor, swa þæt him ðæs slæpes ofþuhte.

Þa ða he mid swiðlicum luste his lifes gewilnode, þa het he hine ferigan ofer ða ea Jordanen,
ðær þær wæron gehæfde hate baðu, þe wæron halwende gecwedene adligendum lichaman. Wearð
105 þa eac his læcum geðuht þæt hi on wlacum ele hine gebeðedon; ac ða ða he wæs in ðissere beðunge
geled, þa wearð se lichama eal toslopen, swa þæt his eagan wendon on gelicnysse sweltendra
manna, and he læg cwydeleas butan andgite. Eft, ða ða he com, þa het he hine ferigan to ðære
byrig Hiericho.

Þa þa he wearð his lifes orwene, þa gelaðode he him to ealle ða Judeiscan ealdras of gehwilcum
110 burgum, and het hi on cwearterne beclysan. And gelangode him to his swustor Salome and hire
wer Alexandrum, and cwæð: 'Ic wat þæt ðis Judeisce folc micclum blissigan wile mines deaðes, ac
Ic mæg habban arwurðfulle licðenunge of heofigendre menigu, gif ge willað minum bebodum
gehyrsumian. Swa ricene swa Ic gewite, ofsleað ealle ðas Judeiscan ealdras ðe Ic on cwearterne
beclysde; þonne beoð heora siblingas to heofunge geneadode, þa ðe wyllað mines forðsiðes fægnian.'
115 He ða his cempan to ðam slege genamode, and het heora ælcum fiftig scyllinga to sceatte syllan,
þæt hi heora handa fram ðam blodes gyte ne wiðbrudon. Þa ða he mid ormætre angsumnysse wæs
gecwylmed, þa het he his agenne sunu Antipatrem arleaslice acwellan, toeacan þam twam þe he
ær acwealde.

Æt nextan, ða ða he gefredde his deaðes nealæcunge, þa het he him his seax aræcan to
120 screadigenne ænne æppel, and hine sylfne hetelice ðyde þæt him on acwehte. Þyllic wæs Herodes
forðsið, þe manfullice ymbe þæs heofenlican Æþelinges tocyme syrwde, and his efenealdan

Christ, was able to suffer for Christ. They were witnesses of the Saviour, although they did not know him yet. They were not ripened for slaying, but yet they blessedly died into life. Blessed was their birth because they met that eternal life on the threshold of this present life. They were seized from maternal breasts, but they were entrusted straightaway to angelic bosoms. The criminal persecutor could not so greatly favour the little ones with any service as much as he favoured them with the violent persecution of hatred.

They are called blossoms of martyrs, because they were just like blossoms springing up in the midst of the chill of unbelief, withered as it were by a certain frost of persecution. Blessed are the wombs that bore them, and the breasts that likewise suckled them. Truly, the mothers suffered from their children's martyrdom: that sword which pierced the children's limbs entered the hearts of the mothers; and it is necessary that they will be partakers of the eternal reward since they were companions in the suffering. They were killed when young and unreasoning, but they shall arise at the public judgement in full growth and heavenly wisdom. We shall all come to one age in the universal resurrection although we now depart from this world at various ages.

The gospel says that Rachel wept for her children, and would not be comforted because they were not. Jacob the patriarch's wife was called Rachel, and she symbolized God's congregation, which weeps for her spiritual children; but she will not be comforted that they returned again to worldly strife who once through victorious death overcame the earth and escaped its miseries in order to be crowned in glory with Christ.

Truly, the impious Herod did not enjoy his kingdom in lasting good health, but without delay, divine vengeance came upon him which afflicted him with manifold miseries, and also clearly revealed what torments he would suffer eternally after death. Indescribable disease seized him: his body burned externally with incessant heat; and internally, at the same time, he was all inflamed and ulcerated. He very much desired food yet no food could satisfy his gluttony. He shook, and coughed terribly, and painfully drew sighs so that he could breathe only with difficulty. Dropsy attacked him beneath the belt to the extent that his genitals seethed with maggots and stinking poison flowed continuously from his swollen feet. Unbearable itches spread over his entire body and unbelievable bloating afflicted his stomach. Foul-smelling breath came out of his mouth such that any physician could only approach him with difficulty. He killed many of the physicians: they said they were able to heal him, and they did not. Continuous sleeplessness afflicted him so that, wide awake, he endured the night without sleep. And if he dozed a little, he was immediately troubled by nightly hallucinations, so that he was dissatisfied with that sleep.

Then, when he longed for his life with an intense desire, he commanded that he be carried over the River Jordan to where hot baths were situated which were said to be a curative for diseased bodies. It then also seemed a good thing to his physicians that they bathe him in lukewarm oils; but when he was placed in that bath, his body became completely paralysed, so that his eyes changed in appearance like those of dead men, and he lay speechless without consciousness. Later, when he had come to, he commanded that he be carried to the city of Jericho.

Then when he despaired of his life, he summoned all the Jewish elders to him from every city, and commanded them to be locked up in prison. And he summoned his sister, Salomi, and her husband, Alexander, to him, and said: 'I know that this Jewish nation will greatly rejoice at my death, but I may have a worthy funeral with a grieving multitude, if you will obey my commands. As soon as I depart, slay all the Jewish elders whom I shut up in prison; then their relatives will be driven to grief, those who will otherwise rejoice at my death.' Then he appointed his warriors to this killing, and commanded each of them to be given fifty shillings as a payment so that they might not withdraw their hands from the shedding of blood. Then, when he was afflicted with intense pain, he wickedly commanded that his own son, Antipater, should be killed, in addition to the two he had killed previously.

Finally, when he felt the approach of his death, he ordered them to reach for a knife to peel an apple, and violently stabbed himself so that it shook in him. Such was the death of Herod who sinfully plotted about the coming of the heavenly Prince and wickedly killed the innocent little ones who were his equals in age.

Behold then, after Herod's death, God's angel appeared to Joseph in a dream in Egypt, saying this: 'Rise up and take the child together with his mother and return again to Israel. Truly, those who plotted

lytlingas unscæððige arleaslice acwealde.

Efne ða Godes engel, æfter Herodes deaðe, æteowode Josepe on swefnum on Egypta lande, þus cweðende: 'Aris and nim þæt cild and his moder samod, and gewend ongean to Israhela lande. Soðlice hi sind forðfarene ða ðe ymbe þæs cildes feorh syrwdon.' He ða aras, swa swa se engel him bebead, and ferode þæt cild mid þære meder to Israhela lande. Þa gefran Joseph þæt Archelaus rixode on Judea lande æfter his fæder Herode, and ne dorste his neawiste genealæcan. Þa wearð he eft on swefne gemynegod þæt he to Galilea gewende for ðan ðe se eard næs ealles swa gehende þam cyninge, þeah ðe hit his rice wære. Þæt cild ða eardode on þære byrig þe is gehaten Nazareth, þæt seo witegung wære gefylled þe cwæð þæt he sceolde beon Nazarenisc geciged. Se engel cwæð to Josepe: 'Þa sind forðfarene þe embe ðæs cildes feorh syrwdon.' Mid þam worde he geswutelode þæt ma ðæra Judeiscra ealdra embe Cristes cwale smeadon; ac him getimode swiðe rihtlice þæt hi mid heora arleasan hlaforde ealle forwurdon.

Nelle we ðas race na leng teon, þy læs ðe hit eow æðryt þince; ac biddað eow þingunge æt þysum unscæððigum martyrum. Hi sind ða ðe Criste folgiað on hwitum gyrlum swa hwider swa he gæð. And hi standað ætforan his ðrymsetle butan ælcere gewemmednysse, hæbbende heora palmtwigu on handa, and singað þone niwan lofsang þam Ælmihtigum to wurðmynte, se þe leofað and rixað a butan ende. Amen.

against the child's life are dead.'[16] He then rose up, just as the angel commanded him, and went with the child and his mother to Israel. Then Joseph learned that Archelaus ruled in Israel after his father Herod, and he did not dare approach his district. Then he was reminded again in a dream that he should go to Galilee because that land was not at all near to the king although it was in his kingdom. That child then lived in the town called Nazareth, and so the prophecy that said that he would be called a Nazarene was fulfilled.[17] The angel said to Joseph: 'Those who plotted against the life of the child are dead.' With these words, he revealed that more of the Jewish elders deliberated about Christ's death; but it happened very justly that they all perished with their wicked lord.

We will not draw out this narrative any longer, in case you might think it tedious; but you should pray for intercession from these innocent martyrs. They are those who follow Christ in white garments wherever he goes. And they stand before his throne without any defilement having in their hands palm branches, and singing the new hymn in honour to the Almighty, he who lives and reigns without end. Amen.

---

16 Matthew 2.20.

17 Matthew 2. 23.

Old English Preface to his *Lives of Saints*

Ælfric compiled his *Lives of Saints* between 990 and 1002, after completing the two series of *Catholic Homilies*. In his Preface, he relates that he embarked on the collection of translations and adaptations from the original Latin into Old English as a result of the requests of his patrons, Æthelweard and his son Æthelmær. In the Latin Preface to the collection, Ælfric explains that 'We have not been able, in this translation, to render always word for word, but, nevertheless, we have tried to translate carefully giving sense for sense, just as we find it in holy writing, through such simple and straightforward phrases as may benefit our listeners.' Ælfric's aim in this work is, as always, didactic and edificatory.

The lives selected by Ælfric in this collection repre-sent those belonging to saints honoured by monastic communities at that time. The *Lives of Saints*, or parts of it, survives in a number of manuscripts; the most important is London, British Library, Cotton Julius E. vii, dated to the early eleventh century. Many of the texts within the collection were copied with other works into manuscripts as late as the second half of the twelfth century.[18] The intactness of Ælfric's work, an issue that he felt was important enough to mention in his Old English Preface, was not maintained either by the compiler of Julius E. vii, or by later manuscript compilers.

Ælfric's *Lives of Saints* begins with a Preface in both Latin and Old English, of which only the latter is edited below (from folios 1 verso to 2 recto).[19]

Old English Preface to his *Lives of Saints*

Ælfric gret eadmodlice Æðelwerd ealdorman, and Ic secge þe, leof, þæt Ic hæbbe nu gegaderod on þyssere bec þæra halgena þrowunga, þe me to onhagode on Englisc to awendene, for þan þe ðu, leof swiðost, and Æðelmær swylcera gewrita me bædon, and of handum gelæhton eowerne geleafan to getrymmenne mid þære gerecednysse, þe ge on eowrum gereorde næfdon ær. Þu wast, leof,

5 þæt we awendon on þam twam ærrum bocum þæra halgena þrowunga and lif þe Angelcynn mid freolsdagum wurþað. Nu gewearð us þæt we þas boc be þæra halgena ðrowungum and life gedihton þe mynstermenn mid heora þenungum betwux him wurðiað.

Ne secge we nan þincg niwes on þissere gesetnysse, for þan ðe hit stod gefyrn awriten on Ledenbocum, þeah þe þa læwedan men þæt nyston. Nelle we eac mid leasungum þyllic liccetan,

10 for þan þe geleaffulle fæderas and halige lareowas hit awriton on Ledenspræce to langum gemynde and to trymmincge þam towerdum mannum.

Sum witega clypode þurh þone Halgan Gast and cwæð: *Mirabilis Deus in sanctis suis, et cetera*: 'Wundorlic is God on his halgum: he sylf forgifð mihte and strengðe his folce. Gebletsod is he, God.' We awritað fela wundra on þissere bec, for þan þe God is wundorlic on his halgum, swa swa

15 we ær sædon, and his halgena wundra wurðiað hine, for þan þe he worhte þa wundra þurh hi. An woruldcynincg hæfð fela þegna and mislice wicneras; he ne mæg beon wurðful cynincg buton he hæbbe þa geþincðe þe him gebyriað, and swylce þeningmen þe þeawfæstnysse him gebeodon. Swa is eac þam ælmihtigan Gode þe ealle þincg gesceop: him gerisð þæt he hæbbe halige þenas, þe his willan gefyllað, and þæra is fela on mannum anum, þe he of middanearde geceas, þæt nan

20 bocere ne mæg, þeah þe mycel cunne, heora naman awriten, for þan þe hi nat nan man. Hi synd ungeryme swa swa hit gerisð Gode; ac we woldon gesettan be sumum þas boc mannum to getrymminge and to munde us sylfum, þæt hi us þingion to þam ælmihtigan Gode swa swa we on worulde heora wundra cyðað.

Ic bidde nu on Godes naman, gif hwa þas boc awritan wille, þæt he hi wel gerihte be þære

25 bysne, and þær na mare betwux ne sette þonne we awendon.

Vale in Domino.

18   For the textual history and extant manuscripts of the *Lives of Saints*, see J. Hill, 'The Dissemination of Ælfric's *Lives of Saints*: A Preliminary Study', in *Holy Men and Holy Women: Old English Prose Saints' Lives and their Contexts*, ed. P. E. Szarmach (Albany, NY, 1996), pp. 235–59.

19   The Latin Preface with a translation can be found in the stand-ard scholarly edition of the *Lives*: W. W. Skeat, ed., *Ælfric's Lives of Saints*, EETS o.s. 76, 82, 94, 114 (London, 1889–1900; repr. as 2 vols, 1966), II, pp. 2–7. All of Ælfric's Prefaces to his works, together with other epistolary material, can be found in Wilcox, *Ælfric's Prefaces*.

Old English Preface to his *Lives of Saints*

Ælfric humbly greets ealdorman Æðelweard, and I say to you, my beloved man, that I have now gathered into this book the passions of the saints that were fitting for me to translate into English, because you, most beloved, and Æðelmær asked me for such writings, and received them from my hands for the confirmation of your faith by means of these stories, which you had never had before in your own language. You know, dear man, that we translated in the two previous books[20] the passions and lives of the saints that the English people honoured with feast days. Now it occurred to us that in this book we should write of the sufferings and lives of those saints whom monks honour among themselves in their services.

We say nothing new in this composition, because it has stood written down before in Latin books, though laymen did not know that. Neither shall we feign such a thing with falsehoods, because devout fathers and holy teachers wrote it in Latin language as a lasting memorial, and as confirmation for future people.

A certain prophet called out through the Holy Ghost, and said: *Mirabilis Deus in sanctis suis, et cetera*: 'Wonderful is God in his saints: he shall give power and strength to his people. Blessed is he, God.' We shall write about many wonders in this book, because God is wonderful in his saints, just as we said before, and the wonders of his saints honour him, because he performed those wonders through them. A worldly king has many servants and various stewards; he cannot be an honourable king unless he has the things that befit him, and such serving men to offer him their obedience. So it is also with almighty God who created all things: it is fitting for him that he should have holy servants who may fulfil his will, and of these there are many from mankind alone, whom he chose out of the world, so that no scribe can, though he knows much, write their names, because no man knows them. They are countless as is fitting for God; but we wanted to compile this book about some of them for the encouragement of people and as security for us ourselves, so that they could intercede for us with almighty God, just as we in this world make their miracles known.

I pray now in the name of God, if anyone wishes to copy this book, that he correct it well according to the exemplar; and place within it no more than we have translated.

Farewell in the Lord.

---

20   The two former books are the two series of *Catholic Homilies*.

PASSION OF SAINT EDMUND

The *Passion of Saint Edmund* is part of Ælfric's sequence the *Lives of Saints*, designed to commemorate the feast-day of the saint (20 November). The text celebrates the life and death of King Edmund of East Anglia, killed by Viking invaders in 869. His martyrdom and subsequent sanctity were confirmed by a number of posthumous miracles, and the first hagiography dedicated to him was that of Abbo of Fleury,[21] written a century after Edmund's death. Ælfric is careful to inform us about his direct source, Abbo, and the veracity of that account. The Old English version curtails the Latin source and is rather more homiletic in focus than Abbo's text.

The *Passion of Saint Edmund* contains all the usual ingredients of the medieval martyred saint's hagiography: the absolute piety and nobility of the saint, the polarization of good and evil, a torture sequence (abbreviated in Ælfric's version in comparison with Abbo's), a decapitation, miracles, and a confirmation of the veneration of the saint by Christians. The saint is not individualized in any realistic way, and thus becomes something of a type of holy character whose actions can be admired and

subsequently emulated by the text's audience. This text has a particular resonance for Ælfric's contemporary audience, harrassed as they were by the Vikings, and awaiting the new millennium with trepidation. In addition, this is a native English subject saint, one whose patriotism and resolution in the face of adversity would encourage a patriotic response in many English listeners or readers.

Ælfric's prose style at the time of writing the *Lives of Saints* is sophisticated and confident. Alliteration dominates the style, creating a rhythm and emphasis on key words similar to that in Old English poetry. Indeed, Skeat, who published an edition of the *Lives of Saints*, printed the texts as poetry (his edition, although late nineteenth-century in date, is still the standard scholarly text: see p. 130, n. 19).

A number of versions of the text survive from the early eleventh to the twelfth centuries. This edition is based on the earliest extant manuscript version contained in London, British Library, Cotton Julius E. vii, folios 203 recto to 207 recto.

Passion of Saint Edmund

XII Kalens Decembres: Passio Sancti Edmundi, Regis et Martyris

Sum swyðe gelæred munuc com suþan ofer sæ fram Sancte Benedictes stowe on Æþelredes cynincges dæge to Dunstane ærcebisceope þrim gearum ær he forðferde, and se munuc hatte Abbo. Þa wurdon hi æt spræce oþþæt Dunstan rehte be Sancte Eadmunde, swa swa Eadmundes swurdbora hit rehte Æþelstane cyninge þa þa Dunstan iung man wæs. And se swurdbora wæs forealdod
5   man. Þa gesette se munuc ealle þa gereccednysse on anre bec, and eft ða þa seo boc com to us binnan feawum gearum, þa awende we hit on Englisc swa swa hit heræfter stent. Se munuc þa Abbo binnan twam gearum gewende ham to his mynstre, and wearð sona to abbode geset on þam ylcan mynstre.

Eadmund se eadiga East-Engla cynincg wæs snotor and wurðfull and wurðode symble mid
10   æþelum þeawum þone ælmihtigan God. He wæs eadmod and geþungen, and swa anræde þurhwunode, þæt he nolde abugan to bysmorfullum leahtrum, ne on naþre healfe he ne ahylde his þeawas, ac wæs symble gemyndig þære soþan lare: 'Þu eart to heafod-men geset? Ne ahefe þu ðe ac beo betwux mannum swa swa an man of him.' He wæs cystig wædlum and wydewum swa swa fæder and mid wel-willendnysse gewissode his folc symle to rihtwisnysse, and þam reþum
15   styrde, and gesæliglice leofode on soþan geleafan.

Hit gelamp ða æt nextan þæt þa Deniscan leode ferdon mid sciphere hergiende and sleande wide geond land swa swa heora gewuna is. On þam flotan wæron þa fyrmestan heafod-men, Hinguar and Hubba, geanlæhte þurh deofol, and hi on Norðhymbralande gelendon mid æscum and aweston þæt land, and þa leoda ofslogon. Þa gewende Hinguar east mid his scipum, and Hubba belaf on
20   Norðhymbralande gewunnenum sige mid wælhreownysse. Hinguar þa becom to East-Englum rowende on þam geare þe Ælfred æðelincg an and twentig geare wæs (se þe West-sexena cynincg siþþan wearð mære); and se foresæda Hinguar færlice swa swa wulf on lande bestalcode and þa leode sloh, weras and wif and þa ungewittigan cild, and to bysmore tucode þa bilewitan Cristenan.

He sende ða sona syððan to þam cyninge beotlic ærende, þæt he abugan sceolde to his manrædene,
25   gif he rohte his feores. Se ærendraca com þa to Eadmunde cyninge and Hinguares ærende him

21   M. Winterbottom, *Three Lives of English Saints* (Toronto, 1972).

Passion of Saint Edmund

20 November: The Passion of Saint Edmund, King and Martyr

A certain very learned monk come south over the sea from Saint Benedict's place in the days of King Æthelred to Archbishop Dunstan, three years before Dunstan died, and the monk was called Abbo. Then they fell into conversation until Dunstan explained about Saint Edmund, just as Edmund's swordbearer had explained it to King Æthelstan, when Dunstan was a young man and the swordbearer was an old man. Then the monk wrote that entire story in one book and then, when the book came to us within a few years, we translated it into English, just as it stands here. Then the monk Abbo returned homewards to his monastery within two years, and was immediately made abbot in the same monastery.

Edmund the blessed, king of the East Anglians, was wise and honourable and always exalted almighty God with noble habits. He was humble and virtuous and persisted so resolutely that he would not bow to shameful sins, nor on the other hand deviate from his good practices, but was always mindful of the true doctrine: 'Are you established as a leader of men? Do not raise yourself up, but be among men just as if you were one of them.'[22] He was generous with beggars and widows just like a father and he always guided his people with benevolence to righteousness, and punished the cruel, and happily lived in the true faith.

It happened eventually that the Danish people went with a fleet ravaging and attacking far and wide just as their custom is. In that fleet were the foremost leaders Hinguar and Hubba, united through the devil, and they landed their ships in Northumbria and wasted that land and murdered the people. Then Hinguar went east with his ships and Hubba remained in Northumberland, having gained victory with cruelty. Hinguar then came in boats to East Anglia, in the year in which noble Alfred was twenty-one (he who would afterwards become glorious as king of the West Saxons); and, like a wolf, the aforesaid Hinguar quickly stalked on land and killed the people, men and women and innocent children, and tormented the innocent Christians disgracefully.

Then immediately afterwards, he sent a boastful message to the king that he should bow down in tribute if he valued his life. The messenger came to King Edmund then and quickly delivered Hinguar's message to him: 'Hinguar, our king, keen and victorious on sea and on land, has power over many people

---

ardlice abead: 'Hinguar ure cyning cene and sigefæst on sæ and on lande hæfð fela þeoda gewyld, and com nu mid fyrde færlice her to lande þæt he her wintersetl mid his werode hæbbe. Nu het he þe dælan þine digelan goldhordas and þinra yldrena gestreon ardlice wið hine, and þu beo his under-kyning, gif ðu cucu beon wylt, for ðan þe ðu næfst þa mihte þæt þu mage him wiðstandan.'

30   Hwæt, þa Eadmund clypode ænne bisceop þe him þa gehendost wæs, and wið hine smeade hu he þam reþan Hinguare andwyrdan sceolde. Þa forhtode se bisceop for þam færlican gelimpe and for þæs cynincges life, and cwæþ þæt him ræd þuhte þæt he to þam gebuge þe him bead Hinguar. Þa suwode se cynincg and beseah to þære eorþan and cwæþ þa æt nextan cynelice him to: 'Eala, þu bisceop, to bysmore synd getawode þas earman landleoda, and me nu leofre wære þæt Ic on feohte

35   feolle wið þam þe min folc moste heora eardes brucan.' And se bisceop cwæþ: 'Eala, þu leofa cyning, þin folc lið ofslagen and þu næfst þone fultum þæt þu feohtan mæge. And þas flotmen cumað and þe cucenne gebindað butan þu mid fleame þinum feore gebeorge oððe þu þe swa gebeorge þæt þu buge to him.' Þa cwæþ Eadmund cyning swa swa he ful cene wæs: 'Þæs Ic gewilnige and gewisce mid mode, þat Ic ana ne belife æfter minum leofum þegum þe on heora

40   bedde wurdon mid bearnum and wifum færlice ofslægene fram þysum flotmannum. Næs me næfre gewunelic þæt Ic worhte fleames; ac Ic wolde swiðor sweltan, gif Ic þorfte, for minum agenum earde; and se ælmihtiga God wat þæt Ic nelle abugan fram his biggengum æfre, ne fram his soþan lufa, swelte Ic, lybbe Ic.'

   After þysum wordum he gewende to þam ærendracan þe Hinguar him to sende, and sæde him

45   unforht: 'Witodlice þu wære wyrðe sleges nu, ac Ic nelle afylan on þinum fulum blode mine clænan handa, for ðan þe Ic Criste folgie þe us swa gebysnode; and Ic bliðelice wille beon ofslagen þurh eow, gif hit swa God foresceawað. Far nu swiþe hraðe, and sege þinum reþan hlaforde "Ne abihð næfre Eadmund Hingware on life hæþenum heretogan, buton he to Hælende Criste ærest mid geleafan on þysum lande gebuge."'

50   Þa gewende se ærendraca ardlice aweg, and gemette be wæge þone wælhreowan Hingwar mid eallre his fyrde fuse to Eadmunde, and sæde þam arleasan hu him geandwyrd wæs. Hingwar þa bebead mid bylde þam sciphere þæt hi þæs cynincges anes ealle cepan sceoldon þe his hæse forseah, and hine sona bindan. Hwæt, þa Eadmund cynincg mid þam þe Hingwar com stod innan his healle þæs Hælendes gemyndig and awearp his wæpna: wolde geæfenlæcan Cristes gebysnungum

55   þe forbead Petre mid wæpnum to winnenne wið þa wælhreowan Judeiscan. Hwæt, þa arleasan þa Eadmund gebundon and gebysmrodon huxlice, and beoton mid saglum. And swa syððan læddon þone geleaffullan cyning to anum eorðfæstum treowe, and tigdon hine þærto mid heardum bendum, and hine eft swuncgon langlice mid swipum; and he symble clypode betwux þam swinglum mid soðan geleafan to Hælende Criste; and þa hæþenan þa for his geleafan wurdon wodlice yrre for þan

60   þe he clypode Crist him to fultume. Hi scuton þa mid gafelucum swilce him to gamenes to oðþæt he eall wæs besæt mid heora scotungum swilce igles byrsta, swa swa Sebastianus wæs. Þa geseah Hingwar, se arlease flotman, þæt se æþela cyning nolde Criste wiðsacan, ac mid anrædum geleafan hine æfre clypode, het hine þa beheafdian and þa hæðenan swa dydon. Betwux þam þe he clypode to Criste þa git, þa tugon þa hæþenan þone halgan to slæge, and mid anum swencge slogon him of þæt

65   heafod, and his sawl siþode gesælig to Criste. Þær wæs sum man gehende gehealden þurh God behyd þam hæþenum þe þis gehyrde eall, and hit eft sæde swa swa we hit secgað her.

   Hwæt, ða se flothere ferde eft to scipe, and behyddon þæt heafod þæs halgan Eadmundes on þam þiccum bremelum þæt hit bebyrged ne wurde. Þa æfter fyrste syððan, hi afarene wæron, com þæt landfolc to þe þær to lafe wæs þa þær heora hlafordes lic læg butan heafde, and wurdon swiðe

70   sarige for his slege on mode, and huru þat hi næfdon þæt heafod to þam bodige. Þa sæde se sceawere þe hit ær geseah þæt þa flotmen hæfdon þæt heafod mid him, and wæs him geðuht (swa swa hit wæs ful soð) þæt hi behyddon þæt heafod on þam holte forhwega.

   Hi eodon þa secende ealle endemes to þam wuda, secende gehwær geond þyfelas and bremelas gif hi ahwær mihton gemeton þæt heafod. Wæs eac micel wundor þæt an wulf wearð asend þurh

75   Godes wissunge to bewerigenne þæt heafod wið þa oþre deor ofer dæg and niht. Hi eodon þa

and now comes quickly here with an army to land so that he might have winter quarters here with his troop. Now he commands you to share your secret treasure and the wealth of your ancestors with him immediately, and you are to be his under-king if you wish to stay alive, for you do not have enough power to be able to withstand him.'

Indeed, then King Edmund summoned the bishop who was nearest to him, and considered with him how he should answer the cruel Hinguar. The bishop was fearful of this sudden event and for the king's life, and said that it seemed advisable to him that he should submit to what Hinguar demanded from him. Then the king fell silent and looked to the ground and said regally to him next: 'Sadly, bishop, the wretched people of this land are treated too miserably, and I would rather fall in battle now as long as my people might enjoy their homeland.' And the bishop said, 'Alas, dear king, your people lie dead, and you do not have help to enable you to fight, and the Vikings will come and will bind you alive, unless you save your life by flight, or you save yourself by submitting to them.' Then King Edmund said, very brave as he was: 'I desire and wish in my mind that I do not remain alone after my beloved thanes who, with their children and women, have been quickly killed in their beds by these Vikings. It has never been my custom to take flight; I would rather die if I must for my own homeland; and almighty God knows that I will never deviate from his service, or from his true love, whether I die, or I live.'

After these words he turned to the messenger that Hinguar had sent and said to him, unafraid: 'Truly, you deserved to die now, but I will not defile my clean hands in your foul blood, because I follow Christ who set us such an example; and I will happily be killed by you, if God ordains it so. Go very quickly now and tell your cruel lord "Edmund will never yield in this life to Hinguar, the heathen commander, unless he will first submit with faith in this land to Christ the Saviour."'

Then the messenger went away quickly and met on the way the bloodthirsty Hinguar with all his army hurrying towards Edmund, and he told the dishonourable man how he had been answered. Hinguar then arrogantly commanded the fleet that they should all seize only the king, who had rejected his command, and immediately bind him. Then, when Hinguar arrived, King Edmund stood in his hall, mindful of the Saviour, and discarded his weapons: he wanted to imitate Christ's example when he forbade Peter to struggle with weapons against the bloodthirsty Jews. Indeed then, the dishonourable men bound Edmund and mocked him shamefully and beat him with staffs. Then afterwards they led the faithful king to a sturdy tree and tied him to it with firm chains, and again beat him with whips for a long time; and Edmund continually called out with true faith to Christ the Saviour in between the blows; and then the heathens became insanely angry because of his faith, because he called out to Christ to support him. Then they shot at him with missiles, too, as if it were a game to them, until he was entirely covered with their missiles just like the bristles of a hedgehog, as Sebastian was.[23] When Hinguar, the cruel Viking, saw that the noble king would not forsake Christ, but continually called out with resolute faith, he ordered him to be beheaded, and the heathens did just that. While he called out to Christ even then, the heathens took the holy man to kill him and with one blow they struck off his head, and his happy soul journeyed to Christ. Nearby, there was a certain man, kept hidden from the heathens by God, who heard all this and repeated it just as we repeat it here.

In truth, the Vikings then went again to their ships and hid the head of the holy Edmund in thick brambles so that it could not be buried. Then, after a while, after they had departed, the people of the area, those of them who were left, came to where their lord's body lay without its head, and were very sorrowful in spirit because of his death, and especially because they did not have the head to go with the body. Then the eyewitness, who saw it previously, said that the Vikings had the head with them, and it seemed to him (as indeed it proved to be true) that they had hidden that head somewhere in the wood.

Then they all went together into the wood, through bushes and brambles, seeking where, if anywhere, they might find that head. It was also a great miracle that a wolf had been sent through God's guidance to protect that head day and night from the other wild animals. Then they went looking and continually calling, as is customary with those who often go into the woods, 'Where are you now, friend?' and the head answered them, 'Here! Here! Here!' and so frequently called out, answering them all as often as any of them shouted, so that they all came to it because of the shouting. There lay the grey

23 Sebastian was martyred in the late classical period when Christians were frequently persecuted by the Romans.

secende and symle clypigende, swa swa hit gewunelic is þam ðe on wuda gað oft: 'Hwær eart þu
nu gefera?' And him andwyrde þæt heafod 'Her, her, her!' and swa gelome clypode, andswarigende
him eallum swa oft swa heora ænig clypode, oþþæt hi ealle becomen þurh ða clypunga him to. Þa
læg se græga wulf þe bewiste þæt heafod, and mid his twam fotum hæfde þæt heafod beclypped:
80   grædig and hungrig, and for Gode ne dorste þæs heafdes abyrian, ac heold hit wið deor. Þa
wurdon hi ofwundrode þæs wulfes hyrdrædenne, and þæt halige heafod ham feredon mid him,
þancigende þam Ælmihtigan ealra his wundra. Ac se wulf folgode forð mid þam heafde oþþæt hi
to tune comon, swylce he tam wære, and gewende eft siþþan to wuda ongean. Þa landleoda þa
siþþan ledon þæt heafod to þam halgan bodige, and bebyrigdon hine swa swa hi selost mihton on
85   swylcere hrædinge, and cyrcan arærdan sona him onuppon.

Eft þa on fyrste, æfter fela gearum, þa seo hergung geswac and sibb wearð forgifen þam
geswenctan folce, þa fengon hi togædere, and worhton ane cyrcan wurðlice þam halgan, for þan ðe
gelome wundra wurdon æt his byrgene, æt þam gebædhuse þær he bebyrged wæs. Hi woldon þa
ferian mid folclicum wurðmynte þone halgan lichaman, and læcgan innan þære cyrcan. Þa wæs
90   micel wundor þæt he wæs eall swa gehal swylce he cucu wære, mid clænum lichaman, and his
swura wæs gehalod þe ær wæs forslagen, and wæs swylce an seolcen þræd embe his swuran, ræd,
mannum to sweotelunge hu he ofslagen wæs. Eac swilce þa wunda, þe þa wælhreowan hæþenan
mid gelomum scotungum on his lice macodon, wæron gehælede þurh þone heofonlican God; and
he liþ swa ansund oþ þisne andwerdan dæg, andbidigende æristes and þæs ecan wuldres. His
95   lichama us cyð, þe lið unformolsnod, þæt he butan forligre her on worulde leofode, and mid
clænum life to Criste siþode.

Sum wudewe wunode, Oswyn gehaten, æt þæs halgan byrgene on gebedum and fæstenum
manega gear syððan. Seo wolde efsian ælce geare þone sanct, and his næglas ceorfan syferlice mid
lufe, and on scryne healdan to haligdome on weofode. Þa wurðode þæs landfolc mid geleafan þone
100   sanct, and Þeodred bisceop þearle mid gifum on golde and on seolfre gegodode þæt mynster, þam
sancte to wurðmynte.

Þa comon on sumne sæl ungesælige þeofas, eahta on anre nihte, to þam arwurðan halgan,
woldon stelan þa maðmas þe men þyder brohton, and cunnodon mid cræfte hu hi in cumon
mihton. Sum sloh mid slecge swiðe þa hæpsan; sum heora mid feolan feolode abutan; sum eac
105   underdealf þa duru mid spade; sum heora mid hlæddre wolde unlucan þæt ægðyrl; ac hi swuncon
on idel and earmlice ferdon swa þæt se halga wer hi wundorlice geband, ælcne swa he stod,
strutigende mid tole, þæt heora nan ne mihte þæt morð gefremman, ne hi þanon astyrian; ac
stodon swa oð mergen. Men þa þæs wundrodon hu þa weargas hangodon: sum on hlæddre, sum
leat to gedelfe, and ælc on his weorce wæs fæste gebunden. Hi wurdon þa gebrohte to þam
110   bisceope ealle, and he het hi hon on heagum gealgum ealle; ac he næs na gemyndig hu se mildheorta
God clypode þurh his witegan þas word þe her standað: Eos qui ducuntur ad mortem eruere ne cesses:
Þa þe man læt to deaðe alys hi ut symble. And eac þa halgan canones gehadodum forbeodað, ge
bisceopum ge preostum, to beonne embe þeofas, for þan þe hit ne gebyraþ þam þe beoð gecorene
Gode to þegnigenne þæt hi geþwærlæcan sceolon on æniges mannes deaðe, gif hi beoð Drihtnes
115   þenas. Eft þa Ðeodred bisceop, sceawode his bec syððan, behreowsode mid geomerunge þæt he
swa reðne dom sette þam ungesæligum þeofum, and hit besargode æfre oð his lifes ende; and þa
leode bæd georne þæt hi him mid fæstan fullice þry dagas, biddende þone Ælmihtigan þæt he
him arian scolde.

On þam lande wæs sum man Leofstan gehaten, rice for worulde, and unwittig for Gode, se rad
120   to þam halgan mid riccetere swiðe, and het him æteowian orhlice swiðe þone halgan sanct hwæþer
he gesund wære; ac swa hraðe swa he geseah þæs sanctes lichaman, þa awedde he sona and
wælhreowlice grymetede, and earmlice geendode yfelum deaðe.

Þis is ðam gelic þe se geleaffulla Papa Gregorius sæde on his gesetnysse be ðam halgan Laurentie
ðe lið on Rome byrig: þæt menn woldon sceawian symle hu he lage, ge gode ge yfele, ac God hi
125   gestilde, swa þæt þær swulton on þære sceawunge ane seofon menn ætgædere, þa geswicon þa
oþre to sceawigenne þone martyr mid menniscum gedwylde.

wolf that guarded the head and embraced the head with his two feet: greedy and hungry, he dared not for God's sake taste the head but he protected it against the wild animals. Then they all marvelled at the guardianship of the wolf, and carried the holy head home with them, thanking the Almighty for all his miracles. But the wolf went after those with the head, as if he were tame, until they came to the village, and then he turned back again to the woods. Then the people afterwards laid that head on the holy body and buried it as best as they could in such haste, and immediately raised up a church above it.

Then again, after a period of time, after many years, when the harrying had ceased, and peace was restored to the oppressed people, then they came together, and built a church worthy of the saint, because miracles frequently occurred at his burial-place, even at the chapel where he was buried. Then they wanted to carry the holy body with popular honour, and lay it within the church. Then there was a great miracle in that he was as entirely whole as if he had been alive, with an uncorrupt body, his neck that had previously been cut through was healed, and there was, as it were, a silken thread about his neck, red, as if to show men how he had been killed. In addition, the wounds, which the bloodthirsty heathen had made in his body by their repeated shots, had been healed by the heavenly God; and so he lies uncorrupt until this present day, awaiting the resurrection and eternal glory. His body, which lies undecayed, shows us that he lived without fornication here in this world, and by a pure life passed to Christ.

A certain widow, who was called Oswyn, lived near the saint's burial-place in prayers and fastings for many years after. Every year, she would cut the saint's hair, and trim his nails properly and lovingly, and keep them in a shrine as relics on the altar. So the people of the land faithfully honoured the saint, and Bishop Theodred magnificently honoured the church with gifts in gold and silver, in the saint's honour.

Then it happened at a certain time that some sinful thieves came, eight in one night, to the worthy saint, wishing to steal the treasures which people had brought there, and they attempted to get in by craft. One struck violently at the bolt with a hammer; one of them filed around it with a rasp; one dug under the door with a spade; one of them with a ladder wanted to unlock the window; but they worked in vain, and did miserably, because the holy man miraculously tied them up, each as he stood, working with his tool, so that none of them could do that evil deed, or move from there; but there they stood until morning. People were amazed then at how the wretches hung there: one on a ladder, one bent down in digging, and each in his task was completely tied up. Then they were all brought to the bishop, and he commanded all of them to be hung on a high gallows; but he did not recall how the merciful God spoke through his prophet with the words which remain here: *Eos qui ducuntur ad mortem eruere ne cesses*: Do not fail to save those who are led to death.[24] And also the holy canons prohibit clerics, both bishops and priests, to be concerned about thieves, because it does not become those who are chosen to serve God to consent to any man's death, if they are the Lord's servants. Then Theodred the bishop, after he had searched his books, repented with sadness that he had given such a cruel judgement to these unhappy thieves, and he always regretted it until the end of his life; and he earnestly asked the people to fast with him for the whole of three days, praying the Almighty that he would pardon him.

In that land was a certain man called Leofstan, wealthy in worldly things, and ignorant towards God, who rode to the saint's shrine with great arrogance, and very insolently commanded them to show him the holy saint, and whether he were incorrupt; but as soon as he saw the saint's body he immediately went mad and roared horribly, and was miserably ended by an evil death.

This is like that which the faithful Pope Gregory said in his writings about the holy Lawrence who is buried in the city of Rome: that men, both good and evil, constantly wanted to see how he lay dead, but God stopped them. When a band of seven men there died together while looking, then the others ceased in looking at the martyr with human error.

We have heard of many miracles in people's talk about the holy Edmund that we will not commit to writing here; but every one knows about them. By this saint, and by others like him, it is shown that almighty God can raise man up whole again on doomsday from the earth, he who preserved Edmund whole in his body until that great day, though he was made of earth. That place is honoured because of the worthy saint so that men should venerate it, and provide it fittingly with God's pure servants, in Christ's service, because the saint is greater than men can imagine.

24 Proverbs 24.11.

Fela wundra we gehyrdon on folclicre spræce be þam halgan Eadmunde þe we her nellaþ on gewrite settan; ac hi wat gehwa. On þyssum halgan is swutel, and on swilcum oþrum, þæt God ælmihtig mæg þone man aræran eft on domes dæg andsundne of eorþan, se þe hylt Eadmunde
130   halne his lichaman oð þone micclan dæg, þeah ðe he of moldan come. Wyrðe is seo stow for þam wurðfullan halgan þæt hi man wurþige, and wel gelogige mid clænum Godes þeowum to Cristes þeowdome, for þan þe se halga is mærra þonne men magon asmeagan.

Nis Angelcynn bedæled Drihtnes halgena, þonne on Engla landa licgaþ swilce halgan swylce þæs halga cyning is, and Cuþberht se eadiga, and sancte Æþeldryð on Elig, and eac hire swustor,
135   ansunde on lichaman, geleafan to trymminge. Synd eac fela oðre on Angelcynne halgan þe fela wundra wyrcað, swa swa hit wide is cuð, þam Ælmihtigan to lofe þe hi on gelyfdon. Crist geswutelaþ mannum þurh his mæran halgan þæt he is ælmihtig God þe macað swilce wundra, þeah þe þa earman Judei hine eallunge wiðsocen, for þan þe hi synd awyrgede swa swa hi wiscton him sylfum.

Ne beoð nane wundra geworhte æt heora byrgenum, for ðan þe hi ne gelyfað on þone lifigendan
140   Crist; ac Crist geswutelað mannum hwær se soða geleafa is, þonne he swylce wundra wyrcð þurh his halgan wide geond þas eorðan. Þæs him sy wuldor a mid his heofonlican Fæder and þam Halgan Gaste, a buton ende, Amen.

The English nation is not deprived of the Lord's saints, since in the land of the English lie such saints as this holy king, and the blessed Cuthbert, and saint Æthelthryth in Ely, and also her sister, whole in body, for the encouragement of faith. There are also many other saints who work many miracles, as is widely known, to the praise of the Almighty in whom they believed. Christ demonstrates to men, through his illustrious saints, that he is almighty God who does such miracles, though the wretched Jews altogether denied him, wherefore they are damned, as they wished upon themselves. There are no miracles performed at their shrines, because they do not believe in the living Christ; but Christ shows men where true faith is, as he performs such miracles through his saints widely throughout the earth. To him, therefore, be glory always with his heavenly Father, and with the Holy Ghost, for ever and ever, Amen.

The Battle of Maldon

The Battle of Maldon is the best example of a short heroic poem to survive from Anglo-Saxon England, and its survival is due to very good fortune: that before 1731, John Elphinston or David Casley transcribed the poem from the manuscript London, British Library, Cotton Otho A. xii. The manuscript itself was subsequently very badly burnt in the fire at Robert Cotton's library in Ashburnham House in 1731. Under Cotton's ownership, the volume had been assembled by bringing together originally separate manuscripts: the Old English poem, a number of Latin saints' lives, and Asser's Latin life of King Alfred with two charms in Latin and Old English.[1] Of the fourteen original texts that formed the composite Otho A. xii only ten survived in a poor state of legibility after the fire, and *The Battle of Maldon* was completely destroyed. The poem is therefore known only from the transcript at pp. 7–12 of Oxford, Bodleian Library, Rawlinson B. 203. It appears that when the text was copied, the beginning and end of the poem had been lost and thus only an incomplete text survives.

The poem may have been written in the late tenth, or early eleventh, century in the East Anglian region.[2] It describes, with considerable poetic licence, the events of the historical Battle of Maldon in 991, in which the English force under the command of Byrhtnoth of Essex fought with the Vikings who had been attacking the coast of southern England. *The Anglo-Saxon Chronicle* and other later sources provide some evidence for the battle itself. The D version of the *Chronicle*, for example, contained in London, British Library, Cotton Tiberius B. iv, written at Worcester in the eleventh century,[3] has the following entry for the year 991: 'In this year, Ipswich was raided, and very quickly after that, Ealdorman Byrhtnoth was killed at Maldon. And in that year, it was first advised that tribute should be paid to the Danes because of the great terror that they made along the sea coast. That was

at first ten thousand pounds. Archbishop Sigeric advised on the decision.'

The Battle of Maldon opens with the English force ready to engage in battle with the Viking army at the river Pante (modern-day Blackwater). The Vikings are separated from their enemies by the high tide and, when their demand for tribute is refused, they ask to cross the causeway to meet the English. Byrhtnoth allows them to do this *for his ofermode* (line 89b, 'because of his pride').[4] A full-scale battle ensues in which Byrhtnoth, the courageous Christian leader, is killed. Some of his retainers choose to flee the battlefield at this point, demonstrating a cowardice that is completely unacceptable within the heroic code. The remainder of the *comitatus* holds out valiantly in the conflict, but is ultimately defeated, and it is their loyal words and actions, contrasting sharply with the flight of the cowards, that form the focus of the second part of the poem. These warriors chose glory and revenge for their lord's death over the saving of their own lives. Thus in the final hour of the defeat of the English, the poem nevertheless celebrates the spirit of the heroes' courage and commitment in adversity. *The Battle of Maldon* is therefore regarded as one of the finest expressions of the ideal, but, by the tenth century, archaic, heroic ethos. In the face of national turmoil in England during this period, the poem becomes a battle-call against the Danes, propaganda to unite the people against the enemy.[5] As Caie puts it so effectively: 'Its [the Germanic ideal's] emergence in the tenth century … is undoubtedly connected with political needs of the Saxon rulers to create a united kingdom by claiming a common Germanic heritage with a great past and ideals of loyalty to God and king. It nourished a sense of nostalgia for a time of fixed beliefs when men could be heroes and heroes were immortal. A time that never was – yet will be forever.'[6]

1 For all of this information on the manuscript and transcript, see D. G. Scragg, ed., *The Battle of Maldon* (Manchester, 1981), pp. 1–8. Emendations in the present edition are based on Scragg.
2 Ibid., pp. 27–8.
3 See G. P. Cubbin, ed., *MS D. The Anglo-Saxon Chronicle: A Collaborative Edition* 6 (Woodbridge, 1996).
4 See H. Gneuss, 'The Battle of Maldon 89b: Byrhtnoth's *ofermod*

Once Again', in *Old English Shorter Poems: Basic Readings*, ed. K. O'Brien O'Keeffe (New York, 1994), pp. 149–72, for the interpretations of this crucial phrase.
5 G. Caie, 'The Shorter Heroic Verse', in *Companion to Old English Poetry*, eds H. Aertsen and R. H. Bremmer Jr (Amsterdam, 1994), p. 93.
6 Ibid., p. 93.

The Battle of Maldon

. . . brocen wurde.

Het þa hyssa hwæne   hors forlætan,
feor afysan   and forð gangan,
hicgan to handum   and to hige godum.
5   Þa þæt Offan mæg   ærest onfunde
þæt se eorl nolde   yrhðo geþolian,
he let him þa of handon   leofne fleogan
hafoc wið þæs holtes,   and to þære hilde stop;
be þam man mihte oncnawan   þæt se cniht nolde
10   wacian æt þam wige,   þa he to wæpnum feng.
Eac him wolde Eadric   his ealdre gelæstan,
frean to gefeohte,   ongan þa forð beran
gar to guþe.   He hæfde god geþanc
þa hwile þe he mid handum   healdan mihte
15   bord and brad swurd;   beot he gelæste
þa he ætforan his frean   feohtan sceolde.

    Ða þær Byrhtnoð ongan   beornas trymian,
rad and rædde,   rincum tæhte
hu hi sceoldon standan   and þone stede healdan,
20   and bæd þæt hyra randas   rihte heoldon
fæste mid folman,   and ne forhtedon na.
Þa he hæfde þæt folc   fægere getrymmed,
he lihte þa mid leodon   þær him leofost wæs,
þær he his heorðwerod   holdost wiste.

25   Þa stod on stæðe,   stiðlice clypode
wicinga ar,   wordum mælde,
se on beot abead   brimliþendra
ærænde to þam eorle,   þær he on ofre stod:
'Me sendon to þe   sæmen snelle,
30   heton ðe secgan   þæt þu most sendan raðe
beagas wið gebeorge;   and eow betere is
þæt ge þisne garræs   mid gafole forgyldon
þon we swa hearde   hilde dælon.
Ne þurfe we us spillan,   gif ge spedaþ to þam;
35   we willað wið þam golde   grið fæstnian.
Gyf þu þat gerædest,   þe her ricost eart,
þæt þu þine leoda   lysan wille,
syllan sæmannum –   on hyra sylfra dom –
feoh wið freode,   and niman frið æt us,
40   we willaþ mid þam sceattum   us to scype gangan,
on flot feran,   and eow friþes healdan.'
Byrhtnoð maþelode;   bord hafenode,
wand wacne æsc,   wordum mælde
yrre and anræd,   ageaf him andsware:
45   'Gehyrst þu, sælida,   hwæt þis folc segeð?
Hi willað eow to gafole   garas syllan,
ættrynne ord   and ealde swurd,
þa heregeatu   þe eow æt hilde ne deah.
Brimmanna boda,   abeod eft ongean,
50   sege þinum leodum   miccle laþre spell:
þæt her stynt unforcuð   eorl mid his werode,

The Battle of Maldon

. . . may have become broken.
Then he commanded each one of the warriors to let his horse go,
to drive it far away and to advance on foot,
to turn thoughts to hands and to be of good courage.
5 Then when Offa's kinsman first found
that the earl would not endure cowardice
he let fly from his hands his beloved
hawk into the wood, and stepped into battle;
by that a man might perceive that the warrior would not
10 weaken at that battle when he took up his weapons.
In addition to him, Eadric wanted to serve his leader,
his lord in the fight, so he began then to carry forward
his spear into battle. He had a firm mind
as long as he could hold with his hands
15 his shield and broad sword; he fulfilled his boast
when he was obliged to fight in front of his lord.

Then Byrhtnoth began to encourage the warriors there,
he rode about and gave them advice, taught the warriors
how they should stand and maintain the position,
20 and urged them to hold their shields properly,
securely with their hands, and not to be afraid at all.
When he had suitably arrayed that host,
he dismounted among the men where it was most pleasing to him to be,
where he knew his retainers to be most loyal.

25 Then there stood on the bank, and fiercely called out
a messenger of the Vikings, he spoke with words,
he announced in a boast a message of the seafarers
to the earl where he stood on the bank of the river:
'Bold seamen have sent me to you,
30 they command me to tell you that you must quickly send
rings in return for protection; and it will be better for you
that you buy off this storm of spears with a tribute
than that we should take part in such a hard battle.
We will not need to destroy one another if you are sufficiently wealthy;
35 we will establish a truce in exchange for that gold.
If you, the one who is most powerful here, decide upon this,
that you want to ransom your people,
give the seamen – what they judge for themselves –
money for peace, and accept protection from us,
40 and we will go to our ships with that tribute,
set sail and maintain that peace with you.'
Byrthnoth made a speech; he lifted his shield,
shook his slender ash spear, spoke forth with words
angry and resolute, and gave him an answer:
45 'Do you hear, seafarer, what this army says?
They will give you spears as tribute,
the poisoned spear-tip and ancient swords,
that war-gear that will not be of use to you in battle.
Messenger of the seamen, report back again,
50 tell your people a much more hateful message:
that here stands, with his troop, an earl of untainted reputation,

þe wile gealgean   eþel þysne,
Æþelredes eard,   ealdres mines,
folc and foldan.   Feallan sceolon
55 hæþene æt hilde.   To heanlic me þinceð
þæt ge mid urum sceattum   to scype gangon
unbefohtene   nu ge þus feor hider
on urne eard   in becomon.
Ne sceole ge swa softe   sinc gegangan:
60 us sceal ord and ecg   ær geseman,
grim guðplega,   ær we gofol syllon.'
    Het þa bord beran,   beornas gangan,
þæt hi on þam easteðe   ealle stodon.
Ne mihte þær for wætere   werod to þam oðrum;
65 þær com flowende   flod æfter ebban
lucon lagustreamas.   To lang hit him þuhte
hwænne hi togædere   garas beron.
Hi þær Pantan stream   mid prasse bestodon,
Eastseaxena ord   and se æschere;
70 ne mihte hyra ænig   oþrum derian
buton hwa þurh flanes flyht   fyl genname.
Se flod ut gewat;   þa flotan stodon gearowe,
wicinga fela,   wiges georne.
Het þa hæleða hleo   healdan þa bricge
75 wigan wigheardne   se wæs haten Wulfstan,
cafne mid his cynne   (þæt wæs Ceolan sunu)
þe ðone forman man   mid his francan ofsceat
þe þær baldlicost   on þa bricge stop.
Þær stodon mid Wulfstane   wigan unforhte,
80 Ælfere and Maccus,   modige twegen,
þa noldon æt þam forda   fleam gewyrcan,
ac hi fæstlice   wið ða fynd weredon
þa hwile þe hi wæpna   wealdan moston.
Þa hi þæt ongeaton   and georne gesawon
85 þæt hi þær bricgweardas   bitere fundon,
ongunnon lytegian, þa   laðe gystas:
bædon þæt hi upgangan   agan moston,
ofer þone ford faran,   feþan lædan.
Ða se eorl ongan   for his ofermode
90 alyfan landes to fela   laþere ðeode.
Ongan ceallian þa   ofer cald wæter,
Byrhtelmes bearn –   beornas gehlyston:
'Nu eow is gerymed,   gað ricene to us
guman to guþe;   God ana wat
95 hwa þære wælstowe   wealdan mote.'
    Wodon þa wælwulfas;   for wætere ne murnon
wicinga werod.   West ofer Pantan,
ofer scir wæter,   scyldas wegon;
lidmen to lande   linde bæron.
100 Þær ongean gramum   gearowe stodon
Byrhtnoð mid beornum.   He mid bordum het
wyrcan þone wihagan   and þæt werod healdan
fæste wiþ feondum.   Þa wæs feohte neh,
tir æt getohte;   wæs seo tid cumen

who will defend this native land,
the country of Æthelred, my lord's
people and ground. The heathens
55 will fall in battle. It seems too shameful to me
that you should go to your ships with our tribute
without a fight now that you have come this far
here into our land.
You shall not get treasure so easily:
60 weapon-tip and edge shall arbitrate between us first,
the fierce game of battle, before we give you tribute.'
    Then he commanded the warriors to advance bearing shields,
so that they all stood on the bank of the river.
One army could not get at the other because of the water there;
65 where the tide came flowing after the ebb
streams of water enclosed the land. It seemed too long to them
until they could brandish spears together.
They stood there alongside the River Pante in military formation,
the East Saxon vanguard and the Viking army;
70 not one of them was able to injure any other
unless someone received death from the flight of a missile.
The tide went out; the seamen stood ready,
many Vikings, eager for battle.
Then the protector of the heroes commanded the causeway to be defended
75 by a warrior fierce in war called Wulfstan,
as brave as all his family (he was Ceola's son),
who with his spear shot the first man
who stepped most boldly onto that causeway.
There stood with Wulfstan fearless warriors,
80 Ælfere and Maccus, two brave men,
who would not take flight from that ford,
but they firmly resisted the enemy
as long as they were able to brandish their weapons.
When the Vikings perceived this and saw plainly
85 that they had found there fierce causeway-defenders,
they began to use cunning, the hateful strangers:
they requested that they should be allowed a passage to land,
to travel over the ford, to lead the foot-soldiers.
Then the earl, because of his pride, began
90 to allow too much land to a more hateful nation.
He began to call out then over the cold water,
this son of Byrhtelm – the warriors listened:
'Now a passage is granted to you, come quickly to us
as men to battle; God alone knows
95 who will be allowed to control the place of slaughter.'
    The wolves of slaughter advanced; they did not care about the water,
that host of Vikings. West over the Pante,
over the shining water, they bore their shields;
the sailors carried their lime-wood shields to land.
100 There against the hostile ones stood ready
Byrhtnoth with his men. He commanded the army
to make a battle-wall with shields and to hold fast
against the enemies. The battle was near then,
glory in the fray; the time had come

<pre>
105   þæt þær fæge men   feallan sceoldon.
           Þær wearð hream ahafen;   hremmas wundon,
           earn æses georn;   wæs on eorþan cyrm.
           Hi leton þa of folman   feolhearde speru,
           gegrundene   garas fleogan;
110   bogan wæron bysige,   bord ord onfeng.
           Biter wæs se beaduræs;   beornas feollon
           on gehwæðere hand,   hyssas lagon.
           Wund wearð Wulfmær,   wælræste geceas,
           Byrhtnoðes mæg;   he mid billum wearð,
115   his swuster sunu,   swiðe forheawen.
           Þær wærð wicingum   wiþerlean agyfen.
           Gehyrde Ic þæt Eadweard   anne sloge
           swiðe mid his swurde –   swenges ne wyrnde –
           þæt him æt fotum feoll   fæge cempa,
120   þæs him his ðeoden   þanc gesæde,
           þam burþene,   þa he byre hæfde.
           Swa stemnetton   stiðhicgende,
           hysas æt hilde,   hogodon georne
           hwa þær mid orde   ærost mihte
125   on fægean men   feorh gewinnan,
           wigan mid wæpnum.   Wæl feol on eorðan.
           Stodon stædefæste;   stihte hi Byrhtnoð,
           bæd þæt hyssa gehwylc   hogode to wige
           þe on Denon wolde   dom gefeohtan.
130   Wod þa wiges heard,   wæpen up ahof,
           bord to gebeorge,   and wið þæs beornes stop.
           Eode swa anræd   eorl to þam ceorle:
           ægþer hyra oðrum   yfeles hogode.
           Sende ða se særinc   suþerne gar
135   þæt gewundod wearð   wigena hlaford;
           he sceaf þa mid ðam scylde   þæt se sceaft tobærst,
           and þæt spere sprengde   þæt hit sprang ongean.
           Gegremod wearð se guðrinc;   he mid gare stang
           wlancne wicing   þe him þa wunde forgeaf.
140   Frod wæs se fyrdrinc;   he let his francan wadan
           þurh ðæs hysses hals;   hand wisode
           þæt he on þam færsceaðan   feorh geræhte.
           Ða he oþerne   ofstlice sceat,
           þæt seo byrne tobærst;   he wæs on breostum wund
145   þurh ða hringlocan;   him æt heortan stod
           ætterne ord.   Se eorl wæs þe bliþra.
           Hloh þa, modi man,   sæde Metode þanc
           ðæs dægweorces   þe him Drihten forgeaf.
           Forlet þa drenga sum   daroð of handa,
150   fleogan of folman,   þæt se to forð gewat
           þurh ðone æþelan   Æþelredes þegen.
           Him be healfe stod   hyse unweaxen,
           cniht on gecampe,   se full caflice
           bræd of þam beorne   blodigne gar,
155   Wulfstanes bearn,   Wulfmær se geonga.
           Forlet forheardne   faran eft ongean;
           ord in gewod   þæt se on eorþan læg
</pre>

105   that fated men should fall there.
An outcry was raised there; ravens circled in the air,
the eagle eager for carrion; there was uproar on earth.
Then from their hands they let fly spears as hard as files,
sharpened missiles;
110   bows were busy, the shield received the sword-point.
Bitter was the rush of battle; warriors fell
on either side, soldiers lay dead.
Wulfmær was wounded, he chose death in battle,
the kinsman of Byrhtnoth, son of his sister:
115   he was cruelly cut down with swords.
Requital was given to the Vikings there.
I heard that Eadweard killed one
fiercely with his sword – he did not withhold the blow –
so that at his feet a doomed warrior fell,
120   for which his lord gave thanks
to his chamberlain when he had the chance.
So those resolute in purpose stood firm,
young warriors in battle, eagerly they concentrated there
on whoever might win the life of a doomed man
125   first with the spear-point,
those soldiers with their weapons. The dead of battle fell to the earth.
They stood steadfast; Byrhtnoth urged them on,
he asked that each soldier should focus on the battle,
whoever wished to get glory from the Danes in battle.
130   Then one fierce in battle advanced, raised his weapon up,
used his shield as protection, and marched towards that man.
The earl moved towards that peasant just as resolutely:
each of them intended ill-harm to the other.
Then the Viking threw a spear of southern make
135   so that the lord of the warriors was wounded;
he shoved with his shield then so that the shaft shattered
and that spear quivered as it sprang back out.
The warrior became enraged; he struck with a spear
the proud Viking who had given him that wound.
140   That warrior was old and wise; he made his spear go
through the neck of the soldier; his hand guided it
so that he took the life from that sudden attacker.
Then he quickly threw another
so that his mail-coat burst; he was wounded in the breast
145   through the ringmail shirt; positioned in his heart
was the poison-tipped spear. The earl was the happier.
The bold man laughed then, he gave thanks to the Creator
for the day's work that the Lord had granted to him.
Then a certain warrior sent a light spear from his hands,
150   let it fly from his clutches, so that it went forwards
through the noble thane of Æthelred.
By his side stood a youth not fully grown,
a boy in the battle, who very bravely
pulled out the bloody spear from that warrior,
155   this was the son of Wulfstan, the young Wulfmær.
He let the exceedingly hard spear journey back again;
the point penetrated so that he who had severely wounded

þe his þeoden ær   þearle geræhte.
    Eode þa gesyrwed   secg to þam eorle;
160   he wolde þæs beornes   beagas gefecgan,
reaf and hringas   and gerenod swurd.
Þa Byrhtnoð bræd   bill of sceðe,
brad and bruneccg,   and on þa byrnan sloh.
To raþe hine gelette   lidmanna sum,
165   þa he þæs eorles   earm amyrde.
Feoll þa to foldan   fealohilte swurd;
ne mihte he gehealdan   heardne mece,
wæpnes wealdan.   Þa gyt þæt word gecwæð
har hilderinc,   hyssas bylde,
170   bæd gangan forð   gode geferan.
Ne mihte þa on fotum leng   fæste gestandan;
he to heofenum wlat:
'Geþance þe,   ðeoda Waldend,
ealra þæra wynna   þe Ic on worulde gebad.
175   Nu Ic ah, milde Metod,   mæste þearfe
þæt þu minum gaste   godes geunne,
þæt min sawul to ðe   siðian mote
on þin geweald,   Þeoden engla,
mid friþe ferian.   Ic eom frymdi to þe
180   þæt hi helsceaðan   hynan ne moton.'
Ða hine heowon   hæðene scealcas,
and begen þa beornas   þe him big stodon,
Ælfnoð and Wulmær   begen lagon,
ða onemn hyra frean   feorh gesealdon.
185   Hi bugon þa fram beaduwe   þe þær beon noldon.
Þær wurdon Oddan bearn   ærest on fleame,
Godric fram guþe,   and þone godan forlet
þe him mænigne oft   mear gesealde.
He gehleop þone eoh   þe ahte his hlaford,
190   on þam gerædum,   þe hit riht ne wæs,
and his broðru mid him   begen ærndon,
Godwine and Godwig: guþe ne gymdon,
ac wendon fram þam wige   and þone wudu sohton,
flugon on þæt fæsten   and hyra feore burgon,
195   and manna ma   þonne hit ænig mæð wære,
gyf hi þa geearnunga   ealle gemundon
þe he him to duguþe   gedon hæfde.
Swa him Offa on dæg   ær asæde
on þam meþelstede,   þa he gemot hæfde,
200   þæt þær modelice   manega spræcon
þe eft æt þearfe   þolian noldon.
    Þa wearð afeallen   þæs folces ealdor,
Æþelredes eorl;   ealle gesawon
heorðgeneatas   þæt hyra heorra læg.
205   Þa ðær wendon forð   wlance þegenas,
unearge men   efston georne:
hi woldon þa ealle   oðer twega,
lif forlætan   oððe leofne gewrecan.
Swa hi bylde forð   bearn Ælfrices,
210   wiga wintrum geong,   wordum mælde,

his lord before lay dead on the ground.
    Then the armed man went towards the earl;
160   he wanted to fetch the warrior's ornaments,
the armour and rings, and decorated sword.
Then Byrhtnoth pulled his sword from its sheath
broad and shiny edged, and struck against the mail-coat.
Too swiftly one of the Vikings prevented him,
165   when he wounded the earl's arm.
The golden-hilted sword fell to the ground:
he could not hold the hard blade,
or wield his weapon. And yet the hoary warrior
said these words, encouraged the young soldiers,
170   urged them to go forwards as good companions.
He could not stand fast on his feet any longer;
he looked up to heaven:
'I thank you, Lord of nations,
for all of the joys that I have experienced in this world.
175   Now I have, merciful God, most need
that you grant a benefit to my spirit,
that my soul might journey to you
into your power, Lord of angels,
to travel in peace. I beg you
180   that thieves from hell will not be permitted to injure it.'
The heathen warriors cut him down,
and both the men who stood beside him,
Ælfnoð and Wulmær both lay slain,
they gave their lives beside their lord.
185   Then those who did not want to be there turned away from battle.
There the sons of Odda became the first to flee,
Godric turned from the battle, and abandoned the good man
who had often given him many a horse.
He leapt onto the horse that his lord had owned,
190   into those trappings, which was not right,
and his brothers, Godwine and Godwig,
both ran with him: they did not care about the battle,
but escaped from that fight and sought the woods,
fled into the place of safety and saved their own lives,
195   as did many more than was in any way appropriate,
if they recalled all the benefits
that Byrhtnoth had done to their advantage.
So earlier in the day Offa had said
in that meeting place, when they held a council,
200   that many spoke bravely there
who would not hold out afterwards when there was need.
    So the leader of the people had fallen,
Æthelred's earl; the retainers
all saw that their lord lay dead.
205   Then proud thanes came forward there,
the undaunted men hastened eagerly:
they wanted one of two things,
to give up their life or to avenge their beloved lord.
The son of Ælfric urged them forth,
210   a warrior young in years, spoke words,

Ælfwine þa cwæð,   he on ellen spræc:
'Gemunaþ þa mæla   þe we oft æt meodo spræcon,
þonne we on bence   beot ahofon,
hæleð on healle,   ymbe heard gewinn;
215 nu mæg cunnian   hwa cene sy.
Ic wylle mine æþelo   eallum gecyþan,
þæt Ic wæs on Myrcon   miccles cynnes;
wæs min ealda fæder   Ealhelm haten,
wis ealdorman,   woruldgesælig.
220 Ne sceolon me on þære þeode   þegenas ætwitan
þæt Ic of ðisse fyrde   feran wille
eard gesecan,   nu min ealdor ligeð
forheawen æt hilde.   Me is þæt hearma mæst:
he wæs ægðer min mæg   and min hlaford.'
225 Þa he forð eode,   fæhðe gemunde,
þæt he mid orde   anne geræhte
flotan on þam folce,   þæt se on foldan læg
forwegen mid his wæpne.   Ongan þa winas manian,
frynd and geferan,   þæt hi forð eodon.
230 Offa gemælde,   æscholt asceoc:
'Hwæt þu, Ælfwine,   hafast ealle gemanode
þegenas to þearfe.   Nu ure þeoden lið,
eorl on eorðan,   us is eallum þearf
þæt ure æghwylc   oþerne bylde,
235 wigan to wige,   þa hwile þe he wæpen mæge
habban and healdan,   heardne mece,
gar and god swurd.   Us Godric hæfð,
earh Oddan bearn,   ealle beswicene:
wende þæs formoni man,   þa he on meare rad,
240 on wlancan þam wicge,   þæt wære hit ure hlaford;
forþan wearð her on felda   folc totwæmed,
scyldburh tobrocen.   Abreoðe his angin,
þæt he her swa manigne   man aflymde!'
Leofsunu gemælde,   and his linde ahof,
245 bord to gebeorge;   he þam beorne oncwæð:
'Ic þæt gehate,   þæt Ic heonon nelle
fleon fotes trym,   ac wille furðor gan
wrecan on gewinne   minne winedrihten.
Ne þurfon me embe Sturmere   stedefæste hælæð
250 wordum ætwitan   nu min wine gecranc,
þæt Ic hlafordleas   ham siðie,
wende fram wige;   ac me sceal wæpen niman,
ord and iren.'   He ful yrre wod,
feaht fæstlice;   fleam he forhogode.
255 Dunnere þa cwæð,   daroð acwehte,
unorne ceorl,   ofer eall clypode,
bæd þæt beorna gehwylc   Byrhtnoð wræce:
'Ne mæg na wandian   se þe wrecan þenceð
frean on folce   ne for feore murnan.'
260 Þa hi forð eodon,   feores hi ne rohton.
Ongunnon þa hiredmen   heardlice feohtan,
grame garberend,   and God bædon
þæt hi moston gewrecan   hyra winedrihten

Ælfwine then said, and he bravely uttered:
'Remember the words that we often spoke over mead,
when we raised a vow at our bench,
heroes in the hall, about the hard battle;
215 now it will be tested who is brave.
I will reveal my noble lineage to everyone,
that I was from a great family in Mercia;
my grandfather was called Ealhelm,
a wise ealdorman, prosperous and happy in this world.
220 The thanes of that people will not reproach me
that I want to go from this army
to seek my homeland, now that my lord lies dead
cut down in battle. To me that is the greatest of sorrows:
he was both my kinsman and my lord.'
225 Then he stepped forward, mindful of the feud,
so that with his spear he reached one
Viking in that army, such that he lay dead on the ground
killed by his weapon. Then he began to exhort his comrades,
friends and companions, that they should go forward.
230 Offa spoke, the ash spear shook:
'Indeed, Ælfwine, you have exhorted all
the thanes at this time of need. Now our lord lies dead,
the earl on the ground, there is a need for us all
that each of us encourage the other,
235 warriors into battle, as long as he may
have and hold a weapon, the hard blade,
a spear and good sword. Godric,
the cowardly son of Odda, has betrayed us all:
very many men thought, when he rode away on that horse,
240 on that noble steed, that it was our lord;
therefore the army on this field became divided,
the shield-wall broken. May his venture fail,
that he caused so many men to flee here!'
Leofsunu spoke out, and he raised his lime-wood shield
245 as protection; he answered the warrior:
'I pledge this, that from here I shall not
flee one footstep, but I mean to go further onwards
to avenge my beloved lord in battle.
The resolute heroes around Sturmer will have no need
250 to condemn me with words, now my lord has died,
that I should go home lordless,
turn away from battle; rather a weapon shall take me,
the spear-tip and iron sword.' Very angry, he advanced,
fought bravely; he scorned flight.
255 Dunnere then spoke, he shook his light spear,
a simple peasant, he called out over everyone,
and urged that each warrior should avenge Byrhtnoth:
'He who thinks to avenge his lord upon that people
cannot draw back or fear for his life.'
260 They went forwards then, they did not care about their lives.
The retainers started to fight fiercely,
hostile spear-carriers, and prayed God
that they could avenge their beloved lord

and on hyra feondum   fyl gewyrcan.
265   Him se gysel ongan   geornlice fylstan;
he wæs on Norðhymbron   heardes cynnes,
Ecglafes bearn,   him wæs Æscferð nama.
He ne wandode na   æt þam wigplegan,
ac he fysde forð   flan genehe;
270   hwilon he on bord sceat,   hwilon beorn tæsde;
æfre embe stunde   he sealde sume wunde
þa hwile ðe he wæpna   wealdan moste.
Þa gyt on orde stod   Eadweard se langa;
gearo and geornful,   gylpwordum spræc
275   þæt he nolde fleogan   fotmæl landes,
ofer bæc bugan,   þa his betera leg.
He bræc þone bordweall   and wið þa beornas feaht,
oðþæt he his sincgyfan   on þam sæmannum
wurðlice wrec,   ær he on wæle læge.
280   Swa dyde Æþeric,   æþele gefera,
fus and forðgeorn,   feaht eornoste,
Sibyrhtes broðor,   and swiðe mænig oþer,
clufon cellod bord,   cene hi weredon.
Bærst bordes lærig,   and seo byrne sang
285   gryreleoða sum.   Þa æt guðe sloh
Offa þone sælidan   þæt he on eorðan feoll,
and ðær Gaddes mæg   grund gesohte.
Raðe wearð æt hilde   Offa forheawen;
he hæfde ðeah geforþod   þæt he his frean gehet,
290   swa he beotode ær   wið his beahgifan
þæt hi sceoldon begen   on burh ridan,
hale to hame,   oððe on here crincgan,
on wælstowe   wundum sweltan.
He læg ðegenlice   ðeodne gehende.
295   Ða wearð borda gebræc.   Brimmen wodon,
guðe gegremode.   Gar oft þurhwod
fæges feorhhus.   Forð ða eode Wistan,
Þurstanes suna,   wið þas secgas feaht;
he wæs on geþrang   hyra þreora bana,
300   ær him Wigelmes bearn   on þam wæle læge.
Þær wæs stið gemot.   Stodon fæste
wigan on gewinne.   Wigend cruncon,
wundum werige;   wæl feol on eorþan.
Oswold and Eadwold   ealle hwile,
305   begen þa gebroþru,   beornas trymedon,
hyra winemagas   wordon bædon
þæt hi þær æt ðearfe   þolian sceoldon,
unwaclice   wæpna neotan.
Byrhtwold maþelode,   bord hafenode,
310   se wæs eald geneat,   æsc acwehte;
he ful baldlice   beornas lærde:
'Hige sceal þe heardra,   heorte þe cenre,
mod sceal þe mare,   þe ure mægen lytlað.
Her lið ure ealdor   eall forheawen,
315   god on greote.   A mæg gnornian
se ðe nu fram þis wigplegan   wendan þenceð.

and bring death to their enemies.
265 The hostage eagerly began to help them;
he was from a hardy family from Northumbria,
the son of Ecglaf, his name was Æscferth.
He did not draw back at all in that battle-game,
but he frequently shot forth darts;
270 sometimes he shot into a shield, sometimes he lacerated a warrior;
always within a short time he caused some wound
as long as he was able to wield weapons.
Also in the vanguard stood Eadweard the tall;
ready and eager, he spoke determined words
275 that he would not flee one foot of ground,
retreat back, while his better man lay dead.
He broke the shield-wall and fought against the warriors,
until, among those Vikings, he avenged his treasure-giver
honourably, before he himself lay among the dead.
280 So did Ætheric, a noble companion,
keen and eager to advance, he fought committedly,
this brother of Sigebryht, and very many others,
they split the embossed shield, they defended themselves bravely.
The rim of the shield burst, and the mail-coat sang
285 a song of terror. Then in the battle
Offa struck a Viking so that he fell dead on the earth,
and there this kinsman of Gad sought the ground.
Offa was quickly cut down in battle;
he had, though, accomplished what he promised his lord,
290 when he pledged before with his ring-giver
that they should both ride into the nobleman's dwelling,
ride unharmed into the home, or fall in conflict,
die from wounds in the place of slaughter.
He lay loyally next to his lord.
295   Then shields were broken. The seafarers advanced
incensed by the battle. The spear often pierced
the body of the fated man. Wistan then went forward,
the son of Thurstan, he fought against the men;
he was the slayer of three of them in the throng
300 before Wigelm's son lay before him among the dead.
It was a fierce encounter there. They stood fast,
warriors in the battle. Warriors died
overcome by wounds; the slain fell to the ground.
Oswold and Eadwold all the while,
305 the two brothers, encouraged the warriors,
they entreated their dear kinsmen with their words
that they should hold out there in this time of need,
use their weapons unfailingly.
Byrhtwold spoke out, raised his shield,
310 he was an old retainer, he shook his ash spear;
very boldy he instructed the men:
'The mind must be tougher, the heart the bolder,
resolve shall be greater, as our strength becomes less.
Here lies our lord all cut down,
315 a good man in the dust. He who thinks to turn away
from this battle-play now will always regret it.

Ic eom frod feores;   fram Ic ne wille,
ac Ic me be healfe   minum hlaforde,
be swa leofan men,   licgan þence.'
320   Swa hi Æþelgares bearn   ealle bylde,
Godric to guþe.   Oft he gar forlet,
wælspere windan   on þa wicingas,
swa he on þam folce   fyrmest eode,
heow and hynde,   oðþæt he on hilde gecranc.
325   Næs þæt na se Godric   þe ða guðe forbeah.

I am experienced in life; I will not go away,
but by the side of my lord,
of such a dear man, I intend to lie.'
320 Godric, Æthelgar's son, encouraged them all
to battle. He sent a spear often,
a deadly spear to fly into the Vikings;
so he advanced first into that army;
he cut down and killed, until he perished in that conflict.
325 He was not that Godric who fled from the battle.

The *Beowulf*-Manuscript

London, British Library, Cotton Vitellius A. xv, chrono-logically the third of the four major poetic codices from the Anglo-Saxon period, is dated to the beginning, or first quarter, of the eleventh century.[1] The manuscript as it now exists is a composite volume containing, in the eleventh-century portion, three Old English prose works (an incomplete *Life of St Christopher*, *Marvels of the East* and *The Letter from Aristotle to Alexander*) preceding *Beowulf*, and the incomplete Old English poem *Judith*, which follows. None of these texts, of course, is provided with a title in the manuscript; the same is true of nearly all Old English poetry. Titles of texts have been supplied following the suggestions of nineteenth-century editors in most cases.

Folios 4–93 of Cotton Vitellius A. xv date to the mid-twelfth century, and include the Old English trans-lation of Augustine's *Soliloquies*, part of the Gospel of Nicodemus, the prose *Solomon and Saturn*, and the open-ing of a homily on Saint Quintin. The second part of the manuscript includes the pre-Conquest material, and is generally referred to as 'the *Beowulf*-Manuscript' or 'the Nowell Codex' (after the sixteenth-century antiquarian Laurence Nowell, who had possession of the manuscript at some point in his career); the first part of the manu-script is usually labelled 'the Southwick Codex' as its medieval provenance appears to be Southwick Priory.

The place of origin of the *Beowulf*-manuscript remains unknown. The texts were copied by two scribes, the sec-ond taking over at line 1939b of *Beowulf*. It is thought now that the manuscript may represent a thematically unified compilation with the emphasis being, among other things, on monsters or the marvellous.[2] And while little is known about the geographical origins of the manuscript, so too is little known about the date of com-position of the texts within it.

While kept in the library of Sir Robert Cotton, the *Beowulf*-manuscript, together with many other manu-scripts now held in the British Library, was damaged in the fire at Ashburnham House in 1731. Fortunately, the damage was restricted to the margins of the text; but this has resulted in numerous letters in the outer mar-gins of the pages being lost. Scholars have, until recently, been dependent on two nineteenth-century transcripts of *Beowulf*, known as Thorkelin A and B, that were cop-ied before subsequent further crumbling of the pages' edges occurred. Within the last decade, however, Kevin Kiernan's work on the manuscript, examining it with the aid of new technology, has advanced the reclamation of the text. His work will be available in CD-Rom for-mat as *The Electronic Beowulf*. Scholars of *Judith*, mean-while, are dependent on the readings of Edward Thwaites's 1698 edition of the text published before the fire at Ashburnham House.

---

1 There is a large body of critical work relating to the date of the *Beowulf* manuscript. See especially K. S. Kiernan, *Beowulf and the Beowulf Manuscript*, 2nd edn (London, 1996), and D. N. Dumville, '*Beowulf* Come Lately: Some Notes on the Palaeography of the Nowell Codex', *Archiv* 225 (1988), 49–63.

2 See A. Orchard, *Pride and Prodigies: Studies in the Monsters of the Beowulf Manuscript* (Cambridge, 1995).

BEOWULF

Beowulf, at 3,182 lines, is the longest, and arguably the greatest, surviving English poem from the earlier medieval period. It is contained at folios 132 recto to 201 verso of Cotton Vitellius A. xv, where it is divided into forty-three fitts (or sections) indicated in the text by roman numerals. The poem regularly generates a substantial amount of critical literature: more is written on *Beowulf* in any given year than on the whole of Old English prose, for example. The reasons behind this unceasing interest in the work stem from its many mysteries: who composed the poem, when was it composed, and for what audience? What was the poet's aim in depicting the magnificent feats of the hero, Beowulf? Is the work substantially a glorification of pagan heroism, or is it ultimately an implicit condemnation of pre-Christian Germanic society? Indeed, what are the implications for our understanding of *Beowulf* of the numerous religious references in the text?[3]

The framework of *Beowulf* can be divided into two sections both concerning the exploits of its hero. Lines 1–2199 relate Beowulf's arrival in Denmark from Geatland. He has come to Denmark in the hope of defeating the monster Grendel, who has been terrorizing the court of the Danish king, Hrothgar, for twelve years (lines 320–1250, the extract printed below). Beowulf also has to fight the mother of the monster in this first part of the poem. The second section begins fifty years later when Beowulf, as king of Geatland, has to fight a dragon that is destroying his kingdom, after which Beowulf dies. Although this summary suggests that the poem is chiefly made up of heroic action, these three fights are surrounded by speeches, by digressions focusing on historic and legendary episodes, and by description of the settings. And while the narrative of the poem is fundamentally chronological in its concentration on the hero's exploits, the poet ranges across time by foreshadowing events to come, and by the careful integration of relevant past events that link characters and deeds into a larger, historical scheme.

It may be that the poem, or elements of it, existed for centuries before its commital to written form in the *Beowulf*-manuscript or its exemplar, and that the complete work represents an accretion of legends moulded

to create a narrative relating the major exploits of the greatest of heroes. The poet certainly draws on a wide range of materials to provide the setting and themes of *Beowulf*: Germanic, Old Testament and historical and legendary sources, among others. For example, included or mentioned within the narrative are Sigemund, the legendary dragon-slayer of the later Old Norse *Volsungasaga*; Hygelac (uncle of Beowulf and king of the Geats), an historical figure, who existed in the sixth century; Cain and Abel, the sons of Adam and Eve; the mythical flying dragon which kills Beowulf; and Weland, the legendary Germanic smith (for whom see also *Deor*). Lines 1068–1124 represent a digression about Finn and Hildeburh, in which the noble Danish woman Hildeburh is given in marriage to Finn in order to settle a dispute between the Danes and the Frisians. A visit from her brother Hnæf results in a pitched battle between the two sides in which Hildeburh and Finn's son and Hnæf are killed. A subsequent fight results in the death of Finn, following which Hildeburh is taken back to her own people. This important digression highlights the inevitability of conflict despite the attempts to settle feuds by a political marriage (such as that which Hrothgar and Wealhtheow have in mind for their own daughter, Freaware). The narrative in *Beowulf* can be supplemented by the Old English poem known as *The Fight at Finnsburh*; it survives only in a transcription made by George Hickes, and published in 1705.[4] In this poem, the details leading up to the fight between the Danes and Frisians at Finn's stronghold and Hnæf's death are recounted, providing valuable evidence for the circulation of the story in Anglo-Saxon England, and demonstrating that the *Beowulf*-poet drew on a wide range of legendary tales in the composition of his poem.

There is little doubt that *Beowulf* is a magnificent achievement weaving together a number of legends around a central heroic character to produce a coherent work of a scope unsurpassed in English in the Anglo-Saxon period. The poem repays close examination. No extract can be representative of the whole text, and this is particularly true of *Beowulf*; students should therefore seek out one of the numerous editions of the text to gain the full effect of this epic work.

---

3   For an excellent discussion of these and other aspects of the text, see the most recently published edition of the poem: B. Mitchell and F. C. Robinson, eds, *Beowulf: An Edition* (Oxford, 1998). The editors comment (at pp. 33–4) that: 'The significance of the Christian elements is a topic on which the authors do not see eye to eye. This is made clear by the fact that where, in the first sentence of our foreword, we speak of "*Beowulf* with its complex blend of heroic and Christian", the word "complex" is a compromise between

FCR[obinson]'s "subtle" and BM[itchell]'s "baffling".' The debate about the essence of *Beowulf*, its dominant Germanic setting and themes, and its sporadic, but integral, Christian aspects, is one that will never cease to generate very different responses.

4   *The Fight at Finnsburh* is included by most editors of *Beowulf*. The most recent editions of it are G. Jack, ed., *Beowulf: A Student Edition* (Oxford, 1995), and Mitchell and Robinson, *Beowulf: An Edition*.

Beowulf

V

320
Stræt wæs stanfah,   stig wisode
gumum ætgædere.   Guðbyrne scan
heard hondlocen,   hringiren scir
song in searwum.   Þa hie to sele furðum
in hyra gryregeatwum   gangan cwomon,

325
setton sæmeþe   side scyldas,
rondas regnhearde,   wið þæs recedes weal,
bugon þa to bence.   Byrnan hringdon,
guðsearo gumena;   garas stodon,
sæmanna searo,   samod ætgædere,

330
æscholt ufan græg: wæs se irenþreat
wæpnum gewurþad.   Þa ðær wlonc hæleð
oretmecgas   æfter æþelum frægn:
   'Hwanon ferigeað ge   fætte scyldas,
græge syrcan   ond grimhelmas,

335
heresceafta heap?   Ic eom Hroðgares
ar ond ombiht.   Ne seah Ic elþeodige
þus manige men   modiglicran.
Wen Ic þæt ge for wlenco,   nalles for wræcsiðum,
ac for higeþrymmum,   Hroðgar sohton.'

340
   Him þa ellenrof   andswarode,
wlanc Wedera leod   word æfter spræc,
heard under helme: 'We synt Higelaces
beodgeneatas;   Beowulf is min nama.
Wille Ic asecgan   sunu Healfdenes,

345
mærum þeodne,   min ærende,
aldre þinum,   gif he us geunnan wile
þæt we hine swa godne   gretan moton.'
   Wulfgar maþelode   – þæt wæs Wendla leod;
wæs his modsefa   manegum gecyðed,

350
wig ond wisdom: 'Ic þæs wine Deniga,
frean Scildinga,   frinan wille,
beaga bryttan,   swa þu bena eart,
þeoden mærne,   ymb þinne sið,
ond þe þa andsware   ædre gecyðan

355
ðe me se goda   agifan þenceð.'
   Hwearf þa hrædlice   þær Hroðgar sæt,
eald ond anhar,   mid his eorla gedriht.
Eode ellenrof   þæt he for eaxlum gestod
Deniga frean: cuþe he duguðe þeaw.

360
Wulfgar maðelode   to his winedrihtne:

Beowulf

(The extract provided below opens with the imminent arrival of Beowulf at the court of Hrothgar, king of the Danes. After an opening describing the funeral of Scyld Scefing, the founder of the Scyldings (that is the Danes), the poet describes the building of the magnificent hall of Heorot by Hrothgar, and the subseqent attacks of the cannibalistic monster Grendel, who, we are told at line 107, is descended from Cain, the first murderer, and an enemy of God. Beowulf, the great heroic warrior, wants to destroy Grendel and end his twelve-year reign of terror; Beowulf, the Geat, comes to Heorot with a band of his men in order to effect this.)

V

320	The street was paved with stone, the path guided
	the men together. War-corslet shone,
	hard, hand-linked, bright ring-iron
	sang in the harness. When they first came
	marching to the hall in their terrible armour,
325	the sea-weary ones placed broad shields,
	wondrously hard shield-bosses, against the wall of the hall,
	and then sat on benches. Mailcoats rang,
	the battle-gear of men; spears stood,
	the equipment of seamen, united together,
330	the ash-grove grey from above: the armed troop
	was dignified with weapons. There a proud hero
	asked the warriors about their ancestry:
	'From where do you carry gold-plated shields,
	grey mailshirts and masked helmets,
335	a mass of battle-spears? I am Hrothgar's
	herald and officer. I have not seen among foreigners
	so many men of more brave an appearance.
	I believe that from daring, and not because of exile at all,
	but from boldness of heart, you have come to seek Hrothgar.'
340	Then the one famed for courage answered him,
	the proud leader of the Geats spoke these words after,
	hard under his helmet: 'We are Hygelac's
	table-companions; Beowulf is my name.
	I want to declare to Healfdane's son,[5]
345	that famous prince, my message,
	to your lord, if he will grant us
	that we may approach him, the good man.'
	Wulfgar spoke – he was a prince of the Vandels;
	his character was known to many
350	for courage in war and wisdom: 'I will ask
	the friend of the Danes, the lord of the Scyldings,[6]
	the giver of rings, the famous ruler,
	as you request, about your venture,
	and I will quickly announce the answer to you
355	which the good man thinks to give back to me.'
	He then turned quickly to where Hrothgar sat,
	old and very grey, with his company of warriors.
	The man famed for courage went so that he stood before the shoulder
	of the lord of the Danes: he knew the custom of court.
360	Wulfgar spoke formally to his friend and lord:

---

5 i.e. Hrothgar.

6 The Scyldings, and variant forms of this, are the Danes.

'Her syndon geferede,　feorran cumene
ofer geofenes begang　Geata leode;
þone yldestan　oretmecgas
Beowulf nemnað;　hy benan synt
365　þæt hie, þeoden min,　wið þe moton
wordum wrixlan.　No ðu him wearne geteoh
ðinra gegncwida,　glædman Hroðgar:
hy on wiggetawum　wyrðe þinceað
eorla geæhtlan;　huru se aldor deah,
370　se þæm heaðorincum　hider wisade.'

VI

Hroðgar maþelode,　helm Scyldinga:
'Ic hine cuðe　cnihtwesende;
wæs his ealdfæder　Ecgþeo haten,
ðæm to ham forgeaf　Hreþel Geata
375　angan dohtor.　Is his eafora nu
heard her cumen,　sohte holdne wine.
Ðonne sægdon þæt　sæliþende,
þa ðe gifsceattas　Geata fyredon
þyder to þance,　þæt he þritiges
380　manna mægencræft　on his mundgripe
heaþorof hæbbe.　Hine halig God[7]
for arstafum　us onsende,
to West-Denum,　þæs Ic wen hæbbe,
wið Grendles gryre.　Ic þæm godan sceal
385　for his modþræce　madmas beodan.
Beo ðu on ofeste,　hat in gan
seon sibbegedriht　samod ætgædere;
gesaga him eac wordum　þæt hie sint wilcuman
Deniga leodum.'
390　　　　　　　Word inne abead:
'Eow het secgan　sigedrihten min,
aldor East-Dena,　þæt he eower æþelu can,
ond ge him syndon　ofer sæwylmas
heardhicgende　hider wilcuman.
395　Nu ge moton gangan　in eowrum guðgetawum
under heregriman　Hroðgar geseon;
lætað hildebord　her onbidan
wudu wælsceaftas　worda geþinges.'
　　　Aras þa se rica,　ymb hine rinc manig,
400　þryðlic þegna heap;　sume þær bidon
heaðoreaf heoldon,　swa him se hearda bebead.
Snyredon ætsomne,　þa secg wisode
under Heorotes hrof
heard under helme,　þæt he on heoðe gestod.
405　Beowulf maðelode　– on him byrne scan,
searonet seowed　smiþes orþancum:

7　None of the words for God (Lord, Ruler, etc.) is capitalized in the manuscript. By choosing to capitalize the noun in modern editing, the editor is implying that the noun represents the Christian God. Readers should be aware that it is equally possible in the case of these particular nouns that the poet is merely being monotheistic, indicating some higher being, and not referring specifically to the Christian deity.

'Here they are brought, arrived from afar
over the expanse of the sea from the people of the Geats;
the leader of the warriors
is called Beowulf; they are petitioners,
365   my lord, that they might be allowed to
exchange words with you. Do not bestow on them the refusal
of your answer, gracious Hrothgar:
they seem worthy in their war-equipment
of the respect of men; indeed the leader is mighty,
370   he who has led the warriors here.'

VI

Hrothgar, protector of the Scyldings, spoke:
'I knew him as a boy;
his late father was called Ecgtheow,
to whom Hrethel of the Geats gave in marriage
375   his only daughter. This is his son now,
who has come here bold, sought out a true friend.
Furthermore it was said by seafarers,
those who carried a gift of treasure from the Geats
to this place in thanks, that he had the strength
380   of thirty men in his handgrip,
brave in battle. Holy God,
as a sign of grace, has sent him to us,
to the West-Danes, as I might have hope,
against the terror of Grendel. To that good man
385   I shall offer treasures for his daring.
Be hasty, command that band of kinsmen
to come in all together for me to see;
tell them also in as many words that they are welcome
among the Danish people.'
390   Then he announced these words from inside:
'My victorious lord, the chief of the East-Danes,
commands me to tell you that he knows your noble descent,
and you are welcome to him here,
brave-minded ones from over the surging of the sea.
395   Now you may go in your battlegear,
under your masked helmets, to see Hrothgar;
leave the shields and wooden deadly shafts
to await the outcome of the speeches here.'
The leader rose up, around him were many men,
400   a mighty band of thanes; some stayed there
to guard the battlegear, just as the bold one ordered them.
They hastened together, the man guided them
under Heorot's roof,
brave under helmet, until he stood in the hall.
405   Beowulf spoke – his corslet shone,
the mail-coat linked by the skill of a smith:

'Wæs þu, Hroðgar, hal!   Ic eom Higelaces
mæg ond magoðegn.   Hæbbe Ic mærða fela
ongunnen on geogoþe.   Me wearð Grendles þing
410   on minre eþeltyrf   undyrne cuð;
secgað sæliðend   þæt þæs sele stande,
reced selesta,   rinca gehwylcum
idel ond unnyt   siððan æfenleoht
under heofenes hador   beholen weorþeð.
415   Þa me þæt gelærdon   leode mine,
þa selestan   snotere ceorlas,
þeoden Hroðgar,   þæt Ic þe sohte,
forþan hie mægenes cræft   minne cuþon;
selfe ofersawon   ða Ic of searwum cwom,
420   fah from feondum,   þær Ic fife geband,
yðde eotena cyn,   ond on yðum slog
niceras nihtes,   nearoþearfe dreah,
wræc Wedera nið   (wean ahsodon),
forgrand gramum;   ond nu wið Grendel sceal,
425   wið þam aglæcan,   ana gehegan
ðing wið þyrse.   Ic þe nu ða,
brego Beorht-Dena,   biddan wille,
eodor Scyldinga,   anre bene:
þæt ðu me ne forwyrne,   wigendra hleo,
430   freowine folca,   nu Ic þus feorran com,
þæt Ic mote ana,   ond minra eorla gedryht,
þes hearda heap,   Heorot fælsian.
Hæbbe Ic eac geahsod   þæt se æglæca
for his wonhydum   wæpna ne recceð.
435   Ic þæt þonne forhicge,   swa me Higelac sie,
min mondrihten,   modes bliðe,
þæt Ic sweord bere   oþðe sidne scyld,
geolorand to guþe;   ac Ic mid grape sceal
fon wið feonde   ond ymb feorh sacan,
440   lað wið laþum;   ðær gelyfan sceal
Dryhtnes dome   se þe hine dead nimeð.
Wen Ic þæt he wille,   gif he wealdan mot
in þæm guðsele,   Geotena leode
etan unforhte,   swa he oft dyde,
445   mægen hreðmanna.   Na þu minne þearft
hafalan hydan,   ac he me habban wile
dreore fahne,   gif mec dead nimeð;
byreð blodig wæl,   byrgean þenceð,
eteð angenga   unmurnlice,
450   mearcað morhopu;   no ðu ymb mines ne þearft
lices feorme   leng sorgian.
Onsend Higelace,   gif mec hild nime,
beaduscruda betst   þæt mine breost wereð,
hrægla selest;   þæt is Hrædlan laf,
455   Welandes geweorc.   Gæð a wyrd swa hio scel.'

'Hail to you, Hrothgar! I am Hygelac's
kinsman and young thane. I have undertaken many glorious
deeds in my youth. The matter of Grendel

410   became openly known to me in my native land;
the seafarers say that this hall stands,
the best of buildings, empty and useless
to every warrior once the evening light
has become hidden under the vault of heaven.

415   Then my people advised me,
the best of the wise men,
Prince Hrothgar, that I should seek you out,
because they knew my power of strength;
they themselves looked on when I came from battle,

420   bloodstained from enemies, where I bound five,
destroyed a race of giants, and killed in the waves
water monsters at night, suffered dire hardship,
avenged the persecution of the Geats (they asked for trouble),
crushed the hostile ones; and now with Grendel

425   I shall a hold a meeting, alone
with that monster. So now
I want to request from you, lord of the Bright-Danes,
protector of the Scyldings, one favour:
that you do not refuse me, protector of warriors,

430   noble friend of the people, now that I have come this far,
that I alone, with my company of nobles,
this bold troop of men, might cleanse Heorot.
    I have also learned that the fierce monster
out of recklessness does not care for weapons.

435   So that Hygelac, my liege lord,
will be joyful in mind, I will then scorn
to carry a sword or broad shield,
a yellow shield, to battle; but with my grip
I shall grapple against the enemy and contend about life,

440   foe against foe; there one must trust
in God's judgement, he whom death takes.
I expect that he intends, if he is allowed to prevail
in that battle-hall, to devour fearlessly
the people of the Geats, as he often has done,

445   the might of glorious warriors. Nor will you need
to cover my head, for he will want to have me,
stained with dripping blood, if death takes me;
he will carry off the bloody corpse, intending to taste it,
the one who goes alone will eat ruthlessly,

450   staining his retreat in the moor; nor will you have need
to worry any longer about the sustenance of my body.
If battle takes me, send to Hygelac
the best of battle-gear that defends my breast,
the best of garments; it is Hrethel's heirloom,

455   the work of Weland.[8] Fate must always go as it will.'

---

8   The legendary Germanic smith referred to in *Deor*.

VII

Hroðgar maþelode,   helm Scyldinga:
'For gewyrhtum þu,   wine min Beowulf,
ond for arstafum   usic sohtest.
Gesloh þin fæder   fæhðe mæste,
460   wearþ he Heaþolafe   to handbonan
mid Wilfingum;   ða hine Wedera cyn
for herebrogan   habban ne mihte.
Þanon he gesohte   Suð-Dena folc
ofer yða gewealc,   Ar-Scyldinga.
465   Ða Ic furþum weold   folce Deniga
ond on geogoðe heold   gimme rice,
hordburh hæleþa;   ða wæs Heregar dead,
min yldra mæg   unlifigende,
bearn Healfdenes.   Se wæs betera ðonne Ic.
470   Siððan þa fæhðe   feo þingode –
sende Ic Wylfingum   ofer wæteres hrycg,
ealde madmas;   he me aþas swor.
Sorh is me to secganne   on sefan minum
gumena ængum   hwæt me Grendel hafað
475   hynðo on Heorote   mid his heteþancum,
færniða gefremed;   is min fletwerod,
wigheap gewanod;   hie wyrd forsweop
on Grendles gryre.   God eaþe mæg
þone dolsceaðan   dæda getwæfan.
480   Ful oft gebeotedon   beore druncne
ofer ealowæge   oretmecgas
þæt hie in beorsele   bidan woldon
Grendles guþe   mid gryrum ecga.
Ðonne wæs þeos medoheal   on morgentid
485   drihtsele dreorfah   þonne dæg lixte,
eal bencþelu   blode bestymed,
heall heorudreore.   Ahte Ic holdra þy læs,
deorre duguðe   þe þa deað fornam.
Site nu to symle,   ond on sæl meoto
490   sigehreð secgum,   swa þin sefa hwette.'
    Þa wæs Geatmæcgum   geador ætsomne
on beorsele   benc gerymed;
þær swiðferhþe   sittan eodon,
þryðum dealle.   Þegn nytte beheold,
495   se þe on handa bær   hroden ealowæge,
scencte scir wered;   scop hwilum sang
hador on Heorote;   þær wæs hæleða dream,
duguð unlytel   Dena ond Wedera.

VIII

Unferð maþelode,   Ecglafes bearn,
500   þe æt fotum sæt   frean Scyldinga,
onband beadurune: wæs him Beowulfes sið,
modges merefaran,   micel æfþunca,
forþon þe he ne uþe   þæt ænig oðer man

VII

Hrothgar spoke, protector of the Scyldings:
'In return for past deeds, my friend Beowulf,
and for kindnesses you have sought us.
Your father began the greatest of feuds when he struck that blow,
460   when he killed Heatholaf with his own hand
among the Wylfings; then the people of the Geats
could not keep him because of the fear of war.
From there he went to the South-Danish people,
the Honour-Scyldings, over the rolling waves.
465   Then I first ruled the Danish people
and in my youth held the precious kingdom,⁹
the rich stronghold of warriors; then Heorogar¹⁰ was dead,
my elder kinsman no longer living,
son of Healfdane. He was better than I.
470   Afterwards I settled the feud with money –
I sent to the Wylfings over the crest of the water
ancient treasures; he swore oaths to me.
It is sorrowful for me to say in my heart
to any man what Grendel has done to me
475   in his humiliations on Heorot with his thoughts of hate,
his sudden attacks; my hall-troop,
the band of warriors, has waned; fate swept them off
in the horror of Grendel. God can easily
hinder the deeds of the wild ravager.
480   Very often warriors, drunk with beer,
vowed over the ale-cups
that in the beer-hall they intended to wait for
Grendel's attack with the ferocity of swords.
Then in the morning, this mead-hall,
485   the noble hall, was bloodstained when day shone forth,
all the bench-planks were drenched with blood,
the hall with blood of battle. I had the fewer loyal men,
dear experienced warriors, since death took those away.
Sit now to feast, and in due time attend
490   to the glory of victory to men, just as your heart urges.'
    Then for the men of the Geats all together
a bench in the beer-hall was cleared;
there the stout-hearted ones went to sit,
proud in their strength. A thane performed his duty,
495   he who in his hands carried the ornate ale-cups,
and poured out the bright sweet drink; at times the scop sang
clearly in Heorot; there was the joy of heroes,
no small body of Danish and Geatish retainers.

VIII

Hunferth spoke, Ecglaf's son,
500   who sat at the feet of the lord of the Scyldings,
unbound a secret hostility: the undertaking of Beowulf,
the courageous seafarer, was a great cause of displeasure to him,
because he would not allow that any other man on earth

---

9   i.e. the country's treasury.   10   Elder brother of Hrothgar, and king before him.

æfre mærða þon ma   middangeardes,
505 gehedde under heofenum,   þonne he sylfa:
'Eart þu se Beowulf   se þe wið Brecan wunne,
on sidne sæ   ymb sund flite?
Ðær git for wlence   wada cunnedon,
ond for dolgilpe   on deop wæter
510 aldrum neþdon;   ne inc ænig mon,
ne leof ne lað,   belean mihte
sorhfullne sið   þa git on sund reon.
Þær git eagorstream   earmum þehton,
mæton merestræta,   mundum brugdon,
515 glidon ofer garsecg.   Geofon yþum weol,
wintrys wylmum;   git on wæteres æht
seofon niht swuncon.   He þe æt sunde oferflat,
hæfde mare mægen.   Þa hine on morgentid
on Heaþo-Ræmas   holm up ætbær;
520 ðonon he gesohte   swæsne eþel,
leof his leodum,   lond Brondinga,
freoðoburh fægere,   þær he folc ahte,
burh ond beagas.   Beot eal wið þe
sunu Beanstanes   soðe gelæste.
525 Ðonne wene Ic to þe   wyrsan geþingea,
ðeah þu heaðoræsa   gehwær dohte
grimre guðe,   gif þu Grendles dearst
nihtlongne fyrst   nean bidan.'
Beowulf maþelode,   bearn Ecgþeowes:
530 'Hwæt, þu worn fela,   wine min Unferð,
beore druncen   ymb Brecan spræce,
sægdest from his siðe.   Soð Ic talige
þæt Ic merestrengo   maran ahte,
earfeþo on yþum,   ðonne ænig oþer man.
535 Wit þæt gecwædon   cnihtwesende
ond gebeotedon   (wæron begen þa git
on geogoðfeore)   þæt wit on garsecg ut
aldrum neðdon,   ond þæt geæfndon swa.
Hæfdon swurd nacod   þa wit on sund reon,
540 heard on handa;   wit unc wið hronfixas
werian þohton;   no he wiht fram me
flodyþum feor   fleotan meahte,
hraþor on holme;   no Ic fram him wolde.
Ða wit ætsomne   on sæ wæron
545 fif nihta fyrst   oþþæt unc flod todraf:
wado weallende,   wedera cealdost,
nipende niht,   ond norþanwind
heaðogrim ondhwearf;   hreo wæron yþa.
Wæs merefixa   mod onhrered:
550 þær me wið laðum   licsyrce min,
heard hondlocen,   helpe gefremede,
beadohrægl broden   on breostum læg
golde gegyrwed.   Me to grunde teah
fah feondscaða,   fæste hæfde

beneath the heavens, could ever care more about
505 glorious deeds than he himself did:
'Are you that Beowulf who struggled against Breca,
who competed at swimming in the open sea?
There, for pride, you two tackled the waters,
and because of a foolish boast ventured your lives
510 in the deep water; nor could any man,
neither dear nor hostile to you, dissuade you two
from the dangerous venture when you both rowed into the sea.
There you two embraced the sea-current with your arms,
traversed the seaways, moved quickly with your hands,
515 glided over the ocean. The sea surged in waves,
in the swellings of winter; you two toiled for seven nights
in the possession of the water. He overcame you at swimming,
he had the greater strength. Then in the morning
the sea carried him up to the Heaþo-Reames;[11]
520 from there he went to his own beloved native land,
dear to his people, the land of the Brondings,
a beautiful stronghold, where he possessed people,
a stronghold, and rings. All of that vow against you
this son of Beanstan faithfully fulfilled.
525 Therefore I expect of you a worse outcome,
though in the storm of battle and grim war
you have prevailed everywhere, if you dare
to wait nearby for Grendel for the duration of a night's length.'
Beowulf spoke, the son of Ecgtheow:
530 'Indeed my friend Hunferth, drunk with beer as you are,
you speak a great deal about Breca,
you talk about his ventures. The truth I maintain
is that I possessed the greater strength in the sea,
in the hard struggles in the waves, than any other man.
535 We two agreed as youths
and vowed (we were both then still
in our youth) that we would venture our lives
out in the ocean, and we did just that.
We had unsheathed swords when we rowed in the sea,
540 secure in our hands; we both thought to protect ourselves
against whales; nor was he able to float
far from me at all in the sea-waves,
or more quickly in the sea; nor did I want to go away from him.
Then we two were in the sea together
545 for the duration of five nights until the sea drove us apart:
the surging waters, the coldest of weather,
the night growing dark, and the north wind,
turned against us, battle-grim; the waves were fierce.
The ocean fish was roused to anger:
550 there against the hostile ones my body-armour,
hard, hand-linked, provided help to me,
the woven mail-shirt lay on my breast
adorned with gold. A hostile, destructive foe
dragged me to the bottom, held me secure

11 A people living in south-east Norway.

555   grim on grape;   hwæþre me gyfeþe wearð
        þæt Ic aglæcan   orde geræhte
        hildebille;   heaþoræs fornam
        mihtig meredeor   þurh mine hand.

VIIII

        Swa mec gelome   laðgeteonan
560   þreatedon þearle;   Ic him þenode
        deoran sweorde,   swa hit gedefe wæs.
        Næs hie ðære fylle   gefean hæfdon,
        manfordædlan,   þæt hie me þegon,
        symbel ymbsæton   sægrunde neah;
565   ac on mergenne   mecum wunde
        be yðlafe   uppe lægon,
        sweordum aswefede,   þæt syðþan na
        ymb brontne ford   brimliðende
        lade ne letton.   Leoht eastan com,
570   beorht beacen Godes;   brimu swaþredon,
        þæt Ic sænæssas   geseon mihte,
        windige weallas.   Wyrd oft nereð
        unfægne eorl   þonne his ellen deah.
        Hwæþere me gesælde   þæt Ic mid sweorde ofsloh
575   niceras nigene.   No Ic on niht gefrægn
        under heofones hwealf   heardran feohtan,
        ne on egstreamum   earmran mannon;
        hwaþere Ic fara feng   feore gedigde,
        siþes werig.   Ða mec sæ oþbær,
580   flod æfter faroðe   on Finna land,
        wudu weallendu.   No Ic wiht fram þe
        swylcra searoniða   secgan hyrde,
        billa brogan.   Breca næfre git
        æt heaðolace,   ne gehwæþer incer,
585   swa deorlice   dæd gefremede
        fagum sweordum,   no Ic þæs fela gylpe,
        þeah ðu þinum broðrum   to banan wurde,
        heafodmægum;   þæs þu in helle scealt
        werhðo dreogan,   þeah þin wit duge.
590   Secge Ic þe to soðe,   sunu Ecglafes,
        þæt næfre Grendel swa fela   gryra gefremede,
        atol æglæca,   ealdre þinum,
        hynðo on Heorote,   gif þin hige wære,
        sefa swa searogrim   swa þu self talast;
595   ac he hafað onfunden   þæt he þa fæhðe ne þearf
        atole ecgþræce   eower leode
        swiðe onsittan   Sige-Scyldinga.
        Nymeð nydbade;   nænegum arað
        leode Deniga,   ac he lust wigeð,
600   swefeð ond sendeþ,   secce ne weneþ
        to Gar-Denum.   Ac Ic him Geata sceal
        eafoð ond ellen   ungeara nu
        guþe gebeodan.   Gæþ eft se þe mot
        to medo modig,   siþþan morgenleoht
605   ofer ylda bearn   oþres dogores,

555   and hard in its grip; however it was granted to me
that I hit the fierce assailant with the point
of my battle-sword; the storm of battle destroyed
the mighty sea-beast through my hand.

VIIII

Thus, often, hateful ravagers
560   severely harassed me; I served them
with an excellent sword, as it was fitting.
They did not have a feast of joy there,
the wicked destroyers, such that they could consume me,
sat round in a feast near the sea-bed;
565   but in the morning wounded with swords
they lay above the shoreline, dead,
killed with the sword, so that afterwards
they never hindered the passage of seafarers
across the high sea. Light came from the east,
570   the bright beacon of God; the waters grew calm,
so that I was able to see the headlands,
the windy cliffs. Fate often saves
the man who is not doomed to die when his courage is good.
Nevertheless, it happened to me that with the sword I killed
575   nine water monsters. I have not heard during an evening
under the vault of heaven of a harder fight,
nor of a more wretched man in the sea-streams;
however, I survived the grasp of foes with my life,
weary from the venture. Then the sea carried me off,
580   the sea with its current, the tossing ship,
onto the land of the Lapps. I have not heard anything about you
recounted concerning such skilful contests,
the terror of swords. Breca never yet
at the sport of battle, or either of you two,
585   accomplished such bold deeds
with shining swords, nor do I boast much of it,
though you proved to be the slayer of your brother,
your chief kinsman; for that in hell you will
suffer damnation, though your wit may be good.
590   In truth I say to you, son of Ecglaf,
that Grendel, that terrible monster, would never have accomplished
so much horror against your leader,
such humiliations in Heorot, if your resolve and spirit
were as fierce in battle as you maintain;
595   but he has discovered that he need fear no feud,
no terrible storm of swords, from your people,
the Victory-Scyldings.
He takes an enforced toll; he shows mercy to none
of the Danish people, but he gets pleasure,
600   he kills and dispatches, he expects no struggle
from the Spear-Danes. But I intend to show him
the strength and courage of the Geats in battle
soon now. He who wants to will go once more,
high-spirited, to mead, when the morning light
605   of another day shines from the south,

sunne sweglwered   suþan scineð.'
      Þa wæs on salum   sinces brytta,
gamolfeax ond guðrof;   geoce gelyfde
brego Beorht-Dena;   gehyrde on Beowulfe

610 folces hyrde   fæstrædne geþoht.
Ðær wæs hæleþa hleahtor;   hlyn swynsode,
word wæron wynsume.   Eode Wealhþeow forð,
cwen Hroðgares,   cynna gemyndig:
grette goldhroden   guman on healle,

615 ond þa freolic wif   ful gesealde
ærest East-Dena   eþelwearde,
bæd hine bliðne   æt þære beorþege,
leodum leofne.   He on lust geþeah
symbel ond seleful,   sigerof kyning.

620 Ymbeode þa   ides Helminga
duguþe ond geogoþe   dæl æghwylcne,
sincfato sealde,   oþþæt sæl alamp
þæt hio Beowulfe,   beaghroden cwen,
mode geþungen,   medoful ætbær.

625 Grette Geata leod,   Gode þancode
wisfæst wordum   þæs ðe hire se willa gelamp,
þæt heo on ænigne   eorl gelyfde
fyrena frofre.   He þæt ful geþeah,
wælreow wiga,   æt Wealhþeon,

630 ond þa gyddode   guþe gefysed,
Beowulf maþelode,   bearn Ecgþeowes:
      'Ic þæt hogode   þa Ic on holm gestah,
sæbat gesæt   mid minra secga gedriht,
þæt Ic anunga   eowra leoda

635 willan geworhte,   oþðe on wæl crunge
feondgrapum fæst.   Ic gefremman sceal
eorlic ellen,   oþðe endedæg
on þisse meoduhealle   minne gebidan.'
Ðam wife þa word   wel licodon,

640 gilpcwide Geates.   Eode goldhroden
freolicu folc-cwen   to hire frean sittan.
      Þa wæs eft swa ær   inne on healle
þryðword sprecen,   ðeod on sælum,
sigefolca sweg,   oþþæt semninga

645 sunu Healfdenes   secean wolde
æfenræste;   wiste þæm ahlæcan
to þæm heahsele   hilde geþinged
siððan hie sunnan leoht   geseon meahton
oþðe nipende   niht ofer ealle,

650 scaduhelma gesceapu   scriðan cwoman
wan under wolcnum.   Werod eall aras.
Gegrette þa   guma oþerne,
Hroðgar Beowulf,   ond him hæl abead,
winærnes geweald,   ond þæt word acwæð:

655 'Næfre Ic ænegum men   ær alyfde,
siþðan Ic hond ond rond   hebban mihte,
ðryþærn Dena   buton þe nu ða.
Hafa nu ond geheald   husa selest:

from the sun clad in its radiance, over the children of men.'
    Then the bestower of treasure was joyful,
grey-haired and brave in war; the leader of the Bright-Danes
counted on this help; the protector of the people
heard from Beowulf of his firmly resolved intent.
There was the laughter of heroes; a din rang out,
words were joyful. Wealhtheow went forwards,
Hrothgar's queen, mindful of courtesy:
gold-adorned, she greeted the men in the hall,
and the noble woman gave a cup
first to the guardian of the native land of the East-Danes,
enjoined him to be joyful at the beer-drinking,
dear to the people. He partook with pleasure
in the feast and the hall-cup, a victorious king.
The lady of the Helmings then went around
the experienced warriors and the youth in each section,
offered costly vessels, until the time came
that the ring-adorned queen, excellent in mind,
carried the mead-cup to Beowulf.
She greeted the man of the Geats, thanked God
with wise words for the fact that her wish had been fulfilled,
that she could count on some warrior for
relief from wicked deeds. He received that cup
from Wealhtheow, a warrior fierce in war,
eager for the battle, and then he spoke,
Beowulf, the son of Ecgtheow, made a formal speech:
    'I resolved when I set out to sea,
sat in the sea-vessel with my company of men,
that I would fulfil completely the wish
of your people, or fall in the slaughter
held fast in the enemy's grasp. I shall accomplish
an heroic deed of courage, or else experience
my last day in this mead-hall.'
Those words were pleasing to the woman,
the vaunting speech of the Geat. She went, gold-adorned,
a noble queen of the people, to sit by her lord.
    Then again, just as before, within the hall
brave words were spoken, people in happiness,
the sound of victorious people, until soon
the son of Healfdane wanted to go to
his night's rest; he knew that a battle had been planned
by the monster in the lofty hall
from the time when they had been able to see the sun's light
until the night grew dark over all,
and shapes under concealing shadows came stalking
dark under the clouds. The company of men arose.
Hrothgar saluted the other man, Beowulf, then,
and wished him luck,
the mastery of the wine-hall, and he spoke these words:
    'I have never entrusted to any man before,
since I could lift my hand and shield,
this mighty house of the Danes except to you now.
Have and hold this best of houses now:

610

615

620

625

630

635

640

645

650

655

gemyne mærþo,   mægen-ellen cyð,
660   waca wið wraþum.   Ne bið þe wilna gad
gif þu þæt ellenweorc   aldre gedigest.'

X

Ða him Hroþgar gewat   mid his hæleþa gedryht,
eodur Scyldinga   ut of healle;
wolde wigfruma   Wealhþeo secan
665   cwen to gebeddan.   Hæfde Kyning-wuldor
Grendle togeanes,   swa guman gefrungon,
seleweard aseted;   sundornytte beheold
ymb aldor Dena,   eotonweard abead.
Huru Geata leod   georne truwode
670   modgan mægnes,   Metodes hyldo.
Ða he him of dyde   isernbyrnan,
helm of hafelan,   sealde his hyrsted sweord
irena cyst   ombihtþegne,
ond gehealdan het   hildegeatwe.
675   Gespræc þa se goda   gylpworda sum,
Beowulf Geata,   ær he on bed stige:
'No Ic me an herewæsmun   hnagran talige
guþgeweorca   þonne Grendel hine;
forþan Ic hine sweorde   swebban nelle,
680   aldre beneotan,   þeah Ic eal mæge.
Nat he þara goda,   þæt he me ongean slea,
rand geheawe,   þeah ðe he rof sie
niþgeweorca;   ac wit on niht sculon
secge ofersittan,   gif he gesecean dear
685   wig ofer wæpen,   ond siþðan witig God
on swa hwæþere hond,   halig Dryhten,
mærðo deme,   swa him gemet þince.'
Hylde hine þa heaþodeor;   hleorbolster onfeng
eorles andwlitan,   ond hine ymb monig
690   snellic særinc   selereste gebeah.
Nænig heora þohte   þæt he þanon scolde
eft eardlufan   æfre gesecean,
folc oþðe freoburh   þær he afeded wæs;
ac hie hæfdon gefrunen   þæt hie ær to fela micles
695   in þæm winsele   wældeað fornam,
Denigea leode.   Ac him Dryhten forgeaf
wigspeda gewiofu,   Wedera leodum,
frofor ond fultum,   þæt hie feond heora
ðurh anes cræft   ealle ofercomon,
700   selfes mihtum.   Soð is gecyþed,
þæt mihtig God   manna cynnes
weold wideferhð.   Com on wanre niht
scriðan sceadugenga.   Sceotend swæfon,
þa þæt hornreced   healdan scoldon,
705   ealle buton anum.   Þæt wæs yldum cuþ
þæt hie ne moste,   þa Metod nolde,
se scynscaþa   under sceadu bregdan;

think of glory, reveal your mighty valour,
660   be watchful against enemies. Nor will you lack good things
if you survive this task of courage with your life.'

X

Then Hrothgar departed with his company of men,
the protector of the Scyldings went out of the hall;
the war-leader wanted to go to Wealhtheow
665   as a bed-fellow to the queen. The King of glory,[12]
as men heard, had appointed a hall-guardian
against Grendel; he fulfilled a special task
for the lord of the Danes, offered a guard against the giant.
Indeed, the Geatish man firmly trusted
670   in his brave strength, the favour of the Creator.
    Then he took off his iron mail-coat,
and the helmet from his head, gave his decorated sword
of the best iron to an attendant thane,
and commanded him to guard the war-equipment.
675   The good man, Beowulf of the Geats,
uttered some vaunting words before he climbed into bed:
'I do not consider myself in warlike stature and in battle-deeds
any poorer than Grendel himself;
therefore I do not wish to kill him with a sword,
680   to deprive him of life so, though I easily could do that.
He does not know the skills, inasmuch as he might strike against me,
cut through a shield, even though he may be strong
in hostile deeds; but tonight we two shall
forgo the sword, if he dares to seek
685   battle without a weapon, and afterwards, the wise God
the holy Lord, will judge glory
on whichever side, as it seems fitting to him.'
    Then the man brave in battle lay down; the pillow
received the face of the warrior, and around him many
690   brave seamen lay down on beds in the hall.
None of them thought that he would ever
reach his beloved homeland again,
his people and noble stronghold where he was brought up;
but they had learned that far too many before them
695   had been carried off in slaughter from that wine-hall,
from among the Danish people. But the Lord granted to them,
the people of the Geats, the fortune of success in war,
comfort and aid, so that they entirely overcame
their enemy through the power of one man,
700   and his own might. The truth is well known,
that mighty God rules the race of men
for ever. In the dark night came
stalking a walker in shadows. The warriors slept,
those who had to guard the gabled hall,
705   all except one. It was known to men
that the demonic ravager could not,
when the Creator did not wish it, drag them under the shadows;

---

12   This may also refer to 'the glorious king'; i.e. Hrothgar.

ac he wæccende　　wraþum on andan,
bad bolgenmod　　beadwa geþinges.

XI

710　Ða com of more　　under misthleoþum
Grendel gongan.　　Godes yrre bær.
Mynte se manscaða　　manna cynnes
sumne besyrwan　　in sele þam hean.
Wod under wolcnum　　to þæs þe he winreced,
715　goldsele gumena　　gearwost wisse,
fættum fahne.　　Ne wæs þæt forma sið
þæt he Hroþgares　　ham gesohte;
næfre he on aldordagum,　　ær ne siþðan,
heardran hæle　　healðegnas fand.
720　　　Com þa to recede　　rinc siðian,
dreamum bedæled.　　Duru sona onarn,
fyrbendum fæst,　　syþðan he hire folmum gehran.
Onbræd þa bealohydig,　　ða he gebolgen wæs,
recedes muþan.　　Raþe æfter þon
725　on fagne flor　　feond treddode,
eode yrre-mod;　　him of eagum stod
ligge gelicost　　leoht unfæger.
Geseah he in recede　　rinca manige,
swefan sibbegedriht　　samod ætgædere,
730　magorinca heap.　　Þa his mod ahlog;
mynte þæt he gedælde,　　ærþon dæg cwome,
atol aglæca,　　anra gehwylces
lif wið lice　　þa him alumpen wæs
wistfylle wen.　　Ne wæs þæt wyrd þa gen
735　þæt he ma moste　　manna cynnes
ðicgean ofer þa niht.　　Þryðswyð beheold
mæg Higelaces　　hu se manscaða
under færgripum　　gefaran wolde.
Ne þæt se aglæca　　yldan þohte,
740　ac he gefeng hraðe　　forman siðe
slæpendne rinc,　　slat unwearnum,
bat banlocan,　　blod edrum dranc,
synsnædum swealh;　　sona hæfde
unlyfigendes　　eal gefeormod,
745　fet ond folma.　　Forð near ætstop,
nam þa mid handa　　higeþihtigne,
rinc on ræste,　　ræhte ongean
feond mid folme;　　he onfeng hraþe
inwitþancum　　ond wið earm gesæt.
750　Sona þæt onfunde　　fyrena hyrde
þæt he ne mette　　middangeardes,
eorþan sceata,　　on elran men
mundgripe maran.　　He on mode wearð
forht on ferhðe;　　no þy ær fram meahte.
755　Hyge wæs him hinfus,　　wolde on heolster fleon
secan deofla gedræg;　　ne wæs his drohtoð þær
swylce he on ealderdagum　　ær gemette.
　　Gemunde þa se goda　　mæg Higelaces,

but he, watching, hostile in anger,
enraged awaited the outcome of battle.

XI

710 Then from the moor under the misty slopes came
Grendel advancing. He bore God's anger.
The evil ravager intended to ensnare one
of the race of men in that lofty hall.
He advanced under the clouds to where he most clearly recognized
715 the wine-hall, the gold-hall of men,
gleaming with gold plating. Nor was that the first time
that he had come to Hrothgar's home;
never in the days of his life, before or after,
did he meet hall-thanes with worse fortune.
720   He came then to the hall, a warrior making his way,
deprived of joys. The door sprang open,
the secure forged bars, when he touched it with his hands.
He was enraged then, intending destruction,
he pulled open the door of the hall. Quickly after that
725 the enemy stepped on the decorated floor,
he advanced angry at heart; from his eyes gleamed
an ugly light, most like a flame.
He saw many warriors in the hall,
a sleeping band of kinsman all together,
730 a troop of young warriors. Then his spirit laughed;
the terrible monster intended to sever
the life from the body of each one
before day came since the expectation of a lavish feast
had presented itself to him. But it was not fated
735 that he would be permitted to take still more
of the race of men after that night. The mighty kinsman of Hygelac
waited to see how the wicked ravager
would proceed with the sudden grip of attack.
Nor did that fierce assailant intend to delay,
740 but at the first opportunity he quickly seized
a sleeping warrior, tore at him without restraint,
bit into the muscles, drank the blood from the veins,
swallowed the sinful morsels; soon he had
completely consumed the unliving man,
745 feet and hands. Forward nearer he stepped,
seized with his hands the strong-hearted man,
the warrior in bed, the fiend reached out
with his hands; Beowulf quickly seized him
with hostile purpose and sat up, leaning on his arm.
750 At once the master of evil deeds discovered that
he had not encountered in the world,
in the regions of the earth, another man
with a greater hand-grip. He became in his heart
fearful in spirit; none the sooner could he get away.
755 His mind was eager to escape, he wanted to flee into the darkness,
to seek the company of devils; nor was his experience there
such as he had encountered before in the days of his life.
    When the brave kinsman of Hygelac remembered

æfenspræce,   uplang astod

760 ond him fæste wiðfeng;   fingras burston –
eoten wæs utweard –   eorl furþur stop.
Mynte se mæra,   þær he meahte swa,
widre gewindan,   ond on weg þanon
fleon on fenhopu;   wiste his fingra geweald

765 on grames grapum.   Þæt wæs geocor sið
þæt se hearmscaþa   to Heorute ateah!
Dryhtsele dynede;   Denum eallum wearð,
ceasterbuendum,   cenra gehwylcum,
eorlum ealuscerwen.   Yrre wæron begen,

770 reþe renweardas.   Reced hlynsode:
þa wæs wundor micel   þæt se winsele
wiðhæfde heaþodeorum,   þæt he on hrusan ne feol,
fæger foldbold;   ac he þæs fæste wæs
innan ond utan   irenbendum

775 searoþoncum besmiþod.   Þær fram sylle abeag
medubenc monig,   mine gefræge,
golde geregnad,   þær þa graman wunnon.
Þæs ne wendon ær   witan Scyldinga
þæt hit a mid gemete   manna ænig,

780 betlic ond banfag,   tobrecan meahte,
listum tolucan,   nymþe liges fæþm
swulge on swaþule.   Sweg up astag
niwe geneahhe;   Norð-Denum stod
atelic egesa,   anra gehwylcum

785 þara þe of wealle   wop gehyrdon,
gryreleoð galan   Godes ondsacan,
sigeleasne sang,   sar wanigean
helle hæfton.   Heold hine fæste,
se þe manna wæs   mægene strengest

790 on þæm dæge   þysses lifes.

XII

Nolde eorla hleo   ænige þinga
þone cwealmcuman   cwicne forlætan,
ne his lifdagas   leoda ænigum
nytte tealde.   Þær genehost brægd

795 eorl Beowulfes   ealde lafe;
wolde freadrihtnes   feorh ealgian,
mæres þeodnes,   ðær hie meahton swa.
Hie þæt ne wiston   þa hie gewin drugon
heardhicgende   hildemecgas

800 ond on healfa gehwone   heawan þohton
sawle secan,   þone synscaðan
ænig ofer eorþan   irenna cyst,
guðbilla nan,   gretan nolde;
ac he sigewæpnum   forsworen hæfde

805 ecga gehwylcre.   Scolde his aldorgedal
on ðæm dæge   þysses lifes
earmlic wurðan,   ond se ellorgast

the evening's speech, he stood upright
760 and grasped him firmly; fingers cracked –
the giant was trying to escape – the warrior stepped closer.
The infamous one intended, if he was able,
to escape further off, and flee from there on his way
to his fen-retreat; he knew the power of those fingers
765 in the grasp of the hostile man. That was a bitter journey
that the grievous foe undertook to Heorot!
The noble hall resounded; to all of the Danes,
the fortress-dwellers, among each of the brave,
the warriors, there were ale-showers.[13] Both were furious,
770 fierce guardians of the hall. The hall echoed:
it was a great wonder that the wine-hall
withstood those brave in battle, that the beautiful building
did not fall to the ground; but it was so securely
and skilfully forged inside and out
775 with iron bands. Many mead-benches there
were turned over on the floor, as I have heard,
gold-adorned, where the hostile ones fought.
The wise men of the Scyldings did not previously think
that any one of humankind would ever shatter it,
780 by any means, excellent and adorned with bones at it was,
or by cunning destroy it, unless the embrace of fire
swallowed it in flames. Sound rose up
anew often; horrible terror came upon
the North-Danes, on each one of them
785 who heard the wailing from the wall,
God's adversary chanted a song of terror,
a song without victory, the captive of hell
bewailing his wound. He held him firmly,
he who of men was the strongest in strength
790 in those days of this life.

XII

The warriors' protector would not by any means
let the murderous visitor go alive,
nor did any of the people consider his life-days
to be of use. There many of Beowulf's men
795 brandished ancient heirlooms;[14]
they wanted to protect their lord's life,
the renowned prince, if they were able to do so.
These warriors resolute in mind did not know
when they engaged in the conflict
800 and thought to strike on each side
to seek its life, that the evil ravager
could not be touched by any war-sword
or by any of the finest swords on earth;
but he had made weapons of victory, every blade,
805 useless by a spell. His severing from life
in those days of this existence would
needs be miserable, and the alien being

---

13 ale-showers, i.e. terror.

14 i.e. swords passed down from generation to generation.

on feonda geweald   feor siðian.

    Ða þæt onfunde,   se þe fela æror
810   modes myrðe   manna cynne,
fyrene gefremede   – he fag wið God –
þæt him se lichoma   læstan nolde,
ac hine se modega   mæg Hygelaces
hæfde be honda;   wæs gehwæþer oðrum
815   lifigende lað.   Licsar gebad
atol æglæca: him on eaxle wearð
syndolh sweotol,   seonowe onsprungon,
burston banlocan.   Beowulfe wearð
guðhreð gyfeþe;   scolde Grendel þonan
820   feorhseoc fleon   under fenhleoðu
secean wynleas wic;   wiste þe geornor
þæt his aldres wæs   ende gegongen,
dogera dægrim.   Denum eallum wearð
æfter þam wælræse   willa gelumpen:
825   hæfde þa gefælsod   se þe ær feorran com,
snotor ond swyðferhð,   sele Hroðgares,
genered wið niðe;   nihtweorce gefeh,
ellenmærþum.   Hæfde East-Denum
Geatmecga leod   gilp gelæsted,
830   swylce oncyþðe   ealle gebette
inwidsorge   þe hie ær drugon,
ond for þreanydum   þolian scoldon,
torn unlytel.   Þæt wæs tacen sweotol,
syþðan hildedeor   hond alegde,
835   earm ond eaxle   – þær wæs eal geador
Grendles grape –   under geapne hrof.

XIII

Ða wæs on morgen,   mine gefræge,
ymb þa gifhealle   guðrinc monig;
ferdon folctogan   feorran ond nean
840   geond widwegas   wundor sceawian,
laþes lastas.   No his lifgedal
sarlic þuhte   secga ænegum
þara þe tirleases   trode sceawode,
hu he werig-mod   on weg þanon,
845   niða ofercumen,   on nicera mere
fæge ond geflymed   feorhlastas bær.
Ðær wæs on blode   brim weallende,
atol yða geswing   eal gemenged
haton heolfre,   heorodreore weol;
850   deaðfæge deog   siððan dreama leas
in fenfreoðo   feorh alegde
hæþene sawle;   þær him hel onfeng.
    Þanon eft gewiton   ealdgesiðas,
swylce geong manig   of gomenwaþe
855   fram mere modge   mearum ridan,
beornas on blancum.   Ðær wæs Beowulfes
mærðo mæned;   monig oft gecwæð
þætte suð ne norð   be sæm tweonum,

was to make a journey far away into the power of fiends.
    Then he discovered, he who had previously
810 committed many afflictions of the heart, wicked deeds
against mankind – he fought against God –
that his body would not be of service,
but the courageous kinsman of Hygelac
had him in his hands; each was loathsome to the other
815 while living. The terrible fierce assailant
suffered physical pain: in his shoulder was
made visible a mortal wound, sinews sprang apart,
muscles burst. To Beowulf was granted
triumph in battle; Grendel had to flee from there
820 fatally wounded under the fenland slopes
to go to a joyless dwelling; he knew the more surely
that his life had reached its end,
his days were numbered. The desire of the Danes
had been fulfilled after that deadly onslaught:
825 he who had come from far away,
wise and resolute, had cleansed Hrothgar's hall,
saved it from the affliction; he rejoiced in the night's work,
in the heroic deeds. The leader of the Geats
had fulfilled his vow to the East-Danes,
830 he also entirely remedied the grief,
for those who had previously endured evil sorrows,
and been forced to suffer dire distresses,
no small affliction. That was a clear sign,
when the man brave in battle placed the hand,
835 the arm and shoulder – there all together was
Grendel's grasp – under the broad roof.

XIII

Then in the morning, as I have heard,
around the gift-hall were many warriors;
the leaders of the people travelled far and near
840 through the distant regions to look at the wonder,
the tracks of the hostile one. His severing from life
did not seem at all painful to any of the men
who looked at the footprints of the inglorious one,
how he, weary-hearted on the way from there,
845 overcome in battle, bore his life-tracks
into the mere of water-monsters, doomed and put to flight.
There the water was surging with blood,
the terrible swirling of waves all mingled
with hot blood, welled up with battle-gore;
850 the one who was doomed to die when deprived of joy hid,
he laid down his life in the fen-refuge,
heathen soul; there hell received him.
    The old retainers departed again from there,
also many young ones from the joyous journey,
855 rode on their horses from the lake, high-spirited,
heroes on horses. There Beowulf's glory
was related; many often said
that south or north between the seas,

ofer eormengrund   oþer nænig
860   under swegles begong   selra nære
rondhæbbendra,   rices wyrðra;
ne hie huru winedrihten   wiht ne logon,
glædne Hroðgar,   ac þæt wæs god cyning.
Hwilum heaþorofe   hleapan leton,
865   on geflit faran   fealwe mearas
ðær him foldwegas   fægere þuhton
cystum cuðe.   Hwilum cyninges þegn,
guma gilphlæden,   gidda gemyndig,
se ðe ealfela   ealdgesegena
870   worn gemunde,   word oþer fand
soðe gebunden.   Secg eft ongan
sið Beowulfes   snyttrum styrian,
ond on sped wrecan   spel gerade,
wordum wrixlan.   Welhwylc gecwæð
875   þæt he fram Sigemunde   secgan hyrde,
ellendædum,   uncuþes fela,
Wælsinges gewin,   wide siðas,
þara þe gumena bearn   gearwe ne wiston,
fæhðe ond fyrena,   buton Fitela mid hine,
880   þonne he swulces hwæt   secgan wolde,
eam his nefan,   swa hie a wæron
æt niða gehwam   nydgesteallan;
hæfdon ealfela   eotena cynnes
sweordum gesæged.   Sigemunde gesprong
885   æfter deaðdæge   dom unlytel,
syþðan wiges heard   wyrm acwealde,
hordes hyrde.   He under harne stan,
æþelinges bearn,   ana geneðde
frecne dæde,   ne wæs him Fitela mid.
890   Hwæþre him gesælde   ðæt þæt swurd þurhwod
wrætlicne wyrm   þæt hit on wealle ætstod,
dryhtlic iren;   draca morðre swealt.
Hæfde aglæca   elne gegongen
þæt he beahhordes   brucan moste
895   selfes dome;   sæbat gehleod,
bær on bearm scipes   beorhte frætwa,
Wælses eafera.   Wyrm hat gemealt.
Se wæs wreccena   wide mærost
ofer werþeode,   wigendra hleo
900   ellendædum (he þæs ær onðah),
siððan Heremodes   hild sweðrode,
eafoð ond ellen.   He mid Eotenum wearð
on feonda geweald   forð forlacen,
snude forsended.   Hine sorhwylmas
905   lemede to lange.   He his leodum wearð,
eallum æþellingum   to aldorceare;
swylce oft bemearn   ærran mælum

over the spacious earth none other
860   under the expanse of the sky was ever a better
shield-bearer, more worthy of a kingdom;
nor indeed did they find fault with the friend and lord,
gracious Hrothgar, but that was a good king.
At times, those brave in battle were allowed to gallop,
865   to ride in a contest of the bay mares
where the paths seemed attractive to them
and were known for their excellence. At times the king's thane,
a man filled with eloquent speech, recalling stories,
he who could remember a multitude, many
870   traditional tales, devised other words
truly linked. The man began again
to recite Beowulf's exploit with skill,
and to compose a skilful tale with success,
to vary it with words. He recounted everything
875   that he had heard said about Sigemund,
of brave deeds, of many things not known,
of Wælsing's[15] conflict, of far journeys,
of things the children of men did not know fully,
except for Fitela[16] who was with him, of feuds and wicked deeds,
880   when he wanted to say something of such a matter,
as uncle to his nephew, so they were always
comrades at need in every battle;
they had killed with swords very many
of the race of giants. Sigemund's glory
885   spread forth not a little after his death-day,
since, hardened in war, he killed a dragon,
a guardian of treasure. Under a grey stone he,
the son of a prince, alone ventured on
the daring deed, nor was Fitela with him.
890   Nevertheless, it happened to him that the sword pierced through
the wondrous serpent so that it remained fast in the skin,
the lordly sword; the dragon had died by violent assault.
The fierce warrior had brought it about with courage
that he was able to enjoy the treasure-hord
895   at his own choice; he loaded the sea-vessel,
carried bright adornments into the hold of the ship,
this son of Wæls. The serpent had melted away in the heat.
He was the most famous of exiles far and wide
over the nations, the protector of warriors,
900   because of his deeds of courage (he had prospered from that previously),
since Heremod's prowess in battle diminished,
his strength and bravery. He was betrayed, along with the Jutes,
into the power of the enemies,
quickly put to death. Surging sorrows
905   oppressed him for too long. He became to his people,
to all the noblemen, a great anxiety;
also many wise men had often lamented in earlier times

---

15   Wælsing (son of Wæls) is another name for Sigemund, the dragon slayer.

16   Fitela was both Sigemund's son and his nephew in the Old Norse *Volsungasaga*.

swiðferhþes sið   snotor ceorl monig,
se þe him bealwa to   bote gelyfde,
910   þæt þæt ðeodnes bearn   geþeon scolde,
fæderæþelum onfon,   folc gehealdan,
hord ond hleoburh,   hæleþa rice,
eþel Scyldinga.   He þær eallum wearð
mæg Higelaces   manna cynne
915   freondum gefægra;   hine fyren onwod.
Hwilum flitende   fealwe stræte
mearum mæton.   Ða wæs morgenleoht
scofen ond scynded.   Eode scealc monig
swiðhicgende   to sele þam hean
920   searowundor seon;   swylce self cyning
of brydbure,   beahhorda weard,
tryddode tirfæst   getrume micle,
cystum gecyþed,   ond his cwen mid him
medostigge mæt   mægþa hose.

XIIII

925   Hroðgar maþelode,   he to healle geong,
stod on stapole,   geseah steapne hrof
golde fahne,   ond Grendles hond:
'Ðisse ansyne   Alwealdan þanc
lungre gelimpe.   Fela Ic laþes gebad
930   grynna æt Grendle.   A mæg God wyrcan
wunder æfter wundre,   wuldres Hyrde.
Ðæt wæs ungeara   þæt Ic ænigra me
weana ne wende   to widan feore
bote gebidan,   þonne blode fah
935   husa selest   heorodreorig stod,
wea widscofen   witena gehwylcum,
ðara þe ne wendon   þæt hie wideferhð
leoda landgeweorc   laþum beweredon,
scuccum ond scinnum.   Nu scealc hafað
940   þurh Drihtnes miht   dæd gefremede
ðe we ealle   ær ne meahton
snyttrum besyrwan.   Hwæt, þæt secgan mæg
efne swa hwylc mægþa   swa ðone magan cende
æfter gumcynnum,   gyf heo gyt lyfað,
945   þæt hyre Ealdmetod   este wære
bearngebyrdo.   Nu Ic, Beowulf, þec,
secg betsta,   me for sunu wylle
freogan on ferhþe;   heald forð tela
niwe sibbe;   ne bið þe nænigre gad
950   worolde wilna   þe Ic geweald hæbbe.
Ful oft Ic for læssan   lean teohhode,
hordweorþunge   hnahran rince,
sæmran æt sæcce.   Þu þe self hafast
dædum gefremed   þæt þin dom lyfað
955   awa to aldre.   Alwalda þec
gode forgylde,   swa he nu gyt dyde.'

at the way of life of the strong-minded man,[17]
many a man who had counted on him to remedy afflictions,
910 and that this son of a prince should have prospered,
received a father's nobility, protected his people,
the treasure and stronghold, the kingdom of heroes,
the native land of the Scyldings. There
the kinsman of Hygelac became the dearer to friends
915 and to all the race of people; sin entered Heremod's heart.
    At times competing on the sandy road
they travelled on horses. Then the morning light was
advanced and hastened. Many a retainer went
resolute in mind to the hall of the high man
920 to see the curious wonder; also the king himself,
the guardian of the hoard of rings, stepped from the marriage-chamber
glorious with his great troop,
renowned for his good attributes, and his queen with him
crossed the path to the mead-hall with a troop of women.

XIIII

925 Hrothgar spoke, he went to the hall,
stood on the steps, saw the lofty roof
gleaming with gold, and Grendel's hand:
'For this sight thanks to the Ruler of all
should be given at once. I have endured many hateful
930 afflictions from Grendel. God always brings about
wonder after wonder, the Shepherd of glory.
It was only recently that I did not ever expect
myself to live to see a remedy for any of the miseries,
when, stained with blood,
935 the best of houses stood gory from battle,
a widespread misery to each of the wise ones,
of those who did not expect that they would ever
defend the people's stronghold from enemies,
demons and evil spirits. Now a warrior,
940 has carried out the deed through the power of the Lord
which we all could not previously
accomplish with our skills. Indeed, it might be said
that whichever woman gave birth to this son
among the race of men, if she is still living,
945 that the God of old was gracious to her
in child-bearing. Now Beowulf,
the best of men, I will love you as my son
in my heart; I will from now on keep well
the new kinship; nor will you lack any
950 desirable things of the world over which I have control.
Very often I have assigned reward for less,
honouring with gifts a more lowly man,
a weaker one in battle. You yourself have
performed deeds so that your glory will live
955 for ever and ever. The Ruler of all
will reward your goodness, as he even now has done.'

17   i.e. Heremod, a previous Danish king.

Beowulf maþelode,   bearn Ecþeowes:
'We þæt ellenweorc   estum miclum,
feohtan fremedon,   frecne geneðdon
960   eafoð uncuþes.   Uþe Ic swiþor
þæt ðu hine selfne   geseon moste
feond on frætewum   fylwerigne.
Ic hine hrædlice   heardan clammum
on wælbedde   wriþan þohte
965   þæt he for mundgripe   minum scolde
licgean lifbysig,   butan his lic swice.
Ic hine ne mihte,   þa Metod nolde,
ganges getwæman,   no Ic him þæs georne ætfealh,
feorhgeniðlan;   wæs to foremihtig
970   feond on feþe.   Hwæþere he his folme forlet
to lifwraþe   last weardian,
earm ond eaxle.   No þær ænige swa þeah
feasceaft guma   frofre gebohte;
no þy leng leofað   laðgeteona,
975   synnum geswenced,   ac hyne sar hafað
mid nidgripe   nearwe befongen,
balwon bendum;   ðær abidan sceal
maga mane fah   miclan domes,
hu him scir Metod   scrifan wille.'
980   Ða wæs swigra secg,   sunu Eclafes,
on gylpspræce   guðgeweorca,
siþðan æþelingas   eorles cræfte
ofer heanne hrof   hand sceawedon,
feondes fingras;   foran æghwær wæs
985   stedenægla gehwylc   style gelicost,
hæþenes handsporu   hilderinces
eg unheoru.   Æghwylc gecwæð
þæt him heardra nan   hrinan wolde
iren ærgod   þæt ðæs ahlæcan
990   blodge beadufolme   onberan wolde.

XV

Ða wæs haten hreþe   Heort innanweard
folmum gefrætwod;   fela þæra wæs
wera ond wifa   þe þæt winreced
gestsele gyredon.   Goldfag scinon
995   web æfter wagum,   wundorsiona fela
secga gehwylcum   þara þe on swylc starað.
Wæs þæt beorhte bold   tobrocen swiðe,
eal inneweard   irenbendum fæst,
heorras tohlidene;   hrof ana genæs
1000   ealles ansund   þe se aglæca
fyrendædum fag   on fleam gewand,
aldres orwena.   No þæt yðe byð
to befleonne   (fremme se þe wille),
ac gesecan sceal   sawlberendra
1005   nyde genydde   niþða bearna,
grundbuendra   gearwe stowe,
þær his lichoma   legerbedde fæst

Beowulf, the son of Ecgtheow, spoke:
'We carried out that courageous deed,
that fight, with good will, daringly risked against
960   the strength of the unknown. I should have wished rather
that you yourself could have seen
the enemy in trappings wearied to the point of death.
I thought to bind him quickly with
a tight grip upon his death-bed
965   so that he should lie struggling for life
because of my hand-grip, unless his body escaped.
I could not prevent him from going,
the Creator did not wish it, neither could I grasp him firmly enough,
the deadly foe; he was too powerful
970   an enemy in going. However, he left his hand
to remain behind in order to protect his life,
his arm and shoulder. Even so the wretched being
will not have gained any comfort there;
nor will the hateful ravager live the longer,
975   afflicted with sins, for his pain will have
seized him tightly in its inexorable grip,
its deadly fetters; there he must await
the great judgement, a man stained with crime,
how the resplendent Creator will judge him.'
980   Then the man, the son of Ecgtheow was more silent
in vaunting speech of warlike deeds,
after the noblemen looked at the hand,
the strength of the warrior, on the high roof,
the enemy's fingers; at every position of the tip
985   each of the firm nails was most similar to steel,
the heathen warrior's claw
a monstrous spike. Each of the hardy men
said that no sword of proven worth
would touch him or would injure that
990   bloody battle-hand of the fierce assailant.

XV

Then orders were quickly given that Heorot
should be decorated inside by hands; many
men and women prepared that wine-hall
and guest-hall. Tapestries shone,
995   adorned with gold along the walls, a number of wondrous sights
for each person who gazed on them.
That bright building was much damaged,
though it was all secured within by iron bands,
hinges sprang apart; the roof alone survived
1000   wholly unharmed when the fierce assailant
stained with wicked deeds turned in flight,
despairing of his life. Nor was it that easy
to flee (let him try it who will),
but compelled by necessity, he is obliged to seek out
1005   the place prepared for the children of men,
for earth-dwellers having a soul,
where his body held fast in the death-bed

swefeþ æfter symle.   Þa wæs sæl ond mæl
þæt to healle gang   Healfdenes sunu;
1010   wolde self cyning   symbel þicgan.
Ne gefrægen Ic þa mægþe   maran weorode
ymb hyra sincgyfan   sel gebæran.
Bugon þa to bence   blædagande,
fylle gefægon;   fægere geþægon
1015   medoful manig   magas þara
swiðhicgende   on sele þam hean,
Hroðgar ond Hroþulf.   Heorot innan wæs
freondum afylled;   nalles facenstafas
Þeod-Scyldingas   þenden fremedon.
1020   Forgeaf þa Beowulfe   brand Healfdenes,
segen gyldenne   sigores to leane,
hroden hildecumbor,   helm ond byrnan;
mære maðþumsweord   manige gesawon
beforan beorn beran.   Beowulf geþah
1025   ful on flette;   no he þære feohgyfte
for sceotendum   scamigan ðorfte.
Ne gefrægn Ic freondlicor   feower madmas
golde gegyrede   gummanna fela
in ealobence   oðrum gesellan.
1030   Ymb þæs helmes hrof   heafodbeorge
wirum bewunden   wala utan heold,
þæt him fela laf   frecne ne meahton
scurheard sceþðan   þonne scyldfreca
ongean gramum   gangan scolde.
1035   Heht ða eorla hleo   eahta mearas
fætedhleore   on flet teon
in under eoderas;   þara anum stod
sadol searwum fah   since gewurþad.
Þæt wæs hildesetl   heahcyninges,
1040   ðonne sweorda gelac   sunu Healfdenes
efnan wolde;   næfre on ore læg
widcuþes wig   ðonne walu feollon.
Ond ða Beowulfe   bega gehwæþres
eodor Ingwina   onweald geteah,
1045   wicga ond wæpna;   het hine wel brucan.
Swa manlice   mære þeoden,
hordweard hæleþa,   heaþoræsas geald
mearum ond madmum   swa hy næfre man lyhð
se þe secgan wile   soð æfter rihte.

XVI

1050   Ða gyt æghwylcum   eorla drihten
þara þe mid Beowulfe   brimlade teah
on þære medubence   maþðum gesealde,
yrfelafe,   ond þone ænne heht
golde forgyldan   þone ðe Grendel ær
1055   mane acwealde,   swa he hyra ma wolde,

sleeps after the feast. Then it was the season and time
that the son of Healfdene went to the hall;
1010 the king himself wanted to participate in the feast.
I have not heard of a greater company of people
behaving better around their treasure-giver.
They sat down on benches enjoying glory,
rejoiced at the feast; the resolute kinsmen,
1015 Hrothgar and Hrothulf, graciously accepted
many a cup of mead
in that lofty hall. The inside of Heorot
was filled with friends; not then were the
people of the Scyldings engaged in wicked acts at all.
1020 Then Hrothgar gave Beowulf Healfdene's sword,
a golden standard as a reward for victory,
a decorated battle-banner, a helmet and corslet;
many saw the renowned treasure-sword
carried before the warrior. Beowulf drank
1025 from a cup in the hall; nor did he need to feel ashamed there
of the costly gifts given in front of the warriors.
I have not heard of four treasures
adorned with gold given by many men to another
on the ale-benches in a more friendly way.
1030 Around the crown of that helmet as a head-guard, a crest
bound with wires gave protection on the exterior,
so that the remnants of files, hard in battle,
might not injure him severely when the shield-warrior
had to advance against hostile men.[18]
1035   The protector of warriors then ordered eight horses
with gold-plated bridles to be led in onto the floor
through the courtyard; on one of them was
a saddle decorated with skill, enriched with treasure.
That had been the battle-seat of the high king,
1040 when Healfdene's son wanted to engage in
the contests of swords; the courage of the renowned man
never failed in the front when those killed fell.
And so the protector of the Ingwine conferred both of the things
into the possession of Beowulf,
1045 the horses and weapons; he told him to enjoy them well.
Thus, manfully, the famous lord,
treasure-guarder of the warriors, repaid the storms of battle
with horses and treasures so that no one would ever find fault with them
among those who are inclined in fairness to speak the truth.

XVI

1050 Furthermore, the lord of warriors gave treasures,
an heirloom, to each of those on the mead-benches
who undertook the sea-passage with Beowulf,
and ordered that one man
should pay compensation of gold for the one whom Grendel
1055 had previously killed through wickedness, as he would have done

---

18   See the picture of the reconstructed helmet that was excavated   Mitchell, ed., *An Invitation to Old English* (Oxford, 1994), p. 115.
at Sutton Hoo, the seventh-century East Anglian ship burial, in B.

nefne him witig God   wyrd forstode
ond ðæs mannes mod.   Metod eallum weold
gumena cynnes,   swa he nu git deð.
Forþan bið andgit   æghwær selest,
1060   ferhðes foreþanc;   fela sceal gebidan
leofes ond laþes   se þe longe her
on ðyssum windagum   worolde bruceð.
     Þær wæs sang ond sweg   samod ætgædere
fore Healfdenes   hildewisan,
1065   gomenwudu greted,   gid oft wrecen
ðonne healgamen   Hroþgares scop
æfter medobence   mænan scolde
Finnes eaferum.   Ða hie se fær begeat,
hæleð Healf-Dena,   Hnæf Scyldinga,
1070   in Freswæle   feallan scolde.
Ne huru Hildeburh   herian þorfte
Eotena treowe;   unsynnum wearð
beloren leofum   æt þam lindplegan,
bearnum ond broðrum;   hie on gebyrd hruron,
1075   gare wunde.   Þæt wæs geomuru ides.
Nalles holinga   Hoces dohtor
meotodsceaft bemearn   syþðan morgen com,
ða heo under swegle   geseon meahte
morþorbealo maga   þær heo ær mæste heold
1080   worolde wynne.   Wig ealle fornam
Finnes þegnas   nemne feaum anum,
þæt he ne mehte   on þæm meðelstede
wig Hengeste   wiht gefeohtan,
ne þa wealafe   wige forþringan
1085   þeodnes ðegne.   Ac hig him geþingo budon
þæt hie him oðer flet   eal gerymdon,
healle ond heahsetl,   þæt hie healfre geweald,
wið Eotena bearn   agan moston;
ond æt feohgyftum   Folcwaldan sunu
1090   dogra gehwylce   Dene weorþode,
Hengestes heap   hringum wenede,
efne swa swiðe   sincgestreonum
fættan goldes,   swa he Fresena cyn
on beorsele   byldan wolde.
1095   Ða hie getruwedon   on twa healfa
fæste frioðuwære.   Fin Hengeste
elne unflitme   aðum benemde
þæt he þa wealafe   weotena dome
arum heolde,   þæt ðær ænig mon
1100   wordum ne worcum   wære ne bræce,
ne þurh inwitsearo   æfre gemænden,
ðeah hie hira beaggyfan   banan folgedon

to more of them if the wise God and the courage of that man
had not prevented that fate. The Creator had power over all
of the race of men, as he does even now.
Therefore, the best thing is always to have understanding,
1060   forethought of mind; he who long partakes
of these days of strife within the world here
shall experience much that is dear and hateful.
    There was song and music together
in the presence of Healfdene's battle-leader,[19]
1065   the mirth-wood[20] was touched, a tale often recited
when Hrothgar's scop[21] related the entertainment in the hall
along the mead-benches
concerning the sons of Finn. When the sudden attack came upon them,
the hero of the Half-Danes, Hnæf of the Scyldings,
1070   was to perish in the Frisian slaughter.
Indeed, Hildeburh had no need to praise
the loyalty of the Jutes; guiltless, she was
deprived of her dear sons and brothers
in that shield-play; fated, they fell
1075   wounded by the spear. That was a sad woman.[22]
Not at all without cause did the daughter of Hoc
mourn the decree of fate when the morning came,
when she was able to see under the sky
the slaughter of kinsmen where she had previously had
1080   the greatest joy in the world. The war had taken away
all the retainers of Finn except for a few only,
so that in that meeting-place he could not fight the battle to a finish
with Hengest, the prince's thane,
or force out in war those that remained
1085   from the disaster. But they[23] offered them a truce,
that they would completely clear out another building for them,
a hall and a high-seat, so that they might control half of it,
could possess it along with the sons of the Jutes;
and that at the treasure-givings the son of Folcwalda[24]
1090   should honour the Danes each time,
should present rings to the company of Hengest,
treasures plated with gold,
just as he would encourage the people of the Frisians
in the beer-hall in the same way.
1095   Then on the two sides they confirmed
the peace-treaty firmly. Finn declared
oaths with undisputed courage to Hengest
that he would honourably hold to the judgement of counsellors
from among the disaster's survivors, that there no man
1100   would break the treaty with words or deeds,
or ever complain through malice,
although they served the murderer of their ring-giver

19   i.e. Hrothgar.
20   Lyre. See also s.v. Musical Instruments in M. Lapidge, J. Blair, S. Keynes and D. Scragg, eds, *The Blackwell Encyclopaedia of Anglo-Saxon England* (Oxford, 1998).
21   i.e. poet; teller of oral tales.
22   See Joyce Hill, ' "þæt wæs geomuru ides!": A Female Stereo-type Examined', in *New Readings on Women in Old English Literature*, eds H. Damico and A. Hennessy Olsen (Bloomington, IN, 1990), pp. 235–47.
23   The Finns.
24   i.e. Finn.

ðeodenlease,   þa him swa geþearfod wæs;
gyf þonne Frysna hwylc   frecnan spræce

1105 ðæs morþorhetes   myndgiend wære,
þonne hit sweordes ecg   syððan scolde.
      Að wæs geæfned   ond icge gold
ahæfen of horde.   Here-Scyldinga
betst beadorinca   wæs on bæl gearu;

1110 æt þæm ade wæs   eþgesyne
swatfah syrce,   swyn ealgylden,
eofer irenheard,   æþeling manig
wundum awyrded;   sume on wæle crungon.
Het ða Hildeburh   æt Hnæfes ade

1115 hire selfre sunu   sweoloðe befæstan,
banfatu bærnan,   ond on bæl don
eame on eaxle.   Ides gnornode,
geomrode giddum.   Guðrinc astah.
Wand to wolcnum   wælfyra mæst,

1120 hlynode for hlawe.   Hafelan multon,
bengeato burston   ðonne blod ætspranc,
laðbite lices.   Lig ealle forswealg,
gæsta gifrost,   þara ðe þær guð fornam
bega folces;   wæs hira blæd scacen.

XVII

1125 Gewiton him ða wigend   wica neosian,
freondum befeallen,   Frysland geseon,
hamas ond heaburh.   Hengest ða gyt
wælfagne winter   wunode mid Finne
eal unhlitme;   eard gemunde,

1130 þeah þe he ne meahte   on mere drifan
hringedstefnan.   Holm storme weol,
won wið winde;   winter yþe beleac
isgebinde   oþðæt oþer com
gear in geardas,   swa nu gyt deð,

1135 þa ðe syngales   sele bewitiað
wuldortorhtan weder.   Ða wæs winter scacen:
fæger foldan bearm;   fundode wrecca,
gist of geardum;   he to gyrnwræce
swiðor þohte   þonne to sælade,

1140 gif he torngemot   þurhteon mihte
þæt he Eotena bearn   inne gemunde.
Swa he ne forwyrnde   woroldrædenne
þonne him Hunlafing   hildeleoman,
billa selest   on bearm dyde

1145 þæs wæron mid Eotenum   ecge cuðe.
Swylce ferhðfrecan   Fin eft begeat
sweordbealo sliðen   æt his selfes ham,
siþðan grimne gripe   Guðlaf ond Oslaf
æfter sæsiðe   sorge mændon,

1150 ætwiton weana dæl;   ne meahte wæfre mod
forhabban in hreþre.   Ða wæs heal roden
feonda feorum,   swilce Fin slægen,
cyning on corþre,   ond seo cwen numen.

without a prince, which was imposed on them by necessity;
if a certain one of the Frisians spoke recklessly then
1105 and was reminded of the murderous hate,
then afterwards it had to be the sword's edge.
    The oath was carried out, and splendid gold
was brought from the hoard. The best of the warriors
of the Scylding army was prepared for the pyre;
1110 easily visible at that funeral pyre was
the bloodstained mail-coat, the all-gold boar image,
the boar as hard as iron, and many a nobleman
destroyed by wounds: some men fallen in slaughter.
Hildeburh then requested her own son
1115 to be committed to the blaze at Hnæf's pyre,
to burn the bodies, and in the fire to be placed
at his uncle's shoulder. The woman mourned,
lamented a dirge. The warrior was raised aloft.
The greatest of funeral fires curled to the clouds,
1120 roared in front of the burial mound. The heads melted,
wound-gashes, the grievous wounds of the body, burst
when the blood spurted out. The fire, the greediest of spirits,
completely swallowed up those who had been carried off in war there
from both nations; their glory had passed away.

XVII

1125 The warriors departed, deprived of friends,
to go to their dwelling-places, to see Friesland,
their homes and great strongholds. Hengest still
remained the slaughter-stained winter with Finn
entirely ill-fated; he thought of his homeland,
1130 although he was not able to sail his ring-prowed ship
on the sea. The sea surged with storms,
contended with winds; winter locked the waves
in icy bonds until another year came
to the dwellings, as it still does,
1135 and those times of gloriously bright weather always observe
their proper seasons. Then the winter departed:
the bosom of the earth grew beautiful; the exile and stranger
longed to go from those dwellings; he thought more
about revenge for injury than upon the sea-journey,
1140 if he could bring about a hostile encounter
so that he could bear in mind the sons of the Jutes.
So it was that he did not refuse the law of the world
when Hunlafing placed on his lap
a battle-light, the best of swords,
1145 the edges of which were known to the Jutes.
Thus, a cruel death by the sword afterwards
befell the bold-spirited Finn at his own home,
when Guthlaf and Oslaf, after their sea-journey,
spoke of the savage attack and their sorrows,
1150 blamed him for their share of woes; nor could his restless spirit
be restrained within his heart. Then the hall was made red
with the lives of the enemies, Finn was also killed,
the king among his troop, and the queen was taken.

Sceotend Scyldinga　　to scypon feredon

1155　eal ingesteald　　eorðcyninges,

swylce hie æt Finnes ham　　findan meahton

sigla searogimma.　　Hie on sælade

drihtlice wif　　to Denum feredon,

læddon to leodum.　　Leoð wæs asungen,

1160　gleomannes gyd.　　Gamen eft astah,

beorhtode bencsweg,　　byrelas sealdon

win of wunderfatum.　　Þa cwom Wealhþeo forð

gan under gyldnum beage　　þær þa godan twegen

sæton suhtergefæderan;　　þa gyt wæs hiera sib ætgædere,

1165　æghwylc oðrum trywe.　　Swylce þær Unferþ þyle

æt fotum sæt frean Scyldinga;　　gehwylc hiora his ferhþe treowde –

þæt he hæfde mod micel –　　þeah þe he his magum nære

arfæst æt ecga gelacum.　　Spræc ða ides Scyldinga:

'Onfoh þissum fulle,　　freodrihten min,

1170　sinces brytta.　　Þu on sælum wes,

goldwine gumena,　　ond to Geatum spræc

mildum wordum,　　swa sceal man don.

Beo wið Geatas glæd,　　geofena gemyndig

nean ond feorran　　þe þu nu hafast.

1175　Me man sægde　　þæt þu ðe for sunu wolde

hererinc habban.　　Heorot is gefælsod,

beahsele beorhta;　　bruc þenden þu mote

manigra medo,　　ond þinum magum læf

folc ond rice　　þonne ðu forð scyle

1180　metodsceaft seon.　　Ic minne can

glædne Hroþulf　　þæt he þa geogoðe wile

arum healdan　　gyf þu ær þonne he,

wine Scildinga,　　worold oflætest;

wene Ic þæt he mid gode　　gyldan wille

1185　uncran eaferan,　　gif he þæt eal gemon,

hwæt wit to willan　　ond to worðmyndum

umborwesendum ær　　arna gefremedon.'

Hwearf þa bi bence　　þær hyre byre wæron,

Hreðric ond Hroðmund,　　ond hæleþa bearn,

1190　giogoð ætgædere;　　þær se goda sæt,

Beowulf Geata,　　be þæm gebroðrum twæm.

XVIII

Him wæs ful boren,　　ond freondlaþu

wordum bewægned,　　ond wunden gold

estum geeawed:　　earmreade twa,

1195　hrægl ond hringas,　　healsbeaga mæst

þara þe Ic on foldan　　gefrægen hæbbe.

Nænigne Ic under swegle　　selran hyrde

hordmaðum hæleþa,　　syþðan Hama ætwæg

to þære byrhtan byrig　　Brosinga mene,

1200　sigle ond sincfæt;　　searoniðas fealh

Eormenrices;　　geceas ecne ræd.

Þone hring hæfde　　Higelac Geata,

The Scylding warriors carried to their ships
1155   all of the property belonging to that country's king,
whatever precious gems and jewels they could find
at Finn's home. They carried the noble lady
on a sea-journey to the Danes,
brought her to her people. A lay was sung,[25]
1160   the tale of a minstrel. Revelry arose again,
the noise of the benches resounded brightly, the cup-bearers gave
wine from wondrous vessels. Then Wealhtheow came forward
under a golden circlet to where the two good men,
nephew and uncle, sat; there was peace between them still,
1165   each was true to the other. The spokesman Unferth was also there
sat at the feet of the lord of the Scyldings; each of them trusted his spirit –
that he had great courage – even though he had not been
merciful to his kinsmen in the play of the sword's edge. The lady of the Scyldings spoke:
    'Take this cup, my noble lord,
1170   giver of treasure. Be joyful,
gold-giving friend of men, and speak to the Geats
with well-disposed words, as a man should do.
Be gracious to the Geats, mindful of the gifts
that you now have from near and afar.
1175   Someone told me that you would have this warrior
as a son. Heorot is cleansed,
the bright ring-hall; make use of the many rewards
while you can, and leave the people and kingdom
to your kinsmen when you have to pass on
1180   to discover your destiny. I know that
my gracious Hrothulf will treat the youths
honourably if you leave the world
earlier than he does, friend of the Scyldings;
I believe that he will generously repay our sons
1185   with goodness, if he recalls it all,
what we two previously did in the way of favours
for pleasure and for honour when he was a child.'
    Then she turned to the bench where her two sons were,
Hrethric and Hrothmund, and the sons of warriors,
1190   a band of young warriors together; the good man,
Beowulf of the Geats, sat there by the two brothers.

XVIII

The cup was carried to him, and a friendly invitation
was offered in words, and twisted gold
was presented with good will: two arm-ornaments,
1195   a garment and rings, the greatest neck-ring
on earth that I have heard of.
I have not heard of better heroes' treasures
under the sky, since Hama carried off
the Brosings' necklace, the jewel and precious setting,
1200   to the magnificent city; he endured the cunning hostility
of Eormenric; he chose eternal gain.
Hygelac of the Geats, grandson of Swerting,

---

25   The action returns to Hrothgar's hall.

nefa Swertinges, nyhstan siðe
siðþan he under segne sinc ealgode,
1205 wælreaf werede; hyne wyrd fornam
syþðan he for wlenco wean ahsode:
fæhðe to Frysum. He þa frætwe wæg,
eorclanstanas ofer yða ful
rice þeoden; he under rande gecranc.
1210 Gehwearf þa in Francna fæþm feorh cyninges,
breostgewædu ond se beah somod;
wyrsan wigfrecan wæl reafeden
æfter guðsceare; Geata leode,
hreawic heoldon. Heal swege onfeng.
1215 Wealhðeo maþelode; heo fore þæm werede spræc:
'Bruc ðisses beages, Beowulf leofa,
hyse, mid hæle, ond þisses hrægles neot,
þeodgestreona, ond geþeoh tela,
cen þec mid cræfte, ond þyssum cnyhtum wes
1220 lara liðe. Ic þe þæs lean geman.
Hafast þu gefered þæt ðe feor ond neah
ealne wideferhþ weras ehtigað,
efne swa side swa sæ bebugeð,
windgeard weallas. Wes þenden þu lifige
1225 æþeling eadig. Ic þe an tela
sincgestreona. Beo þu suna minum
dædum gedefe, dream healdende.
Her is æghwylc eorl oþrum getrywe,
modes milde, mandrihtne hold;
1230 þegnas syndon geþwære, þeod ealgearo,
druncne dryhtguman, doð swa Ic bidde.'
  Eode þa to setle. Þær wæs symbla cyst,
druncon win weras. Wyrd ne cuþon,
geosceaft grimne, swa hit agangen wearð
1235 eorla manegum syþðan æfen cwom
ond him Hroþgar gewat to hofe sinum
rice to ræste. Reced weardode
unrim eorla, swa hie oft ær dydon.
Bencþelu beredon; hit geondbræded wearð
1240 beddum ond bolstrum. Beorscealca sum
fus ond fæge fletræste gebeag.
Setton him to heafdon hilderandas,
bordwudu beorhtan; þær on bence wæs
ofer æþelinge yþgesene
1245 heaþosteapa helm, hringed byrne,
þrecwudu þrymlic. Wæs þeaw hyra
þæt hie oft wæron an wig gearwe,
ge æt ham ge on herge ge gehwæþer þara
efne swylce mæla swylce hira mandryhtne
1250 þearf gesælde. Wæs seo þeod tilu.

had that necklace with him on his last expedition
when he defended the treasure under the standard,
1205 protected the booty from the slain; fate carried him off
after he sought out trouble because of his pride:
a feud with the Frisians. The mighty prince took those adornments,
those precious stones over the cup of the waves;
he died under his shield.
1210 The body of the king passed into the hands of the Franks,
the corslet and the circlet too;
less worthy warriors plundered those killed
after the slaughter of battle; the people of the Geats
occupied the place of corpses. The hall was filled with sound.
1215 Wealhtheow made a speech; she spoke before the company:
'Enjoy this circlet, beloved young Beowulf,
and with luck, use this mail-coat,
the people's treasure, and prosper well,
show yourself with strength, and be kind to my boys
1220 with your advice. I shall remember your reward for this.
You have brought it about that you will be praised among men
near and far for ever,
even as widely as the sea, the home of the wind,
flows round the cliffs. Be fortunate for as long as you live,
1225 prince. I wish well for you
a wealth of treasures. Be kind in the things you do
for my sons, joyful man.
Here, every warrior is true to the other,
kind in heart, loyal to their liege lord;
1230 the thanes are united, the troop is fully prepared,
the noble warriors, having drunk to it, will do as I ask.'
    Then she went to her seat. There was the best of feasts,
men drank wine. They did not know the fate,
the grim destiny, that was to come about
1235 for many of the warriors once evening came,
and once Hrothgar, the powerful one, had gone
to his dwelling to his place of rest. The hall was guarded
by a countless number of warriors, just as they had often done before.
The benches were cleared; bedding and pillows
1240 were spread over the floor. One beer-drinker,
ripe for death, lay down on a couch in the hall.
They set their shields by their heads,
their shining shields; there on the bench,
above a nobleman, was clearly seen
1245 a helmet towering in battle, a corslet formed of rings,
and a mighty spear. It was their custom
that they should be constantly ready for war,
both at home and abroad, and any time,
wherever their liege lord
1250 had need of them. It was a good nation.

JUDITH

The Old English heroic poem *Judith* immediately follows *Beowulf* in London, British Library, Cotton Vitellius A. xv, folios 202 recto to 209 verso, and is written by the same scribe who writes *Beowulf* lines 1939b to 3182. It seems likely that *Beowulf* and *Judith* were not always together in the same manuscript, but were bound together later in their history. As part of the *Beowulf* manuscript, *Judith* suffered damage in the fire at Cotton's library in 1731, but in 1698, Edward Thwaites had published an edition of the poem from which many manuscript letters, now damaged, can be supplied. The date of original composition of *Judith*, as with so much Old English poetry, is not known, but it has been suggested that this poem was written in the later part of the tenth century.[26] The poem adapts the story of the Old Testament heroine from the Deuterocanonical book Judith, chapters xii.10–xvi.1, although as now extant, *Judith* is incomplete at the beginning. The Old English *Judith* is divided up in the manuscript into sections, and begins towards the end of the section number IX. Scholars have debated the extent of the loss of material, and it is possible that very little of the poem (perhaps a hundred lines or so) is, in fact, missing.[27] In the biblical version of the text, the Hebrew city of Bethulia is besieged by Holofernes, a general of the Assyrian king, Nebuchadnezzar. A devout widow named Judith leaves the city to enter the camp of the Assyrians, in an attempt to destroy Holofernes. When she has been with the Assyrians for four days, she recognizes the opportunity to kill Holofernes following a feast in which he and his men have become incapacitated through drinking too much. She beheads Holofernes and

returns triumphantly to her people, urging them to take up arms. The Assyrians, discovering what has happened the following morning, flee and are pursued by the victorious Hebrews.

From this, the Old English poet adapts his source in a number of ways; for example, the number of characters in the biblical account are reduced in the poem to the two main protagonists, Judith and Holofernes (plus the minor role played by Judith's maidservant), in order to polarize the roles and characters of the holy and the damned. In the poem, Judith is Christianized, praying to the Holy Trinity (line 86), and the emphasis appears to be very much on her purity and intellectual capacity, creating a prudent and seemingly more virginal figure than the Old Testament exemplar.[28] The poet also expands the section concerning the Hebrews' attack on the Assyrians into a major battle in the poem that incorporates conventional Germanic heroic vocabulary and motifs (the beasts of battle, for instance, at lines 205–12). In this way, the poem becomes a fine example of the Anglo-Saxon poet's skill in depicting the heroic code within a religious context. *Judith* is certainly one of the most interesting poems from the perspective of the depiction of women in Anglo-Saxon literature. Along with the poems *Elene* and *Juliana*, *Judith* is the only verse text with an eponymous heroine. Judith is unlike her female literary counterparts in that she is the only character to engage actively in wielding a weapon, and yet it is her wisdom and God-given strength of character that are most prominent in the text.

Judith

       . . . tweode gifena
in ðys ginnan grunde;   heo ðær ða gearwe funde
mundbyrd æt ðam mæran Þeodne,   þa heo ahte mæste þearfe
hyldo þæs hehstan Deman,   þæt he hie wið þæs hehstan brogan
5   gefriðode, frymða Waldend.   Hyre ðæs Fæder on roderum
torhtmod tiðe gefremede,   þe heo ahte trumne geleafan
a to ðam Ælmihtigan.   Gefrægen Ic ða Olofernus
winhatan wyrcean georne   ond eallum wundrum þrymlic
girwan up swæsendo;   to ðam het se gumena baldor
10   ealle ða yldestan ðegnas.   Hie ðæt ofstum miclum
ræfndon rondwiggende;   comon to ðam rican þeodne
feran, folces ræswan.   Þæt wæs þy feorðan dogore

---

26 See B. J. Timmer, ed., *Judith* (London, 1952; repr. 1966), pp. 1–16, for a discussion of the issues of date, language and sources. See also M. Griffith, ed., *Judith* (Exeter, 1998).

27 See D. Chamberlain, '*Judith*: A Fragmentary and Political Poem', in *Anglo-Saxon Poetry: Essays in Appreciation for John C. McGalliard*, eds L. E. Nicholson and D. Warwick Frese (Notre Dame, IN, 1975), pp. 135–59, for a detailed account of this issue.

28 On the use of key terminology describing Judith, see P. A. Belanoff, 'Judith: Sacred and Secular Heroine', in *Heroic Poetry in the Anglo-Saxon Period: Studies in Honor of Jess B. Bessinger, Jr.*, eds H. Damico and J. Leyerle (Kalamazoo, 1993), pp. 247–64.

Judith

. . . She doubted
gifts in this wide earth; there she readily found
protection from the glorious Lord, when she had most need
of favour from the highest Judge, so that he, the Lord of creation,
5   defended her against the greatest terror. The glorious Father in the skies
granted her request, since she always possessed true faith
in the Almighty. I have heard then that Holofernes
eagerly issued invitations to a feast and provided all types of
magnificent wonders for the banquets; to it the lord of men summoned
10   the most experienced retainers. The warriors obeyed
with great haste; they came to the powerful lord and
proceeded to the leader of people. That was the fourth day

þæs ðe Judith hyne,   gleaw on geðonce,
ides ælfscinu,   ærest gesohte.

X

15   Hie ða to ðam symble   sittan eodon,
wlance to wingedrince,   ealle his weagesiðas,
bealde byrnwiggende.   Þær wæron bollan steape
boren æfter bencum gelome,   swylce eac bunan ond orcas
fulle fletsittendum.   Hie þæt fæge þægon,

20   rofe rondwiggende,   þeah ðæs se rica ne wende,
egesful eorla dryhten.   Ða wearð Olofernus,
goldwine gumena,   on gytesalum.
Hloh ond hlydde,   hlynede ond dynede,
þæt mihten fira bearn   feorran gehyran

25   hu se stiðmoda   styrmde ond gylede;
modig ond medugal,   manode geneahhe
bencsittende   þæt hi gebærdon wel.
Swa se inwidda,   ofer ealne dæg,
dryhtguman sine   drencte mid wine,

30   swiðmod sinces brytta,   oðþæt hie on swiman lagon,
oferdrencte his duguðe ealle,   swylce hie wæron deaðe geslegene,
agotene goda gehwylces.   Swa het se gumena aldor
fylgan fletsittendum,   oðþæt fira bearnum
nealæhte niht seo þystre.   Het ða niða geblonden

35   þa eadigan mægð   ofstum fetigan
to his bedreste,   beagum gehlæste,
hringum gehrodene.   Hie hraðe fremedon,
anbyhtscealcas,   swa him heora ealdor bebead,
byrnwigena brego.   Bearhtme stopon

40   to ðam gysterne   þær hie Judithe
fundon ferhðgleawe,   ond ða fromlice
lindwiggende   lædan ongunnon
þa torhtan mægð   to træfe þam hean,
þær se rica hyne   reste on symbel

45   nihtes inne,   Nergende lað,
Olofernus.   Þær wæs eallgylden
fleohnet fæger   ymbe þæs folctogan
bed ahongen,   þæt se bealofulla
mihte wlitan þurh,   wigena baldor,

50   on æghwylcne   þe ðærinne com
hæleða bearna,   ond on hyne nænig
monna cynnes,   nymðe se modiga hwæne
niðe rofra   him þe near hete
rinca to rune gegangan.   Hie ða on reste gebrohton

55   snude ða snoteran idese.   Eodon ða stercedferhðe,
hæleð heora hearran cyðan   þæt wæs seo halige meowle
gebroht on his burgetelde.   Þa wearð se brema on mode
bliðe, burga ealdor: þohte ða beorhtan idese
mid widle ond mid womme besmitan.   Ne wolde þæt wuldres Dema

60   geðafian, þrymmes Hyrde,   ac he him þæs ðinges gestyrde,
Dryhten, dugeða Waldend.   Gewat ða se deofulcunda,

after Judith, prudent in mind,
this woman of elfin beauty,[29] first visited him.

X

15 They went into the feast to sit down,
proud men at the wine-drinking, bold mail-coated warriors,
all his companions in misfortune. There, along the benches,
deep bowls were carried frequently; full cups and pitchers
were also carried to the sitters in the hall. They received those, doomed to die,
20 brave warriors, though the powerful man did not expect it,
that terrible lord of heroes. Then Holofernes,
the gold-giving friend of his men, became joyous from the drinking.
He laughed and grew vociferous, roared and clamoured,
so that the children of men could hear from far away,
25 how the fierce one stormed and yelled;
arrogant and excited by mead, he frequently admonished
the guests that they enjoy themselves well.
So, for the entire day, the wicked one,
the stern dispenser of treasures,
30 drenched his retainers with wine until they lay unconscious,
the whole of his troop were as drunk as if they had been struck down in death,
drained of every ability. So, the men's lord commanded
the guests to be served, until the dark night approached
the children of men. Then corrupted by evil,
35 he commanded that the blessed maiden should be hastily fetched
to his bed, adorned with bracelets,
decorated with rings. The retainers quickly did
as their lord, the ruler of warriors,
commanded them. They stepped into the tumult
40 of the guest-hall where they found the wise Judith,
and then quickly
the warriors began to lead the
illustrious maiden to the lofty tent,
where the powerful man Holofernes, hateful to the Saviour,
45 rested himself during the night.
There was a beautiful
all-golden fly-net that the commander
had hung around the bed, so that the wicked one
the lord of warriors, could look through
50 on each of those sons of men who came in there,
but not one of the race of mankind could look
on him, unless, brave man, he commanded one
of his very iniquitous men to come
nearer to him for secret consultation. They quickly brought to bed
55 the prudent woman. Then the resolute heroes
went to inform their lord that the holy maiden
had been brought into his tent. Then the notorious one, that lord of cities,
became happy in his mind: he intended to violate
the bright woman with defilement and with sin. The Judge of glory,
60 the majestic Guardian, the Lord, Ruler of hosts, would not consent to that,
but he prevented him from that thing. Then the diabolical one,

29 See Belanoff, 'Judith', for a discussion of the meaning of *ælfscinu*,
and other key words in this poem.

galferhð gumena ðreate
bealofull his beddes neosan,   þær he sceolde his blæd forleosan
ædre binnan anre nihte.   Hæfde ða his ende gebidenne
65   on eorðan unswæslicne,   swylcne he ær æfter worhte,
þearlmod ðeoden gumena,   þenden he on ðysse worulde
wunode under wolcna hrofe.   Gefeol ða wine swa druncen
se rica on his reste middan,   swa he nyste ræda nanne
on gewitlocan.   Wiggend stopon
70   ut of ðam inne   ofstum miclum,
weras winsade,   þe ðone wærlogan,
laðne leodhatan,   læddon to bedde
nehstan siðe.   Þa wæs Nergendes
þeowen þrymful   þearle gemyndig
75   hu heo þone atolan   eaðost mihte
ealdre benæman,   ær se unsyfra,
womfull, onwoce.   Genam ða wundenlocc
Scyppendes mægð,   scearpne mece,
scurum heardne,   ond of sceaðe abræd
80   swiðran folme.   Ongan ða swegles Weard
be naman nemnan,   Nergend ealra
woruldbuendra,   ond þæt word acwæð:
    'Ic ðe, frymða God   ond frofre Gæst,
Bearn Alwaldan,   biddan wylle
85   miltse þinre   me þearfendre,
Ðrynesse ðrym.   Þearle ys me nu ða
heorte onhæted,   ond hige geomor,
swyðe mid sorgum gedrefed.   Forgif me, swegles Ealdor,
sigor ond soðne geleafan   þæt Ic mid þys sweorde mote
90   geheawan þysne morðres bryttan.   Geunne me minra gesynta,
þearlmod Þeoden gumena: nahte Ic þinre næfre
miltse þon maran þearfe.   Gewrec nu, mihtig Dryhten,
torhtmod tires Brytta,   þæt me ys þus torne on mode,
hate on hreðre minum.'   Hi ða se hehsta Dema
95   ædre mid elne onbryrde,   swa he deð anra gehwylcne
herbuendra   þe hyne him to helpe seceð
mid ræde ond mid rihte geleafan.   Þa wearð hyre rume on mode,
haligre hyht geniwod.   Genam ða þone hæðenan mannan
fæste be feaxe sinum,   teah hyne folmum wið hyre weard
100   bysmerlice,   ond þone bealofullan
listum alede,   laðne mannan,
swa heo ðæs unlædan   eaðost mihte
wel gewealdan.   Sloh ða wundenlocc
þone feondsceaðan   fagum mece,
105   heteþoncolne,   þæt heo healfne forcearf
þone sweoran him,   þæt he on swiman læg,
druncen ond dolhwund.   Næs ða dead þa gyt,
ealles orsawle.   Sloh ða eornoste
ides ellenrof   oþre siðe
110   þone hæðenan hund,   þæt him þæt heafod wand
forð on ða flore.   Læg se fula leap
gesne beæftan;   gæst ellor hwearf
under neowelne næs   ond ðær genyðerad wæs,
susle gesæled   syððan æfre,

the wanton and wicked man, departed
with a troop of his men to find his bed, where he would lose his life
forthwith within that one night. He had attained his violent end
65   on earth, just as he had previously deserved,
this severe lord of men, since he had dwelled under the roof
of clouds in this world. The mighty man then fell into the middle
of his bed, so drunk with wine that he possessed no sense
in his mind. The warriors stepped
70   out from that place with great haste,
men sated with wine, who led the traitor,
that hateful tyrant, to bed
for the last time. Then the Saviour's
glorious handmaiden was very mindful
75   of how she could deprive the terrible one
of life most easily, before the impure and
foul one awoke. Then the Creator's maiden,
with her braided locks, took a sharp sword,
a hard weapon in the storms of battle, and drew it from the sheath
80   with her right hand. She began to call the Guardian of heaven
by name, the Saviour of all
the inhabitants of earth, and said these words:
    'God of creation, Spirit of comfort,
Son of the Almighty, I want to beseech you
85   for your mercy on me in my time of need,
glorious Trinity. My heart is intensely
inflamed within me now, and my mind is troubled,
greatly afflicted with sorrows. Give me, Lord of heaven,
victory and true belief so I might cut down this bestower of torment
90   with this sword. Grant me my salvation,
mighty Lord of men: I have never had more need
of your mercy than now. Avenge now, mighty Lord,
eminent Bestower of glory, that which is so grievous in my mind,
so fervent in my heart.' Then the highest Judge
95   inspired her immediately with great zeal, as he does to each
of the dwellers on earth who seek help from him
with reason and with true faith. Then she felt relief in her mind,
hope was renewed for the holy woman. She seized the heathen man
securely by his hair, pulled him shamefully towards her
100   with her hands, and skilfully placed
the wicked and loathsome man
so that she could most easily manage the miserable one
well. Then, the woman with braided locks struck
the enemy, that hostile one,
105   with the shining sword, so that she cut through half
of his neck, such that he lay unconscious,
drunk and wounded. He was not dead yet,
not entirely lifeless. The courageous woman
struck the heathen hound energetically
110   another time so that his head rolled
forwards on the floor. The foul body lay
behind, dead; the spirit departed elsewhere
under the deep earth and was oppressed there
and fettered in torment forever after,

115 wyrmum bewunden, witum gebunden,
 hearde gehæfted in hellebryne
 æfter hinsiðe. Ne ðearf he hopian no,
 þystrum forðylmed, þæt he ðonan mote
 of ðam wyrmsele, ac ðær wunian sceal
120 awa to aldre butan ende forð
 in ðam heolstran ham, hyhtwynna leas.

XI

 Hæfde ða gefohten foremærne blæd
 Judith æt guðe, swa hyre God uðe,
 swegles Ealdor, þe hyre sigores onleah.
125 Þa seo snotere mægð snude gebrohte
 þæs herewæðan heafod swa blodig
 on ðam fætelse þe hyre foregenga,
 blachleor ides, hyra begea nest;
 ðeawum geðungen þyder on lædde,
130 ond hit þa swa heolfrig hyre on hond ageaf,
 higeþoncolre, ham to berenne,
 Judith gingran sinre. Eodon ða gegnum þanonne
 þa idesa ba ellenþriste,
 oðþæt hie becomon, collenferhðe,
135 eadhreðige mægð, ut of ðam herige
 þæt hie sweotollice geseon mihten
 þære wlitegan byrig weallas blican,
 Bethuliam. Hie ða beahhrodene
 feðelaste forð onettan,
140 oð hie glædmode gegan hæfdon
 to ðam wealgate. Wiggend sæton,
 weras wæccende wearde heoldon
 in ðam fæstenne, swa ðam folce ær
 geomormodum Judithe bebead,
145 searoðoncol mægð, þa heo on sið gewat,
 ides ellenrof. Wæs ða eft cumen
 leof to leodum, ond ða lungre het
 gleawhydig wif gumena sumne
 of ðære ginnan byrig hyre togeanes gan,
150 ond hi ofostlice in forlæton
 þurh ðæs wealles geat; ond þæt word acwæð
 to ðam sigefolce: 'Ic eow secgan mæg
 þoncwyrðe þing þæt ge ne þyrfen leng
 murnan on mode. Eow ys Metod bliðe,
155 cyninga Wuldor. Þæt gecyðed wearð
 geond woruld wide þæt eow ys wuldorblæd
 torhtlic toweard ond tir gifeðe
 þara læðða þe ge lange drugon.'
 Þa wurdon bliðe burhsittende
160 syððan hi gehyrdon hu seo halige spræc
 ofer heanne weall. Here wæs on lustum,
 wið þæs fæstengeates folc onette,
 weras wif somod, wornum ond heapum,
 ðreatum ond ðrymmum þrungon ond urnon
165 ongean ða Þeodnes mægð þusendmælum,

115   wound round with serpents, bound with punishments,
cruelly imprisoned in hell-fire
after his departure. Enveloped in darkness,
he had no need at all to hope that he should get out from
that serpent-hall, but there he must remain
120   always and forever, henceforth without end,
in that dark home deprived of the joy of hope.

XI

Judith had won illustrious glory
in the battle as God, the Lord of heaven,
granted it so when he gave her her victory.
125   Then the prudent woman immediately placed
the warrior's head still bloody
into the sack in which her attendant,
a woman of pale complexion, an excellent handmaiden,
had brought food for them both; and then Judith
130   put it, all gory, into the hands of her
thoughtful servant to carry home.
Then both the courageous women
went from there straightaway,
until the triumphant women, elated,
135   got away out from that army
so that they could clearly see
the beautiful city walls of Bethulia
glitter. Then, ring-adorned,
they hurried forwards along the path
140   until, glad at heart, they had reached
the rampart gate. Warriors were sitting,
men watching, and keeping guard
in that stronghold, just as Judith the wise maiden
had asked, when she had previously
145   departed from the sorrowful people,
the courageous woman. The beloved woman had returned again
to the people, and the prudent woman
soon asked one of the men
from the spacious city to come towards her,
150   and hastily to let them in
through the gate of the city-wall; and she spoke these words
to the victorious people: 'I am able to tell you
a memorable thing so that you need no longer
mourn in your minds. The Ruler, the Glory of kings,
155   is well disposed towards you. It had become revealed
throughout this wide world that glorious and triumphant success
is approaching and that honour has been granted by fate to you
because of the afflictions that you have long suffered.'
    Then the city-dwellers were joyful
160   when they heard how the holy one spoke
over the high city-wall. The army was joyous
and people hurried to the fortress gate,
men and women, in multitudes and crowds,
groups and troops pressed forward and ran
165   towards the Lord's maiden in their thousands,

ealde ge geonge.   Æghwylcum wearð
men on ðære medobyrig   mod areted
syððan hie ongeaton   þæt wæs Judith cumen
eft to eðle;   ond ða ofostlice

170   hie mid eaðmedum   in forleton.
    Þa seo gleawe het,   golde gefrætewod,
hyre ðinenne   þancolmode
þæs herewæðan   heafod onwriðan
ond hyt to behðe   blodig ætywan

175   þam burhleodum   hu hyre æt beaduwe gespeow.
Spræc ða seo æðele   to eallum þam folce:
'Her ge magon sweotole,   sigerofe hæleð,
leoda ræswan,   on ðæs laðestan
hæðenes heaðorinces   heafod starian,

180   Olofernus   unlyfigendes,
þe us monna mæst   morðra gefremede,
sarra sorga,   ond þæt swyðor gyt
ycan wolde;   ac him ne uðe God
lengran lifes   þæt he mid læððum us

185   eglan moste.   Ic him ealdor oðþrong
þurh Godes fultum.   Nu Ic gumena gehwæne
þyssa burgleoda   biddan wylle,
randwiggendra,   þæt ge recene eow
fysan to gefeohte,   syððan frymða God,

190   arfæst Cyning,   eastan sende
leohtne leoman.   Berað linde forð,
bord for breostum   ond byrnhomas,
scire helmas,   in sceaðena gemong;
fyllan folctogan   fagum sweordum,

195   fæge frumgaras.   Fynd syndon eowere
gedemed to deaðe,   ond ge dom agon,
tir æt tohtan,   swa eow getacnod hafað
mihtig Dryhten   þurh mine hand.'
    Þa wearð snelra werod   snude gegearewod,

200   cenra to campe.   Stopon cynerofe
secgas ond gesiðas;   bæron sigeþufas;
foron to gefeohte   forð on gerihte,
hæleð under helmum,   of ðære haligan byrig
on ðæt dægred sylf.   Dynedan scildas,

205   hlude hlummon.   Þæs se hlanca gefeah
wulf in walde,   ond se wanna hrefn,
wælgifre fugel;   wistan begen
þæt him ða þeodguman   þohton tilian
fylle on fægum;   ac him fleah on last

210   earn ætes georn,   urigfeðera,
salowigpada;   sang hildeleoð,
hyrnednebba.   Stopon heaðorincas,
beornas to beadowe,   bordum beðeahte,
hwealfum lindum,   þa ðe hwile ær

215   elþeodigra   edwit þoledon,
hæðenra hosp.   Him þæt hearde wearð
æt ðam æscplegan   eallum forgolden,
Assyrium,   syððan Ebreas

old and young. The mind of each one of the people
in that rejoicing city was gladdened
when they perceived that Judith had returned
to her native land; and then hastily

170 and reverently, they let her in.
    Then the prudent woman, adorned with gold, asked
her attentive handmaiden
to uncover the warrior's head
and to display it, bloodied, as proof

175 to the citizens of how she had been helped in battle.
Then the noble woman spoke to all the people:
'Victorious heroes, here you can gaze clearly
on the leader of the people, on this head
of the most hateful of heathen warriors,

180 of the unliving Holofernes,
who, among men, inflicted on us the worst torments,
grievous afflictions, and wished to add to these
even more; but God would not grant him
a longer life so that he could plague us

185 with wrongs. I deprived him of life
through God's help. Now I intend to ask
each of the men of these citizens,
each of the warriors, that you immediately
hasten to battle, as soon as the God of creation,

190 that glorious King, sends his radiant beam of light
from the east. Go forward carrying shields,
shields in front of your breasts and corslets,
gleaming helmets, into the troop of enemies;
fell the commanders, those leaders doomed to die

195 with shining swords. Your enemies
are condemned to death, and you will possess glory,
honour in conflict, just as mighty God has
given you that sign by my hand.'
    Then a host of brave and keen men prepared quickly

200 for the battle. Noble warriors and retainers
stepped out; they carried triumphant banners;
heroes in helmets went forward to battle straightaway
from that holy city
at dawn of that same day. Shields clashed,

205 resounded loudly. The lean wolf rejoiced
in the forest, as did the dark raven,
a bloodthirsty bird: they both knew
that the warriors intended to provide them
with a feast from those doomed to die; but behind them flew

210 the eagle eager for food, dewy-winged
with dark plumage; the horn-beaked bird
sang a battle-song. The warriors advanced,
men to battle, protected by shields,
hollow wooden shields, those who previously

215 had suffered the insolence of foreigners,
the insult of heathens. In the spear-play,
that was all grievously requited to
the Assyrians, when the Israelites

under guðfanum   gegan hæfdon
220   to ðam fyrdwicum.   Hie ða fromlice
leton forð fleogan   flana scuras,
hildenædran   of hornbogan,
strælas stedehearde.   Styrmdon hlude
grame guðfrecan,   garas sendon
225   in heardra gemang.   Hæleð wæron yrre,
landbuende,   laðum cynne,
stopon styrnmode,   stercedferhðe,
wrehton unsofte   ealdgeniðlan
medowerige.   Mundum brugdon
230   scealcas of sceaðum   scirmæled swyrd,
ecgum gecoste,   slogon eornoste
Assiria   oretmæcgas,
niðhycgende.   Nanne ne sparedon
þæs herefolces,   heanne ne ricne,
235   cwicera manna   þe hie ofercuman mihton.

XII

Swa ða magoþegnas   on ða morgentid
ehton elðeoda   ealle þrage,
oðþæt ongeaton   ða ðe grame wæron,
ðæs herefolces   heafodweardas,
240   þæt him swyrdgeswing   swiðlic eowdon
weras Ebrisce.   Hie wordum þæt
þam yldestan   ealdorþegnum
cyðan eodon,   wrehton cumbolwigan
ond him forhtlice   færspel bodedon,
245   medowerigum   morgencollan,
atolne ecgplegan.   Þa Ic ædre gefrægn
slegefæge hæleð   slæpe tobredon,
ond wið þæs bealofullan   burgeteldes
weras werigferhðe   hwearfum þringan,
250   Olofernus.   Hogedon aninga
hyra hlaforde   hilde bodian,
ær ðon ðe him se egesa   on ufan sæte,
mægen Ebrea.   Mynton ealle
þæt se beorna brego   ond seo beorhte mægð
255   in ðam wlitegan træfe   wæron ætsomne:
Judith seo æðele,   ond se galmoda,
egesfull ond afor.   Næs ðeah eorla nan
þe ðone wiggend   aweccan dorste
oððe gecunnian   hu ðone cumbolwigan
260   wið ða halgan mægð   hæfde geworden,
Metodes meowlan.   Mægen nealæhte,
folc Ebrea;   fuhton þearle
heardum heoruwæpnum,   hæste guldon
hyra fyrngeflitu,   fagum swyrdum,
265   ealde æfðoncan.   Assyria wearð
on ðam dægeweorce   dom geswiðrod,
bælc forbiged.   Beornas stodon
ymbe hyra þeodnes træf   þearle gebylde,
sweorcendferhðe.   Hi ða somod ealle

under their battle-banners had gone
220   to that camp. Then they boldly
let showers of arrows fly forwards,
battle arrows from horned bows,
firm arrows. Angry warriors
roared loudly, sent spears
225   into the midst of the cruel ones. The native heroes
were angry against the hateful race,
resolute, they marched, determined,
they violently aroused their ancient enemies
who were drunk with mead. With their hands,
230   the retainers drew brightly adorned swords from their sheaths,
excellent sword-edges, zealously killed
the Assyrian warriors,
those evil schemers. They did not spare one
man's life from that army, neither the
235   lowly nor the powerful whom they could overcome.

XII
So, in the morning, the retainers
pursued the foreign people the entire time,
until the chief leaders of that army,
of those who were the enemies, perceived
240   that the Hebrew men had shown violent sword-brandishing
to them. They went to reveal
all that in words to the most
senior retainers, and they aroused the warriors
and announced fearfully to those drunk with mead
245   the dreadful news, the morning's terror,
the terrible battle. Then, I have heard, immediately
the warriors, doomed to perish, cast off sleep,
and the subdued men thronged in crowds
to the tent of the wicked man,
250   Holofernes. They intended to announce
the battle to their lord at once,
before the terrible force of the Israelites
came down on them. They all supposed
that the leader of the warriors and the bright maiden
255   were together in that beautiful tent:
Judith the noble one, and the licentious one,
terrible and fierce. There was not a single one of the men
who dared to wake the warrior
or inquire how the warrior
260   had got on with the holy maiden,
the Lord's woman. The armed force of the Israelites
approached; they fought vigorously
with hard swords, violently requited
their ancient grudges, that old conflict,
265   with shining swords. The Assyrians'
glory was destroyed in that day's work,
their pride humbled. Warriors stood
about their lord's tent very uneasy
and sombre in spirit. Then together they all

270
ongunnon cohhetan,   cirman hlude
ond gristbitian,   gode orfeorme,
mid toðon torn þoligende.   Þa wæs hyra tires æt ende,
eades ond ellendæda.   Hogedon þa eorlas
aweccan hyra winedryhten;   him wiht ne speow.

275
      Þa wearð sið ond late   sum to ðam arod
þara beadorinca   þæt he in þæt burgeteld
niðheard neðde,   swa hyne nyd fordraf.
Funde ða on bedde   blacne licgan
his goldgifan   gæstes gesne,

280
lifes belidenne.   He þa lungre gefeoll
freorig to foldan,   ongan his feax teran,
hreoh on mode,   ond his hrægl somod,
ond þæt word acwæð   to ðam wiggendum
þe ðær unrote   ute wæron:

285
'Her ys geswutelod   ure sylfra forwyrd,
toweard getacnod,   þæt þære tide ys
mid niðum neah geðrungen,   þe we sculon nu losian,
somod æt sæcce forweorðan.   Her lið sweorde geheawen,
beheafdod healdend ure.'   Hi ða hreowigmode

290
wurpon hyra wæpen ofdune,   gewitan him werigferhðe,
on fleam sceacan.   Him mon feaht on last,
mægeneacen folc,   oð se mæsta dæl
þæs heriges læg   hilde gesæged
on ðam sigewonge,   sweordum geheawen

295
wulfum to willan   ond eac wælgifrum
fuglum to frofre.   Flugon ða ðe lyfdon,
laðra linde.   Him on laste for
sweot Ebrea,   sigore geweorðod,
dome gedyrsod.   Him feng Dryhten God

300
fægre on fultum,   Frea ælmihtig.
Hi ða fromlice   fagum swyrdum,
hæleð higerofe,   herpað worhton
þurh laðra gemong;   linde heowon,
scildburh scæron.   Sceotend wæron

305
guðe gegremede,   guman Ebrisce,
þegnas on ða tid   þearle gelyste
gargewinnes.   Þær on greot gefeoll
se hyhsta dæl   heafodgerimes
Assiria   ealdorduguðe,

310
laðan cynnes.   Lythwon becom
cwicera to cyððe.   Cirdon cynerofe,
wiggend on wiðertrod,   wælscel on innan,
reocende hræw.   Rum wæs to nimanne
londbuendum   on ðam laðestan,

315
hyra ealdfeondum   unlyfigendum
heolfrig herereaf,   hyrsta scyne,
bord ond bradswyrd,   brune helmas,
dyre madmas.   Hæfdon domlice
on ðam folcstede   fynd oferwunnen

320
eðelweardas,   ealdhettende,

270 began to cough, to cry out loudly,
to gnash their teeth, suffering grief,
to no avail. Then their glory, success and brave deeds
were at an end. The men considered how to awaken
their lord; it did them no good.
275   It got later and later when one of the warriors
became bold in that he daringly risked going
into the tent, as need compelled him to.
He found on the bed his pale lord,
lying deprived of spirit,
280 devoid of life. Immediately, he fell
frozen to the floor, and began to tear at his hair
and clothing, wild in mind,
and he spoke these words to the warriors
who were outside, dejected:
285 'Here our own destruction is made clear,
the future signified, that the time of troubles
is pressing near when we shall now lose,
shall perish at the battle together. Here lies our protector
cut down and beheaded by the sword.' Sorrowful, they
290 threw their weapons down then, and departed from him weary-spirited
to hasten in flight. The mighty people[30]
fought them from behind, until the greatest part
of the army lay destroyed in battle
on that field of victory, cut down by swords
295 as a pleasure for the wolves and also as a joy
to bloodthirsty birds. Those who still lived fled
from the wooden weapons of their enemies. Behind them
came the army of the Hebrews, honoured with victory,
glorified with that judgement. The Lord God, the almighty Lord,
300 helped them generously with his aid.
Then quickly the valiant heroes
made a war-path through the hateful enemies
with their shining swords; cut down shields,
and penetrated the shield-wall. The Hebrew missile-throwers
305 were enraged in the battle,
the retainers at that time greatly desired
a battle of spears. There in the sand fell
the greatest part of the total number
of leaders of the Assyrians,
310 that hateful nation. Few returned
alive to their native land. The brave warriors
turned back to retreat among the carnage,
the reeking corpses. There was an opportunity for
the native inhabitants to seize from the most hateful
315 ancient enemies, the unliving ones,
bloody plunder, beautiful ornaments,
shield and broad sword, shining helmets,
precious treasures. The guardians of the country
had gloriously conquered their foes,
320 the ancient enemy, on that battlefield,

---

30 The Israelites follow after those who are fleeing.

swyrdum aswefede.   Hie on swaðe reston,
þa ðe him to life   laðost wæron
cwicera cynna.   Þa seo cneoris eall,
mægða mærost,   anes monðes fyrst,
325   wlanc, wundenlocc,   wægon ond læddon
to ðære beorhtan byrig   Bethuliam,
helmas ond hupseax,   hare byrnan,
guðsceorp gumena   golde gefrætewod,
mærra madma   ma þonne mon ænig
330   asecgan mæge   searoþoncelra.
Eal þæt ða ðeodguman   þrymme geeodon,
cene under cumblum   ond compwige
þurh Judithe   gleawe lare,
mægð modigre.   Hi to mede hyre
335   of ðam siðfate   sylfre brohton,
eorlas æscrofe   Olofernes
sweord ond swatigne helm,   swylce eac side byrnan
gerenode readum golde,   ond eal þæt se rinca baldor
swiðmod sinces ahte   oððe sundoryrfes,
340   beaga ond beorhtra maðma;   hi þæt þære beorhtan idese
ageafon gearoþoncolre.   Ealles ðæs Judith sægde
wuldor weroda Dryhtne,   þe hyre weorðmynde geaf,
mærðe on moldan rice,   swylce eac mede on heofonum,
sigorlean in swegles wuldre,   þæs ðe heo ahte soðne geleafan
345   to ðam Ælmihtigan.   Huru æt ðam ende ne tweode
þæs leanes þe heo lange gyrnde.   Þæs sy ðam leofan Dryhtne
wuldor to widan aldre,   þe gesceop wind ond lyfte,
roderas ond rume grundas,   swylce eac reðe streamas
ond swegles dreamas   þurh his sylfes miltse.

executed them with swords. Those who had been
the most hateful of living men while alive
rested in their tracks. Then the entire nation,
the greatest of tribes, the proud braided-haired ones,
325 for the space of one month carried and led
to the bright city of Bethulia
helmets and hip-swords, grey corslets,
men's armour decorated with gold,
more illustrious treasures than any man
330 among the wise could say.
All of that was earned by the warriors' glory,
bold under the banners and in battle
through the prudent counsel of Judith,
the daring maiden. The brave warriors
335 brought as her reward from that expedition
the sword of Holofernes and his gory helmet,
and likewise his ample mail-coat
adorned with red gold, and everything that the arrogant
lord of warriors owned by way of treasures or personal heirlooms,
340 rings and bright riches; they gave that to the bright
and ready-witted woman. For all of this Judith said
thanks to the Lord of hosts, who had given her honour
and glory in the kingdom of this earth, and also as her reward in heaven,
the reward of victory in heaven's glory, because she possessed true faith
345 in the Almighty. Indeed, at the end she did not doubt
in the reward which she had long yearned for. For that be glory
to the beloved Lord for ever and ever, who created wind and air,
the heavens and spacious earth, likewise the raging seas
and joys of heaven through his own individual grace.

The Junius Manuscript

Oxford, Bodleian Library, Junius 11, is one of the four extensive poetic Old English codices. The manuscript, which is fully illustrated up to p. 88, with blank spaces left for illustrations thereafter, is divided into two books: the first contains three Old Testament poems, *Genesis*, *Exodus* and *Daniel*, and extends to p. 212; the second part, up to p. 229, contains New Testament material in the poem *Christ and Satan*. The texts in book 1 are numbered into sections by roman numerals. Junius 11 represents two separate scribal enterprises bound together to create a single volume within the late Anglo-Saxon pe-

riod. It is possible to see in the manuscript the unifying theme of salvation history.

The date of the manuscript's creation is the first decade of the eleventh century or slightly later, and it may have been written at Malmesbury, or at Christ Church, Canterbury.[1] The seventeenth-century Dutch scholar Franciscus Junius thought that the author of the Old Testament poems was Cædmon, but this is not now regarded as the case. The manuscript is, nevertheless, sometimes referred to as 'the Cædmon manuscript'.[2]

Exodus

Exodus occurs at pp. 143–71 of Junius 11, and takes as its main inspiration the events of Exodus 13:20–14. The poet, though, handles the material very freely, drawing on a wide number of other biblical books, the liturgy (possibly that for Holy Saturday when Christians renewed their baptismal vows, and when the second lesson is from Exodus 14, 15), and the heroic tradition to create his masterpiece. The New Testament, patristic writings and commentaries, such as those of Augustine of Hippo and Isidore of Seville, may have influenced the multi-layered, allusive depiction of the Israelites and Egyptians meeting at the Red Sea; for example, St Paul in I Corinthians 10.1–2 interprets the passage through the Red Sea as typologically foreshadowing baptism and, thereby, salvation.

Many scholars regard *Exodus* as one of the most difficult Old English texts to interpret: there are gaps in the text (after lines 141 and 446); there is a large number of *hapax legomena* (otherwise unrecorded words) that makes interpretation problematic; and the themes and style are very complex. The poem has thus attracted a great deal of critical attention that varies from seeing the poem as a coherent allegory depicting the universal struggle be-

tween good and evil, to regarding the text as an imaginative, heroic narrative of the Old Testament events with numerous allegorical allusions (see the bibliography). The theme of the poem may be as Lucas deduces:[3] one of 'Salvation by Faith and Obedience', where the obedience of the Israelites to God provides their means of salvation. As such, the text is exemplary, showing Christians that to obey the commandments of God, and to be loyal to him while in this world, are the keys to ensuring entry into heaven.

While *Exodus* is certainly difficult to interpret, then, and while it demands close reading, it is one of the most exciting and creative poems to survive from Anglo-Saxon England. The extracts edited below are lines 1–134 and 447–590 of the poem: these deal with the introduction of Moses, the tenth plague visited on the Egyptians, and the flight of the Israelites from their captives; the drowning of the Egyptians in the Red Sea and the subsequent rejoicing by Moses and the Israelites. The poem ends with the Israelites obtaining the booty washed up on shore from the Egyptians drowned by God's miracle.

---

1 For which see the excellent edition by P. J. Lucas, ed., *Exodus*, Exeter Medieval English Texts and Studies (Exeter, 1977; rev. edn 1994), pp. 2–5.

2 A facsimile of the manuscript is introduced by I. Gollancz, *The*

'Cædmon Manuscript' of Anglo-Saxon Biblical Poetry (London, 1927).

3 Lucas, *Exodus*, p. 61.

Exodus

{Lines 1–134}

XLII

Hwæt, we feor ond neah   gefrigen habbað
ofer middangeard   Moyses domas,
wræclico wordriht,   wera cneorissum:
in uprodor   eadigra gehwam
5   æfter bealusiðe,   bote lifes
lifigendra gehwam   langsumne ræd,
hæleðum secgan.   Gehyre se ðe wille!

    Þone on westenne   werode Drihten,
soðfæst Cyning,   mid his sylfes miht
10   gewyrðode,   ond him wundra fela,
ece Alwalda,   in æht forgeaf.
He wæs leof Gode,   leoda aldor,
horsc ond hreðergleaw,   herges wisa,
freom folctoga.   Faraones cyn,
15   Godes andsacan,   gyrdwite band,
þær him gesealde,   sigora Waldend,
modgum magoræswum   his maga feorh,
onwist eðles   Abrahames sunum.

Heah wæs þæt handlean   ond him hold Frea,
20   gesealde wæpna geweald   wið wraðra gryre,
ofercom mid þy campe   cneomaga fela,
feonda folcriht.   Ða wæs forma sið
þæt hine weroda God   wordum nægde,
þær he him gesægde   soðwundra fela,
25   hu þas woruld worhte   witig Drihten,
eorðan ymbhwyrft   ond uprodor;
gesette sigerice,   ond his sylfes naman,
ðone yldo bearn   ær ne cuðon,
frod fædera cyn,   þeah hie fela wiston.
30   Hæfde he þa geswiðed   soðum cræftum
ond gewurðodne   werodes aldor,
Faraones feond,   on forðwegas.
Þa wæs ungeare   ealdum witum,
deaðe gedrenced   drihtfolca mæst,
35   hordwearda hryre,   heaf wæs geniwad,
swæfon seledreamas,   since berofene.
Hæfde mansceaðan   æt middere niht
frecne gefylled,   frumbearna fela,
abrocene burhweardas.   Bana wide scrað,
40   lað leodhata;   land drysmyde
deadra hræwum;   dugoð forð gewat.

Exodus

{Lines 1–134}

XLII

Listen, far and near we have heard
throughout the middle-earth of the ordinances of Moses,
the wonderful written laws, to generations of men:
in heaven to each of the blessed
5   after the dangerous journey, the reward of life,
for each of the living ones a long-lasting counsel,
heroes tell us. He who can should listen![4]
    In the wilderness the Lord of hosts,
the righteous King, with his own power
10   exalted him, and gave to him[5] many wonders,
the eternal Ruler, into his possession.
He was loved by God, commander of the people,
alert and prudent, leader of the army,
a valiant commander. The tribe of Pharoah,
15   the enemy of God,[6] he bound with the punishment of Moses's rod,
where to him he gave, the Lord of victories,
to the valiant leader, the life of his kinsmen,
the inhabitation of a homeland to the sons of Abraham.
Divine was that reward and the Lord was loyal to him,
20   he gave him the power of weapons against the hostile terror;
thus he overcame in battle many tribes,
the authority of his enemies. That was the first time
that the God of hosts spoke words to him,
where he told him many true marvels,
25   how the wise Lord made the world,[7]
the earth's circuit and the sky;
he established a victorious kingdom, and his own name,
which the children of men did not know before,
nor the experienced kin of patriarchs, though they knew much.
30   God had strengthened then with true power
and honoured the leader of the host,
the enemy of Pharaoh, in the onward journey.
Then there was soon ancient punishment,
the greatest number of the nation was soaked in death,
35   the death of treasure-hoarders, as lamentation was renewed.
the joys of hall-life, bereft of treasure, passed away.[8]
In the middle of the night he had severely struck down
the wicked oppressors, many firstborn children,
and destroyed the city-dwellers. A slayer ranged everywhere,
40   a terrible persecutor of the people; the land suffocated
with the corpses of the dead; the warriors departed forth.

---

4 Lines 1–7 provide an epic opening that effectively iterates the major themes of the poem: the flight of the Israelites from the Egyptians; the covenant between Moses and God that has lasting significance for all humans; and one of the possible allegorical parallels between the Exodus and the Christian's spirtual journey through life.

5 i.e. Moses.

6 A reference to the Egyptians that identifies them with the devil.

7 This broadening of the time-scheme of the poem opens up the allegorical possibilities of interpreting the poem in the light of the whole of salvation history.

8 These lines, referring to the Plagues, are reminiscent of similar lines in other Old English texts (*The Wanderer*, for example), lamenting the decline of past glories. Such images emphasize the transitory nature of temporal splendour.

Wop wæs wide,   worulddreama lyt,
wæron hleahtorsmiðum   handa belocene,
alyfed laðsið   leode gretan;
45   folc ferende;   feond wæs bereafod.
Hergas on helle   (heofon þider becom)
druron deofolgyld.   Dæg wæs mære
ofer middangeard   þa seo mengeo for.
Swa þæs fæsten dreah   fela missera,
50   ealdwerige,   Egypta folc,
þæs þe hie wideferð   wyrnan þohton
Moyses magum,   gif hie Metod lete,
on langne lust   leofes siðes.
    Fyrd wæs gefysed;   from se ðe lædde,
55   modig magoræswa,   mægburh heora.
Oferfor he mid þy folce   fæstena worn,
land ond leodweard   laðra manna,
enge anpaðas,   uncuð gelad,
oðþæt hie on guðmyrce   gearwe bæron
60   (wæron land heora   lyfthelme beþeaht).
Mearchofu mor heald;   Moyses ofer þa
fela meringa,   fyrde gelædde.

XLIII

Heht þa ymb twa niht   tirfæste hæleð,
siððan hie feondum   oðfaren hæfdon,
65   ymbwicigean   werodes bearhtme
mid ælfere   Æthanes byrig,
mægnes mæste,   mearclandum on.
Nearwe genyddon   on norðwegas:
wiston him be suðan   Sigelwara land,
70   forbærned burhhleoðu,   brune leode,
hatum heofoncolum.   Þær halig God
wið færbryne   folc gescylde,
bælce oferbrædde   byrnendne heofon,
halgan nette   hatwendne lyft.
75   Hæfde wederwolcen   widum fæðmum
eorðan ond uprodor   efne gedæled,
lædde leodwerod,   ligfyr adranc,
hate heofontorht;   hæleð wafedon,
drihta gedrymost.   Dægscealdes hleo
80   wand ofer wolcnum.   Hæfde witig God
sunnan siðfæt   segle ofertolden,
swa þa mæstrapas   men ne cuðon,
ne ða seglrode   geseon meahton
eorðbuende   ealle cræfte,
85   hu afæstnod wæs   feldhusa mæst,
siððan he mid wuldre   geweorðode

Anguish was widespread, there were few worldly joys,
the hands of the laughter-smiths were clasped shut,
the people, the travelling multitude, were allowed to
45   undertake the hated journey;[9] the enemy was bereaved.
The shrines of hell (the divine power came there),
the gilded idols, fell. It was a glorious day
over this middle-earth when the multitude went forth.
So with captivity for many half-years
50   the Egyptian people, accursed from old, suffered
because they intended forever to prevent
the kinsmen of Moses, if the Lord had permitted them,
in their long-lasting desire for the cherished journey.
      The army was prepared; valiant was the one who led them,
55   a noble leader of their people.
With the people he passed by numerous inaccessible places,
lands and territories of hostile peoples,
narrow lonely tracks, unknown paths,
until they came bearing arms upon warlike border-dwellers
60   (their lands were covered with cloud).
The wilderness contained borderland dwellings; over those Moses
led the army, over the numerous borderlands.

XLIII

Then about two days after they had escaped
from their enemies, the glorious hero ordered,
65   by the sounding of the troop, the whole host
to encamp around the town of Etham,
the greatest armed force, in the borderland.
Difficulties forced them onto the northerly route:
they knew that south of them was the land of the Ethiopians,
70   a brown people, scorched on the hillsides
by the hot burning sun. There holy God
shielded the people from the terrible heat
with a canopy that covered over the burning heaven,
and the sweltering sky with a holy veil.
75   A cloud with a broad embrace had
evenly divided earth and heaven,
and led the host of people, and quenched the sun's flaming fire,
heaven-bright in its heat; the heroes looked on amazed,
the most joyful of troops. The protection of the day-shield
80   moved over the sky. Wise God had
covered over the sun's course with a sail,[10]
so that men did not have knowledge of the mast-ropes,
nor could the sailyard be seen
by earth-dwellers for all their skill,
85   nor how that greatest of tents was fastened,
when he honoured with glory

9   The 'hated journey' is that of the Egyptians on the way to hell. This contrasts with line 53, where the 'cherished journey' of the Israelites represents the road to salvation. Alternatively, it could refer to Pharaoh's decision to let the people of Israel go, following the last plague. See Exodus 12.31–4.

10   This reference to the cloud as a sail, and the subsequent nautical references in the text, problematize interpretation: the Israelites are allegorically and typologically depicted as sailing the ship that represents *ecclesia* (the church), and that alludes to the Christian's journey through life. Lucas, *Exodus*, pp. 89–90, sees the sail as relating to the veil covering the Ark of the Covenant, and the sailyard as representing also the Cross of Christ.

Þeodenholde.   Þa wæs þridda wic
folce to frofre.   Fyrd eall geseah
hu þær hlifedon   halige seglas,
90   lyftwundor leoht;   leode ongeton,
dugoð Israhela,   þæt þær Drihten cwom
weroda Drihten,   wicsteal metan.
Him beforan foran   fyr ond wolcen
in beorhtrodor,   beamas twegen,
95   þara æghwæðer   efngedælde
heahþegnunga   Haliges Gastes,
deormodra sið   dagum ond nihtum.
      Þa Ic on morgen gefrægn   modes rofan
hebban herebyman   hludan stefnum,
100   wuldres woman.   Werod eall aras,
modigra mægen,   swa him Moyses bebead,
mære magoræswa,   Metodes folce,
fus fyrdgetrum.   Forð gesawon
lifes latþeow   lifweg metan.
105   Segl siðe weold,   sæmen æfter
foron flodwege.   Folc wæs on salum,
hlud herges cyrm.   Heofonbeacen astah
æfena gehwam,   oðer wundor;
syllic æfter sunnan   setlrade beheold,
110   ofer leodwerum   lige scinan,
byrnende beam.   Blace stodon
ofer sceotendum   scire leoman,
scinon scyldhreoðan.   Sceado swiðredon,
neowle nihtscuwan   neah ne mihton
115   heolstor ahydan.   Heofoncandel barn;
niwe nihtweard   nyde sceolde
wician ofer weredum,   þy læs him westengryre,
har hæðbroga,   holmegum wederum
on ferclamme   ferhð getwæfde.
120   Hæfde foregenga   fyrene loccas,
blace beamas;   bellegsan hweop
in þam hereþreate,   hatan lige,
þæt he on westenne   werod forbærnde,
nymðe hie modhwate   Moyses hyrde.
125   Scean scirwerod,   scyldas lixton;
gesawon randwigan   rihte stræte,
segn ofer sweoton,   oðþæt sæfæsten
landes æt ende   leodmægne forstod,
fus on forðweg.   Fyrdwic aras:
130   wyrpton hie werige;   wiste genægdon
modige meteþegnas,   hyra mægen beton.
Bræddon æfter beorgum,   siððan byme sang,
flotan feldhusum.   Þa wæs feorðe wic,
randwigena ræst,   be þan Readan Sæ.

those loyal to the Lord. This third camp was
a comfort to the people. The entire army saw
how the holy sails towered there,
90   a bright miracle in the air; people perceived,
these Israelite warriors, that their Lord had come,
the Lord of troops, to mark out the camping-place.
In front of them proceeded fire and cloud
in the bright sky, two pillars,
95   each of them equally divided
in the exalted service of the Holy Ghost,
the journey of the brave ones by day and night.
    Then in the morning, I heard, strong in mind
they lifted up the trumpets with loud voices,
100   a battle-cry of glory. The entire army arose,
a troop of the valiant, just as Moses the glorious leader
commanded them, the people of the Lord,
an eager force of warriors. In front they saw
their life's guide mark out the way of life.
105   The sail controlled the journey, the sailors travelled
the road of the sea after it. The people were joyful,
the clamour of the army loud. The heavenly beacon rose up
every evening, this the other miracle;
glorious after the sun's setting it remained,
110   shining with fire over the people,
a burning pillar. Bright rays shone
above the warriors, a gleaming ray of light,
so that their shields shone. Shadows melted away,
the low-lying night shadows near by could not
115   conceal their hiding place. The heavenly candle burned;[11]
it was necessary for this new night-guardian
to stay above the troops, in case the terror of the desert,
the grey heath-terror, might put an end to
life with the sudden terrifying grasp of the storms of the seas.
120   The herald had fiery locks,
bright rays; it threatened the terror of fire
on that troop, hot flame,
such that it would consume the troop in the desert,
unless they listened, brave-hearted, to Moses.
125   It shone enveloped in brightness, shields gleamed,
the soldiers could see the straight path,
the banner above the troops, until the barrier of the sea
at the end of the land stood in the way of the people's army,
eager for the way forward. A camp was set up:
130   the weary revived themselves; stewards approached
the noble ones with food, and restored their strength.
When the trumpet sounded, the sailors spread out
tents on the slopes. That was the fourth camp,
the warriors' place of rest, by the Red Sea.

11   A possible allegorical allusion to the paschal candle lit on Holy
Saturday when the new members of the church were baptised.

{*Lines 447–590*}

XLVIIII

Folc wæs afæred;   flodegsa becwom
gastas geomre,   geofon deaðe hweop.
Wæron beorhhliðu   blode bestemed:
450   holm heolfre spaw,   hream wæs on yðum,
wæter wæpna ful,   wælmist astah.
Wæron Egypte   eft oncyrde,
flugon forhtigende;   fær ongeton.
Woldon herebleaðe   hamas findan,
455   gylp wearð gnornra.   Him ongen genap
atol yða gewealc,   ne ðær ænig becwom
herges to hame;   ac behindan beleac
wyrd mid wæge.   Þær ær wegas lagon
mere modgode,   mægen wæs adrenced.
460   Streamas stodon,   storm up gewat
heah to heofonum,   herewopa mæst;
laðe cyrmdon,   lyft up geswearc
fægum stæfnum.   Flod blod gewod.
Randbyrig wæron rofene,   rodor swipode
465   meredeaða mæst.   Modige swulton,
cyningas on corðre.   Cyre swiðrode
sæs æt ende;   wigbord scinon.
Heah ofer hæleðum   holmweall astah,
merestream modig.   Mægen wæs on cwealme
470   fæste gefeterod,   forðganges weg,
searwum æsæled.   Sand basnodon,
witodre fyrde,   hwonne waðema stream,
sincalda sæ,   sealtum yðum,
æflastum gewuna   ece staðulas,
475   nacud nydboda,   neosan come,
fah feðegast,   se ðe feondum geneop.
Wæs seo hæwene lyft   heolfre geblanden.
Brim berstende   blodegesan hweop,
sæmanna sið,   oðþæt soð Metod
480   þurh Moyses hand   mod gerymde:
wide wæðde,   wælfæðmum sweop.
Flod famgode,   fæge crungon,
lagu land gefeol,   lyft wæs onhrered.
Wicon weallfæsten,   wægas burston,
485   multon meretorras   þa se Mihtiga sloh
mid halige hand,   heofonrices Weard,
werbeamas,   wlance ðeode.
Ne mihton forhabban   helpendra pað,

(Lines 135 to 446 concern the approach of Pharoah's army against the Israelites, camped by the Red Sea. Described in Germanic heroic terms, the arrival of the Egyptians causes great fear among the fugitive nation, who, on the subsequent morning, wait anxiously for the advice of Moses. Moses speaks of the mercy of God, and the Red Sea parts for the journey of the tribes of Israel, which are described by the poet crossing the dry bed of the sea. From line 362 to 446, the stories of Noah and the Ark, and Abraham and Isaac, are described, demonstrating God's mercy and salvation for those who obey him and are loyal to him.)

{*Lines 447–590*}

XLVIIII

The people were terrified; terror of the flood came upon
their sorrowful spirits, as the sea threatened death.
The steep slopes were spattered with blood:
450 the sea spewed gore, there was tumult within the waves,
the water was full of weapons, the deadly mist rose up.
The Egyptians were turned back,
they fled terrified; they had experienced sudden disaster.
Cowardly, they wanted to seek out their homes;
455 their boast became less optimistic. It grew dark against them,
a terrible rolling of the waves, and there not one of the
army came home; but from behind, fate
shut them in with waves. Where before paths had lain
the sea raged, the army was drowned.
460 Surges of water mounted up, a tempest rose up
high to the heavens, the greatest cry of an army;
the enemies cried out, the sky above grew dark
with the voices of those doomed to die. Blood saturated the flood.
The water's ramparts were broken, the sky was lashed
465 by the mightiest of sea-deaths. Bold men perished,
kings in their troop. The choice grew less
at the border of the sea; battle-shields shone.
High over the men the ocean-wall rose up,
the raging waters of the sea. That army was fettered
470 securely in death, without the power of a way forward,
held down by armour. The sand waited for
the appointed course of events, when the surge of the waves,
the perpetually cold sea accustomed to change of course,
the mottled warlike spirit, which dragged down the enemies,
475 the naked messenger of inevitable distress, would come to discover,
its everlasting foundations with its salty waves.
The blue sky was blended with blood.
The bursting waters, the terror of blood, threatened
the journey of the seamen, until the true Ruler
480 through Moses's hand manifested his will:
widely it hunted, swept with its deadly clutches.
The flood seethed, those doomed to die fell dying,
the sea-water fell on the land, the air was disturbed.
The ramparts gave way, the waves crashed,
485 the towers of sea-water melted when the Almighty,
the Guardian of the heavenly kingdom,
of the covenant-pillar, killed with his holy hand the proud nation.[12]
Nor could they restrain the course of the helpers,[13]

---

12   i.e. the Egyptians crossing the Red Sea.   13   The 'helpers' are the waves that assisted the Israelites.

merestreames mod,   ac he manegum gesceod
490 gyllende gryre.   Garsecg wedde,
up ateah, on sleap,   egesan stodon,
weollon wælbenna,   witrod gefeol
heah of heofonum,   handweorc Godes,
famigbosma;   Flodweard gesloh
495 unhleowan wæg   alde mece,
þæt ðy deaðdrepe   drihte swæfon,
synfullra sweot.   Sawlum lunnon
fæste befarene,   flodblac here,
siððan hie onbugon   brimyppinge,
500 modewæga mæst.   Mægen eall gedreas
ða þe gedrecte,   dugoð Egypta,
Faraon mid his folcum.   He onfond hraðe,
siððan grund gestah,   Godes andsaca,
þæt wæs mihtigra   mereflodes Weard:
505 wolde heorufæðmum   hilde gesceadan,
yrre ond egesfull.   Egyptum wearð
þæs dægweorces   deop lean gesceod,
forðam þæs heriges   ham eft ne com
ealles ungrundes   ænig to lafe,
510 þætte sið heoro   secgan moste,
bodigean æfter burgum   bealospella mæst,
hordwearda hryre,   hæleða cwenum:
ac þa mægenþreatas   meredeað geswealh,
spelbodan eac.   Se ðe sped ahte
515 ageat gylp wera.   Hie wið God wunnon.
Þanon Israhelum   ece rædas
on merehwearfe   Moyses sægde,
heahþungen wer,   halige spræce,
deop ærende.   Dægweorc nemnað
520 swa gyt werðeode   on gewritum findað
doma gehwilcne,   þara ðe him Drihten bebead
on þam siðfate   soðum wordum.
Gif onlucan wile   lifes wealhstod,
beorht in breostum,   banhuses weard,
525 ginfæsten god   Gastes cægon,
run bið gerecenod,   ræd forð gæð.
Hafað wislicu   word on fæðme,
wile meagollice   modum tæcan
þæt we gesne ne syn   Godes þeodscipes,
530 Metodes miltsa.   He us ma onlyhð
nu us boceras   beteran secgað
lengran lifwynna.   Þis is læne dream,
wommum awyrged,   wreccum alyfed,
earmra anbid.   Eðellease
535 þysne gystsele   gihðum healdað.
Murnað on mode,   manhus witon
fæst under foldan,   þær bið fyr ond wyrm,
open ece scræf   yfela gehwylces,
swa nu regnþeofas   rice dælað:

490

the will of the sea-waters, but he destroyed many
with shrieking terror. The sea raged,
drew up, glided upon them, fears arose,
the deadly bonds of the sea seethed, fell on the path of battle
from high in the heavens, the handiwork of God,
foamy-breasted; the Guardian of the flood struck

495

the unprotective wave[14] with an ancient sword,
so that with that death-blow troops passed away,
the company of the sinful. They parted from their souls
firmly surrounded, the flood-pale army,
when they bowed down to the sea-manifestation,

500

the greatest of wilful waves. The entire troop fell,
those who afflicted, the Egyptian host,
Pharoah with his people. He quickly discovered
when he reached the bottom of the sea, this adversary of God,
that the Guardian of the surging sea was the mightier:

505

he[15] intended to decide the battle with deadly embraces,
angry and terrifying. For the Egyptians
the reward decided on for that day's work was deep,
because from that entire immense army
not one came home again as a survivor

510

so that he could report their misfortune,
might announce through the cities the most grave news,
the death of the treasure-guardians, to the queens of those men:
sea-death had swallowed up those powerful troops,
the messenger also. He who possessed the power

515

poured out[16] the boast of those men. They had fought against God.
After that, Moses, the illustrious man,
announced to the Israelites on the seashore
holy words, eternal counsels,
a profound message. The day's work is related

520

as people still find in the scriptures
each of the ordinances, those which the Lord commended
with his true words on that journey.
If the interpreter of life, bright in the heart,
the guardian of the body, wishes to unlock

525

the ample good with the keys of the Spirit,
the mystery will be explained, wisdom will come forth.[17]
It has wise words in its embrace,
it earnestly wishes to teach our minds
so that we might not be lacking in the fellowship of God,

530

in the mercy of the Lord. He will grant us more
now that writers can tell us of better,
more long-lasting, heavenly joys. This current joy is transitory,
corrupted by sins, granted to exiles,
the wretched ones' time of anticipation. Without a homeland

535

we occupy this hall of visitors[18] with sorrows.
We are anxious in spirit, aware of the place of wickedness
constant under the world, where there is the fire and serpent,
the open eternal pit of every evil,
just as now the arch-thieves share power:

---

14 An ironic reference to the destructive sea.
15 i.e. God.
16 Or 'destroyed'.

17 These four lines (523–6) invite the audience to engage with the poem's potential allegorical meanings.
18 i.e. world.

540   yldo oððe ærdeað.   Eftwyrd cymeð
      mægenþrymma mæst   ofer middangeard,
      dæg dædum fah.   Drihten sylfa
      on þam meðelstede   manegum demeð,
      þonne he soðfæstra   sawla lædeð,
545   eadige gastas,   on uprodor,
      þær leoht ond lif,   eac þon lissa blæd,
      dugoð on dreame   Drihten herigað,
      weroda Wuldorcyning,   to widan feore.
          Swa reordode   ræda gemyndig,
550   manna mildost,   mihtum swiðed,
      hludan stefne.   Here stille bad
      witodes willan;   wundor ongeton,
      modiges muðhæl.   He to mænegum spræc:
      'Micel is þeos menigeo,   Mægenwisa trum,
555   fullesta mæst,   se ðas fare lædeð.
      Hafað us on Cananea   cyn gelyfed,
      burh ond beagas,   brade rice;
      wile nu gelæstan   þæt he lange gehet
      mid aðsware,   engla Drihten,
560   in fyrndagum   fæderyncynne:
      gif ge gehealdað   halige lare
      þæt ge feonda gehwone   forð ofergangað,
      gesittað sigerice   be sæm tweonum,
      beorselas beorna;   bið eower blæd micel.'
565   Æfter þam wordum   werod wæs on salum.
      Sungon sigebyman,   segnas stodon,
      fægerne sweg.   Folc wæs on lande.
      Hæfde wuldres beam   werud gelæded,
      halige heapas,   on hild Godes.
570   Lindwigan life gefegon   þa hie oðlæded hæfdon
      feorh of feonda dome,   þeah ðe hie hit frecne geneðdon,
      weras under wætera hrofas.   Gesawon hie þær weallas standan,
      ealle him brimu blodige þuhton,   þurh þa heora beadosearo wægon.
      Hreððon hildespelle   siððan hie þam herge wiðforon;
575   hofon hereþreatas   hlude stefne,
      for þam dædweorce   Drihten heredon,
      weras wuldres sang.   Wif on oðrum,
      folcsweota mæst,   fyrdleoð golan
      aclum stefnum,   eallwundra fela.
580   Þa wæs eðfynde   Afrisc meowle
      on geofones staðe   golde geweorðod.
      Handa hofon   halswurðunge,
      bliðe wæron,   bote gesawon.
      Heddon herereafes,   hæft wæs onsæled.
585   Ongunnon sælafe   segnum dælan
      on yðlafe,   ealde madmas,
      reaf ond randas.   Heo on riht sceodon
      gold ond godweb,   Josepes gestreon,
      wera wuldorgesteald.   Werigend lagon
590   on deaðstede,   drihtfolca mæst.

540 old age and an early death. A later fate comes,
the greatest of powers, over the earth,
a day of wrath for deeds done. The Lord himself
in that meeting-place will judge the many,
when he leads the righteous souls,
545 the blessed spirits, into heaven,
where there is light and life, as well as an abundance of grace,
the company in happiness will praise the Lord,
the troops' King of glory, for evermore.
Thus he spoke mindful of counsels,
550 the mildest of men, strengthened by powers,
in a loud voice. The army quietly waited for
the will of the appointed one; they recognized the miracle,
salvation from the mouth of the spirited one. He spoke to the throng:
'Great is this multitude, and strong their Leader,
555 the greatest of help, he who leads this journey.
He has granted to us the tribe of the Canaanites,
their cities and treasures, a broad kingdom;
now, the Lord of angels intends to carry out
that which he promised long ago with the swearing of oaths
560 in the days of old to our forefathers' race:
if you will keep the holy instructions
then you will subdue each one of your enemies in future,
and will occupy the victorious kingdom in entirety,
the beer-hall of warriors; your glory will be great.'
565 After these words the army was joyful.
The trumpets of victory sang as the battle-standards stood,
a delightful sound. The people were on land.
The pillar of glory had led the army,
the holy troops, in the protection of God.
570 The warriors rejoiced in living, that they had brought away
their life from the power of the enemies, even though they had daringly risked it,
men under the roofs of the waters. They saw the walls rise up there,
all the waters seemed bloody to them, through those they had carried their war-gear.
They exulted in a song of battle after they had escaped from the army;[19]
575 the troops and the people raised up a loud voice,
they praised the Lord for that achievement
in a song of glory. The women among the others,
the greatest of hosts, sung a battle-song
about the many wonders with voices excited by awe.
580 Then it was easy to find the Ethiopian woman[20]
on the sea's shore ennobled with gold.
Hands lifted up necklaces,
they were happy, they perceived their reward.
They took charge of the booty – their captivity was unloosed.
585 The sea-survivors proceeded to share out
the ancient treasures among the tribes on the shore,
rings and shields. In the proper manner they divided
gold and fine purple cloth, the treasure of Joseph,
the glorious possessions of the men. The protectors[21] lay
590 in the place of death, the greatest of peoples.

---

19 i.e. the Egyptian army.
20 The woman may be Moses's wife.

21 An ironic reference to the Egyptians.

Wulfstan's *Sermo Lupi ad Anglos*

This sermon, written by Wulfstan (died 1023), is one of the most famous pieces of Old English religious prose. Wulfstan, like Ælfric, was a product of the second generation of Benedictine reformers, building on the work of earlier tenth-century monastic figures such as Oswald and Æthelwold. During his prolific and influential career, Wulfstan was bishop of London, and, from 1002, he was bishop of Worcester and archbishop of York. As well as being a homilist, Wulfstan also had a hand in composing the law-codes of Kings Æthelred and Cnut, and he wrote a number of other legal and administrative works. The *Sermo Lupi ad Anglos* represents his least characteristic work (its title incorporates Wulfstan's *nom de plume Lupus* ('wolf')).[1] It was written in *c*.1014 and is preserved in five manuscripts. These are London, British Library, Cotton Nero A. i, folios 110–15 (early eleventh century), Cambridge, Corpus Christi College, 201, pp. 82–6 (mid-eleventh century), Cambridge, Corpus Christi College, 419, pp. 95–112 (first half of the eleventh century), Oxford, Bodleian Library, Hatton 113, folios 84 verso to 90 verso (third quarter of the eleventh century), and Oxford, Bodleian Library, Bodley 343, folios 143 verso to 144 verso, of the second half of the twelfth century. These five versions form two redactions of the original text.[2]

This edited version of the *Sermo* is based on the text in Cotton Nero A. i, a manuscript which is associated with either Worcester or York. In the sermon, the concerns of Wulfstan are very apparent: he believes that the attacks of the Vikings upon the English, which reached crisis point in 1014, represent divine retribution for the sins of the English nation. He allies himself with the Welsh author, Gildas, who wrote a passionate work against the sins of the Britons in the sixth century. Wulfstan here laments the decline of Christian morals among the English, and catalogues in detail the various sins he sees being practised. Wulfstan was absolutely committed to rectifying the wrongs of his people, to re-establishing morality and Christian behaviour, and to appeasing God, and to these ends all his powerful rhetoric is aimed.

Wulfstan's prose is pragmatic, addressing very contemporary concerns with an urgency reflected in the intensity of emotion behind the exhortation and admonition. The theme of the first paragraph, the need for repentance by the English people for the sins committed by them, is clarified and exemplified by the catalogue of sins that follows. Repetition is a major rhetorical device found at every level of the discourse: the word, the clause, the phrase. It aims to emphasize the key themes of the sermon such as the necessity for *bote*, 'a remedy', to avoid *Godes yrre* 'God's anger', and to obey *lagu*, 'the law'. This remedy needs to be kept in mind to prevent the horrors of preceding years; when *inne and ute* ('within and without') dreadful episodes recurred in England *oft and gelome* ('often and frequently'). Repetition ensures that Wulfstan's message will reach every one of his audience, and that the extreme sense of urgency that Wulfstan himself feels can be conveyed effectively. Reinforcing this repetition and structural clarity is the rhythmic nature of the prose, consisting of regular two-stress phrases. The stresses themselves often fall on alliterating syllables, reminiscent of Old English poetic half-lines, and adding to the aural effectiveness of the text (for example, *þurh morðdæda and þurh mandæda, þurh gitsunga and þurh gifernessa*; *here and hete*, etc.).

Sermo Lupi ad Anglos

Sermo Lupi ad Anglos quando Dani maxime persecuti sunt eos, quod fuit anno millesimo xiiii ab incarnatione domini nostri Jesu Cristi

Leofan men, gecnawað þæt soð is: ðeos worold is on ofste, and hit nealæcð þam ende, and þy hit is on worolde aa swa leng swa wyrse. And swa hit sceal nyde for folces synnan ær Antecristes tocyme yfelian swyþe; and huru hit wyrð þænne egeslic and grimlic wide on worolde. Understandað eac georne þæt deofol þas þeode nu fela geara dwelode to swyþe, and þæt lytle getreowþa wæran mid

5   mannum, þeah hy wel spæcan, and unrihta to fela ricsode on lande. And næs a fela manna þe smeade ymbe þa bote swa georne swa man scolde, ac, dæghwamlice, man ihte yfel æfter oðrum and unriht rærde and unlaga manege ealles to wide gynd ealle þas þeode. And we eac forþam habbað fela byrsta and bysmara gebiden, and, gif we ænige bote gebidan scylan, þonne mote we þæs to Gode ernian bet þonne we ær þysan dydan. Forþam mid miclan earnungan we geearnedan

---

1 See D. Bethurum, ed., *The Homilies of Wulfstan* (Oxford, 1957), pp. 355–6. See also A. Orchard, 'Wulfstan the Homilist', in *The Blackwell Encyclopaedia of Anglo-Saxon England*, eds M. Lapidge, J. Blair, S. Keynes and D. Scragg (Oxford, 1998), p. 495, for a summary of Wulfstan's life and work.

2 D. Whitelock discusses the relationship between the texts in her edition of the *Sermo Lupi Ad Anglos*, 3rd edn (London, 1963; repr. Exeter, 1976).

Sermo Lupi ad Anglos

The sermon of 'Wolf' to the English when the Danes persecuted them most, that was in the year 1014 from the birth of our Lord Jesus Christ

Beloved men, know what the truth is: this world is in haste, and it approaches the end, and therefore it is ever worse and worse within the world. And so it shall necessarily become very much worse because of the people's sins before the arrival of the Antichrist; and then it will be especially dreadful and terrible throughout the world. You must also understand well that the devil has now led this people astray for many years, and that there has been little loyalty among men, though they might speak well, and too many injustices have prevailed in the land. And there were never many men who thought about the remedy as eagerly as they might have, but, daily, men have increased one evil after another and established injustice and violations of the law all too widely throughout this entire nation. And therefore we have also experienced many injuries and insults, and, if we are to have any remedy, then we must earn it

10   þa yrmða þe us on sittað, and mid swyþe micelan earnungan we þa bote motan æt Gode geræcan,
gif hit sceal heonanforð godiende weorðan. La hwæt, we witan ful georne þæt to miclan bryce
sceal micel bot nyde, and to miclan bryne wæter unlytel, gif man þæt fyr sceal to ahte acwencan.
And micel is nydþearf manna gehwilcum þæt he Godes lage gyme heonanforð georne and Godes
gerihta mid rihte gelæste. On hæþenum þeodum ne dear man forhealdan lytel ne micel þæs þe

15   gelagod is to gedwolgoda weorðunge; and we forhealdað æghwær Godes gerihta ealles to gelome.
And ne dear man gewanian on hæþenum þeodum inne ne ute ænig þæra þinga þe gedwolgodan
broht bið and to lacum betæht bið; and we habbað Godes hus inne and ute clæne berypte. And
Godes þeowas syndan mæþe and munde gewelhwær bedælde; and gedwolgoda þenan ne dear
man misbeodan on ænige wisan mid hæþenum leodum, swa swa man Godes þeowum nu deð to

20   wide þær Cristene scoldan Godes lage healdan and Godes þeowas griðian.

Ac soð is þæt Ic secge þearf is þære bote, forþam Godes gerihta wanedan to lange innan þysse
þeode on æghwylcan ænde. And folclaga wyrsedan ealles to swyþe, and halignessa syndan to
griðlease wide, and Godes hus syndan to clæne berypte ealdra gerihta and innan bestrypte ælcra
gerisena. And wydewan syndan fornydde on unriht to ceorle, and to mænege foryrmde and gehynede

25   swyþe. And earme men syndan sare beswicene and hreowlice besyrwde and ut of þysan earde wide
gesealde swyþe unforworhte fremdum to gewealde. And cradolcild geþeowede þurh wælhreowe
unlaga for lytelre þyfþe wide gynd þas þeode. And freoriht fornumene and þrælriht genyrwde and
ælmæsriht gewanode. And, hrædest is to cweþenne, Godes laga laðe and lara forsawene. And þæs
we habbað ealle þurh Godes yrre bysmor gelome, gecnawe se þe cunne. And se byrst wyrð gemæne,

30   þeh man swa ne wene, eallre þysse þeode, butan God beorge.

Forþam hit is on us eallum swutol and gesene þæt we ær þysan oftor bræcan þonne we bettan,
and þy is þysse þeode fela onsæge. Ne dohte hit nu lange inne ne ute, ac wæs here and hunger,
bryne and blodgyte on gewelhwylcan ende oft and gelome. And us stalu and cwalu, stric and
steorfa, orfcwealm and uncoþu, hol and hete and rypera reaflac derede swyþe þearle, and ungylda

35   swyðe gedrehtan, and us unwedera foroft weoldan unwæstma. Forþam on þysan earde wæs, swa
hit þincan mæg, nu fela geara unrihta fela and tealte getrywða æghwær mid mannum. Ne bearh
nu foroft gesib gesibban þe ma þe fremdan, ne fæder his bearne, ne hwilum bearn his agenum
fæder, ne broþor oþrum. Ne ure ænig his lif ne fadode swa swa he scolde, ne gahadode regollice,
ne læwede lahlice. Ac worhtan lust us to lage ealles to gelome, and naþor ne heoldan ne lare ne

40   lage Godes ne manna swa swa we scoldan. Ne ænig wið oþerne getrywlice þohte swa rihte swa he
scolde, ac mæst ælc swicode and oþrum derede wordes and dæde; and huru unrihtlice mæst ælc
oþerne æftan heaweþ mid sceandlican onscytan, do mare gif he mæge. Forþam her syn on lande
ungetrywþa micle for Gode and for worolde, and eac her syn on earde on mistlice wisan
hlafordswican manege. And ealra mæst hlafordswice se bið on worolde þæt man his hlafordes

45   saule beswice; and ful micel hlafordswice eac bið on worolde þæt man his hlaford of life forræde,
oððon of lande lifiendne drife. And ægþer is geworden on þysan earde: Eadweard man forrædde
and syððan acwealde and æfter þam forbærnde. And godsibbas and godbearn to fela man forspilde
wide gynd þas þeode; and ealles to manege halige stowa wide forwurdan þurh þæt þe man sume
men ær þam gelogode, swa man na ne scolde, gif man on Godes griðe mæþe witan wolde. And

50   Cristenes folces to fela man gesealde ut of þysan earde nu ealle hwile. And eal þæt is Gode lað,
gelyfe se þe wille. And scandlic is to specenne þæt geworden is to wide, and egeslic is to witanne
þæt oft doð to manege þe dreogað þa yrmþe: þæt sceotað togædere and ane cwenan gemænum
ceape bicgað gemæne, and wið þa ane fylþe adreogað, an æfter anum, and ælc æfter oðrum,
hundum geliccast þe for fylþe ne scrifað. And syððan wið weorðe syllað of lande feondum to

55   gewealde Godes gesceafte and his agenne ceap þe he deore gebohte.

Eac we witan georne hwær seo yrmð gewearð þæt fæder gesealde bearn wið weorþe, and bearn
his modor, and broþor sealde oþerne fremdum to gewealde; and eal þæt syndan micle and egeslice
dæda, understande se þe wille. And gyt hit is mare and eac mænigfealdre þæt dereð þysse þeode:
mænige synd forsworene and swyþe forlogene, and wed synd tobrocene oft and gelome; and þæt

60   is gesyne on þysse þeode þæt us Godes yrre hetelice on sit, gecnawe se þe cunne.

And la, hu mæg mare scamu þurh Godes yrre mannum gelimpan þonne us deð gelome for

better from God than we have previously done. Thus we have deserved the miseries that now afflict us as just deserts, and it is with very great merits that we might obtain the remedy from God, if it is to improve from now on. Indeed, we know very well that a great violation requires a great remedy, and a great fire not a little water, if one is to extinguish that fire at all. And it is very necessary for each man that he eagerly cares about God's law henceforth and pays God's dues properly. Among the heathen people no man dares to withhold little or much of that which is ordained in the worship of false gods; and everywhere we withhold God's dues all too often. And not one of the heathen people dares lessen inside or outside any of the things that are brought to the false gods and are appointed as sacrifices; and we have completely despoiled God's house inside and out. And God's servants are deprived of reverence and protection everywhere; and not one of the heathen people dares mistreat the ministers of false gods in any manner, such as one does now to God's servants too widely where Christians should keep God's law and protect God's servants.

But it is the truth when I say that there is need for a solution, because God's laws have dwindled for too long among this nation in each province. And public laws have declined all too greatly, and sanctuaries are too widely unprotected, and the houses of God are entirely despoiled of ancient rights and stripped of all that is decent inside. And widows are unjustly forced to marry, and too many are impoverished and greatly shamed. And poor men are sorely deceived and cruelly enslaved and, entirely innocent, are widely sold out of this land into the power of strangers. And children in the cradle are enslaved for minor theft widely throughout this nation because of cruel injustice. And the rights of freemen are taken away and the rights of a slave curtailed and the rights to alms are curtailed. And it can all be said most briefly that God's laws are hated and his teachings despised. And through God's anger we are all frequently shamed, understand this whoever is able to. And, although one might not think so, the loss will become universal to this entire nation unless God protect us.

Therefore it is clear and apparent in all of us that previously we more often transgressed than we made amends, and thus many things attack this nation. Nothing has prospered for a long time now either within or without, but there is devastation and hunger, burning and bloodshed in every region often and frequently. And stealing and death, sedition and pestilence, cattle plague and disease, malice and persecution and the plundering of robbers have injured us very severely, and excessive tax has oppressed us greatly, and storms have often caused us crop failures. Therefore, so it now appears, there have been for many years now many injustices in this nation and wavering loyalties among men everywhere. Now very often a kinsman will not protect a kinsman more than he would a stranger, nor a father his son, nor sometimes a son his own father, nor one brother the other. Nor has any one of us ordered his life just as he ought to, either those in the religious orders, or the layman according to the law. But lust has been made a law to us all too frequently, and we have kept neither the teachings nor the laws of God or men as we should. Nor has anyone thought loyally toward the other as justly as he should, but almost all have been treacherous and have betrayed others by words and by deeds; and indeed, almost all wrongfully slander others with shameful assault, and will do more, if he can. Therefore, there are great disloyalties towards God and towards the world throughout the land, and also there are here within the land those who are traitors to their lord in many various ways. And of all the treachery in the world to the lord the greatest is that a man should betray his lord's soul; and it is also a very great betrayal of one's lord in the world that a man should treacherously kill his lord or drive his lord, living, from the land. And both have happened in this land: Edward was betrayed and afterwards killed and afterwards he was burned.[3] And godparents and godchildren have been killed far and wide through this country; and far and wide too many holy establishments have been destroyed because of certain men who had been placed there previously, as they ought not to have been if man had wanted to show respect in God's sanctuary. And all the while now, too many Christian people have been sold out of this land. And all of this is hateful to God, believe it if you will. And it is shameful to speak of that which has widely happened, and it is fearful to know what often many people do who commit that crime: that is, they club together and buy one woman in common as a joint purchase, and with the one they commit filth, one after the other, and each after the other, most like dogs who do not care about filth. And afterwards, they sell for money out of the land and into the power of enemies the creature of God and his own purchase, which he so dearly bought.

3   Edward, the martyred son of King Edgar, murdered in 978.

agenum gewyrhtum? Ðeh þræla wylc hlaforde æthleape and of Cristendome to Wicinge weorþe, and hit æfter þam eft geweorþe þæt wæpngewrixl weorðe gemæne þegene and þræle, gif þræl þæne þegen fullice afylle, licge ægylde ealre his mægðe. And gif se þegen þæne þræl þe he ær ahte
65   fullice afylle, gylde þegengylde. Ful earhlice laga and scandlice nydgyld þurh Godes yrre us syn gemæne, understande se þe cunne.

And fela ungelimpa gelimpð þysse þeode oft and gelome. Ne dohte hit nu lange inne ne ute, ac wæs here and hete on gewelhwilcan ende oft and gelome, and Engle nu lange eal sigelease and to swyþe geyrigde þurh Godes yrre. And flotmen swa strange þurh Godes þafunge þæt oft on gefeohte
70   an feseð tyne, and hwilum læs, hwilum ma, eal for urum synnum. And oft tyne oððe twelfe, ælc æfter oþrum, scendað to bysmore þæs þegenes cwenan, and hwilum his dohtor oððe nydmagan, þær he on locað, þe læt hine sylfne rancne and ricne and genoh godne ær þæt gewurde. And oft þræl þæne þegen þe ær wæs his hlaford cnyt swyþe fæste, and wyrcð him to þræle þurh Godes yrre. Wala þære yrmðe and wala þære woroldscame þe nu habbað Engle, eal þurh Godes yrre!
75   Oft twegen sæmæn, oððe þry hwilum, drifað þa drafe Cristenra manna fram sæ to sæ, ut þurh þas þeode, gewelede togædere, us eallum to woroldscame, gif we on eornost ænige cuþon ariht understandan. Ac ealne þæne bysmor þe we oft þoliað we gyldað mid weorðscipe þam þe us scendað: we him gyldað singallice, and hy us hynað dæghwamlice; hy hergiað and hy bærnað, rypað and reafiað, and to scipe lædað. And la, hwæt is ænig oðer on eallum þam gelimpum butan
80   Godes yrre ofer þas þeode swutol and gesæne?

Nis eac nan wundor þeah us mislimpe, forþam we witan ful georne þæt nu fela geara mænn na ne rohtan foroft hwæt hy worhtan wordes oððe dæde. Ac wearð þes þeodscipe, swa hit þincan mæg, swyþe forsyngod þurh mænigfealde synna and þurh fela misdæda: þurh morðdæda and þurh mandæda, þurh gitsunga and þurh gifernessa, þurh stala and þurh strudunga, þurh mannsylena
85   and þurh hæþene unsida, þurh swicdomas and þurh searacræftas, þurh lahbrycas and þurh æswicas, þurh mægræsas and þurh manslyhtas, þurh hadbrycas and þurh æwbrycas, þurh siblegeru and þurh mistlice forligru. And eac syndan wide, swa we ær cwædan, þurh aðbricas and þurh wedbrycas and þurh mistlice leasunga forloren and forlogen ma þonne scolde. And freolsbricas and fæstenbrycas wide geworhte oft and gelome. And eac her syn on earde apostatan abroþene and cyrichatan
90   hetole and leodhatan grimme ealles to manege, and oferhogan wide godcundra rihtlaga and Cristenra þeawa, and hocorwyrde dysige æghwær on þeode oftost on þa þing þe Godes bodan beodaþ, and swyþost on þa þing þe æfre to Godes lage gebyriað mid rihte.

And þy is nu geworden wide and side to ful yfelan gewunan þæt menn swyþor scamað nu for goddædan þonne for misdædan, forþam to oft man mid hocere goddæda hyrweð and godfyrhte
95   lehtreð ealles to swyþe, and swyþost man tæleð and mid olle gegreteð ealles to gelome þa þe riht lufiað and Godes ege habbað be ænigum dæle. And þurh þæt þe man swa deð – þæt man eal hyrweð þæt man scolde heregian and to forð laðet þæt man scolde lufian – þurh þæt man gebringeð ealles to manege on yfelan geþance and on undæde, swa þæt hy ne scamað na, þeh hy syngian swyðe and wið God sylfne forwyrcan hy mid ealle. Ac for idelan onscytan hy scamað þæt hy betan
100   heora misdæda swa swa bec tæcan, gelice þam dwæsan, þe for heora þrytan, lewe nellað beorgan ær hy na ne magan þeh hy eal willan.

Her syndan þurh synleawa, swa hit þincan mæg, sare gelewede to manege on earde. Her syndan mannslagan and mægslagan and mæsserbanan and mynsterhatan; and her syndan manswaran and morþorwyrhtan; and her syndan myltestran and bearnmyrðran and fule forlegene horingas manege;
105   and her syndan wiccan and wælcyrian; and her syndan ryperas and reaferas and woroldstruderas; and, hrædest is to cweþenne, mana and misdæda ungerim ealra. And þæs us ne scamað na, ac us scamað swyþe þæt we bote aginnan swa swa bec tæcan, and þæt is gesyne on þysse earman forsyngodan þeode. Eala, micel magan manege gyt hertoeacan eaþe beþencan þæs þe an man ne mehte on hrædinge asmeagan, hu earmlice hit gefaren is nu ealle hwile wide gynd þas þeode. And
110   smeage huru georne gehwa hine sylfne and þæs na ne latige ealles to lange. Ac la, on Godes naman, utan don swa us neod is: beorgan us sylfum swa we geornost magan, þe læs we ætgædere ealle forweorðan.

Also we know well where the crime has happened that a father sold his son for a price, and a son his mother, and one brother gave another into the power of foreigners; and all of these are great and terrible deeds, understand that if you are able. And yet there are greater and more various things that harm this nation: many are forsworn and greatly perjured, and pledges are broken often and frequently; and it is visible among this people that God's anger is violently upon us, know this if you able.

Indeed, how can more shame occur to men through God's anger than frequently does to us because of our own deeds? If any slave runs away from a lord and, leaving Christendom, becomes a Viking, and it happens afterwards that a hostile encounter occurs between the nobleman and the slave, if the slave should completely kill the nobleman, he will lie without wergild[4] to any of his family. And, if the nobleman should completely kill the slave that he previously owned, he will have to pay the wergild of a nobleman. Through God's anger, very cowardly laws and shameful forced payments are common among us, understand that if you are able.

And many misfortunes occur to this nation often and frequently. For long now, both within and without, nothing has prospered, but there has been devastation and persecution in every place often and frequently, and the English have now for a long time been completely victory-less and greatly disheart-ened because of God's anger. And the sailors are so strong because of God's permission that often in the battle one will rout ten, sometimes less, sometimes more, and all because of our sins. And often ten or twelve, each one after the other, shamefully insult the wife of a nobleman, and sometimes his daughter or close kinswoman, there where he, who considered himself important and powerful and brave enough before that happened, looks on. And often the slave binds fast the nobleman who was his lord previously, and makes him a slave because of God's anger. Alas for the misery and alas for the great disgrace that now happens to the English, all because of God's anger!

Often two sailors, or sometimes three, will drive a band of Christian men out from this nation from sea to sea, huddled together as a great disgrace to us all, if we in earnest might properly feel any. But all this disgrace which we often suffer we repay with honour to those that injure us: we continually pay them, and they humiliate us daily; they ravage and they burn, plunder and rob, and carry it to their ships. And listen, what are any of all of these occurrences except God's clear and visible anger towards the nation?

It is also no wonder, though, that things go wrong for us, because we know full well that now for many years men have frequently not cared what they did in word or in deed. Rather, so it seems, this nation has become very sinful through various sins and through many misdeeds: through deadly sins and through crimes, through avarice and through greediness, through theft and pillaging, through selling men and through heathen vices, through deceit and through fraud, through breach of the law and through sedition, through attacks on relatives and through manslaughter, through injury to those in holy orders and through adultery, through incest and through various fornication. And also widely, as we said before, more people than should be are abandoned and lost through perjury and through viola-tion of one's pledge and through various falsehoods. And non-observance of festivals and fasts happens widely, often and frequently. And also there are here in this land all too many degenerate apostates and violent persecutors of the church and fierce tyrants, and those who despise the divine just laws and the customs of Christians are widespread, and everywhere in this nation are those ignorant people who most often deride those things which God's messengers command, and most especially those things which always, with justice, belong to God's law.

And therefore far and wide such very evil habits have now arisen that men are more shamed for good deeds than for misdeeds, because too often good deeds are vilified and the pious are reviled all too greatly, and most men blame and greet with contempt all too frequently those who love justice and fear God in any event. And because of that which they do thus – that they blame those whom they should praise and furthermore hate those men that they should love – through that they bring all too many evil thoughts and misdeeds, so that they are not ashamed though they sin greatly and commit wrong against God himself. But because of attacks of idleness they are ashamed to seek remedy for their misdeeds just as the book teaches, like the foolish who, because of their pride, will not protect against injury, until they are not able to do so even though they would wish to.

4 The payment made to a murdered person's immediate kin by
the perpetrators of the crime. This varied according to the status of
the victim.

An þeodwita wæs on Brytta tidum, Gildas hatte, se awrat be heora misdædum: hu hy mid heora synnum swa oferlice swyþe God gegræmedan þæt he let æt nyhstan Engla here heora eard
115   gewinnan and Brytta dugeþe fordon mid ealle. And þæt wæs geworden, þæs þe he sæde, þurh ricra reaflac, and þurh gitsunge wohgestreona, þurh leode unlaga and þurh wohdomas, þurh biscopa asolcennesse, and þurh lyðre yrhðe Godes bydela, þe soþes geswugedan ealles to gelome and clumedan mid ceaflum þær hy scoldan clypian. Þurh fulne eac folces gælsan and þurh oferfylla and mænigfealde synna, heora eard hy forworhtan and selfe hy forwurdan.
120   Ac wutan don swa us þearf is: warnian us be swilcan. And soþ is þæt Ic secge: wyrsan dæda we witan mid Englum þonne we mid Bryttan ahwar gehyrdan. And þy us is þearf micel þæt we us beþencan and wið God sylfne þingian georne. And utan don swa us þearf is: gebugan to rihte, and be suman dæle unriht forlætan, and betan swyþe georne þæt we ær bræcan. And utan God lufian and Godes lagum fylgean, and gelæstan swyþe georne þæt þæt we behetan þa we fulluht
125   underfengan, oððon þa þe æt fulluhte ure forespecan wæran. And utan word and weorc rihtlice fadian, and ure ingeþanc clænsian georne, and að and wed wærlice healdan, and sume getrywða habban us betweonan butan uncræftan. And utan gelome understandan þone miclan dom þe we ealle to sculon, and beorgan us georne wið þone weallendan bryne helle wites, and geearnian us þa mærþa and þa myrhða þe God hæfð gegearwod þam þe his willan on worolde gewyrcað. God ure
130   help. Amen.

As it might appear, here are too many in this land who are sorely injured by the defilement of sin. Here are murderers and the killers of kinsmen, and the killers of priests and the persecutors of monasteries; and here are perjurers and murderers; and here are harlots and child-killers and many foul adulterous fornicators; and here are witches and sorceresses; and here are robbers and plunderers and spoliators; and, it is briefest to say, a countless number of crimes and misdeeds. And this is not shameful to us, yet we are too ashamed to begin the atonement such as the book teaches, and that is clearly visible in this wretched nation, ruined by sin. Alas, many might easily recall yet more besides, about which one man could not treat of in haste, which would indicate how miserably it has proceeded all the time now widely throughout this nation. And indeed, let each earnestly examine himself and not delay entirely for too long. But listen, in God's name, let us do what is necessary for us: defend ourselves as best we can, unless we all perish together.

There was a historian in the time of the Britons called Gildas,[5] who wrote about their misdeeds: how through their sins they angered God so very excessively that at last he allowed the army of the English to conquer their land and they destroyed the power of the Britons completely. And that happened, so he said, because of robbery by the powerful, and through the coveting of ill-gotten acquisitions, through the unlawfulness of the people, and through unjust judgements, through the idleness of bishops, and through the wicked cowardice of God's preachers, who kept silent about the truth all too often and mumbled with their jaws where they should have called out. Also, through the foul pride of the people and through gluttony and numerous sins, they forfeited their country and they themselves perished.

But let us do what is necessary for us: take warning from such things. And what I say is true: we know about worse deeds among the English than we heard anywhere among the Britons. And therefore it is absolutely essential that we reflect among ourselves and earnestly pray to God himself. And let us do what is necessary for us: bow to justice and to some extent abandon injustice, and atone very earnestly for what we violated before. And let us love God and follow the laws of God, and very earnestly perform what we promised when we received baptism, or those who were our sponsors promised at baptism. And let us arrange words and works properly, and earnestly cleanse our conscience, and carefully hold oath and pledge, and have some loyalty between us without deceit. And let us often consider the great judgement to which we all must come, and eagerly defend ourselves against the boiling fire of hell-torment, and earn for ourselves those glories and those joys that God has prepared for those who perform his will in the world. May God help us. Amen.

---

5   Gildas wrote the *De excidio Britanniae* in the sixth century, in which he laments the horrors that had happened to the Britons as a result of their sinfulness.

Apollonius of Tyre

This prose text is the earliest surviving Romance in English. It is copied from an Old English exemplar into the mid-eleventh century English manuscript, Cambridge, Corpus Christi College, 201, pp. 131–45. Corpus 201 is a manuscript more famous for its connections with Archbishop Wulfstan's legal and homiletic works than for its inclusion of this piece; all the texts in this manuscript, with the exception of *Apollonius of Tyre*, are sermons and other religious materials, or law-codes. This makes the manuscript context of this classical Romance very curious and one might wonder how the person responsible for the manuscript's compilation viewed the text.

As it is now extant, there is a substantial portion of *Apollonius* missing in the manuscript: the equivalent of half the Latin account of Apollonius's adventures. It is fortunate that the omission occurs where it does, because even without this middle section, the story is essentially intelligible, and the main events – Apollonius's exile, his marriage and the reclamation of his inheritance – are all present.

Apollonius of Tyre is based on the Latin *Historia Apollonii regis Tyri*, a legend that retained its popularity throughout the medieval and Renaissance periods, forming the storyline for Shakespeare's *Pericles*. While many Latin versions of the Apollonius legend survive, no direct source for the Old English has been identified. P. Goolden in his edition, *The Old English 'Apollonius of Tyre'*, edits a collated Latin text for comparative purposes. It is evident from this that the Old English translation is very close to the Latin in its inclusion of major episodes, but is not identical in minor details.[1] This similarity between the Old English and its source text is the probable cause of the text's neglect by scholars, together with the fact that it is written in prose (always the poor relation of poetry), and is a very late example of Old English. This neglect has been redressed somewhat by A. Riedinger's article,[2] which reappraises the differences between the Old English text and the Latin to show that the translator does adapt his source to account for contemporary English expectations and cultural mores. Arcestrate, for example, the daughter of one king and wife of Apollonius, becomes a less notable and remarkable character in the Old English text.

This text, then, is an important and early witness to the emergence of Romance as a vernacular genre, a literary phenomenon that was to flourish from the twelfth century onwards. All the characteristics of the genre are present: adventure, the quest of the hero, the love interest, loyalty, exile and return, disguise, and the aristocratic focus of the narrative. This text, though, is also particularly interesting for its depiction of the varied relationships between fathers and daughters. The author illustrates in Antiochus and his incestuous relationship with his daughter the irredeemable evil of the wicked monarch; this is sharply contrasted with the loving and mutually respectful relationship of Arcestrates and his daughter Arcestrate, and Apollonius and Thasia. The emphasis on innate nobility, no matter how high- or low-born, is also demonstrated throughout the text, in the behaviour of both the eponymous hero, and many of those with whom he has contact, such as the fisherman and Hellanicus. In this way, the author moralizes while he entertains; the comic incidents surrounding Arcestrates and his dealings with the suitors of his daughter add to this lively narrative and serve to underline the text's essentially positive celebration of perseverance and honour in the face of adversity.

Apollonius of Tyre

Her onginneð seo gerecednes be Antioche, þam ungesæligan cingce, and be Apollonige þam Tiriscan.

I

An Antiochia þare ceastre wæs sum cyningc Antiochus gehaten: æfter þæs cyninges naman wæs seo ceaster Antiochia geciged. Þises cyninges cwen wearð of life gewiten, be ðare he hæfde ane swiðe wlitige dohter ungelifedlicre fægernesse. Mid þi þe heo becom to giftelicre yldo, þa gyrnde hyre mænig mære man, micele mærða beodende. Ða gelamp hit sarlicum gelimpe: þa ða se fæder
5   þohte hwam he hi mihte healicost forgifan, þa gefeol his agen mod on hyre lufe mid unrihtre gewilnunge, to ðam swiðe þæt he forgeat þa fæderlican arfæstnesse and gewilnode his agenre dohtor him to gemæccan. And þa gewilnunge naht lange ne ylde, ac sume dæge on ærne mergen þa he of slæpe awoc, he abræc into ðam bure þar heo inne læg, and het his hyredmen ealle him

1   See P. Goolden, ed., *The Old English 'Apollonius of Tyre'* (Oxford, 1958), pp. xx–xxv, for a discussion of the vernacular variant readings.

2   A. Riedinger, 'The Englishing of Arcestrate: Women in *Apollonius* of Tyre', in *New Readings on Women in Old English Literature*, eds H. Damico and A. Hennessey Olsen (Bloomington, IN, 1990), pp. 292–306.

Apollonius of Tyre

Here begins the story about Antiochus, the wicked king, and about Apollonius the Tyrenian.

I

In the city of Antioch there was a certain king called Antiochus: the city was called Antioch after the king's name. This king's queen, by whom he had a very beautiful daughter of marvellous beauty, had departed from life. When she came to a marriageable age, many a powerful man desired her, and offered many treasures. Then a grievous thing occurred: when the father thought about who of the highest status he might give her, he fell in love with her in his own mind with illegal desire, in such a way that he forgot the duty proper to a father and desired his own daughter as a wife. And that desire was not long delayed, but on a certain day at daybreak when he awoke from sleep, he broke into the chamber where she lay and ordered all his servants to go away from him, as if he wanted to hold a secret conversation

aweg gan, swilce he wið his dohtor sume digle spæce sprecan wolde. Hwæt he ða on ðare manfullan
10   scilde abisgode, and þa ongeanwinnendan fæmnan mid micelre strengðe earfoðlice ofercom, and
þæt gefremede man gewilnode to bediglianne.

II

Ða gewearð hit þæt þæs mædenes fostormodor into ðam bure eode and geseah hi ðar sittan on
micelre gedrefednesse, and hire cwæð to: 'Hwig eart þu, hlæfdige, swa gedrefedes modes?' Þæt
mæden hyre andswerode: 'Leofe fostormodor, nu todæg forwurdon twegen æðele naman on þisum
15   bure.' Seo fostormodor cwæð: 'Hlæfdige, be hwam cwist þu þæt?' Heo hyre andwirde and cwæð:
'Ær ðam dæge minra bridgifta, Ic eom mid manfulre scilde besmiten.' Ða cwæð seo fostormodor:
'Hwa wæs æfre swa dirstiges modes þæt dorste cynges dohtor gewæmman ær ðam dæge hyre
brydgifta, and him ne ondrede þæs cyninges irre?' Ðæt mæden cwæð: 'Arleasnes þa scilde on me
gefremode.' Seo fostormodor cwæð: 'Hwi ne segst þu hit þinum fæder?' Ðæt mæden cwæð: 'Hwar
20   is se fæder? Soðlice on me, earmre, is mines fæder nama reowlice forworden, and me nu forðam
deað þearle gelicað.' Seo fostormodor soðlice þa ða heo gehyrde þæt þæt mæden hire deaðes girnde,
ða cliopode heo hi hire to mid liðere spræce and bæd þæt heo fram þare gewilnunge hyre mod
gewænde, and to hire fæder willan gebuge, þeah ðe heo to geneadod wære.

III

On þisum þingum soðlice þurhwunode se arleasesta cyngc Antiochus, and mid gehywedan mode
25   hine sylfne ætywde his ceastergewarum swilce he arfæst fæder wære his dohtor, and betwux his
hiwcuðum mannum he blissode on ðam þæt he his agenre dohtor wer wæs, and to ðam þæt he hi
þe lengc brucan mihte his dohtor arleasan bridbeddes, and him fram adryfan þa ðe hyre girndon
to rihtum gesynscipum, he asette ða rædels, þus cweðende: 'Swa hwilc man swa minne rædels riht
aræde onfo se mynre dohtor to wife, and se ðe hine misræde sy he beheafdod.'
30   Hwæt is nu mare ymbe þæt to sprecanne buton þæt cyningas æghwanon coman and ealdormen
for ðam ungelifedlican wlite þæs mædenes, and þone dead hi oferhogodon and þone rædels
understodon to arædenne. Ac gif heora hwilc þonne þurh asmeagunge boclicre snotornesse, þone
rædels ariht rædde, þonne wearð se to beheafdunge gelæd swa same swa se ðe hine ariht ne rædde.
And þa heafda ealle wurdon gesette on ufeweardan þam geate.

IV

35   Mid þi soðlice Antiochus, se wælreowa cyningc, on þysse wælreownesse þurhwunode, ða wæs
Apollonius gehaten sum iung man, se wæs swiðe welig and snotor and wæs ealdorman on Tiro þare
mægðe; se getruwode on his snotornesse and on ða boclican lare, and agan rowan oðþæt he becom to
Antiochian. Eode þa into ðam cyninge and cwæð: 'Wes gesund cyningc! Hwæt, Ic becom nu to
ðe swa swa to godum fæder and arfæstum. Ic eom soðlice of cynelicum cynne cumen, and Ic bidde
40   þinre dohtor me to gemæccan.' Ða ða se cyngc þæt gehyrde þæt he his willes gehyran nolde, he
swiðe irlicum andwlitan beseah to ðam iungan ealdormen, and cwæð: 'Þu iunga mann, canst
ðu þone dom mynra dohtor gifta?' Apollonius cwæð: 'Ic can þone dom and Ic hine æt þam
geate geseah.' Ða cwæð se cyningc mid æbilignesse: 'Gehir nu þone rædels: "*Scelere vereor, materna
carne vescor.*"' Ðæt is on Englisc: 'Scylde Ic þolige, moddrenum flæsce Ic bruce.' Eft he cwæð: '"*Quaero
45   patrem meum, meae matris virum, uxoris meae filiam nec invenio.*"' Ðæt is on Englisc: 'Ic sece minne
fæder, mynre modor wer, mines wifes dohtor, and Ic ne finde.' Apollonius þa soðlice onfangenum
rædelse, hine bewænde hwon fram ðam cyninge, and mid þy þe he smeade ymbe þæt ingehyd he hit
gewan mid wisdome, and mid Godes fultume he þæt soð arædde. Bewænde hine þa to ðam cynincge
and cwæð: 'Þu goda cyningc, þu asettest rædels; gehyr ðu þa onfundennesse. Ymbe þæt þu cwæde
50   – þæt þu scilde þolodest – ne eart ðu leogende on ðam. Beseoh to ðe silfum. And þæt þu cwæde
"moddrenum flæsce Ic bruce" – ne eart ðu on ðam leogende. Beseoh to þinre dohtor.'

with his daughter. Indeed, then he occupied himself in that evil crime, and overcame the resisting woman with difficulty by his greater strength, and he wanted to conceal the sin that he committed.

II

Then it happened that the maiden's foster-mother[3] went into the chamber and saw her sitting there in great distress, and said to her: 'Lady, why are you so anxious in mind?' The maiden answered her: 'Dear foster-mother, now today two noble names have been destroyed in this chamber.' The foster-mother said: 'Lady, about whom do you say that?' She answered her and said: 'Before my wedding day, I am defiled with evil sin.' Then the foster-mother said: 'Who was ever so presumptuous that he would dare to defile the king's daughter before her wedding day, and not fear the king's anger?' The girl said: 'Wickedness has committed this sin on me.' The foster-mother said: 'Why do you not reveal this to your father?' The maiden said: 'Where is this father? Certainly, within me, a wretch, the name of my father has been grievously destroyed, and because of this, death would now be very pleasing to me.' Truly, when the foster-mother heard that the maiden wished for her death, she implored her with calm talk and beseeched that she should turn her mind from that desire, and submit to her father's will, even though she might be forced in that.

III

In truth, the wicked king Antiochus persisted in these affairs, and with a false mind he showed himself to his citizens as if he were a devoted father to his daughter, and among his domestic servants he rejoiced in that he was a husband to his own daughter, and in order that he could enjoy for longer the wicked bridal bed of his daughter, and drive those who desired her in proper marriage away from him, he set them a riddle, saying: 'Whichever man interprets my riddle correctly will receive my daughter as his wife, and he who misinterprets it will be beheaded.'

What more can be said about this now except that kings and noblemen came from all regions because of the maiden's marvellous beauty, and they disdained death and resolved to interpret the riddle. However, if any of them interpreted the riddle correctly through the examination of scholarly wisdom, then he was taken to be beheaded just the same as those who did not interpret it correctly. And the heads of all of them were set on the highest part of the gate.

IV

During the time that Antiochus, the cruel king, actually persisted in this cruelty, there was a young man called Apollonius, who was very wealthy and intelligent and was a nobleman in the region of Tyre; he trusted in his intelligence and in scholarly learning, and set about journeying by sea until he arrived in Antioch. He went into the king and said: 'Be of good health, king! Indeed, I have come now to you just as to a good and devout father. Truly, I am descended from a royal family, and I ask to have your daughter as my wife.' When the king heard that he would not be subject to his desire, he looked at the young nobleman with a very angry expression, and said: 'You, young man, do you know the case of my daughter's betrothal?' Apollonius said: 'I know the case and I saw it at the gate.' Then the king spoke in anger: 'Listen to the riddle now: "*Scelere vereor, materna carne vescor.*"' That is in English: 'I suffer wickedness, I enjoy the flesh of the mother.' Again he said: '"*Quaero patrem meum, meae matris virum, uxoris meae filiam nec invenio.*"' That is in English: 'I seek my father, the husband of my mother, the daughter of my wife, and cannot find them.' When, truly, Apollonius received the riddle, he turned away slightly from the king, and when he had thought about the meaning he solved it with wisdom, and with God's help he interpreted the truth. He turned to the king then and said: 'Good king, you set the riddle; listen to the solution then. About what you said – that you suffer crime – you are not lying about that. Look to yourself. And in that you said "I enjoy a mother's flesh" – you are not lying in that. Look to your daughter.'

---

3 The female servant.

V

Mid þy þe se cyningc gehirde þæt Apollonius þone rædels swa rihte arædde, þa ondred he þæt hit
to widcuð wære. Beseah ða mid irlicum andwlitan to him, and cwæð: 'Ðu iunga man, þu eart feor
fram rihte; þu dwelast and nis naht þæt þu segst; ac þu hæfst beheafdunge geearnad. Nu læte Ic
55   ðe to þrittigra daga fæce þæt þu beþence ðone rædels ariht, and ðu siððan onfoh minre dohtor to
wife, and gif ðu þæt ne dest, þu scealt oncnawan þone gesettan dom.' Ða wearð Apollonius swiðe
gedrefed, and mid his geferum on scip astah and reow oðþæt he becom to Tirum.

VI

Soðlice, æfter þam þa Apollonius afaren wæs, Antiochus se cyningc him to gecigde his dihtnere se
wæs Thaliarcus gehaten: 'Thaliarce, ealre mynra digolnessa myn se getrywesta þegn, wite þu þæt
60   Apollonius ariht arædde mynne rædels. Astih nu rædlice on scip and far æfter him, and þonne þu
him to becume, þonne acwel ðu hine mid isene oððe mid attre þæt þu mage freodom onfon þonne
þu ongean cymst.' Thaliarcus sona swa he þæt gehyrde, he genam mid him ge feoh ge attor and
on scip astah, and for æfter þam unscæððian Apollonie oððæt he to his eðle becom. Ac Apollonius
þeahhwæðre ær becom to his agenan, and into his huse eode and his bocciste untynde and asmeade
65   þone rædels æfter ealra uðwitena and Chaldea wisdome. Mid þi þe he naht elles ne onfunde buton
þæt he ær geþohte, he cwæð þa to him silfum: 'Hwæt dest þu nu, Apolloni? Ðæs cynges rædels
þu asmeadest, and þu his dohtor ne onfenge; forðam þu eart nu fordemed þæt þu acweald wurðe.'
And he þa ut eode and het his scip mid hwæte gehlæstan and mid micclum gewihte goldes and
seolfres and mid mænifealdum and genihtsumum reafum, and swa mid feawum þam getrywestum
70   mannum on scip astah on ðare þriddan tide þare nihte, and sloh ut on ða sæ.

VII

Þa ðy æftran dæge wæs Apollonius gesoht and geacsod, ac he ne wæs nahwar fundon. Ðar wearð
ða micel morcnung and ormæte wop, swa þæt se heaf swegde geond ealle þa ceastre. Soðlice, swa
micele lufe hæfde eal seo ceasterwaru to him þæt hi lange tid eodon ealle unscorene and sidfeaxe
and heora waforlican plegan forleton and heora baða belucon. Ða ða þas þingc ðus gedone wæron
75   on Tiron, ða becom se foresæda Thaliarcus, se wæs fram Antiocho þam cynincge asænd to ðam
þæt he scolde Apollonium acwellan. Þa he geseah þæt ealle þas þingc belocene wæron, þa cwæð
he to anum cnapan: 'Swa ðu gesund sy, sege me for hwilcum intingum þeos ceaster wunige on swa
micclum heafe and wope.' Him andswerode se cnapa and þus cwæð: 'Eala, hu manful man þu eart,
ðu þe wast þæt þu æfter axsast: oððe hwæt is manna þe nyte þæt þeos ceasterwaru on heafe
80   wunað forðam ðe Apollonius se ealdorman færinga nahwar ne ætywde siððan he ongean com fram
Antiochio þam cyninge.' Ða þa Thaliarcus þæt gehyrde, he mid micclan gefean to scipe gewænde
and mid gewisre seglunge binnon anum dæge com to Antiochian, and eode in to þam cynge and
cwæð: 'Hlaford cyngc, glada nu and blissa, forðam þe Apollonius him ondræt þines rices mægna
swa þæt he ne dear nahwar gewunian.' Ða cwæð se cyningc: 'Fleon he mæg, ac he ætfleon ne
85   mæg.' He þa Antiochus se cyningc gesette þis geban þus cweðende: 'Swa hwilc man swa me
Apollonium lifigendne to gebringð, Ic him gife fifti punda goldes; and þam ðe me his heafod to
gebringð, Ic gife him c punda goldes.' Þa ða þis geban þus geset wæs, þa wæron mid gitsunge
beswicene – na þæt an his find ac eac swilce his frind – and him æfter foran and hine geond ealle
eorðan sohton, ge on dunlandum, ge on wudalandum ge on diglum stowum; ac he ne wearð
90   nahwar fundon.

VIII

Ða het se cyngc scipa gegearcian and him æfter faran; ac hit wæs lang ær ðam þe ða scipa gegearcode
wæron, and Apollonius becom ær to Tharsum. Ða sume dæge eode he be strande, þa geseah hine
sum his cuðra manna, se wæs Hellanicus genemnod, se þa ærest þider com. Þa eode he to
Apollonium and cwæð: 'Wel gesund, hlaford Apolloni!' Ða forseah he Apollonius cyrlisces mannes
95   gretinge æfter ricra manna gewunan. Hellanicus hine eft sona gegrette and cwæð: 'Wes gesund,

V

When the king heard that Apollonius had interpreted the riddle correctly in this way, he dreaded that it might become known too widely. He looked at him then with an angry expression, and said: 'You are far from right, young man; you are wrong and it is not at all as you say; therefore you have warranted beheading. Now I will let you have thirty days' grace so that you can consider the riddle correctly, and afterwards you will receive my daughter to wife, and if you do not do that you must acknowledge the established judgement.' Then Apollonius was very troubled, and boarded his ship with his companions and sailed until he came to Tyre.

VI

Truly, after Apollonius had gone, Antiochus the king called his steward who was called Thaliarcus to him: 'Thaliarcus, of all my secrets you are my most trustworthy servant, and you know that Apollonius has correctly interpreted my riddle. Quickly now board a ship and sail after him, and when you come to him, then kill him with a sword or with poison so that you might receive your freedom when you come back again.' As soon as Thaliarcus heard that, he took with him both money and poison and boarded a ship, and journeyed after the unwitting Apollonius until he came to his native land. But Apollonius nevertheless had previously arrived at his own land, and he went into his house and opened his book and considered the riddle in the manner of all the philosophers and wisdom of the Chaldeans. When he could find nothing else except that which he had previously guessed, he said to himself: 'Now what do you do, Apollonius? You have interpreted the king's riddle and you have not received his daughter; because of this you are now sentenced such that you will be killed.' And then he went out and ordered that his ship be loaded with wheat and with a substantial amount of gold and silver and with various and plentiful garments, and so with a few of his most trustworthy men he boarded the ship at the third hour of the night and cast out to sea.

VII

Then on the day after, people looked and asked for Apollonius, but he could be found nowhere. Then there was a great deal of sorrow and intense weeping, so that the crying echoed throughout the entire city. Truly, such great love had all the citizens for him that for a long time they went about completely unshaven and long-haired and their theatrical entertainments were neglected and their baths locked. As these things were being done in this way in Tyre, the aforesaid Thaliarcus, who was sent from Antioch by the king so that he might kill Apollonius, arrived there. When he saw that all these things were locked, he said to a boy: 'In order that you remain in good health, tell me for what cause does this city reside in such great sorrow and misery?' The boy answered and said this to him: 'Alas, how wicked a man you are, you who know what it is you ask after: for what man does not know that these city-dwellers remain in sorrow because Apollonius the nobleman has suddenly not been seen since he came back from Antiochus the king?' When Thaliarcus heard that, he went back to the ship with much joy, and with certain sailing within one day arrived at Antioch, and went into the king and said: 'Lord king, be glad now and rejoice, because Apollonius dreads the might of your power so that he does not dare remain anywhere.' Then the king said: 'He might run away, but he cannot escape.' Then Antiochus the king made this decree saying this: 'Whichever man brings Apollonius to me living, I will give him fifty pounds of gold; and to him who brings me his head, I will give a hundred pounds of gold.' When this decree was made in this way, then there were those who were overcome with avarice – not only his enemies but also his friends – and they went after him and searched for him through the entire earth, both in open country and in woodland and in secluded places; but he could not be found anywhere.

VIII

Then the king commanded that ships be prepared and journey after him; but it was a long while before the ships were ready, and Apollonius had already arrived at Tarsus. When he walked along the beach one day, he saw a man who was known to him, who was called Hellanicus and who had come to that place first. He went to Apollonius and said: 'Be of good health, Lord Apollonius!' Then Apollonius scorned the churlish man's greeting as is the custom of more powerful men. Hellanicus greeted him again

Apolloni, and ne forseoh ðu cyrliscne man þe bið mid wurðfullum þeawum gefrætwod. Ac gehyr nu fram me þæt þu silfa nast. Þe is soðlice micel þearf þæt þu ðe warnige forðam þe ðu eart fordemed.' Ða cwæð Apollonius: 'Hwa mihte me fordeman, minre agenre þeode ealdorman?' Hellanicus cwæð: 'Antiochus se cyngc.' Apollonius cwæð: 'For hwilcum intingum hæfð he me
100 fordemed?' Hellanicus sæde: 'Forðam þe þu girndest þæt þu wære þæt se fæder is.' Apollonius cwæð: 'Micclum Ic eom fordemed?' Hellanicus sæde: 'Swa hwilc man swa ðe lifigende to him bringð onfo se fiftig punda goldes; se ðe him bringe þin heafod onfo se hundteontig punda goldes. Forðam Ic ðe lære þæt þu fleo and beorge þinum life.'

Æfter þysum wordum, Hellanicus fram him gewænde, and Apollonius het hine eft to him
105 geclipian, and cwæð to him: 'Þæt wyrreste þingc þu didest þæt þu me warnodest. Nym nu her æt me hundteontig punda goldes, and far to Antiocho þam cynge and sege him þæt me sy þæt heafod fram þam hneccan acorfen, and bring þæt word þam cynge to blisse: þonne hafast þu mede and eac clæne handa fram þæs unscæðþigan blodes.' Ða cwæð Hellanicus: 'Ne gewurðe þæt, hlaford, þæt Ic mede nime æt ðe for þisum þingum, forðon þe mid godum mannum nis naðer ne
110 gold ne seolfor wið godes mannes freondscipe wiðmeten.' Hi toeodon þa mid þisum wordum.

IX

And Apollonius sona gemette oðerne cuðne man ongean hine gan þæs nama wæs Stranguilio gehaten. 'Hlaford geong Apolloni, hwæt dest ðu þus gedrefedum mode on þisum lande?' Apollonius cwæð: 'Ic gehirde secgan þæt Ic wære fordemed.' Stranguilio cwæð: 'Hwa fordemde þe?' Apollonius cwæð: 'Antiochus se cyngc.' Stranguilio cwæð: 'For hwilcum intingum?' Apollonius sæde: 'Forðam
115 þe Ic bæd his dohtor me to gemæccan, be þare Ic mæg to soðe secgan þæt heo his agen gemæcca wære. Forðam gif hit gewurðan mæg, Ic wille me bedihlian on eowrum eðle.' Ða cwæð Stranguilio: 'Hlaford Apolloni, ure ceaster is þearfende and ne mæg þine æðelborennesse acuman, forðon ðe we þoliað þone heardestan hungor and þone reðestan, and minre ceasterwaru nis nan hælo hiht, ac se wælreowesta ende stent ætforan urum eagum.' Ða cwæð Apollonius: 'Min se leofesta freond
120 Stranguilio, þanca Gode þæt he me fliman hider to eowrum gemæran gelædde. Ic sille eowrum ceastergewarum hundteontig þusenda mittan hwætes gif ge minne fleam bedigliað.' Mid þi þe Stranguilio þæt gehirde, he hine astrehte to his fotum and cwæð: 'Hlaford Apolloni, gif ðu þissere hungrige ceasterwaran gehelpest, na þæt an þæt we willað þinne fleam bediglian, ac eac swilce, gif þe neod gebirað, we willað campian for ðinre hælo.'

X

125 Ða astah Apollonius on þæt domsetl on ðare stræte and cwæð to ðam andweardan ceasterwarum: 'Ge Tharsysce ceasterwaran, Ic, Apollonius se Tirisca ealdorman, eow cyðe þæt Ic gelife þæt ge willan beon gemindige þissere fremfulnesse and minne fleam bediglian. Wite eac þæt Antiochus se cyngc me aflimed hæfð of minum earde, ac for eowre gesælðe, gefultumigendum Gode, Ic eom hider cumen. Ic sille eow, soðlice, hundteontig þusenda mittan hwætes to ðam wurðe þe Ic hit
130 gebohte on minum lande.'

Ða ða þæt folc þæt gehirde, hi wæron bliðe gewordene and him georne þancodon and to geflites þone hwæte up bæron. Hwæt, ða Apollonius forlet his þone wurðfullan cynedom and mangeres naman þar genam ma þonne gifendes, and þæt wyrð þe he mid þam hwæte genam he ageaf sona agean to ðare ceastre bote. Þæt folc wearð ða swa fagen his cystignessa and swa þancful
135 þæt hig worhton him ane anlicnesse of are; and on ðare stræte stod and mid þare swiðran hand þone hwæte heold and mid þam winstran fet þa mittan træd; and þaron þus awriten: 'Ðas gifu sealde seo ceasterwaru on Tharsum Apollonio þam Tiriscan, forðam þe he folc of hungre alesde and heora ceastre gestaðolode.'

XI

Æfter þisum, hit gelamp binnon feawum monðum þæt Stranguilio and Dionisiade his wif gelærdon
140 Apollonium ðæt he ferde on scipe to Pentapolim, þare Ciriniscan birig, and cwædon þæt he mihte þar bediglad beon and þar wunian. And þæt folc hine þa mid unasecgendlicre wurðmynte to scipe gelæddon, and Apollonius hi bæd ealle greton and on scip astah. Mid þi þe hig ongunnon

immediately and said: 'Be of good health, Apollonius, and do not scorn a churlish man who is favoured with honourable manners. But hear from me now that which you yourself do not know. There is a truly great need that you watch out for yourself because you have been condemned.' Then Apollonius said: 'Who can condemn me, a nobleman among his own people?' Hellanicus said: 'Antiochus the king.' Apollonius said: 'For what cause has he condemned me?' Hellanicus said: 'Because you desire to be what the father is.' Apollonius said: 'How severely have I been condemned?' Hellanicus said: 'Whichever man brings you to him living will receive fifty pounds of gold; he who brings your head will get a hundred pounds of gold. Because of this I advise that you flee and save your life.'

After these words Hellanicus went from him, and Apollonius asked him to be called back to him, and said to him: 'That is the worst thing that you have done by warning me. Here, take from me now a hundred pounds of gold, and travel to Antiochus the king and tell him that my head has been cut off from my neck, and bring these words for the king's delight: then you will have reward and also clean hands from the blood of the innocent.' Then Hellanicus said: 'It cannot be honourable, lord, that I should take reward from you for such a thing, because among good men neither gold nor silver can compare with a good man's friendship.' Then with these words they separated.

IX

And straightaway Apollonius met coming towards him another man he knew, the name of whom was Stranguillo. 'Young Lord Apollonius, what are you doing in this land so disturbed in mind?' Apollonius said: 'I heard it said that I was condemned.' Stranguillo said: 'Who has condemned you?' Apollonius said: 'Antiochus the king.' Stranguillo said: 'For what cause?' Apollonius said: 'Because I asked for his daughter in marriage, about whom I may say truly that she was his own wife. Because of this, I will, if I am able, hide myself in your country.' Then Stranguillo said: 'Lord Apollonius, our city is poor and will not be able to support your nobility, because we are suffering the hardest and most cruel famine, and for my citizens, there is no hope of salvation, but the most cruel of deaths looms before our eyes.' Then Apollonius said: 'My dearest friend Stranguillo, thank God that he led me here as a fugitive to your territory. I can give to your citizens a hundred thousand measures of wheat if you will conceal my flight.' As soon as Stranguillo heard that, he prostrated himself at his feet and said: 'Lord Apollonius, if you help these hungry citizens, not only will we conceal your flight, but in addition, if the need arises, we will fight for your salvation.'

X

Then Apollonius ascended the judgement seat in that street and said to those citizens present: 'You people of Tarsus, I, Apollonius the prince of Tyre, inform you that I believe that you will be mindful of this generosity and will conceal my flight. You also know that Antiochus the king has made me flee from my country, but with the help of God, for your happiness I have come here. Certainly, I will give you a hundred thousand measures of wheat at the price for which I bought it in my country.'

When the people heard that, they became joyful and eagerly thanked him and avidly off-loaded the wheat. Indeed then Apollonius cast off his noble status and took there the name of a merchant rather than a benefactor, and that price which he took for the wheat he immediately gave back again to benefit the city. Then the people were so pleased at his munificence and so thankful that they made a bronze statue of him; and it stood in the street, and in the right hand it held the wheat and with the left foot trod on the measure; and they wrote this upon it: 'This gift was given by the citizens of Tarsus to Apollonius the Tyrenian, because he released the people from hunger and restored their city.'

XI

After this, it happened within a few months that Stranguillo and Dionysias his wife instructed Apollonius that he should travel by ship to Pentapolis, the Cyrenaican town, and said that he might be hidden there and should stay there. And then the people led him to the ship with indescribable honour, and Apollonius bade them all farewell and boarded the ship. Once they had begun to sail and had gone forward on their

þa rowan and hi forðwerd wæron on heora weg, þa wearð ðare sæ smiltnesse awænd færinga betwux twam tidum and wearð micel reownes aweht swa þæt seo sæ cnyste þa heofonlican tungla
145   and þæt gewealc þara yða hwaðerode mid windum. Þar toeacan coman east-norðerne windas and se angrislica suð-westerna wind him ongean stod, and þæt scip eal tobærst.

XII

On ðissere egeslican reownesse Apollonius geferan ealle forwurdon to deaðe, and Apollonius ana becom mid sunde to Pentapolim þam Ciriniscan lande, and þar upeode on ðam strande. Þa stod he nacod on þam strande, and beheold þa sæ and cwæð: 'Eala, þu sæ, Neptune, manna bereafigend
150   and unscæððigra beswicend, þu eart wælreowra þonne Antiochus se cyngc. For minum þingum þu geheolde þas wælreownesse þæt Ic þurh ðe gewurðe wædla and þearfa, and þæt se wælreowa cyngc me þy eaðe fordon mihte. Hwider mæg Ic nu faran? Hwæs mæg Ic biddan, oððe hwa gifð þam uncuðan lifes fultum?' Mid þi þe he þas þingc wæs sprecende to him silfum, þa færinga geseah he sumne fiscere gan, to þam he beseah, and þus sarlice cwæð: 'Gemiltsa me þu ealda man,
155   sy þæt þu sy; gemildsa me, nacodum, forlidenum, næs na of earmlicum birdum geborenum. And ðæs ðe ðu gearo forwite hwam ðu gemiltsige, Ic eom Apollonius, se Tirisca ealdorman.' Ða sona swa se fiscere geseah þæt se iunga man æt his fotum læg, he mid mildheortnesse hine upahof and lædde hine mid him to his huse and ða estas him beforan legde þe he him to beodenne hæfde. Þa git he wolde be his mihte maran arfæstnesse him gecyðan, toslat þa his wæfels on twa and sealde
160   Apollonige þone healfan dæl, þus cweðende: 'Nim þæt Ic þe to sillenne habbe and ga into ðare ceastre. Wen is þæt þu gemete sumne þæt þe gemiltsige. Gif ðu ne finde nænne þe þe gemiltsian wille, wænd þonne hider ongean and genihtsumige unc bam mine litlan æhta, and far ðe on fiscnoð mid me. Þeahhwæðre Ic mynegie þe, gif ðu fultumiendum Gode becymst to ðinum ærran wurðmynte, þæt þu ne forgite mine þearfendlican gegirlan.' Ða cwæð Apollonius: 'Gif Ic
165   þe ne geþence þonne me bet bið, Ic wisce þæt Ic eft forlidennesse gefare and þinne gelican eft ne gemete.'

XIII

Æfter þisum wordum he eode on ðone weg þe him getæht wæs oððæt he becom to þare ceastre geate, and ðar ineode. Mid þi þe he þohte hwæne he byddan mihte lifes fultum, þa geseah he ænne nacodne cnapan geond þa stræte yrnan; se wæs mid ele gesmerod and mid scitan begird and
170   bær iungra manna plegan on handa to ðam bæðstede belimpende, and cliopode micelre stæfne and cwæð: 'Gehyre ge ceasterwaran, gehyre ge ælðeodige, frige and þeowe, æðele and unæðele; se bæðstede is open.' Ða ða Apollonius þæt gehirde, he hine unscridde þam healfan scicilse ðe he on hæfde and eode in to ðam þweale, and mid þi þe he beheold heora anra gehwilcne on heora weorce, he sohte his gelican, ac he ne mihte hine þar findan on ðam flocce. Ða færinga com
175   Arcestrates, ealre þare þeode cyningc, mid micelre mænio his manna and ineode on þæt bæð. Ða agan se cyngc plegan wið his geferan mid þoðere; and Apollonius hine gemægnde, swa swa God wolde, on ðæs cyninges plegan, and yrnende þone ðoðor gelæhte, and mid swiftre rædnesse geslegene ongean gesænde to ðam plegendan cynge. Eft he agean asænde; he rædlice sloh swa he hine næfre feallan ne let. Se cyngc ða oncneow þæs iungan snelnesse þæt he wiste þæt he næfde his
180   gelican on þam plegan, þa cwæð he to his geferan: 'Gað eow heonon. Þes cniht, þæs þe me þingð, is min gelica.' Ða ða Apollonius gehyrde þæt se cyning hyne herede, he arn rædlice and genealæhte to ðam cynge and mid gelæredre handa he swang þone top mid swa micelre swiftnesse þæt se cyng wæs geþuht swilce he of ylde to iuguðe gewænd wære; and æfter þam on his cynesetle he him gecwemlice ðenode. And þa ða he ut eode of ðam bæðe, he hine lædde be þare handa, and
185   him þa siððan þanon gewænde þæs weges þe he ær com.

XIV

Ða cwæð se cyningc to his mannum siððan Apollonius agan wæs: 'Ic swerige þurh ða gemænan hælo þæt Ic me næfre bet ne baðode þonne Ic dide todæg, nat Ic þurh hwilces iunges mannes þenunge.' Ða beseah he hine to anum his manna and cwæð: 'Ga and gewite hwæt se iunga man sy þe me todæg swa wel gehirsumode.' Se man ða eode æfter Apollonio. Mid þi þe he geseah þæt he way, the calmness of the sea quickly turned within two hours and became agitated by a great storm so that the sea beat against the heavenly stars and the swelling of the waves roared with winds. Furthermore, north-easterly winds came there and the horrible south-westerly wind stood against them, and the ship completely broke asunder.

XII

In this awful storm all of Apollonius's companions died, and, alone, by swimming, Apollonius came to Pentapolis in the Cyrenaican land, and there he went up onto the beach. Then on the beach he stood naked, and looked out to sea and said: 'Alas you sea, Neptune, ravager of men and betrayer of the innocent, you are more bloodthirsty than Antiochus the king. You have saved this cruelty for my deeds so that because of you I would become poor and needy, and so that that savage king might destroy me more easily. Where can I go now? For what might I ask or who will give comfort to this unknown man?' While he was saying these things to himself, suddenly he saw a fisherman advancing, at whom he looked, and sadly said this: 'Have pity on me, you old man, whoever you may be; have pity on me, naked, shipwrecked, who was not born of low birth. And in order that you may clearly understand in advance on whom it is that you take pity, I am Apollonius, prince of Tyre.' Then as soon as the fisherman saw that the young man lay at his feet, with kind-heartedness, he lifted him up and led him with him to his house and laid before him the delicacies that he could give him. Since he wanted to show him yet more kindness as much as was in his power, he then tore his cloak into two and gave a half part to Apollonius, saying this: 'Take what I have to give you and go into the city. By chance you might meet a person who will pity you. If you do not find someone who will pity you, come back here and my few possessions can suffice for us both, and you can come with me in my fishing. Nevertheless, I exhort you, if with the help of God you return to your former honour, that you do not forget my poor garment.' Then Apollonius said: 'If I do not remember you when life is better for me, I wish that I might again be shipwrecked but do not meet one like you next time.'

XIII

After these words he went on the path that he had been shown until he came to the gate of the city, and he went in there. As he considered who he could ask for help in living, he saw a naked boy run through the street; he was smeared with oil and clothed by a towel and bore in his hands equipment for young men's games belonging to the gymnasium, and called out in a loud voice and said: 'Listen you citizens, listen you foreigners, free and enslaved, noble and low-born; the gymnasium is open.' Then when Apollonius heard that, he took off the half a cloak that he had on and went into the bath, and as he looked at each one of them at their work, he sought his equal, but he was not able to find him there in that crowd. Then straightaway Arcestrates, king of all the people, came with a large host of his men and went into the bath. Then the king began to play with a ball with his companions; and Apollonius took part in the king's game, just as God wished it, and running he caught the ball, and with swifter speed struck it and sent it back to the playing king. Again he sent it back; he quickly struck it so that he never let it fall. When the king could see the young man's agility so that he perceived that he did not have his equal in that game, he said to his companions: 'Go away from here. This young man, it seems to me, is my equal.' When Apollonius heard that the king praised him, he ran quickly and approached the king and with an accomplished hand he struck the top with such a great swiftness that it appeared to the king just as though he had turned from old age to youth; and after that, on his throne, he served him agreeably. And then when he went out from the bath, he took him by the hand, and then went the way that he had come from before.

XIV

Then the king said to his men after Apollonius had gone: 'I swear through common salvation that I have never bathed better than I did today, I know not through which young man's service.' Then he looked at one of his men and said: 'Go and discover who the young man might be who obliged me so well today.' The man then went after Apollonius. As soon as he saw that he was clothed with a dirty cloak, he

190   wæs mid horhgum scicelse bewæfed, þa wænde he ongean to ðam cynge and cwæð: 'Se iunga man
þe þu æfter axsodest is forliden man.' Ða cwæð se cyng: 'Þurh hwæt wast ðu þæt?' Se man him
andswerode and cwæð: 'Þeah he hit silf forswige, his gegirla hine geswutelað.' Ða cwæð se cyngc:
'Ga rædlice and sege him þæt se cyngc bit ðe þæt ðu cume to his gereorde.' Ða Apollonius þæt
gehyrde, he þam gehyrsumode and eode forð mid þam men oðþæt he becom to ðæs cynges healle.

195   Ða eode se man in beforan to ðam cynge and cwæð: 'Se forlidene man is cumen þe ðu æfter
sændest, ac he ne mæg for scame ingan buton scrude.' Ða het se cyngc hine sona gescridan mid
wurðfullan scrude, and het hine ingan to ðam gereorde. Ða eode Apollonius in, and gesæt þar him
getæht wæs, ongean ðone cyngc. Ðar wearð ða seo þenung in geboren, and æfter þam cynelic
gebeorscipe, and Apollonius nan ðingc ne æt, ðeah ðe ealle oðre men æton and bliðe wæron; ac he

200   beheold þæt gold and þæt seolfor and ða deorwurðan reaf and þa beodas and þa cynelican þenunga.
Ða ða he þis eal mid sarnesse beheold, ða sæt sum eald and sum æfestig ealdorman be þam cynge.
Mid þi þe he geseah þæt Apollonius swa sarlice sæt and ealle þingc beheold and nan ðingc ne æt,
ða cwæð he to ðam cynge: 'Ðu goda cyngc, efne þes man þe þu swa wel wið gedest; he is swiðe
æfestful for ðinum gode.' Ða cwæð se cyngc: 'Þe misþingð. Soðlice, þes iunga man ne æfestigað

205   on nanum ðingum ðe he her gesihð, ac he cyð þæt hæfð fela forloren.' Ða beseah Arcestrates se
cyngc bliðum andwlitan to Apollonio and cwæð: 'Ðu iunga man, beo bliðe mid us and gehiht on
God þæt þu mote silf to ðam selran becuman.'

XV

Mid þi ðe se cyning þas word gecwæð, ða færinga þar eode in ðæs cynges iunge dohtor, and cyste
hyre fæder and ða ymbsittendan. Þa heo becom to Apollonio, þa gewænde heo ongean to hire

210   fæder and cwæð: 'Ðu goda cyningc, and min se leofesta fæder, hwæt is þes iunga man þe ongean
ðe on swa wurðlicum setle sit mid sarlicum ondwlitan? Nat Ic hwæt he besorgað.' Ða cwæð se
cyningc: 'Leofa dohtor, þes iunga man is forliden and he gecwemde me manna betst on ðam
plegan; forðam Ic hine gelaðode to ðysum urum gebeorscipe. Nat Ic hwæt he is ne hwanon he is,
ac gif ðu wille witan hwæt he sy, axsa hine, forðam þe gedafenað þæt þu wite.' Ða eode þæt

215   mæden to Apollonio and mid forwandigendre spræce cwæð: 'Ðeah ðu stille sy and unrot, þeah Ic
þine æðelborennesse on ðe geseo. Nu þonne gif ðe to hefig ne þince, sege me þinne naman and þin
gelymp arece me.' Ða cwæð Apollonius: 'Gif ðu for neode axsast æfter minum namon, Ic secge þe
Ic hine forleas on sæ. Gif ðu wilt mine æðelborennesse witan, wite ðu þæt Ic hig forlet on Tharsum.'
Ðæt mæden cwæð: 'Sege me gewislicor þæt Ic hit mæge understandan.'

XVI

220   Apollonius þa soðlice hyre arehte ealle his gelymp, and æt þare spræcan ende him feollon tearas of
ðam eagum. Mid þy þe se cyngc þæt geseah, he bewænde hine ða to ðare dohtor and cwæð: 'Leofa
dohtor, þu gesingodest; mid þy þe þu woldest witan his naman and his gelimp, þu hafast nu
geedniwod his ealde sar. Ac Ic bidde þe þæt þu gife him swa hwæt swa ðu wille.' Ða ða þæt
mæden gehirde þæt hire wæs alyfed fram hire fæder þæt heo ær hyre silf gedon wolde, ða cwæð

225   heo to Apollonio: 'Apolloni, soðlice þu eart ure. Forlæt þine murcnunge; and nu Ic mines fæder
leafe habbe, Ic gedo ðe weligne.' Apollonius hire þæs þancode, and se cyngc blissode on his
dohtor welwillendnesse, and hyre to cwæð. 'Leofa dohtor, hat feccan þine hearpan, and gecig ðe to
þinum frynd, and afirsa fram þam iungan his sarnesse.' Ða eode heo ut and het feccan hire hearpan;
and sona swa heo hearpian ongan, heo mid winsumum sange gemægnde þare hearpan sweg. Ða

230   ongunnon ealle þa men hi herian on hyre swegcræft, and Apollonius ana swigode. Ða cwæð se
cyningc: 'Apolloni, nu ðu dest yfele, forðam þe ealle men heriað mine dohtor on hyre swegcræfte,
and þu ana hi swigende tælst.' Apollonius cwæð: 'Eala, ðu goda cyngc, gif ðu me gelifst, Ic secge
þæt Ic ongite þæt soðlice þin dohtor gefeol on swegcræft, ac heo næfð hine na wel geleornod. Ac
hat me nu sillan þa hearpan; þonne wast þu nu þæt þu git nast.' Arcestrates se cyning cwæð:

235   'Apolloni, Ic oncnawe soðlice þæt þu eart on eallum þingum wel gelæred.' Ða het se cyng sillan
Apollonige þa hearpan. Apollonius þa ut eode and hine scridde and sette ænne cynehelm uppon
his heafod, and nam þa hearpan on his hand and in eode and swa stod, þæt se cyngc and ealle þa

returned to the king and said: 'The young man whom you asked about is a shipwrecked man.' Then the king said: 'Through what do you know that?' The man answered him and said: 'Though he would conceal it himself, his garment clearly shows it.' Then said the king: 'Go quickly and tell him that the king asks that you come to his feast.' When Apollonius heard that, he obeyed and went forward with the man until he came to the king's hall. Then the man went in before him to the king and said: 'The shipwrecked man after whom you sent has arrived, but he cannot, for shame, come in without clothes.' Then the king immediately ordered him to be clothed with decent clothing and asked him to come in to the feast. Then Apollonius went in and sat where he was instructed, opposite the king. Then the dishes were carried in there, and after that a royal meal, and Apollonius did not eat anything though all the other men ate and were happy; but he looked at the gold and the silver and the precious clothes and the tables and the royal serving dishes. Then when he was looking at all of this with sadness, a certain old and somewhat envious ealdorman sat by the king. When he noticed that Apollonius sat so sorrowfully and looked at all the things and ate nothing, he said to the king: 'You good king, look at this man whom you have behaved to so well; he is greatly envious because of your possessions.' Then said the king: 'You are wrong. Certainly, this young man does not envy anything that he sees here, but he makes it known that he has lost a great deal.' Then Arcestrates the king looked towards Apollonius with a cheerful expression and said: 'You young man, be happy with us and hope in God that you might arrive at better times yourself.'

XV

When the king had said these words, then suddenly there entered the king's young daughter, and she kissed her father and those who sat around him. When she came to Apollonius, she turned back to her father and said: 'Good king, and my most beloved father, who is this young man who sits opposite you in such an honoured position with a sorrowful expression? I do not know what troubles him.' Then the king said: 'Dear daughter, this young man is shipwrecked and he pleased me when he was the best man in the games; because of this I invited him to this feast of ours. I do not know who he is nor from where he came, but if you want to know who he may be, ask him, because it is reasonable that you should know.' Then that young woman went to Apollonius and respectfully said: 'Even though you are quiet and sad, I see in you your nobility. Now then, if it does not seem too burdensome to you, tell me what your name is and tell me what happened to you.' Then Apollonius said: 'If because of some necessity you ask about my name, I can tell you that I lost it at sea. If you want to know about my nobility, know that I abandoned it in Tarsus.' The maiden said: 'Tell me more explicitly so that I might be able to understand.'

XVI

Apollonius then related to her all about his situation truly, and at the end of the speech tears fell from his eyes. When the king saw that, he turned to his daughter there and said: 'Dear daughter, you have erred; by wanting to know his name and his situation, you have now renewed his original sorrow. But I pray that you give him whatever you desire.' When the young woman heard that she was allowed by her father to do what she herself had already wished, then she said to Apollonius: 'Apollonius, truly you are one of us. Forget your grief; and now I have my father's permission, I will make you wealthy.' Apollonius thanked her for this, and the king was gladdened by his daughter's goodness, and he said to her: 'Beloved daughter, ask for your harp to be fetched and summon your friends and rid the young man of his sadness.' Then she went out and asked her harp to be fetched; and as soon as she began to pluck the strings, she combined the sound of the harp with delightful singing. Then all the men began to praise her for her musical accomplishment, and Apollonius alone remained silent. Then the king said: 'Apollonius, now you do wrong, because all the men praise my daughter for her musical accomplishment and you alone insult her by being silent.' Apollonius said: 'Alas, good king, if you can forgive me, I will say that I can see that truly your daughter has fallen into music-making, but she has not learned it well. But command the harp to be given to me now; then you will know what you do not yet know.' Arcestrates the king said: 'Apollonius, truly I know that you are well instructed in all things.' Then the king commanded that the harp be given to Apollonius. Apollonius then went out and clothed himself and put a garland on his head, and took the harp in his hand and went in and then stood, so that the king

ymbsittendan wendon þæt he nære Apollonius ac þæt he wære Apollines, ðara hæðenra god. Ða
wearð stilnes and swige geworden innon ðare healle. And Apollonius his hearpenægl genam, and
240   he þa hearpestrengas mid cræfte astirian ongan, and þare hearpan sweg mid winsumum sange
gemægnde. And se cyngc silf and ealle þe þar andwearde wæron micelre stæfne cliopodon and
hine heredon. Æfter þisum forlet Apollonius þa hearpan and plegode and fela fægera þinga þar
forð teah þe þam folce ungecnawen wæs and ungewunelic, and heom eallum þearle licode ælc
þara þinga ðe he forð teah.

XVII

245   Soðlice, mid þy þe þæs cynges dohtor geseah þæt Apollonius on eallum godum cræftum swa wel
wæs getogen, þa gefeol hyre mod on his lufe. Ða æfter þæs beorscipes geendunge, cwæð þæt
mæden to ðam cynge: 'Leofa fæder, þu lyfdest me litle ær þæt Ic moste gifan Apollonio swa hwæt
swa Ic wolde of þinum goldhorde.' Arcestrates se cyng cwæð to hyre: 'Gif him swa hwæt swa ðu
wille.' Heo ða sweoðe bliðe ut eode and cwæð: 'Lareow Apolloni, Ic gife þe, be mines fæder leafe,
250   twa hund punda goldes, and feower hund punda gewihte seolfres, and þone mæstan dæl deorwurðan
reafes, and twentig ðeowa manna.' And heo þa þus cwæð to ðam þeowum mannum: 'Berað þas
þingc mid eow þe Ic behet Apollonio, minum lareowe, and lecgað innon bure beforan minum
freondum.' Þis wearð þa þus gedon æfter þare cwene hæse, and ealle þa men hire gife heredon ðe
hig gesawon. Ða soðlice geendode þe gebeorscipe, and þa men ealle arison and gretton þone
255   cyngc and ða cwene, and bædon hig gesunde beon, and ham gewændon. Eac swilce Apollonius
cwæð: 'Ðu goda cyngc and earmra gemiltsigend, and þu cwen, lare lufigend, beon ge gesunde.'
He beseah eac to ðam þeowum mannum þe þæt mæden him forgifen hæfde, and heom cwæð to:
'Nimað þas þing mid eow þe me seo cwen forgeaf, and gan we secan ure gesthus þæt we magon us
gerestan.'
260   Ða adred þæt mæden þæt heo næfre eft Apollonium ne gesawe swa raðe swa heo wolde, and
eode þa to hire fæder and cwæð: 'Ðu goda cyningc, licað ðe wel þæt Apollonius, þe þurh us todæg
gegodod is, þus heonon fare, and cuman yfele men and bereafian hine?' Se cyngc cwæð: 'Wel þu
cwæde. Hat him findan hwar he hine mæge wurðlicost gerestan.' Ða dide þæt mæden swa hyre
beboden wæs, and Apollonius onfeng þare wununge ðe hym getæht wæs, and ðar in eode, Gode
265   þancigende ðe him ne forwyrnde cynelices wurðscipes and frofres.

XVIII

Ac þæt mæden hæfde unstille niht, mid þare lufe onæled þara worda and sanga þe heo gehyrde æt
Apollonige, and na leng heo ne gebad ðonne hit dæg wæs, ac eode sona swa hit leoht wæs and
gesæt beforan hire fæder bedde. Ða cwæð se cyngc: 'Leofa dohtor, for hwi eart ðu þus ær wacol?'
Ðæt mæden cwæð: 'Me awehton þa gecnerdnessan þe Ic girstandæg gehyrde. Nu bidde Ic ðe
270   forðam þæt þu befæste me urum cuman Apollonige to lare.' Ða wearð se cyningc þearle geblissod,
and het feccan Apollonium and him to cwæð: 'Min dohtor girnð þæt heo mote leornian æt ðe ða
gesæligan lare ðe þu canst, and gif ðu wilt þisum þingum gehyrsum beon, Ic swerige ðe þurh
mines rices mægna þæt swa hwæt swa ðu on sæ forlure Ic ðe þæt on lande gestaðelige.' Ða ða
Apollonius þæt gehyrde, he onfengc þam mædenne to lare, and hire tæhte swa wel swa he silf
275   geleornode.

XIX

Hyt gelamp ða æfter þisum binnon feawum tidum þæt Arcestrates se cyngc heold Apollonius
hand on handa and eodon swa ut on ðare ceastre stræte. Þa æt nyhstan comon ðar gan ongean hy
þry gelærede weras and æþelborene, þa lange ær girndon þæs cyninges dohtor. Hi ða ealle þry
togædere anre stæfne gretton þone cyngc. Ða smercode se cyng and heom to beseah and þus
280   cwæð: 'Hwæt is þæt þæt ge me anre stæfne gretton?' Ða andswerode heora an and cwæð: 'We
bædon gefirn þynre dohtor, and þu us oft rædlice mid elcunge geswænctest. Forðam we comon
hider todæg þus togædere. We syndon þyne ceastergewaran, of æðelum gebyrdum geborene. Nu
bidde we þe þæt þu geceose þe ænne of us þrym hwilcne þu wille þe to aðume habban.' Ða cwæð
se cyngc: 'Nabbe ge na godne timan aredodne. Min dohtor is nu swiðe bisy ymbe hyre leornunga,

and all those sitting about thought that he was not Apollonius but that he was Apollo, the god of the heathens. Then within the hall there was quiet and silence. And Apollonius took his harp-pluck and began to play the harp-strings with skill, and he combined the sound of the harp with a delightful song. And the king himself and all of those who were present there called out with a loud voice and praised him. After this Apollonius put the harp down and played and performed many pleasing things there that were unknown and unusual to the people, and each of the things that he performed pleased them all very much.

XVII

Truly, when the king's daughter saw that Apollonius was so well instructed in all useful skills, then her mind fell in love with him. Then after feast's end, the young woman said to the king: 'Beloved father, you allowed a little while ago that I could give Apollonius whatever I wished from your hoard of treasure.' Arcestrates the king said to her: 'Give him whatever you wish.' Then she went out very happily and said: 'Master Apollonius, I give you, with my father's acquiescence, two hundred pounds of gold and four hundred pounds of silver, and a substantial amount of precious clothing, and twenty servants.' And then she said this to the servants: 'Carry with you these things that I have promised to Apollonius, my master, and put them in the chamber in front of my friend.' This was then done in the manner of the princess's request, and all those men praised her gifts when they saw them. Then indeed the feast ended, and all the people rose up and greeted the king and the princess, and prayed that they would fare well, and went home. Likewise Apollonius said: 'Good king and pitier of the wretched, and you princess, lover of learning, be of good health.' He also looked towards the servants that the young woman had given him, and said to them: 'Take these things that the princess has given me with you, and we can go and find our lodgings so that we can rest.'

Then the maiden feared that she might not see Apollonius again as quickly as she desired, and she went to her father then and said: 'Good king, are you happy that Apollonius, whom we have benefited today, has gone from here in this way, and that evil men might come and rob him?' The king said: 'You have spoken up well. Ask them to find him a place where he may rest the most comfortably.' Then the young woman did as she had been asked, and Apollonius took the dwelling as he was instructed, and went in there, thanking God who had not deprived him of his royal honour and comfort.

XVIII

But that young woman had a disturbed night, excited by love of the words and songs that she heard from Apollonius, and she could wait no longer when it became day, but went immediately as soon as it was light and sat at the foot of her father's bed. Then the king said: 'Beloved daughter, why are you awake this early?' The maiden said: 'I was kept awake by the achievements that I heard yesterday. So now I ask of you that you commend me to our guest Apollonius for tuition.' Then the king was very happy, and commanded Apollonius to be fetched and said to him: 'My daughter is eager to be taught by you in the fortunate skills that you know, and if you would be amenable to this, I swear to you through the power of my kingdom that whatever you lost at sea I will replace for you on land.' When Apollonius heard that, he accepted the young woman for tuition and taught her as well as he himself had been taught.

XIX

Then it happened within a few hours of this that Arcestrates the king held Apollonius by the hand and in this manner went out into the city street. Next then there came walking towards them three learned and noble men, who for a long time had previously desired the king's daughter. Then all three of them greeted the king in unison with one voice. Then the king smiled and looked at them and said this: 'What is it that you greet me with one voice?' Then one of them answered and said: 'We asked for your daughter some time ago and you have frequently distressed us with delay. Because of this we come here today together in this way. We are your citizens, born of noble descent. Now we beseech you that you choose which one of us three you wish to have as a son-in-law.' Then the king said: 'You have not chosen a good time. My daughter is now very busy about her studies, but in case I should delay you any longer,

285   ac þe læs þe Ic eow a leng slæce, awritað eowre naman on gewrite and hire morgen-gife; þonne
      asænde Ic þa gewrita minre dohtor þæt heo sylf geceose hwilcne eowerne heo wille.' Ða didon ða
      cnihtas swa, and se cyngc nam ða gewrita and geinseglode hi mid his ringe and sealde Apollonio,
      þus cweðende: 'Nim nu, lareow Apolloni, swa hit þe ne mislicyge, and bryng þinum
      lærincgmædene.'

XX

290   Ða nam Apollonius þa gewrita and eode to ðare cynelican healle. Mid þam þe þæt mæden geseah
      Apollonium, þa cwæð heo: 'Lareow, hwi gæst ðu ana?' Apollonius cwæð: 'Hlæfdige, næs git yfel
      wif! Nim ðas gewrita ðe þin fæder þe sænde and ræd.' Ðæt mæden nam and rædde þara þreora
      cnihta naman, ac heo ne funde na þone naman þar on þe heo wolde. Ða heo þa gewrita oferræd
      hæfde, ða beseah heo to Apollonio and cwæð: 'Lareow, ne ofþingð hit ðe gif Ic þus wer geceose?'
295   Apollonius cwæð: 'Na, ac Ic blissige swiðor ðæt þu miht, ðurh ða lare þe þu æt me underfenge, þe
      silf on gewrite gecyðan hwilcne heora þu wille. Min willa is þæt þu ðe wer geceose þar ðu silf
      wille.' Þæt mæden cwæð: 'Eala, lareow, gif ðu me lufodest þu hit besorgodest.' Æfter þisum
      wordum heo, mid modes anrædnesse, awrat oðer gewrit and þæt geinseglode and sealde Apollonio.
      Apollonius hit þa ut bær on ða stræte and sealde þam cynge. Ðæt gewrit wæs þus gewriten: 'Þu
300   goda cyngc, and min se leofesta fæder, nu þin mildheortnesse me leafe sealde þæt Ic silf moste
      ceosan hwilcne wer Ic wolde, Ic secge ðe to soðan, þone forlidenan man Ic wille. And gif ðu
      wundrige þæt swa scamfæst fæmne swa unforwandigendlice ðas word awrat, þonne wite þu þæt
      Ic hæbbe þurh weax aboden, ðe nane scame, ne can þæt Ic silf ðe for scame secgan ne mihte.'

XXI

      Ða ða se cyningc hæfde þæt gewrit oferræd, þa niste he hwilcne forlidenne heo nemde. Beseah ða
305   to ðam þrim cnihtum and cwæð: 'Hwilc eower is forliden?' Ða cwæð heora an se hatte Ardalius:
      'Ic eom forliden.' Se oðer him andwirde and cwæð: 'Swiga ðu; adl þe fornime þæt þu ne beo hal ne
      gesund. Mid me þu boccræft leornodest, and ðu næfre buton þare ceastre geate fram me ne come.
      Hwar gefore ðu forlidennesse?'
      Mid ði þe se cyngc ne mihte findan hwilc heora forliden wære, he beseah to Apollonio and
310   cwæð: 'Nim ðu, Apolloni, þis gewrit and ræd hit. Eaðe mæg gewurðan þæt þu wite þæt Ic nat ðu
      ðe þar andweard wære.' Ða nam Apollonius þæt gewrit and rædde, and sona swa he ongeat þæt he
      gelufod wæs fram ðam mædene his andwlita eal areodode. Ða se cyngc þæt geseah, þa nam he
      Apollonies hand and hine hwon fram þam cnihtum gewænde, and cwæð: 'Wast þu þone forlidenan
      man?' Apollonius cwæð: 'Ðu goda cyning, gif þin willa bið, Ic hine wat.' Ða geseah se cyngc þæt
315   Apollonius mid rosan rude wæs eal oferbræded, þa ongeat he þone cwyde and þus cwæð to him:
      'Blisa, blissa, Apolloni, forðam þe min dohtor gewilnað þæs ðe min willa is! Ne mæg, soðlice, on
      þillicon þingon nan þinc gewurðan buton Godes willan.' Arcestrates beseah to ðam þrym cnihtum
      and cwæð: 'Soð is þæt Ic eow ær sæde, þæt ge ne comon on gedafenlicre tide mynre dohtor to
      biddanne; ac þonne heo mæg hi fram hyre lare geæmtigan, þonne sænde Ic eow word.' Ða
320   gewændon hie ham mid þissere andsware.

XXII

      And Arcestrates se cyngc heold for ðon Apollonius hand and hine lædde ham mid him, na swilce
      he cuma wære, ac swilce he his aðum wære. Ða æt nyxstan forlet se cyng Apollonius hand and
      eode ana into ðam bure þar his dohtor inne wæs, and þus cwæð: 'Leofe dohtor, hwæne hafast þu ðe
325   gecoren to gemæccan?' Ðæt mæden þa feol to hyre fæder fotum and cwæð: 'Ðu arfæsta fæder,
      gehyr þinre dohtor willan. Ic lufige þone forlidenan man ðe wæs þurh ungelymp beswicen; ac þi
      læs þe þe tweonige þare spræce, Apollonium Ic wille, minne lareow, and gif þu me him ne silst þu
      forlætst ðine dohtor.' Se cyng ða soðlice ne mihte aræfnian his dohtor tearas, ac arærde hi up and
      hire to cwæð: 'Leofe dohtor, ne ondræt þu ðe æniges þinges. Þu hafast gecoren þone wer þe me wel
330   licað.' Eode ða ut and beseah to Apollonio and cwæð: 'Lareow Apolloni, Ic smeade minre dohtor

write your names and her marriage-gift in a letter; then I will send the letters to my daughter so that she herself can choose which of you she desires.' Then the young men did just this, and the king took the letters and sealed them with his ring and gave them to Apollonius, saying this: 'Take and carry these to your student now, Master Apollonius, as long as this does not displease you.'

XX

Then Apollonius took the letters and went to the royal hall. When the maiden saw Apollonius she said: 'Master, why do you come alone?' Apollonius said: 'Lady, you are not yet a wicked woman! Take these letters which your father has sent you and read them.' The maiden took them and read the three young men's names, but she could not find the name she desired there. When she had looked over the letters, then she looked round at Apollonius and said: 'Master, would it not offend you if I were to choose a husband in this way?' Apollonius said: 'No, but I would be much happier if you were able, because of the tuition that you have received from me, yourself to reveal in writing which one of them you desire. My wish is that you choose a husband whom you desire for yourself.' The maiden said: 'Alas, master, if you loved me, you would grieve about this.' After these words, determined of mind, she wrote another letter and sealed it and gave it to Apollonius. Then Apollonius took it out into the street and gave it to the king. That letter was written like this: 'You good king, and my most beloved father, now that your loving kindness has given me leave that I myself might choose whichever husband I desired, I say to you in truth that I want the shipwrecked man. And if you wonder that such a modest woman wrote these words so unhesitatingly, then you should know that I have announced by means of wax, which does not know any shame, what for shame I could not tell you myself.'

XXI

When the king had read through the letter, he did not know which shipwrecked man she referred to. Then he looked round at the three young men and said: 'Which of you is shipwrecked?' Then said that one of them who was called Ardalius: 'I was shipwrecked.' The other answered him and said: 'You shut up; a plague take you so that you become neither healthy nor sound. With me you studied scholarship, and you have never been outside the city gates without me. Where did you suffer a shipwreck?'

When the king could not discover which of them was shipwrecked, he looked round to Apollonius and said: 'Take this letter, Apollonius, and read it. It may easily be the case that you know what I do not since you were present there.' Then Apollonius took that letter and read it, and as soon as he perceived that he was loved by that young woman his face went completely red. When the king saw that, he took Apollonius's hand and turned with him away from the young men, and said: 'Do you know the ship-wrecked man?' Apollonius said: 'You good king, if it is your wish, I do know him.' When the king saw that Apollonius's blushing had spread over his entire face, then he understood the comment and said this to him: 'Be happy, be happy, Apollonius, for my daughter desires that which is my desire! In truth, nothing can happen in such things except with God's will.' Arcestrates looked round at the young men and said: 'It is true what I said to you before, that you did not come at the right time to ask for my daughter; but when she may be at leisure from her studies, then I shall send you word.' Then they went home with this answer.

XXII

So Arcestrates the king held Apollonius's hand and led him home with him, not as though he were a guest, but as though he were his son-in-law. Then at last the king let go of Apollonius's hand and went alone into the bedroom in which his daughter was and said this: 'Beloved daughter, whom have you chosen for your husband?' The young woman then fell to her father's feet and said: 'You kind father, hear your daughter's desire. I love the shipwrecked man who was betrayed by misadventure; but in case you hesitate about this statement, it is Apollonius that I want, my teacher, and if you will not give him to me you abandon your daughter.' Then the king, in truth, could not stand his daughter's tears, but raised her up and said to her: 'Beloved daughter, do not be frightened about anything. You have chosen a man who is very pleasing to me.' He went out then and looked at Apollonius and said: 'Master Apollonius, I have thought about my

modes willan. Ða arehte heo me mid wope betweox oðre spræce þas þingc, þus cweðende: "Þu geswore Apollonio, gif he wolde gehirsumian minum willan on lare, þæt þu woldest him geinnian swa hwæt swa seo sæ him ætbræd. Nu, for ðam þe he gehyrsum wæs þinre hæse and minum willan, Ic for æfter him . . .

XLVIII

335   Ða wæs hyre gecyd, þe ðar ealdor wæs, þæt þar wære cumen sum cyngc mid his aðume and mid his dohtor mid micclum gifum. Mid þam þe heo þæt gehirde, heo hi silfe mid cynelicum reafe gefrætwode and mid purpran gescridde and hire heafod mid golde and mid gimmon geglængde, and, mid micclum fæmnena heape ymbtrimed, com togeanes þam cynge. Heo wæs soðlice þearle wlitig, and for ðare micclan lufe þare clænnesse, hi sædon ealle þæt þar nære nan Dianan swa gecweme swa heo. Mid þam

340   þe Apollonius þæt geseah, he mid his aðume and mid his dohtor to hyre urnon, and feollon ealle to hire fotum, and wende þæt heo Diana wære seo giden for hyre micclan beorhtnesse and wlite. Þæt haliern wearð ða geopenod, and þa lac wæron ingebrohte; and Apollonius ongan ða sprecan and cweðan: 'Ic fram cildhade wæs Apollonius genemnod, on Tirum geboren. Mid þam þe Ic becom to fullon andgite, þa næs nan cræft ðe wære fram cynegum began oðða fram æðelum mannum þæt Ic ne

345   cuðe. Ic arædde Antiochus rædels þæs cynges to þon þæt Ic his dohtor underfenge me to gemæccan; ac he silfa wæs mid þam fulestan horwe þar to geþeod, and me þa sirwde to ofsleanne. Mid þam þe Ic þæt forfleah, þa wearð Ic on sæ forliden and com to Cyrenense. Ða underfengc me Arcestrates se cyngc mid swa micelre lufe þæt Ic æt nyhstan geearnode þæt he geaf me his acænnedan dohtor to gemæccan. Seo for ða mid me to onfonne minon cynerice; and þas mine dohtor, þe Ic beforan ðe Diana geandweard

350   hæbbe, acænde on sæ, and hire gast alet. Ic þa hi mid cynelican reafe gescridde, and mid golde and gewrite on ciste alegde, þæt se þe hi funde hi wurðlice bebirigde. And þas mine dohtor befæste þam manfullestan mannan to fedanne. For me þa to Egipta lande feowertene gear, on heofe. Ða Ic ongean com, þa sædon hi me þæt min dohtor wære forðfaren, and me wæs min sar eal geedniwod.'

XLIX

Mid þam þe he ðas þingc eal areht hæfde, Arcestrate, soðlice his wif, up aras and hine ymbclypte.

355   Ða niste na Apollonius ne ne gelifde þæt heo his gemæcca wære, ac sceaf hi fram him. Heo ða micelre stæfne clipode and cwæð mid wope: 'Ic eom Arcestrate þin gemæcca, Arcestrates dohtor þæs cynges, and þu eart Apollonius, min lareow, þe me lærdest; þu eart se forlidena man ðe Ic lufode, na for galnesse ac for wisdome. Hwar is min dohtor?' He bewænde hine þa to Thasian and cwæð: 'Þis heo is.' And hig weopon ða ealle and eac blissodon, and þæt word sprang geond eal þæt

360   land þæt Apollonius, se mæra cyngc, hæfde fundon his wif; and þar wearð ormæte blis, and þa organa wæron getogene and þa biman geblawene, and þar wearð bliðe gebeorscipe gegearwod betwux þam cynge and þam folce. And heo gesette hyre gingran þe hire folgode to sacerde; and mid blisse and heofe ealre þare mægðe on Efesum heo for mid hire were and mid hire aðume and mid hire dohtor to Antiochian, þar Apollonio wæs þæt cynerice gehealden.

daughter's heart's desire. She told me with tears these things, saying this, among other comments: "You promised Apollonius, if he would consent to my wish for tuition, that you would give back to him whatever the sea had taken from him. Now, because he was compliant to your command and my desire, I went after him . . .

(There are a number of folios missing from the manuscript here. The story proceeds as follows: Apollonius marries Arcestrates's daughter, Arcestrate, and discovers that Antiochus, his persecutor, has died, and that he himself has succeeded to the kingdom of Tyre. He sails to Antioch, but on the way, in a storm, Arcestrate gives birth prematurely to a daughter, and appears to die post-labour. Arcestrate's body is placed in a chest and cast overboard, eventually being washed up in Ephesus. Here, she is found to be alive, and she becomes a priestess in Diana's temple.

Meanwhile, Apollonius lands at Tarsus and puts Thasia, his daughter, into the safekeeping of Dionysias and Stranguillo. Years later, Dionysias orders that Thasia be killed as she is more attractive than her own daughter, Philothemia. The steward, who is to execute her, allows her to pray on the beach before her death, at which point, Thasia is captured by pirates and sold to a brothel in Mitylene. Apollonius happens to put in to Mitylene having been informed that his daughter is dead, and Thasia is sent to comfort him. The father and daughter rediscover one another, and Thasia, who has retained her virginity throughout her ordeal, is married to Athenagoras, a prince of Mitylene.

On the way to Tyre, Apollonius and his party are inspired to visit the temple of Diana at Ephesus, where they ask to see the priestess.)

XLVIII

Then it was revealed to her, there where she was the leader, that a king had arrived with his son-in-law and his daughter with splendid gifts. When she heard that, she adorned herself with regal clothes and with purple garments and decorated her head with gold and gemstones, and, surrounded by a substantial group of women, she came towards the king. She was truly very beautiful and, because of her great love of purity, they all said that no one there was as pleasing as she was to Diana. When Apollonius saw that, he ran to her with his son-in-law and daughter, and they all fell at her feet, and thought that she was Diana the goddess because of her great brightness and beauty. Then the temple was opened and the gifts were brought in; and then Apollonius began to speak and say: 'From childhood I was called Apollonius, born in Tyre. When I arrived at full understanding, then there was no skill that was cultivated by kings or by noblemen that I did not know. I interpreted Antiochus the king's riddle so that I could have his daughter as my wife; but he himself was associated with the foulest defilement there, and then contrived to kill me. When I fled from that, I became shipwrecked at sea and arrived at Cyrene. Then Arcestrates the king accepted me with so great a love that in time I earned his giving to me of his only born daughter as a wife. She travelled with me then to obtain my kingdom; and this daughter of mine, who is presented in front of you Diana, she gave birth to while at sea, and she gave up her spirit. Then I dressed her in noble clothes and I laid her in a chest with gold and a letter, so that the person who found her would be able to bury her honourably. And I put my daughter into the safekeeping of the most evil people. Then I travelled for fourteen years in the land of Egypt, in mourning. Then when I came back, they told me that my daughter had died, and my sorrow was entirely renewed for me.'

XLIX

When he had narrated all these things, Arcestrate, truly his wife, rose up and embraced him. Then Apollonius did not know nor did he believe that she was his wife, but he shoved her away from him. Then she cried out with a loud voice and said with tears: 'I am Arcestrate your wife, Arcestrates the king's daughter, and you are Apollonius, my teacher, who taught me; you are the shipwrecked man that I loved, not because of lust but because of wisdom. Where is my daughter?' Then he looked round at Thasia and said: 'This is she.' And then they all cried and also rejoiced, and that word spread throughout the entire land that Apollonius, the glorious king, had found his wife; and there was huge joy, and the organs were played and the trumpets were blown, and a joyous feast was made ready between the king and the people. And she established her follower who served her as priestess; and to the joy and crying of all that region of Ephesus she travelled with her husband and son-in-law and daughter to Antioch, where the kingdom was held for Apollonius.

L

365 For ða siððan to Tirum and gesette þar Athenagoras, his aðum, to cynge. For ða soðlice þanon to Tharsum mid his wife and mid his dohtor and mid cynelicre firde, and het sona gelæccan Stranguilionem and Dionisiadem and lædan beforan him þar he sæt on his þrimsetle. Ða ða hi gebrohte wæron, þa cwæð he beforan ealre þare gegaderunge: 'Ge Tharsysce ceastergewaran, cweðe ge þæt Ic, Apollonius, eow dide æfre ænigne unþangc?' Hi ða ealle anre stæfne cwædon: 'We

370 sædon æfre þæt þu ure cyng and fæder wære and for ðe we woldon lustlice swiltan, forðam þe þu us alysdest of hungre.' Apollonius þa cwæð: 'Ic befæste mine dohtor Stranguilionem and Dionisiade, and hi noldon me þa agifan.' Ðæt yfele wif cwæð: 'Næs þæt wel, hlaford, þæt þu silf aræddest þa stafas ofer hire birgene?' Ða clipode Apollonius swiðe hlude and cwæð: 'Leofe dohtor Thasia, gif ænig andgit sy on helle, læt þu þæt cwicsuslene hus and gehir ðu ðines fæder stæfne.' Ðæt mæden

375 ða forðeode mid cynelicum reafe ymbscrid and unwreah hire heafod and cwæð hulde to þam yfelan wife: 'Dionisia, hal wes þu. Ic grete þe nu, of helle geciged.' Ðæt forscildgode wif þa eallum limon abifode þa ða heo hire onlocode; and ceastergewaru wundrode and blissode. Ða het Thasia beforan gelædan Theophilum, Dionisiades gerefan, and him to cwæð: 'Theophile, to þon þæt þu ðe gebeorge, sege hluddre stæfne hwa ðe hete me ofslean.' Se gerefa cwæð: 'Dionisia, min

380 hlæfdige.' Hwæt seo burhwaru þa gelæhton Stranguilionem and his wif and læddon ut on ða ceastre, and ofstændon hi to deaðe, and woldon eac Theophilum ofslean, ac Thasia him þingode and cwæð: 'Buton þes man me þone first forgeafe þæt Ic me to Gode gebæde, þonne ne become Ic to þissere are.' Heo ræhte þa, soðlice, hire handa him to and het hine gesund faran; and Philothemian, þare forscildgodan dohtor, Thasia nam to hyre.

LI

385 Apollonius þa soðlice forgeaf þam folce micele gifa to blisse, and heora weallas wurdon geedstaðelode. He wunode þa þar six monðas and for siððan on scipe to Pentapolim, þare Cireniscan birig, and com to Arcestrates þam cynge; and se cyng blissode on his ylde þæt he geseah his nefan mid hire were. Hi wunodon togædere an gear fullice and se cyning siððan, Arcestrates, fulfremedre ylde, forðferde betwux him eallum, and becwæð healf his rice Apollonio, healf his dohtor.

390 Ðisum eallum ðus gedonum, eode Apollonius, se mæra cyngc, wið ða sæ. Þa geseah he þone ealdan fiscere þe hine ær nacodne underfengc. Þa het se cyngc hine færlice gelæccan and to ðare cynelican healle gelædan. Ða ða se fiscere þæt geseah þæt hine þa cæmpan woldon niman, þa wende he ærest þæt hine man scolde ofslean; ac mid þam þe he com into ðæs cynges healle, þa het se cyningc hine lædan toforan þare cwene, and þus cwæð: 'Eala, þu eadige cwen, þis is min

395 tacenbora þe me nacodne underfenc, and me getæhte þæt Ic to þe becom.' Ða beseah Apollonius se cyng to ðam fiscere and cwæð: 'Eala, welwillenda ealda, Ic eom Apollonius se Tirisca, þam þu sealdest healfne þinne wæfels.' Him geaf ða se cyngc twa hund gildenra pænega and hæfde hine to geferan þa hwile þe he lifede. Hellanicus eac þa to him com, se him ær cydde hwæt Antiochus cync be him gedemed hæfde, and he cwæð to þam cynge: 'Hlaford cyng, gemun Hellanicus,

400 þinne þeow.' Ða genam hine Apollonius be þare hand and arærde hine up and hine cyste, and hine weligne gedide and sette hine him to geferan.

Æfter eallum þisum, Apollonius se cyngc sunu gestrynde be his gemæccan, þone he sette to cynge on Arcestrates cynerice his ealdefæder. And he sylfa welwillendlice lifede mid his gemæccan seofon and hundseofonti geara, and heold þæt cynerice on Antiochia and on Tyrum and on Cirenense;

405 and he leofode on stilnesse and on blisse ealle þa tid his lifes æfter his earfoðnesse. And twa bec he silf gesette be his fare, and ane asette on ðam temple Diane, oðre on bibliotheca.

Her endað ge wea ge wela Apollonius þæs Tiriscan. Ræde se þe wille. And gif hi hwa ræde, Ic bidde þæt he þas awændednesse ne tæle, ac þæt he hele swa hwæt swa þar on sy to tale.

L

Then afterwards he travelled to Tyre and established Athenagoras, his son-in-law, there as king. Indeed, then he went from there to Tarsus with his wife and with his daughter and with a kingly army, and commanded Stranguillo and Dionysias to be captured immediately and brought before him where he sat on his throne. When they had been brought, he spoke in front of the entire gathered crowd: 'You citizens of Tarsus, would you say that I, Apollonius, ever did you any harm?' Then they all said with one voice: 'We have always said that you were our king and father and that for you we would happily die, because you saved us from hunger.' Then Apollonius said: 'I put my daughter into the safe keeping of Stranguillo and Dionysias, and they have not given her back to me.' That evil woman said: 'Do you not recall well, lord, that you yourself read the lettering over her grave?' Then Apollonius shouted out very loud and said: 'Beloved daughter Thasia, if there might be any perception in hell, you leave that house of torment and hear your father's voice.' That maiden then advanced clothed in noble robes and uncovered her head and said loudly to that evil woman: 'Dionysias, be of good health. I greet you now, called upon from hell.' That guilty woman then trembled throughout her limbs when she looked on her; and the citizens wondered and rejoiced. Then Thasia ordered Theophilus, Dionysias's steward, to be brought before her, and she said to him: 'Theophilus, so that you can protect your life, reveal with a loud voice who instructed you to murder me.' The steward said: 'Dionysias, my lady.' Indeed then the citizens took Stranguillo and his wife and led them out of the city and stoned them to death, and they wanted to kill Theophilus too, but Thasia interceded for him and said: 'Unless this man had given me the time so that I could pray to God, then I should not have come to this prosperous position.' Then truly she reached out her hand to him and told him to go in safety; and Philothemia, the evil woman's daughter, Thasia took to herself.

LI

Truly then Apollonius gave the people many gifts to make them happy, and their walls were rebuilt. Then he remained there for six months and afterwards journeyed by ship to the Cyrenaican town Pentapolis, and came to Arcestrates the king; and the king in his elderly age rejoiced that he could see his grand-daughter with her husband. They remained together for an entire year and afterwards Arcestrates the king died, very old, surrounded by them all, and he left half his kingdom to Apollonius and half to his daughter.

All of this having been done in this way, Apollonius, the renowned king, walked by the sea. Then he saw the old fisherman who had taken him in before when he had been naked. Then the king ordered him to be quickly taken and led to the royal hall. When the fisherman saw that the soldiers wanted to take him, he thought first of all the men were going to kill him; but then when he came into the king's hall, the king instructed him to be brought before the queen, and he said this: 'My blessed queen, this is my guide who took me in when I was naked, and directed me so that I came to you.' Then Apollonius the king looked round at the fisherman and said: 'Oh benevolent old man, I am Apollonius the Tyrenian, to whom you gave half your garment.' Then the king gave him two hundred gold coins and kept him as a servant for as long as he lived. Then Hellanicus also came to him, the man who had revealed to him before what Antiochus the king had ordained concerning him, and he said to the king: 'Lord king, remember Hellanicus, your servant.' Then Apollonius took him by the hand and raised him up and kissed him, and made him wealthy and established him as one of his servants.

After all of this, Apollonius the king had a son by his wife, whom he established as king in the kingdom of Arcestrates his grandfather. And he himself lived happily with his wife for seventy-seven years, and ruled the kingdom in Antioch and in Tyre and in Cyrene; and he lived in peace and in happiness throughout his lifetime after his misfortune. And he himself wrote two books about his journey, and put one in the temple of Diana, and the second in the library.

Here ends both the grief and the happiness of Apollonius the Tyrenian. Read it whoever wishes to. And if anyone does read it, I ask that he might not speak ill of the translation, but that he will keep quiet about whatever may be derided in it.

The Peterborough Chronicle

The Peterborough Chronicle, Oxford, Bodleian Library, Laud Misc. 636, is one of several manuscripts that are often collectively entitled *The Anglo-Saxon Chronicle*. In relation to these other manuscripts, the Peterborough version is known as Manuscript E. It is the latest of the *Chronicle* manuscripts in date, and the annals entered into it continue up to AD 1154; an Anglo-Norman *Chronicle* is also entered in the margins of the last few folios. As *The Peterborough Chronicle* is a rare piece of original composition in English in the first half of the twelfth century, it is rightly considered one of the most important pieces of transitional English writing. It is of substantial interest to historians, literary scholars and linguists alike.[1]

The last two 'Continuations' in this *Chronicle* were made by monastic scribes at Peterborough Abbey who were contemporary with the details that they record about the reigns of Henry I and King Stephen. The first scribe wrote the manuscript up until the end of annal 1131; the second scribe continued the *Chronicle* from this point up to 1154, writing retrospectively, and occasionally amalgamating events from different years under one annal entry. The extract below, which is edited from the manuscript Laud Misc. 636, folios 88 recto to 90 recto, depicts the years 1131–7, during which Henry I died and his nephew Stephen ruled. It is also the time immediately preceding the civil war between the factions that supported Stephen's claim to the throne, and those who

favoured Henry I's daughter and declared heir, Matilda. In the edited piece below, nothing is said of Matilda, though she appears in the annals from 1139 onwards as the 'empress'.

The monks who wrote this part of the *Chronicle* show both local and national concerns. In the description of the behaviour of Abbot Henry of Angely towards the monks of Peterborough, and its contrast with the pious behaviour of Abbot Martin, the native interests of the monks are evident. In the lamentation of the hardships suffered during King Stephen's reign in many parts of England, and in the chronicling of the rebellions against Stephen, national affairs are at the forefront of the monks' agenda. Chronology in the annals by the second scribe is not always followed, and in the entries below from 1132–7 is the short account of Saint William of Norwich's martyrdom entered under 1137, but actually occurring in 1144. Its inclusion, along with the notable references to the need for God's help, and the seeming abandonment of the English people by Christ and his saints during the reign of Stephen, reflects the obvious religious concerns of the monastic writers. The language of the piece is transitional Old to Middle English. Among other things, the inflectional system of Old English is beginning to break down, word order is usually Subject-Verb-Object, and there are numerous French loanwords.

Annals 1131–7

mcxxxi Ðis gear, æfter Cristesmesse on an Moneniht æt þe forme slæp, wæs se heovene o ðe norð half eall swilc hit wære bærnende fir, swa þet ealle ðe hit sægon wæron swa offæred swa hi næfre ær ne wæron: þet wæs on iii Idus Januarii. Ðes ilces geares, wæs swa micel orfcwalm swa hit næfre ær ne wæs on manne gemynd ofer eall Engleland. Þet wæs on næt and on swin swa þet
5 on þa tun þa wæs tenn ploges oðer twelfe gangende, ne belæf þær noht an; and se man þa heafde twa hundred oðþe ðre hundred swin, ne beleaf him noht an. Þæræfter swulten þa hennefugeles. Þa scyrte ða flescmete and se ceose and se butere. God hit bete þa his wille beð! And se Kyng Heanri com ham to Engleland toforen hervest æfter Sancte Petres messe þe firrer.

Ðes ilces geares, for se Abbot Heanri toforen Eastren fram Burch ofer sæ to Normandi, and
10 þær spreac mid þone kyng and sæide him þet se abbot of Clunni heafde him beboden þet he scolde cumen to him and betæcen him þone abbotrice of Angeli, and siðþen he wolde cumen ham be his læfe. And swa he ferde ham to his agen mynstre and þær wunode eall to Midsumerdæi. And ðes oðer dæies æfter Sancte Johannis messedæi, cusen þa muneces abbot of hemself and brohten him into cyrce mid processionem; sungen *Te deum laudamus*, ringden þa belle, setten
15 him on þes abbotes settle, diden him ealle hersumnesse swa swa hi scolden don here abbot. And se eorl and ealle þa heafedmenn and þa muneces of þa mynstre flemden se oðer abbot, Heanri, ut of þa mynstre. Hi scolden nedes: on fif and twenti wintre ne biden hi næfre an god dæi. Her him

---

1 The whole text is available in facsimile (ed. D. Whitelock, *The Peterborough Chronicle*, EEMF (Copenhagen, 1954)), in edition (ed. C. Clark, *The Peterborough Chronicle 1070–1154*, 2nd edn (Oxford, 1970)) and in translation (trans. and ed. M. Swanton, *The Anglo-Saxon Chronicle* (London, 1996)).

Annals 1131–7

1131   This year, after Christmas on a Sunday night at the earliest period of sleep, the entire northern side of heaven was just as though it was burning fire, so that all those who saw it were more afraid than they had ever been before: that was on 11 January. This same year, there was a great plague over England, more than it had ever been before within the living memory of people. That affected animals and pigs so that in the settlement where there were ten or twelve ploughs going, not one was left; and the man who had two hundred or three hundred pigs, had not one left. After this the hens died. Then there was a shortage of meat and cheese and butter. God remedy it as he sees fit! And King Henry came home to England before harvest after the earlier mass of Saint Peter.

This same year, Abbot Henry travelled before Easter from Peterborough to Normandy, and there he spoke with the king and told him that the abbot of Cluny had instructed him that he must come to him and give back the abbacy of Angely, and afterwards he would come home, with his permission.[2] And afterwards he journeyed home to his own monastery and stayed there until Midsummer Day. And on the second day after Saint John's feast day, the monks chose an abbot from among themselves and brought him into the church with a procession; they sang the *Te deum laudamus*, rang the bells, set him in the abbot's throne, and paid him all obedience just as they ought to do to their abbot. And the earl and all the senior men and the monks of the monastery banished the other abbot, Henry, out of the monastery. They had to, from necessity: for twenty-five years they had never experienced one good day. Here all his

---

2   Henry was (illegally) abbot of both Angely and Peterborough, and had promised Abbot Peter of Cluny that he would relinquish the former abbey in favour of Peterborough. This he did not do, but attempted to retain both.

trucode ealle his mycele cræftes; nu him behofed þet he crape in his mycele codde in ælc hyrne, gif þær wære hure an unwreste wrenc þet he mihte get beswicen anes Crist and eall Cristene folc.

20 Þa ferde he into Clunni, and þær man him held þet he ne mihte na east na west. Sæide se abbot of Clunni þet hi heafdon forloron Sancte Johannis mynstre þurh him and þurh his mycele sotscipe. Þa ne cuþe he him na betre bote bute behet hem and aðes swor on halidom þet gif he moste Engleland secen, þet he scolde begeton hem ðone mynstre of Burch, swa þet he scolde setten þær prior of Clunni and circeweard and hordere and reilþein, and ealle þa ðing þa wæron wiðinne

25 mynstre and wiðuten, eall he scolde hem betæcen. Þus he ferde into France and þær wunode eall þet gear. Crist ræde for þa wrecce muneces of Burch and for þet wrecce stede nu hem behofeð Cristes helpe and eall Cristenes folces.

mcxxxii Ðis gear, com Henri King to þis land. Þa com Henri Abbot and uureide þe muneces of Burch to þe king forþi ðat he uuolde underþeden ðat mynstre to Clunie; sua ðat te king wæs wel

30 neh bepaht, and sende efter þe muneces; and þurh Godes milce and þurh þe biscop of Seresbyri and te biscop of Lincol and te oþre rice men þe þer wæron, þa wiste þe king ðat he feorde mid suicdom. Þa he nammor ne mihte, þa uuolde he ðat his nefe sculde ben abbot in Burch, oc Crist it ne uuolde. Was it noht suithe lang þerefter þat te king sende efter him, and dide him gyven up ðat abbotrice of Burch and faren ut of lande; and te king iaf ðat abbotrice an prior of Sancte Neod,

35 Martin wæs gehaten. He com on Sancte Petres messedei mid micel wurscipe into the minstre.

mcxxxv On þis gære, for se King Henri over sæ æt te Lamasse. And ðat oþer dei, þa he lai an slep in scip, þa þestrede þe dæi over al landes, and uuard þe sunne suilc als it uuare thre niht ald mone, an sterres abuten him at middæi. Wurþen men suiðe ofuundred and ofdred, and sæden ðat micel þing sculde cumen hereafter; sua dide, for þat ilc gær, warth þe king ded ðat oþer dæi efter

40 Sancte Andreas massedæi on Normandi. Þa þestre sona þas landes, for ævric man sone rævede oþer þe mihte. Þa namen his sune and his frend and brohten his lic to Englelande, and bebiriend in Redinge. God man he wes, and micel æie wes of him: durste nan man misdon wið oðer on his time; pais he makede men and dær; wuasua, bare his byrthen gold and sylvre, durste nan man sei to him naht bute god.

45 Enmang þis was his nefe cumen to Englelande, Stephne de Blais, and com to Lundene; and te Lundenisce folc him underfeng, and senden efter þe aercebiscop Willelm Curbuil, and halechede him to kinge on Midewintre dæi. On þis kinges time wes al unfrið and yfel and ræflac, for agenes him risen sona þa rice men þe wæron swikes: alre fyrst Balduin de Redvers, and held Execestre agenes him; and te king it besæt; and siððan Balduin acordede. Þa tocan þa oðre and helden her

50 castles agenes him. And David King of Scotland toc to uuerrien him; þa, þohuuethere þat here sandes feorden betwyx heom, and hi togædere comen and wurðe sæhte, þoþ it litel forstode.

mcxxxvii Ðis gære, for þe King Stephne ofer sæ to Normandi, and ther wes underfangen forþi ðat hi uuenden ðat he sculde ben alsuic alse the eom wes, and for he hadde get his tresor; ac he todeld it and scatered sotlice. Micel hadde Henri King gadered gold and sylver – and na god ne

55 dide me for his saule tharof.

Þa þe King Stephne to Englalande com, þa macod he his gadering æt Oxeneford, and þar he nam þe biscop Roger of Serebyri, and Alexander, biscop of Lincol, and te canceler Roger – hise neves – and dide ælle in prisun til hi iafen up here castles. Þa the suikes undergæton ðat he milde man wæs, and softe and god, and na justise ne dide, þa diden hi alle wunder. Hi hadden him

60 manred maked and athes suoren, ac hi nan treuthe ne heolden. Alle he wæron forsworen and here treothes forloren for ævric rice man his castles makede and agænes him heolden, and fylden þe land ful of castles. Hi suencten suyðe þe uurecce men of þe land mid castelweorces; þa þe castles uuaren maked, þa fylden hi mid deovles and yvele men. Þa namen hi þa men þe hi wenden ðat ani god hefden, bathe be nihtes and be dæies, carlmen and wimmen, and diden heom in prisun, and

65 pined heom efter gold and sylver untellendlice pining; for ne uuæren nævre nan martyrs swa

great skills failed him; now he was forced to creep into his great bag[3] in every corner, if there were at least one cunning trick with which he might yet deceive Christ and all Christian people. Then he travelled into Cluny, and there he was held so that he could not go east or west. The abbot of Cluny said that they had lost the abbey of Saint Jean through him and through his stupidity. Then he did not know of a better solution for himself and for them other than to promise them and swear oaths on relics that, if he was able to go to England, he would get the abbey of Peterborough for them, so that he could establish there a prior of Cluny and sacristan and treasurer and wardrobe-keeper, and all the things that were inside and outside the abbey he would deliver in total to them. So he went into France and stayed there all that year. May Christ guide the wretched monks of Peterborough and that wretched place now they require the help of Christ and all Christian people.

1132   This year, King Henry came to this land. Then Abbot Henry arrived and accused the monks of Peterborough to the king because he wanted to subjugate that monastery to Cluny; by that action the king was almost deceived, and sent after the monks; but through God's mercy and through the bishop of Salisbury and the bishop of Lincoln and the other powerful men who were there, the king knew that he[4] behaved with deception. When he could do no more, then he wanted his nephew to be abbot in Peterborough, but Christ did not desire it. It was not very long after this that the king sent after him, and made him give up that abbacy of Peterborough and go out of the land; and the king gave that abbacy to a prior of Saint Neot's, who was called Martin. He arrived on the feast day of Saint Peter with great honour into the monastery.

1135   In this year, King Henry journeyed over the sea at Lammas. And on that second day, as he lay asleep on the ship, the day grew dark over all the land, and the sun was like a three-night-old moon, with stars about it at midday. People became very amazed and frightened, and said that some great thing would happen after this; so it did, for that same year, the king died on the next day after Saint Andrew's feast day in Normandy. Then, straightaway, this land grew dark, because every man who was able to immediately robbed another. Then Henry's son and his friends took and brought his body to England, and buried it in Reading. He was a good man, and was held in great awe: no man dared wrong any other during his time; he made peace for men and animals; no man dared say any thing but good things to whosoever carried their cargo of gold and silver.

Amongst all this, Henry's nephew, Stephen of Blois, came to England, and arrived in London; and the people of London welcomed him and sent after the archbishop William Corbeil, and ordained him as king on midwinter's day. In this king's time it was all conflict and evil and robbery, for against him immediately rose the powerful men who were traitors: first of all Baldwin de Redvers, who held Exeter against him; and the king besieged it, and afterwards Baldwin capitulated. Then the others seized and held their castles against him. And David, king of Scotland, took to war against him; then, nevertheless, their messengers travelled between them and they came together and became reconciled, though it stood for little.

1137   This year, King Stephen journeyed over the sea to Normandy, and was received there because they thought he would be just as the uncle had been, and because he still had his treasury; but he gave it out and scattered it foolishly. King Henry had gathered a great amount of gold and silver – and no good was done with it for his soul.

Then when King Stephen came to England he held an assembly at Oxford, and there he seized Bishop Roger of Salisbury and Alexander, bishop of Lincoln, and the chancellor Roger – his nephews – and he put them all in prison until they gave up their castles. Then when the traitors perceived that he was a mild man, soft and good, and had not imposed a judgement, they all committed horrors. They had paid tribute to him and sworn oaths, but they did not hold that pledge. They were all forsworn and their promises were broken because every powerful man built his castles and held them against him and filled the land full of castles. They oppressed the wretched men of the land greatly with the making of castles; then these castles that had been made were filled with devils and evil men. Then they took men who

---

3 'bag of tricks' (see Swanton, *Anglo-Saxon Chronicle*, p. 262).   4 'he' being Abbot Henry.

pined alse hi wæron. Me henged up bi the fet and smoked heom mid ful smoke. Me henged bi the
þumbes other bi the hefed, and hengen bryniges on her fet. Me dide cnotted strenges abuton here
hæved, and uurythen it ðat it gæde to þe hærnes. Hi diden heom in quarterne þar nadres and
snakes and pades wæron inne, and drapen heom swa. Sume hi diden in crucethur, ðat is, in an
70   cæste þat was scort and nareu and undep; and dide scærpe stones þerinne, and þrengde þe man
þærinne, ðat him bræcon alle þe limes. In mani of þe castles wæron lof and grin, ðat wæron
rachenteges ðat twa oþer thre men hadden onoh to bæron onne. Þat was sua maced ðat is fæstned
to an beom, and diden an scærp iren abuton þa mannes throte and his hals ðat he ne myhte
nowiderwardes, ne sitten ne lien ne slepen, oc bæron al ðat iren. Mani þusen hi drapen mid
75   hungær.

   I ne can ne I ne mai tellen alle þe wunder ne alle þe pines ðat hi diden wrecce men on þis land;
and ðat lastede þa xix wintre wile Stephne was king, and ævre it was uuerse and uuerse. Hi læiden
gæildes on the tunes ævre umwile, and clepeden it 'tenserie'. Þa þe uurecce men ne hadden
nammore to gyven, þa ræveden hi and brendon alle the tunes ðat wel þu myhtes faren al a dæis
80   fare, sculdest thu nevre finden man in tune sittende, ne land tiled. Þa was corn dære, and flec and
cæse and butere, for nan ne wæs o þe land. Wrecce men sturven of hungær. Sume ieden on ælmes
þe waren sum wile rice men; sume flugen ut of lande. Wes nævre gæt mare wreccehed on land, ne
nævre hethen men werse ne diden þan hi diden. For oversithon ne forbaren hi nouther circe ne
cyrceiærd, oc namen al þe god ðat þarinne was, and brenden sythen þe cyrce and al tegædere. Ne
85   hi ne forbaren biscopes land ne abbotes ne preostes, ac ræveden munekes and clerekes, and ævric
man other þe overmyhte. Gif twa men oþer iii coman ridend to an tun, al þe tunscipe flugæn for
heom, wenden ðat hi wæron ræveres. Þe biscopes and lered men heom cursede ævre, oc was heom
naht þarof, for hi uueron al forcursæd and forsuoren and forloren. War sæ me tilede, þe erthe ne
bar nan corn, for þe land was al fordon mid suilce dædes, and hi sæden openlice ðat Crist slep, and
90   his halechen. Suilc, and mare þanne we cunnen sæin, we þolenden xix wintre for ure sinnes.

   On al þis yvele time heold Martin Abbot his abbotrice xx wintre and half gær and viii dæis,
mid micel suinc; and fand þe munekes and te gestes al þat heom behoved, and heold mycel carited
in the hus, and þoþwethere wrohte on þe circe, and sette þarto landes and rentes, and goded it
suythe, and læt it refen, and brohte heom into þe neuuæ mynstre on Sancte Petres mæssedæi mid
95   micel wurtscipe; ðat was *anno ab incarnatione domini mcxl, a combustione loci xxiii.* And he for to
Rome, and þær wæs wæl underfangen from þe pape Eugenie, and begæt thare privilegies – an of
alle þe landes of þabbotrice, and an oþer of þe landes þe lien to þe circewican; and gif he leng
moste liven alse he mint to don of þe horderwycan. And he begæt in landes þat rice men hefden
mid strengthe. Of Willelm Malduit, þe heold Rogingham þæ castel, he wan Cotingham and
100   Estun; and of Hugo of Waltervile he uuan Hyrtlingbyri and Stanewig, and lx solidos of Aldewingle
ælc gær. And he makede manie munekes, and plantede winiærd, and makede mani weorkes, and
wende þe tun betere þan it ær wæs; and wæs god munec and god man, and forþi him luveden God
and gode men.

   Nu we willen sægen sumdel wat belamp on Stephnes Kinges time. On his time þe Judeus of
105   Noruuic bohton an Cristen cild beforen Estren, and pineden him alle þe ilce pining ðat ure
Drihten was pined; and on Lang Fridæi him on rode hengen for ure Drihtines luve, and sythen
byrieden him wenden ðat it sculde ben forholen; oc ure Dryhtin atywede ðat he was hali martyr;
and to munekes him namen, and bebyried him heglice in þe minstre, and he maket þur ure
Drihtin wunderlice and manifældlice miracles; and hatte he Sanct Willelm.

they thought had any wealth both by day and by night, churls and women, and put them in prison and tortured them for their gold and silver with unspeakable torture; for no martyrs were ever tortured as they were. They hung them up by the feet and smoked them with foul smoke. They hung them up by the thumbs or by the head, and hung coats of mail on their feet. They knotted ropes hung about their heads and twisted until it went into their brains. They put them into prison in which there were adders and snakes and toads, and killed them in this way. Some they put into a crucet-house, that is, in a chest that was short and narrow and shallow; and put sharp stones in there, and squashed the man therein, so that all his limbs were broken. In many of the castles were 'lof and grin', these were chains of which two or three men had enough of a time to carry one. That was done in such a way that it was fastened to a beam, and a sharp iron was put about the man's throat and neck so that he could not move anywhere, nor sit nor lie not sleep, through carrying all that iron. Many thousands they killed by starvation.

I cannot, nor will I, tell of all the horrors nor all the tortures that they performed on the wretched people of this land; and that lasted nineteen years while Stephen was king, and it always became worse and worse. They laid taxes on the villages all the while, and called it 'tenserie'. Then when the wretched people had no more to give, they robbed them and burned all the villages so that you might journey all of a day's journey, but you would never find a person living in a village, nor land tilled. Then corn was expensive, and meat and cheese and butter, because there was none in the land. Wretched people starved of hunger. Some lived by alms of those who were at one time powerful men; some fled from the land. There was never a more wretched time in the land, nor did the heathen men[5] do any worse things than they did. On far too many occasions they did not spare either the church or the churchyard, but took all of the valuable things that were in there, and afterwards burned the church and everything altogether. Neither did they spare the land of bishops nor abbots nor priests, but robbed monks and clerics, and every other man they could overcome. If two or three men came riding to a village, all the villagers fled from them, thinking that they were robbers. The bishops and educated men always cursed them, but that was nothing to them, because they were entirely condemned and despised and lost. Wherever men tilled, the earth bore no corn, because the land was entirely ruined by such deeds, and they said openly that Christ slept, as did his saints. Such things, and more than we can say, we suffered for nineteen years for our sins.

Within this evil time, Abbot Martin held his abbacy for twenty years, six months and eight days, with a great deal of work; and he supplied all that was needed for the monks and the guests, and maintained great charitable work in that house, and even so he worked on the abbey, and established lands and income for it, and benefited it greatly, and organized its roofing, and brought them into the new monastery on the feast day of Saint Peter with great honour; that was in the year of our lord 1140, twenty-three years since the burning of the place.[6] And he journeyed to Rome, and there he was well received by the pope, Eugenius, and he obtained privileges there – one for all of the land of the abbacy, and the second for the land that belongs to the sacrist; and if he had lived longer he thought also to have done the same for the treasurer. And he obtained lands that powerful men had held because of their power. From William Maudit, who held Rockingham castle, he won Cottingham and Easton; and from Hugh of Waterville he got Irthlingborough and Stanwick, and sixty shillings each year from Aldewinckle. And he established many monks and planted vineyards, and built many buildings, and changed the village so that it was better than it was before. And he was a good monk and a good man, and because of that God and good men loved him.

Now we will relate something that happened in King Stephen's time. In his time,[7] the Jews of Norwich bought a Christian child before Easter, and completely tortured him with all the same torments with which our Lord was tortured; and on Good Friday, they hung him on a cross for the love of our Lord, and afterwards buried him. They thought that it would have remained hidden, but our Lord revealed that he was a holy martyr; and the monks took him and buried him honourably in the abbey, and he performs through the Lord wonderful and various miracles; and he is called Saint William.

5   The Vikings.   7   In 1144.
6   Peterborough Abbey was burnt down in 1116.

The Life of Saint Margaret

The Life of Saint Margaret is contained in Cambridge, Corpus Christi College 303, at pp. 99–107. Corpus 303 is an extensive religious manuscript containing saints' lives and sermons; it is written entirely in English, and was produced at Rochester towards the middle of the twelfth century. The *Life*, as it occurs in this volume, is unique in many of the details it includes. An earlier, eleventh-century Old English *Life* that exists in London, British Library, Cotton Tiberius A. iii,[1] is similar, but not identical. An early Middle English version of the *Life* that also differs from the Old English *Lives* was composed as part of the Katherine Group of texts in the early thirteenth century.[2]

Margaret (or Marina as she was also known) was a popular medieval saint, patron of women in childbirth, and her feast day was 20 July until 1969, when she was decanonized. She was martyred for her faith during the reigns of the Emperors Diocletian and Maximian in 305–13 because she refused to worship the pagan gods of Olibrius, reeve of Antioch. He desired her as his wife or concubine, depending on her status, whereas she intended to retain her virginity at all costs. After a number of different tortures and encounters with two demons, Margaret was beheaded. Her legend arose from a brief fifth-century account of her life and its subsequent expansion into the relatively lengthy Latin *Passio* that survives in many manuscripts. While the other vernacular *Lives* of Margaret are relatively close to Latin accounts of her acts, the *Life* in Corpus 303 appears to be the work of an English translator who adapts the source to eliminate the more fantastic details from the story in an attempt to produce a cogent narrative. For example, in other versions of the *Life*, Margaret is swallowed by the first demon, a dragon. She emerges unharmed from the creature once she has made the sign of the Cross. In the Corpus version, she makes the sign of the Cross, at which point the dragon disintegrates. The Corpus adaptor also ap-pears to have created the text intending it to be delivered to a contemporary lay audience.[3] In addition, the emphasis in the text on Margaret's personal and loving connection with God suggests a concern to demonstrate the possibilities for the individual to develop a close relationship with God and Christ that is part of a twelfth-century development in worship. As such, this *Life* can be seen to be an important witness not only to the continued use of English in the post-Conquest period, but also to the adaptation of texts to illustrate contemporary issues.

From a critical perspective, the *Life* is an excellent example of its genre: the female martyred saint's life. Many of the texts associated with this type, such as the Old and Middle English *Juliana*, Old English *Agatha* and the Middle English *Katherine*, are partially formulaic and thus share features (the nobility of the saint, her desire to fend off a lecherous male persecutor, her lengthy prayers and her decapitation). Like these other texts, *The Life of Saint Margaret* provides an exemplar for the audience of a female Christian who will undergo physical and verbal abuse gladly in order to protect her virginity and die for the love of Christ. This saintly epitome of determination and complete devotion suffers passively whatever persecutions come her way, but she is paradoxically simultaneously active in her resolute faith. Margaret's speeches demonstrate a courage and belief in God's assistance for his saints that mark her out as 'a soldier of Christ' as well as a 'bride of Christ', a particular type of Christian determination to be emulated by the audience of the text.

The language of the text is essentially late West Saxon but with some Kentish features. Transitional elements of Old to early Middle English are also present (for example, the levelling of inflections and confusion about grammatical gender), but are not predominant.

The Life of Saint Margaret

Passio Beate Margarete Virginis et Martyris

Efter Drihtnes þrowunge and his æriste þæt he of deaðe aras, hælend Crist, on þan dagum his halgan geþrowodon for his þæra micclan leofan lufan. Eac þa gewearð hit þæt þa halga seagntes ofercomen þa deofla þe wið heom gewunnon. And þa ricem þe on þan dagum wæron hæfdon heom geworht godes of golde and of seolfre, þa wæron dumbe and deafe and blinde, and eal þæt
5   hæþan folc swiðe gelefdon on þan godum.

1 See M. Clayton and H. Magennis, eds, *The Old English Lives of St Margaret*, Canbridge Studies in Anglo-Saxon England 9 (Cambridge, 1994).

2 See B. Millett and J. Wogan-Browne, eds, *Medieval English Prose for Women: Selections from the Katherine Group and Ancrene Wisse* (Oxford, 1990; rev. edn 1992).

3 See H. Magennis, '"Listen Now All and Understand": Adaptation of Hagiographical Material for Vernacular Audiences in the Old English Lives of St Margaret', *Speculum* 71 (1996), 27–42.

The Life of Saint Margaret

The passion of Blessed Margaret, virgin and martyr

After the Lord's suffering and his resurrection when the saviour Christ rose from death, in those days his saints suffered because of their very dear love of him. Also it happened that the holy saints overcame the devils who fought against them. And those who were powerful in those days had made for themselves gods of gold and silver which were dumb and deaf and blind,[4] and all the heathen people greatly believed in those gods.

---

4   The manufactured idols of the heathens are contrasted with the living God throughout this text. This is supplemented by an emphasis on the use of Margaret's senses as opposed to Olibrius's metaphorical blindness and deafness. Biblical text such as Matthew 13.14–15 and Acts 18.24–8 provides the inspiration for this feature of the *Life*.

Sum land is Anthiochia gehaten: on þam lande wæs an Godes þeowa se wæs Theothimus gehaten; he wæs swiðe gelæred man. And þær on lande wæs sum hæþen cyningc, Theodosius gehaten, and his cwen mid him. Hit gewearð swa þæt heo bearn gestreonedon and þæt wearð geboren mædencild. And se hæþene cing (his fæder) hit het ut aweorpan, and men swa dyde. And se Godes þeowe Theochimus gefand þæt cild and he hit up anam, and hit wel befæste to fedenne; and þa hit andgeat hæfde, he him nama gesette and þæt wæs Margareta. And hi syððan to lare befæste and hi þæron wel geþeah.

Ðis eadiga mæden se arwurða Godes þeowa Theochimus fedde and lærde and forðbrohte oðþæt hi xv wintre eald wæs. Dæghwamlice, hi hire utsanges and hire gebedu georne gefylde, and þæt ungelærde folc swiðe mynegode to ures Drihtones hersumnesse, hælendes Cristes, and þus cwæð: 'Geheraðme earma þeoda, ægþer ge weres ge wifes, ge cnihtes ge mægdenes, and healdað fæste on eowre heorta þæt þe Ic eow secge and wissige: forwyrpað þa deadan godas þe ge her beforen to gebugan þe beoð mid mannes handen gegrafena, and gebegeð eow to ure Sceppende Gode almihtigne, Sancte Marian sunu, hælende Criste. And Ic eow behata and on handselle, þæt ge sculon finden reste eowre sawlen mid Gode and mid his gecorenan innan Paradyses myrhþe.'

Seo eadiga Margareta wæs Theodosius dohtor, se gehersumode þan deofle, and hi gehersamedo Gode and ealle his halgan. Ða geherde seo eadiga Margareta, and hi hit on bocum fand, þæt þa cinges and þa ealdormenn and þa yfela gerefan ofslogen æfre and bebyrodon ealle þa Godes þeowas þe þær on lande wæron. Sumne hi mid wæpnum acwealdon, and sumne mid hætum wætere; sumne hi onhengon be þan fotum, and sumne be þan earmum; sumne hi pinedon mid wallende leade and mid hatum stanum; sumne heo mid sweorde ofslogen, sumne mid spiten betweon felle and flæsce þurhwræcon. Eall þæt Godes þeowan geþafodon and geþrowodon for Godes deoran lufan. And þa seo eadiga Margareta þis eall geherde and geseah, hi hi þæs þe swiðor to Gode gebæd, and þus cwæð: 'Domine Deus omnipotens, ego sum ancilla tua. Drihten God ælmihtig,' heo cwæð, 'Ic eom þin þeowa clæna, and ungewæmmed fram eallum mannum þe geborene bið. Þe Ic me betæce ungewæmmode þæt þu me gehealde togeanes þæs deofles costnung strange and staþolfæste on þinre þære sweteste lufa, forþanþe to þe nu is and æfre wæs and þurh þin help æfre beon sceal min hiht and min hope and min soþe lufu.'

Ða gewearð hit on anum dæge, þæt hire fostermoder hi het gan mid oþrum fæmnum on feld sceap to hawienne, and hi swa dydo spinnende. Ða ferde Olibrius, se heahgerefa, fram Asia þæra burh to Anthiochiam, axiende hwær þa wæron þe heora godan here noldan. Ða he on his wege rad, þa beseah he on þæt eadigan mæden þær þe hi sæt, wlitig and fæger, onmang hire geferan. Ða cwæð he to his cnihtum: 'Ridað hraþe to þære fæmnan and axiað hire gif hi seo frig, and gif hi is, þonne wille Ic hi habban me to wife; and gif hi is þeowa, þonne wille Ic gifen fih for hire and hæbban hi me to cefase, and hire scel beon wel mid me þurh hire fægernesse and hire fægre wlite.'

And þa cnihtes hire þa to comen, and hire to spræcon eall swa heom gehaten wæs. Ða Sancta Margareta heo to eorþan gestrehte and hi hire georne to Gode gebæd, and þus cwæð: 'Miserere mei Deus, miserere mei. Gemiltse me Drihten, gemiltse me þæt min sawle ne seo awæmmod þurh þisum hæþenum mannum. And Ic þe wille biddan þæt deofle mine sawle ne beswican, ne mine treowðe fram þe ahwerfan, ne minne clæne lichamen gefylan. Drihten leof, æfre Ic þe lufode, and þu Wuldorcyning ne læt þu me naht beswican, ne næfre min gewit fram þe gehwerfan, ne min mægþhad afylan. Ac asænd me, leofa Drihten, þinne halga engel to fultume þæt Ic min gewitt and minne wisdom forðhealdan mote, forþon Ic eom gesett betweonen þisum folce swa swa sceap betweonon wulfum, and Ic eam befangan eal swa spearwe on nette, and eall swa fisc on hoce, and eal swa hra mid rape. Nu help þu me, leofa Drihten, gehelp þu me.'

And þa cerdon þa cnihtas to heora hlaforde and cwædon: 'Nis þin mægn naht wið hire forþonþe hi lufað þone God þe þine eldran aheongan on rode.' And þa wearð se gerefa swiðe yrre, and het hi niman and him to gebringan, and he hire to cwæð and hire axode of hwilcere þeode hi wære and hwæder hi wære Cristen, and frig oððe þeowe. And seo eadiga Margareta him andwyrde and cwæð: 'Ic eom frig and Cristen.' And se cniht hire to cwæð: 'On hwilcum godum is þin geleafa þe þu on gelefst, and forð wilt get gelefan?' Seo eadiga Margarete him þa geandswarede: 'Ic lufige God ælmihtigne,' cwæð hi, 'and on him Ic gelefa þe is Fæder and Sunu and Halig Gast, þone þe min mægþhad fægre and wel gehealdon hæfð. Þæt is se þe þine yldran ahengan, and þurh þære

There is a certain land called Antioch: in that land was a servant of God called Theothimus; he was a very learned man. And there on that land was a heathen king called Theodosius, and his queen with him. It happened that she gave birth to a child and it was born a girl. And the heathen king (her father) commanded that she be thrown out, and so it was done. And God's servant, Theochimus, found that child and took her up, and made sure that she was fed well; and when she was able to understand, he gave her a name and that was Margaret. And afterwards, he made sure that she learned and she did that well.

This blessed maiden was fed and taught and raised by Theochimus, the worthy servant of God, until she was fifteen years old. Daily, she said her psalms and eagerly completed her prayers, and she often prompted the unlearned people in praise of our Lord, the saviour Christ, and said this: 'Listen to me you wretched people, whether you are men or women, boys or girls, and hold fast in your heart that which I say to you and know: turn away from the dead gods engraved by the hands of men which you previously bowed to here, and pray to our Creator, God almighty, Saint Mary's son, our saviour Christ. And I promise you and assure you that you shall find rest for your souls with God and with his chosen in the joy of Paradise.'

This blessed Margaret was the daughter of Theodosius who worshipped the devil, and she worshipped God and all his saints. Then the blessed Margaret heard, and found it in books, that the kings and the eorldormen and the evil reeves always killed and buried all of the servants of God who were in that land. Some they killed with weapons, and some with boiling water; some they hung by the feet, and some by the arms; some they tortured with boiling lead and some with hot stones; some they killed with the sword and some by means of a spit thrust through the skin and flesh. All this was endured and suffered by the servants of God for God's dear love. And when the blessed Margaret heard and saw all this she prayed all the more eagerly to God and said this: 'Lord God almighty, I am your handmaiden. Lord God almighty,' she said, 'I am your pure servant, and undefiled by all men who are born. I entrust myself to you undefiled so that you might protect me against the devil's strong treachery and keep me steadfast in your sweetest love, because to you now is and ever was and through your help ever shall be my joy and my hope and my true love.'

Then it happened on a certain day that her foster-mother asked her to go with the other women in to the fields to look after the sheep, and she did that task while spinning. Then Olibrius, the high reeve, journeyed from the town of Asia to Antioch, asking where those were who would not obey their gods. As he rode on his way, he saw that blessed maiden there where she sat, beautiful and fair, among her companions. Then he said to his soldiers: 'Ride quickly to that woman and ask her if she is free, and if she is, then I want to have her as my wife; if she is a slave, then I will give money for her and have her as my mistress, and she will do well by me because of her beauty and her fair complexion.'

And the soldiers came to her then, and related to her all that had been commanded to them. Then Saint Margaret stretched herself out on the earth, saying this: 'Have mercy on me God, have mercy on me. Have mercy on me Lord, have mercy on me so that my soul is not defiled by these heathen men. And I pray you that the devil will not betray my soul, nor turn my pledge from you, nor defile my pure body. Dear Lord, I have always loved you, and King of glory, do not allow me to be betrayed at all, nor my mind turned from you, nor my virginity defiled. But send me, dear Lord, your holy angel to help me so that I might hold fast my understanding and my wisdom, because I am set between these people just like a sheep between wolves, and I am entirely caught like a sparrow in a net, and like a fish on a hook, and just as a body with rope. Now help me, dear Lord, you must help me.'

And then the soldiers returned to their lord and said: 'Your power is nothing at all with her because she loves the God whom your ancestors hung on the Cross.' And then the reeve became very angry, and commanded that she be seized and brought to him. And he spoke to her and asked her of which nation she was and whether she was a Christian, and free or a slave. And the blessed Margaret answered him and said: 'I am free and Christian.' And the soldier said to her: 'Which god do you put your faith in and believe, and will yet believe in in times to come?' The blessed Margaret answered him: 'I love God almighty,' she said, 'and in him I believe who is the Father and Son and Holy Ghost – he who has protected my fair virginity well. This is he whom your ancestors hung, and through that deed they had to lose, because he is King and his kingdom will never have an end.'

And then Olibrius became very angry and commanded that the beautiful woman be taken and locked dæde hi losian sculon, forþonþe he is Cyning and his rice ne wurð næfre nan ænde.'

60   And þa wearð Olibrius swiðe yrre and het þa fægre fæmne genimen and innon his carcerne beluccan, þær nan liht inne cumen ne mihte: and men swa dyde. Ða þis gedon wæs, þa for se gerefa Olibrius to Antiochia þære byrig to his godan him to gebiddenne. And he þanen to his gereorde eode and amang þan þe he æt, he to his þegnum spræc, and þus cwæð: 'On hwilca wisa ræde ge me hu Ic muge þis mæden bismærian?' And hi ealle þa swigedon. Ða se gerefa het hi utlædon of
65   þan carcerne, and þæt wæs on þan oðre dæge, and het hi bringan beforen him, and he hire to cwæð: 'Ðu earma fæmna, læt beon þin mycela mod þe þu to me hæfst, and gemiltse þinum fægreran lichamen and gebide þe to minum gode, and Ic þe gife ælc god genoh, and þu scealt eal mines godes wealden mid me selfum.'

Sancta Margareta him andswerode and þus cwæð: 'Drihten hit wat þæt Ic min mægþhad wel
70   þurh him gehealdan habbe, and ne miht þu me beswican ne þu ne miht me becyrran of minum rihtan geleafan, ne fram minne rihte Hlaforde. And Ic eom geara,' cwæð hi, 'on Drihten to gelefanne þe gesceop heofonas and eorðan; and he sæ bedraf þær þe heo wrohtað dæges and nihtes.' Olibrius þa cwæð: 'Gif þu nylt to minum gode þe gebiddan, min swyrd sceal þinne þone fægran lichamen eall to styccan forcyrfan, and þine liemen ealle to sindrian, and þine ban Ic sceal ealle forbærnan.
75   And gif þu woldest me lufian and to minum godum þe gebiddan, þe sceolde beon eall swa wel eall swa me selfan.' And seo eadiga Margareta him answerode and cwæð: 'Ic habbe minne licchamen and mine sawla Gode bebodan, for he is min Hlaford and min help, and min Werigend and min fultum wið þe and wið eallum þinum leasum gewitum. Crist hine selfne to þan geeadmedde þæt he for mancynne micele þrowunge geþrowode, and na for his gewyrhtum ac for ure alesednesse.
80   And Ic wille,' cwæð hi, 'for his leofan wille bliðelice þrowian.'

Ða het se gerefa hi niman, and het hi be þan fotan uppahon and mid greatum roddum beaton. And seo eadiga Margareta hire handan uppahof and hi to Gode gebæd, and þus cwæð: 'On þe Ic gelefa, leofa Drihten, and þæt Ic þe bidde þæt þu ne þole þæt Ic næfre forwurþe, ne þæt me mine feond næfre oferswiðan ne moten, forþan min hiht is to þe, leofe Drihten.' And hi þa get hire
85   clæne gebedu forðhild, and þus cwæð: 'Æfre wunu þu mid me, leofa Drihten, heofonlice Cyng. Miltse me and genere me of deofles anwealde.'

Ealle þa men þe hire abutan stodon to hire cleopoden and þus cwædon: 'Hwi nelt þu, earme fæmne, gelefan on ure gode and to ure hlaforde þe gebugan and lutan? Æle, fægre fæmne, ealle we þe bemænað sarlice, forþonþe we geseoð þe swa nacode sittan, and þinne fægra lichamen to
90   wundre macian. And us þæt þincþ þæt he ah þines gewald, hwæþer swa he wille to deaðe oððe to life. Gelef on ure gode, þonne most þu mid us lif habban.' Seo eadiga Margareta heom andswerode: 'Æle, ge geleasan witan, gað hraðe to eowrum weorce forþanðe min God is mid me on fultume. Hwæt? Wene ge þæt þæt ofþynce þæt min lichame þrowige? Ic wat þæt min sawle is þæs þe clænre mid Gode. Ac earme þeode, gelefað get on minum Gode, and for he is strang and mihtful,
95   and ealle þan mannen gefultumað þe mid rihte farað and mid clænre heorte him to gebiddað and he heom geofð in Paradise eardingstowe. Ne þurfe ge næfre þæs wenen þæt Ic æfre eowrum godum me to gebidde, forþonþe hi syndon dumbe and deafe and blinde and mid drycræfte geworhte.'

Ða wearð se gerefa eorre geworþan and cwæð to hire: 'Ðu wyrcest þines fæðeres weorc þæt is se
100   deofol self.' And seo fæmne andswaro geaf: 'Hwæt þu nu, earming, mid leasunge færst, and me is min Drihten on fultume.' Ða cwæð se gerefa: 'Hwær is se God þe mæg þe gebeorgan of mine handan?' Seo eadiga Margareta him to cwæð: 'Geswiga þu earmingc! Ne hæfþ þu nan þingc on me to donne, ac eall þu eart full, and þu scealt faran into þære nigenda niþhelle, and þu scealt þær onfon þa yfelan geweorc þe þu her gefremest and grefremed hæst.'

105   Ða het se gerefa hio nimon and be þan fexe upahon, and bæd wyrcan scearpa piles and het wrecen betweon flæsce and bane. And seo eadiga Margareta hire handa upahof and hi georne to Drihtne gebæd, and þus cwæð: 'Ðu Drihten leof, beo þu me on fultume for me beoð abuton

in his prison, there where no light might come: and men did just that. And when this was done, then the reeve Olibrius journeyed to the town of Antioch to worship his gods. And he went from there to a feast and he spoke to his noblemen among those who ate, and said thus: 'What would you advise me on how I might ill-treat this maiden?' And they were all silent. Then the reeve commanded her to be led out of the prison, and that was on the second day, and commanded her to be brought before him, and he said to her: 'You wretched woman, abandon this proud mind which you have towards me, and have mercy on your beautiful body and pray to my god, and I will give you enough of everything that is good, and you shall possess all of my benefits with me myself.'

Saint Margaret answered him and said: 'The Lord knows that I have protected my virginity well through him, and you cannot defile me nor can you turn me from my true faith, nor from my true Lord. And I am ready,' she said, 'to believe in the Lord who made heaven and earth and surrounded it by sea there, who made day and night.' Olibrius then said: 'If you will not pray to my god, my sword shall cut into pieces the whole of your fair body, and your body will be entirely cut into pieces, and I shall completely burn your bones. But if you will love me and pray to my gods, then all shall be as well with you as it is with me myself.' And the blessed Margaret answered him and said: 'I have commended my body and soul to God, for he is my Lord and my help, and my Protector and my support against you and against all your false advice. Christ humbled himself so that he might endure great suffering for mankind, and not for his own service but for our salvation. And I shall,' she said, 'happily suffer for his dear will.'

Then the reeve commanded her to be seized and raised up by the feet and beaten with great rods. And the blessed Margaret lifted her hands up and prayed to God, saying: 'I believe in you, dear Lord, and I pray you that you do not allow me ever to weaken, or that my enemy will ever be able to overcome me; therefore my hope is in you, dear Lord.' And then she still kept up her innocent prayers, saying thus: 'Dear lord, heavenly King, always stay with me; have mercy on me and save me from the devil's power.'

Then all the men who stood about her called out to her and said this: 'Wretched woman, why will you not believe in our god, and bow and kneel to our lord? Alas, fair lady, we all lament sadly because we see you sitting so naked, and your fair body made so wounded. And it seems to us that he has all of the power over you, whether he wishes you to die or to live. Believe in our god: then you will have life with us.' The blessed Margaret answered them: 'Alas, you faithless men, go quickly to your work because my God is with me in support. What? Do you imagine that I grieve about the suffering of my body? I know that my soul is the purer with God. But wretched people, believe yet in my God, for he is strong and powerful and supports all the people who journey in truth and pray to him with pure hearts, and he offers them a resting place in Paradise. Nor need you ever imagine that I will pray to your gods, because they are dumb and deaf and blind and are made by witchcraft.'

Then the reeve became angry and said to her: 'You perform your father's work who is the devil himself.' And the woman gave this answer: 'Listen now, you wretched thing, you act with deceit; and my Lord is a support to me.' Then the reeve said: 'Where is this God who can save you from my hands?' The blessed Margaret said to him: 'Be quiet wretch! You have done nothing to me, but you are totally foul, and you shall go into the ninth hateful hell,[5] and there you shall receive the evil deeds that you perform here and have performed before.'

Then the reeve commanded that she be seized and hung up by the hair, and demanded that sharp spikes be made and commanded them to be driven between the flesh and the bone. And the holy Margaret lifted her hands up and prayed earnestly to the Lord, saying this: 'Beloved Lord, be a help to me, for there are so many hounds around me, and they wish to reduce my body to bits. Beloved Lord, judge my soul and release my body, for I am not interested in this false suffering. You must help me Lord, and send me support, so that I can fight against my enemies, so that I can see you with my two eyes in your kingdom.'

Then the wretched ones greatly tormented her, and the reeve said to her: 'Choose, wretched woman, me and my god, and if you will not, you shall become yet more wounded.' The blessed Margaret answered him: 'If I submitted my body to you, then you will have to go into the boiling pitch, in hell's

---

5   The ninth hell is part of the apocryphal tradition depicting hell as a set of different torments depending on the sins committed during life.

hundes swa manega, and heo willeð minne lichamen to sticcan gebringan. Drihten leof, deme mine sawla and ðu genere minne lichome, for Ic ne recce þise leasere þrowunge. Gehelp þu me
110   Drihten, and sænd me fultum, þæt Ic wið minum feondum fihtan muge, þæt Ic mid minum eagne twam þe geseon mote on þine rice.'

Ða þa leasan gewiten hi swiðe gepinedon, and se gerefa hire to cwæð: 'Gecer, earme fæmne, to me and to minum gode, and gif þu nelt, þu scealt to wundre gewurðan.' Seo eadiga Margareta him andswerode: 'Gif Ic minne lichamen to þe geeadmede, þonne scealt þu inne þæt wallende
115   pic, into hellewite, þær þu scealt wunian æfre; þonne miht þu habban minne lichamen þe to gæmene, and God hæfð mine sawle fram þe generod.'

Ða wearð se gerefa swiðe yrre and het hi inne þan carcerne belucen. And hi ineode into þan carcerne, and mid Cristes rodetacne hi hi gebletsode. And hi seofon tide þæs dæges þærinne gesæt, and hi to Gode gebæd, and þus cwæð: 'Drihten leof, þe Ic þancige þeoses domes þe þu me
120   in sændest, for þu eart ælces mannes fultum þe on þe gelefað, and þu eart Fæder ealra þære þe fæderlease syndon, and ne geswic þu me næfre, Drihten leof, ac help þu me, þæt Ic me bewerige wið minum feondum. And ne læt þu me næfre mine sawle beswican, for þu eart ealre demena Dema, and nu betweon me and heom.'

Þa com hire fosterfæder gan to hire and þurh an eahþyrl he hire to spræc, and he hire brohte
125   bread and wæter; þæs wæteres hi gebreac, and nanes breades. And he hire þrowunge fægre sette on Godes bocum. And hit þa færunge gewearð sona æfter þan, þæt þær inneode an grislic deofol; his nama wæs Ruffus. And he wæs swiðe mycel on dracan heowe: and eall he wæs nædderfah, and of his toþan leome ofstod eal swa of hwiten swurde; and of his eagan swilces fyres lyg; and of his nasþyrlum smec and fyr ormæte mycel; and his tunge þrecowe his sweore belygde.

130   Sancta Margareta hi to eorðan gestrehte and hire rihtwise gebedu to Gode gesænte, and þus cwæð: 'Drihten God ælmihtig, georne Ic þe bæd þæt Ic hine geseage, and nu Ic þe eft gebidde þæt Ic hine ofercumen mote.' And hi þa upparas and hire earmes eastweard aðeonode, and þus cwæð: 'Drihten God ælmihtig, þu þe gesceope heofona and eorþa and eal mancyn and heora lif þe on heom syndon, and þa þu on rode wære gehangen, and þu to helle astige, and þu þine halgan ut
135   gedydost and þone mycele deofol Sathan fæste gebunde, gehelp þu me, leofe Drihten, þæt Ic þisne deofol fæste mote gebindan.' And se deofol him þa abalhc and þa fæmne forswelgan wolde; and seo eadiga fæmne sona mid hire swiðre hand wið þonum sceocca wel gebletsode, and on hire forhæfde rodetacna mærcode, and swa wið þonne draca wel generode. And seo eadiga fæmne hal and gesund fram him gewænte, and eall sticmælum toðwan se draca ut of þan carcerne, and hi nan
140   yfel on hire ne gefelde.

Ac hi sona to eorðan gestrehte, and hi geornlice to Gode gebæd and þus cwæð: 'Drihten leof, lof sy þe selfum and wuldor ealra þære goda þe þu me dest and gedon hæfst, and get is min hopa þæt þu don wille, aa in ealra worulda woruld.'

And þa hi hire gebedu gefyld hæfde, þa beseah hio hio on þære wynstre healfe þæs carcernes,
145   and hi oþerne deofol sittan geseah, sweart and unfæger swa him gecynde wæs. And he þa up aras and to hire weard eode. Þa seo fæmne on him beseah, þa cwæð hi to þan deofle: 'Ic wat hwæt þu þæncst, ac geswic þu þæs geþohtes forþon Ic wat eall þin yfel geþanc.' And se deofol hire answerode and cwæð: 'Ic minne broþor Rufonem to þe gesænde on dracan gelice þæt he sceolde þe fordon, and nu hæfst þu hine mid Cristes rodentacn ofslagen, and Ic wat þæt þu me mid þinum gebedum
150   ofslean wilt.'

Seo eadiga Margareta upparas and þone deofol be þan fexe gefeng and hine niþer to eorðan gewearp, and hi hirne swiðre fot uppon his swire gesette, and him to cwæð: 'Geswic þu earming! Ne miht þu to nahte minne mægþhad me to beswicenne, for Ic hæbbe minne Drihten me to fultume, and Ic eam his þeowa and he is min Hlaford, and Ic eom him beweddod þe gehalgod is
155   aa in ealra worulda woruld.'

Ða hi þis gecwedon hæfde, þa þærinne com Drihtnes engel, and þær wearð inne swa mycel leoht swa hit beoð on middæg, and he hæfde Cristes rodentacen on hande. Ða wearð Sancta

torment, where you shall dwell for ever; then you might have had my body to play with, but God will have my soul, saved from you.'

Then the reeve became very angry and commanded her to be locked in the prison. And she entered into the prison, and with the sign of the Cross of Crist she blessed herself. And she sat inside there until the seventh hour of the day, and she prayed to God, and said this: 'Dear Lord, I give thanks to you for this judgement that you sent to me, for you are the help of all people who believe in you, and you are the father of all those who are fatherless, and do not leave me ever, beloved Lord, but help me, so that I may defend myself against my enemies. And do not ever let my soul be betrayed, for you are the Judge of all judges, and are now between me and them.'

Then her foster-father came to her and he spoke to her through a window, and he brought her bread and water; she took some water, but none of the bread. And he effectively inscribed her sufferings in God's book. And then it suddenly happened immediately after that that a grisly devil came in there; his name was Ruffus. And he was very like a dragon; and underneath he was entirely stained like an adder, and from his teeth a light came out just like a white sword; and his eyes were just like the light of a fire; and from his nostrils came smoke and a great and intense fire; and his tongue's pressure lay round his neck.[6]

Saint Margaret stretched herself on the earth and her just prayers sent to God, saying thus: 'Lord God almighty, I prayed you earnestly that I might see him, and now I again pray you that I might overcome him.' And then she rose up and stretched out her arms eastwards, and said thus: 'Lord God almighty, you who shaped heaven and earth and all humanity and the lives which are in them, and you were then hung on the Cross, and you descended to hell, and you got your saints out, and bound fast the great devil Satan, you must help me, dear Lord, that I might bind fast this devil.' And then the devil became irritated and wanted to swallow the maiden; and the blessed maiden immediately blessed herself completely against the devil with her right hand, and on her forehead she made the mark of the Cross, and thus she protected herself well against the dragon. And the blessed woman turned from him whole and sound, and bursting into pieces, the dragon disappeared out of the prison, and no evil befell her.

But she stretched herself on the ground and she eagerly prayed to God, saying this: 'Dear Lord, praise is due to you and for all the glories which you do and have done for me, and it is my hope that you will continue to do for me yet, for ever and ever.'

And when she had completed her prayers, then she looked in the left half of the prison and saw another devil sitting there, black and ugly as was typical of his kind. And he rose up then and went towards her. Then the woman looked upon him and said to that devil: 'I know what you are thinking, but cease those thoughts because I know all your evil intent.' And the devil answered her and said: 'I sent my brother Ruffus to you in the guise of a dragon so that he could undo you, and now you have killed him with the sign of Christ's Cross, and I know that you will kill me with your prayers.'

The holy Margaret rose up and seized the devil by the hair and threw him down to the earth, and she put her left foot upon his neck and said to him: 'Yield you wretch! You will not be able to overcome my virginity at all for I have my Lord to help me, and I am his servant and he is my Lord, and I am betrothed to him who is worshipped throughout all this world and in all worlds.'

When she had said this, then the Lord's angel came in there and there was as much light as if it were midday, and he had Christ's Cross in his hand. Then Saint Margaret was overjoyed, and she thanked God for all that which she previously and afterwards, frequently and often, had seen through God.

And then, the woman had words with the devil and she said thus: 'Tell me, wretch, what are you and from where have you come?' The devil said to her: 'I pray you, because you are a saintly woman, take your foot from my neck, and I will tell you all that I have done.' And then the blessed Margaret lifted her foot up and he told her all that he knew and said: 'After Satan had been bound, I had always dwelt since among people, and I turned many of the servants of God away from God, and no human could ever overcome me except you alone. You killed my brother and you possess power entirely over me because I can see that God is with you, and yet I will tell you more of my deeds, all individually.

For I took plenty of people who believed in God: from some I took their speech, from some their hearing; from some their feet, and from some their hands, and they became crippled because of that; I

6   On the portrayal of the dragon, see J. Price, 'The Virgin and the
Dragon: The Demonology of *Seinte Marherete*', *Leeds Studies in English*
16 (1985), 337–57.

Margareta swiðe bliðe, and hio þancode Gode eall þæt hi ær and sioððon þurh Gode ofte and gelome gesegon hæfde.

160 And hi þa, seo fæmne, wið þone deofol wordum dælde and þus cwæð: 'Sege me earmingc, hwanan eart þu oððe hwanon come þu?' Se deofol hire to cwæð: 'Ic þe gebidde, forþonþe þu eart gehalgod fæmne, þæt þu þinne fot of minum sweorum alihte, and Ic þe secgan wille eall þæt Ic gedon hæbbe.' And hio þa, seo eadiga Margareta, hire fot upahof, and he hire sæde eall þæt he wiste, and cwæð: 'Siððan Sathan gebunden wearð, siððan Ic mid mannum æfre gewunode, and
165 manega Godes þeowas Ic gehwearf fram Gode, and næfre ne mihte me nan man ofercumen buton þu ane. Minne broþor þu ofsloge, and þu mines eall geweald ahst forþan Ic geseo þæt God is mid þe, and get Ic þe mare secge of minum dædum, ealle syndrige.

For Ic nam ealle wæstmes fram mancynne þe on Gode gelefdon: sume Ic spræce benam, and sume heora hlyste; sumen heora fet, and sume heora handa, and heo þurh þæt creopeles wurðon;
170 sumum Ic eagen benam, and sumum his gewittes; sume Ic slæpende beswac, and sume eac wacigende; sume mid winde, and sume mid wætere; sume mid mæte, and sume mid drænce, ofte þonne hio ungebletsodon wæren; sume mid slehte, and sume on some; sume on morððædum, and sume mid oðres mannes wife gehæmdon; sume mid feowerfoted nytene for minum willen gefremedon; and sume heora eldran mid wordon gegræmedon. Eal þis Ic me ane wat, and þæt me
175 nu hearde hreowð. Þin fæder and þin modor mine wæron, and þu ane fram fæder and fram modor and fram eallum þine cynne to Gode þu gehwurfe.'

And seo eadiga fæmna him to cwæð: 'Hwanen wearð eow þæt ge mihton ahan Godes þeowes to beswicenne?' And þa se deofol hire to cwæð: 'Sege me hwanen is þin lif Margareta? And hwanen beoð þine liman? And hwu and on hwilce wise is Crist mid þe? And Ic þe secge eall þæt
180 Ic wat.' And þa seo fæmne to þan deofle cwæð: 'Nelle Ic hit þe secgan forþonþe þu ne eart þæs wurþe þæt Ic wið þe wordum dæle: for God is swiðe god, and him sy geþancod, for Ic eam his nu and æfre ma beon wille.'

Se deofol hire to cwæð: 'Sathana, urne cyning, hine gewræc Drihten of Paradises myrhþe, and him þa twa land agæf; an is Gamne and oðer is Mambre. And þider he gebrincð ealle þa þe he
185 begeton mæig of mancynne. Nu Ic soðlice þe to sprece and for þi ne mæig Ic na læng beon, forþon Ic geseo þæt God is mid þe. Ac Ic þe bidde, eadige fæmne, þæt Ic wið þe an word dælan mote, and Ic þe hælsige þurh þinne God and þurh his Sunu and his þone Halgan Gast, þe þu onbelefst, þæt þu me na mare yfel ne do and Ic þe behate and þæt þe gelæste þæt Ic næfre ma nænne mon on þisum life ne beswice, and þæt Ic þin bebod fæste gehealdan wille.' And seo eadiga fæmne
190 him andswarode: 'Gewit þe heonon on weig, and seo eorðe þe forswelge, and þu þær wunige to Domesdæge.'

And þa þæs oðres dæges, se gerefa het þæt me him þæt mæden toforen brohte, and þa seo fæmne ut of þan carcerne gelæd wæs. Hio hy sona seneda þa hio uteode and me þær forworhte men of Antiochia þære burh gesamnoden, þæt hi þa fæmne geseon woldan. And þa se gerefa to
195 þære fæmne cwæð: 'Wilt þu me get geheran and to minum gode þe gebiddan?' And hi þa andswera ageaf: 'Ne þe ne þinum godum Ic næfre ne lufige, ac þe wel gerisde þæt þu minnen Gode wel geherdest and lufodest, þane þe lufað ælc þære manna þe hine mid inweardre heortan lufiað.'

Ða het se gerefa hio genimon, and bead heom hire claðes ofnimen and hi upahon bi þan fotum; and he het wallende stanes on hire fægre lichamen geworpan. And heo þa leasan gewitan eac swa
200 dydon. And þa cwæð se gerefa to þære fæmne: 'And nylt þu me get lufian, ne to minum gode þe gebugan ne þe to him gebiddan?' And seo eadiga fæmne nolde him andswarigen nan word. Ða wærð se gerefa swiðe eorre, and het mycel fyr onælan and ænne cytel þærofer gesettan, and bæd þære fæmne fet and handan tosomne gebindon, and innen þonne weallende cetel gesetton. And seo eadiga Margareta heo georne to Gode gebæd, and þus cwæð: 'Ic þe wille biddan, leofa Drihten
205 Cyning, þæt þæt wæter gewurðe me to fulluhtes bæðe and to clænsunge ealra minum synnum.' And þa þær com fleogan Drihtnes ængel, and he þa gehalgode þæt wallende wæter to fonte, and þa halga fæmne genam be þære swiðre hand and of þan wætere þa fæmne gesette, and hire on þan wætere na lað ne gewearð.

Ða þæt geherdon and geseagon þe hire ymbstodon, wundor heom þuhte. Hio geherdon stefne
210 of heofone clypion to þære fæmne þus: 'Ic eom þin godfæder and þu min goddohtor, and Ic

seized the sight of some, and from some their wits; some I deceived sleeping, also some that were awake; some by means of wind, some by water; some by food, some through drink – often they were themselves unblessed; some through battle, and some in peace; some because of murder, and some because of adultery with other men's wives; some performed sex with four-footed animals because of my will; and some reviled their elders in speech. All this I alone knew and that distresses me greatly now. Your father and your mother were mine, and you alone from your father and mother and from all your family turned to God.'

And the blessed woman said to him: 'When did you possess the power to betray God's servants?' And the devil said to her: 'Tell me where is your life from Margaret? And where is your body from? And how and in what ways is Christ with you? And I will tell you all that I know.' And the woman said to the devil: 'I will not tell you any of it because you are not worthy for me to speak with: for God is very good, and he should be thanked because I am his now and will be for ever more.'

Then the devil said to her: 'Satan, our king, was expelled by the Lord himself from the joy of Paradise, and he was given two lands; one is Gamne and the other is Mambre. And there he brought all those who he had been able to get from humanity. Now I speak truthfully to you and because of that I will not last long, for I see that God is with you. But I pray you, blessed lady, that I might have a few words with you, and I beseech you, through your God and through his Son and the Holy Spirit in which you believe, that you do no more evil to me and I promise you, and will perform that for you, that I will never more betray any person in this life, and that I will hold fast your command.' And the blessed woman answered him: 'Depart from here on your way, and may the earth swallow you, and may you dwell there until Judgement Day.'

And then the following day the reeve commanded men to bring the maiden before him, and then the woman was led out of prison. She immediately blessed herself as she was led out, and sinful men of Antioch gathered together there because they wanted to see the woman. And the reeve said to the woman: 'Will you hear me yet and pray to my god?' And she gave the answer: 'I will never love you or your gods, but it is entirely fitting for you to hear my God and love him well, he who loves each person who loves him with a sincere heart.'

Then the reeve commanded her to be taken and instructed them to take off her clothes and hang her up by the feet; and he commanded that boiling stones be thrown at her fair body. And then the faithless men did just that. And then the reeve said to the woman: 'And will you not love me yet, nor bow to my god, nor pray to him?' And the blessed woman would not answer one word to him. Then the reeve grew very angry, and commanded a great fire to be lit and a cauldron to be placed over it, and he instructed the woman's hands and feet to be bound together, and her to be placed in the boiling cauldron. And the blessed Margaret prayed earnestly to God, saying thus: 'I want to pray you, dear Lord King, that the water becomes a baptismal bath for me to cleanse all of my sins.' And the Lord's angel came flying down there, and he blessed that boiling water as holy water, and he took the holy woman by the right hand and he set her in that water, and that water was not harmful to her.

When those who stood about her heard and saw this, it seemed a miracle to them. They heard a voice from heaven call out to the woman thus: 'I am your godfather and you are my goddaughter, and I will favour all those who believe in you. Blessed are you, holy lady Saint Margaret, because you hold your heart and hands pure, and suffer greatly for my love.' And after a little while – it was not long – it also immediately happened through that woman's suffering that five thousand men bowed to God there.

Then the reeve grew very angry and he commanded that all those who believed in God should be executed. And the reeve said to his servant Malchus (the same who secretly served God): 'Draw your sword,' said the reeve, 'and kill the woman.' And then God's enemies seized the woman, dragged her out of the city violently, and then they came to where they would kill her. And the heathen men spoke to Malchus and said: 'Draw your sword quickly, and kill the woman.' And then Malchus spoke to her secretly and eagerly asked her, saying thus: 'Remember me, a wretched man, in your prayers.' And the blessed woman said to him: 'I will pray for you.' And then she stretched herself on the ground saying thus: 'Lord God almighty, you who made heaven and earth and all that men live by, hear my prayer: that each of the people who read of my suffering should be forgiven their sins, and each of those people who will hear it for the love of God. And yet I will ask you, dear Lord, that each person who raises a church in my name and those who seek me with their candles, or with other alms, and those who write of my

eallum gearige þe on þe gelefað. Eadig eart þu, halig fæmna Sancta Margareta, forþonþe þu þine hande and þinne hige clæne gehylde, and for minre lufu mycel geþrowodest.' And embe lytle fece, næs hit lang to þan, eac hit sona gewearð þurh þære fæmne þrowunge, þæt þær to Gode gebugan fif þusend manna.

215   Þa wearð se gerefa swiðe eorra and he het ealle ofslean þa þe on Gode gelefdon. And se gerefa cwæð to his þeowum Malcum (se ilca dernunga Gode geþenode): 'Gedrah þu þin swurd,' cwæð se gerefa, 'and þa fæmne þu ofsleah.' And þa Godes wiðerwinnan þa fæmnan genamon ut of þære byrig ungerædelice hi togoden, and þa hi þær becomen þær me hio slean scolde. And þa leasan witan to Malcum spræcan and cwædon: 'Drah hraþa þin swurd and þa fæmna þu ofsleah.' And

220   hire þa to leat Malcus swa dreohlice and hire georne bæd and þus cwæð: 'Gemune þu me, earminge, on þinum gebedum.' And seo eadige fæmne him to cwæð: 'Ic wille þe forebiddan.' And hio hio to eorþan gestrehte and þus cwæð: 'Drihten God ælmihtig, þu þe heofones gescope and eorþe and eall þæt men bi libbað, geher þu mine bene: þæt ælc þære manna synne sy forgiofene þe mine þrowunge rædeð, and ælcum þære mannu þe hi for Godes lufu geheran willæð. And get Ic þe,

225   leofa Drihten, biddan wille, þæt þu ælc þæra manna þe on minum naman cirice arære, and þan þe me mid heora lihte gesecan willað and mid oðrum ælmessan, and þan þe mine þrowunge gewritað oððe mid heora figa gebicgað, þæt inne heora husum nan unhal cild sy geboren: ne crypol, ne dumb, ne deaf, ne blind, ne ungewittes. Ac forgif þu, leofa Drihten, ealle heora synna for þinra þære mycele ara and for þinum godcundum wuldre and for þinre þære mycelen mildheortnesse.'

230   And hio hi eft niðer gestrehte and heore hleor wið þæra eorþan gelegde, and þa ealle þe hire ymbstodan feollan heom on cneowgebedum.

And þa ure Drihten him self com of heofonum to eorþan astigan, and hire sona to cwæð: 'Ic þe geofa and behate swa hwæt swa þu bidst and gebeden hæfst, eal hit is þe gytyðed.' And eft cwæð ure Drihten: 'Ælc þæra þe on þinre lufa me to gebiddað and ælmessan bringað, oððe mid leohte

235   secað, oððe þine þrowunge rædað oððe write, oððe mid his fige gebycge oððe inne his huse hæbbe, ne sceal nan yfel næfre on him becumen, and ælc þære þe his synne forgifennesse habban wille on þinre lufan, eall hit sio forgifen. Eadig eart þu, Margareta, and ealle þa þurh þe on me gelefdon and gelefan willað.'

And þa seo eadiga Margareta uparas of hire gebedum, feagre gefrefred, and cwæð to eallum þan

240   þe hire ymbstodan: 'Geherað me, mine gebroðra and swustra, ealda and geunga, ealle gemænelice: Ic eow bidde þæt ge gelefan on Drihten God ælmihtige and on his Sunu and on his Halgan Gaste; and Ic eow bidde þæt ge me on eowrum bedum gemunnen, forþan Ic eam swiðe synfull.'

Þa þa hi hire gebedu gefylled hæfde, þa cleopode hi swiðe hlude þone þe hi slean sceolde and cwæð: 'Malche, nim nu þin swurd and do þæt þe gehaten is, for nu is min time gecuman.' Malcus

245   hire to cwæð: 'Nylle Ic þe ofslean forþon Ic geseo þæt Crist is mid þe, and Ic geherde hu he spræc to þe and cwæð þæt þu his fæmne wære.' And seo fæmne him to cwæð: 'Gif þu nylt me ofslean, nafa þu nan hlot mid me on heofene rice.' And he þa Malcus to hire fotum gefyll, and þus cwæð: 'Ic þe bidde, leofa eadige fæmne, þæt þu gebidde for me and forgif þu me þas wite, for min Drihten hit wat þæt Ic hit unwillende do þæt Ic æfre þas dæda gefremme.' And þa seo fæmne hi

250   to Gode gebæd, and þus cwæð: 'Drihten leof, forgif þu him ealle þa synne þe he gefremeð hæfð.'

And he þa Malcus his swurd adroh and þæra eadigra fæmne þæt heafod of asloh. And seo eadiga fæmne Margareta hire sawle Gode agef, and Malcus on hire swiðran, uppan his swurda feol, and his sawle Godes ængles underfeongan, and þurh þæra eadigra fæmne bene Gode and betæhton.

255   Ða hit geherdon ealle þa untruman þe wæron þær on lande, ealle hi hire lic gesohton and heora hæle þer gefetton: sume hi wæron blinde and deafa, and sume crypeles; and sume dumbe and sume ungewitfulle. Ealle hi heora hæle æt þære halgan fæmnan onfenge. And mycel mancyn, ealle þa þe unhale wære and þære fæmnen lic gesohton, ealle hi hale and gesunde on heora wege ham gewænton, and ures Drihtnes ænglæs þider comen and þa sawla underfengon, and heo on

260   heofone rice gebrohton. And nu hi is mid Gode and mid eallum his halgum, and þær hi wunað nu and æfre wunian sceal in ealra worulda woruld a buton ænde. Amen.

sufferings or buy it with their money, that within their house no disabled child be born: neither crippled nor dumb nor deaf nor blind nor mentally ill. But forgive, dear Lord, all their sins for your great grace and for your divine glories and for your great mercy.' And she again stretched herself down on the ground and laid her face on the earth, and all those who stood around her fell to their knees in prayer.

And then our Lord himself came from heaven down to the earth, and immediately said to her: 'I grant and promise that whatever you ask and have prayed for, it will be granted to you.' And again our Lord said: 'Each of those who prays to me in your love and bring alms, or comes with a light, or reads your passion or writes it, or buys it with their money, or has one in the house, no evil shall come on them, and each of those who will have their sins forgiven through your love, all of this will be forgiven. Blessed are you Margaret, as are all those who believed in me and will believe through you.'

And then the blessed Margaret rose up from her prayers, greatly refreshed, and said to all of those who stood about her: 'Hear me my brothers and sisters, old and young, all of you individually: I pray you that you believe in the Lord God almighty and in his Son and in the Holy Spirit; and I pray you that you remember me in your prayers because I am very sinful.'

When she had completed her prayer, she called out loudly to him who had to kill her, saying: 'Malchus, take your sword now and do what is commanded to you, for now my time has come.' Malchus said to her: 'I will not kill you because I see that Christ is with you, and I heard how he spoke to you and he said that you were his maiden.' And the maiden said to him: 'If you will not kill me, you cannot have any part with me of the kingdom of heaven.' And then Malchus fell to her feet and said this: 'I pray you, dear blessed lady, that you pray for me and forgive me this punishment, for my Lord knows it that I am unwilling to do this of all the deeds that I ever performed.' And the lady prayed to God and said thus: 'Dear Lord, forgive him all those sins that he has done.'

And then Malchus drew his sword and cut off the head of the woman. And the blessed woman Margaret gave her soul to God and Malchus, on her right hand, fell upon his sword, and God's angel received his soul, and delivered it to God because of the prayer of the blessed woman.

When the unwell who were in that land heard all this, they all sought her body and there received healing: some were blind and deaf, and some were crippled; some were dumb and some mentally ill. All of them received healing from that holy woman. And many people, those who were ill and sought the woman's body, all went on their way home whole and sound, and our Lord's angels came there and received her soul, and brought it into the kingdom of heaven. And now she is with God and all his saints, and she dwells there now and ever shall dwell there, world of all worlds without end. Amen.

The *Hymns* of Saint Godric

Saint Godric (died 1170), a hermit who lived at Finchale near Durham, composed three hymns which were recorded in his Latin *vita* written by Reginald of Coldingham. The three texts are found together on folio 85 recto of London, British Library, Royal 5 F. vii, where the musical notation for the pieces is also included. The order in which the hymns are written in this manuscript is that of Burgwine, Mary and Nicholas. Versions of one or two of the hymns exist in a number of manuscripts ranging in date from the late twelfth century to the sixteenth century, where they are also usually found within the context of a Latin chronicle.

Saint Godric had led a varied life before his decision to become a hermit: he had been a pedlar, and travelled widely as the master of a ship and as a pilgrim. His level of literacy was basic, and although he could read a Latin psalter, rather like Cædmon some five hundred years previously, his inspiration for his *Hymns* came divinely, and not through learning. These three hymns, attributed to Godric, are the result of the visitations of Saint Mary, Godric's dead sister Burgwine, and Saint Nicholas. The hymn to Mary represents one of the earliest such Marian lyrics, and illustrates the personal devotion afforded to this saint that was burgeoning by the last decades of the twelfth century. The hymn of Burgwine, sung by her in a vision to Godric in which she thus reassured her brother that she was saved, refers to the *scamel* or 'footstool', a metaphorical allusion to the altar of a church based on the psalter. The hymn to Nicholas resulted from a visitation by that saint in which Godric accompanied him in singing. It is no surprise that Godric, himself a seafaring man once, should have an especial devotion to the patron saint of sailors. Each of these texts represents an early manifestation of the religious vernacular lyric. The language of each is Northern.

Hymn of Godric's Sister, Burgwine

Crist and Sainte Marie swa on scamel[1] me iledde   *footstool (altar)*
Þat Ic on þis erðe ne silde wið mine bare fote itredie.   *should*

Hymn to Saint Mary

Sainte Marye, Virgine,
Moder Jesu Cristes Nazarene,
Onfo, schild, help þin Godric,   *receive; shield*
Onfang, bring heʒilich wið þe in Godes ric.   *honourably; kingdom*

5   Sainte Marye, Cristes bur,   *bower*
Maidenes clenhad, moderes flur,   *purity; flower*
Dilie mine sinne, rixe in min mod,   *blot out; reign; mind*
Bring me to winne wið þe self God.   *bliss; self-same*

Hymn to Saint Nicholas

Sainte Nicholas, Godes druð,   *darling*
Tymbre us faire scone hus,   *Build; beautiful*
At þi burth, at þi bare,   *funeral*
Sainte Nicholæs, bring us wel þare.   *there*

---

1   Psalm 98.5: 'Exalt ye the Lord our God; and adore his footstool; for it is holy.'

The *Orrmulum*

The *Orrmulum*, written in the last quarter of the twelfth century by an Augustinian canon called Orrm (a Scandinavian name that means 'serpent'), survives only in the autograph manuscript, Oxford, Bodleian Library, Junius 1. It is likely that Orrm lived in, or was closely associated with, the Arroaisian Abbey at Bourne, a twelfth-century foundation in Lincolnshire.[1] The *Orrmulum* was composed with pastoral care in mind, recognizing a need for teaching in the vernacular a generation before the Fourth Lateran Council in 1215, which stipulated that basic doctrine and catechesis were to be performed in the native language.

The work as a whole in its surviving form is some 20,000 lines long, and consists of a chronological sequence of homilies based on the gospel readings of the mass, and relating to the life of Christ and the acts of the Apostles. Orrm's exegesis is based on the *Glossa Ordinaria*, a twelfth-century Latin work that provided a commentary on the scriptures.[2] Orrm relates that he undertook the work as a result of the request of his brother Walter in order to benefit the English congregation, and there is little doubt that the clarity of his exposition would have aided the understanding of the laity. The modern-day critical response to the content of the *Orrmulum* is less than enthusiastic. It has been labelled 'soporific' and 'tedious',[3] for example, though it is unlikely that this would have been a contemporary response for those who only had to listen to a portion of it being read aloud on the appropriate occasion. The fact that it survives in only one, quite remarkable manuscript, despite the fact that Orrm gave instructions to subsequent copyists, may suggest that its popularity was limited.

Nevertheless, the Dedication and Preface, edited below, is an interesting illustration of the author's claim to humility, his aims and intentions, as well as his methodology in writing his text. Orrm is at pains repeatedly to inform us that he wrote his work to bring English people to salvation; and he urges them constantly to perform God's teaching in thought, word and deed. Adopting a cataloguing method, Orrm takes us through the seven benefits that Christ performed on earth: from his arrival in a human form, to his Passion, Harrowing of Hell, Resurrection, Ascension, and ultimately his return on doomsday. Thus Orrm, through lists and wholesale repetition, encapsulates essential Christian teaching in his text. This extract finishes with a typical motif, asking the audience of the text to pray for him in his endeavours.

Whether or not the *Orrmulum* is satisfying aesthetically, the work itself is of significant value to linguists and dialectologists working in the early Middle English field. Orrm attempts to represent the way the words were meant to be pronounced through his system of orthography. The doubling of consonants is part of this phonetic system: they indicate that the vowel preceding them is a short vowel sound. There are numerous Scandinavian words in the text (such as *þeȝȝ*, 'they', *skill*, and *till*, 'until, towards') that probably reflect his own dialect usage. As well as the appropriateness of his language for his chosen didactic intent, his versification has fifteen syllables to every pair of lines (as edited here), a rhythm that would allow for a rapid, and almost incantatory, delivery to the audience.

Dedication and Preface

Nu broþerr Wallterr, broþerr min	
affterr þe flæshess kinde,	
annd broþerr min i Crisstenndom	
þurrh fulluhht, annd þurrh trowwþe,	*baptism; belief*
5 annd broþerr min i Godess hus	
ȝet o þe þridde wise,	*third*
þurrh þatt witt hafenn takenn ba	*both*
an reȝhellboc to follȝhenn –	*rule-book*
unnderr kanunnkess had annd lif,	*canons' order*
10 swa summ Sannt Awwstin sette –	*just as Saint Augustine established*
Icc hafe don swasumm þu badd,	*asked*

1 For this information, and for an excellent analysis of the script and date of the *Orrmulum* manuscript, see M. B. Parkes, 'On the Presumed Date and Possible Origin of the Manuscript of the *Orrmulum*: Oxford, Bodleian Library, MS Junius 1', in M. B. Parkes, *Scribes, Scripts and Readers: Studies in the Communication, Presentation and Dissemination of Medieval Texts* (London, 1991), pp. 187–200.

2 See J. A. W. Bennett, *Middle English Literature*, ed. and comp. D. Gray (Oxford, 1986; repr. 1990), pp. 30–1.

3 Bennett, *Middle English Literature*, pp. 31, 32, 33.

annd forþedd te þin wille.   *furthered*
Icc hafe wennd inntill Ennglissh   *translated into*
goddspelless hallȝhe lare,   *the gospels' holy teaching*
15   affterr þatt little witt þatt me   *intelligence; that*
min Drihhtin hafeþþ lenedd.[4]   *Lord; granted*
Þu þohhtesst tatt itt mihhte wel
till mikell frame turrnenn,   *to great benefit*
ȝiff Ennglissh folk, forr lufe off Crist,
20   itt wollde ȝerne lernenn;   *eagerly*
annd folȝhenn itt, annd fillenn itt   *follow*
wiþþ þohht, wiþþ word, wiþþ dede,
annd forrþi ȝerrndesst tu þatt Icc   *therefore desired*
þiss werrc þe shollde wirrkenn.   *compose*
25   Annd Icc itt hafe forþedd te,
acc all þurrh Cristess hellpe;
annd unnc birrþ baþe þannkenn Crist   *it obliges both of us*
þatt itt iss brohht till ende.
Icc hafe sammnedd o þiss boc   *gathered*
30   þa Goddspelless neh alle,   *almost*
þatt sinndenn o þe messeboc   *are in the mass-book*
inn all þe ȝer att messe;   *year*
annd aȝȝ affterr þe Goddspell stannt   *always; occurs*
þatt tatt te Goddspell meneþþ,   *means*
35   þatt mann birrþ spellenn to þe follc   *preach*
off þeȝȝre sawle nede;   *their*
annd ȝet tær tekenn mare inoh   *enough*
þu shallt tæronne findenn,   *therein*
off þatt tatt Cristess hallȝhe þed   *people*
40   birrþ trowwenn wel annd follȝhenn.   *believe*
Icc hafe sett her o þiss boc
amang Goddspelless wordess,
all þurrh me sellfenn, maniȝ word   *self; many*
þe rime swa to fillenn;   *fill out*
45   acc þu shallt findenn þatt min word,
eȝȝwhær þær itt iss ekedd,   *everywhere; added*
maȝȝ hellpenn þa þatt redenn itt
to sen annd t'unnderrstanndenn
all þess te bettre hu þeȝȝm birrþ   *it obliges them*
50   þe Goddspell unnderrstanndenn;
annd forrþi trowwe Icc þat te birrþ
wel þolenn mine wordess,   *endure*
eȝȝwhær þær þu shallt findenn hemm
amang Goddspelless wordess.
55   Forr whase mot to læwedd follc   *For whoever must to unlearned*
larspell off Goddspell tellenn,   *doctrine*
he mot wel ekenn maniȝ word   *add*
amang Goddspelless wordess.
Annd Icc ne mihhte nohht min ferrs   *verse*
60   aȝȝ wiþþ Goddspelless wordess
wel fillenn all, annd all forrþi

---

4   Orrm here uses a very common modesty topos employed by many
authors in the Middle Ages.

shollde Icc well offte nede
amang Goddspelless wordess don
min word, min ferrs to fillenn.

65   Annd te bitæche Icc off þiss boc,   *I entrust to you*
heh wikenn alls itt semeþþ,   *important duties*
all to þurrhsekenn illc an ferrs,   *search*
annd to þurrhlokenn offte,   *look through*
þatt upponn all þiss boc ne be
70 nan word ȝæn Cristess lare,   *against*
nan word tatt swiþe wel ne be
to trowwenn annd to follghenn.
Witt shulenn tredenn unnderr fot
annd all þwerrtut forrwerrpenn: *completely rejected*
75 þe dom off all þatt laþe flocc   *judgement; hateful crowd*
þatt iss þurrh niþ forrblendedd,   *malice; blinded*
þatt tæleþþ þatt to lofenn iss   *blame; which should be praised*
þurrh niþfull modiȝnesse.   *pride*
Þeȝȝ shulenn lætenn hæþeliȝ   *prevent; contemptuously*
80 off unnkerr swinnc, lef broþerr.   *work; dear*
Annd all þeȝȝ shulenn takenn itt
onn unnitt annd onn idell;   *unprofitable things*
acc nohht þurrh skill, acc all þurrh niþ,
annd all þurrh þeȝȝre sinne.   *their*
85 Annd unnc birrþ biddenn Godd tatt he   *we are obliged to pray*
forrȝife hemm here sinne;
annd unnc birrþ baþe lofenn Godd
off þatt itt wass bigunnenn.
Annd þannkenn Godd tatt itt iss brohht
90 till ende þurrh hiss hellpe:
forr itt maȝȝ hellpenn alle þa
þatt bliþelike itt herenn,   *happily*
annd lufenn itt, annd follȝhenn itt
wiþþ þohht, wiþþ word, wiþþ dede.
95   Annd whase wilenn shall þiss boc
efft oþerr siþe writenn,   *again; afterwards*
himm bidde Icc þatt he't write rihht,   *he*
swasumm þiss boc himm tæcheþþ: *just as; instructs*
all þwerrtut affterr þatt itt iss
100 uppo þiss firrste bisne,   *example*
wiþþ all swillc rime alls her iss sett,   *such*
wiþþ all se fele wordess;   *many*
annd tatt he loke wel þatt he
an bocstaff write twiȝȝess,   *letters; twice*
105 eȝȝwhær þær itt uppo þiss boc   *everywhere*
iss writenn o þatt wise.   *manner*
Loke he wel þatt het write swa,   *so*
forr he ne maȝȝ nohht elless
onn Ennglissh writenn rihht te word,
110 þatt wite he wel to soþe.   *knows; in truth*
Annd ȝiff mann wile witenn whi   *inquire*
Icc hafe don þiss dede,
whi Icc till Ennglissh hafe wennd   *translated*
Goddspelless hallȝhe lare:

115	Icc hafe itt don forrþiþatt all	*because*
	Crisstene follkess berrhless	*salvation*
	iss lang uppo þatt an, þatt teȝȝ	*dependent; one thing; they*
	Goddspelless hallȝhe lare	
	wiþþ fulle mahhte follȝhe rihht	*strength*
120	þurrh þohht, þurrh word, þurrh dede.	
	Forr all þatt æfre onn erþe iss ned	
	Crisstene follc to follȝhenn	
	i trowwþe, i dede, all tæcheþþ hemm	*in*
	Goddspelless hallȝhe lore.	
125	Annd forrþi whase lerneþþ itt	
	annd follȝheþþ itt wiþþ dede,	
	he shall onn ende wurrþi ben	*worthy*
	þurrh Godd to wurrþenn borrȝhenn.	*glory; saved*
	Annd tærfore hafe Icc turrnedd itt	
130	inntill Ennglisshe spæche,	
	forrþatt I wollde bliþeliȝ	
	þatt all Ennglisshe lede	*people*
	wiþþ ære shollde lisstenn itt,	*ears*
	wiþþ herrte shollde itt trowwenn,	
135	wiþþ tunge shollde spellenn itt,	
	wiþþ dede shollde itt follȝhenn,	
	to winnenn unnderr Crisstenndom	
	att Godd soþ sawle berrhless.	
	Annd ȝiff þeȝȝ wilenn herenn itt,	
140	annd follȝhenn itt wiþþ dede,	
	Icc hafe hemm hollpenn unnderr Crist	
	to winnenn þeȝȝre berrhless.	
	Annd I shall hafenn for min swinnc	*work*
	god læn att Godd onn ende,	*reward*
145	ȝiff þatt I, forr þe lufe off Godd	
	annd forr þe mede off heffne,	*bliss; heaven*
	hemm hafe itt inntill Ennglissh wennd	
	forr þeȝȝre sawle nede.	
	Annd ȝiff þegg all forrwerrpenn itt,	*reject*
150	itt turrneþþ hemm till sinne,	
	annd I shall hafenn addledd me	*deserved*
	þe Laferrd Cristess are,	*mercy*
	þurrh þatt Icc hafe hemm wrohht tiss boc	
	to þeȝȝre sawle nede;	
155	þohh þatt teȝȝ all forrwerrpenn itt	*even if*
	þurrh þeȝȝre modiȝnesse.	
	Goddspell onn Ennglissh nemmnedd iss	*called*
	'god word', annd 'god tiþennde',	*tidings*
	'god errnde', forrþi þatt itt wass	*message*
160	þurrh hallȝhe Goddspell wrihhtess	*writers*
	all wrohht annd writenn uppo boc	
	off Cristess firrste come:	
	off hu soþ Godd wass wurrþenn mann[5]	*became*

---

5 What follows in the text is a summary of the Nicene Creed,
outlining the central doctrine about Christ's Passion and Resurrection and the inevitability of doomsday.

	forr all mannkinne nede;	
165	annd off þatt mannkinn þurrh hiss dæþe	*from that; death*
	wass lesedd ut off helle;	*released*
	annd off þatt he wisslike ras	*wisely; arose*
	þe þridde daʒʒ off dæþe;	
	annd off þatt he wisslike stah	*ascended*
170	þa siþþenn upp till heffne;	*afterwards*
	annd off þatt he shall cumenn efft	*again*
	to demenn alle þede,	*judge; people*
	annd forr to ʒeldenn iwhillc mann	*repay; each*
	affterr hiss aʒhenn dede.	*own*
175	Off all þiss God uss brinngeþþ word	
	annd errnde annd god tiþennde	
	Goddspell, annd forrþi maʒʒ itt wel	
	god errnde ben ʒehatenn.	*called*
	Forr mann maʒʒ uppo Goddspellboc	
180	godnessess findenn seffne,	*seven*
	þatt ure Laferrd Jesu Crist	
	uss hafeþþ don onn erþe,	
	þurrh þatt he comm to manne, annd þurrh	
	þatt he warrþ mann onn erþe.	
185	Forr an goodnesse uss hafeþþ don	
	þe Laferrd Crist onn erþe,	
	þurrh þatt he comm to wurrþenn mann	
	forr all mannkinne nede.	
	Oþerr godnesse uss hafeþþ don	*The second*
190	þe Laferrd Crist onn erþe,	
	þurrh þatt he was i flumm Jorrdan	*River*
	fullhtnedd forr ure nede;	*baptised*
	forr þatt he wollde uss waterrkinn	*by the nature of water*
	till ure fulluhht hallʒhenn,	*sanctify*
195	þurrh þatt he wollde ben himmsellf	
	onn erþe i waterr fullhtnedd.	
	Þe þridde god uss hafeþþ don	
	þe Laferrd Crist onn erþe,	
	þurrh þatt he ʒaff hiss aʒhenn lif	
200	wiþþ all hiss fulle wille,	
	to þolenn dæþe o rodetre	*suffer; rood-tree (Cross)*
	sacclæs wiþþutenn wrihhte,	*guiltless; stain*
	to lesenn mannkinn þurrh hiss dæþ	*release*
	ut off þe defless walde.	*devil's power*
205	Þe ferþe god uss hafeþþ don	
	þe Laferrd Crist onn erþe,	
	þurrh þatt hiss hallʒhe sawle stah	*descended*
	fra rode dun till helle,	
	to takenn ut off helle wa	*misery*
210	þa gode sawless alle,	
	þatt haffdenn cwemmd himm i þiss lif	*pleased*
	þurrh soþ unnshaþiʒnesse.	*righteousness*
	Þe fifte god uss hafeþþ don	
	þe Laferrd Crist onn erþe,	
215	þurrh þatt he ras forr ure god	*rose*
	þe þridde daʒʒ off dæþe,	

	annd let te posstless sen himm wel	*Apostles*
	inn hiss mennisske kinde;	*human incarnation*
	forr þatt he wollde fesstnenn swa	*establish*
220	soþ trowwþe i þeȝȝre brestess;	*faith*
	off þatt he, wiss to fulle soþ,	
	wass risenn upp off dæþe,	
	annd i þatt illke flæsh þatt wass	
	forr uss o rode naȝȝledd.	*nailed*
225	Forr þatt he wollde fesstnenn wel	
	þiss trowwþe i þeȝȝre brestess,	
	he let te posstless sen himm wel	
	well offtesiþe onn erþe,	*frequently*
	wiþþinnenn daȝȝess fowwerrtig[6]	*days; forty*
230	fra þatt he ras off dæþe.	
	Þe sexte god uss hafeþþ don	
	þe Laferrd Crist onn erþe,	
	þurrh þatt he stah forr ure god	*ascended*
	upp inntill heffness blisse,	
235	annd sennde siþþenn Haliȝ Gast	
	till hise Lerninngcnihhtess,[7]	*disciples*
	to frofrenn annd to beldenn hemm	*comfort; encourage*
	to stanndenn ȝæn þe defell;	*against*
	to gifenn hemm god witt inoh	*knowledge*
240	off all hiss hallȝhe lare,	
	to gifenn hemm god lusst, god mahht,	*desire; strength*
	to þolenn alle wawenn,	*suffer; miseries*
	all forr þe lufe off Godd, annd nohht	
	forr erþliȝ loff to winnenn.	*praise*
245	Þe seffnde god uss shall ȝet don	*seventh; yet*
	þe Laferrd Crist onn ende,	
	þurrh þatt he shall o Domessdaȝȝ	*Judgement Day*
	uss gifenn heffness blisse,	
	ȝiff þatt we shulenn wurrþi ben	
250	to findenn Godess are.	*mercy*
	Þuss hafeþþ ure Laferrd Crist	
	uss don godnessess seffne,	
	þurrhþatttatt he ta manne comm	
	to wurrþenn mann onn erþe.	
255	Annd o þatt hallȝhe boc þatt iss	
	Apokalypsis nemmnedd,	*Book of Revelations*
	uss wrat te posstell Sannt Johan,	
	þurrh Haliȝ Gastess lare,	
	þatt hee sahh upp inn heffne an boc	
260	bisett wiþþ seffne innseȝȝless,	*seals*
	annd sperrd swa swiþe wel þatt itt	*closed so firmly*
	ne mihhte nan wihht oppnenn,	*creature; open*
	wiþþutenn Godess hallȝhe Lamb	*except*
	þatt he sahh ec inn heffne.	*saw; also*
265	Annd þurrh þa seffne innseȝȝless wass	
	rihht swiþe wel bitacnedd	*signified*

6   The period between the Resurrection and the Ascension.
7   At Pentecost.

þatt sefennfald godleggc þatt Crist   *benefit*
uss dide þurrh hiss come;
annd tatt nan wihht ne mihhte nohht   *creature*
270   oppnenn þa seffne innseȝȝless,
wiþþutenn Godess Lamb, þatt comm,
forr þatt itt shollde tacnenn   *betoken*
þatt nan wihht, nan enngell, nan mann,
ne naness kinness schaffte,   *creature known*
275   ne mihhte þurrh himmsellfenn þa
seffne goodnessess shæwenn   *show*
o mannkinn, swa þatt itt mannkinn   *on*
off helle mihhte lesenn,
ne gifenn mannkinn lusst, ne mahht,
280   to winnenn heffness blisse.
    Annd all allswase Godess Lamb,   *just as*
all þurrh hiss aȝhenn mahhte,
lihhtlike mihhte annd wed inoh   *little; easily*
þa seffne innseȝȝless oppnenn,
285   all swa þe Laferrd Jesu Crist,
all þurrh hiss aȝhenn mahhte,
wiþþ Faderr annd wiþþ Haliȝ Gast
an Godd annd all an kinde,
allswa rihht he lihhtlike inoh
290   annd wel wiþþ alle mihhte
o mannkinn þurrh himm sellfenn
seffne godnessess shæwenn,
swa þatt he mannkinn wel inoh
off helle mihhte lesenn,
295   annd gifenn mannkinn lufe annd lusst,
annd mahht annd witt annd wille,
to stanndenn inn to cwemenn Godd,   *please*
to winnenn heffness blisse.
    Annd forr þatt haliȝ Goddspellboc
300   all þiss godnesse uss shæweþþ,
þiss sefennfald godleȝȝc þatt Crist
uss dide þurrh hiss are;
forrþi birrþ all Crisstene follc   *therefore it obliges*
Goddspelless lare follȝhenn.
305   Annd tærfore hafe Icc turrnedd itt
inntill Ennglisshe spæche,
forr þat i wollde bliþeliȝ
þatt all Ennglisshe lede
wiþþ ære shollde lisstenn itt,
310   wiþþ herrte shollde itt trowwenn,
wiþþ tunge shollde spellenn itt,
wiþþ dede shollde itt follȝhenn,
to winnenn unnderr Crisstenndom
att Crist soþ sawle berrhless.
315   Annd Godd allmahhtiȝ ȝife uss mahht
annd lusst annd witt annd wille
to follȝhenn þiss Ennglisshe boc
þatt all iss haliȝ lare,
swa þatt we motenn wurrþi ben

320   to brukenn heffness blisse.   *enjoy*
               Amæn. Amæn. Amæn.

           Icc þatt tiss Ennglissh hafe sett
           Ennglisshe menn to lare,
           Icc was þær þær I crisstnedd wass,   *christened*
325   Orrmin bi name nemnmedd.
           Annd Icc Orrmin full inwarrdliȝ   *earnestly*
           wiþþ muþ annd ec wiþþ herrte
           her bidde þa Crisstene menn,   *beseech*
           þatt herenn oþerr redenn
330   þiss boc, hemm bidde Icc her þatt teȝȝ
           forr me þiss bede biddenn,   *prayer pray*
           'Þatt broþerr þatt tiss Ennglissh writt
           allr æresst wrat annd wrohhte,   *first wrote and created*
           þatt broþerr forr hiss swinnc to læn   *as a reward*
335   soþ blisse mote findenn.'   *might*
              Amæn.

Cambridge, Trinity College B. 14. 52

Cambridge, Trinity College B. 14. 52, is a composite manuscript containing thirty-four sermons datable to the end of the twelfth century, and the *Poema Morale*, datable to the second half of the twelfth century. The manuscript has a south-eastern origin, perhaps in Suffolk or Essex.[1] Two scribes write the majority of the manuscript: the first scribe writes the *Poema Morale* and some of the homilies; the second writes the remaining homilies. A third scribe writes pp. 156–7. The *Poema Morale* is found in seven medieval manuscripts, ranging from this early version to a late thirteenth-century text in Cambridge, Fitzwilliam Museum, McClean 123. A few small snippets of the text also exist in other manuscripts. Its popularity seems to have been confined to the earlier Middle English period, up to *c.*1300.

The *Poema Morale* and five of the homiletic texts in Trinity College B. 14. 52 are also included, in somewhat variant versions, in another important manuscript: London, Lambeth Palace 487, dated to *c.*1200. Unlike the latter collection, though, the Trinity Homilies themselves do not seem to draw on Old English sources for some of the included material. Instead, Wells suggests,[2] it might be that a twelfth-century collection of Latin homilies may have proved the inspiration for these early Middle English pieces. The Trinity Homilies are arranged very loosely according to the sequence of the church year, but it is difficult to ascertain any central theme other than a general admonitory tone and an emphasis on repentance of sins. Most of these sermons are not specifically designed as expositions on particular gospel pericopes, nor do they always follow the usual homiletic form of providing clear exempla to illustrate a theme. Instead, sin and virtue form the main focus of many of the texts, together with an intention to teach simply the principal doctrinal points of the Catholic church. In the fourth text on the Creed, for example, the preacher directly addresses his audience, stating: 'You all know your Creed, as I suppose, though you do not all know what it signifies. But listen now, and attend to it, and I will teach you.'[3]

The sermons are not particularly well structured at times, but even so, the techniques used by the author are those seen in many other medieval didactic texts. There are, for example, frequent Latin quotations to provide authority in the text; enumeration or cataloguing of major points to aid the retention of details; rhetorical question and direct address that seek to engage the audience. It may be that the author of these homilies created his collection partially from memory, or was not as well trained in the composition of homilies as some of his contemporaries. It may also be that these tracts represent the more 'average' sermon delivered by a parish priest than those that usually survive from the period. It is certainly the case that these texts in Trinity B. 14. 52 are not as highly regarded by modern-day scholars as the English homilies in other contemporary manuscripts (such as Lambeth 487, or London, British Library, Cotton Vespasian A. xxii).

In the texts edited below, the first scribe writes the *Poema Morale*; the second writes most of Homily 33, with the exception of the portion that runs from line 58 *and seið* to line 74 *forleten*.

---

1   See M. Laing's important article, 'Anchor Texts and Literary Manuscripts in Early Middle English', in *Regionalism in Late Medieval Manuscripts and Texts: Essays Celebrating the Publication of 'A Linguistic Atlas of Late Mediaeval English'*, ed. F. Riddy (Cambridge, 1991), pp. 27–52.

2   J. E. Wells, *A Manual of the Writings in Middle English, 1050–1400, with First, Second and Third Supplements* (New Haven, CT, 1926), pp. 280–1.

3   R. Morris, ed., *Old English Homilies of the Twelfth Century*, EETS o.s. 53 (Oxford, 1873), p.16. Morris edits the whole manuscript.

POEMA MORALE

The *Poema Morale*, or a *Moral Ode*, occurs in Trinity College, B. 14. 52, at folios 2 recto to 9 verso, and without a title. The title was assigned to the poem by eighteenth-century scholars, but recently, the more appropriate title of 'Conduct of Life' has been proposed.[4]

In this manuscript version, the poem is 400 lines long, of which 156 lines are edited below. The *Poema Morale* is an homiletic explication of the awareness of sin by someone who is advanced in years, and very aware of the imminence of death. Didactic in aim, and admonitory in tone, it incorporates many themes seen in homilies and later penitential lyrics, including the *contemptus mundi* motif ('contempt of the world'), and eschatalogical concerns of death, Judgement Day and the afterlife. Line 156 precedes a detailed description of doomsday, and a list of those who sin on earth (liars, corrupt officials, adulterers), followed by a description of hell which is full of 'adders and snakes, newts and ferrets' (line 277). The poem concludes with a lengthy exposition of good Christian behaviour, and how one must act to gain salvation. The 'broad street and open way' must be avoided, and the 'narrow and green way' followed to attain heavenly bliss.

In the extract below, the poet opens with a statement indicating an awareness of personal sinfulness, thus providing the impetus for what follows. The personal statement is opened up to apply to all humanity who tend not to think about the afterlife, but rather to focus on the joys of the world, and on the accretion of worldly wealth, thinking little of the horrors that ultimately befall the sinful. The poet's timely reminder about repenting of sins and keeping one's thoughts fixed on heaven seeks to create a sense of responsibility in the audience for their actions. And the series of rhetorical questions and quotidian details at lines 93–106 and 144–8 respectively attempt to draw the audience into the text and make the didacticism of the text individually applicable.

The syntax of the text, with many end-stopped lines forming complete grammatical units, lends an air of gnomic wisdom to the work, but also makes for a somewhat stilted rhythm at times. The versification is septenary rhyming couplets with fifteen syllables to the line (though the last syllable is usually the unstressed <e>). The regular beat, like that of the *Orrmulum*, makes this an ideal rhythm for oral delivery, and it may be that this text is a verse homily, much more than it is 'poetry' as we tend to think of it. The manuscript context of the *Poema Morale* in Trinity College, B. 14. 52, would certainly suggest that the work is intended to form part of a selection of vernacular pastoral materials for a preacher, perhaps, to use in tending to the spiritual needs of his congregation.

Poema Morale

	Ich am nu elder þan Ich was a wintre and a lore.	*older; in years and learning*
	Ich wealde more þan I dude, mi wit oh to be more	*have in my power; ought*
	To longe Ich habbe child iben a worde and a dade.	*deeds*
	Þeih I bie a winter eald, to jung Ich am on rade.	*wisdom*
5	Unnet lif Ich habbe ilad, and ʒiet me þincheð ilade	*idle; still seem to lead*
	Þan I biðenche me þaron, wel sore I me adrade.	*When; dread*
	Mast al Ich habbe idon is idelnesse and chilce.	*Most; childish*
	Wel late Ich habbe me biþoht, bute me God do milce.	*repented; mercy*
	Fele idel word Ich habbe ispeken seðen Ich speken cuðe,	*since*
10	And fele ʒeunge dade I don, þe me ofðinkeð nuðe.	*childish deeds; repent*
	Al to lome Ich habbe igult a werke and a worde.	*often; sinned; in*
	Al to muhel Ic habbe ispend, to litel ileid on horde.[5]	*laid; treasury*
	Mast al þat me likede ar nu, hit me mislicað:	*before; now it displeases me*
	Þe muchel folʒeð his iwil, himselfen he biswicað.	*He who; deceives*
15	Ich mihte habben bet idon, hadde Ich þo iselðe;	*better; good sense*
	Nu Ich wolde, ac I ne mai, for elde and for unhalðe.	*want to; poor health*
	Elde me is bistolen on ar Ich hit iwiste,	*stolen up; knew*
	Ne mai Ich isien bifore me for smeche ne for miste.	*see; because of smoke*
	Arʒe we beð to don god, to uvel al to þriste;	*slow; evil all too ready*
20	More eie stondeð man of man þan him do of Criste.	*awe has man for man*

---

4 See B. Hill, 'The Twelfth-Century *Conduct of Life*, formerly the *Poema Morale* or *A Moral Ode*', *Leeds Studies in English* 9 (1977), 97–144.

5 cf. Matthew 6.19–20: 'Lay not up to yourselves treasure on earth . . . But lay up to yourselves treasure in heaven.'

Þe wel ne deð þe hwile he mai, wel ofte hit sal him rewen *Those; shall; regret*
Þan alle men sulle ripen þat hie ar sewen: *When; reap; sowed*
Do al to Gode þat he muʒe ech, þe hwile he beð alive. *for; may; as long as*
Ne liþne no man to muchel to childe ne to wive; *trust; woman*

25   Þe þe himselfe forʒiet for wive oðer for childe, *For; he; forgets*
He sal cumen on evel stede, bute him God be milde. *place; unless*
Sende god biforen him man þe hwile he mai to hevene, *send some good*
For betre is on almesse biforen þan ben after sevene. *one alms; afterwards*
Ne bie þe levere þan þe self ne þi mæi ne þi mowe,[6]

30   Sot is þe is oðer mannes frend betere þan his owen. *Fool*
Ne hopie wif to hire were ne were to his wive, *hope in; husband*
Be for himself afric man þe hwile he beð alive. *every*
Wis þe himselve biðencheð þe hwile he mot libben, *Wise; thinks of; live*
For sone willeð him forʒiete þe fremde and þe sibbe. *forget; stranger; family*

35   Þe wel ne doð þe hwile he mai ne sal he þan he wolde. *He who; when; wants to*
For manimannes sore iswinc habbeð ofte unholde.[7]
Ne solde no man don a furst ne laten wel to done, *put off or delay good work*
For maniman bihoteð wel þat hi forʒieteð sone. *promises well that which*
Þe man þe wile siker ben to habben Godes blisse, *wishes to be sure*

40   Do wel himself þe hwile he mai, þanne haveð hes mid iwisse. *it for certain*
  Þe riche men weneð siker ben þurch wallen and thurh dichen; *thinks to be safe; by*
He deð his aihte an siker stede þe hit sent to heveriche.[8]
For þer ne þarf he ben ofdrad of fure ne of þieve, *need; fearful; fire*
Þar ne mai hit him binime þe loðe ne þe lieve, *taken; by enemy; friend*

45   Þar ne þarf he habben care of here ne of ʒielde: *worry; gifts; rewards*
Þider we sendeð and ec bereð to litel and to selde. *There; also; seldom*
Þider we solden drawen, and don wel ofte and ilome; *make our way*
For þar ne sal me us naht binime mid wrongwise dome.[9]
Þider we solde ʒierne drawen, wolde ʒie me ileven, *eagerly; believe*

50   For ne mai hit us binime, no king ne no syrreve. *rob us of it; sheriff*
Al þat beste þat we habbeð her, þider we solde sende,
For þar we mihte finden eft, and habben abuten ende. *again; without*
Se þe her doð ani god for to haben Godes ore *mercy*
Al he hit sal eft finde þar, and hundredfealde more. *shall; hundredfold*

55   Se þe aihte wile holde wel þe hwile hes muʒe wealden, *wealth; can enjoy it*
Ʒieve hes for Godes luve, þanne doð hes wel ihealden.[10]
For ure swinch and ure tilðe is ofte wuned to swinde, *labour; inclined to lessen*
Ac al þat we ʒieveð for Godes luve, al we hit sulen eft finden. *give; shall*
Ne sal þar non evel ben unboht, ne god unforʒolden: *unpunished; not repaid*

60   Evel we doð al to muchel, and god lasse þan we solden. *less*
Se þe mast doð nu to gode, and se last to lothe, *most; least; evil*
Eiðer to litel and to muchel hem sal þunche boðe. *seem to him*
Þar me sal ure werkes weiʒen bifore þan heven Kinge *our works will be weighed*
And ʒieven us ure werkes lean after ure erninge. *reward; merits*

65   Africh man mid þat he haveð mai bugge heveriche: *buy; the heavenly kingdom*
Þe þe more haveð and þe þe lasse, boðe iliche; *he who; both alike*
Alse on mid his peni se oðer mid his punde – *Even; one; or another*
Þis is þet wunderlukeste ware þat animan funde. *most wonderful; bargain*
And se þe more ne mai don mid his gode iþanke, *can give of good will*

---

6   Do not prefer yourself to your own kinsman or kinswoman.   9   For there no one can steal from us with iniquitous judgements.

7   Many a man's work often profits his enemies.   10   Give it away for the love of God, and then he possesses it well.

8   He who puts his treasure in heaven puts it in a more secure place.

70   Alse wel se þe þe haved goldes fele manke.
                                                                    Just as well; piles
     And ofte God can more þanc þan þe him ȝieveð lasse;
                                                                    will thank more; give
     Al his werkes and his weies is milce and rihtwisnesse.
                                                                    ways; mercy; righteousness
     Litel loc is Gode lef þe cumeð of gode wille,
                                                                    gift; dear to
     And eðlate muchel ȝieve þan his herte is ille.[11]

75   Hevene and erðe he oversihð, his eien beð ful brihte,
                                                                    oversees; eyes
     Nis him no þing forholen, swo muchel is his mihte:
                                                                    hidden from; power
     Ne bie hit no swo derne idon ne on swo þuster nihte,
                                                                    whether it is secret; dark
     He wot hwat þencheð and hwat doð alle quike wihte.
                                                                    each thinks; living creatures
     Nis loverd swilch is Crist, ne king swilch ure Drihte,
                                                                    like
80   Boðe giemeð þe his bien bi daie and bi nihte.
                                                                    pay heed
     Hevene and erðe, and al þat is, biloken is in his honden,
                                                                    are enclosed
     He doð al þat his wille is a watere and a londe:
                                                                    on
     He makeð þe fisses in þe sa, þe fueles on þe lofte;
                                                                    sea; birds; air
     He wit and wealdeð alle þing and he sop alle safte.[12]

85   He is ord abuten ord, and ende abuten ende,
                                                                    beginning
     He is one afre on eche stede, wende þar þu wende;
                                                                    go wherever you will
     He is buven us and bineðen, biforen and bihinde,
                                                                    above; beneath
     Þe Godes wille doð aihware he maiȝ him finde.
                                                                    He who; everywhere
     Elche rune he hereð, and he wot alle dade,
                                                                    secret; knows; deeds
90   He þurhsihð elches mannes þanc. Wi hwat sal us to rade
     We þe brekeð Godes has and gulteð swo ilome?[13]
     Hwat sulle we seggen oðer don ate muchele dome,
                                                                    great judgement
     We þe luveden unriht and evel lif ladden?
                                                                    wrong; led
     Hwat sulle we seggen oðer don þar ængles beð ofdradde?
                                                                    when; afraid
95   Hwat sulle we beren us biforen, mid hwan sulle we iqueme,
                                                                    carry; what; please
     We þe nafre god ne duden, þan hevenliche Deme?
                                                                    did; to the; Judge
     Þar sulle ben deflen swo fele þat willeð us forwreien,
                                                                    devils so many; accuse
     Nabbeð hie no þing forȝieten of þat hie her iseien:
                                                                    forgotten; here saw
     Al þat hie iseien her hie willeð cuðen þare,
                                                                    make known there
100 Bute we haben hit ibet þe hwile we here waren;
                                                                    Unless; remedied; were
     Al hie habbeð on here write þat we misduden here,
                                                                    documents; did wrong
     Þeih we hes ne niseien hie waren ure iferen.
                                                                    did not see; our companions
     Hwat sullen horlinges don, þes wichen and þe forsworene?
                                                                    pimps, traitors, perjurers
     Wi swo fele beð icleped swo fewe beð icorene?
                                                                    called; chosen
105 Wi hwi waren hie biȝiete, to hwan waren hie iborene,
                                                                    conceived; why; born
     Þe sulle ben to deaðe idemd and afremo ferlorene?
                                                                    damned; abandoned
     Elch man sal þar biclepien himselfen and ec demen,
                                                                    accuse; also condemn
     His oȝen werc and his þanc to witnesse he sal temen;
                                                                    thoughts; summon
     Ne mai him no man alse wel demen ne alse rihte
                                                                    as; judge; or as properly
110 For non ne cnoweð hine alse wel buten one Drihte.
                                                                    knows; alone
     Man wot himself best, his werkes and his wille:
                                                                    knows; intent
     Se þe last wot he seið ofte mast, se þit al wot is stille.[14]
     Nis no witnesse alse muchel se mannes oȝen hierte:
                                                                    great; own heart
     Hwo se seiþ þat hie beð hol, himself wot his smierte;
                                                                    whole; pain
115 Elch man sal himselfen demen to deaðe oðer to live –
     Þe witnesse of his oȝen werc to oðer þan hine sal drive.
                                                                    to that shall force him
     Al þat afri man haveð idon seðen he cam to manne
                                                                    since he became an adult
     Swo he hit iseie a boc iwrite, he sal hit þenche þanne;
                                                                    saw it; written; seem

---

11   And worthless are those substantial gifts when the heart is evil.
12   He protects and controls all things, and he created all creation.
13   He sees through each man's mind. What shall be the advice for us / We who break God's commands and sin so frequently?
14   He who knows least often says most, he who knows everything is silent.

Ac Drihte ne demeð no man after his biginninge,   *by his beginning in life*
120 Ac al his lif sal ben teald after his endinge.   *accounted for; death*
Ʒief þe endinge is god al hit is god, and evel ʒief evel is þe ende.
God ʒieve þat ure ende be god, and ʒieve þat he us lende.   *grant; lent us*
Se man þe nafre nele don god, ne nafre god lif lade,   *led*
Are deað and dom cumeð to his dure, he maiʒ him sore adrade   *Before; door; fear*
125 Þat he ne muʒe þanne bidden ore – for þat itit ilome;[15]
Forþi he is wis þe bit and biʒiet and bet bifore dome.   *watches; prays; repents*
Þanne þe deað is ate dure, wel late he biddeð ore;   *When; too late; mercy*
Wel late he lateþ evel werc þan he hit ne mai don no more.   *hates*
Senne lat þe and þu nah him, þan þu hit ne miht do no more;   *abandon sin;*
130 Forþi he is sot þe swo abit to habben Godes ore.   *foolish; waits*
Þeihhweðere we hit leveð wel, for Drihte self hit sade,   *Even so; believe; said*
Elche time sal þe man ofþunche his misdade,   *every; repents; wrongs*
Oðer raðer oðer later, milce he sal imete.[16]
Ac þe þe her naveð ibet, muchel he haved to bete.   *here has not repented*
135 Maniman seið hwo reche pine þe sal habben ende: *considers the torment*
'Ne bidde Ich no bet bie Ich alesed a domesdai of bende?'[17]
Litel wot he hwat is pine, and litel he cnoweð
Hwilch hit is þar sowle wunieð, hwu biter wind þar bloweð;   *soul will live*
Hadde he ben þar on oðer two bare tiden   *one or two mere hours*
140 Nolde he for al middeneard þe þridde þar abiden.   *world; third; stay*
Þat habbeð isaid þe come þanne þit wiste mid iwisse.   *from there; truly know*
'Wo wurðe soreʒe seve ʒier for seve nihte blisse;
And ure blisse þe ende haveþ for endeléase pine!'[18]
Betere is wori water þan atter imengd mid wine.   *muddy; poison mixed*
145 Swines brade is wel swete, swo is of wilde diere;   *pig's meat; wild deer*
Ac al to diere he hit abuið þe ʒiefð þarfore his swiere.   *dear; buys; gives; neck*
Ful wombe mai lihtliche speken of hunger and of fasten,   *stomach; fasting*
Swo mai of pine þe not hwat is pine þe sal ilasten.[19]
Hadde he fonded sume stunde he wolde seggen oðer: *experienced; time; say*
150 Eðlate him ware wif and child, suster and fader and broðer.   *Worthless then would be*
Al he wolde oðerluker don and oðerluker þenche,   *differently*
Þan he biðohte an helle fur þat nowiht ne mai quenche;   *If; fire; never; put out*
Afre he wolde her in wo and in wane wunien   *anxiety live*
Wið þan he mihte helle fur biflen and bisunien.   *So that; flee from; avoid*
155 Eðlate him ware al wele and erðeliche blisse   *joy and earthly*
For to þe muchele blisse cume, þis murie mid iwisse.   *great; joy with certainty*

---

15 He cannot then pray for mercy – as happens so often;

16 Rather sooner than later, mercy he shall find.

17 Can I not pray better to be released from the bonds at Judgement Day?

18 'It is misery to have seven years' sorrow for seven nights' bliss; / And our bliss which has an end-result of endless torment!'

19 So can one [speak lightly] of torment who does not know how long that torment will last.

Trinity Homily 33

The sermon edited here is the penultimate in Trinity College B. 14. 52; it occurs at pp. 148–53, and is incorporated into the sequence with no title. This exposition of Psalm 119, verse 10, has been labelled as 'exceedingly curious'.[20] The author's impetus for the sermon comes from the idea alluded to in Psalm 119 of the devil hunting mankind through a series of traps. In this sermon, then, the world is conceived of as a wilderness inhabited by potential sinners whose motives are more bestial than pious; and the preacher likens these desires of men to those of foxes, wolves, bears and lions, all predatory animals.

The author fixes upon four traps of the devil: idleness, drunkenness, commerce, and bad behaviour in church. Each of these is treated in turn with some interesting observations that may reflect contemporary practices witnessed by the author among his congregation; for example, the behaviour of some parish priests who do not hold services or speak out about wrongdoing when they should forms a subject for critical commentary at lines 68ff. The timely giving of tithes by the congregation, and the requirement that they assist in the purchasing of new materials for the church, reminds good Christians of their financial responsibilities towards the church, but also serves as a piece of self-advertising on the part of the preacher. Much about his sermon is commonplace in medieval didactic and admonitory texts, but seems here to have specific applicability. The drunkard who incites others to drink is reminiscent of the irresponsible actions of Holofernes in the Old English poem *Judith*; the vendor who attempts to cheat his customer looks forward to the miller in Chaucer's *Reeve's Tale*; and the priest who fails in his duties towards his flock, or who flirts with his female parishioners (like Absolon in *The Miller's Tale*), indicates this author's comments on some of his less committed colleagues. This text, with its lively and detailed accounts of sinful behaviour, is an effective admonitory work, and certainly deserves a more positive review than its simply being 'curious'. The language of the text is East Midland in character.[21]

Trinity Homily 33

Posuerunt peccatores laqueum michi et de mandatis tuis non erravi: 'Þe sinfulle haveð leid grune me to henten, and Ich ne forlet þine bode.' Ure fo fareð on hunteð and leið grune in a wilderne to henten þe deor þe wunieð þerinne. Ute we berȝen us and bidden God þat he us filste and shilde þerwið, þat he us ne shrenche; and seien mid þe prophete: *Custodi me a laqueo quem statuerunt michi*: 'Loverd

5   shild me wið þat grune þat hie leid haven me to henten.'

Listeð nu and Ich ȝiu wile seggen, and undernimeð hit on heorte, and habbeð hit on minde ȝiu is ned michel, wi þe devel is nemd 'sinful' and 'hunte', and þis woreld 'wilderne', and liðere lahtres 'grune', and þes men 'deor'. Þe devel is cleped 'sinful' for he þurh his oregel fulliche sineȝede þo þe he sundrede himselven fro Gode. He is cleped 'mannes fo' for he 'fode' þe forme

10   man wið God; þat was Adam and al his ofspring – þat is, al mankin. He is cleped 'hunte' forþanþe he waiteð ure ech and cunneð te bringen us on liðere lahtres þe beð his grunen; and þerone henteð us, alse hunte driveð deor to grune oðer to nette and swo hentcð. And of þis hunte specð þe prophete, and seið: *Anima nostra sicut passer erepta de laqueo venantium*: 'Ure soule is abroiden of þe hunte grune.'

15   Holi boc cleped þis woreld 'wildren' for þe fewe men þe wunieð þerone þe ben temed and wend to Godes hond his wille to don; ac alle mest hie beð iwileȝeð and habbeð geres after wilde deore. And for is ech man efned to þe deore þe he nimeð after geres: sum fox, sum wulf, sum bere, sum leun. And ech man me nemneð after þan þe his geres beoð; and alse þe michele deor heneð þe little and bi hem libbeð on þe wilderne, swo heneð and astruȝeð þe riche men þe wrecches, and

20   naðeles libbeð bi hem on þis worelde.

In hoc deserto sunt quattuor saltus quos bestie deserti frequentant scilicet corea cervisia forum monasterium: 'On þis wilderne ben fuȝer lages þat mest alle wilde deor to secheð: þat on is pleȝe, þat oder drinch, þe þridde chepinge, þe ferðe chirche.' *In primo saltu ponunt venantes laqueum vanitatis, in secundo impietatis*. On þis fuwer laȝes leið ure fo fuwer grunes us mide to henten. Crist us shilde

25   þerwið ȝif his wille beo. At pleȝe he teldeð þe grune of idelnesse, for al hit is idel þat me at pleȝe bihalt, and listeð, and doð and unqueme Gode and unbiheve þe soule; and swinch þe lichame, þih

20   By Morris, *Old English Homilies*, p. x, who edits this homily with a translation.

21   See M. Laing and A. McIntosh, 'Cambridge, Trinity College, MS 335: Its Texts and their Transmission', in *New Science out of Old Books: Studies in Manuscripts and Early Printed Books in Honour of A. I. Doyle*, eds R. Beadle and A. J. Piper (Aldershot, 1995), pp. 14–47.

Trinity Homily 33

Posuerunt peccatores laqueum mihi et de mandatis tuis non erravi: 'The sinful have laid a trap to catch me, and I have not erred from your commandments.' Our enemy goes hunting and lays a trap in the wilderness to catch the animals that live there. Let us protect ourselves and pray God that he will help us and shield us from that, so that we might not be deceived; and we should say with the prophet: *Custodi me a laqueo quem statuerunt mihi*: 'Lord, protect me from the traps that are laid to catch me.'

Listen now and I will tell you, take it into your heart, and keep it in mind as you have much need to, why the devil is called 'sinful' and 'hunter', and this world a 'wilderness', and hateful sins 'traps', and these men 'wild animals'. The devil is called sinful because through his pride he sinned wickedly when he separated himself from God. He is called man's foe, for he 'foe-ed'[22] the first man against God; that was Adam, and all his offspring – that is, all of mankind. He is called 'hunter' because he lies in wait for each of us and is able to persuade us into hateful sins which are his traps; and he catches us in these, just as the hunter drives wild animals into the trap or into the net and so catches them. And the prophet speaks about this hunter, and says, *Anima nostra sicut passer erepta est de laqueo venantium*: 'Our soul is snatched out of the snare of the hunter.'

The holy book calls this world 'wilderness' because few men who live in it are 'tamed' and turn to God's side to do his will; but most of all of them are wilful and have desires just like wild animals. And therefore each man is compared to the wild animal whose desires he takes after: some a fox, some a wolf, some a bear, some a lion. And each man is named after the one that his desires represent; and just as the strong animals catch the little ones and live off them in the wilderness, so rich men trap and destroy the poor, and furthermore, live off them in this world.

In hoc deserto sunt quattuor saltus quos bestie deserti frequentant; scilicet, corea, cervisia, forum, monasterium: 'In this wilderness are four dens which all wild animals seek most: the first is play, the second is drink, the third commerce, and the fourth church.' *In primo saltu ponunt venantes laqueum vanitatis, in secundo impietatis*. In these four lairs our enemy lays four traps with which to catch us. May Christ shield us from these, if it is his will. At play he sets the trap of idleness, for everything that is seen, heard, and done at play is idle, and it is displeasing to God and unprofitable for the soul; and the body labours, thighs and calves

---

22 'made an enemy of'. One of this author's techniques throughout his writings is to attempt (usually erroneous) etymological ex-
planations for particular words.

and shonkes and fet oppieð, wombe gosshieð, and shuldres wrenchieð, armes and honden frikieð; herte biðencheð þat hie seggen shal on songe; tunge and teð and lippe word shuppieð; muð sent ut þe stefne. And ech man þe þerto cumeþ pleie to toten, oðer to listen oðer to bihelden, ʒif he him wel likeð he beð biseid and hent on þe grune of idelnesse þe þe werse þere haveð itelded. Of þis grune specð þe prophete, and seið: *Non sedi cum concilio vanitatis et cum iniqua gerentibus non introibo*: 'ne held Ich nefre wel mid hem þe gon to idelnesse.'

    Secundus saltus huius deserti est compotatorium: 'Þat oðer laʒe on þis wilderne is drinch.' Þere teldeð þe werse þe grune of unrihte, for þere ne doð no man riht, ac ech man doð þere unriht toʒenes Gode and toʒenes his aʒene soule, and toʒenes his emcristene. Toʒenes Gode he doð unriht, þat is his Loverd, and halt his lif and his hele (þe wile he hit haveð) and doð him al þat he bi beð, and bid him þerof beten his nede and bereʒen him wið overdede; and naðeles ne wile don þat God him het, ac doð þat God forbed, and doð þat þe devel het. And swo unwurðeð God and wurðeð þene devel, and agilt wið Gode and quemeð þe devel, and forgilt hevene wele and haveð helle wowe. Unriht he doð ec toʒenes his soule unwille, and awlencð his lichame and walt his soule, and hefieð his lichame and heneð his soule; and þe lichame, þe sholde ben þe soule hihtliche bure, makeð hire to ateliche quarterne. And þerinne nevre twisteð mid overdede and untimliche drinche, þat hire beoð wo þat hie sal þerinne wunien, and þerefore wilneð ut. Unriht heo doð ec toʒenes his emcristene þenne he hine laðeð to drinken more – noht þe him beo wille oðer queme – ac þenne him ned were. And bringeð uppen him birden more þene bere muʒe, and spilleð on him þat he sholde spelien wrecche men; oðer raðer helden hit ut þene me þermide fordrenchen, and noht sheden Godes shafte, ne spenen on uniðor þat God shop mannen to helpe, ne swo unwurðin Godes handiwerc. Þis beoð at drinche.

    And oðer unriht inoh: þere beð ollende word, and idele lehtres, and winrede bruwes and buweð wenliche þe beð bispeke ewebruche; and oðer unriht inoh – wicching and swikedom, stale and leoð, and lesing, and refloc, and alle þe luðere lastes þe man hafeð þurch devles lore. Of þis grisliche grune specð þe prophete, and seið: *Cum iniqua gerentibus non introibo*: 'Nelle Ich nefre gon þider in þere me swich unriht drigeð.' Þe lif holi man þe wiste Godes wille swic drinch wiðqueð, and þe luðere wune, and þe stede þer me swo one drinkeð.

    Tercius saltus huius deserti est forum ubi ponunt laqueum malignitatis: 'Þe þridde laʒe on þis wilderne is cheping, þere teldeð þe werse þe grune of hindre', þat is, of bipeching; for þenne man bipecheð oðer he him makeð to ben bihinden of þat he weneð to ben biforen. Þat is ure alre wune þe biggeð and silleð. Þe sullere loveð his þing dere and seið þat it is wel wurð oðer betere. Þe beger bet litel þarfore and seið þat hit nis noht wurð, and ligeð boðe. Þe sullere lat sumdel of his lofe, and swereð þat he hit nele lasse selle; þe beggere ecneð his bode and swereð þat he nele more geven. Þanne cumeð þe werse and runeð wið here eiðeres þanc, and doð þe sullere lasse to nimende þanne he swore, and þanne þe biggere more to gevende þanne he swore. And gif hit chepinge be þe me schule meten oðer weien, þe sullere doð narewere þane he sholde, and te biggere rumluker þan he sholde. And þesse wise beswikeð her aiðer oðer, and beð þanne bisaid in þe grune of hinder: on is leasing, oðer is monoð, þe þridde swikedom; and mid þis grune henteð þe werse alle þo þe þus biggeð and sulleð. Þarefore seið þe prophete: *Odivi ecclesiam malignantium*: 'Me is andsete þe samninge of þe hinderfulle, for Ich wot þat hie ben loðe God.'

    Quartus saltus huius deserti est monasterium ubi ponuntur laquei impietatis: 'Ðe feorðe laʒe of þisse wilderne is chireche, þare teldeð ðe werse þe grune of oregelnesse', and bisaið þarone hwile hodede, and hwile lewede, and hwile boðe. Ðe hodede henteð mid þis grune, hwile ofeald, hwile twifeald, þanne he makeð þat þe hodede lat his chireche stonde wiðuten tide þane hit time beð to done þe tiden; and alse swo ofte swo he spekeð in chireche þat he ne sholde, oðer swikeð of þat he sholde: þat is þe sinfule wel tachen and minigen þo þe ben slowe to chireche, and to weldede þat he be snel þarto, and lehtrie þo þe on sinne lið to forleten and mid milde worde to frefrien, and eche heʒe dai fede mid Godes worde þe hungrie soule þe haveð to witen. And alse fele þing swo Ich iteld habbe þat he ine chirche speken sholde; ʒif he nele oðer ne can, oðer ne reccheð, mid alse fele folde grunen þe werse hine biseið and henteð. And ʒif he wliteð mid stefne for to liken wel wimmannen, oðer ledeð hem his life eʒen for to sechen hire loke, þenne beð he laht for to leden to helle.

and feet hop, the belly shakes, and shoulders twist about, and hands and arms flail; the heart assumes that it must sing a song; tongue, teeth and lips shape words; the mouth sends out the voice. And each man that comes there to observe this play, or to hear it, or to see it, if it is very pleasing to him, is entrapped and caught in the trap of idleness that the devil has established there. Of this trap the prophet speaks, and says: *Non sedi cum concilio vanitatis et cum iniqua gerentibus non introibo*: 'I have never condoned those that go to idleness.'

Secundus saltus huius deserti est compotatorium: 'The second den in this wilderness is drink.' There the devil sets the trap of wrongdoing, for there no man does what is right, but there each man does what is not right against God and against his own soul, and against his fellow Christian. He does wrong against God, who is his Lord, and who protects his life and his health (as long as he has it) and gives him everything that he lives by, and asks him through this to satisfy his needs and keep himself from excess; but even so, he will not do what God commands of him, but does what God proscribes, and does that which the devil has commanded. And in this way he dishonours God and honours the devil, and sins against God and pleases the devil, and gives up the prosperity of heaven and obtains the woe of hell. He also does wrong to his soul's displeasure, and beautifies his body and disempowers his soul, and lauds his body and oppresses his soul; and he makes the body, that should be the soul's joyful chamber, a horrible prison for it. And in there the soul can never turn because of excessive and unreasonable drinking, so that it is miserable because it must live in there, and therefore it wants to get out. He also wrongs his fellow Christian when he leads them to drink more – not that which they wanted to or that which was enjoyable – than was necessary for them. And he brings upon them a greater burden than they can bear, and wastes on them what he should spare for poor men; or he should rather pour it out than make men drunk with it, and he ought not to waste what God has made, nor use without benefit what God created to help men, nor should he dishonour God's handiwork in this way. This is drinking.

And there are many other wrongs: there are offensive words, and idle sins, and wine-red brows, and they bend joyfully to vices that are to do with adultery; and many other wrongs – witchcraft and deceit, theft and song, and lying, and spoliation, and all the hateful sins that man possesses through the devil's teaching. The prophet speaks of this dreadful trap, and says: *Cum iniqua gerentibus non introibo*: 'I will never go in there where such wrong is done.' In life the holy man who knew God's will spoke against such drink, and that hateful habit, and the place in which one drinks in this manner.

Tertius saltus huius deserti est forum ubi ponunt laqueum malignitatis: 'The third den in this wilderness is trade, where the devil sets the trap of hindering', that is, of deceit; for when a man tricks another he makes him fall behind what he had expected to be previously. That is the habit of all of us that buy and sell. The vendor values his item expensively, and says it is well worth that price or better. The buyer offers a little for it and says it is not worth that price, and they both lie. The vendor reduces his price by an amount, and insists that he will not sell it for less; the buyer raises his offer, and insists he will not give more. Then the devil arrives and communicates secretly with the minds of each of them, and makes the vendor take less than he insisted on, and then makes the buyer give more than he said. And if it is merchandise that has to be measured or weighed, the vendor makes it a smaller amount than he should, and the buyer makes it larger than he should. And in this way, they defraud each other here, and are then caught in the trap that is deceit: one is lying, the second perjury, the third fraud; and with this trap the devil catches all those who buy and sell in this way. About this the prophet said: *Odivi ecclesiam malignantium*: 'The assembly of the deceitful is hateful to me, for I know that they are hateful to God.'

Quartus saltus huius deserti est monasterium ubi ponuntur laquei impietatis: 'The fourth den of this wilderness is the church, in which the devil sets up the trap of pride', and catches in it sometimes the clergy, and sometimes the laity, and sometimes both. The clergy he catches in this trap, sometimes once and sometimes twice when he causes the cleric to allow his church to stand without a service when it is time to perform the services; and similarly, as often as he speaks in church that which he should not, or when he is silent about what he ought not to be: that is, he should teach the sinful effectively and caution those that are slow in coming to church, and advise that they should be diligent in good works, and that those who lie in sin should cease their wickedness, and he should comfort them with kind words, and on each feast day he should feed the hungry souls whom he has to protect with God's word. And so he should speak in church the many things I have spoken of in this way; if he will not or can not, or does not care, then the devil will trap and catch him with many snares. And if he sings with his voice to be well

80   Þe lewede men henteð þe werse ine chirche mid his grune on þre wise: þanne prest specð inne chirche of chirche neode, and mineʒeð þat me niwe cloðes oðer elde bete, boc, oðer belle, calch, oðer messeref, oðer waferiht, oðer oðre cloðes, þenne cumeð þe werse to þe mannes heorte, and wið his þonc sunderune halt, þus queðinde: 'Wi sholdest þu þis finden þe noht ne fost þerof; ac he fohð al þat þere cumeð, he finde þis nu.' Swo ne andswerede noht Moyses ure Drihten þo he bad

85   him minster maken; and he hit al wel forðede, þeh he noht þeroffe fenge. Alse dide Saleman þe God sende his writ to; swo hoh ech chirche socne don þenne hie nede sen.

Þenne þe prest þe meneʒeð rihtliche teðien, þenne cumeð þe werse to sume mannes heorte, and mineʒeð hine þat he swo ne do, and runeð wið þe mannes þonc and þus him misredeð: 'ʒif þu þe prest bitechest alle þine teðinge, nele he hit delen alse he don sholde, ac wile hit dere sellen and

90   spenen on uniðor. Do þu almes þerof, and del sum wrecche men.' Þus he hine bipecheð þat he chirche bireveð. On þe helde laʒe, het ure Drihten þat me ne sholde none man bitechen bute he were teid to menden chirche. *Undecim generationes iusse sunt a domino solis levitis decimas solvere.* Þanne heh dai cumeð, man hoh herien God mid rihte leve, and mid soðe luve; and of þan þe God him haveð lend loc to chirche bringen, and wurðin þermide Godes borde alse his have beð. Þenne

95   cumeð þe werse to sumes mannes heorte and runeð wið his heorte, and doð hine his loc to wiðteonde, and þus queð: 'Þis chirche is riche inoh, and fele men ben wrecches; þe nes riche non nod, ac wrecches habben michele; wiðteo nu here þi loc and del hit wrecches. *Sed ait in evangelio, hec oportuit facere, et illa non omittere.* Eiðer bihoveð þat man do þe wile loc to chirche bringe, and helpe wrecche men, and þermide hine aleseð ʒif he laht beð on þe orelese grune. Þenne mai he seggen

100   mid te salm wirhte David: *Oculi mei semper ad domino, et cetera*: 'Evre beo mine eʒene opene to ure Drihten, for Ich triste þat he nele neng bi mine wrihte, ac for his milde wille of þis werses grune mine fet breiden.' Swo do he ure alre, þe liveð and rixleð. Amen.

admired by women, or if he voluntarily directs his eyes to them to seek their looks, then he will be caught in order to be led to hell.

The devil catches the laity in church with his traps in three ways: when the priest speaks in church of the church's requirements, and that they should find new garments or repair the old ones, a book, or a bell, a chalice, or a mass-surplice, or an altarcloth, or other garments, then the devil enters the man's heart, and holds a secret conversation in his thoughts, saying this: 'Why do you have to find this of which you will get nothing; for he that receives everything that comes there, he should find this thing now.' Moses did not answer our Lord like this when God asked him to build a church; and he furnished all of it well, although he did not himself get anything from that. Likewise did Solomon to whom God sent his message; so ought each congregation to do when they see that it is necessary.

When the priest urges them to give tithes properly, then the devil enters a man's heart and advises him not to do this, and converses secretly with the man's mind and misleads him in this way: 'If you give the priest all your tithes, he will not distribute them as he should do, but he will sell them at a profit and spend that wastefully. Give from your alms yourself, and distribute some to poor men.' In this way, he encourages him to steal from the church. According to the old law, our Lord instructed that no one should hand anything over to any man, unless he was obliged to mend the church. *Undecim generationes iusse sunt a domino solis levitis decimas solvere.* When the feast day comes, God ought to be praised with proper belief, and with true love; and from that which God has lent him, one should bring a gift to the church, and honour God's table with it, according to what the person possesses. Then the devil enters a man's heart and secretly converses with his heart, and makes him withhold his gift, saying this: 'This church is rich enough, and many men are poor; the rich have no need, but the poor have much; withhold your gift here now, and donate it to the poor.' *Sed ait in evangelio, hec oportuit facere, et illa non omittere.* A man is obliged both to bring a gift to the church and also to help poor men, and by that he shall free himself if he should be caught in the wicked one's trap. Then may he say with the psalmist David: *Oculi mei semper ad domino, etc.*:[23] 'Ever will my eyes be open to our Lord', for I trust that he will not punish me according to my deeds, but will, in his mercy, release my feet loose from the devil's trap. May he do this for all of us, he who lives and reigns. Amen.

23 Psalm 25.15.

Hali Meiðhad

Oxford, Bodleian Library, Bodley 34, is dated to c.1225, and contains, in order, the following texts: *The Life of Saint Katherine*, *The Life of Saint Margaret*, *The Life of Saint Juliana*, *Hali Meiðhad* and *Sawles Warde*.[1] Three of these texts (*Katherine*, *Hali Meiðhad* and *Sawles Warde*) are also found, together with the *Ancrene Riwle* and *Þe Wohunge of Ure Laverd*, in the slightly earlier manuscript, London, British Library, Cotton Titus D. xvii, dated to c.1220. The saints' lives and *Sawles Warde* are also found in London, British Library, Royal 17 A xxvii, dated to c.1220–30.

Each of these texts was probably intended for a female audience, and the emphasis in them is on providing the role model for women of the virgin or chaste religious female. With the exception of the *Ancrene Riwle*, the texts in Bodley 34 have been grouped together under the label 'The Katherine Group'.[2] This grouping is partially thematic, and partially linguistic. The texts all appear to have originated in the West Midlands, somewhere between Herefordshire and South Shropshire, and share features of their language, a literary dialect that has become known as AB language.[3] Features of this dialect include a relatively consistent orthography; the use of *ha*, *ham*, *hare* for 'they', 'them' and 'their'; *ȝe* for 'you'; other dialectal features; and a variable alliterative prose style. There are also a number of French loanwords in some of these texts; for example, *servise*, *cuntasse* and *degrez*.

These prose works are all of great importance for many reasons. They represent the tradition of writing English prose in the West Midlands that appears to have continued, at Worcester for example, from the Norman Conquest with the copying and adaptation of Old English manuscripts. They also demonstrate the utility of the vernacular in religious texts aimed at instructing women. As women usually would not have the same access to Latin, in particular, as their male counterparts were afforded, English was to become an important literary and educational medium for them. As it is highly likely that in the first instance the audience of these texts would be women, the way in which the authors' write also becomes a matter for examination: how are the women portrayed through these texts? What educative techniques does the author use? What can these texts tell us about the career choices women might have had in this period? As we know little about the authors[4] of 'The Katherine Group', much has to be surmised from the texts and manuscripts. In all cases, the authors probably belonged to a religious order, as the religious training is evident in the texts, as are the many religious sources used to compile the texts.

Hali Meiðhad exists in two manuscript versions both dated to around the third decade of the thirteenth century, with Bodley 34 the slightly later of the two. The edition of extracts given below is taken from Bodley 34, folios 52 verso to 71 verso.[5] The title of the text is given at folio 51 recto as *Epistel of meidenhad meidene froure*, 'A letter on virginity for the encouragement of virgins'. This is an apt description of the text, as it takes the form of an address to an individual or group of individuals, spoken to using the second person personal pronoun *þu* by the author.

The text itself may date to the last decade of the twelfth, or first decades of the thirteenth, century; there was certainly one copy of the text prior to those that survive. It is a prose work dedicated to persuading women either to choose a religious life of virginity over a life in the world as a wife, or to remain in a religious life once the choice had been made. Little is known about the audience, though it has been assumed that it would be nuns or recluses. Textual evidence shows that at least one of the texts in Bodley 34 (*The Life of Saint Margaret*) is designed with an audience of virgins in mind, but this need not preclude a wider audience of other women. The fact that the intended recipients of 'The Katherine Group' texts, and *Hali Meiðhad* in particular, are women has important implications for the way in which the text is read. To a degree, these works demonstrate how women could be educated religiously in this period: through the vernacular; with an emphasis on clarity of explanation that does not presuppose a high level of education; and with a view to persuading them that the best role model that they could adopt is that of the virgin, the bride of Christ.

---

1   A facsimile of this manuscript is edited by N. R. Ker, *Facsimile of Bodley 34*, EETS o.s. 247 (London, 1960).

2   For this, and much more information, see the edition and translation of *Hali Meiðhad*, *Saint Margaret*, *Ancrene Wisse* books 7 and 8, and *Sawles Warde* in B. Millett and J. Wogan-Browne, eds, *Medieval English Prose for Women from the Katherine Group and 'Ancrene Wisse'* (Oxford, 1992). For an essential guide to and bibliography of these texts, see B. Millett, *Annotated Bibliographies of Old and Middle English Literature II: Ancrene Wisse, the Katherine Group, and the Wooing Group* (Cambridge, 1996).

3   After J. R. R. Tolkien's essay '*Ancrene Wisse* and *Hali Meiðhad*', *Essays and Studies* 14 (1929), 104–26. This theory, of a literary dia-

lect shared by these texts, has generated a considerable amount of research since 1929. It is currently being reappraised by Bella Millett, and dialectologists working on *The Linguistic Atlas of Early Middle English*.

4   It is not likely that the author of any of these works was a woman, not necessarily because women did not usually have access to the same level of education as men, but because a woman – even a woman in religious orders – would not, to my mind, write about women in the way that the *Hali Meiðhad* author, for one, does.

5   The whole text is edited and translated by Millett and Wogan-Browne (see n.2 above). *Hali Meiðhad* is also edited by B. Millett, ed., *Hali Meiðhad*, EETS o.s. 284 (London, 1982).

This emphasis on virginity and its spiritual benefits is one with which many modern readers have difficulty in empathizing. In the medieval period, however, a substantial amount of patristic writing and religious literature was concerned to highlight the preferred state of the Christian as that of the virgin. Building on the words of Saint Paul, then later, Saint Jerome, the development of the argument in favour of Christianity centred on the retention of the purity of the body, and the denial of the desires of the flesh.[6] Some male authors viewed women as indirectly responsible for the Fall of Man because of Eve's inability to control her desires, and one of the myths about women was that their lust was uncontrollable. Perhaps partially as a result of the suspicion surrounding women, particularly the distrust shown by religious writers, the exemplar of the virgin figure is often the central role model for women in religious texts such as hagiography, and here, in the *Hali Meiðhad*: by remaining a virgin and dedicating her life to God, the woman could attain salvation and the love of Christ. Simultaneously, the lustful impulses of the female were controlled and curtailed.

The *Hali Meiðhad* author aims to persuade and encourage, and his style reflects these aims. He often writes in alliterative prose, which, rather like Old English homiletic prose, provides a regular rhythm to the text if read aloud. The author also employs effective rhetorical figures, such as visual description, simile, metaphor, repetition and hyperbole,[7] to sustain the reader's interest and make his prose more dramatic. Probably the most famous, and without doubt the most startling, passage from this text deals with the miseries of marriage in comparison to the joys of being the bride of Christ. Here the skill of this author's rhetoric is employed to full effect.

Hali Meiðhad

Epistel of Meidenhad Meidene Froure

Avdi, filia, et vide, et inclina aurem tuam; et obliviscere populum tuum et domum patris tui. Dauið þe psalmwruhte spekeð i þe Sawter towart Godes spuse; þet is, euch meiden þet haueð meið þeawes – ant seið: 'Iher me, dohter, bihald ant bei þin eare; ant forʒet ti folc ant tines feader hus.'

Nim ʒeme hwet euch word beo sunderliche to seggen. 'Iher me, dohter', he seið. 'Dohter' he
5　cleopeð hire forþi þet ha understonde þet he hire luueliche lives luue leareð, as feader ah his dohter; ant heo him as hire feader þe bliþeluker lustni. 'Iher me, deore dohter'; þet is, 'ʒeornne lustne me wið earen of þin heauet.' 'Ant bihald'; þet is, 'Opene to understonde me þe ehnen of þin heorte.' 'Ant bei þin eare'; þet is, 'Beo buhsum to mi lare.' Ha mei ondswerien ant seggen, 'Ant hwet is nu þis lare þet tu nimest se deopliche, ant learst me se ʒeorne?' Low, þis: 'Forʒet ti folc ant
10　tines feader hus.' 'Þi folc', he cleopeð, Dauið, þe ʒederunge inwið þe of fleschliche þonkes, þe leaðieð þe ant dreaieð wið hare procunges to flesliche fulðen, to licomliche lustes, ant eggið þe to brudlac ant to weres cluppunge; ant makieð þe to þenchen hwuch delit were þrin, hwuch eise i þe richedom þet þeos leafdis habbeð, hu muche god mahte of inker streon awakenin. A, fals folc of swikel read: as þi muð uleð, as þu schawest forð al þet god þuncheð, ant helest al þet bittri bale
15　þet is þerunder ant al þet muchele lure þer terof ariseð. 'Forʒet al þis folc, mi deorewurðe dohter', seið Dauið þe witege; þet is, 'Þes þonkes warp ut of þin heorte.' Þis is Babilones folc, þe deofles here of helle, þet is umbe for te leaden into þe worldes þeowdom Syones dohter.

'Syon' wes sumhwile icleopet þe hehe tur of Jerusalem; ant 'Syon' seið ase muchel on Englische ledene ase 'heh sihðe'. Ant bitacneð þis tur þe hehnesse of meiðhad, þe bihald, as of heh, alle
20　widewen under hire, ant weddede baðe. For þeos, ase flesches þrealles, beoð i worlddes þeowdom, ant wunieð 'lahe' on eorðe; ant meiden stont þurh heh lif i þe tur of Jerusalem. Nawt of lah on eorðe, ah of þe hehe in heouene þe is bitacnet þurh þis, of þet Syon ha bihalt al þe worlt under hire; ant þurh englene liflade ant heouenlich þet ha lead, þah ha licomliche wunie upon eorðe, ha stiheð gasteliche, ant is as i Syon, þe hehe tur of heouene, freo ouer alle from worldliche weanen.
25　Ah Babilones folc þet Ich ear nempnede, þe deofles here of helle, þet beoð flesches lustes ant feondes eggunge, weorrið ant warpeð eauer towart tis tur for te keasten hit adun ant drahen into þeowdom þet stont se hehe þerin, ant is icleopet forþi Syones dohter. Ant nis ha witerliche akeast ant into þeowdom idrahen, þe of se swiðe heh stal, of se muche dignete, ant swuch wurðschipe as hit is to beo Godes spuse, Jesu Cristes brude, þe Laverdes leofmon þet alle þinges buheð, of al þe

6　See E. Amt, ed., *Women's Lives in Medieval Europe* (London, 1993), for many of these key texts in translation.

7　See Millett, *Hali Meiðhad*, pp. lii–vi, for an analysis of the prose style.

Hali Meiðhad

A Letter on Virginity for the Encouragement of Virgins

Listen, daughter, and see, and incline your ear; and forget your people and your father's house.[8] David the psalm-writer speaks in the Psalter to God's bride; that is, every virgin who has the qualities of virginity – and says: 'Hear me, daughter, behold and incline your ear; and forget your people and your father's house.'

Pay attention to what each word means individually. 'Hear me, daughter', he says. 'Daughter' he calls her in order that she might understand that he is teaching her lovingly about love, as a father should to his daughter; and so that she might listen to him as her father the more happily. 'Hear me, beloved daughter'; that is, 'Listen eagerly to me with the ears in your head.' 'And behold'; that is, 'Open the eyes of your heart in order to understand me.' 'And incline your ear'; that is, 'Be obedient to my teaching.' She might answer and say, 'And what now is this teaching that you take so seriously, and teach me so earnestly?' Indeed, it is this: 'Forget your people and your father's house.' 'Your people', David says, are the fleshly thoughts gathering in your mind, which goad you and draw you with their goadings to fleshly filth, to physical lusts, and egg you on towards marriage and the embrace of a husband; and make you think what delight there would be in them, what ease in the riches those ladies have, how much good might come into being from your offspring. Ah, false people with treacherous advice: when your mouths flatter so, you speak forth all that seems good, and conceal all that bitter harm which is underneath and all the great loss which will arise from it. 'Forget all this people, my precious daughter', says David the prophet; that is, 'Throw out these thoughts from your heart.' This is the people of Babylon, the devil's host from hell, who want to lead Zion's daughter into the world's bondage.

'Zion' was at one time what the high tower of Jerusalem was called; and 'Zion' means the same as 'high vision' in English. And this tower symbolizes the highness of virginity, which sees, as if from on high, all widows beneath it, and those who are married too. For these, as slaves of the flesh, are in the bondage of the world, and live low on earth; and the virgin stands through her high life in the tower of Jerusalem. Not from low on earth, but from the height in heaven which is symbolized by this, from that Zion she looks on the entire world beneath her; and through the angelic and heavenly life that she leads, even though she lives physically on earth, she ascends spiritually, and is as if in Zion, the high tower of heaven, free above all from worldly troubles.

But the people of Babylon that I named before, the devil's host from hell, who are lusts of the flesh and the fiend's temptation, always make war on and attack this tower, so as to cast it down and draw into bondage she who stands so high within it, and is therefore called the daughter of Zion. And is she

8 Psalm 44.11.

30   worlt leafdi, as he is of al Laverd? Ilich him in halschipe, unwemmet as he is, ant þet eadi meiden
his deorrewurðe moder; ilich his hali engles ant his heste halhen; se freo of hireseolven ha nawiht
ne þearf of oðer þing þenchen bute ane of hire leofmon wið treowe luve cwemen. For he wule carie
for hire þet ha haveð itake to of al þet hire bihoveð hwil ha riht luveð him wið soðe bileave. Nis ha
þenne sariliche, as Ich seide ear, akeast ant into þeowdom idrahen, þe of se muchel hehschipe ant

35   se seli freodom schal lihte se lahe into a monnes þeowdom, swa þet ha naveð nawt freo of hireseolven;
ant trukien for a mon of lam þe heovenliche Laverd; ant lutlin hire leafdischipe ase muchel as hire
leatere were is leasse wurð ant leasse haveð þen hefde ear hire earre? Ant of Godes brude ant his
freo dohter, for ba togederes ha is, bikimeð þeow under mon, ant his þrel, to don al ant drehen þet
him likeð, ne sitte hit hire se uvele. Ant of se seli sikernesse as ha wes ant mahte beon under Godes

40   warde, deð hire into drechunge, to dihten hus ant hinen, ant to se monie earmden; to carien for se
feole þing, teonen þolien ant gromen, ant scheomen umbe stunde; drehen se moni wa for se wac
hure as þe worlt forʒelt eaver ed ten ende. Nis þeos witerliche akeast? Nis þis þeowdom inoh,
aʒein þet ilke freolec þet ha hefde hwil ha wes Syones dohter? Ant þah nis inempnet her nawt of
heovenliche luren, þe passið alle wiðuten evenunge.

45   Sikerliche, swa hit feareð: serve Godd ane, ant alle þing schule þe turne to gode; ant tac þe to
him treowliche, ant tu schalt beo freo from alle worldliche weanen, ne mei nan uvel hearmi þe; for
as Seinte Pawel seið, alle þing turneð þen gode to gode. Ne mei na þing wonti þe þe berest him
þet al wealt inwið þi breoste. Ant swuch swettnesse þu schalt ifinden in his luve ant in his servise,
ant habbe se muche murhðe þrof ant licunge i þin heorte, þet tu naldest changin þet stat þet tu

50   livest in for te beo cwen icrunet. Se hende is ure Laverd, þet nule he nawt þet his icorene beon her
wiðute mede. For se muchel confort is in his grace þet al ham sit þet ha seoð, ant þah hit þunche
oþre men þet ha drehen hearde, hit ne derveð ham nawt ah þuncheð ham softe, ant habbeð mare
delit þrin þen ei oðer habbe i licunge of þe worlt. Þis ure Laverd ʒeveð ham her as on earnnesse of
eche mede þet schal cume þrefter. Þus habbeð Godes freond al þe frut of þis worlt þet ha forsaken

55   habbeð, o wunderliche wise, ant heovene ed ten ende.

Nu þenne on oðer half, nim þe to þe worlde; ant eaver se þu mare havest, se þe schal mare
trukien. Ant servin hwen þu naldest Godd þes fikele worlt ant frakele, ant schalt beo sare idervet
under hire as hire þreal on a þusent wisen. Aʒeines an licunge, habben twa ofþunchunges, ant se
ofte beon imaket earm of an eðlich mon þet tu list under, for nawt oðer for nohtunge, þet te schal

60   laði þi lif. Ant bireowe þi sið, þet tu eaver dudest te into swuch þeowdom for worldliche wunne
þet tu wendest to biʒeotene, ant havest ifunden weane þrin ant wontreðe rive. Al is þet tu wendest
golt iwurðe to meastling; al is nawt þet ti folc, of hwam I spec þruppe, biheten þe to ifinden. Nu
þu wast þet ha habbeð bichearret te as treitres; for under weole, i wunnes stude, þu havest her ofte
helle, ant bute ʒef þu wiðbreide þe, þu bredest te þet oðer as doð þes cwenes, þes riche cuntasses,

65   þeos modie leafdis of hare liflade. Soðliche, ʒef ha biþenceð ham riht ant icnawlecheð soð, Ich
habbe ham to witnesse ha lickið honi of þornes. Ha buggeð al þet swete wið twa dale of bittre, ant
þet schal forðre i þis writ beon openliche ischawet. Nis hit nower neh gold, al þat ter schineð; nat
þah na mon bute hamseolfen hwet ham sticheð ofte.

certainly not cast down and drawn into bondage, who from so very high a place, of so much dignity, and such honour as it is to be God's spouse, the bride of Jesus Christ, the sweetheart of the Lord to whom all things bow down, lady of the entire world as he is Lord of all? She is like him in wholeness, as immaculate as he is, and that blessed virgin his adored mother; like his holy angels and his highest saints; so free in herself she does not need to think of anything other than pleasing her sweetheart with true love. For he whom she has taken as her lover will take care of all that she might require while she loves him properly with true belief. Is she not then, as I said before, sorrowfully cast down and drawn into bondage, who from so much dignity and so blessed a freedom shall descend so low into a man's service, so that she has nothing that is freely her own; and abandon the heavenly Lord for a man of clay; and decrease her rank as a lady by as much as her latter husband is worth less, and has less, than had her former husband? And from being God's bride and his free daughter, for she is both together, she becomes a slave to a man, and his servant, to do and suffer all that pleases him, however badly that might suit her. And from so happy a security as she had and might have under God's guardianship, she gives herself to vexation, to supervising a house and servants, and to so many troubles; to care for so many things, to suffer torments and irritations, and, on some occasions, shames; to endure so many woes for so few wages as the world will always pay in the end. Is she not truly cast down? Is not this bondage sufficient in comparison with that same freedom that she had while she was the daughter of Zion? And yet here no mention is made of the heavenly losses, which pass all without equal.

Certainly, it goes like this: serve only God, and all things will turn to good for you; and give yourself to him faithfully, and you will be free from all worldly miseries, nor may any evil harm you; for as Saint Paul says, all things turn from good to better.[9] And you will want for nothing when you bear him who rules all things inwardly in your heart. And such sweetness will you discover in his love and his service, and have so much joy and pleasure from it in your heart, that you would not change that manner in which you live if you were crowned a queen. So noble is our Lord that he would not want his chosen to be here on earth without reward. For there is so much comfort in his grace that all that they see is pleasing to them, and though it seems to other people that they suffer hardship, it does not trouble them but seems easy to them, and they have more delight in it than any other person might have in the pleasure of this world. Our Lord gives them here a pledge of eternal reward that will come afterwards. Thus God's friends have all the benefit of this world that they have forsaken, and, in a wonderful way, heaven in the end.

Now then on the other hand, take the world; and ever the more you have, the more it will desert you. And serve this fickle and worthless world when you would not serve God, and you shall be sorely afflicted by it as its slave in a thousand ways. For every pleasure, you will have two griefs, and be made wretched so frequently by the worthless man whom you are under, for nothing or for a trifle, that your life will be loathsome to you. And you will regret your course of action, that you ever put yourself into such bondage for the worldly joy that you hoped to gain, and have instead found misery in it and all manner of hardship. All that you thought was gold has transformed into brass; everything that your people, of whom I spoke above, promised you would find is nothing. Now you know that they have betrayed you like traitors; for underneath the prosperity, in place of joy, you frequently have hell here on earth, and unless you withdraw from it, you are preparing that other hell for yourself as do those queens, those rich countesses, those proud ladies, because of their way of life. Truly, if they thought about it properly and recognized the truth, I would have them as witnesses that they are licking honey off thorns. They pay for all that sweetness with twice that amount of bitterness, and that will be clearly shown further on in this letter. It is nowhere near gold, all that shines there; yet there is no one but themselves who knows what pain they must frequently be caused.

(The author goes on to say how awful things are for the poor, before turning his attention to the act of sexual intercourse and comparing it ('that burning itch') to the pure state of virginity. The Devil assails the virgin in order to tempt her out of virginity: lechery is an attacker against which the virgin must defend herself. Marriage has been made lawful so that those who are not strong enough to be virgins can have a legitimate means of indulging in intercourse. In the following extract, the three states, of virginity, marriage and widowhood are examined.)

9   Romans 8.28.

{The Three States of Women}

70   Al as Ich seide ear, folhið ure Laverd, ant tah nawt overal; for i þe menske of meiðhad ant in hire mihte ne muhten nane folhin him, ne þet eadi meiden, englene leafdi ant meidenes menske, bute meidnes ane. Ant forþi is hare aturn se briht ant se schene bivoren alle oþre þet ha gad eaver nest Godd hwider se he turneð. Ant alle ha beoð icrunet þe blissið in heovene wið kempene crune; ah þe meidnes habbeð, upo þeo þe is to alle iliche imeane, a gerlondesche schenre þen þe sunne, *aureola* ihaten o Latines ledene. Þe flurs þe beoð idrahe þron, ne þe ʒimmes þrin, ne tellen of hare

75   evene nis na monnes speche. Þus, feole privileges schawið ful sutelliche hwucche beoð þer meiðnes, ant sundrið ham from þe oðre wið þus feole mensken world buten ende.

ʒef of þes þreo hat, meiðhad ant widewehad, ant wedlac is þe þridde, þu maht bi þe degrez of hare blisse icnawen hwuch ant bi hu muchel þe an passeð þe oþre. For wedlac haveð hire frut þrittifald in heovene; widewehad, sixtifald; meiðhad, wið hundretfald, overgeað baþe. Loke þenne

80   herbi, hwa se of hire meiðhad lihteð into wedlac, bi hu monie degrez ha falleð dunewardes. Ha is an hundret degrez ihehet towart heovene hwil ha meiðhad halt, as þe frut preoved; ant leaped into wedlac, þet is, dun neoðer to þe þrittuþe, over þrie twenti ant ʒet ma bi tene. Nis þis ed en cherre a muche lupe dunewart? Ant tah hit is to þolien, ant Godd haved ilahet hit, as Ich ear seide, leste hwa se leope ant þer ne edstode lanhure, nawt nere þet kepte him, ant drive adun swirevorð

85   wiðuten ikepunge deope into helle. Of þeos nis nawt to speokene for ha beod iscrippet ut of lives writ in heovene.

Ah schawi we ʒet witerluker, as we ear biheten, hwet drehen þe iweddede, þet tu icnawe þerbi hu murie þu maht libben, meiden, i þi meiðhad over þet heo libbeð; to eche þe murhðe ant te menske in heovene þet muð ne mei munnen. Nu þu art iweddet, ant of se heh se lahe iliht: of

90   englene ilicnesse, of Jesu Cristes leofmon, of leafdi in heovene, into flesches fulðe, into beastes liflade, into monnes þeowdom, ant into worldes weane. Sei nu hwet frut, ant for hwuch þing meast? Is hit al forþi, oðer ane dale þervore, beo nu soðcnawes, for te keli þi lust wið fulðe of þi licome?[10] For Gode, hit is speatewile for te þenche þron, ant for te speoken þrof ʒet speatewilre. Loke þenne, hwuch beo þet seolve þing ant þet dede to donne. Al þet fule delit is wið fulðe aleid

95   as þu turnest þin hond; ah þet ladliche least leafeð ant lest forð, ant te ofþunchunge þrof, longe þrefter. Ant te unseli horlinges þe unlaheliche hit hantið habbeð in inwarde helle for þet hwilinde lust endelese pine, bute ʒef heo hit leaven, ant hit on eorðe under schrift bitterliche beten. Forhohe for te don hit, þet te þuncheð uvel of ant eil for te heren. For hwen hit is þullich, ant muchele ladluker þen ei wel-itohe muð for scheome mahe seggen, hwet makeð hit iluvet bituhhe beasteliche

100   men bute hare muchele unþeaw, þet bereð ham ase beastes to al þet ham lusteð, as þah ha nefden wit in ham, ne tweire schad as mon haveð, ba of god ant of uvel, of kumelich ant unkumelich, na mare þen beastes þet dumbe neb habbeð? Ah leasse þen beastes ʒet, for þeos doð hare cunde, bute wit þah ha beon, in a time of þe ʒer. Moni halt him to a make ne nule efter þet lure neaver neomen oþer. Ant mon, þet schulde habbe wit, ant don al þet he dude efter hire wilnunge, folheð þet fulðe

105   in eavereuch time, ant nimeð an efter an; ant moni þet is wurse monie toʒederes. Lo nu hu þis unþeaw ne eveneð þe nawt ane to wittlese beastes, dumbe ant broke-rugget, ibuhe towart eorðe (þu þet art i wit wraht to Godes ilicnesse, ant iriht bodi up ant heaved towart heovene; forþi þet tu schuldest þin heorte heoven þiderwart as þin eritage is, ant eorðe forhohien), nim ʒeme hu þis unþeaw ne makeð þe nawt ane evening ne ilich ham, ah deð muchel eateluker ant mare to witen

110   þe forschuptest te seolf willes ant waldes into hare cunde.

Þe leoseð þenne se heh þing, þe mihte ant te biheve of meidhades menske, for se ful fulðe as is ischawet þruppe, hwa se of engel lihteð to iwurðen lahre þen a beast for se ladli cheaffere, loki hu ha spede. 'Nai,' þu wult seggen, 'for þet fulðe nis hit nawt; ah monnes elne is muche wurð, ant me bihoveð his help to fluttunge ant te fode. Of wif ant weres gederunge worldes weole awakeneð,

---

10   The Titus manuscript has in addition here 'for te habbe delit of þi fleschliche wil of monnes imeane' (to have satis-   faction of your fleshly desire through intercourse with a man). It may be that the Bodley 34 scribe is censoring his text here.

{The Three States of Women}

All[11] that I have spoken of before, follow our Lord, and yet not completely; for in the honour of virginity and in its virtue no one may follow him, or that blessed virgin, lady of angels and maidens' glory, except virgins alone. And therefore their garments are so bright and so shining beyond all others that they always go next to God whichever way he turns. And all those who rejoice in heaven are crowned with the victor's crown; but the virgins have, over and above what is the same for all, a golden crown more bright than the sun, called an *aureola* in Latin. The flowers that are engraved there on it, and the jewels in it, no one could tell in human speech of their quality. Thus, the many privileges reveal most clearly which are the virgins there, and separate them from the others with so many honours in perpetuity.

Yet of these three orders, virginity and widowhood, and marriage is the third, you may know by the degrees of their bliss which one surpasses the others, and by how much. For marriage has its benefit thirtyfold in heaven; widowhood, sixtyfold; virginity, with a hundredfold, surpasses both. Understand from this then that whoever should descend into marriage from her virginity, by how many degrees she falls downwards. She is lifted up a hundred degrees towards heaven while she retains her virginity, as the benefits prove; and leaps into marriage, that is, down below to the thirtieth, over sixty and yet more by ten. Is this not at one time a great leap downward? But even so, it is to be allowed, and God has made it law, as I said previously, because in the case of someone leaping who did not at least stop there, nothing there would hold him back, and he would be driven downwards head-first without restraint deep into hell. Of these people nothing is to be said because they are scratched out of the book of life in heaven.

But let us show still more clearly, as we promised before, what those who are married endure, so that by this you may perceive, maiden, how joyfully you might live in your virginity in comparison to how they live; for to each of you will be joy and dignity in heaven that no mouth can speak. Now you are married, and have descended so low from so high: from similarity to the angels, from Jesus Christ's beloved, from a lady in heaven, into the filth of the flesh, into the animal's lifestyle, into a man's bondage, and into the world's woe. Say now what its benefit is, and for what main reason? Be truthful now: is it entirely because, or partly because, you want to cool your lust with the fouling of your body? For God's sake, it is disgusting to think about it, and to speak about it is yet more disgusting.[12] Look then, what it is to perform that very same thing. All that foul pleasure is filled with filth in the time it takes to turn your hand; but that loathsome sin remains and lasts forth, along with regret for it, for a long time after. And those unblessed lechers who unlawfully perform it have endless pain in deepest hell for that transitory lust, unless they abandon it, and repent it bitterly under confession while on earth. Scorn to do it, that which seems to you evil and repugnant to hear about. For when it is such, and even more hateful than anyone respectable can describe for shame of it, what makes it loved among beastly men but their substantial lack of control, that makes them carry on like animals to do all that pleases them, as though they had no power of reason within them, or the ability that people have to discriminate between two things, the one good, the other evil, the one decent and the other indecent, any more than animals which do not have the power of speech? But they are even less than animals, because animals act upon their nature, except they lack reason, at one season in the year. Many restrict themselves to one mate and will never take another after they have lost that one. And man, who should have the power of reason, and do all that he did with reason's agreement, follows that filthiness every time, and takes one after another; and what is worse is that many will take many together. Look now how this lack of control not only equates you with reasonless animals, dumb and hunch-backed, bowed down towards the earth (you who are made with reason in God's likeness, and made upright with body and head towards heaven; therefore you should lift your heart towards heaven where your heritage is, and scorn the earth), but pay attention to how this wantonness does not only make you their equal or similar to them, but makes you much more odious and more responsible for changing yourself willingly and voluntarily into their nature.

Whoever loses this highest thing, then, the virtue and the advantage of virginity's dignity, for so foul

11   Married women and virgins.

12   It may be disgusting to speak about it, but the author still goes ahead. His view of marriage, while just about within the bounds of orthodoxy, is quite extreme. He calls married people engaged in sexual practice 'lechers', and 'without reason', seemingly equating them with those engaged in illegal sexual activity. He is not, however, the only medieval author to exaggerate his case in this way. See Millett, *Hali Meiðhad*, pp. xxx–xxxviii, for the development of these ideas, sources and orthodox views on sex within marriage.

115 ant streon of feire children þe gleadieð muchel þe ealdren.' Nu þu havest iseid tus, ant þuncheð
þet tu havest iseid soð; ah Ich chulle schawin hit al wið falsschipe ismeðet. Ah on alre earst, hwet
weole oðer wunne se þer eaver of cume, to deore hit bið aboht þet tu þe seolf sulest fore, ant ȝevest
þin beare bodi to tukin swa to wundre ant feare wið se scheomeliche, wið swuch uncoverlich lure
as meiðhades menske is ant te mede, for worldlich biȝete. Wa wurðe þet cheaffeare: for ei hwilinde
120 weole sullen meiðhad awei, þe cwen is of heovene. For alswa as of þis lure nis nan acoverunge,
alswa is euch wurð unwurð hertowart.

{On Marriage}

Þus, wummon, ȝef þu havest were efter þi wil, ant wunne ba of worldes weole, þe schal nede
itiden. Ant hwet ȝef ha beoð þe wone þet tu nabbe þi wil wið him ne weole nowðer? Ant schalt
grenin godles inwið westi wahes, ant te breades wone brede þi bearn-team. Ant teke þis, liggen
125 under laðest mon þet þah þu hefdest alle weole, he went hit te to weane. For beo hit nu þet te beo
richedom rive, ant tine wide wahes wlonke ant weolefule, ant habbe monie under þe hirdmen in
halle, ant ti were beo þe wrað, oðer iwurðe þe lað, swa þet inker eiðer heasci wið oþer. Hwet
worltlich weole mei beo þe wunne?

Hwen he bið ute, havest aȝein his cume sar care ant eie. Hwil he bið et hame, alle þine wide
130 wanes þuncheð þe to nearewe. His lokunge on ageasteð þe; his ladliche nurð ant his untohe bere
makeð þe to agrisen. Chit te ant cheoweð þe ant scheomeliche schent te; tukeþ þe to bismere as
huler his hore; beateð þe ant busteð þe as his ibohte þrel ant his eðele þeowe. Þine banes akeð þe
ant ti flesch smeorteð þe; þin heorte wiðinne þe swelleð of sar grome, ant ti neb utewið tendreð ut
of teone.

135 Hwuch schal beo þe sompnunge bituhen ow i bedde? Me, þeo þe best luvieð ham tobeoreð ofte
þrin, þah ha na semblant ne makien ine marhen; ant ofte, of moni nohtunge, ne luvien ha ham
neaver swa, bitterliche bi hamseolf teonið eiðer oþer. Heo schal his wil muchel hire unwil wið
muche weane ofte. Alle his fulitoheschipes ant his unhende gomenes, ne beon ha neaver swa wið
fulðe bifunden, nomeliche i bedde ha schal, wulle ha, nulle ha, þolien ham alle. Crist schilde euch
140 meiden to freinin oþer to wilnin for te witen hwucche ha beon; for þeo þe fondið ham meast,
ifindeð ham forcuðest. Ant cleopieð ham selie iwiss þe nuten neaver hwet hit is, ant heatieð þet ha
hantið. Ah hwa se lið i leifen deope bisuncken, þah him þunche uvel þrof, he ne schal nawt up
acoverin hwen he walde. Bisih þe, seli wummon; beo þe cnotte icnut eanes of wedlac, beo he
cangun oðer crupel, beo he hwuch se eaver beo, þu most to him halden.

145 Ȝef þu art feier, ant wið gleade chere bicleopest alle feire, ne schalt tu o nane wise wite þe wið
unword ne wið uvel blame. Ȝef þu art unwurðliche ilatet þu maht ba to oþre ant to þi were
iwurðen þe unwurðre. Ȝef þu iwurðest him unwurð, ant he as unwurð þe, oðer ȝef þu him muche
luvest ant he let lutel to þe, hit greveð þe se swiðe þet tu wult inohreaðe, ase monie doð, makien
him poisun, ant ȝeoven bale i bote stude. Oðer hwa se swa nule don medi wið wicchen ant
150 forsaken, for te drahen his luve towart hire, Crist ant hire Cristendom ant rihte bileave. Nu hwet
blisse mei þeos bruken þe luveð hire were wel, ant ha habbe his laððe, oþer cunqueari his luve o
þulliche wise?

a filth as is shown above, whoever descends from the likeness of an angel to become lower than a beast for so bad a transaction, look how she prospers. 'No,' you will say, 'for that filth it is not worth anything; but a man's strength is worth much, and I am obliged to his help for support and food. From a man and woman united springs worldly wealth, and a family of fine children who bring much joy to their parents.' Now you have said this, and it seems that you have said the truth; but I shall show it to be entirely glossed over with falsehood. But in the first instance, whatever wealth or joy ever comes from it, it is too dearly bought when you sell yourself for it, and give your bare body to be so awfully ill-treated and dealt with so shamefully, with such irreparable loss as the honour of virginity and its reward, for worldly benefit. This is a miserable transaction: for temporary wealth to give virginity away, which is queen of heaven. For in the same way that there is no reparation from this loss, so is each valuable thing valueless compared with this.

(The author goes on to describe the many aspects of marriage that one would imagine to be pleasurable, emphasizing that inevitably, pleasure brings pain.)

{On Marriage}

So woman, if you have a husband after your own desire, and joy also in worldly wealth, this is what will necessarily happen to you. And what if they are lacking so that you do not have what you would wish with him, or wealth either? And you will become pale with poverty within bare walls, and when you give birth to your children, it will be to a lack of bread. And apart from this, you will be subject to the most loathsome man so that even if you had every wealth, he would turn it to woe for you. For it might be now that you have plentiful riches, and your wide walls are proud and prosperous, and you have many servants under you in the hall, but your husband is angry with you, or has become hateful to you so that each of you is angry with the other. What worldly wealth may then give you joy?

When he is out, you have sorrow and anxiety and fear of his returning. While he is at home, all your wide rooms seem too narrow to you. His looking at you scares you; his loathsome noise and his ill-mannered behaviour horrifies you. He chides you and reviles you and scolds you shamefully; he treats you disgracefully as a lecher does his whore; he beats you and hits you like his bought slave and his family servant. Your bones ache and your flesh smarts; your heart swells within you from grievous anger, and outwardly your expression becomes inflamed with anger.

What will your coupling together in bed be like? Even those who love each other best have frequent differences there, although they may give no indication of it in the morning; and often, from minor matters, though they might love one another a great deal, either one or the other will suffer bitterly on their own. She must often do his will much against her own will with great sorrow. All his lechery and his indecent games she must put up with in bed, however obscenely devised, whether she wants to or not. May Christ preserve every maiden from asking or desiring to know what they are; for those who experience them most, find them to be most hateful. And call those women truly happy who have never known what they are, and who hate what such women practise. But if someone lies sunken deep into the mire, though it seems evil to him there, he cannot climb up from it when he wants to. Think about it, blessed woman, for once that knot of marriage is knotted, whether he is a fool or a cripple, whatever he might be, you must remain with him.

If you are pretty, and you speak to everyone pleasantly with a glad disposition, you will not be able to shield yourself in any manner against malicious talk and harmful blame. If you are plain or ill-tempered you might become worthless both to other people and to your husband. If you become less esteemed by him, and he becomes as less esteemed by you, or if you love him a great deal and he thinks little of you, it will grieve you so greatly that you will readily, as many do, make poison for him, and give suffering in the place of a cure. Another woman who does not wish to do such a thing will pay witches and forsake Christ and her Christianity and true belief in order to attract his love towards her. Now what happiness may this woman who loves her husband well enjoy, if she is hateful to him, or wins his love in this manner?

{On sex and pregnancy}

For Gode, þah hit nere neaver for Godes luve, ne for hope of heovene, ne for dred of helle, þu ahtest, wummon, þis werc for þi flesches halschipe, for þi licomes luve, ant ti bodies heale, over
155 alle þing to schunien. For ase Seinte Pawel seið, euch sunne þet me deð is wiðute þe bodi bute þis ane. Alle þe oþre sunen ne beoð bute sunnen; ah þis is sunne ant ec uncumelecheð þe ant unwurdgeð þi bodi, suleð þi sawle ant makeð schuldi towart Godd, ant fuleð þi flesch ec. Gulteð o twa half: wreaðest þen Alwealdent wið þet suti sunne, ant dest woh to þe seolf ant tu al willes se scheomeliche tukest. Ga we nu forðre, ant loki we hwuch wunne ariseð þrefter i burðerne of bearne, hwen þet
160 streon in þe awakeneð ant waxeð. Ant hu monie earmðen anan awakeneð þerwið, þe wurcheð þe wa inoh, fehteð o þi seolve flesch, ant weorrið wið feole weanen o þin ahne cunde? Þi rudie neb schal leanin, ant ase gres grenin; þine ehnen schule doskin ant underneoðe wonnin; ant of þi breines turnunge þin heaved aken sare. Inwið i þi wombe, swel in þi butte þe bereð þe forð as a weater-bulge; þine þearmes þralunge ant stiches i þi lonke; ant i þi lendene sar eche rive; hevinesse
165 in euch lim, þine breostes burþerne o þine twa pappes ant te milc-strunden þe þerof strikeð. Al is wið a weolewunge þi wlite overwarpen; þi muð is bitter, ant walh al þet tu cheowest; ant hwet se þi mahe hokerliche underveð (þet is wið unlust) warpeð hit eft ut. Inwið al þi weole ant ti weres wunne, forwurðest a wrecche. Þe carest aȝein þi pinunge þrahen bineomeð þe nahtes slepes. Hwen hit þenne þerto kimeð – þet sore sorhfule angoise, þet stronge ant stikinde stiche, þet
170 unroles uvel, þet pine over pine, þet wondrinde ȝeomerunge, hwil þu swenchest terwið, ant þine deaðes dute – scheome teke þet sar wið þe alde wifes scheome creft þe cunnen of þet wa-sið, hwas help þe bihoveð, ne beo hit neaver se uncumelich. Ant nede most hit þolien þet te þerin itimeð. Ne þunche þe nan uvel of, for we ne edwiteð nawt wifes hare weanen, þet ure alre modres drehden on us seolven; ah we schawið ham forð for te warni meiðnes þet ha beon þe leasse efterwart swuch
175 þing, ant witen herþurh þe betere hwet ham beo to donne.

{Concluding exhortation on virginity}

Forþi, eadi meiden, Godes sunes spuse, ne beo þu nawt to trusti ane to þi meidhad, wiðuten oðer god ant þeawfule mihtes ant, over al, miltschipe ant meokeschipe of heorte, efter þe forbisne of þet eadi meiden over alle oðre, Marie, Godes moder. For þa þe hehengel Gabriel grette hire ant brohte hire to tidinge of Godes akennesse, loke hu lah ha lette hire þa ha ontswerede þus bi
180 hireseolven: 'Efter þi word', quoð ha, 'mote me iwurðen. Low, her mi Laverdes þrel.' Ant tah ha ful were of alle gode þeawes, ane of hire meokelec ha seide ant song to Elizabeth: 'For mi Laverd biseh þis þuftenes meokelec, me schulen cleopien', quoð ha, 'eadi alle leoden.'

Nim ȝeme, meiden, ant understont herbi þet mare for hire meokelec þen for hire meiðhad ha lette þet ha ifont swuch grace ed ure Laverd. For al meiðhad, meokelec is muche wurð; ant meiðhad
185 wiðuten hit is eðelich ant unwurð, for alswa is meiden i meiðhad bute meokeschipe as is widute liht eolie in a lampe. Eadi Godes spuse, have þeos ilke mihte þet tu ne þunche þeostri ah schine ase sunne i ti weres sihðe. Feahe þi meiðhad wið alle gode þeawes þe þuncheð him feire. Have eaver i þin heorte þe eadieste of meidnes ant meiðhades moder, ant bisech hire aa þet ha þe lihte,

(The author now turns his attention to child-bearing and the woes that befall the mother whether her child is born healthy or not. Pregnancy, naturally arising from intercourse, and labour form the focus of the following section.)

{On Sex and Pregnancy}

For God's sake, even if it were never for God's love, or for the hope of heaven, or for the dread of hell, you ought, woman, for the wholeness of your flesh, for the respect of your body, and for your body's health, to shun this above all things. For as Saint Paul says, each sin that people do is external to the body except this alone.[13] All the other sins are but sin; yet this is a sin and it also ruins you and disgraces your body, sullies your soul and makes you guilty before God, and it also defiles your flesh. You are guilty in two ways: you make the Almighty angry with that dirty sin, and you do harm to yourself so that you entirely voluntarily injure yourself shamefully. Let us proceed further now, and look at what joy arises after this in the carrying of a child, when that child within you comes into being and grows. And how many afflictions come into being at once with this, which make you miserable enough, contend with your flesh itself, and war on your own nature with many sorrows? Your rosy face will grow lean, and become as green as grass; your eyes will grow dim and their underneath will shadow; and from your brains' churning your head will ache sorely. Within your stomach, swelling in your womb will make you expand out like a water-bag; your bowels will be painful and cause stitches in your side; and in your loins the pain will be plentiful. There will be heaviness in every limb, and weight from your breasts and your two nipples because of the streams of milk that flow from them. With a pallor your beauty is entirely eliminated; your mouth tastes bitter, and all that you eat is nauseating; and whatever your stomach scornfully receives (and that is with disgust), it throws up again. In the middle of all your joy and your husband's happiness, you deteriorate into a wretch. You are anxious about your pains in labour which deprives you of sleep at night. Then when it comes to that – that pain and sorrowful anguish, that persistent and wounding cramp, that unceasing pain, that pain beyond pain, that restless moaning, while you are labouring from this, as well as your fear of death – you have shame in addition to that pain with the shameful craft of the old wives who know of that painful experience, whose help you are obliged to have, whether it is immodest or not. And in there by necessity you have to endure it whatever the outcome for you. Do not consider any of this as evil, for we do not blame women at all for their miseries which all our mothers endured for us ourselves; but we show them in order to warn virgins so that they might pursue such things the less, and perceive through this what they should do for the better.

(The author now begins to move towards his conclusion, reiterating for emphasis many points he has made about love, marriage and children. He advises the virgin to give birth to the spiritual children, such as prudence and moderation. At all costs, though, the virgin must avoid the sin of pride in her achievement as a pure maiden: a humble married woman or widow is spiritually superior to a proud virgin.)

{Concluding exhortation on virginity}

Therefore blessed maiden, bride of God's son, do not put too much trust in your virginity only, without other good and virtuous merits, and, above all, mildness and meekness of heart, following the example of the virgin blessed over all others, Mary, God's mother. For when the archangel Gabriel greeted her and brought her tidings of God's conception, look how humbly she thought of herself when she answered this about herself: 'As it is according to your word, may it so happen. Look, here is the handmaiden of my Lord.' And though she was filled with all good virtues, she spoke of her meekness alone, and sang to Elizabeth: 'Because my Lord has looked on his handmaiden's meekness, all peoples', she said, 'will call me blessed.'[14]

Take note, virgin, and understand by this that she thought it was more for her meekness than her virginity that she had found grace with our Lord. In the case of all virginity, meekness is very valuable; and virginity without it is a worthless and unesteemed thing, for a virgin in a life of virginity without

13   I Corinthians 6.18.   14   Luke 1.38, 48.

ant ȝeove luve ant strengðe for te folhin i meiðhad hire þeawes. Þench o Seinte Katerine, o Seinte
190 Margarete, Seinte Enneis, Seinte Juliene, ant Seinte Cecille, ant o þe oþre hali meiðnes in heovene:
hu ha nawt ane ne forsoken kinges sunes ant eorles, wið alle worldliche weolen ant eorðliche
wunnen, ah þoleden stronge pinen ear ha walden neomen ham ant derf deað on ende. Þench hu
wel ham is nu, ant hu ha blissið þervore bituhe Godes earmes, cwenes of heovene.

Ant ȝef hit eaver timeð þet ti licomes lust, þurh þe false feont, leaðie þe towart flesliche fulðen,
195 ontswere i þi þoht þus: 'Ne geineð þe nawt, sweoke! Þullich Ich chulle beon in meidenes liflade
– ilich heovene engel. Ich chulle halde me hal, þurh þe grace of Godd, as cunde me makede, þet
Paraise selhðe undervo me al swuch as weren, ear ha agulten, his eareste heamen. Allunge swuch
Ich chulle beon as is mi deore leofmon, mi deorewurðe Laverd, ant as þet eadi meiden þe he him
cheas to moder. Al swuch Ich chulle wite me treowliche unwemmet, as Ich am him iweddet. Ne
200 nulle Ich nawt for a lust of ane lutle hwile, þah hit þunche delit, awei warpe þet þing hwas lure
Ich schal biremen, widuten coverunge ant wið eche brune abuggen in helle. Þu wrenchwile ful
wiht! Al for nawt þu prokest me to forgulten, ant forgan þe blisse upo blisse, þe crune upo crune
of meidenes mede; ant willes ant waldes warpe me as wrecche i þi leirwite; ant for þet englene
song of meidhades menske, wið þe ant wið þine greden aa ant granin i þe eche grure of helle.'

205 Ȝef þu þus ontswerest to þi licomes lust ant to þe feondes fondunge, he schal fleo þe wið
scheome. Ant ȝef he alles efter þis inohreaðe etstonde ant halt on to eili þi flesch ant prokie þin
heorte, ti Laverd Godd hit þeaveð him to muchli þi mede. For as Seinte Pawel seið, ne bið nan
icrunet bute hwa se treoweliche i þulli feht fehte, ant wið strong cokkunge overcume hireseolf.
For þenne is þe deofel, wið his ahne turn, scheomeliche awarpen, hwen þu, as þe apostle seið, ne
210 schalt tu beon icrunet bute þu beo asailet. Ȝef Godd wule cruni þe, he wule leote ful wel þe
unwiht asaili þe, þet tu earni þerþurh kempene crune. Forþi hit is þe meast god þet hwen he
greved þe meast ant towart te wið fondunge wodeluker weorreð, ȝef þu wel wrist te under Godes
wengen. For þurh his weorre he ȝarkeð þe, unþonc in his teð, þe blisse ant te crune of Cristes
icorene.

215 Ant Jesu Crist leve hire, þurh þi blescede nome, alle þeo þe leaveð luve of lami mon for te beon
his leofmon. Ant leve ham swa hare heorte halden to him þet hare flesches eggunge, ne þe feondes
fondunge, ne nan of his eorðliche limen ne wori hare heorte wit ne wrenche ham ut of þe wei þet
ha beoð in iȝongen. Ant helpe ham swa in him to hehin towart heovene, aþet ha beon istihe þider
as hare brudlac schal, in al þet eaver sel is, wið þene seli brudgume þet siheð alle selhðe of sitten
220 buten ende. Amen.

meekness is like oil in a lamp without being lit. Blessed bride of God, possess this same virtue so that you might not appear dark but will shine like the sun in your husband's sight. Adorn your virginity with all the good virtues that appear fair to him. Have ever in your heart the most blessed of virgins and mother of virginity, and beseech her to enlighten you always, and give you love and strength to follow her virtues in virginity. Consider Saint Catherine, Saint Margaret, Saint Agnes, Saint Juliana, and Saint Cecilia, and the other holy virgins in heaven: how they not only forsook kings' sons and noblemen, with all their worldly wealth and earthly joys, but prefered to suffer cruel tortures and a painful death in the end, rather than receive them. Think how fortunate they are now, and how they rejoice because of this in the arms of God as queens of heaven.

And if it ever occurs that your bodily lust, because of the false enemy, might encourage you towards physical filth, answer in your thoughts like this: 'It is no use, traitor! I shall stay like this in the life of a virgin – like a heavenly angel. I shall hold myself whole, through the grace of God, as nature has made me, so that Paradise's bliss will receive me just as they, those first inhabitants, were before their sin. I shall be entirely like this as is my beloved sweetheart, my dear Lord, and as is that blessed virgin whom he chose as his mother. I shall maintain myself entirely like this, truly innocent, as I am now married to him. And I will not for a fleeting moment, though it might seem joyful, throw away that thing the loss of which I shall rue; for it is without recovery and I would pay for it with eternal burning in hell. You devil, eager to deceive! All for nothing you urge me to sin, and give up the bliss upon bliss, the crown upon crown of a virgin's reward; and willingly and voluntarily throw myself as a wretch into your punishment for fornication; and in place of that angels' song of virginity's virtue, with you and with yours lament and groan forever in the perpetual horror of hell.'

If you answer your physical lust and the fiend's encouragement like this, he will flee from you in shame. And if after this he resists at all and holds on to afflict your flesh and incite your heart, your Lord God permits him to do it to increase your reward. For as Saint Paul says, none is crowned except she who overcomes herself faithfully in such a fight, and with a strong battle. For then the devil, with his own strategy, is shamefully overthrown, since you, as the apostle says, will not be crowned unless you have been assailed.[15] If God wants to crown you, he will, without doubt, allow the devil to assail you so that you can earn through that the victor's crown. Therefore it is most beneficial for you that when he troubles you most and fights against you more furiously with his temptations, that you protect yourself well under God's wings. For through his attack he makes ready for you the bliss and the crown of Christ's chosen, in spite of himself.

And may Jesus Christ, through your blessed name, grant this to her, and to all those who forgo the love of a man of clay in order to be his sweetheart. And grant that they hold their hearts for him so that neither their body's incitement, nor the fiend's temptations, nor any of his earthly agents may afflict their hearts, or turn them aside from the way that they have gone. And help them, through him, to hurry towards heaven so that they may rise there where their marriage shall be, in all that will always be blessed, with that blessed bridegroom, who is the fount of all bliss that lasts without end. Amen.

---

15   From 2 Timothy 2.5 and I Corinthians 9. 24–7. The motif here
is that of the 'soldier of Christ', a very common topos in religious
writings seeking to encourage perserverance in Christian practice.

Ancrene Wisse

Ancrene Wisse, 'A Guide to Anchoresses', is also known in some manuscripts as *Ancrene Riwle*, 'The Anchoresses' Rule'. There are eleven manuscript versions of all, or part, of the English text that date from *c.*1225 to the fifteenth century; four versions of the text translated into French; and four manuscripts containing the Latin translation. The fact the work was translated into French and Latin demonstrates the high regard in which it was held; and the total number of copies illustrate the text's longevity and popularity. Of the manuscript versions written in English, Corpus Christi College, Cambridge 402, folios 1 to 117 verso, dated to the middle of the thirteenth century, is considered the closest to the author's final revised text, and it thus forms the basis for the edition of extracts below.

The work was originally conceived by the author in response to a request from three sisters (possibly sisters within a religious order, or, indeed, related sisters) for spiritual guidance as they embarked on the life of an anchoress. This religious undertaking involved the woman (or man, if an anchorite) in cutting herself off from society in an ascetic life dedicated to penitence and the contemplation of God. The anchoress, with the permission of the bishop, would enter a small dwelling attached to the wall of a church or monastery, where she would live out the remainder of her life in her devotions. While this solitary vocation seems quite alien to most modern readers, it was a relatively popular career choice for religiously inclined women and men in the medieval period. This was particularly the case from the later twelfth century onwards, partially as a result of a spiritual movement that reflected a desire for closer communion with God, and a concomitant feeling of contempt for things of the world. Famous anchoresses include Christina of Markyate, Loretta, Countess of Leicester, and Julian of Norwich.

The *Ancrene Wisse* seeks to provide both spiritual and practical assistance to the anchoresses in their choice of religious life. The author divides his work into a Preface and eight books, as he outlines in the Preface edited below. The work deals with essential aspects of daily life including all kinds of detail such as what the anchoresses should wear; how they should deal with their servants; and what prayers they should perform and when. The Preface describes the author's intentions in writing the work, and the way in which rules are to be understood; he also discusses the issue of what religious order the anchoresses might belong to. Books 1 and 8, the Outer

Rule, illustrate how the anchoress should seek to describe her vocation, and how she ought to live from day to day. Books 2–7, the Inner Rule, consist of a thorough description of how the women should develop spiritually: how they should perform their devotions, ward off temptation, be thorough in their confession and repentance, and seek to understand what the love of God entails.

As is the case with the texts of 'The Katherine Group', little is known of the author of the text. He was possibly an Augustinian canon, or, as seems more likely, a member of the Dominican order. He draws widely on patristic and theological writings (some of which may be quite contemporary with the author himself) in the compilation of his text, and reworks them to give an ordered and detailed outline of many aspects of the ascetic religious vocation as he would wish to see it practised. He is a sympathetic and realistic director allowing the women flexibility within the guidelines he lays out, depending on their abilities and strength. He assumes a certain degree of education in some of his audience, but allows for the possibility that some of the anchoresses or their servants will not be literate.

The extracts edited here represent a very small selection from what is a lengthy work.[1] The whole of the Preface, and parts of books 2, 3, 7 and 8 are given. In these extracts, the author's intentions are described in the Preface, together with a discussion of what it means to be an anchoress. Book 2, 'On the Senses', is represented here by the beginning of the author's depiction of sight, and his use of the exemplum of Eve, to warn the anchoresses against the dangers of the senses. Book 3, 'On the Inner Feelings', is illustrated by the exemplum of the pelican that begins this book, with part of the subsequent discussion of anger. From book 7, 'On Love', the extract chosen is the famous extended metaphor of Christ as the lover-knight, and the following explanation of the four kinds of love. The extracts from book 8, the 'Outer Rule', include part of the author's instructions concerning the women's clothing, together with the concluding advice on how the anchoresses should treat their servants, and read from the *Ancrene Wisse* often.

While the work as originally conceived was designed for three aristocratic sisters embarking on an anchoritic life, the text in Corpus 402 has been adapted by the author to include a larger group of religious solitaries. A late twelfth-century inscription at folio 1 recto of the manuscript indicates that this volume was given to

1   The whole work is edited diplomatically by J. R. R. Tolkien, ed., *Ancrene Wisse Edited from MS. Corpus Christi College Cambridge 402*, EETS o.s. 249 (London, 1962). Books 7 and 8 are edited and translated in Millett and Wogan-Browne, *Medieval English Prose for*

Women. Books 6 and 7 are edited by G. Shepherd, ed., *Ancrene Wisse* (London, 1959). The entire work is translated by M. Salu, *The Ancrene Riwle* (London, 1955), and by H. White, *Ancrene Wisse: Guide for Anchoresses*, Penguin Classics (London, 1993).

Wigmore Abbey in Herefordshire for the religious community there.

Ancrene Wisse is related by its language and stylistic elements to works in 'The Katherine Group'. The language is essentially that known as AB language, a relatively consistent literary dialect originating in the West Midlands.[2] There is a higher proportion of French loanwords in this text than in those of 'The Katherine Group'; for example, *grace, ordre, religiun, chapitres, parlurs, chastete, prisun, leattres, saluz* and *deboneirte*. Stylistically, this author frequently uses homiletic techniques such as biblical exegesis, incorporating excerpts from the Bible in Latin which are usually translated into English immediately afterwards; and the rhetorical devices of repetition, rhetorical questions, metaphor and simile, exhortation, admonition, and direct address in order to assist the understanding of his audience and to seek their engagement with the text.[3] The alliterative prose of the author provides a regular rhythm consisting of a regular two-stress phrase that is especially effective when read aloud. The author's tone is one of patient encouragement and guidance rather than the vigorous persuasive tone of the author of *Hali Meiðhad*. A flexible approach also underlies the *Ancrene Wisse* author's attitude to his audience, rather than the hyperbole, antitheses, negative examples and successive polemic statements of the *Hali Meiðhad* author.

Ancrene Wisse

Preface

In þe Feaderes and i þe Sunes ant i þe Hali Gastes nome, her biginneð *Ancrene Wisse. Recti diligunt te (in Canticis sponsa ad sponsum). Est rectum grammaticum, rectum geometricum, rectum theologicum, et sunt differencie totidem regularum. De recto theologico sermo nobis est, cuius regule due sunt: una circa cordis directionem; altera versatur circa exteriorum rectificationem. Recti diligunt te.* 'Laverd', seið Godes spuse
5   to hire deorewerðe spus, 'þe rihte luvieð þe.' Þeo beoð rihte þe luvieð efter riwle. Ant ȝe, mine leove sustren, habbeþ moni dei icravet on me after riwle. Monie cunne riwlen beoð, ah twa beoð bimong alle þet Ich chulle speoken of, þurh ower bone, wið Godes grace. Þe an riwleð þe heorte ant makeð efne ant smeðe, wiðute cnost ant dolc of woh inwit ant of wreiȝende, þe segge: 'Her þu sunegest', oþer 'Þis nis nawt ibet ȝet ase wel as hit ahte.' Þeos riwle is eaver inwið ant rihteð þe
10   heorte. *Et hec est caritas quam describit Apostolus de corde puro et consciencia bona et fide non ficta.* Þeos riwle is chearite of schir heorte ant cleane inwit ant treowe bileave. *'Pretende,' inquit Psalmista, 'misericordiam tuam scientibus te' per fidem non fictam, 'et iusticiam tuam', id est, vite rectitudinem, 'hiis qui recto sunt corde', qui scilicet omnes voluntates suas dirigunt ad regulam divine voluntatis. Isti dicuntur boni 'antonomasice'. Psalmista: 'Benefac, Domine, bonis et rectis corde'; istis dicitur ut glorientur testimonio*
15   *videlicet bone consciencie: 'Gloriamini omnes recti corde', quos scilicet rectificavit regula illa suprema rectificans omnia; de qua Augustinus: 'Nichil petendum preter regulam magisterii'; et Apostolus: 'Omnes in eadem regula permaneamus.'*
      Þe oþer riwle is al wiðuten ant riwleð þe licome ant licomliche deden. Þe teacheð al hu me schal beoren him wiðuten: hu eoten, drinken, werien, singen, slepen, wakien. *Et hec est exercitio corporis*
20   *que iuxta Apostolum modicum valet, et est quasi regula recti mechanici quod geometrico recto continetur.* Ant þeos riwle nis nawt bute forte servi þe oþer. Þe oþer is as leafdi; þeos as hire þuften. For al þet me eaver deð of þe oþer wiðuten, nis bute forte riwlin þe heorte wiðinnen.
      Nu easki ȝe hwet riwle ȝe ancren schulen halden. Ȝe schulen alles weis wið alle mihte ant strengðe wel witen þe inre, ant te uttre for hire sake. Þe inre is eaver ilich, þe uttre is mislich, for
25   euch schal halden þe uttre efter þet ha mei best wið hire servi þe inre. Nu þenne, is hit swa þet alle ancren mahen wel halden an riwle *'quantum ad puritatem cordis circa quam uersatur tota religio'*; þet is, alle mahen ant ahen halden a riwle onont purte of heorte; þet is cleane ant schir inwit – *consciencia* – wiðuten weote of sunne þet ne beo þurh schrift ibet. Þis makeð þe leafdi riwle þe

2   It is possible that the original text of the *Ancrene Wisse* may have originated further north in the Midlands area. See Millett, *Annotated Bibliographies of Old and Middle English Literature*, pp. 8–13, for the debate on the language and origins of the text. Millett (p. 13) suggests that there may be a connection between the author and the Dominican priory at Shrewsbury, in Shropshire.

3   G. Shepherd provides an excellent and detailed analysis of the rhetoric of books 6 and 7 in *Ancrene Wisse*, pp. lix–lxxiii.

Ancrene Wisse

Preface

In the name of the Father, and of the Son, and of the Holy Spirit, here begins *Ancrene Wisse.* The right-eous love you (the bride to the bridegroom in Canticles).[4] There is a grammatical rule, a geometrical rule, a theological rule, and there are as many differences in the rules for each of them. Our discourse concerns the theological rule, for which there are two rules: one deals with the directing of the heart; the other with the rectifying of exterior things. 'The righteous love you.' 'Lord,' says God's bride to her precious husband, 'the righteous love you.' They are righteous who love according to the rule. And you, my beloved sisters, have for many days desired a rule from me. There are many kinds of rule, but there are two things concerning them all about which I shall speak because of your request, with God's grace. The one rules the heart and makes it even and smooth, without the bumps and pits of a harmful conscience and self-accusation, which says: 'Here you are sinning', or 'This is not remedied as well as it ought to be.' This rule is always within and guides the heart. It is the charity that the Apostle describes, which comes from a pure heart and a good conscience and true faith.[5] This rule is the charity of a pure heart and clean conscience and true faith. 'Extend', says the Psalmist, 'your mercy to those that know you' by true faith, 'and thy justice', that is, righteous life, 'to those that are right in heart',[6] that is to say, those who direct all their will to the rule of the divine will. These are called good antonomastically. The Psalmist: 'Do good, Lord, to those who are good and to the right in heart';[7] it is said to them that they should rejoice in the witness of a good conscience: 'Glory, all you of right heart',[8] that is, those who have been set right by the supreme rule that guides everything right; on which Augustine: 'Noth-ing must be sought against the rule of authority'; and the Apostle: 'We should all continue in the same rule.'[9]

The other rule is entirely external and rules the body and physical actions. It gives instruction all about how people should bear themselves externally: how to eat, drink, dress, sing, sleep, wake. And this is bodily exercise that, according to the Apostle, is moderately beneficial,[10] and is similar to the rule of correct mechanics, which is contained within correct geometry. And this rule is for nothing except to serve the other. The other is like a lady; this one is her handmaiden. For all that is ever done for the second, outer rule is only in order to rule the heart within.

Now you ask what rule you anchoresses should follow. You must in every way, with all your power and strength, keep the inner rule well, and the outer for its sake. The inner rule is always the same, the outer

---

4   Canticle of Canticles 1.3.
5   Saint Paul in I Timothy 1.5.
6   Psalm 35.11.
7   Psalm 124.4.
8   Psalm 31.11.
9   Saint Paul in Philippians 3.16.
10 Saint Paul in I Timothy 4.8.

riwleð ant rihteð ant smeðeð þe heorte ant te inwit of sunne, for nawt ne makeð hire woh bute
30   sunne ane. Rihten hire ant smeðin hire is of euch religiun ant of euch ordre þe god ant al þe
strengðe. Þeos riwle is imaket nawt of monnes fundles, ah is of Godes heaste. Forþi ha is eaver ant
an wiðute changunge, ant alle ahen hire in an eaver to halden. Ah alle ne mahe nawt halden a
riwle, ne ne þurue nawt ne ne ahe nawt halden on a wise þe uttre riwle, *quantum scilicet ad observantias*
corporales; þet is, onont licomliche locunges, efter þe uttre riwle, þet Ich þuften cleopede ant is
35   monnes fundles, for na þing elles istald bute to servi þe inre. Þe makeð feasten, wakien, calde ant
hearde werien, swucche oþre heardschipes þet moni fles mei þolien, moni ne mei nawt. Forþi mot
þeos changin hire misliche efter euchanes manere ant efter hire evene: for sum is strong, sum
unstrong, ant mei ful wel beo cwite ant paie Godd mid leasse. Sum is clergesse, sum nawt ant mot
te mare wurchen ant on oðer wise seggen hire bonen. Sum is ald ant eðelich ant is þe leasse dred
40   of; sum is ȝung ant luvelich ant is neod betere warde. Forþi schal euch ancre habben þe uttre riwle
efter hire schriftes read; ant hwet se he bit ant hat hire in obedience þe cnaweð hire manere ant
wat hire strengðe. He mei þe uttre riwle changin efter wisdom as he seið þet te inre mahe beo best
ihalden.

Nan ancre, bi mi read, ne schal makien professiun, þet is, bihaten ase heast, bute þreo þinges:
45   þet beoþ obedience, chastete, ant stude steaðelvestnesse, þet ha ne schal þet stude neaver mare
changin bute for nede ane; as strengðe ant deaðes dred, obedience of hire bischop oðer of his herre.
For hwa se nimeð þing on hond ant bihat hit Godd as heast forte don hit, ha bint hire þerto, ant
sunegeð deadliche i þe bruche ȝef ha hit brekeð willes. Ȝef ha hit ne bihat nawt, ha hit mei do þah
ant leaven hwen ha wel wule, as of mete, of drunch, flesch forgan oðer fisch, alle oþer swucche
50   þinges; of werunge, of liggunge, of ures, of oþre beoden, segge swa monie oðer o swucche wise.
Þeos ant þulliche oþre beoð alle ifreo wil, to don oðer to leten hwil me wule ant hwen me wule,
bute ha beon bihaten. Ah chearite – þet is luve ant eadmodnesse ant þolemodnesse, treoweschipe
ant haldunge of þe alde ten heastes, schrift ant penitence – þeos ant þulliche oþre, þe beoð summe
of þe alde lahe, summe of þe neowe, ne beoð nawt monnes fundles ne riwle þet mon stalde; ah
55   beoð Godes heastes. Ant forþi euch mon mot ham nede halden, ant ȝe over alle, for þeos riwleð þe
heorte. Of hire riwlunge is almeast þet Ich write, bute i þe frumðe of þis boc, ant i þe leaste ende.

Þe þinges þet Ich write her of þe uttre riwle, ȝe ham haldeð alle, mine leove sustren, ure Laverd
beo iþonket, ant schulen þurh his grace se lengre se betere. Ant þah nulle Ich nawt þet ȝe bihaten
ham as heaste to halden, for as ofte as ȝe þrefter breken eni of ham, hit walde to swiðe hurten ower
60   heorte ant makien ow swa offearet, þet ȝe mahten sone, þet Godd forbeode ow, fallen i desesperance;
þet is, in an unhope ant an unbileave forte beon iborhen. Forþi þet Ich write ow, mine leove
sustren, of uttre þinges i þe earste dale of ower boc of ower servise, ant nomeliche i þe leaste, ȝe ne
schule nawt bihaten hit; ah habbeð hit on heorte ant doð hit as þah ȝe hit hefden bihaten.

Ȝef ei unweote easkeð ow of hwet ordre ȝe beon, as summe doð, ȝe telleð me, þe siheð þe gneat
65   ant swolheð þe flehe, ondswerieð 'Of Sein James, þe wes Godes apostel, ant for his muchele
halinesse icleopet Godes broðer.' Ȝef him þuncheð wunder ant sullich of swuch ondswere, easkið
him hwet beo 'ordre' ant hwer he funde in hali writ religiun openlukest descrivet ant isutelet þen
is in Sein James canonial epistel. He seiþ 'What is Religiun? Hwuch is riht ordre?' *Religio munda*
et immaculata apud Deum et Patrem hec est: visitare pupillos et viduas in necessitate sua, et immaculatum se
70   *custodire ab hoc seculo.* Þet is 'Cleane religiun ant withute wem is iseon ant helpen wydues ant
feaderlese children, ant from þe world witen him cleane ant unwemmet.' Þus Sein Jame descriveþ
religiun ant ordre. Þe leatere dale of his sahe limpeð to reclusen, for þer beoþ twa dalen to twa
manere þe beoð of religiuse: to eiðer limpeð his dale as ȝe mahen iheren. Gode religiuse beoð i þe
world summe, nomeliche prelaz ant treowe preachurs þe habbeð þe earre dale of þet Sein Jame
75   seide; þet beoð, as he seið, þe gað to helpen wydewes ant faderlese children. Þe sowle is widewe þe
haveð forloren hire spus, þet is, Jesu Crist, wið eni heaved sunne. Þe is alswa federles þe haveð
þurh his sunne forloren þe Feader of heovene. Gan iseon þulliche ant elnin ham ant helpen wið
fode of hali lare, þis is riht religiun, he seið Sein Jame. Þe leatere dale of his sahe limpeð to ower
religiun, as Ich ear seide, þe witeð ow from þe worlt over oþre religiuse cleane ant unwemmet.

is variable, and each person shall maintain the outer in a way that may best serve the inner. Now then, it is the case that all anchoresses can hold one rule well 'with respect to purity of heart with which all religion is concerned'; that is, all can and ought to maintain a rule in respect of purity of heart; that is, with a clean and spotless conscience – *consciencia* – without awareness of sin that has not been absolved through confession. This is what the lady rule does, that rules and corrects and smooths the heart and the conscience of sin, for nothing makes the heart crooked except sin alone. Making it right and smoothing it, is, as far as each religious person and each order is concerned, good and their strength entirely. This rule is not made from man's imagination, but is from God's commands. Therefore it is permanent and the same, without changing, and all ought to keep it the same always. But all are not able to maintain the one rule, and need not, and ought not to hold to the same outer rule in one manner, 'with respect, that is, to observances concerning the body'; that is, with respect to physical observances, according to the outer rule that I have called the handmaiden and which is an invention of man, established only to serve the inner. It discusses fasting, keeping vigil, wearing cold or uncomfortable things, and such other hardships which the flesh of many can endure, but which many cannot. Therefore this rule may be changed variously according to the condition and abilities of each person; for one is strong, one is weak, and may very well be excused and may please God with less. One person is scholarly, one is not and must do more work and say her prayers in other ways. One is old and feeble and is the less to be feared for; one is young and lovely and needs to be better guarded. Therefore each anchoress shall observe the outer rule according to her confessor's advice; and do what he asks or demands of her under obedience, he who knows her situation and her strength. He may change the outer rule as his wisdom sees it, so that the inner rule may best be maintained.

No anchoress, by my advice, will make a profession, that is, make promises of obligation, except to three things: these are obedience, chastity, and stability of place, so that they should never more change their place of living except for necessity alone; such as by force and fear of death, or in obedience to her bishop or to his superior. For whoever takes such a thing in hand and promises to God that she will do it as if it were a command, binds herself by that, and sins mortally in its breaking, if she breaks it of her own free will. If she promises none of that though, she may do it and cease whenever she wishes, such as in her eating, drinking, forgoing meat or fish, or all such other things; with clothing, resting, saying her hours with other prayers, saying as many or in whatever way. These, and other such things, are all left to free will, to do or to leave them while one wants to and when one wants to, unless they have been promised. But charity – that is, love and humility and patience, loyalty and the keeping of the ten old commandments, confession and penitence – these, and other such matters, some belonging to the old law, some to the new, are not the creation of man or a rule established by man; but they are God's commands. And for that reason each person must by necessity keep them, and you above all, because these rule the heart. Virtually all my writing is about the ruling of the heart, except at the beginning of this book, and at the very end.

The things that I write about here concerning the outer rule, you keep them all, my dear sisters, our Lord be thanked, and may you continue to do so, for the longer the better. And yet I would not want you to hold them as commands, for after that, as often as you broke any of them, it would cause too much hurt to your hearts and make you so very afraid, that you might soon, and may God prevent you from it, fall into despair; that is, into a lack of hope and trust in your salvation. Therefore, what I write for you, my beloved sisters, about external things in the first part of your book about your devotions, and certainly in the last part, you should not promise; but have it in your heart and do it as though you had promised them.

If any ignorant person should ask you of which order you are, as some people do, so you tell me, who strain the gnat[11] and swallow the fly, answer 'Of Saint James, who was God's Apostle, and for his great holiness is called God's brother.' If such an answer seems a wonder to him, ask him what an 'order' is and where he is able to find in the holy scriptures religion more openly described and plainly put than in Saint James's canonical epistle. He says 'What is religion? Which is the true order?' Religion clean and undefiled before God and the Father is this: to visit the fatherless and widows in their tribulation, and to keep oneself unspotted from this world.[12] That is 'Pure and spotless religion is to visit and help widows

---

11   i.e. strain the liquid in order to get rid of any gnats in it.   12   James 1.27.

80   Þus þe apostle Sein Jame, þe descriveð religiun, nowðer hwit ne blac ne nempneð he in his ordre.
Ah moni siheð þe gneat ant swolheð þe flehe; þet is, makeð muche strengðe þer as is þe leaste.
Pawel þe earste ancre, Antonie ant Arsenie, Makarie ant te oþre, neren ha religiuse ant of Sein
James ordre? Alswa Seinte Sare ant Seinte Sincletice, ant monie oþre swucche, wepmen ba ant
wummen, wið hare greate matten ant hare hearde heren, neren ha of god ordre? Ant hweðer hwite

85   oðer blake, as unwise ow easkið, þe weneð þet ordre sitte i þe curtel? Godd wat, noðeles, ha weren
wel baðe. Nawt tah onont claðes, ah as Godes spuse singeð bi hireseolven '*Nigra sum, sed formosa.*'
'Ich am blac ant tah hwit', ha seið: unseowlich wiðuten, schene wiðinnen. O þis wise ondswerieð
to þe easkeres of ower ordre hweðer hwite oðer blake; seggeð ȝe beoð ba twa, þurh þe grace of
Godd, ant of Sein James ordre, þet he wrat leatere: *Inmaculatum se custodire ab hoc seculo*; þet is þet

90   Ich seide ear, from þe worlt witen him cleane ant unwemmet. Herin is religiun: nawt i þe wide
hod ne i þe blake cape, ne i þe hwite rochet ne i þe greie cuuel. Þer as monie beoð igedered
togederes, þer for anrednesse, me schal makie strengðe of annesse of claðes, ant of oþer hwet of
uttre þinges þet te annesse wiðuten bitacni þe annesse of a luve ant of a wil þet ha alle habbeð i
meane wiðinnen. Wið hare habit, þet is an, þet euch haveð swuch as oþer, ant alswa of oðer hwet,

95   ha ȝeiȝeð þet ha habbeð alle togederes a luve ant a wil, euch alswuch as oþer. Loke þet ha ne lihen.
Þus hit is i cuvent; ah hwer se wummon liveð oðer mon bi him ane, hearmite oðer ancre, of þinges
wiðuten hwer of scandle ne cume nis nawt muche strengðe. Hercne Michee: *Indicabo tibi, o homo,
quid sit bonum et quid Deus requirat a te: utique facere judicium et justiciam et sollicite ambulare cum
Domino Deo tuo.* 'Ich chulle schawi þe, mon,' seið þe hali Michee, Godes prophete, 'Ich chulle

100 schawi þe soðliche hwet is godd, ant hwuch religiun ant hwuch ordre, hwuch halinesse Godd
easkeð of þe.' Low þis. Understond hit. Do wel ant dem wac eaver þe seolven, ant, wið dred ant
wið luve, ga mid Godd ti Laverd. Þer as þeose þinges beoð, þer is riht religiun; þer is soð ordre;
ant do al þet oðer ant lete þis nis bute trichunge ant a fals gile. *Ve vobis, scribe et pharisei, ypocrite, qui
mundatis quod deforis est calicis et parapsidis, intus autem pleni estis omni spurcitia similes sepulcris dealbatis.*

105 Al þet gode religiuse doð oþer werieð efter þe uttre riwle, al togedere is hervore. Al nis bute ase
tole to timbrin her towart; al nis bute as þuften to servi þe leafdi to riwlin þe heorte.
Þis an boc is todealet in eahte leasse bokes.
Nu mine leove sustren, þis boc Ich todeale on eahte destinctiuns, þet ȝe cleopieð dalen, ant
euch, wiðute monglunge, spekeð al bi himseolf of sunderliche þinges; ant þah euch an riht falleð

110 efter oðer, ant is þe leatere eaver iteiet to þe earre.
Þe earste dale spekeð al of o wer servise.
Þe oðer is hu ȝe schulen þurh ower fif wittes witen ower heorte þet ordre ant religiun ant sawle
lif is inne. I þis destinctiun aren chapitres five, as fif stuchen efter fif wittes þe witeð þe heorte as
wakemen hwer se ha beoð treowe; ant spekeð of euch wit sunderlepes o rawe.

115 Þe þridde dale is of anes cunnes fuheles þe Davið i þe sawter eveneð himseolf to as he were
ancre; ant hu þe cunde of þe ilke fuheles beoð ancren iliche.
Þe feorðe dale is of fleschliche fondunges, ant gasteliche baðe, ant confort aȝeines ham ant of
hare salven.
Þe fifte dale is of schrift.

120 Þe seste dale is of penitence.
Þe seoveðe of schir heorte: hwi me ah ant hwi me schal Jesu Crist luvien, ant hwet binimeð us
his luve ant let us him to luvien.
Þe eahtuðe dale is al of þe uttre riwle: earst of mete ant of drunch, ant of oþre þinges þet falleð
þerabuten; þrefter of þe þinges þe ȝe mahen undervon ant hwet þinges ȝe mahen witen oðer

125 habben; þrefter of ower claðes ant of swucche þinges as þerabuten falleð; þrefter of ower werkes, of
doddunge ant of blodletunge, of ower meidnes riwle. Aleast hu ðe ham schulen leofliche learen.

and fatherless children, and to keep yourself pure and unspotted from the world.' In this way Saint James describes religion and order. The second part of his saying applies to recluses, for there are two parts for the two kinds of religion: to each applies its own part, as you may hear. There are some good religious in the world, namely prelates and faithful preachers who have the first part of what Saint James said; that is, as he says, they are those who go to the help of widows and fatherless children. The soul is the widow who has lost her spouse, that is, Jesus Christ, with any mortal sin. Likewise, the fatherless is he who has lost his heavenly Father through his sin. To go to visit such as these, and to comfort and help them with the nourishment of holy teaching, this is true religion, as says Saint James. The second part of his saying applies to your religion, as I said before, which protects you from the world, beyond those other religious, pure and spotless. In this way, the apostle Saint James, when he describes religion, does not mention anything about white or black in his order.

But there are many that strain the gnat and swallow the fly; that is, they use great strength where there is the least need. Paul, the first anchorite, Antony and Arsenius, Macarius and the others, were they not religious and of the order of Saint James? And Saint Sarah and Saint Syncletica, and many other such people, both men and women, with their coarse mattresses and their uncomfortable hairshirts, were not they of a good order? And what does it matter whether it was white or black, as those foolish people ask who think that an order is dictated by the habit? God knows even so, these saints were both. Not, however, concerning their clothes, but as God's bride sings about herself, 'I am black and yet comely.'[13] 'I am black and yet white', she says: unattractive externally but pure within. In this way answer those who ask of what order you are, whether white or black; say you are both of them, through the grace of God, and of Saint James's order, as he wrote in the latter part: 'To keep oneself unspotted in this world.'[14] In this lies religion: not in a wide hood or a black cape, nor in a white surplice nor in a grey cowl. Where many are gathered together for stability there, one ought to place some importance on the uniformity of clothing, and of other matters concerning exterior things so that the exterior uniformity symbolizes the unity of one love and of one will that they all have in common on the inside. With their one, similar habit, each will have the same as the other, and also in other things, they proclaim that they all have together the one love and the one will, each in the same way as another. Make sure that they do not lie. This is how it is in a community; but where the woman or a man lived by themselves, as a hermit or an anchoress, things on the outside, from which no scandal can come, are not very important. Listen to Micah: 'I will show thee, O man, what is good and what the Lord requires of you: truly, to do judgement and justice, and to walk solicitous with the Lord thy God.'[15] 'I shall show you, man,' says the holy Micah, God's prophet, 'I shall show you truly what is good and what religion and what order, and what holiness God asks of you.' Perceive this. Understand it. Do well, and judge yourself to be weak always, and, with fear and with love, walk with God your Lord. Where these things are, there is true religion; there is the true order; and to do all the rest and not do this is but trickery and a false deceit. Woe to you, scribes and Pharisees, hypocrites, who make clean the outside of the cup and the dish, but within yourselves are full of all uncleanness, similar to whitened sepulchres.[16]

All that good religious people do or wear following the outer rule, all of it together is laid out here. All this is nothing except as a tool to build towards this; all of it is only as a handmaiden to assist the lady to rule the heart.

This book is divided into eight smaller books.

Now my dear sisters, I am dividing this book into eight distinctions, which you call parts, and each, without overlapping, speaks all on its own about individual things; and even so, each one suitably comes after the other, and the subsequent one is linked to the former.

The first part is entirely about your devotions.

The second is about how you should, through your five senses, protect your heart in which order and religion and the life of the soul resides. In this part are five chapters, like five pieces concerning the five

---

13 Canticles 1.4. The Middle English author uses 'white' as a translation in contrast to *nigra* (black), but also to reinforce the argument about the type of order to which the anchoresses belong: both black *and* white.

14 James 1.27.

15 Micah 6.8.

16 Matthew 23.25, 27.

Book 2

Her Biginneð þe oþer dale of þe heorte warde þurh þe fif wittes

Omni custodia serva cor tuum quia ex ipso vita procedit. 'Wið alles cunnes warde dohter,' seið Salomon, 'wite wel þin heorte for sawle lif is in hire', ʒef ha is wel iloket. Þe heorte wardeins beoð þe fif wittes: sihðe ant herunge, smecchunge ant smeallunge, ant euch limes felunge. Ant we schulen
130 speoken of alle, for hwa se wit þeose wel he deð Salomones bode; he wit wel his heorte ant his sawle heale. Þe heorte is a ful wilde beast ant makeð moni liht lupe, as Seint Gregoire seið: *Nichil corde fugatius.* 'Na þing ne etflid mon sonre þen his ahne heorte.' Davið, Godes prophete, meande i sum time þet ha wes etsteart him: *Cor meum dereliquit me*; þet is 'Min heorte is edflohe me.' Ant eft he blisseð him ant seið þet ha wes icumen ham: *Invenit servus tuus cor suum.* 'Laverd,' he seið,
135 'min heorte is icumen aʒein eft. Ich hire habbe ifunden.' Hwen se hali mon, ant se wis ant se war, lette hire edstearten, sare mei an oðer of hire fluht carien. Ant hwer edbrec ha ut from Davið þe hali king, Godes prophete? Hwer? Godd wat, ed his ehþurl, þurh a sihðe þet he seh þurh a bihaldunge, as ʒe schulen efter iheren.

Forþi, mine leove sustren, þe leaste þet ʒe eaver mahen luvieð ower þurles. Alle beon ha lutle,
140 þe parlurs least ant nearewest. Þe clað in ham beo twafald: blac þet clað, þe cros hwit, wiðinnen ant wiðuten. Þet blake clað bitacneð þet ʒe beoð blake ant unwurð to þe world wiðuten, þet te soðe sunne haveð utewið forculet ow ant swa wiðuten as ʒe beoð unseowlich imaket ow þurh gleames of his grace. Þe hwite cros limpeð to ow, for þreo crosses beoð read, ant blac, ant hwit. Þe reade limpeð to þeo þe beoð for Godes luve wið hare blod schedunge irudet ant ireadet as þe
145 martirs weren; þe blake cros limpeð to þeo þe makieð i þe worlt hare penitence for ladliche sunnen; þe hwite limpeð ariht to hwit meidenhad ant to cleannesse, þet is muche pine wel forte halden. Pine is ihwer þurh cros idon to understonden. Þus bitacneð hwit cros þe warde of hwit chastete, þet is muche pine wel to biwitene. Þe blake clað alswa, teke þe bitacnunge, deð leasse eil to þe ehnen, ant is þiccre aʒein þe wind, ant wurse to seon þurh, ant halt his heow betere for wind
150 ant for oðerhwet. Lokið þet te parlures beo on eaver euch half feaste ant wel itachet; ant witeð þer ower ehnen leaste þe heorte edfleo ant wende ut as of Davið, ant ower sawle seccli sone se heo is ute. Ich write muchel for oþre þet nawiht ne rineð ow, mine leove sustren. For nabbe ʒe nawt te nome (ne ne schulen habben þurh þe grace of Godd) of totilde ancres, ne of tollinde locunges ne lates, þet summe oðerhwiles, weilawei, uncundeliche makieð. For aʒein cunde hit is ant unmeað
155 sulli wunder þet te deade dotie ant wið cwike worltmen wede þurh sunne.

senses which guard the heart like watchmen wherever they are faithful; and it speaks of each of the senses separately, in turn.

The third part is about types of bird to which David in the Psalter compared himself as if he were an anchorite; and how the nature of those birds is like that of anchorites.

The fourth part is about both fleshly and spiritual temptations, and how to comfort oneself against them, and about the remedies for them.

The fifth part is about confession.

The sixth is about penance.

The seventh is about purity of heart: why one ought to and must love Jesus Christ, and what deprives us of his love and prohibits us from loving him.

The eighth part is all about the outer rule; first about eating and drinking, and other things which fall into this category; thereafter, about the things that you may receive, and what things you can keep or have; after that, about your clothes and such things which fall into this area; after that, about your work, about cutting hair and blood-letting, about your servants' rule. Lastly, how you should treat them lovingly.

Book 2

Here begins the second part about guarding the heart through the five senses

'With all watchfulness keep thy heart, because life issues out from it.'[17] 'With all kinds of protection, daughter,' says Solomon, 'guard your heart well, for in it is the life of the soul', if it is well locked up. The heart's guardians are the five senses: sight and hearing, taste and smell, and feeling in every part of the body. And we shall speak of them all, for whoever protects these well does Solomon's command; he guards his heart well and the health of his soul. The heart is a very wild animal and makes many a sprightly leap, as Saint Gregory says: 'Nothing is more likely to escape than the heart.'[18] 'Nothing escapes from a man sooner than does his own heart.' David, God's prophet, grieved on one occasion that it had fled from him: 'My heart has forsaken me';[19] that is, 'My heart has fled from me.' And later he rejoiced and said that it had come home again, 'Your servant has found his heart.'[20] 'Lord,' he said, 'my heart has come back again. I have found it.' When so holy a man, so wise, and so wary allowed it to escape, others may be sorely afraid that theirs may escape. And where did it break out from David, the holy king, God's prophet? Where? God knows, at the window of his eye, through a sight that he looked on, as you shall hear afterwards.[21]

Therefore, my dear sisters, love your windows as little as you possibly can. Let them all be small, the parlour windows smallest and narrowest. The curtains in them should be twofold: a black cloth, the cross white, both inside and outside. The black cloth signifies that you are black and worthless to the outside world, and that the true sun has scorched you outwardly and made you unattractive on the outside in this way, through the light of his grace. The white cross belongs to you, for there are three crosses, red, and black, and white. The red belongs to those who, for the love of God, are made red and ruddy with the shedding of their blood as the martyrs were; the black cross belongs to those who do their penance in this world for loathsome sins; the white belongs fittingly to white virginity and to purity, which it is very painful to maintain well. By the cross this suffering is always to be perceived. In this way, the white cross symbolizes the guarding of pure chastity, which is protected with much suffering. The black cloth, likewise, in addition to its symbolism, does less harm to the eyes, and is thicker against the wind, and more difficult to see through, and it retains its colour better against the wind and other things. Look that the parlour window is always fastened and locked securely on both sides; and guard your eyes there, lest your heart escapes and goes out, as did David's, and your soul sickens as soon as it has gone out. Much of what I write is for others than you, my dear sisters, and does not touch you in any way. For you have not the reputation (nor shall you have it, by the grace of God) of anchoresses

17   Proverbs 4.23.
18   Gregory's *Pastoral Care*, 3.14.
19   Psalm 39.13.
20   2 Kings 7.27.

21   This refers to 2 Kings 11. When David saw Bathsheba, he was so overcome with lust that he committed adultery with her. This episode is used later in book 2 to demonstrate the danger of sight.

'Me leove sire,' seið sum, 'ant is hit nu se over uvel forte totin utwart?' ʒe hit is, leove suster, for
uvel þe þer kimeð of hit is uvel, ant over uvel to eaver euch ancre, nomeliche to þe ʒunge. Ant to
þe alde forþi þet ha to þe ʒungre ʒeoveð uvel forbisne, ant scheld to werien ham wið. For ʒef ei
edwit ham, þenne seggeð ha anan: 'Me sire, þeo deð alswa, þet is betere þen Ich am ant wat betere
160   þen Ich hwet ha haveð to donne.' Leove ʒunge ancre, ofte a ful haher smið smeoðeð a ful wac cnif:
þe wise folhe i wisdom, ant nawt i folie. An ald ancre mei do wel þet te þu dest uvele; ah totin ut
wiðuten uvel ne mei ower nowðer. Nim nu ʒeme hwet uuel beo icumen of totunge: nawt an uvel
ne twa; ah al þe wa þet nu is ant eaver ʒete wes ant eaver schal iwurðen, al com of sihðe. Þet hit beo
soð, lo her preove.

165   Lucifer, þurh þet he seh ant biheold on himseolf his ahne feiernesse, leop into prude ant bicom
of angel eatelich deovel. Of Eve, ure alde moder, is iwriten on alre earst in hire sunne hefde inʒong
of hire ehsihðe: *Vidit igitur mulier quod bonum esset lignum ad vescendum et pulcrum oculis aspectu que
delectabile et tulit de fructu eius et comedit deditque viro suo*; þet is, Eve biheold o þe forboden eappel ant
seh hine feier, ant feng to delitin i þe bihaldunge, ant toc hire lust þer toward, ant nom ant et
170   þrof, ant ʒef hire laverd. Low hu hali writ spekeð, ant hu inwardliche hit teleð hu sunne bigon.
Þus eode sihðe bivoren ant makede wei to uvel lust, ant com þe dede þrefter þet al moncun ifeleð.

Þes eappel, leove suster, bitacneð alle þe þing þet lust falleð to ant delit of sunne. Hwen þu
bihaldest te mon, þu art in Eve point: þu lokest o þe eappel. Hwa se hefde iseid to Eve þa ha weorp
earst hire ehe þron: 'A, Eve, went te awei þu warpest ehe o þi deað.' Hwet hefde ha iondsweret?
175   'Me, leove sire, þu havest woh. Hwerof chalengest tu me? Þe eappel þet Ich loki on is forbode me
to eotene, ant nawt to bihalden.' Þus walde Eve inohreaðe habben iondsweret. O mine leove
sustren, as Eve haveð monie dehtren þe folhið hare moder þe ondswerieð o þisse wise. 'Me wenest
tu,' seið sum, 'þet Ich wulle leapen on him þah Ich loki on him?' Godd wat, leove suster, mare
wunder ilomp. Eve þi moder leop efter hire ehnen; from þe ehe to þe eappel, from þe eappel i
180   Parais dun to þer eorðe, from þe eorðe to helle, þer ha lei i prisun fowr þusent ʒer ant mare, heo
ant hire were ba, ant demde al hire ofsprung to leapen al efter hire to deað wiðuten ende. Biginnunge
ant rote of al þis ilke reowðe wes a liht sihðe. Þus ofte, as me seið, of lutel muchel waxeð. Habbe
þenne muche dred, euch feble wummon, hwen þeo þe wes riht ta iwraht wið Godes honden, wes
þurh a sihðe biswiken ant ibroht into brad sunne þet al þe world overspreadde.

Book 3

{On the nature of birds and anchorites}

185   Mine leove sustren, alswa as ʒe witeð wel ower wittes utewið, alswa over alle þing, lokið þet ʒe
beon inwið softe ant milde, ant eadmode, swete ant swote iheortet, ant þolemode aʒein woh of
word þet me seið ow, ant werc þet me misdeð ow, leste ʒe al leosen. Aʒein bittre ancres Davið seið
þis vers: *Similis factus sum pellicano solitudinis, et cetera*. 'Ich am,' he seið, 'as pellican þe wuneð bi
him ane.' Pellican is a fuhel se weamod ant se wreaðful þet hit sleað ofte o grome his ahne briddes
190   hwen ha doð him teone, ant þenne sone þrefter hit wurð swiðe sari, ant makeð swiðe muche man,
ant smit himseolf wið his bile þet he sloh ear his briddes wið, ant draheð blod of his breoste, ant
wið þet blod acwikeð eft his briddes isleine.

Þis fuhel, pellican, is þe weamode ancre; hire briddes beoð hire gode werkes þet ha sleað ofte

who peep out, or use enticing looks and behaviour, as some do unnaturally on occasion, sadly. For it is against nature and an immoderate, amazing wonder that the dead[22] might adore those living men of the world, and become mad through sin.

'But, dear sir,' say some, 'and is it then so very evil to peep out?' Yes, it is, dear sister, because the evil that comes from that is evil, and it is always especially evil in each anchoress, especially in the young. And in the old this is because they set an evil example to the younger ones, and a shield with which they will be able to defend themselves. For if anyone admonishes them, they will say immediately: 'But, sir, she does it as well, she who is better than I am and knows better than I do what she ought to have done.' Beloved young anchoress, often a very skilful smith makes a very weak knife: follow the wise in wisdom, and not in folly. An old anchoress may do something that is fine for her which would be evil for you; but peeping out without any evil cannot be done by either of you. Pay attention now to what evil came about through looking: not one evil or two; for all the woe that is now and ever was, and ever shall be, all this came from sight. That this is the truth, look here at the proof.

Lucifer, because he saw and looked upon his own beauty, leapt into pride and from an angel he became a loathsome devil. Of Eve, our first mother, it is written that in all, the first place that her sin had entry was through her eyesight: 'And the woman saw that the tree was good to eat, and fair to the eyes, and fair to look at, and delightful to behold, and she took of the fruit of it, and ate it, and gave to her husband';[23] that is, Eve looked on the forbidden apple and saw that it was fair, and began to delight in looking at it, and directed her desire towards it there, and she took and ate some of it, and gave it to her lord. Look how the holy scripture speaks about this, and how it says that sin began within. In this way, sin went before and created the way for evil desire, and then came the deed afterwards that all mankind feels.

This apple, my beloved sister, symbolizes all the things on which desire and delight in sin alight. When you see a man, you are in Eve's situation: you are looking on the apple. Someone may have said to Eve, when her eyes lit upon it first: 'Ah, Eve, turn away, you cast your eyes on your death.' What would she have answered? 'But, dear Sir, you are wrong. Why are you accusing me? The apple at which I look is forbidden for me to eat, and not to look at.' In this way, Eve would perhaps have answered. Oh, my beloved sisters, indeed Eve has many daughters who follow their mother and answer in this manner. 'Do you think,' says someone, 'that I shall leap upon a man if I even look at him?' God knows, my beloved sisters, more wondrous things have happened. Eve, your mother, leapt after her eyes; from the eye to the apple, from the apple in Paradise down to the earth, from the earth to hell, where she lay in prison for four thousand years and more, both her and her husband, and damned all her children to leap after her to a death without end. The beginning and root of all this same misery was a quick look. So it is, as they say, that from little, much often grows. Have great fear then, every feeble woman, when she who had been created directly by God's hands, was betrayed through this sight, and brought into that substantial sin that has since spread over the entire world.

Book 3

{On the nature of birds and anchorites}

My beloved sisters, just as you protect your senses on the outside well, so above all things, look that you are soft and mild, and humble on the inside, sweet and gentle of heart, and endure the misery from words that people say to you, and from deeds that are wrongly done to you, in case you should lose everything. Against bitter anchoresses David gives this verse: 'I have become like a pelican in the wilderness, etc.'[24] 'I am,' he says, 'like a pelican that lives by itself.' The pelican is a bird so passionate and so full of anger that often in anger it kills its own chicks when they annoy it, and then soon after that it becomes very sorry, and makes a very loud moan, and strikes itself with its beak with which it killed the chicks before, and draws blood from its breast, and with that blood brings back to life again its dead chicks.

---

22 Anchoresses are, to all intents and purposes, the living dead once they are enclosed in their dwelling. Further on in book 2, the author asks 'For what is the anchor-house except her grave?'

23 Genesis 3.6.

24 Psalm 101.7.

wið bile of scharp wreððe. Ah hwen ha swa haveð idon, do as deð þe pellican; ofþunche hit swiðe
195   sone, ant wið hire ahne bile beaki hire breoste, þet is, wið schrift of hire muð þet ha sunegede wið
ant sloh hire gode werkes, drahe þet blod of sunne ut of hire breoste; þet is, of þe heorte þet sawle
lif is inne. Ant swa schulen eft acwikien hire isleine briddes, þet beoð hire gode werkes. Blod
bitacneð sunne, for alswa as a mon bibled is grislich ant eatelich i monnes ehe, alswa is þe sunfule
bivore Godes ehe. On oðer half, na mon ne mei juggi wel blod ear hit beo icolet. Alswa is of
200   sunne. Hwil þe heorte walleð inwið of wreaððe, nis þer na riht dom; oðer hwil þe lust is hat
toward eani sunne, ne maht tu nawt te hwiles deme wel hwet hit is ne hwetter wule cumen of. Ah
let lust overgan, ant hit te wule likin. Let þet hate acolin as deð þe wule iuggi blod, ant tu schalt
demen ariht þe sunne ful ant ladlich, þet te þuhte feier. Ant uvel se muchel cumen þrof ʒef þu hit
hefdest idon hwil þet hate leaste, þet tu schalt deme wod te seolf þa þu þer toward þohtest. Þis is
205   of euch sunne soð, hwi blod hit bitacneð, ant nomeliche of wreaððe.

Impedit ira a nimum ne possit cernere verum. 'Wreaððe,' hit seið, 'hwil hit least, ablindeð swa þe
heorte þet ha ne mei soð icnawen.' *Maga quedam est, transformans naturam humanam.* Wreaððe is a
forschuppilt, as me teleð i spelles, for ha reaveð mon his wit ant changeð al his chere, ant forschuppeð
him from mon into beastes cunde. Wummon wrað is wulvene; mon wulf, oðer liun, oðer unicorne.
210   Hwil þet eaver wreaððe is i wummone heorte, ʒef versaili, oðer segge hire ures, *Aves, Pater nostres,*
ne deð ha bute þeoteð. Naveð ha bute as þeo þet is iwent to wulvene i Godes ehnen, wulvene
stevene in his lihte earen. *Ira furor brevis est.* 'Wreaððe is a wodschipe', wrað men nis he wod? Hu
lokeð he? Hu spekeð he? Hu feareð his heorte inwið? Hwucche beoð utewið alle hise lates? He ne
cnaweð na mon. Hu is he mon þenne? *Est enim homo animal mansuetum natura.* Mon cundelich is
215   milde. Sone se he leoseð mildheortnesse, he leoseð monnes cunde, ant wreaððe, þe forschuppilt,
forschuppeð him into beast, as Ich ear seide. Ant hwet ʒef eni ancre, Jhesu Cristes spuse, is
forschuppet into wulvene? Nis þet muche sorhe? Nis þer bute sone forwarpe þet ruhe fel abute þe
heorte, ant wið softe sahtnesse makien hire smeðe ant softe, as is cundeliche wummone hude, for
wið þet wulvene fel na þing þet ha deð nis Gode licwurðe.

Book 7

{On love}

220   Godd haveð ofgan ure luve on alle cunne wise. He haveð muchel idon us, ant mare bihaten.
Muchel ʒeove ofdraheð luve; me al þe world he ʒef us in Adam, ure alde feader, ant al þet is i þe
world he weorp under ure fet, beastes ant fuheles, ear we weren forgulte. *Omnia subiecisti sub
pedibus eius, oves et boves universas insuper et pecora campi volucres, celi et pisces maris qui perambulant
semitas maris.* Ant ʒet al þet is, as is þruppe iseid, serveð þe gode to sawle bihove. ʒet to uvele
225   servið eorðe, sea ant sunne. He dude ʒet mare: ʒef us nawt ane of his, ah dude al himseolven. Se
heh ʒeove nes neaver iʒeven to se lahe wrecches. *Apostolus: Christus dilexit ecclesiam et dedit semet
ipsum pro ea.* 'Crist,' seið Seinte Pawel, 'luvede swa his leofmon þet he ʒef for hire þe pris of
himseolven.' Neomeð nu gode ʒeme, mine leove sustren, for hwi me ah him to luvien. Earst as a
mon þe woheð, as a king þet luvede a gentil poure leafdi of feorrene londe, he sende his sonden
230   bivoren – þet weren þe patriarches ant te prophetes of þe alde testament – wið leattres isealet. On
ende he com himseolven ant brohte þe godspel as leattres iopenet, ant wrat wið his ahne blod
saluz to his leofmon: luve gretunge forte wohin hire wið, ant hire luve wealden. Herto falleð a
tale, a wrihe forbisne.

A leafdi wes mid hire fan biset al abuten, hire lond al destruet, ant heo al poure inwið an
235   eorðene castel. A mihti kinges luve wes þah biturnd up on hire swa unimete swiðe þet he for

This bird, the pelican, is the passionate anchoress; her chicks are her good works that she kills frequently with the beak of sharp anger. But when she has done that, she should do as the pelican does; regret it immediately, and with her own beak peck her breast, that is, with confession from her mouth that she sinned with and killed her good works, draw that blood of sin out from her breast; that is, from the heart in which the life of the soul dwells. And so shall her dead chicks be brought back to life, which are her good works. Blood symbolizes sin, for just as a bloodstained man is horrible and terrible in the eyes of men, so is the sinful one before the eyes of God. Furthermore, no one can examine blood well before it is cooled. So it is with sin. While the heart swells within from anger, there can be no proper judgement; or while the desire is hot in the direction of any sin, you cannot judge well at that moment what it is, or what might come of it. But let that desire pass away, and it will be pleasing to you. Let the heat cool, as does someone who wishes to examine blood, and you will properly judge the sin to be foul and loathsome that appeared attractive to you. And so much evil would have come from that if you had done it while the heat lasted, that you will judge yourself to have been mad when you thought in that way. This is true of each sin, and is why blood symbolizes it, and, in particular, anger.

'Anger impedes the soul so that it is not possible to recognize the truth.' 'Anger,' it says, 'while it lasts, so blinds the heart that it is unable to recognize the truth.' 'It is a type of sorceress, that transforms human nature.' Anger is a shape-changer, as we are told about in stories, for it deprives a man of his reason and entirely changes his disposition, and transforms him from a man into the nature of a beast. An angry woman is a she-wolf; a man is a wolf, or a lion, or a unicorn. While there is ever anger in a woman's heart, if she is saying versicles, or her hours, *Aves*, *Pater nosters*, she is doing nothing but howling. It is as if she has changed into a she-wolf in God's eyes, the voice of a she-wolf in his sensitive ears. 'Anger is a brief madness.'[25] 'Wrath is a madness', for is not an angry man mad? How does he look? How does he speak? How is his heart proceeding on the inside? What is all his behaviour like on the outside? He does not know any man. How is he a man then? 'And man is a gentle-natured animal.' Man is mild by nature. As soon as he loses mildness, he loses man's nature, and anger, the shape-changer, transforms him into a beast, as I said before. And what if any anchoress, Jesus Christ's bride, is transformed into a she-wolf? Would that not be a great sorrow? There she can but rapidly discard that rough pelt around her heart, and with gentle agreement make herself smooth and soft, as is a woman's skin naturally, for with that skin of a she-wolf nothing that she does is agreeable to God.

Book 7

{On love}

God has deserved our love in all manner of ways. He has done a great deal for us, and promised us more. A great gift attracts love; but all the world he gave us in Adam, our ancient father, and all that is in the world he put under our feet, the animals and the birds, before we were found guilty of sin: 'You have subjected all things under his feet, all sheep and oxen, moreover the beasts of the field, the birds of the air, and the fish of the sea that pass through the paths of the sea.'[26] And all that remains even now, as is said above, serves the good people to the advantage of their souls. Furthermore, the evil are served by the earth, the sea and the sun. He did yet more: he gave us not only what was his, but he gave us himself entirely. Such a high gift was never given to such low wretches. 'The Apostle: Christ loved the church and gave himself up for it.'[27] 'Christ,' Saint Paul says, 'so loved his beloved that he gave for her the price of himself.' Now pay good attention, my dear sisters, to why we ought to love him. First, like a man who woos, as a king who loved a well-bred poor lady living in a foreign land, he sent his envoys before him – they were the patriarchs and prophets of the Old Testament – with sealed letters. Finally, he came himself and brought the gospel as a letters patent,[28] and wrote with his own blood salutations to his beloved: a love greeting in order to woo her, and gain her love. There is a story here, a parable with a concealed meaning.

A lady was besieged all around by her enemies, her land entirely destroyed, and she was completely

---

25 Horace, *Epistles*, I.ii.62.

26 Psalm 8.8–9.

27 Saint Paul in Ephesians 5.25.

28 An open letter, available for all to read (as opposed to a letters close, that is, sealed and private).

wohlech sende hire his sonden, an efter oðer, ofte somet monie; sende hire beawbelez baðe feole
ant feire sucurs of liveneð, help of his hehe hird to halden hire castel. Heo underfeng al as on
unrecheles, ant swa wes heard iheortet þet hire luve ne mahte he neaver beo þe neorre. Hwet wult
tu mare? He com himseolf on ende, schawde hire his feire neb as þe þe wes of alle men feherest to
240 bihalden. Spec se swiðe swoteliche ant wordes se murie þet ha mahten deade arearen to live.
Wrahte feole wundres ant dude muchele meistries bivoren hire ehsihðe: schawde hire his mihte,
talde hire of his kinedom, bead to makien hire cwen of al þet he ahte. Al þis ne heold nawt. Nes
þis hoker wunder? For heo nes neaver wurðe forte beon his þuften. Ah swa þurh his deboneirte,
luve hefde overcumen him þet he seide on ende: 'Dame, þu art iweorret, ant þine van beoð se
245 stronge þet tu ne maht nanes weis wiðute mi sucurs edfleon hare honden þet ha ne don þe to
scheome deað efter al þi weane. Ich chulle, for þe luve of þe, neome þet feht up o me ant arudde þe
of ham þe þi deað secheð. Ich wat, þah, to soðe, þet Ich schal bituhen ham neomen deaðes wunde,
ant Ich hit wulle heorteliche forte ofgan þin heorte. Nu þenne, biseche Ich þe, for þe luve þet Ich
cuðe þe, þet tu luvie me lanhure efter þe ilke dede dead, hwen þu naldest lives.' Þes king dude al
250 þus: arudde hire of alle hire van, ant wes himseolf to wundre ituket ant islein on ende. Þurh
miracle aras þah from deaðe to live. Nere þeos ilke leafdi of uveles cunnes cunde, ȝef ha over alle
þing ne luvede him her efter?

Þes king is Jhesu, Godes sune, þet al o þisse wise wohede ure sawle þe deoflen hefden biset. Ant
he, as noble wohere, efter monie messagers ant feole goddeden, com to pruvien his luve, ant
255 schawde þurh cnihtschipe þet he wes luve wurðe, as weren sumhwile cnihtes iwunet to donne.
Dude him i turneiment ant hefde for his leoves luve his scheld i feht, as kene cniht, on euche half
iþurlet. His scheld, þe wreah his Goddhead, wes his leove licome þet wes ispread o rode: brad as
scheld buven in his istrahte earmes, nearow bineoðen, as þe an fot, efter monies wene, set up o þe
oðer. Þet þis scheld naveð siden is for bitacnunge þet his deciples, þe schulden stonden bi him ant
260 habben ibeon his siden, fluhen alle from him ant leafden him as fremede, as þe godspel seið:
Relicto eo, omnes fugerunt. 'Þis scheld is iȝeven us aȝein alle temptatiuns', as Jeremie witneð: *Dabis
scutum cordis, laborem tuum.* Nawt ane þis scheld ne schilt us from alle uveles, ah deð ȝet mare:
cruneð us in heovene *scuto bone voluntatis.* 'Laverd,' he seið Davið, 'wið þe scheld of þi gode wil þu
havest us icrunet.' 'Scheld' he seið, 'of god wil', for willes he þolede al þet he þolede: Ysaias:
265 *Oblatus est quia voluit.*

'Me laverd,' þu seist, 'hwerto? Ne mahte he wið leasse gref habben arud us?' Ȝeoi, iwiss, ful
lihtliche; ah he nalde. 'For hwi?' For te bineomen us euch bitellunge aȝein him of ure luve þet he
se deore bohte. Me buð lihtliche þing þet me luveð lutel. He bohte us wið his heorte blod – deorre
pris nes neaver – forte ofdrahen of us ure luve toward him þet costnede him se sare. I scheld beoð
270 þreo þinges: þe treo ant te leðer ant te litunge. Alswa wes i þis scheld: þe treo of þe rode, þet leðer
of Godes licome, þe litunge of þe reade blod þet heowede hire so feire. Eft þe þridde reisun: efter
kene cnihtes deað, me hongeð hehe i chirche his scheld on his mungunge. Alswa is þis scheld, þet
is þe crucifix, i chirche iset, i swuch stude þer me hit sonest seo, forte þenchen þerbi o Jesu Cristes
cnihtschipe þet he dude o rode. His leofmon bihalde þron hu he bohte hire luve: lette þurlin his
275 scheld, openin his side to schawin hire his heorte, to schawin hire openliche hu inwardliche he
luvede hire, ant to ofdrahen hire heorte.

Fowr heaved luven me ifind i þis world: bitweone gode iferen; bitweone mon ant wummon;
bitweone wif ant hire child; bitweone licome ant sawle. Þe luve þet Jesu Crist haveð to his deore
leofmon overgeað þeos fowre, passeð ham alle. Ne teleð me him god fere, þe leið his wed i Giwerie
280 to acwitin ut his fere? Godd almihti leide himseolf for us i Giwerie ant dude his deorewurðe bodi
to acwitin ut his leofmon of Giwene honden. Neaver fere ne dude swuch fordede for his fere.

Muche luve is ofte bitweone mon ant wummon. Ah þah ha were iweddet him, ha mahte iwurðen
se unwreast ant swa longe ha mahte forhorin hire wið oþre men þet, þah ha walde aȝein cumen, he
ne kepte hire nawt. Forþi Crist luveð mare, for þah þe sawle, his spuse, forhori hire wið þe feond
285 under heaved sunne feole ȝeres ant dahes, his mearci is hire eaver ȝarow hwen ha wule cumen ham

impoverished inside an earthen castle. However, a powerful king had fallen in love with her so inordinately that in order to woo her he sent her his messengers, one after the other, often many at the same time; he sent her expensive presents, goods to assist her, the help of his noble army to retain her castle. She received it all as if she could not care less, and so hard-hearted was she that he could never get any nearer to gaining her love. What more would you want? He came himself in the end, showed her his beautiful face since he was the most beautiful of all men to look on. He spoke so very gently and with such joyful words that they were able to raise the dead to life. He performed many miracles and did great actions before her eyes: he demonstrated his power to her, told her of his kingdom, promised to make her queen of everything he owned. All this served no purpose. Was this scorn not an amazing thing? For she was never worthy to be his handmaiden. But through his gentleness, love overcame him so that finally he said: 'Madam, you are under attack, and your enemies are so strong that there is no way without my help for you to escape coming into their hands, and being put to a shameful death after all your miseries. I shall, because of my love for you, take that fight upon myself and free you from those who seek your death. I know, though, too truly, that I shall be mortally wounded in fighting against them, and I shall joyfully accept that in order to gain your heart. Now then, I beseech you, for the love that I have made known to you, that at least you love me after that same deed when I am dead, since you would not while I lived.' This king did all of this: he freed her from all her enemies, and was himself shamefully ill-treated and executed in the end. Through a miracle, however, he arose from death to life. Would not this same lady have an evil nature, if, above all things, she did not love him after this?

This king is Jesus, God's Son, who entirely in this way wooed our souls which devils had attacked. And he, as a noble suitor, after many messengers and many acts of goodness, came to prove his love, and demonstrated by his knightly behaviour that he was worthy of love, as knights were once accustomed to doing. He performed in the tournament, and, like a courageous knight, had each part of his shield pierced in the fight for the love of his beloved. His shield, which concealed his divinity, was his dear body that was spread on the cross: broad as a shield at the top where his arms were stretched out, narrow beneath, where the one foot, as many think, was set upon the other. That this shield has no sides is to symbolize that his disciples, who should have stood by him and been his sides, all fled from him and abandoned him as a stranger, as the gospel says: 'All leaving him, they fled.'[29] 'This shield is given to us against all temptations,' as Jeremiah testifies: 'You will give your labour as a shield for the heart.'[30] Not only does this shield protect us from all evils, but it does yet more: it crowns us in heaven 'with a shield of good will'.[31] 'Lord,' says David, 'with the shield of your good will you have crowned us.' 'Shield', he says, 'of good will', for willingly he suffered all that he suffered: Isaiah: 'He was offered because it was his own will.'[32]

'But, lord,' you say, 'what for? Could he not have freed us with less pain?' Yes, certainly, very easily; but he did not want that. 'Why?' In order to deprive us of any excuse against him for our love that he had bought so dearly. You buy cheaply the thing that you care little for. He bought us with his heart's blood — there was never a dearer price — to draw our love towards himself that cost him so much pain. In a shield there are three things: the wood and the leather and the painting. So it is in this shield: the wood of the cross, that leather of God's body, the painting of the red blood that coloured it so attractively. Then the third reason: after the courageous knight's death, his shield is hung high in church in his memory. Likewise is this shield, that is the crucifix, placed in the church, in a position where it can be seen most obviously, in order thereby for people to contemplate Jesus Christ's knightly courage that he showed on the Cross. His beloved should there consider how he bought her love: he allowed his shield to be pierced, his side to be opened to show her his heart, to show her clearly how earnestly he loved her, and to attract her heart to him.

There are four chief loves that one finds in this world: between good companions; between a man and a woman; between a woman and her child; between the body and the soul. The love that Jesus Christ has for his beloved is greater than these four, surpasses them all. Can he not be counted a good friend, who lays a pledge with the Jews to get his friend acquitted? God almighty laid himself out as a pledge for us

29 Matthew 26.56.

30 Lamentations 3.65.

31 Psalm 5.13.

32 Isaiah 53.7.

ant leten þen deovel. Al þis he seið himseolf þurh Jeremie: *Si dimiserit vir uxorem suam, et cetera. Tu autem fornicata es cum multis amatoribus; tamen revertere ad me, dicit Dominus.* ʒet he ʒeiʒeð al dei: 'Þu þet havest se unwreaste idon, biturn þe ant cum aʒein. Welcume schalt tu beo me.' *Immo et occurrit prodigo venienti.* 'ʒet he eorneð,' hit seið, 'aʒein hire ʒein cume ant warpeð earmes anan abuten hire
290   swire.' Hweat is mare milce? ʒet her gleadfulre wunder. Ne beo neaver his leof forhoret mid se monie deadliche sunnen, sone se ha kimeð to him aʒein, he makeð hire neowe meiden. For as Seint Austin seið, swa muchel is bitweonen bituhhen Godes neoleachunge ant monnes to wummon, þet monnes neoleachunge makeð of meiden wif ant Godd makeð of wif meiden. *Restituit, inquit Job, in integrum.* Gode werkes ant treowe bileave – þeose twa þinges beoð meiðhad i sawle.

295   Nu of þe þridde luve. Child þet hefde swuch uvel þet him bihofde beað of blod ear hit were ihealet, muchel þe moder luvede hit þe walde þis beað him makien. Þis dude ure Laverd us, þe weren se seke of sunne ant swa isulet þerwið þet na þing ne mahte healen us ne cleansin us bute his blod ane, for swa he hit walde. His luve makeð us beað þrof: iblescet beo he eavre. Þreo beaðes he greiðede to his deore leofmon forte weschen hire in ham, se hwit ant se feier þet ha were wurðe
300   to his cleane cluppunges. Þe earste beað is fulluht. Þe oðer beoð teares, inre oðer uttre, efter þe forme beað ʒef ha hire suleð. Þe þridde is Jesu Cristes blod, þet halheð ba þe oþre, as Sein Juhan seið i þe Apocalipse: *Qui dilexit nos et lavit nos in sanguine suo.* Þet he luveð us mare þen eani moder hire child, he hit seið himseolven þurh Ysaie: *Nunquid potest mater oblivisci filii uteri sui? Et si illa obliviscatur, ego non obliviscar tui.* 'Mei moder,' he seið, 'forʒeoten hire child? Ant þah heo do, Ich ne
305   mei þe forʒeoten neaver.' Ant seið þe resun efter: *In manibus meis descripsi te.* 'Ich habbe,' he seið, 'depeint te i mine honden.' Swa he dude mid read blod upo þe rode. Me cnut his gurdel to habben þoht of a þing; ah ure Laverd, for he nalde neaver forʒeoten us, dude mearke of þurlunge in ure munegunge i ba twa his honden.

Nu þe feorðe luve. Þe sawle luveð þe licome swiðe mid alle, ant þet is etscene i þe twinnunge,
310   for leove freond beoð sari hwen ha schulen twinnin. Ah ure Laverd willeliche totweamde his sawle from his bodi forte veien ure baðe togederes, world buten ende, i þe blisse of heovene. Þus, lo, Jesu Cristes luve toward his deore spuse, þet is hali chirche oðer cleane sawle, passeð alle ant overkimeð þe fowr measte luven þet me ifind on eorðe.

with the Jews, and gave his precious body to acquit his beloved from the hands of the Jews. A friend never did such a favour for his friend.

Much love is often between a man and a woman. But, even if she were married to him, she might become so depraved and for so long she might prostitute herself with other men that, though she might want to come back again, he would have nothing to do with her. Therefore Christ loves more, for though the soul, his wife, prostitutes herself with the devil in capital sin for many years, his mercy is always ready for her when she wishes to come home and abandon the devil. All this he says himself through Jeremiah: 'If a man can put away a wife, etc. But you have prostituted yourself to many lovers. Nevertheless, return to me, says the Lord.'[33] Still he cries out all day: 'You who have been so wicked, turn around and come back. You will be welcome to me.' 'He even runs to meet the prodigal as he comes.'[34] 'Still he runs,' it says, 'to meet her as she comes back and throws his arms about her neck.' What could be more merciful? Yet here is a more joyful miracle. It never matters how much his beloved has prostituted herself with so many deadly sins, for as soon as she comes to him again, he makes her a new virgin. For, as Saint Augustine says, there is so great a difference between God's approach and a man's to a woman, that a man's approach creates a woman from a virgin, and God creates a virgin from a woman. 'He makes whole again, says Job.' Good works and true belief – these two things are virginity in the soul.

Now about the third love. If a child had such an illness that it was obliged to have a bath of blood before it could be healed, the mother who would make this bath for it would love it very much. This our Lord did for us, who were so sick from sin and so dirtied with it that nothing could heal us or clean us other than his blood alone, for so he wished it. His love makes for us a bath of blood: blessed be he for ever. He got three baths ready for his dear sweetheart in order for her to wash herself in them, so white and so beautiful that she would be worthy of his clean embraces. The first bath is baptism. The second is tears, inner or outer, after the first bath if she stains herself. The third is Jesus Christ's blood, which makes both the others holy, as Saint John says in the Apocalypse: 'Who has loved us and washed us from our sins in his own blood.'[35] That he loves us more than any mother does her child, he says it himself through Isaiah: 'Can a mother forget the son from her womb? And if she should forget, yet will I not forget you.'[36] 'May a mother,' he says, 'forget her child? And though she might do, I can never forget you.' And he says the reason after: 'I have engraved you in my hands.'[37] 'I have,' he says, 'painted you in my hands.' This he did with red blood upon the Cross. People tie a knot in their girdle to remind them of something; but our Lord, because he did not ever want to forget us, put pierce marks to remind him of us in both his hands.

Now the fourth love. The soul loves the body most of all, and that is made clear at their separation, for beloved friends are sorry when they have to part. But our Lord willingly separated his soul from his body in order to join ours both together, world without end, in the bliss of heaven. In this way, see, Jesus Christ's love for his beloved wife, that is, holy church, or the pure soul, surpasses and overcomes all the four greatest loves that can be found on earth.

(The author then illustrates Christ's love of the soul through a series of images (for example, Christ as wooer of a beloved lady who responds with only tepid affection; and the love of Christ, and spiritual love, as Greek fire) and concludes with a depiction of the power of love.)

---

33 Jermiah 3.1.
34 Refer to Luke 15.20.
35 Revelations 1.5.

36 Isaiah 49.15.
37 Isaiah 49.16.

Book 8

{The Outer Rule}

Forþi þet wepmen ne seoð ow, ne ȝe ham, wel mei don of ower clað beo hit hwit, beo hit blac, bute
315 hit beo unorne, warm ant wel iwraht, felles wel itawet; ant habbeð ase monie as ow to neodeð to
bedde ant to rugge.

Nest flesch ne schal nan werien linnene clað bute hit beo of hearde ant of greate heorden.
Stamin habbe hwa se wule; hwa se wule beo buten. Ȝe schulen in an hetter ant igurd liggen, swa
leoðeliche þah þet ȝe mahen honden putten þerunder. Nest lich nan ne gurde hire wið na cunne
320 gurdles bute þurh schriftes leave, ne beore nan irn ne here, ne ilespiles felles, ne ne beate hire
þerwið ne wið scurge ileadet, wið holin ne wið breres ne biblodgi hireseolf, wiðute schriftes leave.
Nohwer ne binetli hire, ne ne beate bivoren, ne na keorvunge ne keorve, ne ne neome ed eanes to
luðere disciplines temptatiuns forte acwenchen. Ne, for na bote aȝein cundeliche secnesses, nan
uncundelich lechecreft ne leve ȝe ne ne fondin wiðuten ower meistres read, leste ow stonde wurse.
325 Ower schon i winter beon meoke, greate ant warme. I sumer ȝe habbeð leave bearvot gan ant
sitten ant lihte scheos werien. Hosen wiðute vampez ligge in hwa se likeð. Ischeoed ne slepe ȝe
nawt, ne nohwer bute i bedde. Sum wummon inohreaðe wereð þe brech of here ful wel icnottet,
þe streapeles dun to þe vet ilacet ful feaste. Ah eaver is best þe swete ant te swote heorte; me is
leovere þet ȝe þolien wel an heard word þen an heard here.
330 Ȝef ȝe muhen beo wimpelles ant ȝe wel wullen beoð bi warme cappen ant þeruppon hwite oðer
blake veiles. Ancren summe sungið in hare wimplunge na leasse þen leafdis. Ah þah seið sum þet
hit limpeð to euch wummon cundeliche forte werien wimpel. Nai. Wimpel ne heaved-clað nowðer
ne nempneð hali writ, ah 'wriheles' ane: *Ad Corinthios: Mulier velet caput suum.* 'Wummon,' seið þe
apostle, 'schal wreon hire heaved.' 'Wrihen' he seið, nawt 'wimplin'. Wrihen ha schal hire scheome
335 as Eve sunfule dohter i mungunge of þe sunne þet schende us on earst alle, ant nawt drahe þe
wriheles to tiffunge ant to prude. Eft, wule þe apostle þet wummon wreo i chirche hire neb
ȝetten, leste uvel þoht arise þurh hire onsihðe: *et hoc est propter angelos.* Hwi þenne, þu chirch ancre,
iwimplet openest þi neb to wepmonnes ehe? Toȝeines þe sist men spekeð þe apostle, ȝef þu þe ne
hudest; ah ȝef þet ei þing wriheð þi neb from monnes ehe, beo hit wah, beo hit clað i wel itund
340 windowe, wel mei duhen ancre of oðer wimplunge. Toȝeines þe þe þus ne dest spekeð þe apostle,
nawt toȝeines oþre þet hare ahne wah wriheð wið euch monnes sihðe. Þer awakenið ofte wake
þohtes of ant werkes oðerhwiles. Hwa se wule beon isehen, þah ha atiffi hire nis nawt muche
wunder; ah to Godes ehnen ha is lufsumre þe is for þe luve of him untiffet wiðuten.
Ring ne broche ne habbe ȝe, ne gurdel imembret, ne gloven ne nan swuch þing þet ow ne deh
345 to habben. A meoke surpliz ȝe mahen in hat sumer werien. Eaver me is leovere se ȝe doð greattre
werkes.

Book 8

{The Outer Rule}

(The author begins by detailing when the anchoresses should take communion, when they should eat, and how they should not host elaborate entertainment, being instead like Mary, the sister of Martha.[38] The anchoress is enjoined not to keep any animals except a cat, or a cow (but only if she has to), nor to engage in trade, nor to allow a man to sleep in her dwelling.)

Since men do not see you, nor you them, it matters not whether your clothes are white or black, except that they are plain, warm and well made with skins well cured; and have as many as you need on your bed and to wear. Next to the flesh no one must wear linen cloth unless it is of hard and coarse material. Whoever wants to can have a stamin;[39] whoever wants can do without.

You must sleep in a robe with a belt, so loosely fitted, though, that you are able to put your hands under it. No one should gird herself with any kind of belt except with her confessor's permission, or wear any iron or hair, or hedgehog skins, or beat herself with these or with a lead whip, or make herself bloody with holly or brambles, without her confessor's permission. Nowhere should she sting herself with nettles, or beat herself on her front, or carve herself with cuts, or take at one time disciplines to quench temptations that are too hard. Do not, for a cure for natural illnesses, attempt any unnatural treatment, or even try it, unless your director gives you permission, in case you should get worse.

Let your shoes in winter be soft, large and warm. In summer you have permission to go and to sit barefoot and to wear light shoes. Whoever wishes can lie down in stockings without feet. Do not sleep with shoes on, or anywhere except in bed. Some women are quite ready to wear drawers of haircloth knotted very firmly, the laces very tightly tied down to the feet. But always the best thing is the gentle and pleasant heart; I would prefer you to suffer a harsh comment well than a harsh hairshirt.

If you can manage without wimples and are very willing to, use warm caps and over them white or black veils. Some anchoresses sin in their practice of wearing wimples no less than ladies do. But, however, someone might say that it is natural for every woman to wear a wimple. No. The holy scripture does not mention a 'wimple' or a 'headcloth' either, but only a 'covering': 'To the Corinthians: Let a woman cover her head.'[40] 'A woman,' says the Apostle, 'must cover her head.' 'Cover', he says, not 'wimple'. She has to cover her shame as Eve's sinful daughter in memory of the sin that caused us all destruction in the beginning, and not make the covering into an adornment and proud thing. Again, the Apostle wishes that a woman should cover her face in church too, in case evil thoughts might arise through being looked at: 'and this is because of the angels'.[41] Why, then, you church anchoress, do you wear a wimple so that your face is open to a man's eye? The Apostle speaks against those of you who see men, if you do not conceal yourself; but if anything conceals your face from a man's eye, whether it is a wall, whether it is a cloth in a firmly shut window, an anchoress can manage without other wimpling. In this way, the Apostle speaks against you who act like this, not against the others where their own wall conceals them from every man's sight. There, often weak thoughts and sometimes deeds awaken. Whoever wishes to be seen, it is not a great surprise if she adorn herself; but in God's eyes she is the lovelier who, for the love of him, is unadorned on the outside.

Do not have a ring or a brooch, or a girdle with links of precious metal, or gloves or any such thing that you ought not to have. In a hot summer you may wear a light white linen gown. Always, the plainer you make things, the more I prefer it.

---

38   This refers to Luke 10.38–42, which concerns a visit by Christ to the house of a woman called Martha. She busied herself providing Christ with refreshments while her sister, Mary, simply sat at his feet listening to him talk. When Martha complained that her sister was not helping, Christ replied: 'Martha, Martha, you are careful and are troubled about many things; But one thing is necessary. Mary has chosen the best part which shall not be taken away from her.' This text was interpreted, especially in the twelfth century, as indicating that a contemplative life was preferable to an active life, however religious the latter might be. See G. Constable, *Three Studies in Medieval Religious and Social Thought* (Cambridge, 1995), esp. ch. 1.

39   A vest of coarse cloth.

40   Saint Paul to the Corinthians I 11.6.

41   I Corinthians 11.10.

Nan ancre servant ne ahte bi riht to easkin iset hure, bute mete ant hure þet ha mei flutte bi, ant Godes milce. Ne misleve nan Godd, hwet se tide of þe ancre, þet he hire trukie. Þe meidnes wiðuten, ȝef ha servið þe ancre alswa as ha ahen, hare hure schal beon þe hehe blisse of heovene. Hwa se haveð ehe of hope toward se heh hure gleadliche wule ha servin ant lihtliche alle wa ant alle teone þolien. Wið eise ant wið este ne buð me nawt blisse.

350

ȝe ancres ahen þis leaste stucche reden to ower wummen euche wike eanes aþet ha hit cunnen. Ant muche neod is þet ȝe neomen to ham muche ȝeme, for ȝe mahen muchel beon þurh ham igodet ant iwurset. On oðer half, ȝef þet ha sungið þurh ower ȝemeles, ȝe schule beo bicleopet þrof bivore þe hehe Deme. Ant forþi, as ow is muche neod ant ham ȝet mare, ȝeornliche leareð ham to halden hare riwle, ba for ow ant for hamseolf, liðeliche ant luveliche; for swuch ah wummone lare to beonne luvelich ant liðe ant selthwenne sturne. Ba is riht þet ha ow dreden ant luvien, ant þah þet ter beo eaver mare of luve þen of drede. Þenne schal hit wel fearen. Me schal healden eoli ant win ba i wunden efter Godes lare, ah mare of softe eoli þen of bitinde win; þet is, mare of liðe wordes þen of suhinde. For þerof kimeð þinge best; þet is, luve eie. Lihtliche ant sweteliche forȝeoveð ham hare gultes hwen ha ham icnaweð ant bihateð bote.

355

360

Ase forð as ȝe mahen of mete ant of claðes ant of oþre þinges þet neode of flesch easkeð, beoð large toward ham, þah ȝe nearowe beon ant hearde to owseolven. Swa deð þe wel blaweð: went te nearewe of þe horn to his ahne muð ant utward þet wide. Ant ȝe don alswa, as ȝe wulleð þet ower beoden bemin wel ant dremen i Drihtines earen, nawt ane to ower ahnes ah to alle folkes heale, as ure Laverd leve þurh þe grace of himseolf þet hit swa mote. Amen.

365

Hwen ower sustres meidnes cumeð to ow to froure, cumeð to ham to þe þurl earunder ant overunder eanes oðer twien, ant gað aȝein sone to ower note gastelich; ne bivore Complie ne sitte ȝe nawt for ham over riht time, swa þet hare cume beo na lure of ower religiun, ah gastelich biȝete. ȝef þer is eani word iseid þet mahte hurten heorte, ne beo hit nawt iboren ut ne ibroht to oþer ancre þet is eð hurte. To him hit schal beon iseid þe lokeð ham alle. Twa niht is inoh þet ei beo edhalden, ant þet beo ful seldene: ne for heom ne breoke silence ed te mete, ne for blodletunge, bute ȝef sum muche god oðer neod hit makie.

370

Þe ancre ne hire meiden ne plohien worldliche gomenes ed te þurle, ne ne ticki togederes; for ase seið Seint Beornard, unwurðe þing is to euch gastelich mon, ant nomeliche to ancre, euch swuch fleschlich froure, ant hit binimeð gastelich; þet is wiðute met utnume murhðe. Ant þet is uvel change, as is iseid þruppe.

375

Of þis boc redeð hwen ȝe beoð eise euche dei, leasse oðer mare. Ich hopie þet hit schal beon ow, ȝef ȝe hit redeð ofte swiðe, biheve, þurh Godes muchele grace, elles Ich hefde uvele bitohe mi muchele hwile. Me were leovere, Godd hit wite, do me toward Rome, þen forte biginnen hit eft forte donne. ȝef ȝe findeð þet ȝe doð alswa as ȝe redeð, þonckið Godd ȝeorne; ȝef ȝe ne doð nawt, biddeð Godes are, ant beoð umben þeronuven þet ȝe hit bet halden efter ower mihte.

380

Feader, Sune, Hali Gast, an almihti Godd, wite ow in his warde. He gleadie ow ant frouri ow, mine leove sustren, ant for al þet ȝe for him dreheð ant dreaieð, ne ȝeove ow neaver leasse þen altogedere himseolven. Beo he aa iheiet from world into worlde aa on ecnesse. Amen.

385

Ase ofte as ȝe habbeð ired eawiht heron, greteð þe Leafdi wið an *Ave* for him þet swonc herabuten. Inoh meaðful Ich am þe bidde se lutel. *Explicit.*

(This instruction goes on to say that the anchoress must only make clothing of use to the church and the poor, and must remain busy to ward off temptation. She is to look after herself physically, and to supervise her servants, whose behaviour is outlined by the author.)

No anchoress's servant ought by right to ask for set wages, unless it is food and the wage that she can support herself with, and God's mercy. No one should mistrust God, whatever happens to the anchoress, and suspect that he will fail her. The maids outside, if they serve the anchoress exactly as they ought to, will find their wages are the high bliss of heaven. She who has the eye of hope directed towards such high wages will gladly serve and suffer all misery and all discomfort lightly. With ease and comfort one cannot buy bliss.

You anchoresses ought to read this last section to your women once each week until they know it. And there is a great need that you give much attention to them, for through them you can derive great benefit and great harm. Furthermore, if they sin because of your neglect, you will be called to answer for that in front of the high Judge. And therefore, as is very necessary for you and yet more for them, devoutly teach them to maintain their rule, both for you and for themselves, gently and lovingly; for in this way ought women's teaching to be loving and gentle, and rarely stern. It is right that they should both fear and love you, and yet, there should be more of love than of fear. Then things will proceed well. Both oil and wine should be poured into wounds following God's teaching, but more of gentle oil than of biting wine; that is, more of gentle words than of sharp ones. For from that come the best things; that is, fear caused by love. Easily and sweetly forgive them their sins when they recognize them and promise to make amends.

As far as you are able, be generous towards them in food and clothing and in other things that the needs of the flesh demand, though you be sparing and hard on yourselves. This is how the good trumpeter acts: he turns the narrow end of the horn to his own mouth and outwards he turns the wide end. And you should act just like this, as you desire that your prayers trumpet well and resound in the Lord's ears, not only for your own but for all people's salvation, as our Lord grant, through his own grace, that it may be so. Amen.

When your sisters' maids come to you as a comfort, come to them at the window in the morning and the afternoon once or twice, and then return soon to your spiritual work; and before Compline do not sit beyond the proper time on account of them so that their visiting will cause no loss to your religious observance, but rather, be a spiritual benefit. If any words are said there that might cause hurt feelings, it should not be borne or brought to another anchoress who is hurt easily. It must be repeated to him who looks after all of them.[42] Two nights are enough for anyone to stay with you, and that should be very seldom: do not break silence for them when you are eating, nor for bloodletting, unless some great benefit or need makes you.

The anchoress and her maid should not play worldly games at the window, or play games of 'touch' together; for, as Saint Bernard says, every such fleshly comfort is an unworthy thing for every spiritual person, and especially for an anchoress, and it deprives them of the spiritual; that is, immoderate mirth without moderation. And that is a poor exchange, as is said above.

From this book read when you are at leisure each day, less or more. I hope that it will be to you, if you read it very often, beneficial, through God's great grace, otherwise I have wasted the long time that it took me. I would rather, God knows it, set off for Rome, than have to begin to do it again. If you find that you do just as you read, thank God eagerly; if you do not do it, ask for God's mercy, and be better at observing it in future according to your ability.

Father, Son, Holy Ghost, one almighty God, protect you in his guardianship. May he gladden you and comfort you, my beloved sisters, and for all that you suffer and endure for him, may he give you nothing less than his whole self. May he be glorified from this world to the next world, always in perpetuity. Amen.

As often as you have read anything in this, greet the Lady with an *Ave* for him who worked on it. I am reasonable enough in asking for so little. The End.

42 The confessor.

Oxford, Bodleian Library, Digby 86

Oxford, Bodleian Library, Digby 86, is one of the most important manuscripts surviving from the period. It was compiled for a lay owner in the last quarter of the thirteenth century. The manuscript contains 101 texts written in French, Latin and English that range from forms of confession, prayers, charms and psalms to religious lyrics, miracles of the saints, romances and 'titbits of useful information';[1] these create a varied collection designed both for private religious instruction and for entertainment. Of the texts, twenty-two are written in English, and they occur from folio 119 forward where they are interspersed with French material. Among these texts are religious verse such as *The Harrowing of Hell* and *The Sayings of St Bernard*, and lyrics such as *Stond wel, moder, Ounder Rode*; and secular verse such as *The Thrush and the Nightingale*, *The Fox and the Wolf*, *Dame Siriþ*, and lyrics such as *Love is Sofft*. In addition, *The Proverbs of Hending* and *The Names of the Hare* demonstrate further the variety of material incorporated into the volume.

There appears to be little thematic order to the manuscript as it is now extant, but, as explained by the editors of the recent facsimile, the texts were originally copied into quires which were kept unbound before being sewn together into the volume. Thus it appears that the first part of the manuscript containing religious prose texts, and the second part, in which the English texts occur, 'contain[ing] secular verse texts for edification or education including some devotional texts', were originally two separate collections, which were sewn together with additional material (which includes a section from folios 65 to 112 that comes in between the two original collections).[2] Digby 86 shares some of its texts with other manuscripts including the contemporary Cambridge, Trinity College, B. 14. 39; and London, British Library, Cotton Caligula A. ix; as well as the fourteenth-century manuscript London, British Library, Harley 2253. While none of the texts in Digby 86 is directly copied from these other manuscripts, the fact that these volumes have texts in common suggests some English poems were relatively well known and popular in the thirteenth and fourteenth centuries, with a wide circulation. The scribe, a layman,[3] and probably the earliest owner of the manuscript, seems to have included material from a number of different sources to create a single, extensive collection, copied over a period of time, that best suited his literary and devotional interests. The manuscript, then, is particularly important for the information it can provide about the interests of a late thirteenth-century literate person, as well as the access that such a person appears to have had to a variety of source texts.

In the fourteenth century, the manuscript belonged to the Underhill family, who lived in Worcestershire. This localization is consonant with the linguistic evidence of the texts, which consists of dialectal forms belonging to south Worcestershire or Gloucestershire.[4]

UBI SOUNT QUI ANTE NOS FUEROUNT?

The English verse *Ubi Scount Qui Ante Nos Fuerount?* (Where are those who went before us?) begins at folio 126 verso of Digby 86, as item 44. Previous editors of the text have anglicized or summarized the title to 'Where ben they before us were'[5] and 'Contempt of the World'.[6] The lyric occurs in four later manuscripts including the Auchinleck manuscript (see p. 465). In these other versions, some verses are omitted or moved around, or form part of a larger text.

The poem is based on the popular and widespread 'ubi sunt?' motif (the same motif occurs also in the Old English poem *The Wanderer* and in Vercelli Homily X). This involves a lament for the passing of those who lived before the present, and a realization that life with all its wealth and glories is transitory. The best hope for the living, then, is not to dwell on temporal riches and the trappings of success, but rather to seek eternal life by avoiding the temptations of this world, and by focusing on the potential treasures of the next.

Ubi Sount Qui Ante Nos Fuerount?

Were beþ þey biforen us weren,
Houndes ladden and hauekes beren,   *led; hawks; carried*

1 J. Tschann and M. B. Parkes, intro., *Facsimile of Oxford, Bodleian Library, MS Digby 86*, EETS s.s. 16 (Oxford, 1996), p. xi.
2 All of this information on the manuscript's compilation can be found in Tschann and Parkes, *Facsimile of Digby 86*, pp. xlii–xlvii.
3 Possibly a man called Richard de Grimhill. See Tschann and Parkes, *Facsimile of Digby 86*, p. lvii.

4 See M. Laing, *A Catalogue of Sources for a Linguistic Atlas of Early Middle English* (Cambridge, 1993), pp. 129–30, at p. 130.
5 T. G. Duncan, ed., *Medieval English Lyrics 1200–1400* (London, 1995), p. 62
6 R. T. Davies, ed., *Medieval English Lyrics: A Critical Anthology* (London, 1963), p. 56

And hadden feld and wode?   *owned*
Þe riche levedies in hoere bour,   *ladies; their; chambers*
5   Þat wereden gold in hoere tressour,   *head-dress*
Wiþ hoere briȝtte rode,   *faces*

Eten and drounken and maden hem glad,   *entertained themselves*
Hoere lif was al wiþ gamen ilad;   *spent in pleasure*
Men keneleden hem biforen.
10   Þey beren hem wel swiþe heye,   *bore; proudly*
And, in a twincling of on eye,
Hoere soules weren forloren.   *lost*

Were is þat lawing and þat song,   *laughter*
Þat trayling and þat proude ȝong,   *trailing robes; walk*
15   Þo hauekes and þo houndes?
Al þat joye is went away,   *has gone*
Þat wele is comen te weylaway,   *happiness; misery*
To manie harde stoundes.   *times*

Hoere paradis hy nomen here,   *took*
20   And now þey lien in helle ifere,   *together*
Þe fuir hit brennes hevere: *burns; forever*
Long is 'ay' and long is 'ho',   *'ah' (also 'forever'); 'oh'*
Long is 'wy' and long is 'wo';   *'alas'*
Þennes ne comeþ þey nevere.   *From there*

25   Dreȝy here, man, þenne, if þou wilt   *Suffer*
A luitel pine þat me þe bit,   *a little torment that is asked of you*
Wiþdrau þine eyses ofte,   *withdraw; comforts*
Þey þy pine he ounrede;   *though; severe*
And þou þenke on þi mede,   *If; reward*
30   Hit sal þe þinken softe.   *seem*

If þat fend, þat foule þing,   *fiend*
Þorou wikke roun, þorou fals egging,   *counsel; incitement*
Neþere þe haveþ icast,   *downwards; has cast*
Oup and be god chaunpioun!
35   Stond, ne fal namore adoun
For a luytel blast.   *At a little blast of wind*

Þou tak þe rode to þi staf,   *cross*
And þenk on him þat þereonne yaf   *gave*
His lif þat wes so lef,   *dear*
40   He it ȝaf for þe; þou yelde hit him,   *repay him for it*
Aȝein his fo þat staf þou nim,   *take*
And wrek him of þat þef.   *avenge*

Of riȝtte bileve þou nim þat sheld   *belief; shield*
Þe wiles þat þou best in þat feld   *while; are*
45   Þin hond to strenkþen fonde;   *try*
And kep þy fo wiþ staves ord,   *at the staff's point*
And do þat traytre seien þat word.   *make*
Biget þat murie londe   *Gain; happy*

Þereinne is day wiþhouten niȝt
50   Wiþouten ende, strenkþe and miȝt,
And wreche of everich fo;   *vengeance*
Mid God himselwen eche lif,   *eternal*
And pes and rest wiþoute strif,
Wele wiþouten wo.   *joy*

55   Mayden, moder, hevene quene,
Þou miȝt and const and owest to bene   *ought; be*
Oure sheld aȝein þe fende;   *devil*
Help ous sunne for to flen,   *sin; flee*
Þat we moten þi sone iseen   *might; son*
60   In joye wiþouten hende. Amen.

Stond Wel, Moder, Ounder Rode

This well-known religious lyric, *Chauncoun de nostre dame*, begins at folio 127 recto, immediately following *Ubi Sount Qui Ante Nos Fuerount?*. It survives in a number of manuscripts, including London, British Library, Royal 12. E. 1, where music is supplied for the text, suggesting, as Davies points out,[7] that it may originally have been intended to be performed in church. The ultimate source of the lyric may be a Latin narrative of the Crucifixion in which the Virgin Mary speaks to St Anselm, or to St Bernard.[8] Here, the dialogue takes place between Christ on the Cross and his mother, standing at the foot of the Cross. Unlike versions of this lyric in other manuscripts, the Digby 86 copy does not include the final two stanzas concerning Christ's resurrection and Mary's role as intercessor for sinners. The two stanzas, as copied in the British Library manuscript, Harley 2253, version are:[9]

When he ros þo fel hire sorewe,
Hire blisse sprong þe þridde morewe,
Blyþe moder wer þou þo.
Levedy, for þat ilke blisse,
Bysech þi sone of sunnes lisse,
Þou be oure sheld aȝeyn oure fo.

Blessed be þu, ful of blysse,
Let us never hevene misse,
Þourh þi suete sones myht.
Loverd, for þat ilke blode
Þat þou sheddest on þe rode,
Þou bryng us into hevene lyht.
Amen.

In the text from Digby 86, without these two stanzas, we are left with a bleaker conclusion focusing on the sacrifice of Christ, and Mary's anguish as a witness of her son's death. This emphasis on mankind's debt to Christ is continued in the subsequent text in the manuscript, editorially entitled 'Sinners Beware'.

Stond wel, moder, ounder rode

'Stond wel, moder, ounder rode,   *the Cross*
Bihold þi child wiþ glade mode,   *heart*
Moder bliþe miȝt þou be.'   *happy; might*
'Sone, hou may Ich bliþe stonde?
5   Ich se þine fet and þine honde
Inayled to þe harde tre.'

'Moder, do wey þi wepinge;   *stop*
Ich þolie deþ for monnes kuinde,   *suffer; because of; nature*
Wor mine gultes ne þolie I non.'   *For; sins*

7   Davies, *Medieval English Lyrics*, p. 317.
8   C. Brown, ed., *English Lyrics of the Thirteenth Century* (Oxford, 1932; repr. 1971), p. 204.
9   For which see B. Dickins and R. M. Wilson, eds, *Early Middle English Texts* (London, 1951), pp. 129–30.

10   'Sone, Ich fele þe deþes stounde: *time*
     Þat swerd is at min herte grounde,   *the bottom of my heart*
     Þat me byheyte Simeon.'[10]   *promised*

     'Moder, do wei þine teres,
     Þou wip awey þe blodi teres,   *wipe*
15   Hy doþ me worse þene my deþ.'   *They*
     'Sone, hou miȝtte Ich teres werne?   *restrain*
     I se þine blodi woundes herne   *run*
     From þin herte to þi fot.'

     'Moder, nou I may þe seye,   *say*
20   Betere is þat Ich one deye   *alone*
     Þen all monkun to helle go.'   *mankind*
     'Sone, I se þi body iswonge,   *beaten*
     Þine honde, þine fet, þi bodi istounge,   *pierced*
     Hit nis no wonder þey me be wo.'   *distressed*

25   'Moder, if Ich þe dourste telle,   *dare*
     If Ich ne deye þou gost to helle: *will go*
     I þolie deþ for monnes sake.'
     'Sone, þu me bihest so milde,   *to me; are; mild*
     Icomen hit is of monnes kuinde   *It stems from human nature*
30   Þat Ich sike and serewe make.'   *sigh; sorrow*

     'Moder, merci, let me deye,
     For Adam out of helle beye,   *buy*
     And monkun þat is forlore.'   *mankind; lost*
     'Sone, wat sal me to stounde?   *Son, what shall I do then?*
35   Þine pinen me bringeþ to þe grounde,   *torments*
     Let me dey þe bifore.'

     'Swete moder, nou þou fondest   *experience*
     Of mi pine þer þou stondest;
     Wiþhoute mi pine nere no mon.'
40   'Sone, I wot, I may þe telle,   *know*
     Bote hit be þe pine of helle,   *unless*
     Of more pine ne wot I non.'   *I do not know of greater torment*

     'Moder, of moder þus I fare   *journey*
     Nou þou wost wimmanes kare;   *know about women's sorrow*
45   Þou art clene mayden on.'   *pure; alone*
     'Sone, þou helpest alle nede   *in need*
     Alle þo þat to þe wille grede,   *cry out*
     May and wif and fowel wimmon.'   *maiden; foul*

     'Moder, I ne may no lengore dwelle.
50   Þe time is comen I go to helle;
     I þolie þis for þine sake.'
     'Sone, iwis I wille founde,   *truly; go*
     I deye almest, I falle to grounde,
     So serwful deþ nes never non.'

10   Luke 2.25–35.

THE FOX AND THE WOLF

The Fox and the Wolf is included uniquely in Digby 86 at folios 138 recto to 140 recto immediately following *The Thrush and the Nightingale* and preceding *The Proverbs of Hending*. It is the only pre-Chaucerian beast fable to have survived, and relates the story, in octosyllabic rhyming couplets, of the deceit practised by the fox (Reynard) on the wolf (Sigrim). The Middle English fable may have been derived from a French exemplar, part of the *Roman de Renart* episodes, but if so, the source is non-extant. It appears that the Middle English version combined two episodes from this French sequence into one poem.[11] The beast fable genre itself has an ancient history, the most famous example being, of course, Æsop's Fables, and was a particularly popular continental literary type throughout the Middle Ages. Its rarity in English literature of this period makes this particular poem especially important, and this version is unique in some of the details it includes; for example, the nearby house is a friary instead of an abbey as in the French version.

The Fox and the Wolf

	A vox gon out of þe wode go,	
	Afingret so þat him wes wo;	*Hungry*
	He nes nevere in none wise	
	Afingret erour half so swiþe.	*before; much*
5	He ne hoeld nouþer wey ne strete,	*held to*
	For him wes loþ men to mete;	
	Him were levere meten one hen,	
	Þen half an oundred wimmen.	
	He strok swiþe overal,	*went*
10	So þat he ofsei ane wal;	*caught sight of*
	Wiþinne þe walle wes on hous,	*a*
	The wox wes þider swiþe wous,	*eager to go to*
	For he þohute his hounger aquenche,	
	Oþer mid mete, oþer mid drunche.	*food*
15	Abouten he biheld wel ȝerne;	*eagerly*
	Þo eroust bigon þe vox to erne.	*only then; run*
	Al fort he come to one walle,	
	And som þerof wes afalle,	
	And wes þe wal overal tobroke,	*broken*
20	And on ȝat þer wes iloke.	*gate; lock*
	At þe furmeste bruche þat he fond,	*opening*
	He lep in, and over he wond.	*went*
	Þo he wes inne, smere he lou,	*scornfully; laughed*
	And þerof he hadde gome inou:	*enjoyment*
25	For he com in wiþouten leve	
	Boþen of haiward and of reve.	*hedge-keeper*
	On hous þer wes, þe dore was ope,	*One*
	Hennen weren þerinne icrope,	*crept*
	Five – þat makeþ anne flok,	
30	And mid hem sat on kok.	
	Þe kok him wes flowen on hey,	
	And two hennen him seten ney.	*near*
	'Wox,' quod þe kok, 'wat dest þou þare?	
	Go hom, Crist þe ȝeve kare.	*sorrow*
35	Houre hennen þou dest ofte shome.'	*Our; injury*

11   See J. A. W. Bennett, *Middle English Literature*, ed. and comp. D. Gray (Oxford, 1986; repr. 1990), pp. 12–14. F. Mossé, *A Handbook of Middle English*, trans. J. A. Walker (Baltimore, 1952), edits Branch IV of the *Roman de Renart* at pp. 178–87 for comparison with the Middle English.

'Be stille, Ich hote, a Godes nome!' *order*
Quaþ þe wox, 'Sire Chauntecler,
Þou fle adoun, and com me ner.
I nabbe don her nout bote goed: *good*
40 I have leten þine hennen blod;
Hy weren seke ounder þe ribe, *sick*
Þat hy ne miȝtte non lengour libe, *live*
Bote here heddre were itake, *their; life-blood*
Þat I do for almes sake.
45 Ich have hem letten eddre-blod,
And þe, Chauntecler, hit wolde don goed.
Þou havest þat ilke ounder þe splen, *same; spleen*
You nestes nevere daies ten: *survive*
For þine lifdayes beþ al ago, *gone*
50 Bote þou bi mine rede do. *Unless; advice*
I do þe lete blod ounder þe brest,
Oþer sone axe after þe prest.'¹² *ask*
'Go wei,' quod þe kok, 'wo þe bigo!
Þou havest don oure kunne wo. *family*
55 Go mid þan þat þou havest nouþe; *now*
Acoursed be þou of Godes mouþe!
For were I adoun, bi Godes nome,
Ich miȝte ben siker of oþre shome. *confident*
Ac weste hit houre cellerer¹³
60 Þat þou were icomen her,
He wolde sone after þe ȝonge, *go*
Mid pikes and stones and staves stronge.
Alle þine bones he wolde tobreke;
Þene we weren wel awreke.' *avenged*
65 He wes stille, ne spak namore,
Ac he werþ aþurst wel sore. *thirsty*
Þe þurst him dede more wo
Þen hevede raþer his hounger do. *had; before*
Overal he ede and sohvte: *went*
70 On aventure his wiit him brohute *as it happened*
To one putte wes water inne, *well*
Þat wes imaked mid grete ginne. *skill*
Tuo boketes þer he founde
Þat oþer wende to þe grounde, *both*
75 Þat wen me shulde þat on opwinde, *people; wind up*
Þat oþer wolde adoun winde.
He ne hounderstod nout of þe ginne,
He nom þat boket, and lep þerinne, *took*
For he hopede inou to drinke.
80 Þis boket biginneþ to sinke,
To late þe vox wes biþout, *realized*
Þo he was in þe ginne ibrout. *trap; taken*
Inou he gon him biþenche,
Ac hit ne halp mid none wrenche; *device*
85 Adoun he moste, he wes þerinne,
Ikaut he wes mid swikele ginne. *treacherous*

---

12 i.e. for the last rites.   13 But our steward will know about this

Hit miȝte han iben wel his wille
To lete þat boket hongi stille.
Wat mid serewe and mid drede,   *sorrow*
90 Al his þurst him overhede.   *disappeared*
Al þus he come to þe grounde,
And water inou þer he founde.
Þo he fond water, ȝerne he dronk: *When; eagerly*
Him þoute þat water þere stonk,
95 For hit wes toȝeines his wille!   *against*
'Wo worþe,' quaþ þe vox, 'lust and wille,
Þat ne con meþ to his mete.   *moderation*
ȝef Ich nevede to muchel iete,   *too*
Þis ilke shome neddi nouþe,   *same injury; I should not have*
100 Nedde lust iben of mine mouþe.   *Had not*
Him is wo in euche londe,
Þat is þef mid his honde;   *thief*
Ich am ikaut mid swikele ginne,
Oþer soum devel me broute herinne.
105 I was woned to ben wiis,   *accustomed*
Ac nou of me idon hit hiis.'
    Þe vox wep and reuliche bigan;   *piteously*
Þer com a wolf gon after þan,
Out of þe depe wode blive,   *quietly*
110 For he wes afingret swiþe.   *hungry*
Noþing he ne founde in al þe niȝte
Wermide his honger aquenche miȝtte.
He com to þe putte, þene vox iherde,
He him kneu wel bi his rerde,   *voice*
115 For hit wes his neiȝebore,
And his gossip, of children bore.   *kinsman*
Adoun bi þe putte he sat.
Quod þe wolf, 'Wat may ben þat
Þat Ich in þe putte ihere?
120 Hertou Cristine oþer er mi fere?   *friend*
Say me soþ, ne gabbe þou me nout,   *lie*
Wo haveþ þe in þe putte ibrout?'
    Þe vox hine ikneu wel for his kun,
And þo eroust kom wiit to him;   *only then; an idea*
125 For he þoute mid soumme ginne   *ingenuity*
Himself houpbringe, þene wolf þerinne.
Quod þe vox, 'Wo is nou þere?
Ich wene hit is Sigrim þat Ich here.'
'Þat is soþ,' þe wolf sede,
130 'Ac wat art þou, so God þe rede?'
    'A!' quod þe vox, 'Ich wille þe telle,
On alpi word Ich lie nelle,   *single; will not lie*
Ich am Reneuard, þi frend;
And ȝif Ich þine come hevede iwend,   *would have expected*
135 Ich hedde so ibede for þe,   *prayed*
Þat þou sholdest comen to me.'
    'Mid þe?' quod þe wolf, 'War-to?
Wat shulde Ich ine þe putte do?'
Quod þe vox, 'Þou art ounwiis,

140	Her is þe blisse of Paradiis:	
	Her Ich mai evere wel fare,	
	Wiþouten pine, wiþouten kare;	*torment*
	Her is mete, her is drinke,	
	Her is blisse wiþouten swinke;	*labour*
145	Her nis hounger nevermo,	
	Ne non oþer kunnes wo;	*kinds of*
	Of alle gode her is inou.'	
	Mid þilke wordes þe volf lou:	*laughed*
	'Art þou ded, so God þe rede,	
150	Oþer of þe worlde?' þe wolf sede.	
	Quod þe wolf, 'Wenne storve þou,	*starved*
	And wat dest þou þere nou?	
	Ne beþ nout ȝet þre daies ago	
	Þat þou and þi wif also,	
155	And þine children, smale and grete,	
	Alle togedere mid me hete.'	*ate*
	'Þat is soþ,' quod þe vox,	
	'Gode þonk, nou hit is þus,	
	Þat Ihc am to Criste vend;	*gone*
160	Not hit non of mine frend.	
	I nolde, for al þe worldes goed,	
	Ben ine þe worlde, þer Ich hem fond.	*them*
	Wat shuld Ich ine þe worlde go,	
	Þer nis bote kare and wo,	*Where there is nothing*
165	And livie in fulþe and in sunne?	*filth; sin*
	Ac her beþ joies fele cunne,	*many*
	Her beþ boþe shep and get.'	*goats*
	Þe wolf haveþ hounger swiþe gret,	
	For he nedde ȝare iete,	*for a long time*
170	And þo he herde speken of mete,	*when*
	He wolde bleþeliche ben þare.	*gladly*
	'A!' quod þe wolf, 'Gode ifere,	*companion*
	Moni goed mel þou havest me binome,	*meals; taken*
	Let me adoun to þe kome,	
175	And al Ich wole þe forȝeve.'	*forgive*
	'Ȝe,' quod þe vox, 'were þou isrive,	*absolved*
	And sunnen hevedest al forsake,	*sins*
	And to klene lif itake,	
	Ich wolde so bidde for þe	*ask*
180	Þat þou sholdest comen to me.'	
	'To wom shuld Ich,' þe wolf seide,	
	'Ben iknowe of mine misdede?	*confessed*
	Her nis noþing alive,	
	Þat me kouþe her nou srive.	*absolve*
185	Þou havest ben ofte min ifere,	
	Woltou nou mi srift ihere,	*confession*
	And al mi liif I shal þe telle?'	
	'Nay,' quod þe vox, 'I nelle.'	
	'Neltou?' quod þe wolf, 'Þin ore,	*Won't you?; have pity*
190	Ich am afingret swiþe sore;	
	Ich wot toniȝt Ich worþe ded,	*will be*
	Bote þou do me somne reed.	*give; assistance*

For Cristes love, be mi prest.'

Þe wolf bey adoun his brest,   *bowed*

195   And gon to siken harde and stronge.   *began; sigh*

'Woltou,' quod þe vox, 'srift ounderfonge,   *receive*

Tel þine sunnen on and on,

Þat þer bileve never on.'   *omit*

'Sone,' quod þe wolf, 'wel ifaie!   *gladly*

200   Ich habbe ben qued al mi lif-daie: *wicked*

Ich habbe widewene kors,   *widows' curse*

Þerfore Ich fare þe wors.

A þousent shep Ich habbe abiten,

And mo ʒef hy weren iwriten,   *recorded*

205   Ac hit me ofþinkeþ sore.   *sorrowful*

Maister, shal I tellen more?'

'ʒe,' quod þe vox, 'al þou most sugge,   *say*

Oþer elleswer þou most abugge.'   *pay for it*

'Gossip,' quod þe wolf, 'forʒef hit me,   *Friend*

210   Ich habbe ofte sehid qued bi þe.   *said; wicked things*

Men seide þat þou on þine live

Misferdest mid mine wive: *Misbehaved*

Ich þe aperseivede one stounde,   *observed; occasion*

And in bedde togedere ou founde.

215   Ich wes ofte ou ful ney,

And in bedde togedere ou sey.   *saw*

Ich wende, also oþre doþ,   *thought, as others do*

Þat Ihc iseie were soþ,   *What*

And þerfore þou were me loþ.   *loathsome*

220   Gode gossip, ne be þou nohut wroþ.'   *angry*

'Vuolf,' quod þe vox him þo,

'Al þat þou havest herbifore ido,

In þohut, in speche, and in dede,

In euche oþeres kunnes quede,

225   Ich þe forʒeve at þisse nede.'   *necessity*

'Crist þe forʒelde!' þe wolf seide,   *reward*

'Nou Ich am in clene live,

Ne recche Ich of childe ne of wive.   *care*

Ac sei me wat I shal do,

230   And ou Ich may comen þe to.'   *how*

'Do?' quod þe vox, 'Ich wille þe lere.   *instruct*

Isiist þou a boket hongi þere?

Þer is a bruche of hevene blisse,   *opening*

Lep þerinne, mid iwisse,   *for certain*

235   And þou shalt comen to me sone.'

Quod þe wolf, 'Þat is liʒt to done.'   *easy*

He lep in, and way sumdel: *a good deal*

Þat weste þe vox ful wel.

Þe wolf gon sinke, þe vox arise,

240   Þo gon þe wolf sore agrise;   *to be afraid*

Þo he com amidde þe putte,

Þe wolf þene vox opward mette.

'Gossip,' quod þe wolf, 'Wat nou?

Wat havest þou imunt? Weder wolt þou?' *in mind; to where*

245   'Weder Ich wille?' þe vox sede,

'Ich wille oup, so God me rede,
And nou go doun wiþ þi meel –
Þi biȝete worþ wel smal.   *profit*
Ac Ich am þerof glad and bliþe,
250   Þat þou art nomen in clene live.   *taken*
Þi soule-cnul Ich wille do ringe,   *death-knell*
And masse for þine soule singe.'
      Þe wrecche bineþe noþing ne vind   *find*
Bote cold water, and hounger him bind.
255   To colde gistninge he wes ibede,   *guest-house*
Wroggen haveþ his dou iknede.   *Frogs; dough; kneaded*
      Þe wolf in þe putte stod,
Afingret so þat he ves wod.   *mad*
Inou he cursede þat þider him broute;
260   Þe vox þerof luitel route.   *cared*
      Þe put him wes þe house ney,
Þer freren woneden swiþe sley.   *friars; lived; crafty*
Þo þat hit com to þe time,
Þat hoe shulden arisen ine
265   For to suggen here houssong,   *say; matins*
O frere þer wes among,
Of here slep hem shulde awecche,   *From their; awake*
Wen hoe shulden þidere recche.   *go*
He seide, 'Ariseþ, on and on,
270   And komeþ to houssong hevereuchon.'   *everyone*
      Þis ilke frere heyte Ailmer,   *same; was called*
He wes hoere maister curtiler.   *gardener*
He wes hofþurst swiþe stronge,   *thirsty*
Riȝt amidward here houssonge.   *in the middle of*
275   Alhone to þe putte he hede   *Alone; went*
For he wende bete his nede.   *remedy*
He com to þe putte and drou,   *drew up*
And þe wolf wes hevi inou.
Þe frere mid al his maine tey   *strength pulled*
280   So longe þat he þene wolf isey.   *the*
For he sei þene wolf þer sitte,   *saw*
He gradde: 'Þe devel is in þe putte!'   *cried out*
      To þe putte hy gounnen gon,   *began*
Alle mid pikes and staves and ston,
285   Euch mon mid þat he hedde,
Wo wes him þat wepne nedde.   *weapons had not*
Hy comen to þe putte, þene wolf opdrowe,
Þo hede þe wreche fomen inowe   *Then; enemies*
Þat weren egre him to slete   *eager; bait with dogs*
290   Mid grete houndes, and to bete.
Wel and wroþe he wes iswonge,   *beaten*
Mid staves and speres he was istounge.   *stabbed*
Þe wox bicharde him, mid iwisse,   *deceived*
For he ne fond nones kunnes blisse,   *kind of*
295   Ne hof duntes forȝevenesse. *Explicit.*   *had of blows*

Dame Siriþ

Dame Siriþ, the only English fabliau outside Chaucer's works, occurs uniquely at folios 165 recto to 168 recto of Digby 86, where it is preceded by a Latin text on truths and followed by an English charm listing seventy-seven names for a hare. It appears that the text was originally part of a separate booklet inserted into its current place in the manuscript when the volume was bound.[14] *Dame Siriþ* is based on a traditional story that has analogues in a number of different languages, and that might ultimately have been oriental in origin. As a fabliau (*fablel*, 'little story' in the manuscript title), it is bawdy, and the action revolves around a trick (or *cointise*, 'stratagem') played upon one of the characters, an illicit love interest, localized action, and non-aristocratic protago-nists. As Bennett and Gray point out, there is very little narrative description in the text; instead, its dynamic is dialogue.[15] *Dame Siriþ* might have been performed orally by a poet reading the different roles in different voices with identifiable props; in some ways, then, it could be considered as a proto-dramatic text. This text is written in tail rhyme stanzas, made up of three- or four-beat lines. In the earlier part of the manuscript text, letters placed in the margin indicate a change of speaker in the text; these are reproduced here as *Testator* (T), *Clericus* (C), *Uxor* (U) and *Femina* (F), representing the narrator, Wilekin, Margeri and Dame Siriþ respectively.[16] Within this edition, I have used þ in place of the manuscript z where it occurs.

Dame Siriþ

Ci comence le fablel e la cointise de Dame Siriþ

Here begins the fabliau and the stratagem of Dame Siriþ

	As I com bi an waie,	(T)	road
	Hof on Ich herde saie		Of; a certain person
	Ful modi mon and proud.		high-spirited
	Wis he wes of lore,		in; learning
5	And gouþlich under gore,		handsome; clothing
	And cloþed in fair sroud.		clothes
	To lovien he bigon		
	On weddod wimmon;		a certain; married
	Þerof he hevede wrong.		did
10	His herte hire wes al on,		
	Þat reste nevede he non,		had no
	Þe love wes so strong.		
	Wel ʒerne he him biþoute		eagerly; thought about
	Hou he hire gete moute		could
15	In ani cunnes wise.		sort of; way
	Þat befel on an day		happened
	Þe loverd wend away		husband
	Hon his marchaundise.		On; business
	He wente him to þen inne		house
20	Þer hoe wonede inne,		she; lived
	Þat wes riche won;		house
	And com into þen halle,		
	Þer hoe wes srud wiþ palle,		dressed; expensive dress
	And þus he bigon:		began

---

14   Tschann and Parkes, *Facsimile of Digby 86*, pp. xliii–xliv.
15   Bennett, *Middle English Literature*, p. 18.
16   As suggested by J. A. W. Bennett and G. V. Smithers, eds,

Early Middle English Verse and Prose, with a glossary by N. Davis, 2nd edn (Oxford, 1968), p. 306.

25	'God almiȝtten be herinne!'	(C)
	'Welcome, so Ich ever bide wenne,'	(U) *may experience; joy*
	Quod þis wif.	
	'His hit þi wille, com and site,	*if it is; sit*
	And wat is þi wille let me wite,	*wish; know*
30	Mi leve lif.	*My dear*
	Bi houre Loverd, heveneking,	*our*
	If I mai don aniþing	
	Þat þe is lef,	*pleasing*
	Þou miȝtt finden me ful fre:	*might; generous*
35	Fol bleþeli will I don for þe	*happily*
	Wiþhouten gref.'	*ungrudgingly*
	'Dame, God þe forȝelde,	(C) *reward*
	Bote on þat þou me nout bimelde	*Provided that you do not inform against me*
	Ne make þe wroþ,	*angry*
40	Min hernde will I to þe bede.	*purpose; announce*
	Bote wraþþen þe for ani dede	*But; to anger; deed*
	Were me loþ.'	*to me; hateful*
	'Nai iwis, Wilekin,	(U) *certainly*
	For noþing þat ever is min,	
45	Þau þou hit ȝirne,	*Even if; might desire*
	Houncurteis ne will I be;	*Discourteous*
	Ne con I nout on vilte,	*know; meanness*
	Ne nout I nelle lerne.	*will not; learn*
	Þou mait saien al þine wille,	*can; say*
50	And I shal herknen and sitten stille	*listen*
	Þat þou have told;	*To what*
	And if þat þou me tellest skil,	*something reasonable*
	I shal don after þi wil –	
	Þat be þou bold.	*You may be confident about that*
55	And þau þou saie me ani same,	*shameful thing*
	Ne shal I þe nouiȝt blame	*not*
	For þi sawe.'	*words*
	'Nou Ich have wonne leve,	(C) *permission*
	Ȝif þat I me shulde greve	*feel unhappy*
60	Hit were hounlawe.	*wrong*
	Certes, dame, þou seist as hende	*courteously*
	And I shal setten spel on ende	*come to the point*
	And tellen þe al:	
	Wat Ich wolde, and wi Ich com.	*why*
65	Ne con Ich saien non falsdom,	*lie*
	Ne non I ne shal.	
	Ich habbe iloved þe moni ȝer,	*years*
	Þau Ich nabbe nout ben her	*here*
	Mi love to schowe.	*declare*

70	Wile þi loverd is in toune,	*husband*
	Ne mai no mon wiþ þe holden roune	*private conversation*
	Wiþ no þewe.	*propriety*
	3urstendai Ich herde saie,	*Yesterday*
	As Ich wende bi þe waie,	
75	Of oure sire.	*your*
	Me tolde me þat he was gon	*Someone*
	To þe feire of Botolfston	*Boston*
	In Lincolneschire.	
	And for Ich weste þat he ves houte,	*knew; was; out*
80	Þarfore Ich am igon aboute	*have taken steps*
	To speken wiþ þe.	
	Him burþ to liken wel his lif	*It befits him*
	Þat miʒtte welde secc a vif	*rule; such*
	In privite.	*In private*
85	Dame, if hit is þi wille,	
	Boþ dernelike and stille	*secretly; quietly*
	Ich wille þe love.'	
	'Þat wold I don for non þing, (U)	
	Bi houre Loverd, hevene King,	
90	Þat ous is bove.	
	Ich habe mi loverd þat is mi spouse,	
	Þat maiden broute me to house	
	Mid menske inou.	*honour*
	He loveþ me and Ich him wel:	
95	Oure love is also trewe as stel,	
	Wiþhouten wou.	*Truly (lit. without wrong)*
	Þau he be from hom on his hernde,	*business*
	Ich were ounseli if Ich lernede	*unhappy*
	To ben on hore.	*whore*
100	Þat ne shal nevere be	
	Þat I shal don selk falsete,	*deceit*
	On bedde ne on flore.	
	Nevermore his lifwile,	*during his lifetime*
	Þau he were on hondred mile	
105	Biʒende Rome,	*Beyond*
	For noþing ne shuld I take	
	Mon on erþe to ben mi make	*lover*
	Ar his homcome.'	*Before*
	'Dame, dame, torn þi mod, (C)	*turn; mind*
110	Þi curteisi wes ever god,	
	And ʒet shal be:	
	For þe Loverd þat ous haveþ wrout,	*made*
	Amend þi mod, and torn þi þout,	*Change; thought*
	And rew on me!'	*pity*

115	'We, we! Oldest þou me a fol?	(U)	Oh; Consider
	So Ich ever mote biden ʒol,		must wait for Christmas
	Þou art ounwis.		foolish
	Mi þout ne shalt þou never wende.		turn
	Mi loverd is curteis mon and hende,		gracious
120	And mon of pris;		excellence
	And Ich am wif boþe god and trewe –		
	Trewer womon ne mai no mon cnowe		know
	Þen Ich am.		
	Þilke time ne shal never bitide		That; come
125	Þat mon for wouing ne þoru prude		wooing; arrogance
	Shal do me scham.'		
	'Swete lemmon, merci!	(C)	dear one
	Same ne vilani		Shame
	Ne bede I þe non;		ask of
130	Bote derne love I þe bede,		secret
	As mon þat wolde of love spede,		succeed
	And finde won.'		great quantity
	'So bide Ich evere mete oþer drinke,	(U)	await; food
	Her þou lesest al þi swinke.		lose; labour
135	Þou miʒt gon hom, leve broþer,		may as well
	For wille Ich þe love ne non oþer		
	Bote mi wedde houssebonde.		
	To tellen hit þe ne wille Ich wonde.'		hesitate
	'Certes, dame, þat me forþinkeþ,	(C)	I am sorry to hear it
140	An wo is þe mon þat muchel swinkeþ		too much
	And at þe laste leseþ his sped.		loses; success
	To maken menis his him ned.		It is necessary for him to enlist support
	Bi me I saie, ful iwis,		As for myself
	Þat love þe love þat I shal mis.		That I love the love that I shall be without
145	An, dame, have nou godnedai!		good day
	And þilke Loverd, þat al welde mai,		that same; rules
	Leve þat þi þout so tourne		Grant; might change
	Þat Ich for þe no leng ne mourne.'		longer
	Drerimod he wente awai,	(T)	Sad at heart
150	And þoute boþe niʒt and dai		
	Hire al forto wende.		change
	A frend him radde forto fare,		advised; go
	And leven al his muchele kare,		great; sorrow
	To Dame Siriþ þe hende.		courteous
155	Þider he wente him anon		
	So suiþe so he miʒtte gon,		As fast as
	(No mon he n'imette)		met
	Ful he wes of tene and treie;		grief; pain
	Mid wordes milde and eke sleie		crafty
160	Faire he hire grette.		greeted

'God þe iblessi, Dame Siriþ!   (C)
Ich am icom to speken þe wiþ,   *with*
For ful muchele nede.
And Ich mai have help of þe,   *And if*
165   Þou shalt have, þat þou shalt se,
Ful riche mede.'   *reward*

'Welcomen art þou, leve sone.   (F)   *dear*
And if Ich mai oþer cone   *can*
In eni wise for þe do,
170   I shal strengþen me þerto.   *try*
Forþi, leve sone, tel þou me
Wat þou woldest I dude for þe.'

'Bote, leve nelde, ful evele I fare,   (C)   *old woman*
I lede mi lif wiþ tene and kare.
175   Wiþ muchel hounsele Ich lede mi lif,   *unhappiness*
And þat is for on suete wif   *sweet*
Þat heiȝtte Margeri.   *is called*
Ich have iloved hire moni dai,
And of hire love hoe seiþ me nai;   *she*
180   Hider Ich com forþi.   *therefore*

Bote if hoe wende hire mod,   *mind*
For serewe mon Ich wakese wod   *must; grow mad*
Oþer miselve quelle.   *kill*
Ich hevede iþout miself to slo;   *slay*
185   Forþ þen radde a frend me go   *advised*
To þe, mi sereue telle.   *sorrow*

He saide me, wiþhouten faille,
Þat þou me couþest helpe and vaile,   *could; assist*
And bringen me of wo   *from*
190   Þoru þine crafftes and þine dedes.   *skills*
And Ich wile ȝeve þe riche mede,   *give; rich*
Wiþ þat hit be so.'   *On condition*

'Benedicite be herinne!   (F)   *God bless us!*
Her havest þou, sone, mikel senne.   *sin*
195   Loverd, for his suete nome,   *name*
Lete þe þerfore haven no shome!
Þou servest affter Godes grome,   *wrath*
Wen þou seist on me silk blame.   *of; such; accusation*
For Ich am old, and sek, and lame,   *sick*
200   Seknesse haveþ maked me ful tame.   *subdued*
Blesse þe, blesse þe, leve knave!   *boy*
Leste þou mesaventer have   *misadventure*
For þis lesing þat is founden   *lying tale*
Oþþon me, þat am harde ibonden.   *pressed (i.e. in difficulty)*
205   Ich am on holi wimon;
On wicchecrafft nout I ne con,   *know*
Bote wiþ gode men almesdede   *men's alms (i.e. donations)*

Ilke dai mi lif I fede,   *Each*
And bidde mi paternoster and mi crede,   *say*
210   Þat Goed hem helpe at hore nede   *in; their*
Þat helpen me mi lif to lede,
And leve þat hem mote wel spede.   *grant; succeed*
His lif and his soule worþe ishend   *shall be destroyed*
Þat þe to me þis hernde haveþ send.   *Who; business*
215   And leve me to ben iwreken   *avenged*
On him þis shome me haveþ speken.'

'Leve nelde, bilef al þis!   (C)   *cease old lady*
Me þinkeþ þat þou art onwis.   *seems; unwise*
Þe mon þat me to þe taute   *directed*
220   He weste þat þou hous couþest saute.   *knew; us; reconcile*
Help, Dame Siriþ, if þou maut,   *are able*
To make me wiþ þe sueting saut;   *darling*
And Ich wille geve þe gift ful stark,   *large*
Moni a pound and moni a mark,
225   Warme pilche and warme shon,   *fur coat; shoes*
Wiþ þat min hernde be wel don.   *When*
Of muchel godlec miȝt þou ȝelpe,   *benefit; boast*
If hit be so þat þou me helpe.'

'Liȝ me nout, Wilekin! Bi þi leute,   (F)   *Lie; good faith*
230   Is hit þin hernest þou tellest me?   *serious intention*
Lovest þou wel Dame Margeri?'

'Ȝe, nelde, witerli,   (C)   *truly*
Ich hire love; hit mot me spille   *will; destroy*
Bote Ich gete hire to mi wille.'   *Unless*

235   'Wat God, Wilekin, me reweþ þi scaþe   (F)   *pity; suffering*
Houre Loverd sende þe help raþe!   *quickly*
Weste Hic hit miȝtte ben forholen,   *If I knew; hidden*
Me wolde þunche wel folen   *seem; directed*
Þi wille forto fullen.   *fulfil*
240   Make me siker wiþ word on honde   *Give me assurance with your pledged word*
Þat þou wolt helen, and I wile fonde   *keep silent; try*
If Ich mai hire tellen.
For al þe world ne wold I nout
Þat Ich were to chapitre ibrout   *ecclesiastical court*
245   For none selke werkes.   *such*
Mi jugement were sone igiven
To ben wiþ shome somer-driven   *shame; driven on a pack-horse*
Wiþ prestes and wiþ clarkes.'   *By*

'Iwis, nelde, ne wold I   (C)   *old lady*
250   Þat þou hevedest vilani   *dishonour*
Ne shame for mi goed.   *benefit*
Her I þe mi trouþe pliȝtte: *pledge*
Ich shal helen bi mi miȝtte,   *conceal*
Bi þe holi roed.'   *cross*

255 'Welcome, Wilekin, hiderward. (F) *here*
Her havest imaked a foreward *you have; agreement*
Þat þe mai ful wel like. *very*
Þou maizt blesse þilke siþ, *occasion*
For þou maizt make þe ful bliþ: *happy*
260 Ðar þou namore sike. *Need; sigh*
To goder-hele ever come þou hider; *your advantage*
For sone will I gange þider *go*
And maken hire hounderstonde.
I shal kenne hire sulke a lore *teach; lesson*
265 Þat hoe shal lovien þe mikel more *much*
Þen ani mon in londe.'

'Al so havi Godes griþ, (C) *I have; peace*
Wel havest þou said, Dame Siriþ,
And goder-hele shal ben þin. *prosperity*
270 Have her twenti shiling,
Þis Ich zeve þe to meding, *reward*
To buggen þe sep and swin.' *buy; mutton and pork*

'So Ich evere brouke hous oþer flet, (F) *enjoy; floor*
Neren never pones beter biset *pennies; employed*
275 Þen þes shulen ben.
For I shal don a juperti, *venture*
And a ferli maistri, *marvellous feat*
Þat þou shalt ful wel sen.
Pepir nou shalt þou eten; *Pepper; you (i.e. her dog)*
280 Þis mustart shal ben þi mete, *food*
And gar þin eien to rene. *cause; eyes; run*
I shal make a lesing *lying tale*
Of þin heie renning,
Ich wot wel wer and wenne.' *know*

285 'Wat! Nou const þou no god! (C) *can do*
Me þinkeþ þat þou art wod: *mad*
Zevest þou þe welpe mustard?' *Give; dog*

'Be stille, boinard! (F) *fool*
I shal mit þis ilke gin *with; trick*
290 Gar hire love to ben al þin. *Cause*
Ne shal Ich never have reste ne ro *peace*
Til Ich have told hou þou shalt do.
Abid me her til min homcome.' *Await*

'Zus, bi þe somer blome, (C) *Yes, until the summer blooms*
295 Heþen null I ben binomen *From here; taken away*
Til þou be azein comen.'

Dame Siriþ bigon to go
As a wrecche þat is wo, *miserable*
Þat hoe com hire to þen inne *until; house*
300 Þer þis gode wif wes inne.

	Þo hoe to þe dore com,	
	Swiþe reuliche hoe bigon:	*pitifully*
	'Loverd,' hoe seiþ, 'wo is holde wives, (F)	
	Þat in poverte ledeþ ay lives;	*always*
305	Not no mon so muchel of pine	*Knows not; suffering*
	As poure wif þat falleþ in nausine.	*distress*
	Þat mai ilke mon bi me wite,	*each; know*
	For mai I nouþer gange ne site,	*walk*
	Ded wold I ben ful fain.	*I should very gladly be dead*
310	Hounger and þurst me haveþ nei slain:	*almost*
	Ich ne mai mine limes onwold	*limbs; control*
	For mikel hounger and þurst and cold.	
	Warto liveþ selke a wrecche?	*To what end*
	Wi nul Goed mi soule fecche?'	*won't*

'Seli wif, God þe hounbinde! (U)   *Poor; unbind*
315 Todai wille I þe mete finde.
For love of Goed
Ich have reuþe of þi wo,   *pity*
For evele icloþed I se þe go
320 And evele ishoed.
Com herin, Ich wile þe fede.'

'Goed almiȝtten do þe mede, (F)
And þe Loverd þat wes on rode idon,   *Cross; killed*
And faste fourti daiis to non,   *ninth hour*
325 And hevene and erþe haveþ to welde;   *rule*
As þilke Loverd þe forȝelde.'   *same; may repay*

'Have her fles and eke bred, (U)   *meat*
And make þe glad, hit is mi red.   *advice*
And have her þe coppe wiþ þe drinke,   *cup*
330 Goed do þe mede for þi swinke.'   *reward; labours*

Þenne spac þat holde wif –   *old*
Crist awarie hire lif –   *damn*
'Alas, alas, þat ever I live! (F)
Al þe sunne Ich wolde forgive   *sin*
335 Þe mon þat smite of min heved.   *cut; head*
Ich wolde mi lif me were bireved!'   *wish; taken from*

'Seli wif, what eilleþ þe?' (U)   *Poor; ails*

'Bote eþe mai I sori be. (F)   *easily*
Ich hevede a douter feir and fre,   *noble*
340 Feiror ne miȝtte no mon se.
Hoe hevede a curteis hossebonde,
Freour mon miȝtte no mon fonde.   *Nobler*
Mi douter lovede him al to wel;
Forþi mak I sori del.   *Therefore; lament*
345 Oppon a dai he was out wend,
And þarþoru wes mi douter shend.   *thereby; shamed*

	He hede on ernde out of toune,	*had; certain; business*
	And com a modi clarc wiþ croune	*arrogant; tonsure*
	To mi douter his love beed,	*offered*
350	And hoe nolde nout folewe his red;	*follow; advice*
	He ne miȝtte his wille have,	
	For noþing he miȝtte crave.	*beg*
	Þenne bigon þe clerc to wiche,	*use sorcery*
	And shop mi douter til a biche.	*made; into; bitch*
355	Þis is mi douter þat Ich of speke;	
	For del of hire min herte breke.	*sorrow; breaks*
	Loke hou hire heien greten,	*eyes; weep*
	On hire cheken þe teres meten.	
	Forþi, dame, were hit no wonder	
360	Þau min herte burste assunder.	*If*
	A wose ever is ȝong houssewif,	*whoso*
	Ha loveþ ful luitel hire lif,	*She*
	And eni clerc of love hire bede,	*If; offer*
	Bote hoe grante and lete him spede.'	*have his way*

365	'A, Loverd Crist! Wat mai þenne do?	(U)	*might I*
	Þis enderdai com a clarc me to		*other day*
	And bed me love on his manere,		
	And Ich him nolde nout ihere.		
	Ich trouue he wolle me forsaþe.		*believe; transform*
370	Hou troustu, nelde, Ich moue ascape?'		*believe you; old woman; might*

	'God almiȝtten be þin help	(F)	
	Þat þou ne be nouþer bicche ne welp!		
	Leve dame, if eni clerc		
	Bedeþ þe þat love werc,		
375	Ich rede þat þou grante his bone		*advise; request*
	And bicom his lefmon sone;		*sweetheart*
	And if þat þou so ne dost,		
	A worse red þou ounderfost.'		*undertake*

	'Loverd Crist! þat me is wo	(U)	
380	Þat þe clarc me hede fro		*went*
	Ar he me hevede biwonne!		*Before; had; won*
	Me were levere þen ani fe		*preferable; money*
	That he hevede enes leien bi me,		*once*
	And efftsones bigunne.		*immediately*
385	Evermore, nelde, Ich wille be þin,		
	Wiþ þat þou feche me Willekin,		*On consideration*
	Þe clarc of wam I telle.		*whom*
	Giftes will I geve þe		
	Þat þou maiȝt ever þe betere be,		
390	Bi Godes houne belle.'		*own*

	'Soþliche, mi swete dame,	(F)	*Truly*
	And if I mai wiþhoute blame,		
	Fain Ich wille fonde.		*I should be glad to try*
	And if Ich mai wiþ him mete		

395	Bi eni wei oþer bi strete;	
	Nout ne will I wonde.	*hesitate*
	Have goddai, dame! Forþ will I go.'	
	'Allegate loke þat þou do so	(U) *By all means*
	As Ich þe bad.	*requested*
400	Bote þat þou me Wilekin bringe,	
	Ne mai never lawe ne singe	*may I; laugh*
	Ne be glad.'	
	'Iwis, dame, if I mai,	(F) *Certainly*
	Ich wille bringen him ȝet todai,	
405	Bi mine miȝtte.'	
	Hoe wente hire to hire inne	*house*
	Þer hoe founde Wilekinne,	*she*
	Bi houre Driȝtte!	*By our Lord!*
	'Swete Wilekin, be þou nout dred,	(F)
410	For of þin hernde Ich have wel sped.	*business; prospered*
	Swiþe com forþ þider wiþ me,	*Quickly*
	For hoe haveþ send affter þe.	
	Iwis nou maiȝt þou ben above,	*now; succeed*
	For þou havest grantise of hire love.'	*grant*
415	'God þe forȝelde, leve nelde,	(C) *reward*
	Þat hevene and erþe haveþ to welde.'	*rule*
	Þis modi mon bigon to gon	*arrogant*
	Wiþ Siriþ to his levemon	*sweetheart*
	In þilke stounde.	*that same; time*
420	Dame Siriþ bigon to telle,	
	And swor bi Godes ouene belle,	
	Hoe hevede him founde.	
	'Dame, so have Ich Wilekin sout,	(F) *sought*
	For nou have Ich him ibrout.'	
425	'Welcome, Wilekin, swete þing,	(U)
	Þou art welcomore þen þe king.	
	Wilekin þe swete,	
	Mi love, I þe bihete	*promise*
	To don al þine wille.	
430	Turnd Ich have mi þout,	*Changed*
	For I ne wolde nout	
	Þat þou þe shuldest spille.'	*destroy*
	'Dame, so Ich evere bide noen,	(C) *await the ninth hour*
	And Ich am redi and iboen	*prepared*
435	To don al þat þou saie.	
	Nelde, par ma fai!	*Old woman, by my faith*
	Þou most gange awai,	
	Wile Ich and hoe shulen plaie.'	*While; amuse ourselves*

<table>
<tr><td></td><td>'Goddot so I wille;</td><td>(F)</td><td>*God knows*</td></tr>
<tr><td>440</td><td>And loke þat þou hire tille</td><td></td><td>*work on her*</td></tr>
<tr><td></td><td>And strek out hire þes.</td><td></td><td>*stretch; thighs*</td></tr>
<tr><td></td><td>God 3eve þe muchel kare</td><td></td><td>*sorrow*</td></tr>
<tr><td></td><td>3eif þat þou hire spare</td><td></td><td></td></tr>
<tr><td></td><td>Þe wile þou mid hire bes.</td><td></td><td>*are*</td></tr>
</table>

<table>
<tr><td>445</td><td>And wose is onwis,</td><td>*whoever*</td></tr>
<tr><td></td><td>And for non pris</td><td>*price*</td></tr>
<tr><td></td><td>Ne con geten his levemon,</td><td></td></tr>
<tr><td></td><td>I shal, for mi mede,</td><td>*reward*</td></tr>
<tr><td></td><td>Garen him to spede,</td><td>*Cause; succeed*</td></tr>
<tr><td>450</td><td>For ful wel I con.'</td><td></td></tr>
</table>

LOVE IS SOFFT

This unique secular lyric, *Ci comence la manere quele amour est pur assaier*, begins at folio 200 verso of Digby 86, immediately after three English lyrics about doomsday. Carleton Brown refers to it as a 'Definition of Love' poem and comments on its simplicity and antithetical style.[17]

Love is Sofft

<table>
<tr><td></td><td>Love is sofft, love is swet, love is goed sware;</td><td>*good; response*</td></tr>
<tr><td></td><td>Love is muche tene, love is muchel kare.</td><td>*trouble; care*</td></tr>
<tr><td></td><td>Love is blissene mest, love is bot 3are;</td><td>*joy; remedy; quick*</td></tr>
<tr><td></td><td>Love is wondred and wo, wiþ forto fare.</td><td>*misery; to live with*</td></tr>
<tr><td>5</td><td>Love is hap wo hit haveþ, love is god hele;</td><td>*good luck; whoever; fortune*</td></tr>
<tr><td></td><td>Love is lecher and les, and lef forto tele.</td><td>*lecher; false; ready; betray*</td></tr>
<tr><td></td><td>Love is douti in þe world, wiþ forto dele;</td><td>*adventurous; deal with*</td></tr>
<tr><td></td><td>Love makeþ in þe lond moni hounlele.</td><td>*unfaithful*</td></tr>
<tr><td></td><td>Love is stalewarde and strong to striden on stede;</td><td>*stalwart; stride; horse*</td></tr>
<tr><td>10</td><td>Love is loveliche a þing to wommone nede.</td><td>*of necessity*</td></tr>
<tr><td></td><td>Love is hardi and hot as glouinde glede;</td><td>*brutal; glowing; ember*</td></tr>
<tr><td></td><td>Love makeþ moni mai wiþ teres to wede.</td><td>*become mad*</td></tr>
<tr><td></td><td>Love had his stiuart bi sti and bi strete;</td><td>*steward; paths*</td></tr>
<tr><td></td><td>Love makeþ moni mai hire wonges to wete.</td><td>*maiden; cheeks*</td></tr>
<tr><td>15</td><td>Love is hap wo hit haveþ, hon forto hete;</td><td>*one to inflame*</td></tr>
<tr><td></td><td>Love is wis, love is war and wilfful an sete.</td><td>*vigilant; wilful (one); suitable (one)*</td></tr>
<tr><td></td><td>Love is þe softeste þing in herte mai slepe;</td><td></td></tr>
<tr><td></td><td>Love is craft, love is goed wiþ kares to kepe.</td><td>*sorrows; heed*</td></tr>
<tr><td></td><td>Love is les, love is lef, love is longinge;</td><td>*false; dear*</td></tr>
<tr><td>20</td><td>Love is fol, love is fast, love is frowringe;</td><td>*foolish; firm; comfort*</td></tr>
<tr><td></td><td>Love is sellich an þing, wose shal soþ singe.</td><td>*wonderful; whoever; truth*</td></tr>
<tr><td></td><td>Love is wele, love is wo, love is gleddede,</td><td>*joy; gladness*</td></tr>
<tr><td></td><td>Love is lif, love is deþ, love mai hous fede.</td><td>*us; sustain*</td></tr>
</table>

17 *English Lyrics of the Thirteenth Century*, pp. 208–9.

Were love also londdrei as he is furst kene   *long-lasting*

25 Hit were þe wordlokste þing in werlde were, Ich wene *worthiest; that could be; suppose*

Hit is isaid in an song, soþ is isene —   *seen*

Love comseþ wiþ kare and hendeþ wiþ tene,   *commences; ends; trouble*

Mid lavedi, mid wive, mid maide, mid quene.   *lady; woman*

Arundel 292: *The Bestiary*

The unique copy of the Middle English *Bestiary*, or *Physiologus*, survives in London, British Library, Arundel 292, folios 4 recto to 10 verso. This manuscript, comprised of texts in Latin, French, and English, is dated to c.1275–1300, with later material from c.1350. The manuscript was part of the collection at Norwich Cathedral in the fourteenth century.[1] As well as *The Bestiary*, the manuscript contains six other contemporary English religious texts including the Creed, *Pater Noster*, and *Ave Maria*. *The Whale*, which is edited below, is found at folio 8, among the other beasts in this *Bestiary*, such as the Lion, Serpent, Eagle, Stag, Spider, Mermaid and Panther.[2]

The Bestiary represents an ancient tradition of viewing beasts as signifying something other than their simple nature. Within the text, the characteristics and habits of each creature are outlined, before the spiritual signification is elucidated. The popularity of the *Physiologus* throughout the medieval period can be demonstrated by the inclusion in the tenth-century Old English Exeter Book of three creatures: *The Panther*, *The Whale* and *The Partridge* (see pp. 54–9).

The Middle English text is adapted, perhaps via an intermediary source, from the eleventh-century Latin verse *Physiologus* of Thetbaldus. Rather like this Latin text, the English poet varies the versification adopted for the different beasts.[3] *The Whale* is written in rhyming couplets, and the language can be ascribed dialectally to West Norfolk.

The Whale

Natura Cetegrandie

	Cethegrande is a fis,	*The whale*
	Ðe moste ðat in water is,	*largest*
	Ðat ðu wuldes seien get,	*say yet*
	Gef ðu it soge wan it flet,	*saw; floated*
5	Ðat it were a neilond	*an island*
	Ðat sete one ðe se-sond.	*sat; sea-shore*
	Ðis fis ðat is unride,	*unwieldy*
	Ðanne him hungreð he gapeð wide;	
	Ut of his ðrote it smit an onde,	*emits; breath*
10	Ðe swetteste ðing ðat is o londe,	
	Ðerfore oðre fisses to him dragen.	*draw near*
	Wan he it felen he aren fagen;	*feels; happy*
	He cumen and hoven in his muð;	*stays*
	Of his swike he arn uncuð.	*Of the whale's deceit it is unaware*
15	Ðis cete ðanne his chaveles lukeð,	*whale; jaws lock*
	Ðise fisses alle in sukeð.	
	Ðe smale he wile ðus biswiken,	*deceive*
	Ðe grete maig he nogt bigripen.	*grip*
	Ðis fis wuneð wið ðe se-grund,	*lives near the sea-bottom*
20	And liveð ðer evre heil and sund,	*hale and hearty*
	Til it cumeð ðe time	
	Ðat storm stireð al ðe se.	*sea*
	Ðanne sumer and winter winnen	*contest with each other*
	Ne mai it wunen ðerinne,	*live*
25	So drovi is te sees grund;	*turbulent*
	Ne mai he wunen ðer ðat stund,	*at that time*
	Oc stireð up and hoveð stille.	*rises up*

1 M. Laing, *A Catalogue of Sources for a Linguistic Atlas of Early Middle English* (Cambridge, 1993), p. 68.

2 J. A. W. Bennett and G. V. Smithers, eds, *Early Middle English Verse and Prose*, with a glossary by N. Davis, 2nd edn (Oxford, 1968; repr. 1982), pp. 165–73, edit the *Eagle*, the *Ant*, the *Stag* and the *Whale*.

3 See Bennett and Smithers, *Early Middle English*, pp. 165–6.

Wiles ðat weder is so ille
Ðe sipes ðat arn on se fordriven,   *ships; driven*
30   Loð hem is deð and lef to liven,   *hateful; death; desirable*
Biloken hem, and sen ðis fis;   *look around*
A neilond he wenen it is.   *they presume*
Ðerof he aren swiðe fagen,
And mid here migt ðarto he dragen   *strength*
35   Sipes on festen,   *onto the 'island' for mooring*
And alle up gangen,   *go up*
Of ston mid stel in ðe tunder   *tinder*
Wel to brennen one ðis wunder,   *to build a fire on*
Warmen hem wel, and heten and drinken.   *eat*
40   Ðe fir he feleð, and doð hem sinken: *causes them to sink*
For sone he diveð dun to grunde;   *immediately*
He drepeð hem alle wiðuten wunde.   *kills; wound*

Significacio[4]

Ðis devel is mikel wið wil and magt,   *great; strength*
So witches haven in here craft.   *Just as; their*
45   He doð men hungren and haven ðrist,   *makes; thirst*
And mani oðer sinful list;   *desires*
Tolleð men to him wið his onde,   *He entices; breath*
Woso him folgeð, he findeð sonde: *follows; shame*
Ðo arn ðe little, in leve lage;   *Those who are little or weak in faith*
50   Ðe mikle ne maig he to him dragen;
Ðe mikle I mene ðe stedefast   *the steadfast*
In rigte leve mid fles and gast.   *In true faith both body and soul*
Woso listneð develes lore,   *teaching*
On lengðe it sal him rewen sore;   *will repent it sorely at length*
55   Woso festeð hope on him   *fastens*
He sal him folgen to helle dim.   *follow*

---

4   The allegorical interpretation of the whale.

Oxford, Jesus College 29

Oxford, Jesus College 29, is probably most famous for its inclusion of one of the two copies of *The Owl and the Nightingale* among its twenty-seven English texts. One scribe wrote the entire volume, probably in the last quarter of the thirteenth century.[1] This manuscript's English texts are predominantly religious verses of a penitential and devotional nature, and *The Proverbs of Alfred*, a moral and instructive set of precepts, is also among its contents. Many of the texts in Jesus 29 are also included in London, British Library, Cotton Caligula A. ix. Neither manuscript is directly copied from the other, but it does seem that the two manuscripts shared a common exemplar from which the texts may have been selected.[2] This suggests that an extensive compendium, or a number of such volumes, of the most popular English works was circulating in the thirteenth century.

The language of the scribe of Jesus 29 can be localized dialectally to south-east Herefordshire or north-west Gloucestershire.[3]

THE *LOVE-RON* OF FRIAR THOMAS HALES

The *Love-Ron* or 'Love Song' of Thomas Hales is uniquely contained in Jesus 29 at folios 187 recto to 188 verso, after a lyric entitled *Hwi Ne Serve We Crist*, and immediately prior to the *Song of the Annunciation*. The *Love-Ron* was probably composed before 1272, since it mentions King Henry III, who died in that year. Thomas Hales provides us with some information about himself in the Latin *incipit* of the work: 'Here begins that song composed by brother Thomas of Hales of the order of the Franciscan Friars at the request of a certain female servant of God.' This, plus the first stanza of the poem, shows that a female religious, probably a nun, asked for this devotional song to be written, presumably as an encouragement to her in her chosen life as a virgin. Further information about the poet comes in the mention of a certain Thomas de Hales in a letter written by a Franciscan friar, Adam Marsh, who died in the late 1250s; this provides valuable historical evidence.[4] Hales itself is a place in Gloucestershire and may very well be where Thomas Hales originated from. This would make Thomas Hales's poem the product of a local man, if the ascription of the dialect of the scribe of Jesus 29 to Herefordshire or Gloucestershire can be taken to indicate the area in which the manuscript was actually written. It is possible that this same Thomas Hales was also responsible for a number of Latin sermons and an Anglo-Norman sermon;[5] such literary activity is very much in keeping with the pastoral work of the friars in the thirteenth century.

The *Love-Ron* is written in stanzas of eight lines, rhyming abababab, with four stresses to each line. Hales utilizes contemporary imagery of Christ the lover-knight, and of virginity as a something to be well protected, to assist in the explanation of the incomparable value of virginity. Indeed, many aspects of this work are reminiscent of, among other things, *Hali Meiðhad* and *Ancrene Wisse*: for example, the image of the virgin protecting the castle of the body against the temptations of the flesh (line 152); the concept of virginity as the greatest of treasures, and as a cure for the wounds of love (lines 153–6); the description of the virgin as the lover of Christ (line 120 etc.); and the revelation of God's holy teaching on virginity coming in the form of an 'open' letter 'wiþute sel' (line 194). The poem's emphasis on the transience of earthly wealth, and the inevitability of death, is also a theme common in much religious writing in the medieval period.[6] The *ubi sunt*? motif and the topos of contempt for worldly things are also familiar, and are aimed at inspiring the recipient of the poem to look heavenward for joy and happiness.[7] The request at the end of the text (lines 195–6) that the religious woman learns the work by heart tells us something also about the importance of memorization as part of the process of education in this period. This virgin is then to take on the role of the educator, in teaching other religious women what the poem contains (lines 197–8).

1   For this scribe's work, see N. R. Ker, ed., *The Owl and the Nightingale: Reproduced in Facsimile from the Surviving Manuscripts, Jesus College, Oxford 29, and British Museum, Cotton Caligula A. ix*, EETS 251 (London, 1963), where a facsimile of that poem is included. There has been some debate about the date of Jesus 29. Ker, pp. ix and xvi, implies a dating of the last couple of decades of the thirteenth century. See also B. Hill, 'The History of Jesus College, Oxford, MS 29', *Medium Ævum* 32 (1963), 203–13.

2   This is certainly the case with the copies of *The Owl and the Nightingale*, which were made from the same exemplar. See N. Cartlidge, 'The Date of *The Owl and the Nightingale*', *Medium Ævum* 65 (1996), 230–47, at pp. 233–4.

3   See M. Laing, *A Catalogue of Sources for a Linguistic Atlas of Early Middle English* (Cambridge, 1993), p. 147.

4   See C. Brown, ed., *English Lyrics of the Thirteenth Century* (Oxford, 1932; repr. 1971), pp. 198–9.

5   See B. Dickins and R. M. Wilson, eds, *Early Middle English Texts* (London, 1951), p. 103.

6   For example, in many religious lyrics; and in *The Wanderer* and *The Seafarer*.

7   See also *Ubi Sount Qui Ante Nos Fuerount?*, for example, one of the many religious lyrics contained in Digby 86, above.

The *Love-Ron* of Friar Thomas Hales

Incipit quidam cantus quem composuit frater Thomas de Hales de ordine fratrum Minorum, ad instanciam cuiusdam puelle Deo dicate.

A mayde Cristes me bit yorne	*of Christ; asked; earnestly*
Þat Ich hire wurche a luve-ron,	*make; love song*
For hwan heo myhte best ileorne	*So that; learn*
To taken onoþer soþ lefmon,	*another; true; sweetheart*
Þat treowest were of alle berne	*men*
And best wyte cuþe a freo wymmon.	*protect; know how to; noble*
Ich hire nule nowiht werne;	*in any way refuse*
Ich hire wule teche as Ic con.	
Mayde, her þu myht biholde	
Þis worldes luve nys bute o res	*but a thing of distraction*
And is byset so fele volde,	*many ways*
Vikel and frakel and wok and les.	*Fickle; deceitful; weak; false*
Þeos þeines þat her weren bolde	*thanes (men)*
Beoþ aglyden so wyndes bles;	*passed away; wind's blast*
Under molde hi liggeþ colde	*earth; lie*
And faleweþ so doþ medewe gres.	*decay; meadow*
Nis no mon iboren o lyve	
Þat her may beon studevest,	*steadfast*
For her he haveþ seorewen ryve,	*sorrows plentiful*
Ne tyt him never ro ne rest.	*befalls; peace*
Toward his ende he hyeþ blyve	*hurries quickly*
And lutle hwile he her ilest;	*lasts*
Pyne and deþ him wile ofdryve	*Pain; drive away*
Hwenne he weneþ to libben best.	*expects*
Nis non so riche ne non so freo	
Þat he ne schal heonne sone away;	*from here; soon*
Ne may hit never his waraunt beo,	*protection*
Gold ne seolver, vouh ne gray.	*patterned or grey fur*
Ne beo he no þe swift, ne may he fleo,	*whether he's swift; flee*
Ne weren his lif enne day.	*save; one*
Þus is þes world, as þu mayht seo,	
Also þe schadewe þat glyt away.	*glides*
Þis world fareþ hwilynde,	*proceeds transiently*
Hwenne on cumeþ anoþer goþ;	*one*
Þat wes bifore nu is bihynde;	
Þat er was leof nu hit is loþ.	*beloved; hateful*
Forþi he doþ as þe blynde	
Þat in þis world his luve doþ.	
Ye mowen iseo þe world aswynde	*might see; vanish*
Þat wouh goþ forþ, abak þat soþ.	*evil; backwards*
Þeo luve þat ne may her abyde,	
Þu treowest hire myd muchel wouh;	*trust; with*
Also hwenne hit schal toglide,	*disappear*

5

10

15

20

25

30

35

40

	Hit is fals and mereuh and frouh	*weak; fragile*
45	And fromward in uychon tide.	*unreliable; each hour*
	Hwile hit lesteþ is seorewe inouh;	*enough*
	An ende, ne werie mon so syde,	*In; defend; ever so expansively*
	He schal todreosen so lef on bouh.	*decay; as; bough*
	Monnes luve nys buten o stunde:	*but a short moment*
50	Nu he luveþ, nu he is sad,	*tired*
	Nu he cumeþ, nu wile he funde,	*go*
	Nu he is wroþ, nu he is gled.	
	His luve is her and ek a lunde,	*also; elsewhere*
	Nu he luveþ sum þat he er bed;	*previously offered to fight*
55	Nis ne never treowe ifunde	*faithful*
	Þat him tristeþ he is amed.	*trusts; mad*
	Yf mon is riche of worldes weole,	*wordly wealth*
	Hit makeþ his heorte smerte and ake;	*hurt*
	If he dret þat me him stele,	*fears; men; steal from*
60	Þenne doþ him pyne nyhtes wake.	
	Him waxeþ þouhtes monye and fele	*come into his mind*
	How he hit may witen wiþuten sake.	*defend; conflict*
	An ende hwat helpeþ hit to hele?	*conceal*
	Al deþ hit wile from him take.	
65	Hwer is Paris and Heleyne	
	Þat weren so bryht and feyre on bleo,	*face*
	Amadas and Ideyne,	
	Tristram, Yseude and alle þeo,[8]	
	Ector, wiþ his scharpe meyne,	*retinue*
70	And Cesar, riche of wordes feo?[9]	*wealth*
	Heo beoþ iglyden ut of þe reyne	*disappeared; world*
	So þe schef is of þe cleo.	*sheaf; hillside*
	Hit is of heom also hit nere;	*never was*
	Of heom me haveþ wunder itold.	
75	Nere hit reuþe for to heren	*pity*
	How hi were wiþ pyne aquold,	*killed*
	And hwat hi þoleden alyve here?	*suffered*
	Al is heore hot iturnd to cold	
	Þus is þes world of false fere:	*appearance*
80	Fol he is þe on hire is bold.	*A fool; it; trusting*
	Þeyh he were so riche mon	
	As Henry ure kyng,[10]	
	And also veyr as Absalon[11]	*fair*
	Þat nevede on eorþe non evenyng,	*equal*
85	Al were sone his prute agon,	

8 Loyal lovers of medieval French Romance: Amadas and Idoine and Tristram and Isolde.

9 Hector of Troy and Julius Caesar, together with Alexander the Great, were the three Worthies of the classical period. There were nine Worthies, considered the greatest of heroes; the other six are Joshua, David and Judas Maccabeus (Old Testament), Charlemagne, Arthur and Godfrey of Bouillon (Christian). This list was not definitive: see, for example, Shakespeare's *Love's Labour's Lost*, Act V, scene ii.

10 Henry III.

11 The Absolon of the Old Testament (2 Samuel 14.26) was renowned for his beauty.

Hit nere on ende wurþ on heryng.   *worth a herring*
Mayde, if þu wilnest after leofmon   *desire*
Ich teche þe enne treowe king.

A swete, if þu iknowe
90   Þe gode þewes of þisse childe: *qualities; noble youth*
He is feyr and bryht on heowe,
Of glede chere, of mode mylde,   *character*
Of lufsum lost, of truste treowe,   *lovely desire*
Freo of heorte, of wisdom wilde,   *strong*
95   Ne þurhte þe never rewe,   *need; regret*
Myhtestu do þe in his ylde.   *If you might be; protection*

He is ricchest mon of londe,
So wide so mon spekeþ wiþ muþ;   *As*
Alle heo beoþ to his honde,   *in his power*
100   Est and west, norþ and suþ.
Henri, king of Engelonde,
Of hym he halt and to hym buhþ.   *holds as a vassal; bows*
Mayde, to þe he send his sonde   *messengers*
And wilneþ for to beo þe cuþ.   *to be made known*

105   Ne byt he wiþ þe lond ne leode,   *demands as dowry*
Vouh ne gray ne rencyan ;   *Furs; fine cloth*
Naveþ he þerto none neode,   *need*
He is riche and weli man.
If þu him woldest luve beode   *offer*
110   And bycumen his leovemon,   *lover*
He brouhte þe to suche wede   *garments*
Þat naveþ king ne kayser non.   *emperor*

Hwat spekestu of eny bolde   *temple*
Þat wrouhte þe wise Salomon
115   Of jaspe, of saphir, of merede golde,   *refined*
And of mony onoþer ston?
Hit is feyrure of feole volde   *in many ways*
More þan Ich eu telle con;
Þis bold, mayde, þe is bihote   *promised*
120   If þat þu bist his leovemon.

Hit stont uppon a treowe mote   *hill*
Þar hit never truke ne schal;   *fail*
Ne may no mynur hire underwrote,   *miner; undermined*
Ne never false þene grundwal.   *weaken; foundation*
125   Þarinne is uich balewes bote,   *every sorrow's remedy*
Blisse and joye and gleo and gal;   *glee; song*
Þis bold, mayde, is þe bihote
And uych o blisse þar wyþal.   *as well*

Þer ne may no freond fleon oþer,   *leave*
130   Ne non furleosen his iryhte;   *lose; rights*
Þer nys hate ne wreþþe nouþer,   *anger; either*
Of prude ne of onde, of none wihte.   *envy; creature*

Alle heo schule wyþ engles pleye,
Some and sauhte in heovene lyhte.   *Together; reconciled*

135   Ne beoþ heo, mayde, in gode weye   *good position*
        Þat wel luveþ ure Dryhte?

        Ne may no mon hine iseo,
        Also he is in his mihte,   *As*
        Þat may wiþuten blisse beo

140   Hwanne he isihþ ure Drihte.   *sees*
        His sihte is al joye and gleo,
        He is day wyþute nyhte.
        Nere he, mayde, ful seoly   *Would (s)he not be; joyful*
        Þat myhte wunye myd such a knyhte?   *dwell*

145   He haveþ bitauht þe o tresur   *entrusted*
        Þat is betere þan gold oþer pel,   *expensive purple cloth*
        And bit þe luke þine bur,   *asks that you guard it in your chamber*
        And wilneþ þat þu hit wyte wel   *protect*
        Wyþ þeoves, wiþ reveres, wiþ lechurs.   *Against; robbers*

150   Þu most beo waker and snel;   *vigilant; brave*
        Þu art swetture þane eny flur
        Hwile þu witest þene kastel.   *protect*

        Hit is ymston of feor iboren,   *gemstone; from afar carried*
        Nys non betere under heovene grunde,

155   He[12] is tofore alle oþre icoren,   *before; chosen*
        He heleþ alle luve wunde.
        Wel were alyve iboren   *born*
        Þat myhte wyten þis ilke stunde;   *protect; state of being*
        For habbe þu hine enes forloren,   *once; deprived of*

160   Ne byþ he never eft ifunde.

        Þis ilke ston þat Ich þe nemne   *name*
        Maydenhod icleoped is.   *Virginity is called*
        Hit is o derewurþe gemme,   *precious*
        Of alle oþre he berþ þat pris,   *carries off first prize*

165   And bryngeþ þe wiþute wemme   *blemish*
        Into þe blysse of Paradis
        Þe hwile þu hyne witest under þine hemme,   *as long as; dress*
        Þu ert swetture þan eny spis.   *sweeter; spice*

        Hwat spekstu of eny stone

170   Þat beoþ in vertu oþer in grace:
        Of amatiste, of calcydone,   *amethyst; chalcedon*
        Of lectorie and tupace,   *cock-stone; topaz*
        Of jaspe, of saphir, of sardone,   *sardonyx*
        Smaragde, beril and crisopace?   *Emerald; beryl; crysosprace*

175   Among alle oþre ymstone,
        Þes beoþ deorre in uyche place.   *dearer; every*

12   i.e. virginity.

Mayde, also Ich þe tolde,
Þe ymston of þi bur
He is betere an hundredfolde

180 Þan alle þeos in heore culur.   *those; brilliance*
He is idon in heovene golde   *It is set*
And is ful of fyn amur.   *fin amor (pure love)*
Alle þat myhte hine wite scholde,   *can should guard it*
He schyneþ so bryht in heovene bur.

185 Hwen þu me dost in þine rede   *consulting*
For þe to cheose a leofmon,   *chose*
Ich wile don as þu me bede,   *ask*
Þe beste þat Ich fynde con.
Ne doþ he, mayde, on uvele dede,   *does he not do; evil deed*

190 Þat may cheose of two þat on,
And he wile wiþute neode   *If one*
Take þet wurse, þe betere let gon?

Þis rym, mayde, Ich þe sende,   *verse*
Open and wiþute sel,   *seal*
195 Bidde Ic þat þu hit untrende   *unroll*
And leorny bute bok uych del   *learn by heart; part*
Herof þat þu beo swiþe hende   *courteous*
And tech hit oþer maydenes wel.
Hwoso cuþe hit to þan ende,   *knows*

200 Hit wolde him stonde muchel stel.   *very good stead*

Hwenne þu sittest in longynge,
Drauh þe forþ þis ilke wryt;   *take out; same text*
Mid swete stephne þu hit singe,   *voice*
And do also hit þe byt.   *instructs*
205 To þe he haveþ send one gretynge;
God almyhti þe beo myd,   *be with you*
And leve cumen to his brudþinge   *may he allow you; bridal chamber*
Heye in heovene þer he sit.

And yeve him god endynge,
210 Þat haveth iwryten þis ilke wryt. Amen.

THE PROVERBS OF ALFRED

The Proverbs of Alfred survives in its most extensive version as a collection of thirty-four moral sayings. It is extant in four independent recensions. The earliest text is a fragment of only three pages in London, British Library, Cotton Galba A. xix, a manuscript dated to the early thirteenth century, but which is very badly damaged as a result of the fire at the Cotton Library in 1731. Maidstone Museum A. 13, dated to the first half of the thirteenth century, contains another text that may have originated in the Northampton area. Cambridge, Trinity College, B. 14. 39, dated to *c.*1275–1300, contains the most extensive text. Oxford, Jesus College, 29, dated to the last quarter of the thirteenth century, contains twenty-four of the *Proverbs* at folios 189 recto to 192 recto.[13] It is probably the version that most accurately represents the original text, and is thus used for the edition below.[14]

While all the surviving manuscripts of this text are thirteenth-century, *The Proverbs of Alfred* itself is thought to be twelfth-century in origin, dating perhaps from as early as 1150.[15] As some of the *Proverbs* occur in *The Owl and the Nightingale*, this has been seen as further evidence for supposing the *Proverbs* to be twelfth-century in origin, as, until recently, *The Owl and the Nightingale* was thought to date from sometime between 1189 and 1215. It is possible, however, that *The Owl and the Nightingale* can itself be dated to the final quarter of the thirteenth century.[16] If this is the case, then it makes the proposed twelfth-century date for the *Proverbs* less convincing, although the four surviving versions differ to the extent that it seems likely some time must have intervened between the creation of the original text and its transmission into the forms in which it now exists. Also, in addition to *The Owl and the Nightingale* alluding to the *Proverbs*, Laȝamon's *Brut* may also draw on the text, albeit infrequently. Indeed, the *Brut's* possible allusion to the *Proverbs* may simply result from the commonplace nature of much proverbial literature.

The form of the *Proverbs* is alliterative verse, with some rhyming couplets; and it is quite freely composed.[17] It may be that the non-extant original text was comprised of long alliterative lines, like Old English poetry and Laȝamon's *Brut*, but during the transmission of the text,

the scribes have evidently misunderstood the nature of the verse and the precise form of the original has been lost. As edited, the verse is laid out as half-lines, as also the case with The *Orrmulum*. The dialect of the original text may have been south-eastern, but it too has been overlaid with the dialectal forms of the various scribes. Jesus College 29, for example, is predominantly composed in a West Midlands dialect.

The claim of the *Proverbs* to authorship by King Alfred (who died in 899) is almost certainly spurious. The purpose behind such a claim is probably to lend authority to the text, using a king who was famed for his wisdom to the extent that Alfred could be compared to Solomon. The setting is a meeting of the king and his *witan*, or counsellors, in Seaford in Sussex, at which time Alfred advises his subjects on the best ways to govern, and to live moral and happy lives. These *Proverbs* are drawn from many sources, including the Old Testament and proverbial collections such as *The Dicts of Cato*.[18] For example, much of *Proverb* 9 may be derived from *The Dicts of Cato*, i. 18; while the idea of *Proverb* 12 is a commonplace derived ultimately from the Old Testament Book of Wisdom 7.30: 'but no evil can overcome wisdom'. *Proverb* 4 is reminiscent of Alfred's division of society into three orders, 'those who pray, those who fight, and those who labour', in his addition to the translation of Boethius's *Consolation of Philosophy*, which outlines his thoughts on the nature of government. The *Proverbs* are didactic and moralistic, and admonitory (as in *Proverbs* 10 and 11, which warn against hoarding treasure while on earth, for example). *Proverbs* 14–17 warn men to be careful in choosing a wife, for women can be attractive on the outside, but of bad character underneath; women irritated by their spouses deliberately deride them in public; a woman will always follow her mother's example; and so on. This set of *Proverbs* repeats stereotypical anti-feminist material found often in medieval literature as diverse as homilies, proverbial collections, and Chaucer's *Prologue* of the Wife of Bath. Other common themes seen in the *Proverbs* reflect the prevalent concerns of medieval authors; for example, the transience of life, the need to choose friends carefully, and the essential requirement to trust in God and do his will.

13   For all of this information and a discussion of the manuscript's history and relationship, see the complete edition of *The Proverbs of Alfred*, ed. O. Arngart, 2 vols (Lund, 1955), II, 1–64.
14   Edited *en face* with the other three versions in Arngart, *The Proverbs of Alfred*, but also edited separately as the Appendix in that same volume at pp. 135–50.
15   See Arngart, *The Proverbs of Alfred*, pp. 55–7.
16   See Cartlidge, 'The Date of *The Owl and the Nightingale*'.

17   Arngart, *The Proverbs of Alfred*, pp. 225–32, analyses the metre and verse form in detail.
18   Of which, interestingly, three copies survive from the period *c.*1100–50, written in transitional English. These survivals, together with *The Proverbs of Alfred* and other similar vernacular texts, suggest the popularity of this form of moralistic writing in the twelfth and thirteenth centuries, in particular.

The Proverbs of Alfred

Incipiunt documenta Regis Alvredi

At Sevorde[19]
Sete þeynes monye, *thanes*
Fele biscopes,
And feole bok-ilered, *scholars*
5 Eorles prute, *noble*
Knyhtes egleche. *valiant*
Þar wes þe Eorl Alvrich,
Of þare lawe swiþe wis, *law; very*
And ek Ealvred, *also Alfred*
10 Englene hurde, *protector of the English*
Englene durlynge; *darling*
On Englenelonde he wes kyng.
  Heom he bigon lere, *He began to teach them*
So ye mawe ihure, *As you might hear*
15 How hi heore lif *their lives*
Lede scholden. *Lead*
Alvred, he wes in Englenelond
An king wel swiþe strong.
He wes king, and he wes clerek,[20] *scholar*
20 Wel he luvede Godes werk.
He wes wis on his word
And war on his werke; *prudent*
He wes þe wysuste mon *wisest*
Þat wes Englelande on.

2

25 Þus queþ Alvred
Englene frouer: *comforter*
  'Wolde ye mi leode *people*
Lusten eure loverde. *Listen to your lord*
He ou wolde wyssye *you; teach*
30 Wisliche þinges: *Wise*
How ye myhte worldes
Wurþscipes welde; *Honour; possess*
And ek eure saule *also your*
Somnen to Criste.' *Assemble*
35   Wyse were þe wordes
Þe seyde þe King Alvred:
  'Mildeliche Ich munye *warn*
Myne leove freond, *dear*
Poure and riche,
40 Leode myne,
Þat ye alle adrede *fear*
Ure Dryhten Crist: *Lord*
Luvyen hine and lykyen *him; please*
For he is Loverd of lyf.

19 Seaford in Sussex.
20 'clerek' here has the meaning of *clericus*, that is, 'literate', 'learned'.

45   He is one God
         Over alle godnesse;
         He is one gleaw   *wise*
         Over alle glednesse;   *Above all joy*
         He is one blisse
50   Over alle blissen;
         He is one monne,
         Mildest mayster;
         He is one folkes fader
         And frouer;   *protector*
55   He is one rihtwis,   *righteous*
         And so riche king,
         Þat him ne schal beo wone   *lacking*
         Nouht of his wille,   *Nothing*
         Wo hine her on worlde   *Whoever*
60   Wurþie þencheþ.'   *Intends to worship*

3
Þus queþ Alvred,
Englene vrouer: *comforter*
    'Ne may non ryhtwis king   *There may be no*
Under Criste seolven,
65 Bute if he beo
In boke ilered;   *learned*
And he his wyttes   *learning*
Swiþe wel kunne;   *knows*
And he cunne lettres,
70 Lokie himseolf one: *And can examine*
How he schule his lond
Laweliche holde.'   *Lawfully*

4
Þus queþ Alvred:
    'Þe eorl and he eþelyng   *nobleman*
75 Ibureþ under godne king,   *belong*
Þat lond to leden
Myd lawelyche deden.
And þe clerek and þe knyht
He schulle demen evelyche riht;   *administer justice fairly*
80 Þe poure and þe ryche
Demen ilyche.   *similarly*
Hwych so þe mon soweþ   *Whatever*
Al swuch he schal mowe;   *Likewise; reap*
And everuyches monnes dom   *every; judgement*
85 To his owere dure churreþ.   *door; returns*
    Þan knyhte bihoveþ   *is obliged*
Kenliche on to fone,   *Courageously to go into battle*
For to werie þat lond   *defend*
Wiþ hunger and wiþ heriunge   *Against; invasion*
90 Þat þe chireche habbe gryþ,   *So that; security*
And þe cheorl beo in fryþ   *common person; peace*
His sedes to sowen,
His medes to mowen;   *meadows*

And his plouh beo idryve   *driven*
95   To ure alre bihove.   *need*
Þis is þes knyhtes lawe:
Loke he þat hit wel fare.'   *goes well*

5

Þus queþ Alvred:
   'Þe mon þe on his youhþe
100   Yeorne leorneþ   *Diligently*
Wit and wisdom
And iwriten reden,   *to read documents*
He may beon on elde   *old age*
Wenliche lorþeu.   *An excellent teacher*
105   And þe þat nule one youhþe   *in*
Yeorne leorny
Wit and wysdom
And iwriten rede,
Þat him schal on elde
110   Sore rewe.   *Sorely regret it*
Þenne cumeþ elde   *When*
and unhelþe,   *ill-health*
Þenne beoþ his wene   *Then; hopes*
Ful wroþe isene.   *evil; seen to be*
115   Boþe heo beoþ biswike   *deceived*
And eke hi beoþ aswunde.'   *also; perished*

6

Þus queþ Alvred:
   'Wyþute wysdome
Is weole wel unwurþ;   *wealth; worthless*
120   For þey o mon ahte   *For though a man possessed*
Hunt-seventi acres,   *seventy*
And he hi hadde isowen
Alle myd reade golde,   *red*
And þat gold greowe
125   So gres doþ on eorþe,   *grass does*
Nere he for his weole   *He would not*
Never þe furþer,   *Get any the further*
Bute he him of frumþe   *Unless; entertainment*
Freond iwurche.   *perform for his friends*
130   For hwat is gold bute ston
Bute if hit haveþ wis mon?'   *Unless it is owned by a wise man?*

7

Þus queþ Alvred:
   'Ne scolde never yong mon
Howyen to swiþe,   *Care too much*
135   Þeih him his wyse   *situation*
Wel ne lykie;
Ne þeih he ne welde   *possess*
Al þat he wolde.   *would like to*
For God may yeve,   *give*
140   Þenne he wule,   *wishes*

God after uvele,   *benefits*
Weole after wowe.   *misfortune*
Wel is him þat hit ischapen is.'   *Happy is he for whom that is destined*

8

Þus seyþ Alvred:
145   'Strong hit is to reowe   *difficult; row*
Ayeyn þe see þat floweþ;   *sea*
So hit is to swynke   *labour*
Ayeyn unylimpe.   *misfortune*
Þe mon þe on his youhþe
150   Swo swinkeþ,
And worldes weole
Her iwinþ   *wins*
Þat he may on elde   *So that*
Idelnesse holde;   *have*
155   And ek myd his worldes weole   *But also*
God iqueme er he quele,   *satisfy; dies*
Youþe and al þat he haveþ idrowe   *performed*
Is þenne wel bitowe.'   *employed*

9

Þus queþ Alvred:
160   'Mony mon weneþ   *Many a man thinks*
Þat he wene ne þarf   *need not expect*
Longes lyves;
Ac him lyeþ he wrench.   *deceives; trick*
For þanne his lyf   *when*
165   Alre best luvede,   *loved best of all*
Þenne he schal leten   *depart from*
Lyf his owe.
For nys no wurt vexynde   *herb; growing*
A wude ne a velde,   *field*
170   Þat ever muwe þas feye   *might; when fated to die*
Furþ upholde.   *Life; support*
Not no mon þene tyme   *No man knows*
Hwanne he schal heonne turne;   *turn away from here*
Ne no mon þene ende   *end result*
175   Hwenne he schal heonne wende.   *leave from here*
Dryhten hit one wot,   *The Lord alone knows it*
Doweþes Loverd,   *Lord of Hosts*
Hwanne ure lif
Leten schule.   *We shall leave*

10

180   Þus queþ Alvred:
'Yf þu seolver and gold
Yefst and weldest in þis world,   *give up; possess*
Never upen eorþe
To wlonk þu ny-wurþe.   *Too proud; may not become*
185   Ayhte nys non ildre istreone   *Property is no ancestors' gain*
Ac hit is Godes lone.   *alone*
Hwanne hit is his wille

Þarof we schulle wende,   *From it; go*
And ure owe lyf
190   Mydalle forleten.   *Entirely lose*
Þanne schulle ure ifon   *foes*
To ure vouh gripen;   *wealth seize*
Welden ure maþmes   *Gain control; treasure*
And leten us byhinde.'   *leave*

11

195   Þus queþ Alvred:
    'Ne ilef þu nouht to fele   *believe; too much*
Uppe þe see þat floweþ,   *sea*
If þu hafst madmes   *treasures*
Monye and inowe,   *Many and sufficient*
200   Gold and seolver;
Hit schal gnyde to nouht,   *crumble*
To duste hit schal dryven;   *pass*
Dryhten schal libben evere.   *The Lord shall live for ever*
Mony mon for his gold
205   Haveþ Godes urre;   *anger*
And for his seolver
Hymseolve foryemeþ,   *neglects*
Foryeteþ and forleseþ.   *Forgets and ruins*
Betere him bycome   *It is better that*
210   Iboren þat he nere.'   *He had never been born*

12

Þus queþ Alvred:
    'Lusteþ ye me leode,   *Listen; people*
Ower is þe neode: *Yours; need*
And Ich eu wille lere   *teach*
215   Wit and wisdom:
Þat alle þing overgoþ.   *pass away*
Syker he may sitte   *secure*
He hyne haveþ to ivere;   *He who has wit as a companion*
For þeyh his eyhte him ago,   *possessions*
220   His wit ne agoþ hym never mo;
For ne may he forvare   *perish*
Þe hyne haveþ to vere,
Þe wile his owe lyf   *As long as*
Ileste mote.'   *Might last*

13

225   Þus queþ Alvred:
    'If þu havest seorewe,
Ne seye þu hit nouht þan arewe.   *don't tell; to a deceiver*
Seye hit þine sadelbowe,   *saddlebow*
And ryd þe singinde forþ.
230   Þenne wile wene,   *he expect*
Þet þine wise ne con,   *who your situation does not know*
Þat þe þine wise   *your situation*
Wel lyke.   *Pleases you well*
Serewe if þu havest

235	And þe erewe hit wot,	*knows*
	Byfore he þe meneþ,	*In front of you he consoles you*
	Byhynde he þe teleþ.	*Behind your back he reviles you*
	Þu hit myht segge swyhc mon	*reveal; to the very*
	Þat þe ful wel on,	*Who would wish it on you*
240	Wyþute echere ore	*any pity*
	He on þe muchele more.	*much*
	Byhud hit on þire heorte,	*Conceal*
	Þat þe eft ne smeorte;	*So that it will not harm you again*
	Ne let þu hyne wite	*And do not let him know*
245	Al þat þin heorte bywite.'[21]	*may care about*

14
Þus queþ Alvred:

	'Ne schaltu nevere þi wif	*should you; your wife*
	By hire wlyte cheose,	*looks choose*
	For never none þinge	*And never for anything*
250	Þat heo to þe bryngeþ.	*she*
	Ac leorne hire custe,	*character*
	Heo cuþeþ hi wel sone.	*will reveal; very soon*
	For mony mon for ayhte	*wealth*
	Uvele iauhteþ,	*bargains badly*
255	And ofte mon of fayre	*for beauty*
	Frakele icheoseþ.	*Chooses what is worthless*
	Wo is him þat uvel wif	
	Bryngeþ to his cotlyf;	*dwelling*
	So him is alyve	*As it is for him in life*
260	Þat uvele ywyveþ.	*Who marries badly*
	For he schal uppen eorþe	
	Dreori iwurþe.	*Miserable become*
	Mony mon singeþ	
	Þat wif hom bryngeþ;	
265	Wiste he hwat he brouhte	*If he knew*
	Wepen he myhte.'	*Weep*

15
Þus queþ Alvred:

	'Ne wurþ þu never so wod	*be; mad*
	Ne so wyn-drunke,	*drunk with wine*
270	Þat evere segge þine wife	*tell*
	Alle þine wille.	*desires*
	For if þu iseye þe bivore	*in front of you*
	Þine ivo alle,	*enemies*
	And þu hi myd worde	*her*
275	Iwreþþed hevedest,	*Angered*
	Ne scholde heo hit lete	*she omit*
	For þing lyvyinde,	*for any living thing*
	Þat heo ne scholde þe forþ upbreyde	*reprove*
	Of þine baleusyþes.	*misfortunes*
280	Wymmon is word-wod,	*word-mad (wild in speech)*

---

21 Compare these lines to *The Wanderer*, lines 11b–14, where the speaker comments that it is a noble custom in a nobleman that he binds his heart fast, holds his heart, and thinks as he will (without revealing his thoughts).

And haveþ tunge to swift;   *too*
Þeyh heo wel wolde,   *Even if she really wanted to*
Ne may heo hi nowiht welde.'   *in no way control*

16
Þus queþ Alfred:
285   'Idelschipe   *Vanity*
And over-prute   *excessive pride*
Þat lereþ yong wif   *teaches*
Uvele þewes,   *Bad habits*
And ofte þat wolde
290 Do þat heo ne scholde.
Þene unþeu lihte   *Then bad habits easily*
Leten heo myhte,   *she might give up*
If heo ofte a swote   *in a sweat*
Forswunke were.   *Was exhausted with hard work*
295 Þeyh hit is uvel to buwe   *Yet it is difficult to bend*
Þat beo nule treowe;   *That which refuses to be straight*
For ofte museþ þe kat
After hire moder.[22]
Þe mon þat let wymmon   *allows*
300 His mayster iwurþe,   *to become*
Ne schal he never beon ihurd   *listened to*
His wordes loverd;   *As the lord of his own words*
Ac heo hine schal steorne   *cruelly*
Totrayen and toteone,   *torment; harass*
305 And selde wurþ he blyþe and gled   *seldom will he*
Þe mon þat is his wives qued.   *wretch*
Mony appel is bryht wiþute   *shiny on the outside*
And bitter wiþinne;
So is mony wymmon
310 On hyre fader bure   *father's house*
Schene under schete,   *Beautiful; sheet*
And þeyh heo is schendful.   *yet; shameless*
So is mony gedelyng   *knight in arms*
Godlyche on horse,   *Splendid*
315 And is þeyh lutel wurþ: *yet worth little*
Wlonk bi þe glede,   *Brave by the hearth*
And uvel at þare neode.'   *Useless in time of need*

17
Þus queþ Alvred:
    'Evre þu bi þine lyve   *Don't ever in your life*
320 Þe word of þine wyve
To swiþe þu ne arede.   *Too quickly heed as advice*
If heo beo iwreþþed   *angered*
Myd worde oþer myd dede,   *With*
Wymmon wepeþ for mode   *rage*
325 Oftere þan for eny god;   *More often; good reason*
And ofte lude and stille   *quiet*

---

22 'For often the cat [or kitten] will catch a mouse in the way that
its mother did.' All women take after their mothers.

For to vordrye hire wille.   *get her own way*
Heo wepeþ oþer hwile   *at other times*
For to do þe gyle.   *a trick*
330   Salomon hit haveþ ised
Þat wymmon can wel uvelne red.   *well knows evil counsel*
Þe hire red foleweþ,   *He who*
Heo bryngeþ hine to seorewe.
For hit seyþ in þe loþ[23]   *song*
335 As cuenes forteoþ.   *How women deceive*
Hit is ifurn iseyd   *said long ago*
Þat cold red is quene red;   *That a woman's advice is cold*
Hu he is unlede   *miserable*
Þat foleweþ hire rede.
340 Ich hit ne segge nouht forþan   *I do not say therefore*
Þat god þing ys god wymmon,
Þe mon be hi may icheose   *When a man can choose her*
And icovere over oþre.'   *win her over the others*

18

Þus queþ Alvred:
345   'Mony mon weneþ   *thinks*
Þat he weny ne þarf   *should not trust*
Freond þat he habbe:
Þar me him vayre bihat,   *promises*
Seyþ him vayre bivore   *in front of him*
350 And frakele bihynde.   *evilly behind his back*
So me may þane loþe   *enemy*
Lengust lede.   *Longest delude*
Ne ilef þu never þane mon   *believe*
Þat is of feole speche;   *many speeches*
355 Ne alle þe þinge
Þat þu iherest singe.
Mony mon haveþ swikelne muþ,   *deceitful*
Milde and monne forcuþ;   *Gentle but wicked to men*
Nele he þe cuþe   *He will not reveal to you*
360 Hwenne he þe wule bikache.'   *deceive*

19

Þus queþ Alvred:
'Þurh sawe mon is wis,   *proverbs*
And þurh hiselþe mon is glev;   *goodness; prudent*
Þurh lesinge mon is loþ,   *lying; hateful*
365 And þurh luþre wrenches unwurþ;   *evil tricks worthless*
And þurh hokede honde þat he bereþ,   *thieving hands*
Himseolve he forvareþ: *He ruins himself*
From lesynge þu þe wune;   *Get out of the habit of lying*
And alle unþewes þu þe bischune,   *bad habits; shun*
370 So myht þu on þeode   *among men*
Leof beon in alle leode.   *Dear; among all people*
And luve þyne nexte –   *neighbour*
He is at þe neode god;   *useful*

23　The Book of Proverbs.

At chepynge and at chyreche	*market; church*

375 Freond þu þe iwurche, *obtain*
Wyþ povere and wiþ riche, *Among*
Wiþ alle monne ilyche. *equally*
Þanne myht þu sikerliche *securely*
Sely sytte; *Happily*
380 And ek faren over londe *journey*
Hwider so beoþ þi wille.' *Wherever you want to*

20

Þus queþ Alvred:
  'Alle world ayhte *possessions*
Schulle bicumen to nouhte;
385 And uyches cunnes madmes *kind of treasure*
To mixe schulen imulten. *dung; dwindle*
And ure owe lif
Lutel hwile ileste: *lasts*
For þeyh o mon wolde *wanted*
390 Al þe worlde,
And al þe wunne *joys*
Þe þarinne wunyeþ, *dwelled*
Ne myhte he þarmyde his lif *therewith*
None hwile holde; *retain for no period of time*
395 Ac al he schal forleten *lose*
On a litel stunde. *while*
And schal ure blisse
To balewe us iwurþe, *evil; become*
Bute if we wurcheþ *perform*
400 Wyllen Cristes.
Nu biþenche we *consider*
Þanne us sulve, *ourselves*
Ure lif to leden
So Crist us gynneþ lere. *begins; to teach*
405 Þanne mawe we wenen *hope*
Þat he wule us wurþie, *honour*
For so seyde Salomon þe wise:
Þe mon þat her wel deþ *does well*
He cumeþ þar he lyen foþ *will be received*
410 On his lyves ende,
He hit schal avynde.' *find out*

21

Þus queþ Alvred:
  'Ne gabbe þu ne schotte, *mock; quarrel*
Ne chid þu wyþ none sotte, *quarrel; fool*
415 Ne myd manyes cunnes tales, *many kinds of*
Ne chid þu wiþ nenne dwales. *idiots*
Ne never þu ne bigynne
To telle þine tyþinges *news*
At nones fremannes borde. *franklin's table*
420 Ne have þu to vale worde: *many*
Mid fewe worde wismon
Fele biluken wel con, *to enclose*

And sottes bolt is sone ischote.   *And a fool's arrow is soon shot*
Forþi Ich holde hine for dote,   *weak-minded fool*
425   Þat sayþ al his wille
Þanne he scholde beon stille.   *quiet*
For ofte tunge brekeþ bon   *bone*
Þeyh heo seolf nabbe non.'[24]

22

Þus queþ Alvred:
430   'Wis child is fader blisse,
If hit so bitydeþ   *happens*
Þat þu bern ibidest   *son have*
Þe hwile hit is lutel.
Ler him mon þewes   *Teach; good habits*
435   Þanne hit is wexynde;   *growing*
Hit schal wende þarto   *proceed along those lines*
Þe betere hit schal iwurþe,   *become*
Ever buven eorþe.   *on*
Ac if þu him lest welde   *neglect to control*
440   Wexende on worlde,
Lude and stille
His owene wille.   *He will do what he pleases*
Hwanne cumeþ ealde,   *old age*
Ne myht þu hyne awelde;   *manage*
445   Þanne deþ hit sone   *Then the child soon does*
Þat þe biþ unqueme;   *displeasing*
Oferhoweþ þin ibod   *He despises; command*
And makeþ þe ofte sorymod.   *sorrowful*
Betere þe were
450   Iboren þat he nere;
For betere is child unbore   *unborn*
Þane unbuhsum.   *disobedient*
Þe mon þe spareþ yeorde   *rod*
And yonge childe,
455   And let hit arixlye   *have its own way*
Þat he hit areche ne may,   *control*
Þat him schal on ealde
Sore reowe.   *Sorely regret*

Amen. *Expliciunt dicta Regis Alvredi.*

---

24   i.e. the tongue can (indirectly) break bones, though it has no
bones itself.

London, British Library, Cotton Caligula A. ix

London, British Library, Cotton Caligula A. ix, is a manuscript dated to the last quarter of the thirteenth century that is made up of two, originally separate, manuscripts. Part I, folios 3 recto to 194 verso, contains the verse chronicle, Laȝamon's *Brut*. Part II, folios 195 recto to 261 verso, contains *The Owl and the Nightingale* and seven English religious texts, as well as a number of French texts, both religious and historical. The religious texts, such as *Death's Winter-Clench*, *The Last Day* and *Dooms-*day, warn of the inevitability of death, and admonish the audience to serve Christ. *A Lutel Soth Sermon* is a satirical poem dealing with abuses in contemporary England, and again, attempting to urge the sinful to repent in order to achieve salvation. Caligula A. ix shares these texts and others with another contemporary manuscript, Oxford, Jesus College 29. The manuscript, like Jesus 29, is thought to have originated in the West Midlands region.

LAȝAMON'S *BRUT*

Laȝamon's *Brut*, a 16,000-line alliterative verse chronicle narrating the history of Britain, is contained in London, British Library, Cotton Caligula A. ix, folios 3 recto to 194 verso, and London, British Library, Cotton Otho C. xiii, folios 1 recto to 146 verso. Both of these manuscripts can be dated to the last quarter of the thirteenth century, though the text itself is earlier in date than these manuscript copies. The *Brut* in Otho C. xiii is shorter than Caligula A. ix's text, and also differs linguistically, but it seems that both copies were derived from a common exemplar.[1]

Laȝamon himself was a priest at Areley Kings in Worcestershire, as he reveals in his Preface to his text. He wrote the work at the beginning of the thirteenth century, or a little earlier.[2] His main source was the *Roman de Brut*, a verse history written in Anglo-Norman by Wace in the middle of the twelfth century, which Wace presented to Eleanor of Aquitaine, queen of Henry II. Wace, in turn, used for his source the prose *Historia Regum Britanniae* composed in Latin by Geoffrey of Monmouth in the first half of the twelfth century. It is in Geoffrey that the legend of King Arthur of the Britons finds its literary genesis,[3] and, indeed, Arthur was to become one of the greatest heroes of many medieval Romances and chronicles in English and French. Laȝamon's *Brut*, although deriving its structure and its episodes from the antecedent *Brut* of Wace, and thus, indirectly, from Geoffrey, is longer than both of these works, and expands considerably on the source material in some parts of the story, such as the Arthurian section which forms almost half of Laȝamon's text where it is only one-fifth of Geoffrey's.[4] The medieval concept of history as witnessed in these three works is not that which we would tend to think of as the iteration of historical facts. In Geoffrey, Wace and Laȝamon, 'history' becomes a mixture of true events, of legend and of myth. Anachronistic elements are integrated into the process of compilation,[5] and one is as likely to encounter a fairy[6] or magical prophecies as an historical figure.

Laȝamon composed his text using the alliterative verse line comprised of two linked half-lines, often with regular stress, which is reminiscent of Old English verse. Within some verse lines, Laȝamon is also influenced by the French-inspired couplet form incorporating rhyme at the ends of half-lines; for example, line 11442 'Timber me lete *biwinnen* and þat beord *biginnen*' (Timber was brought and that table was started). He also seems deliberately to employ archaisms and an overall style that Barron suggests is 'a self-consciously literary effort to devise a medium appropriate to his view of his subject, a national chronicle breathing the spirit of the heroic age'.[7] Certainly much of his treatment of Arthur in the Round Table episode edited below recalls aspects of heroic poetry such as *Beowulf*. In particular, the description of the feasting in Arthur's court recalls that of the feasting in Heorot; the emphasis on Arthur as the most noble of kings, unsurpassed in the world at that time, is similar to the superlative description of Beowulf; and the concept that the fame of past heroes survives because of their glory and the world's memory of that glory is of fundamental importance in both poems.

The extracts from the *Brut* that are edited here are

---

1 All of this information can be obtained from W. R. J. Barron and S. C. Weinberg, eds, *Laȝamon's Brut* (London, 1995). This is a full edition of the Caligula text with *en face* translation. Much of the information given here in my introduction derives from the Introduction in Barron and Weinberg, pp. ix–xx.

2 See Barron and Weinberg, *Laȝamon's Brut*, p. ix. See also J. A. W. Bennett, *Middle English Literature*, ed. and comp. D. Gray (Oxford, 1986; repr. 1990), pp. 68–89 for a detailed reading of the *Brut*.

3 Although as Bennett points out (*Middle English Literature*, p. 88) with regard to *English* literature: 'Layamon's most important role

lies in establishing the Matter (or Myth) of Britain, and of Arthur.'

4 Barron and Weinberg, *Laȝamon's Brut*, p. xvi.

5 The reign of Athelstan, the tenth-century king and grandson of Alfred, is, for example, made contemporary with the reign of Cadwallader, the seventh-century king.

6 For example, at Arthur's birth (lines 9604–15), the *alven*, 'fairies', receive him and endow him with qualities that make him outstanding among men.

7 W. R. J. Barron, *English Medieval Romance* (London, 1987), pp. 134–5.

Laȝamon's Preface, in which he tells us something about himself and his methodology in composing his work (lines 1–35); and the creation of Arthur's Round Table (lines 11345–517), which is probably Laȝamon's own addition to the thirteen-line description he found in Wace. The Round Table episode occurs after Arthur, king of the Britons, has succeeded in conquering the Saxons, and subduing a number of kingdoms including Ireland, Iceland, Scotland and Jutland; he is thus in the process of becoming the most powerful king in Europe. When his subjects arrive to celebrate the Christmas season, a fight breaks out between them because each thinks he should have precedence over the others. Arthur meets a skilled carpenter who suggests that he should be permitted to construct the Round Table to facilitate peace among the subject kings and their entourages when they are at court. Laȝamon ends this section of the text by emphasizing Arthur's supremacy as a knight and king, his long-lasting fame, and the prophecy of Merlin, still believed by the Britons in Laȝamon's day, that Arthur will return to his people, even though he appeared to have died.

Laȝamon's *Brut*

Incipit Hystoria Brutonum

An preost wes on leoden, Laȝamon wes ihoten;
He wes Leovenaðes sone: liðe him beo Drihten.
He wonede at Ernleȝe, at aeðelen are chirechen
Uppen Sevarne staþe (sel þar him þuhte)
5 Onfest Radestone. Þer he bock radde.
   Hit com him on mode and on his mern þonke
Þet he wolde of Engle þa æðelæn tellen,
Wat heo ihoten weoren and wonene heo comen
Þa Englene londe ærest ahten
10 Æfter þan flode þe from Drihtene com,
Þe al her aquelde quic þat he funde,
Buten Noe and Sem, Japhet and Cham,
And heore four wives þe mid heom weren on archen.
   Laȝamon gon liðen wide ȝond þas leode,
15 And biwon þa æðela boc þa he to bisne nom.
He nom þa Englisca boc þa makede Seint Beda.
Anoper he nom on Latin þe makede Seinte Albin
And þe feire Austin þe fulluht broute hider in.
Boc he nom þe þridde, leide þer amidden,
20 Þa makede a Frenchis clerc,
Wace wes ihoten, þe wel coupe writen;
And he hoe ȝef þare æðelen Ælienor
Þe wes Henries quene þes heȝes kinges.
Laȝamon leide þeos boc and þa leaf wende;
25 He heom leofliche biheold: liþe him beo Drihten!
Feþeren he nom mid fingren and fiede on boc-felle,
And þa soþere word sette togadere,
And þa þre boc þrumde to are.
   Nu biddeð Laȝamon
30 Alcne æðele mon, for þene almiten Godd,
Þet þeos boc rede and leornia þeos runan,
Þat he þeos soðfeste word segge tosumne

Laȝamon's *Brut*

Here begins the history of the Britons

A priest was among the people, Laȝamon he was called;
He was Leovenath's son: may God be merciful to him.
He lived at Areley, by a noble church
Upon the bank of the Severn (it seemed good to him there),
Close to Redstone. There he read books.
    It came into his mind as an excellent idea
That he would tell of the noble English,
What they were called and from where they came
Those who first had possession of the land of the English,
After the flood which came from God,
Which killed all those which it found living,
Except Noah and Shem, Japhet and Ham
And their four wives who were with them in the ark.
    Laȝamon went travelling widely throughout the land,
And got the noble books which he took as examples.
He took the English book made by Saint Bede;[8]
Another one he took in Latin was made by Saint Albin
And the blessed Augustine who brought baptism here.[9]
He took a third book, and laid it amidst the others,
That was created by a French cleric
Whose name was Wace,[10] he could write well;
And he gave it to the noble Eleanor[11]
Who was Henry's queen, that great king.
Laȝamon opened this book and turned the leaves;
He looked at them joyfully: God be merciful to him.
He took feathers with his fingers and wrote on book-skins[12]
And the true words put together,
And the three books were joined into one.
    Now Laȝamon asks
That each good man, for the sake of almighty God,
That this book reads and learns its secrets,
That he these true words he should say in full

8 Bede's *Ecclesiastical History of the English People*, an eighth-century history and major source for all subsequent historians.
9 Albin was archbishop of Canterbury 708–32; Augustine brought Christianity to the southern English people at the end of the sixth century. This book to which Laȝamon refers is unknown now.
10 Wace's *Roman de Brut*, written by 1155.
11 Eleanor of Aquitaine, wife of Henry II.
12 He picked up a quill and began writing on parchment made from the skin of sheep.

For his fader saule   þa hine forðbrouhte,
And for his moder saule   þa hine to monne iber,

35   And for his awene saule   þat hire þe selre beo. Amen.

Lines 11345–517

{The Establishment of the Round Table and The Prophecy of Merlin}

11345   Ich mai sugge hu hit iwarð,   wunder þæh hit þunche.
Hit wes in ane ȝeol-dæie   þat Arður in Lundene lai,
Þa weoren him to icumen   of alle his kinerichen –
Of Brutlonde, of Scotlonde,   of Irlonde, of Islonde,
And of al þan londe   þe Arður hæfede an honde –

11350   Alle þa hæxte þeines   mid horsen and mid sweines.
Þer weoren seoven kingene sunes   mid seoven hundred cnihten icumen,
Wiðuten þan hired   þe herede Arðure.
Ælc hafede an heorte   leches heȝe,
And lette þat he weore   betere þan his ivere.

11355   Þat folc wes of feole londe;   þer wes muchel onde
Forþe an hine talde hæh,   þe oðer muche herre.
     Þa bleou mon þa bemen   and þa bordes bradden;
Water me brohte an uloren   mid guldene læflen,
Seoððen claðes soften   al of white seolke.

11360   Þa sat Arður adun   and bi him Wenhaver þa quene;
Seoððen sete þa eorles   and þerafter þa beornes;
Seoððen þa cnihtes,   al swa mon heom dihte.
Þa heȝe iborne   þene mete beoren
Æfne forðrihten   þa to þan cnihten,

11365   Þa touward þan þæinen,   þa touward þan sweinen,
Þa touward þan bermonnen   forð at þan borden.
Þa duȝeðe wærð iwraðfed;   duntes þer weoren rive:
Ærest þa laves heo weorpen   þa while þa heo ilæsten;
And þa bollen seolverne   mid wine iuulled;

11370   And seoððen þa vustes   vusden to sweoren.
     Þa leop þer forð a ȝung mon   þe ut of Winetlonde com,
He wes iȝefen Arðure   to halden to ȝisle,
He wes Rumarettes sune,   þas kinges of Winette.
Þus seide þe cniht þere   to Arðure Kinge:

11375   'Laverd Arður, buh raðe   into þine bure,
And þi quene mid þe,   and þine mæies cuðe,
And we þis comp scullen todelen   wið þas uncuðe kempen.'
     Æfne þan worde   he leop to þan borde
Þer leien þa cnives   biforen þan leod-kinge;

11380   Þreo cnifes he igrap,   and mid þan anæ he smat
I þere swere þe cniht   þe ærest bigon þat ilke fiht
Þat his hefved i þene flor   hælde to grunde.
Sone he sloh ænneoðer,   þes ilke þeines broðer;
Ær þa sweordes comen,   seovene he afelde.

11385   Þer wes fæht swiðe græt;   ælc mon oðer smat;
Þer wes muchel blodgute;   balu wes an hirede.
     Þa com þe king buȝen   ut of his buren,
Mid him an hundred beornen   mid helmen and mid burnen;
Ælc bar an his riht hond   whit stelene brond.

For his father's soul who brought him forth,
And for his mother's soul who bore him as a male-child,

35   And for his own soul that it might be better for it. Amen.

Lines 11345–517

[The Establishment of the Round Table and The Prophecy of Merlin]

11345   I can relate how it happened, though it will seem a wonder.
It was on a day in Yuletide when Arthur lay in London,
When there came to him from all of his kingdoms –
From Britain, from Scotland, from Ireland, from Iceland,
And from all the lands that Arthur controlled in his hands –

11350   All the highest thanes with horses and servants.
There seven kings' sons with seven hundred knights arrived,
Not including the servants who served Arthur.
Each had noble feelings in his heart,
And considered that he was better than his companions.

11355   Those people were from many lands; there was a great deal of envy
Because the one counted himself high, and the other much higher.
    Then trumpets were blown and the tables were spread;
Water was brought in bowls adorned with gold,
Then the soft cloths that were made entirely from white silk.

11360   Then Arthur sat down and Quinevere the queen sat by him;
Then the earls sat down and after them the noblemen;
Then the knights, just as they were instructed.
Then the nobles carried the food
Immediately to the knights,

11365   Then to the thanes, then to the household men,
Then to the servants alongside the table.
The noble-retainers were angry then; there were plentiful blows;
First loaves were thrown as long as they were in supply;
And then silver bowls filled with wine;

11370   And afterwards fists were thrust at necks.
    Then a young man, who came from Winetland, leapt forwards there,
He was given to Arthur to keep as a hostage,
He was the son of Rumareth, the king of Winetland.
There the knight said to King Arthur in this way:

11375   'Lord Arthur, go quickly into your chamber,
And take the queen with you, and your known kinsmen,
And we shall separate this fight between these foreign warriors.'
    With these words he leapt onto the table
Where knives lay in front of the people's king;

11380   He gripped three knives, and with one he struck
In the neck the knight who had started that same fight
So that his head fell down on the ground.
Immediately, he struck another, this same thane's brother;
Before swords arrived, he had killed seven.

11385   There was very great conflict; each man struck the other;
There was substantial bloodshed; the court was in turmoil.
    Then the king came hurrying out of his chamber,
With a hundred knights with helmets and mailcoats;
Each carried in his right hand a bright steel sword.

11390   Þa cleopede Arður,   aðelest kingen:
    'Sitteð, sitteð swiðe,   elc mon bi his live!
    And waswa þat nulle don   he scal fordemed beon.
    Nimeð me þene ilke mon   þa þis feht ærst bigon,
    And doð widðe an his sweore   and draȝeð hine to ane more,
11395   And doð hine in an ley ven   þer he scal liggen;
    And nimeð al his nexte cun   þa ȝe maȝen ivinden
    And swengeð of þa hafden   mid breoden eouwer sweorden.
    Þa wifmen þa ȝe maȝen ifinden   of his nexten cunden,
    Kerveð of hire neose   and heore wlite ga to lose,
11400   And swa Ich wulle al fordon   þat cun þat he of com.
    And ȝif Ich averemare   seoððen ihere
    Þat æi of mine hirede,   of heȝe na of loȝe,
    Of þissen ilke slehte   æft sake arere,
    Ne sculde him neoðer gon fore   gold ne na gærsume,
11405   Hæh hors no hære scrud   þat he ne sculde beon ded,
    Oðer mid horsen todraȝen   þat is elches swiken laȝen.
    Bringeð þene halidom   and Ich wulle swerien þeron,
    Swa ȝe scullen cnihtes   þe weoren at þissen fihte,
    Eorles and beornes,   þat ȝe hit breken nulleð.'
11410   Ærst sweor Arður,   aðelest kingen,
    Seoððen sworen eorles,   seoððen sweoren beornes,
    Seoððen sweoren þeines,   seoððen sweoren sweines
    Þat heo naveremare   þe sake nulde arere.
    Me nom alle þa dede   and to leirstowe heom ladden.
11415   Seoððen me bleou bemen   mid swiðe murie dremen;
    Weoren him leof weoren him læð,   elc þer feng water and clæð,
    And seoððen adun seten   sæhte to borden,
    Al for Arðure æiȝe,   aðelest kingen.
    Birles þer þurngen,   gleomen þer sungen,
11420   Harpen gunnen dremen;   duȝeþe wes on selen;
    Þus fulle seoveniht   wes þan hirede idiht.
      Seoððen, hit seið in þere tale,   þe king ferde to Cornwale.
    Þer him com to anan   þat wæs a crafti weorcmon,
    And þene king imette   and feiere hine grætte:
11425   'Hail seo þu, Arður,   aðelest kinge.
    Ich æm þin aȝe mon;   moni lond Ich habbe þurhgan.
    Ich con of treowrekes   wunder feole craftes.
    Ich iherde suggen   biȝeonde sæ neowe tidende
    Þat þine cnihtes   at þine borde gunnen fihte;
11430   A Midewinteres dæi   moni þer feollen.
    For heore mucchele mode   morðgomen wrohten,
    And for heore hehȝe cunne   ælc wolde beon wiðinne.
    Ah Ich þe wulle wurche   a bord swiðe hende
    Þat þer maȝen sitten to   sixtene hundred and ma
11435   Al turn abuten   þat nan ne beon wiðuten;
    Wiðuten and wiðinne   mon toȝæines monne.
    Whenne þu wult riden   wið þe þu miht hit leden,
    And setten hit whar þu wulle,   after þine iwille.
    And ne dert þu navere adrede   to þere worlde longen

11390 Then Arthur called out, the noblest of kings:
          'Sit, sit quickly, each man at risk of his life!
          And whoever does not sit down shall be condemned.
          Seize that same man, who started this fight first,
          And put a rope around his neck and drag him to a moor,
11395   And put him in a boggy fen where he shall lie;
          And seize all his next of kin that you can find,
          And cut off their heads with your broad swords.
          The women who are his closest kin that you can find,
          Cut off their noses so their looks go to ruin,
11400   And in this way I will destroy that family from which he came.
          And if I ever hear afterwards
          That any of my household, either noble or common,
          Should raise this same fight after the conflict,
          He shall be ransomed by neither gold nor precious stones,
11405   Neither tall horses nor battle garments shall prevent him from being killed,
          Or drawn with horses which is each traitor's penalty.
          Bring the relics and I shall swear upon them,
          So shall you knights that were at this fight,
          Earls and noblemen, so that you will not break it.'
11410   First Arthur swore, the noblest of kings,
          After the earls swore, after the knights swore,
          Then the thanes swore, then the retainers swore
          That they would never more raise that conflict.
          The dead were all taken and carried to the burial ground.
11415   Afterwards, trumpets were blown with a very merry sound;
          Whether they were dear or hateful to one another, each shared the water and towel,[13]
          And then sat down in friendship at the table,
          All in awe of Arthur, the noblest of kings.
          Cupbearers thronged there, minstrels sang there,
11420   Harps began to sound joy; the crowd was in good spirits;
          For an entire week the court was maintained like this.
              Afterwards, it says in the tale, the king went to Cornwall.
          There a man who was a skilled craftsman came to him,
          And he met the king and pleasantly greeted him:
11425   'Good health to you, Arthur, most noble king,
          I am your own man; I have travelled through many lands.
          I know many marvellous skills of carpentry.
          I heard beyond the sea fresh news
          That your knights had begun a fight at your table;
11430   On Midwinter's Day many fell there.
          Because of their great pride they created a murderous game,
          And because of their high ancestry each wanted to be included.
          But I shall create for you a very noble table
          So that sixteen hundred and more might sit
11435   Around the extent of it so that none is excluded;
          Man will sit facing man on the outside and inside.
          When you wish to leave you can take it with you,
          And put it wherever you want to, as you prefer.
          And you need not fear, as long as the world lasts,

13   Washed their hands and dried them, as was customary before
feasting.

11440   Þat ævere ænie modi cniht   at þine borde makie fiht,
For þer scal þe hehȝe   beon æfne þan loȝe.'
    Timber me lete biwinnen   and þat beord biginnen;
To feouwer wikene virste   þat wrec wes ivorðed.
    To ane heȝe dæie   þat hired wes isomned,
11445   And Arður himseolf beh   sone to þan borde,
And hehte alle his cnihtes   to þan borde forðrihtes.
Þo alle weoren iseten   cnihtes to heore mete,
Þa spæc ælc wið oðer   alse hit weore his broðer;
Alle heo seten abuten   nes þer nan wiðuten.
11450   Ævere ælches cunnes cniht   þere wes swiðe wel idiht;
Alle heo weoren bi ane,   þa hehȝe and þa laȝe.
Ne mihten þer nan ȝelpen   for oðere kunnes scenchen
Oðer his iveren   þe at þan beorde weoren.
    Þis wes þat ilke bord   þat Bruttes of ȝelpeð,
11455   And sugeð feole cunne lesinge   bi Arðure þan kinge.
Swa deð averalc mon   þe oðer luvien con
Ȝif he is him to leof   þenne wule he liȝen,
And suggen on him wurðscipe   mare þenne he beon wurðe;
Ne beo he no swa luðer mon   þat his freond him wel ne on.
11460   Æft ȝif on volke   feondscipe arereð
An æveræi time   bitweone twon monnen,
Me con bi þan læðe   lasinge suggen;
Þeh he weore þe bezste mon   þe ævere æt at borde,
Þe mon þe him weore lað   him cuðe last finden.
11465   Ne al soh ne al les   þat leodscopes singeð,
Ah þis is þat soððe   bi Arðure þan kinge:
Nes næver ar swulc king   swa duhti þurh alle þing;
For þat soðe stod a þan writen   hu hit is iwurðen
Ord from þan ænden   of Arðure þan kinge
11470   No mare no lasse   buten alse his laȝen weoren.
Ah Bruttes hine luveden swiðe   and ofte him on liȝeð,
And suggeð feole þinges   bi Arðure þan kinge
Þat nævere nes iwurðen   a þissere weorlde-richen.
Inoh he mai suggen,   þe soð wule vremmen,
11475   Seolcuðe þinges   bi Arðure Kinge.
Þa wes Arður swiðe heh,   his hired swiðe hende,
Þat nas na cniht wel itald   no of his tuhlen swiðe bald,
Inne Wales no in Ænglelond,   inne Scotlond no in Irlond,
In Normandie no inne France,   inne Flandres no inne Denemarc,
11480   No in navere none londe   þe a þeos halfe Mungiu stondeð,
Þet weoren ihalde god cniht,   no his deden itald oht
Bute he cuðe of Arður   and of aðelen his hirede,
His wepnen and his weden   and his horsleden,
Suggen and singen   of Arður þan ginge,
11485   And of his hired-cnihten   and of heȝe heore mihten,
And of heore richedome   and hu wel hit heom bicomen.
Þenne weore he wilcume   a þissere weorlde-richen,
Come þer he come,   and þeh he weore i Rome.
    Al þat iherde   of Arðure telle
11490   Heom þuhte muchel seollic   of selen þan kinge.
And swa hit wes ivuren iboded   ær he iboren weoren,
Swa him sæide Merlin,   þe witeȝe wes mære,

11440 That any proud knight will ever create conflict at your table,
For there the high will be even with the low.'
  Timber was brought and that table was started;
In the space of four weeks that work was finished.
  On a feast day the court was gathered together,
11445 And Arthur himself went immediately to the table,
And commanded all his knights to come to the table straight away.
When they were all seated as knights about their feast,
Then each spoke with the other just as if he were his brother;
They all sat around, and not one of them was excluded there.
11450 Each and every kind of knight was very well established there;
They were all as one, the high and the low.
Nor could any of them brag that he had a different kind of food
Other than his companions had who were at the table.
  This was that same table that the Britons boast of,
11455 And say many kinds of fictitious things about Arthur the king.
Every man who feels love for another does this too
If he is too dear to him then he will lie,
And say more in worship of him than the beloved man is worthy of;
There is no man so hateful that his friend will not speak well of him.
11460 Again, if hatred arises between people
At anytime between two men,
Lies will be told about the one who is hated;
Even though he were the best man who was ever at a table,
The man who hated him would be able to find fault with him.
11465   Not everything that minstrels sing is all truth or all lies,
But this is the truth about Arthur the king:
There was never such a king before, so courageous in all things;
For that truth has remained in writing always, about how it happened
For Arthur the king, from beginning to end,
11470 No more, no less, other than as his deeds were.
For the Britons loved him greatly and often tell lies about him,
And say numerous things about Arthur the king
That never occurred in this worldly kingdom.
It is sufficient for one to say in speaking the truth
11475 The wonderful things about King Arthur.
Arthur was very great, his court very noble,
So that no knight was respected or his deeds thought courageous,
Not in Wales or in England, in Scotland or in Ireland,
In Normandy or in France, in Flanders or in Denmark,
11480 Or in any land which stands on this side of the Alps,
Who was held to be as good a knight, nor would his deeds count for anything
Unless he knew of Arthur and of his noble court,
His weapons and his armour and his cavalry,
And could relate in song of Arthur the youth
11485 And of his courtly knights and their noble strength,
And of their splendour and how well it became them.
Then he would be welcome anywhere in this worldly kingdom,
Come wherever he might, even if he were in Rome.
  All that heard tell of Arthur
11490 Thought it a great wonder about that noble king.
And so it had been prophesied before he had been born,
As Merlin the famous prophet had said about him,

Þat a king sculde cume   of Uðere Pendragune
Þat gleomen sculden wurchen burd   of þas kinges breosten,
11495   And þerto sitten,   scopes swiðe sele,
And eten heore wullen   ær heo þenne fusden,
And winscenches ut teon   of þeos kinges tungen
And drinken and dreomen   daies and nihtes;
Þis gomen heom sculde ilasten   to þere weorlde longe.
11500   And ȝet him seide Marlin   mare þat wes to comene:
Þat al þat he lokede on   to foten him sculde buȝen.
Þa ȝet him sæide Mærlin   a sellic þe wes mare:
Þat sculde beon unimete care   of þas kinges forðfare
And of þas kinges ende   nulle hit na Brut ileve,
11505   Buten hit beon þe leste dæð   at þan muchele Dome
Þenne ure Drihte   demeð alle volke;
Ælles ne cunne we demen   of Arðures deðen,
For he seolf sæide   to sele his Brutten –
Suð inne Cornwale   þer Walwain wes forfaren,
11510   And himseolf wes forwunded   wunder ane swiðe –
Þat he varen wolde   into Avalune,
Into þan æitlonde,   to Argante þere hende,
For heo sculde mid haleweie   helen his wunden,
And þenne he weore al hal   he wolde sone come heom.
11515   Þis ilefde Bruttes   þet he wule cumen þus,
And lokieð a whenne   he cume to his londe
Swa he heom bihahte   ar he heonne wende.

That a king would issue from Uther Pendragon,
That poets would make a table of food from that king's breast
11495 And sit there at it, the best of great poets,
And eat to their desire before they left that place,
And draw wine out from that king's tongue
And drink and be joyful by day and by night;
This feasting would last them as long as the world did.
11500 And furthermore Merlin said of him that more was to come:
That all those he looked upon would bow down to his feet.
Furthermore Merlin said of him a more wondrous thing:
That there would be unending sorrow at the king's passing
And the Britons would not believe the king's death,
11505 Unless it were the final death at the great Judgement
When our Lord will judge all people;
Or else we cannot judge of Arthur's death,
For he himself said to his noble Britons –
South in Cornwall where Gawain died
11510 And he himself was injured with a very great wound –
That he would journey into Avalon,[14]
Onto that island, to the noble Argante,[15]
For she would heal his wounds with healing ointment,
And when he was entirely whole he would come to them immediately.
11515 The Britons believe that he will come just like this,
And are always looking for when he will come to this land
As he promised them before he went from here.

14 An island otherworld inhabited by fairies where death does not   15 The queen of the fairies.
exist (compare the fairy kingdom in *Sir Orfeo*).

THE OWL AND THE NIGHTINGALE

The Owl and the Nightingale survives in two similar, but independent versions, in the manuscripts London, British Library, Cotton Caligula A. ix, and Oxford, Jesus College 29. N. K. Ker, in his parallel facsimile edition, dates both manuscripts to the second half of the thirteenth century, and perhaps as late as the last quarter of that century.[16] The author of the poem is not known, although it has been proposed that the Nicholas of Guildford to whom the birds defer judgement in the debate may be the author himself. There is little evidence, however, to justify this attribution. Whoever the author was, he or she was certainly well educated and keenly aware of contemporary concerns about religion, love and marriage, among other things. Precisely what the contemporary context was for this poem, though, is currently itself a matter for debate. The original poem, as distinct from the date of copying of the manuscripts, has usually been dated to *c*.1189–1216, on the grounds of tentative internal evidence at lines 1091–2: 'Þat underyat þe king Henri: / Jesus his soule do merci!' These lines have generally been taken to refer to Henry II, who died in 1189. Neil Cartlidge has suggested in a recent important article that the text itself should be regarded as later than this: as from the second half of the thirteenth century. The reference in the text, if it refers to a king at all, might then perhaps refer to Henry III, who died in 1272.[17]

The poem is an entertaining and humorous account of a debate between two birds, overheard by the narrator. Unlike some other English debates of the period, there is no solution provided in this text; we do not know which of the birds is intended to be the winner. This problematizes the text to an extent, and forces the onus of interpretation onto the reader. Perhaps this is the point of the poem: to entertain, educate and engage the reader as the two protagonists progress in their argument, and moreover, to emphasize the issues raised in the text and their importance in life. The birds do cover a great deal of ground, discussing marriage, love, religion, song, toilet manners, and a number of other fundamental topics during the course of their debate; but the text's difficulties, caused by the lack of closure, has inevitably led to an array of interpretations proposed by scholars.[18] Each interpretation has its merits; they range from exegetical readings which base an interpretation of the poem on

the potential medieval response to Biblical references to the Owl, in particular, to viewing the poem as a text concerned with the teaching of debate itself within the grammar school *trivium*.[19] Other scholars have proposed that the text should be viewed as an implicit commentary on historical events and characters; and still others hold the view that the poem is a satire on the contentiousness of humanity.[20] The variety of interpretation at once indicates the difficulties of the text and the manner in which it demands a reader's response in order to gain meaning.

The manuscript context of both poems might provide some clues to the way in which the text itself was viewed at the time of its copying. Cotton Caligula A. ix and Jesus College 29 share a number of texts that suggest a common source manuscript at some point in the texts' transmission. Both manuscripts contain monitory and satirical pieces that warn against sin and that stress the need to avoid damnation. It may be that *The Owl and the Nightingale* should be read within this religious and didactic context in which the textual emphases are the transience of life, inevitability of death, and imminence of doomsday. In this case, the poem's symbolism could be more potent than such a humorous text may at first suggest. On the other hand, the historical aspects of the poem – the reference to a King Henry and the contemporary resonances throughout – might be foregrounded by the immediate context of *The Owl and the Nightingale* in Cotton Caligula A. ix, where it is preceded by Laȝamon's *Brut*, a verse chronicle outlining the history of the Britons.

This edition of *The Owl and the Nightingale* is based on the Cotton Caligula manuscript, folios 233 recto to 246 recto. The verse form of the text is the octosyllabic couplet, a form derived from French versification. In its most simplistic terms, the language of the text operates on two levels. The dialect of the author appears to have been southern, possibly showing an origin in Surrey (and this would tie in with the reference to Nicholas of Guildford) or Dorset. The second dialectal level is found in the scribe's forms that were superimposed on the original during the copying process. These forms show a West Midlands influence. Thus, in the text, spellings such as *ho* ('she'), *mon* ('man') and *sunne* ('sin') are West Midlands forms.

---

16   N. R. Ker, ed., *The Owl and the Nightingale: Reproduced in Facsimile from the Surviving Manuscripts, Jesus Cllege, Oxford 29, and British Museum, Cotton Caligula A. ix*, EETS o.s. 251 (London, 1963; repr. 1993), pp. ix and xvi. Note that in the facsimile, folio 234 verso is placed before folio 234 recto.

17   N. Cartlidge, 'The Date of *The Owl and the Nightingale*', *Medium Ævum* 65 (1996), 230–47

18   See especially R. Barton Palmer, 'The Narrator in *The Owl and the Nightingale*: A Reader in the Text', *Chaucer Review* 22 (1988), 305–21, for a discussion of the difficulties in interpreting the text,

and the vacillation of the narrator.

19   The *trivium* is the first part of the scholar's education, covering rhetoric, grammar, and logic. Learning to debate skilfully and to prepare and deliver an argument cogently was part of the training undertaken by the scholar.

20   See K. Hume, *The Owl and the Nightingale: The Poem and its Critics* (Toronto, 1975), for a synopsis of all the various interpretations of the poem up to 1976, and for her own view that the text is a burlesque-satire.

The Owl and the Nightingale[21]

Ich was in one sumere dale,	*valley*
In one suþe diȝele hale,	*very secluded nook*
Iherde Ich holde grete tale	*held; debate*
An Hule and one Niȝtingale.	
5 Þat plait was stif and starc and strong,	*pleading; violent*
Sum wile softe and lud among;	
An aiþer aȝen oþer sval,	*either; swelled up angrily*
And let þat uvole mod ut al.	*offensive; temper*
And eiþer seide of oþeres custe	*character*
10 Þat alre-worste þat hi wuste:	*she; knew*
And hure and hure of oþeres songe	*especially*
Hi holde plaiding suþe stronge.	*law-suit*
Þe Niȝtingale bigon þe speche	
In one hurne of one breche,	*corner*
15 And sat up one vaire boȝe,	
Þar were abute blosme inoȝe,	*enough*
In ore waste þicke hegge	*one*
Imeind mid spire and grene segge.	*Interspersed; reeds; sedge*
Ho was þe gladur vor þe rise,	*She; branch*
20 And song a vele cunne wise:	*sang in many kinds of song*
Bet þuȝte þe dreim þat he were	*rather; seemed; sound*
Of harpe and pipe þan he nere;	*than otherwise*
Bet þuȝte þat he were ishote	*shot forth*
Of harpe and pipe þan of þrote.	*throat*
25 Þo stod on old stoc þar biside,	*tree-stump*
Þar þo Ule song hire tide,	*canonical hours*
And was mid ivi al bigrowe.	
Hit was þare Hule eardingstowe.	*dwelling-place*
Þe Niȝtingale hi iseȝ,	
30 And hi bihold and overseȝ,	*looked down on*
And þuȝte wel vul of þare Hule,	*seemed; loathsome*
For me hi halt lodlich and fule.	*men; her; hold*
'Unwiȝt,' ho sede, 'awei þu flo!	*Monster*
Me is þe wurs þat Ich þe so.	*see*
35 Iwis for þine vule lete,	*Indeed; behaviour*
Wel oft Ich mine song forlete;	
Min horte atfliþ and falt mi tonge,	*flies aways; fails*
Wonne þu art to me iþrunge.	*when you thrust yourself on me*
Me luste bet speten þane singe	*spit*
40 Of þine fule ȝoȝelinge.'	*hooting*
Þos Hule abod fort hit was eve,	*waited until*
Ho ne miȝte no leng bileve,	*hold back*
Vor hire horte was so gret	
Þat wel neȝ hire fnast atschet,	*breath; shot out*
45 And warp a word þarafter longe;	*threw out*
'Hu þincþe nu bi mine songe?	
Wenst þu þat Ich ne cunne singe	
Þeȝ Ich ne cunne of writelinge?	*warbling*
Ilome þu dest me grame,	*Often; injury*

21 The version of the text in Oxford, Jesus College 29, folio 156 recto, provides the title: 'Incipit Altercatio inter filomenam et Bubonem' (Here begins the altercation between the Owl and the Nightingale).

50	And seist me boþe tone and schame.	*vex*
	3if Ich þe holde on mine vote –	*feet*
	So hit bitide þat Ich mote –	*As it so happens that I could*
	And þu were ut of þine rise,	*branch*
	Þu sholdest singe anoþer wise.'	*manner*
55	Þe Niȝtingale ȝaf answare:	
	'3if Ich me loki wit þe bare,	*guard; open*
	And me schilde wit þe blete,	*against; being exposed*
	Ne reche Ich noȝt of þine þrete;	*care*
	3if Ich me holde in mine hegge,	
60	Ne recche Ich never what þu segge.	
	Ich wot þat þu art unmilde	*unmerciful*
	Wiþ hom þat ne muȝe from þe schilde;	*those who cannot*
	And þu tukest wroþe and uvele	*pluck*
	Whar þu miȝt, over smale fuȝele.	*birds*
65	Vorþi þu art loþ al fuelkunne,	*Because; types of birds*
	And alle ho þe driveþ honne,	
	And þe bischricheþ and bigredet,	*screech around; cry out at*
	And wel narewe þe biledet;	*pursue*
	And ek forþe þe sulve mose,	*titmouse itself*
70	Hire þonkes wolde þe totose.	*willingly; rip to shreds*
	Þu art lodlich to biholde,	
	And þu art loþ in monie volde:	*in many respects*
	Þi bodi is short, þi swore is smal,	*neck*
	Grettere is þin heved þan þu al;	*head*
75	Þin eȝene boþ col-blake and brode,	*big*
	Riȝt swo ho weren ipeint mid wode;	*woad*
	Þu starest so þu wille abiten	*bite to death*
	Al þat þu miȝt mid clivre smiten.	*claws*
	Þi bile is stif and scharp and hoked,	*beak*
80	Riȝt so an owel þat is croked;	*hook*
	Þarmid þu clackest oft and longe,	*With that*
	And þat is on of þine songe.	
	Ac þu þretest to mine fleshe,	
	Mid þine clivres woldest me meshe.	*crush*
85	Þe were icundur to one frogge	*You; more natural*
	Þat sit at mulne under cogge	*mill; cog-wheel*
	Snailes, mus, and fule wiȝte,	*creatures*
	Boþ þine cunde and þine riȝte.	*Accord with your nature*
	Þu sittest adai and fliȝst aniȝt,	*at night*
90	Þu cuþest þat þu art on unwiȝt.	*monster*
	Þu art lodlich and unclene,	
	Bi þine neste Ich hit mene,	
	And ek bi þine fule brode,	*foul brood*
	Þu fedest on hom a wel ful fode.	*offspring*
95	Vel wostu þat hi doþ þarinne:	
	Hi fuleþ hit up to þe chinne,	
	Ho sitteþ þar so hi bo bisne.	*both blind*
	Þarbi men segget a vorbisne:	*proverb*
	"Dahet habbe þat ilke best	*Bad luck to those*
100	Þat fuleþ his owe nest."	
	Þat oþer ȝer a faukun bredde,	
	His nest noȝt wel he ne bihedde.	

Þarto þu stele in o dai,
And leidest þaron þi fole ey.   *foul egg*
105 Þo hit bicom þat he haȝte,   *hatched*
And of his eyre briddes wraȝte;   *eggs; chicks; had brought to life*
Ho broȝte his briddes mete,
Bihold his nest, iseȝ hi ete;   *saw*
He iseȝ bi one halve
110 His nest ifuled uthalve.   *on the outside*
Þe faucun was wroþ wit his bridde,
And lude ȝal and sterne chidde: *yelled*
"Segget me, wo havet þis ido?   *who*
Ov nas never icunde þarto.   *You; natural inclination*
115 Hit was idon ov a loþe custe.   *way*
Seggeþ me ȝif ȝe hit wiste."
Þo quaþ þat on and quad þat oþer:
"Iwis it was ure oȝer broþer,
Þe ȝond þat haved þat grete heved:
120 Wai þat hi nis þarof bireved!   *It's a pity; deprived*
Worp hit ut mid þe alre vurste   *Throw; worst of all*
Þat his necke him to-berste!"
Þe faucun ilefde his bridde,   *believed*
And nom þat fule brid amidde,   *took*
125 And warp hit of þan wilde bowe,
Þar pie and crowe hit todrowe.   *magpie*
Herbi men segget a bispel,   *moral tale*
Þeȝ hit ne bo fuliche spel;   *fully; fiction*
Also hit is bi þan ungode   *low-born person*
130 Þat is icumen of fule brode,
And is meind wit fro monne,   *brought together; noble*
Ever he cuþ þat he com þonne,
Þat he com of þan adel eye,   *addled egg*
Þeȝ he a fro neste leie.   *noble*
135 Þeȝ appel trendli from þon trowe   *might roll*
Þar he and oþer mid growe,
Þeȝ he bo þarfrom bicume,
He cuþ wel whonene he is icume.'
    Þos word aȝaf þe Niȝtingale,
140 And after þare longe tale
He song so lude and so scharpe,
Riȝt so me grulde schille harpe.   *plucked*
Þos Hule luste þiderward,   *listened*
And hold hire eȝe noþerward,   *downwards*
145 And sat tosvolle and ibolwe,   *swollen*
Also ho hadde one frogge isuolȝe,   *swallowed*
For ho wel wiste and was iwar
Þat ho song hire a-bisemar.   *in mockery of her*
And noþeles ho ȝaf andsuare:
150 'Whi neltu flon into þe bare,   *open*
And sewi ware unker bo   *which of us both*
Of briȝter howe, of uairur blo?'   *fairer; complexion*
    'No, þu havest wel scharpe clawe,
Ne kep Ich noȝt þat þu me clawe.   *I have no wish*
155 Þu havest clivers suþe stronge,

	Þu tuengst þarmid so doþ a tonge.	*pinch; tongs*
	Þu þoȝtest, so doþ þine ilike,	
	Mid faire worde me biswike.	*betray*
	Ich nolde don þat þu me raddest,	*advised*
160	Ich wiste wel þat þu me misraddest.	*misadvised*
	Schamie þe for þin unrede.	*poor advice*
	Unwroȝen is þi svikelhede!	*Revealed; deceitfulness*
	Schild þine svikeldom vram þe liȝte,	*deceit*
	And hud þat woȝe among þe riȝte.	*hide the crookedness*
165	Þane þu wilt þin unriȝt spene,	*wickedness; put to use*
	Loke þat hit ne bo isene.	*be*
	Vor svikedom haved schome and hete,	
	Ȝif hit is ope and underȝete.	*perceived*
	Ne speddestu noȝt mid þine unwrenche,	*did you succeed; trickery*
170	For Ich am war and can wel blenche.	*get out of the way*
	Ne helpþ noȝt þat þu bo to þriste:	*bold*
	Ich wolde viȝte bet mid liste	*cunning*
	Þan þu mid al þine strengþe.	
	Ich habbe, on brede and eck on lengþe,	*also*
175	Castel god on mine rise:	
	"Wel fiȝt þat wel fliȝt," seiþ þe wise.	*fought; takes flight*
	Ac lete we awei þos cheste,	*brawling*
	Vor suiche wordes boþ unwreste;	*petty*
	And fo we on mid riȝte dome,	*let us begin; judgement*
180	Mid faire worde and mid ysome.	*peaceable words*
	Þeȝ we ne bo at one acorde,	
	We muȝe bet mid fayre worde,	*rather*
	Witute cheste, and bute fiȝte,	
	Plaidi mid foȝe and mid riȝte;	*Plead; relevance*
185	And mai hure eiþer wat hi wile	
	Mid riȝte segge and mid sckile.'	*reason*
	Þo quaþ þe Hule: 'Wu schal us seme,	*reconcile*
	Þat kunne and wille riȝt us deme?'	*will be able; judge*
	'Ich wot wel,' quaþ þe Niȝtingale,	
190	'Ne þaref þarof bo no tale.	*There's no need*
	Maister Nichole of Guldeforde,[22]	
	He is wis an war of worde;	*careful*
	He is of dome suþe gleu,	*very prudent*
	And him is loþ evrich unþeu.	*vice*
195	He wot insiȝt in eche songe,	*a deep understanding*
	Wo singet wel, wo singet wronge;	
	And he can schede vrom þe riȝte	*distinguish*
	Þat woȝe, þat þuster from þe liȝte.'	*What is wrong, the dark*
	Þo Hule one wile hi biþoȝte,	
200	And after þan þis word upbroȝte:	
	'Ich granti wel þat he us deme,	
	Vor þeȝ he were wile breme,	*wild for a while*
	And lof him were Niȝtingale,	*beloved*
	And oþer wiȝte gente and smale,	*high-born*
205	Ich wot he is nu suþe acoled.	*greatly cooled down*

---

22   Master Nicholas of Guildford, the judge in this debate, is seen
by some critics as being the possible author of the poem.

	Nis he vor þe noȝt afoled,	*because of; fooled*
	Þat he, for þine olde luve,	
	Me adun legge and þe buve;	*lay down; raise up*
	Ne schaltu nevre so him queme,	*please*
210	Þat he for þe fals dom deme.	
	He is him ripe and fastrede,	*mature; secure in advice*
	Ne lust him nu to none unrede;	*does not like; foolishness*
	Nu him ne lust na more pleie,	
	He wile gon a riȝte weie.'	
215	Þe Niȝtingale was al ȝare,	
	Ho hadde ilorned wel aiware:	*everywhere*
	'Hule,' ho sede, 'seie me soþ,	*truly*
	Wi dostu þat unwiȝtis doþ?	*monsters*
	Þu singist aniȝt and noȝt adai,	
220	And al þi song is "wailawai".	*"woe and alas"*
	Þu miȝt mid þine songe afere	*frighten*
	Alle þat ihereþ þine ibere.	*cries*
	Þu schrichest and ȝollest to þine fere,	*screech; companions*
	Þat hit is grislich to ihere.	
225	Hit þincheþ boþe wise and snepe	*seems; to fools*
	Noȝt þat þu singe, ac þat þu wepe.	
	Þu fliȝst aniȝt and noȝt adai:	
	Þarof Ich wundri and wel mai,	
	Vor evrich þing þat schuniet riȝt,	*shuns*
230	Hit luveþ þuster and hatiet liȝt;	*darkness*
	And evrich þing þat is lof misdede,	*beloved of*
	Hit luveþ þuster to his dede.	*for*
	A wis word, þeȝ hit bo unclene,	
	Is fele manne a muþe imene,	*many; common among*
235	For Alvred King hit seide and wrot:	
	"He schunet þat hine vul wot."[23]	
	Ich wene þat þu dost also,	
	Vor þu fliȝst niȝtes ever mo.	
	An oþer þing me is a wene,	*think*
240	Þu havest aniȝt wel briȝte sene;	*vision*
	Bi daie þu art stareblind,	*quite blind*
	Þat þu ne sichst ne bov ne rind.	*bough nor bark*
	Adai þu art blind oþer bisne,	*or sightless*
	Þarbi men segget a vorbisne:	
245	"Riȝt so hit farþ bi þan ungode	*goes*
	Þat noȝt ne suþ to none gode,	*sees*
	And is so ful of uvele wrenche	*tricks*
	Þat him ne mai no man atprenche,	*elude*
	And can wel þane þustre wai,	*knows; dark*
250	And þane briȝte lat awai."	*abandons*
	So doþ þat boþ of þine cunde:	
	Of liȝte nabbeþ hi none imunde.'	*concern*
	Þos Hule luste suþe longe,	
	And was oftoned suþe stronge.	*offended*
255	Ho quaþ: 'Þu hattest Niȝtingale,	*are called*
	Þu miȝtest bet hoten galegale,	*chatterbox*

23 He who knows himself to be foul shrinks away.

Vor þu havest to monie tale.
Lat þine tunge habbe spale!   *rest*
Þu wenest þat þes dai bo þin oȝe;   *own*
260 Lat me nu habbe mine þroȝe.   *turn*
Bo nu stille and lat me speke,
Ich wille bon of þe awreke.   *be; avenged*
And lust hu Ich con me bitelle   *listen; defend*
Mid riȝte soþe, witute spelle.   *fiction*
265   Þu seist þat Ich me hude adai,
Þarto ne segge Ich "nich" ne "nai".
And lust, Ich telle þe warevore,   *what for*
Al wi hit is and warevore.
Ich habbe bile stif and stronge,
270 And gode clivers scharp and longe,   *claws*
So hit bicumeþ to hauekes cunne;   *hawk's*
Hit is min hiȝte, hit is mi wune,   *delight; joy*
Þat Ich me draȝe to mine cunde,   *I take after*
Ne mai no man þarevore schende.   *put to shame*
275 On me hit is wel isene,
Vor riȝte cunde Ich am so kene.   *nature; bold*
Vorþi Ich am loþ smale foȝle
Þat floþ bi grunde an bi þuvele: *fly; thicket*
Hi me bichermet and bigredeþ,   *scream at; cry out at*
280 And hore flockes to me ledeþ.
Me is lof to habbe reste
And sitte stille in mine neste:
Vor nere Ich never no þe betere   *would not*
Yif Ich mid chavling and mid chatere   *bickering*
285 Hom schende and mid fule worde,   *scolded*
So herdes doþ oþer mid schitworde.   *shitty words*
Ne lust me wit þe screwen chide;   *like; shrewish; debate*
Forþi Ich wende from hom wide.   *thus; turned*
Hit is a wise monne dome,   *judgement*
290 And hi hit segget wel ilome,   *very often*
Þat me ne chide wit þe gidie,   *people; foolish*
Ne wit þan ofne me ne ȝonie.   *oven; should one; gape*
At sume siþe herde I telle   *occasion*
Hu Alvred sede on his spelle:
295 "Loke þat þu ne bo þare
Þar chavling boþ and cheste ȝare:
Lat sottes chide and vorþ þu go."[24]
And Ich am wis and do also.
And ȝet Alvred seide an oþer side
300 A word þat is isprunge wide:
"Þat wit þe fule haveþ imene,   *has dealings with*
Ne cumeþ he never from him cleine."
Wenestu þat haueck bo þe worse   *Do you think*
Þoȝ crowe bigrede him bi þe mershe,   *cry out at*
305 And goþ to him mid hore chirme   *screeching*
Riȝt so hi wille wit him schirme?   *fight*

24   Where bickering and strife are at hand / Let idiots get on with
it, and off you go.

Þe hauec folзeþ gode rede,   *advice*
And fliзt his wei and lat him grede.   *lets; cry*
   Зet þu me seist of oþer þinge,
310 And telst þat Ich ne can noзt singe;
Ac al mi rorde is woning,   *voice; lamentation*
And to ihire grislich þing.   *hear*
Þat nis noзt soþ, Ich singe efne,   *smoothly*
Mid fulle dreme and lude stefne.   *sound; voice*
315 Þu wenist þat ech song bo grislich,
Þat þine pipinge nis ilich.   *like*
Mi stefne is bold and noзt unorne;   *wretched*
Ho is ilich one grete horne,
And þin is ilich one pipe,
320 Of one smale wode unripe.   *half-grown*
Ich singe bet þan þu dest:
Þu chaterest so doþ on Irish prost.
Ich singe an eve a riзte time,
And soþþe won hit is bedtime,   *after*
325 Þe þridde siþe ad middelniзte,   *time*
And so Ich mine song adiзte.   *prepare*
Wone Ich iso arise vorre   *see; far away*
Oþer dairim oþer daisterre.   *daybreak; morning star*
Ich do god mid mine þrote,
330 And warni men to hore note.[25]   *advantage*
Ac þu singest alle longe niзt,
From eve fort hit is dailiзt,   *until*
And evre seist þin o song   *one*
So longe so þe niзt is long;
335 And evre croweþ þi wrecche crei,   *throat*
Þat he ne swikeþ niзt ne dai.   *is not silent*
Mid þine pipinge þu adunest   *deafen*
Þas monnes earen þar þu wunest,   *dwell*
And makest þine song so unwurþ
340 Þat me ne telþ of þar noзt wurþ.   *count it; value*
Evrich murзþe mai so longe ileste   *mirth; last*
Þat ho shal liki wel unwreste: *badly*
Vor harpe, and pipe, and fuзeles song
Mislikeþ, зif hit is to long.
345 Ne bo þe song never so murie,
Þat he ne shal þinche wel unmurie
Зef he ilesteþ over unwille: *beyond displeasure*
So þu miзt þine song aspille.   *waste*
Vor hit is soþ, Alvred hit seide,
350 And me hit mai ine boke rede:
"Evrich þing mai losen his godhede   *excellence*
Mid unmeþe and mid overdede."   *excess*
Mid este þu þe miзt overquatie,   *gratification; overindulge*
And overfulle makeþ wlatie;   *superfluity; produces disgust*
355 An evrich mureзþe mai agon,   *pleasure; vanish*
Зif me hit halt evre forþ in on,   *one; persists; continually*

---

25   The Owl describes, at lines 323ff, the monastic hours at which
she sings: vespers (*an eve*), compline (*bedtime*), Matins (*ad middelniзte*)
and Lauds (*dairim*). See E. G. Stanley, ed., *The Owl and the Nightingale* (London, 1960; repr. 1981), p. 113.

	Bute one, þat is Godes riche,	*Except; kingdom*
	Þat evre is svete and evre iliche.	*the same*
	Þeȝ þu nime evre oþþan lepe,	*take; basket*
360	Hit is evre ful bi hepe;	*fully heaped*
	Wunder hit is of Godes riche,	
	Þat evre spenþ and ever is iliche.	*is used*
	Ȝut þu me seist anoþer shome:	
	Þat Ich am on mine eȝen lome,	*crippled*
365	An seist, for þat Ich flo bi niȝte,	
	Þat Ich ne mai iso bi liȝte.	*see*
	Þu liest! On me hit is isene	
	Þat Ich habbe gode sene:	*vision*
	Vor nis non so dim þusternesse	
370	Þat Ich ever iso þe lasse.	
	Þu wenest þat Ich ne miȝte iso,	
	Vor Ich bi daie noȝt ne flo.	*fly*
	Þe hare luteþ al dai,	*hides*
	Ac noþeles iso he mai:	
375	Ȝif hundes urneþ to himward,	*run towards it*
	He gengþ wel suiþe awaiward,	*goes very quickly*
	And hokeþ paþes sviþe narewe,	*turns this way and that along*
	And haveþ mid him his blenches ȝarewe,	*dodges; prepared*
	And huppþ and stard suþe cove,	*hops and leaps; fast*
380	An secheþ paþes to þe grove;	
	Ne sholde he vor boþe his eȝe	
	So don, ȝif he þe bet niseȝe.	*could not see*
	Ich mai ison so wel so on hare,	
	Þeȝ Ich bi daie sitte an dare.	*remain hidden*
385	Þar aȝte men boþ in worre,	*valiant; are*
	An fareþ boþe ner an forre,	
	An overvareþ fele þode,	*overrun; countries*
	An doþ bi niȝte gode node,	*service*
	Ich folȝi þan aȝte manne,	
390	An flo bi niȝte in hore banne.'	*troop*
	Þe Niȝtingale in hire þoȝte	
	Athold al þis and longe þoȝte	*Considered*
	Wat ho þarafter miȝte segge,	
	Vor ho ne miȝte noȝt alegge	*refute*
395	Þat þe Hule hadde hire ised,	
	Vor he spac boþe riȝt an red.	*good sense*
	An hire ofþuȝte þat ho hadde	
	Þe speche so for vorþ iladde,	*led*
	An was oferd þat hire answare	
400	Ne wurþe noȝt ariȝt ifare.	
	Ac noþeles he spac boldeliche,	
	Vor he is wis þat hardeliche	*resolutely*
	Wiþ is vo berþ grete ilete,	*enemy; puts on a great show*
	Þat he vor areȝþe hit ne forlete:	*cowardice; yield*
405	Vor suich worþ bold ȝif þu fliȝst,	*For such a one becomes*
	Þat wule flo ȝif þu isvicst;	*fight*
	Ȝif he isiþ þat þu nart areȝ,	*coward*
	He wile of bore wurchen bareȝ.	*boar; piglet*
	And forþi, þeȝ þe Niȝtingale	

410	Were aferd, ho spac bolde tale.
	'Hule,' ho seide, 'wi dostu so?
	Þu singest a-winter "wolawo"!
	Þu singest so doþ hen a snowe,	*as; in*
	Al þat ho singeþ hit is for wowe.
415	A wintere þu singest wroþe and ȝomere,	*angrily and dolefully*
	An evre þu art dumb a sumere.
	Hit is for þine fule niþe	*hatred*
	Þat þu ne miȝt mid us bo bliþe,	*happy*
	Vor þu forbernest wel neȝ for onde	*are consumed; spite*
420	Wane ure blisse cumeþ to londe.
	Þu farest so doþ þe ille,	*evil man*
	Evrich blisse him is unwille:
	Grucching and luring him boþ rade,	*grumbling and scowling*
	Ȝif he isoþ þat men boþ glade.
425	He wolde þat he iseȝe
	Teres in evrich monnes eȝe;
	Ne roȝte he þeȝ flockes were	*would care*
	Imeind bi toppes and bi here.	*Entangled; tufts; hair*
	Also þu dost on þire side:	*your*
430	Vor wanne snou liþ þicke and wide,
	An alle wiȝtes habbeþ sorȝe,	*creatures*
	Þu singest from eve fort amorȝe.	*until morning*
	Ac Ich alle blisse mid me bringe,
	Ech wiȝt is glad for mine þinge,
435	And blisseþ hit wanne Ich cume,
	And hiȝteþ aȝen mine kume.	*anticipates with hope; arrival*
	Þe blostme ginneþ springe and sprede,
	Boþe ine tro and ek on mede:	*also; field*
	Þe lilie mid hire faire wlite	*appearance*
440	Wolcumeþ me, þat þu hit wite,	*know*
	Bit me mid hire faire blo	*Greets; complexion*
	Þat Ich shulle to hire flo.
	Þe rose also mid hire rude,	*red hue*
	Þat cumeþ ut of þe þorne wode,
445	Bit me þat Ich shulle singe
	Vor hire luve one skentinge.	*amusing song*
	And Ich so do þurȝ niȝt and dai,
	Þe more Ich singe þe more I mai,	*can*
	An skente hi mid mine songe,	*amuse*
450	Ac noþeles noȝt overlonge.
	Wane Ich iso þat men boþ glade,
	Ich nelle þat hi bon to sade.	*are too weary of it*
	Þan is ido vor wan Ich com,	*Then is done what I came here to do*
	Ich fare aȝen and do wisdom.	*go*
455	Wane mon hoȝeþ of his sheve,	*considers; sheaves*
	An falewi cumeþ on grene leve,	*green leaves become fallow*
	Ich fare hom and nime leve:	*take; my leave*
	Ne recche Ich noȝt of winteres reve.	*plunder*
	Wan Ich iso þat cumeþ þat harde,	*hard season*
460	Ich fare hom to min erde,	*native land*
	An habbe boþe luve and þonc
	Þat Ich her com and hider swonk.	*worked*

Þan min erende is ido,

Sholde Ich bileve? Nai, warto? *remain here; what for*

465 Vor he nis noþer ȝep ne wis, *clever*

Þat longe abid þar him nod nis.' *doesn't need to*

Þos Hule luste, and leide an hord

Al þis mot, word after word, *argument*

An after þoȝte hu he miȝte

470 Ansvere vinde best mid riȝte: *find*

Vor he mot hine ful wel biþenche, *ponder*

Þat is aferd of plaites wrenche. *tricks of pleading*

'Þu aishest me,' þe Hule sede, *ask*

'Wi Ich a winter singe and grede. *cry out*

475 Hit is gode monne iwone, *customary*

An was from þe worlde frome, *world's beginning*

Þat ech god man his frond icnowe,

An blisse mid hom sume þrowe *rejoice; for some time*

In his huse at his borde, *table*

480 Mid faire speche and faire worde.

And hure and hure to Cristesmasse, *especially*

Þane riche and poure, more and lasse,

Singeþ cundut niȝt and dai; *carols*

Ich hom helpe what Ich mai.

485 And ek Ich þenche of oþer þinge

Þane to pleien oþer to singe. *or*

Ich habbe herto gode ansuare

Anon iredi and al ȝare: *prepared*

Vor sumeres tide is al to wlonc, *heedless*

490 An doþ misreken monnes þonk: *to go astray; thoughts*

Vor he ne recþ noȝt of clennesse,

Al his þoȝt is of golnesse. *wantoness*

Vor none dor no leng nabideþ, *animal; will not wait*

Ac evrich upon oþer rideþ;

495 Þe sulve stottes ine þe stode *horses themselves; stud*

Boþ boþe wilde and merewode. *Are; mad for the mares*

And þu sulf art þar among, *yourself*

For of golnesse is al þi song,

An aȝen þet þu wilt teme *expecting; breed*

500 Þu art wel modi and wel breme. *full of spirit; wild*

Sone so þu havest itrede, *As soon as; copulated*

Ne miȝtu leng a word iqueþe; *longer; speak*

Ac pipest also doþ a mose, *titmouse*

Mid chokeringe, mid stevne hose. *hoarse voice*

505 Ȝet þu singst worse þon þe heisugge, *hedge-sparrow*

Þat fliȝþ bi grunde among þe stubbe:

Wane þi lust is ago,

Þonne is þi song ago also.

A sumere chorles awedeþ *go mad*

510 And vorcrempeþ and vorbredeþ: *cramp and contort themselves (i.e. have sex)*

Hit nis for luve noþeles,

Ac is þe chorles wode res; *violent impulse*

Vor wane he haveþ ido his dede,

Ifallen is al his boldhede; *valour*

515 Habbe he istunge under gore, *poked; clothing*

Ne last his luve no leng more.
Also hit is on þine mode:
So sone so þu sittest a brode,   *lose; tunes*
Þu forlost al þine wise.

520   Also þu farest on þine rise,   *branch*
Wane þu havest ido þi gome,   *sport*
Þi stevne goþ anon to shome.   *voice; ruin*
   Ac wane niʒtes cumeþ longe,
And bringeþ forstes starke an stronge,   *frosts*

525   Þanne erest hit is isene
War is þe snelle, war is þe kene.   *active one; bold one*
At þan harde me mai avinde   *hard times; discover*
Wo geþ forþ, wo liþ bihinde.
Me mai ison at þare node,   *one; necessary time*

530   Wan me shal harde wike bode.   *From whom; ask for service*
Þanne Ich am snel and pleie and singe,
And hiʒte me mid mi skentinge: *rejoice in myself*
Of none wintere Ich ne recche,   *care*
Vor Ich nam non asunde wrecche.   *a feeble*

535   And ek Ich frouri vele wiʒte   *comfort; creatures*
Þat mid hom nabbed none miʒtte: *in themselves; power*
Hi boþ hoʒfule and uel arme,   *anxious; wretched*
An secheþ ʒorne to þe warme.   *eagerly*
Oft Ich singe vor hom þe more

540   For lutli sum of hore sore.   *to lessen; sorrow*
Hu þincþ þe? Artu ʒut inume?   *answered*
Artu mid riʒte overcume?'
   'Nay, nay!' sede þe Niʒtingale,
'Þu shalt ihere anoþer tale:

545   ʒet nis þos speche ibroʒt to dome.   *judgement*
Ac bo wel stille, and lust nu to me.
Ich shal mid one bare worde
Do þat þi speche wurþ forworþe.'   *becomes worthless*
   'Þat nere noht riʒt,' þe Hule sede,

550   'Þu havest bicloped also þu bede, *brought a charge; requested*
An Ich þe habbe iʒive ansuare;
Ac ar we to unker dome fare,   *before; our*
Ich wille speke toward þe
Also þu speke toward me;

555   An þu me ansuare ʒif þu miʒt.
   Seie me nu, þu wrecche wiʒt,
Is in þe eni oþer note
Bute þu havest schille þrote?   *Except; shrill*
Þu nart noʒt to non oþer þinge,

560   Bute þu canst of chateringe:
Vor þu art lutel an unstrong,
An nis þi reʒel noþing long.   *dress*
Wat dostu godes among monne?   *of benefit*
Na mo þe deþ a wrecche wranne.   *wren*

565   Of þe ne cumeþ non oþer god,
Bute þu gredest suich þu bo wod;   *cry out; are*
An bo þi piping overgo,   *finished*
Ne boþ on þe craftes na mo.   *of skill; no more*

Alvred sede, þat was wis —

570 He miȝte wel, for soþ hit is:

"Nis no man for is bare songe

Lof ne wurþ noȝt suþe longe: *Praised or honoured*

Vor þat is a forworþe man   *useless*

Þat bute singe noȝt ne can."   *other than; knows*

575 Þu nart bute on forworþe þing: *a*

On þe nis bute chatering.

Þu art dim an of fule howe,

An þinchest a lutel soti clowe;   *seem like; sooty bundle*

Þu nart fair, no þu nart strong,

580 Ne þu nart þicke, ne þu nart long;

Þu havest imist al of fairhede,   *missed out on; beauty*

An lutel is al þi godede.   *excellence*

An oþer þing of þe Ich mene: *complain*

Þu nart vair, ne þu nart clene.

585 Wane þu comest to manne haȝe,   *hedges*

Þar þornes boþ and ris idraȝe,   *branches drawn together*

Bi hegge and bi þicke wode,

Þar men goþ oft to hore node   *need*

Þarto þu draȝst, þarto þu wunest,   *approach; dwell*

590 An oþer clene stede þu schunest.

Þan Ich flo niȝtes after muse,

I mai þe vinde ate rumhuse;   *you; toilet*

Among þe wode, among þe netle,

Þu sittest and singst bihinde þe setle.   *seat*

595 Þar me mai þe ilomest finde,   *most often*

Þar men worpeþ hore bihinde.   *thrust out; behinds*

Ȝet þu atuitest me mine mete,   *upbraid*

An seist þat Ich fule wiȝtes ete.   *foul creatures*

Ac wat etestu, þat þu ne liȝe,   *and don't you lie*

600 Bute attercoppe and fule vliȝe,   *spiders; flies*

An wormes, ȝif þu miȝte finde

Among þe volde of harde rinde?   *bark*

Ȝet Ich can do wel gode wike,   *services*

Vor Ich can loki manne wike;   *protect; dwellings*

605 An mine wike boþ wel gode,

Vor Ich helpe to manne vode.   *food*

Ich can nimen mus at berne,   *catch*

An ek at chirche ine þe derne: *dark*

Vor me is lof to Cristes huse,

610 To clansi hit wiþ fule muse,   *cleanse; from*

Ne schal þar nevre come to

Ful wiȝt, ȝif Ich hit mai ivo.   *catch*

An ȝif me lust one mi skentinge   *like*

To wernen oþer wunienge,   *reject; dwellings*

615 Ich habbe at wude tron wel grete,   *tree*

Mit þicke boȝe no þing blete,   *not at all bare*

Mid ivi grene al bigrowe,

Þat evre stont iliche iblowe,   *in leaf*

An his hou never ne vorlost,   *appearance; changes*

620 Wan hit sniuw ne wan hit frost.

Þarin Ich habbe god ihold,   *refuge*

A winter warm, a sumere cold.
Wane min hus stont briȝt and grene, *stands*
Of þine nis noþing isene.
625   Ȝet þu me telst of oþer þinge,
Of mine briddes seist gabbinge: *chicks; lies*
Þat hore nest nis noȝt clene.
Hit is fale oþer wiȝte imene, *many; common*
Vor hors a stable and oxe a stalle
630 Doþ al þat hom wule þar falle. *Allow*
An lutle children in þe cradele,
Boþe chorles an ek aþele, *noble*
Doþ al þat in hore ȝoeþe *youth*
Þat hi vorleteþ in hore duȝeþe. *abandon; adulthood*
635 Wat! Can þat ȝongling hit bihede? *young one; prevent*
Ȝif hit misdeþ, hit mod nede: *does wrong; must by necessity*
A vorbisne is of olde ivurne, *proverb; from ancient times*
Þat node makeþ old wif urne. *necessity; run*
    An ȝet Ich habbe anoþer andsware.
640 Wiltu to mine neste vare *go*
An loki hu hit is idiȝt? *made*
Ȝif þu art wis lorni þu miȝst. *learn*
Mi nest is holȝ and rum amidde, *hollow; spacious*
So hit is softest mine bridde.
645 Hit is broiden al abute, *woven*
Vrom þe neste vor wiþute:
Þarto hi god to hore node; *go*
Ac þat þu menest Ich hom forbode. *complain about; forbid*
We nimeþ ȝeme of manne bure, *example; bowers*
650 An after þan we makeþ ure: *following*
Men habbet, among oþer iwende, *alternatives*
A rumhus at hore bures ende, *toilet*
Vor þat hi nelleþ to vor go, *will not; too far*
An mine briddes doþ also.
655 Site nu stille, chaterestre! *chatterbox*
Nere þu never ibunde vastre; *secured; faster*
Herto ne vindestu never andsware.
Hong up þin ax! Nu þu miȝt fare!' *can*
    Þe Niȝtingale at þisse worde
660 Was wel neȝ ut of rede iworþe, *good ideas*
An þoȝte ȝorne on hire mode *eagerly; mind*
Ȝif ho oȝt elles understode, *anything*
Ȝif ho kuþe oȝt bute singe, *knew how to do; except*
Þat miȝte helpe to oþer þinge. *for anything else*
665 Herto ho moste andswere vinde,
Oþer mid alle bon bihinde: *be*
An hit is suþe strong to fiȝte *difficult*
Aȝen soþ and aȝen riȝte. *Against*
He mot gon to al mid ginne, *at; cunning*
670 Þan þe horte boþ on winne; *When the heart is troubled*
An þe man mot onoþer segge, *something different*
He mot bihemmen and bilegge, *hem round; explain away*
Ȝif muþ wiþute mai biwro *outwardly; conceal*
Þat me þe horte noȝt niso. *cannot see*

675	An sone mai a word misreke	*go astray*
	Þar muþ shal aȝen horte speke;	
	An sone mai a word misstorte	*misstart*
	Þar muþ shal speken aȝen horte.	
	Ac noþeles ȝut upe þon,	
680	Her is to red wo hine kon:	*a sound plan; for those who know it*
	Vor never nis wit so kene	*sharp*
	So wane red him is a wene.	*plan; in doubt*
	Þanne erest kumed his ȝephede	*first; comes; astuteness*
	Wone hit is alre mest on drede.	*most of all; jeopardy*
685	For Alvered seide of olde quide,	*saying*
	An ȝut hit nis of horte islide:	*mind; slipped*
	'Wone þe bale is alre hecst,	*calamity; highest of all*
	Þonne is þe bote alre necst.'	*solution; nearest of all*
	Vor wit west among his sore,	*prospers; trouble*
690	An for his sore hit is þe more.	
	Vorþi nis nevere mon redles	*without plan*
	Ar his horte bo witles;	*Until*
	Ac ȝif þat he forlost his wit,	
	Þonne is his redpurs al toslit;	*bag of good ideas; split*
695	Ȝif he ne kon his wit atholde,	*retain*
	Ne vint he red in one volde.	*ideas; fold*
	Vor Alvred seide, þat wel kuþe	*was skilled*
	(Evre he spac mid soþe muþe):	
	'Wone þe bale is alre hecst,	
700	Þanne is þe bote alre nest.'	
	Þe Niȝtingale al hire hoȝe	*mind*
	Mid rede hadde wel bitoȝe;	*employed*
	Among þe harde, among þe toȝte,	*strained circumstances*
	Ful wel mid rede hire biþoȝte,	
705	An hadde andsuere gode ifunde	
	Among al hire harde stunde.	*moments*
	'Hule, þu axest me,' ho seide,	
	'Ȝif Ich kon eni oþer dede	
	Bute singen in sume tide,	
710	An bringe blisse for and wide.	*far*
	Wi axestu of craftes mine?	
	Betere is min on þan alle þine,	*single one*
	Betere is o song of mine muþe	
	Þan al þat evre þi kun kuþe.	*kind; could do*
715	An lust? Ich telle þe warevore.	*what for*
	Wostu to wan man was ibore?	*Do you know; for what*
	To þare blisse of hovene riche,	*the heavenly kingdom*
	Þar ever is song and murȝþe iliche.	
	Þider fundeþ evrich man	*sets out*
720	Þat eni þing of gode kan.	
	Vorþi me singþ in holi chirche,	*people*
	An clerkes ginneþ songes wirche,	*begin; compose*
	Þat man iþenche bi þe songe	*considers*
	Wider he shal, and þar bon longe:	*shall go*
725	Þat he þe murȝþe ne vorȝete,	*forget*
	Ac þarof þenche and biȝete,	*obtain*
	An nime ȝeme of chirche stevene,	*take note; voice*

Hu murie is þe blisse of hovene.

Clerkes, munekes, and kanunes, *canons*

730 Þar boþ þos gode wicketunes, *dwelling places*

Ariseþ up to midelniȝte,

An singeþ of þe hovene liȝte; *heavenly light*

An prostes upe londe singeþ, *in the country*

Wane þe liȝt of daie springeþ.

735 An Ich hom helpe wat I mai,

Ich singe mid hom niȝt and dai,

An ho boþ alle for me þe gladdere, *are*

An to þe songe boþ þe raddere. *comes the quicker*

Ich warni men to hore gode *their*

740 Þat hi bon bliþe on hore mode, *should be; mind*

An bidde þat hi moten iseche *entreat; must seek*

Þan ilke song þat ever is eche. *same; eternal*

Nu þu miȝt, Hule, sitte and clinge;

Her among nis no chateringe.

745 Ich graunti þat we go to dome

Tofore þe sulfe þe Pope of Rome. *self-same*

Ac abid ȝete, noþeles,

Þu shalt ihere anoþer þes; *thing*

Ne shaltu, for Engelonde,

750 At þisse worde me atstonde. *withstand*

Wi atuitestu me mine unstrengþe, *do you twit on about*

An mine ungrete and mine unlengþe, *small size*

An seist þat Ich nam noȝt strong,

Vor Ich nam noþer gret ne long?

755 Ac þu nost never wat þu menst, *do not know; mean*

Bute lese wordes þu me lenst: *Only false; proffer*

For Ich kan craft and Ich kan liste, *skill; shrewdness*

An þarevore Ich am þus þriste. *bold*

Ich kan wit and song mani eine, *many a one*

760 Ne triste Ich to non oþer maine; *trust; strength*

Vor soþ hit is þat seide Alvred:

"Ne mai no strengþe aȝen red." *good advice*

Oft spet wel a lute liste *speeds; little*

Þar muche strengþe sholde miste; *Where; fail*

765 Mid lutle strengþe, þurȝ ginne, *ingenuity*

Castel and burȝ me mai iwinne; *can be won*

Mid liste me mai walles felle,

An worpe of horsse kniȝtes snelle. *throw; bold*

Uvel strengþe is lutel wurþ, *Force of*

770 Ac wisdom ne wurþ never unwurþ. *is never*

Þu myht iseo þurh alle þing

Þat wisdom naveþ non evening. *equal*

An hors is strengur þan a mon;

Ac, for hit non iwit ne kon, *has no understanding*

775 Hit berþ on rugge grete semes, *back; burdens*

An draȝþ bivore grete temes, *before it*

An þoleþ boþe ȝerd and spure, *suffers; stick*

An stont iteid at mulne dure. *mill door*

An hit deþ þat mon hit hot: *does what; commands*

780 An forþan þat hit no wit not,

Ne mai his strenþe hit ishilde   *prevent*
Þat hit nabuȝþ þe lutle childe.   *yield to*
Mon deþ mid strengþe and mid witte
Þat oþer þing nis non his fitte.   *That no other thing equals him*
785   Þeȝ alle strengþe at one were,   *as one*
Monnes wit ȝet more were;
Vorþe mon mid his crafte,   *And so*
Overkumeþ al orþliche shafte.   *earthly creatures*
Also Ich do mid mine one songe
790   Bet þan þu al þe ȝer longe: *year*
Vor mine crafte men me luvieþ,
Vor þine strengþe men þe shunieþ.
Telstu bi me þe wurs forþan   *Do you account me*
Þat Ich bute anne craft ne kan?
795   Ȝif tueie men goþ to wraslinge,   *two*
An eiþer oþer faste þringe,   *presses against*
An þe on can swenges suþe fele,   *knows many holds*
An kan his wrenches wel forhele,   *tricks; hide*
An þe oþer ne can sweng but anne,   *one hold*
800   An þe is god wiþ eche manne,   *a good one against*
An mid þon one leiþ to grunde
Anne after oþer a lutle stunde,   *within a short time*
Wat þarf he recche of a mo swenge,   *need he care about*
Þone þe on him is swo genge?   *one of his; effective*
805   Þu seist þat þu canst fele wike,   *services*
Ac ever Ich am þin unilike.   *dissimilar*
Do þine craftes alle togadere,
Ȝet is min on horte betere.   *one essentially*
Oft þan hundes foxes driveþ
810   Þe kat ful wel himsulve liveþ,
Þeȝ he ne kunne wrench bute anne;
Þe fox so godne ne can nanne,   *does not know any as good*
Þeȝ he kunne so vele wrenche,
Þat he wenþ eche hunde atprenche.   *hopes; to elude*
815   Vor he can paþes riȝte and woȝe,   *straight and crooked*
An he kan hongi bi þe boȝe,   *bough*
An so forlost þe hund his fore,   *scent*
An turnþ aȝen eft to þan more.   *returns; moor*
Þe vox kan crope bi þe heie,   *creep; hedge*
820   An turne ut from his forme weie,
An eft sone kume þarto;
Þonne is þe hundes smel fordo:
He not, þurȝ þe imeinde smak,   *knows not; variety of smells*
Weþer he shal avorþ þe abak.
825   Ȝif þe vox mist of al þis dwole,   *escapes; trickery*
At þan ende he cropþ to hole;   *creeps*
Ac naþeles mid alle his wrenche,
Ne kan he hine so biþenche,   *arrange it*
Þeȝ he bo ȝep an suþe snel,   *is clever; quick*
830   Þat he ne lost his rede vel.   *pelt*
Þe cat ne kan wrench bute anne
Noþer bi dune ne bi venne: *both by hill; fen*
Bute he kan climbe suþe wel,

	Þarmid he wereþ his greie vel.	keeps wearing
835	Also Ich segge bi mi solve,	about
	Betere is min on þan þine twelve.'	one skill
	'Abid! Abid!' Þe Ule seide,	
	'Þu gest al to mid swikelede:	deceit
	Alle þine wordes þu bileist	explain away
840	Þat hit þincþ soþ al þat þu seist;	seems true
	Alle þine wordes boþ isliked,	slick
	An so bisemed an biliked,	seem likely and possible
	Þat alle þo þat hi avoþ,	those that hear them
	Hi weneþ þat þu segge soþ.	
845	Abid! Abid! Me shal þe зene.	respond
	Nu hit shal wurþe wel isene	
	Þat þu havest muchel iloзe,	lied
	Wone þi lesing boþ unwroзe.	falsehoods; uncovered
	Þu seist þat þu singist mankunne,	
850	And techest hom þat hi fundieþ honne	should seek to go forward
	Up to þe songe þat evre ilest:[26]	lasts
	Ac hit is alre wunder mest	
	Þat þu darst liзe so opeliche.	
	Wenest þu hi bringe so liзtliche	
855	To Godes riche al singinge?	kingdom
	Nai, nai, hi shulle wel avinde	
	Þat hi mid longe wope mote	weeping must
	Of hore sunnen bidde bote,	Pray for a remedy for their sins
	Ar hi mote ever kume þare.	
860	Ich rede þi þat men bo зare,	counsel; prepared
	An more wepe þane singe,	
	Þat fundeþ to þan Hoven-kinge;	
	Vor nis no man witute sunne.	
	Vorþi he mot, ar he wende honne,	
865	Mid teres an mid wope bete,	make amends
	Þat him bo sur þat er was swete.	sour; previously
	Þarto Ich helpe, God hit wot!	
	Ne singe Ich hom no foliot:	to them; of any foolishness
	For al me song is of longinge,	
870	An imend sumdel mid woninge,	partly mixed; lamentation
	Þat mon bi me hine biþenche	
	Þat he groni for his unwrenche.	faults
	Mid mine songe Ich hine pulte,	assail
	Þat he groni for his gulte.	guilt
875	Зif þu gest herof to disputinge,	go about
	Ich wepe bet þane þu singe.	
	Зif riзt goþ forþ, and abak wrong,	
	Betere is mi wop þane þi song.	
	Þeз sume men bo þurзut gode,	thoroughly
880	An þurзut clene on hore mode,	
	Hon longeþ honne noþeles.	to go from here
	Þat boþ her, wo is hom þes,	thus
	Vor þeз hi bon homsolve iborзe,	are themselves saved
	Hi ne soþ her nowiзt bote sorwe;	see nothing here

26 i.e. that mankind should seek the eternal song of heaven.

885	Vor oþer men hi wepeþ sore,	
	An for hom biddeþ Cristes ore.	*mercy*
	Ich helpe monne on eiþer halve,	*both sides*
	Mi muþ haveþ tweire kunne salve:	*two kinds saved*
	Þan gode Ich fulste to longinge,	*help*
890	Vor þan hin longeþ, Ich him singe:	
	An þan sunfulle Ich helpe alswo,	
	Vor Ich him teche þare is wo.	
	Ʒet Ich þe ʒene in oþer wise:	*counter you; ways*
	Vor þane þu sittest on þine rise,	*branch*
895	Þu draʒst men to fleses luste,	*desires of the flesh*
	Þat wulleþ þine songes luste;	*listen to*
	Al þu forlost þe murʒþe of hovene,	
	For þarto nevestu none stevene.	*voice*
	Al þat þu singst is of golnesse,	*lust*
900	For nis on þe non holinesse,	
	Ne wened na man for þi pipinge	*thinks*
	Þat eni preost in chircce singe.	
	Ʒet I þe wulle anoder segge,	*another thing*
	Ʒif þu hit const ariht bilegge:	*explain*
905	Wi nultu singe anoder þeode,	*people*
	Þar hit is muchele more neode?	
	Þu neaver ne singst in Irlonde,	
	Ne þu ne cumest noʒt in Scotlonde.	
	Hwi nultu fare to Noreweie,	
910	An singin men of Galeweie?	*Galloway*
	Þar beoð men þat lutel kunne	
	Of songe þat is bineoð þe sunne.	
	Wi nultu þare preoste singe,	*to the priests*
	An teche of þire writelinge,	*by your chirping*
915	An wisi hom mid þire stevene	*instruct*
	Hu engeles singeð ine heovene?	
	Þu farest so doð an ydel wel	*idle*
	Þar springeþ bi burne þar is snel,	*by a stream*
	An let fordrue þe dune,	*the hill dry up*
920	And flohþ on idel þar adune.	
	Ac Ich fare boþe norþ and suþ:	
	In eaverevch londe Ich am cuuþ;	
	East and west, feor and neor,	
	I do wel faire mi meoster,	*follow my calling*
925	An warni men mid mine bere,	*behaviour*
	Þat þi dweole song heo ne forlere.	*heretical; does not misguide*
	Ich wisse men mid mine songe,	
	Þat hi ne sunegi nowiht longe.	*do not sin*
	I bidde hom þat heo iswike,	*abandon*
930	Þat heomseolve ne biswike:	*betray*
	For betere is þat heo wepen here	
	Þan elleshwar to beon deovlene fere.'	*elsewhere; devils' companions*
	Þe Niʒtingale was igremet,	*furious*
	An ek heo was sumdel ofchamed,	*ashamed*
935	For þe Hule hire atwiten hadde	*reproached*
	In hwucche stude he sat an gradde,	*place; cried*

Bihinde þe bure, among þe wede, *chamber*
Þar men goð to here neode; *when necessity calls*
An sat sumdel, and heo biþohte,
940 An wiste wel on hire þohte
Þe wraþþe binimeþ monnes red. *deprives; judgement*
For hit seide þe King Alfred:
'Selde endeð wel þe loþe, *hated person*
An selde plaideð wel þe wroþe.' *angry*
945 For wraþþe meinþ þe horte blod
Þat hit floweþ so wilde flod, *in a*
An al þe heorte overgeþ, *overwhelms*
Þat heo naveþ noþing bute breþ,
An so forleost al hire liht,
950 Þat heo ne siþ soþ ne riht. *does not see*
Þe Niȝtingale hi understod,
An overgan lette hire mod. *allowed her mood to pass*
He mihte bet speken a sele *in a happy mood*
Þan mid wraþþe wordes deale.
955   'Hule,' heo seide 'lust nu hider:
Þu schalt falle, þe wei is slider. *slippery*
Þu seist Ich fleo bihinde bure:
Hit is riht, þe bur is ure. *ours*
Þar laverd liggeþ and lavedi *where; lie*
960 Ich schal heom singe and sitte bi.
Wenstu þat uise men forlete,
For fule venne, þe riȝtte strete? *mud*
Ne sunne þe later shine,
Þeȝ hit bo ful ine nest þine?
965 Sholde Ich, for one hole brede,
Forlete mine riȝte stede,
Þat Ich ne singe bi þe bedde
Þar loverd haveþ his love ibedde? *as a bed-fellow*
Hit is mi riȝt, hit is mi laȝe,
970 Þar to þe hexst Ich me draȝe; *highest*
Ac ȝet þu ȝelpst of þine songe
Þat þu canst ȝolle wroþe and stronge,
An seist þu visest mankunne,
Þat hi biwepen hore sunne. *bewail; sins*
975 Solde euch mon wonie and grede *lament; cry out*
Riȝt suich hi weren unlede, *miserable*
Solde hi ȝollen also þu dest, *as*
Hi miȝte oferen here prost. *frighten; priest*
Man schal bo stille and noȝt grede,
980 He mot biwepe his misdede; *must*
Ac þar is Cristes heriinge, *praise*
Þar me shal grede and lude singe: *a person*
Nis noþer to lud ne to long, *neither*
At riȝte time chirche-song.
985 Þu ȝolst and wones, and Ich singe: *weep*
Þi stevene is wop, and min skentinge. *lamentation; entertainment*
Ever mote þu ȝolle and wepen
Þat þu þi lif mote forleten, *must foresake*

An ʒollen mote þu so heʒe

990   Þat ut berste bo þin eʒe.   *both*

We[þ]er is betere of twere twom: *the two*

Þat mon bo bliþe oþer grom?   *angry*

So bo hit ever in unker siþe,   *our case*

Þat þu bo sori and Ich bliþe.

995   ʒut þu aisheist wi Ich ne fare   *journey*

Into oþer londe and singe þare?

No! Wat sholde Ich among hom do   *them*

Þar never blisse ne com to?

Þat lond nis god, ne hit nis este,   *pleasant*

1000 Ac wildernisse hit is and weste:

Knarres and cludes hoventinge,   *Crags and rocky hills reaching the skies*

Snou and haʒel hom is genge.   *hail; common*

Þat lond is grislich and unvele,   *ghastly and wretched*

Þe men boþ wilde and unisele,   *unhappy*

1005 Hi nabbeþ noþer griþ ne sibbe: *peace nor truce*

Hi ne reccheþ hu hi libbe.   *care*

Hi eteþ fihs an flehs unsode,   *uncooked fish and meat*

Suich wulves hit hadde tobrode: *As if; ripped apart*

Hi drinkeþ milc and wei þarto,

1010 Hi nute elles þat hi do;   *know not any other way*

Hi nabbeþ noþer win ne bor,   *beer*

Ac libbeþ also wilde dor;   *live like; animals*

Hi goþ bitiʒt mid ruʒe velle,   *clothed; rough pelts*

Riʒt suich hi comen ut of helle.

1015 Þeʒ eni god man to hom come,

So wile dude sum from Rome,[27]   *on one occasion; a certain one*

For hom to lere gode þewes,   *teach; habits*

An for to leten hore unþewes,   *abandon; vices*

He miʒte bet sitte stille,

1020 Vor al his wile he sholde spille: *time; waste*

He miʒte bet teche ane bore   *bear*

To weʒe boþe sheld and spere,   *carry*

Þan me þat wilde folc ibringe

Þat hi me wolde ihere singe.

1025 Wat sol Ich þar mid mine songe?   *would I do*

Ne sunge Ich hom never so longe,

Mi song were ispild ech del: *entirely*

For hom ne mai halter ne bridel

Bringe vrom hore wude wise,   *Dissuade; mad ways*

1030 Ne mon mid stele ne mid ire.   *iron*

Ac war lond is boþe este and god,   *pleasant*

An þar men habbeþ milde mod,

Ich noti mid hom mine þrote,   *use*

Vor Ich mai do þar gode note,   *service*

1035 An bringe hom love tiþinge,   *welcome tidings*

Vor Ich of chirche songe singe.

Hit was iseid in olde laʒe,

27   A possible allusion to the work of a papal missionary such as
Cardinal Vivian, who journeyed in 1176 to Scotland, Ireland and
Norway; or Cardinal Guala, who travelled to Scotland in 1218.

An ȝet ilast þilke soþsaȝe, *that same true saying*
Þat man shal erien an sowe, *plough*
1040 Þar he wenþ after sum god mowe: *hopes; reap*
For he is wod þat soweþ his sed *mad*
Þar never gras ne sprinþ ne bled.' *blossoms*
　　Þe Hule was wroþ, to cheste rad, *eager for strife*
Mid þisse worde hire eȝen abrad: *widened*
1045 'Þu seist þu witest manne bures, *protect men's*
Þar leves boþ and faire flores,
Þar two ilove in one bedde *lovers*
Liggeþ biclopt and wel bihedde. *embraced; watched over*
Enes þu sunge, Ic wod wel ware, *Once; know*
1050 Bi one bure, and woldest lere *teach*
Þe lefdi to an uvel luve, *lady*
An sunge boþe loȝe and buve, *low and high*
An lerdest hi to don shome
An unriȝt of hire licome. *do wrong with her body*
1055 Þe loverd þat sone underȝat, *soon perceived*
Liim and grine and wel eiwat, *Bird-lime; snares; all manner of things*
Sette and ledde þe for to lacche. *laid; you; catch*
Þu come sone to þan hacche, *casement*
Þu were inume in one grine, *trapped*
1060 Al hit aboȝte þine shine: *paid for; shins*
Þu naddest non oþer dom ne laȝe, *judgement; law*
Bute mid wilde horse were todraȝe. *drawn*
Vonde ȝif þu miȝt eft misrede, *Try; again lead astray*
Waþer þu wult, wif þe maide: *Whichever*
1065 Þi song mai bo so longe genge *effective*
Þat þu shalt wippen on a sprenge.' *dangle; snare*
　　Þe Niȝtingale at þisse worde
Mid sworde an mid speres orde, *point*
ȝif ho mon were, wolde fiȝte: *a man*
1070 Ac þo ho bet do ne miȝte *because*
Ho vaȝt mid hire wise tunge: *fought*
'Wel fiȝt þat wel specþ,' seiþ in þe songe.
Of hire tunge ho nom red: *took advice*
'Wel fiȝt þat wel specþ', seide Alvred.
1075 'Wat! Seistu þis for mine shome
Þe loverd hadde herof grame? *suffered from this*
He was so gelus of his wive,
Þat he ne miȝte for his live
Iso þat man wiþ hire speke, *Sees*
1080 Þat his horte nolde breke.
He hire bileck in one bure, *locked*
Þat hire was boþe stronge and sure: *for her*
Ich hadde of hire milse an ore, *mercy and pity*
An sori was for hire sore,
1085 An skente hi mid mine songe *amused*
Al þat Ich miȝte, raþe an longe. *quickly and lengthily*
Vorþan þe kniȝt was wiþ me wroþ, *Therefore*
Vor riȝte niþe Ich was him loþ. *downright malice; loathsome*
He dude me his oȝene shome, *placed on*
1090 Ac al him turnde it to grome. *grief*

	Þat underyat þe king Henri:[28]	*perceived*
	Jesus his soule do merci!	
	He let forbonne þene kniзt,	*ordered to be outlawed*
	Þat hadde idon so muchel unriзt	
1095	Ine so gode kinges londe;	
	Vor riзte niþe and for fule onde	*ill-will*
	Let þane lutle fuзel nime	*To allow the little bird to be taken*
	An him fordeme lif an lime.	*condemned it in life and limb*
	Hit was wurþsipe al mine kunne,	*came back to the honour of*
1100	Forþon þe kniзt forles his wunne,	*Because of this; lost; joys*
	An зaf for me an hundred punde;	
	An mine briddes seten isunde,	*soundly*
	An hadde soþþe blisse and hiзte,	*joy*
	An were bliþe, and wel miзte.	
1105	Vorþon Ich was so wel awreke,	*avenged*
	Ever eft Ich dar þe bet speke:	*more easily*
	Vor hit bitidde ene swo,	*happened; once; like this*
	Ich am þe bliþur ever mo.	
	Nu Ich mai singe war Ich wulle,	
1110	Ne dar me never eft mon agrulle.	*annoy*
	Ac þu, ereming! Þu wrecche gost!	*wretch*
	Þu ne canst finde, ne þu nost,	*know not*
	An holз stok þar þu þe miзt hude,	*stump; hide*
	Þat me ne twengeþ þine hude.	*pinch; skin*
1115	Vor children, gromes, heme and hine,[29]	
	Hi þencheþ alle of þire pine:	*torment*
	Зif hi muзe iso þe sitte,	
	Stones hi doþ in hore slitte,	*place; pockets*
	An þe totorved and toheneþ,	*pelt and stone to pieces*
1120	An þine fule bon tosheneþ.	*break*
	Зif þu art iworpe oþer ishote,	*hit or shot*
	Þanne þu miзt erest to note;	*at last be useful*
	Vor me þe hoþ in one rodde,	*people hang you on a rod*
	An þu, mid þine fule codde,	*belly*
1125	An mid þine ateliche swore,	*horrible neck*
	Biwerest manne corn vrom dore.	*Guard men's corn against animals*
	Nis noþer noзt, þi lif ne þi blod:[30]	
	Ac þu art shueles suþe god.	*scarecrow*
	Þar nowe sedes boþe isowe,	*new; are*
1130	Pinnuc, golfinc, rok, ne crowe	*Sparrow, goldfish*
	Ne dar þar never cumen ihende,	*near*
	Зif þi buc hongeþ at þan ende;	*carcass*
	Þar tron shulle a зere blowe,	*trees; every year*
	An зunge sedes springe and growe,	
1135	Ne dar no fuзel þarto vonge,	*ravage them*
	Зif þu art þarover ihonge.	
	Þi lif is evre luþer and qued,	*worthless and wicked*
	Þu nard noзt bute ded.	*are worthless unless*

28   This reference could be to Henry I, II or III. Most critics have assumed it refers to Henry II. 'Jesus, his soule do merci!' suggests the relevant king is dead, and many have used this as evidence for dating the poem: Henry I died in 1135; Henry II in 1189; and Henry III in 1272.

29   Village boys and monastic boys, villagers and members of a monastery [are all united in pursuing the Owl]. See Stanley, *The Owl and the Nightingale*, pp. 132–3.

30   As a thing of flesh and blood (i.e. alive), you are worthless.

	Nu þu miȝt wite sikerliche	*truly*
1140	Þat þine leches boþ grisliche	*looks*
	Þe wile þu art on lifdaȝe;	
	Vor wane þu hongest islaȝe,	*slaughtered*
	Ȝut hi boþ of þe ofdradde,	*frightened*
	Þe fuȝeles þat þe er bigradde.	*cried out at before*
1145	Mid riȝte men boþ wiþ þe wroþe,	
	For þu singist ever of hore loþe:	*troubles*
	Al þat þu singst, raþe oþer late,	*early*
	Hit is ever of manne unwate.	*ill luck*
	Wane þu havest aniȝt igrad	*at night*
1150	Men boþ of þe wel sore ofdrad.	
	Þu singst þar sum man shal be ded:	
	Ever þu bodest sumne qued.	*prophesy; misfortune*
	Þu singst aȝen eiȝte lure,[31]	
	Oþer of summe frondes rure,	*friend's ruin*
1155	Oþer þu bodes huses brune,	*burning*
	Oþer ferde of manne, oþer þoves rune;	*invasion; the hue and cry for a thief*
	Oþer þu bodest cualm of oreve,	*plague of cattle*
	Oþer þat londfolc wurþ idorve,	*will become stricken*
	Oþer þat wif lost hire make,	*will lose her mate*
1160	Oþer þu bodest cheste an sake.	*conflict and strife*
	Ever þu singist of manne hareme,	*harm*
	Þurȝ þe hi boþ sori and areme;	*wretched*
	Þu ne singst never one siþe	*time*
	Þat hit nis for sum unsiþe.	*mishap*
1165	Hervore hit is þat me þe shuneþ,	
	An þe totorveþ and tobuneþ	*beat severely*
	Mid stave, and stoone, and turf, and clute,	*clods*
	Þat þu ne miȝt nowar atrute.	*escape*
	Dahet ever suich budel in tune	*Cursed be; town-crier*
1170	Þat ever bodeþ unwreste rune,	*bad news*
	An ever bringeþ uvele tiþinge,	
	An þat ever specþ of uvele þinge!	
	God Almiȝti wurþe him wroþ,	*be angry with him*
	An al þat werieþ linnene cloþ!'[32]	*linen clothes*
1175	Þe Hule ne abod noȝt swiþ longe,	*did not wait*
	Ah ȝef ondsware starke and stronge:	
	'Wat,' quaþ ho, 'hartu ihoded?	
	Oþer þu kursest al unihoded?[33]	
	For prestes wike Ich wat þu dest;	*functions; perform*
1180	Ich not ȝef þu were ȝavre prest,	*did not know; previously*
	Ich not ȝef þu canst masse singe:	
	Inoh þu canst of mansinge.	*Enough; know; excommunication*
	Ah hit is for þine alde niþe,	*ancient malice*
	Þat þu me akursedest oþer siðe.[34]	*a second time*
1185	Ah þarto is lihtlich ondsware:	*easy*
	"Drah to þe!" cwað þe cartare.	*Slow down; carter*

---

31 You sing in expectation of the loss of possessions.

32 Only the relatively well-to-do wore linen. Neither monks nor the poor wore such underclothing.

33 'What,' she said, 'are you hooded, Or do you curse without a hood?' Only the 'hooded', priests, were able to perform excommunication. The Owl refers to ecclesiastical law here.

34 The Nightingale curses the Owl at lines 99 and 1169.

Wi attwitestu me mine insihte,   *insight*
An min iwit and mine miȝte?   *wisdom*
For Ich am witi, ful iwis,   *wise, certainly*
1190   An wod al þat to kumen is: *know*
Ich wot of hunger, of hergonge,   *invasions*
Ich wot ȝef men schule libbe longe,
Ich wat ȝef wif luste hire make,   *will lose*
Ich wat þar schal beo niþ and wrake,   *vengeance*
1195   Ich wot hwo schal beon anhonge,
Oþer elles fulne deþ afonge.   *receive*
Ȝef men habbeþ bataile inume,   *undertaken judicial combat*
Ich wat hwaþer schal beon overkume.   *defeated*
Ich wat ȝif cwalm scal comen on orfe,   *plague; cattle*
1200   An ȝif dor schul ligge astorve;   *wild animals; dead*
Ich wot ȝef treon schule blowe,
Ich wat ȝef cornes schule growe,
Ich wot ȝef huses schule berne,
Ich wot ȝef men schule eorne oþer erne,[35]   *run or ride*
1205   Ich wot ȝef sea schal schipes drenche,   *cause to founder*
Ich wot ȝef smiþes schal uvele clenche.   *poorly rivet*
An ȝet Ich con muchel more: *know*
Ich con inoh in bokes lore,   *scholarship*
An eke Ich can of þe goddspelle
1210   More þan Ich nule þe telle;
For Ich at chirche come ilome,   *often*
An muche leorni of wisdome.
Ich wat al of þe tacninge,   *divining the future*
An of oþer feole þinge.   *many*
1215   Ȝef eni mon schal rem abide,   *raise a hue and cry*
Al Ich hit wot ear hit itide.   *before it happens*
Ofte, for mine muchele iwitte,
Wel sorimod and worþ Ich sitte: *sad at heart; angry*
Wan Ich iseo þat sum wrechede   *grief*
1220   Is manne neh, innoh Ich grede;   *near; cry out*
Ich bidde þat men beon iwarre,   *beseech; aware*
An habbe gode reades ȝarre.   *counsels prepared*
For Alfred seide a wis word,
Euch mon hit schulde legge on hord: *store up as treasure*
1225   "Ȝef þu isihst er he beo icume,   *see before it (grief)*
His strencþe is him wel neh binume."[36]   *taken from*
An grete duntes beoþ þe lasse,   *blows*
Ȝef me ikepþ mid iwarnesse,   *take heed by being aware*
An fleo schal toward misȝenge,   *arrow; miss its mark*
1230   Ȝef þu isihst hu fleo of strenge;   *it flew from the string*
For þu miȝt blenche wel and fleo,   *dodge; flee*
Ȝif þu isihst heo to þe teo.   *it proceeding towards you*
Þat eni man beo falle in odwite,   *Though; shame*
Wi schal he me his sor atwite?   *sorrow; blame*
1235   Þah Ich iseo his harm bivore,
Ne comeþ hit noȝt of me þarvare.   *derives; therefore*

---

35   The owl knows who will be poor, and go on foot; or rich, and ride on horseback.

36   If you know about coming trouble, the impact it has will be lessened.

Þah þu iseo þat sum blind mon,
Þat nanne rihtne wei ne con,   *does not know*
To þare diche his dweole fulied,   *error follows*
1240   An falleþ, and þarone sulied,   *is made dirty by it*
Wenest þu, þah Ich al iseo,
Þat hit for me þe raþere beo?   *because of me happened quicker*
    Alswo hit fareþ bi mine witte: *Likewise*
Hwanne Ich on mine bowe sitte,
1245   Ich wot and iseo swiþe brihte   *clearly*
An summe men kumed harm þarrihte.   *To; straight away*
Schal he, þat þerof noþing not,   *knows*
Hit wite me for Ich hit wot?   *blame*
Schal he his mishap wite me,
1250   For Ich am wisure þane he?
Hwanne Ich iseo þat sum wrechede
Is manne neh, inoh Ich grede,
An bidde inoh þat hi heom schilde,
For toward heom is harm unmylde.   *harsh*
1255   Ah þah Ich grede lude an stille,
Al hit itid þurþ Godes wille.   *through*
Hwi wulleþ men of me hi mene,   *complain*
Þah Ich mid soþe heo awene?   *vex them*
Þah Ich hi warni al þat ȝer,
1260   Nis heom þerfore harem no þe ner.   *the nearer*
Ah Ich heom singe for Ich wolde
Þat hi wel understonde schulde
Þat sum unselþe heom is ihende,   *misfortune; near*
Hwan Ich min huing to heom sende.   *hooting*
1265   Naveþ no man none sikerhede   *certainty*
Þat he ne mai wene and adrede   *expect*
Þat sum unhwate neþ him beo,   *calamity*
Þah he ne conne hit iseo.
Forþi seide Alfred swiþe wel,
1270   And his worde was goddspel,
Þat evereuch man, þe bet him beo,   *better he may be*
Eaver þe bet he hine beseo;   *should look to himself*
Ne truste no mon to his weole   *wealth*
To swiþe, þah he habbe veole: *a great deal*
1275   "Nis nout so hot þat hit na coleþ,   *cool*
Ne noȝt so hwit þat hit ne soleþ,   *soil*
Ne noȝt so leof þat hit ne aloþeþ,   *beloved; become hateful*
Ne noȝt so glad þat hit ne awroþeþ;   *become angry*
Ac eavereeuch þing þat eche nis,   *is not eternal*
1280   Agon schal, and al þis worldes blis."   *Shall pass away*
    Nu þu miȝt wite readliche   *know*
Þat eavere þu spekest gideliche,   *foolishly*
For al þat þu me seist for schame,
Ever þe seolve hit turneþ to grome.   *to your own harm*
1285   Go so hit go, at eche fenge   *round of the fight*
Þu fallest mid þine ahene swenge;   *swing*
Al þat þu seist for me to schende,   *revile*
Hit is mi wurschipe at þan ende.
Bute þu wille bet aginne,   *go about things*

1290	Ne shaltu bute schame iwinne.'	
	Þe Niȝtingale sat and siȝte,	*sighed*
	And hohful was, and ful wel miȝte,	*thoughtful*
	For þe Hule swo ispeke hadde,	
	An hire speche swo iladde.	*conducted*
1295	Heo was hoþful, and erede	*unsure*
	Hwat heo þarafter hire sede:	
	Ah neoþeles heo hire understod.	*understood (the Owl's words)*
	'Wat!' heo seide, 'Hule, artu wod?	
	Þu ȝeolpest of seolliche wisdome,	*boast; strange*
1300	Þu nustest wanene he þe come,	
	Bute hit of wicchecrefte were.[37]	
	Þarof þu, wrecche, moste þe skere	*must clear your name*
	Ȝif þu wult among manne beo,	
	Oþer þu most of londe fleo.	*flee into exile*
1305	For alle þeo þat þerof cuþe,	*those that are familiar with it*
	Heo were ifurn of prestes muþe	*previously*
	Amanset: swuch þu art ȝette,	*Excommunicated; still*
	Þu wiecchecrafte neaver ne lete.	*abandoned*
	Ich þe seide nu lutel ere,	*a little while before*
1310	An þu askedest ȝef Ich were	
	A bisemere to preost ihoded:	*mockery*
	Ah þe mansing is so ibroded,	*excommunication; widespread*
	Þah no preost a londe nere,	*were in the land*
	A wrecche neoþeles þu were,	
1315	For eavereuch child þe cleopeþ fule,	*calls foul*
	An evereuch man a wrecche hule.	
	Ich habbe iherd, and soþ hit is,	
	Þe mon mot beo wel storrewis,[38]	*star-wise*
	And wite innoþ of wucche þinge kume,	*enough of what things might happen*
1320	So þu seist þe is iwune.	*customary*
	Hwat canstu, wrecche þing, of storre,	*do you know; of the stars*
	Bute þat þu bihalst hi feorre?	*Except; look on them; far off*
	Alswo deþ mani dor and man,	
	Þeo of swucche nawiht ne con.	*such things; know nothing*
1325	On ape mai a boc bihalde,	
	An leves wenden and eft folde;	*turn; close*
	Ac he ne con þe bet þarvore	
	Of clerkes lore top ne more.	*from beginning to end*
	Þah þu iseo þe steorre alswa,	
1330	Nartu þe wisure neaver þe mo.	
	Ah ȝet þu, fule þing, me chist	*chide*
	An wel grimliche me atwist	*reproach*
	Þat Ich singe bi manne huse,	
	An teache wif breke spuse.	*marriage vows*
1335	Þu liest iwis, þu fule þing,	
	Þurh me nas neaver ischend spusing.	*a marriage broken*
	Ah soþ hit is, Ich singe and grede	
	Þar lavedies beoþ and faire maide;	
	And soþ hit is of luve Ich singe,	

37   You don't know where your wisdom came from, / Unless it was   38   The man would have to be very knowledgeable about the stars.
from witchcraft.

1340	For god wif mai i spusing	
	Bet luvien hire oȝene were,	*man*
	Þane awe hire copenere;	*anywhere else; lover*
	An maide mai luve cheose	
	Þat hire wurþschipe ne forleose,	*honour; abandon*
1345	An luvie mid rihte luve	
	Þane þe schal beon hire buve.	*The one (Christ); above*
	Swiche luve Ich itache and lere,	
	Þerof beoþ al mine ibere.	*cries*
	Þah sum wif beo of nesche mode,	*tender*
1350	For wummon beoþ of softe blode,	
	Þat heo, for sume sottes lore	*fool's teaching*
	Þe ȝeorne bit and sikeþ sore,	*eagerly beseeches; sighs*
	Misrempe and misdo sume stunde,	*Go astray; on occasion*
	Schal Ich þarvore beon ibunde?	*made responsible*
1355	Ȝif wimmen luvieþ unrede,	*ill-advisedly*
	Hwitistu me hore misdede?	*Why blame me*
	Ȝef wimmon þencheþ luvie derne,	*intend; secretly*
	Ne ne mai Ich mine songes werne.	*Not at all; deny*
	Wummon mai pleie under cloþe,	
1360	Weþer heo wile, wel þe wroþe:	*honestly or dishonestly*
	And heo mai do bi mine songe	
	Hwaþer heo wule, wel þe wronge.	
	For nis a worlde þing so god	
	Þat ne mai do sum ungod	*evil*
1365	Ȝif me hit wule turne amis.	*a person*
	For gold and seolver, god hit is:	
	An noþeles þarmid þu miȝt	
	Spusbruche buggen and unriȝt.	*Buy adultery*
	Wepne beoþ gode griþ to halde,	*Weapons; peace*
1370	Ah neoþeles þarmide beoþ men acwalde	*killed*
	Aȝeines riht an fale londe,	*Against the law in many lands*
	Þar þeoves hi bereð an honde.	
	Alswa hit is bi mine songe,	
	Þah heo beo god, me hine mai misfonge	*it; misuse*
1375	An drahe hine to sothede,	*convert it to folly*
	An to oþre uvele dede.	
	Ah schaltu wrecch, luve tele?	*blame*
	Bo wuch ho bo, uich luve is fele	*Be as it may be, each love is good*
	Bitweone wepmon and wimmane;	
1380	Ah ȝef heo is atbroide, þenne	*snatched away*
	He is unfele and forbrode.	*improper and perverted*
	Wroþ wurþe heom þe holi rode,	*May the holy Cross be angry with those*
	Þe rihte ikunde swo forbreideþ!	*Who pervert proper nature like this*
	Wunder hit is þat heo na wedeþ:	*do not go mad*
1385	An swo heo doþ, for heo beoþ wode	
	Þe bute nest goþ to brode.	*Who go and breed without a nest*
	Wummon is of nesche flesche,	*tender*
	An flesches lustes is strong to cwesse;	*suppress*
	Nis wunder nan þah he abide,	*he persists*
1390	For flesches lustes hi makeþ slide.	*will make her yield*
	Ne beoþ heo noþt alle forlore,	
	Þat stumpeþ at þe flesches more,	*stumbles over; root*

For moni wummon haveþ misdo
Þat aris op of þe slo. *mire*
1395   Ne beoþ noþt ones alle sunne, *of one kind; sins*
Forþan hi beoþ tweire kunne: *types*
Sun arist of þe flesches luste,
An sum of þe gostes custe. *spirit's character*
Þar flesch draheþ men to drunnesse, *drunkenness*
1400   An to wrovehede and to golnesse, *perverseness; lechery*
Þe gost misdeþ þurch niþe an onde, *malice and envy*
And seoþþe mid murhþe of monne shonde, *after; joy in man's shame*
An ȝeoneþ after more and more, *longs with open mouth for*
An lutel rehþ of milce and ore; *cares about mercy and pity*
1405   An stiȝþ on heþ þurþ modinesse, *ascends; pride*
An overhoheð þanne lasse. *derides; humble man*
Sei me sooþ, ȝef þu hit wost, *know*
Hweþer deþ wurse, flesch þe gost?
Þu miȝt segge, ȝef þu wult,
1410   Þat lasse is þe flesches gult:
Moni man is of his flesche clene,
Þat is mid mode deovel imene. *in mind, a companion of the devil*
Ne schal non mon wimman bigrede, *speak out against*
An flesches lustes hire upbreide; *reproach*
1415   Swuch he may tellen of golnesse *reprove; lechery*
Þat sunegeþ wurse i modinesse. *sins; through pride*
Hwet ȝif Ich schulde a luve bringe *to love*
Wif oþer maide hwanne Ich singe?
Ich wolde wiþ þe maide holde, *side*
1420   Ȝif þu hit const ariht atholde. *understand*
Lust nu, Ich segge þe hwarvore,
Up to þe toppe from þe more: *bottom*
Ȝef maide luveþ dernliche *secretly*
Heo stumpeþ and falþ icundeliche; *by natural instinct*
1425   For þah heo sum hwile pleie,
Heo nis nout feor ut of þe weie;
Heo mai hire guld atwende *guilt escape from*
A rihte weie þurþ chirche bende, *In the; bonds*
An mai eft habbe to make
1430   Hire leofmon wiþute sake, *sweetheart; blame*
An go to him bi daies lihte
Þat er stal to bi þeostre nihte. *stole away to; dark*
An ȝunling not hwat swuch þing is,
His ȝunge blod hit draȝeþ amis,
1435   An sum sot mon hit tihþ þarto *foolish; leads*
Mid alle þan þat he mai do:
He comeþ and fareþ and beod and bid, *commands and beseeches*
An heo bistant and oversid, *harrasses; neglects*
An bisehþ ilome and longe. *pleads; often*
1440   Hwat mai þat chil þah hit misfonge? *child do, though it is wrong*
Hit nuste neaver hwat hit was;
Forþi hit þohte fondi þas, *Thus she thought to try it*
An wite iwis hwuch beo þe gome *for certain what the game is*
Þat of so wilde makeþ tome. *a tame one*
1445   Ne mai Ich for reoþe lete, *pity refrain*

Wanne Ich iseo þe tohte ilete · strained face
Þe luve bring on þe ӡunglinge,
Þat Ich of murӡþe him ne singe. · for pleasure for her
Ich teache heom bi mine songe
1450 Þat swucch luve ne lest noӡt longe; · lasts
For mi song lutle hwile ilest, · rest for a moment
An luve ne deþ noӡt bute rest · rest for a moment
On swuch childre, and sone ageþ, · departs
An falþ adun þe hote breþ. · declines; passion
1455 Ich singe mid heom one þroӡe, · for a while
Biginne on heh and endi laӡe,
An lete mine songes falle · allow; to fall away
An lutle wile adun mid alle. · completely
Þat maide wot, hwanne Ich swike, · stop
1460 Þat luve is mine songes iliche;
For hit nis bute a lutel breþ
Þat sone kumeþ, and sone geþ. · goes
Þat child bi me hit understond, · by my example
An his unred to red wend, · her foolishness; turns to good sense
1465 An iseӡþ wel, bi mine songe, · she sees
Þat dusi luve ne last noӡt longe. · foolish
Ah wel Ich wule þat þu hit wite:
Loþ me beoþ wives utschute; · Hateful; immoderation
Ah wif mai of me nime ӡeme, · take example
1470 Ich ne singe naþt hwan Ich teme. · mate
An wif ah lete sottes lore, · ought to abandon a fool's teaching
Þah spusingbendes þuncheþ sore. · marriage ties; seem
Wundere me þungþ wel starc and stor, · It seems to me a wonder; severe
Hu eni mon so eavar for · behaved
1475 Þat he his heorte miӡte drive
An do hit to oþers mannes wive: · another
For oþer hit is of twam þinge,
Ne mai þat þridde no man bringe;
Oþar þe laverd is wel aht, · able
1480 Oþer aswunde, and nis naht. · feeble
Ӡef he is wurþful and aht man, · honourable and valiant
Nele no man, þat wisdon can, · no one that is wise will want to
Hure of is wive do him schame: · bring shame on him through his wife
For he mai him adrede grame, · be fearful of harm
1485 An þat he forleose þat þer hongeþ, · lose; depends on that
Þat him eft þarto noӡt ne longeþ. · long for
An þah he þat noӡt ne adrede,
Hit is unriӡt and gret sothede
An misdon one gode manne, · do wrong to
1490 An his ibedde from him spanne. · bed-fellow; urge
Ӡef hire laverd is forwurde, · enfeebled
An unorne at bedde and at borde, · useless
Hu miӡte þar beo eni luve
Wanne a swuch cheorles buc hire ley buve? · churl's body lies above her
1495 Hu mai þar eni luve beo
Þar swuch man gropeþ hire þeo? · thigh
Herbi þu miӡt wel understonde
Þat on is aren, þat oþer schonde, · harm; shame

To stele to oþres mannes bedde;

1500   For ʒif aht man is hire bedde,   *able; bed-fellow*
Þu miʒt wene þat þe mistide,   *anticipate; it may get bad results*
Wanne þu list bi hire side.   *lie*
An ʒef þe laverd is a wercche,   *wretch*
Hwuch este miʒtistu þar vecche?   *pleasure; get*

1505   ʒif þu biþenchest hwo hire ofligge,   *may have lain with her*
Þu miʒt mid wlate þe este bugge.   *disgust; buy*
Ich not hu mai eni freoman   *man of standing*
For hire sechen after þan.
ʒef he biþencþ bi hwan he lai,   *whom*

1510   Al mai þe luve gan awai.'
Þe Hule was glad of swuche tale;
Heo þoʒte þatte Nihtegale,
Þah heo wel speke atte frume,   *the beginning*
Hadde at þen ende misnume,   *gone wrong*

1515   An seide: 'Nu Ich habbe ifunde
Þat maidenes beoþ of þine imunde: *concern*
Mid heom þu holdest, and heom biwerest,   *protect*
An overswiþe þu hi herest.   *immoderately; praise*
Þe lavedies beoþ to me iwend,   *turned*

1520   To me heo hire mode send.
For hit itit ofte and ilome   *happens; frequently*
Þat wif and were beoþ unisome;   *at odds*
And þerfore þe were gulte,   *is guilty*
Þat leof is over wummon to pulte,   *Who likes; to assail*

1525   An speneþ on þare al þat he haveþ,   *her*
An siveþ þare þat no riht naveþ,   *follows*
An haveþ attom his riʒte spuse,   *at home*
Wowes weste, and lere huse,   *Desolate walls and empty*
Wel þunne ischrud and ived wroþe,   *scantily clothed and fed badly*

1530   An let heo bute mete and cloþe.   *abandons her without*
Wan he comeþ ham eft to his wive,
Ne dar heo noʒt a word ischire;   *utter*
He chid and gred swuch he beo wod,   *mad*
An ne bringþ hom non oþer god.

1535   Al þat heo deþ him is unwille,   *displeasing to*
Al þat heo spekeþ hit is him ille;
An oft hwan heo noʒt ne misdeþ,   *does no wrong*
Heo haveþ þe fust in hire teþ.   *his fist*
Nis nan mon þat ne mai ibringe   *send*

1540   His wif amis mid swucche þinge: *astray*
Me hire mai so ofte misbeode   *mistreated*
Þat heo do wule hire ahene neode.   *attend to her own needs*
La, Godd hit wot, heo nah iweld,   *is not responsible*
Þa heo hine makie kukeweld.   *a cuckold*

1545   For hit itit lome and ofte,
Þat his wif is wel nesche and softe,   *tender*
Of faire bleo and wel idiht: *complexion; shaped*
Wi, hit is þe more unriht
Þat he his luve spene on þare

1550   Þat nis wurþ one of hire heare.   *hairs*
An swucche men beoþ wel manifolde,   *numerous*

Þat wif ne kunne noþt ariȝt holde.
Ne mot non mon wiþ hire speke;   *thinks; immediately break*
He veneð heo wule anon tobreke   *thinks; immediately break*
1555   Hire spusing, ȝef heo lokeþ
Oþer wiþ manne faire spekeþ.
He hire biluþ mid keie and loke: *locks up*
Þarþurh is spusing ofte tobroke;   *marriage*
For ȝef heo is þarto ibroht,   *brought to that*
1560   He deþ þat heo nadde ear iþoht.   *what she had not thought of previously*
Dahet þat to swuþe hit bispeke,   *Cursed be; speaks about*
Þah swucche wives heom awreke!   *avenge themselves*
Herof þe lavedies to me meneþ   *lament*
An wel sore me ahweneþ;   *they grieve*
1565   Wel neh min heorte wule tochine,   *break asunder*
Hwon Ich biholde hire pine.   *torment*
Mid heom Ich wepe swiþe sore,
An for heom bidde Cristis ore,   *pity*
Þat þe lavedi sone aredde   *may rescue*
1570   An hire sende betere ibedde.
     Anoþer þing Ich mai þe telle,
Þat þu ne schald, for þine felle,   *should; skin*
Ondswere none þarto finde;
Al þi sputing schal aswinde.   *contention; fail*
1575   Moni chapmon and moni cniht   *merchants*
Luveþ and hald his wif ariht,
An swa deþ moni bondeman.   *peasants*
Þat gode wif deþ after þan,   *acts in response to that*
An serveþ him to bedde and to borde   *in*
1580   Mid faire dede and faire worde,
An ȝeorne fondeþ hu heo muhe   *eagerly; tries; might*
Do þing þat him beo iduȝe.   *may do him good*
Þe laverd into þare þeode
Fareþ ut on þare beire nede,   *both of their needs*
1585   An is þat gode wif unbliþe   *unhappy*
For hire laverdes houdsiþe,   *departure*
An sit and sihð wel sore oflonged,   *in longing*
An hire sore an horte ongred;   *grieves*
Al for hire loverdes sake
1590   Haveþ daies kare and niȝtes wake,
An swuþe longe hire is þe hwile,   *to her*
An euch steape hire þunþ a mile.   *seems*
Hwanne oþre slepeþ hire abute,
Ich one lust þar wiðþute,   *alone*
1595   An wot of hire sore mode,
An singe a niȝt for hire gode:
An mine gode song, for hire þinge,
Ich turne sundel to murnige.   *in part; mourning*
Of hure seorhe Ich bere sume,   *sorrow*
1600   Forþan Ich am hire wel welcume:
Ich hire helpe hwat I mai,
For hoȝeþ þane rehte wai.   *Being mindful of*
Ah þu me havest sore igramed   *annoyed*
Þat min heorte is wel neh alamed,   *paralysed*

1605	Þat Ich mai unneaþe speke;	*Such that; uneasily*
	Ah ʒet Ich wule forþure reke.	*proceed further*
	Þu seist þat Ich am manne loð,	
	An evereuch man is wið me wroð,	
	An me mid stone and lugge þreteþ,	*sticks*
1610	An me tobusteþ and tobeteþ,	
	An hwanne heo habeþ me ofslahe,	*killed*
	Heo hongeþ me on heore hahe,	*hedge*
	Þar Ich aschewele pie an crowe	*scare away the magpie*
	Fron þan þe þar is isowe.	*that which there is sown*
1615	Þah hit beo soþ, Ich do heom god,	
	An for heom Ich chadde mi blod.	*shed*
	Ich do heom god mid mine deaþe,	
	Warvore þe is wel unneaþe.	
	For þah þu ligge dead and clinge,	*shrivel up*
1620	Þi deþ nis naþt to none þinge:	*nothing*
	Ich not neaver to hwan þu miʒt,	*I don't know what you are useful for*
	For þu nart bute a wrecche wiʒt.	*are nothing; creature*
	Ah þah mi lif me beo atschote,	*shot out of*
	Þe ʒet Ich mai do gode note:	*service*
1625	Me mai up one smale sticke	
	Me sette a wude ine þe þicke,	*thicket*
	An swa mai mon tolli him to	*attract*
	Lutle briddes and ivo,[39]	*trap them*
	An swa me mai mid me biʒete	*one can get with me*
1630	Wel gode brede to his mete.	*roast meat for his food*
	Ah þu nevre mon to gode	
	Lives ne deaþes stal ne stode:	*In life or death you were no use*
	Ich not to hwan þu breist þi brod,	*for what reason; breed*
	Lives ne deaþes ne deþ hit god.'	
1635	Þe Nihtegale iherde þis,	
	An hupte uppon on blowe ris,	*hopped; blossoming branch*
	An herre sat þan heo dude ear:	*higher; earlier*
	'Hule,' heo seide, 'beo nu wear,	
	Nulle Ich wiþ þe plaidi na more,	*debate*
1640	For her þe mist þi rihte lore:	*fails; skill*
	Þu ʒulpest þat þu art manne loþ,	*boast*
	An evereuch wiht is wið þe wroþ;	
	An mid ʒulinge and mid igrede	*yelling; crying out*
	Þu wanst wel þat þu art unlede.	*know; vile*
1645	Þu seist þat gromes þe ifoð,	*boys; catch*
	An heie on rodde þe anhoð,	*rod; hang*
	An þe totwichet and toschakeð,	*pluck and shake to pieces*
	An summe of þe schawles makeð.	*a scarecrow*
	Me þunch þat þu forleost þat game,	
1650	Þu ʒulpest of þire oʒe schame;	
	Me þunch þat þu me gest an honde,	*you are submitting to me*
	Þu ʒulpest of þire oʒene schome.'	
	Þo heo hadde þeos word icwede,	
	Heo sat in one faire stude,	*place*

39   Small birds are attracted to the carcass of the Owl and can thus
be caught in traps.

1655	An þarafter hire stevene dihte,	*voice attuned*
	An song so schille and so brihte,	*clearly*
	Þat feor and ner me hit iherde.	
	Þarvore anan to hire cherde	*turned*
	Þrusche and þrostle and wudewale,	*throstle; woodpecker*
1660	An fuheles boþe grete and smale;[40]	
	Forþan heom þuhte þat heo hadde	
	Þe Houle overcome, vorþan heo gradde	*because she cried out*
	An sungen alswa vale wise;	*and likewise, they sang many songs*
	An blisse was among þe rise.	
1665	Riȝt swa me gred þe manne a schame	
	Þat taveleþ and forleost þat gome.	*gambles*
	Þeos Hule, þo heo þis iherde,	
	'Havestu,' heo seide, 'ibanned ferde?	*summoned an army*
	An wultu, wreche, wið me fiȝte?	
1670	Nai! Nai! Navestu none miȝte!	
	Hwat gredeþ þeo þat hider come?	
	Me þuncþ þu ledest ferde to me.	
	Ȝe schule wite, ar ȝe fleo heonne,	*should know; from here*
	Hwuch is þe strenþe of mine kunne;	*What; kindred*
1675	For þeo þe haveþ bile ihoked,	*hooked beaks*
	An clivres charpe and wel icroked,	*sharp talons*
	Alle heo beoþ of mine kunrede,	
	An walde come ȝif Ich bede.	*ask them*
	Þe seolfe coc, þat wel can fiȝte,	
1680	He mot mid me holde mid riȝte,	
	For boþe we habbeþ stevene briȝte,	
	An sitteþ under weolkne bi niȝte.	*the clouds*
	Schille Ich an utest uppen ow grede,	*If I shall call a hue and cry on you*
	Ich schal swo stronge ferde lede	
1685	Þat ower proude schal avalle.	*pride; fall*
	A tort ne ȝive Ich for ow alle!	*turd*
	Ne schal, ar hit beo fulliche eve,	
	A wreche feþer on ow bileave.	*leave*
	Ah hit was unker voreward,	*our agreement*
1690	Þo we come hiderward,	
	Þat we þarto holde scholde,	*should agree to hold to*
	Þar riht dom us ȝive wolde.	*proper judgement given*
	Wultu nu breke foreward?	
	Ich wene dom þe þingþ to hard:	*I expect; seems to you too hard*
1695	For þu ne darst domes abide,	*wait for*
	Þu wult nu, wreche, fiȝte and chide.	
	Ȝet Ich ow alle wolde rede,	*counsel*
	Ar Ich utheste uppon ow grede,	*call out a hue and cry*
	Þat ower fihtlac leteþ beo,	*your quarrel*
1700	An ginneþ raþe awei fleo;	*begin quickly*
	For bi þe clivres þat Ich bere,	
	Ȝef ȝe abideþ mine here,	*wait for; army*
	Ȝe schule on oþer wise singe,	
	An acursi alle fiȝtinge;	*curse*

---

40 This coming together of the birds at the end of the debate is
also conventional in other debate texts.

1705	Vor nis of ow non so kene,	*bold*
	Þat durre abide mine onsene.'	*face*
	Þeos Hule spac wel baldeliche,	
	For þah heo nadde swo hwatliche	*as quickly*
	Ifare after hire here,	*Gone*
1710	Heo walde neoþeles ȝefe answere	*to give an answer to*
	Þe Niȝtegale mid swucche worde.	
	For moni man mid speres orde	*point*
	Haveþ lutle strencþe, and mid his chelde,	*or with; shield*
	Ah neoþeles in one felde,	*on one battlefield*
1715	Þurh belde worde an mid ilete,	*bold; behaviour*
	Deþ his ivo for arehþe swete.	*Makes his enemy sweat for cowardice*
	Þe Wranne, for heo cuþe singe,	*Wren*
	Þar com in þare moreȝeninge	
	To helpe þare Niȝtegale;	
1720	For þah heo hadde stevene smale,	
	Heo hadde gode þrote and schille,	
	An fale manne song a wille.	*And sang to please many men*
	Þe Wranne was wel wis iholde,	*held to be*
	For þeg heo nere ibred a wolde,	*though; raised in the forest*
1725	Ho was itoȝen among mankenne,	*brought up*
	An hire wisdom brohte þenne.	
	Heo miȝte speke hwar heo walde,	
	Tovore þe king þah heo scholde.	*Before; she wanted*
	'Lusteþ,' heo cwaþ, 'lateþ me speke.	
1730	Hwat! Wulle ȝe þis pes tobreke,	*peace*
	An do þanne kinge swuch schame?	
	ȝe! Nis he nouþer ded ne lame.	
	Hunke schal itide harm and schonde,	*On you both; will arise*
	ȝef ȝe doþ griþbruche on his londe.	*breach of the peace*
1735	Lateþ beo, and beoþ isome,	*united*
	An fareþ riht to ower dome,	*go straight*
	An lateþ dom þis plaid tobreke,	*decide this debate*
	Alswo hit was erur bispeke.'	*earlier agreed*
	'Ich an wel,' cwað þe Niȝtegale,	*grant that readily*
1740	'Ah, Wranne, naþt for þire tale,	*because of*
	Ah do for mire lahfulnesse:	*I do so; lawfulness*
	Ich nolde þat unrihtfulnesse	*I should not want unlawfulness*
	Me at þen ende overkome.	
	Ich nam ofdrad of none dome.	*afraid; any*
1745	Bihote Ich habbe, soþ hit is,	*Promised*
	Þat Maister Nichole, þat is wis,	
	Bituxen us deme schule,	*Between*
	An ȝet Ich wene þat he wule.	
	Ah, war mihte we hine finde?'	*where can we find him*
1750	Þe Wranne sat in ore linde;	*a linden tree*
	'Hwat! Nuste ȝe,' cwaþ heo, 'his hom?	*Don't you know*
	He wuneþ at Porteshom,	*Portesham*
	At one tune ine Dorsete,	*town; Dorset*
	Bi þare see in ore utlete:	*Near; inlet*
1755	Þar he demeþ manie riȝte dom,	
	An diht and writ mani wisdom,	*composes and writes*
	An þurh his muþe and þurh his honde	*because of his*

Hit is þe betere into Scotlonde. *Things are; as far as*
To seche hine is lihtlich þing, *easy*
1760 He naveþ bute one woning. *dwelling*
Þat his bischopen muchel schame, *is to the bishops*
An alle þan þat of his nome *to all those; name*
Habbeþ ihert, and of his dede. *heard*
Hwi nulleþ hi nimen heom to rede, *will they not take as advice*
1765 Þat he were mid heom ilome *might be; frequently*
For teche heom of his wisdome, *In order to*
An ʒive him rente a vale stude, *income from many places*
Þat he miʒte heom ilome be mide?' *be with them*
   'Certes,' cwaþ þe Hule, 'þat is soð:
1770 Þeos riche men wel muche misdoð,
Þat leteþ þane gode mon,
Þat of so feole þinge con, *knows*
An ʒiveþ rente wel misliche, *income very irregularly*
An of him leteþ wel lihtliche. *respect*
1775 Wið heore cunne heo beoþ mildre *kin; more lenient*
An ʒeveþ rente litle childre: *income to*
Swo heore wit hi demþ a dwole, *intelligence judges them as in error*
Þat ever abid Maistre Nichole.[41]
Ah ute we þah to him fare, *let us*
1780 For þar is unker dom al ʒare.' *prepared*
   'Do we,' þe Niʒtegale seide;
'Ah wa schal unker speche rede, *who; our; present*
An telle tovore unker deme?' *relate it; judge*
   'Þarof Ich schal þe wel icweme,' *please*
1785 Cwaþ þe Houle, 'for al, ende of orde, *from beginning to end*
Telle Ich con, word after worde. *am able*
An ʒef þe þincþ þat Ich misrempe, *go amiss*
Þu stond aʒein and do me crempe.' *offer opposition; make me stop*
   Mid þisse worde forþ hi ferden,
1790 Al bute here and bute verde, *without army; troops*
To Portesham þat heo bicome. *arrived*
Ah hu heo spedde of heore dome *succeed in their judgement*
Ne can Ich eu na more telle: *you*
Her nis na more of þis spelle. *story*

---

41 That Master Nicholas is kept in expectation (of preferment).

Lyrics from Cambridge, Trinity College B. 14. 39

Cambridge, Trinity College B. 14. 39 (or manuscript 323 as it is also known), is dated to the last quarter of the thirteenth century, and is written by up to five different scribes.[1] It is an extensive collection of Latin, Anglo-Norman and English texts, of which the last number over forty individual works. The majority of the English pieces are penitential and devotional lyrics and hymns, but the manuscript also contains a *Life of Saint Margaret*, a homily for Saint Nicholas's feast day, and *The Proverbs of Alfred*. It seems that the language of the manuscript may point to an origin in West Worcestershire,[2] and judging by the texts included in the volume, it may have been intended for private devotion and, perhaps, for religious instruction.

Of the six lyrics edited here, three are included in other, contemporary manuscripts, indicating that a stock of religious verse circulated in England in this period, and particularly in the West of England where these manuscripts themselves originate. *Of One That Is So Fair and Bright,* occurring at folio 24 verso, is also found in London, British Library, Egerton 613; *When I Think on Domesday*, occurring at folio 43, is also in London, British Library, Caligula A. ix, Oxford, Jesus College, 29, and Oxford, Bodleian Library, Digby 86; *An Orison to Our Lady* (that is, a prayer of penitence), contained at folios 81 verso to 82 recto, is also found in Caligula A. ix, Jesus College 29, and London, British Library, Royal 2 F. viii.

The remaining three edited lyrics are unique to Trinity B. 14. 39. *When the Turf is Thy Tower* and *A Saying of Saint Bernard*[3] both occur at folio 47 verso, and *I Sing of One That Is Matchless* occurs at folio 81 verso.[4]

The themes discussed in these lyrics are those seen in twelfth- and earlier thirteenth-century religious poems: themes that are also prominent in much Old English religious verse and prose. For example, the transience of life is the dominant concern in *When the Turf is Thy Tower*, and demonstrates the reductive nature of death, affecting all of humankind. The knowledge that life is transitory leads the poet of *When I Think on Domesday* to contemplate the final judgement, and the fear engendered in those who are to be judged by Christ. Stanzas four and five dwell on the futility of wealth and warfare; such temporal things will not save the sinner. This poem, like those dedicated to the Virgin Mary, seeks the Virgin's intercession for the speaker in helping the good Christian to attain salvation. Devotion to Mary forms the focus in *Of One That Is So Fair and Bright*, *An Orison to our Lady* and *I Sing of One That Is Matchless*, where the beauty and purity of the virgin-figure are juxtaposed with her mildness and excellence as a mother, both aspects of her character being contrasted with the sinfulness of Eve. In *A Saying of Saint Bernard*, the wealth of temporal kingship is countered by the humble surroundings of Christ's birth, the antithesis serving effectively to highlight the futility of worldly wealth.

Of One That Is So Fair and Bright[5]

For on þat is so feir ant brist		one; bright
Velud maris stella,		*Like the star of the sea*
Bristore þen þe daiis list,		*Brighter; day's light*
Parens et puella;		*Mother and maiden*
5 I crie þe grace of þe,		
Levedi, priie þi sone for me,		*pray*
Tam pia,		*So devoted*
Þat I mote come to þe,		*might*
Maria.		
10 Levedi, best of alle þing,		
Rosa sine spina,		*Rose without thorns*

---

1   It is bound with the fourteenth- and fifteenth-century manuscript B. 14. 40.

2   See M. Laing, *A Catalogue of Sources for a Linguistic Atlas of Early Middle English* (Cambridge, 1993), p. 37.

3   My own title for this piece, derived from the nature of its Latin source.

4   Carleton Brown, ed., *English Lyrics of the Thirteenth Century* (Oxford, 1932; repr. 1971) edits most of the lyrics in Trinity B. 14. 39, in all their variant versions. I have adopted his modern titles. For

When the Turf is Thy Tower and *A Saying of Saint Bernard*, Brown prints the Latin texts which precede these short English lyrics and which appear to be direct sources. Some of the lyrics from the Trinity manuscript are also edited in R. Davies, ed., *Medieval English Lyrics: A Critical Anthology* (London, 1963; repr. 1981).

5   In this macaronic poem, Latin verse-lines complete the sense of the English; where the Latin verse-line is comprised of only one word, the emphasis created is striking.

Þou bere Jhesu, hevene King,   *bore*
Gratia divina.   *Through divine grace*
Of alle þou berest þat pris,
15   Heie quen in Parais   *Paradise*
Electa,   *Chosen*
Moder milde ant maidan ec   *also*
Efecta.   *Proven*

In car ant consail þou art best   *sorrow*
20   *Felix fecundata*;   *Fortunate and fertile*
To alle weri þou art rest,   *the weary*
Mater honorata.   *Honoured mother*
Bihold tou him wid milde mod
Þat for us alle scedde is blod   *shed his*
25   *In cruce,*   *On the Cross*
Bidde we moten come to him   *Pray*
In luce.   *In the light*

Al þe world it wes furlorn   *completely lost*
Þoru *Eva peccatrice*   *Through Eve the sinner*
30   Toforn þat Jhesu was iborn   *Before*
Ex te genitrice;   *From you the mother*
Þorou *Ave* e wende awei   *Ave Maria it*
Þe þestri nist ant com þe dai   *dark*
Salutis.   *Of salvation*
35   Þe welle springet out of þe
Virtutis.   *Of virtue*

Wel þou wost he is þi sone   *know*
Ventre quem portasti;   *Whom you bore in your womb*
He nul nout werne þe þi bone   *He will not deny you your prayer*
40   *Parvum quem lactasti.*   *When you suckled him as a little one*
So god ant so mild e is,
He bringet us alle into is blis
Superni;   *Of heaven*
He havet idut þe foule put   *shut the foul pit*
45   *Inferni.*   *Of hell*

When I Think on Domesday

Wenne hi þenche on Domesdai, ful sore I me adrede;
Þer scal efter his werec huc mon fongon mede.   *receive; reward*
Hic habbe Criste agult wid þonc and wid dede,   *I; sinned; in thought*
Lovered Helende, Godis sone, what scal me to rede?   *do as remedy*

5   Þat fuir sal comen in þis world on one sonen-nist,   *fire; Saturday night*
Firbernen al þis middeherd so Crist hit wole disten,   *Burn; earth; command*
Boþen watir and þed-lond, þe flurs þat beit briste;   *land; flowers that are bright*
Hiheriet bo ure Loverd, muchel is his miththe.   *Praise be; might*

Foure engles in þe dairet blouit here bemen,   *dawn; will blow their trumpets*
10   Þenne comit Jhesus Crist his domes forto demen,   *judgements; judge*

Ne helpit hit noþinc þenne to wepen ne to remen,   *cry out*
To him þat lutel havet idon þat Criste was iqueme.   *pleasing to*

From þat Adam was iwrout þat comet Domesday,   *from the time; created; until*
Monie of þe riche men þat werden fou and gray,   *wore patterned and grey fur*
15   Riden uppe steden and uppe palefray;   *fine horses*
Ha sculen atte Dome singen weilaway.   *alas*

Ne sculen heo þer nout fisten wid sceldes ne wid sperre,   *fight; with shields*
Wid helme ne wid brunie ne wid none gerren;   *mail-coats; war-gear*
Ne sal no mon oþeir wid wise worde werren;   *attack*
20   Bote here almesdeden þat hore herinde sal beren.   *Only their alms; petitions; forward*

Ho sculen isen þene kyng þat al þe world wroutte,   *see; created*
And oppe þe suete rode wid stronge pine bocðthe;   *sweet Cross; pain; redeemed*
Adam and is ofspring, in helle he hem southe,   *sought*
To bidden þenne milse to late heo beoit biþoutthe.   *ask; mercy; too; had considered*

25   He sulen isen þat maiden þat Jhesus Crist inne kennede,   *bore*
Bituenen hire ermes sueteliche hine wende.   *embraced*
Þe wile þat we misten, to lutel we hire sende,   *were able; too little*
Þat makede þe worse, so woule he us ablende.   *devil; completely; blinded*

Þer sulen þe riswise ben on Godis rist honde,[6]   *righteous; right*
30   And þe sunfulle sulen ateliche stonden,   *sinful shall in fear stand*
Wid here sunnes iwriten, þat is muchel sconde;   *sins documented; shame*
Alle heo sullen hem isen þat liveden in londe.   *All; shall see; who lived*

To þe riswise he spekit wordes suiþe suete: *will speak; very gentle*
'Comit heir mine frents, yeure sunnes for te lete;   *come here; friends; abandon*
35   Hi mine fadeir huse hou is imakit sete,   *made an eternal dwelling*
Þerinne sculen engles sueteliche greten.'

To þe sunfule he spekit so ye mouin iheren: *as you might hear*
'Gooid, ye awariede, wid funden iwere,   *Depart; damned; devils as companions*
Into berninde fur; of blisse ye beoit scere   *burning; will be deprived*
40   Forþi þat ge oure sunnen ut of þis worild beren.'   *Because; carry*

Bidde we ure levedye, suetis alre þinge,   *sweetest of all things*
Þat heo beore ure herinde to þen hevene Kinge,   *carry our petition*
Þat for is holie nome, and for hire herendinge,   *his holy name; intercession*
Þat he ure soule into heoveneriche bringe.   *heavenly kingdom*

When the Turf is Thy Tower

Wen þe turuf is þi tuur,   *turf; tower*
And þi put is þi bour,   *grave; bedroom*
Þi wel and þi wite þrote,   *skin; white throat*
Ssulen wormes to note.   *be good for*
5   Wat helpit þe þenne
Al þe worilde wunne?   *world's joys*

6   Matthew 25.34–46.

A Saying of Saint Bernard

Of one stable was is halle,	*his*
Is kenestol on occe stalle	*throne; ox's*
Sente Marie is burnes alle.	*royal court*

I Sing of One That Is Matchless

Nu þis fules singet and maket hure blisse,	*birds sing*
And þat gres up þringet and leved þe ris;	*thrusts; leaves grow on branches*
Of on Ic wille singen þat is makeles,	*without comparison*
Þe King of halle kinges to moder he hire ches.	*all; as a mother; chose*

5 Heo his wituten sunne and wituten hore,	*without sin; defilement*
Icumen of kinges cunne of Gesses more;	*Descended; lineage; Jesse's*
Þe Loverd of monkinne of hire was yboren	*from her*
To bringen us hut of sunne, elles wue weren forlore.	*or else we would have been lost*

Gabriel hire grette and saide hire, 'Ave,	*Hail*
10 Marie, ful of grace, ure Loverd be uit þe,	*with*
Þe frut of þire wombe ibleset mot id be:	
Þu sal go wit chide, for sout Ic suget þe.'	*be with child; truth I say*

And þare gretinke þat angle havede ibrout,	*greeting*
He gon to biþenchen and meinde hire þout,	*She began to consider; it disturbed*
15 He saide to þen angle: 'Hu may tiden þis?	*How did this happen?*
Of monnes ymone nout Y nout, iuis.'	*company none; truly*

Mayden heo was uid childe and maiden her biforen,	*Virgin*
And maiden ar sothent hire chid was iboren;	*before and after*
Maiden and moder nas never non wimon boten he,	*no woman was ever but she*
20 Wel mitte he berigge of Goddes sune be.	*bearer*

Iblessed beo þat suete chid and þe moder ec,	
And þe suete broste þat hire sone sec;	*sucked*
Ihered ibe þe time þat such chid uas iboren,	*Praised be*
Þat lesed al of pine þat arre was forlore.	*released; pain; before; lost*

An Orison to Our Lady

On hire is al mi lif ylong	*desire*
Of vam Ic wille singen;	*whom*
And herien him þeramong,	*praise*
Þad gon us bote bringen	*That; remedy*
5 Of helle-pine þat is strong,	*From hell torment*
Ant brut us blisse þat is so long	*brought; eternal*
Al þurut hire childinke.	*labour*
We biddit hire in ure song,	*We pray*
He yef us god hendinke,	*She might give; ending*
10 Þau ve don wrong.	*Though we*

Al þis world hid sal agon	*it shall depart*
Wid serve and wid sore,	*sorrow; pain*

And al þis blisse Ic mot forgon,
Nofþingit me so sore.   *Does not seem*

15   Þis world nis bute ure fo,   *enemy*
Þarfor Ic wille henne gon   *from here*
And lernin Godis lore;   *teaching*
Þis worldis blis nis wurd a slo.   *is not worth; sloe-berry*
I bidde, God, þin hore,   *mercy*

20   Nu and hevermore.

To longe Ic abbe sot iben   *have foolish*
Ful sorre Y me adrede;   *fear*
Ylovid Ic abbe gomin and gle   *games and fun*
And hevir fayre wedin.   *always lovely clothes*

25   Al þad nis nout, ful wel Ic seo,
Þerfore we sulin ur sunnis flen   *we should flee from our sins*
And ure sothede.   *foolishness*
We biddit hire us to seo,
Þad con wissin and redin,   *guide and advise*

30   Þat is so fre.   *noble*

Heo is hele and lif ond licte   *She; health; light*
And helpit al moncunene;
Ho us havet ful vel idiit,   *governed*
Ho yaf us wele and winne.   *happiness and joy*

35   Þu brutis us day, and Eve nith,   *brought; night*
Heo brout wou, þu brout rid,   *woe; right*
Þu almesse, and heo sunne.   *alms; sin*
Þu do us merci, lavedi brit,   *lady*
Wene we sulin henne:

40   Ful wel þu mit.   *As; might*

Agult Ic have, waylaway,   *Sinned; alas*
Sunful Ic am a wreche,
Þu do me merci, lavedi brit,
Ar det me henne wecche.   *Before death fetches me from here*

45   Yif me þi love, Ic am redi,   *Give*
Let me live and amendi,   *make amends*
Þad fendes me ne letten.   *fiends; prevent*
Of mine sunnin Ic am sori,
Of my lif Ic ne recche,   *care*

50   Lavedi, merci.

The South English Legendary

The *Life of Saint Wulfstan* and *The Invention of the Cross* are two of the texts in the cycle of saints' lives and sermons included in the extensive collection *The South English Legendary*.[1] This legendary contains as a whole some ninety verse texts that could have been read out to celebrate any saint's day or feast day, and which are generally organized chronologically according to the date of the feast day. The hagiographic and homiletic collection survives in twenty-five complete manuscripts, nineteen fragments and, in selected forms, eighteen other manuscripts. Among the earlier complete manuscripts are London, British Library, Harley 2277, dated to *c*.1300; Cambridge, Corpus Christi College 145, dated to *c*.1310–20, and written, possibly, in Worcester; and Oxford, Bodleian Library, Ashmole 43, dated from between 1300 and 1330. The transmission of this text in all its variant forms is highly complicated, and as yet, there are many unanswered questions about the work: its authorship, the texts' relationships, and the localization of the manuscripts.[2] In its origins, *The South English Legendary* may date to the end of the thirteenth century, and it was copied throughout the fourteenth and fifteenth centuries in the south and Midlands areas of England, reflecting the importance of the cult of the saints in this period and region.

Major influences on the compilation of *The South English Legendary* may have been liturgical texts providing the service of worship for a particular saint's feast day. In addition, Latin legendaries such as that by Jacobus de Voragine (compiler of the thirteenth-century *Legenda Aurea*) might also have provided the impetus for a vernacular collection. From texts such as these, the compiler of *The South English Legendary* in its earliest form may have derived some of the saints' lives that were common to much of the Catholic church at this time; for example, the *Lives* of the evangelists, the early martyred saints, and the late classical confessors. There are also, though, in many manuscripts of *The South English Legendary*, English saints whose *Lives* are not recorded in the universal Latin collections and which may point to the geographical origins of individual manuscripts in which these *Lives* occur. Certain religious institutions, for example, often had an especial veneration for patron saints; a saint whose relics were held there; and also for saints who were directly connected to those institutions by having been a founder or having served there. Worship of the saint on the appropriate day was of central importance to the church throughout the medieval period, and *The South English Legendary* is one of the key witnesses to this religious phenomenon.

THE LIFE OF SAINT WULFSTAN

About twenty Middle English copies of the *Life of Saint Wulfstan* survive in the various manuscripts of *The South English Legendary*. In Cambridge, Corpus Christi College 145, the *Life* is the fifth item, occurring at folios 3 verso to 6 recto. His feast day of 19 January dictates this early positioning. The text describes the life of the last of the Anglo-Saxon bishops, Wulfstan of Worcester, who lived from 1008 to 1095. He was appointed to Worcester where he was a monk in 1062, and became the longest-surviving Anglo-Saxon bishop after the Norman Conquest in 1066. He was canonized in 1203, and was the patron saint of King John, who asked to be buried at Worcester next to Wulfstan.

The verse *Life* is written in long alliterative lines, a form common to many texts from the west and north Midlands in this period. The source of the *Life* may have been the Latin liturgy used for the feast day of Saint Wulfstan found in London, British Library, Cotton

Vespasian E. ix,[3] which itself may have been derived from legends circulating about Saint Wulfstan. Wulfstan's life is well documented, and the first hagiographic text was Coleman's *Life*, written at the end of the eleventh century in English by a monk at Worcester. Although this text is now non-extant, William of Malmesbury translated it into the Latin *Vita Wulfstani* at the request of Worcester monks in the twelfth century. Other Latin *Lives* followed as the cult of Saint Wulfstan grew, but none is identical to the English *Life* in *The South English Legendary*. Certain legends are easily attributed, such as the legend of the staff that Wulfstan thrusts into the stone of King Edward's tomb in defiance of William the Conqueror (lines 115–35). Osbert of Clare's twelfth-century *Life of King Edward* first relates this story as an imaginary adaptation of the historical dispute between Wulfstan and William the Conqueror about lands belonging to the see of Worcester.[4] Likewise, the legend of

1 See C. D'Evelyn and A. Mill, eds, *The South English Legendary*, EETS o.s. 235, 246 (London, 1956).
2 See M. Görlach, *The Textual Tradition of the South English Legendary*, Leeds Texts and Monographs 6 (Leeds, 1974), pp. viii–ix.
3 Görlach, *The Textual Tradition of the South English Legendary*, p. 34.

4 See E. Mason, *St Wulfstan of Worcester, c.1008–1095* (Oxford, 1990), for Wulfstan's life and for the subsequent *Lives* written about him.

Wulfstan waking up the monks who had fallen asleep while performing prayers over his coffin is related in the *Vita Wulfstani* of William of Malmesbury.[5]

The English *Life* draws, then, on well-attested legends of its hero saint, and creates a cogent account of the bishop: his early piety as a child, his dedication to his role as monk and bishop, his miraculous abilities, his defiance of King William and Archbishop Lanfranc, his healing powers, and his longevity. In this legend, Wulfstan's ascetic lifestyle and devotion to God in word, thought and deed are vividly related. His simplicity, a characteristic of earlier accounts of his life, is transformed here into a depiction of a saint who, while not very learned, is nevertheless the holiest of men,[6] and thus an example of how to live a pious Christian life. Perhaps most interesting in this English account is the obvious anti-Norman bias of the writer. Other manuscript versions, such as Oxford, Bodleian Library, Laud Misc. 108, expand this aspect of the text, and it is possible that in the edited account below, taken from Corpus 145, the poet has excised some of the more explicit criticisms of the conquerors. The Englishness of the text remains, though, and may reflect its origins in the Worcester area, where a sense of being English characterized this region throughout the post-Conquest period. The *Life* becomes, in a way, similar to the later poem *Athelston*, as much a political and historical statement as a text venerating an ideal Christian.

De Sancto Wolstano {Of Saint Wulfstan}

	Sein Wolston bissop of Wircetre	was her in Engelonde	*Worcester*
	Swuþe holyman al is lif he was,	as Ich understonde,	*Great; his*
	Þe wile he was a ȝong child,	god lif he ladde inou;	
	Wanne oþere children eode pleie,	toward chirche he drou.	*drew*
5	Seint Edward[7] was þo owre king	þat nouþe in hevene is;	*then; now*
	And þe bissop of Wircestre,	Briȝteiȝe het ywis.[8]	
	Of þis bissop Briȝteiȝe,	Sein Wolston is ordre nom	*took*
	Ech after oþer as it bivel,	so þat he preost bicom.	
	Þis bissop underveng hym suþþe,	and monk him made iwis,	*received; honourably*
10	In þe priorie of Wircetre,	þat gret hous and hei is,	*esteemed*
	Swuþe wel is ordre he held	in þe priorie,	*his*
	And al is wille was to paie	God and Seinte Marie.	
	In none bed he nolde come	ac wanne oþer ȝeode þerto,	*when others went*
	Tovore an auter he wolde go	his orisons to do;	*altar; prayers*
15	Wanne þe dede slep hym overcom,	þat he ne miȝt fer gon,	
	His heved he wolde legge adoun	upe a hard ston	
	On a degre byvore þe auter,	oþer is bok þerunder do,	*step; put*
	And ligge a stonde in dwellinge;	al is slep was so.	
	He nolde þre dawes in þe wike	noþing ete wiþalle,[9]	
20	Ne noþing speke bote is beden,	for noȝt þat miȝte bivalle;	*prayers; happen*
	Þe oþer dawes wel lite he spak,	and wel lite et also,	*little; eat*
	Bote a lite gruwel oþer porreie,	holde he wolde þerto.	*gruel; porridge*
	So longe he was at Wircetre	in holy lyf þus stille,	
	Þat me made hym prior of þe hous,	muche aȝen is wille.	*he was made*
25	Is covent he weste wel,	and to alle godnesse ham drou	*oath*
	Of God and al gode men,	love he hadde inou.	
	Þe priorie of Wircetre	Sein Oswold[10] bygan er —	*previously*
	Þat was bivore sein Wolston	aboute an hondred ȝer —	
	And þat Seint Oswold bigan er	Sein Wolston vulde iwis,	
30	So þat þoru hore beire werk	strang and hei it is.	
	As þis holyman Sein Wolston	a time let arere	*ordered to be built*

5   Mason, *St Wulfstan*, p. 258.

6   Saint Wulfstan was, in fact, quite well educated.

7   Edward the Confessor, king of England, who died in 1066.

8   Bishop Brihtheah of Worcester, who died in 1038.

9   For three days in the week he would eat nothing at all.

10   Saint Oswald, bishop of Worcester (961–92), was one of the main church leaders in the tenth-century Benedictine Reform. He did not found Worcester, but he did re-establish it as a cathedral monastery.

An hey belhous of strang werk   þe bellen to honge þere;[11]
And masons above and byneþe   þeraboute were,
And bi laddren clomme up and doun   and stones up bere;
35 A man clam upward bi a laddre,   and þo he was up an hey   *when; high*
Fram eorþe mo þan fourti vet,   as al þat folk ysey,   *more than forty feet*
Dounward he vel as he misstep   (men were sore agaste).   *fell*
Sein Wolston stod and byheld   hou he com dounward vaste,   *fast*
He made him þe signe of þe crois   as he vel to gronde:
40 Harmles he vel and hol inou,   his lymes hol and sonde,   *whole; limbs*
And aros up and dude is werk   as hym noþing nere.   *as if nothing had happened*
Loverd, muche is þi miȝte,   as þou kuddest þere,   *great; revealed*
Þat he so harde fram heie vel,   and of eche harm was sker: *escaped*
Þou ert God þat wonder dest –   as seiþ þe sauter.   *miracles performs; Psalter*
45   So þat Briȝteiȝe, þe bissop   of Wircetre, was ded,
A clerk was bissop after hym,   þat me clupede Aldred,[12]
Þat Seint Wolston lovede wel,   and he hym also:
For ech god man wol lovie oþer,   it were elles misdo.
Suþþe hit bicom þat þe erchebissop   of Everwik was ded,   *After; occurred; York*
50 Erchebissop hy made þer   þis bissop Aldred;
And þe bissopriche of Wircestre   vacant was and lere   *empty*
Sein Wolston was sone ichose,   and bissop imad þere.   *chosen*
   Bissop him made þe holyman   Seint Edward oure kyng,
And aveng him in is dignete,   and tok him crois and ryng;   *received*
55 His bissopriche he weste wel   and ek is priorie,   *knew*
And aforcede him to servi wel   God and Seinte Marie.
Four ȝer he hadde bissop ibe,   and noȝt follich fyve,   *fully*
To seint Edward þe holy king   wende out of þis live,   *departed*
To gret ruþe to al Engelonde,   so weilawei þe stonde,   *pity; alas the times*
60 For strange men þer come suþþe   and broȝte Engelond to gronde.   *foreign*
   Vor Harald was suþþe kyng,   wiþ traison, alas,   *treachery*
Þe croune he bar of Engelond,   wuch wile so it was;
Ac Willam Bastard, þat was þo   duk of Normandie,
Þoȝte to wynne Engelond   þoru strengþe and felonye.   *Intended*
65 He let him greiþe folk inou   and gret poer wiþ hym nom,   *prepare; brought*
Wiþ gret strengþe in þe se hym dude,   and to Engelond com;   *put out to sea*
He let ordeiny is feorde wel,   and is baner up arere,   *army; raised up*
And let destruye al þat he vond,   and þat lond sore aferde.   *people were sorely afraid*
   Harald hurde herof telle,   þe kyng of Engelonde,
70 He let ȝarke vaste is ost   aȝen him forto stonde;   *prepared quickly; army*
Þe baronie of Engelonde   iredy was wel sone
Þe kyng to helpe and eke amsulve,   as wone was to done.   *themselves; accustomed*
Þe worre was þo in Engelonde   deolvol and strang inou,   *miserable*
And hore eiþer of oþeres men   al to gronde slou.   *each of the others'; killed*
75   No strengþe nadde þe stronge men   þat icome were so niwe
Aȝen þe baronie of Engelond,   þe wile hi wolde be triwe;
Ac alas þe tricherie   þat þo was and ȝute is   *yet*
Þat broȝte þo Engelonde   al to grounde ywis: *then; certainly*
Vor Englisse barons bycome somme   untriwe and fals also,
80 To bitraie homsulf and hore kyng   þat so muche triste ham to.   *trust*

---

11   Wulfstan actually had the entire cathedral rebuilt between 1084
and 1089.
12   Ealdred was bishop of Worcester from 1046 to 1062. The hagi-
ographer has omitted Bishop Lyfing, who was appointed to the see
after Brihtheah in 1038 only to be deprived of it in 1040–1. Elfric,
archbishop of York, held Worcester during 1040–1.

Þe Normans and þe Englisse men   day of bataille nome,
Þare as is þe Abbei of Bataille,   a day togadere ycome;
To gronde hy smite and slouwe also,   as God ȝaf þat cas,
Willam Bastard was above,   Harald byneþe was;
85   For hy þat Harald triste to,   faillede him wel vaste,
So þat he was byneþe ibroȝt,   and overcome attelaste.
Þis Willam Bastard þat was kyng,   suþþe hym understod,
Þat he mid unriȝt hadde yssad   so many mannes blod,   *spilled*
And þere as þe bataille was   an abbey he let rere,   *erected*
90   Þat me clupeþ Abbey of þe Bataille,   þat noble stont ȝut þere.   *call; stands*
     As sone so he was king ymad,   and al Engelond bysette   *subdued*
As he wolde mid strange men,   ac no man ne miȝte hym lette,   *allow*
Þis holy Sein Wolston   wel ofte him wiþsede,   *spoke against*
Þat he wiþ unriȝt hadde ido   a such uvel dede;   *wrong*
95   And spak aȝen hym baldeliche,   and ne sparede for no drede,   *boldly*
For he was þe kundeste Englisseman   þat was of eny manhede,   *best kind; man*
(For alle oþer were deserited ney)[13]   þe kyng was wiþ him wroþ   *angry*
Þat he dradde so lite of hym,   he swor anon is oþ   *feared; oath*
To pulte him of is bissopriche;   he let him somni also   *deprive; summoned*
100   To Westmistre to answerie hym   of þat he hadde misdo.   *done wrong*
Nou nas noȝt Sein Wolston   wel gret clerk in lore,   *learning*
For wan he scholde to scole go   at churche he was more.
To Westmestre he com to is daie,   as he was isomned er,
Þis king was in grete wraþþe   wel prest aȝen hym þer,   *ill-disposed*
105   And þe erchebissop of Kanterburi,   Lanfranc[14] was is name,
And þe bissop Gondolf of Roucetre,[15]   alle to don hym ssame.
     Sein Wolston tovore hom com,   þat aȝen him were so stronge,   *before them*
As a þeof tovore a justice   his dom for to avonge.[16]
Þe king and þe erchebissop ek   speke wordes grete
110   Þat he ssolde as he worþe was   his bissopriche forlete;[17]
For to holde such dignete   to lite he couþe of lore,   *too little he knew*
And hy hym hadde to lange iþoled,   and þo nolde hi namore;   *endured*
And foles hy were þat such fol   vurst broȝte in such miȝte,   *foolish; fool; first*
And if he was follich undervonge,   adoun he ssolde wiþ riȝte.   *admitted; step down*
115   Sein Wolston stod wel mildeliche,   and hurde al þat hy sede,   *peaceably; heard*
Nadde he no man bote God   to answerie ne to rede: *except; think about*
'Sires', he sede, 'riȝt it is   þat Ich ȝoure heste do,   *command*
For, sire king, þou ert mi soverein,   and þou erchebissop also.
Þe crois Ich habbe ȝare ybore   þat ȝe seoþ her, lo,   *readily carried*
120   I knowe Ich am and wel Ichot   þat Ynam noȝt worþe þerto.   *I believe; I am not*
Wanne ȝe wolleþ þat Ich me bileve   as man þat unworþe is,   *I believe myself to be*
Wel vawe Ichelle ȝoure heste do,   as mine sovereins iwis.   *vow; indeed*
In obedient to Holy Churche   iwis Ich nel be noȝt,
To ȝulde up as ȝe me hoteþ   Ich me habbe here ibroȝt;   *yield; order; been brought*
125   Ac for ȝe ne toke hyne me noȝt,   I nelle ȝou take non   *because; chose; choose*
Ac him þat hine me bitok;   byvore ȝou everichon   *entrusted it*
Þe godeman[18] þat hit me bitok   ȝend he liþ wel stille,   *lies*
Ichelle him take up aȝen   þanne do Ich ȝoure wille.'

13   For all other English men were nearly destroyed.
14   Lanfranc became archbishop of Canterbury from 1070, and was, in fact, not only Wulfstan's superior, but also his ally.
15   Gundulf was bishop of Rochester 1077–1108.

16   And as a thief in front of a judge to receive his judgement.
17   That he should, if he were honourable, resign from his bishopric.
18   The 'good man' Edward the Confessor, who appointed Wulfstan.

To Seinte Edwardes tombe he wende, þat was in marbelston,
130 And nom is crois wel mildeliche, and smot þe point þeron; *took; struck*
Þe staf smot in þe marbelston as it were in nesse sonde *soft sand*
And he was inne deop inou, þe godeman let hym stonde.
'Nou', he sede, 'Ich him habbe bitake þat bitok it me, *entrusted it to him*
And tovore ȝou here I ȝoulde up al þulke dignete. *all that status*
135 Takeþ nou wam þat ȝe wolleþ, somme þat be bet in lore, *is better educated*
And habbeþ goday everichon: ȝe ne mowe me esse namore.'
Þis holyman hym wende vorþ amang ham alle wel softe,
Þe volk stod as hy were inome and biheld þe crois wel ofte: *stunned*
Hou he stod in þe marbelston so deope and so vaste;
140 Of þe miracle hom wondred alle and were somdel agaste. *somewhat afraid*
Somme of hom wende þerto sone þe crois up to drawe,
Ac þer nas non so strang of ham þat miȝte hure enes wawe. *move*
Hy porveide þer Sire Gondolf, bissop of Roucetre, *procured*
Þat he were after Sein Wolston byssop of Wircetre.[19]
145 Þe erchebissop him het arise and nyme þe crois anon, *to get up and take*
Þe bissop aros wel baldeliche and þuderward gan gon.
Þe crois he nom and faste drou uppon þe marbelston – *quickly*
He ne miȝte hure wawe noȝt – þat folk wondrede echon. *each one*
And þareaboute wel þicke drou þat wonder for to se; *drew round; miracle*
150 Þe king and þe erchebissop iseye þat it ne miȝte oþer be. *could not be otherwise*
Hy repentede of hore dede, and after Sein Wolston sende, *their*
In vaire manere þat hy wolde hore trespas amende.
Þe messagers iredi were, after hym sone wende;
Ȝute þis holyman for al ȝare gult is herte to ham bende, *guilt*
155 And sede: 'Ich mot nede do mine sovereines wille.'
To court he wende aȝen mid hom wel mildeliche and stille. *quiet*
Þo he was to court icome hy arise aȝen him anon, *When; they got up*
Þe kyng and þe erchebissop ek, and oþere þat were is fon, *enemies*
In grete noblesse hy clupede him vorþ, and forȝifnesse hym bede, *called*
160 And bede to amendy aȝen him al hore misdede; *asked; redress*
And bede him nyme aȝe þe crois, and do by hore rede,
For he was best worþe þerto þanne eni oþer hy sede. *said*
'Nay certes, sire', quaþ Sein Wolston, 'þat nere noȝt to do,
For Ich wot ȝe sede soþ, Inam noȝt worþe þerto; *the truth; I am not*
165 Ac nymeþ wan ȝoure wille be, anoþer þat conne more.' *appoint; knows*
Þe king and þe erchebissop ek cride him milce and ore, *mercy and pity*
And sede þer nas non oþer þat so worþe were þerto.
Longe it was ar þis holiman hore wille wolde do; *before; their will*
Ac for to obeie is sovereins, he wende vorþ attelaste,
170 And nom þis crois wel mildeliche þat stikede er so faste. *stuck before*
As liȝtliche as he wolde hymsulf þe crois he gan up drawe,
Þat so mani men vondede er and ne miȝte noȝt enes wawe, *had tried; move*
Þicke orn þat folk aboute hym – and no wonder hit nas – *In a crowd ran*
Þe miracle was sone ikud þat so apert was. *revealed; clear*
175 Me honurede þis holyman as muche as me miȝte: *men could*
His poer þat him was bynome, he tok aȝen wiþ riȝte; *power; taken from*
And aȝen to is bissopriche wiþ gret honour drou,
Is covent underveng hym faire, and honurede him inou. *monastery; very well*
Þis holyman ladde al is lyf in god lyf and clene.

---

19 Gundulf was never bishop of Worcester.

180	In syknesse wel vewe þer were þat man wolde ofmene	*few; complain to*
	Þat he ne broȝte to hele anon, þoru oure Loverdes grace;	*did not make whole*
	Sike men wel þicke come to him in eche place,	
	Deve and dombe and eke blinde, and ech maner sike also,	*deaf; all sorts of*
	He helde þoru oure Loverdes grace wanne bicome hym to.	*healed; came*
185	So longe he livede an eorþe her þat a was of gret elde,	*he; age*
	His body bygan to hevegy al, gret feblesse he velde.	*grow heavy; felt*
	A slou fevere him com on, þat nom hym noȝt to stronge,	*made*
	Þat made is body multe awey, þat laste swuþe long.	*fail away; very*
	Seveniȝt byvore þat he deide, his breþeren let vecche alle,	*died; he let be fetched*
190	And let him al his riȝtes do,²⁰ and sede wat ssolde bivalle.	
	Out of þis lyf to hevene he wende, as he ssel byleve,	
	In the monþe of Geniver, a Sein Fabianes eve;	*19 January; on*
	A þousond ȝer and nyenty and five þer byvore	
	It was þat oure swete Loverd an eorþe was ibore;	
195	In þe teþe ȝer it was also of þe kyngdom	*tenth*
	Of Willam þe rede kyng, þat after Willam Bastard com.	*William Rufus*
	He hadde ar he hanne wende voure and þritti ȝer	
	And four monþes and four dawes bissop ibeo her.	
	Vour score ȝer he was old and sevene also ney,	*almost eighty-seven*
200	Ar he wende out of þis lyf to þe joie of hevene an hey.	*Before*
	Þo þis holyman was ded, þis monekes come sone	*When; soon*
	In þe priorie of Wircetre and dude wat was to done:	
	Wesse þat body as it was riȝt and to churche it bere.	*Washed*
	Þe monkes alle wiþ gret honur, þat is breþeren were,	
205	Þe servise þer aboute dede, as it was wel riȝt,	
	And to segge hore sauter ek, þeraboute hy woke al niȝt.	*Psalter; also*
	Þo hit was wel wiþinne niȝt, as hy sede in hore boke,	*spoke from*
	Hom luste slepe swuþe wel, unneþe hi miȝte loke,	*greatly desired; hardly*
	And somme ne miȝte noȝt forbere, ac leiȝe and slepe vaste,	*lay; slept fast*
210	Somme as it were in dwellinge, hore eiȝne togadere caste.	*shut their eyes*
	Þis holy body þat lay þer ded bytwene hom in þe bere,	*coffin*
	Aros him up wel mildeliche as it alyve were;	*as if he were alive*
	And aweiȝte hom everichon, and bigan atte on ende,	*woke them up; one*
	And bygan al along þe rewe þoruout þe quer wende.	*row; through; quire*
215	And evere as he aweiȝte hom, he gan hom somdel chide,	*somewhat*
	Þat hy nolde wiþ hore slep hore riȝte time abide.	*their proper time await*
	So muche was is holy herte þe ordre for to wite,	*the monastic order; protect*
	Þat he nolde noȝt, þei he were ded, is breþeren forȝute.	*forget*
	Þis miracle was wide ikud, as riȝt was þat he were,	*widely known*
220	At Wircestre he was ibured, and issrined is nou þere.	*enshrined*
	For him me may þer al day many fair miracle ise;	*witness*
	Nou God leove þat we mote wiþ hym in þe joie of hevene be!	

---

20   He had all his last rites performed.

THE HISTORY AND INVENTION OF THE TRUE CROSS AND THE LIFE OF SAINT QUIRIAC

Virtually all of the major surviving manuscripts of *The South English Legendary* contain *The History and Invention of the True Cross*, with its subsequent brief martyrdom of Saint Quiriac. In Cambridge, Corpus Christi College 145, these texts are the thirty-eighth and thirty-ninth items, occurring at folios 63 recto to 67 verso. The feast day of The Invention of the Cross is 3 May, and that of Quiriac is 4 May. The whole text is divided into three related parts. The first part is the early history of the Cross, describing its origin from three seeds of an apple from the Tree of Knowledge in the Garden of Eden, to its use as the instrument of Christ's death. The second part details the Invention, or finding, of the Cross by Helena, mother of the Emperor Constantine in the first quarter of the fourth century. The final part is the short Passion of Quiriac, the Jew who discovered the place of the Cross, and who subsequently converted to Christianity, becoming bishop of Jerusalem.

The legend of the Cross, and the various accretions to it, was a popular religious story in the medieval period,[21] emphasizing the miracles associated with God and the Cross on which he suffered; and reinforcing the image of the Cross as the symbol of humankind's salvation. The finding of the Cross meant that pieces of it were among the most treasured relics in this period: numerous religious institutions claimed to have a fragment of the true Cross that pilgrims would visit, bringing with them increased revenues for that particular church. The popularity of the Cross, and legends associated with it, can also be evidenced by the extant literature. From the Anglo-Saxon period, for example, there are two anonymous Old English prose versions of *The Invention of the Cross*; and more famously, perhaps, the Old English poem, *Elene*, which relates the story of Constantine's mother and her discovery of the Cross and nails. Ælfric, too, in his second series of *Catholic Homilies*, composed a short account of the event; and in *The Dream of the Rood*, the Cross itself explains how it was found.

The texts concerning the history of the Cross and the subsequent Passion of Quiriac edited below are written in the same long, alliterative, rhyming couplet lines as the *Life of Saint Wulfstan* and the other pieces in *The South English Legendary*. The action is rapid, and the accounts of both the Cross's history and the death of the saint are lively and dramatic. The source for the first part, the early history of the Cross, is, in its origin, an eleventh-century Latin legend.[22] *The Invention of the Cross* is ultimately derived from the *Acta Quiriaci*, the Acts of Saint Quiriac,[23] but the version edited here may also have been influenced by the Sarum liturgy used for the feast day celebrating the finding of the Cross. Saint Quiriac's martyrdom, as found appended to this text, is derived from a version similar to that in the thirteenth-century *Legenda Aurea*, the extensive collection of Latin legends attributed to Jacobus de Voragine.

The History and Invention of the True Cross

De sancto ligno

Þe holy rode, þe swete tre,	riȝt is to habbe in munde,	*mind*
Þat haþ fram strange deþ ibroȝt	to lyve al mankunde:	*strong*
Þoru þulke tre we were forlore,	and ferst ibroȝt to gronde,	*lost*
And þoru tre suþþe to lyve ibroȝt,	yherd be þulke stonde;	*praised; time*
5 Al it com of one more	þat us to deþe broȝte	*tree*
And þat us broȝte to lyve aȝen	þoru Jesus þat us boȝte.	*redeemed*
Of þe appel tre þat oure vader	þe luþer appel of nom,	*evil; took*
In þe manere þat Ich wol nou telle,	þe swete rode com.	*Cross*
Þo Adam oure verste vader	þe sunne hadde ydo,[24]	*sin; committed*
10 Idrive was out of Parais,	and Eve is wif also.	*Driven; his*
After milce ȝeorne he cride,	þei it to late were,	*mercy; earnestly*
And biheste hadde of oure Loverd,	þo me drof him out þere.	*promise*
Þat wanne þe time were volveold,	oure Loverd him wolde biþenche,	*fulfilled; consider*
And mid oile of milce smurie him,	and is sunne quenche;	*anoint; his*
15 Gret hope hadde he to þis biheste	Adam evere mo,	

21   See for example, the texts in R. Morris, ed., *Legends of the Holy Rood: Symbols of the Passion and Cross-Poems*, EETS o.s. 46 (London, 1881; repr. 1969).
22   Görlach, *The Textual Tradition of the South English Legendary*, pp. 164–6.
23   Printed in translation by D. G. Calder and M. J. B. Allen, *Sources and Analogues of Old English Poetry* (Cambridge, 1976), pp. 59–69.
24   The following lines relate Genesis 3–4.

In þe valeie of Ebron   he livede in teone and wo.[25]
                Tweie sones he hadde suþþe,   Caim and Abel,   *after*
Þe on slou þe oþer for envie,   as 3e witeþ wel;   *killed; know*
Þo Caim hadde is broþer aslawe,   iflemd he was þervore.   *When; exiled*
20   Þo Adam isei þat he hadde   boþe is sones forlore,   *saw; lost*
He wep and made deol inou: 'Loverd', he sede, 'þin ore: *lamentation; pity*
Ney womman Ich habbe to muche ibe,   Inel come hure nei more.   *I shan't; her; near*
Þre harmes Ich habbe þoru hure iheved: misulf ferst forlore,   *suffered; myself*
And nou my sones boþe alas,   and of al womman is more.'[26]
25   Nolde þo Adam come nei is wif   to hondred 3er and more,   *Would not*
For wo þat he hadde for hure,   and evere he livede in sore.   *sorrow*
Suþþe he hadde toknyng of oure Loverd   þat he ssolde to is wif wende,   *sign; turn*
Ne derste he no3t be þer a3en,   an sone he hadde attenende;   *son; in the end*
Suþþe he het is name nemne,   and suþþe he hadde mo.   *Seth he called him*
30   Al is lif þe sely man   livede in teone and wo.   *wretched*
Þo he was of vif hondred 3er   and to and þritti old,[27]   *five; year; thirty*
Þe strengþe him failede of is lymes,   is bodi bicom al cold.   *limbs*
He ne mi3te no3t swinke aboute þe eorþe,   þe weodes up to drawe,   *work; weeds*
Of is lif he was anuyd,   he wilnede be of dawe.   *weary; to be dead*
35   He sat and carede of is lyf;   he clupede is sone Seþ,   *worried; called*
Sone he sede: 'Icham weri ylived,   Ich wilny muche mi deþ.   *wish*
Þo Ich was idrive of Parays,   oure Loverd byhet me þere,   *promised*
To smure me wiþ þe oil of milce,   wanne it tyme were.   *anoint; mercy*
So lange Ich habbe abide þerafter   þat I ne may libbe namore,   *waited*
40   To Parais þou most þerafter go,   and bidde him milce and ore.   *pray; pity*
Þe angel þou sselt þare finde   þat drof me out atte 3ete,   *shall; the gate*
Sey Ich abide þulke biheste,   me þincþ it comþ wel late,   *await; promise*
And þat elde me haþ overcome: þat I ne may no3t libbe longe,   *old age; live*
Bidde him þat Ich deie mote,   and þe oil of milce avonge.'   *might; receive*
45   'I ne can nanne wei', quaþ þis sone,   'Þuderward Ich wene.'   *know; think*
'Leve sone', quaþ Adam,   'þe wei is wel ysene: *Beloved*
Wanne þou comst to þe ende of þis valeie,   a grene wey þou sselt wende,   *shall proceed*
Þat ri3t evene estward geþ   to Parais last þe on ende.   *directly*
Þerbi wende þi moder and Ich,   þo Ich Parais forlet;   *lost*
50   Everich stude þat we on stepte,   forbarnde under oure vet.   *place; burned*
Ne mi3te þer nevere eft gras on growe,   and al þe oþer wei is grene,   *again*
For þe voule sunne þat we dude   oure stappes beoþ evere sene;   *foul sin; steps*
Þerby wiþoute defaute   to Parais evene gon.'   *directly*
Seþ nom is fader blessinge,   and wende him forþ anon.   *took*
55   Þe stappes he vond forwelwed,   as is fader him sede;   *found withered*
Þo he to þe 3ete com,   he ne derste go ner for drede.   *dared; near*
An angel com to þe 3ate,   and esste wat he so3te,   *asked*
He sede þat to him an erande   fram is fader he bro3te: *message*
Þat he was old and weri ilyved,   and þat him longede sore
60   After þe swete oil of milce,   for he ne mi3te libbe namore.
        '3e', quaþ þe angel, 'is he so?   He ne ssel þerof no3t doute: *fear*
Put in þi heved atte 3ate,   and stond þisulf wiþoute.'   *head; yourself*
He putte in is heved as he bad,   and bihuld al aboute,   *asked; looked*
So murie ne þo3te him nevere in stude,   þei he stode himsulf wiþoute.   *joyful; place*
65   So gret delit he hadde and joie   of þe foules murie song,   *birds'*

---

25   In the valley of Hebron he lived in grief and woe.
26   Adam attributes all his miseries to the actions of Eve.

27   Other accounts give the age of Adam as nine hundred and thirty-two years.

Of þe swote mede also   and of þe floures þer among,   *meadow*
Of ech maner frut þat he sey   þat smulde al so swote,   *smelled*
Þat of eche maner uvel as him þo3te   a man mi3te habbe þerof bote.   *evil; remedy*
Him þo3te 3if he moste þere   biholde in eny stonde,   *at any time*
70 Everemo he mi3te in joie be,   his limes hol and sonde.   *whole*
Amidde þe place þat was so fair   he sei a vair welle,   *fair*
Of wan al þe wateres comþ an eorþe   (as þe boc[28] us deþ telle);   *from which*
Over þe welle þer stod a tre   wiþ bowes brode and lere,   *empty*
Ac it ne bar noþer lef ne rinde,   as it forolded were;   *bark; decayed*
75 An addre it hadde biclupt aboute,   al naked wiþoute skynne,   *adder; entwined*
Þat was þe tre and þe addre   þat made Adam ferst do sunne.   *caused; first*
    Efsone he biheld in atte 3ete   þat tre him þo3te he sey,   *As soon as; saw*
Fair ileved and ywoxe   up to hevene an hey;   *growing; high*
A 3ong child he sey upe þe tre   in smale cloþes iwonde;   *wrapped*
80 Þe more of þe tre him þo3te tilde   þoruout helle gronde;   *root; reached*
His broþer soule Abel ek,   him þo3te in helle he sey;   *brother's soul*
Þe angel him drof þo fram þe 3et   þat he nas namore þer ney: *gate; near*
    'Þe child', he sede, 'þat þou iseie   anouwarde þe tre,   *upward in*
Godes sone it was þat wol an eorþe   for þi vader sunne be,   *father's sin*
85 And þe oil of milce wiþ him bringe,   wanne þe time in eld is,   *ages*
And smurie þerwiþ and bringe of pine   þi vader and alle his.'   *torment*
Þe angel wende to þulke tre,   an appel þerof he nom,   *the same*
And tok Seþ þerof þre curnels   þo he to him com,   *seeds*
And bad him þulke curnels legge   under is faderes tonge,   *lay*
90 And burie him wanne he were ded   and loke wat þerof spronge.   *bury; grew*
    Seth wende a3en as he com   for þe wey was wel isene,   *returned*
For þe stappes were al forbarnd,   and þe oþer wey grene.
Þo he was hom a3en icome   is fader he vond ded;   *found*
Þe curnels he dude under is tonge,   as þe angel hadde ised,
95 And suþþe he burede him as ri3t was,   in þe valeie of Ebron,   *buried; properly*
And ofswonk is mete,   he nuste no betere ywon.   *worked for; food*
    Wiþinne an vewe 3er þerafter   þis curnels gonne to springe,   *few years*
Þre faire 3eorden þere woxe of,   vaire þoru alle þinge;   *staffs*
Þo hy were ywoxe to þe lengþe   of an elne, Ich wene,   *ell; I guess*
100 In þulke stat hy stode longe,   and everemore grene.   *position*
Forte Moyses þe prophete   aboute 3eode in þe londe: *Until; went*
To lede þat fok of Israel   and he þe 3erden sei stonde.   *staffs; standing*
'Lo her!' he sede, 'Gret toknynge   of þe Holy Trinite,   *symbol*
Fader and Sone and Holy Gost   of þis 3eorden þre.'
105   Op he is nom wiþ gret honur,   and in a vair cloþ is wonde,   *Up; covered*
A swote smul þer com out of   þat smulde into al þe londe;   *smell*
To confermy þe bet is lawe,   he bar hom vorþ in is hond,   *confirm; better*
Ech sik man þat þerto hopede   his hele anon he vond.   *sick; healing*
To teche þe volk þe ri3te lawe   þe 3erden aboute he ber,   *staffs; carried*
110 And eke to hele sike men,   to and fourti 3er.
Suþþe þo he deie ssolde   þe 3erden he sette er   *earlier*
Under þe hul of Tabour,[29]   and deide himsulf þer.   *hill; died*
    Þere stode þis 3eorden grene   mo þanne a þousond 3er,
For Sein Davit þe kyng   þat was of so gret poer,   *Until; power*
115 So þat he was, þoru þe Holy Gost,   yhote forto hie   *told; hasten*
To þe hul of Tabor,   in þe lond of Arabie,

---

28 The Bible, at Genesis 2.6   29 Mount Tabor in Arabia.

	Þat þulke ȝerden þre vette, and wiþ him nome:	*fetch; take*
	Nie dawes he was þuderward ar he þuder come.	*Nine days*
	Wiþ gret honur he nom is up þo he þe ȝerden vonde,	*them*
120	Þe swotnesse þat þerof com velde al þe londe.	*filled*
	Wiþ gret melodie of is harpe Sein Davi þe ȝerden nom,	
	And to Jerusalem ladde is hom þe niþe day hom he com;	*ninth*
	In a deorne stude he is sette, for it was in þe evenynge,	*secret*
	Forte amorwe þat he iseie woder he miȝte is bringe.	*Until; where*
125	Amorwe þo he com þerto to one hy were alle ycome,	*into one*
	And ymored so vaste also, þat hy ne miȝte awey bynome,	*rooted; taken*
	Þat alle þre bicome to on, wat bitokneþ þis,	*signifies*
	Bote Vader and Sone and Holy Gost al o God it is?	*one*
	Sein Davit aboute þis holy ȝeorde a strong wal let rere,	*staff; had erected*
130	And nome gode ȝeme ho longe hy woxe fram ȝere to ȝere,	*heed; tall*
	Wiþ a cercle of selver he bond ech ȝer is stude þere,	*tied; position*
	Þat he miȝte attelaste iwite hou hold þat tre were.	*eventually know*
	So þat wiþinne þritti ȝer þis tre wax wel heie,	
	Ac it ne wax nanmore þer afterward, as hi weste bi þe selveren beye;	*knew; bond*
135	Ac everemo þereafterward vaire it stod,	
	Sein Davit it honurede wel, for he weste it was god.	
	Þo Sein Davit hadde ido þe sunne of lecherie,	*committed*
	And man slaȝt þo he let sle for is owe wif, Urie;[30]	*murder*
	And oure Loverd nom þerof wreche gret, swuþe sori he bicom,	*grief*
140	His penance he dude under þis tre þat he þerevore nom.	
	Þere he makede ek þane sauter is sunne forto bete,	*Psalter; absolve*
	Þe watloker it him was forȝive for þe holy tre so swete.	*quicker*
	Þo bigan he ek for is sunne þe holy temple to rere,	*build*
	Swuþe noble in Jerusalem, ac he deide in þe vourteþe ȝere.	*fourteenth*
145	Þe king Salamon is sone, þat king was subþe þere,	*son; after*
	After him þe temple bulde þat he ȝare were:	*it was ready*
	To and þritti ȝer he was þereaboute and is fader fortene also,	*fourteen*
	So þat it was sixe and fourti ȝer ar þat work were ido.	*before; finished*
	Þo þe work was almest ido, hom faillede a vair tre:	*needed*
150	Þat holy tre was fairost þo, þat hi miȝte awer ise.	*anywhere be seen*
	Salamon he let fulle and hewe as queinteliche as he miȝte,[31]	
	And let it mete and make more bi a vot þanne is riȝte,[32]	*measured; foot*
	And broȝte it to is riȝte stude, and lasi wolde it þer;	*tied*
	Þo was it by a vot to ssort as evene as hy mete it er,	*too short*
155	Þe carpenters it lete adoun in strong wraþþe and grete,	*anger*
	To noþing þat hi it broȝte to hi ne miȝte it make ymete.[33]	*fit*
	A brugge over an olde dich hy made it attelaste,	*bridge; at last*
	Þo hy ne miȝte in þe temple to non oþer werk it caste.[34]	
	Þereover ȝeode many a man þe wile it þere lay,	*went; while*
160	Nuste noȝt al wat it was þat defoulede it aday.	*trampled on*
	Þe Quene of Saba[35] com þer vorþ, and anon so he it isey,	*as soon as she*
	Honourede it faire and sat akne, he nolde come þer ney;	*knelt down*
	By anoþer wey he wende vorþ, to Salamon he com,	*she went*

---

30 2 Kings 11 tells how David committed adultery with Bathsheba, and wishing to marry her, he ordered that her husband, Uriah, be placed in a position in battle where he was most likely to die. When Uriah was killed, David married Bathsheba.

31 Solomon had it felled and hewn as neatly as he could.

32 It was measured and cut but was a foot too long.

33 When the tree is cut and replaced it is a foot too short to fit into its place.

34 When they could not use it in the temple, it served no other purpose than to become a bridge over a ditch.

35 The Queen of Sheba.

	And he him hadde wide yso3t to leorny of him wisdom.	*learn from*
165	Þoru grace þat oure Loverd hure 3af, to Salamon he sede	*gave her; she*
	Þat þe tre ne ssolde no3t ligge þer, 3if he dude by hure rede;	*lie; advice*
	For þere ssolde 3ute a man deie on þulke tre,	*will; yet*
	Þoru wan al þe lawe of Giwes destrud ssolde be.	*whom; Jews*
	Salamon it let nyme sone, and under eorþe it caste,	*had it taken*
170	Wel deope ver fram alle men, and burede it swuþe vaste;	*far; buried; fast*
	So longe so it þer after were, a vair welle þere sprong,	
	And a vair water suþþe wiþ gret fiss, boþe deop and long.	*lake; fish*
	Somme sike men þat þere come and hore vet wesse þere,	*sick; feet washed*
	Oþer honden, oþer baþede al, pur hol anon were;	*entirely whole*
175	Þat water hi honurede muche, and wolde þerinne wade,	
	Ac hy nuste noþing of þe tre þat al þe vertue made.	*knew nothing*
	Suþþe it was þer afterward longe þat oure Loverd an eorþe com,	*Then*
	And þat folk byspeke is deþ, and hore red þerof nom.[36]	
	Þat treo bigan to vleote anon, as it oure Loverd is wille was,	*float*
180	Þe Giwes come and fonde þis tre vleotinge þere bi cas,	*floating; by chance*
	Hy nome it up for it was foul and ileye hadde þer longe,	*lain*
	And made þer of þe holy rode oure Loverd on to honge;	*Cross*
	For þat treo was vil and old, and to vyly oure Louerd also,	*defile*
	And 3ute ham þo3te þe tre to vair þat he were þeron ido.	*too; killed*
185	Þe crois after oure Loverdes deþ under eorþe hy caste,	
	Þere as hi him to deþe dude, and burede it þere vaste.	*fast*
	And boþe crois eke þerewiþ þat þe þeves honge on er:	*thieves; before*
	Þere hy leie as hi were ifonde more þanne to hondred 3er.	*two*
	Þo Titus and Vaspasian Jerusalem nome,[37]	*When; captured*
190	And destrude al þe Giwes þat never eft þer hi ne come,[38]	*destroyed*
	Al þat lond was ibro3t in þe emperor is hond of Rome,	*emperor's control*
	And mid is men al biset to nyme þerto gome.	*besieged; heed*
	Suþþe þer com an emperor þat het Adrian,	*Hadrian*
	Swuþe heþene and luþer ek, and worrede ech Cristene man;	*also; persecuted*
195	He weste ware þe rode lay þat God was on ido,	*knew*
	And þat Cristene men þen stude honurede wanne hi mi3te come þerto;	
	He let a temple of maumetis in þulke stude arere,	*idolatry; built*
	Þat me ne vond noþing to loute to bote maumetis þere.	*pray to except*
	Wanne Cristene men mi3te þuder stele, hy ne durste for doute,	*fear*
200	And eke a3en hore heorte it was to eny maumet aloute.	*against; bow down*
	Hy bilevede also þulke stude and muche del for fere,	*left; great part*
	So þat wiþinne a vewe 3er, no Cristen man ne com þere;	*few years*
	So þat þulke stude was forlete many a day,	*abandoned*
	Þat no Cristene man ne pain nuste war þe rode lay.	*pagan knew*

De invencione Sancte Creucis[39]

205	A noble emperor þer com suþþe þat het Constantin,	*was called*
	In bataille he was so muche þat þer nas of no fin;	*great; end*
	Suþþe come is fon and wonne muche del of is londe,	*foes; part*

---

36 That people demanded his death, and their advice was taken there.

37 Vespasian (emperor AD 69–79) and Titus (emperor AD 79–81) brought about the subjugation of Judea. The Temple of Jerusalem was destroyed in AD 70.

38 Referring to the Great Diaspora, though it was under Hadrian, line 193 (emperor AD 117–38), that the final dispersal of the Jews took place in 132–5.

39 The finding of the holy Cross.

	He ȝarkede a day is ost aȝen hom forto stonde.	*prepared; army*
	As he touward bataile wende,⁴⁰ he bihuld up an hey,	*looked; high*
210	Hym þoȝte þat a vair crois up in hevene he sey;	*saw*
	Lettres he sei þeron iwrite, he is bigan to rede:	*read*
	'Wiþ þeos signe þou sselt maister be' þulke lettres sede.	*symbol*
	Þe emperor þis understod, þei he heþene were,	*heathen*
	A crois he let make sone þat is men tovore him bere	*had made; carried*
215	In stude of is baner; to bataille he wende anon,	*place*
	And þoru vertu of þe holy crois he overcom is fon,	*through*
	And þe maistrie wan of al is lond in a lite stonde þere;	*won; short time*
	Muche afterward he þoȝte suþþe wat þulke signe were.	*then; that*
	Þe wisoste men of al is lond bivore him he let bringe,	*wisest*
220	And enquerede of þe crois, wat were þe toknynge.	*asked; meaning*
	Hi sede þat at Jerusalem God was ido on rode,	*They; killed; Cross*
	And þat þe Giwes hudde þulke crois, as hi understode.	*hid*
	'Wanne Ich habbe þer þoru', quaþ þe emperor, 'my fon ibroȝt to gronde,	*through it; foes*
	Ne worþ Ich nevere bliþe of herte, ar þe holy crois be fonde.'	*will; happy*
225	Elyne þat is moder was to Jerusalem he sende	
	To seche after þe holi crois, and he gladliche forþ wende.	*she; went*
	Þo he com þuder heo let crie, as heo hadde hure red inome,	*advice taken*
	Þat alle þe Giwes of þe cite bivore hure ssolde come.	*Jews*
	Þo þe Giwes ysomned were, hy hadde ssortliche gret fere,	*gathered; fear*
230	Gret conseil hy nome þerof wat þe encheson were.	*cause might be*
	Þo sede on þat het Judas: 'Ich wene þat Ich wot	*Then; one called*
	Wat þis somonce amonte ssal gif þat Ich telle mot.	*summons amounts to*
	Ich wene þe quene enqueri wolle, as he haþ iþoȝt,	*think; enquire; she*
	After þe rode þat Jesu Crist to deþe was on ybroȝt.	
235	Þat non of ȝou ne be so wod þat þerof iknowe be,	*mad; may know*
	Ichelle ȝou telle in conseil þat my fader tolde me.	*confidence what*
	Þo my vader Symeon in is deþ uvel lay,	*When; miserably*
	In conseil he was to me iknewe þo he þane deþ isay:	*revealed; saw*
	"Judas", he sede, "leve sone, gif it bitideþ so,	*dear; happens*
240	Þat me enqueri after þe rode þat Jesus was on ido,	*people; Cross*
	Loke þat þou be iknewe þerof, raþer þanne me þe quelle."	*informed; sooner; kill*
	Þat Zache my fader tolde me, in conseil Ichelle þe telle:	*What; I will*
	He sede me a lite bivore is deþ þat he was atte dede	*little; that*
	To burie in Calvari hul, þe rode þoru comun rede.	*Calvary hill; assent*
245	"Leve fader", Ich sede þo, "wat eileþ ȝou alas?	*worries; sadly*
	Wy wolde ȝe him to deþe do wanne þat he God was?"	*kill; when*
	He sede þoru me nas it noȝt, ac for þat he⁴¹ wiþsede	*nothing; contradicted*
	Mine felawes of hore lawe, hi him broȝte to dede.	*their; consigned to death*
	Suþþe hy broȝte him in sepulcre, ac he aros to lyve	*tomb*
250	Fram deþe þe þridde day, mid is wonden vive;	*wounds five*
	Þane fortiþe day þerafterward, to hevene he wende an hey,	*fortieth*
	In þe lond of Galile, as al þat folk ysey.⁴²	
	Twelf monþe it was þer afterward, and half ȝer and more,	
	Þat Stevene, þat was my broþer,⁴³ prechede of is lore.	*teaching*
255	Þe Giwes him ladde wiþoute toun, and hende him wiþ stones,	*led; killed*
	And to stronge deþe him broȝte inou, and debrusede al is bones.	*broke*

---

40   The Battle of Milvian Bridge in 312, where Constantine defeated the northern tribes.

41   Christ.

42   The Ascension, forty days after the Resurrection.

43   This is an anachronism creating a familial bond between the
first martyr, Stephen, who was stoned to death, and Judas.

Þe morwe after Midwinter day[44] to deþe hi him broȝte,
And nou he is in þe joie of hevene þat he þo aboȝte.' *purchased*
 Þo Judas hadde þis tale itold, þe Giwes sede as hi stode: *said*
260 'Telle ne hurde we nevere er þus muche of þe rode.' *before*
Þo þe tyme was icome tofore þe quene hy come, *When*
'Chooseþ anon', quaþ þe quene, 'on of þeos tweie dome: *Choose; judgements*
Lyf and deþ ȝou is bivore, cheseþ weþer ȝe wolle; *which; want*
Bote ȝe me vinde þe swete rode, brenne echon ȝe ssolle.' *Unless; find; burn*
265 Greot fur he let make tovore hore alre eiȝe, *fire; before; eyes*
Þe Giwes bigonne to crie loude þo hi þat fur yseye: *when; saw*
'ȝyf eny mon wot þerof', hi sede, 'þanne wot Judas, *knows*
For Zache is fader of gret poer was *Zacharias; power*
Þulke tyme þat Jesus was on þe rode ydo.' *At the time*
270 Þe quene let nyme þo Judas, and alle þe oþer let go, *had Judas seized*
And bad him be knewe anon, he nolde for none þinge. *asked*
Þe quene him let wel faste bynde, and in strang prison bringe. *securely bound*
Þere wiþoute mete and drinke seve dawes he lay; *food; a week*
For honger he gan crie loude þe seveþe day,
275 And sede: 'Bringeþ me of þis wo, and Ichelle ȝou lede *Release; lead*
Þere Ich wene þe rode be, as my fader me sede.' *Where; believe*
Þo he out of prison com mid muche volk he wende
To þe place as þe rode was, as is fader him kende. *revealed*
 Þo he to þe place com, he sat adoun akne: *on his knees*
280 'Loverd', he sede, 'ȝif it is soþ þat þou man and God be, *true*
And þat þou of Marie were ibore, send us her þi grace *born*
And toknynge þat we mote finde þe rode in þis place.' *sign*
Anon so Judas hadde þis bone to oure Loverd ibede,
Þe hul bigan to quake, and out of one stude *hill; place*
285 Þer sprong out a smoke and wende an hei, and muche place fulde – *filled*
Swettore þing ne miȝte be þanne þe smoke smulde. *smelled*
 Þo Judas þis isay, loude he gan to crie: *saw; began*
'Jesus is sone of almiȝti God, ibore of maide Marie.
Wod is þat biluveþ oþer, as Ich habbe many o day, *Mad; he who*
290 Take Ichelle to Cristendom, and forsake þe Giwes lay.' *Convert; law*
He let him ssrive hasteliche, and þo he issrive was, *confess*
He let him nemne Quiriac þat er het Judas. *took the name*
 Þo nome hi spade and ssovele, and ner þe place wende; *took; went*
Deope hy gonne to delve þer as þe smoke out wende, *dig*
295 So þat hy fonde roden þre þo hi hadde idolve longe – *three crosses*
Oure Loverdes rode and oþer to þat þe þeves were on anhonge *two*
Biside oure Loverd him to ssende; þo nuste hi of þe þre *shame; not know*
Þe holi crois þat hi soȝte wuch it miȝte be; *which*
And naþeles hy nome alle þre, and toward toune bere *But even so*
300 To Eleyne þe gode quene wiþ wel glade chere.
Bi þe wey atte heie non me gan aȝen hom bringe, *noon*
A ded ȝonge man up a bere toward buringe; *bier; burial*
Curiac nom is owe rode, and efsone is oþer, *one; immediately*
And leide up þis dede man, ac he ne aros for noþer; *neither*
305 Hi leide þe þridde him upon, and he aros wel blyve, *happy*
And bigan to þonke Godes sone þat broȝte him fram deþe to lyve.
 Þo com þe devel ȝollinge forþ, loude he gan grede: *yelling; cry out*

---

44 Saint Stephen's Day, 26 December.

'Alas, nou is mi miȝte ido   evere mo!' he sede.   *power undone*
'Jesus! Jesus! Wat þencstou   al folk to þe lede?

310   Þou hast here man in ward iȝive   þing þat Ich mest ofdrede,   *into his keeping*
Þoru wan Ich was ferst overcome   and nou Ich am al at gronde,   *whom; defeated*
Alas, þulke sori wille,   þat he evere was ifonde!
For Inabbe poer non so gret   an eorþe amang manne,   *I have not; power*
ȝif hi makeþ þe forme of þe crois   þat I ne mot anon þanne,

315   Þervore Ichot þat echmon   wole þat soþe ise,   *I know; see*
Þat þe crois me haþ overcome,   and al bileve me.   *will abandon*
Alas, alas, þis tyme!   Nou Ich worþ al forsake,   *will be*
Judas, Judas, wat was þe   wi wostou þus on take?   *would you*
Þoru on þat Judas was ihote,   Jesus to deþe I broȝte;   *one; called*

320   And þoru Judas Icham overcome,   and ibroȝt to noȝte;   *nought*
Me ne tit nevere eft strengþe non,   bote enyman wole wiþ wille   *soon; again*
Servi me to paie is fleiss   is soule forto spille.   *please; lose*
Wanne my strengþe me is bynome,   fondy Ich mot mid gynne   *deprived; traps*
And wiþ traison lif Ich may   eny man to me wynne.   *treacherous*

325   I ne may here no leng bileve,   for þis me þencheþ longe,   *stay; too long*
For þe crois þat me is so ney   in pine Ich am wel stronge.'   *near; pain*
'Go hanne anon!' quaþ Judas,   'Ne com her nevere eft more.   *from here*
Ifonde he is þe it late be   þat overcomþ al þi lore.   *let; teaching*
He þat here þis dede man   fram deþe broȝte to lyve

330   Pulte þe wiþ is poer   into helle gronde blyve.'   *Thrusts; his power*
Muche was þe joie of þe crois   þat men made þo þere,
Wiþ gret song and procession   þe quene hi is bere.   *to; it is carried*
Judas nom þo Cristendom,   and þo he ibaptized was,   *took*
He let him nenme Curiac   þat er her het Judas.

335   Þe quene of selver and of gold   a riche ssrine wroȝte,   *shrine; made*
And of ȝymmes precious,   and þe rode þeron broȝte;   *gems*
Upe þe hul of Calvari   þere hi þe rode fonde,   *hill*
A noble churche he let rere,   ihered be þulke stonde.[45]   *had built; praised*
Þo desirede þe quene muche   after þe nailes þre,   *three nails*

340   Warewiþ oure Loverd was   ynailed to þe tre.   *With which*
Quiriac (þat het er Judas)   wende to þe place
As þe crois ifonde was,   and bad oure Loverdes grace   *Where; prayed*
Þat he, ȝif is wille were,   þe þre nailes him sende;
Þe nailes wiþ gret liȝtinge   out of þe eorþe wende.   *easiness*

345   Quiriac þonkede oure Loverd Crist –   wiþ gret joie he is nom –   *seized*
And tok is Eleine, þe gode quene,   þo he to hure com.   *took them to*

De Sancto Quiriaco

Seyn Quiriak þat bissop was   prechede Godes lawe.
Julian, þe luþer emperor,[46]   broȝte him suþþe of dawe,   *after; from life*
For þe swete rode þat he vond,   and for he men þerto drou   *found; drew*
350   To biluve on Jesu Crist,   for he it held al wou.   *wrong*
Sein Quiriak was þo bivore   þe emperor ibroȝt,   *then*
He het biluve in hore maumetes,   and he nolde noȝt.[47]

---

45   The Church of the Holy Sepulchre that still stands in Jerusalem.
46   'Julian, the evil emperor' is Julian the Apostate, who ruled AD 360–3.
47   He commanded him to put his faith in idols, but he would not.

His riȝt hond he let smite of ferst: 'Ic do', he sede 'þis,   *cut*
'For þou hast ofte iwrite þerwiþ   aȝen oure lawe, iwis.'   *written with it*
355 'Þou gidi hound!' quaþ Sein Quiriak,   'Wel hastou do by me   *foolish dog; done*
Of a god dede, þou were wel understonde,   wel aȝte Ich blessy þe: *ought; to bless*
For þou bynome me þulke lyme   þat me haveþ ofte to sunne idrawe,   *deprived; limb*
For Ich habbe ofte iwrite þerwiþ   aȝen Cristes lawe
Þe wile Ich was a luþer Giu,   and on him biluvede noȝt.'   *evil Jew; believed*
360   Þo þis emperor isei,   þat he nolde noȝt turne is þoȝt,   *change his mind*
He made him drinke led iweld   and in is mouþ huld it þere;   *molten lead; hold*
Evere sat þis gode man   as him noþing nere.   *as if it were*
Op a gridil he leide him suþþe,   over a gret fur and strong,   *Upon a griddle*
To rosty as me deþ veirss fleyss,   grece was þer among;   *roast; fresh flesh*
365 For þat fur was al of grece and col   and salt was eke þerto,   *coal; also*
And of is fleiss þat was forbarnd,   þe wonden hi sulte also.   *salted the wounds*
Þo he ne miȝte þerwiþ turne is þoȝt,   ne to deþe him bringe,   *Julian*
He þoȝte ȝif he miȝte him turne   mid eny oþer þinge.
   'Quiriak,' he sede, 'biþench þe bet,   and do after mi lore,   *consider; remedy*
370 Ȝif þou nelt oure godes honure,   bote þou wolt do more: *unless*
Seie þat þou nert Cristene noȝt,   and Ichelle debonere be,   *are not; gracious*
Þat murie lif þou sselt lede,   and þat þou sselt ise.'   *shall; see*
   Þe gode man nolde do after him þo,   a caudron he let fulle
Wiþ seoþinge eoly vol inou,   and let hym þerinne pulle.   *flowing; oil foul*
375 Þerinne he seþ þe gode man,   forte he weri was,   *until*
Þe gode man herede oure Loverd Crist,   and nevere þe worse him nas.   *praised*
Þo þat þe emperor isei   þat he ne miȝte him overcome,
Wiþ a swerd he smot him þoru þe herte   þo he was out inome.   *struck; taken*
And is soule to hevene wende   after þis tormentynge;
380 God, for love of Sein Quiriak,   to þulke joie us bringe.   *the same*

Cursor Mundi

Cursor Mundi, or 'The Over-Runner of the World', is a 30,000-line versification of the Christian history of the world.[1] It is contained in whole or in part in ten manuscripts, the earliest of which is probably thirteenth-century (Cambridge University Library, Gg. IV. 27). Other manuscript versions date from the fourteenth to the fifteenth centuries. The most complete version is found in the late fourteenth-century London, British Library, Cotton Vespasian A. iii, a text thought to have originated in the north or north-east Midlands. Certainly, the work's origins are northern English. The extract below is from Göttingen University Library, Theol. 107r, folios 68 recto to 69 verso. This particular version is dated to the first quarter of the fourteenth century. The dialect of this extract is probably from south-east Lincolnshire; after line

11000, the language of the text becomes distinctly northern.[2]

The *Cursor Mundi* is mostly composed of short couplets, though at times the verse-lines become longer, especially when the subject matter is complex and dense (as in Christ's Passion, for example). In the excerpt below, the author has drawn on Bishop Grosseteste's thirteenth-century *Chasteau D'Amour* for his depiction of the Castle of Love and Grace. This is part of the fifth age of the world (there are seven ages altogether), in which the prophecies concerning Christ take place, and his conception, birth and baptism are related. This parable of the castle follows the prophecy of Isaiah and precedes the conception of Christ, providing an allegory of the virtues of Mary.

Lines 9879–10120: The Castle of Love and Grace

	In a castel semly sett,	*beautifully*
9880	Strenthed wele widuten lett	*neglect*
	Þis castel es of love and grace.	*is*
	Both of socure and of solace;	*succour*
	Apon þe marche it standes traist,	*secure*
	Of enmye dredis it na fraist,	*enemy; fears*
9885	It es hy sett apon a cragg,	
	Gray and hard, widuten hagg.	*without*
	Dounward es it polischt bright,	
	Þat it may neyhe na warid wiht,	*near; criminal; person*
	Ne na maner gin of were	*engine; war*
9890	May cast þartill it forto dere,	*to it; harm*
	Wid wallis closid four of stan,	
	Þat fayrer in þis world es nan.	*none*
	Baylis has þis castel thre,	*Baileys*
	Wid wallis thrinne, semly to se,	*three*
9895	As ȝe sal siþen here divyse,	*afterwards*
	Bot wel fayrer on many wise	*ways*
	Þan tung may tell, or hert thinc,	
	Or any clerc may write wid ink.	
	A depe dick þar es aboute	*ditch*
9900	Wele wroght, widuten doute;	*made*
	Wid kirneles es umset ful wele,	*battlements; set about*
	Schroud on ilk a side wid sele;	*Covered; good*
	Seven barbicans er þar dight,	*arranged*
	Þat er made wid mekil slight,	*are; great*
9905	Ilkan þai have bath ȝate and toure,	*Each one; gate*
	Þat never mare may fayle socoure.	*succour*
	Wid mislike sal he never be ledd,	*disease*
	Þe man þat þiþerward es fledd.	

1   R. Morris, ed., *Cursor Mundi*, EETS o.s. 57, 59, 62, 66, 68, 99, 101 (London, 1874–93; repr. 1961–6).

2   See M. Laing, *A Catalogue of Sources for a Linguistic Atlas of Early Middle English* (Cambridge, 1993), p. 56.

Þis castel es noght for to hide,   *So that this castle is not hidden in any way*

9910   Es payntid on þe uter syde   *exterior*

Wid thre colouris of sundri hewe,

Þe grund wal neyst, þat es so trew,   *bottom; next*

Metand wid þat roche of stan   *Meeting; rock*

Of gret suetnes þai wantis nan;   *sweetness*

9915   For suete grennes, I dar wele say,   *green*

His hew he haldis lastand ay.   *holds; lasting; always*

Þe toþer hew neist to finde,   *other; next*

Es all of blew men cals Ynde,   *blue*

Þe midward heu es þat I mene,   *middle*

9920   To sight it es ful selcuth schene;   *astonishingly; beautiful*

Þe thrid colour over mast of all,

Þat þe kirnelis er paynt widall,

It cestis lem over all sua bright,   *casts; light; so*

Þat rechis to þe donwar light,   *reaches; lowest*

9925   As rose rede es in spring,

And semes als a brinand thing.   *burning*

Waried wight nan comes þar never,   *Criminal*

Bot suetnes es þar lastand ever

Widin þat castel þat sua es tift,

9930   Þat queþer es þan snau on drift,   *whiter; snow*

Þat castel brightnes so unnede,

Overall þat contre on lenth and brede.

Midward þe hiest tour itelle,

Þar springes of clere water a well;

9935   Þarfra rennys four stremes suete,   *From it*

Thoru þat gravel and þat grete,   *grit*

And þarwid fillis ilk a dicke,   *each one; ditch*

Qua þarbi es, wele may þaim like;   *Who; by it*

Qua miht þaim wid þat water wass,   *wash*

9940   He miht have hele of all his fless.   *body*

    Widin þis tour þat es forsayd

Es sett a trone of yvor graid,   *ivory*

Þat es of gretter light and lem

Þan someres day es sunnes bem;

9945   Craftyly castin wid compas,   *made*

Climband up wid seven pas,   *Climbing; steps*

Ilkan es wid þair mesur mett,   *Each one; their; well-proportioned*

Ful semely þar þan er þai sett.

Þe lem of light ay lendis new,   *beam; sends forth*

9950   Þat mengis wid þa coluris hew.   *mingles*

Was never ȝit king ne cayser,   *emperor*

Þat ever satt in suilk a chayer.   *chair*

Bot fayrer was, widuten ende,

Þe stede þar God himselven wald lende,   *place; would*

9955   Þat was þar never suilk a hald,

Ne nan wylyer in world to wald,   *wiser; control*

Ne never bes made wid manes witt,   *be; knowledge*

For God himself divysed itt,

To his bihove sundri and sere,   *advantage; various*

9960   Forþi we awe to hald it dere.   *ought; hold*

    Þis castel es of beld and bliss,   *joy*

	Þar myrth es never mar to miss,	*more; lack*
	Castel bath of hope and hald,	*both; honour*
	Hir grith to have þai may be bald.	*peace; bold*
9965	Þat es þe bodi of þat berde,	*lady*
	Had never womman so blissed werde,	*become*
	Ne never sua many maners gode,	*qualities*
	As Mari mayden, mylde of mode.	*heart*
	It es up sett as in þe marche,	
9970	And standis us fore schild and targe,	*small shield*
	Agaynes all ur feloun fa,	*foe*
	Þat waytis us ay for to sla.	*kill*
	Þe roche þat es þolichit so sliht	*polished; skilfully*
	Es mayden Mari hert ful bright,	
9975	Þat nehyes never to wic dede;	*thought; wicked*
	Bot ever scho lyves in maydenhede,	*she*
	Þat scho hir ches þe first day,	*chose*
	Scho ȝemed it in mekenes ay.	*kept*
	Þe fundement þat first es laid	*foundation*
9980	Nest þe roche, as it es said,	*Next to*
	Þat paynted es wid grenne hew,	*green*
	And þat lastes ever elike new,	
	Þat es end of þat mayden clene,	
	Lyghtand hir haly herte schene.	*Lighting; resplendent*
9985	Þe grennes lastand ever and ay,	
	Bitakins ending of þat may,	*It betokens; maiden*
	For gode ending of al and all,	
	Of al vertus es grund wal.	*bottom*
	Þe midward hew þat es of Ynde,	
9990	Es na man þat may fayrer fynde,	
	Þat es takening of all sothfaste,	*symbol; sincerely true*
	Of tendernes and trouth stedfast;	
	Scho servid in our Laverd of miht,	
	In mekenes suete, day and niht.	
9995	Þe colour overmast of all,	
	It coverys all aboute þe wall,	
	And it es rede as any blode,	
	Of all þir oþer es nan sua gode,	*these; so*
	Þat es þat haly charite,	
10000	Was kindlyd in þat lefdy fre.	*lady; noble*
	Sua umlayd wid love so clene,	*surrounded; pure*
	Scho was gevyn to serve God bidene.	*God's command*
	Þe foure trettis on hy er sett,	*turrets*
	Þe castel with fra saght to gett,	*harm; protect*
10005	Þat er four vertus principalys,	
	Þe quilk men callis cardinalys;[3]	*Those; which; call*
	All oþer vertus of þaim has hald,	*from these; held*
	Forþi er þay hefd vertus tald:	*chief*
	Þat es rightwisnes, and meth,	*righteousness; moderation*
10010	Forsiht, and strenth, to tell er eth.	*perception*
	At þe ȝatis foure er four porteris,	*gates*
	Þat nathing may cum in þat deris.	*doors*

---

3 The four cardinal virtues.

Þe baylis thre of þat castell,   *baileys*
Þat es sua wele wroght cernel,   *made with battlements*

10015   Þat es in cumpas wroght aboute,
And weris all þat werk fra doute;   *protect*
Þat on þe overmast stage es sett,
Hir maydenhede es graythly gett,
Þat never was wemmyd, was a dele,   *defiled*
10020   For scho was filde wid þe grace so wele.   *filled*
Þe bayle midilmast of þe thre,   *in the middle*
Betakins wele hir chastite.
Þe overmast, widuten fayle,
May wele bitakin hir sposayle,
10025   Name of bayli it hatt forþi,   *has; therefore*
For it hir held as in bayly,
Þat makles es hir self, I say,   *matchless*
Spousid, and moder, and clene may;   *Spouse; pure maiden*
He most wend thoru an of þir thre,   *go; one; these*
10030   Þat in þis world wil saved be.

    Þe barbicans seven þat es aboute,
Þer standis thre baylis widute,
Þat wele kepis þat castel,   *protect*
For arw, schott, and quarel,   *From arrow; crossbow bolt*
10035   Þat er þe seven vertus to tell,
Þe sevyn sinnes er sett to quell.
Ʒe sal þaim here, widuten bide.   *shall; them; hear*
Þe first of þaim men clepis pride,   *call*
Þat es overcomin and mad ful mate   *in every way*
10040   Þer buxumnes may hald hir state;   *humility*
Charite ever fordos envye;   *destroys*
Abstinence fordos glutrie;   *gluttony*
Þe chastite of þis levedy   *lady*
Overcumes all lust of lichery;   *lechery*
10045   Al gredines of everilkan,   *everyone*
Hir fredam all fordos it þan;   *generosity*
Miht never in hir be wreth ne hete,   *anger; hate*
Hir tholemodnes it was so grete;   *meekness*
Gastly gladnes was hir emydd,   *Spiritual; within*
10050   Þat al ille hevynes it fordidd.

    Þe welle of grace springes þarin,   *within her*
Þat fynis never mare to rine.
God gaf his grace to al his dere,   *beloved*
And delt it all wid mesur sere;   *variously*
10055   Bot scho þat was his aun to wale,   *own; choose*
To hir he gaf his grace al hale.   *completely*
Bot of þe grace þat of hir brestis,
Over all þis world þat grace it kestis.   *casts*
Forþi scho es cald in ilka place   *called*
10060   Moder of pyte and als of grace.   *pity*

    And quat may we call þa dikes   *what; ditches*
Bot wilful povert þat man in likes?
Ne may na gynne in erde be wroght,   *traps; earth*
May cast to dere þis castel aght,   *harm*
10065   Quarthoru þe feind, þe warid wiht,   *Through which; enemy; criminal*
Overcomen es and has tint his miht,   *lost; power*

Þat had sua mekil miht biforn,
Þat was na man of moder born
Miht were him fra þat fend sua fell, *terrible*
10070 Þat he ne him putt to þe pine of hell. *torment*
For þis ilk levedi forsoth es scho, *same*
Þat Godd said of þe nedder unto,
Þat suilk a womman ȝit suld spring,
Þat suld ful sare his hevid thring. *should; sorrow*
10075   Now blissid be þat blisful berde, *lady*
Þe worthiest an of all in werlde,
Þat King of all þat ay has bene,
His sete made in hir saule clene, *soul*
To gestyn in hir lele body, *stay; true*
10080 To save his folk fra sinne and foly,
And bring þaim ute of presun strang *prison*
Þat þai had liggen in sua lang. *lain*
Ful lef was us, þis levedy lele, *beloved*
Þat bountes in hir bar sua fele, *goodness; much*
10085 Mare þan any schaft þat es;
Bot þe Sone of hir rightwisnes,
Þat in hir lovely bodi light
Made hir a thousand sith so bright. *times*
He cam in at þe ȝate sperd,
10090 And sua it was quen he forth ferd, *when*
As þe sune gas thoru þe glas, *goes*
He miht do quat his willis was.
    'Mi saule es cumyn, levdi, þe to, *has come*
And callis at þe ȝate þe unto,
10095 Knockand it fynis noght to crie,
Levdy suete, þu have mercy!
Undo, undo, levdy, þin are *grace*
To þis caytif, castin in care. *pleader*
Widuten þi castel I am umsett, *beset*
11000 Hard wid thre famen thrett: *foes*
Þis world, mi fless, þe fend als, *devil; too*
Þat fylus me wid fandyng fals, *fills; testing*
To ger me fall in fylthes fele, *make; filthy*
All agaynes mi saule hele. *salvation*
11005 A gadring held þai gret togider, *gathering*
Þe fend formast he cam thider
Wid thre werkis bunden bi his side, *bound*
Þat es slawnes, envie, and pride; *sloth*
Þe world has tuynne to his ascyse, *two; service*
11010 Þat es avaris, and covaytise; *avarice; covetousness*
Þe fless has ful redily him by
Lechury, and eke glutry. *gluttony*
Thoru þis þan am I driven dun, *down*
And lijs forcastin as crachun. *wretch*
11015 I drede me sare lang for to ly, *sorely; lie*
Bot if þi grace me helpe, levdy.
Þat þu þe wayke es wont to cover, *trust*
Do me to passe þa dykes over, *ditches*
Þar þe castel standis so stabil,
11020 And charite es so comunabil.'

Robert Mannyng of Brunne

HANDLYNG SYNNE

Handlyng Synne is extant in ten manuscripts. Among these the chief witnesses to the whole work are London, British Library, Harley 1701, dated to the second half of the fourteenth century, and Oxford, Bodleian Library, Bodley 415, dated to the end of the fourteenth century.[1] In addition to the manuscripts in which all or parts of the work survive, extracts deliberately selected by later compilers survive in other manuscripts, demonstrating the usefulness of *Handlyng Synne*, with its 'short story' format. The number of manuscript witnesses to Mannyng's work attests to its popularity in the later medieval period. The appeal of Mannyng's text contrasts with that of Dan Michel of Northgate's, whose autograph manuscript of the *Aȝenbite of Inwit* is the only extant copy of this didactic work.

Robert Mannyng probably came originally from Bourne in Lincolnshire, where he was born in the second half of the thirteenth century. He attended Cambridge University in the early fourteenth century, and then appears to have made his career in religious orders, possibly as a canon; he was certainly living with the Gilbertine order at Sempringham by the time he began *Handlyng Synne* in 1303, but may have moved elsewhere later in his career. Much of this information is contained in the Prologue to *Handlyng Synne*. Mannyng states that he lived for fifteen years at Sempringham (lines 63–6), and then he lived for five years with Dan John of Clinton (lines 71–2).

The aim of *Handlyng Synne* is to inspire the Christian congregation to learn to 'handle' their sin: by not engaging in sinful deeds or words, by learning what sin consists of, and by confessing regularly and performing penance. The work is in the same tradition of penitential and instructive works as the *Aȝenbite of Inwit*. This tradition extends back to the early centuries of Christianity, but was particularly inspired in the later Middle Ages by the ordinance of the Fourth Lateran Council in 1215 that those responsible for the cure of souls should use the vernacular in confessional practices and in instruction. Numerous French and English manuals of sins and virtues survive, and *Handlyng Synne* is itself an adaptation and translation of the *Manuel des Pechiez*, a confessional work assigned, perhaps erroneously, to William of Waddington.

Mannyng's text is organized along the same lines as his source, and as the *Aȝenbite of Inwit*. He reveals his scheme in the Prologue: first, the Ten Commandments,

and how these are sinned against; then the seven capital sins, which demonstrate how 'þe fende us wynnes' (line 20); the seven sacraments, that show the way to heaven; the twelve aspects and graces of confession; and the twelve articles of faith. Mannyng makes clear the fact that:

> For lewde men Y undyrtoke
> On Englyssh tunge to make þys boke
> For many ben of swyche manere   *such a manner*
> Þat talys and rymys wyl bleþly here;   *tale and rhymes*
> Yn games and festys, and at þe ale,
> Love men to lestene trotevale: *listen to tale-telling*
> Þat may falle ofte to vylanye,
> To dedly synne, or oþer folye.[2]

His intention is clearly a pastoral one, educating the unlearned in the ways of salvation, and encouraging regular confession. To this didactic end, Mannyng writes in octosyllabic rhyming couplets, using verse, not only because his source did, but also to reflect the fact that the most popular contemporary literary mode was poetic: if one hopes to inspire and to teach, one must entertain. Indeed, Orrm chose the same approach in his twelfth-century homiletic work, the *Orrmulum*. Mannyng also incorporates exempla in the form of tales to illustrate each aspect of his scheme. These tales are most often derived directly from the *Manuel des Pechiez*, but there are also a number which seem to be Mannyng's own, or which are derived from alternative sources. Mannyng is though, much more than a translator; he adds to his source, alters the emphasis, omits what he believes to be extraneous material, and creates a lively work that very much reflects his own fourteenth-century society. For example, in his discussion of envy, Mannyng adds that English men are renowned particularly for being envious, while the French are renowed for their lechery. He therefore advises the English to be especially on their guard against backbiting, envy, lying and being treacherous.[3]

The extracts edited below from Harley 1701 are taken from the explanation and illustration of 'Sloth, the Fourth Deadly Sin'. The complete account of this sin includes a general introduction, 'The Tale of the English Squire Who Left his Repentance Too Late', 'A Warning against Tournaments', 'The Tale of a Minstrel Killed for Disturbing a Bishop', 'Why Bishop Grosseteste Loved Music', 'The Tale of a Father Who Would Not Chastise his Child', 'The Tale of "Sire Ely"' and 'The Tale of Carpus's

---

1   Edited by F. J. Furnivall, *Robert of Brunne's 'Handlyng Synne'*, EETS o.s. 119, 123 (London, 1901–3); and I. Sullens, *Robert Mannyng of Brunne: 'Handlyng Synne'*, MRTS 14 (Binghamton, 1983).

2   Furnivall, *Handlyng Synne*, pp. 2–3, lines 43–50.
3   Lines 4149–66.

Vision'. Each of these exempla demonstrates in different ways the dangers of a slothful life. His examples, his focus and his language are all geared towards making the uneducated understand the dreadful outcome of their sin.

Edited here are the introduction, 'A Warning against Tournaments', 'The Tale of a Minstrel Killed for Disturbing a Bishop' and 'Why Bishop Grosseteste Loved Music'. Of these, Mannyng expands considerably on the introduction he found in his French source; and he includes the story of Bishop Robert Grosseteste of Lincoln, which is not in the source.

Handling Synne

Sloth, the Fourth Deadly Sin

	Now shul we speke of sloghnes,	*sloth*
	Among þe toþer ful wyk hyt es;	*wicked*
	Þe vourþe hyt ys of dedly synnes,	*fourth*
4240	Alle þese ryche men hyt wynnes.	*enjoy*
	Moche ys a man for to blame	
	Þat kan nat wurschep Goddys name	
	With *Pater Noster* no wyþ Crede:	
	Þys beleve shuld hym to hevene lede.	
4245	Ful slogh he ys þat wyl nat lere	*learn*
	Þat yche frame blessed preyere;	*same benefit from*
	And also he ys ful of slownes	
	Þat may, and wyl nat, here hys messe,	*hear his Mass*
	Specyaly on þe Sunday,	
4250	He trespasyþ þe more yn þe lay.	*religion*
	Yn þe woke, o day, þurgh ryght,	*week*
	Þe Sunday, ys a day of myȝt.	
	How sey þese men þat are þus so slowe,	*slothful*
	Þat oute of mesure slepe a throwe?	*beyond moderation; while*
4255	Whan he heryþ a belle rynge,	
	To holy cherche men kallyng,	
	Þan may he nat hys bedde lete	*leave*
	But þan behoveþ hym to lygge and swete,	*obliges him; sweat*
	And take þe mery mornyng slepe;	
4260	Of matynes ryche men take no kepe.	*Matins; pay no heed*
	Ȝyf þey mowe aryse at tyme of messe	*must get up*
	For þe matynes, noþer more ne lesse,	
	Þan ys þys Terlyncels skylle:	*the demon's*
	'Slepe þou long, and Y shal hele.'	*conceal it for you*
4265	He putteþ hevenys yn hys yȝe,	*heaviness; eyes*
	And makeþ hym lenger for to lye;	
	And seyþ 'Al betyme mayst þou ryse,	
	Whan þey do þe messe servyse;	
	A messe ys ynogh for þe;	
4270	Þe touþer gyblot, late hyt be;	*giblet (pointless extras)*
	Here mayst þou bettyr slepe a throwe	
	Þan sytte and loke uppon a wowe.'	*wall*
	Þys ys þe cunsel of Terlyncel;	*advice*
	Yn alle slownesse he bereþ þe bel;	
4275	He ys a devyl of þat myster,	*profession*
	To slownes he ys cunseler.	
	Þan cumþ one aboute pryme	*first thing in the morning*
	'Rys up,' he seyþ, 'now ys tyme.'	

	Þan begynneþ he to klawe and to raske,	scratch; stretch
4280	And зyveþ Terlyncel hys taske.	
	He klawyþ, he shrubbyþ, wel at hys pay,	rubs; to his satisfaction
	And makyþ to Terlyncel a lay;	
	To hym þat kalled, he spekeþ stoutly:	
	'What devyl, why haþ þe prest swych hy?	haste
4285	Byd hym þat he abyde algate;	nevertheless
	Hym dar nat syng зyt over late.'	
	For hym shal so Goddys servyse abyde	
	Tyl hyt be passed over þe tyde.	
	зyt peraventure, at hys rysyng,	perhaps
4290	Of God spekeþ he no þyng,	
	But зyf hyt be of sum vanyte,	frivolous thing
	Þat renþ yn hys þoght, þat spekeþ he.	runs through his thoughts
	And when he cumþ unto þe messe,	
	Þer behoveþ hym hys heer dresse.	hair (penitential garment)
4295	Ful fewe bedys are yn hys mouþe,	prayers
	He usyþ none; þey are uncouthe.[4]	uses
	And зyf a frere cum for to preche,	friar
	Of a dyner were bettyr speche.	meal
	Þan seyþ he: 'God shal alle save;	
4300	Do wel; wel shalt þou have.'	
	Certys þat ys nat ynow,	In truth; enough
	For doþ he noþyng to prow.	for the common good
	But зyf he wulde lestene þe frere,	
	To do weyl þan myзt he lere.	well; learn
4305	зyf hyt be nat þan redy, hys dyner,	
	Take furþe þe chesse or þe tabler;	game of chess or backgammon
	So shal he pley tyl hyt be none,	noon (or the hour of nones)
	And Goddys servyse be al done.	finished
	Alas, wykkedly he dyspendyþ	wastes
4310	Alle þe lyfe þat God hym sendyth.	
	Aftyr þe none, þan shal he do	
	As he dede before none so.	
	Swyche a lyfe þan shal he lede:	
	Noght þat he shal have to mede.	Nothing shall he have as reward
4315	Yn alle hys lyfe shal he nat fynde	
	Oght þat nay hym of pyne unbynde.	Anything that could loose him from torment
	No more he halt to God cunnaunt,	keeps to; covenant
	But weyl more to Termagaunt;[5]	the devil
	He ys no more a Crystyn man	
4320	Þan whoso kallyþ a blak oxe 'swan'.	
	Y dar weyl seye to hygh and logh,	the high and the low
	Yn Goddys servyse are swych men slogh;	
	Swych synne men kalle 'accyde'	accidie (sloth)
	Yn Goddes servyse slogh betyde.	sloth happens
4325	Lord! What shal swych men seye	
	Yn þat poynt when þey shul deye?	At that point
	Yn alle here lyfe ne reyght þey noght	they did not care
	Of hym þat hem ful dere boght.	For him who so dearly redeemed them
	Ful gretly shul þey hem repente	

---

4 *bedys* can mean prayers or rosary beads here.   5 Termagaunt is a fictional Islamic deity.

4330 Whan þe Dome ys aȝens hem went; — *Judgement goes against them*
But þan mow þey do no bote; — *might make no remedy then*
Ylyche logh lyþ boþe hande and fote. — *Similar to*
    Many swyche mow have no grace
To repentaunce, no to space; — *nor any time*
4335 Hyt ys no wundyr þogh þey have noun,
Þey wyl nat graunte þey have mysdoun — *done wrong*
Yn here lyfe, whyle þey have myght. — *have the ability*
And þan shal God ȝelde alle with ryght. — *repay*
Ful slogh þey were when þey shuld wyrk,
4340 Yn tyme of traveyle were þey yrk, — *work-time; slow*
Þey þoght nat of þat men spelle, — *words*
Þat God seyþ yn þe Gospelle:
'Beþ wakyng,' he seyþ, to men alle; — *'Be vigilant'*
'What tyme þat ȝoure Lorde wyl kalle,
4345 For þat tyme þat ȝe leste wene — *you least know*
He wul ȝow kalle. Loke ȝe be clene;
For ȝyf ȝe slepe at hys kallyng,
Ȝe shul nat come yn at þe weddyng.'[6]
    Þys yche Lorde kalleþ us every day, — *same*
4350 Wyþ þe prechour, alle þat he may.
Ȝe are slogh, and lyen to slepe,
Whan ȝe aȝens þe prechur þrepe. — *the preacher rebukes you*
Ȝe mow nat come ynto þe weddyng –
Hevene blys ys þe menyng –
4355 For ȝe slepe yn wykked wyl,
And wyl nat shryve ȝow of ȝoure yl. — *be confessed; wickedness*
Ȝe wene þat God shal ȝow ȝeve — *think; give*
Yn wykkednes, long to leve; — *live*
And ȝe here seye þat sum whyle,
4360 Yn swyche hope goþ moche gyle.[7] — *evil*
    A lytyl tale Y shal ȝow undo — *reveal*
Of a man þat hoped so,
As tellyþ þe holy man, Seynt Bede,
Yn gestys of Ingland þat men rede. — *tales*

(There follows a tale from Bede's Ecclesiastical History, *V.3, of a squire who put off his confession and repentance until it was too late, and he was condemned to hell. This is succeeded by 'A Warning against Tourmaments'.)*

A Warning against Tournaments

Of tournamentys þat are forbede — *forbidden*
Yn holy cherche, as men rede,
Of tournamentys Y preve þerynne, — *prove*
Sevene poyntes of dedly synne:
4575 Fyrst ys pryde, as þou wel wost,
Avauntement, bobaunce, and bost; — *Boasting; showing off; bragging*
Of ryche atyre ys here avaunce, — *promotion*
Prykyng here hors with olypraunce. — *Spurring; ostentation*
Wete þou wel þyr ys envye — *know; there*

---

6 Matthew 24.42.

7 People hope to leave their confession until the last minute.

4580	Whan one seeþ anoþer more maystrye,	*more superior*
	Oþer yn wurdys, oþer yn dedys,	
	Envye moste of alle hem ledys.	
	Yre and wraþþe may þey nat late;	*anger; leave off*
	Ofte are tournamentys made for hate.	
4585	ȝyf every knyȝt lovede oþer weyl,	
	Tournamentes shulde be never a deyl;	
	And certys þey falle yn sloghnes,	
	Þey love hyt more þan God or messe.	
	And þerof ys hyt no doute,	
4590	Þey dyspende more gode þeraboute,	*in this*
	(þat ys ȝeve al to folye)	*folly*
	Þan to any dede of mercy.	
	And ȝyt may nat, on no wyse,	*in any way*
	Be forȝete Dame Coveytyse,	*forgotten*
4595	For she shal fonde, on alle wyse,	*attempt*
	To wynne hors and harnyse.	
	And ȝyt shal he make sum robbery,	
	Or bygyle hys hoste þer he shal lye.	*be a guest*
	Glotonye also ys hem among,	
4600	Delycyus metes to make hem strong;	*food*
	And drynke þe wyne þat he were lyght,	
	Wyþ glotonye to make hym wyght.	*brave*
	ȝyt ys þere Dame Lecherye:	
	Of here cumþ alle here maystrye.	
4605	Many tymes, for wymmen sake,	
	Knyghteys tournamentys make;	
	And whan he wendyþ to þe tournament	*go*
	She sendyþ hym sum pryvy present,	*secret*
	And byt hym do for hys lemman	*sweetheart*
4610	Yn vasselage alle þat he kan;	*prowess*
	So ys he bete þere, for here love,	*beaten*
	Þat he ne may sytte hys hors above,	
	Þat peraventure, yn alle hys lyve,	
	Shal he never aftyr þryve.	*thrive*
4615	Loke now whedyr swyche tourneours	*jousters*
	Mow be kalled turmentours:	*tormentors*
	For þey turmente alle with synne;	
	Þere tourment ys, þer shul þey ynne,	*where*
	But þey leve swyche myschaunce,	*Unless*
4620	And for here synne do penaunce.	
	Also Y telle by justyng,	*about*
	Þerof cumþ myschefful þyng:	
	Alle ys þe toon with þe touþer	*one with the other*
	As a shyppe þat ys turned with þe roþer.	*rudder*
4625	And þese bourdys of þese squyers,	*games*
	Also have þey made for swyche maners	*habits*
	Of pryde, hate, and envye;	
	Sloghnes, coveytyse, and glotonye;	
	Lecherye makþ hem alle to bygynne:	
4630	Þese wymmen are partyners of þere synne.	
	A clerk of order þat haþ þe name,	
	ȝyf he juste, he ys to blame,	*joust*

Hyt were wurþy þat had þe gre,   *as well; prize*
Brokyn þe arme, or lege, or thee;   *leg; thigh*
4635   Hyt ys forsoþe, ȝyf he so werche,
Aȝens þe state of holy cherche.
   Hyt ys forbode hym, yn þe decre,[8]
Myracles for to make or se;   *miracle plays*
For myracles ȝyf þou bygynne,
4640   Hyt ys a gaderyng, a syght of synne.   *gathering*
He may yn þe cherche, þurgh þys resun,
Pley þe resurreccyun,
Þat ys to seye, how God ros,   *rose*
God and man yn myȝt and los,   *glory*
4645   To make men be yn beleve gode   *true belief*
Þat he ros with flesshe and blode.
And he may pleye withoutyn plyght   *guilt*
Howe God was bore yn ȝole nyght,   *Christmas*
To make men to beleve stedfastly
4650   Þat he lyght yn þe Vyrgyne Mary.
   Ȝif þou do hyt yn weyys or grevys,   *in roads or; graveyards*
A syght of synne truly hyt semys.
Seynt Isidre, Y take to wyttnes,   *Saint Isidore*
For he hyt seyþ, þat soþe hyt es:
4655   Þus hyt seyþ, yn hys boke,
Þey forsake þat þey toke,
God and here Crystendam,
Þat make swyche pleyys to any man
As myracles and bourdys,   *games*
4660   Or tournamentys of grete prys.
Þese are þe pompes þat þou forsoke,
Fyrst whan þou þy Crystendam toke.   *i.e. baptism*
At þe fonte, seyþ þe lewed man: *uneducated*
'Y forsake þe, here, Satan,
4665   And alle þy pompes and all thy werkys':[9]
Þys ys þy lore, aftyr þe clerkys.
Haldyst þou forward, e, certys nay,
Whan þou makyst swyche adray?   *a disturbance*
Aȝens God þou brekest cunnaunt,
4670   And servyst ȝoure syre, Termagaunt.
Seynt Ysodre seyþ yn hys wrytyng:
'Alle þo þat delyte to se swyche þyng,
Or hors or harneys lenyþ þartyl;   *give to that*
Ȝyt have þey gylt of here peryl.'   *at their peril*
4675   Ȝyf prest or clerk lene vestement   *grant*
Þat halwed ys þurgh sacrament,
More þan ouþer þey are to blame,
Of sacrylege þey have þe fame;
Fame, for þey falle yn plyght,
4680   Þey shuld be chastysed þerfor with ryȝt.
   Daunces, karols, somour games,   *summer*

---

8   i.e. church canons.
9   The words spoken by the person undergoing the baptismal
rite.

Of many swych come many shames;
Whan þou stodyyst to make þyse,   *study; these*
Þou art slogh yn Goddys servyse;   *slothful*
4685   And þat synnen yn swych þurgh þe,
For hem þou shalt acouped be.   *accused of an offence*
　　　What seye ʒe by every mynstral,
Þat yn swyche þynges delyte hem alle?
Here doyng ys ful perylous,
4690   Hyt loveth noþer God ne Goddys house.
Hem were lever here of a daunce,   *they would rather hear*
Of bost, and of olypraunce,   *boasting; ostentation*
Þan any gode of God of hevene,
Or ouþer wysdom þat were to nevene.   *to speak of*
4695   Yn foly ys alle þat þey gete,
Here cloth, here drynke, and here mete.
And, for swych þyng, telle Y shal,
What byfyl onys of a mynstral.   *happened once to*
Seynt Gregorye telleþ yn hys spell: *story*
4700   How hyt of a mynstral fell.

The Tale of the Minstrel Killed for Disturbing a Bishop

A mynstralle, a gulardous,   *teller of ribald tales*
Come onys to a bysshopes hous
And asked þere þe charyte;
Þe porter lete hym have entre.
4705   　　At tyme of mete, þe bourde was leyd,   *table was laid*
And þe benesun shuld be seyd,   *grace*
Þys mynstral made hys melody
With grete noyse, and loude, and hy.
Of þe bysshope þe fame ran
4710   Þat he was an holy man;
Þe bysshope sette hym at þe bourde,
And shuld have blessed hyt with wurde.
So was he sturbled with þe mynstral,   *prevented by*
Þat he hadde no grace to sey withalle   *been given no time*
4715   His graces ryght devoutely
For þe noyse of þe mynstralsy.
　　Þe bysshope pleyned hym ful sore,   *complained*
And seyd to alle þat were þore,   *there*
Þat he ne shulde make hys nycete   *foolishness*
4720   Before the graces of þe charyte.
He sagh hyt weyl, þurgh þe Spyryt,
Þat þer shuld come veniaunce astyt.   *vengeance; at once*
'ʒyveþ hy þe charyte, and latyþ hym go
Hys deþ ys nygh, þat shal hym slo.'   *kill*
4725   He toke charyte, and toke hys gate,   *leave*
And as he passed out at þe ʒate,
A stone fyl down of þe wal,
And slogh þere þe mynstral.   *killed*
　　Þat betokened þat God was noght
4730   Payd of þat þe mynstral wroght;   *Pleased with*
Þat he desturbled þe benesoun

And þe gode mannys devocyoun.

Þys tolde Y for þe glemennes sake,   *singers of tales*
To loke whan þey here gle shul make;
4735 And also for þo þat shuld hyt here,   *those that might hear it*
Þat þey love hyt nat so dere;
Ne have þerynne so grete lykyng,
Þe lesse to wurschyp hevene Kyng.

Why Bishop Grosseteste Loved Music

Y shall ȝow telle, as Y have herd,
4740 Of þe bysshope Seynt Roberd;[10]
Hys toname ys 'Grostest
Of Lynkolne', so seyþ þe gest.   *story*
He loved moche to here þe harpe,
For mannys wytte hyt makyþ sharpe;
4745 Next hys chaumbre, besyde hys stody,   *study*
Hys harpers chaumbre was fast þerby.
Many tymes, be nyȝtys and dayys,
He had solace of notes and layys.
One asked hym onys, resun why
4750 He hadde delyte yn mynstralsy.
He answerede hym on þys manere,
Why he helde þe harpe so dere:
'Þe vertu of þe harpe, þurgh skylle and ryȝt,
Wyl destroye þe fendes myȝt;   *the devil's power*
4755 And to þe croys by gode skylle
Ys þe harpe lykened weyle.

Anoþer poynt cumforteþ me,
Þat God haþ sent unto a tre   *piece of wood*
So moche joye to here with eere;   *ears*
4760 Moche þan more joye ys þere
With God hymselfe, þere he wonys.   *dwells*
Þe harpe þerof me ofte mones   *reminds*
Of þe joye and of þe blys
Where God hymself woneþ and ys.
4765 Þarefor, gode men, ȝe shul lere,   *learn*
Whan ȝe any glemen here,   *songsters*
To wurschep God at ȝoure powere,
As Davyd seyþ yn þe sautere: *Psalter*
"Yn harpe, yn thabour, and symphan gle,   *drum; cymbals (?)*
4770 Wurschepe God, yn troumpes, and sautre,   *sautrie (stringed instrument)*
Yn cordys, yn organes, and bellys ryngyng,   *stringed instrument*
Yn al þese, wurschepe ȝe hevene Kyng."[11]
ȝyf ȝe do þus, Y sey hardly,   *boldly*
ȝe mow here ȝoure mynstralsy.
4775 ȝyf þou lygge long yn synne,
And wylt nat ryse, ne þerof blynne,   *turn aside*

---

10 Robert Grosseteste was a bishop of Lincoln in the thirteenth century. He was concerned with pastoral care, promulgated numerous canons to further pastoral work, particularly through the medium of the vernaculars, and wrote, among other things, the *Chasteau D'Amour*.

11 Psalm 150.

Certeynly, for every oure   *hour*
Þou shalt ȝelde acounte ful soure.   *give a painful account*
For every oure þat þou þeryn lay
4780 Yn purgatorye þou gest þy pay.
Hyt ys sloghnes, and kalled "accyde",
Fro Goddys servyse so long þe hyde.
    And some, alle þe ȝere wyllyn abyde   *year; wait*
Of shryfte tyl þe Lentyn tyde;   *for Lent before confession*
4785 And nygh tyl Lentyn be al gone   *almost*
Mede for fastyng gete þey none;[12]   *Reward*
Þat ys, for sloghnes þey wyl nat ryse;
Lyggyng yn synne ys lore servyse.
    And sum men, yn alle here lyve,
4790 Clenly ne wyle þey hem shryve;   *Thoroughly; confess*
For þey synne alle yn hope of grace
At here endyng, wene þey have space.   *time*
Þan þenke þey to shryve hem clene:
To swyche men, God sheweþ hys tene.   *anger*
4795 Hyt ys seyd al day, for þys skyl: *reason*
"He þat wyl nat whan he may,
He shal nat, when he wyl, have pay."
And þer byþ many one ful evyl to wynne
To any godenes fro vyle synne.   *vile*
4800 Evyl tokyn hyt ys of swyche a man;   *sign*
God hym deme, for Y ne kan.   *God will judge him*
    And þyr are ouþer þat mysdous,   *do wrong*
As a best, for defaute þat goþ lous.   *animal; gets loose*
But whan men teche hem þe wey,
4805 And þey wyl do as men hem sey,
A tokyn hyt ys, þey shul have grace
To come to God, and have space.
And he may hope of evyl endyng
Þat none may to Gode brynge.
4810   A slogh messagere, hys wylland,   *consent*
Þat charged ys wyþ lordes erand,
Ȝyf he go nat as he ys sent,
He ys wurþy to be shent.   *disgraced*
Man þat wel spedyþ hym yn dede,
4815 And messager smart at nede,
Þey shul stonde byfore þe Kyng,
And have mede to here askyng.
    A persone ys slogh yn holy cherche   *parson*
Þat on hys shepe wyl nat werche
4820 How þey shul hemself ȝeme,   *take care of themselves*
And God and holy cherche to queme.   *please*
Þe hyghe Shepard shal hym blame
How he lateþ hem go to shame.
    Ȝyf he se yn anyþyng
4825 Þat þey have defaute of chastysyng,

---

12 If sinners wait until Lent, the time when confession was man-
datory, they are slothful; but they are more so if they wait until Lent
is nearly over so that they do not have to perform the full Lenten
penance of fasting.

But he teche hem and chastyse so   *Unless*
Þat þey forward better do,
For hem he shal, at þe assyse,   *assize (court)*
Be ponysshed before þe hygh Justyse.
4830   Also behoveþ hym, for hem pray,
Þat God, of grace, wysse hem þe wey.   *instruct*
    3yf any of hem defaute has,
And he may helpe hem yn þat kas,   *case*
And wyl nat, for unkyndhede,   *conduct against his nature as a priest*
4835   But late hem perysshe þer for nede,   *their need*
Ful harde acounte shal he 3elde   *yield*
Þat he ne my3t helpe whan he welde.   *governed them*
    3yf he kyndly undyrstode,
Of hem he haþ al hys gode.
4840   For God seyþ yn þe gospel þys,
Upbreydyng hem when þey do mys,   *wrong*
Þe mylke, þe wulle, þey wyl receyve;
And syþþen þe shepe þey wyle late weyve,   *stray*
Holy wryte swyche men holdes
4845   As wylde wulves brekyng foldes.   *sheep-folds*
Swyche a persone ys ful slogh,
Be he hygh, or be he logh.
    Man or womman þat haþ a chylde
Þat wyþ unþewys wexyþ wylde,   *bad habits; grows up*
4850   Þat wyl boþe myssey and do,   *speak and act badly*
Chastysment behoveþ þarto;   *is required*
But 3e hem chastyse at 3oure my3t,
3e falle, ellys, for hem yn ply3t.
Better were þe chylde unbore
4855   Þan fayle chastysyng, and syþþen lore.
Þus seyth þe wys kyng Salamonn
To men and wymmen everychonn: *each one*
    "Wyle 3e þat 3oure chylder be aferd,   *children*
3eveþ hem þe smert ende of þe 3erde;   *stick*
4860   And techeþ hem gode þewys echone;   *habits*
3yt dur 3ow breke hem no bone." '   *But don't dare break any bones*

THE CHRONICLE

Robert Mannyng's *Chronicle* is extant in three manuscripts, all of which are considerably later than the date of the text itself, which was finished in 1338, according to Mannyng's closing lines. The manuscripts are London, Inner Temple Library, Petyt 511, vol. 7, dated to the last quarter of the fourteenth century, which may have originated in the Lincolnshire area; London, Lambeth Palace, Lambeth 131, dated to the second quarter of the fifteenth century; and the fragment, Oxford, Bodleian Library, Rawlinson Misc. D. 913, which may date to *c.* 1400.[13]

The earliest manuscript, Petyt 511, is written in a south Lincolnshire dialect, which accords with what Mannyng tells us about himself: that he lived within the Gilbertine order at Sempringham, having originally come from Bourne in Lincolnshire.[14] He began his translation of *The Chronicle* some time after beginning his work on *Handlyng Synne*, perhaps in the 1320s. His main sources for his historical verse narrative were the Anglo-Norman *Brut* of Wace, originally written in the middle of the twelfth century, and Pierre Langtoft's early fourteenth-century French *Chronicle*, though Mannyng also consulted other historical sources available to him. The most extensive manuscript of Mannyng's national *Chronicle* has just over 24,000 lines of verse covering the events of English monarchical history. This history extends from the Flood in the Old Testament Book of Genesis, followed by Brutus's settlement in England after the fall of Troy, up to the year 1338 in the reign of Edward III.

Two short extracts are edited here. The first is lines 1–202, of which lines 1–198 occur uniquely in Petyt 511. In this extract, essentially a Prologue, Mannyng outlines his sources, and thereby demonstrates his knowledge of the tradition in which he writes; and his reasons for compiling his narrative. He reveals that he is writing for 'love of the unlearned person' out of a desire to make accessible the deeds of the greatest of British and English kings. By inscribing his intentions, his methods and sources, and his name into the narrative, Mannyng shows that he is highly conscious of his role as writer. He uses octosyllabic rhyming couplets in this first part of *The Chronicle* where he is following Wace's form in the *Brut*. Longer verse rhyming couplets occur in part II, where he generally follows Langtoft. He criticizes earlier English verse writers whose style is difficult to understand.

From the second section of the poem, the Battle of Hastings and coronation of William is edited below. The excerpt follows the Battle of Stamford Bridge, in which Harold defeats the invading Norsemen, immediately prior to the Battle of Hastings. Mannyng stops at this point in his *Chronicle* to reiterate why Harold and William fought over the crown of England after Edward the Confessor's death.

The Chronicle

Lines 1–202

	Lordynges þat be now here,	
	If ȝe wille listene and lere	*learn*
	Alle þe story of Inglande	
	Als Robert Mannyng wryten it fand,	*found it written*
5	And on Inglysch has it schewed,	
	Not for þe lerid, bot for þe lewed;	*learned; uneducated*
	For þo þat in his land won	*live*
	Þat þe Latyn no Frankys con,	*that know no*
	For to haf solace and gamen	*entertainment*
10	In felawschip when þai sitt samen.	*together*
	And it is wisdom forto wytten	
	Þe state of þe land and haf it wryten:	
	What manere of folk first it wan	
	And of what kynde it first began.	
15	And gude it is for many thynges	
	For to here þe dedis of kynges –	
	Whilk were foles and whilk were wyse,	*Which; fools*
	And whilk of þam couth mast quantyse,	*intelligence*

---

13 Edited recently by I. Sullens in a parallel text version: *Robert Mannyng of Brunne: The Chronicle*, MRTS 153 (Binghampton, 1996). Detailed information about Mannyng himself, the manuscripts, his sources, language and influence can be found in Sullens's Introduction, pp. 1–76.

14 Sullens, *The Chronicle*, pp. 4–5.

And whilk did wrong and whilk ryght,

20 And whilk mayntend pes and fyght.

Of þare dedes salle be my sawe;   *speech*

And what tyme and of what lawe

I salle ȝow schewe fro gre to gre   *step by step*

Sen þe tyme of Sir Noe,   *After; Noah*

25 Fro Noe unto Eneas,

And what betwix þam was.

And fro Eneas tille Brutus tyme,

Þat kynde he telles in þis ryme,

Fro Brutus tille Cadwaladres,[15]

30 Þe last Bryton þat þis lande lees: *lost*

Alle þat kynde and alle þe frute

Þat come of Brutus, þat is þe *Brute*.   *The* Brut *of Wace*

And þe ryght *Brute* is told nomore

Þan þe Brytons tyme wore;   *When; had passed*

35 After þe Bretons þe Inglis camen,

Þe lordschip of þis lande þai namen.   *seized*

South and north, west and est,

Þat calle men now þe Inglis gest: *geste or chronicle*

When þai first amang þe Bretons

40 Þat now ere Inglis, þan were Saxons.

Saxons, Inglis hight alle oliche,   *similarly*

Þai aryved up at Sandwyche

In þe kynges tyme, Vortogerne[16]

Þat þe lande walde þam not werne,   *controlled; prevented*

45 Þat were maysters of alle þe togider:

Hengist he hight, and Hors his broþire,[17]

Þes were hede, als we fynde,

Whereof is comen oure Inglis kynde.

A hundreth and fifty ȝere þai com

50 Or þai receyved Cristendom;   *Before*

So lang woned þai þis lande in

Or þai herde out of Saynt Austyn.[18]

Amang þe Bretons with mykelle wo,   *great*

In sclaundire, in threte, and in thro,   *strife*

55 Þes Inglis dedes ȝe may here

As Pers telles alle þe manere.   *Pierre Langtoft*

One mayster Wace þe Frankes telles

Þe Brute, alle þat þe Latyn spelles,   *narrative (of Geoffrey of Monmouth)*

Fro Eneas tille Cadwaladre.

60 Þis mayster Wace þer leves he;

And ryght as mayster Wace says,

I telle myn Inglis þe same ways,

For mayster Wace þe Latyn alle rymes

Þat Pers overhippis many tymes.   *skips over*

65 Mayster Wace þe Brute alle redes,   *describes*

And Pers tellis alle þe Inglis dedes;

Þer Mayster Wace of þe Brute left,

---

15   Brutus, legendary founder of Britain; Cadwalader, a seventh-century king of the Britons.

16   A king of the Britons at the end of the Roman rule in Britain.

17   Hengist and Horsa, the two Saxon chiefs who, according to Bede's *Ecclesiastical History*, arrived as mercenaries in the fifth century.

18   Saint Augustine arrived in 597 and began the Christianization of the Anglo-Saxons in the kingdom of Kent.

Ryght begynnes Pers eft,   *after*
And tellis forth þe Inglis story,
70   And as he says þan say I.   *then so*
    Als þai haf wryten and sayd
Haf I alle in myn Inglis layd
In symple speche, as I couth,
Þat is lightest in mannes mouth.
75   I mad noght for no disours,   *story tellers*
Ne for no seggers, no harpours,   *minstrels*
Bot for þe luf of symple men
Þat strange Inglis can not ken.   *understand*
For many it here þat strange Inglis
80   In ryme, wate never what it is;   *don't know*
And bot þai wist what it mente,   *unless*
Ellis me thoght it were alle schente;   *pointless*
I made it not forto be praysed,
Bot at þe lewed men were aysed.   *eased*
85   If it were made in ryme couwee,   *tail rhyme verse*
Or in strangere or enterlace,   *stanzas; complicated rhyme*
Þat rede Inglis it ere inowe
Þat couthe not haf coppled a kowe,   *completed a couplet*
Þat outhere in couwee or in baston,   *stanza*
90   Som suld haf ben fordon,   *come to grief*
So þat fele men þat it herde   *many*
Suld not witte howe þat it ferde.   *went*
I see in song, in sedgeyng tale   *a written tale*
Of Erceldoun and of Kendale:[19]
95   Non þam says as þai þam wroght,
And in þer sayng it semes noght.
Þat may þou here in Sir Tristrem,[20]
Over gestes it has þe steem   *worth*
Over alle þat is or was,
100   If men it sayd as made Thomas.
Bot I here it no man so say
Þat of som copple, som is away.   *couplets*
So þare fayre sayng here beforn,
Is þare travayle nere forlorn;   *work; wasted*
105   Þai sayd it for pride and nobleye
Þat non were suylk as þei,   *such*
And alle þat þai wild overwhere,   *would; everywhere*
Alle þat ilk wille now forfare.   *same*
Þai sayd in so quante Inglis   *quaint*
110   Þat manyone wate not what it is;   *many did not know*
Þerfore hevyed wele þe more   *weighed down*
In strange ryme to travayle sore;   *labour sorrowfully*
And my witte was ovre thynne,   *knowledge was ever scanty*
So strange speche to travayle in.
115   And forsoth I couth noght   *could not do*
So strange Inglis as þai wroght.
And men besoght me many a tyme   *asked*

---

19   Minstrels of Erceldoune and Kendale who spoil their stories by elaborate versification and expression.

20   The Middle English Romance.

To turne it bot in light ryme;

Þai sayd if I in strange it turne,

120   To here it manyon suld skurne,   *scorn*

For it ere names fulle selcouth   *words; peculiar*

Þat ere not used now in mouth.

    And þerfore for þe comonalte   *common person*

Þat blythely wild listen to me,

125   On light lange I it began   *language*

For luf of þe lewed man;   *love of the common man*

To telle þam þe chaunces bolde   *them; events*

Þat here before was don and tolde.

For þis makyng I wille no mede   *desire no reward*

130   Bot gude prayere when ȝe it rede.

Þerfore ȝe lordes lewed

For wham I haf þis Inglis schewed,

Prayes to God he gyf me grace: *Praise; give me grace*

I travayled for ȝour solace.

135   Of Brunne I am if any me blame,

Robert Mannyng is my name.

Blissid be he of God of heven

Þat me, Robert, with gude wille neven.   *nephew*

In þe thrid Edwardes tyme was I   *Edward III's*

140   When I wrote alle þis story.

In þe hous of Sixille I was a throwe;²¹   *while*

Danȝ Robert of Malton, þat ȝe know,

Did it wryte for felawes sake

When þai wild solace make.

145   Dares þe Freson of Troie first wrote   *Dares the Phrygian*

And putt it in buke þat we now wote;

He was a clerk and a gude knyght.

When Troie was lorn, he sawe þat fight.   *lost*

Alle þe barons wele he knewe:

150   He tellis þer stature and þer hewe,

Long or schorte, whyte or blak,

Alle he telles gude or lak.   *bad*

Alle þer lymmes how þai besemed,   *limbs; appeared*

In his buke has Dares demed,   *judged*

155   Both of Troie and of Grece,

What kyns schappe was ilka pece.   *What shape; bit*

Of manyon he reknes and sayes,

Both of Troiens and of Gregeis,   *Trojans; Greeks*

Þat it were over long to telle;

160   And many wald not þerin duelle   *remain*

Þare names alle for to here.

    Bot þe Latyn is fayre to lere:

Geffrey Arthure of Minumue²²

Fro Breton speche he did remue   *extract*

165   And made it alle in Latyn

Þat clerkes haf now knawyng in.

In Gloucestre was fonden a buke

---

21 The Gilbertine house at Sixhills in Lincolnshire where Mannyng   22 Geoffrey of Monmouth, the twelfth-century writer of the *Historia*
went after his years at Sempringham.   *Regum Brittaniae.*

Þat þe Inglis couthe not rede no luke.
On þat langage þai knew no herde,
170 Bot an erle þat hyght Roberde,
He prayed þat ilk clerk Geffrey
To turne it fro þat speche away
Into Latyn, as it mente
Þat þe Inglis mot know þe entente;   *purpose*
175 For Geffrey knew þe langage wele,
In Latyn he broght it ilka dele.   *each section*
     Siþen com a clerk, Mayster Wace,
To make romance had he grace,
And turned it fro Latyne
180 And rymed it in Frankis fyne,
Unto þe Cadwaladres –
No forer, þer makes he ses.   *further; the end*
Als Geffrey in Latyn sayd,
So Mayster Wace in Frankis layd.
185 Þe date of Criste was þan þis lyve,
A thousand ʒere fifty and fyve.
Than com out of Brydlyngton
Pers of Langtoft, a chanon.   *Pierre; canon*
Als Mayster Wace þe same he says,
190 Bot he rymed it oþer ways.
He begynnes at Eneas,
Of alle þe *Brute* he tellis þe pas.   *each step*
And siþen alle þe Inglis dedis:
Feyrere langage non ne redis.
195 After þe Inglis kynges, he says þer pris,   *chief examples*
Þat alle in metir fulle wele lys.   *metrical poetry*
     And I, Robert, fulle fayn wald bringe   *very happily*
In Ynglis tonge þer faire saiynge.
God gyf me grace wele to spede
200 Þis ryme on Inglis forto rede.
Now of þe story wille we gynne
When God toke wreke of Caym synne.[23]   *revenge for Cain's sin*

{The Battle of Hastings}[24]

Listen and I salle rede why þe misaventoure
1665 On Harald side gan sprede þorgh William Conqueroure.   *afterwards began*
The duke of Normundie, William is his name,
Wolnoth, Haraldes broþer he had in prisoun at Kame,   *Caen*
And his nevow, Hakon, in preson was him with –   *nephew*
I ne wote for what reson so fer out of þer kith.   *their country*
1670   Harald, whan he was ʒonge, he went unto France,
Þe cuntre forto see, and forto here of chance.   *events*
All his mishappyng felle, he com in to Pountif,   *misadventure*
To Richere þat was erle, men told it fulle rif.   *correctly*
Þis lord of Pountif, Richer le Fitʒ Jhoun
1675 He tok þis ilk Harald and did him in presoun;   *put*

---

23 Cain's sin of fratricide ultimately resulted in the Flood. This,   24 Part II of the *Chronicle*.
then, is Mannyng's starting point.

Þe bode of him sone kam to þe duke of Normundie. *news*
   Þe duke went to Pountif and toke him with maistrie *authority*
And brouht Harald home and seid þorgh curteisie:
'Harald, haf now þin eyse in alle my seignorie.' *ease; domain*

1680
Now has Harald his eyse at reson in alle þing:
Þe meyne in alle þing plesed him next þe kyng.[25] *servants; William*
   William and Harald went þam for to play, *entertain themselves*
Tales togider þei tald, ilk on a gode palfray. *each; horse*
Whan þei had wele riden þat þam þouht right lang,

1685
Þei lighted and abiden biside a water strang. *remained*
'Harald,' said William, 'listen to my resoun,
What right þat I have of Inglond þe coroun
After Edwardes dede, if it so betide *death; happens*
Þat God haf ordeynd, so I after him abide. *remain*

1690
Whan þat we were ȝonge, Edward þe kyng and I,
He was in my fader courte exiled, I ne wote whi, *I don't know why*
Out of Inglond; þan suore he to me,
If he þe coroun mot wynne, his heyre suld I be. *heir should I be*
Þerof he mad me skrite, his hote to mak leale, *document; decision; legal*

1695
And for to sikere his dede, set þerto his seale. *authenticate*
   Harald, whan þou ses tyme, do þi help þerto;
I salle delyver þi broþer and þi nevow also,
And Marie, my douhter, to wife I wille þe gyve.
A man I salle þe make richely forto lyve,

1700
Or my chefe justise, þe lawes to mend and right;
Þi sistere I salle gyve a riche prince of myght.'
   'Sire,' said Harald, 'I shalle, if þat I may,
Help þe þe coroun to hald if ever I se þat day. *to the crown*
My broþer delyver þou me, my nevow þou me grante,

1705
And hold þi certeynte and salle hold covenante.' *agreement; promise*
   Þe presons forth were fette tille Harald or he foore; *prisoners; before long*
To hold þat he had hette, on þe boke he suore. *promised*
Now gos he home, Harald, and has overcomen his tene;[26] *grief*
Þe othe þat he suld hold, it is forgeten clene.

1710
   Edward is dede, allas; messengers overwent
To William; Harald was þorgh comon assent
Was corouned nobly and for kyng þei him helde; *crowned*
Bot þe duke of Normundie, to William felle þe schelde. *symbol of government*
Þe duke wrote to þe kyng, in luf withouten loth, *hatred*

1715
Bisouht him over alle þing þat he wild hold his oth *keep to his oath*
And ȝeld him þe coroun of Inglond ilka dele, *yield him all*
Or Marie to warisoun, wed hir and joy it wele. *Before marrying*
And if he wild not so, he suld mak him oknowen *acknowledge*
He suld wynne it, fordo in right as for his owen. *or be destroyed*

1720
   Harald wrote ageyn and seid he never þouht
Marie to wedde certeyn, þe lond hight him nouht; *he did not promise*
And if he wild it wynne with dynt als duke hardie, *battle as a*
He suld fynd þerinne Kyng Harald redie.
Ȝit is Harald, I say, regnand in myght and mayn;

1725
Þe kyng of Norway in bataile has he slayn.

---

25 William had been made heir to Edward the Confessor, king of England.

26 Grief (or anger) at not being heir, presumably, and being forced into a promise of assistance to William.

Þe duke forto geten his riȝt of þat Harald hette,   *get his right; promised*
Now is he in þe see with saile on mast upsette;
Toward þis lond þei drouh to aventure his chance   *chance this event*
With Normandes inouh and of Flandres and of France.   *enough Normans*
1730   He had redy sailyng þat to þe lond him ledde,
And at his rivyng, þe lond non him forbedde.   *arriving; prohibit*
    His folk went up to lond, himselven was þe last;
To bank over þe sond, plankes þei over kast.   *As a; shore*
Als William þeron suld go, he stombled at a nayle,
1735   Into þe waise þam fro, he tombled top over taile.   *mire; head over heels*
His knyghtis up him lyft and did him eft atire,
William was oglyft, his helm was fulle of myre;   *afraid; helmet; slime*
William was not paied, þat falle mad him ofright.   *pleased*
He stode alle dismaied, þan said tille him a knyght:
1740   'Discomfort noþing þe, so faire happe never þou fond;   *such good luck*
Stoupe and þou may se, þi helm has wonne lond.   *Bend down; won the*
Þat þe lond is þin, þi helm schewes it þe.
Forsuorn is Harald, he salle no dure.'   *will not be daring enough*
    Whan William alle was dight and to þe boun,   *equipped; armed*
1745   Redy with him to fight, he fond Harald fulle sone.   *quickly*
He fond fulle wele and sone þat Harald nouht ne slepe;   *had not slept*
To prove with dede to done, fulle wakand on him lepe.   *alertly; leapt*
To bataile haf þei mynt, Harald and William,   *intent*
Bot non stode Harald dynt þat bifor him kam;[27]   *withstood; blows*
1750   Þe rouht of þare rascaile he did it rere and ryme,[28]
Normanȝ and Flemmyng taile he kutted many tyme.   *vanguard*
To while þat he was fresch, þei fond him fulle austere;
Þei felt of his pruesse, als knyght did his devere,   *prowess; duty*
For he was over prest and egre to assaile,   *ever advancing; eager*
1755   He wild haf no rest tille he myght travaile.   *while he could labour*
    Allas for Sir Harald, for him was mikelle reuth;   *a great pity*
Fulle wele his awen suld hald, if he had kept his treuth.   *kept*
Bot þat he was forsuorn, mishappyng þerfor he fond,   *because; lied; bad luck*
Suld he never els haf lorn for William no lond,   *lost because of*
1760   Ne we bien in þat bondage þat brouht was over þe se;
Now ere þei in servage, fulle fele þat or was fre.[29]
Our fredom þat day forever toke þe leve;   *its leave*
For Harald it went away, his falshed did us greve.[30]   *lie caused us harm*
    He was so fer in presse, so fele wer him about,   *advanced; were*
1765   Him befor alle þei ches þat he suld not skape out.   *chased; escape*
Normanȝ and Burgolons with lance, suerd, and mace
Bare Sir Harald doun; allas, he had no grace.   *was given no mercy*
So douhty knyght of dede was non of noiþer sides;   *bold; either*
Þore to dede he ȝede als man forsuorn betides.[31]
1770   Nien monethes beforn kept Harald þe regalle,   *monarchy*
Bot þat he was forsuorn, þerfor he lost alle.   *because; committed perjury*
Out of þe stoure þar stode tuo man skaped ware,   *combat*
Of Sir Haraldes blode, Eadwyn and Morkare.
Þei tok þe Quene Edith for doute of treson,   *in fear of accusations*

27   Harold and William intended battle. No one could withstand
Harold's blows as he advanced.
28   He forced the foot soldiers (rascaile = rabble) to withdraw and
retreat.

29   Now they are in servitude, very many who were previously free.
30   This is a very pro-English response to the Conquest.
31   There in action he went forward as a man who had happened to
perjure himself (or been renounced).

1775	Was Kyng Edwardes wif, led hir to Kelion.	*Carlisle*
	Wele was scho þer to hold prive sojorne;	*temporary stay*
	Eadwyn and Morkare to London gan þei turne,	
	Unto þe Londreis þei told þat þei had fonden an hayre,	*Londoners; heir*
	Was Edmund kosyn þe kyng; þe Londreis wer in speyr	*of the king; hope*
1780	Him for þar kyng uplift, his name was kald Edgar.	*elect as king*
	For William þei wer oglift and said: 'Þat we ne dar;	*afraid; dare*
	For slayn is Kyng Harald, and in lond may non be	*no one can stay here*
	Bot he of William hald for homage and feaute.'	*unless; fealty*
	Morkar recleymed es, as es þe faukon fre,	*falcon*
1785	And Eadwyn com to pes, he mot no better se;	*peace; no alternative*
	Þe burgeis of London þar conseile wild it nouht	*citizens; would not agree*
	To gif Edgar þe coroun þat for heyr þei brouht.	
	William þe Conquerour to London has he þouht,	
	Þer þe bataile was stoure, an abbay wild he haf wrouht;	*fought; have built*
1790	Þer he and Harald mette, þer standes þe kirke,[32]	*where*
	For blode þat þer was gette, to praie þei suld not irke.	*spilt; shirk*
	To London com William his 3ole feste to hold,	*Christmas (Yuletide)*
	His barons with him nam, knyghtes þat wer bold.	*took*
	Wardeyns of tour and toun, and oþer þat ne wold	
1795	Þar landes les alle doun, for tynt wer þei told;	*lay; destruction*
	To Frankis and Norman3 for þar grete laboure,	
	To Flemmynges and Pikardes þat wer with him in stoure,	
	He gaf londes bityme, of whilk þer successoure	
	Hold 3it þe seysyne with fulle grete honoure.	*Hold yet legal possession*
1800	Fair grace William fond, his chance fulle wele him satte,	
	Þe reame of Inglond so graciously he gatte.	*obtained*
	Þe Archbisshop Stigand, of Inglond primate,	*chief ecclesiastic*
	Þat tyme was suspended, þe Pape reft him þe state;[33]	*deprived*
	And abbot and prioure, men of religion,	*prior*
1805	And oþer men of honour, archdecane and person,	*parson*
	Wer prived of þar office, of woulfes had renoun	*deprived; wolves*
	For lichorie, þat vice, wer many als don doun.	
	Þe archbisshop of 3ork com with devocioun,	
	Þorgh William praiere com to London toun.	
1810	Bifor þe barons brouht, he gaf William þe coroun;	
	To chalange was he nouht, Sir Stigand was don doun.	
	Whan William was coruned kyng so solemply	
	And had taken homage of barons bi and bi,	
	He turned over þe se unto Normundi;	
1815	Dam Helienore, quene was sche, scho bare him company.	
	When he had duelled þore, at Pask he com ageyn,	*stayed there; Easter*
	And Dam Helianore, with many knyght and sueyn,	*retainers*
	To London alle þei went, þe courte holy alle pleyn.	
	For þe archbishop þei sent, messengers 3ede tueyn.	*two*
1820	Elred, þe archbisshop of 3ork, had þe se;	*diocese*
	Þe kyng him bisouht als clerk of dignite:	*asked*
	'To coroune Helianore, þat biseke I þe.'	
	Þe bisshop corouned hir þore bifor þat faire semble.	*noble crowd*

---

32   Battle Abbey in Sussex.
33   Stigand was deprived of his archiepiscopacy by the Conqueror.
Lanfranc, abbot of Bec in Normandy, replaced him.

Whan þe folk had bien at þe coronment ilk dele,

1825 · Boþe þe kyng and þe quene þe barons paied wele. *repaid*

Þe kyng and þe clergie ordeynd þat ilk seele *royal document*

Þe pes to ȝeme and gyve with lawes trewe als stele. *preserve*

The Land of Cockayne

The Land of Cockayne was probably composed in Ireland originally, and has associations with both Waterford and Kildare. The poem is included in London, British Library, Harley 913, folios 3 recto to 6 verso, dated to *c*.1330.[1] The manuscript may have been put together by a Franciscan friar, and this might go a long way to explaining the satirical references to monks and nuns in *The Land of Cockayne*. There are numerous Latin texts in the manuscript, but among the other English texts is a 'Satire on the People of Kildare', and a number of didactic and catechetical works.

The Land of Cockayne, written in couplets, may be classified as a parody of Utopian texts that dwell on the wondrous nature of the ideal world. There are both French and Dutch analogous texts, but much of the detail belongs to the Middle English adaptor. Here, essentially, the characteristics of Utopian texts are turned around to produce a dystopic view of an earthly Paradise: one where rivers flow with medicinal drinks; the abbey is constructed from edible materials; roast geese fly about calling 'Geese, all hot!'; monks can fly like birds of prey; and monks and nuns have regular orgies. The poem is a lively depiction of a topsy-turvy contemporary world, but is one that draws on common motifs and language to create its effect; for example, the penance undertaken by those wishing to enter the Land of Cockayne is to wade for seven years in pig dung; to stand eternally in dung was, in non-orthodox homiletic literature, a punishment of one hell set aside especially for liars. Whether this text is more comedic than didactic is a matter for debate: its tone and content are certainly amusing, but its emphases and manuscript context suggest that the intention of the author was both to entertain and to moralize.

The Land of Cockayne

	Fur in see bi west Spayngne	*Far*
	Is a lond ihote Cockaygne:	*called*
	Þer nis lond under hevenriche	*heavenly kingdom*
	Of wel, of godnis, hit iliche.	*like*
5	Þoȝ Paradis be miri and briȝt,	
	Cockaygn is of fairir siȝt.	
	What is þer in Paradis	
	Bot grasse and flure and grene ris?	*branch*
	Þoȝ þer be joi and gret dute,	*pleasure*
10	Þer nis met bote frute;	*food*
	Þer nis halle, bure, no bench,	*bedroom*
	Bot watir manis þurst to quench;	
	Beþ þer no men bot two,	
	Hely and Enok also;	*Elijah*
15	Elinglich mai hi go	*Miserably*
	Whar þer woniþ men no mo.	*live*
	In Cokaigne met and drink	
	Wiþute care, how, and swink.	*care; work*
	Þe met is trie, þe drink is clere,	*excellent*
20	To none, russin, and sopper.	*midday meal; light evening meal*
	I sigge forsoþ, boute were,	*say*
	Þer nis lond on erþe is pere;	*equal*
	Under heven nis lond, iwisse,	*certainly*
	Of so mochil joi and blisse.	
25	Þer is mani swete siȝte:	
	Al is dai, nis þer no niȝte.	
	Þer nis baret noþer strif,	*conflict*
	Nis þer no deþ, ac ever lif;	
	Þer nis lac of met no cloþ,	*clothing*

1   See M. Laing, *A Catalogue of Sources for a Linguistic Atlas of Early Middle English* (Cambridge, 1993), p. 90.

30	Þer nis man no womman wroþ;	*angry*
	Þer nis serpent, wolf, no fox,	
	Hors no capil, kowe no ox;	*nag*
	Þer nis schepe no swine no gote	
	No non horwȝ, la, God it wote,	*dirt*
35	Noþer harace, noþer stode:	*stud farm; stud*
	Þe lond is ful of oþer gode.	
	Nis þer flei, fle, no lowse	*flea*
	In cloþ, in toune, bed, no house;	
	Þer nis dunnir, slete, no hawle,	*thunder*
40	No non vile worme no snawile,	*snail*
	No non storme, rein, no winde,	
	Þer nis man no womman blinde.	
	Ok al is game, joi, and gle –	*But*
	Wel is him þat þer mai be.	
45	Þer beþ rivers gret and fine	
	Of oile, melk, honi, and wine.	
	Watir serviþ þer to noþing	
	Bot to siȝt and to waiissing.	*washing*
	Þer is mani maner frute;	
50	Al is solas and dedute.	*pleasure*
	Þer is a wel fair abbei	
	Of white monkes and of grei;	
	Þer beþ bowris and halles:	
	Al of pasteiis beþ þe walles,	*pasties*
55	Of fleis, of fisse, and rich met,	*flesh*
	Þe likfullist þat man mai et.	
	Fluren cakes beþ þe schingles alle	*Flour; shingles*
	Of cherch, cloister, boure, and halle;	
	Þe pinnes beþ fat podinges,	*nails*
60	Rich met to princeȝ and kinges.	
	Man mai þerof et inoȝ,	*enough*
	Al wiþ riȝt and noy wiþ woȝ.	*misery*
	Al is commune to ȝung and old,	
	To stoute and sterne, mek and bold.	
65	Þer is a cloister, fair and liȝt,	
	Brod and lang, of sembli siȝt;	*beautiful*
	Þe pilers of þat cloister alle	
	Beþ iturned of cristale,	
	Wiþ har bas and capitale	*their; base*
70	Of grene jaspe and rede corale.	
	In þe praer is a tre	*meadow*
	Swiþe likful for to se:	
	Þe rote is gingevir and galingale,	*ginger; aromatic root*
	Þe siouns beþ al sedwale;	*shoots; jedoary (a plant)*
75	Trie maces beþ þe flure,	*Excellent*
	Þe rind canel of swet odur;	*bark; cinammon*
	Þe frute gilofre of gode smakke,	*cloves; flavour*
	Of cucubes þer nis no lakke.	*spicy berries*
	Þer beþ rosis of rede ble,	*hue*
80	And lilie likful forto se;	
	Þai faloweþ never dai no niȝt	
	Þis aȝt be a swet siȝt.	*is bound to*

	Þer beþ iiii willis in þe abbei	*wells*
	Of triacle and halwei,	*ointment; medicine*
85	Of baum, and ek piement;	*balsam; spiced wine*
	Ever ernend to riȝt rent	*running; profit*
	Of þai stremis al þe molde –	*earth*
	Stonis preciuse, and golde.	
	Þer is saphir and uniune,	*pearl*
90	Carbuncle and astiune,	*astrion*
	Smaragde, lugre, and prassiune,	*Emerald; ligure; prasine²*
	Beril, onix, topasiune,	*topaz*
	Ametist and crisolite,	
	Calcedun and epetite.	*Chalcedony; red gems*
95	Þer beþ briddes mani and fale:	*birds; various*
	Þrostil, þruisse, and niȝtingale,	*thrush*
	Chalandre, and wodwale,	*lark*
	And oþer briddes wiþout tale	*number*
	Þat stinteþ never bi har miȝt,	
100	Miri to sing dai and niȝt.	
	Ȝite I do ȝow mo to witte:	*let you know*
	Þe gees irostid on þe spitte	*roasted*
	Fleeȝ to þat abbai, God hit wot,	
	And grediþ: 'Gees, al hote, al hot!'	*cry out*
105	Hi bringeþ garlek, gret plente,	
	Þe best idiȝt þat man mai se.	*dressed*
	Þe leverokes, þat beþ cuþ,	*larks*
	Liȝtiþ adun to manis muþ	
	Idiȝt in stu ful swiþe wel,	*Prepared*
110	Pudrid wiþ gilofre and canel.	*Seasoned with cloves and cinammon*
	Nis no spech of no drink,	*talk*
	Ak take inoȝ wiþute swink.	
	Whan þe monkes gooþ to masse,	
	Al þe fenestres þat beþ of glasse	*windows*
115	Turneþ into cristal briȝt	
	To ȝive monkes more liȝt.	
	Whan þe masses beþ iseiid,	
	And þe bokes up ileiid,	
	Þe cristal turniþ into glasse	
120	In state þat hit raþer wasse.	*was*
	Þe ȝung monkes euch dai	
	Aftir met goþ to plai.	*food*
	Nis þer hauk no fule so swifte	
	Bettir fleing bi þe lifte	*at flying; air*
125	Þan þe monkes, heiȝ of mode,	*high in spirit*
	Wiþ har slevis and har hode.	*sleeves; hood*
	Whan þe abbot seeþ ham flee,	
	Þat he holt for moch glee;	*reckons*
	Ak naþeles, al þeramang,	*thereamong*
130	He biddiþ ham liȝt to evesang.	*come down*
	Þe monkes liȝtiþ noȝt adun;	
	Ac furre fleeþ in o randun.	*fly further; in a rush*
	Whan þe abbot him iseeþ	

---

2   All of these are precious stones.

Þat is monkes fram him fleeþ,

135 He takeþ maidin of þe route, *girls; crowd*

And turniþ up hir white toute *buttocks*

And betiþ þe taburs wiþ is hond *drums*

To make is monkes liʒt to lond.

Whan is monkes þat iseeþ,

140 To þe maid dun hi fleeþ;

And goþ þe wench al abute,

And þakkeþ al hir white toute; *thwacks*

And siþ aftir her swinke *then*

Wendiþ meklich hom to drink, *Go*

145 And goþ to har collacione: *evening meal*

A wel fair processione.

Anoþer abbei is þerbi:

Forsoþ, a gret fair nunnerie,

Up a river of swet milke,

150 Whar is gret plente of silk.

Whan þe someris dai is hote,

Þe ʒung nunnes takiþ a bote *remedy*

And doþ ham forþ in þat river,

Boþe wiþ oris and wiþ stere. *oars; rudder*

155 Whan hi beþ fur fram þe abbei,

Hi makiþ ham nakid forto plei;

And lepiþ dune into þe brimme *water*

And doþ ham sleilich forto swimme.

Þe ʒung monkes þat hi seeþ,

160 Hi doþ ham up and forþ hi fleeþ, *fly*

And commiþ to þe nunnes anon,

And euch monke him takeþ on, *one*

And snellich beriþ forþ har prei *quickly; prey*

To þe mochil grei abbei;

165 And techiþ þe nunnes an oreisun *prayer*

Wiþ jambleve up and dun. *a raised leg*

Þe monke þat wol be stalun gode *stallion*

And kan set ariʒt is hode,

He schal hab wiþoute danger

170 xii wives euch ʒere:

Al þroʒ riʒt and noy þroʒ grace, *by right*

Forto do himsilf solace.

And þilk monke þat slepiþ best,

And doþ his likam al to rest, *body*

175 Of him is hoppe, God hit wote,

To be sone vadir abbot. *father*

Whose wil com þat lond to,

Ful grete penance he mot do:

Seve ʒere in swineis dritte *pigs' dung*

180 He mote wade, wol ʒe iwitte,

Al anon up to þe chynne,

So he schal þe lond winne.

Lordinges gode and hend, *noble*

Mot ʒe never of world wend,

185 Fort ʒe stond to ʒure cheance *Until; risk*

And fulfille þat penance

Þat ʒe mote þat lond ise,
And nevermore turne aʒe.   *away*
Prey we God go mote hit be,
190   Amen, pur seint charite.   *through*

The Auchinleck Manuscript

Edinburgh, National Library of Scotland, Advocates 19. 2. 1, is one of the most famous manuscripts surviving from the medieval period. It is an extensive collection of Middle English, containing forty-four texts, seventeen of which are Romances, but some of which are incomplete (such as *Kyng Alisaunder*). A facsimile of the entire manuscript has an excellent introduction in which the manuscript's creation, contents and history are discussed.[1] Compiled around 1330–40 and copied by six scribes, it was probably made in London in what has been termed a 'bookshop'.[2] It is possible that not only was this bookshop responsible for the copying of the volume, but also some of the texts were actually composed there;[3] some of the texts included in the manuscript are almost certainly by the same author, who may have been commissioned to translate and versify specific works for this collection. The recipients of the manuscript evidently wished to be both instructed and entertained; hence the representation in the codex of Romances, hagiographies, homilies, a chronicle and satirical verse, among other items. Of the hagiographies, for example, both Saint Katherine and Saint Margaret are represented; the Romances include *Amis and Amiloun*, *The King of Tars*, *Guy of Warwick*, *Kyng Alisaunder* and *Sir Orfeo*. As Pearsall and Cunningham state: 'The taste that it appeals to and is designed for is that of the aspirant middle-class citizen, perhaps a wealthy merchant.'[4]

From this manuscript are edited *Sir Orfeo* and *The Four Foes of Mankind*. *Kyng Alisaunder* is also edited below, but is taken from a different manuscript.

SIR ORFEO

Sir Orfeo occurs at folios 299 recto to 303 recto in the Auchinleck Manuscript, immediately after the Romance *Sir Tristrem*, and followed by *The Four Foes of Mankind*. The text itself may well have been composed in the first quarter of the fourteenth century. It occurs in variant versions in two other manuscripts besides the Auchinleck volume: London, British Library, Harley 3810, a manuscript dated to the fifteenth century with an origin in Warwickshire; and Oxford, Bodleian Library, Ashmole 61, a late fifteenth- and early sixteenth-century volume, possibly of north-east Midlands origin. As the first thirty-eight lines are missing in the version in the Auchinleck manuscript, these have to be supplied from later in the manuscript where they reappear as the introduction to another Romance, *The Lay le Freyne*, and from the versions of *Sir Orfeo* in the two later manuscripts.[5]

The poem is a Breton lay, a sub-genre of Romance. Marie de France, a twelfth-century poet, was the first to commit the Breton lay to a written format. Usually the lay would have been accompanied by music and sung by a minstrel, as we are indeed told is the case in *Sir Orfeo* (lines 19–20). Arranged in rhyming couplets, the text has a lyrical quality to it that may reflect the musical origins of the genre. Themes of Breton lays vary from those that revolve around Arthurian knights (such as *Sir Degaré*) to those which involve classical matter. *Sir Orfeo* is a medievalized account of the classical legend of Orpheus and Eurydice, told by Virgil and Ovid, and later recontextualized by Boethius in his *Consolation of Philosophy*.[6] The Middle English version takes this classical legend and transforms it, favouring a happy resolution instead of the tragic, and avoiding the explicit allegorical interpretation placed on the legend by Boethius.

There are numerous proposed sources for parts of *Sir Orfeo*, including a non-extant French lay about the hero. Celtic sources may have played a formative role in the narrative composition, particularly in the account of the fairies and the Otherworld. The poet creates from his sources a contemporary and lively account of the legend, setting the poem in Winchester and identifying it with Thrace; making Orfeo a medieval king with a steward and parliament; and creating a court of the fairies, who enjoy the same noble pursuits as fourteenth-century aristocrats.

The elements of the Breton lay are, among others, love and loyalty, exile and return, the appearance of the supernatural, and the testing of the hero. The poet of *Sir Orfeo* employs each of these elements to great effect, and demonstrates powerful descriptive abilities. Arguably one of the most startling passages in Middle English poetry is the catalogue depiction of the mutilated bodies of the Taken in the Otherworld incongruously positioned within the beautiful, if artificial, palace. Similarly, the anguish of Heurodis in the narration of her capture by the fairy king is touchingly answered by Orfeo's loving speech.

1   D. Pearsall and I. C. Cunningham, intro., *The Auchinleck Manuscript: National Library of Scotland Advocates' MS 19. 2. 1* (London, 1977).

2   Pearsall and Cunningham, *Auchinleck Manuscript*, p. viii.

3   For example, as Pearsall and Cunningham discuss at p. xi, it is likely that *The Seven Sages*, *Arthour and Merlin*, *Kyng Alisaunder* and *Richard* are by the same author.

4   Pearsall and Cunningham, *Auchinleck Manuscript*, p. viii.

5   See A. J. Bliss, ed., *Sir Orfeo* (Oxford, 1954), p. xv.

6   See the excerpts from King Alfred's translation of the *Consolation of Philosophy* towards the beginning of this volume, pp. 16–19.

While the poem ends with the restoration of the right-ful order in Winchester, the kingdom of the fairies persists, and it is this that lends the poem its slightly perturbing aspect. The fragility of human happiness is apparent throughout the text – the 'Ubi Sunt?' passage at lines 241–60 lending a homiletic tone – and no more so than at the happy ending.

Sir Orfeo

	We redeþ ofte and findeþ ywrite,	
	And þis clerkes wele it wite,	*well; know*
	Layes þat ben in harping	
	Ben yfounde of ferli þing.	*composed; marvellous*
5	Sum beþe of wer and sum of wo,	*war*
	And sum of joie and mirþe also,	
	And sum of trecherie and of gile	
	Of old aventours þat fel while,	*events*
	And sum of bourdes and ribaudy,	*jests; ribaldry*
10	And mani þer beþ of fairy:	
	Of al þinges þat men seþ	
	Mest o love for soþ þai beþ.	*of*
	In Breteyne þis layes were wrouȝt,	*made*
	First yfounde and forþ ybrouȝt	
15	Of aventures þat fel bi dayes,	
	Wherof Bretouns made her layes.	
	When kinges miȝt our yhere	*anywhere; hear*
	Of ani mervailes þat þer were,	
	Þai token an harp in gle and game,	*revelry*
20	And maked a lay and ȝaf it name.	
	Now of þis aventours þat weren yfalle	
	Y can tel sum, ac nouȝt alle.	
	Ac herkneþ, lordinges þat beþ trewe,	
	Ichil ȝou telle of Sir Orfewe.	*I will*
25	Orfeo mest of ani þing	
	Loved þe gle of harping;	
	Siker was everi gode harpour	*Sure*
	Of him to have miche honour.	*much*
	Himself he lerned forto harp	
30	And leyd þeron his wittes scharp;	
	He lerned so, þer noþing was	
	A better harpour in no plas.	*place*
	In al þe warld was no man bore	*born*
	Þat ones Orfeo sat before,	
35	And he miȝt of his harping here,	
	Bot he schulde þenche þat he were	
	In on of þe joies of Paradis,	
	Swiche melody in his harping is.	
	Orfeo was a king	
40	In Inglond, an heiȝe lording,	
	A stalworþ man and hardi bo,	*as well*
	Large and curteys he was also.	*Generous*
	His fader was comen of King Pluto,	
	And his moder of King Juno,	
45	Þat sumtime were as godes yhold	
	For aventours þat þai dede and told.	

Þis king sojournd in Traciens,   *lived*
Þat was a cité of noble defens: *fortifications*
For Winchester was cleped þo   *called; then*
50   Traciens, wiþouten no.   *denial*
      Þe king hadde a quen of priis   *precious*
Þat was ycleped Dame Herodis,
Þe fairest levedi for þe nones   *lady*
Þat miȝt gon on bodi and bones,   *walk*
55   Ful of love and of godenisse;
Ac no man may telle hir fairnise.
      Bifel so in þe comessing of May,   *beginning*
When miri and hot is þe day,
And oway beþ winter schours,
60   And everi feld is ful of flours,
And blosme breme on everi bouȝ   *bright*
Overal wexeþ miri anouȝ,   *grows; enough*
Þis ich quen, Dame Heurodis,   *same*
Tok to maidens of priis,
65   And went in an undrentide   *late morning*
To play bi an orchard side,
To se þe floures sprede and spring,
And to here þe foules sing.
Þai sett hem doun all þre
70   Under a fair ympe-tre,[7]   *grafted tree*
And wel sone þis fair quene
Fel on slepe opon þe grene.
Þe maidens durst hir nouȝt awake,
Bot lete hir ligge and rest take.   *lie*
75   So sche slepe til after none,
Þat undertide was al ydone.   *gone*
Ac as sone as sche gan awake
She crid, and loþli bere gan make: *loathsome outcry*
Sche froted hir honden and hir fet,   *rubbed*
80   And crached hir visage, it bled wete;   *face*
Hir riche robe hye al torett   *tore to pieces*
And was reveyd out of hir wit.   *driven*
Þe tuo maidens hir biside
No durst wiþ hir no leng abide,   *dared*
85   Bot ourn to þe palays ful riȝt   *ran; straight*
And told boþe squier and kniȝt
Þat her quene awede wold,   *had gone mad*
And bad hem go and hir at-hold.   *urged; restrain*
Kniȝtes urn, and levedis also –
90   Damisels sexti and mo.
In þe orchard to þe quen hye come,   *they*
And her up in her armes nome   *took*
And brouȝt hir to bed atte last,
And held hir þere fine fast;
95   Ac ever sche held in o cri,   *persisted*
And wold up and owy.   *away*
When Orfeo herd þat tiding,

---

7   The 'ympe-tree' was renowned for its attraction of fairies.

Never him nas wers for noþing. *worse; nothing (i.e. any reason)*
He come wiþ kniʒtes tene *ten*
100   To chaumber riʒt bifor þe quene,
And biheld, and seyd wiþ grete pité:
'O lef liif, what is te, *dear*
Þat ever ʒete hast ben so stille,
And now gredest wonder schille? *cries out; shrilly*
105   Þi bodi þat was so white ycore *excellently*
Wiþ þine nailes is al totore; *torn to pieces*
Allas, þi rode þat was so red *complexion*
Is al wan as þou were ded; *as if*
And also þine fingres smale
110   Beþ al blodi and al pale.
Allas, þi lovesom eyʒen to *beautiful*
Lokeþ so man doþ on his fo. *as*
A, dame, Ich biseche, merci!
Lete ben al þis reweful cri,
115   And tel me what þe is, and hou, *is wrong; how it happened*
And what þing may þe help now.'
    Þo lay sche stille atte last
And gan to wepe swiþe fast, *very*
And seyd þus þe king to:
120   'Allas, mi lord Sir Orfeo,
Seþþen we first togider were, *Since*
Ones wroþ never we nere, *were not*
Bot ever Ich have yloved þe
As mi liif, and so þou me;
125   Ac now we mot delen ato *must be split apart*
Do þi best, for Y mot go.'
    'Allas!' quaþ he, 'Forlorn Icham! *I am*
Whider wiltow go, and to wham? *will you; whom*
Whider þou gost Ichil wiþ þe, *I will*
130   And whider Y go þou schalt wiþ me.'
    'Nay, nay, sir, þat nouʒt nis; *cannot be*
Ichil þe telle al hou it is.
As Ich lay þis undertide
And slepe under our orchard side,
135   Þer come to me to faire kniʒtes
Wele yarmed al to riʒtes, *properly*
And bad me comen an heiʒing *in haste*
And speke wiþ her lord þe king; *their*
And Ich answerd at wordes bold, *with*
140   Y no durst nouʒt, no Y nold. *dared not; would not*
Þai pricked oʒain as þai miʒt drive. *They rode again as fast as they could*
Þo com her king also blive *immediately*
Wiþ an hundred kniʒtes and mo,
And damisels an hundred also,
145   Al on snowe-white stedes;
As white as milke were her wedes. *clothes*
Y no seiʒe never ʒete bifore *saw*
So faire creatours ycore. *excellent*
Þe king hadde a croun on hed,
150   It nas of silver no of gold red, *was not*

Ac it was of a precious ston;
As briȝt as þe sonne it schon.
And as son as he to me cam,   *soon*
Wold Ich, nold Ich, he me nam,   *Whether I wanted to or not, he took me*
155   And made me wiþ him ride
Opon a palfray bi his side;
And brouȝt me to his palays,
Wele atird in ich ways,   *adorned; each*
And shewed me castels and tours,
160   Rivers, forestes, friþ wiþ flours,   *woodland*
And his riche stedes ichon,   *estates; each one*
And seþþen me brouȝt oȝain hom   *after*
Into our owhen orchard,   *own*
And said to me þus afterward:
165   "Loke, dame, tomorwe þatow be   *that you*
Riȝt here under þis ympe-tre,   *grafted tree*
And þan þou schalt wiþ ous go
And live wiþ ous evermo;
And ȝif þou makest ous ylet,   *cause; hindrance*
170   Whar þou be, þou worst yfet,   *Wherever; will; be fetched*
And totore þine limes al,   *limbs*
Þat noþing help þe no schal;
And þei þou best so totorn,   *even though; will be*
Ȝete þou worst wiþ ous yborn."'   *will be; carried*
175   When King Orfeo herd þis cas,   *event*
'O we!' quaþ he, 'Allas, allas!   *woe*
Lever me were to lete mi liif   *Rather; lose*
Þan þus to lese þe quen mi wiif.'
He asked conseyl at ich man,
180   Ac no man him help no can.
Amorwe þe undertide is come   *On the next day*
And Orfeo haþ his armes ynome   *taken*
And wele ten hundred kniȝtes wiþ him,
Ich yarmed stout and grim,   *Each*
185   And wiþ þe quen wenten he
Riȝt unto þat ympetre.   *grafted tree*
Þai made scheltrom in ich a side,   *shield wall*
And sayd þai wold þere abide
And dye þer everichon,
190   Er þe quen schuld fram hem gon;
Ac ȝete amiddes hem ful riȝt   *straight away*
Þe quen was oway ytuiȝt,   *snatched*
Wiþ fairi forþ ynome:
Men wist never wher sche was bicome.   *knew; disappeared*
195   Þo was þer criing, wepe and wo;
Þe king into his chaumber is go,
And oft swoned opon þe ston,   *stone floor*
And made swiche diol and swiche mon   *sorrow; lamentation*
Þat neiȝe his liif was yspent.
200   Þer was non amendement.   *remedy*
He cleped togider his barouns,   *called*
Erls, lordes of renouns;
And when þai al ycomen were,

'Lordinges,' he said, 'bifor ʒou here

205 Ich ordainy min heiʒe steward *appoint*

To wite mi kingdom afterward. *rule*

In mi stede ben he schal *place*

To keþe mi londes over al;

For now Ichave mi quen ylore, *I have; lost*

210 Þe fairest levedi þat ever was bore,

Never eft Y nil no woman se. *again*

Into wildernes Ichil te *I will; go*

And live þer evermore

Wiþ wilde bestes in holtes hore. *grey woods*

215 And when ʒe understond þat Y be spent, *dead*

Make ʒou þan a parlement

And chese ʒou a newe king. *choose*

Now doþ ʒour best wiþ al mi þing.' *goods*

 Þo was þer wepeing in þe halle,

220 And grete cri among hem alle;

Unneþe miʒt old or ʒong *Scarcely*

For wepeing speke a word wiþ tong.

Þai kneled adoun al yfere *together*

And praid him, ʒif his wille were,

225 Þat he no schuld nouʒt fram hem go.

'Do way!' quaþ he, 'It schal be so!' *Enough*

Al his kingdom he forsoke,

Bot a sclavin on him he toke: *Only; pilgrim's mantle*

He no hadde kirtel no hode, *short coat*

230 No schert, no noþer gode; *other*

Bot his harp he tok algate *at any rate*

And dede him barfot out atte ʒate; *went (word-play on 'dead'?); gate*

No man most wiþ him go.

 O, way! What þer was wepe and wo *alas*

235 When he þat hadde ben king wiþ croun

Went so poverlich out of toun. *in poverty*

Þurth wode and over heþ *Through*

Into þe wildernes he geþ. *goes*

Noþing he fint þat him is ays, *finds; comfort*

240 Bot ever he liveþ in gret malais. *discomfort*

He þat hadde ywerd þe fowe and griis, *worn; patterned fur; grey fur*

And on bed þe purper biis, *purple; fine linen*

Now on hard heþe he liþ,

Wiþ leves and gresse he him wriþ. *covers*

245 He þat hadde had castels and tours,

River, forest, friþ wiþ flours, *woodland*

Now, þei it comenci to snewe and frese, *though; begins*

Þis king mot make his bed in mese. *moss*

He þat had yhad kniʒtes of priis

250 Bifor him kneland, and levedis, *kneeling*

Now seþ he noþing þat him likeþ,

Bot wilde wormes bi him strikeþ. *snakes; glide*

He þat had yhad plenté

Of mete and drink, of ich deynté,

255 Now may he al day digge and wrote *root around*

Er he finde his fille of rote. *root*

In somer he liveþ bi wild frut,
And berien bot gode lite;　　　　　　　　　　　*And berries of only little good*
In winter may he noþing finde
260　Bot rote, grases and þe rinde.　　　　　　　　　*bark*
Al his bodi was oway duine　　　　　　　　　　　*wasted away*
For missays, and al tochine.　　　　　　　　　　*hardship; scarred*
Lord, who may telle þe sore　　　　　　　　　　　*sorrow*
Þis king sufferd ten ȝere and more?
265　His here of his berd, blac and rowe,　　　　　　*unkempt*
To his girdelstede was growe.　　　　　　　　　　*waist*
His harp, whereon was al his gle　　　　　　　　　*revelry*
He hidde in an holwe tre,
And when þe weder was clere and briȝt
270　He toke his harp to him wel riȝt,　　　　　　　*straight away*
And harped at his owhen wille.
Into alle þe wode þe soun gan schille,　　　　　　*to resound*
Þat alle þe wilde bestes þat þer beþ
For joie abouten him þai teþ,　　　　　　　　　　*approach*
275　And alle þe foules þat þer were　　　　　　　　*may be*
Come and sete on ich a brere　　　　　　　　　　*branch*
To here his harping afine –
So miche melody was þerin;　　　　　　　　　　　*much*
And when he his harping lete wold,　　　　　　　*stop*
280　No best bi him abide nold.　　　　　　　　　　*stay*
　　　He miȝt se him bisides,　　　　　　　　　　*moreover*
Oft in hot undertides,
Þe king o fairy wiþ his rout　　　　　　　　　　　*company*
Com to hunt him al about
285　Wiþ dim cri and bloweing,　　　　　　　　　　*faint*
And houndes also wiþ him berking;
Ac no best þai no nome,　　　　　　　　　　　　*caught*
No never he nist whider þai bicome.　　　　　　　*where; went*
And oþerwhile he miȝt him se　　　　　　　　　　*sometimes*
290　As a gret ost bi him te,　　　　*What seemed to be a great army go by him*
Wele atourned, ten hundred kniȝtes,　　　　　　　*equipped*
Ich yarmed to his riȝtes,　　　　　　　　　　　*properly*
Of cuntenaunce stout and fers,　　　　　　　　　*fierce*
Wiþ mani desplaid baners,
295　And ich his swerd ydrawe hold;
Ac never he nist whider þai wold.　　　　　　　　*were going*
And oþerwhile he seiȝe oþer þing:
Kniȝtes and levedis com daunceing
In queynt atire, gisely,　　　　　　　　　　　　*elegant; skilfully*
300　Queynt pas and softly.　　　　　　　　　　　*pace*
Tabours and trunpes ȝede hem bi,　　　　　　　　*trumpets*
And al maner menstraci.　　　　　　　　　　　　*revelry*
　　　And on a day he seiȝe him biside　　　　　　*moreover*
Sexti levedis on hors ride,
305　Gentil and jolif as brid on ris.　*Charming and cheerful as a bird on a twig*
Nouȝt o man amonges hem þer nis;
And ich a faucon on hond bere,　　　　　　　　　*falcon*
And riden on haukin bi o rivere.　　　　　　　　*hawking*
Of game þai founde wel gode haunt,　　　　　　　*abundance*

310	Maulardes, hayroun and cormeraunt.	*Mallards*
	Þe foules of þe water ariseþ;	
	Þe faucouns hem wele deviseþ;	*aim at*
	Ich faucoun his pray slouȝ.	*killed*
	Þat seiȝe Orfeo and louȝ.	*laughed*
315	'Parfay!' quaþ he, 'þer is fair game;	*Indeed*
	Þider Ichil, bi Godes name:	*There I will (go)*
	Ich was ywon swiche werk to se.'	*accustomed*
	He aros and þider gan te.	*went*
	To a levedi he was ycome,	
320	Biheld and haþ wele undernome,	*recognized*
	And seþ bi al þing þat it is	
	His owhen quen, Dam Heurodis.	*own*
	Ȝern he biheld hir, and sche him eke,	*Eagerly; also*
	Ac noiþer to oþer a word no speke.	
325	For messais þat sche on him seiȝe,	*discomfort; saw*
	Þat had ben so riche and so heiȝe,	
	Þe teres fel out of her eiȝe.	
	Þe oþer levedis þis yseiȝe	
	And maked hir oway to ride;	
330	Sche most wiþ him no lenger abide.	*could*
	'Allas,' quaþ he, 'now me is wo.	
	Whi nil deþ now me slo?	*kill*
	Allas, wroche, þat Y no miȝt	*wretch*
	Dye now after þis siȝt.	*sight*
335	Allas, to long last mi liif,	
	When Y no dar nouȝt wiþ mi wiif,	
	No hye to me, o word speke.	
	Allas, whi nil min hert breke?	
	Parfay,' quaþ he, 'tide wat bitide,	*what will happen will happen*
340	Whider so þis levedis ride,	
	Þe selve way Ichil streche –	*same; go*
	Of liif no deþ me no reche.'	*care*
	His sclavain he dede on also spac	*put; at once*
	And henge his harp opon his bac,	
345	And had wel gode wil to gon;	
	He no spard noiþer stub no ston.	*stopped for; tree trunk*
	In at a roche þe levedis rideþ	*rock*
	And he after, and nouȝt abideþ.	
	When he was in þe roche ygo	
350	Wele þre mile oþer mo,	
	He com into a fair cuntray	
	As briȝt so sonne on somers day,	
	Smoþe and plain and al grene,	*flat*
	Hille no dale nas þer non ysene.	
355	Amidde þe lond a castel he siȝe,	*saw*
	Riche and real and wonder heiȝe.	*royal*
	Al þe utmast wal	
	Was clere and schine as cristal;	
	An hundred tours þer were about,	
360	Degiselich and bataild stout;	*Wonderful; crenellated*
	Þe butras com out of þe diche	*buttress; moat*
	Of rede gold yarched riche;	

Þe vousour was avowed al *vaulting; decorated*

Of ich maner divers aumal. *enamel*

365 Wiþin þer wer wide wones *dwelling-places*

Al of precious stones;

Þe werst piler on to biholde *pillar*

Was al of burnist gold. *burnished*

Al þat lond was ever liȝt,

370 For when it schuld be þerk and niȝt, *dark*

Þe riche stones liȝt gonne *shone*

As briȝt as doþ at none þe sonne. *noon*

No man may telle no þenche in þouȝt *think*

Þe riche werk þat þer was wrouȝt. *made*

375 Bi al þing him þink þat it is *it seems to him*

Þe proude court of Paradis.

In þis castel þe levedis aliȝt;

He wold in after ȝif he miȝt. *he wished (to go)*

    Orfeo knokkeþ atte gate;

380 Þe porter was redi þerate *at it*

And asked what he wold have ydo.

'Parfay,' quaþ he, 'Ich am a minstrel, lo!

To solas þi lord wiþ mi gle, *minstrelsy*

Ȝif his swete wille be.'

385 Þe porter undede þe ȝate anon *undid*

And lete him in to þe castel gon.

    Þan he gan bihold about al,

And seiȝe liggeand wiþin þe wal *lying*

Of folk þat were þider ybrouȝt,

390 And þouȝt dede and nare nouȝt. *seemed; were not*

Sum stode wiþouten hade, *head*

And sum non armes nade,

And sum þurth þe bodi hadde wounde,

And sum lay wode ybounde, *mad*

395 And sum armed on hors sete, *sat*

And sum astrangled as þai ete, *choked; ate*

And sum were in water adreynt, *drowned*

And sum wiþ fire al forschreynt. *shrivelled*

Wives þer lay on child-bedde,

400 Sum ded and sum awedde, *gone mad*

And wonder fele þer lay bisides *many*

Riȝt as þai slepe her undertides. *morning nap*

Eche was þus in þis warld ynome, *taken*

Wiþ fairi þider ycome.

405 Þer he seiȝe his owhen wiif,

Dame Heurodis, his lef liif, *dear*

Slepe under an ympe-tre; *grafted tree*

Bi her cloþes he knewe þat it was he. *she*

    And when he hadde bihold þis mervails alle *marvel*

410 He went in to þe kinges halle;

Þan seiȝe he þer a semly siȝt,

A tabernacle blisseful and briȝt, *canopied dais*

Þerin her maister king sete, *lord*

And her quen, fair and swete.

415 Her crounes, her cloþes schine so briȝt

Þat unneþe bihold he hem miȝt.   *scarcely*
When he hadde biholden al þat þing,
He kneled adoun bifor þe king.
'O lord,' he seyd, 'ȝif it þi wille were,
420   Mi menstraci þou schust yhere.'   *should*
Þe king answerd: 'What man artow
Þat art hider ycomen now?
Ich, no non þat is wiþ me,   *Neither I nor those with me*
No sent never after þe.
425   Seþþen þat Ich here regni gan,   *Since; reign*
Y no fond never so folehardi man
Þat hider to ous durst wende   *come*
Bot þat Ic him wald ofsende.'   *Unless I desired to send for him*
'Lord,' quaþ he, 'trowe ful wel,   *believe*
430   Y nam bot a pover menstrel,
And, sir, it is þe maner of ous
To seche mani a lordes hous;
Þei we nouȝt welcom no be,
ȝete we mot proferi forþ our gle.'   *offer*
435   Bifor þe king he sat adoun
And tok his harp so miri of soun,   *sound*
And tempreþ his harp as he wele can,   *tunes*
And blisseful notes he þer gan,
Þat al þat in þe palays were
440   Com to him forto here,
And liggeþ adoun to his fete,   *lie; at*
Hem þenkeþ his melody so swete.   *It seems to them*
Þe king herkneþ and sitt ful stille,   *listens*
To here his gle he haþ gode wille.
445   Gode bourde he hadde of his gle,   *entertainment*
Þe riche quen also hadde he.   *she*
When he hadde stint his harping   *stopped*
Þan seyd to him þe king:
'Menstrel, me likeþ wele þi gle.
450   Now aske of me what it be,
Largelich Ichil þe pay.   *Generously*
Now speke and tow miȝt asay.'   *if you can test (me)*
      'Sir,' he seyd, 'Ich biseche þe
Þatow woldest ȝive me
455   Þat ich levedi, briȝt on ble,   *same; complexion*
Þat slepeþ under þe ympe-tre.'
'Nay,' quaþ þe king, 'þat nouȝt nere!   *cannot be*
A sori couple of ȝou it were,   *miserable; would be*
For þou art lene, rowe and blac,   *unkempt*
460   And sche is lovesum wiþouten lac.   *beautiful; blemish*
A loþlich þing it were forþi   *loathsome; therefore*
To sen hir in þi compayni.'
      'O sir,' he seyd, 'gentil king,
ȝete were it a wele fouler þing   *sorrier*
465   To here a lesing of þi mouþe.   *falsehood*
So, sir, as ȝe seyd nouþe,   *just now*
What Ich wold aski have Y schold,   *ask*
And nedes þou most þi word hold.'   *keep*

Þe king seyd, 'Seþþen it is so,
470   Take hir bi þe hond and go.
Of hir Ichil þatow be bliþe.'   *I hope; happy*
He kneled adoun and þonked him swiþe.   *greatly*
His wiif he tok bi þe hond
And dede him swiþe out of þat land.   *went; quickly*
475   And went him out of þat þede;   *country*
Riȝt as he come, þe way he ȝede.
So long he haþ þe way ynome
To Winchester he is ycome
Þat was his owhen cité;
480   Ac no man knewe þat it was he.
No forþer þan þe tounes ende   *further*
For knoweleche no durst he wende;   *recognition*
Bot wiþ a begger ybilt ful narwe   *lodged; poorly*
Þer he tok his herbarwe   *lodging*
485   To him and to his owhen wiif,
As a minstrel of pover liif,
And asked tidinges of þat lond
And who þe kingdom held in hond.
Þe pover begger in his cote   *cottage*
490   Told him everich a grot: *single; detail*
Hou her quen was stole owy
Ten ȝer gon wiþ fairy,   *years*
And hou her king en exile ȝede,   *went*
Bot no man nist in wiche þede,   *country*
495   And hou þe steward þe lond gan hold,
And oþer mani þinges him told.
    Amorwe, oȝain nonetide,   *The following day, towards noon*
He maked his wiif þer abide;
Þe beggers cloþes he borwed anon
500   And heng his harp his rigge opon,   *back*
And went him into þat cité
Þat men miȝt him bihold and se.
Erls and barouns bold,
Burjays and levedis him gun bihold.   *Townsmen*
505   'Lo,' þai seyd, 'swiche a man!
Hou long þe here hongeþ him opan!
Lo, hou his berd hongeþ to his kne!
He is yclongen also a tre!'   *shrivelled*
And as he ȝede in þe strete,
510   Wiþ his steward he gan mete,
And loude he sett on him a crie:
'Sir steward,' he seyd, 'merci!
Ich am an harpour of heþenisse;   *foreign parts*
Help me now in þis destresse.'
515   Þe steward seyd, 'Com wiþ me, come;
Of þat Ichave þou schalt have some.
Everich gode harpour is welcom me to
For mi lordes love, Sir Orfeo.'   *For the love of my lord*
    In þe castel þe steward sat atte mete,   *meal*
520   And mani lording was bi him sete;
Þer were trompours and tabourers,   *drummers*

Harpours fele, and crouders.   *many; fiddlers*
Miche melody þai maked alle,
And Orfeo sat stille in þe halle
525   And herkneþ; when þai ben al stille
He toke his harp and tempred schille.   *tuned it clearly*
Þe blissefulest notes he harped þere   *most delightful*
Þat ever ani man yherd wiþ ere: *ear*
Ich man liked wele his gle.
530   Þe steward biheld and gan yse,
And knewe þe harp als blive: *immediately*
'Menstrel,' he seyd, 'so mot þou þrive,
Where hadestow þis harp and hou?
Y pray þat þou me telle now.'
535   'Lord,' quaþ he, 'in uncouþe þede,   *unknown; land*
Þurth a wildernes as Y ȝede,
Þer Y founde in a dale
Wiþ lyouns a man totorn smale,   *torn into small pieces*
And wolves him frete wiþ teþ so scharp,   *gnawed*
540   Bi him Y fond þis ich harp,   *same*
Wele ten ȝere it is ygo.'
'O', quaþ þe steward, 'now me is wo!
Þat was mi lord Sir Orfeo.
Allas, wreche, what schal Y do
545   Þat have swiche a lord ylore?   *lost*
A, way, þat Ich was ybore!   *woe; born*
Þat him was so hard grace yȝarked   *a fate; appointed*
And so vile deþ ymarked!'   *marked out*
Adoun he fel aswon to grounde.   *in a swoon*
550   His barouns him tok up in þat stounde   *time*
And telleþ him hou it geþ: *goes*
It nis no bot of mannes deþ.   *There is no remedy for man's death*
     King Orfeo knewe wele bi þan   *this*
His steward was a trewe man
555   And loved him as he auȝt to do,   *ought*
And stont up and seyt þus: 'Lo!   *stands; says*
Steward, herkne now þis þing:
Ȝif Ich were Orfeo þe king,
And hadde ysuffred ful ȝore   *long ago*
560   In wildernisse miche sore,   *sorrow*
And hadde ywon mi quen owy
Out of þe lond of fairy,
And hadde ybrouȝt þe levedi hende   *courteous*
Riȝt here to þe tounes ende,
565   And wiþ a begger her in ynome,
And were miself hider ycome
Þoverlich to þe, þus stille,   *In poverty*
Forto asay þi gode wille,   *test*
And Ich founde þe þus trewe,
570   Þou no schust it never rewe.   *should; regret*
Sikerlich, for love or ay,   *Certainly; fear*
Þou schust be king after mi day.
And ȝif þou of mi deþ hadest ben bliþe,   *happy*
Þou schust have voided also swiþe.'   *been banished; just as quickly*

575	Þo al þo þat þerin sete	Then; those
	Þat it was King Orfeo underȝete,	perceived
	And þe steward him wele knewe:	
	Over and over þe bord he þrewe	table
	And fel adoun to his fet;	
580	So dede everich lord þat þer sete,	
	And al þai seyd at o criing:	one
	'ȝe beþ our lord, sir, and our king!'	
	Glad þai were of his live.	
	To chaumber þai ladde him als bilive,	immediately
585	And baþed him, and schaved his berd,	
	And tired him as a king apert.	dressed; without disguise
	And seþþen, wiþ gret processioun,	then
	Þai brouȝt þe quen in to þe toun	
	Wiþ al maner menstraci.	revelry
590	Lord, þer was grete melody!	
	For joie þai wepe wiþ her eiȝe	
	Þat hem so sounde ycomen seiȝe.	safe; returned
	Now King Orfeo newe coround is,	crowned
	And his quen Dame Heurodis,	
595	And lived long afterward,	
	And seþþen was king þe steward.	
	Harpours in Bretaine after þan	
	Herd hou þis mervaile bigan,	
	And made herof a lay of gode likeing,	delight
600	And nempned it after þe king.	named
	Þat lay 'Orfeo' is yhote –	called
	Gode is þe lay, swete is þe note.	
	Þus com Sir Orfeo out of his care:	sorrow
	God graunt ous alle wele to fare! Amen.	

THE FOUR FOES OF MANKIND

The lyric, *The Four Foes of Mankind*, occurs immediately after *Sir Orfeo* in the Auchinleck manuscript, at folio 303. The four foes referred to are the world, the flesh, the devil and death, and the poem's admonitory tone seeks to instruct Christians against these enemies of salvation. The inevitability of misery while on earth is emphasized by the antitheses of stanzas two and three; the fragility of happiness is demonstrated by the mutability of all things. Death is also an inevitable consequence of life, and the poet warns his audience to beware that death does not come before we are prepared. The poet advises the audience to avoid the pitfalls of sinning and of focusing too much on obtaining the joys and wealth of the world. The poem closes with an injunction that while steering clear of the four foes that are on every path one might chose to take, one should deliberately seek out allies. The poem is therefore ultimately a penitential lyric: advising good Christians to repent of and abandon their sins and seek to lead a better life to obtain lasting happiness thereafter.

The Four Foes of Mankind

	Þe siker soþe whoso seys,	sure
	Wiþ diol dreye we our days,	sorrow; suffer
	And walk mani wil ways	wrong
	As wandrand wiȝtes.	wandering; creatures
5	Al our games ous agas,	disappear
	So mani tenes ous tas	afflictions; attack
	Þurch fonding of fele fas,	temptation; foes

Þat fast wiþ ous fiȝtes.   *insistently; fight*
Our flesche is fouled wiþ þe fende,   *corrupted; fiend*
10   Þer we finde a fals frende,
Þei þai heven up her hende   *Though; might raise*
Þai no hold nouȝt her hiȝtes.   *uphold; promises*
Þis er þre þat er þra,   *are; three; persistent*
ȝete þe ferþ is our fa,   *Yet; foe*
15   Deþ þat derieþ ous swa   *injures; so*
And diolely ous diȝtes.   *dolefully; prepares*

Þis world wileþ þus, Y wat,   *beguiles; know*
Þurch falsschip of fair hat;   *deceitfulness; promise*
Where we go bi ani gat   *road*
20   Wiþ bale he ous bites.   *pain*
Now kirt, now care,   *peace*
Now min, now mare,   *less*
Now sounde, now sare,   *healthy; in pain*
Now song, now sites,   *sorrows*
25   Now nouȝt, now ynouȝ,   *nothing; enough*
Now wele, now wouȝ,   *joy; distress*
Now is in longing þat louȝ,   *laughed*
Þat o þis liif lites;   *trusts*
Now geten, now gan   *gone*
30   Y tel it bot a lent lan,   *consider; lent; loan*
When al þe welþ of our wan   *dwelling*
Þus oway wites.   *departs*

Now under, now over,
Now cast, now cover,   *taken off*
35   Now plente, now pouer,
Now pine, now plawe,   *suffering; play*
Now heþen, now here,   *hence*
Now feble, now fere,   *ailing; healthy*
Now swift, now swere,   *sluggish*
40   Now snelle, now slawe,   *quick*
Now nouȝt, now ynouȝ,
Now fals, now frouȝ   *false; untrustworthy*
Þe warld tirneþ ous touȝ   *roughly*
Fram wawe to wawe,   *misery*
45   Til we be broyden in a brayd,   *snatched; moment*
Þat our lickham is layd   *body*
In a grave þat is grayd   *prepared*
Under lame lawe.   *earth; low*

When derne deþ ous haþ ydiȝt,   *secret; prepared*
50   Is non so war no so wiȝt   *watchful; brave*
Þat he no felles him in fiȝt,   *destroys; fight*
As fire dos in tunder.   *tinder*
Þer nis no letting at lite   *There is no counting on delay*
Þat he no tittes til him tite,   *pull; to; quickly*
55   Þat he haþ sammned in site   *assembled; position*
Sone wil he sunder.   *separate*
Noiþer he stintes no stokes,   *stops; holds back*

Bot ay prickes and prokes *thrusts*

Til he unclustri al þe lokes *might unfasten; locks*

60 Þat liif ligges under. *lies*

When Y tent til him take *When I pay heed to him*

How schuld Ich ani mirþe make *could; rejoicing*

Or wele in þis warld wake? *joy; summon up*

Ywis it were wonder. *Certainly*

65 Deþ þat deries ous ȝete *injures*

And makes mani wonges wete, *cheeks*

Þer nis no liif þat he wil lete *neglect*

To lache when him list. *seize; pleases*

When he is lopen out of les, *escaped; leash*

70 No pray no man after pes; *peace*

For non giftes þat ges *may be acceptable*

Mai no man til him trist. *to; trust*

Our gode frendes has he fot, *fetched*

And put þe pouer to þe pot, *abyss of hell*

75 And over him yknett his knott *tied*

Under his clay kist. *chest*

Derne deþ, opon þe ȝong *young*

Wiþ þe to strive it is strong: *contend*

Y wold be wreken of mi wrong, *avenged*

80 Ȝif Y way wist. *a way; might know*

When þou has gaderd and yglened, *gleaned*

Long lyowen and lened, *lent; given out*

Sparely þi gode spened *spent*

And loþ forto lete, *reluctant; let go*

85 Þe war lever swelt under sword *watchful; rather; die*

Þan parti of þi peni hord, *distribute*

Þou wringest mani wrang word *force out; false*

Wiþ wanges ful wete. *cheeks*

And deþ dinges o þi dore *beats*

90 Þat nedes schal be þi neiȝebore, *inevitably*

And fett þe to fen-fore, *fetch; an earthen trench*

Foule under fete. *corrupted*

For al þe craft þat þou can, *skill; can do*

And al þe wele þatow wan, *wealth; that you; acquired*

95 Þe mock and þe mad man *riches; mad*

No schul þai never mete.

Seþþen font ous fra filþ wesche, *after; washed*

Our fa have founde we our flesche, *enemy*

Wiþ mani fondinges and fresche *temptations; dangers*

100 And four-sum of fendes. *four together*

Is nan so þra of hem þre *persistent*

Þat ma merres þan me; *hinders; myself*

Bisier mai nan be

To bring ous on bendes. *(into) bonds*

105 Man, mene þou þi mis, *lament; wrongdoing*

Trowe trustly on þis: *Believe*

Þou no wat never, ywis, *knows*

In world whare þou wendes,   *pass*
No wat gat þatow gas,   *road; might go*
110   Þis four er redi on þi pas.   *way*
Now have yfounden þi fas,   *enemies*
Finde tow þi frendes!   *friends*

London, British Library, Harley 2253

London, British Library, Harley 2253, contains over one hundred religious and secular texts written in French, English and Latin. The manuscript itself can be dated to *c*.1340,[1] though many of the texts will have originated earlier. It was compiled by a scribe in the Marches region, probably someone working in the town of Ludlow in Shropshire, who may have had native connections with Leominster.[2] This same scribe was also responsible for another collection of texts in London, British Library, Royal 12 C. xii, and appears to have had access to a large number of exemplars in Latin, French and English.[3] He drew on a number of these exemplars for the compilation of Harley 2253, which appears to have been compiled for edification and for entertainment, probably as a lay-person's volume. Among the non-English contents in Harley 2253 are fabliaux, hagiographies, prayers, directions for religious observances, biblical stories, historical texts, and descriptions of the Holy Land. The fifty-one English texts, which include *King Horn*, are all verse with the exception of some prose recipes. This makes the collection in Harley 2253 one of the most important medieval manuscripts for the study of lyrical poems. It is a vital witness to secular poetic texts composed in English in particular, for as Derek Pearsall states: 'It contains unique copies of poems and groups of poems whose loss would wipe out our knowledge of whole areas of English poetry, some of it the very best of its kind, in a critical time of change . . . there is no other manuscript of any of the secular love-poems or political poems.'[4]

There appears to be little thematic structuring of the material in Harley 2253; rather, the English lyrics are interspersed with French and Latin texts, and are not themselves organized into groupings such as 'religious', 'secular' or 'political', as the poems edited below demonstrate.

The lyrics edited here are *Earth upon Earth*, *Alysoun*, *Spring*, *Advice to Women*, *An Old Man's Prayer*, *Blow, Northerne Wynd*, *The Death of King Edward I*, *I Syke when Y Singe* and *An Autumn Song*. The lyrics from *Spring* to *Edward I* occur in sequence from folio 71 verso to folio 73 recto, demonstrating the apparent lack of thematic organization to this manuscript's items. The titles of the lyrical texts given here are those supplied by Brook and by Ker in his facsimile.[5] Following these lyrics is *King Horn*, a lengthy verse Romance.

EARTH UPON EARTH

Earth upon Earth, found at folio 59 verso, is a well-known penitential quatrain that depends on its condensed form and punning for its effective *contemptus mundi* theme. According to Duncan, this 'riddle-like poem is a punning elaboration of the Biblical text, *Memento homo quod cinis in cinerem reverteris*, "Remember man that you are dust and to dust you shall return", used in the Ash Wednesday liturgy'.[6] This version is the original text that may date from the thirteenth century; the many later versions often expand these four lines.

Earth upon Earth

Erþe toc of erþe erþe wyþ woh,	
Erþe oþer erþe to þe erþe droh;	*added*
Erþe leyde erþe in erþene þroh.	*grave*
Þo hevede erþe of erþe erþe ynoh.	*had*

1 N. R. Ker, intro., *Facsimile of British Museum MS. Harley 2253*, EETS o.s. 255 (London, 1965), p. xxi. Ker's *Facsimile* includes folios 49–140, all of the work of the main scribe.
2 M. Samuels, 'The Dialect of the Scribe of the Harley Lyrics', in *Middle English Dialectology: Essays on Some Principles and Problems*, eds A. McIntosh, M. L. Samuels and M. Laing (Aberdeen, 1989), pp. 256–63.

3 See Ker, *Facsimile*, pp. xx–xxi.
4 D. Pearsall, *Old English and Middle English Poetry*, Routledge History of English Poetry I (London, 1977), p. 120.
5 G. L. Brook, ed., *The Harley Lyrics* (Manchester, 1940); Ker, *Facsimile of British Museum MS. Harley 2253*.
6 T. G. Duncan, ed., *Medieval English Lyrics, 1200–1400* (London, 1995), p. 208.

ALYSOUN

This secular love lyric, contained at folio 63 verso, opens with the *reverdie*, the traditional description of spring, that here leads into a revelation that the poet is suffering for love. The burden, or refrain, with its double alliteration, is a joyful song that through its careless abandon serves to emphasize the contrasting love-sickness of the speaker in the stanzas. Alysoun herself is described in terms of courtly love, which run through the second and third stanzas interspersed with the poet's melancholic musings. Alysoun is the superlative example of womankind as one might expect, but there is individualization here with the giving of her name at least.

Alysoun

	Bytuene Mersh ant Averil,	
	When spray biginneþ to sprynge,	*shoots*
	Þe lutel foul haþ hire wyl	*desire*
	On hyre lud to synge.	*song*
5	Ich libbe in love-longinge	*live*
	For semlockest of alle þynge:	*most seemly*
	He may me blisse bringe;	*She*
	Icham in hire baundoun.	*power*
	An hendy hap Ichabbe yhent,	*fair fortune; received*
10	Ichot from hevene it is me sent;	*I know*
	From alle wymmen mi love is lent,	*gone*
	Ant lyht on Alysoun.	*alighted*
	On heu hire her is fayr ynoh,	*hue; hair*
	Hire browe broune, hire eзe blake;	*eyebrows*
15	Wiþ lossum chere he on me loh,	*lovely; countenance; she; laughed*
	Wiþ middel smal ant wel ymake.	
	Bote he me wolle to hire take	*she*
	Forte buen hire owen make,	*be; mate*
	Longe to lyven Ichulle forsake	
20	Ant, feye, fallen adoun.	*fated to die*
	An hendy hap etc.	
	Nihtes when Y wende ant wake,	*turn; lie awake*
	Forþi myn wonges waxeþ won,	*cheeks; grow*
	Levedi, al for þine sake,	
25	Longinge is ylent me on.	*arrived*
	In world nis non so wyter mon	*wise*
	Þat al hire bounte telle con:	*goodness*
	Hire swyre is whittore þen þe swon,	*neck; swan*
	Ant feyrest may in toune.	*maid*
30	An hendi hap etc.	
	Icham for wowyng al forwake,	*wooing; weary with waking*
	Wery so water in wore,	*weir*
	Lest eny reve me my make	*rob*
	Ychabbe yзyrned зore.	*yearned; for a long time*
35	Betere is þolien whyle sore	*to suffer; sorely*
	Þen mournen evermore.	
	Geynest under gore,	*loveliest; clothing (i.e. in body)*
	Herkne to my roun.	*Listen; song*
	An hendi hap etc.	

SPRING

This secular love lyric, at folio 71 verso of Harley 2253, like the previous and following ones, begins with the *reverdie*. Here, though, it opens into an extended and amusing discussion of the joys of the world of animals, who woo and make love, while the poet must contend with his equally amorous desires and desperation to find a lover.

Spring

	Lenten ys come wiþ love to toune,	*Spring*
	Wiþ blosmen ant wiþ briddes roune,	*song*
	Þat al þis blisse bryngeþ.	
	Dayeseʒes in þis dales,	*Daisies*
5	Notes suete of nyhtegales,	
	Uch foul song singeþ.	
	Þe þrestelcoc him þreteþ oo;	*thrush; brawls continuously*
	Away is huere winter woo	*their*
	When woderove springeþ.	*woodruff*
10	Þis foules singeþ ferly fele,	*in wonderful profusion*
	Ant wlyteþ on huere wynne wele	*warble; abundant joy*
	Þat al þe wode ryngeþ.	

Þe rose rayleþ hire rode, — *puts on; redness*
Þe leves on þe lyhte wode
15 Waxen al wiþ wille. — *willingness*
Þe mone mandeþ hire bleo; — *sends forth; beams*
Þe lilie is lossom to seo, — *lovely*
Þe fenyl ant þe fille. — *chervil*
Wowes þis wilde drakes, — *Woo*
20 Miles murgeþ huere makes — *Animals; delight; mates*
Ase strem þat strikeþ stille. — *flows; softly*
Mody meneþ, so doþ mo; — *Passionate men; complain; many*
Ichot Ycham on of þo — *those*
For love þat likes ille. — *badly*

25 Þe mone mandeþ hire lyht,
So doþ þe semly sonne bryht
When briddes singeþ breme. — *brightly*
Deawes donkeþ þe dounes, — *Dews; soak*
Deores wiþ huere derne rounes — *Animals; secret*
30 Domes forte deme. — *Wishes; declare*
Wormes woweþ under cloude, — *clod*
Wymmen waxeþ wounder proude — *wonderfully*
So wel hit wol hem seme. — *suit/befit*
ʒef me shal wonte wille of on, — *lack; my desire; from one of them*
35 Þis wunne weole Y wole forgon, — *wealth of joy; forego*
Ant wyht in wode be fleme. — *as a creature; banished*

Advice to Women

As in the previous two examples, this lyric, found at folio 71 verso, begins with a reminder that spring is the time of renewed interest in love. Although there are numerous formulaic phrases here (*Ase ledies þat beþ bryht in bour* etc.) there is more to this work than mere convention. The return of spring prompts the speaker to engage in advising women to beware of the treachery of men who will want them only for their money and their virginity. The second stanza seems deliberately to employ the plural pronoun with its inherent ambiguity (men or women?) to cast aspersions on not only men's traitorous habits, but women's falseness too. In the light of the last three lines of the poem, this makes for an intriguing explanation of the poet's seeming philanthropy.

Advice to Women

	In May hit murgeþ when hit dawes	*makes us merry; dawns*
	In dounes wiþ þis dueres plawes,	*animals; play*
	Ant lef is lyht on lynde;	*linden tree*
	Blosmes bredeþ on þe bowes,	*spring forth*
5	Al þis wylde wyhtes wowes,	*creatures; woo*
	So wel Ych under-fynde.	*perceive*
	Y not non so freoli flour	*do not know; noble*
	Ase ledies þat beþ bryht in bour,	
	Wiþ love who mihte hem bynde.	
10	So worly wymmen are by west;	*worthy*
	One of hem Ich herie best	*praise*
	From Irlond in to Ynde.	*India*
	Wymmen were þe beste þing,	
	Þat shup oure heȝe hevene Kyng –	*formed; high*
15	Ȝef feole false nere;	*many; were not*
	Heo beoþ to rad upon huere red	*They; too hasty; counsel*
	To love þer me hem lastes bed,	*one; vices; offers*
	When heo shule fenge fere.	*take; a companion*
	Lut in londe are to leve,	*Few; be believed*
20	Þah me hem trewe trouþe ȝeve,	*Though one might give them a true pledge*
	For tricherie to ȝere.	*For treachery (men are) too ready*
	When trichour haþ is trouþe yplyht,	*traitor; his*
	Byswyken he haþ þat suete wyht,	*Deceived; sweet; creature*
	Þah he hire oþes swere.	*oaths*
25	Wymmon, war þe wiþ þe swyke	*guard; treacherous one*
	Þat feir ant freoly ys to fyke:	*freely; flatter*
	Ys fare is o to founde.	*practice; ever; found wanting*
	So wyde in world ys huere won,	*dwelling*
	In uch a toune untrewe is on	*one*
30	From Leycestre to Lounde.	*London*
	Of treuþe nis þe trichour noht,	*nothing at all*
	Bote he habbe is wille ywroht	*Unless; performed*
	At stevenyng umbe stounde.	*an assignation; for a short time*
	Ah, feyre levedis, be onwar!	
35	To late comeþ þe ȝeyn-char,	*repentance*
	When love ou haþ ybounde.	*you*
	Wymmen bueþ so feyr on hewe,	*hue*
	Ne trow Y none þat nere trewe	*believe*
	Ȝef trichour hem ne tahte.	*taught*

40	Ah, feyre þinges, freoly bore,	*creatures; nobly*
	When me ou woweþ, beþ war bifore	*men; aware*
	Whuch is worldes ahte.	*About; possessions*
	Al to late is send aȝeyn	*return*
	When þe ledy liht byleyn	*lies; deflowered*
45	Ant lyveþ by þat he lahte;	*which she; received*
	Ah, wolde lylie-leor in lyn	*lily-face; linen*
	Yhere levely lores myn,	*willingly; advice*
	Wiþ selþe we weren sahte.	*happiness; reconciled*

AN OLD MAN'S PRAYER

At folio 72 recto is a penitential lyric which is a poignant reflection on a sinful life by a speaker who believes he is nearing death. The desire to atone for sins committed, and the realization that it is only by repentance that salvation might be gained, is evident in many other lyrics. In this poem, however, the detail of the suffering of the subject and the personal nature of his revelations (the names he is called, for example, in lines 16–17) makes this a powerful and moving expression of regret, tempered throughout by a longing for days gone by.

An Old Man's Prayer

	Heȝe Loverd, þou here my bone,	*High; prayer*
	Þat madest middelert ant mone	*earth*
	Ant mon of murþes munne.	*joys; to think*
	Trusti kyng ant trewe in trone,	*throne*
5	Þat þou be wiþ me sahte sone,	*reconciled*
	Asoyle me of sunne.	*Absolve; sin*
	Fol Ich wes in folies fayn,	*eager*
	In luthere lastes Y am layn,	*wicked; vices*
	Þat makeþ myn þryftes þunne,	*gains; meagre*
10	Þat semly sawes wes woned to seyn,	*speeches; accustomed*
	Nou is marred al my meyn,	*virtue*
	Away is al my wunne.	*joy*
	Unwunne haveþ myn wonges wet,	*Sadness; cheeks*
	Þat makeþ me rouþes rede;	*lamentations; utter*
15	Ne semy nout þer Y am set,	*suits me; sat*
	Þer me calleþ me 'fulleflet',	*'floor-filler'*
	Ant 'waynoun wayteglede'.	*'good-for-nothing; fire-gazer'*
	Whil Ich wes in wille wolde,	*pleasure's; power*
	In uch a bour among þe bolde	*every; noble*
20	Yholde wiþ þe heste;	*In keeping; highest*
	Nou Y may no fynger folde,	*bend*
	Lutel loved ant lasse ytolde,	*less; esteemed*
	Yleved wiþ þe leste.	*Believed to be; among*
	A goute me haþ ygreyþed so,	*gout; grieved*
25	Ant oþer eveles monye mo,	
	Y not whet bote is beste.	*remedy*
	Þat er wes wilde ase þe ro,	*before; wild; roe*
	Nou Y swyke, Y mei nout so,	*desist*
	Hit siweþ me so faste.	*pursues*

30   Faste Y wes on horse heh,
       Ant werede worly wede;   *expensive; clothes*
       Nou is faren al my feh,   *gone; property*
       Wiþ serewe þat Ich hit ever seh;   *sorrow; saw*
       A staf ys nou my stede.   *steed*

35   When Y se steden styþe in stalle,   *strong*
       Ant Y go haltinde in þe halle,   *halting*
       Myn huerte gynneþ to helde.   *sink*
       Þat er wes wildest inwiþ walle,   *within*
       Nou is under fote yfalle
40   Ant mey no fynger felde.
       Þer Ich wes luef Icham ful loht,   *loved; loathed*
       Ant alle myn godes me atgoht,   *disappeared*
       Myn gomenes waxeþ gelde;   *pleasures; barren*
       Þat feyre founden me mete ant cloht, *Those who kindly; food*
45   Hue wrieþ awey as hue were wroht;   *turn; angry*
       Such is evel ant elde.   *evil; old age*

       Evel ant elde ant oþer wo
       Foleweþ me so faste,
       Me þunkeþ myn herte brekeþ a-tuo,
50   Suete God, whi shal hit swo?   *so*
       Hou mai hit lengore laste?

       Whil mi lif wes luþer ant lees   *wicked; false*
       Glotonie mi glemon wes,   *minstrel*
       Wiþ me he wonede a while;   *lived*
55   Prude wes my plowe-fere,   *play-fellow*
       Lecherie my lauendere,   *laundress (i.e. mistress)*
       Wiþ hem is gabbe ant gyle.   *mockery; guile*
       Coveytise myn keyes bere,   *Covetousness; carried off*
       Niþe ant onde were mi fere,   *Anger; envy; companions*
60   Þat bueþ folkes fyle;   *vile*
       Lyare wes mi latymer,   *translator*
       Sleuthe ant slep mi bedyver,   *Sloth; sleep; bed-fellows*
       Þat weneþ me unbewhile.   *entertained; from time to time*

       Umbewhile Y am to whene,   *cheered up*
65   When Y shal murþes meten;   *merriment; meet*
       Monne mest Y am to mene.   *Of men; most; to be pitied*
       Lord, þat hast me lyf to lene,   *grant*
       Such lotes lef me leten.   *behaviour; abandon*

       Such lyf Ich have lad fol ȝore   *led; for a long time*
70   Merci, Loverd, Y nul namore,
       Bowen Ichulle to bete.   *amendment*
       Syker hit siweþ me ful sore –   *Truly; pursues*
       Gabbes, les, ant luþere lore: *lies; wicked; teaching*
       Sunnes bueþ unsete.   *Sins; unprofitable*
75   Godes heste ne huld Y noht,   *commands; held*
       Bote ever aȝeyn is wille Y wroht   *did (what)*
       Mon lereþ me to lete.   *I am taught to leave off*

Such serewe haþ myn sides þurhsoht		*pierced*
Þat al Y weolewe away to noht		*waste away*
80 When Y shal murþes mete.		

To mete murþes Ich wes wel fous		*eager*
Ant comely mon ta calle;		*And a fine man to be called*
Y sugge by oþer ase bi ous,		*I speak about others just as of us*
Alse ys hirmon halt in hous,		*As a; servant; of high rank*
85 Ase heved-hount in halle.		*head-hound*

Dredful deþ, why wolt þou dare		
Bryng þis body þat is so bare		
Ant yn bale ybounde?		*misery*
Careful mon ycast in care,		*Anxious*
90 Y falewe as flour ylet forþfare,		*fade; to die*
Ychabbe myn deþes wounde:		
Murþes helpeþ me no more.		
Help me, lord, er þen Ich hore,		*grow grey*
Ant stunt my lyf a stounde;		*stop; soon*
95 Þat ʒokkyn haþ yʒyrned ʒore,		*Who with lustful desire has yearned long since*
Nou hit sereweþ him ful sore		
Ant bringeþ him to grounde.		

To grounde hit haveþ him ybroht;		
Whet ys þe beste bote?		*remedy*
100 Bote heryen him þat haht us boht,		*But; praise*
Ure Lord þat al þis world haþ wroht,		
Ant fallen him to fote.		*to his feet*

Nou Icham to deþe ydyht		*prepared*
Ydon is al my dede,		
105 God us lene of ys lyht,		*grant*
Þat we of sontes habben syht		*saints; sight*
Ant hevene to mede. Amen.		*reward*

BLOW, NORTHERNE WYND

This secular love song, contained at folio 72 verso, is a good example of the later thirteenth- or early fourteenth-century poet's ability to combine the conventions of courtly love poetry with a lyrical refrain that may have been extracted from a popular song. The simplicity of the burden is in sharp contrast to the elaborate rhetoric of the verses. Among the devices and motifs is formulaic description (*A burde of blod ant bon*), the courtly personification of emotions, the love-sickness of the suitor, and the non-individualized, and occasionally highly artificial, references to the woman. This poetic display suggests *Blow, Northerne Wynd* is designed as a general or public lyric.

Blow Northerne Wynd

Blow, northerne wynd,
Send þou me my suetyng!
Blow, norþerne wynd,
Blou, blou, blou!

5	Ichot a burde in boure bryht	*I know; lady*
	Þat fully semly is on syht,	
	Menskful maiden of myht,	*Graceful*
	Feir ant fre to fonde;	*charming; to find*
	In al þis wurhliche won	*noble; dwelling*
10	A burde of blod ant of bon	
	Never ȝete Y nuste non	*knew*
	Lussomore in londe.	*More lovely*
	Blow, etc.	
	Wiþ lokkes lefliche ant longe,	*lovely*
15	Wiþ frount ant face feir to fonde,	*forehead*
	Wiþ murþes monie mote heo monge,	*joys; many (people); cheer*
	Þat brid so breme in boure.	*maiden; bright*
	Wiþ lossom eye grete ant gode,	
	Wiþ browen blysfol under hode,	*hood*
20	He þat reste him on þe rode	*Christ*
	Þat leflich lyf honoure!	
	Blou, etc.	
	Hire lure lumes liht	*face; shines*
	Ase a launterne a nyht,	
25	Hire bleo blykyeþ so bryht;	*hue; shines*
	So feyr heo is ant fyn.	
	A suetly suyre heo haþ to holde,	*neck*
	Wiþ armes, shuldre ase mon wolde,	
	Ant fyngres feyre forte folde;	*clasp*
30	God wolde hue were myn!	*she*
	Middel heo haþ menskful smal,	*Waist; gracefully*
	Hire loveliche chere as cristal,	*countenance*
	Þeȝes, legges, fet ant al	*Thighs*
	Ywraht wes of þe beste.	*Made*
35	A lussum ledy lasteles	*faultless*
	Þat sweting is, ant ever wes;	
	A betere burde never nes,	
	Yheryed wiþ þe heste.	*To be praised; highest*
	Heo is dereworþe in day,	*precious*
40	Graciouse, stout, ant gay,	*stoutly*
	Gentil, jolyf so þe jay,	*lively; as*
	Worhliche when heo wakeþ.	*Noble*
	Maiden murgest of mouþ;	*merriest*
	Bi est, bi west, by norþ ant souþ,	
45	Þer nis fiele ne crouþ	*fiddle; viol*
	Þat such murþes makeþ.	
	Heo is coral of godnesse,	
	Heo is rubie of ryhtfulnesse,	*righteousness*
	Heo is cristal of clannesse,	*purity*
50	Ant baner of bealte;	*beauty*
	Heo is lilie of largesse,	*generosity*
	Heo is parvenke of prouesse,	*periwinkle; excellence*

Heo is solsecle of suetnesse,   *marigold*
Ant ledy of lealte.   *loyalty*

55   To Love, þat loflich is in londe,
Y tolde him, as Ych understonde,
Hou þis hende haþ hent in honde   *courteous one; seized*
On huerte þat myn wes:
Ant hire knyhtes me han so soht,   *sought*
60   Sykyng, Sorewyng ant Þoht,   *Sighing*
Þo þre me han in bale broht   *misery*
Aȝeyn þe poer of Pees.   *authority*

To Love Y putte pleyntes mo,   *complaints*
Hou Sykyng me haþ siwed so;   *pursued*
65   Ant eke Þoht me þrat to slo   *threatens; kill*
Wiþ maistry ȝef he myhte.   *force*
Ant Serewe sore in balful bende   *grievous; captivity*
Þat he wolde, for þis hende,
Me lede to my lyves ende
70   Unlahfulliche, in lyhte.   *Unlawfully, plainly*

Hire Love me lustnede uch word   *listened*
Ant beh him to me over bord,   *leaned; table*
Ant bed me hente þat hord   *instructed; to take; treasure*
Of myne huerte hele: *cure*
75   'Ant bisecheþ þat swete ant swote,   *sweet and gentle one*
Er þen þou falle ase fen of fote,   *mud*
Þat heo wiþ þe wolle of bote   *as a remedy*
Dereworþliche dele.'   *Affectionately behave*

For hire love Y carke ant care,   *fret*
80   For hire love Y droupne ant dare,   *droop; falter*
For hire love my blisse is bare,   *poor*
Ant al Ich waxe won.   *grow*
For hire love in slep Y slake,   *grow weak*
For hire love al nyht Ich wake,
85   For hire love mournyng Y make,
More þen eny mon.

THE DEATH OF KING EDWARD I

At folio 73 recto is this lament on Edward I's death in 1307. It is one of a number of unique political poems surviving from Harley 2253.[7] It is a loose translation of a French text, mourning the king's passing, and selectively emphasizing Edward as a crusading king, fighting (and, incidentally, losing) his holy wars. Its religious emphasis suggests that its original author may have been a cleric, but this national event is given international significance by drawing into the text the king of France (an enemy of Edward), cardinals, knights, and the pope (an ally of Edward). A sermon recently discovered in a Vatican manuscript was delivered as a eulogy on Edward to Pope Clement V in 1307.[8] The existence of this text lends historical substance to the poem included in Harley 2253.

The Death of King Edward I

	Alle þat beoþ of huerte trewe	
	A stounde herkneþ to my song:	*while*
	Of duel þat deþ haþ diht us newe,	*sorrow; prepared*
	Þat makeþ me syke ant sorewe among;	*sigh; at times*
5	Of a knyht þat wes so strong,	
	Of wham God haþ don ys wille.	
	Me þuncheþ þat deþ haþ don us wrong	*It seems to me*
	Þat he so sone shal ligge stille.	*lie*
	All Englond ahte forte knowe	*ought*
10	Of wham þat song is þat Y synge:	
	Of Edward, kyng þat liþ so lowe,	*lies*
	ȝent all þis world is nome con sprynge;	*Through; name*
	Trewest mon of alle þinge,	*in*
	Ant in werre war ant wys.	*prudent*
15	For him we ahte oure honden wrynge –	
	Of Christendome he ber þe pris.	*prize*
	Before þat oure kyng wes ded	
	He spek ase mon þat wes in care:	*anxious*
	'Clerkes, knyhtes, barouns', he sayde,	
20	'Y charge ou by oure sware	*you; oath*
	Þat ȝe to Engelonde be trewe.	
	Y deȝe, Y ne may lyven na more:	
	Helpeþ mi sone ant crouneþ him newe,	
	For he is nest to buen ycore.	*next; chosen*
25	Ich biqueþe myn herte aryht,	*bequeath; properly*
	Þat hit be write at mi devys,	*plan*
	Over þe see þat hue be diht,	*it; sent*
	Wiþ fourscore knyhtes al of pris	*esteem*
	In were þat buen war ant wys,	
30	Aȝein þe heþene forte fyhte	
	To wynne þe crois þa lowe lys;	*low; lies*
	Myself Ycholde ȝef þat Y myhte.'	*I would*

7   For this and others, see P. Coss, intro., *Thomas Wright's Political Songs of England from the Reign of John to that of Edward II* (Cambridge, 1996).

8   See M. T. Clanchy, *England and its Rulers*, 2nd edn (Oxford, 1998), p. 210, n. 15, and p. 211.

King of Fraunce, þou hevedest sunne,   *sin*
Þat þou þe counsail woldest fonde   *try*
To latte þe wille of Kyng Edward   *prevent*
To wende to þe Holy Londe: *go*
Þat oure kyng hede take on honde   *had; taken*
Al Engelond to ȝeme ant wysse   *rule; guide*
To wenden into þe Holy Londe
To wynnen us heveriche blisse.   *heavenly*

Þe messager to þe Pope com,
Ant seyde þat oure King was ded.
Ys oune hond þe lettre he nom –   *to his; own; took*
Ywis, is herte wes ful gret.   *very*
Þe Pope himself þe lettre redde,
Ant spec a word of gret honour:
'Alas!' he seide, 'Is Edward ded?
Of Christendome he ber þe flour.'

Þe Pope to is chaumbre wende,
For del ne mihte he speke namore;   *sorrow*
Ant after cardinals he sende,
Þat muche couþen of Christes lore   *knew; teaching*
Boþe þe lasse ant eke þe more,
Bed hem boþe rede ant synge.   *Asked; to; conduct services*
Gret deol me myhte se þore,   *sorrow; men; there*
Mony mon is honde wrynge.

Þe Pope of Peyters stod at is masse,   *Poitiers*
Wiþ ful gret solempnete,
Þer me con þe soule blesse –   *began*
'King Edward, honoured þou be.
God lene þy sone, come after þe,   *grant; son*
Brynge to ende þat þou hast bygonne:
Þe holy crois, ymad of tre,   *wood*
So fain þou woldest hit han ywonne.   *much*

Jerusalem, þou hast ilore   *lost*
Þe flour of al chivalerie
Nou King Edward liveþ na more.
Alas! Þat he ȝet shulde deye,
He wolde ha rered up ful heyȝe   *raised*
Oure baners þat bueþ broht to grounde.   *have been*
Wel longe we mowe clepe ant crye   *might; call out*
Er we a such king han yfounde.'

Nou is Edward of Carnarvan
King of Engelond al aplyht.   *in truth*
God lete him ner be worse man
Þen is fader, ne lasse of myht: *strength*
To holden is pore men to ryht,   *justice*
Ant understonde good consail,
Al Engelond forte wisse ant diht;   *guide; instruct*
Of gode knyhtes darh him nout fail.   *lack*

Þah mi tonge were mad of stel,
Ant min herte yȝote of bras,   *made*
Þe godnesse might Y never telle
Þat wiþ King Edward was.
85   King, as þou art cleped conquerour,   *called*
In uch bataille þou hadest pris,   *each*
God brynge þi soule to þe honour
Þat ever wes ant ever ys,
Þat lesteþ ay wiþouten ende.   *lasts; always*
90   Bidde we God ant oure Ledy,
To þilke blisse Jesus us sende. Amen.   *that same*

I SYKE WHEN Y SINGE

This devotional lyric, found at folio 80 recto, column a, is extraordinarily moving. It creates a vivid visual picture of the crucifixion as viewed through the mind of the narrator singing about Christ. The personal relationship between lyricist, Christ and Mary is emphasized by the movement of the poet, who merely observes in the first two stanzas but then addresses Christ directly in the third stanza, and by the immediacy of the present tense. The use of terms such as *Jhesu, þe suete, Jhesu, mi lemmon, Marie, reweþ þe*, adapted from the courtly love tradition to this religious setting, enhances the theme of love, and makes the love-sickness of the poet the more poignant. The reverie of this love is sharply contrasted with the derisive tone reserved for sinners in the final stanza.

I Syke when Y Singe

I syke when Y singe   *sigh*
For sorewe þat Y se,
When I wiþ wypinge   *weeping*
Biholde upon þe tre,
5   Ant se Jhesu, þe suete,   *sweet*
Is herte blod forlete   *shed*
For þe love of me.
Ys woundes waxen wete   *grow wet*
Þei wepen still and mete –
10   Marie, reweþ þe.   *pity*

Heȝe upon a doune   *hill*
Þer al folk hit se may
A mile from uch toune
Aboute þe midday
15   Þe rode is up arered   *raised*
His frendes aren aferd   *afraid*
And clyngeþ so þe clay;   *shrunken; as*
Þe rode stond in stone.   *cross*
Marie stont hire one   *stands; alone*
20   And seiþ 'Weylaway!'

When Y þe biholde
Wiþ eyȝen bryhte bo,   *both*
And þi bodi colde,
Þi ble waxeþ blo,   *face; leaden*
25   Þou hengest al of blode   *bloody*
So heȝe upon þe rode,

Bituene þeves tuo –
Who may syke more?
Marie wepeþ sore
30 And siht al þis wo. *sees*

Þe naylles beþ to stronge,
Þe smyþes are to sleye, *skilful*
Þou bledest al to longe,
Þe tre is al to heyȝe,
35 Þe stones beoþ al wete:
Alas! Jhesu, þe suete.
For nou frend hast þou non
But Seint Johan mournynde,
And Marie wepynde,
40 For pyne þat þe ys on. *torment; upon*

Ofte when Y sike
And makie my mon, *lamentation*
Wel ille þah me like, *not at all; though*
Wonder is hit non.
45 When Y se honge heȝe
And bittre pynes dreȝe, *torments; suffering*
Jhesu, mi lemmon, *sweetheart*
His wondes sore smerte, *hurting*
Þe spere al to is herte
50 Ant þourh is sydes gon. *through; his*

Ofte when Y syke
Wiþ care Y am þourhsoht; *pierced through*
When Y wake Y wyke, *grow weak*
Of sorewe is al mi þoht.
55 Alas, men beþ wode *mad*
Þat suereþ by þe rode, *swear*
Ant selleþ him for noht
Þat bohte us out of synne;
He bryng us to wynne *joy*
60 Þat haþ us duere boht. *dearly*

AN AUTUMN SONG

At folio 80 recto, column b, is this penitential lyric addressed to the Virgin Mary. It incorporates conventions of the secular love lyric in the seasonal reference of the opening, and in the second stanza that begins as does the *pastourelle* (in which the lover rides out into the countryside in pursuit of pleasure). This is not spring, though, but autumn, when thoughts turn to the inevitable mortality of living things, prompting the poet's penitence. This is a lyric that demonstrates a stylistic self-consciousness, coupled with conventional language and imagery adapted from secular lyrics (of the object of devotion as healer or physician, for example). Its personal theme of repentance is extended in the final stanza into a more general reminder to women that their beauty (unlike the Virgin's) is a passing thing; and that concentrating on eternal life rather than earthly looks would serve a better purpose.

An Autumn Song

	Now shrinkeþ rose ant lylie-flour	*withers*
	Þat whilen ber þat suete savour	*scent*
	In somer, þat suete tide.	*time*
	Ne is no quene so stark ne stour,	*mighty; strong*
5	Ne no levedy so bryht in bour,	
	Þat ded ne shal byglyde.	*creep up on*
	Whose wol fleysh lust forgon	*of fleshly*
	Ant Hevene blis abyde,	*await*
	On Jhesu be is þoht anon	*his; constantly*
10	Þat þerled was ys side.	*pierced*
	From Petresbourh in o morewenyng,	*Peterborough*
	As Y me wende o my pley3yng,	*pleasure*
	On mi folie Y þohte.	*folly (or adultery)*
	Menen Y gon my mournyng	*Express; began*
15	To hire þat ber þe hevene Kyng,	
	Of mercy hire bysohte:	
	'Ledy, preye þi sone for ous,	
	Þat us duere bohte,	*dearly*
	Ant shild us from þe loþe hous	*hateful*
20	Þat to þe fend is wrohte.'	*for; made*
	Mine herte of dedes wes fordred,	*deeds; afraid*
	Of synne þat Y have my fleish fed	
	Ant folewed all my tyme:	
	Þat Y not whider I shal be led,	
25	When Y lygge on deþes bed,	*lie*
	In joie ore into pyne.	*or; torment*
	On o Ledy mine hope is,	
	Moder ant virgyne:	
	We shulen into hevene blis	
30	Þurh hire medicine.	
	Betere is hire medycyn	
	Þen eny mede or eny wyn,	
	Hire erbes smulleþ suete.	*smell*
	From Catenas into Dyvelyn	*Caithness; Dublin*
35	Nis þer no leche so fyn	*physician*
	Oure sorewes to bete.	*cure*
	Mon þat feleþ eny sor,	*grief*

Ant his folie wol lete,   *abandon*
Wiþoute gold oþer eny tresor
40   He mai be sound ant sete.   *at ease*

Of penaunce is his plastre al,   *plaster*
Ant ever serven hire Y shal,
Now ant al my lyve.
Now is fre þat er wes þral,   *slave*
45   All þourh þat levedy, gent ant smal,   *noble; slender*
Heried be hyr joies fyve.[9]   *Praised*
Wherso eny sek is   *sick person*
Þider hye blyve;   *to her; hasten*
Þurh hire beoþ ybroht to blis
50   Bo mayden ant wyve.

For he þat dude is body on tre   *gave*
Of oure sunnes have piete,   *sins; pity*
Þat weldes hevene boures.   *rules*
Wymmon, wiþ þy jolyfte,   *Women; jollity*
55   Þou þench on Godes shoures: *pains*
Þah þou be whyt ant bryth on ble   *bright; of face*
Falewen shule þy floures.   *Wither*
Jesu have merci of us,
Þat al þis world honoures. Amen.

King Horn

King Horn, a 1,552-line Romance, exists in three versions.[10] The manuscripts are Cambridge University Library, Gg. IV. 27 (part II), folios 6 recto to 13 recto, dated to the beginning of the fourteenth century;[11] Oxford, Bodleian Library, Laud Misc. 108, folios 219 verso to 228 recto, dated to *c.*1300; and London, British Library, Harley 2253, folios 83 recto to 92 verso, dated to *c.*1340, and from which the edition below is taken. The fragmentary Cambridge manuscript contains the Romance *Floriz and Blauncheflur*, *King Horn* and a portion of the *Cursor Mundi*; Laud Misc. 108 contains part of *The South English Legendary*, other, shorter religious texts in English, and in its second section the Romances *Havelok the Dane* and *King Horn*. Harley 2253, as described above, contains numerous English secular and religious lyrics, and French and Latin prose and verse. Indeed, the manuscript contexts of *King Horn* vary in such a way as to suggest that the text can be viewed as a Romance that also has potentially didactic or religious themes.

The text of *King Horn* itself is earlier than the dates of the surviving manuscripts suggest. The majority of critics agree that its date of composition is *c.*1225.[12] The

place of origin has been partially obscured by scribal imposition of dialectal forms; Laud Misc. 108, for example, illustrates features consonant with a south-east Surrey, south-west Kent, or north Suffolk origin.[13] The other two manuscripts evidence West Berkshire (Gg. IV. 27) and Herefordshire (Harley 2253) dialectal forms.

King Horn is derived from a non-extant Anglo-Norman exemplar, probably written in the later twelfth century. The story of this prodigious knight and his acts of courage and prowess was a popular 'Matter of Britain' legend, and the three surviving versions attest to this popularity. It is, in many respects, a transitional text; one that contains many thematic elements seen in Old English heroic verse combined with the love interest that inspires so many later Romance heroes. The typical Romance elements of exile and return, heroic conduct in the proving of martial prowess and moral rectitude are seen in Horn himself; and Rymenhild, daughter of the king of Westnesse, provides the love interest. The composition is relatively naive, in that the poet focuses on the actions and events of the narrative, rather than the characterization or thoughts of the protagonists. Horn,

9   The five joys of Mary: the Annunciation, Nativity, Resurrection, Ascension, and Assumption of Mary.
10   J. Hall, ed., *King Horn: A Middle English Romance* (Oxford, 1901).
11   See M. Laing, *A Catalogue of Sources for a Linguistic Atlas of Early Middle English* (Cambridge, 1993), p. 45. See also M. J. Evans, *Re-*

reading Middle English Romance: Manuscript Layout, Decoration, and the Rhetoric of Composite Structure (Montreal, 1995), pp. 86–7.
12   See, for example, W. R. J. Barron, *English Medieval Romance* (London, 1987), p. 65.
13   Laing, *Catalogue of Sources*, p. 137, citing M. L. Samuels.

Rymenhild, Fykenhild and the other major characters are delineated in simplistic terms: bad or good; the best or the worst. Horn is always instantly recognizable as a noble figure, his beauty and goodness representing his inner worth and leadership. This sparsity of detail enables the rapid flow of the poem and provides a conciseness to the episodes. The setting of the poem varies as Horn moves around, although little description of different places is offered; his sea-journeys represent transitions in the action of the text, as well as indicating the progression of his evolution into the most noble of knights. These elements of the text – rapid action incorporating phrasal formulae and repetition – could be considered features of oral composition in the earliest stages of the text's composition. It is certainly the case that the text is a polished performative piece, and one which is most satisfactory when read aloud. The versification is couplets of three stresses per line.

King Horn

Her Bygynneþ þe geste of Kyng Horn

	Alle heo ben blyþe	
	Þat to my song ylyþe,	*listen*
	A song Ychulle ou singe	*I will*
	Of Allof þe gode kynge.	
5	Kyng he wes by weste,[14]	
	Þe whiles hit yleste,	*lasted*
	Ant Godylt his gode quene,	
	No feyrore myhte bene,	
	Ant huere sone hihte Horn,	*their; called*
10	Feyrore child ne myhte be born;	
	For reyn ne myhte byryne,	*touch upon*
	Ne sonne myhte shyne	*shine upon*
	Feyrore child þen he was;	
	Bryht so ever eny glas,	*as*
15	Is so whit so eny lylye flour,	
	So rose red wes his colour.	
	He wes feyr ant eke bold	*also*
	Ant of fyftene wynter old;	
	Nis non his yliche	*equal*
20	In none kinges ryche.	*kingdom*
	Tweye feren he hadde	*companions*
	Þat he wiþ him ladde;	
	Alle riche menne sones,	
	Ant alle swyþe feyre gomes,	*very; young men*
25	Wyþ him for te pleye.	
	Mest he lovede tweye:	*two*
	Þat on wes hoten Athulf Chyld,	*one was called*
	Ant þat oþer Fykenyld.	
	Athulf wes þe beste,	
30	Ant Fykenyld þe werste.	
	Hyt was upon a someres day,	
	Also Ich ou telle may,	
	Allof þe gode kyng,	
	Rod upon ys pleyჳyng	
35	Bi þe see side,	
	Þer he was woned to ryde.	*accustomed*
	Wiþ him ne ryde bote two –	

14 He was king in the west. Allof's kingdom, and Horn's birthplace, is Suddene.

	Al too fewe hue were þo.	*they; then*
	He fond by þe stronde	*shore*
40	Aryved on is lond	*his*
	Shipes fyftene	
	Of Sarazynes kene.[15]	*Saracens*
	He askede whet hue sohten,	
	Oþer on is lond brohten.	*Or*
45	A payen hit yherd,	*pagan*
	Ant sone him onsuerede:	*answered*
	'Þy landfolk we wolleþ slon	*kill*
	Þat ever Crist leveþ on,	*believed in*
	Ant þee we wolleþ ryht anon:	
50	Shalt þou never henne gon.'	*go from here*
	Þy kyng lyhte of his stede,	*dismounted*
	For þo he hevede nede,	*then; had*
	Ant his gode feren tuo:	
	Mid ywis, huem wes ful wo.	*Truly; great woe*
55	Swerd hy gonne gripe	*they; began to grip*
	Ant togedere smyte;	*struck*
	Hy smyten under shelde	
	Þat hy somme yfelde.	
	Þe kyng hade too fewe	
60	Aȝeyn so monie schrewe.	*evil men*
	So fele myhten eþe	*many might easily*
	Bringe þre to deþe.	
	Þe payns come to londe	
	Ant nomen hit an honde;	*And took control of it*
65	Þe folk hy gonne quelle	*kill*
	Ant cherches for to felle.	
	Þer ne myhte libbe	
	Þe fremede ne þe sibbe,	*stranger; relation*
	Bote he is lawe forsoke	*Unless he abandoned his religion*
70	Ant to huere toke.	*theirs*
	Of alle wymmanne	
	Werst wes Godyld þanne:	
	For Allof hy wepeþ sore	*sorely*
	Ant for Horn ȝet more.	
75	Godild hade so muche sore,	*sorrow*
	Þat habbe myhte hue na more.	*she*
	Hue wente out of halle	
	From hire maidnes alle	
	Under a roche of stone,	
80	Þer hue wonede alone.	*lived*
	Þer hue servede Gode	
	Aȝeyn þe payenes forbode;	*forbidding of it*
	Þer hue servede Crist	
	Þat þe payenes hit nust;	*did not know*
85	Ant ever hue bad for Horn Child	*prayed*
	Þat Crist him wurþe myld.	*would be merciful*
	Horn wes in payenes hond	
	Mid is feren of þe lond;	*companions*

---

15   Saracens became the archetypal foes in many Romances.

	Muche wes þe feyrhade	*beauty*
90	Þat Jhesu Crist him made.	
	Payenes him wolde slo,	*wished to kill him*
	Ant summe him wolde flo;	*flay*
	Ʒyf Hornes feyrnesse nere,	*If Horn had not been beautiful*
	Yslawe þis children were.	
95	Þo spec on admyrold,	*Then; commander*
	Of wordes he wes swyþe bold:	
	'Horn, þou art swyþe kene,	*brave*
	Bryht of hewe ant shene;	*fair*
	Þou art fayr ant eke strong	
100	Ant eke eveneliche long;	*also equally tall*
	Yef þou to lyve mote go	*alive; be allowed to*
	Ant þyne feren also,	
	Þat Y may byfalle	*allow to happen*
	Þat ye shule slen us alle.	*kill*
105	Þarefore þou shalt to streme go	*the sea's currents*
	Þou ant þy feren also,	
	To shipe ʒe shule founde	
	Ant sinke to þe grounde.	*bottom of the sea*
	Þe see þe shal adrenche,	*drown*
110	Ne shal hit us ofþenche;	*concern*
	For ʒef þou were alyve	
	Wiþ suerd oþer wiþ knyve	
	We shulden alle deʒe,	*die*
	Þy fader deþ to beye.'	*avenge*
115	Þe children ede to þe stronde	*went*
	Wryngynde huere honde,	*their*
	Ant into shipes borde	*embarked*
	At þe furste worde.	
	Ofte hade Horn be wo	
120	Ah never wors þen him wes þo.	
	Þe see bygon to flowen	
	Ant Horn faste to rowen,	
	Ant þat ship wel swyþe drof,	*was very rapidly driven*
	Ant Horn wes adred þerof:	*fearful*
125	Hue wenden mid ywisse	*They thought with certainty*
	Of huere lyve to misse.	*lose*
	Al þe day ant al þe nyht	
	O þat sprong þe daylyht	*Until*
	Flotterede Horn by þe stronde	
130	Er he seye eny londe.	*saw*
	'Feren', quoþ Horn þe ʒynge,	*young*
	'Y telle ou tydynge:	*good tidings*
	Ich here foules singe,	*birds*
	Ant se þe grases springe.	
135	Blyþe be ʒe alyve;	
	Ur ship is come to ryve.'[16]	*Our; land*
	Of shipe hy gonne founde,	*From; began to leave*
	Ant sette fot to grounde	
	By þe see syde,	

16 Horn and his companions have landed in Westnesse.

140   Hure ship bigon to ryde.
      Þenne spec him Child Horn
      In Sudenne he was yborn:
      'Nou, ship, by þe flode
      Have dayes gode;
145   By þe see brynke
      No water þe adrynke;   *drown*
      Softe mote þou sterye   *steer*
      Þat water þe ne derye.   *injure*
      Ȝef þou comest to Sudenne,
150   Gret hem þat me kenne;   *know*
      Gret wel þe gode
      Quene Godild, mi moder.
      Ant sey þene heþene kyng,   *to the*
      Jhesu Cristes wytherlyng,   *enemy*
155   Þat Ich hol ant fere   *whole and healthy*
      In londe aryvede here,
      Ant say þat he shal fonde
      Þen deþ of myne honde.'
          Þe ship bigon to fleoten   *float away*
160   Ant Horn Child to weopen.
      By dales ant by doune   *hills*
      Þe chidren eoden to toune;
      Metten hue Eylmer þe kyng,
      Crist him ȝeve god tymyng,
165   Kyng of Westnesse.
      Crist him myhte blesse!
      He spec to Horn Childe
      Wordes swyþe myld:
      'Whenne be ȝe gomen,   *From where are you, young men*
170   Þat bueþ her a londe ycomen,   *are*
      Alle þrettene   *thirteen*
      Of bodye swyþe kene?
      By God þat me made,
      So feyr a felawrade   *group*
175   Ne Ich ynever stonde   *never saw standing*
      In Westnesse londe.
      Say me whet ȝe seche.'
      Horn spec huere speche.
      Horn spac for huem alle,   *them*
180   For so hit moste byfalle –   *happen*
      He wes þe wyseste
      And of wytte þe beste:
      'We bueþ of Sudenne,
      Ycome of gode kenne   *kin*
185   Of Cristene blode,
      Of cunne swyþe gode.   *a family*
      Payenes þer connen aryve,   *did*
      Ant Cristine brohten of lyve,   *deprived*
      Slowen ant todrowe   *cut to pieces*
190   Cristine men ynowe.   *enough*
      So Crist me mote rede,   *As Christ may guide me*
      Ous hy duden lede   *Us; did*

Into a galeye
Wiþ þe see to pleye.

195   Day is gone ant oþer   *For one day and another day*
Wiþoute seyl and roþer   *rudder*
Ure ship flet forþ ylome   *floated; constantly*
And her to lande hit ys ycome.
Now þou myht us slen and bynde

200   Oure honde us bihynde;
Ah, ȝef hit is þi wille,   *But*
Help us þat we ne spille.'   *do not die*
      Þo spac þe gode kyng –
He nes never nyþyng: *an evil man*

205   'Sey, Child, whet is þy name?
Shal þe tide bote game.'[17]
      Þe child him onsuerede
So sone he hit yherde:
'Horn Ycham yhote,   *I am called*

210   Ycome out of þis bote
From þe see side.
Kyng, wel þe bitide.'   *may good come to you*
      'Horn Child,' quoþ þe kyng,
'Wel brouc þou þy nome ȝyng.   *suits; young*

215   Horn him goþ so stille   *A horn proceeds quietly*
Bi dales ant by hulles;
Horn haþ loude soune
Þurhout uch a toune.   *every*
So shal þi nome springe

220   From kynge to kynge,
Ant þi feirnesse
Aboute Westnesse.
Horn, þou art so suete,
Ne shal Y þe forlete.'   *abandon*

225   Hom rod Aylmer þe kyng   *Home*
Ant Horn wiþ him, his fundlyng,   *homeless one*
Ant alle his yfere
Þat him were so duere.   *beloved*
Þe kyng com into halle

230   Among his knyhtes alle;
Forþ he clepeþ Aþelbrus,
His stiward, ant him seide þus:
'Stiward, tac þou here
My fundling for to lere   *teach*

235   Of þine mestere   *trade*
Of wode ant of ryvere;
And toggen o þe harp   *teach him to play on*
Wiþ is nayles sharpe.
And tech him alle þe listes   *skills*

240   Þat þou ever wystest: *knew*
Byfore me to kerven,   *carve*
Ant of my coupe to serven;
Ant his feren devyse

17   Only good things shall happen to you.

Wiþ ous oþer servise.
245 Horn Child, þou understond,
Tech him of harpe ant of song.'
Aþelbrus gon leren *began to teach*
Horn and hyse feren;
Horn mid herte lahte *learnt by heart*
250 Al þat mon him tahte.
    Wiþinne court and wiþoute,
Ant overal aboute
Lovede men Horn Child,
Ant most him lovede Rymenyld,
255 Þe kynges oune dohter, *own*
For he wes in hire þohte.
Hue lovede him in hire mod, *She; heart*
For he wes feir and eke god;
Ant, þah hue ne dorste at bord *though; dared; table*
260 Mid him speke ner a word,
Ne in þe halle,
Among þe knyhtes alle,
Hyre sorewe ant hire pyne *torment*
Nolde never fyne *would not ever cease*
265 Bi daye ne by nyhte;
For hue speke ne myhte *she could not speak*
Wiþ Horn þat wes so feir ant fre
Þo hue ne myhte wiþ him be. *When*
In herte hue hade care ant wo, *sorrow*
270 Ant þus hue biþohte hire þo. *thought about that then*
Hue sende hyre sonde *messenger*
Aþelbrus to honde *to bring*
Þat he come hire to
Ant also shulde Horn do
275 Into hire boure, *chamber*
For hue bigon to loure. *Because; sicken*
Ant þe sonde sayde
Þat seek wes þe mayde
Ant bed him come swyþe, *asked him to come quickly*
280 For hue nis nout blyþe. *is not at all happy*
Þe stiward wes in huerte wo, *sorrowful*
For he nuste whet he shulde do *For he did not know that he should do*
What Rymenild bysohte.
Gret wonder him þohte *it seemed to him*
285 Aboute Horn þe ȝinge
To boure forte bringe:
He þohte on is mode
Hit nes for none gode. *It could be for no benefit*
He tok wiþ him anoþer,
290 Aþulf, Hornes broþer:
    'Athulf', quoþ he, 'ryht anon *straight away*
Þou shalt wiþ me to boure gon
To speke wiþ Rymenild stille *quietly*
To wyte hyre wille. *know*
295 Þou art Hornes yliche; *similar to Horn*
Þou shalt hire bysuyke. *deceive*

Sore me adrede
Þat hue wole Horn mysrede.'   *mislead*
　Athelbrus ant Athulf bo   *together*
300   To hire boure beþ ygo.
Upon Athulf Childe
Rymenild con waxe wilde;   *began to grow*
Hue wende Horn it were
Þat hue hade þere.
305   Hue seten adoun stille   *They sat*
Ant seyden hure wille
In hire armes tweye
Athulf he con leye.   *lay*
　'Horn,' quoþ heo, 'wel longe
310   Y have loved þe stronge.
Þou shalt þy treuþe plyhte   *pledge your word*
In myn hond wiþ ryhte
Me to spouse welde   *to have me in marriage*
Ant Ich þe loverd to helde.'   *I will hold you as lord*
315   So stille so hit were,   *As quietly as could be*
Athulf seyde in hire eere:
'Ne tel þou no more speche
May, Y þe byseche.   *Maiden*
Þi tale gyn þou lynne,   *you must stop talking*
320   For Horn nis nout herynne –
Ne be we nout yliche,   *similar*
For Horn is fayr ant ryche;
Fayrore by one ribbe   *rib*
Þen ani mon þat libbe.   *lives*
325   Þah Horn were under molde,   *the earth*
Oþer ellewher he sholde   *Or should be somewhere else*
Hennes a þousent milen,   *A thousand miles from here*
Y nulle him bigilen.'   *betray*
Rymenhild hire bywente   *turned*
330   Ant Athelbrus þus heo shende: *reproached*
'Aþelbrus, þou foule þef,
Ne worþest þou me never lef!   *You will never be beloved of me*
Went out of my boure!   *Get out*
Shame þe mote byshoure,   *May shame fall upon you*
335   Ant evel hap to underfonge,   *And may you receive bad luck*
Ant evele rod on to honge.   *Cross*
Ne speke Y nout wiþ Horne –
Nis he nout so unorne!'   *unattractive*
　Þo Athelbrus a stounde   *Then; immediately*
340   Fel akneu to grounde: *on bended knee*
'Ha, levedy my owe,   *my own lady*
Me lyþe a lutel þrowe,   *listen to me for a while*
Ant list werefore Ych wonde   *hear why I hesitated*
To bringen Horn to honde.
345   For Horn is fayr ant riche,   *Because*
Nis non his ylyche,   *equal*
Aylmer þe gode kyng
Dude him me in lokyng.   *Put him in my care*
Yif Horn þe were aboute   *around*

350	Sore Ich myhte doute	*Dreadfully; fear*
	Wiþ him þou woldest pleye	
	Bitwene ouselven tweye;	*yourselves*
	Þenne shulde, wiþouten oþe,	*doubt*
	Þe kyng us make wroþe.	*would become angry*
355	Ah forзef me þi teone,	*But forgive me for causing you grief*
	My levedy ant my quene:	
	Horn Y shal þe fecche,	
	Whamso hit yrecche.'	*Whoever it might bother*
	Rymenhild, зef heo couþe,	*were able*
360	Con lyþe wyþ hyre mouþe;	*smiled*
	Heo loh ant made hyre blyþe,	*laughed*
	For wel wes hire o lyve.	*in life*
	'Go þou,' quoþ heo, 'sone,	*immediately*
	Ant send him after none	*noon*
365	A skuyeres wyse	*in the manner of a squire*
	When þe king aryse.	
	He shal myd me bileve	*remain*
	Þat hit be ner eve;	*Until*
	Have Ich of him mi wille,	
370	Ne recchi whet men telle.'	
	Athelbrus goþ wiþ alle;	
	Horn he fond in halle	
	Bifore þe kyng o benche,	
	Wyn for te shenche.	*pour*
375	'Horn,' quoþ he, 'þou hende,	*courteous one*
	To boure gyn þou wende	
	To speke wiþ Rymenild þe зynge,	
	Dohter oure kynge.	
	Wordes swyþe bolde	
380	Þin horte gyn þou holde.	
	Horn, be þou me trewe,	
	Shal þe nout arewe.'	*regret it*
	He eode forþ to ryhte	*straight away*
	To Rymenild þe bryhte.	
385	Aknewes he him sette	*Kneeling*
	Ant suetliche hire grette;	
	Of is fayre syhte	*From the fair sight of him*
	Al þat bour gan lyhte.	
	He spak faire is speche,	
390	Ne durþ non him teche:	*needed anyone*
	'Wel þou sitte ant softe,	
	Rymenild, kinges dohter,	
	Ant þy maydnes here	
	Þat sitteþ þyne yfere.	*as your companions*
395	Kynges styward oure	
	Sende me to boure	
	Forte yhere, levedy myn,	
	Whet be wille þyn.'	
	Rymenild up gon stonde	
400	Ant tok him by þe honde.	
	Heo made feyre chere,	
	Ant tok him bi þe swere.	*clasped; neck*

Ofte heo him custe
So wel hyre luste.   *As pleased her best*

405   'Welcome, Horn,' þus sayde
Rymenild þat mayde,
'An even ant amorewe   *At evening and in the morning*
For þe Ich habbe sorewe,
Þat Y have no reste

410   Ne slepe me ne lyste.   *desire*
Horn, þou shalt wel swyþe   *swiftly*
Mi longe serewe lyþe;   *lessen*
Þou shalt wiþoute strive   *difficulty*
Habbe me to wyve.

415   Horn, have of me reuþe,   *pity*
Ant plyht me þi treuþe.'
    Horn þo hym byþohte
Whet he speken ohte: *ought*
'Crist,' quoþ Horn, 'þe wisse,   *will guide you*

420   Ant зeve þe hevene blisse   *give*
Of þine hosebonde,
Who he be a londe.   *in*
Ich am ybore þral,   *in servitude*
Þy fader fundlyng wiþal;

425   Of kunde me ne felde   *It would not be appropriate for me*
Þe to spouse welde.
Hit nere no fair weddyng
Bitwene a þral ant þe kyng!'
    Þo gon Rymenild mislyken,   *became displeased*

430   Ant sore bigon to syken,   *sigh*
Armes bigon unbowe,   *loosen*
Ant doun heo fel yswowe.   *in a swoon*
Horn hire up hente   *picked*
Ant in is armes trente.   *embraced*

435   He gon hire to cusse
Ant feyre forte wisse.   *advise*
'Rymenild,' quoþ he, 'duere,   *beloved*
Help me þat Ych were
Ydobbed to be knyhte,   *Dubbed*

440   Suete, bi al þi myhte
To mi loverd þe kyng,
Þat he me зeve dobbyng;
Þenne is my þralhede   *servitude*
Al wend into knyhthede.   *transformed*

445   Y shal waxe more
Ant do, Rymenhild, þi lore.'   *bidding*
Þo Rymenhild þe зynge
Aros of hire swowenynge: *swoon*
'Nou, Horn, to soþe,   *in truth*

450   Y leve þe by þyn oþe.   *believe*
Þou shalt be maked knyht
Er þen þis fourteniht.
Ber þou her þes coppe,
Ant þes ringe þeruppe

455   To Athelbrus þe styward,

Ant say him he holde foreward.   *tell him to support this agreement*
Sey Ich him biseche
Wiþ loveliche speche,
Þat he for þe falle
460   To þe kynges fet in halle,
Þat he wiþ is worde   *so that; his*
Þe knyhty wiþ sworde.   *Might knight you*
Wiþ selver ant wiþ golde
Hit worþ him wel yȝolde.   *repaid*
465   Nou, Crist him lene spede,   *give*
Þin erndyng do bede.'   *message; announce*
     Horn tok is leve,
For hit wes neh eve.
Athelbrus he sohte
470   Ant tok him þat he brohte,
Ant tolde him þare
Hou he hede yfare.   *had*
He seide him is nede   *told*
Ant him bihet is mede.   *promised his reward*
475   Athelbrus so blyþe
Eode into halle swyþe,
Ant seide: 'Kyng, nou leste,   *listen to*
O tale mid þe beste.
Þou shalt bere coroune
480   Tomarewe in þis toune:
Tomarewe is þi feste,   *feast day*
Þe bihoveþ geste.   *You deserve a special event*
Ich þe rede mid al my myht   *advise*
Þat þou make Horn knyht;
485   Þin armes do him welde.   *allow*
God knyht he shal þe ȝelde.'   *repay*
Þe kyng seide wel sone:
'Hit is wel to done.
Horn me wel quemeþ –   *pleases*
490   Knyht him wel bysemeþ.
He shal have mi dobbyng
Ant be myn oþer derlyng,
Ant hise feren tuelve
He shal dobbe himselve.
495   Alle Y shal hem knyhte
Byfore me to fyhte.'
     Al þat þe lyhte day sprong   *Until*
Aylmere þohte long.
Þe day bigon to springe;
500   Horn com byfore þe kynge
Wiþ his tuelf fere:
Alle þer ywere.
Horn knyht made he
Wiþ ful gret solempnite;
505   Sette him on a stede
Red so eny glede,   *ember*
Smot him a lute wiht,   *Tapped; light touch*
Ant bed him buen a god knyht.

	Athulf vel akne þer	*fell on his knees*
510	Ant þonkede kyng Aylmer:	
	'Nou is knyht Sire Horn,	
	Þat in Sudenne wes yborn.	
	Lord he is of londe	
	Ant of us þat by him stonde.	
515	Þin armes he haveþ ant þy sheld	
	Forte fyhte in þe feld.	
	Let him us alle knyhte	
	So hit is his ryhte.'	
	Aylmer seide ful ywis:	
520	'Nou do þat þi wille ys.'	
	Horn adoun con lyhte,	*dismounted*
	Ant made hem alle to knyhte,	
	For muchel wes þe geste,	*great*
	Ant more wes þe feste.	
525	Þat Rymenild nes nout þere	
	Hire þohte seve ȝere.	*It seemed like seven years to her*
	Efter Horn hue sende;	
	Horn into boure wende.	
	He nolde gon is one;	*alone*
530	Athulf wes hys ymone.	*companion*
	Rymenild welcomeþ Sire Horn	
	Ant Aþulf knyht him biforn.	
	'Knyht, nou is tyme	
	For to sitte by me.	
535	Do nou þat we spake;	
	To þi wyf þou me take.	
	Nou þou hast wille þyne,	
	Unbynd me of þis pyne.'	*Free me from this torment*
	'Rymenhild, nou be stille;	
540	Ichulle don al þy wille.	*I will*
	Ah her hit so bitide,	*But before it happens thus*
	Mid spere Ichulle ryde	
	Ant my knyhthod prove	
	Er þen Ich þe wowe.	*woo*
545	We bueþ now knyhtes ȝonge	
	Alle today yspronge,	
	Ant of þe mestere	*occupation*
	Hit is þe manere	
	Wiþ sum oþer knyhte	
550	For his lemmon to fyhte	*sweetheart*
	Er ne he eny wyf take,	
	Oþer wyþ wymmon forewart make.	*agreement*
	Today, so Crist me blesse,	
	Y shal do pruesse	*excellence through deeds*
555	For þi love mid shelde	
	Amiddewart þe felde.	*In the midst of*
	Ȝef Ich come to lyve,	*return alive*
	Ychul þe take to wyve.'	
	'Knyht, Y may yleve þe;	
560	Why, ant þou trewe be,	
	Have her þis gold ring.	

Hit is ful god to þi dobbyng.   *fitting*
Ygraved is on þe ryng
"Rymenild þy luef þe ȝynge".   *beloved*
565 Nis non betere under sonne
Þat eny mon of conne.   *knows of*
For mi love þou hit were,
Ant on þy fynger þou hit bere.
Þe ston haveþ suche grace   *Divine protection*
570 Ne shalt þou in none place
Deþ underfonge;   *receive*
Ne buen yslaye wiþ wronge   *killed*
Yef þou lokest þeran,
Ant þenchest o þi lemman;   *think*
575 Ant Sire Aþulf þi broþer
He shal han enoþer.
Horn, Crist Y þe byteche   *entrust*
Mid mourninde speche.   *sorrowful*
Crist þe ȝeve god endyng,
580 Ant sound aȝeyn þe brynge.'
    Þe knyht hire gan to cusse,
Ant Rymenild him to blesse.
Leve at hyre he nom,   *took*
Ant into halle he com.
585 Knyhtes eode to table,   *went*
Ant Horn eode to stable.
Þer he toc his gode fole,   *horse*
Blac so ever eny cole.
Wiþ armes he him sredde,   *clothed*
590 Ant is fole he fedde.
Þe fole bigon to springe,
Ant Horn murie to synge.
Horn rod one whyle
Wel more þen a myle;
595 He seh a shyp at grounde   *saw*
Wiþ heþene hounde.   *heathen*
He askede wet hue hadden,
Oþer to londe ladden.   *brought*
An hound him gan biholde
600 Ant spek wordes bolde:
'Þis land we wolleþ wynne
Ant sle þat þer bueþ inne!'   *those that are*
Horn gan is swerd gripe
Ant on is arm hit wype;
605 Þe Sarazyn he hitte so
Þat is hed fel to ys to.   *toes*
Þo gonne þe houndes gone   *approach*
Aȝeynes Horn ys one.   *on his own*
He lokede on is rynge
610 Ant þohte o Rymenyld þe ȝynge.
He sloh þerof þe beste,
An houndred at þe leste;
Ne mihte no mon telle
Alle þat he gon quelle.   *did kill*

615	Of þat þer were oryve	*had come ashore*
	He lafte lut olyve.	*few alive*
	Horn tok þe maister heved	*chief's head*
	Þat he him hade byreved,	*deprived of*
	Ant sette on is suerde	
620	Aboven o þen orde.	*point*
	He ferde hom to halle	
	Among þe knyhtes alle.	
	'Kyng,' quoþ he, 'well þou sitte	
	Ant þine knyhtes mitte.	*with you*
625	Today Ich rod o my pleyyng	
	After my dobbyng;	
	I fond a ship rowen	
	In þe sound byflowen	
	Mid unlondisshe menne	*foreign*
630	Of Sarazynes kenne,	
	To deþe forte pyne	*kill*
	Þe ant alle þyne.	
	Hy gonne me asayly;	*attack*
	Swerd me nolde fayly;	
635	Y smot hem alle to grounde	
	In a lutel stounde.	*short time*
	Þe heved Ich þe bringe	
	Of þe maister kynge.	
	Nou have Ich þe ȝolde	*repaid*
640	Þat þou me knyhten woldest.'	
	Þe day bigon to springe;	
	Þe kyng rod on hontynge	
	To þe wode wyde,	
	Ant Fykenyld bi is syde	
645	Þat fals wes ant untrewe,	
	Whose him wel yknewe.	*To those*
	Horn ne þohte nout him on	
	Ant to boure wes ygon.	
	He fond Rymenild sittynde,	
650	Ant wel sore wepynde	
	So whyt so þe sonne,	
	Mid terres al byronne.	*tears*
	Horn seide, 'Luef, þyn ore:	*Beloved; mercy*
	Why wepest þou so sore?'	
655	Hue seide, 'Ich nout ne wepe,	
	Ah Y shal er Y slepe.	
	Me þohte o my metyng	*It seemed to me in my dream*
	Þat Ich rod o fysshyng	*went out*
	To see my net ycaste;	
660	Ant wel fer hit laste,	*And it was thrown out far*
	A gret fyssh at þe ferste	
	My net made berste.	
	Þat fyssh me so bycahte	
	Þat Y nout ne lahte.	*netted nothing*
665	Y wene Y shal forleose	*think; lose*
	Þat fyssh þat Y wolde cheose.'	*choose*
	'Crist and Seinte Stevene,'	

	Quoþ Horn, 'areche þy swevene.	*interpret; dream*
	No shal Y þee byswyke,	*betray*
670	Ne do þat þe mislyke.	*displeases*
	Ich take þe myn owe	*own*
	To holde ant eke to knowe	
	For everuch oþer wyhte;	*Before; creature*
	Þerto my trouþe Y plyhte.'	
675	Wel muche was þe reuþe	*grief*
	Þat wes at þilke treuþe.	*that same pledge*
	Rymenild wep wel ylle,	
	Ant Horn let terres stille:	*caused the tears to still*
	'Lemmon,' quoþ he, 'dere,	
680	Þou shalt more yhere –	
	Þy sweven shal wende:	*can be interpreted*
	Summon us wole shende.	*Someone; injure*
	Þat fyssh þat brac þy net,	
	Ywis, it is sumwet,	*something*
685	Þat wol us do sum teone.	*injury*
	Ywys, hit worþ ysene.'	*will be seen*
	Aylmer rod by Stoure,	
	Ant Horn wes yne boure.	
	Fykenhild hade envye	
690	Ant seyde þeose folye:	*this lie*
	'Aylmer, Ich þe werne,	*warn*
	Horn þee wole forberne.	*destroy*
	Ich herde wher he seyde,	
	Ant his swerd he leyde,	*laid a bet on*
695	To brynge þe of lyve	
	Ant take Rymenyld to wyve.	
	He lyht nou in boure,	
	Under covertoure,	*bed-covers*
	By Rymenyld þy dohter,	
700	Ant so he doþ wel ofte.	
	Do him out of londe	
	Er he do more shonde.'	*shameful thing*
	Aylmer gon hom turne	
	Wel mody ant wel sturne.	*wrathful*
705	He fond Horn under arme	
	In Rymenyldes barme.	*bosom*
	'Go out,' quoþ Aylmer þe kyng,	
	'Horn, þou foule fundlyng,	
	Forþ out of boures flore;	
710	For Rymenild þin hore,	*Because of*
	Wend out of londe sone;	*Go; immediately*
	Her nast þou nout to done.	
	Wel sone, bote þou flette,	*unless you flee*
	Myd swert Y shal þe sette.'	
715	Horn eode to stable	
	Wel modi for þat fable.	*falsehood*
	He sette sadel on stede;	
	Wiþ armes he gon him shrede;	*clothe*
	His brunie he con lace,	*mail-coat*
720	So he shulde, into place;	

His suerd he gon fonge,   *took up*
Ne stod he nout to longe.
To us suerd he gon teon,   *drew to himself*
Ne durste non wel him seon.   *Nor did any dare at all to see him*
725   He seide, 'Lemmon, derlyng,
Nou þou havest þy swevenyng: *dream*
Þe fyssh þat þyn net rende
From þe me he sende.
Þe kyng wiþ me gynneþ strive;
730   Awey he wole me dryve.
Þarefore have nou godne day.
Nou Y mot founde and fare away   *leave*
Into uncouþe londe   *unknown*
Wel more forte fonde.   *experience*
735   Y shal wonie þere   *stay*
Fulle seve ȝere;
At þe seve ȝeres ende,
Ȝyf Y ne come ne sende,
Tac þou hosebonde:
740   For me þat þou ne wonde.   *Do not hesitate on my account*
In armes þou me fonge,   *take*
Ant cus me swyþe longe.'
Hy custen hem a stounde,   *a while*
An Rymenhild fel to grounde.
745   Horn toc his leve –
He myhte nout byleve.   *remain*
He toc Aþulf is fere   *clasped; companion*
Aboute þe swere   *neck*
Ant seide: 'Knyht so trewe,
750   Kep wel my love newe.
Þou never ne forsoke
Rymenild to kepe ant loke.'   *protect*
His stede he bigan stryde,
Ant forþ he con hym ryde.
755   Aþulf wep wiþ eyȝen,
Ant alle þat hit yseyȝen.   *saw it*
Horn forþ him ferde,   *journeyed*
A god ship he him herde,   *hired*
Þat he shulde passe   *So that*
760   Out of Westnesse.
Þe wynd bigon to stonde   *blow steadily*
Ant drof hem up o londe.[18]
To londe þat hy fletten,   *sailed to*
Fot out of ship hy setten.
765   He fond bi þe weye
Kynges sones tueye: *two*
Þat on wes hoten Aþyld   *called*
Ant þat oþer Beryld.
Beryld hym con preye
770   Þat he shulde seye
What he wolde þere   *wanted*

18   Horn lands in Ireland.

Ant what ys nome were. *name*

   'Godmod,' he seid, 'Ich hote, *am called*

Ycomen out of þis bote

775   Wel fer from by weste

To seche myne beste.'

Beryld con ner him ryde *did*

Ant toc him bi þe bridel:

'Wel be þou, knyht, yfounde;

780   Wiþ me þou lef a stounde. *remain; a while*

Also Ich mote sterve, *as I might die*

Þe kyng þou shalt serve;

Ne seh Y never alyve

So feir knyht her aryve.'

785   Godmod he ladde to halle,

Ant he adoun gan falle

Ant sette him a knelyng

Ant grette þene gode kyng.

Þo saide Beryld wel sone:

790   'Kyng, wiþ him þou ast done —

Þi lond tac him to werie, *take; guard*

Ne shal þe no mon derye, *injure*

For he is þe feyreste man

Þat ever in þis lond cam.'

795   Þo seide þe kyng wel dere:

'Welcome be þou here.

Go, Beryld, wel swyþe, *very swiftly*

Ant make hym wel blyþe,

Ant when þou farest to wowen, *go; woo*

800   Tac him þine gloven. *gloves as a challenge*

Þer þou hast munt to wyve *Where; a mind*

Awey he shal þe dryve;

For Godmodes feyrhede *beauty*

Shalt þou nower spede.' *have success*

805   Hit wes at Cristesmasse,

Nouþer more ne lasse

Þe kyng made feste,

Of his knyhtes beste.

Þer com in at none

810   A geaunt swyþe sone

Yarmed of paynyme *in a pagan manner*

Ant seide þise ryme:

'Site kyng bi kynge,

And herkne my tidynge.

815   Her bueþ paynes aryve,

Wel more þen fyve

Her beþ upon honde,

Kyng, in þine londe.

On þerof wol fyhte *One*

820   Toȝeynes þre knyhtes: *Against*

Ȝef eure þre sleh oure on, *your*

We shulen of eure londe gon;

Ȝef ure on sleh eure þre,

Al þis lond shal ure be. *ours*

825   Tomorewe shal be þe fyhtynge
       At þe sonne upspringe.'
          Þo seyde þe kyng, Þurston,
       'Godmod shal be þat on,   one
       Beryld shal be þat oþer,
830   Þe þridde, Aþyld is broþer;   his
       For hue bueþ strongeste
       Ant in armes þe beste.
       Ah wat shal us to rede?   But; counsel
       Y wene we bueþ dede.'   fear; dead
835   Godmod set at borde
       Ant seide þeose wordes:
       'Sire kyng, nis no ryhte   it is not
       On wiþ þre fyhte;   One against
       Aʒeynes one hounde
840   Þre Cristene to founde.   contend
       Ah, kyng, Y shal alone
       Wiþoute more ymone   another person
       Wiþ my swerd ful eþe   most easily
       Bringen hem alle to deþe.'
845   Þe kyng aros amorewe;
       He hade muche sorewe.
       Godmod ros of bedde;
       Wiþ armes he him shredde.   armed himself
       His brunye he on caste   mail-coat
850   Ant knutte hit wel faste,   knotted
       Ant com him to þe kynge
       At his uprysynge.
       'Kyng,' quoþ he, 'com to felde
       Me forte byhelde,
855   Hou we shule flyten   battle
       Ant togedere smiten.'   fight
          Riht at prime tide,   the first hour
       Hy gonnen out to ryde.
       Hy founden in a grene
860   A geaunt swyþe kene,   bold
       His feren him biside,
       Þat day for to abyde.   await
       Godmod hem gon asaylen;   attack
       Nolde he nout faylen.
865   He ʒef duntes ynowe;   blows
       Þe payen fel yswowe.   unconscious
       Ys feren gonnen hem wiþdrawe,   started to
       For huere maister wes neh slawe.   almost dead
       He[19] seide: 'Knyht, þou reste
870   A whyle ʒef þe leste.   desire
       Y ne hevede ner of monnes hond   had
       So harde duntes in non lond
       Bote of þe kyng Murry,[20]
       Þat wes swiþe sturdy.
875   He wes of Hornes kenne;

---

19   The pagan giant.   20   Horn's father.

Y sloh him in Sudenne.'

 Godmod him gon agryse,   *tremble*
Ant his blod aryse.
Byforen him he seh stonde   *standing*
880 Þat drof him out of londe,   *The one that*
Ant fader his aquelde.   *killed*
He smot him under shelde;   *struck*
He lokede on is rynge
Ant þohte o Rymenild þe ȝynge.
885 Mid god swerd at þe furste
He smot him þourh þe huerte.
Þe payns bigonne to fleon
Ant to huere shype teon.   *took to their ship*
To ship hue wolden erne;   *run*
890 Godmod hem con werne.   *stopped*
Þe kynges sones tweyne
Þe paiens slowe beyne.   *both of them*
Þo wes Godmod swyþe wo,
Ant þe payens he smot so,
895 Þat in a lutel stounde
Þe paiens hy felle to grounde.
Godmod ant is men
Slowe þe payenes everuchen.
His fader deþ ant ys lond
900 Awrek Godmod wiþ his hond.   *Avenged*
Þe kyng wiþ reuþful chere   *sorrowful*
Lette leggen is sones on bere   *bier*
Ant bringen hom to halle.
Muche sorewe hue maden alle.
905 In a chirche of lym ant ston
Me buriede hem wiþ ryche won.   *many riches*
 Þe kyng lette forþ calle
Hise knyhtes alle
Ant seide: 'Godmod, ȝef þou nere,   *had it not been for you*
910 Alle ded we were.
Þou art boþe god ant feyr;
Her Y make þee myn heyr,   *heir*
For my sones bueþ yslawe
Ant ybroht of lyfdawe.   *deprived; life*
915 Dohter Ich habbe one,
Nis non so feyr of blod ant bone:
Ermenild þat feyre may,   *maiden*
Bryht so eny someres day.
Hire wolle Ich ȝeve þe,   *give*
920 Ant her kyng shalt þou be.'
He seyde: 'More Ichul þe serve,
Kyng, er þen þou sterve.   *die*
When Y þy dohter ȝerne,   *desire*
Heo ne shal me noþyng werne.'   *deny*
925 Godmod wonede þere
Full six ȝere;
Ant, þe seveþe ȝer bygon,
To Rymynyld sonde ne sende he non.   *messenger*

Rymenyld wes in Westnesse

930 Wiþ muchel sorewenesse:

A kyng þer wes aryve

Ant wolde hyre han to wyve.

At one were þe kynges   *Of one mind*

Of þat weddynge.

935 Þe dayes were so sherte,

Ant Rymenild ne derste

Latten on none wyse.   *Give up in any way*

A wryt hue dude devyse;

Aþulf hit dude wryte,

940 Þat Horn ne lovede nout lyte.   *That loved Horn not a little*

Hue sende hire sonde

Into everuche londe

To sechen Horn knyhte

Whesoer me myhte.   *Wherever he was able*

945 Horn þerof nout herde

Til o day þat he ferde   *went*

To wode forte shete,   *hunt*

A page he gan mete.

Horn seide: 'Leve fere,   *Dear companion*

950 Whet dest þou nou here?'

'Sire, in lutel spelle

Y may þe sone telle.

Ich seche from Westnesse

Horn knyht of Estnesse,

955 For Rymenild, þat feyre may,

Soreweþ for him nyht ant day.

A kyng hire shal wedde

A Sonneday to bedde,

Kyng Mody of Reynis,

960 Þat is Hornes enimis.

Ich habbe walked wyde

By þe see side;

Ne mihte Ich him never cleche   *get hold of*

Wiþ nones kunnes speche;   *kind of*

965 Ne may Ich of him here

In londe fer no nere.

Weylawey þe while!   *Alas*

Him may hente gyle.'   *Treachery may deceive him*

Horn hit herde wiþ earen

970 Ant spec wiþ wete tearen:

'So wel, grom, þe bitide!   *boy*

Horn stond by þi syde.

Aȝeyn to Rymenild turne,

Ant sey þat hue ne murne: *tell her not to mourn*

975 Y shal be þer bi time

A Sonneday er prime.'   *before the first hour*

Þe page wes wel blyþe,

Ant shipede wel swyþe.   *boarded ship*

Þe see him gon adrynke;   *drowned*

980 Þat Rymenil may ofþinke.   *regret*

Þe see him con ded þrowe

Under hire chambre wowe.   *wall*
Rymenild lokede wide
By þe see syde,
985   3ef heo se3e Horn come   *could see*
Oþer tidynge of eny gome.   *news; young man*
Þo fond hue hire sonde   *When; messenger*
Adronque by þe stronde   *Drowned; shore*
Þat shulde Horn brynge
990   Hire hondes gon hue wrynge.
Horn com to Þurston þe kynge
Ant tolde him þes tidynge;
Ant þo he was biknowe   *recognized*
Þat Rymenild wes ys owe,
995   Ant of his gode kenne
Þe kyng of Sudenne,
Ant hou he sloh afelde   *in battlefield*
Him þat is fader aquelde,
Ant seide: 'Kyng so wyse,
1000   3eld me my service.   *Repay*
Rymenild help me to wynne,
Swyþe, þat þou ne blynne,   *cease*
Ant Y shal do to house   *ensure that at home*
Þy dohter wel to spouse;
1005   For hue shal to spouse have
Aþulf my gode felawe.
He is knyht mid þe beste
Ant on of þe treweste.'
Þe kyng seide so stille:
1010   'Horn, do al þi wille.'
He sende þo by sonde
3end al is londe   *Throughout*
After knyhtes to fyhte
Þat were men so lyhte.   *excellent*
1015   To him come ynowe
Þat into shipe drowe.
     Horn dude him in þe weye   *departed*
In a gret galeye.
Þe wynd bigon to blowe
1020   In a lutel þrowe.   *while*
Þe see bigan wiþ ship to gon;
To Westnesse hem brohte anon.
Hue striken seyl of maste
Ant ancre gonnen caste.   *anchor*
1025   Matynes were yronge,   *Matins bells*
Ant þe masse ysonge
Of Rymenild þe 3ynge
Ant of Mody þe kynge;
Ant Horn wes in watere,
1030   Ne mihte he come no latere.
He let is ship stonde
Ant com him up to londe;
His folk he made abyde
Under a wode syde.

1035	Horn eode forh alone	
	So he sprong of þe stone.	
	On palmer he ymette	*pilgrim*
	Ant wiþ wordes hyne grette:	
	'Palmere, þou shalt me telle,'	
1040	He seyde, 'of þine spelle.	*tidings*
	So brouke þou þi croune,	*So that you keep your head*
	Why comest þou from toune?'	
	Ant he seide on is tale,	
	'Y come from a brudale,	*bridal feast*
1045	From brudale wylde	
	Of maide Remenylde;	
	Ne mihte hue nout dreȝe	*suffer it*
	Þat hue ne wep wiþ eȝe.	
	Hue seide þat hue nolde	
1050	Be spoused wiþ golde:	*married*
	Hue hade hosebonde,	
	Þah he were out of londe.	
	Ich wes in þe halle,	
	Wiþinne þe castel walle.	
1055	Awey Y gon glide –	
	Þe dole Y nolde abyde.	*sorrow*
	Þer worþ a dole reuly;	*pitiful sorrow*
	Þe brude wepeþ bitterly.'	*bride*
	Quoþ Horn, 'So Crist me rede,	
1060	We wolleþ chaunge wede.	
	Tac þou robe myne;	
	Ant I sclaveyn þyne.	*cloak*
	Today Y shal þer drynke	
	Þat summe hit shal ofþynke.'	*repent*
1065	Sclaveyn he gon doun legge	
	Ant Horn hit dude on rugge;	*back*
	Ant toc Hornes cloþes,	
	Þat nout him were loþe.	*hateful*
	Horn toc bordoun ant scrippe,	*staff and bag*
1070	Ant gan to wrynge is lippe;	
	He made foul chere,	
	Ant bicollede is swere.	*blackened*
	He com to þe ȝateward,	*gate-keeper*
	Þat him onsuerede froward.	*forwardly*
1075	Horn bed undo wel softe	*asked him to open the gates very quietly*
	Moni tyme ant ofte;	
	Ne myhte he ywynne	*succeed*
	For to come þerynne.	
	Horn þe wyket puste	*pushed the gate*
1080	Þat hit open fluste.	*So that*
	Þe porter shulde abugge;	*pay for that*
	He þrew him adoun þe brugge	*drawbridge*
	Þat þre ribbes crakede.	
	Horn to halle rakede,	*rushed*
1085	Ant sette him doun wel lowe	
	In þe beggeres rowe.	
	He lokede aboute	

Myd is collede snoute. *blackened nose*
Þer seh he Rymenild sitte
1090 Ase hue were out of wytte,
Wepinde sore;
Ah he seh nower þore *nowhere there*
Aþulf is gode felawe
Þat trewe wes in uch plawe. *event*
1095 Aþulf wes o tour ful heh *tower*
To loke fer ant eke neh
After Hornes comynge,
Ȝef water him wolde brynge.
Þe see he seh flowe,
1100 Ah Horn nower rowe.
He seyde on is songe:
'Horn, þou art to longe.
Rymenild þou me bitoke *commended to me*
Þat Ich hire shulde loke. *look after*
1105 Ich have yloked evere,
Ant þou ne comest nevere.'
Rymenild ros of benche
Þe beer al forte shenche *pour*
After mete in sale, *food; hall*
1110 Boþe wyn ant ale.
An horn hue ber an honde, *drinking horn*
For þat wes lawe of londe.
Hue dronc of þe beere
To knyht ant skyere. *squire*
1115 Horn set at grounde;
Him þohte he wes ybounde. *It seemed that he was made helpless*
He seide: 'Quene so hende, *noble*
To me hyderward þou wende. *turn*
Þou shenh us wiþ þe vurste; *pour for*
1120 Þe beggares bueþ afurste.' *thirsty*
Hyre horn hue leyde adoune
Ant fulde him of þe broune *brown vessel*
A bolle of a galoun; *gallon bottle*
Hue wende he were a glotoun. *She presumed*
1125 Hue seide: 'Tac þe coppe,
Ant drync þis ber al uppe.
Ne seh Y never, Y wene,
Beggare so kene.'
Horn toc hit hise yfere
1130 Ant seide: 'Quene so dere,
No beer nullich I bite *I will not taste*
Bote of coppe white.
Þou wenest Ich be a beggere;
Ywis, Icham a fysshere *Certainly*
1135 Wel fer come by weste
To seche mine beste.
Min net lyht her wel hende *lies; near*
Wiþinne a wel feyr pende. *enclosure*
Ich have leye þere *put it there*
1140 Nou is þis þe seveþe ȝere.

Icham icome to loke
ȝef eny fyssh hit toke;   *caught*
ȝef eny fyssh is þerinne,
Þerof þou shalt wynne.
1145   For Icham come to fyssh,
Drynke null Y of dyssh;
Drynke to Horn of horne,
Wel fer Ich have yorne.'   *journeyed*
     Rymenild him gan bihelde;
1150   Hire herte fel to kelde.   *cold*
Ne kneu hue noht is fysshyng
Ne himselve noþyng;[21]
Ah wonder hyre gan þynke
Why for Horn he bed drynke.   *asked for*
1155   Hue fulde þe horn of wyne,
And dronk to þat pelryne.   *pilgrim*
Hue seide: 'Drync þi felle,   *fill*
Ant seþþen þou me telle   *afterwards*
ȝef þou Horn ever seȝe   *saw*
1160   Under wode leȝe.'
     Horn dronc of horn a stounde
Ant þreu is ryng to grounde,   *the bottom*
Ant seide, 'Quene, þou þench   *consider*
What Y þreu in þe drench.'   *drink*
1165   Þe quene eode to boure
Mid hire maidnes foure;
Hue fond þat hue wolde,   *what she wished for*
Þe ryng ygraved of golde
Þat Horn of hyre hedde.   *from*
1170   Ful sore hyre adredde
Þat Horn ded were,
For his ryng was þere.
Þo sende hue a damoisele
After þilke palmere: *that same*
1175   'Palmere,' quoþ hue, 'so trewe,
Þe ryng þat þou yn þrewe,
Þou sey wer þou hit nome,   *acquired*
Ant hyder hou þou come.'   *here*
He seyde, 'By Seint Gyle,[22]
1180   Ich eode mony a myle   *travelled*
Wel fer ȝent by weste   *away*
To seche myne beste,
Mi mete for te bydde,   *beg*
For so me þo bitidde.   *happened*
1185   Ich fond Horn knyht stonde   *waiting*
To shipeward at stronde;   *To join a ship*
He seide he wolde gesse
To aryve at Westnesse.
Þe ship nom into flode   *sailed*
1190   Wiþ me ant Horn þe gode.

---

21 She did not understand either his allusion to fishing / Or any-   22 Giles, patron saint of beggars.
thing about him himself.

Horn bygan be sek ant deȝe,   *sickened and died*
Ant for his love me preȝe   *beseeched*
To gon wiþ þe rynge
To Rymenild þe ȝynge.
1195 Wel ofte he hyne keste: *kissed it*
Crist ȝeve is soule reste!'
 Rymenild seide at þe firste,
'Herte, nou toberste.
Horn worþ þe no more   *lives for you*
1200 Þat haveþ þe pyned sore.'   *tormented sorrowfully*
Hoe fel adoun a bedde,   *She*
Ant after knyves gredde   *cried out*
To slein mide hire kyng loþe   *With which to kill her hated king*
Ant hireselve boþe
1205 Wiþinne þilke nyhte,
Come ȝef Horn ne myhte.   *If Horn was not able to come*
To herte knyf hue sette.
Horn in is armes hire kepte.   *embraced*
His shurtelappe he gan take,   *the edge of his shirt*
1210 Ant wypede awey þe foule blake
Þat wes opon his swere,
Ant seide: 'Luef so dere,
Ne const þou me yknowe?   *Can you not recognize me?*
Ne am Ich Horn þyn owe?
1215 Ich, Horn of Westnesse,
In armes þou me kesse!'
Yclupten ant kyste   *They embraced*
So longe so hem lyste.   *desired*
'Rymenild,' quoþ he, 'Ich wende   *will go*
1220 Doun to þe wodes ende,
For þer bueþ myne knyhte,
Worþi men ant lyhte,
Armed under cloþe;   *clothing*
Hue shule make wroþe   *furious*
1225 Þe kyng and hise gestes
Þat bueþ at þise festes;
Today Ychulle huem cacche.
Nou Ichulle huem vacche.'   *fetch*
 Horn sprong out of halle;
1230 Ys sclavin he let falle.
Rymenild eode of boure;
Aþulf hue fond loure: *scowling*
'Aþulf, be wel blyþe,
Ant to Horn go swyþe.   *quickly*
1235 He is under wode bowe
Wiþ felawes ynowe.'
Aþulf gon froth springe
For þat ilke tydynge.
Efter Horn he ernde;   *ran*
1240 Him þohte is herte bernde.
He oftok him, ywisse,   *overtook*
Ant custe him wiþ blysse.
Horn tok is preye,   *troop of men*

Ant dude him in þe weye.

1245   Hue comen in wel sone   *immediately*

Þe ȝates weren undone;   *gates*

Yarmed swiþe þicke   *Armed very heavily*

From fote to þe nycke.

Alle þat þer evere weren,

1250   Wiþoute is trewe feren,   *Except for his loyal companions*

Ant þe kyng Aylmare –

Ywis hue hade muche care.   *Truly; sorrow*

Monie þat þer sete,

Hure lyf hy gonne lete.   *did lose*

1255   Horn understondyng ne hede   *had no knowledge*

Of Fykeles falssede.

Hue sworen alle ant seyde

Þat hure non him wreȝede;   *none of them had deceived him*

Ant swore oþes holde

1260   Þat huere non ne sholde

Horn never bytreye   *betray*

Þah he on deþe leye.

Þer hy ronge þe belle

Þat wedlak to fulfulle.   *marriage*

1265   Hue wenden hom wiþ eyse   *ease*

To þe kynges paleyse.

Þer wes þe brudale suete,   *wedding feast*

For richemen þer ete;

Telle ne mihte no tonge

1270   Þe gle þat þer was songe.   *music*

     Horn set in chayere

Ant bed hem alle yhere.

He seyde: 'Kyng of londe,

Mi tale þou understonde.

1275   Ich wes ybore in Sudenne;

Kyng wes mi fader of kenne.

Þou me to knyhte hove;   *exalted*

Of knythod habbe Y prove.

Þou dryve me out of þi lond,

1280   Ant seydest Ich wes traytour strong.

Þou wendest þat Ich wrohte   *presumed; did*

Þat Y ner ne þohte

By Rymenild forte lygge.   *lie*

Ywys, Ich hit wiþsugge,   *deny*

1285   Ne shal Ich hit ner agynne   *begin it*

Er Ich Sudenne wynne.   *Before*

Þou kep hyre me a stounde,   *guard*

Þe while þat Ich founde

Into myn heritage

1290   Wiþ þis Yrisshe page.

Þat lond Ichulle þorhreche   *recover*

Ant do mi fader wreche.   *avenge*

Ychul be kyng of toune

Ant lerne kynges roune.   *learn a king's counsel*

1295   Þenne shal Rymenhild þe ȝynge

Ligge by Horn þe kynge.'

	Horn gan to ship drawe	
	Wiþ hyse Yrisshe felawe;	
	Aþulf wiþ him, his broþer –	
1300	He nolde habbe non oþer.	
	Þe ship bygan to croude;	*move on*
	Þe wynd bleu wel loude.	
	Wyþinne dawes fyve,	
	Þe ship bigan aryve;	
1305	Under Sudennes side,	*shore*
	Huere ship bygon to ryde	
	Aboute þe midnyhte.	
	Horn eode wel rihte.	*went straight away*
	He nom Aþulf by honde	
1310	Ant ede up to londe.	
	Hue fonden under shelde	
	A knyht liggynde on felde.	
	O þe shelde wes ydrawe	
	A croyz of Jhesu Cristes lawe.	*religion*
1315	Þe knyht him lay on slape,	*sleep*
	In armes wel yshape.	
	Horn him gan ytake	
	Ant seide, 'Knyht, awake.	
	Þou sei me whet þou kepest,	*guard*
1320	Ant here whi þou slepest.	
	Me þuncheþ, by crois liste,[23]	*the device of the Cross*
	Þat þou levest on Criste.	*believe*
	Bote þou hit wolle shewe,	
	My suerd shal þe tohewe.'	*split asunder*
1325	Þe gode knyht up aros;	
	Of Hornes wordes him agros.	*trembled*
	He seide, 'Ich servy ille	*unhappily*
	Paynes toзeynes mi wille.	*against*
	Ich was Cristene sumwhile.	*formerly*
1330	Y come into þis yle.	
	Sarazyns loþe ant blake	*hateful*
	Me made Jhesu forsake;	
	To loke þis passage	*guard*
	For Horn þat is of age,	
1335	Þat woneþ her by weste,	*lives*
	God knyht mid þe beste.	
	Hue slowe mid huere honde	*killed*
	Þe kyng of þisse londe,	
	Ant wiþ him mony honder.	*hundreds*
1340	Þerfore me þuncheþ wonder	*It seems a wonder*
	Þat he ne comeþ to fyhte:	
	God зeve him þe myhte	
	Þat wynd him hider dryve	
	To don hem alle of lyve.	*from life*
1345	Ant hue slowen kyng Mury,	*they killed*
	Hornes cunesmon hardy;	*kinsman*

23 The device of the Cross refers to its use as an heraldic emblem
on the shield.

Horn, of londe hue senten,
Twelf children wiþ him wenten.
Wiþ hem wes Aþulf þe gode,
1350   Mi child, myn oune fode.   *child*
3ef Horn is hol ant sounde,
Aþulf tit no wounde.   *suffers*
He lovede Horn wiþ mihte,
Ant he him wiþ ryhte.
1355   3ef Y myhte se hem tueye,
Þenne ne roht I forte deye.'   *care*
    'Knyht, be þenne blyþe
Mest of alle syþe.   *times*
Aþulf ant Horn is fere,
1360   Boþe we beþ here.'
        Þe knyht to Horn gan skippe
Ant in his armes clippe.   *embraced*
Muche joye hue maden yfere
Þo hue togedere ycome were.
1365   He saide wiþ stevene þare: *voice*
'3unge men, hou habbe 3e 3ore yfare?   *previously fared*
Wolle 3e þis lond wynne
Ant wonie þerynne?'   *remain*
He seide: 'Suete Horn child,
1370   3et lyveþ þy moder Godyld.
Of joie hue ne miste   *would not lack*
Olyve 3ef hue þe wiste.'   *If she knew you were alive*
Horn seide on is ryme:
'Yblessed be þe time
1375   Icham icome into Sudenne
Wiþ fele Yrisshemenne.   *many*
We shule þe houndes kecche   *catch*
Ant to þe de3e vecche;   *death fetch*
Ant so we shulen hem teche
1380   To speken oure speche.'
        Horn gon is horn blowe,
Is folc hit con yknowe;
Hue comen out of hurne   *hiding places*
To Horn swyþe 3urne.   *eagerly*
1385   Hue smiten ant hue fyhten   *struck*
Þe niht ant eke þe ohtoun;   *dawn*
Þe Sarazyns hue slowe
Ant summe quike todrowe;   *dismembered alive*
Mid speres ord hue stonge   *edge; pierced*
1390   Þe olde and eke þe 3onge.
        Horn lette sone wurche   *had built*
Boþe chapel and chyrche.
He made belle rynge
Ant prestes masse synge.
1395   He sohte is moder halle   *mother's dwelling*
In þe roche walle;
He custe hire ant grette
Ant into þe castel fette.   *fetched*
Croune he gan werie   *wear*

1400	Ant make feste merye.	
	Murie he þer wrohte,	*He created happiness there*
	Ah Rymenild hit abohte.	*suffered*
	Þe whiles Horn wes oute,	
	Fikenild ferde aboute.	*went*
1405	Þe betere for te spede;	*succeed*
	Þe riche he ȝef mede,	*reward*
	Boþe ȝonge ant olde,	
	Wiþ him forte holde.	
	Ston he dude lade	*had brought*
1410	Ant lym þerto he made.	
	Castel he made sette	*had built*
	Wiþ water by flette,	*surrounded*
	Þat þeryn come ne myhte	
	Bote foul wiþ flyhte;	*birds*
1415	Bote when þe see wiþdrowe,	
	Þer mihte come ynowe.	
	Þus Fykenild gon bywende	*began to proceed*
	Rymenild forte shende.	*shame*
	To wyve he gan hire ȝerne;	*As a wife he desired her*
1420	Þe kyng ne durst him werne,	*reject*
	Ant habbeþ set þe day	
	Fykenild to wedde þe may.	*maiden*
	Wo was Rymenhild of mode:	*heart*
	Terres hue wepte of blode.	
1425	Þilke nyht Horn suete	
	Con wel harde mete	*had an awful dream*
	Of Rymenild his make:	
	Þat into shipe wes take.	
	Þe ship gon overblenche;	*capsize*
1430	Is lemmon shulde drenche.	*His; drown*
	Rymenild mid hire honde	
	Swymme wolde to londe;	
	Fykenild aȝeyn hire pylte	*pushed against her*
	Mid his suerdes hylte.	*hilt*
1435	Horn awek in is bed	
	Of his lemman he wes adred.	*For; fearful*
	'Aþulf,' he seide, 'felawe,	
	To shipe nou we drawe.	
	Fykenild me haþ gon under,	*deceived*
1440	Ant do Rymenild sum wonder.	
	Crist, for his wondes fyve,	
	Tonyht þider us dryve!'	
	Horn gon to shipe ride,	
	His knyhtes bi his side;	
1445	Þe ship bigon to sture	
	Wiþ wynd god of cure;	*preference*
	Ant Fykenild, her þe day springe,	*before*
	Seide to þe kynge	
	After Rymenild þe bryhte	*About*
1450	Ant spousede hyre by nyhte.	*married*
	He ladde hire by derke	
	Into is newe werke.	*castle*

Þe feste hue bigonne
Er þen aryse þe sonne.
1455 Hornes ship atstod in Stoure
Under Fykenildes boure.
Nuste Horn alyve   *Horn was not aware*
Wher he wes aryve:
Þene castel hue ne knewe,
1460 For he was so newe.   *it*
Þe see bigon to wiþdrawe;
Þo seh Horn his felawe,
Þe feyre knyht Arnoldyn,
Þat wes Aþulfes cosyn;
1465 Þat þer set in þat tyde   *sat*
Kyng Horn to abide.   *await*
He seide, 'Kyng Horn, kynges sone,
Hider þou art welcome.
Today haþ Sire Fykenild
1470 Yweddeþ þi wif Rymenild.
White þe nou þis while,   *Protect yourself*
He haveþ do þe gyle: *deceit*
Þis tour he dude make   *tower*
Al for Rymenildes sake;
1475 Ne may þer comen ynne
No mon wiþ no gynne.   *ingenuity*
Horn, nou Crist þe wisse   *direct you to*
Rymenild þat þou ne misse.'
    Horn couþe alle þe listes   *knew; skills*
1480 Þat eni mon of wiste.
Harpe he gon shewe
Ant toc him to felawe
Knyhtes of þe beste
Þat he ever hede of weste.   *from the*
1485 Oven o þe sherte   *over*
Hue gurden huem wiþ suerde.   *armed themselves*
Hue eoden on þe gravele
Towart þe castele.
Hue gonne murie singe
1490 Ant makeden huere gleynge   *music*
Þat Fykenild mihte yhere.
He axede who hit were;
Men seide hit were harpeirs,
Jogelers, ant fyþelers.   *Jugglers*
1495 Hem me dude in lete,   *They were allowed in*
At halle dore hue sete.
Horn sette him a benche;   *sat*
Is harpe he gan clenche.   *pluck*
He make Rymenild a lay,
1500 Ant hue seide 'Weylawey.'   *Alas*
    Rymenild fel y swowe;   *in a swoon*
Þo nes þer non þat lowe.   *laughed*
Hit smot Horn to herte;
Sore con him smerte.   *hurt*
1505 He lokede on is rynge

Ant o Rymenild þe ȝynge.
He eode up to borde;
Mid his gode suorde,   *sword*
Fykenildes croune   *head*
1510   He fel þer adoune,   *cut off*
Ant alle is men a rowe   *in order*
He dude adoun þrowe.
Ant made Arnoldyn kyng þere,
After kyng Aylmere,
1515   To be kyng of Westnesse,
For his mildenesse;
Þe kyng ant is baronage
Ȝeven him truage.   *Gave him tribute*
    Horn toc Rymenild by honde
1520   Ant ladde hire to stronde,   *shore*
Ant toc wiþ him Aþelbrus,
Þe gode stiward of hire fader hous.
Þe see bigan to flowen,
Ant hy faste to rowen;
1525   Hue aryveden under Reme   *at Reynis*
In a wel feyr streme.
Kyng Mody wes kyng in þat lond,
Þat Horn sloh wiþ is hond.   *his*
Aþelbrus he made þer kyng
1530   For his gode techyng;
For Sire Hornes lore   *teaching*
He wes mad kyng þore.
    Horn eode to ryve;   *shore*
Þe wynd him con wel dryve.
1535   He aryvede in Yrlonde,
Þer Horn wo couþe er fonde.   *Where; knew grief previously*
He made þer Aþulf Chyld
Wedde mayden Ermenyld;
Ant Horn corn to Sudenne,
1540   To is oune kenne.   *own*
Rymenild he made þer is quene,
So hit myhte bene.
In trewe love hue lyveden ay,   *always*
Ant wel hue loveden Godes lay.   *law*
1545   Nou hue beoþ boþe dede.
Crist to heovene us lede. Amen.

The *Ayenbite of Inwit*

The prose *Ayenbite of Inwit*, or 'Remorse of Conscience', was translated by Dan Michel of Northgate, a Benedictine monk at Saint Augustine's, Canterbury. It was finished in the year 1340, at which time the author would have been quite elderly. It survives uniquely in the autography copy in London, British Library, Arundel 57, folios 13–94.[1] The manuscript also includes a number of other religious and prophetic texts, the former copied by Michel, the latter by a later scribe.

The *Ayenbite* is translated from the French *Somme le Roi*, many manuscripts of which are extant from the late thirteenth and fourteenth centuries. Michel translated this text into English for the edification of those unable to understand Latin, and to this end, he writes in a style that is accessible by virtue of its straightforwardness, and its contemporary and domestic imagery. In the *Ayenbite*, 'Nature and Reason are the guiding forces: self-knowledge is the first step to perfection',[2] and thus, the ultimate aim is to identify sin, prevent it, and enable salvation. Michel reveals his intentions at the close of the *Ayenbite* proper:

Nou Ich wille þat ye ywyte hou hit is ywent:	*know; translated*
þet þis boc is ywrite mid Engliss of Kent.	
Þis boc is ymad vor lewede men,	*unlearned*
Vor vader and vor moder and vor oþer ken,	*kindred*
Ham vor to berȝe vram alle	
manyere sen,	*save from all kinds of sin*
þet ine hare inwytte ne bleve no	
voul wen.	*conscience; remains; blemish*
'Huo ase God?' is his name	
ysed,	*'Who is like God?'; the author's name*

þet þis boc made – God him yeve þet bread
Of Angles of hevene, and þerto his red,
And ondervonge his saule huanne þet he is
dyad. Amen.[3]   *receive; dead*

As is the case with Robert Mannyng of Brunne's *Handlyng Synne*, the *Ayenbite* forms part of the long tradition of didactic and confessional literature. It is organized into parts that deal with the Ten Commandments, the seven sins (described as the seven 'heads of the beast', with a variety of off-shoots or 'boughs'), the inner virtues, the *Pater Noster*, the four cardinal virtues, and the steps to perfection.[4] Each section is also split into numerical divisions throughout in order to provide mnemonic assistance for the audience, and ease of reference for subsequent users of the text.

Unlike Mannyng's *Handlyng Synne*, the *Ayenbite* appears not to have achieved any substantial popularity, as only the one manuscript survives. Edited below is the complete sin of lechery,[5] the sixth sin to be discussed. Its depiction is considerably shorter and less detailed than those of the other sins.[6] It illustrates many of the usual instructive techniques of other religious texts in this period; for example, the use of biblical exempla to reinforce a particular point, none of which is fully explained within its context, presupposing some level of knowledge in the audience. The numerical listing common to the work as a whole also provides the framework for the logical discussion of the two sub-divisions of lechery: lechery of the heart and of the body; and the fourteen kinds of lecherous deeds (all referring to forbidden sexual relations).

---

1 The text is edited in R. Morris, ed., *The Aȝenbite of Inwit*, EETS o.s. 23 (London, 1866; repr. with corrections 1965). A full Introduction describing the manuscript and the text's sources, and including notes and a glossary, can be found in P. Gradon, *Dan Michel's Ayenbite of Inwit: Volume II, Introduction, Notes and Glossary*, EETS o.s. 278 (London, 1979).

2 J. A. W. Bennett, *Middle English Literature*, ed. and comp. D. Gray (Oxford, 1986; repr. 1990), p. 294.

3 Morris, *Aȝenbite of Inwit*, p. 262, lines 8–18, with modernized punctuation here.

4 Outlined by Michel himself in his Table of Contents, edited by Morris, *Aȝenbite of Inwit*, pp. 1–4.

5 Dan Michel usually uses initial z for words such as *ziȝþe* (sight), *zenne* (sin). I have consistently replaced the z graph with s.

6 This lack of detail about lechery and what it entails is similar in its evasiveness to William Langland's *Piers Plowman*, passus V, where the depiction of lechery is the shortest of those of the sins.

<h1 style="text-align:center">The *Ayenbite of Inwit*</h1>

<h2 style="text-align:center">*Lechery*</h2>

<h3 style="text-align:center">The Sixte Heaved of Þe Beste[7]</h3>

Þe sixte heaved of þe kueade[8] beste is lecherie; þet is, to moche love and desordene ine lost[9] of lenden,[10] oþer ine ulesslich[11] lost. Of þise senne vondeþ[12] þe dyevel in vif maneres, ase sayþ Saynt Gregorie. Averst, ine fole si3þe;[13] efterward ine fole wordes; efterward ine fole takinges;[14] efterward ine fole kessinges; efterward me comþ to þe dede.[15] Vor of fole si3þe me comþ to þe speche, and vram þe speche to þe handlinge; vram þe handlinge to þe kesinge, vram þe kessinge to þe dede. And þous sotilliche makeþ þe dyevel guo[16] vram on to oþer.

Þis senne him todelþ[17] verst ine tuo maneres, vor þer is lecherie of herte, and lecherie of bodie. Þe lecherie of herte suo heþ vour stapes.[18] Vor þe gost of fornicacion, þet serveþ of þe vere[19] of lecherie becleppe[20] þe herten, makeþ verst come þe þo3tes and þe likinges and þe ymaginacions of senne to herte, and makeþ þenche.[21] Efterward, þe herte blefþ[22] ine þe þo3tes, an suo deliteþ, yet ne deþ[23] he na3t þe dede vor noþing. And ine þise blevinge and ine þe ilke lost is þo oþer stape þet may by dyadlich[24] senne. Þe greate senne may by þe lost. Þe þridde stape is þe grauntingge of herte and of þe scele[25] and of þe wylle. And suyche grantinges byeþ alneway deadlich senne. Efter þe grantinge comþ þe wylnynge,[26] and þe greate hete þet hy habbeþ vor to sene3y.[27] And doþ more þanne tuenti sennes yne þe daye ine si3þe of levedys[28] and of maydynes þet sseweþ ham vayre ydi3t,[29] þet ofte hy sseaweþ and di3teþ ham þe more quaynteliche and þe more honesteliche vor to maki musi[30] þe foles to ham, and ne weneþ na3t gratliche sene3y, vor þet hi ne habbeþ no wyl to do þe dede.[31] Ac vorsoþe hy sene3eþ wel grevousliche. Vor be þe ancheysoun[32] of ham byeþ vorlore[33] manye saules. And þer byeþ moche volk ydo to dyaþe and to senne. Vor ase sayþ þe vorbisne[34]: 'Levedi of vaire di3tinge is arblast to þe tour.'[35] Vor hi ne heþ leme ine hire bodye þet ne is a gryn[36] of þe dyevle, ase sayþ Salomon. Þanne behoveþ hit yelde scele ate daye of Dome of þe saules þet be þe ancheaysoun of ham byeþ vorlore; þet is to onderstonde huanne hi yeveþ encheysoun vor to sene3y be hare wytinde.[37]

Lecherie of bodie him todelþ ine lecherie of e3en, of yearen, of mouþe, of honden, an of alle þe wyttes[38] of þe bodye; and specialliche of þe voule dede. And hue is hit voul dede seþþe hit is kendelich?[39] Vor þet God hit vorbyet[40] ine his spelle; and his apostel Pauel þet þus sayþ: 'Ech man habbe his o3ene vor fornicacion';[41] þet ys to sigge, his o3ene wyf. To þe senne belongeþ alle þe þinges huerby[42] þet uless him arist and wylneþ suiche dede,[43] ase byeþ þe mochele drinkeres

---

7 The seven-headed beast is the Apocalyptic dragon, the devil, of Revelations 12.3.
8 evil
9 lust
10 loins
11 carnal
12 tempts
13 sight
14 touching
15 sexual intercourse
16 proceed
17 separates
18 thus has four steps
19 flame
20 embraces (kindles)
21 think (dwell on it)
22 dwells
23 does
24 deadly
25 reason
26 desire
27 sin
28 ladies

29 adorned
30 marvel
31 Women adorn themselves with no sinful intent in order to make the foolish marvel at them. They do not think it a great sin, because they have no desire to encourage sexual advances.
32 cause
33 lost
34 proverb
35 'Lady, your fair adornment [encourages] the crossbow to the tower.' This proverbial phrase metaphorically warns women about unwanted attentions and potential attacks because of their adornment. This is reminiscent of the central metaphor of the 'tower' used in *Hali Meiðhad*.
36 trap
37 knowingly (that is, when women adorn themselves, they are knowingly engaging in sin).
38 senses
39 natural
40 commands
41 Corinthians 7.2
42 as a result of it
43 that his flesh is aroused and desires such things

and eteres; þe softe bed; cloþes likerouses; and alle manyere eyse of bodye out of nyede,[44] and
30   specialliche ydelnesse.

Þe senne of dede of lecherie him todelþ ine vele boʒes be þe stat[45] of þe persones þet hit doþe
and geþ an heʒ[46] vram kuede[47] to worse. Þe verste is of man oþer of wyfman þet ne habbeþ nenne
bend:[48] ne of wodewehod, ne of spoushod, ne of ordre, ne of religioun, ne of oþre manere. Þet is
þe verste senne dyadlich in dede of lecherie. Þe oþer is to wyfmanne commune.[49] Þis senne is
35   more hard vor hi is more ald, and vor þet suyche wyfmen byeþ oþerhuyl wyves, oþer of religon,
and ne vorsakeþ nenne – ne vader, ne broþer, ne sone, ne ken. Þe þridde is of man sengle mid
wodewe, oþer ayeward.[50] Þe verþe is wiþ sengle wifman. Þe vifte is mid wyfman ymarissed þet is
þe senne of spousbreche.[51] Þet is wel kuead vor þer is brekinge of trouþe þet þe on ssel bere to þe
oþre. Efterward þer is a sacrilege huanne me brecþ þe sacrement of spoushod. Hit yvalþ oþerhuyl
40   desertesoun of eyr and valse mariages.[52] Þis senne him dobbleþ oþerhuil huanne hi is of man
yspoused wyþe wymman þet heþ housebounde.

Þe sixte is huanne þe man heþ his oʒe wyf deþ þing þet is vorbode and disordene aye kende of
man, and ordre, and of spoushod.[53] And mid oʒene suorde man may himselve sle.[54] Alsuo may he
mid his oʒene wyve seneʒi dyadliche. Þervore smot God to evele dyaþe onam Jacobis nevu.[55] And
45   þe dyevel þet hette Asmodeus astranglede þe seve houseboundes of þe holy mayde Sare, þet seþþe
wes yonge Thobyes wyf.[56] Vor alle þe sacremens of holi cherche me ssel usi clenliche and mid
greate worþssipe. Þe sevende is of man to his godmoder oþer to his goddoʒter, oþer of godsone to
þe children of his godsyb, oþer of his godsybbe; vor þo children ne moʒe naʒt come togydere
wyþoute dyadlich senne ne be spoushod.[57] Þe eʒtende is of man to his kenne, and þe ilke senne
50   arist, and loʒeþ be þet þe kenrede is nyeʒ oþer ver.[58] Þe neʒende is of þe manne mid þe kenne of
his wyve, oþer ayeward of þe wyve mid þe kenne of hare housebounde. Þe ilke senne is wel
dredvol, vor huanne þe man heþ velaʒrede[59] myd enye wyfmane, he ne may nanmore be spoushod
habbe none of hire kenne.[60] And yef he enye nimþ,[61] þe spoushod ne is naʒt. And yef he nimþ
wyf, and efterward of þe half of hire kenne, ha lyest þe riʒt[62] þet he hedde to his wyve ine suo
55   moche þet he ne may efterward wonye mid hire, bote hy hit ne bidde bevore.

Þe tende is of wyfmen to clerkes yhoded. Þis senne anheʒeþ and loʒeþ by þe hodes and þe
worþssiphede.[63] Þe enlefte is of man of þe wordle to wyfman of religioun, oþer ayeanward of
wyfman of þe wordle to man of religioun. Þe xii is of man of religioun and of wyfman of religion,
and þis senne anheʒeþ and loʒeþ be þe stat of þe persones þet hit doþ. Þe xiii is of prelas þet
60   ssolden bi licnesse and vorbysne of holynesse and of klennesse to al þe wordle.[64]

Þe laste is mest voul an lodlakest þet ne is naʒt to nemny.[65] Þe ilke senne is aye kende, þet þe

---

44   and all kinds of ease for the body, beyond that which is required

45   he divides into many boughs according to the status of the person

46   progressively

47   bad

48   bond

49   The second is adultery with a common woman (prostitute).

50   The third is a single man living with a widow, or vice versa.

51   adultery (with a married woman)

52   This results sometimes in the desertion of the heir and false marriages.

53   The sixth is when a man has his own wife perform things that are forbidden and unnatural against the nature of man, and order, and marriage.

54   kill

55   God killed Onan because of his 'detestable' sin: Genesis 38.8–10, referring to masturbation.

56   Referring to the apocryphal Book of Tobit 3.7–8, in which Sarah, daughter of Raguel, had been given in marriage to seven husbands, all of whom were killed by the demon Asmodaeus before the con-summation of the marriage. After the blessing of God, she married Tobias, son of Tobit.

57   It is equally a deadly sin for sexual relations to take place between those related by baptismal kinship: godparents and godchildren.

58   The eighth is incest, when a man has sexual relations with his relations, and the same sin increases or diminishes according to whether the family member is closely or distantly related.

59   intercourse

60   If a man has sex with a woman he is then forbidden from marrying any of her relations.

61   takes as a wife

62   And if he takes a wife, and afterwards takes another wife from among her family, he truly lies.

63   The tenth is sexual relations between a woman and one ordained as a member of the clergy. The sin increases and lessens depending on the order and the status of the cleric.

64   The thirteenth is the sin of prelates who ought to be the image and example of holiness and of purity for all the world (to see).

65   The last is the most foul and most loathsome such that it cannot be named.

dyevel tekþ[66] to man oþer to wyfman ine vele maneres þet ne byeþ naȝt to nemni vor þe materie þet is to moche abomynable. Ac ine ssrifþe hit ssel nemni þe ilke to huam hit is bevalle.[67] Vor ase moche ase þe senne is more voul and more grislich, þe more is worþ þe ssrifte. Vor þe ssame þet me heþ of þe sigginge is grat del of þe penonce.[68] Þis senne is suo onworþ to Gode þet he dede rine ver berninde and bernston stinkinde ope þe cité of Sodome and of Gomorre,[69] and asenkte vif cites into helle. Þe dyvel himself þet hit porchaceþ,[70] heþ ssame huanne man hit deþ and þe eyr is anvenymed[71] of þe dede.

---

66   teaches
67   But in confession it shall be named by those to whom it has happened.
68   For the result of telling must be a great deal of penance.
69   For the sin is so displeasing to God, that he rained burning fire and stinking brimstone on the cities of Sodom and Gomorrah. See Genesis 19.24–5. Tradition has it that this unspeakable sin is sodomy.
70   causes
71   poisoned

Richard Rolle

Richard Rolle was born in c.1290 in Thornton, Yorkshire, and he died in 1349.[1] He went to the University of Oxford to study, but decided at the age of about nineteen to leave the university and return home. This decision appears to have been a result of Rolle's desire to enter into the life of a hermit. His first hermitage was within the household of John de Dalton; later, after travelling abroad, he became a hermit in various parts of Yorkshire, ending his life at Hampole. He wrote many Latin and English writings that mark him out as one of the most significant medieval English mystics, and that were to assure his fame, both in his own lifetime and in the present day. One of Rolle's primary activities while leading his eremetic life was the provision of devotional and spiritual materials for those of his friends who sought to engage in a religious life themselves. His pastoral work was of great importance to him, and also allows the student of Rolle to see how he regarded and expressed his relationship with God, and the obtaining of spiritual grace.

Rolle's mysticism involved him in an intimate relationship with his Lord, dependent on the contemplative life afforded to him by his relative seclusion. The tradition of mysticism reaches as far back as Augustine and Gregory, Church Fathers of the late classical period; and, in England, was particularly influenced by the Latin writings of Anselm of Canterbury (d. 1109), Aelred of Rievaulx (d. 1167) and their successors. This mystical literature is characterized by the emphasis on the importance of *lufe* (love), and of the effectiveness of an emotional bond with God and his saints. The aim of these writings, to cause emotion or affection, seeks to engage the reader in the sufferings of Christ in his humanity, and to inspire in the reader a fervent devotion.[2] The devotion of mystics, such as Richard Rolle, is very apparent in the effusiveness of the language used, and the desire to represent the feelings caused by the *lufe* of God.

From Rolle's many writings, *Ego Dormio* and *Ghostly Gladness* are edited below.[3] These texts can be assigned to a date in the 1340s. Numerous manuscripts of these works survive (as do numerous versions of Rolle's other writings), bearing witness to his very substantial popularity in the late medieval period, which is also seen in his influence on later mystics such as Julian of Norwich, and the author of *The Cloud of Unknowing*. The *Ego Dormio* is an epistle that was probably written for a female disciple of Rolle's, Margaret Kirkeby, a nun at Yedingham. Written in the first person, the epistle is an admonition against concerns of the world, and a demonstration of the means of attaining a close and personal relationship with Christ. The prose style is occasionally alliterative, and within the prose framework are two lyrical and meditative verse sections. *Ghostly Gladness* is similarly alliterative, and can be regarded as a lyric written in prose. Both of these texts are edited from a manuscript of northern origin, Cambridge University Library, Dd. V. 64, folios 22 verso to 29 recto (*Ego Dormio*), and folio 41 verso (*Ghostly Gladness*).

Ego Dormio

Ego dormio et cor meum vigilat.[4] Þai þat lyste[5] lufe, herken and here of luf. In þe sang of luf it es writen: 'I slepe and my hert wakes.' Mykel[6] lufe he schewes þat never es irk[7] to lufe, bot ay[8] standand,[9] sittand, gangand,[10] or wirkand, es ay his lufe thynkand, and oftsyth þarof es dremande. Forþi þat I lufe, I wow[11] þe, þat I myght have þe als I wolde, noght to me, bot to my Lorde. I will
5 become þat messanger to bryng þe to hys bed þat hase made þe and boght þe, Criste, þe Keyng sonn of heven, for he wil with þe dwelle, if þou will lufe hym. He askes þe na mare bot þi lufe, and, my dere syster in Criste, my wil þou dose, if þou lufe hym. Crist covaytes noght els bot þat

1 Information about the life of Richard Rolle, and his works, can be found in H. E. Allen, ed., *English Writings of Richard Rolle, Hermit of Hampole* (Oxford, 1931; repr. 1963).
2 For an excellent discussion of mysticism in the late eleventh and twelfth centuries, see T. H. Bestul, 'Antecedents: The Anselmian and Cistercian Contributions', in *Mysticism and Spirituality in Medieval England*, eds W. F. Pollard and R. Boenig (Cambridge, 1997), pp. 1–20.
3 See S. J. Ogilvie-Thomson, ed., *Richard Rolle: Prose and Verse, Edited from MS Longleat 29 and Related Manuscripts*, EETS o.s. 293 (Oxford, 1988), for the most recent edition of the English writings.
4 Canticles 5.2: 'I sleep and my heart awakens.' The Song of Songs (Canticles) was a text of immense importance to mystics, as it was to religious readers and writers generally. Saint Bernard of Clairvaux's

thoughts and teaching on the contemplative life are evidenced in his *Sermones in Cantica Canticorum*. As Bestul comments in 'Antecedents: The Anselmian and Cistercian Contributions', 'The intense yearning of the bride for the bridegroom in that book is taken by Bernard, as it was by many other spiritual writers, as a mystical representation of the soul's longing to be united with God.'
5 pleases
6 Much
7 weary
8 always
9 standing (*-and* is the present participle ending).
10 moving
11 woo

þou do his wil, and enforce þe day and nyght þat þou leve al fleschly lufe, and al lykyng þat lettes
þe til lofe Jhesu Crist verraly.[12] For ay, whils þi hert es heldand til lufe any bodely thyng, þou
may nat perfitely be coupuld with God.

In heven er neyn orders of aungels þat er contened in thre ierarchies:[13] þe lawest ierarchi
contenes aungels, archaungels, and vertues; þe mydel ierarchi contenes principates, potestates,
and dominacions; þe heest[14] ierarchi, þat neest es to God, contenes thronos, cherubyn, and seraphyn.
Þe lawest es aungels, þe heest es seraphyn. And þat order þat leste es bryght es seven sythe sa
bryght als þe sonn es bryghtar þan a kandele, þe kandel bryghtar þan þe mone, þe mone bryghtar
þan a sterne;[15] also er þe orders in heven ilk ane bryghter þan other, fra aungels to seraphyn. Þis
I say to kyndel þi hert forto covayte þe felichip[16] of aungels; for al þat er gude and haly, when þai
passe owt of þis worlde, sal be taken intil þies orders: sum intil þe lawest, þat hase lufed mykel;
sum intil þe mydelmast, þat hase lufed mare; oþer intil þe heest, þat maste lufed God, and
byrnandest[17] es in hys lufe. Seraphyn es at say brynand; til þe whilk order þai er receyved þat leest
covaytes in þis worlde, and maste swetnes feles in God, and brynandest hertes hase in his lufe.

Til þe I write specialy for I hope mare godenes in þe þan in another, and þat þou wil gyf þi
thoght to fulfil in dede þat þou seys[18] es maste prophetabel for þi sawle, and þat lif gif þe til in þe
whilk þow may halyest offer þi hert to Jhesu Criste, and leste be in bisynes of þis worlde. For if
þow stabil þi lufe, and be byrnande whils þou lyfes here, withowten dowte, þi settel es ordaynde
ful hegh in heven and joyful before Goddes face amang his haly aungels. For in þe self degre þeir
prowde devels fel downe fra, er meke men and wymen, Criste dowves, sett to have rest and joy
withowten ende, for a litel schort penance and travel[19] þat þai have sufferd for Goddes lufe.

Þe thynk peraventure hard to gife þi hert fra al erthly thynges, fra al ydel speche and vayne, and
fra al fleschly lufe, and to be alane, to walk and pray and thynk of þe joy of heven, and of þe
passyon of Jhesu Criste, and to ymagyn þe payne of hell þat es ordande for synful man. Bot
wyterly, fra þou be used þarin,[20] þe wil thynk it lyghter and swetter þan þou dyd any erthly
thyng or solace. Als sone als þi hert es towched with þe swetnes of heven, þe wil lytel lyst þe
myrth of þis worlde; and when þou feles joy in Criste lufe, þe wil lathe with þe joy and þe
comforth of þis worlde and erthly gamen. For al melody and al riches and delites þat al men in þis
world kan ordayne or thynk sownes bot noy and anger til a mans hert þat verraly es byrnand in þe
lufe of God, for he hase myrth and joy and melody in aungels sang, als þou may wele wyt. If þou
leve al thyng þat þi fleschly lufe list, for the lufe of God, and have na thoght on syb frendes, bot
forsake al for Goddes lufe, and anely gyf þi hert to coveyte Goddes lufe and pay hym, mare joy sal
þou have and fynd in hym þan I can on thynk. How myght þou þan wyt hit? I wate never if any
man be in swilk lufe, for ay þe hegher þe lyfe es, þe fewer folowers it hase here, for many thynges
drawes man fra Goddes lufe, þat þow may here and se; and God comfortes his lufers mare þan þai
wene þat lufes hym noght. Forþi, þof we seme in penance withowten, we sal have mykel joy
within, if we ordayne us wysely to Goddes servyce, and sett in hym al owre thoghtes, and forsake
al vanyte of þis worlde.

Gyf þien entent til understand þis wrytyng, and if þou have sett al þi desyre til lufe God, here
þies thre degrees of lufe,[21] sa þat þou may rise fra ane til another to þou be in þe heest. For I wil
noght layne fra þe þat I hope may turne þe til halynes.[22] Þe fyrst degre of lufe es when a man
haldes þe ten commandementes, and kepes hym fra þe seven dedely synnes, and es stabyl in þe

12   and all pleasure that distracts you in order to love Jesus Christ
truly.

13   hierarchies

14   highest. The three orders of angels is a system of classification
stemming back to Pseudo-Dionysias's angelology.

15   star

16   to desire the fellowship

17   most ardent

18   see

19   For in the same order where proud devils fell down from, men
and women, Christ's doves, are set to have rest and joy without end,
for a little short penance and labour.

20   But certainly, when you are accustomed to doing this.

21   The three degrees of love to which Rolle refers are the 'insuper-
able', the 'inseparable' and the 'singular'. These are derived from
Richard of Saint Victor's four degrees of love, the fourth being 'insa-
tiable', combined by Rolle with the 'singular'. In Rolle, these three
degrees reflect the secular life, the active religious life, and the contemplative life. See W. F. Pollard, 'Richard Rolle and the "Eye of
the Heart" ', in Pollard and Boenig, *Mysticism and Spirituality in Medieval England*, p. 91.

22   For I will not keep from you that which I hope will turn you
towards holiness.

50   trowth of hali kyrke; and when a man wil noght for any erthly thyng wreth God, bot trewly
standes in his servyce, and lastes þarin til his lyves ende. Þis degre of lufe behoves ilk man have
þat wil be safe; for na man may com til heven bot if he lufe God and his neghbor, withowten
pride, ire, envy, or bakbityng, and withowten al other venemus synne, glotony, lichery, and
covayties. For þies vices slaes[23] þe soule, and makes it to depart fra God withowten wham na
55   creature may lyf. For als a man pusonde of a swete morcell takes venome þat slase his body, sa dose
a synful wreche in likynge and luste of hys flesch: destrues his sawle, and brynges it to dede
withowten end. Men thynk it swete to synne, bot þaire mede þat es ordand for þam es bitterer þan
þe galle, sowrar þan þe atter, war þan al þe waa þat we may here, se or fele.[24] Alle perisches and
passes þat we with eghe see; it wanes[25] into wrechednes, þe welth of þis worlde. Robes and ritches
60   rotes in dike; prowde payntyng slakes into sorowe.[26] Delites and drewryse[27] stynk sal ful sone;
þair golde and þaire tresoure drawes þam til dede. Al þe wikked of þis worlde drawes til a dale,
þat þai may se þare sorrowyng, whare waa es ever stabel; bot he may syng of solace þat lufes Jhesu
Criste. Þe wretchesse fra wele falles into hell.

      Bot when þou have wele leved in þe ten comandementes of God, and styfly put þe fra al dedely
65   synnes, and payes God in þat degre, umbethynk þe þat þou wil plese God mare, and do better
with þi sawle, and become perfyte. Þan enters þou into þe toþer degre of lufe, þat es to forsake al
þe worlde, þi fader and þi moder and al þi kyn, and folow Criste in poverte. In þis degre þou sal
stody how clene þou be in hert, and how chaste in body; and gife þe til mekenes, suffryng, and
buxumnes.[28] And loke how fayre þou may make þi saule in vertues, and hate al vices, so þat þi lyf
70   be gastly and noght fleschly. Never mare speke evyl of þi neghbor, ne gyf any evel worde for
another, bot al þat men says, evel or gude, suffer it mekeli in þi hert withowten styrryng of wreth;
and þan sal þou be in rest within and withowte, and so lyghtly sal þou come to þe gastly lyfe, þat
þou sal fynde swettar þan any erthly thyng.

      Perfite life and gastly es to despise þe worlde, and covete þe joy of heven, and destroy thorow
75   Goddes grace al wicked desyres of þe flesch, and forgete þe solace and þe lykyng of þe kynredyn,
and lufe noght bot in God: whethir þai dy or lyfe, or be pore or riche, or seke, or in wa or in hele,
thank þou ay God and blisse hym in al þi werkis. For his domes er so pryve þat na creature may
comprehend þam, and oftsithes some haves þar likyng and þair wil in þis worlde, and hell in þe
toþer; and some men er in pyne and persecucion and anguysch in þis lyfe, and hase heven to þair
80   mede. Forþi, if þi frendes be ay in þaire ese and hele and welth of þis worlde, þou and þai bath may
have þe mare drede þat þai lose noght þe joy of heven withouten end. If þai be in penance and
sekenes, or if þai lyf rightwisly, þei may trayste to come til þe blysse.

      Forþi in þis degre of lufe þou sal be fulfilde with þe grace of þe Haly Gaste þat þou sal noght
have na sorow ne grutchyng bot for gastly thyng, als for þi synnes and other mennes, and after þe
85   lufe of Jhesu Criste, and in thynkyng of his passyon; and I wil þat þou have it mykel in mynde for
it wyll kyndel þi hert to sett at noght al þe gudes of þis worlde and þe joy þarof, and to desyre
byrnandly þe lyght of heven with aungels and halowes.[29] And when þi hert es haly ordande to þe
service of God, and al worldly thoghtes put oute, þan wil þe liste stele bi þe alane to thynk on
Criste, and to be in mykel praying; for thorow gode thoghtes and hali prayers þi hert sal be made
90   byrnand in þe lufe of Jhesu Crist, and þan sal þow fele swetnes and gastely joy, bath in praying
and in thynkyng. And when þou ert by þe alane, gyf þe mykel to say þe psalmes of þe psauter and
Pater Noster and Ave Maria, and take na tent þat þou say many, bot þat þou say þam wele, with
al þe devocion þat þow may, liftand up þi thoght til heven. Better it es to say seven psalmes wyth
desyre of Crystes lufe, havand þi hert of þi praying, þan seven hundreth thowsand suffrand þi
95   thoght passe in vanitees of bodyli thynges. What gude, hopes þou, may come þarof, if þou let þi

23 slay
24 For as a man poisoned by a sweet morsel ingests poison that
kills his body, so does a sinful wretch in pleasure and desire of his
flesh: destroys his soul, and brings it to eternal death. Men think it
sweet to sin, but their reward that is ordained for them is bitterer
than gall, more sour than poison, worse than all the woes that we
may hear, see or feel.

25 vanishes
26 Robes and riches rot in a ditch; proud painting dies down into
sorrow.
27 jewels
28 obedience
29 saints
30 various

tonge blaber on þe boke and þi hert ren abowte in sere³⁰ stedes in þe worlde? Forþi sett þi thoght in Criste, and he sal rewle it til hym, and halde þe fra þe venome of þe worldly bisynesse.

And I pray þe, also þou covaytes to be Goddes lufer, þat þou lufe þis name Jhesu, and thynk it in þi hert sa þat þou forget it never, whareso þou be. And sothely I say þe, þat þou sal fynd mykel
100 joy and comforth þarin, and for þe lufe þat þou lufes Jhesu so tenderly and so specialy, þou sal be fulfild of grace in erth, and be Criste dere servande in heven. For na thyng pays God swa mykel als verray lufe of þis nam Jhesu. If þou luf hit ryght and lastandely, and never let for na thyng þat men may do or say, þou sal be receyved intil a heghar lyfe þan þou can covete. His godenes es sa mykel, þar we inwardly aske hym ane, he wil gyf fyfe, so wele payde es he when we wil sett al oure
105 hert to lufe hym.

In þis degre of lufe þou sal overcome þi enmyse, þe worlde, þe devel, and þi flesche; bot neverþelatter þou sal ever have feghtyng whils þou lyfes. Til þou dye, þe behoves to be bysy to stande, þat þou fal noght intil delites, ne in evel thoghtes, ne in evel wordes, ne in evel warke; forþi grete aght þi ȝernyng be þat þou lufe Criste verrayly. Þi flesche sal þou overcome with
110 haldyng of þi maydenhede for Goddes lufe anely; or if þou be na mayden, thorow chaste lyvyng and resonabel in thoght and dede, and thorow discrete abstinence. Þe world þou sal overcom thorow covaytyng of Cristes lufe and thynkyng on þis swete name Jhesus, and desyre til heven. For als sone als þou feles savoure in Jhesu, þe wil thynk al þe worlde noght bot vanyte and noy for men sawles. Þou will noght covayte þan to be riche, to have many mantels and fayre, many kyrtels
115 and drewryse; bot al þou wil sett at noght, and despise it als noght it ware, and take na mare þan þe nedes. Þe wil thynk twa mantels or ane inogh; þow þat hase fyve or sex, gyf some til Criste, þat gase naked in a pore wede;³¹ and halde noght all, for þou wate noght if þow lif til þai be half gane. Þe devell es overcome when þou standes stabley agaynes al hys fandyngys³² in sothefast charite and mekenes.

120 I wil þat þow never be ydel; but ay owther speke of God, or wirke som notabil warke, or thynk on hym principaly, þat þi thoght be ay havand hym in mynde. And thynk oft on his passyon:³³

My Keyng þe water grette, and blode swette;
Sythen ful sare bette, so þat hys blode hym wette,   *beaten*
When þair scowrges mette.
125 Ful fast þai gan hym dyng, and at þe pyler swyng,   *beat; scourge*
And hys fayre face defowlyng with spittyng.
Þe thorne crownes þe Keyng; ful sare es þat prickyng.
Alas, my joy and my swetyng es demed to hyng.   *condemned*
Nayled was his handes, nayled was hys fete,
130 And thyrled was hys syde, so semely and so swete.   *pierced*
Naked es his whit breste, and rede es his blody syde,
Wan was his fayre hew, his wowndes depe and wyde.
In fyve stedes of his flesch þe blode gan downe glyde
Als stremes of þe strande; hys pyne es noght to hyde.   *torrent; pain*
135 Þis to see es grete pyte, how he es demed to þe dede,   *sorrow*
And nayled on þe rode tre, þe bryght aungels brede.³⁴   *bread*
Dryven he was to dole, þat es owre gastly gude,   *pain*
And alsso in þe blys of heven es al þe aungels fude.   *food*
A wonder it es to se, whasa understude: *whoever*
140 How God of mageste was dyand on þe rude.
Bot suth þan es it sayde þat lufe ledes þe ryng;   *truth*
Þat hym sa law hase layde bot lufe it was na thyng.   *low*
Jhesu, receyve my hert, and to þi lufe me bryng;
Al my desyre þou ert, bot I covete þi comyng.

---

31 clothes
32 temptations
33 A rubric in the margin 'Meditacio de passione Christi' (Medi-

tation on the Passion of Christ) introduces this lyric.
34 Christ is described here as spiritual nourishment.

145   Þow make me clene of synne, and lat us never twyn;   *separate*
        Kyndel me fire within, þat I þi lufe may wyn
        And se þi face, Jhesu, in joy þat never sal blyn.   *cease*
        Jhesu, my saule þou mend; þi lufe into me send,
        Þat I may with þe lend in joy withowten end.   *dwell*

150   In lufe þow wownde my thoght, and lyft my hert to þe;
        My sawle þou dere hase boght, þi lufer make it to be.
        Þe I covete, þis world noght, and for it I fle;
        Þou ert þat I have soght – þi face when may I see?
        Þow make my sawle clere, for lufe chawnges my chere:

155   How lang sal I be here?
        When mai I negh þe nere, þi melody to here?
        Oft to here sang, þat es lastand so lang?   *hear song*
        Þou be my lufyng, þat I lufe may syng.

If þou wil thynk þis ilk day, þou sal fynde swetnes þat sal draw þi hert up, þat sal gar þe fal in
160 gretyng and in grete langyng til Jhesu; and þi thoght sal al be on Jhesu, and so be receyved
aboven all erthly thyng, aboven þe firmament and þe sternes,[35] so þat þe egh of þi hert may loke
intil heven.

    And þan enters þow into þe thirde degre of lufe, in þe whilk þou sal have gret delyte and
comforth, if þow may get grace to come þartill. For I say noght þat þou, or another þat redes þis,
165 sal do it all, for it es at Goddes will to chese wham he will to do þat here es sayde, or els another
thyng on another maner, als he gifes men grace til have þaire hele. For sere[36] men takes seer grace
of oure Lorde Jhesu Criste; and al sal be sett in þe joy of heven, þat endes in charite. Whasa es in
þis degre, wisdom he hase, and discrecion, to luf at Goddes will.

    Þis degre es called contemplatife lyfe, þat lufes to be anely withowten ryngyng or dyn or
170 syngyng or criyng. At þe begynyng, when þou comes þartil, þi gastly egh es taken up intil þe
blysse of heven, and þar lyghtned with grace and kyndelde with fyre of Cristes lufe, sa þat þou sal
verraly fele þe bernyng of lufe in þi hert, ever mare and mare, liftand þi thoght to God, and feland
lufe, joy, and swetnes, so mykel þat na sekenes, anguys, ne schame, ne penance may greve þe, bot
al þi lyf sal turne intyl joy. And þan fore heghnesse of þi hert in prayers turnes intil joyful sange
175 and þi thoghtes to melody. Þan es Jhesu al þi desyre, al þi delyte, al þi joy, al þi solace, al þi
comforth. Al I wate[37] þat on hym ever be þi sang, in hym all þi rest. Þen may þow say: 'I slepe and
my hert wakes. Wha sall tyll my lemman[38] say, for hys lufe me langes ay?'

    Al þat lufes vanytees and specials of þis warlde, and settes þaire hert on any other thynges þan
of God, intyll þis degre þai may noght come, ne intyll other degre of lufe before nevind.[39] And
180 þarfore all worldely solace þe behoves forsake, þat þi hert be heldande til na lufe of any creature,
ne til na bysynes in erth, þat þou may in sylence, be ay stabilly, and stalwortly with þi hert in
Goddes lufe and hys drede.

    Owre Lorde gyfes noght to men fairehede,[40] ritchesse, and delytes forto sette þaire hertes on
and dispend þam in synne, bot for þai sulde knaw hym and lufe hym and thank hym of al hys
185 gyftes. Þe mare es þaire schame if þai wreth[41] hym þat hase gyfen þam gyftes in body and in saule.
Forþi, if we covayte to fle þe payne of purgatory, us behoves restreyne us perfitely fra þe lust and
þe likyng and al þe il delytes and wikked drede of þis worlde, and þat worldely sorow be noght in
us, bot þat we halde owre hope faste in Jhesu Criste, and stande manly agaynes al temptacions.

    Now I write a sang of lufe þat þou sal delyte in when þow ert lovand Jhesu Criste:

190   My sange es in syhtyng, my lyfe es in langynge,   *sighing*
        Til I þe se, my Keyng, so fayre in þi schynyng,

35 stars
36 various
37 know
38 sweetheart

39 named
40 beauty
41 anger

So fayre in þi fayrehede, intil þi lyght me lede,
And in þi lufe me fede, in lufe make me to spede,
Þat þou be ever my mede.   *reward*

195   When wil þou come, Jhesu my joy, and cover me of kare,[42]
And gyf me þe, þat I may se, lifand evermare?
Al my coveytyng war commen, if I myght til þe fare;
I wil na thyng bot anely þe, þat all my will ware.
Jhesu my savyoure, Jhesu my comfortoure,

200   Of al my fayrnes flowre, my helpe and my sokoure,   *comfort*
When may I se þi towre?
When wil þou me kall? Me langes to þi hall
To se þe þan al; þi luf, lat it nat fal.
My hert payntes þe pall þat steds us in stal.[43]

205   Now wax I pale and wan for luf of my lemman.[44]
Jhesu, bath God and man, þi luf þou lerd me þan   *teach*
When I to þe fast ran; forþi now I lufe kan.
I sytt and syng of luf langyng þat in my breste es bredde.
Jhesu, Jhesu, Jhesu, when war I to þe ledde?

210   Full wele I wate þou sees my state; in lufe my thoght es stedde;   *placed*
When I þe se and dwels with þe, þan am I fylde and fedde.
Jhesu, þi lufe es fest, and me to lufe thynk best.   *secure*
My hert, when may it brest to come to þe, my rest?
Jhesu, Jhesu, Jhesu, til þe it es þat I morne

215   For my lyfe and my lyvyng, when may I hethen torne?   *to there turn*
Jhesu, my dere and my drewry, delyte ert þou to syng;   *treasure*
Jhesu, my myrth and melody, when will þow com, my Keyng?
Jhesu, my hele and my hony, my whart and my comfortyng,   *health*
Jhesu, I covayte forto dy when it es þi payng.   *pleasure*

220   Langyng es in me lent þat my lufe hase me sent;
Al wa es fra me went, sen þat my hert es brent   *ardent*
In Criste lufe sa swete, þat never I wil lete;
Bot ever to luf I hete, for lufe my bale may bete,   *sorrow; remedy*
And til hys blis me bryng, and gyf me my ȝernyng.   *desire*

225   Jhesu, my lufe, my swetyng:
Langyng es in me lyght, þat byndes me day and nyght
Til I it hafe in syght, his face sa fayre and bryght.
Jhesu, my hope, my hele, my joy ever ilk a dele,   *in every part*
Þi lufe lat it noght kele þat I þi luf may fele,   *cool so that*

230   And won with þe in wele.   *dwell; prosperity*
Jhesu, with þe I byg and belde; lever me war to dy[45]
Þan al þis worlde to welde and hafe it in maystry.   *control*
When wil þou rew on me, Jhesu, þat I myght with þe be,   *take pity*
To lufe and lok on þe?

235   My setell ordayne for me, and sett þou me þarin,   *seat*
For þen moun we never twyn,   *may; separated*
And I þi lufe sal syng thorow syght of þi schynyng,
In heven withowten endyng. Amen.

Explicit tractatus Ricardi heremite de Hampole, scriptus cuidam moniali de ȝedyngham.

42   shield me from trouble
43   My heart sees the cloth of the Eucharist that is the cause of our
security (i.e. Christ's blood, dispensed at Communion, is the reason
for humankind's salvation).

44   The familiar love-sickness of the Romance lyric is here applied
to the lovelorn Christian.
45   Jesus, with you I dwell and shelter, and I would rather die

Ghostly Gladness

Gastly[46] gladnes in Jhesu, and joy in hert, with swetnes in sawle of þe savor of heven in hope, es helth intil hele,[47] and my lyfe lendes[48] in luf, and lyghtsumnes unlappes[49] my thoght. I drede noght þat me may wyrk wa,[50] sa mykel I wate of wele.[51] It war na wonder if dede war dere[52] þat I mught se hym þat I seke; bot now it es lenthed fra me, and me behoves lyf here til he wil me
5   lese.[53] Lyst and lere of þis lare, and þe sal noght myslike.[54] Lufe make me to melle, and joy gars me jangell.[55] Loke þow lede þi lyf in lyghtsumnes; and hevynes, helde it away. Sarynes, lat it noght sytt wyth þe; bot in gladnes of God, evermare make þow þi gle. Amen.

46	spiritual	51	so much I know of prosperity
47	salvation	52	death were precious
48	lives	53	release
49	cheerfulness embraces	54	Listen and learn of this teaching and it shall not displease you.
50	grief	55	Love makes me speak, and joy makes me chatter.

Kyng Alisaunder

Three manuscript versions of the verse Romance *Kyng Alisaunder* survive. In the Auchinleck manuscript, Edinburgh, National Library, Advocates 19. 2. 1, dated to *c*.1330–40, the last four hundred lines of *Kyng Alisaunder* occur at folios 278–9;[1] Oxford, Bodleian Library, Laud Misc. 622, dated to the late fourteenth century, contains *Kyng Alisaunder* at folios 27 verso to 64 recto; and London, Lincoln's Inn 150, dated to the late fourteenth century, also has the poem at folios 28 recto to 90 recto.[2] Each of these manuscripts contains texts that are historical and religious, as well as this Romance. The context of *Kyng Alisaunder* in Laud Misc. 622 is primarily religious, although the inclusion of *The Siege of Jerusalem* and notes about the Holy Land suggest an interest in tales and legends of the Mediterranean.

Kyng Alisaunder is only one of a number of Middle English texts in verse and prose that celebrated the life and heroic achievements of this Macedonian hero.[3] Born in 356 BC to King Phillip II and Queen Olympias, Alexander was to become one of the greatest leaders of all time, defeating the Persians in the 330s BC, and extending his empire into India. He died from a fever at the age of thirty-two in 323 BC, but his fame was already assured by the extent of his victories, and by the legends that evolved around his deeds.[4] Medieval authors generally used one of the Latin biographies of Alexander in composing their works: *Kyng Alisaunder* is based on a French source, Thomas of Kent's twelfth-century *Le Ro-man de Toute Chevalrie*,[5] itself based on the *Res Gestae Alexandri Magni*, a fourth-century Latin text written by Julius Valerius. By the time *Kyng Alisaunder* was composed, many of the historical details of Alexander's life had been transformed into an imaginative romanticization of the hero, but despite this, the author of the text himself regards his poem as a serious work providing moral education as well as entertainment for the audience.

The extract edited here from Laud Misc. 622[6] narrates the story surrounding Alexander's birth. According to the legend, Alexander was fathered by Nectanebo II, an Egyptian pharaoh who was simultaneously to be identified with the Libyan god Ammon (whom the Greeks regarded as similar to Zeus).[7] This complex combination of two major legends has led to an episode in the text that essentially highlights the divine birth of Alexander, adding to his heroic stature and universal appeal. In *Kyng Alisaunder*, Nectanebo is the Egyptian monarch Neptenabus, who is skilled at magic and astrology, and who, wishing to avenge his defeat at the hands of Phillip II, seduces Olympias and impregnates her. The ensuing sequence of events represents the marvels of Romance at its best. The extract closes with the declaration of Alexander's nobility.

The language of the text is a south-eastern, probably London, dialect of the earlier part of the fourteenth century.

Kyng Alisaunder: Lines 1–672

Divers is þis myddellerde		*earth*
To lewed men and to lerede.		*the educated and uneducated*
Bysynesse, care and sorouȝ		
Is myd man uche morowȝe:		
5 Somme for sekenesse, for smert,		*hurt*
Somme for defaut oiþer povert,		*want*
Somme for þe lyves drede		
Þat glyt away so floure in mede.		*meadow*
Ne is lyves man non so sleiȝe		*capable*
10 Þat he ne þoleþ ofte ennoyȝe		*suffers*
In many cas, on many manere,		
Whiles he lyveþ in werlde here;		
Ac is þere non fole ne wys,		*foolish; wise*

1 Two fragments identified by N. R. Ker as belonging to this manuscript also exist. See G. V. Smithers, ed., *Kyng Alisaunder*, EETS o.s. 227, 237 (London, 1952–7), II, 5.

2 Smithers, *Kyng Alisaunder*, edits the three versions using the Laud manuscript as his base text. I am very grateful to David Salter for his assistance on the Introduction to *Kyng Alisaunder*.

3 Other texts include the *Prose Life* in the Thornton manuscript and *The Wars of Alexander*.

4 See G. Cary, *The Medieval Alexander*, ed. D. J. A. Ross (Cambridge, 1956).

5 See B. Foster, ed., *The Anglo-Norman 'Alexander' (Le Roman de Toute Chevalrie)*, Anglo-Norman Text Society 29 (London, 1976).

6 As Smithers, *Kyng Alisaunder*, pp. 8–13, discusses, this is the more reliable of the two complete fourteenth-century texts.

7 See B. Hill, 'The Alexanderromance: The Egyptian Connection', *Leeds Studies in English* 12 (1981), 185–94.

	Kyng, ne duk, ne kniȝth of prys,	*worth*
15	Þat ne desireþ sum solas	
	For to here of selcouþe cas;	*wonderful events*
	For Caton seiþ, þe gode techer,	*Cato*
	Oþere mannes liif is oure shewer.	*informant*
	Naþeles, wel fele and fulle	
20	Beeþ yfounde in herte, and shulle,	
	Þat hadden lever a ribaudye	*rather; ribald tale*
	Þan here of God oiþer Seint Marie;	
	Oiþer to drynk a copful ale	
	Þan to heren any gode tale:	
25	Swiche Ich wolde weren out bishett,	*kept out*
	For certeynlich it were nett.	*good thing*
	For hii ne habbeþ wille, Ich woot wel,	
	Bot in þe gut and in þe barel.	
	Now pes! Listneþ, and leteþ cheste,	*leave off wrangling*
30	Ȝee shullen heren noble geste,	*story of heroic deeds*
	Of Alisaundre, þe riche kyng,	
	Þat dude by his maistres teching,[8]	
	And overcom, so I fynde,	
	Darrye of Perce and Pere of Ynde,[9]	
35	And many oþere, wiȝth and hende,	*bold and noble*
	In to þe est werldes ende;	
	And þe wondres of worme and beest –	
	Deliciouse it is to ylest.	*listen to*
	Ȝif ȝee willeþ sitten stylle,	
40	Fulfylle Ich wil al ȝoure wille.	
	Whilom clerkes wel ylerede	
	On þre diȝtten þis middelerde,	*divided*
	And cleped hem in her maistrie	
	Europe, Affryke, and Assye;	*Asia*
45	Ac Assye also mychel is	*big*
	As Europe and Affryk, iwys.	*indeed*
	Wise men also founden þere	
	Twelve shedynges in þe ȝere,	*divisions*
	Þe ȝer to lede by riȝth ars.	*scientific calculation*
50	Þe first was ycleped Mars,	
	Þe oþere Averylle, þe þridd May,	
	Þe fierþe June in lengest day;	
	Þe fyfte Jule, þe sexte August,	
	Þe sevenþe Septembre, þou miȝth trust,	
55	Octobre þe eiȝtteþ, þe nynþe Novembre;	
	Þe tienþe moneþ is Decembre.	
	Genever was þe ellevenþe þoo,	
	Feverel þe twelveþ, and nomoo.	
	Names of planetes so beþ yhote;	*called*
60	Summe beeþ chelde, summe beeþ hote.	
	By hem men han þe seysyne	
	To londe, to watre, to corne, to wyne;	
	And alle chaunces, nesshe and hard,	*pleasant and unpleasant*

8   A possible reference to Aristotle, tutor to Alexander.
9   Alexander defeated Darius III of Persia in the 330s BC, and Porus
of India after that.

	Knaweþ by hem men ylerd.	*learned*
65	Whoso wil þe nature ysee,	
	Hii moten yheren Tholome,[10]	
	For I ne may, by Goddes ore,	*grace*
	Þerof now telle nomore.	
	Ac whi Ich habbe hem þus unleke	*discussed*
70	3ee shullen me after her speke.	

    Barouns weren whilom wiis and gode
Þat þis art wel understoode;
Ac on þere was hoten Neptenabus
Wiis in þis ars and maliciouse.

75	Whan kyng oiþer erle com hym to awerre,	*make war upon*
	Quyk he loked in þe sterre.	
	Of wexe he made hym popatrices,	*wax images*
	And dude hem fi3tten myd latrices;	*brick tablets for magical purposes*
	And so he lerned, *jeo vous dy*,	*I tell you*
80	Ay to afelle his enemy.	
	Mid charmes and myd conjurisouns,	
	Þus he assaied þe regiouns	
	Þat hym comen to assaile,	
	In pure manere of bataile.	
85	By clere candel in þe ni3th	
	He dude uche myd oþere fi3th.	
	Þus he lerned, Ich 3ou telle,	
	Hou he sholde his fon afelle,	*enemies*
	Of alle manere naciouns	
90	Comynde by shippe oiþer dromouns.	*large ships*
	At the last, of many londe	
	Kynges hadden of hym grete onde.	*envy*
	Wel a þritty ygadred beeþ,	*thirty nations gathered*
	And bispeken alle his deþ;	
95	Kyng Philippe, of grete þede,	*nation*
	Maister of þat felawrede	*confederation of states*
	(For he was man of mi3tty honde)	
	Myd hym he brou3th of dyvers londe	
	Nyne and twenty riche kynges,	
100	To maken on hym bataillynges.	
	Neptenabus it understood	
	Achaufed so was al his blood –	*boiling*
	He was aferde sore of harme;	
	He made his wexe and cast his charme.	
105	His ymage he made onon,	
	And of his barouns everychon,	
	And afterward of his fon,	
	And dude hem togedre gon	
	In a bacyne, al by charme.	*bowl*
110	He sei3 to hym fel þe harme;	*saw*
	He sei3 þe slau3tte of his barounes,	
	Of hise þe destrucciounes.	
	He loked and knew in þe sterren	
	Of alle kynges þe grete werren,	

10   Ptolemy's *Quadripartitum*, an astrological work.

115 And seiȝ his deþ ȝif he abyde:
Michel sorouȝ was hym myde.
He ne couþe no better diȝtt,   *knew; plan*
Bot out of londe stale by niȝtt.
Nyst þere non þat hym was neiȝ   *near*
120 Whan he out of londe fleiȝ.
He degysed hym onon
Þat hym ne knew frende ne fon.
He fleiȝ away fro toun to toun,
Þorouȝ many straunge regioun;
125 Sojournyng non he nam,   *Place of stay; took*
To Macedoyne forto he cam: *Macedonia*
A riche cite, þou understonde,
In þe herte of Grece londe.
Neptanabus sore is anoyed,
130 For Philippe haþ his londe destroyed,
And he is in Philippes cite,
And þinkeþ ȝelde his iniquite.   *repay*
Of golde he makeþ hym on table   *a*
Al ful of sterren, *saunz fable*,   *without lie*
135 And þenkeþ siggen amonges men   *to tell*
Þat he is an astromyen;
For of astronomye and nygromaunce   *magic*
Couþe non so mychel, *saunz dotaunce*.   *without doubt*
      Averylle is mery and langeþ þe daye:
140 Levedyes dauncen and þai playe;
Swaynes justneþ, kniȝttes tournay;   *Retainers; tournament*
Syngeþ þe niȝttyngale, gradeþ þe jay;   *calls out*
Þe hote sunne clyngeþ þe clay,
As ȝee wel yseen may.
145 In þis tyme, Ich understonde,
Philippe is in Neptenabus londe,
And haveþ ydon to þe swerde
Þem þat nolden myd hym acorde.
Olympyas, as I fynde on bokes,
150 Þe cite of Macedoyne lokes: *looks after*
Kynges Philyppe quene she is,
Of lyvyng ladies she bereþ þe priis.   *she is the best*
Neptenabus in þe cite was.
Ac hereþ now a selcouþ cas: *wonderful event*
155 In þis tyme faire and jolyf,
Olympyas, þat faire wiif,
Wolde make a riche fest
Of kniȝttes and lefdyes honest,
Of burgeys and of jugelers,   *citizens*
160 And of men of uche mesters.   *profession*
For men seiþ by north and south
Wymmen beeþ evere selcouþ: *marvellous*
Mychel she desireþ to shewe hire body,
Her faire here, her face rody,
165 To have loos and ek praisyng,   *glory*
And al is folye, by heven Kyng.
So dude þe dame Olympyas,

For to shewe hire gentyl face.
She hete marshales and kniȝttes
170 Greiþe hem to ryde ononriȝttes;   *prepared; straight away*
And levedyes and damoysele
Quyk hem greiþed, þousandes fele,   *many*
In faire atyre, in dyvers queyntise;
Many þere roode on riche wise.
175 A mule also whyte so mylk
Wiþ sadel of gold, sambu of sylk,   *saddle-cloth*
Was ybrouȝth to þe quene,
Myd many belle of sylver shene
Yfastned on orfreys of mounde,   *gold trappings*
180 Þat hengen neiȝ doune to grounde.
Forþ she ferde myd her route,
A þousande lefdyes of riche soute.   *dress*
A sperver þat was honest   *sparrow-hawk; noble*
So sat on þe lefdyes fyst.
185 Foure trumpes toforne hire blew;   *before*
Many man þat day hire knew,
An hundreþ þousand and ek moo,
Alle alouten hire unto.   *honoured*
Al þe toun byhonged was
190 Aȝeins þe lefdy Olympyas.
Orgnes, chymbes, uche manere glee,   *cymbals; each*
Was dryven aȝein þat levedy free.   *noble*
Wiþouten þe tounes murey   *Outside; wall*
Was arered uche manere pley: *entertainment*
195 Þere was kniȝttes tourneyng,
Þere was maydens carolyng,
Þere was champouns skirmyng,
Of hem, of oþere also, wrestlyng,
Of lyons chace, of bere baityng,
200 Abay of bore, of bole slatyng.   *bull fighting*
Al þe cite was byhonge
Wiþ riche samytes and pelles longe.   *fabrics; fine hangings*
Dame Olympias amonge þis pres   *crowd*
Sengle rood, al mantelles,   *without a mantle*
205 And naked-heved, in one coroune,   *bare-headed*
She rood þorouȝout al þe toun.
Here ȝelewe her was faire atired
Mid riche strenges of golde wyre,
And wriȝed here abouten al   *covered*
210 To her gentile myddel smal.
Briȝth and shene was her face;   *Bright; glowing*
Every fairehede in hir was.   *beauty*
Of þe folk, lewed and lered,
Ȝaven hire priis of þe middlerd.
215 Neptanabus in þe weye stood
Myd polled heved and of his hood;   *shaven*
Of her fairehede, *saunz fayle*,   *without fail*
He had in hert grete mervayle.   *wonder*
In hir he loked stedfastlyk,
220 And she in hym, al outrelyk.   *boldly*

She hym avised among þe pleye,   *observed*
For he was nouȝth of þat contreye.
She asked his beyng in hast:
He was abasched and agast,
225   And þouȝth, ȝif he myd tale duelld,   *lingered*
A þeef he shulde ben yhelde.
    'Dame', he seide, 'be þou nouȝth looþ,   *angry*
Ich am ycome to telle þe sooþ.'
She was adrad he shulde telle
230   Þing of shame, and nolde duelle: *wait*
More she þouȝth þan she spaak.
Away she roode from hym, good shak,   *speed*
And þouȝth she wolde hym yhere
Whan she was of leysere.   *at leisure*
235   Gamen is good whiles it wil last,
Ac it fareþ so wyndes blast
Þe werldelich man, and lesse and maast,
Here leve þereinne so wel waast:
Whan it is beest to þee henne it wil haste.   *from you it will hurry*
240   Me wondreþ þat men ne beeþ agaste,
And þat somme hem by oþere ne chasteþ.   *learn by example*
Olympyas her herte casteþ
After þis game deliciouse;
She þencheþ on Neptanabus.
245   She clepeþ to hir ane sweyn   *servant*
Þat is hire under-chaumberleyn,
And Neptanabus after sendeþ;
Þe chaumberleyn hym after wendeþ.
To hir chaumbre he comeþ on hast,
250   Of her fairehede he was agast.
Toforne hir a knawe he satt,   *Before her on his knees*
And she hym seide onon, myd þat:
    'Me þinkeþ,' she seide, 'maister, iwys,
Þat in þe sterren þou art wys.
255   Saye,' she seide, 'for my love,
Who drouȝ þee so heiȝe above
Swiche maistrie þee to tache?'
'Dame,' he seide, 'I nylle þe nouȝth bicache.   *deceive*
By þe planetes and by þe sterren
260   I can juggen alle þe werren,
Alle pleȝes, alle metynges   *dreams*
On erþe and alle oþere þinges.
Þorouȝ þat art, Ich sygge þee,
I can þe goddes pryvete.'   *I know the gods' private knowledge*
265   And Olympyas hym asked þoo:
'Why bihelde þou me so
Now toforne in þe vys,   *face*
Þoo Ich roode to wynne prys?'
'Oo, madame!' he seide, 'Olympyas,
270   Heiȝe maister in Egipte I was.
On a day, after redyng,   *studying*
To goddes I made sacrifyeyng.
On ansuere me was yseide.

Þou shalt nouȝth þerof ben ennoyed,

275 Ac þank me conne, lefdy free,

Þat Ich com hider to warne þee.'

Þe lefdy liiþ on her bedde,

Yhiled myd a silken webbe.   *covered; woven coverlet*

In a chaysel smok she lay,   *fine linen*

280 And in a mantel of Doway.   *Douai cloth*

Of þe briȝthede of her face

Al aboute schoon þe place.

Selde she spaak, and nouȝth loude,

And so don wymmen þat ben proude.

285 Þat was wel in his herte,

It dude hym good to duelle, certes.

His aristable[11] he took out sone:

Þe cours he tolde of sonne and mone;

Þe cours of þe planetes sevene

290 He tolde also under hevene.

Þe sonne he shewed in hir al

Þat had colour of cristal;

Þe mone in propre nature

Of adamaunt bare þe coloure.

295 Þe lefdy he dude also conne   *reveal*

Hou she took lyȝth of þe sonne.

Mars was swiþe reed fere lyche,   *fire; like*

Venus was þe saphire ylyche,

Mercurye he made gres grene,

300 And Jovyne so metal shene: *Jove*

Þe lefdy seiȝ al þis, *saunz fayle.*

Þereof she had grete mervayle,

And seide to hym: 'Be þou nouȝth looþ

Me to telle of oo þing sooþ.

305 Maistres me habbeþ ytolde, by dome,

Þat whan my lorde is hom ycome

He me wil away dryve,

And taken hym anoþer wyve.'

He loked in his aristable,

310 'It is sooþ,' he seide, '*saunz fable.*

Ac of oo þing I nylle þee nouȝth gabbe,   *lie*

A knave-childe þou shalt arst habbe   *male child; first*

Þat shal be cleped god of londe.   *called*

He shal awreke al þi shonde.   *avenge; shame*

315 Of alle kynges he worþe þe best,

Þe werlde to wynne in to þe est.

Amon, þe god of Lybye,   *Libya*

Shal doune come from þe skye

To þine bed, la, God it wete,

320 And in þine body hym biȝete.   *impregnate you*

Greiþe þee now, and faire þee kepe   *Prepare*

To-niȝth þou seest hym in þi slepe.'

For folye al it helde þe quene,

---

11 A circle which contains the signs of the zodiac, onto which are
placed precious stones representing the planets.

And seide soþe it miȝth nouȝth bene,

325　　And swore, by Adam and by Eve,[12]

　　　She ne wolde it nevere yleve;　　　　　　　　　　*believe*

　　　Ac ȝif she hym seiȝ in metyng

　　　She wolde leve in swiche þing.

　　　His leve took Neptenabus,

330　　To his in, wel yrous.　　　　　　　　　　*enraged? lustful?*

　　　Herbes he took in on herbere,

　　　And stamped hem in a mortere,　　　　　　*mortar (with a pestle)*

　　　And wronge it out in a boxe;　　　　　　　　*wrung*

　　　And after he took virgyne waxe

335　　And made a popet after þe quene;

　　　His aristable he gan unwriȝen;　　　　　　　*uncover*

　　　Þe quenes name in þe wexe he wroot

　　　Whiles it was sumdel hoot.

　　　In a bed he it diȝth,　　　　　　　　　　　　*put*

340　　And al aboute candelliȝth,　　　　　　　　　*candlelight*

　　　And spraynde þereon of þe herbes juse;　　*sprinkled; juice*

　　　And þus charmed Neptenabus.

　　　Þe levedy in her bed lay,

　　　Aboute mydniȝth, ar þe day,

345　　Whiles he made his conjuryng,

　　　She seiȝ ferly in her metyng.　　　　　　　　*vision; dream*

　　　Hire þouȝth a dragoun adoune liȝth　　　*It seemed; alighted down*

　　　To hire chaumbre and made a fliȝth.　　　　*flight*

　　　In he com to hire boure

350　　And crepe under her covertoure.

　　　Many siþe he hire kyste　　　　　　　　　　　*times; kissed*

　　　And fast in his armes þriste,　　　　　　　　*embraced*

　　　And went away so dragon wylde;

　　　Ac gret he lete hir wiþ childe.

355　　Þoo he lete redyng on his book,

　　　Olympyas of slepe awook.

　　　She was agrised for þe nones,　　　　　*aggrieved; for that event*

　　　Þat alle quakeden hire bones.

　　　Anon by a message gent

360　　After Neptanabus she sent;

　　　Al þat she seiȝ she hym telde.

　　　She seide, 'Sir, God þee forȝelde!　　　　　　*requite*

　　　On uche manere it ferd soo.

　　　Fro me shaltou nowhider goo,

365　　Ac loke me and bileve stille

　　　For to Ich wyte þi lordes wille.'　　　　　*Because; know*

　　　　He bileved, wiþoute sorowe,　　　　　　　*remained*

　　　Myd þe lefdy al þe morowe.

　　　Hire bed was made by hym, forsoþe,

370　　Myd pelles and myd riche cloþe;

　　　Þe chaumbre was myd cloþes of golde

　　　Byhenged so þe maister wolde.　　　　　　　*wanted*

　　　He voided þe chaumbre of men uchon,　　　*each one*

12　An obvious Christian invocation, but not one that Olympias
would be likely to make.

For, he seide, þat niȝth Amon
Shulde come to þe levedy,
And ben her leef and her amy;   *lover; friend*
And hymself was kniȝth, and swayn,
And boure-mayde, and chaumberlayn!
Forto it well forþ niȝttes was
In bed wook dame Olympyas,
And aspyed on uche manere
Ȝif she miȝth ouȝth yhere   *anything*
Hou Amon þe god shulde come.
Neptenabus his charme haþ nome,   *taken*
And takeþ hym hames of dragoun,   *skin*
From his shuldre to hele adoun;
His heved and his shuldres fram
He diȝtteþ in fourme of a ram.   *dressed*
Overe hire bed twyes he lepeþ,
Þe þrid tyme and in he crepeþ.
Offe he cast his dragons hame
And wiþ þe lefdy playeþ his game.
She was þolemood and lay stille;   *anxious*
Þe fals god dude al his wille
Also oft so he wolde;
Þat game she refuse nolde.   *did not want to*
Þoo þe cok crowe bigan,
He seide to hir: 'Gentil lemman,   *sweetheart*
Ich habbe biȝeten on þee a kyng
Þat shal be Philippes maisterlyng.   *superior*
On erþe worþe non hym yliche,   *will be; no equal*
He shall conquere many kyngriche.'   *kingdoms*
And afterward, in þe daweyng,   *daybreak*
He makeþ eft his charmyng,
And smyteþ of hire bed in to his,   *went quickly*
So he it nere nouȝth, iwys.
Þoo his charme ydon was,
Up hir stirte Olympyas,   *arose*
And telleþ to Neptanabon
Alle þe affers of Amon,   *circumstances about*
And he to hire – boþe acorde –
Alle þe gestes of Amon his lorde;
Ȝif he faile, mysaventure he have,
For he was lorde and eek knave.
      Olympyas stant tofore Neptanabus
Of her nywe love wel desirous.
So dooþ womman after mysdoyng,
Ne can no shame ne no repentyng,
Er she be lauȝtte in her folye   *captured*
So in þe lyme is þe fleiȝe.   *bird-trap; fly*
She seide to hym, 'Of maistres floure,
Hou shal I take on wiþ myne amoure?
Shal I any more hym yseen,
Shal I anymore aqueynte hym ben?
Ȝif he is god, he is kiynde,
And he wil me often come hende.

375
380
385
390
395
400
405
410
415
420
425

His love is also swete, iwys,
So notemuge oiþer lycorys.   *As; nutmeg*
Erþelich kniȝth ne erþelich kyng
430   Nys so swete, in none þing;
ȝif he is god, he is mylde.
Now he haþ brouȝth me myd childe,
He me wil solace and liþe   *ease*
And in þis care maken me bliþe.'   *happy*
435   'Care þou nouȝth,' quoþ þis losongere,   *trickster*
'Ich am Amonns messagere.
Telle me amorowe þi wille free,
Aniȝth he shal myd þee bee.
Ac it wil gode skylle
440   ȝoure pryvete þat þou hele,   *maintain*
For onde of kniȝth ne baroun,   *envy*
And ne wraþþe þi god Amon.'
     Swiþe bliþe was dame Olympias
Of Neptenabus gilful cas.
445   She maked hym her chaumberleyn
Overe kniȝth and overe sweyn,
And hym bitook alle here kayes,   *keys*
And her kepyng by niȝth and dayes;
Neptenabus al dooþ his wille
450   Wiþ Olympyas, ac evere stille,   *quietly*
Also it were þe god Amon.
Þe lefdy greted wiþ newe bon;   *swelled in pregnancy*
Þe barouns hadden suspecioun,
And senten saie kyng Philippoun.
455   Yhereþ now hou selcouþe liif
Comeþ to shame, sorouȝ, and striif.
     Whan corne ripeþ in hervest-tyde,
Mery it is in felde and hyde.   *countryside*
Synne it is and shame to chide,
460   For shameful dedes springeþ wyde.
Kniȝttes willeþ on huntyng ride –
Þe dere galpeþ by wodesyde.
He þat can his tyme abide
Al his wille hym shal bityde.   *happen*
465   Þe quene greteþ myd quyk bon
By þe fals god Amon.
To Neptenabus she seiþ hire mone,   *lament*
And askeþ what hire be to done:
She dredeþ hire lorde Philippoun
470   Hire wil forsake for þat chesoun.   *cause*
He bad hire make hardy chere,
And seide Amon was of powere
To kepe hire from encombrement: *distress*
'And þi fruyt shal be so gent   *chivalrous*
475   Þat he shal þee so awreke   *avenge*
Þat alle men shullen þereof speke.'
Þe levedy hire conforteþ þus.
     Þat ilk niȝth Neptenabus
Made so stronge sorcery,

480	And adressed it by þe sky,	
	Þat it com to þe pavyloun	
	Þere þat liiþ kyng Philippoun.	
	Also he liiþ in slepe by niȝth,	
	Hym þinkeþ a goshauk in grete fliȝth	
485	Settleþ on his herbergeynge,	*lodging-place*
	And ȝyneþ, and sprat abrode his wenge.	*opened its mouth*
	A dragoun of his denne gan fleiȝe	
	Whan he þat goshauk yseiȝe,	
	And settleþ sone after þas	
490	On stede þere þe quene was.	
	Sone so he þe quene fonde,	
	In hire mouþe he blew a bronde.	*breath*
	Þereafter nouȝth swiþe lang,	
	A lyoun at hire navel out sprang.	
495	Þe lyoun smoot into þe est;	*struck*
	Ne durst hym wiþstonde beest.	
	Þe goshauk of hym was agast,	
	And awook hym wel on hast.[13]	
	Þoo kyng Philippe of sleep awook,	
500	Alle clerkes wise on book	
	He dude ofsende, most and last,	
	And telde hem þis swevene in hast.	*dream*
	On þere was, hiȝth Abyron,	*called*
	Wisest clerk of everychon:	
505	'Sir,' he seide, 'here my stevene.	*voice*
	Swiþe selcouþ is þi swevene.	
	Þe goshauk of whom þe þouȝth	
	Is þiself, wery of-fouȝth.	*after battle*
	Þe dragoun is sum sterne man,	*redoubtable*
510	Oiþer a god, so Ich þee telle can,	
	Þat haþ leyn by þi quene,	
	And biȝeten a sterne strene.	*child*
	He shal be kynges alle above,	
	Bitwene þis and heven-rove.	*heaven's roof*
515	Whan þou comest to þi londe,	
	Þe soþe þou shalt understonde.'	
	Þe kyng herof took grete sorouȝ,	
	And took homward myd his folk amorouȝ.	*in the morning*
	He fonde al sooþ, wiþouten noo,	
520	And asked who hire greiþed soo.	*treated*
	She seide þat she was amye	*the mistress*
	To Amon, þe god of Lybye.	
	Þe kyng was wrooþ – no wonder it nas –	
	Þat his wiif wiþ childe was:	
525	Fewe wordes to hire he seide,	
	Louryng semblaunt on hire he made.	*A scowling expression*
	He þouȝth on hir awreken ben	*to be avenged*
	Whan he miȝth his tyme seen.	
	Þeiȝ Neptenabus nolde speke,	

13 A prophetic dream foreshadowing Alexander's (the lion's) military successes.

530   Wel he þouȝth hire awreke.

                     A day it fel þe kyng a feste   *feast*

                     Wolde helden, swiþe honeste,

                     Of dukes, of princes, of barouns,

                     Of kniȝttes of his regiouns,

535   And after make bymenyng   *complaint*

                     Of his wyves mysdoyng.

                     Þai comen to þe kynges sonde,   *banquet*

                     Gentyl men of fele londe.

                     To þe mete þay weren ysett,

540   Ne miȝtten men ben served bett

                     Noiþer in mete ne in drynk;

                     Bot þereaboute nyl Ich swynk.   *I will not labour*

                     Ac þoo þai shulde bere up þe clooþ,   *carry the table-cloth*

                     Uche of hem so bycom wrooþ,

545   For a dragon þere com in fleen,   *flying*

                     Swithe griselich on to seen.   *gruesome*

                     His tayl was fyve fadem lang;   *fathoms*

                     Þe fyre out at his noseþerles sprang; *nostrils*

                     By þre, by foure, myd þe tayle

550   To þe grounde he smoot *saunz fayle.*   *struck*

                     Wiþ þe mouþe he made a beere   *noise*

                     So al þe halle shulde ben afere.   *afraid*

                     Þe kyng had wel grete hawe;   *anxiety*

                     Alle his barouns to chaumbre drawe.

555   Þe lefdy ȝede unto þe drake   *went; dragon*

                     He lete his rage for hire sake,   *ceased*

                     And laide his heved in hir barme,   *breast*

                     Wiþouten doyng of any harme.

                     Also þis folk abouten prest

560   For to see þis selcouþe beest;   *marvellous*

                     On erne he bycam and out fleiȝ   *he became an eagle*

                     Into þe skyes þat uche man seiȝ.

                     Sone þerafter and nouȝth longe,

                     Fel a chaunce selcouþe and stronge. *A chance happening occurred*

565   Of wilde beestes com a grete pray   *host*

                     Ȝerned þorouȝout þe contray,   *Galloped*

                     And afterward a flok of bryddes,

                     And a fesaunt hem fleiȝ amyddes.

                     An eye he leide, also he fleiȝ,   *egg*

570   Þat fel þe kyng Phelippe neiȝ.   *fell near*

                     Þat eye braak, Ich ȝou telle: *broke*

                     A dragon crepe out of þe shelle.

                     Þe briȝth sonne so hoot shoon

                     Þat þe eyeshelle al toscroon.   *eggshell; split*

575   Þe dragonett lay in þe strate;   *little dragon*

                     Miȝth he nouȝth dure for þe hate. *He could not stay out*

                     He fonded to crepe, Ich ȝou telle,   *tried*

                     Aȝeyn in to þe eyeshelle.

                     It was tobroken, and he ne miȝth,

580   And þere he starf ononriȝth.   *died immediately*

                     Þe kyng it seiȝ and wonder he had:

                     Alle his maistres he ofgrad,   *summoned*

And seide he had þerof dotaunce,   *doubt*
For it was som signifiaunce;
585 And bad hem telle of whiche þing
It miȝth be signifieyng.
On þere was þat hete Antyfon,   *called*
Wyser clerk ne lyved non
In al þis werldes regioun,
590 In art of estallacioun.   *mapping of the stars*
He seide, 'O, sir kyng, *saunfaile*,   *without doubt*
Here is fallen gret merveyle.
By þis ilk litel dragon
Is bitokned þe quenes son:
595 Þe eye rounde shal signifie   *egg*
Þat he shal habbe seignourye   *sovereignty*
Of þis rounde myddellerd
Boþe of lewed and of lerd;
Ac he shal wende of londe fer,
600 To Grece and comen never ner;
He shal be poysond *saunz retours*   *without fail*
Of his owen traytoures.
Þat signifieþ þe dragonett
Ne may recover to his recett.'   *place of refuge*
605   Time is comen þe lefdy shal childe;
She biddeþ þe god be hire mylde.
Þe þrowen hire afongen gynne.   *labour-pains; she began to receive*
Neptanabus biholdeþ his gynne,   *instrument*
And seiþ to þe lefdy aloude:
610 'Wiþholde þe, dame, and aȝeyn croude,   *push*
For ȝif þou childest in þis stounde,   *at this moment*
Þi childe shal be myd sorouȝ bounde, *bound with sorrow*
Coward, feynt, and nouȝth worþ.
Wiþhelde þee ȝut, and bere þee forþ.' *withhold yourself yet*
615 She wiþhelde hire wiþ al hire woo,
So þat she ne childed þoo.   *give birth; then*
Ac sone after a þrowe hire cam,   *contraction*
Anoþer shryke þe quene up nam.   *cry of pain*
'Now is wers,' quoþ Neptanabus,
620 'And þou childe in þis hous,
A shal be a þing uneste –   *repulsive*
Heved of cok, breest of man, croupe of beest.' *backside*
In hire sorouȝ ȝut she louȝ,   *lay*
Of hire childyng and hir wiþdrouȝ;   *confinement*
625 Ac sone þereafter hire was so woo
So þat she ne miȝth goo.   *go on*
And he loked in þe planete,
Þe tyme þoo hym þouȝth swete,
And seide swiftely to þe quene:
630 'Doo, dame, now lete come þi strene;   *child*
For he shal be master of londes,
Gode werroure, miȝtty of hondes,   *warrior*
Þe hardyest of lyvyng man
Shal hym no foo stonde aȝein.'
635 In þat tyme þat he þus grad,   *spoke*

A knave-childe þe quene hadd:
Alisaunder he named was.
In his beryng fel straunge cas: *at his time of birth*
Þe erþe shook, þe cee bycom grene;   *sea*
640 Þe sonne wiþdrouȝ, shynyng shene;
Þe mone hire shewed, and bicom blak;
Þe þonder made many crak;
Þe day bycom derk so niȝth.
Afered was sore every wiȝth.   *creature*
645 Kyng Phelipp seide to þe moder:
'Þou hast brouȝth forþ an yvel fode;   *progeny*
Mote he lybbe and þenne goo
Many man he shal do woo.'
Neptanabus took on bysmare   *took affront*
650 Al þat þe kyng seide þare.
He dude þe childe habbe noryce –   *ensured; nurses*
Gentil levedyes and nouȝth nyce.   *frivolous*
Þe weder bicom mery and briȝth;
At aise hem makeþ lefdy and kniȝth.   *At their pleasure*
655 Þe childe waxeþ a wiȝth ȝongelyng.   *lively little boy*
Now hereþ geste and ȝiveþ listnyng.
    Alisaundre waxeþ a childe of mayn.   *might*
Maistres he haveþ two doseyn:
Somme hym techeþ forþ to gon,
660 Þat oþere his cloþes on to don;
Þe þrid hym techeþ to pleye atte balle,
Þe fierþe afetement of halle;   *manners*
Þe fifte hym tauȝtte to skirme and ryde   *fence*
And to demayne horses bridel;   *control*
665 Þe sevenþe maister techeþ his pars
And þe wytt of þe seven ars –   *liberal arts*
Aristotle was on þerof.
Þis is nouȝth romaunce of skof,   *frivolous stuff*
Ac storye ymade of maistres wyse,
670 Of þis werlde of mest pryse.
Was þere nevere, Ich understonde,
Nobler childe in none londe.

Athelston

Athelston,[1] a verse Romance, is contained only in folios 120 verso to 131 verso of Cambridge, Gonville and Caius College 175, a manuscript dated to the early fifteenth century. This volume also contains other Romances such as *Richard Coeur de Lyon*, *Sir Ysumbras* and *Bevis of Hamptoun*, all of which can be considered didactic Romances. This aspect of the texts, together with the inclusion in the manuscript of the religious texts such as *The Life of Saint Katherine* and *Matutinas de Cruce*, suggests that the compiler of Gonville and Caius 175 thought of *Athelston* as a religiously instructive poem as well as a Romance with demonstrable political overtones.

The date of *Athelston*'s composition is not known, although it can be assigned in all probability to the last few decades of the fourteenth century.[2] It may have been written in East Anglia or the south-east Midlands, the area in which tail rhyme versification was most prevalent, and the area to which some of the dialectal forms in *Athelston* can be ascribed. It is a curious text with no known direct source, although there are some episodes in the text for which there are antecedent analogues. For example, the English Romances the *Sege of Melayne*, the *Earl of Toulouse* and *Amis and Amiloun* all have some parallels with *Athelston*,[3] and the judicial processes described by the poet seem to have their origins in archaic legal codes and procedures. *Athelston* may then be a composite text, formed from a number of commonplace themes found in numerous Romances (loyalty versus treachery,

kingship and brotherhood, justice and mercy) and other medieval legends.

It is intriguing that the poet chooses to use an Anglo-Saxon king as his central protagonist, and the obsolete trial by ordeal.[4] The reasons for this are unclear, but if this text were a didactic treatise on good kingship, for example, or a text with some contemporary political relevance, it would make sense to distance the audience from the text by setting it in a past time-frame. The poem concerns four 'weddyd brothers' sworn in loyalty to each other, but one of whom is a traitor. The treacherous act initiated by this traitor, Wymound, almost causes a major political crisis as the king and archbishop of Canterbury dispute their respective moral and regnal rights. The poem has important fourteenth-century resonances, as both Edward III and Richard II were determined to increase their monarchical powers at the expense of the nobility. In this poem, Athelston reacts furiously to any attempts to undermine his sole authority, even killing his own unborn child in a fit of fury against his wife. Essentially, the poem depicts the personal development of a king, from one who acts tyrannically, to one who learns the value of taking advice and acting with caution. Like so many other Romances, *Athelston* is chiefly an entertaining, relatively fast-paced text, and one that contemporizes fictional past events to make its historical setting identifiable in order to facilitate the absorption of valuable moral lessons.

Athelston

	Lord, þat is off myȝtys most,	*power*
	Fadyr and sone and holy gost,	
	Bryng us out off synne,	
	And lene us grace so forto wyrke,	*grant*
5	To love boþe God and holy kyrke,	
	Þat we may hevene wynne.	
	Lystnes, lordyngys þat ben hende,	*courteous*
	Off falsnesse, hou it wil ende	
	A man þat ledes hym þerin.	*leads*
10	Off foure weddyd breþeryn I wole ȝow tel,	*united*
	Þat wolden yn Yngelond go dwel,	
	Þat sybbe were nouȝt off kyn.	*related; kin*

1   A. McI. Trounce, ed., *Athelston: A Middle English Romance*, EETS o.s. 224 (London, 1951).

2   See E. Ashman Rowe, 'The Female Body Politic and the Miscarriage of Justice in *Athelston*', *Studies in the Age of Chaucer* 17 (1995), 79–98, who believes the poem to post-date Richard II's reign; and E. M. Treharne, 'The Romanticisation of the Past in the Middle English *Athelston*', *Review of English Studies* 50 (1999), 1–21, who does not.

3   See Trounce, *Athelston*, pp. 4–20.

4   Athelstan was a tenth-century king of Wessex, grandson of Alfred the Great. He was the hero of *The Battle of Brunanburh*, and generally in medieval chronicles he was depicted as a wise and courageous king.

And alle foure messangeres þey were,
Þat wolden yn Yngelond lettrys bere,
15   As it wes here kynde.   *occupation*
By a forest gan þey mete
Wiþ a cros, stood in a strete,
Be leff undyr a lynde.   *leaf; linden tree*
And, as þe story telles me,
20   Ylke man was of dyvers cuntre   *Each; country*
(In book iwreten we fynde),
For love of here metyng þare,
Þey swoor hem weddyd breþeryn for evermare,
In trewþe trewely dede hem bynde.   *did*

25   Þe eldeste off hem ylkon,   *each one*
He was hyƷt Athelston,   *called*
Þe kyngys cosyn dere;   *dear*
He was off þe kyngys blood,
Hys eemes sone, I undyrstood;   *uncle's*
30   Þerfore he neyƷyd hym nere.   *was closely related*
And at þe laste, weel and fayr,
Þe kyng hym dyyd withouten ayr;   *heir*
Þenne was þer non hys pere   *equal*
But Athelston, hys eemes sone;
35   To make hym kyng wolde þey nouƷt schone,   *shun*
To corowne hym with gold so clere.

Now was he kyng semely to se:
He sendes afftyr hys breþeryn þre,
And gaff hem here warysoun.   *reward*
40   Þe eldest broþir he made eerl of Dovere
And þus þe pore man gan covere   *recover*
Lord off tour and toun.   *castle*
Þat oþer broþer he made eerl of Stane
Egelond was hys name,
45   A man off gret renoun,
And gaff hym tyl hys weddyd wyff   *as*
Hys owne sustyr, Dame Edyff,
Wiþ gret devocyoun.

Þe ferþe broþir was a clerk,   *fourth; cleric*
50   Mekyl he cowde off Goddys werk: *Much*
Hys name it was Alryke.
Cauntyrbury was vacant
And fel into þat kyngys hand;
He gaff it hym, þat wyke,   *office*
55   And made hym bysschop of þat stede.   *place*
Þat noble clerk, on book cowde rede –
In þe world was non hym lyche.   *like*
Þus avaunsyd he hys broþer þorwƷ Goddys gras,   *grace*
And Athelston hymselven was
60   A good kyng and a ryche.   *powerful*

And he þat was eerl off Stane
(Sere Egeland was hys name)
Was trewe, as ȝe schal here.
Þorwȝ þe myȝt off Goddys gras,

65 He gat upon þe countas   *countess*
Twoo knave-chyldren dere.   *boys*
Þat on was fyfftene wyntyr old,
Þat oþer þryttene, as men me told:
In þe world was non here pere,   *their*

70 Also whyt so lylye-flour,
Red as rose off here colour,
As bryȝt as blosme on brere.   *branch*

Boþe þe eerl and hys wyff,
Þe kyng hem lovede as hys lyff,   *his own*

75 And here sones twoo;
And offtensyþe he gan hem calle   *oftentimes*
Boþe to boure and to halle,
To counsayl whenne þey scholde goo.
Þerat sere Wymound hadde gret envye,

80 Þat eerl off Dovere, wyttyrlye,   *truly*
In herte he was ful woo;
He þouȝte al for here sake   *ruin*
False lesyngys on hem to make,   *lies*
To don hem brenne and sloo.   *To get them burned to death*

85 And þanne sere Wymound hym beþouȝte: *reflected*
'Here love þus endure may nouȝte;   *Their*
Þorwȝ wurd oure werk may sprynge.'   *conversation; move forward*
He bad hys men maken hem ȝare;   *ready*
Unto Londone wolde he fare,   *go*

90 To speke wiþ þe kynge.
Whenne þat he to Londone come,
He mette with þe kyng ful sone.   *immediately*
He sayde: 'Welcome, my derelyng.'
Þe kyng hym fraynyd soone anon   *asked*

95 Be what way he hadde igon,   *arrived*
Wiþouten ony dwellyng: *stay-overs*

'Come þou ouȝt be Cauntyrbery,
Þere þe clerkys syngen mery
Boþe erly and late?

100 Hou faryth þat noble clerk,   *goes*
Þat mekyl can on Goddys werk?
Knowest þou ouȝt hys state?   *at all*
And come þou ouȝt be þe eerl off Stane,
Þat wurþy lord in hys wane?   *dwelling*

105 Wente þou ouȝt þat gate?   *way*
Hou fares þat noble knyȝt,
And hys sones fayr and bryȝt,
My sustyr, ȝiff þat þou wate?'   *know*

'Sere,' þanne he sayde, 'wiþouten les,   *lie*
110   Be Cauntyrbery my way I ches;   *chose*
Þere spak I wiþ þat dere.   *dear man*
Ryȝt weel gretes þee þat noble clerk,
Þat mykyl can off Goddys werk,
In þe world is non hys pere.
115   And also be Stane my way I drowȝ;   *went*
Wiþ Egeland I spak inowȝ,   *quite a lot*
And with þe countesse so clere.   *bright*
Þey fare weel, is nouȝt to layne,   *hide*
And boþe here sones.' Þe king was fayne,   *happy*
120   And in his herte made glad chere.

'Sere kyng,' he sayde, 'ȝiff it be þi wille,
To chaumbyr þat þou woldest wenden tylle   *proceed*
Counsayl forto here,
I schal þe telle a swete tydande;   *news*
125   Þer comen nevere non swyche in þis lande   *such*
Off al þis hundryd ȝere.'
Þe kyngys herte þan was ful woo
Wiþ þat traytour forto goo;
Þey wente boþe forþ in fere –   *together*
130   And whenne þat þey were þe chaumbyr withinne,
False lesyngys he gan begynne
On hys weddyd broþer dere.   *sworn*

'Sere kyng,' he sayde, 'woo were me,
Ded þat I scholde see þe,   *might*
135   So moot I have my lyff.
For by hym þat al þis worl wan,   *world*
Þou hast makyd me a man,
And iholpe me forto þryff.   *thrive*
For in þy land, sere, is a fals traytour;
140   He wole doo þe mykyl dyshonour,
And brynge þe on lyve;   *out of*
He wole deposen þe slyly,
Sodaynly þan schalt þou dy,
Be Crystys woundys fyve.'

145   Þenne sayde þe kyng: 'So moot þou the,
Knowe I þat man, and I hym see?   *seen*
His name þou me telle.'
'Nay,' says þat traytour, 'þat wole I nouȝt,
For al þe gold þat evere was wrouȝt,
150   Be massebook and belle;   *(a common oath)*
But ȝiff þou me þy trowþe wil plyȝt,   *word; pledge*
Þat þou schalt nevere bewreye þe knyȝt   *betray*
Þat þe þe tale schal telle.'
Þanne þe kyng his hand up rauȝte,   *raised*
155   Þat false man his trowþe betauȝte: *pledged*
He was a devyl off helle!

'Sere kyng,' he sayde, 'þou madyst me knyȝt,
And now þou hast þy trowþe me plyȝt
Oure counsayl forto layne: *conceal*
160   Sertaynly, it is non oþir
But Egelane, þy weddyd broþir,
He wolde þat þou were slayne;
He dos þy sustyr to undyrstande   *gives*
He wole be kyng off þy lande,
165   And þus he begynnes here trayne;   *plot*
He wole þe poysoun ryȝt slyly,
Sodaynly þanne schalt þou dy –
Be hym þat suffryd payne.'

Þanne swoor þe kyng be cros and roode:
170   'Meete ne drynk schal do me goode,   *be eaten by me*
Tyl þat he be dede;
Boþe he and hys wyff, hys soones twoo,
Schole þey nevere be no moo
In Yngelond, on þat stede.'
175   'Nay,' says þe traytour, 'I so moot I the,
Ded wole I nouȝt my broþer se;
But do þy beste rede.'   *think*
No lengere þere þen wolde he lende: *remain*
He takes hys leve, to Dovere gan wende.
180   God geve hym schame and dede!

Now is þat traytour hom iwent.
A messanger was afftyr sent   *sent for*
To speke with þe kyng.
I wene he bar his owne name: *think; had*
185   He was hoten Athelstane;   *called*
He was foundelyng.   *orphan*
Þe lettrys were imaad fullyche þare,
Unto Stane forto fare   *journey*
Wiþouten ony dwellyng,   *stopping*
190   To fette þe eerl and his sones twoo,   *fetch*
And þe countasse alsoo,
Dame Edyve, þat swete þyng.

And in þe lettre ȝit was it tolde,
Þat þe kyng þe eerlys sones wolde   *wished to*
195   Make hem boþe knyȝt;
And þerto his seel he sette.
Þe messanger wolde nouȝt lette,   *delay*
Þe way he rydes ful ryȝt.   *straight away*

Þe messanger, þe noble man,
200   Takes hys hors and forþ he wan,   *goes*
And hyes a ful good spede.   *hastens*
Þe eerl in hys halle he fande;
He took hym þe lettre in his hande,
Anon he bad hym rede:
205   'Sere,' he sayde also swyþe,   *at once*

'Þis lettre ouȝte to make þe blyþe: *happy*
Þertoo, þou take good hede.
Þe kyng wole for þe cuntas sake
Boþe þy sones knyȝtes make
210   To London I rede þe spede.   *advise*

Þe kyng wole for þe cuntas sake
Boþe þy sones knyȝtys make,
Þe blyþere þou may be.   *happier*
Þy fayre wyff with þe þou bryng –
215   And þer be ryȝt no lettyng –   *delay*
Þat syȝte þat sche may see.'
Þenne sayde þat eerl with herte mylde:
'My wyff goþ ryȝt gret with chylde
And, forþynkes me,   *it seems*
220   Sche may nouȝt out off chaumbyr wyn   *go*
To speke with non ende off here kyn,   *member*
Tyl sche delyveryd be.'

But into chaumbyr þey gunne wende,
To rede þe lettrys before þat hende,   *lady*
225   And tydyngys tolde here soone.
Þenne sayde þe cuntasse: 'So moot I the,
I wil nouȝt lette tyl I þere be,   *delay*
Tomorwen or it be noone.   *before*
To see hem knyȝtys, my sones fre,   *good*
230   I wole nouȝt lette tyl I þere be:
I schal no lengere dwelle.
Cryst forȝelde my lord þe kyng,   *reward*
Þat has grauntyd hem here dubbyng;   *knighting*
Myn herte is gladyd welle.'

235   Þe eerl hys men bad make hem ȝare;   *instructed; ready*
He and hys wyff forþ gunne þey fare,   *journey*
To London faste þey wente.
At Westemynstyr was þe kyngys wone;   *dwelling*
Þere þey mette with Athelstone,
240   Þat afftyr hem hadde sente.

Þe goode eerl soone was hent,   *seized*
And feteryd faste, verrayment,   *truly*
And hys sones twoo.
Ful lowde þe countasse gan to crye,
245   And sayde: 'Goode broþir, mercy!
Why wole ȝe us sloo?   *you*
What have we aȝens ȝow done,
Þat ȝe wole have us ded so soone?
Me þynkiþ ȝe arn oure foo.'   *are*
250   Þe kyng as wood ferde in þat stede: *mad; behaved; place*
He garte hys sustyr to presoun lede,   *ordered*
In herte he was ful woo.

Þenne a squyer, was þe countasses frende,
To þe qwene he gan wende,
255 And tydyngys tolde here soone.
Gerlondes off chyryes off sche caste, *Garlands; cherries*
Into þe halle sche come at þe laste,
Longe or it were noone. *before*
'Sere kyng, I am before þe come
260 Wiþ a chyld, douȝtyr or a sone;
Graunte me my bone: *request*
My broþir and sustyr þat I may borwe, *act as surety for*
Tyl þe nexte day at morwe,
Out off here paynys stronge. *torments*

265 Þat we mowe wete be comoun sent *may; know; assent*
In þe playne parlement . . .' *full*
'Dame!' he sayde, 'goo fro me!
Þy bone schal nouȝt igrauntyd be,
I doo þe to undyrstande.
270 For, be hym þat weres þe corowne off þorn,
Þey schole be drawen and hangyd tomorn,
Ȝyff I be kyng off lande.'

And whenne þe qwene þese wurdes herde,
As sche hadde be beten wiþ ȝerde, *stick*
275 Þe teeres sche leet doun falle.
Sertaynly, as I ȝow telle,
On here bare knees doun sche felle,
And prayde ȝit for hem alle. *yet*
'A, dame!' he sayde, 'Verrayment,
280 Hast þou broke my comaundement?
Abyyd ful dere þou schalle.' *Pay for that*
Wiþ hys foot (he wolde nouȝt wonde) *hesitate*
He slowȝ þe chyld ryȝt in here wombe: *killed; her*
Sche swownyd amonges hem alle. *fainted*

285 Ladys and maydenys þat þere were
Þe qwene to here chaumbyr bere, *carried*
And þere was a dool inowȝ. *lamentation; much*
Soone withinne a lytel spase *time*
A knave-chyld iborn þer wase, *was*
290 As bryȝt as blosme on bowȝ.
He was boþe whyt and red,
Off þat dynt was he ded – *blow*
Hys owne fadyr hym slowȝ.
Þus may a traytour baret rayse, *trouble*
295 And make manye men ful evele at ayse,
Hymselff nouȝt afftyr it lowȝ. *laughed*

But ȝit þe qwene, as ȝe schole here,
Sche callyd upon a messangere,
Bad hym a lettre fonge; *receive*
300 And bad hym wende to Cauntyrbery,
Þere þe clerkys syngen mery

Boþe masse and evensonge.
'Þis lettre þou þe bysschop take,
And praye hym, for Goddys sake,

305   Come borewe hem out off here bande.   *bail; fetters*
He wole doo more for hym, I wene,   *Athelston; think*
Þanne for me, þouȝ I be qwene,
I doo þe to undyrstande.

An eerldom in Spayne I have of land;

310   Al I sese into þyn hand,   *grant legally*
Trewely, as I þe hyȝt,   *promise*
An hundryd besauntys off gold red.   *gold coins*
Þou may save hem from þe ded   *death*
Ȝyff þat þyn hors be wyȝt.'   *speedy*

315   'Madame, brouke weel þy moregeve,   *use; dowry (of land)*
Also longe as þou may leve –
Þerto have I no ryȝt;
But off þy gold and off þy fee,
Cryst in hevene forȝelde it þe;   *requite*

320   I wole be þere tonyȝt.

Madame, þrytty myles off hard way
I have reden, siþ it was day: *ridden; since*
Ful sore I gan me swynke;   *hard; toiled*
And forto ryde now fyve and twenti þertoo,

325   An hard þyng it were to doo,
Forsoþe, ryȝt as me þynke.
Madame, it is nerhande passyd prime,   *nearly; the first part of the day*
And me behoves al forto dyne,   *it suits me*
Boþe wyn and ale to drynke.

330   Whenne I have dynyd, þenne wole I fare.
God may covere hem off here care,   *recover; anxieties*
Or þat I slepe a wynke.'   *Before*

Whenne he hadde dynyd, he wente his way,
Also faste as þat he may,

335   He rod be Charynge-cros,
And entryd into Flete-strete,
And seþþyn þorwȝ Londone, I ȝow hete,   *afterwards; assure*
Upon a noble hors.
Þe messanger, þat noble man,

340   On Loundone-brygge sone he wan,   *was*
For his travayle he hadde no los   *Because of; loss (in time)*
From Stone into Steppyngebourne.
Forsoþe his way nolde he nouȝt tourne;
Sparyd he nouȝt for myre ne mos.   *mire; bog*

345   And þus hys way wendes he
Fro Osprynge to þe Blee;   *forest of Blean*
Þenne myȝte he see þe toun
Off Cauntyrbery, þat noble wyke,   *town*
Þerin lay þat bysschopryke,   *bishopric*

350   Þat lord off gret renoun.

And whenne þey runggen undernbelle,   *mid-morning bell*
He rod in Londone (as I ȝow telle),   *told*
He was non er redy;   *before*
And ȝit to Cauntyrbery he wan,
Longe or evensong began;
355 He rod mylys fyffty.

Þe messanger noþyng abod;   *waited*
Into þe palays forþ he rod
Þere þat þe bysschop was inne.
360 Ryȝt welcome was þe messanger,
Þat was come from þe qwene so cleer,   *bright*
Was off so noble kynne.
He took hym a lettre ful good speed,
And sayde: 'Sere bysschop, have þis and reed';
365 And bad hym come wiþ hym.   *The bishop; the messenger*
Or he þe lettre hadde halff iredde,
For dool, hym þouȝte, hys herte bledde;   *sorrow*
Þe teeres fyl ovyr hys chyn.

Þe bysschop bad sadele hys palfray:
370 'Also faste as þay may,
Bydde my men make hem ȝare;   *ready*
And wendes before,' þe bysschop dede say,
'To my maneres in þe way;   *manors*
For noþyng þat ȝe spare.
375 And loke, at ylke fyve mylys ende   *each*
A fresch hors þat I fynde,
Schod and noþyng bare;   *without harness*
Blyþe schal I nevere be,
Tyl I my weddyd broþer see,
380 To kevere hym out off care.'   *recover; sorrow*

On nyne palfrays þe bysschop sprong
Ar it was day, from evensong –
In romaunce as we rede.
Sertaynly, as I ȝow telle,
385 On Londone-brygge ded doun felle
Þe messangeres stede.
'Allas,' he sayde, 'þat I was born!
Now is my goode hors forlorn,   *lost*
Was good at ylke a nede;   *every*
390 Ȝistyrday upon þe grounde,
He was wurþ an hundryd pounde,
Ony kyng to lede.'

Þenne bespak þe erchebysschop,
Oure gostly fadyr undyr God,   *spiritual*
395 Unto þe messangere:
'Lat be þy menyng off þy stede,   *complaining*
And þynk uþon oure mykyl nede,   *great*
Þe whylys þat we ben here;
For ȝiff þat I may my broþer borwe,   *bail*

400	And bryngen hym out off mekyl sorwe,	
	Þou may make glad chere;	
	And þy warysoun I schal þe geve,	*reward*
	And God have grauntyd þe to leve	
	Unto an hundryd ȝere.'	
405	Þe bysschop þenne nouȝt ne bod,	*wait*
	He took hys hors, and forþ he rod	
	Into Westemynstyr so lyȝt;	*nimbly*
	Þe messanger on his foot alsoo –	
	Wiþ þe bysschop come no moo,	
410	Neþer squyer ne knyȝt.	
	Upon þe morwen þe kyng aros,	
	And takes þe way to þe kyrke he gos,	
	As man off mekyl myȝt.	
	Wiþ hym wente boþe preest and clerk,	
415	Þat mykyl cowde off Goddys werk,	
	To praye God for þe ryȝt.	*justice*
	Whenne þat he to þe kyrke com;	
	Tofore þe rode he knelyd anon,	*Before*
	And on hys knees he felle:	
420	'God, þat syt in Trynyte,	
	A bone þat þou graunte me:	*request*
	Lord, as þou harewyd helle,	*harrowed*
	Gyltles men ȝiff þat þay be,	*Guilty; people*
	Þat are in my presoun free,	*strong*
425	Forcursyd þere to ȝelle;	*Condemned; shriek*
	Off þe gylt and þay be clene,	*innocent*
	Leve it moot on hem be sene,	*Allow*
	Þat garte hem þere to dwelle.'	*causes*
	And whenne he hadde maad his prayer,	
430	He lokyd up into þe qweer,	*choir*
	Þe erchebysschop sawȝ he stande.	
	He was forwondryd off þat caas,	*amazed; event*
	And to hym he wente apas,	
	And took hym be þe hande.	
435	'Welcome', he sayde, 'þou erchebysschop,	
	Oure gostly fadyr undyr God.'	
	He swoor be God levande:	*Alryke; living*
	'Weddyd broþer, weel moot þou spede,	*fare*
	For I hadde nevere so mekyl nede,	
440	Siþ I took cros on hande.	
	Goode weddyd broþer, now turne þy rede:	*change; mind*
	Doo nouȝt þyn owne blood to dede,	*death*
	But ȝiff it wurþy were.	*Unless; merited*
	For hym þat weres þe corowne off þorn,	
445	Lat me borwe hem tyl tomorn,	
	Þat we mowe enquere;	
	And weten alle be comoun asent	*know; assent*
	In þe playne parlement	*full*

Who is wurþy be schent. *deserving; of execution*
450 And, but ȝiff ȝe wole graunte my bone,
It schal us rewe boþe or none, *grieve*
Be God þat alle þyng lent.' *granted*

Þanne þe kyng wax wroþ as wynde, *grew*
A wodere man myȝte no man fynde *madder*
455 Þan he began to bee.
He swoor oþis be sunne and mone: *oaths*
'Þey schole be drawen and hongyd or none *before*
Wiþ eyen þou schalt see.
Lay doun þy cros and þy staff,
460 Þy mytyr and þy ryng þat I þe gaff; *mitre*
Out off my land þou flee!
Hyȝe þe faste out off my syȝt;
Wher I þe mete, þy deþ is dyȝt; *certain*
Non oþir þen schal it bee.'

465 Þenne bespak þat erchebysschop,
Oure gostly fadyr undyr God,
Smertly to þe kyng: *Angrily*
'Weel I wot þat þou me gaff
Boþe þe cros and þe staff,
470 Þe mytyr and eke þe ryng;
My bysschopryche þou reves me? *deprive of*
And crystyndom forbede I þe: *refuse (i.e. excommunication)*
Preest schal þer non syngge;
Neyþer maydynchyld ne knave
475 Crystyndom schal þer non have; *(i.e. an interdict is placed on England)*
To care I schal þe brynge. *grief*

I schal gare crye þorwȝ ylke a toun *cause; every*
Þat kyrkys schole be broken doun,
And stoken agayn wiþ þorn; *choked*
480 And þou schalt lygge in an old dyke, *lie; ditch*
As it were an heretyke. *heretic*
Allas, þat þou were born.

Ȝiff þou be ded þat I may see,
Asoylyd schalt þou nevere bee; *Absolved*
485 Þanne is þy soule in sorwe.
And I schal wenden in uncouþe lond, *foreign*
And gete me stronge men of hond; *force*
My broþir ȝit schal I borwe. *rescue*
I schal brynge upon þy lond
490 Hungyr and þyrst ful strong,
Cold, drouȝþe, and sorwe;
I schal nouȝt leve on þy lond *leave*
Wurþ þe gloves on þy hond,
To begge ne to borwe.'

495 Þe bysschop has his leve tan, *taken*
By þat his men were comen ylkan: *then; each one*

Þey sayden: 'Sere, have good day.'
He entryd into Flete-strete;
Wiþ lordys off Yngelond gan he mete
500 Upon a nobyl aray.
On here knees þey kneleden adoun,
And prayden hym off hys benysoun; *blessing*
He nykkyd hem wiþ 'Nay'. *He replied to them with 'No'*
Neyþer off cros neyþer off ryng *about*
505 Hadde þey non kyns wetyng; *way; of knowing*
And þanne a knyʒt gan say. *to speak*

A knyʒt þanne spak with mylde voys:
'Sere, where is þy ryng ? Where is þy croys?
Is it fro þe tan?' *taken*
510 Þanne he sayde: 'ʒoure cursyd kyng
Haþ me refft off al my þyng, *deprived*
And off al my worldly wan; *possessions*
And I have entyrdytyd Yngelond: *interdicted*
Þer schal no preest synge masse with hond,
515 Chyld schal be crystenyd non;
But ʒiff he graunte me þat knyʒt,
His wyff and chyldryn fayr and bryʒt:
He wolde with wrong hem slon.' *kill*

Þe knyʒt sayde: 'Bysschop, turne agayn;
520 Off þy body we are ful fayn; *presence; glad*
Þy broþir ʒit schole we borwe. *rescue*
And, but he graunte us oure bone, *unless*
Hys presoun schal be broken soone,
Hymselff to mekyl sorwe.
525 We schole drawe doun boþe halle and boures;
Boþe hys castelles and hys toures,
Þey schole lygge lowe and holewe. *lie*
Þouʒ he be kyng and were þe corown,
We scholen hym sette in a deep dunioun: *dungeon*
530 Oure crystyndom we wole folewe.'

Þanne, as þey spoken off þis þyng,
Þer comen twoo knyʒtys from þe kyng,
And sayden: 'Bysschop, abyde,
And have þy cros and þy ryng,
535 And welcome, whyl þat þou wylt lyng – *remain*
It is nouʒt forto hyde – *It cannot be hidden*
Here he grauntys þe þe knyʒt,
Hys wyff and chyldryn fayr and bryʒt;
Again I rede þou ryde. *advise*
540 He prayes þe pur charyte
Þat he myʒte asoylyd be, *absolved*
And Yngelond long and wyde.'

Hereoff þe bysschop was ful fayn, *glad*
And turnys hys brydyl and wendes agayn;
545 Barouns gunne wiþ hym ryde

Unto þe Brokene-Cros off ston. *a London landmark*
Þedyr com þe kyng ful soone anon, *There*
And þere he gan abyde. *wait*
Upon hys knees he knelyd adoun,
550 And prayde þe bysschop off benysoun;
And he gaff hym þat tyde. *then*
Wiþ holy watyr and orysoun, *prayer*
He asoylyd þe kyng þat weryd þe coroun,
And Yngelond long and wyde.

555 Þenne sayde þe kyng anon ryȝt: *immediately*
'Here I graunte þe þat knyȝt,
And hys sones free,
And my sustyr, hende in halle: *a gracious woman*
Þou hast savyd here lyvys alle.
560 Iblessyd moot þou bee.'
Þenne sayde þe bysschop also soone:
'And I schal geven swylke a dome, *judgement*
Wiþ eyen þat þou schalt see;
Ȝiff þay be gylty off þat dede,
565 Sorrere þe doome þay may drede, *More grievous*
Þan schewe here schame to me.' *the showing; of their*

Whanne þe bysschop hadde sayd soo,
A gret fyr was maad ryȝt þoo – *fire*
In romaunce as we rede.
570 It was set, þat men myȝte knawe,
Nyne plowȝ-lengþe on rawe, *plough-lengths; in succession*
As red as ony glede. *ember*
Þanne sayde þe kyng: 'What may þis mene?'
'Sere, off gylt and þay be clene, *innocent*
575 Þis doom hem thar nouȝt drede.' *i.e. the ordeal by fire*
Þanne sayde þe good Kyng Athelston:
'An hard doome now is þis on:
God graunte us alle weel to spede!'

Þey fetten forþ Sere Egelan, *fetched*
580 A trewere eerl was þer nan,
Before þe fyr so bryȝt.
From hym, þey token þe rede scarlet, *scarlet clothes*
Boþe hosyn and schoon þat weren hym met, *stockings; appropriate*
Þat fel al for a knyȝt.
585 Nyne syþe þe bysschop halewid þe way *times; sanctified*
Þat his weddyd broþer scholde goo þat day,
To praye God for þe ryȝt. *justice*
He was unblemeschyd foot and hand;
Þat sawȝ þe lordes off þe land,
590 And þankyd God off hys myȝt. *power*

Þey offeryd hym with mylde chere *reverently*
Unto Seynt Powlys heyȝe awtere, *altar*
Þat mekyl was off myȝt.
Doun upon hys knees he felle,

595	And þankyd God þat harewede helle, And hys modyr so bryȝt.	
	And ȝit þe bysschop þo gan say: 'Now schal þe chyldryn gon þe way Þat þe fadyr ȝede.'	*went*
600	Fro hem þey tooke þe rede scarlete, Þe hosen and schoon þat weren hem mete, And al here worldly wede.	*clothes*
	Þe fyr was boþe hydous and red,	*awful*
	Þe chyldryn swownyd as þey were ded;	*fainted*
605	Þe bysschop tyl hem ȝede.	*to; went*
	Wiþ careful herte on hem gan look, Be hys hand he hem up took: 'Chyldryn, have ȝe no drede.'	*fear*
	Þanne þe chyldryn stood and lowȝ:	*laughed*
610	'Sere, þe fyr is cold inowȝ.'	
	Þorwȝout þey wente apase.	*quickly*
	Þey weren unblemeschyd foot and hand; Þat sawȝ þe lordys off þe land, And þankyd God off his grace.	
615	Þey offeryd hem with mylde chere	*reverently*
	To Seynt Poulys hyȝe awtere;	*altar*
	Þis myracle schewyd was þere.	
	And ȝit þe bysschop efft gan say: 'Now schal þe countasse goo þe way,	
620	Þere þat þe chyldryn were.'	
	Þey fetten forþ þe lady mylde;	*fetched*
	Sche was ful gret igon with chylde –	*heavily pregnant*
	In romaunce as we rede. Before þe fyr when þat sche come,	
625	To Jesu Cryst he prayde a bone,	*she; request*
	Þat leet his woundys blede: 'Now, God, lat nevere þe kyngys foo	
	Quyk out off þe fyr goo.'	*Alive*
	Þeroff hadde sche no drede.	*fear*
630	Whenne sche hadde maad here prayer, Sche was brouȝt before þe feer	*fire*
	Þat brennyd boþe fayr and lyȝt.	*bright*
	Sche wente fro þe lengþe into þe þrydde;	*first length; third*
	Stylle sche stood þe fyr amydde,	*in the midst*
635	And callyd it merye and bryȝt.	
	Harde schourys þenne took here stronge	*labour-pains*
	Boþe in bak and eke in wombe; And siþþen it fel at syȝt.	*?after the ordeal; the baby; into*
	Whenne þat here paynys slakyd was,	*pains; weakened*
640	And sche hadde passyd þat hydous pas,	*awful; passage*
	Here nose barst on bloode.	*burst*

Sche was unblemeschyd foot and hand;
Þat sawȝ þe lordys off þe land,
And þankyd God on rode.
645 Þey comaundyd men here away to drawe,   *there; move*
As it was þe landys lawe,
And ladyys þanne tyl here ȝode.   *to; went*
Sche knelyd doun upon þe ground,
And þere was born Seynt Edemound:
650 Iblessyd be þat foode!   *child*

And whanne þis chyld iborn was,
It was brouȝt into þe plas;   *place*
It was boþe hool and sound.   *whole*
Boþe þe kyng and bysschop free
655 Þey crystnyd þe chyld, þat men myȝt see,
And callyd it Edemound.
'Halff my land,' he sayde, 'I þe geve
Also longe as I may leve,   *For as; live*
Wiþ markys and with pounde;   *coins*
660 And al afftyr my dede   *everything*
Yngelond to wysse and rede.'   *guide; direct*
Now iblessyd be þat stounde!   *hour*

Þenne sayde þe bysschop to þe kyng:
'Sere, who made þis grete lesyng,   *falsehood*
665 And who wrouȝte al þis bale?'   *created; trouble*
Þanne sayde þe kyng: 'So moot I thee,
Þat schalt þou nevere wete for me,   *know*
In burgh neyþer in sale;   *public; private*
For I have sworn be Seynt Anne
670 Þat I schal nevere bewreye þat manne,   *betray*
Þat me gan telle þat tale.
Þey arn savyd þorwȝ þy red;   *saved; counsel*
Now lat al þis be ded,
And kepe þis counseyl hale.'   *undivulged*

675 Þenne swoor þe bysschop: 'So moot I the,
Now I have power and dignyte
Forto asoyle þe as clene   *absolve; sinless*
As þou were hoven off þe fount-ston;   *raised; font (in baptism)*
Trustly trowe þou þerupon,
680 And holde it for no wene.   *in; doubt*
I swere boþe be book and belle,
But ȝiff þou me his name telle,
Þe ryȝt doom schal I deme: *just; judgement; award*
Þyselff schalt goo þe ryȝte way   *exact*
685 Þat þy broþer wente today,
Þouȝ it þe evele beseme.'

Þenne sayde þe kyng: 'So moot I the,
Be schryffte off mouþe, telle I it þe,   *confessed*
Þerto I am unblyve.   *unhappy*
690 Sertaynly, it is non oþir

But Wymound, oure weddyd broþer;
He wole nevere þryve.'
'Allas,' sayde þe bysschop þan,
'I wende he were þe treweste man,
695   Þat evere ȝit levyd on lyve;
And he wiþ þis ateynt may bee,   *If; found guilty*
He schal be hongyd on trees þree,   *gallows*
And drawen with hors ffyve.'

And whenne þat þe bysschop þe soþe hade –   *truth*
700   Þat þat traytour þat lesyng made –
He callyd a messangere.
Bad hym to Dovere þat he scholde founde,
Forto fette þat eerl Wymounde:
Þat traytour has no þere!
705   'Sere Egelane and hys sones be slawe,   *killed*
Boþe ihangyd and todrawe –   *pulled apart*
Doo as I þe lere!   *Do as I tell you!*
Þe countasse is in presoun done;
Schal sche nevere out off presoun come,
710   But ȝiff it be on bere.'   *bier*

Now wiþ þe messanger was no badde;   *delay*
He took his hors as þe bysschop radde,   *advised*
To Dovere tyl þat he come.
Þe eerl in hys halle he fand;
715   He took hym þe lettre in his hand
On hyȝ, wolde he nouȝt wone: *haste; delay*
'Sere Egelane and his sones be slawe,
Boþe ihangyd and to-drawe:
Þou getyst þat eerldome.
720   Þe countasse is in presoun done;
Schal sche nevere more out come,
Ne see neyþer sunne ne mone.'

Þanne þat eerl made hym glade,
And þankyd God þat lesyng was made: *falsehood; successful*
725   'It haþ gete me þis eerldome.'
He sayde: 'Felawe, ryȝt weel þou bee!
Have here besauntys good plente   *gold coins*
For þyn hedyr-come.'   *coming here*
Þanne þe messanger made his mon: *complaint*
730   'Sere, off ȝoure goode hors lende me on;
Now graunte me my bone.   *grant*
For ȝystyrday deyde my nobyl stede,
On ȝoure arende as I ȝede,   *errand; went*
Be þe way as I come.'

735   'Myn hors be fatte and cornfed,
And off þy lyff I am adred,'   *for*
Þat eerl sayde to hym þan;
'Þanne ȝiff myn hors scholde þe sloo,   *kill*

My lord þe kyng wolde be ful woo

740   To lese swylk a man.'   *lose; such*

Þe messanger ȝit he brouȝte a stede,   *To the; nevertheless*
On off þe beste at ylke a nede,   *for every need*
Þat evere on grounde dede gange.   *did*
Sadelyd and brydelyd at þe beste,

745   Þe messanger was ful preste,   *ready*
Wyȝtly on hym he sprange.   *Vigorously*
'Sere,' he sayde, 'have good day;
Þou schalt come whan þou may;   *are able*
I schal make þe kyng at hande.'   *be prepared*

750   With sporys faste he strook þe stede;   *struck*
To Gravysende he come good spede,
Is fourty myle to fande.   *if tested*

Þere þe messanger þe traytour abood,   *awaited*
And seþþyn boþe insame þey rod   *together*

755   To Westemynstyr wone.   *palace*
In þe palays þere þay lyȝt,   *dismounted*
Into þe halle þey come ful ryȝt,
And mette wiþ Athelstone.
He wolde have kyssyd his lord swete;   *Wymound*

760   He sayde: 'Traytour, nouȝt ȝit! Lete!   *Stop!*
Be God and be Seynt Jhon,
For þy falsnesse and þy lesyng
I slowȝ myn heyr, scholde have ben kyng   *heir*
When my lyf hadde ben gon.'

765   Þere he denyyd faste þe kyng,   *denied strongly to*
Þat he made nevere þat lesyng –
Among hys peres alle.
Þe bysschop has hym be þe hand tan;   *taken*
Forþ insame þey are gan   *together*

770   Into þe wyde halle.   *Great Hall*
Myȝte he nevere with crafft ne gynne   *deceit; trickery*
Gare hym schryven off hys synne,   *Cause; confess*
For nouȝt þat myȝte befalle.   *happen*
Þenne sayde þe goode kyng Athelston:

775   'Lat hym to þe fyr gon,
To preve þe treweþe wiþ alle.'

Whenne þe kyng hadde sayd soo,
A gret fyr was maad þoo –
In romaunce as we rede.

780   It was set, þat men myȝten knawe,
Nyne plowȝ-lenge on rawe,   *succession*
As red as ony glede.   *ember*
Nyne syþis þe bysschop halewes þe way   *times; sanctifies*
Þat þat traytour schole goo þat day:

785   Þe wers hym gan to spede.   *worse; hastily*
He wente fro þe lengþe into þe þrydde,   *first length; third*

And doun he fel þe fyr amydde:
Hys eyen wolde hym nouȝt lede.

Þan þe eerlys chyldryn were war ful smerte,   *aware; cleverly*
790   And wyȝtly to þe traytour sterte,   *quickly; started up*
And out off þe fyr hym hade;
And sworen boþe be book and belle:
'Or þat þou deye, þou schalt telle   *Before*
Why þou þat lesyng made.'

795   'Certayn, I can non oþer red,   *nothing; say*
Now I wot I am but ded: *know*
I telle ȝow noþyng gladde.   *reasonable*
Certayn, þer was non oþer wyte: *blame*
He lovyd hym to mekyl and me to lyte;   *much; little*
800   Þerfore envye I hadde.'

Whenne þat traytour so hadde sayde,
Fyve good hors to hym were tayde,   *tied*
Alle men myȝten see wiþ yȝe.   *eyes*
Þey drowen hym þorwȝ ylke a strete,   *drew; many*
805   And seþþyn to þe Elmes, I ȝow hete,   *after; Tyburn; assure*
And hongyd hym ful hyȝe.
Was þer nevere man so hardy,   *bold*
Þat durste felle hys false body: *cut down*
Þis hadde he for hys lye.
810   Now Jesu, þat is hevene kyng,
Leve nevere traytour have betere endyng,   *Allow*
But swych dome forto dye.   *judgement*
Explicit.

Ywain and Gawain

Ywain and Gawain is contained uniquely in London, British Library, Cotton Galba E. ix, dated to *c*.1400–25, folios 4–25. The text itself is much earlier, and dates from the first half of the fourteenth century. It is the only Romance proper included in the composite manuscript, which otherwise contains historical texts (such as poems by Laurence Minot) and religious texts (for example, *The Prick of Conscience*, *The Gospel of Nicodemus* and *The Seven Sages of Rome*).[1] The manuscript, put together from three separate volumes, has a northern provenance. It is likely that *Ywain and Gawain* is of northern origin, though within the text some north-east Midlands forms impinge on the dominant northern dialectal features.[2]

Ywain and Gawain is an Arthurian Romance, a genre that was prolific throughout the later medieval period from the twelfth century onwards. The fourteenth and fifteenth centuries saw a large number of Arthurian Romances being written in English, either as translations from (usually) French sources, or as adaptations and recontextualizations of adventures that were in circulation, pertaining to particular knights. One of the most popular heroes, apart from Arthur himself, was Gawain, a knight of the Round Table,[3] and he plays a minor role in this poem: the hero in this 4,032-line work is Ywain, a less well-renowned Arthurian knight.

The source of *Ywain and Gawain* is Chrétien de Troyes's *Yvain, Le Chevalier au Lion*, dated to the later part of the twelfth century. It was Chrétien who took the framework of Arthur and his knights created by Geoffrey of Monmouth in his *Historia Regum Britanniae*,[4] and composed a number of tales around individual Arthurian knights. For some of the adventures of Ywain, Chrétien probably turned to Celtic legends. The English version is almost two-thirds shorter than Chrétien's *Yvain* and, written for a different audience, emphasizes different concerns.[5] While the English poet retains the narrative structure and chronology of episodes of the source, there are also numerous areas where the text varies from the French. In particular, in *Ywain and Gawain*, there is far less emphasis on the niceties of courtly and chivalric behaviour; for example, some non-essential narrative material is excised or curtailed to facilitate the rapidity of the action, and to focus on the deeds, not the thoughts, of the knights.[6]

In the extract edited here, lines 1–584, Arthur's court is meeting at Cardiff on Whitsunday. After the feast, Colgrevance, a knight of the Round Table, relates his adventures of six years previously to Ywain, Gawain, Kay, Dedyne, Segramore and Queen Guinevere while they are all sitting guarding the court. Among Colgrevance's exploits is a meeting with the Giant Herdsman, and an encounter with a fearsome knight, the guardian of a magic fountain. Colgrevance's adventures and defeat at the hands of the mysterious knight inspire Ywain to set out on a quest to avenge this knight's dishonour.

Ywain and Gawain

Here bigyns Ywaine and Gawain

Almyghti God þat made mankyn
He schilde his servandes out of syn,
And mayntene þam with might and mayne,
Þat herkens Ywayne and Gawayne.   *listens to*
5   Þai war knightes of þe tabyl rownde,
Þarfore listens a lytel stownde.[7]   *for a time*
        Arthure, þe kyng of Yngland,
Þat wan al Wales with his hand,
And al Scotland, als sayes þe buke,[8]

---

1 There is some debate about the genre of *The Seven Sages of Rome*: whether it should be classified as a Romance or a religious text. See M. J. Evans, *Rereading Middle English Romance: Manuscript Layout, Decoration, and the Rhetoric of Composite Structure* (Montreal, 1995), pp. 90–1.

2 See A. B. Friedman and N. T. Harrington, eds, *Ywain and Gawain*, EETS o.s. 254 (London, 1964; repr. 1981), pp. xxxvi–xlviii, for an analysis of the linguistic forms of the text. In addition to their full edition of the text, an edition with glosses is edited by M. Mills in *Ywain and Gawain, Sir Percyvell of Gales, and The Anturs of Arther* (London, 1992).

3 Who appears, for example, in *Sir Gawain and the Green Knight*, *The Jeaste of Syr Gawayne* and *Syre Gawene and the Carle of Carelyle*.

4 See also the extract from Laȝamon's *Brut* above for the evolution of Arthurian legends in the twelfth century.

5 See Friedman and Harrington, *Ywain and Gawain*, pp. xvi–xxxiv, for a full account of the proximity of the Middle English to the French source.

6 See, for example, W. R. J. Barron, *English Medieval Romance* (London, 1987), pp. 160–3.

7 This introduction is original to the English text.

8 Probably Chrétien's *Yvain*.

10	And mani mo, if men wil luke,	
	Of al knightes he bare þe pryse:	*was the worthiest*
	In werld was none so war ne wise;	
	Trew he was in alkyn thing.	*all kinds*
	Als it byfel to swilk a kyng,	*happened to such*
15	He made a feste, þe soth to say,	
	Opon þe Witsononday	*Whit Sunday*
	At Kerdyf þat es in Wales.	*Cardiff*
	And efter mete þare in þe hales,	*food*
	Ful grete and gay was þe assemble	
20	Of lordes and ladies of þat cuntre,	
	And als of knyghtes war and wyse,	
	And damisels of mykel pryse.	*worth*
	Ilkane with oþer made grete gamin,	*Each one; entertainment*
	And grete solace als þai war samin.	*together*
25	Fast þai carped and curtaysly	*talked*
	Of dedes of armes and of veneri,	*hunting*
	And of gude knightes þat lyfed þen,	
	And how men might þam kyndeli ken	*properly know*
	By doghtines of þaire gude dede	*boldness*
30	On ilka syde wharesum þai ʒede;	*went*
	For þai war stif in ilka stowre,	*strong; battle*
	And þarfore gat þai grete honowre.	
	Þai tald of more trewth þam bitwene	
	Þan now omang men here es sene,	
35	For trowth and luf es al bylaft:	*neglected*
	Men uses now anoþer craft.	
	With worde men makes it trew and stabil,	
	Bot in þaire faith es noght bot fabil;	
	With þe mowth men makes it hale,	*wholesome*
40	Bot trew trowth es nane in þe tale.	
	Þarfore hereof now wil I blyn;	*stop*
	Of þe Kyng Arthure I wil bygin,	
	And of his curtayse cumpany.	
	Þare was þe flowre of chevallry:	
45	Swilk lose þai wan with speres horde,	*renown; spear's point*
	Over al þe werld went þe worde.	*reputation*
	After mete went þe kyng	
	Into chamber to slepeing,	
	And also went with him þe quene;	
50	Þat byheld þai al bydene,	*one and all*
	For þai saw þam never so	
	On high dayes to chamber go.	
	Bot sone, when þai war went to slepe,	
	Knyghtes sat þe dor to kepe:	*defend*
55	Sir Dedyne and Sir Segramore,	
	Sir Gawayn and Sir Kay[9] sat þore,	*there*
	And also sat þare Sir Ywaine,	
	And Colgrevance of mekyl mayn.	*great strength*
	Þis knight þat hight Colgrevance,	

---

9   Foster-brother and steward of Arthur, Kay is a knight renowned
for his discourteousness.

Tald his felows of a chance   *occurrence*
And of a stowre he had in bene;   *fight*
And al his tale herd þe quene.
Þe chamber dore sho has unshet,
And down omang þam scho hir set;   *she sat among them*
Sodainli sho sat downright,   *straight down*
Or ani of þam of hir had sight.   *Before*
Bot Colgrevance rase up in hy,   *pulled himself (in courtesy)*
And þareof had Syr Kay envy,
For he was of his tong a skalde,   *ribald speaker*
And for to boste was he ful balde.
 'Ow Colgrevance,' said Sir Kay,   *You*
'Ful light of lepes has þou bene ay.   *quick to leap up*
Þou wenes now þat þe sal fall   *think; be considered*
For to be hendest of us all.   *most noble*
And þe quene sal understand
Þat here es none so unkunand;   *unsophisticated*
Al if þou rase and we sat styll,   *Even though*
We ne dyd it for none yll,
Ne for no manere of fayntise,   *deceit*
Ne us denyd noght for to rise,
Þat we ne had resen had we hyr sene.'
 'Sir Kay, I wote wele,' sayd þe quene,   *I know that well*
'And it war gude þou left swilk sawes   *speech*
And noght despise so þi felawes.'
 'Madame,' he said, 'by Goddes dome,   *judgement*
We ne wist nothing of þi come;   *arrival*
And if we did noght curtaysly,
Takes to no velany.   *as; villainy*
Bot pray ȝe now þis gentil man
To tel þe tale þat he bygan.'
Colgrevance said to Sir Kay:
'Bi grete God þat aw þis day,   *controls*
Na mare manes me þi flyt   *bothers; quarrelling*
Þan it war a flies byt.
Ful oft wele better men þan I
Has þou desspised desspytusely.
It es ful semeli, als me think,   *appropriate*
A brok omang men for to stynk.   *badger*
So it fars by þe, Syr Kay: *goes with*
Of weked wordes has þou bene ay,   *always*
And sen þi wordes er wikked and fell,   *since; false*
Þis time þarto na more I tell,
Bot of the thing þat I bygan.'
 And sone Sir Kay him answerd þan
And said ful tite unto þe quene: *quickly*
'Madame, if ȝe had noght here bene,
We sold have herd a selly case;   *marvellous*
Now let ȝe us of oure solace.   *you have lost us*
Þarfore, madame, we wald ȝow pray,
Þat ȝe cumand him to say
And tel forth, als he had tyght.'   *intended*
Þan answerd þat hende knight:

60
65
70
75
80
85
90
95
100
105
110

'Mi lady es so avyse,   *prudent*
Þat scho wil noght cumand me
115 To tel þat towches me to ill;
Scho es noght of so weked will.'
   Sir Kai said þan ful smertli:
'Madame, al hale þis cumpani,
Praies ȝow hertly now omell,   *in the interval*
120 Þat he his tale forth might tell;
If ȝe wil noght for oure praying,
For faith ȝe aw unto þe kyng,   *owe it*
Cumandes him his tale to tell,
Þat we mai here how it byfell.'
125   Þan said þe quene, 'Sir Colgrevance,
I prai þe tak to no grevance
Þis kene karping of Syr Kay;
Of weked wordes has he bene ay,
So þat none may him chastise.
130 Þarfore I prai þe, on al wise,
Þat þou let noght for his sawes,   *words*
At tel to me and þi felawes   *But*
Al þi tale, how it bytid: *happened*
For my luf I þe pray and byd.'   *ask*
135 'Sertes, madame, þat es me lath;   *hateful*
Bot for I wil noght mak ȝow wrath,
Ȝowre cumandment I sal fulfill,
If ȝe wil listen me untill,   *to*
With hertes and eres understandes;
140 And I sal tel ȝow swilk tithandes,   *reports*
Þat ȝe herd never none slike   *such*
Reherced in no kynges ryke.   *realm*
Bot word fares als dose þe wind,
Bot if men it in hert bynd;   *Unless*
145 And, wordes woso trewly tase,   *whoever faithfully receives*
By þe eres into þe hert it gase,   *goes*
And in þe hert þare es þe horde   *store*
And knawing of ilk mans worde.
   Herkens, hende, unto my spell,   *nobles; story*
150 Trofels sal I ȝow nane tell,   *Trivialities*
Ne lesinges forto ger ȝow lagh;   *lies; make*
Bot I sal say right als I sagh.
Now als þis time, sex ȝere,   *six years ago*
I rade allane, als ȝe sal here,   *alone*
155 Obout forto seke aventurs,
Wele armid in gude armurs.
In a frith I fand a strete,   *forest; path*
Ful thik and hard, I ȝow bihete,   *I promise you*
With thornes, breres, and moni a quyn.   *gorse*
160 Nerehand al day I rade þareyn,   *Almost*
And thurgh I past with mekyl payn.
Þan come I sone into a playn,
Whare I gan se a bretise brade,   *parapet*
And þederward ful fast I rade.
165 I saw þe walles and þe dyke,   *ditch*

And hertly wele it gan me lyke.   *please*
   And on þe drawbrig saw I stand
A knight with fawkon on his hand.
Þis ilk knight, þat be ȝe balde,   *assured*
170   Was lord and keper of þat halde.   *stronghold*
I hailsed him kindly als I kowth;   *as graciously as I could*
He answerd me mildeli with mowth.
Mi sterap toke þat hende knight
And kindly cumanded me to lyght;   *get down*
175   His cumandment I did onane,   *at once*
And into hall sone war we tane.   *led*
He thanked God, þat gude man,
Sevyn sithes or ever he blan,   *times; before; ceased*
And þe way þat me þeder broght,
180   And als þe aventurs þat I soght.
   Þus went we in, God do him mede,   *give; reward*
And in his hand he led my stede.
When we war in þat fayre palays –
It was ful worthly wroght always –
185   I saw no man of moder born.
Bot a burde hang us biforn,   *sheet of metal*
Was nowther of yren ne of tre,   *wood*
Ne I ne wist whareof it might be,
And by þat bord hang a mall.   *hammer*
190   Þe knyght smate on þarwithall   *struck; at it*
Thrise, and by þen might men se
Bifore him come a faire menȝe,   *company of followers*
Curtayse men in worde and dede;
To stabil sone þai led mi stede.
195   A damisel come unto me,
Þe semeliest þat ever I se:
Lufsumer lifed never in land.   *More lovely*
Hendly scho toke me by þe hand,
And sone þat gentyl creature
200   Al unlaced myne armure.
Into a chamber sho me led,
And with a mantil scho me cled: *dressed*
It was of purpure faire and fine,
And þe pane of rich ermyne.   *trimming*
205   Al þe folk war went us fra,
And þare was none þan bot we twa.
Scho served me hendely te bend;   *close by*
Hir maners might no man amend.
Of tong sho was trew and renable   *eloquent*
210   And of hir semblant soft and stabile.   *appearance; trustworthy*
Ful fain I wald, if þat I might,
Have woned with þat swete wight.   *stayed; creature*
And, when we sold go to sopere,   *had to*
Þat lady with a lufsom chere   *gracious*
215   Led me down into þe hall,
Þare war we served wele at all.   *in everything*
It nedes noght to tel þe mese,   *It's not necessary; courses*
For wonder wele war we at esse.

Byfor me sat þe lady bright
220   Curtaisly my mete to dyght;   *prepare*
Us wanted nowþer baken ne roste.
     And efter soper sayd myne oste
Þat he cowth noght tel þe day   *could not recall*
Þat ani knight are with him lay,   *stayed with him*
225   Or þat ani aventures soght.
Þarfore he prayed me, if I moght,
On al wise when I come ogayne,   *returned*
Þat I sold cum to him sertayne.
I said, "Sir, gladly, yf I may."
230   It had bene shame have said him nay.
     Þat night had I ful gude rest,
And mi stede esed of þe best.
Alsone als it was dayes lyght,
Forth to fare sone was I dyght.   *prepared*
235   Mi leve of mine ost toke I þare,
And went mi way withowten mare,   *more leave-taking*
Aventures forto layt in land.   *seek*
A faire forest sone I fand;
Me thoght mi hap þare fel ful hard,
240   For þare was mani a wilde lebard,
Lions, beres, bath bul and bare,   *both; boars*
Þat rewfully gan rope and rare.   *cry out; roar*
Oway I drogh me, and with þat   *I took myself away*
I saw sone whare a man sat
245   On a lawnd, þe fowlest wight   *glade*
Þat ever ʒit man saw in syght.
He was a lathly creature,   *loathsome*
For fowl he was out of mesure;
A wonder mace in hand he hade,
250   And sone mi way to him I made.
     His hevyd, me thoght, was als grete   *head*
Als of a rowncy or a nete;   *horse; ox*
Unto his belt hang his hare,
And efter þat byheld I mare.
255   To his forhede byheld I þan,
Was bradder þan twa large span;
He had eres als ane olyfant   *elephant*
And was wele more þan geant.   *giant*
His face was ful brade and flat;
260   His nese was cutted als a cat;
His browes war like litel buskes;   *bushes*
And his tethe like bare-tuskes.   *boars' tusks*
A ful grete bulge opon his bak –
Þare was noght made withowten lac[10] –
265   His chin was fast until his brest;
On his mace he gan him rest.
Also it was a wonder wede   *amazing clothes*
Þat þe cherle yn ʒede: *went about in*
Nowther of wol ne of line   *linen*

10   There was nothing about him that was right.

270 Was þe wede þat he went yn.
   When he me sagh, he stode upright;
I frayned him if he wolde fight,   *asked*
For þarto was I in gude will,   *right mind for that*
Bot als a beste þan stode he still.
275 I hopid þat he no wittes kowth,   *I supposed that he had no intelligence*
No reson forto speke with mowth.
To him I spak ful hardily,
And said: "What ertow, belamy?"   *fair friend*
He said ogain: "I am a man."   *replied*
280 I said: "Swilk saw I never nane."   *The like*
"What ertow?" alsone said he.   *are you*
I said: "Swilk als þou here may se."
I said: "What dose þou here allane?"   *alone*
He said: "I kepe þir bestes ilkane."   *look after; each one*
285 I said: "Þat es mervaile, think me;
For I herd never of man bot þe,
In wildernes ne in forestes,
Þat kepeing had of wilde bestes,
Bot þai war bunden fast in halde."   *Unless; bound*
290 He sayd: "Of þire es none so balde
Nowþer by day ne bi night
Anes to pas out of mi sight."
   I sayd, "How so? Tel me þi scill."   *how you do this*
"Parfay," he said, "gladly I will."
295 He said: "In al þis faire foreste
Es þare none so wilde beste
Þat remu dar, bot stil stand,   *dare to move*
When I am to him cumand.
And ay, when þat I wil him fang   *seize*
300 With mi fingers þat er strang,
I ger him cri on swilk manere,   *make*
Þat al þe bestes when þai him here
Obout me þan cum þai all,
And to mi fete fast þai fall,
305 On þaire manere merci to cry.
Bot understand now redyli:
Olyve es þare lifand no ma   *alive; living; others*
Bot I þat durst omang þam ga,
Þat he ne sold sone be al torent.   *should be torn to pieces*
310 Bot þai er at my comandment;
To me þai cum when I þam call,
And I am maister of þam all."
Þan he asked onone right,   *straight away*
What man I was; I said, a knight
315 Þat soght aventurs in þat land,
My body to asai and fande: *to put my body to the test*
"And I þe pray of þi kownsayle,
Þou teche me to sum mervayle."   *direct*
   He sayd: "I can no wonders tell,
320 Bot here bisyde es a well.
Wend þeder and do als I say;
Þou passes noght al quite oway.   *You will not get through easily*

Folow forth þis ilk strete,
And sone sum mervayles sal þou mete.
325   Þe well es under þe fairest tre
Þat ever was in þis cuntre;
By þat well hinges a bacyne   *hangs a bowl*
Þat es of gold gude and fyne,
With a cheyne, trewly to tell,
330   Þat wil reche into þe well.
Þare es a chapel nere þarby,
Þat nobil es and ful lufely.
By þe well standes a stane:
Tak þe bacyn sone onane   *straight away*
335   And cast on water with þi hand,
And sone þou sal se new tithand.   *occurrence*
A storme sal rise and a tempest
Al obout, by est and west;
Þou sal here mani thonor-blast
340   Al obout þe blawand fast.   *blowing*
And þare sal cum slik slete and rayne   *such*
Þat unnese sal þou stand ogayne;   *with difficulty*
Of lightnes sal þou se a lowe.   *lightning; flash*
Unnethes þou sal þiselven knowe.   *With difficulty*
345   And, if þou pas withowten grevance,
Þan has þou þe fairest chance,
Þat ever ȝit had any knyght,
Þat þeder come to kyth his myght."   *display*
      Þan toke I leve and went my way
350   And rade unto þe midday;
By þan I come whare I sold be,
I saw þe chapel and þe tre.
Þare I fand þe fayrest thorne
Þat ever groued sen God was born: *grew since*
355   So thik it was with leves grene,
Might no rayn cum þarbytwene;
And þat grenes lastes ay,   *lasts perennially*
For no winter dere yt may.   *harm*
I fand þe bacyn als he talde,
360   And þe wel with water kalde.
An amerawd was þe stane,   *emerald*
Richer saw I never nane.
On fowre rubyes on heght standand;   *rubies standing on top*
Þaire light lasted over al þe land.
365   And when I saw þat semely syght,
It made me bath joyful and lyght.   *happy*
      I toke þe bacyn sone onane
And helt water opon þe stane.   *poured*
Þe weder wex þan wonder blak,   *grew*
370   And þe thoner fast gan crak.
Þare come slike stormes of hayl and rayn,
Unnethes I might stand þare ogayn;
Þe store windes blew ful lowd,   *fierce*
So kene come never are of clowd.   *Bitter; before*
375   I was drevyn with snaw and slete,

Unnethes I might stand on my fete;
In my face þe levening smate,   *lightning; struck*
I wend have brent, so was it hate.   *I thought I'd burn, it was so hot*
Þat weder made me so will of rede,   *confused*
380   I hopid sone to have my dede;   *expected to meet my death*
And sertes, if it lang had last,
I hope I had never þeþin past.   *thought; from there; get passed*
Bot thorgh his might þat tholed wownd,[11]   *suffered*
Þe storme sesed within a stownde.   *a moment*
385   Þan wex þe weder fayre ogayne,
And þareof was I wonder fayne: *amazingly glad*
For best comfort of al thing
Es solace efter myslikeing.
        Þan saw I sone a mery syght:
390   Of al þe fowles þat er in flyght
Lighted so thik opon þat tre,
Þat bogh ne lefe none might I se.
So merily þan gon þai sing
Þat al þe wode bigan to ring;
395   Ful mery was þe melody
Of þaire sang and of þaire cry.
Þare herd never man none swilk,   *like it*
Bot if ani had herd þat ilk.   *Unless; the same*
And when þat mery dyn was done,
400   Anoþer noyse þan herd I sone,
Als it war of horsmen
Mo þan owþer nyen or ten.
        Sone þan saw I cum a knyght,
In riche armurs was he dight;   *arrayed*
405   And sone, when I gan on him loke,
Mi shelde and spere to me I toke.
Þat knight to me hied ful fast,   *hastened*
And kene wordes out gan he cast.   *bold*
He bad þat I sold tel him tite,   *quickly*
410   Whi I did him swilk despite,
With weders wakend him of rest
And done him wrang in his forest.
"Þarfore," he said, "þou sal aby."   *suffer for it*
And with þat come he egerly
415   And said I had, ogayn resowne,   *against reason*
Done him grete destrucciowne,
And might it never more amend,
Þarfore he bad I sold me fend.   *defend*
And sone I smate him on þe shelde,
420   Mi schaft brac out in þe felde,   *lance*
And þan he bare me sone bi strenkith   *threw; force*
Out of my sadel my speres lenkith.   *length*
        I wate þat he was largely   *greatly*
By þe shuldres mare þan I;   *bigger*
425   And bi þe ded þat I sal thole,   *by the death that I shall suffer*
Mi stede by his was bot a fole.

---

11   Referring to God's grace.

For mate I lay down on þe grownde,   *Thoroughly exhausted*
So was I stonayd in þat stownde.   *stunned; moment*
A worde to me wald he noght say,
430   Bot toke my stede and went his way.
Ful sarily þan þare I sat,
For wa I wist noght what was what.
With my stede he went in hy   *quickly*
Þe same way þat he come by.
435   And I durst folow him no ferr   *further*
For dout me solde bitide werr;   *worse would happen to me*
And also зit, by Goddes dome,
I ne wist whare he bycome.
      Þan I thoght how I had hight   *promised*
440   Unto myne ost, þe hende knyght,
And also til his lady bryght,
To com ogayn if þat I myght.
Mine armurs left I þare ilkane,   *each item*
For els myght I noght have gane.
445   Unto myne in I come by day.
Þe hende knight and þe fayre may   *maiden*
Of my come war þai ful glade,
And nobil semblant þai me made.   *welcome*
In al thinges þai have þam born   *performed*
450   Als þai did þe night biforn.
      Sone þai wist whare I had bene,   *knew*
And said þat þai had never sene
Knyght þat ever þeder come,
Take þe way ogayn home.   *back*
455   On þis wise þat tyme I wroght,
I fand þe folies þat I soght.'   *foolish things*
      'Now sekerly,' said Sir Ywayne,   *truly*
'Þou ert my cosyn jermayne,   *closely related*
Trew luf suld be us bytwene,
460   Als sold bytwyx breþer bene.
Þou ert a fole at þou ne had are   *fool; previously*
Tald me of þis ferly fare,   *wondrous journey*
For sertes I sold onone ryght   *immediately*
Have venged þe of þat ilk knyght;
465   So sal I зit, if þat I may.'
      And þan als smertly sayd Syr Kay –
He karpet to þam wordes grete –   *bragging*
'It es sene now es efter mete: *It is quite clear you have eaten*
Mare boste es in a pot of wyne   *after*
470   Þan in a karcas of Saynt Martyne.   *meat killed at Martinmas*
Arme þe smertly, Syr Ywayne!
And sone, þat þou war cumen ogayne,
Luke þou fil wele þi panele,   *pad placed under saddle*
And in þi sadel set þe wele.
475   And, when þou wendes, I þe pray,   *go*
Þi baner wele þat þou desplay;
And, rede I, or þou wende,   *I advise, before you go*
Þou tak þi leve at ilka frende;
And if it so bytide þis nyght,
480   Þat þe in slepe dreche ani wight   *any creature disturbs you*

Or any dremis mak þe rad, *alarmed*
Turn ogayn and say "I bad!"' *"I will remain"*
 Þe quene answerd with milde mode,
And said: 'Sir Kay, ertow wode? *mad*
485 What þe devyl es þe withyn,
At þi tong may never blyn *cease*
Þi felows so fowly to shende? *injure*
Sertes, Sir Kay, þou ert unhende. *discourteous*
By him þat for us sufferd pine, *pain*
490 Syr, and þe tong war myne, *and if*
I sold bical it tyte of treson, *accuse; quickly*
And so might þou do, by gude reson.
Þi tong dose þe grete dishonowre,
And þarefore es it þi traytowre.'
495 And þan alsone Syr Ywayne
Ful hendly answerd ogayne
(Al if men sayd hym velany, *Because*
He karped ay ful curtaysly):
'Madame,' he said unto þe quene,
500 'Þare sold na stryf be us bytwene.
Unkowth men wele may he shende *be shamed*
Þat to his felows es so unhende.
And als, madame, men says sertayne
Þat, woso flites or turnes ogayne, *rebukes*
505 He bygins al þe melle: *quarrel*
So wil I noght it far by me. *it goes that way for me*
Lates him say halely his thoght,
His wordes greves me right noght.'
 Als þai war in þis spekeing
510 Out of þe chamber come þe kyng.
Þe barons þat war þare, sertayn,
Smertly rase þai him ogayne.
He bad þam sit down al bydene, *one and all*
And down he set him by þe quene.
515 Þe quene talde him fayre and wele,
Als sho kowth, everilka dele,
Ful apertly al þe chance *In front of them all; occurrence*
Als it bifel Syr Colgrevance.
When sho had talde him how it ferd,
520 And þe king hyr tale had herd,
He sware by his owyn crowne
And his fader sowl, Uter Pendragowne,
Þat he sold se þat ilk syght
By þat day þeþin a fowretenight, *within a fortnight*
525 On Saint Johns evyn, þe Baptist,
Þat best barn was under Crist.
 'Swith,' he sayd, 'wendes with me, *Eagerly; come*
Whoso wil þat wonder se.'
Þe kynges word might noght be hid,
530 Over al þe cowrt sone was it kyd; *made known*
And þare was none so litel page
Þat he ne was fayn of þat vayage; *eager*
And knyghtes and swiers war ful fayne;
Mysliked none bot Syr Ywayne.

535	To himself he made grete mane,	*lament*
	For he wald have went allane;	
	In hert he had grete myslykyng	
	For þe wending of þe kyng,	
	Al for he hopid, withowten fayle,	
540	Þat Sir Kay sold ask þe batayle,	
	Or els Sir Gawayn, knyght vailant;	
	And owþer wald þe king grant.	
	Whoso it wald first crave	
	Of þam two, sone might it have.	
545	Þe kynges wil wald he noght bide,	*await*
	Worth of him, what may bityde;	*No matter what happened to him*
	Bi him allane he thoght to wend,	
	And tak þe grace þat God wald send.	
	He thoght to be wele on hys way,	
550	Or it war passed þe thryd day,	*Before*
	And to asay if he myght mete	*discover*
	With þat ilk narow strete,	
	With thornes and with breres set,	
	Þat mens way might lightli let;	*easily; prevent*
555	And also for to fynd þe halde	*stronghold*
	Þat Sir Colgrevance of talde,	
	Þe knyght and þe mayden meke.	
	Þe forest fast þan wald he seke	
	And als þe karl of Kaymes kyn,[12]	*Cain's kin*
560	And þe wilde bestes wirh him,	
	Þe tre with briddes þareopon,	
	Þe chapel, þe bacyn and þe stone.	
	His thoght wald he tel to no frende	
	Until he wyst how it wald ende.	
565	Þan went Ywaine to his yn;	*lodgings*
	His men he fand redy þareyn.	
	Unto a swier gan he say:	
	'Go swith and sadel my palfray,	
	And so þou do my strang stede,	
570	And tak with þe my best wede.	*clothing*
	At ȝone ȝate I wil out ryde,	
	Withowten town I sal þe bide;	
	And hy þe smertly unto me,	*hurry*
	For I most make a jorne,	*journey*
575	Ogain sal þou bring my palfray,	
	And forbede þe oght to say.	
	If þou wil any more me se	
	Lat none wit of my prevete;	*know; secret design*
	And if ani man þe oght frayn,	*should ask*
580	Luke now lely þat þou layn.'	*faithfully; maintain the secret*
	'Sir,' he said, 'with ful gude will,	
	Als ȝe byd, I sal fulfyll;	*command*
	At ȝowre awyn wil may ȝe ride,	
	For me ȝe sal noght be ascryed.'	*given away*

---

12 This is the Giant Herdsman, who, like Grendel in *Beowulf*, is
said to be a descendant of Cain, the first murderer, and outcast.

Wynnere and Wastoure

Wynnere and Wastoure occurs at folios 176 verso to 181 verso of London, British Library, Additional 31042, dated to the first half of the fifteenth century. Unfortunately, this unique text lacks the conclusion, and the poem ends in the middle of the king's pronouncement of judgement on the two protagonists. The manuscript was copied by John Thornton, lord of East Newton in Ryedale, Yorkshire, possibly for the use of his own family.[1] *Wynnere and Wastoure* is the last text in the manuscript, and is preceded by a number of religious, romantic and political-didactic texts such as parts of the *Cursor Mundi*, *The Northern Passion*, *The Sege of Jerusalem*, *Richard the Lionheart* and the alliterative *Parlement of Thre Ages*. These texts were copied from a variety of different sources, but it is the case that the *Parlement of Thre Ages* and *Wynnere and Wastoure* may share a common origin. Trigg is of the opinion that the latter poem, at least, is at some remove from the original composition, and consequently, it illustrates a number of different dialectal forms; the predominant dialect is north Midlands, possibly originating in the Nottinghamshire/Lincolnshire area.[2] The precise date of the poem, like its original authorship and localization, is not known, and has occasioned much critical debate: the modern consensus provides a date of *c.*1352–*c.*1370. It may be that the contemporary issues raised throughout the poem refer to the reign of Edward III. The poem may, in particular, allude to the turbulent years following the Black Death, which saw a significant reduction in the numbers of labourers available for essential agricultural work, and the subsequent demands for higher wages and better conditions.

Wynnere and Wastoure belongs to the genre of complaint and satire, here cast in the form of an alliterative dream-vision, a poetic form seen at its finest in this period in William Langland's *Piers Plowman*. The metre of the poem varies, but generally there are three alliterating syllables in the line, which is itself composed of four or five stressed syllables, with the caesura in the middle of the line providing a pause. The alliterative method of poetic composition underwent a major revival in the fourteenth century, particularly in the west and north-west Midlands areas, and this poem very much belongs to this trend.[3]

The poem is divided into three fitts (lines 1–217; 218–367; and 368 to the end). It begins as if it were a chronicle, but quickly becomes the narrator's complaint at the deterioration of, among other things, standards of wisdom and literary composition. The dream takes place while the narrator sleeps on the banks of a stream on a sunny day. He sees before him two amassed armies: one belonging to Wynnere, and the other to Wastoure. The narrator sees also the king and his messenger, and a wild man of the woods (a 'wodwyse'). The messenger approaches the armies, and describes, on the side of Wynnere, the pope, lawyers, friars and merchants; Wastoure, meanwhile, has only a great number of bowmen. Both leaders appear before the king, who recognizes them as knights in his service; following this, in the second fitt, the debate between Wynnere and Wastoure begins. Wynnere is a personification of economic prudence, or saving, but there is a thin line between this aspect and that of miserly acquisition or hoarding. Wastoure attacks his opponent for these latter features, in particular. For his part, Wastoure can be regarded as prodigality or extravagant spending, but can also be interpreted as the proper usage of God-given produce, and necessary expenditure. Part of Wynnere's attacks on Wastoure dwell on the former characteristics. That these two elements of the economy are essential and yet quite disparate provides for the king's decision to maintain a distance between the two. It seems likely that the poet was very much influenced in his choice of subject matter by the economic changes under way in the fourteenth century.

Wynnere and Wastoure

Here begynnes a tretys[4] and god schorte refreyte[5] bytwixe Wynnere and Wastoure

Sythen that Bretayne was biggede and Bruyttus it aughte		*founded; conquered*
Thurgh the takynge of Troye with tresone withinn,		
There hathe selcouthes bene sene in seere kynges tymes,		*marvels; various*
Bot never so many as nowe by the nyne dele.		*ninth part*
5 For nowe alle es witt and wyles that we with delyn,		*guile; cunning; concerned*
Wyse wordes and slee and icheon wryeth othere.[6]		

1 For this and much more essential information, see S. Trigg's excellent edition, *Wynnere and Wastoure*, EETS o.s. 297 (London, 1990).
2 Trigg, *Wynnere and Wastoure*, pp. xviii–xxi.
3 See T. Turville-Petre, *The Alliterative Revival* (Cambridge, 1977).

4 narrative
5 treatment of a theme
6 Knowing and misleading words, and each one obscuring the other.

Dare never no westren wy,   while this werlde lasteth,   *western man*

Send his sone southewarde   to see ne to here   *hear*

That he ne schall holden byhynde   when he hore eldes.[7]

10   Forthi sayde was a sawe   of Salomon the wyse,   *saying*

It hyeghte harde appone honde,   hope I no noþer,   *comes quickly*

When wawes waxen schall wilde   and walles bene doun,   *waves*

And hares appon herthe-stones   schall hurcle in hire fourme,   *cower; lairs*

And eke boyes of blode   with boste and with pryde   *also*

15   Schall wedde ladyes in londe,   and lede hir at will,   *marry her*

Thene dredfull domesdaye   it draweth neghe aftir.   *soon*

Bot whoso sadly will see   and the sothe telle

Say it newely will neghe   or es neghe here.   *soon; approach*

Whylome were lordes in londe   þat loved in thaire hertis   *Formerly*

20   To here makers of myrthes   þat matirs couthe fynde;   *writers; matters; compose*

And now es no frenchipe in fere   bot fayntnesse of hert,[8]

Wyse wordes withinn   þat wroghte were never   *felt within; expressed*

Ne redde in no romance   þat ever renke herde.[9]   *story; any man*

Bot now a childe appon chere   withowtten chyn-wedys   *in face; a beard*

25   Þat never wroghte thurgh witt   thies wordes togedire,   *created*

Fro he can jangle als a jaye   and japes telle   *Because; chatter*

He schall be lenede and lovede   and lett of a while   *listened to; regarded*

Wele more þan þe man   that made it hymselven.

Bot never þe lattere at the laste   when ledys bene knawen;   *newcomer; men; known*

30   Werke wittnesse will bere   who wirche kane beste.[10]   *Poetic work; compose*

    Bot I schall tell ȝow a tale   þat me bytyde ones   *happened*

Als I went in the weste   wandrynge myn one.   *on my own*

Bi a bonke of a bourne   bryghte was the sonne   *bank; stream*

Undir a worthiliche wodde   by a wale medewe   *great; pleasant*

35   Fele floures gan folde   ther my fote steppede.   *Many; unfold; where*

I layde myn hede one ane hill   ane hawthorne[11] besyde.

The throstills[12] full throly   they threpen togedire;   *vigorously; quarrelled*

Hipped up heghwalles   fro heselis[13] tyll othire;   *Hopped; woodpeckers*

Bernacles with thayre billes   one barkes þay roungen;   *Wild geese; on; gnawed*

40   Þe jay janglede one heghe,   jarmede the foles;   *chirped; birds*

Þe bourne full bremly rane   þe bankes bytwene.   *loudly*

So ruyde were þe roughe stremys   and raughten so heghe   *violent; reached*

That it was neghande nyghte   or I nappe myghte   *nearing; before; sleep*

For dyn of the depe watir   and dadillyng of fewllys.   *twittering; birds*

45   Bot as I laye at the laste   þan lowked myn eghne,   *closed; eyes*

And I was swythe in a sweven   sweped belyve.   *dream; swept; quickly*

    Me thoghte I was in the werlde,   I ne wiste in whate ende,   *seemed; part*

One a loveliche lande   þat was ylike grene,   *equally*

Þat laye loken by a lawe   the lengthe of a myle.   *enclosed; earthworks*

50   In aythere holte was ane here   in hawberkes full brighte,   *grove; army; mail-coats*

Harde hattes appon hedes   and helmys with crestys.   *helmets*

---

7   So that he remains behind while he grows grey with age.

8   But now there is no friendship in meeting with companions, only cowardice in heart.

9   The poet is here decrying the lack of men's desire to hear about serious issues, to participate in true friendship, and to provide wise advice. He thus sets himself up as an authority in these matters.

10   Here, the poet criticizes the poor quality of the work of popular authors who compose 'japes' or jokes, and who are listened to atten-tively; their compositions will ultimately bear witness to their ama-teurism. Again, the contrast serves to highlight this poet's self-ap-pointed authority.

11   The hawthorn is often associated with magic in medieval lit-erature.

12   thrushes

13   hazel bushes

	Brayden owte thaire baners bown forto mete;	*They flourished; ready*
	Schowen owte of the schawes in schiltrons[14] þay felle,	*Marched; woods*
	And bot the lengthe of a launde thies lordes bytwene.	*only; clearing*
55	And alle prayed for the pese till the prynce come	*peace; ruler*
	For he was worthiere in witt than any wy ells:	*other person*
	For to ridde and to rede and to rewlyn the wrothe	*judge; advise; anger*
	That aythere here appon hethe had untill othere.[15]	*either; for the other*
	At the creste of a clyffe a caban was rerede,	*pavilion; erected*
60	Alle raylede with rede the rofe and the sydes	*adorned*
	With Ynglysse besantes full brighte betyn of golde;	*ornaments*
	And ichone gayly umbygone with garters of inde,[16]	*surrounded; indigo*
	And iche a gartare of golde gerede full riche.	*decorated*
	Then were ther wordes in þe webbe werped of heu,	*woven; colour*
65	Payntted of plunket and poyntes bytwene	*light blue; dots*
	Þat were fourmed full fayre appon fresche lettres	
	And alle was it one sawe appon Ynglysse tonge:	*saying*
	'Hethyng have the hathell þat any harme thynkes'.[17]	*Scorn; man*
	Now the kyng of this kythe kepe hym oure Lorde!	*country; may protect*
70	Upon heghe one the holt ane hathell up stondes	*soldier*
	Wroghte als a wodwyse[18] alle in wrethyn lokkes,	*dressed; curled*
	With ane helme one his hede, ane hatte appon lofte,	*cap; on top*
	And one heghe one þe hatte ane hattfull beste,[19]	*wrathful animal*
	A lighte lebarde and a longe lokande full kene	*nimble lion; long one*
75	ʒarked alle of ʒalowe golde in full ʒape wyse.	*Made; yellow; clever*
	Bot that þat hillede the helme byhynde in the nekke	*covered*
	Was casten full clenly in quarters foure:	*divided*
	Two with flowres of Fraunce before and behynde,[20]	
	And two out of Ynglonde with sex grym bestes,[21]	*six fierce*
80	Thre leberdes one lofte and thre on lowe undir.	*on top; underneath*
	At iche a cornere a knoppe of full clene perle	*knob*
	Tasselde of tuly silke tuttynge out fayre.	*fine red; spreading*
	And by þe cabane I knewe the knyghte that I see	*recognized*
	And thoghte to wiete or I went wondres ynewe.	*learn something before*
85	And als I waytted withinn I was warre sone	*aware*
	Of a comliche kynge, crowned with golde,	
	Sett one a silken bynche with septure in honde,	*throne*
	One of the lovelyeste ledis whoso loveth hym in hert	*most attractive men*
	That ever segge under sonn sawe with his eghne.	*a man; eyes*
90	This kynge was comliche clade in kirtill and mantill,	*tunic; mantle*
	Bery-brown was his berde brouderde with fewlys,	*embroidered; birds*
	Fawkons of fyne golde flakerande with wynges;	*Falcons; flapping*
	And ichone bare in ble, blewe als me thoghte	*colour; seemed*
	A grete gartare of ynde gerde full riche.	*adorned*
95	Full gayly was that grete lorde girde in the myddis	*girded in the middle*
	A brighte belte of ble broudirde with fewles;	
	With drakes and with dukkes daderande þam semede	*trembling*

---

14 phalanxes; organized into close units of fighting men

15 This prince or lord is able to make the correct judgement upon the two armies at war who are filled with loathing for each other.

16 The 'garters' of indigo cloth are the heraldic designs of the Order of the Garter.

17 The famous motto of the Order of the Garter, *Honi soit qui mal y pense*.

18 A 'wodwyse' is a wild man of the woods, familiar in medieval literature as representing an uncivilized or marginalized figure.

19 The following description of the accoutrements of the wild man of the woods describes the heraldic devices decorating them.

20 In the top left and bottom right quarters of the shield.

21 A corrupt line where the alliteration has been lost by the inclusion of 'sex grym'.

	For ferdnes of fawkons fete lesse fawked þay were.[22]	*fear; in case seized*
	And ever I sayd to myselfe: 'Full selly me thynke	*marvellous; it seems*
100	Bot if this renke to the revere ryde umbestounde.'[23]	*man; riverbank; at times*
	The kyng biddith a beryn by hym þat stondeth	*asks; knight*
	One of the ferlyeste frekes þat faylede hym never:	*most wonderful; soldiers*
	'Thynke I dubbede the knyghte with dynttis to dele?	*blows; fight*
	Wende wightly thy waye my willes to kythe.	*Go; boldly; proclaim*
105	Go bidd þou 3ondere bolde batell þat one þe bent hoves	*on the battlefield; lingers*
	That they never neghe nerre togedirs;	*come close to fight; nearer*
	For if thay strike one stroke stynte þay ne thynken.'	*cease*
	'3is lorde,' said þe lede, 'while my life dures.'	*Yes; lasts*
	He dothe hym doun one þe bonke and dwellys a while	*comes down*
110	Whils he busked and bown was one his beste wyse:	*prepared; got ready*
	He laped his legges in yren to the lawe bones;	*enclosed; low*
	With pysayne and with pawnce polischede full clene;	*armour for neck and torso*
	With brases of broun stele brauden full thikke;	*arm protection; linked*
	With plates buklede at þe bakke þe body to 3eme;	*protect*
115	With a jupown full juste joynede by the sydes;	*tunic; close-fitting*
	A brod chechun at þe bakke, þe breste had anoþer,	*coat of arms*
	Thre wynges inwith wroghte in the kynde	*made naturalistically*
	Umbygon with a gold wyre. When I þat gome knewe –	*Surrounded; soldier*
	What! He was 3ongeste of 3eris and 3apeste of witt	*in years; sharpest*
120	Þat any wy in this werlde wiste of his age.[24]	*man; knew*
	He brake a braunche in his hande and caughte it swythe,	*quickly*
	Trynes one a grete trotte and takes his waye	*Proceeds*
	There bothe thies ferdes folke in the felde hoves.	*To where; armies'; wait*
	Sayd:[25] 'Loo! The kyng of this kyth, þer kepe hym oure Lorde,	
125	Send his erande by me als hym beste lyketh,	*message; pleases*
	That no beryn be so bolde one bothe his two eghne,	*man; on*
	Ones to strike one stroke, ne stirre none nerre	*Once; move; nearer*
	To lede rowte in his rewme so ryall to thynke	*troop; realm; proudly*
	Pertly with 3oure powers his pese to disturbe.	*Boldly; peace*
130	For this es the usage here and ever schall worthe,	*custom; be*
	If any beryn be so bolde with banere for to ryde	
	Withinn þe kyngdome riche, bot the kynge one,	*powerful; except; alone*
	That he schall losse the londe and his lyfe aftir.[26]	*lose his*
	Bot sen 3e knowe noghte this kyth, ne the kynge ryche,	
135	He will forgiffe 3ow this gilt of his grace one.	*offence; alone*
	Full wyde hafe I walked amonges thies wyes one,	*Very widely; people*
	Bot sawe I never siche a syghte, segge, with myn eghne;	*such; sir*
	For here es alle þe folke of Fraunce ferdede besyde	*gathered; beside*
	Of Lorreyne, of Lumbardye, and of Lawe Spayne;	*Those of*
140	Wyes of Westwale þat in were duellen,	*People of Westphalia*
	Of Ynglonde, of Yrlonde, Estirlynges full many	*Easterlings[27]*
	Þat are stuffede in stele, strokes to dele.	*equipped with; deliver*

22 The king's belt is so realistically embroidered with ducks and drakes that the birds seem to be trembling in fear of being seized by the embroidered falcons of the king's clothing.

23 The poet comments that it would seem incredible if this king were not engaged in hunting at times.

24 I. Gollancz suggested in his edition of the poem (*A Good Short Debate Between Winner and Waster: An Alliterative Poem on Social and Economic Problems in England in the Year 1352, with Modern English Rendering* (London, 1920; repr. Cambridge, 1974) that this soldier

can be identified as the Black Prince, son of Edward III.

25 The messenger said . . .

26 This may be a reference to the Statute of Treasons of 1352, which stated that those who led bands of soldiers against other armed troops were guilty of a felony, or, in some interpretations of the law, treason. This penalty did not apply to foreigners, hence the forgiveness of line 135. See Trigg, *Wynnere and Wastoure*, pp. 25–6.

27 East German merchants.

And ȝondere a baner of blake   þat one þe bent hoves · · · · · *on the battlefield waits*
With thre bulles[28] of ble white   brouden withinn, · · · · · *colour; embroidered*
And iche one hase of henppe   hynged a corde · · · · · *hemp*
Seled with a sade lede,   I say als me thynkes. · · · · · *heavy seal*
That hede es of holy kirke –   I hope he be there – · · · · · *leader*
Alle ferse to the fighte   with the folke þat he ledis. · · · · · *keen; leads*
   Anoþer banere es upbrayde   with a bende of grene, · · · · · *displayed; diagonal stripe*
With thre hedis white-herede   with howes one lofte, · · · · · *lawyers' wigs; high*
Croked full craftyly and   kembid in the nekke. · · · · · *curled; combed*
Thies are ledis of this londe   þat schold oure lawes ȝeme, · · · · · *men; care for*
That thynken to dele this daye   with dynttis full many. · · · · · *fight; blows*
I holde hym bot a fole þat fightis   whils flyttynge may helpe · · · · · *fool; debate*
When he hase founden his frende   þat fayled hym never.
   The thirde banere one bent   es of blee whitte · · · · · *battlefield; colour*
With sexe galegs, I see,   of sable withinn, · · · · · *sandals*
And iche one has a brown brase   with bokels twayne. · · · · · *strap*
Thies are Sayn Franceys folke   þat sayen alle schall fey worthe. · · · · · *be fated to die*
They aren so ferse and so fresche   þay feghtyn bot seldom. · · · · · *brave; bold; fight*
I wote wele for wynnynge   thay wentten fro home, · · · · · *profit*
His purse weghethe full wele   that wanne thaym all hedire. · · · · · *persuaded; here*
   The fourte banere one the bent   was brayde appon lofte · · · · · *raised*
With bothe the brerdes of blake,   a balle in the myddes, · · · · · *borders*
Reghte siche as the sonne es   in the someris tyde · · · · · *Just such; time*
When it hase moste of þe mayne   one Missomer even. · · · · · *its strength*
That was Domynyke this daye   with dynttis to dele; · · · · · *Saint Dominic; blows; fight*
With many a blesenande beryn   his banere es stuffede,[29] · · · · · *splendid knight*
And sythen the pope es so priste   thies prechours to helpe, · · · · · *willing*
And Fraunceys with his folke[30]   es forced besyde,
And alle the ledis of the lande   ledith thurgh witt · · · · · *men; lead*
There es no man appon molde   to machen þaym agayne, · · · · · *earth; against*
Ne gete no grace appon grounde   undir God hymselven. · · · · · *victory*
   And ȝitt es the fyfte appon þe felde   þe faireste of þam alle:
A brighte banere of blee whitte   with three bore hedis. · · · · · *wild boars'*
Be any crafte þat I kan   Carmes thaym semyde · · · · · *know; Carmelites[31]*
For þay are the ordire þat loven   oure lady to serve. · · · · · *order; Virgin Mary*
If I scholde say þe sothe   it semys no nothire · · · · · *nothing else*
Bot þat the freris with othere folke   shall þe felde wynn.
   The sexte es of sendell   and so are þay alle, · · · · · *silk*
Whitte als the whalles bone   whoso the sothe tellys,
With beltys of blake   bocled togedir, · · · · · *fastened*
The poyntes pared off rownde,   þe pendant awaye, · · · · · *trimmed; gone*
And alle the lethire appon lofte   þat one lowe hengeth · · · · · *leather*
Schynethe alle for scharpynynge   of the schavynge iren. · · · · · *razor*
The ordire of þe Austyns,[32]   for oughte þat I wene, · · · · · *know*
For by the blussche of the belte   the banere I knewe. · · · · · *gleam*
And other synes I seghe   sett appon lofte:
Some of wittnesse of wolle   and some of wyne tounnes, · · · · · *in witness; wool; casks*
Some of merchandes merkes,   so many and so thikke · · · · · *merchants'*
That I ne wote in my witt,   for alle this werlde riche, · · · · · *don't know*

---

28 Papal bulls, or letters.
29 The Dominican Friars.
30 The Franciscan Friars.
31 Carmelites are the White Friars.
32 The Augustinian Friars.

586 WYNNERE AND WASTOURE

Whatt segge under the sonne   can the sowme rekken.   *can; total count*
And sekere one þat other syde   are sadde men of armes:[33]   *resolute; determined*
Bolde sqwyeres of blode,   bowmen many,   *bold-hearted squires*
195   Þat if thay strike one stroke   stynt þay ne thynken   *to cease*
Till owthir here appon hethe   be hewen to dethe.   *army; cut*
Forthi I bid ȝow bothe   that thaym hedir broghte   *Therefore; here*
That ȝe wend with me   are any wrake falle   *go; before; misfortune*
To oure comely kyng   that this kythe owethe;   *country owns*
200   And fro he wiete wittirly   where þe wronge ristyth   *knows clearly; fault lies*
Thare nowthir wye be wrothe   to wirche als he doeth.'[34]

    Off ayther rowte ther rode owte   a renke als me thoghte,   *From each troop; man*
Knyghtis full comly   one coursers attyred,   *war-horses*
And sayden: 'Sir, sandisman,   sele the betyde![35]
205   Wele knowe we the kyng,   he clothes us bothe,
And hase us fosterde and fedde   this fyve and twenty wyntere.
Now fare þou byfore   and we schall folowe aftire.'   *go*
And now are þaire brydells upbrayde   and bown one þaire wayes;   *pulled up; ready; journeys*
Thay lighten doun at þe launde   and leved thaire stedis,   *alighted; glade; left*
210   Kayren up at the clyffe   and one knees fallyn,   *went; on*
The kynge henttis by þe handes   and hetys þam to ryse,   *clasps; orders*
And sayde: 'Welcomes, heres, as hyne   of oure house bothen.'   *sirs; servants*
The kynge waytted one wyde   and the wyne askes;   *around*
Beryns broghte it anone   in bolles of silvere.   *Men; bowls*
215   Me thoghte I sowpped so sadly   it sowrede bothe myn eghne,   *drank; deeply; stung*
And he þat wilnes of this werke   to wete any forthire   *desires; know; further*
Full freschely and faste[36]   for here a fitt endes.   *Fill; quickly; soon*

Bot than kerpede the kynge, sayd: 'Kythe what ȝe hatten,   *spoke; Reveal; are called*
And whi the hates aren so hote   ȝoure hertis bytwene;   *enmities*
220   If I schall deme ȝow this day   dothe me to here.'   *judge; let*
'Now certys lorde,' sayde þat one,   'the sothe for to telle,
I hatt Wynnere, a wy   that alle this werlde helpis,   *am called; man*
For I lordes cane lere   thurgh ledyng of witt.   *can teach; instruction*
Thoo þat spedfully will spare   and spende not to grete,   *succesfully; save*
225   Lyve appon littill-whattes   I lufe hym the bettir.   *small amounts*
Witt wiendes me with   and wysses me faire;   *Knowledge comes; guides*
Aye when gadir my gudes   than glades myn hert.   *Whenever; possessions*
Bot this felle false thefe   þat byfore ȝowe standes   *wicked*
Thynkes to strike or he styntt   and stroye me for ever.   *before he might cease*
230   Alle þat I wynn thurgh witt   he wastes thurgh pryde;   *skill/cunning; ostentation*
I gedir, I glene   and he lattys goo sone;   *scrape together; releases*
I pryke and I pryne   and he the purse opynes.   *tie up; sew up*
Why hase this cayteffe no care   how men corne sellen?   *rogue*
His londes liggen alle ley,   his lomes aren solde,   *fallow; tools*
235   Downn bene his dowfehowses,   drye bene his poles.   *dovecotes; pools*
The devyll wounder one the wele   he weldys at home,   *marvels at; wealth; enjoys*
Bot hungere and heghe howses   and howndes full kene.   *rented houses*
Safe a sparthe and a spere   sparrede in ane hyrne,   *Except; axe; hidden; corner*
A bronde at his bede-hede   biddes he no noþer,   *sword; asks*

---

33   Wastoure's army is described in only four lines, 193–6, in comparison to the preceding lengthy description of Wynnere's army.
34   That there neither man will be angry to do as he considers.
35   'Sir, messenger, may prosperity be yours!'
36   The poet demands a full glass before he continues.

240	Bot a cuttede capill to cayre with to his frendes.	*gelding; ride*
	Then will he boste with his brande and braundesche hym ofte –	*threaten; strut about*
	This wikkede weryed thefe that Wastoure men calles –	
	That if he life may longe this lande will he stroye.	*destroy*
	Forthi deme us this daye, for Drightyns love in heven,	*judge; Lord's*
245	To fighte furthe with oure folke to owthire fey worthe.'	*forth; either; may die*
	'Ʒee Wynnere,' quod Wastoure, 'thi wordes are hye,	
	Bot I schall tell the a tale that tene schall the better.	*to annoy*
	When thou haste waltered and went and wakede alle þe nyghte,	*tossed and turned*
	And iche a wy in this werlde that wonnes the abowte,	*lives near you*
250	And hase werpede thy wyde howses full of wolle sakkes,	*filled*
	The bemys benden at the rofe, siche bakone there hynges,	*beams; bacon*
	Stuffed are sterlynges undere stelen bowndes.	*silver pennies; hoops*
	What scholde worthe of that wele if no waste come?	*become; wealth; spending*
	Some rote, some ruste, some ratouns fede.	*rats*
255	Let be thy cramynge of thi kystes, for Cristis lufe of heven;	*chests*
	Late the peple and the pore hafe parte of thi silvere,	
	For if thou wydwhare scholde walke and waytten the sothe,	*far and wide; consider*
	Thou scholdeste reme for rewthe in siche ryfe bene the pore.	*weep; pity; abundance*
	For and thou lengare thus lyfe, leve thou no noþer,	*longer; nothing*
260	Thou schall be hanged in helle for that thou here spareste.	
	For siche a synn haste þou solde thi soule into helle	
	And there es ever wellande woo, worlde withowtten ende.'	*boiling torment*
	'Late be thi worde, Wastoure,' quod Wynnere the riche,	
	'Thou melleste of a mater tho madiste it thiselven.	*complain; grievance; caused*
265	With thi sturte and thy stryffe thou stroyeste up my gudes:	*violence; consume; produce*
	In playinge and in wakynge in wynttres nyghttis,	
	In owttrage, in unthrifte, in angarte pryde.	*extravagance; excessive*
	There es no wele[37] in this werlde to wasschen thyn handes	*wealth*
	That ne es gyffen and grounden are þou it getyn have.	*spent; before granted*
270	Thou ledis renkes in thy rowte wele rychely attyrede;	*lead men; troop*
	Some hafe girdills of golde þat more gude coste	*money*
	Than alle þe faire fre londe that ʒe byfore haden.	*fine*
	Ʒe folowe noghte ʒoure fadirs þat fosterde ʒow alle	*taught*
	A kynde herveste to cache and cornes to wynn	*gather*
275	For þe colde wyntter and þe kene with gleterand frostes	*intense; glittering*
	Sythen dropeles drye in the dede monethe.[38]	*After rainless drought*
	And thou wolle to the taverne byfore þe tonne-hede,	*end of the wine barrel*
	Iche beryne redy with a bolle to blerren thyn eghne;	*each servant; cup; dim*
	Hete the whatte thou have schalte and whatt thyn hert lykes,	*Order*
280	Wyfe, wedowe or wenche þat wonnes thereaboute.	*dwells*
	Then es there bott "fille in" and "feche forthe" florence to schewe[39]	
	"Wee hee" and "worthe up" wordes ynewe;	*"get up"*
	Bot when this wele es awaye the wyne moste be payede fore.	
	Than lympis ʒowe weddis to laye or ʒoure londe selle,	*it befalls to; mortgage*
285	For siche wikked werkes wery the oure Lorde.	
	And forthi God laughte that he lovede and levede þat oþer,	*accepted; left*
	Iche freke one felde ogh þe ferdere be to wirche.	*man; owned; in fear*
	Teche thy men for to tille and tymen thyn feldes,	*harrow*

---

37 A pun on 'well' and the washing of hands.

38 The 'dead month' is March, before the coming of spring. March is traditionally regarded as being a dry month.

39 Then the only words there are 'fill up my glass' and 'pay up' to make you show your gold coins.

	Rayse up thi renthowses, ryme up thi ȝerdes,	*houses for rent; clear*
290	Owthere hafe as þou haste done and hope aftir werse;	*Either; expect*
	Þat es firste þe faylynge of fode and than the fire aftir	
	To brene the alle at a birre for thi bale dedis.	*instantly; wicked*
	The more colde es to come als me a clerke tolde.'⁴⁰	
	' Ȝee, Wynnere,' quod Wastoure, 'thi wordes are vayne,	*empty*
295	With oure festes and oure fare we feden the pore.	
	It es plesynge to the Prynce þat Paradyse wroghte,	*created*
	When Cristes peple hath parte hym payes alle the better	*a share; it pleases*
	Then here ben hodirde and hidde and happede in cofers	*heaped up; covered up*
	That it no sonn may see thurgh seven wyntter ones,	*sun; once*
300	Owthir freres it feche when thou fey worthes	*or; are doomed to die*
	To payntten with thaire pelers or pergett with thaire walles.	*pillars; plaster*
	Thi sone and thi sektours ichone slees othere,	*son; executors; destroys*
	Maken dale aftir thi daye for thou durste never,	*Give gifts; death; dared*
	Mawngery ne myndale ne never myrthe lovediste.	*Feasts nor anniversaries*
305	A dale aftir thi daye dose the no mare	*donation*
	Þan a lighte lanterne late appone nyghte	*lighted*
	When it es borne at thi bakke, beryn, be my trouthe.⁴¹	*man*
	Now wolde God that it were, als I wisse couthe,	*as; devise*
	That thou Wynnere, thou wriche, and Wanhope thi brothir	*wretch; Despair*
310	And eke ymbryne dayes⁴² and evenes of sayntes,	*Ember Days; vigils*
	The Frydaye and his fere one the ferrere syde	*neighbour; other side*
	Were drownede in the depe see there never droghte come,	*where; drought*
	And dedly synn for thayre dede were endityde with twelve	*condemned*
	And thies beryns one the bynches with bonets one lofte	*judges' benches; caps*
315	That bene knowen and kydde for clerkes of the beste,	*recognized*
	Als gude als Arestotle or Austyn the wyse,	*Saint Augustine*
	That alle schent were those schalkes and Scharshull⁴³ itwiste	*shamed; men; together with*
	Þat saide I prikkede with powere his pese to distourbe.⁴⁴	*rode out; peace*
	Forthi, comely kynge, that oure case heris,	*Therefore; listens to*
320	Late us swythe with oure swerdes swyngen togedirs,	*Permit; to meet in battle*
	For nowe I se it es full sothe þat sayde es full ȝore:	*long before*
	"The richere of ranke wele the rathere will drede;	*abundant wealth*
	The more havande þat he hathe the more of hert feble".'	*possessions; faint-hearted*
	Bot than this wrechede Wynnere full wrothely he lukes,	
325	Sayse: 'Þis es spedles speche to speken thies wordes.	*unprofitable*
	Loo, this wrechide Wastoure that wydewhare es knawenn,	*widely*
	Ne es nothir kaysser ne kynge ne knyghte þat the folowes,	*emperor; is loyal to*
	Barone ne bachelere ne beryn that thou loveste,	*knight*
	Bot foure felawes or fyve that the fayth owthe.	*owe allegiance to you*
330	And he schall dighte thaym to dyne with dayntethes so many	*summon*
	Þat iche a wy in this werlde may wepyn for sorowe.	*each man*
	The bores hede schall be broghte with plontes appon lofte,	*vegetables*
	Buktayles full brode in brothes there besyde,	*bucks' hind parts*

---

40 Lines 291–3 implicitly refer to the crop-failure that will result from the lack of agricultural work done by Wastoure and his followers. The result will not simply be a lack of food, though, but inevitable damnation in the fire and ice of hell.

41 Wastoure's argument is that it is better to spend money in this life than to hoard it up so that, after death, relations and executors divide and argue over it, or grasping friars obtain it and use it to decorate.

42 The Ember Days are religious days of fasting.

43 Sir William Shareshull was chief justice 1350–61 and was prominent in assisting in proscriptive legislation that forbade the gathering of armed bands of men. He was despised as a 'hated figure of authority' (Trigg, *Winnere and Wastoure*, p. 37; see further references there).

44 See lines 126–33.

	Venyson with the frumentee and fesanttes full riche,	*wheat boiled with milk*
335	Baken mete therby one the burde sett,	*table*
	Chewettes of choppede flesche, charbinade fewlis,	*Pies; grilled birds*
	And iche a segge þat I see has sexe mens doke.	*man; duck*
	If this were nedles note anothir comes aftir:	*excessive affair*
	Roste with the riche sewes and the ryalle spyces,	*soups; sumptuous*
340	Kiddes cloven by þe rigge, quarterd swannes,	*split; spine*
	Tartes of ten ynche þat tenys myn hert	*it angers*
	To see þe borde overbrade with blasande disches	*spread; piping hot*
	Als it were a rayled rode with rynges and stones.	*decorated cross*
	The thirde mese to me were mervelle to rekken	*course*
345	For alle es Martynmesse mete[45] þat I with moste dele,	*concern myself with*
	Noghte bot worttes with the flesche withowt wilde fowle	*herbs*
	Save ane hene to hym that the howse owethe.	*owns*
	And he will hafe birdes bownn one a broche riche:	*ready; on a skewer*
	Barnakes and buturs and many billed snyppes,	*Geese; bitterns; snipes*
350	Larkes and lyngwhittes lapped in sogoure,	*linnets; syrup*
	Wodcokkes and wodwales full wellande hote,	*woodpeckers; simmering*
	Teeles and titmoyses to take what hym lykes;	*Teals; titmice*
	Caudils of connynges and custadis swete,	*Stews; rabbits; flans*
	Dariols and dische-metis þat ful dere coste,	*Pastries; pies*
355	Mawmene þat men clepen ʒour mawes to fill,	*Meat wine stew; stomachs*
	Iche a mese at a merke bytwen twa men	*course; costs a mark*
	Þat sothe bot brynneth for bale ʒour bowells within.	*stings; pain*
	Me tenyth at ʒour trompers, þay tounen so heghe	*It angers me; resound*
	Þat iche a gome in þe gate goullyng may here;	*loud trumpeting*
360	Þen wil þay say to þamselfe as þay samen ryden,	*together*
	ʒe hafe no myster of the helpe of þe heven Kyng.	*need; benefit*
	Þus are ʒe scorned by skyll and schathed þeraftir	*reason; disgraced*
	Þat rechen for a repaste a rawnsom of silver.	*pay; significant amount*
	Bot ones I herd in a haule of a herdmans tong:	*hall; retainer's*
365	"Better were meles many þan a mery nyghte".'	*riotous*
	And he þat wilnes of þis werke for to wete forthe	*desires; know further*
	Full freschely and faste for here a fit endes.	*Pour*
	'ʒee, Wynnere,' quod Wastour, 'I wote wele myselven	
	What sall lympe of þe, lede, within fewe ʒeris.	*become; a few*
370	Thurgh þe poure plenté of corne þat þe peple sowes	*you; a perfect plenty*
	Þat God will graunte of his grace to growe on þe erthe	
	Ay to appaire þe pris and passe nott to hye,	*always; lower, it passes*
	Schal make þe to waxe wod for wanhope in erthe,	*grow mad; despair*
	To hope aftir an harde ʒere to honge þiselven.[46]	*want*
375	Woldeste þou hafe lordis to lyfe as laddes on fote,	*low-born men*
	Prelates als prestes þat þe parischen ʒemes,	*Bishops; care for*
	Prowde marchandes of pris as pedders in towne?	*merchants; pedlars*
	Late lordes lyfe als þam liste, laddes as þam falles:	*Let; like; it happens*
	Þay þe bacon and beefe, þay botours and swannes;	*bitterns*
380	Þay þe roughe of þe rye, þay þe rede whete;	*fine*
	Þay þe grewell gray, and þay þe gude sewes;	*soups*

---

45 Martinmas (November) is the traditional time of year in which animals are slaughtered for preparation as winter provisions.
46 Wastoure claims that Wynnere always desires a poor harvest so that he can sell his own stock of corn at a higher price. When the harvest yields a good crop, Wynnere will want to hang himself from despair at the loss of profit.

And þen may þe peple hafe parte   in povert þat standes,   *a share; exists*
Sum gud morsell of mete   to mend with þair chere.   *improve; happiness*
If fewlis flye schold forthe   and fongen be never,   *birds; trapped*
385   And wild bestis in þe wodde   wonne al þaire lyve,   *remain*
And fisches flete in þe flode   and ichone ete oþer,   *float*
Ane henne at ane halpeny   by halfe ʒeris ende;   *would cost a half-penny*
Schold not a ladde be in londe   a lorde for to serve.   *There would not be*
Þis wate þou full wele   witterly þiselven: *clearly*
390   Whoso wele schal wyn   a wastour moste he fynde,   *wealth*
For if it greves one gome   it gladdes anoþer.'   *man*

      Now quod Wynner to Wastour: 'Me wondirs in hert   *It amazes me*
Of thies poure penyles men   þat peloure will by,   *furs; might buy*
Sadills of sendale   with sercles full riche.   *Saddles; silk; rings*
395   Lesse ʒe wrethe ʒour wifes   þaire willes to folowe   *Lest; anger*
ʒe sellyn wodd affir wodde   in a wale tyme,   *wood; short*
Bothe þe oke and þe assche   and alle þat þer growes;
Þe spyres and þe ʒonge sprynge   ʒe spare to ʒour children   *seedlings; saplings*
And sayne God wil graunt it his grace   to grow at þe last   *declare*
400   For to save to ʒour sones,   bot þe schame es ʒour ownn,
Nedeles save ʒe þe soyle   for sell it ʒe thynken.[47]   *in vain; earth; plan*
ʒour forfadirs were fayne   when any frende come   *eager*
For to schake to þe schawe   and schewe hym þe estres   *ride; woods; paths*
In iche holt þat þay had   ane hare for to fynde,   *grove*
405   Bryng to the brod launde   bukkes ynewe   *glade; bucks*
To lache and to late goo   to lightten þaire hertis.   *catch*
Now es it sett and solde   my sorowe es þe more,   *leased*
Wastes alle wilfully   ʒour wyfes to paye.   *You waste*
That are had lordes in londe   and ladyes riche   *Those that are held to be*
410   Now are þay nysottes of þe new gett   so nysely attyred   *fools; immoderately*
With syde slabbande sleves   sleght to þe grounde   *wide trailing; let down*
Ourlede all umbtourne   with ermyn aboute   *Trimmed; around*
Þat es as harde, as I hope,   to handil in þe derne   *difficult; dark*
Als a cely symple wenche   þat never silke wroghte.   *innocent; embroidered*
415   Bot whoso lukes on hir lyre,   oure Lady of heven,   *hardship*
How scho fled for ferd   ferre out of hir kythe   *fear; far from; family*
Appon ane amblande asse   withowtten more pride,   *ambling*
Safe a barne in hir barme   and a broken heltre   *except for; child; halter*
Þat Joseph held in hys hande   þat hend for to ʒeme.   *noble one (Christ); protect*
420   All þofe scho walt al þis werlde,   hir wedes wer pore   *Though; ruled; clothes*
For to gyf ensample of siche   for to schewe oþer   *such (humility); teach*
For to leve pompe and pride;   þat poverte ofte schewes.'
      Than þe Wastour wrothly   castes up his eghne
And said: 'Þou Wynner, þou wriche,   me woundirs in hert
425   What hafe oure clothes coste þe,   caytef, to by   *scoundrel; buy*
Þat þou schal birdes upbrayd   of þaire bright wedis,   *ladies; rebuke; clothes*
Sythen þat we vouchesafe   þat þe silver payen?   *Since; allow; pleases you*
It lyes wele for a lede   his lemman to fynde,[48]
Aftir hir faire chere   to forthir hir herte;   *happy mood; to please*
430   Then will scho love hym lelely   as hir lyfe one,   *faithfully*

---

47   Wynnere claims that Wastoure, and other lords of his kind,   48   It is fitting for a man to provide well for his sweetheart.
sell their forests and lands to increase their income and fulfil their
wives' desires.

Make hym bolde and bown   with brandes to smytte   *ready; swords to strike*

To schonn schenchipe and schame   þer schalkes ere gadird.   *avoid; disgrace; men*

And if my peple ben prode   me payes alle þe better   *magnificent*

To see þam faire and free   tofore with myn eghne.   *them; noble*

435   And ȝe negardes appon nyghte,   ȝe nappen so harde,   *misers; sleep*

Routten at ȝour raxillyng,   raysen ȝour hurdes.   *Snore; stretching; buttocks*

Ȝe beden wayte one þe wedir   þen wery ȝe þe while   *give orders to wait; curse*

Þat ȝe nade hightilde up ȝour houses   and ȝour hyne raysed.[49]

Forthi, Wynnere, with wronge   þou wastes þi tyme   *error*

440   For gode day ne glade   getys þou never.   *cheerful*

Þe devyll at þi dede-day   schal delyn þi gudis;   *death-day; distribute*

Þo þou woldest þat it were   wyn þay it never,   *wish; acquire*

Þi skathill sectours   schal sever þam aboute   *wicked executors; disperse*

And þou hafe helle full hotte   for þat þou here saved,

445   Þou tast no tent one a tale   þat tolde was full ȝore.   *pay no heed to*

I hold hym madde þat mournes   his make for to wyn,   *mad; is worried; mistress*

Hent hir þat hir haf schal   and hold hir his while: *would embrace*

Take þe coppe as it comes,   þe case as it falles,   *chance when it comes*

For whoso lyfe may lengeste   lympes to feche   *live; it befalls*

450   Woodd þat he waste schall   to warmen his helys   *Wood; heels*

Ferrere þan his fadir dide   by fyvetene myle.[50]   *Further; miles*

Now kan I carpe no more,   bot Sir Kyng, by þi trouthe,   *speak*

Deme us where we duell schall,   me thynke þe day hyes.   *Judge; live; passes*

Ȝit harde sore es myn hert   and harmes me more

455   Ever to see in my syghte   þat I in soule hate.'

      The kynge lovely lokes   on þe ledis twayne,   *two men*

Says: 'Blynnes, beryns, of ȝour brethe   and of ȝoure brode worde   *Cease; men; bold*

And I schal deme ȝow this day   where ȝe duelle schall,

Aythere lede in a lond   þer he es loved moste.   *Each man; where*

460   Wende, Wynnere, þi waye   over þe wale stremys,   *Go; swift*

Passe forthe by Paris   to þe Pope of Rome,

Þe cardynalls ken þe wele,   will kepe þe ful faire,   *know; nobly*

And make þi sydes in silken   schetys to lygge,   *your body; sheets*

And fede þe and foster þe   and forthir thyn hert   *encourage*

465   As leefe to worthen wode   as þe to wrethe ones.   *Eager; crazed; make angry*

Bot loke, lede, be þi lyfe,   when I lettres sende   *ensure, man*

Þat þou hy þe to me home   on horse or one fote,   *hurry*

And when I knowe þou will come   he[51] schall cayre uttire   *ride further away*

And lenge with anoper lede   til þou þi lefe take.   *stay; leave*

470   For þofe þou bide in þis burgh   to þi beryinge-daye   *though; remain*

With hym happyns þe never   a fote forto holde.   *get a foothold*

And thou, Wastoure, I will   þat þou wonne   *wish; dwell*

Þer moste waste es of wele   and wyng þer untill.   *wealth; hurry there*

Chese þe forthe into þe chepe,   a chambre þou rere,   *Go; market; set up*

475   Loke þi wyndowe be wyde   and wayte þe aboute

Where any potent beryn   þurgh þe burgh passe.   *powerful man*

Teche hym to þe taverne   till he tayte worthe,   *Show; he might be merry*

---

49 'You give orders to wait on the weather and then curse the whole time that you had not prepared your buildings or organized your household.' Wynnere lazily waits to see if the weather will be good before spending money to ensure the proper preparation of his property for storing an abundant crop.

50 Because Wastoure has sold all the wood from his forests, he has to walk further and further to get the wood that remains. Therefore, life should be enjoyed while it lasts because things only become more difficult.

51 Wastoure. The king judges that Wynnere and Wastoure must be separated.

Doo hym drynke al nyȝte   þat he dry be at morow;   *Make; thirsty*
Sythen ken hym to þe crete   to comforth his vaynes,   *introduce; sweet wine; spirit*
480 Brynge hym to Bred Strete,[52]   bikken þi fynger,   *beckon*
Schew hym of fatt chepe   scholdirs ynewe,   *sheep; many forelegs*
"Hotte for þe hungry"[53]   a hen oþer twayne.   *or two*
Sett hym softe one a sege   and sythen send after;   *seat; then send for him*
Bryng out of þe burgh   þe best þou may fynde,
485 And luke thi knafe hafe a knoke   bot he þe clothe sprede.   *servant; blow; unless*
Bot late hym paye or he passe   and pik hym so clene   *let; before; rob*
Þat fynd a peny in his purse   and put owte his eghe.   *That you would find*
When þat es dronken and don   duell þer no lenger,   *spent in drinking*
Bot teche hym owt of the townn   to trotte aftir more.   *direct; run*
490 Then passe to þe pultrie,   þe peple þe knowes,   *poultry-sellers'*
And ken wele þi katour   to knawen þi fode,   *direct; caterer*
The herouns, þe hasteleteȝ,   þe henne wele serve   *roasted meat*
Þe pertrikes, þe plovers,   þe oþer pulled byrddes;   *partridges; plucked*
Þe albus, þis oþer foules,   þe egretes dere,   *bullfinches; egrets*
495 Þe more þou wastis þi wele   þe better þe Wynner lykes.   *waste; wealth*
     And wayte to me, þou Wynnere,   if þou wilt wele chefe: *pay attention; prosper*
When I wende appon werre   my wyes to lede   *war; men*
For at þe proude pales   of Parys þe riche   *palace*
I thynk to do it in ded   and dub þe to knyghte,
500 And giff giftes full grete   of golde and of silver
To ledis of my legyance   þat lufen me in hert.   *men; allegiance*
And sythen kayre as I come   with knyghtes þat me foloen   *ride; are loyal*
To þe kirke of Colayne   þer þe kynges ligges . . . '   *Cologne*

---

52   Bread Street in London.
53   The cry of a food-seller in the street. Compare *The Land of Cockayne*, line 104.

Textual Emendations

The textual emendations included here are often those suggested by the editors of the individual texts; where this is the case, I have generally referenced the particular editor. I have not included a record here of the emendations which occur as a result of a correction in the manuscript by a contemporary or slightly later hand.

Bede's *Ecclesiastical History*

The Settlement of the Angles, Saxons and Jutes

Line 10: þæt hi for sibbe] ms. þæt he for sibbe

The Life of Cædmon

Line 11: gedafenode] ms gedeofanade
Line 14: sceoldon] ms sealde
Line 15: for scome] ms for for scome
Line 21: me aht] ms meaht
Line 34: Gode wyrðes] ms godes wordes
Line 39: þæt him] ms þæt hit
Line 68: nære] ms neah wære
Line 84: swa swa he hluttre] ms swa swa hluttre

Alfred

Preface to the Translation of Gregory's *Pastoral Care*

Line 4: hu] supplied from other mss.
Line 8: don] supplied from another ms.

Translation of Boethius's *Consolation of Philosophy*

PROEM
Line 3: weoroldbisgum] ms. wordum ond bisgum. As emended by Sedgefield, p. 1, from Junius 12.
Line 5: hæfde] ms. hæfe

ON GOVERNMENT
Line 3: tola] ms. la. As emended by Whitelock, *Sweet's Anglo-Saxon Reader*, p. 15
Line 6: ne mæg] ms. ne ne mæg
Line 10: ondweorc] ms. weorc andweorc
Line 15: forgitene] ms. forgifen
Line 20: min gemynd] min supplied from Junius 12. As emended by Whitelock, p. 16

ORFEUS AND EURYDICE
Line 15: Cruerus] ms. Ceruerueruerus (dittography)
Line 27: Tyties] ms. sticces. As emended by Whitelock, p. 14
Line 36: spell] supplied from Bodley 180

Anglo-Saxon Chronicle

Annals 855–78: The death of Edmund, Alfred's battles with the Vikings

Line 12: Frealafing] corrected from ms. Freawining.
Line 25: friþ wiþ] ms. friþ.
Line 48: ærcebiscope] ms. ærcebiscpe.

The reign of Æðelstan and *The Battle of Brunanburh*

Line 57: cumbolgehnastes] ms. culbodgehnades. As emended by Campbell, p. 113, from the other manuscript versions.

The Exeter Book

Advent Lyric VII and VIII (from Christ I)

Line 166: worda] ms. worde

The Wanderer

Line 14: healde] ms. healdne. As Klinck et al.
Line 24: waþema] ms. waþena
Line 28: freondleasne] ms. freondlease
Line 59: modsefa min ne] ms. mod sefan minne
Line 89: deorce] ms. deorcne
Line 102: hrusan] ms. hruse

The Seafarer

Line 25: ne ænig] ms. nænig
Line 49: wlitigiað] ms. wlitigað
Line 56: esteadig] ms. eft eadig
Line 69: tidege] ms. tide ge
Line 72: bið] ms. þæt. As emended by Muir, *The Exeter Book Anthology.*
Line 79: blæd] ms. blæð
Line 109: mon] ms. mod (haplography)
Line 115: swiþre] ms. swire
Line 117: we²] ms. se

Deor

Line 14: Mæðhilde] ms. mæð hilde
Line 16: him] ms. hi
Line 30: earfoða] ms. earfoda

Wulf and Eadwacer

Line 16: earmne] ms. earne

Exeter Book Riddles

RIDDLE 5
Line 6 forwurðe] ms. forwurde

RIDDLE 12
Line 6: beorne] ms. beorn

RIDDLE 26
Line 8: geondsprengde speddropum] ms. geond speddropum
Line 12: hyde] ms. hyþe

RIDDLE 29
Line 2: hornum bitweonum] ms horna abitweonum (homeoteleuton?)
Line 5: atimbran] ms. atimbram
Line 11: onette] ms o netteð

RIDDLE 30
Line 7: onhnigaþ] ms. on hin gaþ

RIDDLE 44
Line 7: efenlang] ms. efe lang. Emended by all editors.

RIDDLE 45
Line 1: weaxan] ms. weax

RIDDLE 55
Line 1: healle] ms. heall

The Wife's Lament

Line 20: hycgendne] ms. hycgende
Line 25: sceal] ms. seal

The Husband's Message

Line 4: settan] ms. setta[.]
Line 8: ofer] ms. [.]fer
Line 8: hafu] ms. hofu. As emended by Klinck, *The Old English Elegies.*
Line 21: læran] ms. læram
Line 38: foldan] ms. folda[.]
Line 50 gehyre] ms. gecyre

The Ruin

Line 4: hrimgeat berofen] ms. hrim geat torras berofen
Line 26: secgrofra] ms. secgrof. Emended here to agree with gen. pl. wera.
Line 33: gefrætwed] ms. gefrætweð

The Vercelli Book

The Fates of the Apostles

Line 1: Hwæt] ms. [.] wæt
Line 4: wæron] ms. woron
Line 84: ealle] ms. ealne
Line 90: halgan] ms. halga
Line 94: lætan] ms. læt
Line 98: standeþ] ms. standaþ
Line 119: gildeð] ms. glideð

Vercelli Homily X

I have adopted many of the emendations suggested by D. G. Scragg in his edition of *The Vercelli Homilies and Related Texts*, EETS o.s. 300 (London, 1992). Students should refer to this work for an introduction to the manuscript, and a description of the sources of Homily X.

Line 19: and feala wundra mannum] omitted in ms.
Line 24: earan] omitted in ms.

Line 28: God] omitted in ms.

Line 34: ne to inwitfulle] ms. ne inwitfulle

Line 35: to fyligenne] omitted in ms.

Line 36: Ne lufien we]: ms. ne lufien

Lines 51–2: þu her somnost . . . werod þe] omitted in ms.

Line 57: min riht is] omitted in ms.

Line 59: Þonne] ms. þonn

Line 64: þe afremdedon] ms. hy afremedon

Line 69: geeadmeddest] ms. gemeddest

Line 70: and mid þine þe æðelan] mid omitted in ms.

Lines 78–9: in þam hatan] ms. hatan

Lines 84: we eft] ms. eft

Line 91: him wæs lað] ms. him lað

Line 92: oððe þam sealde] ms. oððe sealde

Line 95: symle] ms. sylle

Line 95: gehyre . . . sende] omitted in ms.

Line 95: man] omitted in ms.

Line 99: þu] ms. and þu

Line 99: Ac Ic] ms. And Ic

Line 101: geunrotsodest . . . awendest, and] omitted in ms.

Line 104: cwæð] omitted in ms.

Line 107: æghwylce] ms. æghwylc

Line 108: anum] omitted in ms.

Line 109: læstum] ms. leofestum

Line 112: to ðan þæt] ms. to ðan þan þæt

Line 115: For hwan] ms. For

Line 121: sæd læded and onlifan] omitted in ms. to *onlif*

Line 144: mann] ms. mannon

Line 148: ar] omitted in ms.

Line 149: syleð] ms. to forlæteð

Line 150: to forlæteð] ms. syleð

Line 154: hit þonne] ms. hine

Line 159: heofonfyre] ms. hatum fyre

Line 159: and geslægen] omitted in ms.

Line 165: eal astæned] ms. ealne astænen

Lines 165–6: mid seolfrenum . . . beddum] omitted in ms.

Line 174: woruldescriftum] ms. woruldesciriftum

Line 182: of] ms. ofer

Line 187: hwilendlicum] ms. willendlicum

Line 194: Dryhten] ms. gefean

Line 197: heahfædera and witegena] ms. heahfæderas and witegan

Line 201: ham] omitted in ms.

The Dream of the Rood

Line 2: hwæt] ms. hæt

Line 20: sorgum] ms. surgum

Line 59: sorgum] omitted in ms. As emended by Swanton, p. 93, from Ruthwell Cross text.

Line 71: stefn] omitted in ms. Supplied by Swanton et al.

The *Beowulf*-manuscript

Beowulf

This edition, more than that for any other text in this volume, owes a great deal to previous scholarly editions of the text. Among those that I have consulted are C. L. Wrenn, ed., *Beowulf*; G. Jack, ed., *Beowulf: A Student Edition* (whose glossing I have made frequent reference to); M. Alexander, ed., *Beowulf*; and B. Mitchell and F. R. Robinson, eds, *Beowulf: An Edition*. For full introductions, explanatory notes, glosses and glossaries, students should refer to these, and other published, editions of the complete poem. I have generally not referred to the readings from Thorkelin A and B, even where one of those readings has been adopted over the other.

Line 332: æþelum] ms. hæleþum

Line 357: anhar] ms. unhar

Line 375: eafora] ms. eaforan

Line 395: guðgetawum] ms. guð geata wum

Line 418: minne] ms. mine

Line 457: For gewyrhtum] ms. fere fyhtum

Line 461: Wedera] ms. gara

Line 465: Deniga] ms. deninga

Line 499, 530, 1165: Unferð] ms. Hunferð

Line 516: wylmum] ms. wylm

Line 586: fela] omitted in ms. Supplied by Jack, *Beowulf*.

Line 591: Grendel] ms. Gredel

Line 652: Gegrette] ms. grette

Line 684: he] ms. het

Line 702: wideferhð] ms. ferhð. As Mitchell and Robinson, *Beowulf*.

Line 707: scynscaþa] ms. syn scaþa

Line 722: gehran] ms. ehran. As Jack, *Beowulf*.

Line 752: sceata] ms. sceatta

Line 765: wæs] ms. he wæs

Line 780: betlic] ms. hetlic

Line 902: eafoð] ms. earfoð. As all editions.

Line 936: gehwylcum] ms. gehwylce.

Line 949: nænigre] ms. ænigre

Line 954: dom] omitted in ms. Supplied by all editors above.

Line 963: hine] ms. him

Line 965: mundgripe] ms. hand gripe

Line 976: nidgripe] ms. mid gripe

Line 984: æghwær] ms. æghwylc

Line 985: stedenægla] ms. steda nægla. As most editors above.

Line 1004: gesecan] ms. gesacan

Line 1022: hildecumbor] ms. hiltecumbor

Line 1026: sceotendum] ms. scotenum

Line 1031: wala] ms. walan

Line 1051: brimlade] ms. brimleade

Line 1073: lindplegan] ms. hildplegan

Line 1079: heo] ms. he. As Jack, *Beowulf*, etc.

Line 1104: frecnan] ms. frecnen
Line 1117: eame] ms. earme. As most editors above.
Line 1129: eal] ms. l
Line 1130: ne] omitted in ms. As most editors above.
Line 1151: roden] ms. hroden
Line 1174: þe] omitted in ms.
Line 1176: hererinc] ms. hereric
Line 1198: hordmaðum] ms. hordmadmum
Line 1199: þære] ms. here
Line 1218: þeodgestreona] ms. þeogestreona
Line 1229: hold] ms. hol

Judith

Line 15: symble] ms. symle
Line 40: Judithe] ms. Iudithðe
Line 47: ymbe] ms. ond ymbe
Line 85: þearfendre] ms. þearf fendre
Line 87: heorte] ms. heorte ys
Line 134: hie] ms. hie hie
Line 144: Judith] ms. Iudithe
Line 165: þeodnes] ms. þeoðnes
Line 207: wistan] ms. westan
Line 234: ricne] ms. rice
Line 249: werigferhðe] ms. ferhðe. Emendation supplied by Timmer.
Line 251: hilde] ms. hyldo
Line 263: hæste] ms. hæfte
Line 287: nu] supplied by Timmer et al.
Line 297: linde] ms. lind

The Junius Manuscript

Exodus

I have adopted many of the emendations suggested by Lucas. These are noted below.
Line 1: habbað] ms. habað. As Lucas.
Line 15: andsacan] ms. andsaca. As Lucas.
Line 22: feonda] ms. feonda feonda.
Line 33: ungeare] ms. ingere. As Lucas.
Line 55: magoræswa] ms. mago ræwa. As Lucas.
Line 62: meringa] ms. meoringa. As Lucas.
Line 63: tirfæste] ms. tirfæstne.
Lines 81, 105: segl] ms. swegl. As Lucas.
Line 113: sceado] ms. sceaðo. As Lucas.
Lines 118: hæðbroga] ms. hæð. As Lucas.
Lines 119: on ferclamme] ms. ofer clamme; getwæfde] ms. getwæf. As Lucas.
Line 128: leodmægne] ms. leomægne. As Lucas.
Line 471: basnodon] ms. barenodon. As Lucas.
Line 494: Flodweard gesloh] ms. flodwearde sloh. As Lucas.
Line 499: onbugon brimyppinge] ms. on bogum brun yppinge. As Lucas.

Line 502: onfond] ms. on feond. As Lucas.
Line 503: grund] omitted in ms. As Lucas.
Line 505: heorufæðmum] ms. huru fæðmum. As Lucas.
Line 514: eac] omitted in ms.
Line 517: Moyses] ms. Moyse. As Lucas.
Line 538: gehwlyces] ms. gehylces. As Lucas.
Line 540: cymeð] ms. cymð. As Lucas.
Line 556: us on] ms. ufon. As Lucas.
Line 567: fægerne] ms. on fægerne. As Lucas.
Line 570: Lindwigan] omitted in ms. As Lucas.
Line 570: gefegon] ms. gefeon. As Lucas.
Line 574: herge] omitted in ms. As Lucas.
Line 578: golan] ms. galan. As Lucas.
Line 587: sceodon] ms. sceo. As Lucas.

Wulfstan's *Sermo Lupi ad Anglos*

Line 5: spæcan] ms. swæcan
Line 36: getrywða] ms. getryða
Line 38: ne fadode] ms. fadode
Line 76: woroldscame] ms. wolodscame
Line 87: þurh] ms. þur

Apollonius of Tyre

I have followed the section numbering as it appears in Goolden's edition, rather than that of earlier editors.
Rubric: Apollonius] ms. Apolonius
Line 16: twegen] ms. twege
Line 30: æghwanon] ms. æghwano
Lines 36, 42, 46 etc.] Apollonius] ms. apollinius
Line 37: rowan] ms. rowa
Lines 38, 95: Wes] ms. wel
Line 44: vescor] ms. vestor
Line 75: Antiocho] ms. antiochio
Line 119: ende] supplied
Line 121: ceastergewarum] ms. geceasterwarum; mittan] ms. mitta
Line 122: gif] supplied
Line 126: ealdorman] ms. ealdormen
Line 128: gefultumigendum] ms. gefultumigend
Line 133: naman] ms. nama
Line 136: heold] ms. hlod
Line 152: gifð] ms. gif
Line 159: arfæstnesse] ms. fæstnesse
Line 163: Gode] supplied
Line 171: gehyre] ms. gehyran
Line 183: cyng] ms cynge
Line 188: anum] ms. an
Line 198: cynelic] ms. cynelice
Line 215: stille] ms. stilli
Line 229: hearpian] ms heapian
Line 272: plegode] ms. plegod; ungecnawen] ungecnawe

Line 369: unþangc] ms. unþang
Line 386: Pentapolim] ms. Pontaoplim
Line 406: bibliotheca] ms. bibiliotheca

The Peterborough Chronicle

Lines 64–5: and pined heom efter gold and sylver] ms. heom efter gold and sylver and pined heom

The Life of Saint Margaret

Line 132: earmes] ms. carmes
Line 231: cneowgebedum] ms. cweowgebedum

Cambridge, Trinity College B. 14. 32

Poema Morale

Line 19: uvel] ms. juel
Line 24: lipne] ms. lipnie
Line 43: For þer ne þarf] ms. For þarf. Supplied from Lambeth 487.
Line 72: rihtwisnesse] ms. rihtwinesse
Line 108: his] ms. hi
Line 126: is] omitted in ms.
Line 149: he] omitted in ms.

Trinity Homily 33

Line 15: þerone] ms. erone
Line 61: nimende] ms. gevende. Emendation supplied by Morris, *Old English Homilies.*
Line 97: here] ms. ere

Hali Meiðhad

This scribe tends to write ð and d with some degree of interchangeability. I have retained the manuscript reading except in cases where to do so would seriously impair the sense.

Line 2: meið] ms. meiið
Line 4: word] ms. worð
Line 6: lustni] ms. lustin
Line 8: Ha mei . . . seggen] omitted in ms. As emended by Millett.
Line 9: ȝeorne] ms. geone
Line 11: hare] ms. har
Line 13: god] omitted in ms. As emended by Millett.
Line 15: deorewurðe] ms. deorewrðe
Lines 23–4: ha stiheð gasteliche] omitted in ms. As emended by Millett.
Line 28: þe] omitted in ms.

Line 29: al] omitted in ms.
Line 58: ofþunchunges] ms. ofþunchunge
Line 74: aureola] ms. an urle. As emended by Millett.
Line 95: least] ms. beast
Line 96: habbeð] omitted in ms. As supplied by Millett.
Line 104: folheð] ms. foheð
Line 122: þe schal nede] ms. þe ne schal itiden
Line 137: eiðer oþer] ms. eiðer
Line 138: fulitoheschipes] ms. fulitohechipes
Line 176: trusti] ms. trust
Line 179: lah] ms. þah
Line 187: Feahe] ms. Feahi
Line 187: i] ms. ant
Line 194: leaðie þe] ms. leaðie
Line 197: heamen] ms. himen. As emended by Millett.
Line 199: me] omitted in ms.
Line 201: wrenchwile] ms. wrenchfule
Line 207: ti] ms. ant ti

Ancrene Wisse

Line 2: grammaticum] ms. gramaticum
Line 14: suprema] ms. supprema
Line 20: geometrico] ms. geometrio
Line 30: god] ms. goð
Line 38: mot te] ms. moten
Line 64: ȝe] ms. þe
Line 67: descrivet] ms. descriveþ
Line 71: feaderlese] ms. felese
Line 83: Sincletice] ms. Sicleclice
Line 104: spurcitia ms. spursicia
Line 114: wit] ms. hwet
Line 156: hit is, leove] ms. hit leove
Line 167: hefde] omitted in ms.
Line 171: sihðe] ms. sunne
Line 210: ȝef versaili, oðer segge] ms. versaili, segge
Line 226: wrecches] ms. wrecchces
Line 230: prophetes] ms. prophes

Oxford, Bodleian Library, Digby 86

Ubi Sount Qui Ante Nos Fuerount?

Line 33: Neþere] ms. Þere neþere

The Fox and the Wolf

Lines 59, 66, 106, 130, etc.: Ac] ms. At
Line 121: Say] ms. May
Line 199: ifaie] ms. ifare

Dame Siriþ

Line 88: þing] ms. þin
Line 127: lemmon] ms. lenmon
Line 140, 218: þat] ms. þa
Line 142: menis] ms. menig
Line 185, 411: Forþ] ms. For
Line 279: Pepir] ms. Pepis
Line 287: þou] ms. þo
Line 306: nausine] ms. ausine. As emended by Bennett
     and Smithers, *Early Middle English Verse and Prose.*
Line 410: hernde] ms. herde

Love is Sofft

Line 16: sete] ms. wede. As emended by C. Brown, *Eng-*
     lish Lyrics of the Thirteenth Century.
Line 22: gleddede] ms. geddede

Arundel 292: *The Bestiary*

The Whale

Line 28: ðat] ms. ðar
Line 30: deð] ms. ded
Line 47: Tolleð] ms. Colleð

Oxford, Jesus College 29

The *Love-Ron* of Friar Thomas Hales

Line 62, 76: how] ms. hw (ms. reading is correct, but
     emended for ease of reading)
Line 67: Ideyne] ms. Dideyne
Line 86: wurþ] ms. wrþ

The Proverbs of Alfred

Line 15, etc.: How] ms. Hw
Line 18: An] ms. and
Line 32: wurþscipes] ms. wrþscipes
Line 60: wurþie] ms. wrþie
Line 129: iwurche] ms. iwrche
Line 164: lyf] ms. lyves. Emendation suggested by
     Arngart.
Line 168: wurt] ms. wrt
Line 184: wurþe] ms. wrþe
Line 193: maþmes] ms. mayþenes. Emendation suggested
     by Arngart.
Line 280: wod] ms. woþ
Line 335: As cuenes] ms. As scumes. See Arngart, p.
     182, for the convincing argument in favour of this
     emendation.
Line 365: unwurþ] ms. And unwurþ
Line 380: londe] ms. lond le

Line 406: wurþie] ms. wrþie
Line 423: ischote] ms. iscohte
Line 440: wexende] ms. werende. Emendation suggested
     by Arngart.

London, British Library, Cotton Caligula A. ix

Laȝamon's *Brut*

Line 11370: seoððen] ms. seodden
Line 11389: brond] ms. brod
Line 11403: arere] ms. are
Line 11406: oðer] ms. orðer
Line 11416: læð, clæð] ms. læd, clæd
Line 11456: con] ms. ne con
Line 11469, 11482, 11489: Arðure] ms. ardure
Line 11478: Scotlond] ms. Scotland
Line 11482: bute] ms. bute of

The Owl and the Nightingale

Quite often in Cotton Caligula A. ix, the scribe writes *w*
for *wu* or *w* for *wi* (as in *wrþ* for *wurþ*, *wte* for *wite*, for
example). I have emended every relevant instance of
w+consonant to *wu/wi*+consonant. In addition, the
scribe usually places a dot above wynn to distinguish
it from *þ*. On the occasions where the dot has been
omitted, but the graph is clearly meant to be wynn, I
have transcribed it thus.
Line 11: oþeres] ms. oþere
Line 21: Bet] ms. [.]et
Line 25: þo] ms [.]o
Line 29: þe] ms. [.]e
Line 47: Wenst] ms. West
Line 54: wise] ms. wse
Line 62: þe] ms. se
Line 78: miȝt] ms. mist
Line 81: clackest] ms. clackes
Line 86: This line is omitted in Caligula A. ix, and is
     obviously required to complete the couplet. Supplied
     from Jesus 29, as emended by Stanley.
Line 89: fliȝst] ms. fliȝt
Line 115: loþe custe] ms. loþ vviste
Line 116: Seggeþ] ms. Segge
Line 121: alre vurste] ms. alre yrste
Line 134: neste] ms. nest
Line 135: from] ms. fron
Line 144: noþerward] ms. noþervad
Line 149: ȝaf] ms. ȝas
Line 178: unwreste] ms. unwerste
Line 223: schrichest] ms. schirchest
Line 225: þincheþ] ms. þinchest
Line 255: hattest] ms. attest with 'h' added in later hand
Line 280: me] ms. ne

Line 317: bold] ms. blod
Line 340: þat] ms. þa ('t' added)
Line 343: song] ms. songe
Line 405: fliȝst] ms. fliȝste
Line 411: Hule] ms. [.]ule
Line 506: þat] ms. ȝat
Line 548: wurþ] ms. wrht
Line 564: wrecche] ms. wercche
Line 630 and 633: Doþ] ms. [.]oþ
Line 638: þat] ms. [.]at
Line 697: Alvred] ms. Alverid
Line 767: walles] ms. walle
Lines 770–2: ne wurþ . . . wisdom] omitted in ms. Supplied from Jesus 29, as suggested by Stanley.
Line 805: þu] ms. þe
Line 812: fox] ms. for
Line 813: þeȝ] ms. þe. Supplied from Jesus 29.
Line 823: þurȝ] ms. þurs
Line 846: Nu] ms. þu
Line 868: Ich] ms. Ih
Line 920: flohþ] ms. floh
Line 921: suþ] ms. soþ
Line 943: Selde] ms. Sele
Line 955: Hule] ms. þule
Line 970: hexst] ms. herst
Line 978: prost] ms. brost
Line 1011: noþer] ms. noþ
Line 1024: me] ms. me segge
Line 1031: lond] ms. long
Line 1048: biclopt] ms. biclop
Line 1056: grine and] ms. grineþ
Line 1106: dar] ms. dart
Line 1125: swore] ms. spore
Line 1195: anhonge] ms. and honge
Line 1200: astorve] ms. and storve
Line 1221: iwarre] ms. iwarte
Line 1222: ȝarre] ms. ȝarte
Line 1225: er] omitted in ms.
Line 1226: strencþe] ms. strncþe
Line 1254: harm unmylde] omitted in ms. Supplied from Jesus 29, as emended by Stanley.
Line 1279: eavereeuch] ms. eavereeuh
Line 1303: beo] ms. boe
Line 1319: And] ms. An
Line 1320: þe] ms. þer(?)
Line 1322: bihaltst] ms. bihaitest. Emendation as suggested by Stanley.
Line 1336: þurh] ms. þ. Emended from Jesus 29.
Line 1342: awer] ms. awet
Line 1353: Misrempe] ms. Mistempe. Emendation as suggested by Stanley.
Line 1366: For] ms. Eor
Line 1371: an] ms. and
Line 1384: Wunder] ms. Winder
Line 1417: Hwet] ms. Bet. Emended from Jesus 29.

Line 1448: of] ms. os
Line 1449: teache] ms. originally treache
Line 1457: mine] ms. mines
Line 1469: wif mai of me] ms. ȝif mai of of me
Line 1471: sottes] ms. sortes
Line 1475: he] ms. e
Line 1529: ischrud] ms. ischud
Line 1534: hom] ms. heom
Line 1539: Nis] ms. Wis
Line 1562: heom] ms. hire
Line 1567: swiþe] ms. swise
Line 1576: hald his] ms. hlad hif
Line 1592: euch] ms. ek
Line 1635: iherde] ms. ihrde
Line 1642: wroþ] ms. worþ
Line 1694: þingþ] ms. þing. As emended by Stanley.
Line 1697: ȝet] ms. ȝot
Line 1698: Ar Ich] Ms. Ariht. Supplied from Jesus 29.
Line 1718: moreȝeninge] ms. moreȝennge. As emended by Stanley.
Line 1721: þrote] ms. þorte
Line 1725: mankenne] ms. mannenne. As emended by Stanley.
Line 1731: kinge] omitted in both mss. As emended by Stanley.
Line 1748: ȝet] ms. ȝef
Line 1751: nuste] ms. nuȝte
Line 1793: can] ms. chan

Lyrics from Cambridge, Trinity College B. 14. 39

One That Is So Fair and Bright

Line 1: For on] ms. For ou

When the Turf is Thy Tower

Line 6: wunne] ms. wnne

I Sing of One That Is Matchless

Line 4: king] ms. kind
Line 10: loverd] ms. louer
Line 15: hu] ms. þu
Line 20: he] ms. þe

An Orison to Our Lady

Line 9: yef] ms. þef
Line 18: wurd] ms. wrd
Line 34: yaf] ms. þaf
Line 45: yif] ms. þif

The South English Legendary

The Life of Saint Wulfstan

Line 2: he] omitted in ms.
Line 5: þo owre] omitted in ms.
Line 38: dounward] ms. douward
Line 46: Aldred] ms. Alred
Lines 121, 124: me] ms. ine
Line 135: bet] omitted in ms. Given in Ashmole 43.
Line 136: me] omitted in ms. Given in Ashmole 43.
Line 172: vondede] ms. ede
Line 207: wiþinne] ms. iþinne
Line 220: Wircestre] ms. Wicestre

The History and Invention of the True Cross, and the Life of Saint Quiriac

Line 4: tre] omitted in ms.
Line 40: Parais] omitted in ms.
Line 65: of] omitted in ms.
Line 91: aȝen] ms. aȝe
Line 102: Israel] ms Irrael
Line 154: it] omitted in ms.
Line 245: Ich] omitted in ms.
Line 288: of] omitted in ms.
Line 301: me] ms. he
Line 323: strengþe] ms. stregþe
Line 355: hastou] omitted in ms.
Line 356: dede] omitted in ms.
Line 365: of grece and col] ms. of fur and grece. Supplied from Bodleian, Ashmole 43.
Line 377: Þo] ms. So

Cursor Mundi

Line 9890: dere] ms. dede
Line 9914: gret suetnes] emended from ms. suete grennes (haplography?). As in Cotton Vespasian A. iii.
Line 9969: up] ms. us
Line 9974: es] ms. ee
Line 9888: Of] omitted in ms.
Line 10007: has] ms. tas
Line 10072: nedder] ms. moder
Line 10100: wid] ms. we
Line 10107: side] ms. hide
Line 10118: Do] ms. þo

Robert Mannyng of Brunne

Handlyng Synne

Line 4292: þoght] ms. þogh
Line 4302: he] omitted in ms.
Line 4315: nat] omitted in ms.

Line 4319: He ys] ms. He þat ys
Line 4327: reyght] ms. reyghete
Line 4662: Fyrst] ms. Fryst
Line 4669: cunnaunt] ms. cumnaunt
Line 4714: withalle] ms. weylalle
Line 4797: have pay] omitted in ms. Supplied by Furnivall.

The Chronicle

Line 45: togider] ms. toþire
Line 79: here] ms. ere
Line 159: over] ms. oure
Line 193: siþen] ms. sþen
Line 1674: Jhoun] ms. Jȝoun
Line 1682: play] ms. paly
Line 1685: strang] ms. stank
Line 1690: ȝonge] omitted in ms.
Line 1697: þi] ms. þ
Line 1703: if] ms. And
Line 1724: Harald] ms. Halald
Line 1726: þe duke for to geten his riȝt of] ms. þe duke forgeten is he of þing. Emendation supplied from Lambeth ms.
Line 1729: and] ms. omitted
Line 1756: for] ms. for for
Line 1760: we] omitted in ms.
Line 1772: þar] ms. þat

The Land of Cockayne

Line 177: wil] ms. wl

The Auchinleck Manuscript

Sir Orfeo

Line 11: þinges] ms. þingeþ. As Bliss.
Line 57: Bifel] ms. Uifel
Line 140: Y no durst] ms. Y n durst. As Bliss.
Line 219: þo] ms. Lo
Line 388: liggeand] ms. ful liggeand. As Bliss.
Line 406: lef liif] ms. liif liif. As Bliss.
Line 450: aske] ms. alke
Line 521: trompours] ms. trompour

London, British Library, Harley 2253

Spring

Line 11: wynne] ms. wyne
Line 22: doþ] ms. do

King Horn

Line 66: cherches] ms. saraȝyns
Line 550: fyhte ms. fyþte
Line 822: eure] ms. ore
Line 1062: I] ms. ȝe
Line 1230: sclavin] ms. burnie?
Line 1345: Ant hue] ms. Ant
Line 1449: bryhte] ms. brhyte

The *Ayenbite of Inwit*

Line 5: handlinge] ms. hanlinge
Line 13: grauntingge] ms. grauntigge
Line 53: spoushod] ms. spuoshod
Line 55: hire] ms. him. Emendation suggested by
Gradon, p. 131.

Richard Rolle

Ego Dormio

Line 7: þat] ms. at.
Line 10: heven] ms. wham
Line 21: þat] omitted in ms.
Line 22: in] omitted in ms.
Lines 57–8: Alle . . . see] omitted in ms. As emended by
Allen, p. 64.
Line 63: þou] ms. þai
Line 77: his] ms. þi
Line 154: When . . . here] omitted in ms. As emended
by Allen, p. 69.
Line 172: þan fore] ms. þar fore

Kyng Alisaunder

Line 31: riche kyng] ms. rich[.].[.]yng
Line 32: maistres] ms. mais[.]res
Line 115: deþ] ms. de[.]'ed'
Line 217: fayle] ms. fayse. As Smithers.
Line 405: bed] ms. ben
Line 535: bymenyng] ms. bymenyg
Line 607: afongen] ms. afongeþ
Line 631: master] ms. craster

Athelston

Line 6: we] omitted in ms.
Line 12: kyn] ms. kynde
Line 157: knyȝt] ms. kn[. . .]
Line 251: sustyr] ms. [. . . . . .]. As Trounce.
Line 266: playne] ms. playne playne
Line 333: way] ms. w[. . .]

Line 337: hete] ms. h[. . .]
Line 486: lond] ms. [. . . .]
Line 600: hem] ms. hem. As Trounce.
Line 604: ded] ms. d[..]
Line 611: þey] ms. he. As Trounce.
Line 616: hyȝe] ms. þat hyȝe
Line 777: wiþ alle] ms. in dede. Emended by Trounce.

Ywain and Gawain

Line 17: es] omitted in ms. Emendation supplied by
Friedman and Harrington (F&H).
Line 33: bitwene] ms. bitwne
Line 353: thorne] ms. tlorne. As F&H.
Line 436: bitide] ms. bite. As F&H.
Line 575: palfray] ms. palfra

Wynnere and Wastoure

Line 58: hethe] ms. hate. Emendation supplied by Trigg
et al.
Line 64: ther; heu] ms. thre, he. As emended by Trigg.
Line 83: knyghte] ms. kynge
Line 91: as] ms. was
Line 94: gerede full riche] ms. girde in the myddes. As
emended by Trigg.
Line 121: caughte] ms. caughten. Trigg emends to *brayde*,
'seize' or 'reach for'.
Line 127: ne] ms. no
Line 144: bulles] ms. bibulles
Line 157: galegs] ms. galeys. As emended by Trigg.
Line 164: balle] ms. balke or bawe.
Lines 176, 186: Convincingly argued by Trigg to be
transposed in the manuscript.
Line 177: ordire. Trigg and others emend to *ledis*, be-
cause of alliteration, and the plural verb 'loven'. How-
ever, *ordire* has been retained here as semantically
acceptable, and is understood as a collective noun gov-
erning a plural verb.
Line 190: merkes] ms. merke. As emended by Trigg.
Line 201: wye] ms. wyes
Line 236: wounder] ms. wounder one
Line 270: rychely] ms. ryhely
Line 300: Owthir] ms. It
Line 314: bonets] ms. howes. As emended by Trigg.
Line 336: charbinade] ms. charbiande. Emendation sup-
plied by Trigg.
Line 353: Caudils] ms. [. . .]ils
Line 354: Dariols and] This is the emendation supplied
by Trigg et al. However, the manuscript appears to
read [. . .]cilost, a corrupt superlative form, perhaps?
The Middle English superlative tends to be –*est* not –
ost, so this reading remains unclear.

Line 355: Mawmene] ms. [. . .]mene

Line 356: Iche] ms. [. . .]e

Line 357: sothe] ms. sother

Line 358: Me tenyth] ms. [. . .]enyth

Line 359: Þat iche] ms. [. . .]he

Line 364: ones] ms. one

Line 390: moste] ms. moþe

Line 395: Lesse] ms. Lesse and

Line 411: syde] ms. elde. Emended by Trigg et al.

Line 420: wedes] ms. wordes

Line 434: see] ms. fee

Line 445: tast no] ms. tast

Line 454: hert] omitted in ms. Supplied by Trigg et al.

Line 471: to holde] omitted in ms. Supplied by Trigg.

Line 473: þer untill] only partially visible in ms.

Line 476: potent] ms. potet (with a missing abbreviation mark for potent?). Most editors choose to emend ms. *potet* to a variety of other readings. The reading 'potent' has been suggested before by L. M. Rosenfield, 'Wynnere and Wastoure: A Critical Edition' (PhD, Columbia, 1975), cited by Trigg, p. 46.

Line 485: sprede] supplied by Trigg et al. from ms. spr . . .

Line 502: kayre] ms. layren. As emended by Trigg.

Select Bibliography

Language

Baugh, A. C., and T. Cable, *A History of the English Language*, 3rd edn (London, 1978)

Burrow, J. A., and T. Turville-Petre, eds, *A Book of Middle English* (Oxford, 1992)

Cambridge History of the English Language: Volume 1, The Beginnings to 1066, ed. R. M. Hogg; *Volume 2, 1066–1476*, ed. N. F. Blake (Cambridge, 1992)

Campbell, A., *Old English Grammar* (Oxford, 1959; repr. 1997)

Laing, M., *A Catalogue of Sources for a Linguistic Atlas of Early Middle English* (Cambridge, 1993)

Lass, R., *Old English: A Historical Linguistic Companion* (Cambridge, 1994)

Lester, G. A., *The Language of Old and Middle English Poetry* (London, 1996)

McIntosh, A., M. L. Samuels and M. Benskin, *A Linguistic Atlas of Late Medieval English*, 4 vols (Aberdeen, 1986)

Mitchell, B., *Old English Syntax*, 2 vols (Oxford, 1985)

Mitchell, B., and F. C. Robinson, eds, *A Guide to Old English*, 5th edn (Oxford, 1995)

Mossé, F., ed., *A Handbook of Middle English*, trans. J. A. Walker (Baltimore, 1952)

Quirk, R., and C. L. Wrenn, *An Old English Grammar*, 2nd edn (London, 1957; repr. 1989)

Scragg, D. G., *A History of English Spelling* (Manchester, 1974)

Wilson, R. M., 'English and French in England 1100–1300', *History* 28 (1943), 37–60

General

Amt, E., ed., *Women's Lives in Medieval Europe* (London, 1993)

Barnes, G., *Counsel and Strategy in Middle English Romance* (Cambridge, 1993)

Barron, W. R. J., *English Medieval Romance* (London, 1987)

Bennett, J. A. W., *Middle English Literature*, ed. and comp. D. Gray (Oxford, 1986; repr. 1990)

Bennett, J. A. W., and G. V. Smithers, eds, *Early Middle English Verse and Prose*, with a glossary by N. Davis, 2nd edn (Oxford, 1968; repr. 1982)

Blamires, A., ed., *Woman Defamed and Woman Defended: An Anthology of Medieval Texts* (Oxford, 1992)

Carruthers, L., ed., *Heroes and Heroines in Medieval English Literature: A Festschrift Presented to André Crepin on the Occasion of his Sixty-Fifth Birthday* (Cambridge, 1994)

Clark Hall, J. R., *A Concise Anglo-Saxon Dictionary*, supp. H. D. Meritt, 4th edn (Toronto, 1960)

Clemoes, P., *Interactions of Thought and Language in Old English*, Cambridge Studies in Anglo-Saxon England 12 (Cambridge, 1995)

Damico H., and J. Leyerle, eds, *Heroic Poetry in the Anglo-Saxon Period: Studies in Honor of Jess B. Bessinger, Jr.* (Kalamazoo, 1993)

Evans, M. J., *Rereading Middle English Romance: Manuscript Layout, Decoration, and the Rhetoric of Composite Structure* (Montreal, 1995)

Fellows, J., R. Field, G. Rogers and J. Weiss, *Romance Reading on the Book: Essays on Medieval Narrative Presented to Maldwyn Mills* (Cardiff, 1996)

Godden, M., and M. Lapidge, eds, *The Cambridge Companion to Old English Literature* (Cambridge, 1991)

Godden, M., D. Gray and T. Hoad, eds, *From Anglo-Saxon to Early Middle English: Studies Presented to E. G. Stanley* (Oxford, 1994)

Gransden, A., *Historical Writing in England, c.550–1307* (Ithaca, NY, 1974)

Hartung, A. E., ed., *A Manual of Writings in Middle English, 1050–1500* (New Haven, CT, 1986)

Harwood, B. J., and G. R. Overing, eds, *Class and Gender in Early English Literature: Intersections* (Bloomington, IN, 1994)

Korhammer, M., et al., eds, *Words, Texts and Manuscripts: Studies in Anglo-Saxon Culture, Presented to Helmut Gneuss on the Occasion of his Sixty-Fifth Birthday* (Cambridge, 1992)

Kurath, H. and S. M. Kuhn et al., eds, *The Middle English Dictionary* (Ann Arbor, 1956–).

Lapidge, M., and H. Gneuss, eds, *Learning and Literature in Anglo-Saxon England: Studies Presented to Peter Clemoes* (Cambridge, 1985)

Lapidge, M., J. Blair, S. Keynes and D. Scragg, eds, *The Blackwell Encyclopaedia of Anglo-Saxon England* (Oxford, 1998)

Legge, M. D., *Anglo-Norman Literature and its Background* (Oxford, 1963)

Magennis, H., *Images of Community in Old English Poetry*. Cambridge Studies in Anglo-Saxon England 18 (Cambridge, 1996)

Meale, C., ed., *Readings in Medieval English Romance* (Cambridge, 1994)

Meale, C., ed., *Women and Literature in Britain, 1150–1500* (Cambridge, 1996)

Mehl, D., *The Middle English Romances of the Thirteenth and Fourteenth Centuries* (London, 1969)

O'Brien O'Keeffe, K., ed., *Old English Shorter Poems: Basic Readings* (New York, 1994)

O'Brien O'Keeffe, K., ed., *Reading Old English Texts* (Cambridge, 1997)

O'Brien O'Keeffe, K., *Visible Song: Transitional Literacy in Old English Verse*, Cambridge Studies in Anglo-Saxon England 4 (Cambridge, 1992)

Owst, G. R., *Literature and Pulpit in Medieval England*, 2nd edn (Oxford, 1961)

Parsons, D., ed., *Tenth-Century Studies: Essays in Commemoration of the Millennium of the Council of Winchester and 'Regularis Concordia'* (London, 1973)

Pearsall, D., *Old English and Middle English Poetry*, Routledge History of English Poetry I (London, 1977)

Pulsiano, P., and E. M. Treharne, eds, *Anglo-Saxon Manuscripts and their Heritage* (Aldershot, 1998)

Richards, M. P., ed., *Anglo-Saxon Manuscripts: Basic Readings* (New York, 1994)

Roberts, J., et al., eds, *Alfred the Wise: Studies in Honour of Janet Bately on the Occasion of her Sixty-Fifth Birthday* (Cambridge, 1997)

Robinson, F. R., *The Editing of Old English* (Oxford, 1994)

Scragg, D. G., and P. E. Szarmach, eds, *The Editing of Old English: Papers from the 1990 Manchester Conference* (Cambridge, 1994)

Spearing, A. C., *Readings in Middle English Poetry* (Cambridge, 1987)

Spencer, H. L., *English Preaching in the Late Middle Ages* (Cambridge, 1993)

Stanley, E. G., *Continuations and Beginnings: Studies in Old English Literature* (London, 1966)

Szarmach, P. E., ed., *The Garland Medieval Encyclopedia* (New York, 1998)

Szarmach, P. E., and J. T. Rosenthal, eds, *The Preservation and Transmission of Anglo-Saxon Culture* (Kalamazoo, 1997)

Trigg, S., ed., *Medieval English Poetry* (London, 1993)

Wells, J. E., *A Manual of the Writings in Middle English, 1050–1400, with First, Second and Third Supplements* (New Haven, CT, 1926)

Whitelock, D., rev., *Sweet's Anglo-Saxon Reader in Prose and Verse*, 15th edn (Oxford, 1983)

Cædmon

Abbott Conway, C., 'Structure and Idea in Cædmon's Hymn', *Neuphilologische Mitteilungen* 96 (1995), 39–50

Colgrave, B., and R. A. B. Mynors, eds, *Bede's Ecclesiastical History of the English People*, Oxford Medieval Texts (Oxford, 1969)

Robinson, F. C., 'The Accentuation of *Nu* in *Cædmon's Hymn*', in *Heroic Poetry in the Anglo-Saxon Period: Studies in Honor of Jess B. Bessinger, Jr.*, eds, H. Damico and J. Leyerle (Kalamazoo, 1993), pp. 115–20

Alfred

Bately, J., 'Old English Prose Before and During the Reign of Alfred', *Anglo-Saxon England* 17 (1988), 93–138

Colgrave, B., and R. A. B. Mynors, eds, *Bede's Ecclesiastical History of the English People*, Oxford Medieval Texts (Oxford, 1969)

Keynes, S., and M. Lapidge, eds, *Alfred the Great: Asser's Life of King Alfred and Other Contemporary Sources* (London, 1983)

Powell, T. E., 'The "Three Orders" of Society in Anglo-Saxon England', *ASE* 23 (1994), 103–32

Sedgefield, W. J., ed., *King Alfred's Old English Version of Boethius, De Consolatione Philosophiae* (Oxford, 1899)

Wittig, J. S., 'King Alfred's Boethius and its Latin Sources: A Reconsideration', *ASE* 11 (1983), 157–98

The Anglo-Saxon Chronicle

Bately, J., *The Anglo-Saxon Chronicle: Texts and Textual Relationships* (Reading, 1991)

Bately, J., ed., *MS A. The Anglo-Saxon Chronicle: A Collaborative Edition* 3 (Cambridge, 1986)

Campbell, A., ed., *The Battle of Brunanburh* (London, 1938)

Dumville, D. N., *Wessex and England from Alfred to Edgar: Six Essays on Political, Cultural and Ecclesiastical Revival* (Cambridge, 1992)

Parkes, M. B., 'The Palaeography of the Parker Manuscript of the Chronicle, Laws and Sedulius, and Historiography at Winchester in the Late Ninth and Tenth Centuries', *Anglo-Saxon England* 5 (1976), 149–71

Plummer, C., ed., *Two of the Saxon Chronicles Parallel*, rev. J. Earle, 2 vols (Oxford, 1892–9)

Swanton, M., trans. and ed., *The Anglo-Saxon Chronicle* (London, 1996)

The Exeter Book

Chambers, R. W., ed. (Facsimile) *The Exeter Book of Old English Poetry* (London, 1933)

Fell, C., 'Perceptions of Transience', in *The Cambridge Companion to Old English Literature*, eds M. Godden and M. Lapidge (Cambridge, 1991), pp. 172–89

Klinck, A., ed., *The Old English Elegies: A Critical Edition and Genre Study* (London, 1992)

Muir, B., *The Exeter Book Anthology of Old English Poetry: An Edition of Exeter, Dean and Chapter MS 3501*, 2 vols (Exeter, 1994)

Pope, J. C., 'Palaeography and Poetry: Some Solved and Unsolved Problems of the Exeter Book', in *Medieval Scribes, Manuscripts and Libraries: Essays Presented to N. R. Ker*, eds M. B. Parkes and A. G. Watson (London, 1978), pp. 25–65

Advent Lyrics

Burlin, R. B., *The Old English Advent: A Typological Commentary* (New Haven, CT, 1968)

The Wanderer

Harbus, A., 'Deceptive Dreams in *The Wanderer*', *Studies in Philology* 93 (1996), 164–79

Galloway, A., 'Dream Theory in *The Dream of the Rood* and *The Wanderer*', *Review of English Studies* 45 (1994), 475–85

Leslie, R. F., ed., *The Wanderer* (Exeter, 1966; repr. 1985)

The Seafarer

Gordon, I. L., ed., *The Seafarer* (London, 1960)

Greenfield, S. B., 'Sylf, Seasons and Structure in *The Seafarer*', *Anglo-Saxon England* 9 (1981), 199–211

The Physiologus: The Whale

Squires, A., ed., *The Old English Physiologus* (Durham, 1988)

Deor

Hill, J. ed., *Old English Minor Heroic Poems* (Durham, 1983; rev. edn, 1994)

Malone, K., ed., *Deor* (London, 1933; rev. edn Exeter, 1977)

Wulf and Eadwacer

Aertsen, H., '*Wulf and Eadwacer*: A Woman's Cri de Coeur – For Whom? For What?', in *Companion to Old English Poetry*, eds H. Aertsen and R. H. Bremmer (Amsterdam, 1994), pp. 119–44

Baker, P. S., 'The Ambiguity of *Wulf and Eadwacer*', in *Old English Shorter Poems: Basic Readings*, ed. K. O'Brien O'Keeffe (New York, 1994), pp. 393–407

Belanoff, P., 'Women's Songs, Women's Language: *Wulf and Eadwacer* and *The Wife's Lament*' in *New Readings on Women in Old English Literature*, eds H. Damico and A. Hennessey Olsen (Bloomington, IN, 1990), pp. 193–203

Riddles

Irving, E. B., Jr, 'Heroic Experience in the Old English Riddles', in *Old English Shorter Poems: Basic Readings*, ed. K. O'Brien O'Keeffe (New York, 1994), pp. 199–212

Tigges, W., 'Snakes and Ladders: Ambiguity and Coherence in the Exeter Book Riddles and Maxims', in *Companion to Old English Poetry*, eds H. Aertsen and R. H. Bremmer (Amsterdam, 1994), pp. 95–118

Tupper, F., ed., *The Riddles of the Exeter Book* (Darmstadt, 1968)

The Wife's Lament

Horner, S., 'En/Closed Subjects: *The Wife's Lament* and the Culture of Early Medieval Monasticism', *Æstel* 2 (1994), 45–61

Leslie, R. F., ed., *Three Old English Elegies* (Manchester, 1961; repr. 1966)

Strauss, B. R., 'Women's Words as Weapons: Speech as Action in *The Wife's Lament*', in *Old English Shorter Poems: Basic Readings*, ed. K. O'Brien O'Keeffe (New York, 1994), pp. 335–56

Wentersdorf, K. P., 'The Situation of the Narrator in the Old English *Wife's Lament*', in *Old English Shorter Poems: Basic Readings*, ed. K. O'Brien O'Keeffe (New York, 1994), pp. 357–92

The Husband's Message

Leslie, R. F., ed., *Three Old English Elegies* (Manchester, 1961; repr. 1966)

Orton, P., 'The Speaker in *The Husband's Message*', *Leeds*

Studies in English (1981), 43–56

The Ruin

Leslie, R. F., ed., *Three Old English Elegies* (Manchester, 1961; repr. 1966)

Wentersdorf, K., 'Observations on *The Ruin*', *Medium Ævum* 46 (1977), 171–80

Vercelli Book

The Fates of the Apostles

Bjork, R. E., ed., *Cynewulf: Basic Readings*, Basic Readings in Anglo-Saxon England 4 (New York, 1996)

Brooks, K. R., ed., *Andreas and The Fates of the Apostles* (Oxford, 1961)

Rice, R. C., 'The Penitential Motif in Cynewulf's *Fates of the Apostles* and in his Epilogues', *Anglo-Saxon England* 6 (1977), 105–20.

Warwick Frese, D., 'The Art of Cynewulf's Signatures', repr. in *Cynewulf: Basic Readings*, ed. R. E. Bjork, Basic Readings in Anglo-Saxon England 4 (New York, 1996), pp. 323–45.

Woolf, R., ed., *Cynewulf's Juliana*, 2nd edn (Exeter, 1993)

The Vercelli Homilies

Scragg, D. G., 'An Old English Homilist of Archbishop Dunstan's Day', in *Words, Texts and Manuscripts: Studies in Anglo-Saxon Culture, Presented to Helmut Gneuss on the Occasion of his Sixty-Fifth Birthday*, eds M. Korhammer, K. Reichl and H. Sauer (Cambridge, 1992)

Scragg, D. G., ed., *The Vercelli Homilies and Related Texts*, EETS o.s. 300 (London, 1992)

Sisam, C., intro., *The Vercelli Book: A Late Tenth-Century Manuscript Containing Prose and Verse, Vercelli Biblioteca Capitolare CXVIII*, EEMF 19 (Copenhagen, 1976)

Wright, C. D., *The Irish Tradition in Old English Literature*, Cambridge Studies in Anglo-Saxon England 6 (Cambridge, 1993)

The Dream of the Rood

Irvine, M., 'Anglo-Saxon Literary Theory Exemplified in Old English Poems: Interpreting the Cross in *The Dream of the Rood* and *Elene*', in *Old English Shorter Poems: Basic Readings*, ed. K. O'Brien O'Keeffe (New York, 1994), pp. 31–63

Jennings, M., '*Rood* and Ruthwell: The Power of Paradox', *English Language Notes* 31 (1994), 6–12

Swanton, M., ed., *The Dream of the Rood* (Manchester, 1970)

Ælfric

Clark, C., 'Ælfric and Abbo', *English Studies* 49 (1968), 30–6

Clayton, M., 'Homiliaries and Preaching in Anglo-Saxon England', *Peritia* 4 (1985), 207–42

Clemoes, P., ed., *Ælfric's Catholic Homilies: The First Series*, EETS s.s. 17 (Oxford, 1997)

Clemoes, P., 'The Chronology of Ælfric's Works', in *The Anglo-Saxons: Studies in Some Aspects of their History and Culture presented to Bruce Dickins*, ed. P. A. M. Clemoes (London, 1959), pp. 212–47

Eliason, N. E., and P. Clemoes, eds, *Ælfric's First Series of Catholic Homilies: British Museum Royal 7 C. xii*, EEMF 13 (Copenhagen, 1966)

Gatch, M. McC., *Preaching and Theology in Anglo-Saxon England: Ælfric and Wulfstan* (Toronto, 1977)

Godden, M., ed., *Ælfric's Catholic Homilies: The Second Series; Text*, EETS s.s. 5 (London, 1979)

Godden, M., 'Ælfric's Saints' Lives and the Problem of Miracles', *Leeds Studies in English* n.s. 16 (1985), 83–100

Grundy, L., *Books and Grace: Ælfric's Theology*, King's College London Medieval Studies 6 (London, 1991)

Hill, J., 'Ælfric and Smaragdus', *Anglo-Saxon England* 21 (1992), 203–37

Hill, J., 'The Dissemination of Ælfric's *Lives of Saints*: A Preliminary Study', in *Holy Men and Holy Women: Old English Prose Saints' Lives and Their Contexts*, ed. P. E. Szarmach (Albany, NY, 1996), pp. 235–59

Marsden, R., 'Ælfric as Translator: The Old English Prose *Genesis*', *Anglia* 109 (1991), 319–58

Nichols, A. E., 'Ælfric's Prefaces: Rhetoric and Genre', *English Studies* 49 (1968), 215–23

Pope, J. C., ed., *Homilies of Ælfric: A Supplementary Collection*, EETS o.s. 259–60 (London, 1967–8)

Skeat, W. W., ed., *Ælfric's Lives of Saints*, EETS o.s. 76, 82, 94, 114 (London, 1889–1900; repr. as 2 vols, 1966)

Szarmach, P. E., eds, *Holy Men and Holy Women: Old English Prose Saints' Lives and their Contexts* (Albany, NY, 1996)

Szarmach, P. E., and B. F. Huppé, eds, *The Old English Homily and its Background* (Albany, NY, 1978)

Wilcox, J., ed., *Ælfric's Prefaces*, Durham Medieval Texts 9 (Durham, 1994)

Zettel, P. H., 'Saints' Lives in Old English: Latin Manuscripts and Vernacular Accounts: Ælfric', *Peritia* 1 (1982), 17–37

The Battle of Maldon

Blake, N., 'The Genesis of *The Battle of Maldon*', *Anglo-Saxon England* 7 (1978), 119–29.

Gneuss, H., '*The Battle of Maldon* 89b: Byrhtnoth's *ofermod*

Once Again', in *Old English Shorter Poems: Basic Readings*, ed. K. O'Brien O'Keeffe (New York, 1994), pp. 149–72

Richards, M. P., '*The Battle of Maldon* in its Manuscript Context', in *Old English Shorter Poems: Basic Readings*, ed. K. O'Brien O'Keeffe (New York, 1994), pp. 173–84

Scragg, D. G., ed., *The Battle of Maldon* (Manchester, 1981)

Scragg, D. G., ed., *The Battle of Maldon* AD 991 (Oxford, 1991)

The *Beowulf*-Manuscript and *Beowulf*

Baker, P. S., ed., *Beowulf: Basic Readings* (New York, 1995)

Bjork, R. E., 'Speech as Gift in *Beowulf*', *Speculum* 69 (1994), 993–1022

Bruce-Mitford, R., *The Sutton Hoo Ship Burial: A Handbook* , 3rd edn (London, 1979)

Clark Hall, J. R., *Beowulf and the Fight at Finnsburg*, rev. edn by C. L. Wrenn (London, 1940)

Chase, C., ed., *The Dating of Beowulf* (Toronto, 1981)

Dean, P., '*Beowulf* and the Passing of Time: Part I', 'Part II', *English Studies* 75 (1994), 193–209, 293–302

Dumville, D. N., 'Beowulf Come Lately: Some Notes on the Palaeography of the Nowell Codex', *Archiv* 225 (1988), 49–63

Earl, J. W., *Thinking about Beowulf* (Stanford, 1994)

Fulk, R., D., ed., *Interpretations of Beowulf* (Bloomington, IN, 1991)

Griffith, M. S., 'Some Difficulties in *Beowulf*, lines 874–902: Sigemund Reconsidered', *Anglo-Saxon England* 24 (1995), 11–41

Hasenfrantz, R. J., *Beowulf Scholarship: An Annotated Bibliography, 1979–1990* (New York, 1993)

Hill, J. M., *The Cultural World of Beowulf* (Philadelphia, 1995)

Hill, J., '"Þæt wæs geomuru ides!": A Female Stereotype Examined', in *New Readings on Women in Old English Literature*, eds H. Damico and A. Hennessy Olsen (Bloomington, IN, 1990), pp. 235–47

Irving, E. B., *Rereading Beowulf* (Philadelphia, 1989)

Jack, G., ed., *Beowulf: A Student Edition* (Oxford, 1995)

Kiernan, K. S., *Beowulf and the Beowulf Manuscript*, 2nd edn (London, 1996)

Klaeber, F., *Beowulf and the Fight at Finnsburg*, 3rd edn (Boston, 1950)

Lapidge, M., '*Beowulf* and the Psychology of Terror', in *Heroic Poetry in the Anglo-Saxon Period: Studies in Honor of Jess B. Bessinger, Jr.*, eds H. Damico and J. Leyerle (Kalamazoo, 1993), pp. 373–402

Malone, K., ed., *The Nowell Codex*, EEMF 12 (Copenhagen, 1963)

Mitchell, B., ' "Until the Dragon Comes . . . ": Some

Thoughts on *Beowulf*', *Neophilologus* 47 (1963), 126–38; repr. in *On Old English*, B. Mitchell (Oxford, 1988), pp. 3–15

Mitchell, B., and F. C. Robinson, eds, *Beowulf: An Edition* (Oxford, 1998)

Newton, S., *The Origins of Beowulf and the Pre-Viking Kingdom of East Anglia* (Cambridge, 1993)

Nicholson, L. E., ed., *An Anthology of Beowulf Criticism* (Notre Dame, IN, 1963)

Robinson, F. R., *The Tomb of Beowulf* (Oxford, 1993)

Stanley, E. G., *In the Foreground: Beowulf* (Cambridge, 1994)

Tolkien, J. R. R., '*Beowulf*: The Monsters and the Critics', *Proceedings of the British Academy* 22 (1936), 245–9

Zupitza J., *Beowulf Reproduced in Facsimile*, with an introductory note by N. Davis, EETS o.s. 245, 2nd ed. (London, 1959)

Judith

Belanoff, P., 'Judith: Sacred and Secular Heroine', in *Heroic Poetry in the Anglo-Saxon Period: Studies in Honor of Jess B. Bessinger, Jr.*, eds H. Damico and J. Leyerle (Kalamazoo, 1993), pp. 247–64

Chamberlain, D., '*Judith*: A Fragmentary and Political Poem', in *Anglo-Saxon Poetry: Essays in Appreciation for John C. McGalliard*, eds L. E. Nicholson and D. Warwick Frese (Bloomington, IN, 1975), pp. 135–59

De Lacy, P., 'Aspects of Christianisation and Cultural Adaptation in the Old English *Judith*', *Neuphilologische Mitteilungen* 97 (1996), 393–410

Lucas, P. J., 'The Place of *Judith* in the *Beowulf*-manuscript', *Review of English Studies* 41 (1990), 463–78

Magennis, H., 'Contrasting Narrative Emphases in the Old English Poem *Judith* and Ælfric's Paraphrase of the Book of Judith', *Neuphilologische Mitteilungen* 96 (1995), 61–6

Raffel, B., '*Judith*: Hypermetricity and Rhetoric', in *Anglo-Saxon Poetry: Essays in Appreciation for John C. McGalliard*, eds L. E. Nicholson and D. Warwick Frese (Bloomington, IN, 1975), pp. 124–34

Timmer, B. J., ed., *Judith* (London, 1952; repr. 1966)

Exodus

Cross, J. E., and S. I. Tucker, 'Allegorical Tradition and the Old English *Exodus*', *Neuphilologische Mitteilungen* 44 (1960), 122–7

Earl, J. W., 'Christian Tradition in the Old English *Exodus*', *Neuphilologische Mitteilungen* 71 (1970), 541–70

Farrell, R. T., 'A Reading of the Old English *Exodus*', *Review of English Studies* n.s. 20 (1969), 401–17

Gollancz, ed., *The 'Cædmon Manuscript' of Anglo-Saxon Biblical Poetry* (London, 1927)

Hall, J. R., 'The Old English Epic of Redemption: The Theological Unity of MS Junius 11', *Traditio* 32 (1976), 185–208

Helder, W., 'Abraham and the Old English *Exodus*', in *Companion to Old English Poetry*, eds H. Aertsen and R. H. Bremmer (Amsterdam, 1994), pp. 189–200

Irving, E. B., Jr., ed., *The Old English Exodus* (New Haven, CT, 1953; repr. Hamden, CT, 1970)

Kruger, S. F., 'Oppositions and their Operation in the Old English *Exodus*', *Neuphilologische Mitteilungen* 78 (1994), 165–70

Lucas, P. J., ed., *Exodus*, Exeter Medieval English Texts and Studies (Exeter, 1977; rev. edn 1994)

Marsden, R., 'The Death of the Messenger: The 'spelboda' in the Old English *Exodus*', *Bulletin of the John Rylands University Library of Manchester* 77.iii (1995), 141–64

Marsden, R., *The Text of the Old Testament in Anglo-Saxon England*, Cambridge Studies in Anglo-Saxon England 15 (Cambridge, 1995)

Remley, P., *Old English Biblical Verse: Studies in 'Genesis', 'Exodus', and 'Daniel'*, Cambridge Studies in Anglo-Saxon England 16 (Cambridge, 1996)

Wulfstan

Bethurum, D., ed., *The Homilies of Wulfstan* (Oxford, 1957)

Gatch, M. McC., *Preaching and Theology in Anglo-Saxon England: Ælfric and Wulfstan* (Toronto, 1977)

Loyn, H. R., *A Wulfstan Manuscript*, EEMF 17 (Copenhagen, 1971)

Orchard, A., 'Crying Wolf: Oral Style and the *Sermones Lupi*', *Anglo-Saxon England* 21 (1992), 239–64

Whitelock, D., ed., *Sermo Lupi ad Anglos*, 3rd edn (London, 1963; repr. Exeter, 1976)

Wilcox, J., 'The Dissemination of Wulfstan's Homilies: The Wulfstan Tradition in Eleventh-Century Vernacular Preaching', in *England in the Eleventh Century*, ed. C. Hicks, Harlaxton Medieval Studies 2 (Stamford, 1992), pp. 1–18.

Apollonius of Tyre

Archibald, E., *Apollonius of Tyre: Medieval and Renaissance Themes and Variations* (Cambridge, 1991)

Goolden, P., ed., *The Old English 'Apollonius of Tyre'* (Oxford, 1958)

Riedinger, A., 'The Englishing of Arcestrate: Woman in *Apollonius of Tyre*', in *New Readings on Women in Old English Literature*, eds H. Damico and A. Hennessey Olsen (Bloomington, IN, 1990), pp. 292–306

The Peterborough Chronicle

See *The Anglo-Saxon Chronicle*.

The Life of Saint Margaret

Clayton, M., and H. Magennis, eds, *The Old English Lives of St Margaret*, Cambridge Studies in Anglo-Saxon England 9 (Cambridge, 1994)

Magennis, H., '"Listen Now All and Understand": Adaptation of Hagiographical Material for Vernacular Audiences in the Old English Lives of St Margaret', *Speculum* 71 (1996), 27–42

Millett B., and J. Wogan-Browne, eds, *Medieval English Prose for Women: Selections from the Katherine Group and Ancrene Wisse* (Oxford, 1990; rev. edn 1992)

Price, J., 'The Virgin and the Dragon: The Demonology of *Seinte Marherete*', *Leeds Studies in English* 16 (1985), 337–57

Treharne, E. M., 'The Sensibility of the Virtuous and the Old English Life of St Margaret', *Publications of the Medieval and Renaissance Conference* 15 (1992), 195–216

The Hymns of Saint Godric

Rankin, J. W., 'The Hymns of St Godric', *Publications of the Modern Language Association* 38 (1923), 699–711

Zupitza, J., 'Cantus Beati Godrici', *Englische Studien* 11 (1887), 401–32

The Orrmulum

Morrison, S., 'Sources for the *Orrmulum*', *Neuphilologische Mitteilungen* 84 (1983), 410–36

Parkes, M. B., 'On the Presumed Date and Possible Origins of the *Orrmulum*: Oxford, Bodleian Library, MS Junius 1', in *Scribes, Scripts and Readers: Studies in the Communication, Presentation and Dissemination of Medieval Texts*, M. B. Parkes (London, 1991), pp. 187–200

White, R. M., ed., The *Orrmulum*, 2 vols (Oxford, 1852)

Poema Morale

Hill, B., 'The Twelfth-Century *Conduct of Life*, formerly the *Poema Morale* or *A Moral Ode*', *Leeds Studies in English* 9 (1977), 97–144

Laing, M., 'A Linguistic Atlas of Early Middle English: The Value of Texts Surviving in More than One Version', in *History of Englishes: New Methods and Interpretations in Historical Linguistics*, eds M. Rissanen, et al. Topics in English Linguistics 10 (Berlin, 1992), pp.

566–81

Morris, R., ed., *Old English Homilies of the Twelfth Century*, EETS o.s. 53 (Oxford, 1873)

Trinity Homily 33

Laing, M., 'Anchor Texts and Literary Manuscripts in Early Middle English', in *Regionalism in Late Medieval Manuscripts and Texts: Essays Celebrating the Publication of 'A Linguistic Atlas of Late Mediaeval English'*, ed. F. Riddy (Cambridge, 1991), pp. 27–52

Laing, M., and A. McIntosh, 'Cambridge, Trinity College, MS 335: Its Texts and their Transmission', in *New Science out of Old Books: Studies in Manuscripts and Early Printed Books in Honour of A. I. Doyle*, eds R. Beadle and A. J. Piper (Aldershot, 1995), pp. 14–47

Morris, R., ed., *Old English Homilies of the Twelfth Century*, EETS o.s. 53 (Oxford, 1873)

Hali Meiðhad and *Ancrene Wisse*

Barratt, A., 'The Five Wits and their Structural Significance in Part II of *Ancrene Wisse*', *Medium Ævum* 56 (1987), 12–24

Bately, J., 'On Some Aspects of the Vocabulary of the West Midlands in the Early Middle Ages: The Language of the Katherine Group', in *Medieval English Studies Presented to George Kane*, eds E. D. Kennedy, R. Waldron and J. S. Wittig (Cambridge, 1988), pp. 55–77

Fletcher, A. J., 'Black, White and Grey in *Hali Meiðhad* and *Ancrene Wisse*', *Medium Ævum* 62 (1993), 69–78

Innes-Parker, C., 'The Lady and the King: *Ancrene Wisse*'s Parable of the Royal Wooing Re-examined', *English Studies* 75 (1994), 509–22

Ker, N. R., ed., *Facsimile of Bodley 34*, EETS o.s. 247 (London, 1960)

Millett, B., *Annotated Bibliographies of Old and Middle English Literature II: Ancrene Wisse, the Katherine Group, and the Wooing Group* (Cambridge, 1996)

Millett, B., ed., *Hali Meiðhad*, EETS o.s. 284 (London, 1982)

Millett, B., 'The Origins of *Ancrene Wisse*: New Answers, New Questions', *Medium Ævum* 61 (1992), 206–28

Millett B., and J. Wogan-Browne, eds, *Medieval English Prose for Women: Selections from the Katherine Group and Ancrene Wisse* (Oxford, 1990; rev. edn 1992).

Robertson, E., *Early English Devotional Prose and the Female Audience* (Knoxville, 1990)

Potts, J., L. Stevenson and J. Wogan-Browne, eds, *Concordance to Ancrene Wisse: MS Corpus Christi College, Cambridge 402* (Cambridge, 1993)

Shepherd, G., ed., *Ancrene Wisse* (London, 1959)

Tolkien, J. R. R., '*Ancrene Wisse* and *Hali Meiðhad*', *Essays and Studies* 14 (1929), 104–26

White, H., trans., *Rule for Anchoresses*, Penguin Classics (London, 1993)

Wogan-Browne, J., 'The Virgin's Tale', in *Feminist Readings in Middle English Literature: The Wife of Bath and all her Sect*, eds R. Evans and L. Johnson (London, 1994), pp. 165–94

Oxford Bodleian Library, Digby 86

Brown, C., ed., *English Lyrics of the Thirteenth Century* (Oxford, 1932; repr. 1971)

Tschann, J., and M. B. Parkes, intro., *Facsimile of Oxford, Bodleian Library, MS Digby 86*, EETS s.s. 16 (Oxford, 1996)

The Fox and the Wolf

Bercovitch, S., 'Clerical Satire in *Þe Vox and þe Wolf*', *Journal of English and Germanic Philology* 65 (1966), 287–94

Tigges, W., '*The Fox and the Wolf*: A Study in Medieval Irony', in *Companion to Early Middle English Literature*, eds N. H. G. E. Veldhoen and H. Aertsen, 2nd edn (Amsterdam, 1995), pp. 79–91

Von Kreisler, N., 'Satire in *The Fox and the Wolf*', *Journal of English and Germanic Philology* 69 (1970), 650–8

Dame Siriþ

Busby, K., '*Dame Sirith* and *De Clerico et Puella*', in *Companion to Early Middle English Literature*, eds N. H. G. E. Veldhoen and H. Aertsen, 2nd edn (Amsterdam, 1995), pp. 67–78

The Bestiary: The Whale

Bennett, J. A. W., *Middle English Literature*, ed. and comp. D. Gray (Oxford, 1986; repr. 1990), pp. 23–7

Morris, R., ed., *An Old English Miscellany*, EETS o.s. 49 (London, 1872)

White, B., 'Medieval Animal Lore', *Anglia* 72 (1954), 21–30

The *Love-Ron* of Friar Thomas of Hales

Hill, B., 'The History of Jesus College, Oxford, MS 29', *Medium Ævum* 32 (1963), 203–13

Hill, B., 'The "luue-ron" and Thomas de Hales', *Modern Language Review* 59 (1964), 321–30

The Proverbs of Alfred

Arngart, O., ed., *The Proverbs of Alfred*, 2 vols (Lund, 1955)

Laȝamon's *Brut*

Allen, R., trans., *Lawman Brut* (London, 1992)

Barron, W. R. J., and S. C. Weinberg, eds, *Laȝamon's Brut* (London, 1995)

Kennedy, E. D., ed., *King Arthur: A Casebook* (New York, 1996)

Le Saux, F. H. M., *Laȝamon's Brut: The Poem and its Sources* (Cambridge, 1989)

Le Saux, F., ed., *The Text and Tradition of Layamon's Brut*, Arthurian Studies 33 (Cambridge, 1994)

Sayers, W., 'Rummaret de Wenelande: A Geographical Note to Wace's *Brut*', *Romance Philology* 18 (1964), 46–53

Stanley, E. G., 'Layamon's Antiquarian Sentiments', *Medium Ævum* 38 (1969), 23–37

The Owl and the Nightingale

Barratt, A., 'Flying in the Face of Tradition: A New View of *The Owl and the Nightingale*', *University of Toronto Quarterly* 56 (1987), 471–85

Barton Palmer, R., 'The Narrator in *The Owl and the Nightingale*: A Reader in the Text', *Chaucer Review* 22 (1988), 305–21

Cartlidge, N., 'The Date of *The Owl and the Nightingale*', *Medium Ævum* 65 (1996), 230–47

Coleman, J., '*The Owl and the Nightingale* and Papal Theories of Marriage', *Journal of Ecclesiastical History* 38 (1987), 517–68

Djordjevic, I., '*The Owl and the Nightingale* and the Perils of Criticism', *Neuphilologische Mitteilungen* 96 (1995), 367–80

Gottschalk, J., '*The Owl and the Nightingale*: Lay Preachers to a Lay Audience', *Philological Quarterly* 45 (1966), 657–67

Hume, K., *The Owl and the Nightingale: The Poem and its Critics* (Toronto, 1975)

Ker, N. R., ed., *The Owl and the Nightingale: Reproduced in Facsimile from the Surviving Manuscripts, Jesus College, Oxford 29, and British Museum, Cotton Caligula A. ix*, EETS o.s. 251 (London, 1963; repr. 1993)

Lumiansky, R. M., 'Concerning *The Owl and the Nightingale*', *Philological Quarterly* 32 (1953), 411–17

Potkay, M. B., 'Natural Law in *The Owl and the Nightingale*', *Chaucer Review* 28 (1994), 368–83

Reale, N. M., 'Rhetorical Strategies in *The Owl and the Nightingale*', *Philological Quarterly* 63 (1984), 417–29

Stanley, E. G., ed., *The Owl and the Nightingale* (London, 1960; repr. 1981)

Witt, M. A., '*The Owl and the Nightingale* and English Law Court Procedure of the Twelfth and Thirteenth Centuries', *Chaucer Review* 16 (1982), 282–92

The Trinity Lyrics

Brown, C., ed., *English Lyrics of the Thirteenth Century* (Oxford, 1932; repr. 1971)

Duncan, T. G., ed. *Medieval English Lyrics 1200–1400* (London, 1995)

The South English Legendary

D'Evelyn, C., and A. Mill, eds, *The South English Legendary*, EETS o.s. 235, 246 (London, 1956)

Görlach, M., *The Textual Tradition of the South English Legendary*, Leeds Texts and Monographs 6 (Leeds, 1974)

Hamerlinck, R., 'St Kenelm and the Legends of the English Saints in *The South English Legendary*', in *Companion to Early Middle English Literature*, eds N. H. G. E. Veldhoen and H. Aertsen, 2nd edn (Amsterdam, 1995), pp. 19–28

Mason, E., *St Wulfstan of Worcester, c. 1008–1095* (Oxford, 1990)

Cursor Mundi

Horrall, S. M., '"For the commun at understand": *Cursor Mundi* and its Background', in *De Cella in Seculum: Religious and Secular Life and Devotion in Late Medieval England*, ed. M. G. Sergeant (Cambridge, 1989), pp. 97–107

Morris, R., ed., *Cursor Mundi*, EETS o.s. 57, 59, 62, 66, 68, 99, 101 (London, 1874–93; repr. 1961–6)

Robert Mannyng of Brunne

Handlyng Synne

Crosby, R., 'Robert Mannyng of Brunne: A New Biography', *Publications of the Modern Language Association* 57 (1942), 15–28

Furnivall, F. J., ed., *Robert of Brunne's 'Handlyng Synne'*, EETS o.s. 119, 123 (London, 1901–3)

Miller, M., 'Displaced Souls, Idle Talk, Spectacular Scenes: *Handlyng Synne* and the Perspective of Agency', *Speculum* 71 (1996), 606–32

Sullens, I., ed., *Robert Mannyng of Brunne: 'Handlyng Synne'*, MRTS 14 (Binghamton, 1983)

The Chronicle

Furnivall, F. J., ed., *The Story of England by Robert Mannyng of Brunne, AD 1338: Edited from Manuscripts at Lambeth Palace and the Inner Temple*, 2 vols (London, 1887)

Robbins, R. H., ed., *Historical Poems of the Fourteenth and Fifteenth Centuries* (New York, 1959)

Stepsis, R. P., 'The Manuscripts of Robert Mannyng of Brunne's "Chronicle of England"', *Manuscripta* 13 (1969), 131–41

Sullens, I., *Robert Mannyng of Brunne: The Chronicle*, MRTS 153 (Binghamton, 1996)

Taylor, J., *English Historical Literature in the Fourteenth Century* (Oxford, 1987)

Turville-Petre, T., 'Politics and Poetry in the Early Fourteenth Century: The Case of Robert Manning's *Chronicle*', *Review of English Studies* 39 (1988), 1–28

The Land of Cockayne

Henry, P. L., '*The Land of Cockayne*: Cultures in Contact in Medieval Ireland', *Studia Hibernica* 12 (1972), 120–41

Hill, T. D., 'Parody and Theme in the Middle English "Land of Cockayne"', *Notes and Queries* 220 (1975), 55–9

Kuczynski, P., 'Utopie and Satire in *The Land of Cockayne*', *Zeitschrift fur Anglistik und Amerikanistik* 28 (1980), 45–55

Tigges, W., '*The Land of Cockayne*: Sophisticated Mirth', in *Companion to Early Middle English Literature*, eds N. H. G. E. Veldhoen and H. Aertsen, 2nd edn (Amsterdam, 1995), pp. 93–101

The Auchinleck Manuscript

Bliss, A. J., 'Notes on the Auchinleck Manuscript', *Speculum* 26 (1951), 652–8

Loomis, L. H., 'The Auchinleck Manuscript and a Possible London Bookshop of 1330–1340', *Publications of the Modern Language Association* 57 (1942), 595–627

Pearsall, D., and I. C. Cunningham, intro., *The Auchinleck Manuscript: National Library of Scotland Advocates' MS 19. 2. 1* (London, 1977)

Sir Orfeo

Bliss, A. J., ed., *Sir Orfeo* (Oxford, 1954)

Edwards, A. S. J., 'Marriage, Harping and Kingship: The Unity of *Sir Orfeo*', *American Benedictine Review* 32 (1981), 282–91

Hill, D. M., 'The Structure of "Sir Orfeo"', *Medieval Studies* 23 (1961), 136–53

Knapp, J. F., 'The Meaning of *Sir Orfeo*', *Modern Language Quarterly* (1968), 263–73

Kooper, E., 'The Twofold Harmony of the Middle English *Sir Orfeo*', in *Companion to Early Middle English Literature*, eds N. H. G. E. Veldhoen and H. Aertsen, 2nd edn (Amsterdam, 1995), pp. 114–32

Liuzza, R. M., '*Sir Orfeo*: Sources, Traditions, and the Poetics of Peformance', *Journal of Medieval and Renaissance Studies* 21 (1991), 269–84

Lucas, P., 'An Interpretation of *Sir Orfeo*', *Leeds Studies in English* 6 (1972), 1–9

Ronquist, E. C., 'The Powers of Poetry in *Sir Orfeo*', *Philological Quarterly* 64 (1985), 99–117

London, British Library, Harley 2253

Ker, N. R., intro., *Facsimile of British Museum MS. Harley 2253*, EETS o.s. 255 (London, 1965)

The Harley Lyrics

Brook, G. L., ed., *The Harley Lyrics* (Manchester, 1940)

Brown, C., ed., *English Lyrics of the Thirteenth Century* (Oxford, 1932)

Brown, C., ed., *Religious Lyrics of the Fourteenth Century*, 2nd edn rev. G. V. Smithers (Oxford, 1952)

Coss, P., intro., *Thomas Wright's Political Songs of England from the Reign of John to that of Edward II* (Cambridge, 1996)

Samuels, M., 'The Dialect of the Scribe of the Harley Lyrics', in *Middle English Dialectology: Essays on Some Principles and Problems*, eds A. McIntosh, M. L. Samuels and M. Laing (Aberdeen, 1989), pp. 256–63

King Horn

Allen, R., 'Some Textual Cruces in *King Horn*', *Medium Ævum* 53 (1984), 73–7

Childress, D. T., 'Between Romances and Legend: Secular Hagiography in Middle English Literature', *Philological Quarterly* 57 (1978), 311–22

Creek, H. L., 'Character in the Matter of England Romances', *Journal of English and Germanic Philology* 10 (1911), 429–52, 585–609

Hall, J., ed., *King Horn: A Middle English Romance* (Oxford, 1901)

Hearn, M., 'Twins of Infidelity: The Double Antagonists of *King Horn*', *Medieval Perspectives* 8 (1993), 78–86

Hynes-Berry, M., 'Cohesion in *King Horn* and *Sir Orfeo*', *Speculum* 50 (1975), 652–70

Pope, M. K., 'The *Romance of Horn* and *King Horn*', *Medium Ævum* 25 (1955), 164–7

Ziegler, G., 'Structural Repetition in *King Horn*', *Neuphilologische Mitteilungen* 81 (1980), 403–8

The *Ayenbite of Inwit*

Francis, W. N., 'The Original of the *Ayenbite of Inwit*', *Publications of the Modern Language Association* 70 (1937), 983–5

Gradon, P., ed., *Dan Michel's Ayenbite of Inwit: Volume II, Introduction, Notes and Glossary*, EETS o.s. 278 (London, 1979)

Morris, R., ed., *The Aȝenbite of Inwit*, EETS o.s. 23 (London, 1866; repr. with corrections 1965)

Richard Rolle

Allen, H. E., ed., *English Writings of Richard Rolle, Hermit of Hampole* (Oxford, 1931; repr. 1963)

Ogilvie-Thomson, S. J., ed., *Richard Rolle: Prose and Verse Edited from MS Longleat 29 and Related Manuscripts*, EETS o.s. 293 (Oxford, 1988)

Kyng Alisaunder

Cary, G., *The Medieval Alexander*, ed. D. J. A. Ross (Cambridge, 1956)

Foster, B., ed., *The Anglo-Norman 'Alexander' (Le Roman de Toute Chevalrie)*, Anglo-Norman Text Society 29 (London, 1976)

Hill, B., 'The Alexanderromance: The Egyptian Connection', *Leeds Studies in English* 12 (1981), 185–94

Smithers, G. V., ed., *Kyng Alisaunder*, EETS o.s. 227, 237 (London, 1952–7)

Athelston

Ashman Rowe, E., 'The Female Body Politic and the Miscarriage of Justice in Athelston', *Studies in the Age of Chaucer* 17 (1995), 79–98

Pigg, D. F., 'The Implications of Realist Poetics in the Middle English *Athelston*', *English Language Notes* 32 (1994), 1–8

Treharne, E. M., 'The Romanticisation of the Past in the Middle English *Athelston*,' *Review of English Studies* 50 (1999), 1–21

Trounce, A. McI., ed., *Athelston: A Middle English Romance*, EETS o.s. 224 (London, 1951)

Ywain and Gawain

Finlayson, J., '*Ywain and Gawain* and the Meaning of Adventure', *Anglia* 87 (1969), 313–37

Friedman, A. B., and N. T. Harrington, eds, *Ywain and Gawain*, EETS o.s. 254 (London, 1964; repr. 1981)

Mills, M., *Ywain and Gawain, Sir Percyvell of Gales, and The Anturs of Arther* (London, 1992)

Wynnere and Wastoure

Gollancz, I., ed., *A Good Short Debate between Winner and Waster: An Alliterative Poem on Social and Economic Problems in England in the Year 1352, with Modern English Rendering* (London, 1920; repr. Cambridge, 1974)

Harrington, D., 'Indeterminacy in *Winner and Waster* and *The Parliament of the Three Ages*', *Chaucer Review* 20 (1986), 246–57

Salter, E., 'The Timeliness of *Wynnere and Wastoure*', *Medium Ævum* 47 (1978), 40–65

Trigg, S., ed., *Wynnere and Wastoure*, EETS o.s. 297 (London, 1990)

Glossary of Common Hard Words

This glossary provides a very select list of common hard words found in the texts from *c*.1200 onwards. The graphs *i* and *y* are treated as interchangeable. The following abbreviations are used: *adj.* adjective; *adv.* adverb; *conj.* conjunction; *indef.* indefinite; *n.* noun; *prep.* preposition; *pron.* pronoun; *vb.* verb.

a, aa, ay *adv.* always
abide *vb.* await
ac, at *conj.* but
ageyn, aȝeyn *prep.* against, in the presence of
ahte *vb.* ought
andwerian *vb.* to answer
ane *adj.* alone
anon *adv.* immediately
ar *conj.* before
atte *prep.* at the
be *prep.* by
bede *n.* prayer
bede, beode *vb.* offer, order
bifel *vb.* happened
bihoves *vb.* is fitting that
biþenche *vb.* reflect, concern oneself with
ble(e) *n.* colour
bliþe *adj.* happy
bot(e) *conj.* but, unless
bote *n.* remedy
brid *n.* bird, woman
burde *n.* woman
can, con *vb.* can, knows how to
care *n.* anxiety, sorrow
ches, chose *vb.* choose, chose
cleped *vb.* called
con *vb.* know
couþe *vb.* known
dai, deȝe *n.* day
deȝe *vb.* die

demen *vb.* to judge
dere *n.* costly
derne *adj.* hidden, secret
diȝht *vb.* prepared, adorned
dome *n.* doom
domesdai *n.* Doomsday
ec, ek *adv.* also
eft *adv.* again
eȝe(n) *n.* eye(s)
elde *n.* old age
eode, ȝeode *vb.* went
er, ar *adv.* previously, before
everich *adj.* every, each
everichon *pron.* everyone
fader, vader *n.* father
fele *adj.* many
ferly *adj.* marvellous
folde *n.* earth
fole *n.* fool
for, vor *conj.* on account of
forbeode *vb.* forbid
forȝelde *vb.* requite, pay back
forlet *vb.* abandon, give up
forloren *vb.* to be lost
forte, for to *prep.* to, in order to
forþi *conj.* because, therefore
fre(e) *adj.* noble
fro *prep.* from
fro(u)fre *n.* comforter
fugel, fowel *n.* bird

ful *adv.* very
fulluht *n.* baptism
fultume *n.* help, grace
ʒe *pron.* you
ʒede, ʒeode *vb.* went
ʒelde *vb.* pay
ʒeond, ʒond *prep.* through(out)
ʒeorne *adv.* eagerly, earnestly
ʒeve *vb.* give
ʒif, ʒef *conj.* if
ʒure, ʒoure *pron.* your
habban, han *vb.* to have
ham, hem *pron.* them
hare, h(u)ere *pron.* their
he *pron.* he, she
heiʒ, heʒ *adj.* high
hende *adj.* noble, courteous
heo, ho, scho *pron.* she
heoven, heven *n.* heaven
here, yherd *vb.* hear, heard
het *vb.* command
heved *n.* head
hight(e) *vb.* was called, promise
hire, hure *pron.* her
ic, ich, Y *pron.* I
iliche *adj.* alike, similar
ilk *adj.* same
inow, inoʒ *adj.* enough, plenty
iwis *adv.* certainly, indeed
kepe(n) *vb.* guard, attend to
kin, cunne *n.* kin
koude *vb.* could
lede *n.* man
lef, leof *adj.* dear
lefmon, lemmon *n.* sweetheart, lover
lere *vb.* learn, teach
lesinge *n.* falsehood, lie
levedy, lefdy *n.* lady
levere *adv.* rather
lewd, lewed *adj.* uneducated, ignorant
libbe(n) *vb.* live
ligge *vb.* lie (down)
liste *vb.* pleased
lore, lare *n.* teaching
loþ *adj.* hateful
luþer *adj.* wicked
make *n.* mate
me *pron.* me
me *indef.* people, someone
mede *n.* reward
mete *n.* food
micel, mucel *adj.* much, great
middelerd *n.* earth

milce *n.* mercy
mirþe, murþe *adj.* joy
mo, moo *pron.* more
molde *n.* earth
moste *vb.* must
mote *vb.* (I, we) might
nabbe *vb.* have not
namo *pron.* no more
neʒe, neiʒe *prep.* near
nelle, nulle *vb.* will not
nemned *vb.* was named
nim(e), nam *vb.* take
nis *vb.* is not
nolde *vb.* would not
nouþe *adv.* now
on *prep.* on, in
on *n.* one
ones *adv.* once
ore *n.* pity, grace
oþer *adj.* other, second
oþerhwil *adv.* sometimes
oþþe *conj.* or
palfray *n.* horse
pine *n.* torment
plighte *vb.* promise, swear
poure *adj.* poor
pris, prys *adj.* excellent (or *n.* prize)
quaþ, quoþ *vb.* said
recche *vb.* care about
rede *vb.* advise (or *n.* advice)
rode *n.* Cross
sal, ssel, schal *vb.* shall
sawe *n.* saying, proverb
scho *pron.* she
schrift *n.* confession
seʒ, seiʒ *vb.* saw
selcouþe *adj.* wondrous
semely *adj.* fitting, proper
shuld *vb.* should
sigge *vb.* said
sone *adv.* soon
soþ *n.* truth
soþliche *adv.* truly
spell *n.* words, story, gospel
sted(e) *n.* place
stede *n.* horse
stonde *vb.* stand
stonde *adv.* a while
sunne *n.* sin
swa *adj.* so
swich, swilk *adj.* such
swink *n.* work
swiþe, swuþe *adj.* very

sythe *n.* times
syþþe, suþþe *adv.* after
syþþen *conj.* since
tide *n.* time
til *prep.* to, until
tofore *prep.* before, in front of
treuþe, treowþe *n.* truth, faith
trewe *adj.* true, faithful
unneþe *adv.* scarcely, uneasily
þe *pron.* you (or the)
þeah, þoh *conj.* though, even so
þilke, þulke *adj.* that same
þo *conj.* then, when
þoughte *vb.* seemed
vorbisne *n.* example, proverb

welde *vb.* possess, rule over
wele *n.* wealth, prosperity
wende *vb.* went
wene *vb.* think
weste, wiste *vb.* knew
whasa, whase *pron.* whoever
wite, wot *vb.* knows
witerliche *adv.* truly
with *n.* creature
wol, will *vb.* will
wolde *vb.* would, wished
wraþþe, wroþ *adj.* anger
wune *vb.* lived, stayed
wurþe *vb.* become

Index of Manuscripts

General Index

AB language, 293

adultery, in *Ayenbite of Inwit*, 526–9; in *Dame Siriþ*, 338–48; in *The Owl and the Nightingale*, 380–415; in *Kyng Alisaunder*, 537–50

Advent Lyrics, 36–41

Advice to Women, 481, 484

Ælfric, xvi, 116–39, 427; Homily on the Nativity of the Innocents, 122–9; *Passion of Saint Edmund*, 132–9; Old English Preface to his First Series of *Catholic Homilies*, 116–21; Old English Preface to his *Lives of Saints*, 130–1

Æthelwold, bishop of Winchester, xv

Æthelwulf, king of Wessex, 22–3

Æthered, king of Wessex, 24–5

ages of the world, 436

Alexander the Great, 537–50

Alfred, xv, 1, 10–19, 358; Battles with the Vikings, 24–7; *The Proverbs of*, 358–68, 416; Translation of Boethius's *Consolation of Philosophy*, 14–19, 358; *Preface* to the Translation of Gregory's *Pastoral Care*, 10–13

allegory, in *Ancrene Wisse*, 315–23; in bestiary, 54–9, 350–1; in *Cursor Mundi*, 439–43; in *Hali Meiðhad*, 293–6; in *Wynnere and Wastoure* (political allegory), 581–92

alliterative verse, xviii; *see also* Laʒamon's *Brut*, *Wynnere and Wastoure* (and all Old English verse in this volume)

Alysoun, 481, 482

Amis and Amiloun, 465, 551

Ammon-Zeus, 537

anchoresses, xvii, 307–27

Ancrene Riwle, 293, 307–27

Ancrene Wisse, xvii, 307–27, 352

Andreas, 89

Angles, Saxons and Jutes, The Settlement of, 2–5

Anglo-Saxon Chronicle, The, xv, 20–33; *see also The Peterborough Chronicle*

Anglo-Saxons, settlement of, xiv–xv, 2–5, 452

Annunciation, 38–9

Antichrist, 116–21, 226–33

anti-feminism, 358; *see also* women

Apollonius of Tyre, 234–53

Arthur, xvii, 369, 372–9, 569–80

Athelstan, king of Wessex, 551n

Athelston, 551–68

Auchinleck Manuscript, The, 465–80, 537

audience, xviii–xix

Augustine, conversion of Kent, xv

Augustine of Hippo, 213, 530; *Soliloquies*, xv, 10

authorship, xviii–xix; *see also* Ælfric, *Ancrene Wisse*, Cynewulf, Laʒamon's *Brut*, *The Owl and the Nightingale*, Robert Mannyng of Brunne, Wulfstan's *Sermo Lupi ad Anglos*

Autumn Song, An, 481, 494–5

Ayenbite of Inwit, 526–9

Battle of Brunanburh, The, 28–33

Battle of Hastings, 455–9

Battle of Maldon, The, xviii, 141–55

beast fable, 332–7, 380–415

Bede's *Ecclesiastical History*, xv, 1–9, 368n, 444; Cædmon's *Hymn*, 1–3; translation of The Life of Cædmon, 4–9; translation of The Settlement of the Angles, Saxons and Jutes, 2–5

Benedictine reform, xv–xvi

Beowulf, xvi, xviii, 156–95, 369

Beowulf-Manuscript, xvi, 156, 196

Beves of Hamptoun, 551

Black Death, 581

Blickling Homilies, 98, 116

Blow, Northern Wynd, 481, 487–9